W9-BLI-834

MOON HANDBOOKS®

MAINE

THIRD EDITION

KATHLEEN M. BRANDES

AVALON TRAVEL

© AVALON TRAVEL PUBLISHING, INC.

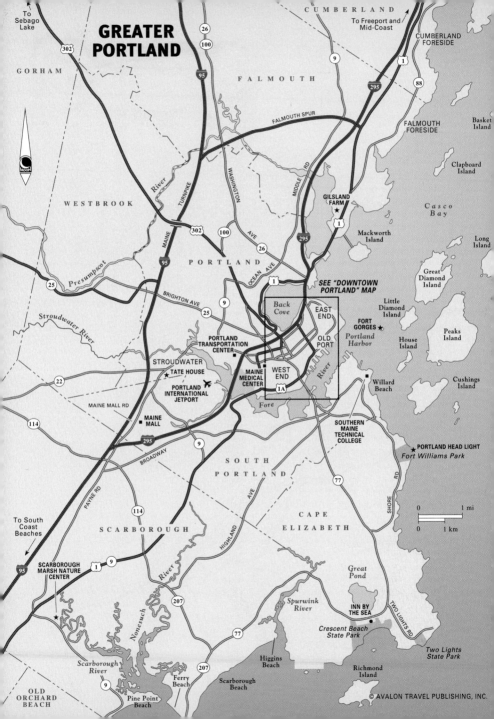

MOUNT DESERT ISLAND/ ACADIA NATIONAL PARK

Porcupine Islands

The Thrumcap

SCHOONER HEAD

Frenchman Bay

Champlain Mountain ▲

INTERNATIONAL FERRY TERMINAL

COLLEGE OF THE ATLANTIC

Bar Island

Bar Harbor

SIEUR DE MONTS ★

Dorr Mountain ▲

Cadillac ▲

PARK LOOP RD

3

Eagle Lake

Hulls Cove

HULLS COVE VISITOR CENTER

Witch Hole Pond

Acadia

Eastern Bay

RD

Lake Wood

233

National

Aunt Betty Pond

Salisbury Cove

NORWAY

DR

Marlboro

CROOKED

198

Sou

Lamoine State Park

3

Town Hill

102

198

Somesville

OAK HILL RD

Lamoine

RD

OAK

Somes Pond

Narrows

102

198

POINT

Blagden Preserve

OAK HILL CROSS RD

Round Pond

102

To Ellsworth

3

✈ AIRPORT

Trenton

THOMPSON ISLAND INFORMATION CENTER

Mount Desert

Indian Point

INDIAN

Squid Cove

Pretty

Alley Island

Green Island

Black Island

Union River Bay

230

Western Bay

Narrows

Bartlett Island

Great Head

Sand Beach

THUNDER HOLE OVERLOOK ★

Gorham Mountain ▲

Otter Cliffs

Park

BLACKWOODS CAMPGROUND ▲

Otter Creek

WILDWOOD STABLES

Day Mountain ▲

Seal Harbor

Mountain

Jordan Pond

THUYA GARDEN ★

Little Long Pond

JORDAN POND HOUSE

Eastern Way

Sutton Island

INFORMATION CENTER

3

Bear Island

Little Cranberry Island

Islesford

Green Nubble

Baker Island

Acadia National Park

Hadlock Ponds

ASTICOU AZALEA GARDEN ★

Norumbega Mountain ▲

Crow Island

3

198

RGENT

DR

Northeast Harbor

Great Cranberry Island

ATLANTIC

und

Western Way

OCEAN

Greening Island

CLARK POINT RD

Acadia Mountain ▲

FERNALD POINT RD

WENDELL GILLEY MUSEUM ★

Southwest Harbor

Manset

Echo Lake

102

Beech Mountain ▲

Southwest Harbor/ Tremont Chamber of Commerce

SOUTHWEST HARBOR/ TREMONT CHAMBER OF COMMERCE

102

Park

SEAWALL CAMPGROUND ▲

102A

Pond

RD

LONG POND RD

Mansell Mountain ▲

Bernard Mountain ▲

WESTERN MOUNTAIN RD

National

Tremont

Bass Harbor

Great Gott Island

Hodgdon Pond

Seal Cove Pond

COVE RD

Bernard

BASS HARBOR HEAD LIGHT

SEAL COVE RD

Acadia

Seal Cove

SWANS ISLAND FERRY TERMINAL

Harbor

Folly Island

West Tremont

102

Blue Hill Bay

Moose Island

2 mi

2 km

0

0

PARK LOOP ROAD

TWO-WAY

ONE-WAY

© AVALON TRAVEL PUBLISHING, INC.

© KATHLEEN M. BRANDES

CONTENTS

Discover Maine

Explore Maine

South Coast and Portland 14

Western Lakes and Mountains.........................498

Know Maine

NEW BRUNSWICK

CANADA

QUÉBEC
CANADA

Moosehead
Lake
○ Greenville

MAP SYMBOLS

Divided Highway
Primary Road
Secondary Road
Railroad
Airport
Interstate Highway
U.S. Highway
State Highway
City/Town
Point of Interest
Accommodation
Restaurant/Bar
Mountain
Unique Natural Feature
Park
Golf Course
Ski Area
Campground
Trailhead
Other Location

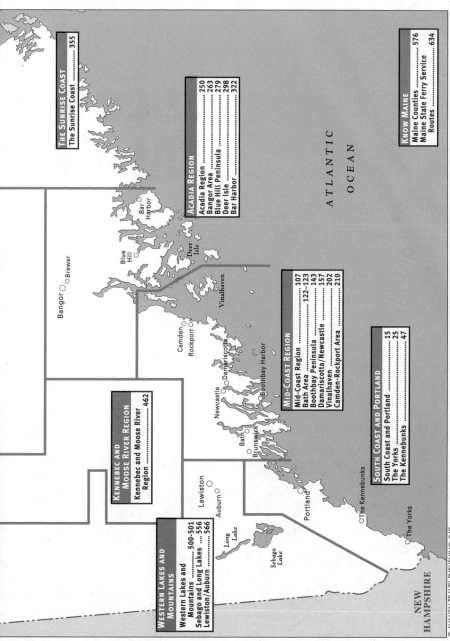

© AVALON TRAVEL PUBLISHING, INC.

Discover
Maine

© KATHLEEN M. BRANDES

A young student of Maine-born author and Smith College professor Mary Ellen Chase once mused, "Maine is different from all other states, isn't it? I suppose that's because God never quite finished it."

Maine may indeed be a work in progress, but it's a masterwork. Tucked into the northeasternmost corner of the United States and comprising 33,215 square miles, Maine boldly promotes itself as "The Way Life Should Be." Not to say that everything's perfect, mind you, but it is an extraordinarily special place.

There's a reason—no, there are lots of reasons—why more than eight million people visit every year, why longtime summer folk finally just pick up stakes and *settle* here, why Maine lobsters are the best, why Maine politicians become national household names. The traditional Maine traits of honesty, thrift, frankness, and ruggedness remain refreshingly appealing.

Also appealing is the state's natural wealth—a major drawing card not only for all the visitors ("people from away") but also for the state's 1.3 million residents. Acadia National Park,

Baxter State Park, more than 30 other state parks and tax-funded public preserves cover well more than half a million acres—and residents and nonresidents alike have full access to all this real estate.

Maine's wrinkled, 5,300-mile coastline, if pulled taut from Eastport southward, would stretch past Florida! Along that coast are 64 lighthouses, thousands of coastal and interior islands, 90 percent of the nation's lobsters, and the eastern seaboard's highest peak.

And if you get enough of the natural highs, you can poke into museums, galleries, boutiques, microbreweries, antiques shops, and playgrounds—and attend any number of concerts, plays, festivals, and county and country fairs.

Maine is a national natural treasure—a fact observed by 19th-century author Harriet Beecher Stowe from her Brunswick home: "It seems to us quite wonderful that in all the ecstasies that have been lavished on American scenery, this beautiful state of Maine should have been so much neglected [by visitors]; for nothing is or can be so wildly and peculiarly beautiful." Within two decades after her rave review, tourism had begun in earnest, Maine could no longer claim neglect, and Stowe's words proved just slightly premature.

WHEN TO GO

Maine has four distinct seasons: summer, fall, winter, and mud. Lovers of spring need to look elsewhere in March, the lowest month on the popularity scale with its mud-caked vehicles, soggy everything, irritable temperaments, tank-trap roads, and often the worst snowstorm of the year.

Summer can be idyllic—with moderate temperatures, clear air, and wispy breezes—but it can also close in with fog, rain, and chills. Prevailing winds are from the southwest. Officially, summer runs from June 21 to September 22 or 23, but June, July, and August is more like it, with temperatures in the Portland area averaging 70°F during the day and in the 50s at night. The normal growing season is 148 days.

A poll of Mainers might well show autumn as the favorite season— days are still warmish, nights are cool, winds are optimum for sailors, and the foliage is brilliant. Fall colors usually begin appearing far to the north, in Fort Kent, about mid-September, reaching their peak in that region by the end of the month. The last of the color begins in late September in the southernmost part of the state and fades by mid-October. Early autumn, however, is also the height of hurricane season, the only potential flaw this time of year.

Winter, officially December 21 to March 20, means deep snow in the western mountains, deep cold in the North Woods, and an unpredictable potpourri along the coast. It also means great alpine skiing and snowboarding at Sugarloaf/USA, Sunday River, Shawnee Peak, Saddleback, and smaller peaks; splendid snowmobiling on a huge network of trails; and such other pursuits as cross-country skiing, ice fishing, snowshoeing, ice-skating, dogsledding, ice-climbing, and winter trekking and camping.

Spring, officially March 20 to June 21, is the frequent butt of jokes. It's an ill-defined season that arrives much too late and departs all too quickly. Ice floes dot inland lakes and ponds until "ice-out", in early to mid-May; spring planting can't occur until well into May; lilacs explode in late May and disappear by mid-June. And just when you finally can enjoy being outside, blackflies stretch their wings and satisfy their hunger pangs. Even the moose head out of the woods and into open spaces when the blackflies show up.

FALL FOLIAGE

The timing of Maine's fall foliage owes much to the summer weather that precedes it, and so does the quality (although the annual spectacle never disappoints). In early September, as deciduous trees ready themselves for winter, they stop producing chlorophyll, and the green begins to disappear from their leaves. Taking its place are the spectacular pigments—brilliant reds, yellows, oranges, and purples—that paint the leaves and warm the hearts of every "leaf-peeper," shopkeeper, innkeeper, and restaurateur in the region.

The colorful display begins slowly, reaches a peak, then fades—starting in the north in early to mid-September and working down to the southwest corner by mid-October. Peak foliage in far-north Aroostook County usually occurs in late September, about three weeks after the colors have begun to appear there. Along the South Coast and Mid-Coast, the peak can occur as late as the middle of October, with the last bits of color hanging on even beyond that.

Trees put on their most magnificent show after a summer of moderate heat and rainfall; a summer of excessive heat and scant rainfall means colors will be less brilliant and disappear more quickly. Throw a September or October northeaster or hurricane into the mix and estimates are up for grabs.

So predictions are imprecise, and you'll need to allow some schedule flexibility to take advantage of the changes in different parts of the state. From mid-September to mid-October, check the state's Department of Conservation website (www.mainefoliage.com) for frequently updated maps, panoramic photographs, and reports on the foliage status (this is gauged by the percentage of leaf drop in every region of the state). Or call the Foliage Hotline: 888/MAINE-45. Another resource for info on driving tours during foliage season is www.visitmaine.com, the official website of the Maine Office of Tourism.

A reminder: Fall-foliage trips are extremely popular and have become more so in recent years, so lodging can be scarce. Plan ahead and make reservations, especially if you're headed for the Kennebunks, Boothbay Harbor, Camden, Bar Harbor, Greenville, Rangeley, and Bethel.

It's a tough, thankless job to single out sightseeing highlights in Maine. There are just *so many*. But, unless you have years to spend, such a big chunk of real estate needs some whittling down to be made explorable. So the following is offered as a list of sites you have to see (or at least sample) before claiming to have "done" Maine.

Acadia National Park

Maine's only national park, 40,000-plus acres, is open all year. It boasts landscapes and seascapes beyond description; barren summits with panoramic vistas; even quiet corners where you can be alone. Plan to drive, bike, hike, cross-country ski, or even snowshoe the park's roads and trails; canoe or kayak the lakes and ponds; swim in its chilly ocean waters; or sail the surrounding bays and harbors.

Monhegan Island

A car-free, carefree gem a dozen miles off the coast, reachable by boat from Port Clyde, New Harbor, and Boothbay Harbor. Pack a picnic and spend a day hiking the wooded, surf-bashed island, the inspiration for artists and photographers for more than a century.

Portland Museum of Art

Maine's premier art museum is smack in the heart of the state's largest city. While you're at it, explore the boutiques, bistros, and bars in the surrounding Downtown Arts District and a few blocks away in the retrofitted Old Port.

L.L. Bean, Inc.

The giant, world-famous sportswear retailer and hub of the hubbub in Freeport—Maine's outlet bonanza (second-largest outlet cluster is in Kittery, on the Maine–New Hampshire border). L.L. Bean also has a factory outlet store in downtown Portland.

Kennebunkport, Camden, and Blue Hill

Okay, we're cheating a little to list three together. These are neck-and-neck on any must-see list; all have historic homes, upscale shops, and waterfront vistas to die for.

Portland Head Light

It's a Cape Elizabeth landmark and Maine's oldest lighthouse (1791), at the edge of 94-acre Fort Williams Park. A great spot for an all-day family outing (don't forget your kite).

Kennebec River White-Water Rafting

It's headquartered in the area around the Forks. Licensed firms take advantage of controlled dam releases on the state's most popular rafting river.

Maine Maritime Museum

Over 10 acres of indoor and outdoor exhibits celebrating the state's nautical heritage. River cruises operate regularly throughout the summer.

Baxter State Park

Camping, hiking, and canoeing in 200,000-plus acres of pristine wilderness owned by the people of Maine, near Millinocket. Centerpiece of the park is mile-high Katahdin.

Sunday River Ski Resort

The state's biggest ski and snowboard area, near Bethel, with 128 well-groomed trails. (In summer, there's mountain biking.)

CITIES, TOWNS, AND VILLAGES

Even the dinkiest Maine hamlet has its own special character, but a handful of communities make good destinations in themselves as well as base camps for day-trips. Except for Portland—which has its own cachet—most still have a unique small-town flavor, although summer traffic sometimes stretches the space limits. Most scenic are Camden/Rockport, Blue Hill/Castine, the Kennebunks, Bar Harbor, and Rangeley. The most historic communities? York, Belfast/Searsport, Damariscotta/Newcastle, Wiscasset, Bethel, Machias, and Greenville. For a little and a lot of everything, head for Portland.

PARKS FOR PICNICS AND HIKES

Best parks for kids of all ages are Bradbury Mountain State Park in Pownal, Camden Hills State Park in Camden, Lily Bay State Park on Moosehead Lake near Greenville, Cobscook Bay State Park near Eastport, Grafton Notch State Park near Bethel, Holbrook Island Sanctuary State Park in Brooksville, and Mount Blue State Park in Weld.

MOUNTAINS TO CLIMB

For climbing challenges that range from easy to moderate to rigorous, best choices are Blue Hill Mountain in Blue Hill, Sargent Mountain on Mount Desert Island, Mount Agamenticus in York, Mount Battie in Camden, Katahdin in Baxter State Park, Borestone Mountain Sanctuary near Monson, Table Rock near Bethel, and Tumbledown Mountain in Weld. Easiest of these is Blue Hill Mountain; toughest is Katahdin.

BEACHES

Warmest water is along lakefronts—such as Sebago Lake State Park—and in southern Maine, such as Ferry Beach State Park in Saco and Ogunquit Beach. Scenic standouts, with chillier water, are Popham Beach State Park in Phippsburg (near Bath) and Sand Beach in Acadia National Park. On hot midsummer days (fairly infrequent in Maine), plan to arrive early at any beach—parking is always at a premium on such occasions.

LIGHTHOUSES CLOSE UP

All of Maine's 64 working lighthouses have now been automated by the U.S. Coast Guard. Their settings inevitably are spectacular, so seek 'em out. Among the easiest to approach are Cape Neddick Light (known as Nubble Light) in York, Portland Head Light in Cape Elizabeth, Pemaquid Point Light near Damariscotta, Marshall Point Light near Port Clyde, Owls Head Light near Rockland, Rockland Breakwater Light, Bass Harbor Head Light on Mount Desert Island, Hockamock Head Light on Swans Island, and West Quoddy Head Light near Lubec. In 1997, more than half of the working lighthouses were deeded by the Coast Guard to the Rockland-based Island Institute, whose Maine Lights Program has turned over individual lights to nonprofit organizations.

MUSEUMS

If museums and history intrigue you, you'll have no dearth of options in Maine. The best museums and sites for kids are the Children's Museum of Maine in Portland, the Maine Discovery Museum in Bangor, the Maine State Museum in Augusta, and Fort Knox State Historic Site near Bucksport.

Best art museums are the Portland Museum of Art, the Farnsworth Art Museum and Wyeth Center

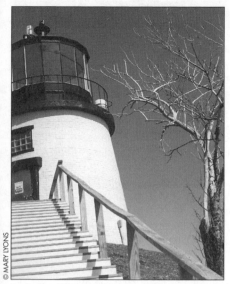

© MARY LYONS

Owls Head lighthouse

has a sprawling collection of historic museum buildings.

Self-explanatory are the collections in the Webb Museum of Vintage Fashion in Island Falls; the Lumberman's Museum in Patten, the Seashore Trolley Museum in Kennebunkport, the Wendell Gilley Museum of Bird Carving in Southwest Harbor, and the Peary-MacMillan Arctic Museum at Bowdoin College in Brunswick.

Music boxes fill the Musical Wonder House in Wiscasset, and operatic costumes fill the Nordica Homestead Museum in Farmington (birthplace of early-20th-century opera diva Madame Lillian Nordica). The Shaker Museum, in New Gloucester, represents the life and work of the nation's only remaining Shaker colony.

in Rockland, and the art museums at Bowdoin College in Brunswick and Colby College in Waterville.

Best marine museums are the Maine Maritime Museum in Bath and the Penobscot Marine Museum (Maine's oldest) in Searsport. The Owls Head Transportation Museum in Owls Head, near Rockland, focuses on wheeled and winged vehicles—it's the best such collection in the state and even beyond.

Maine's most eclectic and one-of-a-kind museums—where every display case holds a surprise—include the Nylander Museum in Caribou, the Wilson Museum in Castine, and the L.C. Bates Museum in Hinckley.

HISTORIC MAINE

Unique history museums include the 1770 Burnham Tavern in Machias, the 1754 Old Fort Western in Augusta, the 1870s Norlands Living History Center in Livermore, and the 1885 Franklin D. Roosevelt Cottage on Campobello Island, near Lubec. The Old York Historical Society also

BOAT TRIPS

Getting on the water is no problem in Maine. You can play mail carrier aboard the Great Pond mailboat in Belgrade Lakes or the Casco Bay mailboat in Portland; watch for whales out of Bar Harbor, Boothbay Harbor, Eastport, or Ogunquit; join the regular commuters on the car ferries to Islesboro, Vinalhaven, and Swans Island; or take a nostalgic trip aboard the paddle wheeler *Songo River Queen II* in Naples, the SS *Katahdin* on Moosehead Lake, or one of the antique and replica windjammer schooners sailing for 3–6 days out of Camden, Rockport, and Rockland.

TRAIN EXCURSIONS

The long hiatus in passenger-train service in Maine has drummed up plenty of interest in excursion trips. The Maine Eastern Railroad has midcoast excursion trips, and the Maine Narrow Gauge Railroad is "the little train that could," running very popular short trips on harborfront track in downtown Portland.

The Lobster Experience

No Maine visit can be considered complete without the "real Maine" experience of a "lobsta dinnah" at a lobster wharf/pound/shack. Keep an eye on the weather, pick a sunny day, and head out.

If you spot a lobster place with "Restaurant" in its name and no outside dining, keep going. What you're looking for is the genuine article; you want to eat outdoors, at a wooden picnic table, with a knockout view of boats and the sea. Whatever place you choose, the drill is much the same, and the "dinners" are served anytime from noon on (some places close as early as 7 PM). First of all, dress very casually so you can manhandle the lobster without messing up your good clothes. If you want beer or wine, call ahead and ask if they serve it; you may need to bring your own, since many such operations don't have beer/wine licenses, much less liquor licenses. In the evening, carry some insect repellent, in case mosquitoes crash the party (many places light citronella candles or dispense Skin-So-Soft to keep the bugs at bay).

THE LOBSTER DINNER

A basic one-pound lobster and go-withs (coleslaw or potato salad, potato chips, and butter or fake butter for dipping) should run just under $20. Depending on your hunger, though, you may want to indulge in a shore dinner (lobster, steamed clams, potato chips, and maybe coleslaw or corn), for which you may have to part with an extra $15. Don't skip dessert in either case; many lobster pounds are known for their homemade pies.

HOW TO EAT A MAINE LOBSTER

Typically, you'll need to survey a chalkboard or whiteboard menu and step up to a window to order. You'll either give the person your name or get a number. A few places have staff to deliver your meal, but usually you head back for the window when your name or number is called. Don your plastic lobster bib and begin the attack. If you're a neophyte, watch a pro at a nearby table. Some pounds have "how-to" info on printed paper placemats. If you're really worried (you needn't be), write ahead to the Maine Lobster Promotion Council, 382 Harlow St., Bangor 04401, www.lobsterfrommaine.com—they publish a brochure with detailed instructions. Don't worry about doing it "wrong"; you'll eventually get what you came for, and it'll be an experience to remember.

WHERE TO GET A MAINE LOBSTER

Here are 22 of the best places to experience lobster. All are described in detail in the regional chapters.

© KATHLEEN M. BRANDES

fresh lobster in Vinalhaven

The South Coast and Portland

Barnacle Billy's Lobster Pound, Perkins Cove, Ogunquit, 207/646-5575.

Chauncey Creek Lobster Pier, Kittery Point, 207/439-1030.

The Lobster Shack, Two Lights Rd., Cape Elizabeth (near Portland), 207/799-1677.

Mid-Coast Region

Boothbay Region Lobstermen's Co-op, Boothbay Harbor, 207/633-4900.

Cod End, Tenants Harbor (near Thomaston), 207/372-6782.

The Lobster House, Small Point (near Bath), 207/389-1596.

The Lobster Pound, Lincolnville Beach, 207/789-5550.

Miller's Lobster Company, Spruce Head (near Rockland), 207/594-7406.

Muscongus Bay Lobster, Round Pond (near Damariscotta), 207/529-5528.

Pemaquid Fishermen's Co-op, Pemaquid Harbor (near Damariscotta), 207/677-2801.

Robinson's Wharf, Southport (near Boothbay Harbor), 207/633-3830.

Round Pond Lobster Co-Op, Round Pond (near Damariscotta), 207/529-5725.

Shaw's Fish & Lobster Wharf, New Harbor (near Damariscotta), 207/677-2200.

South Bristol Fishermen's Co-op, South Bristol (near Damariscotta), 207/644-8224.

Waterman's Beach Lobsters, South Thomaston (near Rockland), 207/596-7819.

Young's Lobster Pound, East Belfast, 207/338-1160.

Acadia Region

Beal's Lobster Pier, Southwest Harbor (Mount Desert Island), 207/244-3202.

Dennett's Wharf, Castine, 207/326-9045.

Eaton's Lobster Pool, Little Deer Isle, 207/348-2383.

Thurston's Lobster Pound, Steamboat Wharf, Bernard (Mount Desert Island), 207/244-7600.

Tidal Falls, Hancock, 207/422-6457.

Trenton Bridge Lobster Pound, Trenton (near Bar Harbor), 207/667-2977.

© MARY LYONS

working dock, South Freeport

Cultural-Heritage "Trails"

Years of requests from visitors for lists of cultural-heritage sites and special-interest activities led to the creation of a whole range of "trails" that cover maritime history, art museums, architecture, outstanding gardens, sculpture, and Wabanaki Indian sites. Several counties and groups have produced their own regional cultural maps and guides. Many of the groups producing the trails and maps received state assistance or help from the Maine Tourism Association, 327 Water St., Hallowell 04347, 207/623-0363, www.maine-tourism.com. For a copy of any of these publications call 800/782-6497, or request from the Maine Office of Tourism website, www.visitmaine.com.

MARITIME HERITAGE TRAIL

Maine's rich maritime history provides this trail—a large-format, two-sided map—with stops around every corner. Among the highlights: boat-building schools, maritime museums, the Portland Fish Exchange (daily fish auctions), historic homes, lighthouses, a restored lake steamer, and the Old Town Canoe Company.

MAINE ART MUSEUM TRAIL

An attractive brochure focuses on the state's seven significant art museums, containing more than 53,000 works of art—ancient to contemporary, painting and sculpture, furniture and textiles. From south to north: Ogunquit Museum of American Art (Ogunquit); Portland Museum of Art (Portland); Bowdoin College Museum of Art (Brunswick); Bates College Museum of Art (Lewiston); Farnsworth Art Museum (Rockland); Colby Museum of Art (Waterville); and the University of Maine Museum of Art (Orono). The trail website is www.maineartmuseums.org. The May–June 2000 issue of *American Art Review* devoted 110 pages to the trail, the museums, and their holdings.

MAINE ARCHIVES AND MUSEUMS DIRECTORY

More than 125 institutions are listed by region in this 72-page directory of museums, historical societies, historic sites, and archives. (The directory includes some of the highlights of the maritime-heritage and art-museum trails.) The website is www.mainemuseums.org.

MAINE ARCHITECTURE TRAIL

From the Revolutionary architecture of Down East Maine to the state's connected farm buildings and covered bridges, this brochure is an education in a few pages. Compelling photography and detailed routing for six architectural discovery trips.

MAINE GARDEN AND LANDSCAPE TRAIL

A handy foldout map lists and locates more than 50 gardens—a huge variety ranging from pocket parks to city parks; formal, English, and experimental gardens; even a monastery and a cemetery. You'll find the finest displays in June and July, when garden tours are also on the agenda. Best of the tours are in Camden, Damariscotta, the Kennebunks, and Mount Desert Island. The "trail" map also lists several dozen garden and plant centers where you can indulge your horticultural habit.

Fads and fashions reach Maine in slow motion from the West Coast or New York, but once they catch on, watch out! Take the microbrewery phenomenon. Maine now has one of the nation's highest numbers of microbreweries per capita, and microbrewing is one of the state's fastest-growing industries. The pioneer of all this micro-entrepreneurship is Portland's D.L. Geary Brewing Company, which began producing Geary's Pale Ale in 1986. Some two dozen other breweries now create more than 100 different ales, stouts, lagers, and porters—along with the occasional seasonal oddities. Brewpubs and even "brewtiques" are sprouting up, and microbrewery tours attract both aficionados and neophytes.

The statewide Maine Brewers Guild, a nonprofit organization created to keep the industry honest, also keeps track of breweries, brewpubs, and beer-related events. Their website is www.drinkmainebeer.com.

Best place to graze through all of the state's award-winning brews is the annual Maine Brewers' Festival, held in Portland the first weekend in November (sort of a belated Oktoberfest). If a November visit doesn't suit you, dozens of restaurants feature Maine beers on tap year-round. Drop in at one of these brewpubs, all affiliated with microbreweries.

South Coast and Portland

Federal Jack's Brewpub (Shipyard Brewing Co.), 8 Western Ave., Kennebunk.
Gritty McDuff's, Lower Main St., Freeport, and 396 Fore St., Portland.

Acadia Region

Bear Brewpub, 36 Main St., Orono (near Bangor).
Lompoc Café and Brewpub, 36 Rodick St., Bar Harbor.
Sea Dog Tavern, 26 Front St., Bangor; 1 Main St., Topsham.

Western Lakes and Mountains

Bray's Brewpub, Rtes. 302 and 35, Naples (Sebago Lake).
Sunday River Brewing Company, 1 Sunday River Rd., Bethel.
Theo's (Sugarloaf Brewing Co.), Sugarloaf Access Rd., Carrabassett Valley.

Explore Maine

South Coast and Portland

Drive over the I-95 bridge from New Hampshire into Maine's South Coast region on a bright summer day and you'll swear the air is cleaner, the sky bluer, the trees greener, the roadside signs more upbeat: Welcome to Maine: The Way Life Should Be. (*Is* it? Or maybe the way life *used* to be?)

Whether you enter southern Maine via I-95 or the parallel U.S. 1, stop first at the Maine Visitor Information Center, 207/439-1319, in Kittery, for maps, brochures, amazingly cheerful staffers, pay phones, clean restrooms, and an outdoor pet-recreation area.

Southernmost York County, part of the Province of Maine, was incorporated in 1636 (only 16 years after the Mayflower pilgrims reached Plymouth, Massachusetts) and reeks of history: ancient cemeteries, musty archives, and architecturally stunning homes and public buildings. Probably the best places to dive into that history are in the seven buildings of the Old York Historical Society in York Harbor.

Most visitors come to this region for the spectacular attractions of the justly world-famous Maine coast. But there's much more here than inlets, islands, and beaches. Any itinerary is enriched by a visit to inland York County—a trove of "best-kept secrets" and

© KATHLEEN M. BRANDES

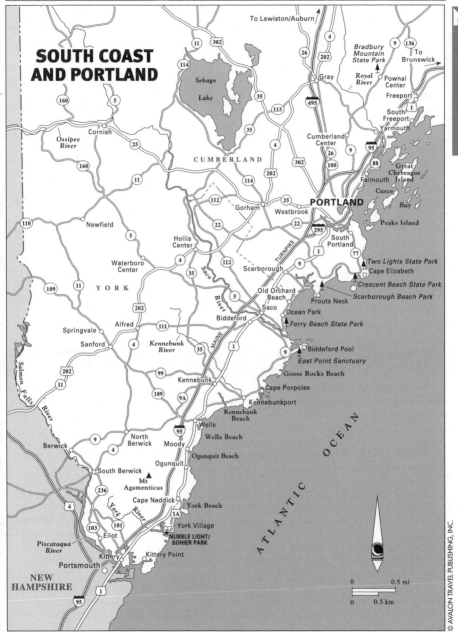

SOUTH COAST AND PORTLAND

© AVALON TRAVEL PUBLISHING, INC.

historic sites (it's home to, among other things, the state's first sawmill and the nation's oldest courthouse records). Inland from the Yorks, the county stretches west and north through farmland and historic towns such as the Berwicks, Waterboro, Newfield, and Alfred, the county seat. When Old Kittery was incorporated, in 1647, Old Berwick was part of it. In 1714, the two areas severed their ties and Berwick incorporated on its own—making it the ninth-oldest incorporated town in Maine. Gradually, it spun off the separate communities of South Berwick in 1814 and North Berwick in 1831. For the history, the architecture, the New England scenery, and the literary past—and a setting made more enjoyable by the dearth of crowds—the region is well worth visiting.

But you can't *not* hit the coast, either. Following U.S. 1 northeast from the Yorks, you'll drive (slowly in midsummer) through Ogunquit, Wells, the Kennebunks, Biddeford, Saco, Old Orchard Beach, and on into Greater Portland. Geological fortune smiled on this 50-mile ribbon, endowing it with a string of sandy beaches—nirvana for sun worshippers, less enchanting to swimmers, who need to steel themselves to spend much time in the ocean (especially in early summer, before the water temperature has reached a tolerable level).

After Labor Day (the first Monday in September), the character of these communities changes markedly. Life goes on, but at a different (and still interesting) pace. Crowds and traffic thin, seasonal attractions go into hibernation, and many lodgings in southern Maine drop their rates dramatically, even though daytime weather and even the ocean can still be comfortably warm.

In Portland, seat of Cumberland County and Maine's premier population center, the pace actually increases after summer. Greater Portland takes in a sprawling area from Scarborough on the south through Westbrook and Gorham to the west and on northward to Falmouth, Cumberland, Yarmouth, and Freeport.

Kittery and Eliot

As well as being a natural point of entry into the state, Kittery also competes with Freeport, farther up the coast, as an outlet-shopping mecca. Kittery boasts more than 120 factory outlets in more than a dozen buildings, lining both sides of U.S. 1. But before or after you overdose on shoes, china, tools, toys, candles, and underwear, take time to explore the back roads of Maine's oldest town—settled in 1623 and chartered in 1647. Maine is home to a lot of well-kept secrets, Kittery being one of them. Parks, a small nautical museum, historic architecture, and three lobster restaurants are only a few of the attractions in Kittery and its "suburb," Kittery Point.

To reach Kittery's shops and services, as well as Eliot's lodgings, from I-95 northbound, take the exit 3 cloverleaf, designated Kittery, Coastal Route 1 North, and continue to Rte. 1. From I-95 southbound, take exit 7, designated Yorks/Berwicks; then take Coastal Route 1 South. Follow signs; the twists and turns can be confusing.

Eliot, once a fishing, farming, and shipbuilding center on the Piscataqua River, now boasts well-preserved homes, wide-open spaces, and a sedate personality.

SIGHTS AND RECREATION
Kittery Historical and Naval Museum
Maritime history buffs shouldn't miss the small but well-stocked Kittery Historical and Naval Museum, Rogers Rd., near the junction of Rtes. 1 and 236, Kittery 03904, 207/439-3080. A large exhibit hall and a small back room contain ship models, fishing gear, old photos and paintings, and an astonishing collection of scrimshaw (carved whale ivory). Open Tues.–Sat. June–mid-Oct., Wed. and

Sat. to late Nov., 10 AM–4 PM, with a Holiday Open House in early Dec. Admission is $3 adults, $1.50 children (7–15), kids under seven free, family maximum $6.

Lady Pepperrell House

Formerly open to the public, the 1760 Georgian Lady Pepperrell House, Pepperrell Rd., Rte. 103, shortly before the Fort McClary turnoff, is now privately owned. Nearby, across from the First Congregational Church, is the area's most-visited burying ground. Old-cemetery buffs should bring rubbing gear here for some interesting grave markers. The tomb of Levi Thaxter (husband of poet Celia Thaxter) bears an epitaph written for him by Robert Browning.

Fort McClary Historic Site

Since the early 18th century, fortifications have stood on this 27-acre headland, protecting Portsmouth Harbor from seaborne foes. Contemporary remnants at Fort McClary, Rte. 103, Kittery Point 03905, 207/439-2845, are several outbuildings, an 1846 blockhouse, granite walls, and earthworks—all with a dynamite view of Portsmouth Harbor. Opposite are the sprawling buildings of the Portsmouth Naval Shipyard. Bring a picnic (covered tables and a lily pond are across the street) and turn the kids loose to run and play. Officially open Memorial Day–Sept. 30, but the site is accessible off season. Admission is $2 adults, $1 children (5–11), free for seniors (over 65) and kids under five. The fort is 2.5 miles east of Rte. 1.

Fort Foster

The only problem with Fort Foster, Pocahontas Rd., off Rte. 103, Gerrish Island, Kittery Point 03905, 207/439-3800, is that it's no secret, so parking can be scarce (and expensive) at this 90-acre municipal park at the entrance to Portsmouth Harbor. On a hot day, arrive early. Then you can swim, hike the nature trails, fish off the pier (no license needed), picnic, and investigate the tide pools. Bring your sailboard and a kite—there's almost always a breeze. From nearby **Seapoint Beach** on a clear day,

there's a wide-open view of the offshore Isles of Shoals, owned jointly by Maine and New Hampshire. The park is open Memorial Day–Labor Day, 10 AM–8 PM, as well as May and September weekends.

Brave Boat Harbor

One of the Rachel Carson National Wildlife Refuge's 10 Maine coastal segments is Brave Boat Harbor, a beautifully unspoiled, 748-acre wetlands preserve in Kittery Point with a four-mile (round-trip) trail. Carry binoculars, wear rubberized boots to maneuver the squishy areas, and slather on the insect repellent. The habitat is particularly sensitive here, so be kind to the environment. Take Rte. 103 to Chauncey Creek Road, continue past the Gerrish Island bridge to Cutts Island Lane. Turn left and park on the left near the small bridge. The trail's left fork leads to an abandoned trolley trestle, overlooking marshlands.

Route 103

The best way to appreciate this part of Maine is to drive or cycle along squiggly Rte. 103 from the Rte. 1 rotary in Kittery through Kittery Point (administratively part of Kittery) and on to Rte. 1A in York. If you're on a bike, the road's narrow in places, but forge ahead. You can even make a day of it, stopping at all the sites mentioned above.

Isles of Shoals

During turf battles in the 17th century, these nine offshore islands were split into two jurisdictions (now the two states of Maine and New Hampshire). Maine received five islands, New Hampshire four. New Hampshire's **Star Island** is now a summer center for religious, artistic, and foreign-affairs conferences. Landings on these windswept islands are restricted, but several excursion boats offer a close-up view. The **Isles of Shoals Steamship Co.,** 315 Market St., P.O. Box 311, Portsmouth, NH 03801, 603/431-5500 or 800/441-4620 offers a "Historic Isles of Shoals, Lighthouses, and Portsmouth Harbor Tour" cruise with two departures a day: 9:55 AM and 1:55 PM. Cost is

$24 adults, $16 children 3–12, free for children under 3. There is a $3 military and senior citizen (65 and over) discount.

ACCOMMODATIONS

Kittery

Built in 1879, the handsome brick **Portsmouth Harbor Inn And Spa,** 6 Water St., Kittery 03904, 207/439-4040, www.innatportsmouth .com, looks out over the Piscataqua River, Portsmouth, and the Portsmouth Naval Shipyard. Owners are Lynn and Nathaniel Bowditch, a grandson of Nathaniel Bowditch, author of the *American Practical Navigator,* which was *the* pre-Loran navigational tool for maritime America. Five attractive Victorian-style rooms have private baths, phones, and wireless internet. Request a back room if you're noise-sensitive, although air-conditioning camouflages traffic noise in summer. Walk across the river to Portsmouth for interesting culinary choices. The historic barn houses a full day spa, massages through manicures. No smoking, pets, or children under 16. Inn rates are $145–210 d May–Oct., $110–145 the rest of the year.

Just over the Memorial Bridge on Rte. 103 (take a right two blocks after the bridge) is the 1890 Princess Anne Victorian **Enchanted Nights B&B,** 29 Wentworth St., Kittery 03904, 207/439-1489, www.enchantednights .org. Innkeepers Peter Lamandia and Nancy Bogenberger have eight guest rooms, two with whirlpools; one of the whirlpool rooms also has a fireplace. Pets are welcome. Year-round rates for the French country–style rooms range from $60–275, with seasonal and holiday variations.

Eliot

Climb a steep, secluded driveway off Rte. 101, 4.5 miles west of Rte. 1, and suddenly you're at **High Meadows Bed & Breakfast,** 4 Brixham Rd., Rte. 101, Eliot 03903, 207/439-0590, the antiques-filled 1736 home of Elaine Michaud. Four rooms have private baths, some have canopied four-poster beds. Lots of comfortable corners for relaxing, including the renovated barn. No pets, no children under 12, and smoking only on the terrace. Complimentary afternoon refreshments. If the atmosphere sways you and a loved one, Elaine's a justice of the peace. Open Apr.–Oct., rates run $85–95 d.

Family-friendly **Farmstead Bed & Breakfast,** 999 Goodwin Rd., Rte. 101, Eliot 03903, 207/748-3145, www.farmstead.qpg.com, even provides coloring placemats to entertain kids during the sumptuous breakfast. Innkeeper John Lippincott, an Air Force retiree, specializes in cheese strata and seven kinds of pancakes. Six guest rooms, $75–100 d, have private baths and air-conditioning. Outside are horseshoes, badminton, a play area, a hammock, a gas grill, and a butterfly garden. Children and pets are welcome. The bed-and-breakfast is six miles west of I-95, near the junction between Rtes. 101 and 236. Open all year.

FOOD

Kittery

Fancy dining isn't a Kittery specialty— there's plenty of that within walking distance in Portsmouth (New Hampshire) or driving distance in York. If you came to Maine to eat lobster, though, Kittery has three good spots for a quick fix. **Chauncey Creek Lobster Pier,** 16 Chauncey Creek Rd., off Rte. 103, Kittery Point 03905, 207/439-1030, has the least pretense and the most character. Grab a table overlooking tidal Chauncey Creek and the woods on the close-in opposite shore. Open daily Mother's Day weekend through Columbus Day, 11 AM–8 PM, after Labor Day to 7 PM, and closed Mon. BYOL. Also in Kittery Point is **Cap'n Simeon's Galley,** 90 Pepperrell Rd., Rte. 103, Kittery Point 03905, 207/439-3655, serving lunch, dinner, and Sunday brunch. Seafood and a spectacular view are the draws here. Nothing particularly unusual—just decent cooking at reasonable prices, and a casual atmosphere conducive to bringing the kids. Fried clams are particularly tasty (market price), and young ones go for the burgers, dogs, subs, and fries. Open daily at 11 AM in summer for lunch and dinner; closed Tues. fall and spring seasons; in winter open Thurs.–Sun. Built on pilings at the edge of the Piscataqua River, **Warren's Lobster House,** 11 Water St., Rte. 1, Kittery 03904, 207/439-1630, www.lobsterhouse.com, began life as a diner in 1940 and has been packing them in ever since. The 60-item salad bar is the proverbial meal in itself. Basic seafood, moderate prices, ample portions, river view, so-so service. Lobster *stuffed with lobster* is a specialty. Open daily 11:30 AM–8:30 PM (to 9 PM Fri.–Sat.).

The best **breakfast** spot is the **Sunrise Grill,** 182 State Rd., Rte. 1, Kittery Traffic Circle, Kittery 03904, 207/439-5748, where you can order waffles, granola, omelettes, or Diana's benedict ($7.25) 6:30 AM–2 PM. Lots of salads, sandwiches, and burgers on the lunch menu, from 11 AM.

If clams are high on your must-have list, you can't do much better than **Bob's Clam Hut,** 315 Rte. 1, Kittery 03904, 207/439-4233, www.bobsclamhut.com, next to the Kittery Trading Post. Using vegetable oil for frying, they turn out everything from scallops to shrimp to calamari to, of course, clams. The Fishwich, five ounces of deep-fried haddock on a bulky roll, with a choice of toppings, is $6.95. And the tartar sauce is their secret weapon. For dessert, there's Ben & Jerry's ice cream. Unlike most lobster pounds and clam shacks, Bob's is open all year, from 11 AM.

For **picnic fare,** pick up a sandwich or salad at the Sunrise Grill or head down Rte. 1 to the bustling **Golden Harvest** (open 9 AM–6:30 PM Mon.–Sat., Sun. to 5 PM) and pick up fruit to accompany lunch specials or a *sfogiatelle* from **Terra Cotta Pasta Company,** directly across Rte. 1. Terra Cotta also sells a near-infinite variety of pasta and sauces in quantity, and is open Mon. 10 AM–6 PM, Tues.–Sat. 9 AM–6:30 PM, and Sun. noon–5 PM. It's a canard that you can't find a bialy in Maine. At **Beach Pea Baking Co.,** 53 State Rd., Rte. 1, 207/439-3555, two types of bialys are part of a wide selection of artisan breads, cakes, and sandwiches, made from ingredients like unbleached or bromated flours, Belgian chocolate, and meats roasted on the premises, available Tues.–Sat. 7:30 AM–6 PM. Or take Rte. 103 to **Frisbee's 1828 Market,** 207/439-0014, in Kittery Point, an experience in itself. Established in 1828, the store has marginally modernized but still earns its label as North America's oldest family store—run by the fifth generation of Frisbees. It's open daily 8 AM–7 PM.

SHOPPING

No question, you'll find bargains at the 120-plus factory outlets at the Kittery Outlets, P.O. Box 357, Kittery 03904, 888/548-8379, www.thekitteryoutlets.com—actually a bunch of mini-malls clustered along both sides of Rte. 1. All the household names are here: Bass, Calvin Klein, Eddie Bauer, J Crew, Mikasa, Esprit, Lenox, Timberland, Tommy Hilfiger, GAP, Villeroy & Boch, and a hundred more. All shops are open daily; hours tend to vary. For information, a free coupon book, or gift certificates, call, go to the website, or stop at one of four information centers: the Reebok Outlet Store at the Tidewater Mall, 207/439-5100; Tanger Outlet Center Mall Office, 207/439-6822; the Welcome Center at the Maine Outlet, 207/439-6666; or the Weathervane Seafood Restaurant, 207/439-0330. There's even the local version of famous Freeport outfitter L.L. Bean: the three-story **Kittery Trading Post,** 301 Rte. 1, P.O. Box 904, Kittery 03904, 888/587-6246, a 1930s-era sporting-goods emporium with 45,000 square feet of old-fashioned flavor and up-to-date wares. Addition of 30,000 more square feet, plus pedestrian walkways, sitting areas, and green space, should be complete in 2006. It's open Mon.–Sat. 9 AM–9 PM, Sun. 10 AM–6 PM. Try to avoid the outlets on weekends, when you might need to take a number for the try-on rooms. Most of the mini-malls have telephones; several have ATMs; all have restrooms.

INFORMATION

The **Greater York Region Chamber of Commerce,** 1 Stonewall La., York 03909, 207/363-4422, www.gatewaytomaine.org, includes the towns of Kittery, Eliot, South Berwick, York Beach, York Village, York Harbor, and Cape Neddick. In addition to the York Visitors' Center, there are two others, one at Short Sands Beach, and one at the Welcome Center at Kittery's Maine Outlet Mall. Kittery hours are: Sun.–Thurs. 10 AM–6 PM and Fri.–Sat. 10 AM–8 PM Jan.–Apr.; Mon.–Sat. 9 AM–8 PM, and Sun. 10 AM–6 PM May 1–Dec. 31.

GETTING AROUND

If you have your own plane, and want to fly in to do your outlet shopping, **Littlebrook Airpark** is located five miles from Portsmouth, New Hampshire, the first airport in Maine after crossing the New Hampshire border. In the town of Eliot, it's off Rte. 236 and Beech Road. Littlebrook is paved, lighted, has three instrument approaches, 10 individual hangars, and tiedowns. For more information, call 603/235-3000.

Inland York County

Several inland pockets in Maine's southwesternmost county too often go overlooked. The Wabanaki once summered here, sustaining themselves with salmon fishing and flourishing crops of corn and beans. The first Europeans who moved in revved up the agricultural output, established year-round trading centers, and built thriving sawmills (including the state's first) and shipbuilding wharves. The area once known as Old Berwick or Barwick incorporated in 1714 and gave birth to South Berwick in 1814 and North Berwick in 1831.

SOUTH BERWICK

Probably the best-known of the area's present-day communities is the riverside town of South Berwick—thanks to a historical and literary tradition dating back to the 17th century, and antique cemeteries to prove it. The 19th- and 20th-century novels of Sarah Orne Jewett and Gladys Hasty Carroll have lured many a contemporary visitor to explore their rural settings—an area aptly described by Carroll as "a small patch of earth continually occupied but never crowded for more than three hundred years."

Also here is the 150-acre hilltop campus of **Berwick Academy,** Maine's oldest prep

school, chartered in 1791 with John Hancock's signature. The coed school's handsome gray-stone William H. Fogg Memorial Library ("The Fogg") is named for the same family connected with Harvard's Fogg Art Museum. The highlight of the library is an incredible collection of dozens of 19th-century stained-glass windows, most designed by Victorian artist Sarah Wyman Whitman, who also designed jackets for Sarah Orne Jewett's books. Thanks to a diligent fundraising effort, the windows were recently restored to their former glory.

Sights and Recreation

Don't blink or you might miss the tiny sign outside the 1774 **Sarah Orne Jewett House,** 5 Portland St., Rtes. 4 and 236, South Berwick 03908, 207/384-2454, smack in the center of town. Park on the street and join one of the tours—you'll learn details of the Jewett family and its star, Sarah (1849–1909), author of *The Country of the Pointed Firs,* a New England classic. Books by and about Sarah are available in the gift shop. Open Fri.–Sun. 11 AM–5 PM June 1–Oct. 15. Tours begin on the hour—last one at 4 PM. Admission is $8 adults, $7 seniors, and $4 children 12 and under. The house is owned by the Boston-based Society for the Preservation of New England Antiquities

South Coast and Portland

© KATHLEEN M. BRANDES

Hamilton House

(SPNEA), also known as Historic New England, 603/436-3205, www.spnea.org.

Dramatically crowning a bluff overlooking the Salmon Falls River and flanked by handsome colonial revival gardens, 18th-century **Hamilton House,** 40 Vaughan's Ln., South Berwick 03908, 207/384-2454, evokes history and tradition. Like the Jewett House, the 35-acre site is owned by SPNEA. Knowledgeable guides relate the house's fascinating history. Open Wed.– Sun. 11 AM–5 PM June 1–Oct. 15. Tours begin only on the hour—last one at 4 PM. Admission is $8 adults, $7 seniors, and $4 children 12 and under. Each Sunday in July, SPNEA hosts **Sunday in the Garden,** a concert on the lawn. ($8 admission, including a free pass to come back and see the house). Pray for sun; the concert is moved indoors on rainy days. From Rte. 236 at the southern edge of South Berwick (watch for a signpost), turn left onto Brattle St. and take the second right onto Vaughan's Lane.

A path connects Hamilton House to adjoining **Vaughan Woods State Park,** 28 Oldfields Rd., South Berwick 03908, 207/384-5160, but it's not easy to find, and there's much more parking space at the main entrance to the 250-acre river's-edge preserve. Three miles of maintained trails wind through this underutilized park, and benches are scattered here and there. There's even a bench looking out over the river and Hamilton House. Picnic tables are located near the parking area, as are outhouses. Open Memorial Day weekend to Labor Day 9 AM–8 PM, but accessible all year. Admission is $2 adults, $1 children (5–11), free for seniors (over 65) and kids under five. As with directions for Hamilton House, take Brattle St. from Rte. 236. (Vine St. and Old South Rd., both off Rte. 236, also will get you there.) Turn left at Old Fields Rd. and continue to the park entrance. Both Hamilton House and Vaughan Woods are easy bike rides from downtown South Berwick along wide, flat Rte. 236.

Based in a onetime cotton-mill building known as the Counting House, the **Old Berwick Historical Society,** Liberty and Main Sts., Rte. 4, P.O. Box 296, South Berwick 03908, 207/384-8041 or 207/384-2251, sees a steady stream of genealogists looking for their roots in one of Maine's oldest settlements. Books and documents are only part of the museum's collection, which includes old photos and tools, boat models and nautical instruments, plus special annual exhibits. The 19th-century **Counting House** is open Sat.–Sun. 1–4 PM in July, Aug., and Sept., and also by appointment. Admission is free, but donations are welcomed.

Festivals and Events

The last Saturday of June, the **Strawberry Festival,** www.southberwickstrawberryfestival.com, is a longtime South Berwick tradition. Over 20,000 people come to enjoy the strawberry shortcake, high-end craft fair, entertainment, food, and fireworks. You can pitch in at Friday morning's "Hulling Party" at the Community Center on Norton Street, 8 AM to about 11 AM, depending on the number of volunteer hullers!

Accommodations

Once the headmaster's residence for nearby Berwick Academy, the elegant, turn-of-the-20th-century **Academy Street Inn Bed & Breakfast,** 15 Academy St., South Berwick 03908, 207/384-5633, boasts crystal chandeliers, leaded-glass windows, working fireplaces, and high-ceilinged rooms full of antiques. Paul and Lee Fopeano's handsome home has five rooms with private baths ($79–89 d). Full breakfast or afternoon lemonade on the 60-foot screened porch is a real treat. No pets, no smoking, no children under 10. Open all year.

Food

A local institution since 1960, **Fogarty's,** 471 Main St., South Berwick 03908, 207/384-8361, looks like your typical takeout place, but its claim to fame is the freshest of fish, lightly fried and not dripping with grease. Opens at 11 AM all year for lunch and dinner, closed Mon.

Information and Services

The best source of local information is the South Berwick Town Office, 180 Main St., South Berwick 03908, 207/384-3300, open all year Mon., Tues., and Fri. 9 AM–5 PM; Thurs. 9 AM–6 PM; closed Wed.

NORTH BERWICK AND BERWICK

As with South Berwick, these historic communities are prime exploration territory for architecture and history buffs—as well as anyone interested in Maine's less crowded corners.

North Berwick

From South Berwick northward along Rte. 4, rolling fields line the roads, and the distinctive summit of Mt. Agamenticus punctures the horizon off to the east. The road is wide and flat—a good cycling route.

In downtown North Berwick, **Lumpy's Pizza & Subs,** Elm St., Rte. 4, North Berwick 03906, 207/676-9020, has picnic tables alongside the unpronounceable Nequtaquet River—right around the corner from the thundering falls on the Great Works River. After your pizza, try one of the 32 Shain's ice-cream flavors. Open daily year-round, 11 AM–9 PM (8 PM in winter).

Berwick

Theatergoers head to the Berwick area for the long-running (since 1972) **Hackmatack Playhouse,** 538 School St. (Rte. 9), Berwick 03901, 207/698-1807, www.hackmatack.org, midway between North Berwick and Berwick. The popular summer theater, based in a renovated barn reminiscent of a past era; has 8 PM performances (comedies and musical comedies) Tues.–Sat. and a 2 PM matinee Thursday. The ambience is relaxed and casual but quality is high, though it's a non-Equity house. From mid-July–mid-Aug., professional-level children's plays go on at 10 AM Fri. and Sat., when all seats are $6. The Hackmatack season runs late June–early Sept. Tickets are $20; discounts for seniors and students except Sat.

ALFRED

The shire town, or county seat, of York County, Alfred (named, incredibly, for Alfred the Great) also has a long history, having broken away from Sanford, five miles to its south, in 1794. The courthouse here (Kennebunk and Main Sts.) claims the nation's oldest court records, dating from 1636.

Festivals and Events

July's **Alfred Festival Day,** an annual community extravaganza, starts with a pancake breakfast and ends with a band concert. In between are a parade, entertainment, bean supper, book sale, food booths, and a craft sale.

Information

Alfred has no chamber of commerce, so the best source of tourism information is the **Town Office,** Saco Rd., opposite the green, Alfred 04002, 207/324-5872, open weekdays, with a noon closing on Fridays. For quickie questions on weekends, try the **Alfred Country Store,** across the street, 207/324-7719.

OTHER AREA ATTRACTIONS

Waterboro Barrens Preserve

Four miles north of Alfred, Waterboro town was incorporated in 1797. In the far northwestern corner of the town limits is one of The Nature Conservancy's newest and least-visited holdings. Central feature of the Waterboro Barrens Preserve is a rare forest of northeastern pitch pine. Easy-to-moderate loop trails provide access to the 2,140-acre pine barrens—where you're apt to spot deer, moose, ruffed grouse, and rare moths and butterflies. The preserve is open year-round for day use only, closing at sunset. Admission is free. No pets or smoking. From downtown Waterboro (Rte. 4/202), take West Rd. six miles west/northwest to Newfield Rd.; turn right and go one mile to Lake Sherburne Rd. Turn right, go one mile to Buff Brook Rd. Turn left, go to the parking lot on the left at end of road. For additional information, contact the Maine chapter of The Nature Conservancy, 14 Maine St., Fort Andross, Brunswick 04011, 207/729-5181.

Willowbrook Museum Village

About six miles northwest of the Waterboro Barrens Preserve (via Newfield Rd.) is tiny Newfield, probably best known for the fascinating 19th-century museum/village known as Willowbrook Museum Village, Main St., just north of Rte. 11, Newfield 04056, 207/793-2784. Plan to spend several hours here, exploring the 37 buildings listed on the National Register of Historic Places. What's to see? A carriage house, firehouse, country store, schoolhouse, a magnificently restored carousel, and incredible collections of farm tools, toys, sewing machines, and musical instruments. Bring a picnic and camera and soak up the history. Open Memorial Day weekend through Columbus Day, daily 10 AM–5 PM. Admission is $8.50 adults, $4 children 6–18, free for kids under six. The gift shop, called Christmas Etcetera, is open daily 11 AM–5 PM from Memorial Day to Columbus Day, thereafter Wed.–Sun. 11 AM–4 PM until Dec. 23.

Also on Main Street just before Willowbrook, is **Barnswallow Pottery,** Elm St., Newfield 04056, 207/793-8044, Barbara O'Brien's barn-based shop. In addition to antiques and Barbara's superb pottery, the shop carries unusual garden art. The shop is open daily in summer 9 AM–5 PM, then weekends through Christmas. This is a small operation, so if you're making a special trip, call ahead to be sure someone will be home.

Back Country Excursions of Maine

Here's major fun for the fat-tire set. Located northwest of Waterboro, Back Country Excursions, 42 Woodward Rd., Parsonsfield 04047, 207/625-8189, www.bikebackcountry.com, has been the state's premier mountain-biking center since 1991. Close-to-Renaissance man Cliff Krolick takes small groups—from neophytes to pros—pedaling over a combined total of 70 miles of logging roads and handmade singletrack. He can keep you going three days without retracing your route. Best of all, he contributes part of his proceeds to environmental causes. Everything's ultra-casual at his rustic, hostel-style lodge, set on a knoll amid 12 acres—adjoining 10,000 acres of public lands. Everyone pitches in here, and the camaraderie is contagious. The hot tub is a welcome magnet at the end of a biking day. Accommodations range from three lodge rooms (sharing two baths) to a 20-foot-diameter yurt (with thick mattresses) to campsites with water. Packages—two nights plus breakfast, lunch, and biking—range $130–170. A half-day biking tour, guided by Cliff, is $20; a full day is $35, including lunch. Mountain-bike rentals are $30 a day; or you can bring your own.

CORNISH

At York County's northernmost inland boundary, Cornish is a charming little town incorporated as Francisborough in 1791. Local historians boast that in the 1850s many of the splendid homes on the main drag were moved by oxen from other parts of town to be close to the stagecoach route.

A great time to visit Cornish is the last Saturday in September, when the annual **Apple Festival,** 207/625-7447, www.cornish-maine .org, held in downtown Cornish, celebrates the area's major crop with music, a crafts fair, and even an apple-pie contest. You can overdose all day on apples and stock up for winter, and do it just as fall foliage is starting to appear. For a spectacular panorama of fall colors along the Ossipee and Saco River Valleys, drive up Towles Hill Rd. (left turn, just west of town).

In the genuinely quaint downtown, shops worth a stop include the **Cornish Trading Company,** 19 Main St., Rte. 25, Cornish 04020, 207/625-8387, a terrific group antiques shop in the handsome Masonic build-

ing. Variety and price range are broad. Open Wed.–Mon. 10 AM–5 PM, Apr.–Oct., weekends till mid-Dec. Around the corner, at 3 Maple St., is **Cornish Hardware,** Maine's oldest continuously operating hardware store. Nearby is **The Bag Lady** factory and store, 16 Old Pike Rd., just off Rte. 25, Cornish 04020, 207/625-8421, a local firm that's gone big-time, marketing Cornish-made handbags and luggage nationally in elegant shops and catalogs. The shop is open daily in summer 10 AM–4 PM, shorter hours off season.

Best source of local information is the Cornish **Town Office,** Maple St., Rte. 25, Cornish 04020, 207/625-4324, fax 207/625-4416. Closed Thurs., open other weekdays all year, but hours vary. Call ahead. On weekends, stop in at any of the local shops and restaurants.

The Yorks

Four villages with distinct personalities—upscale York Harbor, historic York Village, casual York Beach, and semirural Cape Neddick—make up the Town of York. First inhabited by Native Americans, who named it Agamenticus, the area was settled as early as 1624—so history is serious business here. Town high points were the founding, by Sir Ferdinando Gorges, and the arrival of well-to-do vacationers in the 19th century. In between were Indian massacres, economic woes, and population shuffles. Today the town has a winter population of about 10,000 Yorkies; in summer, though, that explodes to 40,000 (pretty obvious in July and August, when you're searching for a free patch of York Beach sand).

History and genealogy buffs can study the headstones in the Old Burying Ground or comb the archives of the Old York Historical Society. For lighthouse fans, there's Cape Neddick Light Station ("Nubble Light") and, six miles offshore, Boon Island. You can go to the top of Mt. Agamenticus for a spectacular view, board a deep-sea fishing boat in York

Harbor, or spend an hour hiking the Cliff Path in York Harbor. For the kids, there's a zoo, a lobsterboat cruise, a taffymaker, or, of course, back to the beach.

SIGHTS
Nubble Light at Sohier Park
The best-known photo op in York is the distinctive 1879 lighthouse known formally as Cape Neddick Light Station and familiarly as **"The Nubble."** Although there's no access to the lighthouse's island, Sohier Park Welcome Center (with restrooms and volunteer-staffed gift shop) provides the perfect viewpoint. Parking is limited, but the turnover is fairly good. Not a bad idea, however, to walk from the Long Sands parking area or come by bike, even though the road has inadequate shoulders. Weekdays, this is also a popular spot for scuba divers. The center is open daily 10 AM–8 PM, Memorial Day weekend–mid-Oct. It's on Nubble Rd., off Rte. 1A, between Long and Short Sands Beaches, York Beach, 207/363-3569.

THE YORKS

To Mt Agamenticus

To Ogunquit

To Ogunquit

To Portland

AGAMENTICUS RD

To Portland

95 TURNPIKE

Chases Pond

RIVER

RD

SHORE

RD

Cape Neddick

Cape

Cape Neddick Beach

Neddick River

MAIN

ST

OCEAN

AVE

ANIMAL PARK RD

RAILROAD AVE

Short Sands Beach

OCEAN AVE EXT

ROGERS RD

YORK'S WILD KINGDOM ★

RAILROAD AVE EXT

Pond

BEACON ST

RD

BROADWAY

NUBBLE RD

SOHIER PARK ★ ★

CHASES

RIDGE RD

OLD POST RD

Long Sands Beach

NUBBLE LIGHT

95

1

York Beach

1A

I-95 ACCESS RD

Long Sands Beach

RD

SANDS

■ **VISITOR CENTER**

ATLANTIC OCEAN

To New Hampshire

1A

YORK

LONG

ST

Lobster Cove

OLD YORK HISTORICAL SOCIETY

ORGANUG RD

BARRELL LN

LINDSAY RD

ST

SENTRY HILL RD

WOODBRIDGE RD

YORK ST

Barrells Mill Pond

Steedman Woods

York Harbor

WIGGLY BRIDGE

★ **SAYWARD-WHEELER HOUSE**

York River

103

Bragdon Island

Harbor Beach

★ **CLIFF PATH**

York Harbor

ORGANUG RD

Harris Island

Stage Neck

To New Hampshire

HARRIS ISLAND RD

0   0.5 mi

0   0.5 km

MOON

© AVALON TRAVEL PUBLISHING, INC.

Old York Historical Society

Based in York Village, the Old York Historical Society, 207 York St. (Rte. 1A), York 03909, 207/363-4974, www.oldyork.org, is the driving force behind a collection of eight colonial and post-colonial buildings (plus a research library) open from early June to Columbus Day weekend. Start at Jefferds' Tavern Visitor Center, Lindsay Rd. and York St. (Rte. 1A), 207/363-4703, where you'll need to purchase tickets for visiting the museum buildings. Free parking is available next to the tavern. Nearby are the Old Gaol and the one-room Schoolhouse (both fun for kids), and the Emerson-Wilcox House. Don't miss the Old Burying Ground, dating from 1735, across the street (rubbings are a no-no). About 0.5 mile down Lindsay Road, on the York River, are the John Hancock Warehouse, where visitors can experience York's seafaring past, and the George Marshall Store Gallery (140 Lindsay Rd.), now operated as a respected contemporary-art gallery. Across the river is the Elizabeth Perkins House, with its recently restored garden. Antiques buffs shouldn't miss the Wilcox and Perkins Houses. Visit some or all of the buildings, at your own pace—no one leads you from one to another. At 196 York St., across from the jail, is the well-stocked Museum Shop (open May–Dec., 10 AM–5 PM Mon.–Sat., closed Sun.). The museum buildings are open Mon.–Sat. 10 AM–5 PM, closed Sun., early June–Columbus Day weekend. Admission is $10 adults, $9 seniors, $5 children (6–16), and $20 for a family. AAA discounts and single building and group rates available.

Sayward-Wheeler House

Owned by the Boston-based Society for the Preservation of New England Antiquities (SPNEA, also called Historic New England), the 1718 Sayward-Wheeler House, 79 Barrell Lane Extension, York Harbor 03911, 207/384-2454, www.spnea.org, occupies a prime site at the edge of York Harbor. In the house are lots of period furnishings—all in pristine condition. The house is open 11 AM–5 PM, June–Oct., on the first Sat. of the month. Tours are on the hour (last tour at 4 PM). Admission is $5 adults, $4 seniors, $2.50 children 12 and under. Take Rte. 1A to Lilac Lane (Rte. 103) to Barrell Lane, then to Barrell Lane Extension.

York's Wild Kingdom

More than 250 animals—tigers, zebras, llamas, deer, lions, elephants, and monkeys—call York's Wild Kingdom home. It's not a state-of-the-art zoo, but it keeps the kids entertained, as does the 90-foot super slide in the amusement-park section. Between the zoo and the rides, it's easy to spend a day here. You can buy a ticket to the zoo, or a combination ticket for the zoo and amusement park. Zoo open daily, weather permitting, from Saturday of Memorial Day weekend through Labor Day. Rates and hours vary widely, call or check website. Located at 23 Railroad Ave., York Beach 03910, 207/363-4911 or 800/456-4911, www.yorkzoo.com. There's also an entrance on Rte. 1, two miles north of I-95's exit 7.

Spooky Sightseeing

Flickering candles and a black-hooded guide get you right in the spirit of things during imaginative evening walking tours of historic York village. **Ghostly Tours,** 250 York St., Rte. 1A, York 03909, 207/363-0000, specializes in ghost stories and 18th-century folklore during its hour-long meanders through burial grounds in the oldest part of town. (Even the phone number is weird.) The candlelight tour begins at 8 PM Tues.–Sat., late June–Labor Day; at 7 PM Fri. and Sat. Sept.–Oct. Cost is $10 per person.

PARKS AND RECREATION

The York Parks and Recreation Department, 186 York St., York 03909, 207/363-1040, www.yorkmaine.org, is a dynamic operation that organizes and sponsors races, tournaments, camps, kayaking, fitness sessions, children's events, and outdoor programs. Plus it supervises the local beaches. Registration for activities may be done in person at the Grant House, Rte. 1, York, or by phone, beginning June 1. York residents have first priority, so some things fill up quickly, but it's worth sending for a copy of the annual Summer Program Guide (available mid-May) to consider the many possibilities.

Walk the Walks

A less strenuous route is known variously as the **Shore Path, Harbor Walk,** or **Fisherman's Walk,** running west along the harbor and river from Stage Neck Road (next to Edwards' Harborside Inn) and passing the Sayward-Wheeler House before crossing the tiny, green-painted Wiggly Bridge—the shortest suspension bridge in the United States—leading into the **Steedman Woods** preserve. Carry binoculars for good boat-watching and birding in the 16-acre preserve, owned by the Old York Historical Society. A one-mile double-loop trail takes less than an hour of easy strolling.

Swimming

Sunbathing and swimming are big draws in York, with four beaches of varying sizes and accessibility. Bear in mind that traffic can be gridlocked along the beachfront (Rte. 1A) in midsummer, so it may take longer than you expect to get anywhere. **Lifeguards** are on duty mid-June–Labor Day 9:30 AM–4 PM at Short Sands Beach, Long Beach, and Harbor Beach, and bathhouses are open daily 9 AM–7 PM in midsummer. The biggest parking space (metered) is at Long Sands, but that 1.5-mile beach also draws the most customers. Scarcest parking is at Harbor Beach, near the Stage Neck Inn, and at Cape Neddick Beach, near the Ogunquit town line.

Mount Agamenticus

Drive to the summit of Mt. Agamenticus and you're at York County's highest point. It's only 692 feet, but it offers panoramic views of ocean, lakes, woods, and sometimes the White Mountains. At the top are a billboard map of the hiking-trail network and a curious memorial to St. Aspinquid, a 17th-century Algonquian Indian leader. Mountain biking is hugely popular on Agamenticus. Take a picnic, a kite,

and binoculars. In the fall, if the wind's from the northwest, watch for migrating hawks; in winter, bring a sled for the best downhill run in southern Maine. Contact the **York Parks and Recreation Department,** 207/363-1040, for info about the trail rides and other activities at the mountain park. Fortunately, in recent years, conservationists have been particularly active here, saving thousands of acres from development. The efforts continue. From Rte. 1 in Cape Neddick, take Mountain Rd. (also called Agamenticus Rd.) 4.2 miles west to the access road.

Bicycling

Rent a bike from **Berger's Bike Shop,** 241 York St., York 03909, 207/363-4070, and you'll probably get around faster in July and August than you would by car. An especially scenic bike route runs eight or nine miles along Rte. 103—very winding, not always well shouldered, but mostly level—from York Village to Kittery Point and Kittery. It's wiser to return the same way, rather than make a loop via Rte. 1, unless you're not intimidated by zooming traffic and shoulder drop-offs. Or cross over I-95 on Rte. 103 and continue the loop via Martin Road.

Beached Wheels, Rte. 1A (near Short Sands Beach), York Beach 03910, 207/363-8021, rents scooters for $25 for the first hour, less for each hour after that. Riders must be over 18. Bike rentals are available for all ages at $5 per hour, $20 per day. Helmets are offered to all, but riders under 16 must wear them. Most credit cards accepted. Open May–Oct., weekends till mid-June, then Mon.–Fri. 10 AM–6 PM.

Getting Afloat

If overdosing on lobsters makes you want to see how they're caught, contact **Capt. Dan Gile,** 207/408-1194, www.budmar.com, who'll take you on a 50-minute tour in the *Holly B,* his 30-foot Down East–style fiberglass lobsterboat, and maybe even let you take the helm. Reservations are advisable, though not necessary. Cost is $12 adult, $11 senior, $8 child, with free parking. Visit the restroom before you board. Departures are on the hour, 8 AM–4 PM Mon.–Fri., June, July, and Aug., check for hours in Apr., May, Sept., and Oct. The lobster trip, and charters or sunset trips with Capt. Gile, leave from Town Dock #2, Harris Island Rd., off Rte. 103 in York Harbor.

Capt. Tom Farnon, 207/363-3234, does private charters by appointment—"anything you'd like to do, from cruising and viewing lighthouses, to fishing with your own gear." Trips accommodate up to six passengers, at a rate of $50 per hour.

For **deep-sea fishing,** also out of Town Dock #2, contact **Capt. Bill Coite,** 207/363-5324. His 22-foot *Shearwater* departs daily at 7:30 AM in July and Aug., for either a full or a half day, to fish for striped bass, bluefish, or mackerel—"mostly stripers." Cost, for a maximum of four people, is $300 for a half day, $350 full. Gear and bait provided; be sure to pack warm clothes, wear sunblock, and don rubber-soled shoes.

Capt. Richard Witham, 207/363-6526, www.mainelyfishingcharterservice.com, takes private charters fishing for bass, bluefish, and mackerel on the 35-ft *Linesider II* in spring, fall, and summer. Additionally, in summer he will take mixed groups of up to six people ($50 pp) on twice-daily trips, 7 AM–noon and 12:30–5 PM. Private charters are $300. Reservations are advisable. Leaves from Town Dock #2.

Capt. Dave Gittins, 207/363-3874, www .maineflyfishing.net, runs **FishTale Charters,** a "strictly charter" operation specializing in fly fishing in a 16-foot Maritime skiff. He will accommodate light-tackle anglers, but does not provide bait. From late May–mid-Oct., the price for one or two people (two is the maximum) to go after striped bass, bluefish, and mackerel is $350 for a full day, $300 for half.

Harbor Adventures, Town Dock #2, P.O. Box 345, York Harbor 03911, 207/363-8466, www.harboradventures.com, offers standard and custom sea-kayak and bike adventures. The Lobster Luncheon includes a paddle in Chauncey Creek and around Kittery Point, and costs $67.

ENTERTAINMENT

Many York restaurants have dinner music or evening entertainment in summer, plus there are concerts in Ellis Park almost every evening in July and August, from 7–9 PM.

For first-rate professional theater, you can't do better than the famed Ogunquit Playhouse, next town north on Rte. 1.

FESTIVALS AND EVENTS

Each year, York produces a *Calendar of Events,* listing activities galore for summer and beyond. It used to be poster size, but now takes up a small book. For a copy (after May 1), contact the Greater York Region Chamber of Commerce, 1 Stonewall La., York 03909, 207/363-4422, www.gatewaytomaine.org. Listed are band concerts, church suppers, walking tours, berry festivals, book sales, art shows, and museum events. Scarcely a day goes by without something on the calendar. In June, Maine's artisans and products are celebrated at the two-day **Made in Maine Products & Seafood Festival.** From late July into early August, **York Days** enliven the town for over a week with fireworks, sports tournaments, sandcastle sculpting, a road race, Walk for Hope, concerts, craft fair, and dog show. One highlight is a Christmas in July celebration at York Beach's Sohier Park, with the Nubble decorated in Christmas lights, and music by the Seacoast Wind Ensemble.

York Village and York Beach's **Annual Harvestfest** takes place 10 AM–4 PM the weekend after Columbus Day and combines colonial crafts and cooking demonstrations, museum tours, entertainment, an ox roast, and beanhole beans. In the evenings, there is a Pumpkin Stroll and a Chocolate Lover's Fling. This is one of the town's most popular events; most activities are free.

SHOPPING

If you're looking for factory outlets, head south on Rte. 1 to Kittery, for more than 120

South Coast and Portland

of them. But York has some unique shopping options of its own.

Gifts and Antiques

York Village Marketplace, 211 York St., Rte. 1A, York 03909, 207/363-4830, www.yorkvillagemarketplace.com, is a group shop with 100 dealer spaces in a c. 1834 historic church. A full spectrum of merchandise includes antiques, crafts, vintage clothes, and model trains. There's lots of tasteful stuff; you can bet you won't leave empty-handed. It's open daily 9:30 AM–5:30 PM, except for Easter, Thanksgiving, and Christmas.

Quilters and quilt lovers will find custom made quilts and 3,000 bolts of fabric at **Knight's, A Working Quilt & Gift Shop,** 1901 Rte. 1, Cape Neddick 03902, 207/361-2500, www.mainequiltshop.com. Closed Tues., open Sun. noon–5 PM, the rest of the week 10 AM–5 PM.

Everything in **Woods to Goods,** 891 Rte. 1, York 03909, 207/363-6001 or 888/966-3724, www.WoodsToGoods.com, comes from inmate woodworkers in Maine and beyond, plus the shop carries Oregon's Prison Blues jeans. Quality and price vary widely, with some genuine bargains and some near-kitsch. Open 10 AM–6 PM daily, but closing at 5 PM between the spring and fall time changes.

Fiona's Porch, 7 York St., York 03909, 207/363-6270, www.fionasporch.com, was named after the niece of one of the owners—before she was even born. The shop is an artful blend of old and new home and garden furnishings, accessories, and gifts. There are lots of handmade pieces, and the stock changes regularly. Holiday workshops are held in December. Open daily, 10 AM–5 PM.

It's hard to know whether Food or Gifts is the right category for **Stonewall Kitchen,** Stonewall Lane, York 03909, 207/351-2713 or 800/207-5267, www.stonewallkitchen .com. This phenomenally successful company has mushroomed from a two-person farmers-market gig to a mammoth award-winning year-round retail and catalog operation famous for imaginative condiments (there are

20 jams) and other food products, about 140 in all. The packages are as outstanding as the tastes. The headquarters building—including a handsome shop with tasting areas, a "viewing gallery" where you can watch it all happen, and a café—is on Stonewall Ln., next to the Yorks Chamber of Commerce building, just off Rte. 1. The viewing gallery is open Mon.–Fri. 9 AM–4 PM, while the store is open Mon.–Thurs. 8 AM–6 PM, Fri. and Sat. 8 AM–7 PM, Sun. 9 AM–6 PM. A café has been added, serving breakfast and lunch to enjoy on premises or take out. In summer, there's a pergola to sit under.

A good spot for unexpected "finds" is **Dusted Things and Daisies,** 69 Old Post Rd., York 03909, 207/363-5929. Since 1998, veteran dealer Lee Regan Jacks has operated this antiques and collectibles shop out of the first floor of her house—a large open area painted to suit the wares. Open Thurs.–Sat. 9 AM–4 PM, May–Oct.

ACCOMMODATIONS

York Harbor

All of the York Harbor lodgings described below are within easy walking distance of Harbor Beach.

You can't miss the **Stage Neck Inn,** 8 Stage Neck Rd., P.O. Box 70, York Harbor 03911, 207/363-3850 or 800/222-3238, www.Stage-Neck.com, occupying its own private peninsula overlooking York Harbor. Modern, resort-style facilities include two pools, tennis courts, fitness center, and spectacular views from balconies and terraces. The formal Harbor Porches restaurant (no jeans; entrées in the low $20s) and the casual Sandpiper Bar & Grille are open to the public. Three-night minimum July, Aug., and holiday weekends, two-night minimum off-season weekends. Rates are $245–255 d (beach-view rooms) and $315–350 d (ocean-view rooms) mid-May–Labor Day, $145–260 d other months (special packages available). No smoking, no pets. Open all year.

Tanglewood Hall, 611 York St., P.O. Box 490, York Harbor 03911, 207/351-1075, has a country-inn feel in an in-town setting. Relax on the broad veranda (or enjoy your Big Breakfast there) and you'll understand. In the spring of 2000, Bill and Bonnie Alstrom bought this former "designer show house," retaining some of the decorators' intriguing features (wonderful painted floors) and adding their own unique touches (a tranquil meditation corner). Six rooms and suites have lots of antiques, wireless Internet access, robes, and journals for comments. Rates are $125–250 d. No smoking, no pets, no children under 12. Open May–Oct.

High on a pretty hill, Paul and Donna Archibald's **Chapman Cottage,** 370 York St., P.O. Box 575, York Harbor 03911, 207/363-2059, www.ChapmanCottageBandB.com, takes the bed-and-breakfast concept to a very high level. The five rooms include two suites with fireplaces in both the huge bed/sitting room, *and* the Jacuzzi bathroom. There are balconies and pleasant common spaces, plus luxuries like turndown service, nightly port and truffles, and fruit baskets on arrival. Rates are $150–250 May–Oct., $100–250 Nov.–Apr. Pets are not permitted, but children over 12 are. Paul is a chef, and an experiment with serving dinner proved so successful that there is now a Chapman Cottage restaurant with a full liquor license, nice wines, and casually elegant dinners, from filet of beef with béarnaise sauce to seafood risotto (lobster, shrimp, and scallops). Full dinners range from $20–30, and are served nightly, 5–10 PM May–Oct; off season, 5–9 PM Thurs.–Sat.

York Harbor Inn, Rte. 1A, P.O. Box 573, York Harbor 03911, 207/363-5119 or 800/343-3869, www.yorkharborinn.com, is an in-town spot with a country-inn flavor and a wide variety of room and package-plan options ($89–299, depending on room, season, specials) throughout the year. The oldest section dates from the 17th century. All 47 rooms have phones and air-conditioning; some have decks, fireplaces, and whirlpools. The glass-walled dining room has an ocean view, and continental entrées from $17–29. The lower-level pub, the **Cellar Pub Grill,** is a favorite local watering hole, featuring live entertainment.

Since 1984, hospitable Sue Antal has operated the **Inn at Harmon Park,** 415 York St., P.O. Box 495, York Harbor 03911, 207/363-2031, a 14-room "cottage" just a block from the water. Having run the chamber of commerce and devoted many hours to community organizations, Sue's a great touring resource. (She's also a justice of the peace, with a price that's right and a long string of weddings under her belt.) In 2000, she turned the tables at her bed-and-breakfast: It's open Sept.–May rather than during the summer, when she rents the entire cottage by the week. Four comfortable guest rooms and a suite have private baths. Rates are $79–129 d. Breakfast is a creative treat, sometimes served on the porch. No credit cards, no smoking, no children under 12. Open all year.

Though not in York Harbor's postal zone, **Dockside Guest Quarters,** P.O. Box 205, York 03909, 207/363-2868, fax 363-1977, faces Stage Neck from Harris Island in the harbor. The Lusty family's inn, on seven prime acres, has five guest rooms in its 1885 Maine House and 16 rooms and suites in four modern buildings with unbeatable views. Everything's open and airy, with a tinge of yachtiness and less formality than the Stage Neck. Bikes and canoes available for guests; marina facilities for boat-owners. Rates range from $130–260 d in season. Kids 12 and under are free in suites and studios. Two-night minimum July, Aug., and Labor Day weekends. No smoking, no pets. Dockside is open early May–late Oct.; eight rooms are available on winter weekends ($100–125 d). The **Restaurant at Dockside,** 207/363-2722, is open to the public for lunch and dinner Tues.–Sun., Memorial Day weekend to mid-Oct., specializing in American contemporary dining. Try for a table on the harbor-view screened deck.

York Beach

The Anchorage Inn, 265 Long Beach Ave., P.O. Box 1329, York Beach 03910, 207/363-5112, www.anchorageinn.com, is close to York

Beach's ground zero, so be prepared for plenty of action. The family resort's 178 modern, motel-style rooms are across the street from Long Sands Beach, but set back a bit for relief from traffic sounds. (The Atrium building, in back, has less street noise but more noise from the interior pool.) Rates are $61–372 d. Facilities include handicapped-accessible rooms, indoor and outdoor pools, fitness center, and restaurant (right on the beach, open daily 9 AM–9 PM in season, closed early in the year). The highest-priced spa suites have private whirlpools. No pets. Open all year.

Everything's casual and flowers are everywhere at the brightly painted **Katahdin Inn,** 11 Ocean Ave. Ext., P.O. Box 193, York Beach 03910, 207/363-1824 (or 363-9625 off season). Built as an inn in 1865, and overlooking the breakers of Short Sands Beach, the inn's classic summer porch feels close enough to dive from. Rae and Bob LeBlanc's eleven first-, second-, and third-floor rooms (nine with water views) have lots of four-poster beds. Private and shared baths. Breakfast is not included, but coffee is always available, the rooms have refrigerators, and several eateries are nearby. Rooms cost $95–125 d, 75–95 off season. No smoking. Open all year.

Barbara and Michael Sheff's **Candleshop Inn,** 44 Freeman St., P.O. Box 1216, York Beach 03910, 207/363-4087 or 888/363-4087, www.CandleshopInn.com, has welcomed guest to York Beach for at least a century, and was once a candle shop. Barbara teaches yoga on the deck and can provide anything needed to use the inn as a holistic retreat center. Of the ten rooms, with shared and private baths, seven have ocean views. The beach is within walking distance, and there is an all-you-can-eat vegetarian breakfast. Families are welcome. Rates are $80–115.

Cape Neddick

Innkeeper Dianne Goodwin is far too young to be anyone's grandmother, but you'll feel like a privileged grandchild at the **Cape Neddick House Bed-and-Breakfast,** 1300 Rte. 1, P.O. Box 70, Cape Neddick 03902, 207/363-2500, www.capeneddickhouse.com. No need for lunch after a breakfast here—and you can even come to Dianne's cooking classes and culinary weekends, or arrange for a six-course dinner cooked on a woodstove. The inn is right on busy Rte. 1, yet out back are 10 acres of gardens and woods for walkers and bird-watchers. Family antiques fill this homey place, which has been in the Goodwin family since it was built in 1885. Five air-conditioned guest rooms (with private baths) are named after New England states. Rates are $100–150 d, lower off-season. No pets, no children under six. Open all year.

Seasonal Rentals

Several companies manage week- or month-long rental properties, usually houses or condos. Weekly rentals begin and end on Saturday. Best is **Seaside Vacation Rentals,** Meadowbrook Plaza, 647 Rte. 1, P.O. Box 2000, York 03909, 207/363-1825, fax 351-1091, a long-time family-operated firm with more than 450 properties in the Yorks, Ogunquit, Wells, Kittery, and Old Orchard Beach.

FOOD

York Village and York

At the **Bagel Basket,** 273 York St., York Village, 207/363-1244, you can breakfast, lunch, or nosh Mon.–Sat. 6 AM–2 PM, Sun. 6:30 AM–1 PM.

Interested in just picking up some fruit? Try **York Corner Gardens,** 381 Rte. 1, 207/363-5900, a singular farm stand with luscious peaches in season. Or get chicken barbeque and groceries at **Hannaford Food and Drug,** 440 Rte. 1, York 03909, 207/363-5357, at the high end of the chain's food chain. Another quick and clever choice is **Anthony's Food Shop,** 679 Rte. 1, York 03909, 207/363-2322, where signature pizzas, burgers, and a wide range of appealing takeout—combo meals $5–7—is complemented by an extensive deli counter. Open daily 6 AM–9 PM, some seasonal variations. For a burger, try **Wild Willy's** "Best Burgers," charbroiled chicken or burgers, eat-in or take-out, certified Angus beef. For accents, there's Gifford Ice Cream and Green Mountain Coffee Roasters coffee. Open Mon.–Thurs. 11 AM–7 PM, Fri.–Sat., 11 AM–8 PM, closed Sun.

The Stonewall Kitchen Café, Stonewall Lane, York 03909, 207/351-2719, www.stonewallkitchen.com, is in the spirit of the company—trendy, with a bistro flavor. Adjoining the shop, it's busy most of the time. Choose from breakfast, lunch, and Sunday brunch, plus a take-out menu and espresso bar.

You can't go wrong at **Food & Co.,** One York St. (U.S. Rte. 1, just south of Rte. 1A), 207/363-0900, a gourmet market and café, where the lunch special might be a reasonably priced melt-in-your mouth spanakopita, with phyllo layers so thin they're transparent. Cheeses of exotic provenance are on hand, there's a coffee bar, assorted gourmet goodies, and a take-out dinner menu. If you call in by 3 PM, you can pick up dinners like Salmon Provencale en Paupiotte at 5 PM. The three-layer chocolate marquise is worth every calorie. Winter hours are 8 AM–6 PM Mon.–Sat. Extended hours in summer, including Sun.

Getting excellent local reviews, as well as a feature in *Gourmet Travel,* **Carla's Bakery & Cafe,** 241 York St., York Village, 207/363-4637, features daily special entrées, soups, fresh pastries, and $6 sandwiches like chicken salad with red grapes and mango chutney. Open Mon.–Fri., 7 AM–3 PM, breakfast till 11 AM, lunch 11 AM–2 PM, Sat. brunch 7 AM till noon. Closed Sun.

Lobster stew is the most popular item on the menu at **Maude Hutchins,** 290E York St. (behind Bragdon Real Estate), York 03909, 207/363-6192, but bisque, chowders, and sandwich specials are no wallflowers. The catering menu includes platters and appetizers like phyllo triangles and mini lobster cakes. The driveway is tricky; try to park on the street.

Or follow the locals to **Norma's Restaurant,** 529 Rte. 1, Ice Pond Mall, York 03909, 207/363-3233, where you can breakfast all day—try the Nubble Light Special, a pancake classic. Hot lunches and sandwiches, as well as Kids Breakfast and Lunch (for 10 and under), are also served in this light-filled, friendly place

where 1930s York postcards and photos cover the walls. Open Mon. and Wed.–Sat. 6 AM–2 PM, Sun. 6 AM–1 PM. No credit cards accepted.

Get lunch packed to go, and chowder with it, at **Finestkind Fish Market & More,** 855 Rte. 1, York 03909, 207/363-5000 or 800/288-8154. In addition to really fresh fish, the store offers an excellent selection of wine and gourmet foods. Open all year, seven days, 9 AM–6 PM.

Ruby's Wood Grill, 433 Rte. 1, a mile south of the I-95 exit, York 03909, 207/363-7980, does a great job with some intriguing pizza combos (pulled pork and barbecue sauce, for instance), and "grill of my dreams" entrées include St. Louis ribs. In nice weather, opt for the enclosed deck. In summer, the kitchen is open Mon.–Thurs. 11:30 AM–10 PM, Fri. and Sat. 11:30 AM–11 PM, and Sun. 11:30 AM–10 PM. Spirit service continues after the kitchen is closed.

White tablecloths, traditional Italian fare from calamari to ravioli du jour, and seasonal selections make **Fazio's Italian Restaurant,** 38 Woodbridge Rd., York Village 03909, 207/363-7019, a favorite family dinner spot—so reserve ahead in July and August. And it's no secret that next-door **La Stalla Pizzeria,** 207/363-1718 (same number for Fazio's take-out fare), under the same ownership, dishes out York's most creative pizza for lunch, dinner, and takeout anytime. Try the 12-inch veggie special ($10.95). Weekdays, there's a pizza buffet for $6. Fazio's opens at 4 PM daily, year-round; La Stalla opens at 11 AM daily.

Since 1972, the **Lobster Barn,** Rte. 1, York 03909, 207/363-4721 or 800/341-4849, www.thelobsterbarn.com, has been drawing a devoted local clientele to its 250-seat roadside site. All the usual suspects are here—fried clams, baked haddock, etc.—plus good steaks. Well-stuffed lobster rolls are "equal to 1¼ lb lobster—picked fresh daily." Open Mon.–Fri. noon–9 PM May–Sept.; open weekends off-season. Closed mid-Dec.–mid-Feb. From Memorial Day weekend to Labor Day, their super-casual outdoor area,

Lobster in the Rough, is a good option, and there's a playground for the kids.

When people mention **J. Ellen's Café and Wine Bar,** Meadowbrook Plaza, 647 Rte. 1, York 03909, 207/363-3751, they note it's not your usual plaza place. And lots of people do mention J. Ellen's when they talk about where to go for exceptional food. Lunch might be duck quesadilla, dinner seared scallops on butternut puree and black trumpet mushrooms. Reviews have been outstanding. Open year-round for dinner Tues.–Fri. 3:30–10 PM, Sat. 4:30–10 PM; and lunch Fri. 11:30 AM–2:30 PM.

York Beach

Just follow your nose to **Mimmo's Ristorante,** 243 Long Beach Ave., York Beach 03910, 207/363-3807—the scent of garlic will meet you halfway down the beach. Moderately priced, well-prepared Italian menu (entrées $16–20). BYOL. It's wildly popular, so reservations are essential in midsummer (try for the patio). Open for dinner daily in summer, closed Mon.–Tues., Oct.–June, and major holidays.

See those people with their faces pressed to the glass? They're all watching the taffymakers inside **The Goldenrod,** 2 Railroad Ave., York Beach 03910, 207/363-2621, www.thegoldenrod.com, where machines spew out 180 Goldenrod Kisses a minute, 65 tons a year—and have been at it since 1896. (They also accept mail orders.) The Goldenrod is an old-fashioned place, with a tearoom, gift shop, old-fashioned soda fountain (135 ice-cream flavors), and casual dining room. Open for breakfast (8 AM), lunch, and dinner late May–Columbus Day.

The wide-open ocean view couldn't be better than at the **Sun 'n' Surf,** Long Beach Ave., Rte. 1A, opposite the Anchorage Inn, York Beach 03910, 207/363-2961, a cut above most fast-food places. Full liquor license, too. Resist the urge to sit outside, or you'll be sharing your lobster roll ($9 with fries) with kamikaze gulls. Open most of the year for lunch and dinner. Call to check in deep winter months.

Lobster Cove Restaurant, 756 York St. (Rte. 1A), York Harbor 03910, 207/351-1100, garnishes breakfast, lunch, and dinner with a view of the Atlantic. Omelettes and eggs Benedict are in the $6 range, dinner entrées, including an array of seafood and lobster dishes, are $10–16 (for a Captain's Platter). Spirited coffees include Calypso and Irish. Open every day except Christmas, 8 AM–8:30 PM, till 9:30 PM Fri.–Sat.

Cape Neddick

Sometimes the line runs right out the door of the low-ceilinged, reddish-brown roadside shack housing **Flo's Steamed Dogs,** Rte. 1, opposite the Mountain Rd. turnoff, Cape Neddick 03902. Founder Flo Stacy died at age 92 in June 2000, but her legend and her family live on—the local institution celebrated its 45th anniversary in 2004, and the secret sauce is now sold retail. No menu here—just steamed hot dogs, buns, chips, and beverages. The secret? The spicy, sweet-sour hot-dog sauce (allegedly once sought by the H.J. Heinz corporation). The cognoscenti order their dogs only with mayonnaise and the special sauce—nothing heretical like mustard. Open all year, Thurs.–Tues. 11 AM–3 PM.

After your hot dog, you can have one of eight varieties of large cookies just down the road at **Pie in the Sky Bakery,** Rte. 1, River Rd., Cape Neddick 03902, 207/363-2656. And then you have to take home dessert—one of the bakery's incomparable handcrafted gourmet pies, weighing in at between four and five pounds of fruit heaven. Pies are 10 inches and cost $22.

Serving "food that loves you back," **Frankie & Johnny's Natural Foods,** 1594 Rte. 1 N., Cape Neddick 03902, 207/363-1909, has a heavy Mediterranean accent—if you don't count the lobster wontons, the bean-curd satay, and the Cajun crab cakes. Best vegetarian menu in York—in a funky, roadside place where you'll need a dinner reservation on summer weekends. No smoking, no credit cards ("plastic is not natural"). BYOL. Open for dinner Wed.–Mon. July–Aug., Fri.–Sun. in spring and fall.

Before heading for the **Cape Neddick Lobster Pound/Harborside Restaurant,** Shore Rd., Cape Neddick 03902, 207/363-5471, www.capeneddick.com, check the tide calendar. The rustic shingled building dripping with lobster-pot buoys has a spectacular harbor view (especially from the deck) at high tide, but a rather drab one at low tide, so plan accordingly. Bouillabaisse with half a lobster goes for $19.95; other entrées are $12–17. Open for dinner Memorial Day weekend to Columbus Day, also for lunch Sat.–Sun. July–Aug.

Higher up the price scale and the ambience level is **Clay Hill Farm,** 220 Clay Hill Rd., Cape Neddick 03902, on the York-Ogunquit town line, 207/361-2272, an attractive country-inn type of place two miles west of Rte. 1. It's convenient from both Ogunquit and York. Predictably good regional American entrées are in the $17–23 range; daily specials tend to be more imaginative. Allow time to wander the beautifully landscaped grounds, popular for weddings. Open all year: daily 5:30–9 PM in summer; closed Mon.–Wed. in winter. Reservations are essential July–Aug.

INFORMATION AND SERVICES

For local info, head for the Shingle-style palace of the **Yorks Chamber of Commerce,** 1 Stonewall La., right off Rte. 1 at the I-95 York exit, York 03909, 207/363-4422, www.gatewaytomaine.org. Inside the elegant hillside building, you'll find racks of brochures, restrooms, and a cheerful staff. Open daily 9 AM–5 PM May 1–Nov. 1. Nov. 1–May 1 open weekdays 9 AM–4 PM, Sat. 10 AM–4 PM, closed Sun. There is a seasonal branch at York Beach—the Short Sands Beach kiosk on Railroad Ave., open daily 10 AM–4 PM weekdays, 11 AM–6 PM weekends. See *Information* under *Kittery and Eliot,* above, for Kittery branch info. The York Public Library, 15 Long Sands Rd., York 03909, 207/363-2818, www.york.lib.me.us, is spacious and well-equipped. Open Wed. 1 PM–7 PM, Thurs.–Fri. 10 AM–5 PM, Sat. 10 AM–1 PM. The local weekly (Wed.) newspapers are *The York Weekly* and *York Independent.* Both produce summer supplements carrying features, ads, calendar listings, and other helpful information.

Emergencies
For emergencies, contact **York Hospital,** 15 Hospital Dr., York 03909 (emergency room 207/351-2157), a respected local institution. The hospital's **Tel-a-Nurse** service, 800/283-7234, provides free over-the-phone advice for minor medical problems around the clock. For **police, fire, or ambulance services,** dial 911.

Kennels
Thee Privileged Pet, LLC, 915 Rte. 1, York 03909, 207/363-5700, www.theeprivilegedpet.com, has heated floors, 24-hour music and staffing, and home-cooked meals. Services include boarding, day care, training, and grooming. Immunizations must be current, and certificates provided. Open Mon.–Fri. 9 AM–11 AM and 4–6 PM, Sat. 9–11 AM, and Sun. 3–5 PM.

Getting Around
The York Trolley Company, LLC, 207/748-3030, www.yorktrolley.com, operates a **trolley-bus service** beginning at 9:15 AM, late June–Labor Day. Every 30 minutes trolleys make a beach loop between Short and Long Sands. A single boarding is $1, 12 for $10; children age 3 and under are free. There's a narrated tour of York hourly; cost is $7 adults, $4 children 10 and under, free for children 3 and under.

Ogunquit and Wells

Ogunquit has been a holiday destination since the indigenous residents named it "beautiful place by the sea." What's the appeal? An unparalleled, unspoiled beach, several top-flight (albeit pricey) restaurants, a dozen art galleries, and a respected art museum with a view second to none. The town has been home to an art colony attracting the glitterati of the painting world starting with Charles Woodbury in 1898. The summertime crowds continue, multiplying the minuscule year-round population of about 930. Besides the beach, the most powerful magnet is Perkins Cove, a working fishing enclave that looks more like a movie set. Best way to approach the cove is via trolley-bus or on foot, along the shoreline Marginal Way from downtown Ogunquit—midsummer parking in the cove is madness.

Wells, once the parent of Ogunquit and since 1980 its immediate neighbor to the north, was settled in 1640. Nowadays, it's best known as a long, skinny, family-oriented community with about 10,000 year-round residents, seven miles of splendid beachfront, and heavy-duty commercial activity: lots of antiques and used-book shops, and a handful of factory outlets. It also claims two spectacular nature preserves worth a drive from anywhere. At the southern end of Wells, abutting Ogunquit, is **Moody,** an enclave named after 18th-century settler Samuel Moody and even rating its own post office.

The Wells Regional Transportation Center, 207/646-2499 or 207/646-2451, was designed to make travel to and from the town easier. Off exit 19 of the Maine Turnpike, it's a regular stop for Amtrak's Downeaster service (800/USA-RAIL, www.amtrakdowneaster.com), making four round-trips between Boston and Portland daily, and for Vermont Transit intercity bus service. The center offers Quik-Trak train ticketing, restrooms with baby-changing stations, pay phone, vending machines, an ATM, and travel and tourism information. The center is some distance from town centers, so make sure you have arrangements in place to get you to your end destination. There are on-call rental services, and many accommodations will pick you up with advance notice.

If swimming isn't your top priority, plan to visit Ogunquit and Wells after Labor Day, when crowds let up, lodging rates drop, weather is still good, and you can find restaurant seats and parking spots.

SIGHTS AND RECREATION
Art and History Museums
Not many museums can boast a view as stunning as the one at the **Ogunquit Museum of American Art (OMAA),** 543 Shore Rd., P.O. Box 815, Ogunquit 03907, 207/646-4909, www.ogunquitmuseum.org, nor can many communities boast such renown as a summer art colony. Overlooking Narrow Cove, 1.4 miles south of downtown Ogunquit, the museum prides itself on its distinguished permanent collection—works of Marsden Hartley, Rockwell Kent, Walt Kuhn, and Louise Nevelson, among others. Special exhibits are mounted each summer, when there is an extensive series of lectures and programs. OMAA has a well-stocked gift shop, wheelchair access, and landscaped grounds with sculptures, a pond, and manicured lawns. Admission is $5 adults, $4 seniors, $3 students, free for kids under 12 and members. Open July 1–Oct. 15 Mon.–Sat. 10:30 AM–5 PM, Sun. 2–5 PM. Closed Labor Day and four days in Aug. for rehanging.

Closer to downtown Ogunquit is the **Barn Gallery,** Shore Rd. and Bourne Ln., P.O. Box 529, Ogunquit 03907, 207/646-8400, www.mainegalleryguide.com, featuring the works of member artists—an impressive group. The Barn is owned by the nonprofit Ogunquit Artists Cooperative and the Ogunquit Art Association (OAA). In addition to showing members' work, it also has a student show, and an open juried regional show. The OAA was established in 1928 by Charles Woodbury, who was inspired to open an art school in Perkins Cove. Special programs throughout the season include an annual chamber-music festival, workshops, gallery talks, and the oldest art auction in the area, held the first Saturday in August. The gallery is open late May–late Sept., 11 AM–5 PM Mon.–Sat. and 1–5 PM Sun. Admission is free.

Right in downtown Ogunquit is the **Captain James Winn House,** 86 Obeds Lane, P.O. Box 723, Oqunquit 03907, 207/646-0296, home of the Oqunquit Heritage Museum. An 18th-century sea captain's home, the Winn House is located among period plantings in Dorothea Grant Common, a new park space. The c. 1780 building retains many of its original components. Saved from demolition, it was opened in 2002, and is the first historical museum in Ogunquit. Hours are 1–4 PM Tues.–Sat., June–Sept.

Right on the historic Post Road that once linked Boston with points north stands the **Historic Meetinghouse Museum,** Buzzell Rd. and Rte. 1, 936 Post Rd., opposite Wells Plaza, P.O. Box 801, Wells 04090, 207/646-4775, www.historicalsocietyof-wellsandogunquit.com, a handsome steepled structure on the site of the town's first church (1643). Preserved and maintained by the Historical Society of Wells & Ogunquit, its displays include old photos, ship models, needlecraft, and local memorabilia. On the premises is the Esselyn Perkins genealogical library where volunteers will help you research your roots. Open Memorial Day–Columbus Day Tues.–Thurs. 10 AM–4 PM. Winter hours are Wed.–Thurs. 10 AM–4 PM. Entrance at rear.

Dozens of vintage vehicles, including a Stanley Steamer, plus a collection of old-fashioned nickelodeons, fill the **Wells Auto Museum,** Rte. 1, Wells 04090, 207/646-9064. From the outside, it just looks like a big warehouse, right on the highway. You can ride in a working antique auto, and the gift shop has car-oriented items. Open daily Memorial Day–Columbus Day 10 AM–5 PM. Adults $5, Children (6–12) $2, under 6 free.

Marginal Way

The best times to appreciate this mile-long, shrub-lined, shorefront walkway in Ogunquit are early morning or when everyone's at the beach. En route are tidal pools, intriguing rock formations, crashing surf, pocket beaches, benches (though the walking's a cinch, even partially wheelchair-accessible), and a marker listing the day's high and low tides. When the surf's up, keep a close eye on the kids—the sea has no mercy. One end of the paved footpath crosses through the Sparhawk Resort (Shore Rd., one block east of Rte. 1) and the other end is next to the Oarweed Cove Restaurant (Shore Rd.) in Perkins Cove. There's also a midpoint access at Israel's Head (behind a sewage plant masquerading as a tiny lighthouse), but getting a parking space is pure luck. Best advice is to stroll the Marginal Way to Perkins Cove for lunch, shopping, and maybe a boat trip, then return to downtown Ogunquit via trolley-bus.

Perkins Cove

Turn-of-the-20th-century photos show Ogunquit's Perkins Cove lined with gray-shingled shacks used by a hardy colony of local fishermen—fellows who headed offshore to make a tough living in little boats. They'd hardly recognize it today. Though the cove remains a working lobster-fishing harbor, several old shacks have been reincarnated as boutiques and restaurants, and photographers go crazy shooting the quaint inlet spanned by a unique little pedestrian drawbridge. In midsummer, you'll waste precious time looking for one of the three or four dozen parking places, so take advantage of the trolley-bus service. In the cove are galleries, gift shops, and a range of eateries, boat excursions, and public restrooms.

Beaches

One of Maine's most scenic and unspoiled sandy beachfronts can be found across the Ogunquit River. The 3.5-mile stretch of strand fringed with seagrass is a major magnet for hordes of sunbathers, spectators, swimmers, surfers, and sandcastle-builders. Getting there means crossing the river via one of three access points. For the **Main Beach**—with a spanking new bathhouse and high crowd content—take Beach Street. To reach **Footbridge Beach,** which is marginally less crowded, either take Ocean St. and the footbridge or take Bourne Ave. to Ocean Ave. in adjacent Wells and walk back toward Ogunquit. **Moody Beach,** at Wells' southern end, technically is private property—a subject of considerable legal dispute. Lifeguards are on duty all summer at the public beaches, and there are restrooms in all three areas. The beach is free, but parking is not; some parking lots charge hefty hourly fees ($4 an hour at the Main Beach; reduced hourly rates after 6 PM) or by the day ($15 a day at Footbridge Beach and Moody Beach), and they fill up early on warm midsummer days. It's far more sensible to opt for the frequent trolley-buses or shank's mare.

Wells' beaches continue where Ogunquit's leave off. **Crescent Beach,** Webhannet Dr., between Eldredge and Mile Rds., is the tiniest, with tidal pools, no facilities, and limited parking. **Wells Beach,** Mile Rd. to Atlantic Ave., is the major (and most crowded) beach, with lifeguards, restrooms, and parking. Around the other side of Wells Harbor is **Drakes Island Beach** (take Drakes Island Rd., across from the post office), a less crowded spot with restrooms and lifeguards. Walk northeast from Drakes Island Beach and you'll eventually reach Laudholm Beach, with great birding along the way. Though fees are less than Ogunquit's, daily nonresident beach-parking fees in Wells can add up; extended-visit deals are available at the lots for lower rates.

Walks and Hikes

Wells National Estuarine Research Reserve, known locally as Laudholm Farm (the name of the restored 19th-century visitors center), 342 Laudholm Farm Rd., Wells 04090, 207/646-1555, www.wellsreserve.org, occupies 1,600 acres of upland fields, woods, beach, and coastal salt marsh on the southern boundary of the Rachel Carson National Wildlife Refuge, just 0.5 mile east of Rte. 1. Seven miles of

trails wind through the property. The best is the Barrier Beach Walk, a 1.4-mile round-trip that goes through multiple habitats all the way to beautiful Laudholm Beach. Allow 1.5 hours. Lyme disease–carrying ticks have been found here, so tuck pant legs into socks and stick to the trails (some of which are wheelchair-accessible). The informative exhibits in the farmhouse visitors center and the new exhibits in the Maine Coastal Ecology Center make a valuable prelude for enjoying the reserve. The reserve is open Mon.–Fri. 10 AM–4 PM Jan. 16–Dec. 15; from Memorial Day weekend to Columbus Day, it's also open Sat. 10 AM–4 PM and Sun. noon–4 PM. Open by appointment Dec. 16–Jan. 15. An extensive program schedule (May–Nov.) includes lectures, nature walks, a bean supper, and family and children's programs. Many programs are free; fees vary for others Financial aid is available. Reservations are required for some space-limited programs. Trails are accessible 7 AM–sunset daily, all year. From Memorial Day weekend to Columbus Day, admission fees are in effect: $1 for children age 6–16, $2 over 16, members free except for some special events.

Ten chunks of coastal Maine real estate—currently more than 5,000 acres, eventually 7,500 acres, between Kittery Point and Cape Elizabeth—make up the **Rachel Carson National Wildlife Refuge,** 321 Port Rd. (Rte. 9), Wells 04090, 207/646-9226, headquartered at the northern edge of Wells, near the Kennebunk town line. Pick up a *Carson Trail Guide* at the refuge office (parking space is very limited) and follow the mile-long walkway (wheelchair-accessible) past tidal creeks, salt pans, and salt marshes. It's a birder's paradise during migration seasons. As with the Laudholm Farm reserve, Lyme disease–carrying ticks have been found here, so tuck pant legs into socks and stick to the trail. Office hours are weekdays 8 AM–4:30 PM, year-round; trails are open sunrise to sunset, year-round.

Municipal Recreation Areas

On Rte. 9A, west of I-95 (take Burnt Mill Rd.), the 70-acre **Wells Recreation Area,**

207/646-5826, has four tennis courts, a fitness trail, basketball courts, baseball field, picnic tables, a large playground, and restrooms. Three-acre **Wells Harbor Community Park,** Lower Landing Rd. (turn off Rte. 1 at the fire station), has a playground, restrooms, and a bandstand (Hope Fenderson Hobbs Memorial Gazebo) where frequent concerts are held during the summer. **Ogunquit Recreational Area,** Agamenticus Rd., west of I-95, Ogunquit, 207/646-3032, has three tennis courts.

Bike Rentals
Wheels and Waves, 579 Post Rd., Rt. 1, Wells 04090, 207/646-5774, rents and services mountain bikes and sells any kind of board that'll ride the surf. Mountain-bike rentals are $25 a day. They're open daily in summer.

Getting Afloat
Depending on your interest, you can go deep-sea fishing, whale-watching, or just gawking out of Perkins Cove, Ogunquit. Between April and mid-November, Capt. Tim Tower runs half-day (departing 4 PM; $45 pp) and full-day (departing 7 AM; $65 pp) **deep-sea-fishing trips** aboard the 40-foot *Bunny Clark,* P.O. Box 837, Ogunquit 03907, 207/646-2214. Reservations are necessary. Tim has a science degree, so he's a wealth of marine-biology information. All gear is provided, and they'll fillet your catch for you; dress warmly, wear sunblock, and bring food and drink.

Perkins Cove (Barnacle Billy's Dock) is also home port for the Hubbard family's **Finestkind Scenic Cruises,** 207/646-5227, www .finestkindcruises.com, offering 1.5-hour Nubble Light cruises (daily at 10 AM, noon, 2, and 4 PM; $16 adults, $10 kids) and one-hour cocktail cruises (daily at 5:45, 7, and 8:15 PM; $11 adults, $7 kids; cash bar) in a sheltered powerboat. A 75-minute breakfast cruise, complete with coffee, juice, and muffin, departs at 9 AM daily ($15 adults, $10 kids). They also do 50-minute lobstering trips (Mon.–Sat. 10:30 AM–3 PM; look and listen—no helping; $11 adults, $7 kids) in a real lobsterboat (no toilets). High season runs July 1–Labor Day; limited schedule May, June, Sept., Oct. Reservations are advisable but usually unnecessary midweek. No credit cards.

Whale-watching is the specialty of the 40-foot *Deborah Ann,* 207/361-9501, departing 8 AM and 1:30 PM daily from Perkins Cove, mid-June–Labor Day. At each end of the season, mid-May–mid-June and Labor Day–Oct, there is one trip a day, from 10 AM–3 PM. Trips last 4.5 hours; reservations are essential. Dress warmly. If you're especially motion-sensitive, plan ahead with appropriate medication. Cost (no credit cards) is $40 adults, $35 seniors (60 and over), $25 children 12 and under.

ENTERTAINMENT
Having showcased topnotch professional theater since the 1930s, the 688-seat **John Lane's Ogunquit Playhouse,** Rte. 1, P.O. Box 915, Ogunquit 03907, 207/646-5511, knows how to do it right: six comedies and musicals each summer, with big-name stars. The air-conditioned building is wheelchair- accessible. The box office is open daily, beginning in May. Performances are June–Sept., Mon.–Fri. at 8 PM, Sat. 8:30 PM; matinees Wed. and Thurs. at 2:30 PM. There are five children's theater performances on Saturdays at noon. Tickets are $29–45, and performances often sell out. There is a large parking lot, but it can sometimes take a good 20 minutes to exit onto two-lane Rte. 1; consider walking the short distance from the Bourne Ln. trolley-bus stop.

An even older local institution is the 640-seat **Leavitt Fine Arts Theatre,** 40 Main St., Ogunquit 03907, 207/646-3123, a handsome landmark since 1923. Nightly first-run films in summer at 8 PM; matinees on rainy days. Tickets are $7.50 adults, $4.50 kids. Down the road in Wells, at the seven-screen **Wells Five Star Cinemas,** Wells Plaza, Rte. 1, Wells 04090, 646-0500, www.fivestarcinemas.com, evening tickets are $7.75 adults, $5.50 for children (11 and under) and seniors.

Ogunquit has several nightspots with good

reputations for food and live entertainment. Best known is **Jonathan's,** 92 Bourne Lane, P.O. Box 1879, Ogunquit 03907, 207/646-4777, www.jonathansrestaurant.com, where national headliners often are on the weekend schedule upstairs. Advance tickets are cheaper than at the door, and dinner guests get preference for seats. Reservations are essential at this popular spot. The informal downstairs restaurant has creative entrées for $18–25. Focus of the dining room is a 600-gallon freshwater aquarium. Open year-round, closed Tues. only in winter. A Saturday morning breakfast and Sunday brunch are served throughout fall and spring.

FESTIVALS AND EVENTS

Harbor Fest, held at Wells Harbor Park, is two July days filled with food, a crafts fair, live entertainment, and children's activities. The **Independence Day Fireworks Display** does a good job of lighting up Ogunquit's Main Beach and awing visitors. Musical entertainment begins at 7:30 PM, fireworks at 9:30 PM.

The **Sidewalk Art Show** in August is a "true sidewalk show," where artists display and sell their work along the streets of Ogunquit Center 9 AM–4:30 PM.

Capriccio is a performing-arts festival, with daytime and evening events held throughout Ogunquit the first week of September. Then, the second weekend that month, Wells National Estuarine Research Reserve (Laudholm Farm) hosts the **Laudholm Nature Crafts Festival,** a two-day juried crafts fair that attracts thousands. This is an especially fine event. And the *third* weekend of September, the **Annual Ogunquit Antique Show** benefits the Historical Society of Wells & Ogunquit. At the Dunaway Center, School St., Ogunquit, 9 AM–4 PM, brunch and lunch in the café.

Christmas by the Sea, the second weekend of December, features caroling, tree lighting, shopping specials, Santa Claus, a chowderfest, and a beach bonfire in Ogunquit.

SHOPPING
Antiques and Antiquarian Books
Antiques are a Wells specialty, so there are plenty of choices, with a huge range of prices. **R. Jorgensen Antiques,** 502 Post Rd., Rte. 1, Wells 04090, 207/646-9444, www.rjorgensen.com, is a phenomenon in itself, filling 11 showrooms in two buildings with European and American 18th- and 19th-century furniture and accessories. Open daily except Wednesday 10 AM–5 PM (noon–5 PM Sun.). **MacDougall-Gionet Antiques,** 2104 Post Rd., Rte. 1, Wells 04090, 207/646-3531, has been here since the mid-1960s, and its reputation is stellar. The 65-dealer shop—in an 18th-century barn—carries American and European country and formal furniture and accessories. Open Tues.–Sun. 9 AM–5 PM, year-round. In the hamlet of Wells Branch is **The Farm,** 294 Mildram Rd., Wells 04090, 207/985-2656, with room-format displays of English and French antiques and early Chinese porcelain in a splendidly renovated barn. Owned by the Crouthamels and Hacketts since 1967. From Rte. 1, take Coles Hill Rd. to Mildram Rd., 2.5 miles west. Open Thurs.–Tues. 10 AM–4 PM, mid-June–Labor Day; Fri.–Sun. Labor Day–Nov.

If you've been scouring antiquarian bookshops for a long-wanted title, chances are you'll find it at **Douglas N. Harding Rare Books,** 2152 Post Rd., Rte. 1, P.O. Box 184, Wells 04090, 207/646-8785, www.hardings-books.com. Well-catalogued and organized, the sprawling bookshop at any given time stocks upwards of 100,000 books, prints, and maps, including a hefty selection of Maine and New England histories. Don't count on leaving empty-handed—there are too many temptations. Open daily 9 AM–5 PM Jan.–June, 9 AM–7 PM July–Aug., 9 AM–6 PM Sept.–Dec. Other Wells antiquarian bookshops are **The Arringtons,** 1908 Post Rd., Rte. 1, P.O. Box 160, Wells 04090, 207/646-4124, specializing in military books (open daily 10 AM–5 PM June–Oct., weekends Nov.–May, and most weekdays, 10 AM–4 PM), and **East Coast Books and Art,** Depot St., P.O. Box 849,

Wells 04090, 207/646-3584, fax 646-0416, open daily 11 AM–5 PM Apr. 1–June 30 and Nov. 1–Nov. 20; daily 10 AM–6 PM July 1–Oct. 31.

Art Galleries

There's no scarcity of the spectacular scenery that drew artists to Ogunquit in the early 20th century, but it's not the artistic magnet it once was. Yet galleries have popped up here and there. Do your art browsing along Shore Road and in Perkins Cove.

Books, Clothing, and Gifts

Several mini-lighthouses stand watch over the **Lighthouse Depot,** 1690 Post Rd., Rte. 1, P.O. Box 1690, Wells 04090, 207/646-0608 or 800/758-1444, www.lighthousedepot.com— a truly amazing mecca for lighthouse aficionados. Imagine this: two floors of lighthouse books, sculptures, videos, banners, sweatshirts, Christmas and lawn ornaments, paintings, and replicas running the gamut from pure kitsch to attractive collectibles. Their *Maine Lighthouse Map and Guide* ($5.95) is particularly helpful for tracking down the state's sentinels. Owners Tim Harrison and Kathy Finnegan also publish the *Lighthouse Digest,* a monthly magazine focusing on North American lighthouses, and produce a large mail-order catalog. Next-door to the Depot is the American Lighthouse Foundation and its museum. Hours are Sun.–Thurs. 9 AM–6 PM, Fri.–Sat. 9 AM–7 PM, July–Labor Day. In Apr., May, and Oct. 12–Dec., hours are 9 AM–5 PM daily. In June and Sept.7–Oct. 11, hours are Mon.–Sat. 9 AM–6 PM, Sun. 9 AM–5 PM. Jan.–Mar., hours are 10 AM–4:30 PM Fri.–Mon., closed other days. Also closed Christmas and Jan. 1–5. The shop is about 1.5 miles north of the junction of Rtes. 1 and 109.

ACCOMMODATIONS

Ogunquit

Motel-style accommodations are everywhere in Ogunquit, most along Rte. 1, yet finding last-minute rooms in July and August can be a challenge, so book well ahead if you'll be here then.

The Seafarer Motel, Rte. 1, P.O. Box 2099, Ogunquit 03907, 207/646-4040 or 800/646-1233, www.seafarermotel.com, is under new ownership, and has added a picnic area for people to grill outside, as well as new furniture, carpets, and kitchens. Half the rooms have double beds and a refrigerator ($129–149 d) and half are queen rooms with kitchens ($139–159 d). There is a heated indoor pool and an outdoor pool and hot tub. All rooms have cable color TV and air-conditioning. The Ogunquit Playhouse is across the street. The clean, well-managed motel is set back a bit from the highway, but if you're noise-sensitive or prefer a woodsy view, ask for a back-facing room. Open May–Oct.

You're almost literally within spitting distance of Perkins Cove at the 37-room **Riverside Motel,** 50 Riverside La., P.O. Box 2244, Ogunquit 03907, 207/646-2741, www.riversidemotel.com, where you can perch on your balcony and watch the action—or, for that matter, join it. Rooms with refrigerators and cable TV are $115–180 d late June–Labor Day, $70–130 d early and late in the season; three-night minimum July and Aug. No pets. Open late Apr.–Oct. 21.

Juniper Hill Inn, 336 Main St., Rte. 1, P.O. Box 2190, Ogunquit 03907, 207/646-4501 or 800/646-4544, www.ogunquit.com/juniperhill, is a particularly well-run motel-style lodging on five acres close to downtown Ogunquit and the beach. Amenities include refrigerators, cable TV, coin-operated laundry, fitness center, and indoor and outdoor pools. No pets. Rooms are $129–224 d late June–early Sept., $84–149 d Sept. 5–Oct. 22, lower other periods. Open all year.

It's not easy to describe the **Sparhawk Oceanfront Resort,** 85 Shore Rd., P.O. Box 936, Ogunquit 03907, 207/646-5562, www.thesparhawk.com, a sprawling, one-of-a-kind place popular with honeymooners, sedate families, and seniors. There's lots of tradition in this thriving, five-acre complex—it's had various incarnations since the turn of the 20th century, and the Happily Filled sign regularly hangs out front. Out back is the Atlantic, with forever views, and the Marginal Way starts right here. Amenities include tennis courts, gardens, and a heated freshwater pool. There's no restaurant, but Ogunquit has plenty of options, and breakfast is included with your room. The 87 rooms vary in the different buildings—from motel-type rooms (best views) and suites to luxury suites and select efficiency apartments; rates run $170–300 d late June–Labor Day (seven-night minimum July–mid-Aug.), $90–265 d other months. No pets. Open mid-Apr.–Oct.

Within walking distance to many Ogunquit attractions, Jane and Fred Garland have created a very warm and welcoming ambience at their bed-and-breakfast **The Morning Dove,** 13 Bourne Ln., P.O. Box 1940, Ogunquit 03907, 207/646-3891, www.themorningdove.com, a restored 1860s farmhouse with lovely gardens. Two suites—one with a fireplace—and three rooms have family quilts, TV, air-conditioning, mini-refrigerators, hair dryers, and private baths. A hearty breakfast is served in the huge living/dining room (with a fireplace in winter) or on the porch. No smoking, no pets, no kids under 16. Rates run $145–185 d in summer, $100–145 d in winter. Open all year.

Conveniently close to the center of town and an easy walk to the beach, **The Nellie Littlefield House,** 27 Shore Rd., Ogunquit 03907, 207/646-1692, www.visit-maine.com/nellielittlefieldhouse, is a handsomely restored 1889 Victorian. Antiques and replicas fill the eight rooms, all named after members of the distinguished 19th-century Littlefield family; the third-floor Grace Littlefield even has a turret. The air-conditioning muffles street noise, but request a back- or side-facing room if you're extremely noise-sensitive. One room is handicapped-accessible. Innkeepers Jorg and Patty Ross whip up an excellent breakfast buffet. Open Apr.–Oct., rates are $165–220 d July–Labor Day; $115–170 Apr.–June 30 and Labor Day–Columbus Day; $115–140 Columbus Day–Oct. 22; three-night minimum holiday weekends. No pets, smoking, or small children.

The Beauport Inn on Clay Hill Road, 339 Agamenticus/Clay Hill Road, PO Box 941, Ogunquit 03907, 207/361-2400 or 800/646-8681, www.beauportinn.com, is a luxurious world unto itself, yet within walking distance of town. Set apart at the end of a long driveway, the English Manor–style inn has a steam room, a pool, and just four rooms and one apartment. Well-traveled, knowledgeable, and attentive hosts Cathy and George Wilson prepare a delicious full breakfast in a kitchen dining room; you can spend time either admiring the great room or looking out the window toward the acres in back, where you can fish for trout from the Josia River. Rooms run $175–235 in season (mid-June–early Sept.), $120–155 various other times; suite is $140–235, depending on season and number of persons. Open all year.

Built in 1899 for a prominent Maine lumbering family, the seaside, shingle-style **Rockmere Lodge,** 150 Stearns Rd., P.O. Box 278, Ogunquit 03907, 207/646-2985, www.rockmere.com, has been restored to its former glory with antiques and the comforts of Old Ogunquit, by hosts and preservationists Andy Antoniuk and Bob Brown. Near the Marginal Way on a peaceful street—an easy walk to town and Perkins Cove—the handsome home has eight very comfortable Victorian guest rooms, all with private baths and cable TV and most with ocean views. Rooms go for $160–215 d late June–Labor Day, $140–190 d other months, and include a generous continental breakfast. A front porch overlooking the ocean, and "The Lookout," a third-floor windowed nook with panoramic views, are both available for guests. The woodwork throughout is gorgeous. Every room has a basket of magazines, and beach towels, chairs, umbrellas, and many other conveniences are provided for guests. No pets, smoking, or children under 16. Open May 1–Nov. 20.

Floors glisten, brass gleams, and breakfast is served on the glass-walled porch at the **Hartwell House,** 312 Shore Rd., P.O. Box 1950, Ogunquit 03907, 207/646-7210 or 800/235-8883, www.hartwellhouseinn.com, where the 13 rooms and three good-size suites (all with private bath and air-conditioning) are divided between two buildings straddling Shore Road. Some of the rooms are suitable for extended stays, with kitchenettes, sleep sofas, and decks or patios. Rooms are beautifully decorated with antiques and reproductions; try for a garden-view room in the main house. No pets, no smoking. Prices run $160–270 d June 20–mid-Sept. (two-night minimum), $120–200 d other months. Weekly rates and packages are available. Open all year. The inn also has a conference center, and the S.W. Swan Bistro is across the street.

Founded in 1872, **The Cliff House Resort & Spa,** Shore Rd., P.O. Box 2274, Ogunquit 03907, 207/361-1000, www.cliffhousemaine .com, sprawls over 70 oceanfront acres at the edge of Bald Head Cliff, midway between the centers of York and Ogunquit. All guestrooms feature picture windows, balconies, and spectacular ocean views. The resort's full-service spa offers an array of traditional and signature treatments such as the Maine Wild Rose Wrap and the Cliff House Stone Massage, which features local stones from Bald Head Cliff. Additional amenities include family pools, a vanishing-edge outdoor pool, whirlpools, tennis courts, and a fitness center. During July and August, complimentary trolley service shuttles guests to Perkins Cove, downtown Ogunquit, and Ogunquit Beach. 2005 rates range from $145–315 per night. The resort offers a "European Plan" and a variety of special packages that pair fine dining with activities such as golf, shopping, and spa services. No pets. Open late Mar.–Dec.

Wells

Like Ogunquit, Wells has a long list of motel-type lodgings, mostly on Rte. 1, and everything fills up in late July and early August. If you're arriving then, don't count on finding last-minute space. You might, however, find a campsite—Wells has 20 campgrounds.

Once a 19th-century salt-marsh farm, the **Beach Farm Inn,** 97 Eldridge Rd., Wells 04090, 207/646-8493, www.beachfarminn .com, is a 2.5-acre oasis in a rather congested area 0.2 mile off Rte. 1. Guests can swim in the pool, relax in the library, or walk 0.5 mile down the road to the beach. A full country breakfast is served daily. Eight rooms (five with private baths and air-conditioning) are $125–135 d in summer, $70–100 d off-season; two cottages (June–Sept. only) go for $650 and $950 a week. There's a two-night minimum for rooms on weekends. No pets, no smoking, no children under 12 except in cottages. Off-season specials, weekend and holiday packages, and special events are all available. Open all year.

FOOD

Ogunquit

Breakfast: The Egg and I 501 Main St., Rte. 1, across from the Ogunquit Lobster Pound, Ogunquit 03907, 207/646-8777, www.eggandibreakfast.com, earns high marks for its omelettes and waffles. You can't miss it—there's always a crowd. It's open year-round at 6 AM daily. Cash only. **Amore Breakfast,** 178 Shore Rd., P.O. Box 725, Ogunquit 03907, 207/646-6661 or 866/641-6661, www.amore-breakfast.com, is another standby, with a palette of eggs Benedicts and omelettes, plus the usual suspects. It's open early 7 AM–1 PM daily spring–mid-Dec. , closed Wed.–Thurs. in the off-season.

Lunch: Picnic fixings and gift baskets, plus a great array of private-label condiments, will catch your eye at **Perkins & Perkins,** 478 Main St., Rte. 1, P.O. Box 2027, Ogunquit 03907, 207/646-0288 or 877/646-0288, www.per-kinsandperkins.com. Their slogan—"Life is short, drink good wine!"—will tempt you to follow their advice; the wine selection is extensive. They also run the Vine Café and Wine Bar. The store is open all year; the café is open mid-May–mid-Sept.

Lobster: In Ogunquit's Perkins Cove is the landmark **Lobster Shack,** 207/646-2941, a converted fishing shanty where they've been turning out first-rate lobster rolls (and chowder) since the 1950s. You'll also find beer, wine, and a few picnic tables. Open only in summer.

Creative marketing, a knockout view, and

efficient service help explain why more than a thousand pounds of lobster bite the dust every summer day at **Barnacle Billy's,** Perkins Cove, Ogunquit, 207/646-5575 or 800/866-5575. For ambience, stick with the original operation; Barnacle Billy's Etc., next door (formerly the Whistling Oyster), is an upmarket version of the same thing. Try for the deck, with a front-row seat on Perkins Cove. Open 11 AM– 9 PM mid-Apr.–Oct.

Second-generation Hancocks now operate the **Ogunquit Lobster Pound,** 504 Main St., Rte. 1, a quarter of a mile north of downtown, Ogunquit 03907, 207/646-2516, the town's oldest lobster place (since 1944). Choose your own lobster from the tank outside; it's cooked in a numbered mesh bag, in sea water, so what you see is what you get. Steak and chicken are also available. Diners can eat indoors (in a rustic log cabin) or outdoors (shaded by pines), and there's a full bar available. Reservations are not accepted, so be prepared to wait on midsummer weekends. Open all year except Dec., daily May–mid-Oct.; otherwise weekends only, 5–9:30 PM.

Candy and Ice Cream: Harbor Candy Shop, 248 Main St., Ogunquit 03907, 207/646-8078 or 800/331-5856, www.harborcandy.com, is packed with the most outrageous chocolate imaginable. Fudge, truffles, and turtles are all made here in the shop. Fortunately (or maybe unfortunately), they also accept mail orders. Open all year.

Kids (and lots of adults) can easily follow the slogan, "Life is short, eat dessert first" at **The Scoop Deck,** 6 Eldredge Rd. just off Rte. 1, Wells 04090, 207/646-5150, www.scoopdeck.com, where over three dozen flavors of ice cream, soft- and hard-serve yogurt, sorbet, and baked goods are most of the menu; for the meal itself, there are cold drinks and steamed hot dogs. Ask about the "almost famous Deck Deal Meal." Takeout only. Open daily late May– Sept.; 11 AM–11 PM in July and Aug.

Moderate to Expensive Restaurants: In addition to the restaurants listed here, there's easy access from Ogunquit to the attractive **Clay Hill Farm** restaurant, in a rural setting west of Rte. 1 on Agamenticus Rd., on the York-Ogunquit town line.

The cocktail invention served in its lounge, the Cosmotini, exemplifies the touch of urban chic **Five-O,** 50 Shore Rd., Ogunquit 03907, 207/646-5001, www.five-oshoreroad.com, brings to its seasonal menus. Entrées, ranging from $21–31, might include Local Day Boat Haddock with pancetta and light horseradish crust, or Rack of Veal rubbed with green peppercorns. Five-O has an impressive wine list and has wine-pairing dinners and special events throughout the year. Open year-round. May 27–Oct.1: daily at 5 PM; Oct. 2–Nov. 13: Thurs., Sun., Mon., 5–9 PM, Fri., Sat. to 10 PM; Nov. 14–May 26: Thurs., Sun. 5–9 PM, Fri., Sat., to 10 PM.

S.W. Swan Bistro 309 Shore Rd., Ogunquit 03907, 207/646-1178, www.swanbistro.com, serves American Bistro cuisine accompanied by a thoughtful wine list. Entrée selections range from a vegetarian pasta at $15, to filet mignon at $27. Open for dinner at 5:30 PM Thurs.–Sun.

The closest thing to an upscale-rustic French country inn is the dining room at **Provence** (also referred to as 98Provence), 262 Shore Rd., Ogunquit 03907, 207/646-9898, www.98provence.com. Chef/owner Pierre Gignac produces the cuisine to match, turning out appetizers such as stewed pheasant in baked tomato and chevre gratin and superb entrées in the $20–35 range. Duck, venison, seafood, veal, and lamb are all represented. There are three seasonal menus a year, and a $48 prix fixe menu. Service is attentive and well-paced. Don't miss it. Open for the season in early Apr., 5:30 PM Wed.–Mon., more limited hours in spring and fall.

Cross the street from Provence and you're in Italy—sort of. Vegetarians and pastafanatics gravitate to **The Impastable Dream,** 261 Shore Rd., Ogunquit 03907, 207/646-3011. Entrée range is $10–18; choices are predictable (ravioli, gnocchi, lasagna, Mediterranean tomato-based sauces over pasta, etc.) in this comfortable, casual spot. Open all year for dinner, with a restricted schedule off-season.

Like several other Ogunquit restaurants, **Poor Richard's Tavern,** 331 Shore Rd., Ogunquit 03907, 207/646-4722, www.poorrichardstavern.com, occupies a former residence. Veteran local restaurateur Richard Perkins has found a marketable mix: sensible prices ($17–24 for entrées), a "comfortable" menu (the $16.95 Yankee pot roast and $18.95 fresh Atlantic haddock are big favorites), longevity (close to 50 years in business), and a reasonable wine list. All this means it's jammed in summer, so be sure to reserve. Open April–New Year's.

Right in downtown Ogunquit, **Gypsy Sweethearts,** 30 Shore Rd., P.O. Box 593, Ogunquit 03907, 207/646-7021, www.gypsysweethearts.com, occupies two floors of a restored house, including an outside deck and garden dining nook with three tables and a fireplace. The creative international menu includes exceptional vegetarian dishes. Entrées range from $16–26. Reservations advised in midsummer. Open mid-May–late Oct. for dinner (5:30–10 PM daily) except Mon. in midsummer, weekends in spring and fall.

Diners (and lodgers) have been stopping at **The Old Village Inn,** 250 Main St., Ogunquit 03907, 207/646-7088, www.theoldvillageinn.com, since 1833; the food, service, and warmth continue to draw crowds. One of the dining rooms in the historic house has only a single table and a fireplace. Entrées are $17–22. Off-season "winter warmer specials" and "spring warmer specials" (5:30–7:30 PM), and summertime early-bird specials (5:30–6:15 PM), are bargains. Midsummer reservations are recommended. Open seven nights a week Feb.–Jan. 1 (closed Jan.).

The Cliff House, Shore Rd., P.O. Box 2274, Ogunquit 03907, 207/361-1000, www.cliffhousemaine.com, sprawls over 70 oceanfront acres at the edge of Bald Head Cliff, midway between the centers of York and Ogunquit. The fourth generation of the same family now runs the Cliff House, which was founded in 1872. The dining room, with fantastic ocean views, is open to the public for breakfast and dinner, plus lunch in July and August. The Sunday-brunch buffet—a favorite with guests and local residents—is served 7:30 AM–1 PM. Reservations are required for dinner. Casual sportswear is acceptable for breakfast and lunch, while business casual is expected for dinner. Entrées range from $19–31. Before or after dining, wander the grounds. Open late Mar.–Dec.

Worthwhile Wallet-Cruncher: Restrain yourself for a couple of days and then splurge on an elegant dinner at **Arrows,** Berwick Rd., about 1.5 miles west of Rte. 1, Ogunquit 03907, 207/361-1100, www.arrowsrestaurant .com, definitely one of the state's finest restaurants. Located in a beautifully restored 18th-century farmhouse overlooking well-tended gardens whose produce is often incorporated into the menu, Arrows does absolutely everything right. Prices are stratospheric by Maine standards (with wine, you can count on paying at least $200 a couple), but worth it. "Innovative" is too tame to describe the menu; entrées are about $44, so the best deal is the six-course Garden Tasting Menu ($95). In spring and fall, there are other options: On Fridays, there is a three-course trattoria and bistro menu for $39.95, and on Sundays, a regional dinner series—a five-course prix fixe for $75. Reservations are essential in midsummer. Jackets preferred for men, no shorts, casual dress discouraged. Open for dinner at 6 PM Apr.–mid-Dec. on the following schedule: Wed.–Sun. in June, Tues.–Sun. July and Aug., Wed.–Sun. Labor Day–mid-Oct, Thurs.–Sun. the rest of Oct; weekends other months, and Thanksgiving Day.

Wells

Breakfast: The best homemade doughnuts in Wells (and beyond), hands down, are at **Congdon's Doughnuts,** Rte. 1, Wells 04090, 207/646-4219, www.congdons.com, which celebrated a half-century of doughnut-making in 2005. Open daily year-round for breakfast (anytime) and lunch. Drive-thru service has been added, too.

Pizza and Inexpensive Fare: No eatery in this category qualifies as heart-healthy, so don't say you weren't forewarned. **Alfredo's Italian Pizzeria,** Rte. 1 (at Rte. 109), opposite the fire station, 207/646-1718, www.alfredositalian-pizzeria.com, has been voted best pizza in Wells/Ogunquit on a regular basis. Sub rolls are baked on the premises, and lunch specials are available.

Long-time favorite **Billy's Chowder House,** 216 Mile Rd., just off Rte. 1, 207/646-7558, www.billyschowderhouse.com, has a prime marsh-view location—with wall-to-wall cars in the parking lot. Open mid-Jan.–early Dec. daily at 11:30 AM for lunch and dinner. **The Hayloft,** Rte. 1, in Moody 04054, 207/646-4400, gets gold stars for hearty seafood chowder (clams, shrimp, and chunks of lobster) and good burgers. It's a casual, popular place, and is great for families, so go early. Open all year, 8 AM–8:30 PM, later in summer. Fried-clam aficionados swear by **Jake's Seafood,** Rte. 1 and Bourne Ave., Moody 04054, 207/646-6771, but you'll also like their clam chowder and onion rings. Open all year for breakfast and lunch; in summer, open for breakfast, lunch, and dinner.

Your basic family-oriented place, **Maine Diner,** 2265 Post Rd., Rte. 1, Wells 04090, 207/646-4441, www.mainediner.com, has a reputation built on lobster pie and award-winning seafood chowder. Beer and wine only. Open Sun.–Thurs. 7 AM–8 PM, Fri. and Sat. 7 AM–9 PM for breakfast (any time of day), lunch, and dinner.

Moderate to Expensive Restaurants: A loyal local clientele patronizes **Litchfield's,** 2135 Post Rd., Rte. 1, Wells 04090, 207/646-5711, so reservations are wise on summer weekends. Blackened rib eye and fried oysters are house specialties, along with Maine seafood primavera. Entrées range from $13–20. Open daily, all year, for lunch 11:30 AM–3 PM and dinner 5–9 PM (to 9:30 PM on weekends). Piano music accompanies dinners Thurs.–Sat. in summer. Weekday early-bird specials (entrées under $11) and a good kids' menu are also available.

Seals and surf are just beyond the windows at **The Grey Gull,** 475 Webhannet Dr., a mile west of Rte. 1, Wells 04090, 207/646-7501, www.thegreygullinn.com, the best restaurant in town. Seafood is a specialty (lobster's always on the menu), but so are Yankee pot roast, creative chicken dishes, pasta entrées, and diet-conscious items; prices range from $12–27. Service is superb, wine list is selective, and there's a kids' menu. Reservations are requested in July and Aug. (ask for a window table). Open for dinner at 5:30 PM July and Aug. Closed Wed. and Thurs. mid-Dec.–mid-Mar. Upstairs, the Grey Gull Inn has five rooms with private baths. Under the same ownership are Clay Hill Farm in the Yorks and the Sea Chambers resort complex in Ogunquit.

INFORMATION AND SERVICES

At the southern edge of town, right next to the Ogunquit Playhouse, the Ogunquit Chamber of Commerce's **Welcome Center,** Rte. 1, Box 2289, Ogunquit 03907, 207/646-2939, www.ogunquit.org, provides all the usual visitor information, including restaurant menus. Ask for the *Touring Map,* showing the Marginal Way, beach locations, and public restrooms. The chamber of commerce's annually published visitor booklet thoughtfully carries a high-tide calendar for the summer months. The info center, which also has restrooms, is open 9 AM–5 PM weekdays all year, plus weekends during the summer.

Just over the Ogunquit border in Wells (actually in Moody) is the **Welcome/Information Center,** Rte. 1 at the Kimball Lane light, P.O. Box 356, Wells 04090, 207/646-2451, www.wellschamber.org. Summer hours are 9 AM–5 PM daily; off-season it's open Mon.–Fri. 9 AM–5 PM.

The handsome fieldstone **Ogunquit Memorial Library,** 166 Shore Rd., Ogunquit 03907, 207/646-9024, is the downtown's only National Historic Register building. Open Mon.–Sat. 9 AM–noon and 2–5 PM, June–Oct.; same hours other months, Tues.–Sat. The **Wells Public Library,** 1434 Post Rd., Rte. 1, Wells 04090, 207/646-8181, www.wells.lib.me.us, offers summer reading programs and special events for residents and vacationers. Open Mon. 10 AM–6 PM, Tues. 1–8 PM, Wed. 10 AM–8 PM, Thurs. 1–6 PM, and Fri.–Sat. 10 AM–5 PM.

The local weekly (Wednesday) newspaper is the *York County Coast Star,* based in Kennebunk but covering the entire county. Each Thursday in summer, the paper produces *Vacation,* a free tabloid supplement covering restaurants, shopping, entertainment, and tide calendar.

Emergencies

The nearest hospital to Ogunquit is **York Hospital,** 15 Hospital Dr., York, 207/363-4321. The nearest to Wells are (to the north) the 150-bed **Southern Maine Medical Center,** 1 Medical Center Dr., Biddeford 04005, emergency room 207/283-7100; and (to the west) **Goodall Hospital,** 25 June St., Sanford 04073, 207/324-4310. All three have round-the-clock emergency rooms. York Hospital's **Tel-a-Nurse** service, 800/283-7234, provides free over-the-phone advice for minor medical problems around the clock. For **Ogunquit** and **Wells** ambulance, police, and fire emergencies, call 911.

Photo Services

Ogunquit Camera Shop and Cricket's Corner,
41 Shore Rd., Ogunquit 03907, 207/646-2261, provides one-hour photo processing, camera repairs, and digital imaging. Part of the shop is Cricket's Corner, with all kinds of last-minute beach-type items, including kites. Open all year, daily in summer.

Getting Around

From the first Sat. of May—weekends only— and then daily mid-May–Columbus Day, a fleet of eight **trolley-buses**—named (ouch) Polly, Holly, Dolly, Jolly, Molly, Polly, Rolly, and Wally—makes the rounds of Ogunquit, with 39 stops (signposted). Each time you board, it'll cost you $1.50, but for the same price you can go the whole route—a great way to get your bearings—in about 40 minutes. Hours are 9 AM– 9 PM mid-May to the first day of summer, then 9 AM–11 PM through Labor Day, and 9 AM–8 PM Labor Day–Columbus Day. Children 10 and under ride free with adult. Wells, too, has regular trolley-bus service via Katie, Kerry, Kelly, and Karen, operating daily 9 AM–10 PM, late June– early Sept. Fare is $1 per trip or $3 for a day pass; a family day pass is $8. The Wells trolleys meet the Ogunquit trolleys at the Wells Welcome/Information Center, Rte. 1, and a trolley is on call for the Regional Transportation Center and also meets all northbound trains.

The Kennebunks

The world may have first learned of Kennebunkport when George Herbert Walker Bush was president, but Walkers and Bushes have owned their summer estate here for three generations. Visitors continue to come to the Kennebunks (the collective name for Kennebunk, Kennebunkport, Cape Porpoise, and Goose Rocks Beach—combined population about 13,500) hoping to catch a glimpse of the former first family, but they also come for the terrific ambience, the bed-and-breakfasts, boutiques, boats, biking, and beaches.

The Kennebunks' earliest European settlers arrived in the mid-1600s. By the mid-1700s, shipbuilding had become big business in the area.

Two ancient local cemeteries—North St. and Evergreen—provide glimpses of the area's heritage. Its Historic District reveals Kennebunk's moneyed past—the homes where wealthy shipowners and shipbuilders once lived, sending their vessels to the Caribbean and around the globe. Today, unusual shrubs and a dozen varieties of rare maples still line Summer St.—the legacy of ship captains in the global trade. Another legacy is the shiplap construction in many houses— throwbacks to a time when labor was cheap and lumber plentiful. Closer to the beach, in Lower Village, stood the workshops of sailmakers, carpenters, and mastmakers whose output drove the booming trade to success.

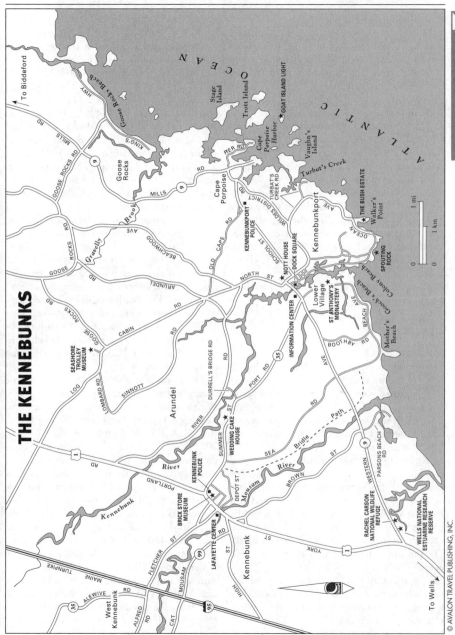

South Coast and Portland

THE KENNEBUNKS

ATLANTIC OCEAN

To Biddeford

Goose Rocks Beach

HWY

S. KING'S

MILLS RD

GOOSE ROCKS RD

9

Goose Rocks

Gravelly Brook

AVE

BEACHWOOD

GOOSE ROCKS RD

GOOSE ROCKS RD

LOG

LOMBARD RD

CABIN RD

SINNOTT RD

Arundel

SEASHORE TROLLEY MUSEUM

ARUNDEL RD

OLD CAPE RD

CAPE MILLS RD

9

Cape Porpoise

PER. RD

KENNEBUNKPORT POLICE

WILDES DISTRICT

SCHOOL ST

NORTH ST

NOTT HOUSE

DOCK SQUARE

Stage Island

Trott Island

GOAT ISLAND LIGHT

Cape Porpoise Harbor

Vaughn's Island

TURBAT'S CREEK RD

Turbut's Creek

Kennebunkport

OCEAN AVE

THE BUSH ESTATE

Walker's Point

SPOUTING ROCK

Colony Beach

Crow's Beach

St Anthony's Monastery

Lower Village

INFORMATION CENTER

BOOTHBY RD

BEACH AVE

Mother's Beach

35

PORT RD

DURRELL'S BRIDGE RD

RIVER RD

River

1

Kennebunk River

KENNEBUNK POLICE

PORTLAND RD

BRICK STORE MUSEUM

LAFAYETTE CENTER

SUMMER ST

WEDDING CAKE HOUSE

DEPOT ST

SEA RD

Mousam River

BROWN ST

Bridle Path

9

WESTERN AVE

RACHEL CARSON NATIONAL WILDLIFE REFUGE

Parsons Beach

PARSONS BEACH RD

WELLS NATIONAL ESTUARINE RESEARCH RESERVE

1

YORK ST

Kennebunk

HIGH ST

MOUSAM ST

FLETCHER ST

99

West Kennebunk

MAINE TURNPIKE

35

ALEWIVE RD

ALFRED RD

CAT RD

95

To Wells

1 mi

1 km

© AVALON TRAVEL PUBLISHING, INC.

While Kennebunkport draws most of the sightseers and summer traffic, Kennebunk feels more like a year-round community. It boasts an interesting, old-fashioned downtown and a mix of shops, restaurants, and attractions. Yes, its beaches, too, are well known, but many visitors drive right through the middle of Kennebunk without stopping to enjoy its assets.

The Kennebunks are communities with conscience—loaded with conservationists working to preserve hikeable, bikeable green space for residents and visitors. Be sure not to miss these trails, bikeways, and offshore islets. Gravestone rubbers will want to check out Evergreen Cemetery, and history buffs should pick up a copy of *Strolling through the Port,* the Kennebunkport Historical Society's well-researched booklet of four self-guided historic walking tours. To appreciate the area another way, climb aboard the Intown Trolley, with regular summertime service and lots of entertaining tidbits from the driver.

SIGHTS

Museums

Occupying four restored 19th-century buildings (including the 1825 William Lord store) in downtown Kennebunk, **The Brick Store Museum,** 117 Main St., Kennebunk 04043, 207/985-4802, www.brickstoremuseum.org, has garnered a reputation for unusual exhibits: a century of wedding dresses; *Made in Kennebunk,* about manufacturing along the Mousam River; a special Civil War display within the permanent exhibition, *Treasures of the Community.* Lately, the museum has put an emphasis on a number of public programs, including lectures and other educational events for both adults and children. During the winter, the museum shows juried exhibits of local artists. Open all year: Tues.–Fri. 10 AM–4:30 PM, Sat. 10 AM–1 PM. Admission is by donation, and free to members. The museum encourages appreciation for the surrounding Kennebunk Historic District with hour-long **architectural walking tours,** available June–mid-Oct. for $5 (members free). The

museum's gift shop also sells a walk-it-yourself booklet, as well as historical publications.

Owned and maintained by the Kennebunkport Historical Society, **The Nott House,** 8 Maine St., Kennebunkport 04046, 207/967-2751, is a mid-19th-century Greek Revival mansion filled with Victorian furnishings. It's open Tues., Wed., Fri. 1–4 PM, Thurs. and Sat. 10 AM–1 PM, mid-June–mid-Oct. Tour tickets are $5 for adults; members and those under age 18 are free. Hour-long architectural walking tours of the Kennebunkport Historic District depart from the Nott House at 11 AM Thurs. and Sat. late June–late Sept. Cost is $5; under 18 and members free.

The **Kennebunkport Historical Society** also owns and maintains a five-building History Center at 125–135 North St. The Town House School, dating from the turn of the 20th century, is the society's research center. The Pasco Exhibit Center, containing the society's offices, also has rotating exhibits of local memorabilia. It's open Tues.–Fri. 10 AM–4 PM June 11–Dec. 2, as well as Sat. 10 AM–1 PM June 11–Oct. 8. Admission is $3 (members and children under 18 are free). Parking is free, and group tours are encouraged.

There's nothing quite like an antique electric trolley to dredge up nostalgia for bygone days. With a collection of more than 225 trolleys, the **Seashore Trolley Museum,** 195 Log Cabin Rd., P.O. Box A, Kennebunkport 04046, 207/967-2712, www.trolleymuseum.org, verges on trolley-mania. Whistles blowing and bells clanging, restored streetcars do nine trips daily (between 10:05 AM and 4:15 PM) on a four-mile loop through the nearby woods. After a ride, you can check out the activity in the streetcar workshop, grab a treat at the Trolley Fare Snack Bar, and go wild in the trolley-oriented gift shop. Special events, like an Ice Cream and Sunset Trolley Ride, are held throughout the summer, and guided tours are available in July and August; call or see their website for the schedule. Tickets are $7.50 adults, $5.50 seniors, $5 kids 6–16, and free for kids five and under. The museum is 1.7 miles southeast of Rte. 1. Open daily 10 AM–5 PM, Memorial Day weekend through Columbus Day; weekends in May and late Oct. It's also open during Christmas Prelude in early Dec.

Walker's Point: The Bush Estate

There's no public access to Walker's Point, but you can join the sidewalk gawkers on Ocean Avenue overlooking George and Barbara Bush's summer compound. The 41st president and his wife lead a low-key, laid-back life when they're here, so if you don't spot them through binoculars, you may well run into them at a shop or restaurant in town. Intown Trolley's regular narrated tours go right past the house—or it's an easy, scenic family walk via Henry Parsons Park from Kennebunkport's Dock Square. On the way, you'll pass **St. Ann's Church,** whose stones came from the ocean floor, and the paths to **Spouting Rock** and **Blowing Cave**—two natural phenomena that create spectacular water fountains if you manage to be there midway between high and low tides.

Wedding Cake House

The Wedding Cake House, 104 Summer St., Kennebunk, is a private residence, so you can't go inside, but it's one of Maine's most-photographed buildings. Driving down Summer St. (Rte. 35), midway between the downtowns of Kennebunk and Kennebunkport, it's hard to miss the yellow and white Federal mansion with gobs of gingerbread and Gothic Revival spires and arches. Built in 1826 by shipbuilder George Bourne as a wedding gift for his wife, the Kennebunk landmark remained in the family until 1983.

Cape Porpoise

When your mind's eye conjures up an idyllic lobster-fishing village, it probably looks a lot like Cape Porpoise—only 2.5 miles from busy Dock Square. Follow Rte. 9 eastward from Kennebunkport; when Rte. 9 turns north, continue straight, and take Pier Rd. to its end. From the small parking area, you'll see lobsterboats at anchor, a slew of working wharves, and 19th-century **Goat Island Light,** now automated, directly offshore. In Cape Porpoise are

a handful of bed-and-breakfasts, restaurants, galleries, historic Atlantic Hall, and the extra-friendly Bradbury Bros. Market.

PARKS AND RECREATION

Thanks to a dedicated coterie of year-round and summer residents, the foresighted **Kennebunkport Conservation Trust** (KCT), founded in 1973, has become a nationwide model for land-trust organizations. The KCT has managed to preserve from development more than a thousand acres of town land (including nearly a dozen small islands off Cape Porpoise Harbor), and most of this acreage is accessible to the public, especially with a sea kayak. The trust has even assumed ownership of 7.7-acre Goat Island, with its distinctive lighthouse visible from Cape Porpoise and other coastal vantage points. Contact the KCT, P.O. Box 7004, Cape Porpoise 04014, for info on its holdings or to volunteer for trail maintenance. Better yet, become a member ($35 a year) and support their efforts.

In addition to all the recreational options listed below, don't miss the Wells National Estuarine Research Reserve or the Rachel Carson National Wildlife Refuge, on Kennebunk's southwestern boundary, or the East Point Sanctuary in Biddeford Pool, northeast of the Kennebunks.

Beaches

Ah, the beaches. The Kennebunks are well endowed with sand but not with parking spaces. Mid-June–mid-Sept., you'll need to buy a **parking pass** ($10 a day, $20 a week, $50 a season) from the Kennebunk Town Hall, 4 Summer St., 207/985-3675; the Kennebunkport Police Station, 101 Main St., 207/967-2454; or the chamber of commerce. (The police station is open 24 hours; other locations are not.) *You need a separate pass for each town.* Many lodgings provide free passes for their guests—be sure to ask when making room reservations. Or you can avoid the parking dilemma altogether by hopping aboard the Intown Trolley, which goes right by the major beaches.

The main beaches in **Kennebunk** (east to west, stretching about two miles) are 3,346-foot-long Gooch's (most popular), Kennebunk (locally called Middle or Rocks Beach), and Mother's (a smallish beach next to Lords Point, where there's also a playground). Lifeguards are on duty at Gooch's and Mother's Beaches July–Labor Day. Mother's Beach is the home of the Kennebunk Beach Improvement Association. Ask locally about a couple of other beach options.

Kennebunkport's claim to beach fame is three-mile-long Goose Rocks Beach, one of the loveliest in the area. Parking spaces are scarce and biking on Rte. 9 can be dicey, so if sun and sand are your primary goals, the best solution is to book a room nearby. You'll be about five miles east of all the downtown action, however. To reach the beach, take Rte. 9 from Dock Square east and north to Dyke Rd. (Clock Farm Corner). Turn right and continue to the end (King's Hwy.).

The prize for tiniest beach goes to Colony (officially Arundel) Beach, located near the Colony resort complex. It's close to many Kennebunkport lodgings and an easy walk from Dock Square.

Vaughn's Island Preserve

Thanks to the Kennebunkport Conservation Trust, 46-acre Vaughn's Island has been saved for posterity. You'll need to do a little planning, tide-wise, since the island is some 600 feet offshore. Consult a tide calendar and aim for low tide close to new moon or full moon (when the most water drains away). Allow yourself an hour or so before and after low tide, but no longer, or you may need a boat rescue. Wear treaded rubber boots, since the crossing is muddy and slippery with rockweed. Keep an eye on your watch and explore the ocean (east) side of the island, along the beach. It's all worth the effort, and there's a great view of Goat Island Light off to the east. From downtown Kennebunkport, take Maine St. to Wildes District Rd. Continue to Shore Rd. (also called Turbat's Creek Rd.), go 0.6 mile, jog left 0.2 mile more, and park in the tiny lot at the end.

Emmons Preserve

Also under the stewardship of the Kennebunkport Conservation Trust, the Emmons Preserve has two trails (blazed yellow and pink) meandering through 146 acres of woods and fields on the edge of Batson's River (also called Gravelly Brook). The yellow trail gives best access to the water. Fall colors here are brilliant, birdlife is abundant, and you can do a loop in half an hour. But why rush? This is a wonderful oasis in the heart of Kennebunkport. From Dock Square, take North St. to Beachwood Ave. (right turn) to Gravelly Brook Rd. (left turn). The trailhead is on the left, about 0.2 mile past the brown-shingled Emmons home.

Picnic Rock

About 1.5 miles up the Kennebunk River from the ocean, Picnic Rock is the centerpiece of the **Butler Preserve,** a 14-acre enclave managed by The Nature Conservancy. Well named, the rock is a great place for a picnic and a swim, but don't count on being alone. A short trail loops through the preserve. Consider bringing a canoe or kayak (or renting one) and paddle with the tide past beautiful homes and the Cape Arundel Golf Course. From Lower Village Kennebunk, take Rte. 35 west and hang a right onto Old Port Rd. When the road gets close to the Kennebunk River, watch for a Nature Conservancy oak-leaf sign on the right. Parking is along Old Port Rd; walk down through the preserve to Picnic Rock, right on the river.

Kennebunk Plains Preserve

Also linked to The Nature Conservancy is the 1,600-acre Kennebunk Plains Preserve, nesting site for the endangered grasshopper sparrow and home to dozens of other bird species. Best time to come is August, when hundreds of acres of blueberries are ripe for the picking and the rare northern blazing star carpets parts of the preserve with purple blossoms. You may even see wild turkeys. Most of the preserve was purchased by the Land for Maine's Future Board, created by a $35 million state bond issue in 1987. To reach Kennebunk Plains, head northwest on Rte. 99 from Rte. 9A in Kennebunk. About two miles west of I-95, watch for a small, signposted parking area.

St. Anthony's Monastery

Long ago, 35,000 Native Americans used this part of town for a summer camp. They knew a good thing. So did a group of Lithuanian Franciscan monks who in 1947 fled war-ravaged Europe and acquired the 200-acre St. Anthony's Franciscan Monastery, 28 Beach Ave., Kennebunk (mailing address: P.O. Box 980, Kennebunkport 04046), 207/967-2011, www .framon.net. From 1956 to 1969, they ran a high school here. The monks occupy the handsome Tudor great house, but the well-tended grounds (sprinkled with shrines) are open to the public sunrise to sunset. A short path leads from the monastery area to a peaceful gazebo overlooking the Kennebunk River. No pets or bikes. Public restrooms are available. The monastery also has a fair-sized **guest house** operation, which it runs mid-May–late Oct. (www .franciscanguesthouse.com, 207/967-4865) in a variety of buildings ranging from basic to very comfortable. Rates vary with accommodation, but are highly reasonable in the local scheme of things. There's even an outdoor saltwater pool, and a complimentary buffet breakfast.

Bicycling

A mandatory stop for anyone interested in bicycles and biking is **Cape-Able Bike Shop,** 83 Arundel Rd., Kennebunkport 04046, 207/967-4382, www.capeablebikes.com, a local institution since 1974. The shop specializes in rentals, tours, sales, and service, and provides a free area bike map and the best insider info. (The bike map is also available at the chamber of commerce.) Daily rentals start at $20, weekly rentals at $80. Map, helmet, and lock are included. It's open seven days a week; call for hours. The shop has a second location in Kennebunk Village.

Local rides include a 10-mile Goose Rocks pedal, an eight-mile Cape Porpoise ride, and, if you can cope with a bit of congestion, an eight-mile route through downtown Kennebunkport and over to Kennebunk Beach.

At the height of midsummer traffic, the safest cycling excursion in the area follows an old trolley-line route called the **bridle path** along the Mousam River in Kennebunk. Easiest places to park are at the shop, on Railroad Ave., or at the Sea Road School when school's not in session. Both just south of Rte. 35. The three-mile path is also a wonderfully easy walk for the whole family, ending up near Kennebunk Beach.

Golf and Tennis

Three 18-hole golf courses make the sport a big deal in the area. **Cape Arundel Golf Club,** 19 River Rd., Kennebunkport, 207/967-3494, established in 1896, is semiprivate, open to nonmembers; call for tee times at least 48 hours in advance. George Bush plays here, and no jeans or sweatpants are allowed. Greens fees are $55. **Webhannet Golf Club,** 26 Golf Club Dr., Kennebunk Beach, 207/967-2061, also over a century old, is open to nonmembers, too; again, call for tee times at least 48 hours in advance. In-season greens fees are $60. In nearby Arundel, **Dutch Elm Golf Course,** 5 Brimstone Rd., Arundel, 207/282-9850, www .dutchelmgolf.com, is a public course with rentals, pro shop, and putting greens. It's open Apr. 15–Nov. 15; fees are $35 weekends, $30 weekdays, from Memorial Day–Labor Day, lower the rest of the season. There's also a driving range and banquet facilities.

Tennis courts are scattered around town: **Kennebunk High School,** Fletcher St., Rte. 35, Kennebunk; **Parsons Field,** Park St., Kennebunk; and **West Kennebunk Recreation Area,** Holland Rd., West Kennebunk. The chamber of commerce can provide additional details.

GETTING AFLOAT

You don't have to swim to enjoy the water in the Kennebunks. Kayaking, whale-watching, sailing, and an excursion on a lobsterboat are all other options. Wear a hat and rubber-soled shoes, dress in layers, use sunblock, and remember that freaky weather can put the kibosh on

South Coast and Portland

your plans at the last minute. Reservations are advisable, sometimes required, for all cruises.

Underwater video is the lure for a scenic eco-cruise onboard the *Atlantic Explorer,* 12 Fairway Dr., Kennebunk 04043, docked at the Nonantum Resort Marina, Ocean Ave., Kennebunkport 04046, 207/967-4784 (info) or 207/967-4050 (reservations), www.scenic-cruise.com.

Whale sightings offshore include finbacks, minkes, and humpbacks. The 80-foot *Nick's Chance,* 4 Western Ave., Lower Village, Kennebunk 04043, 207/967-5507 or 800/767-2628, www.FirstChanceWhaleWatch.com, does two four-hour whale-watch trips daily, from the end of June through Labor Day, weather permitting. The boat operates Memorial Day through Columbus Day, with a limited schedule early and late in the season. Cost is $32 adults, $20 children 3–12.

For day-sailing, the 37-foot yacht *Bellatrix,* Sail-aboard-Bellatrix, Ocean Ave., P.O. Box 2762, Kennebunkport 04046, 207/967-8685, www.sailingtrips.com, based at the Nonantum Resort, charges $40 pp for two hours of sailing. The handsome 55-foot gaff-rigged schooner *Eleanor,* Arundel Wharf, Ocean Ave., P.O. Box 572, Kennebunkport, 207/967-8809, heads out for two-hour sails, weather and tides willing, one to three times daily during the summer. Cost is $38 pp.

Kylie's Chance, 4 Western Ave., Lower Village, Kennebunk 04043, 207/967-5507 or 800/767-2628, under the same ownership as *Nick's Chance,* and docked on the Kennebunk side of the river, at Performance Marine, heads out five times daily in summer for 90-minute lobstering cruises—watching, not eating. Trips take place Memorial Day through Columbus Day, with a limited schedule in place earlier and later in the season. Cost is $15 adults, $10 children 3–12.

KIDS STUFF

Besides all the parks and recreational activities described above, most of which are great for children, there's the **Kennebunk Beach Im-provement Association** (KBIA), 262 Beach Ave., Kennebunk 04043, 207/967-2180, www.kbia.net—a child-oriented membership organization ideal for families spending extended time here. KBIA sponsors a huge array of week-long programs, early July–late Aug., for children 3–18.

Kennebunk Parks and Recreation, 1 Summer St., Kennebunk 04043, 207/985-6890, www.kennebunkmaine.org, also sponsors numerous summer activities, with activity fees but no membership fee. Registration must be done in person (weekdays 8 AM–4:30 PM, closed 1–2 PM) or by mail, beginning in mid- to late May. Programs for tiny tots, kids (art and music camp, theater, golf, track, surfing, field hockey, swimming, tennis, and much more), families (Concerts in the Park, canoe trips), adults (softball, tennis, golf lessons), and 55-plus (field trips). Send for the semiannual catalog, which comes out late in April and August.

Kennebunkport Parks and Recreation, 25 School St., P.O. Box 566, Kennebunkport 04046, 207/967-4304, also has a children's summer program. Call or write for the schedule.

All-day play is the rule at **Parsons Field,** Park St., Kennebunk, a municipal park with tennis courts, picnic tables, baseball and softball field, lighted basketball court, and harbor playground.

ENTERTAINMENT

Live entertainment is featured at Federal Jack's Brewpub, the Kennebunkport Inn, and the Nonantum Resort, among other local hotspots. There is also a monthly "Kennebunk Coffeehouse" at the First Parish Church, usually featuring a nationally renowned folksinger.

River Tree Arts

The area's cultural spearhead is **River Tree Center for the Arts** (RTA), 35 Western Ave., Kennebunk 04043, 207/967-9120, www.rivertreearts.org, an incredibly energetic community-arts organization comprising the Chappell

School of Music, the Irvine School of Art, and the Irvine Gallery of Art, with a professional staff, offering opportunities in the arts for all ages. Check website or newspaper listings for RTCA programs and events, or call the office.

FESTIVALS AND EVENTS

During the month-long **February is for Lovers,** inns and bed-and-breakfasts go all out to create a romantic interlude, with candlelight dinners, afternoon teas, and wine tastings.

In July, **Private Gardens of the Kennebunks** features eight outstanding gardens in an area that takes its gardening seriously. Guides and Master Gardeners are on hand to answer questions.

Thursday evenings mid-July–mid-Aug., the River Tree Center for the Arts presents the **WBACH Summer Concert Series,** "Jazz in the Kennebunks." The **Craft Fair on the Green** brings a juried craft show, food booths, and live entertainment to Kennebunkport one Saturday in August.

Take the kids to the **Teddy Bear Show and Sale,** usually the second Saturday in August, but watch the reactions of all the grown-ups. It happens 9:30 AM–3:30 PM at Kennebunk High School.

The first two weekends of December bracket the **Christmas Prelude,** during which spectacular decorations adorn historic homes, candle-toting carolers stroll through the Kennebunks, stores have special sales, and Santa Claus shows up in a lobsterboat.

SHOPPING

Lots of small, attractive boutiques surround **Dock Square,** the hub of Kennebunkport, so gridlock often develops in midsummer. Avoid driving through here at the height of the season. Take your time and walk, bike, or ride the local trolley-bus.

Art Galleries

Jean Briggs represents nearly 110 artists at her topflight, 26-year-old, **Mast Cove Galleries,** Mast Cove Ln. and Maine St., P.O. Box 2718, Kennebunkport 04046, 207/967-3453, www.mastcove.com, in a handsome Greek Revival house near the Graves Memorial Library. Prices vary widely, so don't be surprised if you spot something affordable. Between early June and late August, the gallery sponsors three-hour Wednesday evening jazz and blues concerts. For winter concerts, call or check the website for a schedule. The gallery is open daily 10 AM–5 PM in spring, summer, and fall, by appointment in winter. Also in the Port is **The Gallery on Chase Hill,** 10 Chase Hill Rd., P.O. Box 2786 Kennebunkport, 207/967-0049, www.maine-art.com A showplace for original artwork, the gallery hosts events throughout the summer season. Representing many of the region's best-known artists, it is housed in the stunningly restored Captain Chase House, next to the Windows on the Water restaurant.

Books

To appreciate the friendly, funky **Kennebunk Book Port,** 10 Dock Square, Kennebunkport 04046, 207/967-3815, www.kbookport.com, climb to the second floor of the antique rum warehouse and read the shop slogan: "Ice cream, candy, children, bare feet, short hair, long hair, no hair, cats, dogs and small dragons are welcome here anytime." This place has character. The inventory is well chosen by owners Rick and Ellen Chasse, and the loft even has a small selection of used books. It's open daily, year-round.

Gifts, Crafts, and Clothing

It's tough to describe the inventory at **Marlows,** 64 Main St., Kennebunk 04043, 207/985-2931, www.marlows-maine.com—there's lots of it, and everything's so interesting. There are home and garden gadgets and gifts, thousands of cards, candles, bath and body unguents, jewelry, gourmet goodies, and on and on. It's open all year Mon.–Sat. 9:30 AM–5:30 PM (to 5 PM Sat.). It's also open Sun. 11 AM–4 PM May–Christmas.

Just a bit south of Marlows, on the opposite side of Main St., **Hearth & Soul,** 35 Main St., Kennebunk 04043, 207/985-7466, is as imaginative as its name. Self-described as "Primarily Primitives," it's a fun place to shop. There are small country furniture pieces, great clocks, and stocking-stuffer tidbits like tin ornaments and candles. Not your usual "country" offerings—you won't find these things at the mall. Open Mon.–Sat. 9:30 AM-"ish"–5 PM-"ish." If you're locked out, go have a coffee up the hill, further south, at Cherie's, across from New Morning.

The reason the VW bug in the middle of the floor at **Carrots & Company,** 19 Ocean Ave., P.O. Box 3114, Kennebunkport 04046, 207/967-5300 or 800/803-2820, www.carrotsandcompany.com, looks real is because it is a real car, right in the middle of the store's "gifts, accessories, and laughter." They say you will never find their unique items anywhere else, and they're probably right. Take a look daily in summer (June–mid-Sept.) 9 AM–9 PM; in spring and fall 9 AM–5 PM; or Fri.–Sun. 10 AM–5 PM in winter (Jan.–Mar.).

Compliments, Dock Square, P.O. Box 567-A, Kennebunkport 04046, 207/967-2269 or 800/248-2269, a design center and gallery of fine American crafts, represents a national group of 250 different artists and offers delightful, museum-quality glass, furniture, and jewelry. Open daily, its open Memorial Day–Columbus Day 10 AM–10 PM, till 7 PM in fall, and 10 AM–5:30 PM the rest of the year.

For artful, vibrant clothing, designed, produced, and sold only in Maine, **Catwear,** 800/270-3592, www.catwear.com, has two retail outlets. One is at 8 Spring St., Kennebunkport 04046, 207/967-5060, the other in Portland's Old Port, 399 Fore St., Portland 04101, 207/772-2668. Both sell comfort clothing for women (with a few soft pieces for the babies). Almost everything is made of first-quality Polarfleece from the worker-oriented Malden Mill.

Natural Foods and Farmers Markets

Lafayette Center, a handsomely restored mill building housing boutiques and eateries, is also home to the **Tom's of Maine Natural Living Store,** Storer St., just off Main St., Kennebunk 04043, 207/985-3874 or 800/985-3974, www.tomsofmaine.com, an ecosensitive local firm that makes natural oral- and body-care products. The store sells Tom's of Maine products as well as other natural body- and baby-care products, books, pet-care items, yoga gear, CDs, natural cleaning supplies, candles, and locally crafted items. "Factory seconds" are real bargains. The store is open Mon.–Sat. 10 AM–5 PM.

If all that intrigues you, head for the Tom's of Maine factory and take a one-hour tour, Mon.–Thurs. at 11 AM and 1 PM in summer. In winter, tours are offered only on Wed. at 11 AM. Reservations are essential (800/775-2388). You'll receive a free sample. From the Natural Living Store, take Rte. 1 South to Rte. 9A (at the fork take a right), then take Rte. 99 to Sanford. At the end of Rte. 99, take a right onto Rte. 109. Then take a right into the Sanford Industrial Estates; follow this to the end, take a sharp right, and continue to the factory. Park in a visitor's spot and a tour guide will meet you in the lobby.

New Morning Natural Foods, 3 York St., Rtes. 1 and 9, Kennebunk 04043, 207/985-6774, is a branch of Paul and Sheila Ouellette's Biddeford market by the same name. It includes a super selection of produce and natural foods.

The **Kennebunk Farmers Market** sets up shop early May–mid-Oct. in the Grove St. parking lot off Rte. 1 (behind the Mobil station). Hours are 8 AM–noon on Sat. Vendors sell flowers, herbs, fresh local produce (including organic), eggs, meats, baked goods, and potted plants; special events, like a Tomato Tasting Day, are sometimes on the agenda.

ACCOMMODATIONS

With about 1,500 beds for rent in the Kennebunks, there's plenty of choice and variety.

However, don't arrive without a reservation in early August or during the Christmas Prelude; you may find yourself facing a sea of No Vacancy signs. If that happens, the best fallback is the Kennebunk/Kennebunkport Chamber of Commerce—the staff has a knack for miracle-working.

Resorts
Graciously dominating its garden-filled spread at the mouth of the Kennebunk River, **The Colony Hotel,** 140 Ocean Ave. at King's Hwy., P.O. Box 511, Kennebunkport 04046, 207/967-3331 or 800/552-2363, www.thecolonyhotel.com, springs right out of a bygone era, yet it's racing ahead as one of the state's foremost "green" resorts—calling itself "Maine's first environmentally responsible hotel," and garnering lots of travel and ecological awards. But green doesn't come cheap; this is a splurge choice. Doubles go anywhere from $145–545, depending on type, location, and season, but there are occasional specials. Higher-priced rooms have ocean views, others have garden views. There's no smoking, a three-night minimum is required on summer weekends and holidays, and pets are allowed ($25 extra per day). There's a special feeling here, with cozy corners for reading, lawns and gardens for strolling, a private beach, heated outdoor saltwater pool, room service, bike rentals, badminton, and croquet. The hotel dining room is open to the public for breakfast, lunch, and dinner; reservations are advisable. The hotel is open mid-May–late Oct.

Established in 1883, the **Nonantum Resort,** 95 Ocean Ave., P.O. Box 2626, Kennebunkport 04046, 207/967-4050 or 800/552-5651, www.nonantumresort.com, preserves the feel of a bygone era. Its enviable location on the Kennebunk River means lobsterboat tours and sailing cruises leave right from its dock, so you haven't far to go to see Maine from the water—or the land—Dock Square is a short walk away. A wide selection is available among the 108 rooms in either the Carriage House Inn or the Portside Lodge; there are four suites. Prices are $129–349 d; take a look at the spe-

cials and packages. In summer the Nonantum's River Jewel restaurant serves breakfast, lunch, and dinner. The resort is open late Apr.–mid-Nov.

The Yachtsman Lodge and Marina
An innovative blend of motel and bed-and-breakfast warrants a separate category for the Yachtsman Lodge and Marina, Ocean Ave., Kennebunkport 04046, 207/967-2511, www.yachtsmanlodge.com. Under the same ownership as the White Barn Inn and Grissini Restaurant, the lodge has a motel-type layout with 30 understatedly elegant rooms with telephones, TV/VCR, air-conditioning, and an in-your-face view of the Kennebunk River. Continental breakfast and afternoon tea are served on a lovely patio between the lodge's two sections. Rates vary by season, from a low of $154 to a high of $325 d; special packages are available in spring and fall, including dinners at the White Barn or Grissini. Bikes are available for guests. No smoking is permitted, but pets are allowed for a $25 fee. Open Apr.–early Dec.

Inns
The homey, low-key, turn-of-the-20th-century **Green Heron Inn,** 126 Ocean Ave., Kennebunkport 04046, 207/967-3315, www.greenheroninn.com, sees many repeat guests. Ten rooms and a two-story cottage for three have televisions, phones, air-conditioning, and private baths. Prices are $149–179 d (cottage is $260) early June–early Oct.; lower rates are available other seasons (open year-round). A two-night minimum is required most weekends. Children are welcome, and pets are permitted in selected rooms. No smoking. Also included is breakfast—one of the best in town—served in the coveside breakfast room.

Inns with Restaurants
Innkeeper (and restaurateur and artist) Jack Nahil seems to have a magic touch with everything he undertakes. Now he's rehabbed the **Cape Arundel Inn,** 208 Ocean Ave.,

Kennebunkport 04046, 207/967-2125, making it (and its restaurant) a prime destination. The fabulous ocean view, overlooking the Bush compound, doesn't hurt, either. The Cape Arundel compound consists of the Shingle-style main inn building (seven rooms, most with water view; $275–345 d late June–mid-Sept.), the Rockbound motel-style building (six rooms with sea-view balconies; $285–295 d in season), and Ocean Bluff, a large suite on the upper floor of the carriage house ($275 d in season). Rates are lower off-season. Continental breakfast is included, and all rooms have private baths. A two-night minimum is required on weekends. No smoking or pets, and children under 12 are not allowed in the main inn. Children are permitted in the Rockbound building. The in is open early Mar.–Jan. 2., and its restaurant earns raves for its intriguingly creative continental cuisine. Entrées range from about $25–35.

If nonstop beaching is your vacation goal, book one of the 22 rooms at **Tides Inn by-the-Sea,** 252 Kings Hwy., Goose Rocks Beach, Kennebunkport 04046, 207/967-3757, www.tidesinnbythesea.com, directly across the street from superb Goose Rocks Beach. Decor at the John Calvin Stevens–designed Victorian inn is funky, whimsical (faux painting, costumed dummies, a resident ghost named Emma), and altogether fun. Next door is **Tides Too,** a modern, condo-type building with two-bedroom efficiencies available by the week ($3,700 for four persons). Antique-decorated rooms, with private baths and individual personalities, go for $195–325 June–Labor Day; a three-night minimum is required. Rates are $145–265 other months. Smoking and pets are not permitted. The inn is open mid-May–mid-Oct. The AAA Three Diamond Belvidere Club Victorian Dining Room is open to the public, serving regional gourmet dinners with an extensive wine list.

Bed-and-Breakfasts

At **The Maine Stay Inn & Cottages,** 34 Maine St., Box 500A, Kennebunkport 04046, 207/967-2117 or 800/950-2117,

www.mainestayinn.com, hospitable innkeepers George and Janice Yankowski are both enhancing tradition and introducing innovations. Descendants of Melville Walker, the sea captain who built the house, have gathered at the inn for a family celebration, and Janice has redecorated the parlor in authentic sea-captain style. And, as a Select Registry distinguished inn and a Passport to New England inn, the innkeepers are collaborating on itineraries with another Passport inn in Camden. In the architecturally eclectic inn (Italianate Victorian) are four rooms and two suites (all with private baths, air-conditioning, and color TVs), plus a flying staircase and elegant furnishings. Across the spacious lawn are 11 modern cottage suites—ideal for families, and cribs are available—where you can even have a breakfast basket delivered to your door. Inn rates, in high season, are $199–279 d (no children under five in inn), lower other months; in-season cottage suite rates are $219–279 d. A two-night minimum is required on most weekends, especially in summer. No pets, no smoking. Open all year.

Ex-Peace Corps volunteer Carolyn McAdams considers it her mission to help guests appreciate the Kennebunks. And, post-sightseeing, she encourages guests at **Lake Brook Bed & Breakfast,** 57 Western Ave., Rte. 9, Kennebunk 04043, 207/967-4069, to relax on the veranda of her comfortable marsh-view farmhouse. The three rooms and one suite all have private baths. A full breakfast is served at 8:30 AM every day. No pets, smoking outdoors only. Rates run $95–150 d in season, $80–110 off-season. A two-night weekend minimum is required on weekends July–Labor Day, and a three-night minimum is required on holidays. Across the street is On the Marsh restaurant. The bed-and-breakfast is open all year, but call ahead off-season.

Breakfast is a highlight at **The Captain Fairfield Inn,** 8 Pleasant St., P.O. Box 3089, Kennebunkport 04046, 207/967-4454 or 800/322-1928, www.captainfairfield.com, an 1813 National Historic Register home where innkeepers Rob and Leigh Blood whip up a four-course morning feast. Nine rooms, filled with antiques and fresh flowers (six with fireplaces, all with air-conditioning, many with "gracefully concealed" TVs), have private baths; there's a garden with comfortable lawn chairs; afternoon tea is served, and one of the rooms is an actual art gallery. It's close to Colony Beach and Dock Square, but on a quiet side of the street. No pets, no smoking, inquire about children. Rates are $119–310 d, the upper end being for the spectacular Library Suite. Two-night minimum holidays and most weekends. Open all year. Quiet season packages, with dinner included, are available.

On a side street near the shops, galleries, and restaurants of Dock Square, Tom and Patti Bond preside over **The Inn on South Street,** 5 South St., P.O. Box 529A, 207/967-5151 or 800/963-5151, www.innonsouthst.com. A gourmet candlelight breakfast is served in an elegant dining room. The inn has three very comfortable rooms ($165–185 d in midsummer, $120–135 d other months) and a three-room suite ($275 d in summer, $185–225 d the rest of the year). The suite overlooks incredible herb gardens. No smoking, no pets. Open all year, but call ahead off-season.

A gracious gourmet breakfast is a hallmark at Marc and Sue Trottier's **1802 House Bed and Breakfast Inn,** 15 Locke St., Box 646-A, Kennebunkport 04046, 207/967-5632 or 800/932-5632, www.1802inn.com, a lovely oasis on a country lane within walking distance (10 minutes) of Dock Square. The breakfast room overlooks the Cape Arundel Golf Club, and the Kennebunk River runs by the property. Five elegant rooms and a suite have private baths, air-conditioning, and TV; most rooms have fireplaces, two of which are wood-burning; $159–269 d for rooms in midsummer, $139–269 off-season. The suite, which has a double Jacuzzi and private deck, and is popular for honeymoons, has a seasonal range of $299–389; two-night minimum. No pets, no smoking, no children under 12. Open all year.

Immediately east of the Wedding Cake House, **The Waldo Emerson Inn,** 108 Summer St., Rte. 35, Kennebunk 04043, 207/985-4250, www.waldoemersoninn.com, has a charming colonial feel—as it should, since the main portion was built in 1784. Poet Ralph Waldo Emerson spent many a summer in this, his great-uncle's home. John and Kathy Daamen's four attractive rooms with private baths start at $95 d. No smoking, no pets, no children under six. Open May–mid-Dec. Quilters, take note: In the barn is **Mainely Quilts,** a well-stocked quilt and gift shop, open daily in summer.

You'll awake to the sound of lobsterboat engines at **The Inn at Harbor Head,** 41 Pier Rd., Cape Porpoise, Kennebunkport 04046, 207/967-5564, www.harborhead.com, an idyllic spot on Cape Porpoise Harbor, 2.5 miles from Dock Square. Hand-painted murals, monogrammed bathrobes, flower bouquets, a superb library, hammocks in the yard, and outstanding views are just a few of the pluses here. Three themed rooms (Ocean Room, Garden Room, and the Greenery) and the Summer Suite are available; all are lush, and all come with private baths. Rates (mid-June–mid-Oct. and holidays) are $195–325 d ($160–275 d other months). No pets, no smoking, no children under 12; two-night minimum. Open Feb.–mid-Dec.

Fifteen landscaped acres surround the AAA Four Diamond **Old Fort Inn,** P.O. Box M, Kennebunkport 04046, 207/967-5353, www.oldfortinn.com, in an area of estates just a block from the ocean. The luxury is implicit in the down-filled comforters, robes, hairdryers, sweet treats, and breakfast buffet. A pool, antique shop, and tennis courts complete the picture. No pets or smoking. A two-day-minimum stay is required July–Labor Day weekends, and during the fall-foliage season. A three-day minimum is required over holiday weekends. In-season rates range from $170–385; off-season they start at $109.

Motels and Cottages

With indoor and outdoor heated pools and a good-size fitness center, the **Rhumb Line Motor Lodge,** Ocean Ave., P.O. Box 3067, Kennebunkport 04046, 207/967-5457 or

800/337-4862, www.rhumblinemaine.com, is a magnet for families. This well-managed two-story establishment in a quiet residential area is 1.5 miles from Dock Square, and has its own trolley-bus stop. Fifty-five large rooms (and four suites) have private balcony or patio, phones, air-conditioning, cable TV, and small refrigerators. Free continental breakfast is also provided. Late May–mid-Sept., weather permitting, there are nightly poolside lobsterbakes. Rates are $149–195 d late June–Labor Day, $79–135 d other months; kids 12 and under stay free. Two- or three-night minimum on holiday weekends. Special packages off season. No pets. Open year-round except Jan.

Seasonal Rentals

Weekly and monthly rentals, like nightly room rates, are fairly steep in the Kennebunks. Several real-estate firms handle seasonal rentals. Start with **Kennebunk Beach Realty,** Rtes. 9 and 35, 25 Western Ave., Kennebunk 04043, 207/967-5481, www.KennebunkBeachRealty.com, or **Port Properties, Ltd.,** 169 Port Rd., Village Marketplace, P.O. Box 799, Kennebunkport 04046, 207/967-4400 or 800/443-7678, www .portproperties.com.

FOOD

Breakfast

All Day Breakfast, 55 Western Ave., Rte. 9, Lower Village, Kennebunk 04043, 207/967-5132, is a favorite meeting spot, offering such specialties as invent-your-own omelettes and crepes, Texas French toast, and the ADB sandwich. No smoking. ADB is open daily year-round, 7 AM–1:30 PM, weekends till 2 PM.

Picnic Fare

Next door to the Kennebunk/Kennebunkport Chamber of Commerce, **H.B. Provisions… a general store,** 15 Western Ave., Rte. 9, Lower Village, Kennebunk 04043, 207/967-5762, www.hbprovisions.com, has an excellent wine selection, along with plenty of picnic supplies, newspapers, and all the typical general-store inventory. Open daily, all year.

People come from all over, bringing their coolers with them, to pick up the prepared and frozen delicacies at **Market Day,** Rte. 35, Lower Village, Kennebunk 04043, 207/967-5577, where Peggy Wagor and Jane Chilton preside with ease and efficiency over a huge selection of wines and cheeses, highly satisfactory sandwiches (try their recommended turkey), and takeout items along the lines of stuffed chicken with boursin, pastitsio, and sweet potato with maple bacon and pear. Try to get a scone when it's still warm—it will make your day. Open all year, daily, 9 AM–6:30 PM (Sun. till 5 PM, except winter).

Outstanding pies, pastries, and other desserts make **Cherie's Sweet Treats and Other Eats,** 7 High St., Kennebunk 04043, 207/985-1200, www.cheriesbakery.com, a mandatory stop for anyone possessing a sweet tooth. Cherie's also has sandwiches and wraps, soups, and a varied selection of prepared foods ranging from pasta salad to pork chops. Bakery hours Mon.–Sat 6 AM–6 PM, Sun 6 AM–1 PM. There's also a restaurant (see below).

Bradbury Bros. Market, P.O. Box 7267, Cape Porpoise 04014, 207/967-3939, www.bradburybrothers.com, is the heart and soul of Cape Porpoise. Here you can collect some gourmet picnic goodies (even house-brand items), hang around for local gossip, even send a fax or use the ATM. Open 7 AM–9 PM in summer, slightly shorter hours in winter. Owner Tom Bradbury is the guiding light of the Kennebunkport Conservation Trust.

Lobster-in-the-Rough

Bush-watchers often head to **Mabel's Lobster Claw,** Ocean Ave., Kennebunkport 04046, 207/967-2562, hoping to spot the former president (the little place is just around the corner from Walker's Point). Try Mabel Hanson's chowder or a lobster roll and see why the restaurant's a favorite. During the summer, it's open daily 11:30 AM–3 PM and 5–9 PM.

Moderate and Informal

Nearest thing to being afloat is sitting at a riverfront deck table at **Arundel Wharf Restau-**

rant, 43 Ocean Ave., Kennebunkport 04046, 207/967-3444, where passing tour and lobsterboats provide plenty of lunchtime entertainment. Service is efficient and friendly. On nasty days, a fireplace warms the indoor dining area. Burgers and fries are always on the menu for kids; adults can enjoy lobster with a touch of class. Open for lunch and dinner beginning of May–mid-Oct., daily from 11:30 AM; dinner reservations are wise. There's a "grazing menu" on the deck between lunch and dinner, 2:30–5 PM.

In an airy, stylish room next to the bakery, **Cherie's Sweet Treats and Other Eats,** 7 High St., Kennebunk 04043, 207/985-1200, www.cheriesbakery.com, serves breakfast, Sunday brunch, and dinner. Breakfast specials include a variety of muffins, scones, and creative egg dishes or waffles. Dinner might begin with PEI mussels or grilled brie for two. Entrées like Seared New Bedford Scallops run about $16–18. There's a Kids' Corner menu, too. Breakfast is served Tues.–Sat 7–11 AM; Sun. brunch 8 AM–1 PM; dinner Thurs., Fri., Sat. 5–9 PM.

If the crowds, even on a quiet day in winter, are anything to go by, **Alisson's Restaurant,** 11 Dock Square, P.O. Box 344, Kennebunkport 04046, 207/967-4841, www.alissons.com, is a good choice for lunch—gourmet burgers in the $7 range, Island Chicken Salad at $9—and dinner, emphasizing seafood in dishes like lobster ravioli. There are lots of entrées in the $14 range. The spacious upstairs room has a great view of Dock Square. When you're not eating at Alisson's, you can see who is, on the webcam. Open daily, year-round.

On tap at **Federal Jack's Restaurant and Brewpub,** 8 Western Ave., Lower Village, Kennebunk 04043, 207/967-4322, are the specialty beers of Kennebunkport Brewing Company, producers of Shipyard beers and ales—Goat Island Light, Blue Fin Stout, and several seasonal ales. An eclectic regional American lunch and dinner menu ($12–20 for entrées, plus plenty of tasty pub food; good burgers) keeps kids and adults happy at Federal Jack's (named after a locally built 19th-century schooner), and the brewery also makes nonalcoholic root beer. Inquire about by-request, reservation-only, brewery tours. The brewpub is open daily for lunch and dinner all year; there's live acoustic music on weekends. A recent addition to the complex is **KBC Coffee and Dry Goods,** where you can pick up gourmet condiments and KBC shirts as well as sip coffee while you check your email on the house laptops.

Moderate to Expensive

Just west of the junction of Rtes. 9 and 35, casually elegant **Grissini Trattoria,** 27 Western Ave., Lower Vilalge, Kennebunk 04043, 207/967-2211, www.restaurantgrissini.com, has drawn nothing but bravos since it opened. Attentive service, an inspired Tuscan menu, moderate prices (entrées $13–33), and a bright, open-beamed space make it a winner. In nice weather, try for the sunken patio. Reservations are highly advisable in summer. Open daily 5:30–9:30 PM, Sat. from 5 PM Apr.–Dec; closes at 9 PM Jan.–Mar.

European country cuisine reigns at **On the Marsh,** 46 Western Ave., Rte. 9, Lower Village, Kennebunk 04043, 207/967-2299, www.onthemarsh.com, a restored barn overlooking marshlands leading to Kennebunk Beach. Entrée range is $19–32. The decor here is astonishing, courtesy of owner Denise Rubin, an interior designer: raspberry exterior, art and antiques on both floors of the interior. Quiet piano music adds to the elegant but unstuffy ambience; service is attentive. Reservations are essential in midsummer. Open for dinner 5:30–9 PM Feb.–Dec.: daily June–Oct.; closed Mon.–Tues. other months.

Winner of a raft of culinary awards, **Windows on the Water,** 12 Chase Hill Rd., Kennebunk 04043, 207/967-3313 or 800/773-3313, has been filling its screened porch, patio, and dining rooms since 1985. Significant entrées are $15–36, the latter for such dishes as lobster ravioli and Thai lobster. Reservations are advisable, and essential in midsummer. Open daily for lunch and dinner in summer; call for winter hours.

Getting rave reviews for chef Peter Morency's inventive cuisine is **Pier 77 Restaurant,**

77 Pier Rd., Cape Porpoise 04014, 207/967-8500, www.pier77restaurant.com, right on the harbor. Lunch might begin with steamed mussels or clams in three styles—Classic, Portuguese, and Provencal—and then continue on to a $12.50 Jonah crab sandwich or North Carolina–style BBQ pork ($7.95). Dinner appetizers might include oysters bingo or field greens, and entrées range from $14 spaghetti Pomodoro to lobster paella at $28. Menus change with the seasons. A private upstairs dining room has a window wall, and the downstairs Ramp Bar & Grille offers casual fare. Open daily June 1–Sept. 30, closed Tues.–Wed. other months. Lunch is offered 11:30 AM–3 PM, dinner 5 –10 PM.

Worthwhile Wallet-Cruncher

One of Maine's biggest and best splurges is the **White Barn Inn,** 37 Beach Ave., P.O. Box 560C, Kennebunkport 04046, 207/967-2321, www.whitebarninn.com—haute cuisine, haute prices, haute-rustic barn. In summer, don't be surprised to run into members of George Bush's clan (probably at the back window table). Soft piano music accompanies impeccable service and an outstanding four-course prix fixe menu ($89 pp, excluding wine). Reservations are essential—well ahead during July and August—and you'll need a credit card (cancel 24 hours ahead or you'll have a charge). No jeans or sneakers, and jackets are required. Maine's only AAA five-diamond restaurant, it's part of the Relais et Chateaux network. Open daily for dinner Feb.–Dec. The adjoining inn's beautifully decorated 16 rooms, nine suites, and three stunning waterfront cottages are $325–725 d in peak season, including breakfast, afternoon tea, bikes, and canoes. Suites have fireplaces and whirlpool baths. Other amenities include sunflower shower heads, and having a champagne bath drawn for you. Staff are attentive and urbane.

INFORMATION AND SERVICES

The **Kennebunk/Kennebunkport Chamber of Commerce,** The Yellow House, 17 Western Ave., Rte. 9, Lower Village, P.O. Box 740, Kennebunk 04043, 207/967-0857, www.visitthekennebunks.com, has an especially helpful staff; inquire about accommodations, restaurant menus, area maps, bike maps, tide calendars, recreation, and beach parking passes. Be sure to request a copy of the handsome annual chamber booklet, available each January and loaded with ads and enough useful information to plan any kind of vacation in the Kennebunks. The office is located next to H.B. Provisions, about midway between Rte. 35 and the Kennebunk River. Office hours are Mon.–Fri. 9 AM–5 PM, and most summer Sat. 10 AM–3 PM.

The handsome **Louis T. Graves Memorial Library,** Maine St., Kennebunkport 04046, 207/967-2778, www.graves.lib.me.us, has a worthwhile ongoing book sale in an adjoining building. Once a bank and customs house, the library has a story hour for children on Fridays in the upstairs children's room, where a 1930 Louis Norton frieze depicts fairy tales in the styles of the original illustrators. In downtown Kennebunk is the **Kennebunk Free Library,** 112 Main St., Kennebunk 04043, 207/985-2173.

Newspapers

The local *York County Coast Star,* based in Kennebunk, comes out every Wednesday. Each issue in summer, the paper produces *Vacation,* a free tabloid supplement covering restaurants, shopping, entertainment, and a tide calendar for York and the Kennebunks.

Daily newspapers covering this area are the *Portland Press Herald* and the Biddeford *Journal-Tribune.*

Emergencies

In an emergency requiring police, fire, and/or ambulance in **Kennebunkport** or **Kennebunk,** call 911. The nearest hospital is **Southern Maine Medical Center,** 1 Medical Center Dr., Biddeford, 207/283-7000 (round-the-clock emergency room: 283-7100). For minor medical problems, head

South Coast and Portland

for the **Kennebunk Walk-In Clinic,** 24 Portland Rd., Rte. 1, Kennebunk, 207/985-6027. York Hospital's **Tel-a-Nurse** service, 800/283-7234, provides free over-the-phone advice for minor medical problems.

Public Restrooms

Public toilets are located at Goose Rocks, Gooch's and Mother's Beaches, as well as at St. Anthony's Monastery and the chamber of commerce building, and in Dock Square.

Laundry

Maytag Laundromat & Dry Cleaners, 169 Port Rd., Village Marketplace, Lower Village, Kennebunk 04043, 207/967-5066, is open daily, all year, except major holidays.

Photo Services

Ocean Exposure, 35 Western Ave., Rte. 9, Lower Village, Kennebunk 04043, 207/967-0500, www.oceanexposure.com, does one-hour processing and on-premises black-and-white and slide processing. It's open all year.

Getting Around

The **Intown Trolley,** 207/967-3686, www .intowntrolley.com, operates trolley-buses throughout Kennebunkport, originating on Ocean Ave. and making regular stops at beaches and other attractions. The entire route takes about 45 minutes, with the driver providing a hefty dose of local history and gossip. Seats are park-bench-style. An all-day ticket is $10 adults.

Biddeford and Saco

Saco and Biddeford have long been upstairs/downstairs sister cities, with wealthy mill owners living in Saco and their workers (and workplaces) located in Biddeford. But even those personalities have always been split—congested, commercial Rte. 1 ("Hamburger Alley") is part of Saco, and exclusive Biddeford Pool is, of course, in below-stairs Biddeford. Saco still has an attractive downtown, with boutiques and stunning homes on Main St. and beyond. One city focus is Saco Island (also called Factory Island or York Hill), in the middle of the Saco River. Once a massive millworks, the sprawling brick buildings are very gradually being retrofitted as shops and offices—an eco-conscious model proven successful in other American cities.

Biddeford's downtown has suffered from the end of the mill era and the big-box store trend, but is also home to the magnificent Biddeford City Theater, the historic McArthur Library, a new wave of ethnic restaurants, and revitalization efforts like the Heart of Biddeford, plus the University of New England is nearby. A new riverfront park and mill space adaptations are help-

ing Biddeford to change its blue-collar mill-town image. Another Biddeford hallmark is its Franco-American tradition—thanks to the French-speaking workers who sustained the textile and shoemaking industries in the 19th century. Never is the heritage more evident than during Biddeford's annual La Kermesse festival in late June.

SIGHTS AND RECREATION

Saco Museum

Founded in 1866, the Saco Museum (formerly the York Institute Museum), 371 Main St., Saco 04072, 207/283-3861, www.saco-museum.org, might also be one of the state's best-kept secrets. It shouldn't be. The outstanding collection includes 18th- and 19th-century paintings, furniture, and natural-history artifacts. The museum features both changing and permanent exhibitions related to decorative arts, regional history, and contemporary artists. Open Tues., Wed., Fri., and Sun. noon–4 PM; Thurs. noon–8 PM. Also open noon–4 PM on Sat. July–Oct. Admission $4 adults, $3 seniors,

$2 students/children, children under 6 free; free admission Thurs. 4–8 PM.

The Heath

Owned by The Nature Conservancy, 1,100-acre Saco Heath Preserve is the nation's southernmost "raised coalesced bog"—where peat accumulated over eons into two above-water dome shapes that eventually merged into a single natural feature. For a bit of esoterica, it's the home of the rare Hessel's hairstreak butterfly. Pick up a map at the parking area and follow the mile-long, self-guided trail through the woods and then into the heath via boardwalk. The best time to come is early to mid-October, when the heath and woodland colors are positively brilliant and insects are on the wane. You're likely to see deer, and perhaps even spot a moose. The preserve entrance is on Rte. 112, Buxton Rd., two miles west of I-95. Open all year, sunrise to sunset, it's also popular with snowshoers and cross-country skiers in winter. For information, contact the **The Nature Conservancy,** 14 Maine St., Fort Andross, Brunswick 04011, 207/729-5181, www.nature.org.

Ferry Beach State Park

When the weather's hot, arrive early at Ferry Beach State Park, Bay View Rd., off Rte. 9, Saco, 207/283-0067, a pristine beach backed by dune grass on Saco Bay. In the 117-acre park are changing rooms, restrooms, a lifeguard, picnic tables, and five easy interconnected nature trails winding through woodlands (with a rare stand of tupelo trees), marshlands, and dunes. (Later in the day, keep the insect repellent handy.) Admission is $3 adults, $1 children 5–11, free for seniors (over 65) and kids under five. Open daily Memorial Day weekend–Sept. 30, but accessible all year. (Trail markers are removed in winter.)

Camp Ellis

Begun as a small fishing village named after early settler Thomas Ellis, Camp Ellis is crowded with longtime summer homes—some precariously close to the shore, courtesy of storm-tossed waves. A nearly mile-long granite jetty—designed to keep silt from clogging the Saco River—has taken the blame for massive beach erosion in the last 20 years. But the jetty is a favorite spot for wetting a line (no fishing license needed) and for panoramic views off toward Wood Island Light (built in 1808) and Biddeford Pool. Camp Ellis Beach is open to the public. Parking—scarce on hot days—is $1 an hour for residents, $2 for nonresidents, $20 for vehicles with trailers. There is a $5 daily boat-launch fee for motorized vessels; those without motors are free.

East Point Sanctuary

Owned by the Maine Audubon Society, the 30-acre East Point Sanctuary is a splendid preserve at the eastern end of Biddeford Pool. Crashing surf, beach roses, bayberry bushes, and offshore Wood Island Light are all features of the two-part perimeter trail here—skirting the golf course of the exclusive Abenakee Club. Allow at least an hour; even in fog, the setting is dramatic. During spring and fall migrations, it's one of southern Maine's prime birding locales, so you'll have plenty of company if you show up then, and the usual streetside parking may be scarce. Open sunrise to sundown, all year. From Rte. 9 (Main St.) in downtown Biddeford, take Rte. 9/208 (Pool Rd.) southeast about five miles to the Rte. 208 turnoff to Biddeford Pool. Go 0.6 mile on Rte. 208 (Bridge Rd.), then left onto Mile Stretch Rd. Continue to Lester B. Orcutt Blvd., turn left, and go to the end. For further information, contact Maine Audubon Society, 20 Gilsland Farm Rd., P.O. Box 6009, Falmouth 04105, 207/781-2330, www.maineaudubon.org.

Hiking

Saco Bay Trails, a local land trust, has produced a very helpful trail guide that includes the Saco Heath, the East Point Sanctuary, and more than a dozen other local trails. The Cascade Falls trail, for example, is a 0.5-mile stroll ending at a hidden waterfall. Copies are available for $5 at a number of Biddeford and Saco locations (including the Dyer Library) or from Saco Bay Trails, P.O. Box 720, Saco 04072. The organization takes an active role in trail building and maintenance and can always use help; check the website for workday events—you needn't be a member.

Golf

Opened in 1922 as a nine-hole course, the **Biddeford-Saco Country Club,** 101 Old Orchard Rd., P.O. Box 448, Saco 04072, 207/282-5883, added a back nine in 1987 (toughest hole on the par-71 course is the 11th). There is a full driving range. Call three days in advance for reservations. Fees are $30–50, depending on the day and the time of year. Open to the public early Apr.–mid-Nov.

KIDS STUFF

Along a three-mile stretch of Rte. 1 in Saco sometimes dubbed "Kids' Alley," Funtown/ Splashtown USA is just south of the Vacationland Bowling Center and the Saco/Portland South KOA campground. The second big attraction, Aquaboggan Water Park, is about three miles farther north.

Funtown/Splashtown USA

Two adjoining amusement parks merged in 1996, creating Funtown/Splashtown USA, 774 Portland Rd., Rte. 1, Saco, 207/284-5139 or 800/878-2900, www.funtownsplashtownusa.com, the largest family-themed water and amusement park in New England, with 29 rides and 13 water slides. The Funtown section has food tents and rides for all ages, including the 100-foot-high Excalibur, Maine's only wooden roller coaster, and the Dragon's Descent Turbo-Drop. The Splashtown section has Thunder Falls Log Flume and the new Pirate's Paradise, the tallest and largest attractions of their kind in New England. There are stage shows and acres of landscaped grounds and flowers. Funtown opens mid-May (weekends only), while Splashtown opens mid-June; everything's up and running daily from then through Labor Day. (Schedules are dependent on the hundreds of young park workers, including a contingent from Russia.) Visitors can

buy combo passes or pay individually for each ride; call or check website for prices.

Aquaboggan Water Park

Three miles north of Funtown/Splashtown USA, Aquaboggan Water Park, Rte. 1, Saco, 207/282-3112, is wet and wild, with such stomach-turners as the Stealth and the Suislide. Wear a bathing suit that won't abandon you in the rough-and-tumble. Also, if you wear glasses, safety straps and plastic lenses are required. Besides all the water stuff, there are shuffleboard courts, mini-golf, picnic tables, and snack bars. Lots of ticket options cover varying numbers of attractions. Open 10 AM– 6 PM late June–Labor Day.

ENTERTAINMENT AND EVENTS

City Theater

Designed by noted architect John Calvin Stevens in 1896, the 500-seat **National Historic Register City Theater**, 205 Main St., P.O. Box 993, Biddeford 04005, 207/282-0849, www.citytheater.org, has been superbly restored, and acoustics are excellent even when Eva Gray, the resident ghost, mixes it up backstage. A respected community theater group mounts a fall and spring drama season and showcases other talent throughout the year. Check local papers, their website, or call for the schedule.

The **Arundel Barn Playhouse,** 53 Old Post Rd., Arundel 04046, 207/985-5552 (seasonal box office), www.arundelbarnplayhouse.com, presents musicals in a restored 1888 barn. Single tickets are $19–29; subscriptions receive a 15 percent discount. Open end of June– Labor Day.

Cinema

You can see as many as 14 first-run films in the stadium seating at **Cinemagic Stadium Theaters,** 779 Portland Rd., Rte. 1, Saco, 207/282-6234, across from Funtown/Splashtown USA and open year-round. Bring large-denomination bills if you intend to buy snacks.

La Kermesse

La Kermesse (the fair or the festival) is Biddeford's summer highlight, and New England's largest Franco-American Festival. About 30,000 visitors pour into town on the last full weekend in June (Thurs.–Sun.) to celebrate the town's Franco-American heritage. Local volunteers go all out to plan a block party, parade, fireworks, games, carnival, live entertainment, and traditional dancing—most of it centered on Biddeford's St. Louis Field. Then there's *la cuisine Franco-Américaine;* you can fill up on *boudin, creton, poutine, tourtière,* and crepes (although your arteries may rebel). The camaraderie is contagious, much of it in a French you never learned in language class. As with revelers on St. Patrick's Day who adopt Irish heritage, everyone instantly becomes Franco-American during La Kermesse, but festival organizers have reached out in recent years to other ethnic groups to make this a multicultural event. For more information, call 207/468-3921, www.biddefordmaine.org.

Generally scheduled for the Saturday of the same weekend, the **Saco Sidewalk Arts Festival** involves dozens of artists exhibiting their work all along Saco's Main St., vying for thousands of dollars in awards and prizes. Strolling musicians, kids' activities, and food booths are all part of the well-organized, day-long event.

In Saco in July, St. Demetrios Orthodox Greek Church presents its Annual Greek Heritage Festival, a weekend of Greek music and dancing, crafts, and authentic Greek food, with Greek coffee and scrumptious homemade pastries for dessert.

SHOPPING
Gifts and Clothing

Stone Soup Artisans, 228 Main St., Saco 04072, 207/283-4715, is a cooperative shop carrying work from more than 60 artisans affiliated with the **Society of Southern Maine Craftsmen.** Open year-round Mon.–Sat. 10 AM–5:30 PM. Open Sun. in summer.

Just down the street is **Saco Bay Classics,** 260 Main St., Saco 04072, 207/283-1400, with a fine selection of high-end, high-quality men's and women's clothing. Open Mon.–Sat. 9 AM–5 PM.

At **Heart's Desire,** 191 Main St., Saco 04072, 207/282-6957, second-time-around fashions are stylishly arranged. It's a good hunting ground for consignment junkies. There are also some brand-new items and a compelling jewelry counter. Summer hours are Tues.–Fri. 10 AM–6 PM (till 7 on Thurs.), Sat. 9 AM–5 PM. Shorter hours in winter.

Nellie's Tea & Gifts at **Pot de Fleur,** 265 Main St., Biddeford 04005, 207/294-3322, is a shop-within-a-shop. Nellie's purveys stylish teas and accouterments, *pot de fleur,* antiques, accessories, and art.

Discount Shopping

Bargain-hunting is encouraged at the **West Point Stevens Bed & Bath Mill Store,** 170 Main St., Biddeford 04005, 207/286-8255, a factory outlet where you can find real deals on mostly irregular towels, comforters, blankets, bedspreads, and sheets, plus remnants for quilters. Be sure to look over the merchandise carefully. Open Mon.–Sat. 9 AM–4:30 PM, all year.

Farmers Market

Every Wednesday and Saturday, 7 AM–noon, from the Saturday before Mother's Day to the end of October, the **Saco Farmers' and Artisans' Market** sets up shop at the Saco Valley Shopping Center, Rte. 1, Saco. A great combination of crafts, seasonal produce, eggs, flowers, plants, glass-bottled milk and cream, meats, and artisanal cheeses are available.

ACCOMMODATIONS

An excellent address in Saco is the **Crown 'n' Anchor Inn,** 121 North St., P.O. Box 228, Saco 04072, 207/282-3829 or 800/561-8865, www.crownnanchor.com. Innkeeper John Barclay will show you around the extraordinary 19-room Thacher-Goodale House, a masterfully restored Greek Revival National Historic Register manse on three in-town acres. Six antiques-filled Victorian guest rooms with private baths are $80 (single room) to $130 (carriage-house honeymoon suite with deck) d. Mid-June–mid-Oct., add $10. However, singles and senior citizens get a $10 reduction. (The Normandy suite even has two fireplaces.) Breakfast is to die for—served by candlelight on bone china to four guests at a time (seatings at 7, 8:30, and 10 AM); plan to skip lunch. Then inn has gained fame for always managing to include ice cream in the breakfast menu; guests have taken photos of the July 4 and Memorial Day red, white, and blue compote (blueberries, strawberries, vanilla ice cream) decorated with a flag. No smoking, but pets are welcome. The inn will also arrange for Portland and Boston airport pickups. Open all year.

Owned by the Pagano family since the 1960s, the basic, well-maintained **Saco Motel,** 473 Main St., Rte. 1, Saco 04072, 207/284-6952, three miles from the beach, has 26 rooms (some efficiencies) with air-conditioning and cable TV. Doubles are $60–85 July–Labor Day, lower rates early and late in the season. Giselle Pagano is a great booster of the area and very helpful with touring suggestions. Open late Apr.–mid-Oct.

The **Holiday Inn Express Hotel & Suites,** 352 North St., Saco Plaza, Saco 04072, 207/286-9600 or 800/HOLIDAY, www.hiexpress.com/sacome, has its own exit from I-95, between the Biddeford and Saco/Old Orchard exits. The hotel has a conference center, heated outdoor pool, complimentary Express Start Breakfast, and complimentary airport/Amtrak/beach shuttle. There are 88 rooms and 21 suites. Convenient to I-95 in Biddeford is the **Comfort Suites Biddeford,** exit 32, 45 Barra Rd., Biddeford 04005, 207/294-2464.

A convenient, well-maintained **campground** is the Saco/Portland South KOA, 814 Portland Rd., Rte. 1, Saco 04072, 207/282-0502 or 800/562-1886, www.sacokoa.com, with 16 cabins and 120 tent and RV sites on 30 acres alongside Rte. 1. It's not remote; request a wooded site back from the highway. Among the facilities are a swimming pool,

laundry, playground, and rec room. Reservations are advisable July–Aug. Nightly rates for two persons are $29–82, depending on requirements and accommodation. The campground is about 1.5 miles from I-95 exit 36. Open May 1–mid-Oct.

FOOD
Saco
Having risen from the ashes of a disastrous fire with strong community support, the Cyr family's **Lily Moon Café & Bakery,** 17 Pepperell Sq., Saco 04072, 207/284-2233 or 888/729-4118, continues to be a popular spot for that community to dine on fresh, thoughtfully prepared breakfasts, Tues.–Fri. 8 AM–11 PM, Sat.–Sun. to 1 PM, and lunches, Mon.–Fri. 11:30 AM–2 PM. The Lily Mooner is an egg and cheese breakfast sandwich ($3.59). There are also breakfast crepes and blintzes ($4.59–5.69), and an interesting selection of salads, plus hot and cold sandwiches for lunch, including grilled crabmeat ($7.99).

Well seasoned after more than half a century, family-oriented **Wormwood's Restaurant,** 16 Bay Ave., Camp Ellis Beach, Saco 04072, 207/282-9679, next to the stone jetty, still draws the crowds and keeps its clientele happy with ample portions and $5–20 entrées. Cajun-style seafood is a specialty. Open daily all year, 11:30 AM–9 PM.

Also at Camp Ellis is **Huot's Seafood Restaurant,** Camp Ellis Beach, Saco 04072, 207/282-1642, a local institution since 1935. Portions are large, prices are not. Open for lunch and dinner.

It's still the summer of 1877 at **The Milliken House,** 65 North St., Saco 04072, 207/283-9691, www.MillikenHouse.com, and the downstairs maid greets you at the door, just before you sit down to enjoy a serious dessert like Key Lime Torte, Berry Lovely Charlotte, or Grandma's German Chocolate Surprise. There are over a dozen dessert options from $3.50–5.45, plus beverages like ice-cream and Italian sodas, fresh breads, scones, and soup. Summer hours (to Labor Day) are Tues.–Thurs.

5–10 PM, Fri.–Sat. 2–10 PM. After Labor Day (to Dec. 10) Fri.–Sat. hours only.

Biddeford

Pool Lobster Co., formerly P.M. Inniss, 18 Yates St., Biddeford Pool 04006, 207/284-5000, www.poollobster.com, claims seniority in the local lobster business, and it's a fine spot for a lobster-roll picnic. Or order a cooked lobster and take it to the beach. Open daily 8 AM–6:30 PM, shorter hours fall and winter.

Produce is super-fresh and all organic at Paul and Sheila Ouellette's **New Morning Natural Foods,** 230 Main St., Biddeford 04005, 207/282-1434, a local institution since 1976. The Ouellettes have added a very popular small café open Mon.–Sat. 11 AM–2 PM, serving a delicious, healthy menu of from-scratch quiche, an array of salads and soups, and wraps. Quiche or other entrée, with a huge salad, is $5.95. Open all year, Mon.–Fri. 9 AM–5:30 PM, Sat. to 5 PM.

Collette's Cup, 146 Alfred St., Biddeford 04005, 207/286-8655, serves Java Tree coffee with bagels and other breakfast goodies amid its arts-and-crafts gallery. There are lots of magazines and a sofa seating area in front of the wood stove. Open Mon.–Thurs. 6:30 AM–4 PM, Fri. 6:30 AM–6 PM, Sat. 8 AM–1 PM.

Bebe's Burritos, 140 Main St., Biddeford 04005, 207/283-4222, the place to go for outstanding Mexican food—everything from nachos to burritos, including heavenly guacamole—typifies the ethnic restaurant trend now brightening Biddeford's downtown. Other ethnic eateries are **Thai Siam Restaurant,** 144 Main St., Biddeford 04005, 207/294-3300, and the **Jewel of India,** 26 Alfred St., Biddeford 04005, 207/283-4200, www.thejewelofindia.com.

INFORMATION AND SERVICES

The **Biddeford-Saco Chamber of Commerce and Industry,** 110 Main St., Ste. 1202, Saco 04072, 207/282-1567, www.biddefordsacochamber.org, oversees development and tourism in the two-town

area. The office, on Saco Island, is open all year, Mon.–Thurs. 8:30 AM–4:30 PM, Fri. 8 AM–4 PM.

The **Dyer Library,** 371 Main St., Saco 04072, 207/283-3861, www.sacomuseum.org, next door to the Saco Museum, attracts scads of genealogists to its vast Maine history collection. Open Tues. and Thurs. 9:30 AM–8 PM, Mon., Wed., and Fri. 9:30 AM–5 PM, Sat. 9:30 AM–12:30 PM.

The **McArthur Public Library,** 270 Main St., Biddeford 04005, 207/284-4181, www.mcarthur.lib.me.us, is the oldest public library in the state, established by the town in 1863. There are more than 27,000 volumes in the children/young adults collection, just one of the library's pluses—others include its stately appearance and spacious interior. Open Mon.–Thurs. 9:30 AM–8 PM, , Fri. 10 AM–5 PM, Sat. 9:30 AM–3:30 PM.

Emergencies

Southern Maine Medical Center, 1 Medical Center Dr., Biddeford 04005, 207/283-7000, is an up-to-date hospital with a fine reputation and round-the-clock emergency-room care. For **police, fire, or ambulance,** dial 911.

Media

The *Journal Tribune,* 207/282-1535, published daily in Biddeford, and the *BiddefordSacoOOB Courier,* 207/282-4337, a free weekly, are the primary local information sources.

Getting Around

Operated by the Biddeford-Saco-Old Orchard Beach Transit Committee, **ShuttleBus,** www.shuttlebus-zoom.com, provides frequent weekday and less-frequent weekend service (except national holidays) between Biddeford and City Hall in downtown Portland. In-between stops are Saco, Old Orchard Beach, Scarborough, and the Maine Mall. One-way fare on the entire one-hour route is $3; kids under five are free; seniors pay half on Tuesdays. A separate route connects Biddeford, Saco, and Old Orchard Beach with frequent weekday and weekend service (except on national holidays). One-way fare on the 30-minute route is $1. Another route, known as Zoom, began operations in 1998 for Biddeford-to-Portland com-muters, via the Maine Turnpike. Travel time is 31 minutes to Monument Square.

The **Amtrak Downeaster** stops at Saco Island

(just south of Main St.) on each of its four round-trips between Boston and Portland.

Taxi standbys are **Twin City,** 207/284-7911 or 800/482-8294, and **Alternative,** 207/284-0269.

Old Orchard Beach

Old Orchard has been vacation-oriented for generations—from the earliest Native Ameri-cans through wealthy, turn-of-the-20th-cen-tury summer folk (including Rose Fitzgerald and Joe Kennedy, who met on these sands in the days when men strolled around in dress suits and women toted parasols) to the T-shirted pleasure-seekers of today.

It's once again possible to come to Old Orchard the way many of the wealthy did—by train. Amtrak's Downeaster has a seasonal stop (May 1–Oct. 31) right next to the new Welcome and Visitors Center, and two blocks from the beach, the amusement park, and the center of town. For more information on the Downeaster, call 800/USA-RAIL.

But the tourist profile began to change a bit when French-Canadian tourism slumped in the late 1980s and early 1990s. (For one thing, shop-owners began to diversify their inventory to cater to the year-round clientele.) You'll still hear French on the streets in summer, but fami-lies are the target now, giving rise to amusements of every stripe—arcades, concerts, festivals, shopping, and more. There's not a kid on earth who wouldn't have fun in Old Orchard—even if parents find it all a bit much.

Town fathers have built brick sidewalks, in-stalled Victorian streetlights, and landscaped the downtown. But the miles-long crescent of white sand is what draws crowds to Old Orchard Beach—and you'd better like people if you stop here, because this town welcomes tourists (the population expands from about 9,500 in winter to about 100,000 in midsummer).

ENTERTAINMENT

The biggest beachfront amusement park, **Pal-ace Playland,** 1 Old Orchard St., Old Or-

chard, 207/934-2001, www.palaceplayland .com, has the works: giant water slide, fun house, bumper cars, Ferris wheel, two roller coasters, and arcade. It opens at 10 AM week-days and 9 AM weekends during the summer season.

The Pier, jutting 475 feet into the ocean, is a mini-mall of shops, arcades, and fast-food outlets. Far longer when it was built in 1898, it's been lopped off gradually by fires and storms. The current incarnation has been here since the late 1970s.

More sedate entertainment is the rule at the southwest end of town, in the **Ocean Park** section. Established in 1881 as a reli-gious summer-cottage community, Ocean Park still offers interdenominational services and vacation Bible school, but it also has an active cultural association that sponsors con-certs, Chautauqua-type lectures, and family events throughout the summer. All are open to the public. The Temple is the venue for the Ocean Park Music Festival's Sunday-night concerts (7:30 PM, $10 adults, group discounts available). For a schedule, contact the Ocean Park Association, 15 Colby Ave., P.O. Box 7296, Ocean Park 04063, 207/934-9068, www.oceanpark.org.

In Old Orchard, the Salvation Army has conducted Camp Meetings since 1873. They are still holding them, along with Bible Study and Pier Praise, but they also offer family entertainment at the comfort-able, covered **Old Orchard Beach Pavil-ion,** Union Ave. and Sixth St., P.O. Box 285, Old Orchard Beach 04064, 207/934-2024, www.oobpavilion.org.

Golf

Covering more than 300 acres, the 18-hole,

par-71 **Dunegrass Golf Club,** 200 Wild Dunes Way, Old Orchard Beach 04064, 207/934-4513 or 800/521-1029, has drawn raves for its challenges. Greens fees are $39–79, depending on season and whether play is before or after 1 PM, when they drop $10. The sprawling modern clubhouse includes a restaurant and pro shop.

FESTIVALS AND EVENTS

Old Orchard's organized fun is about as extensive as anywhere in southern Maine. Here are just a few of the regular events.

Every Monday and Tuesday night, late June–Labor Day, there's free entertainment at 7 PM in the town square. Every Thursday during the same season, fireworks begin at 9:45 PM near the Pier.

One night in August, the Ocean Park community's **Illumination Night** makes the little town a fairyland, with strings of lights, candles, and luminaria punctuating the summer night. A concert and strawberry shortcake sale add the finishing touches. One weekend in mid-August, the **Beach Olympics,** a family festival of games, exhibitions, and music, is held to benefit Maine's Special Olympics program.

ACCOMMODATIONS

Old Orchard has hundreds of beds—mostly in motel-style lodgings. The chamber of commerce is the best resource for motels, cottages, and the area's thousands of campsites. In recent years, the motels and campgrounds have been joined by a sprinkling of inns and bed-and-breakfasts.

On a quiet side street, **The Atlantic Birches Inn,** 20 Portland Ave., Rte. 98, Old Orchard Beach 04064, 207/934-5295 or 888/934-5295, www.atlanticbirches.com, has 10 guest rooms with private baths and air-conditioning in a Victorian house and separate cottage. Breakfast is hearty continental, and there's a swimming pool; smoking is permitted only on the veranda. The beach is an easy walk. No pets, no smoking. Rates run $96–142 d July–Labor

Day, lower other months. Open all year, but call ahead off-season.

The view is everything at Dick and Patte Kessler's **Nautilus By the Sea,** 2 Colby Ave., P.O. Box 7276, Ocean Park 04063, 800/981-7018, www.nautilusbythesea.com, a Victorian bed-and-breakfast located about as close as you can get to the water. Thirteen comfortable rooms and suites (two with shared baths, the rest private) are $75–160 d at the height of summer, $55–115 d other months; three-day minimum in midsummer (or add 10 percent to the rate). No pets, no smoking. Open Apr.–Nov.

Calling itself a bed-and-breakfast but a bit larger than most, the **Old Orchard Beach Inn,** 6 Portland Ave., Old Orchard Beach 04064, 207/934-5834 or 877/700-6624, www.old-orchardbeachinn.com, was rescued from ruin by owner Steve Cecchetti and opened in the summer of 2000. Built in 1730, and most recently known as the Staples Inn, the National Historic Register building seemed destined for the wrecker's ball in 1997. Now it's been transformed, with 18 antiques-filled rooms with private baths, air-conditioning, phones, and TV. Continental breakfast is included in the rates—$109–185 d in peak season, $69–140 d other months; a two-bedroom suite is $175–400, depending on the season. No pets, no smoking. Open all year.

Cristina's Bed & Breakfast, 36 Main Ave., Camp Ellis Beach 04072, 207/282-7483, is part of Saco, like all of Camp Ellis, but it's at the southern end of Old Orchard Beach, and you can walk right to the beach through the garden. A spacious porch and outdoor beach shower reflect the nostalgic atmosphere here, a reminder of how peaceful a seaside vacation can be. But if you want things to do, hospitable innkeepers Cristina and Paul Trahan are part of the local community (he teaches English, she's a sometime teacher, bilingual in Spanish and English, and taking an advanced Spanish studies degree) and can give you the inside dope. Their two cats and a friendly golden retriever don't mind company, but check first. Their full breakfasts are homemade and organic. The bed-

and-breakfast, which celebrated its 10th year in 2005, has three upstairs rooms sharing a bath, and one downstairs room with private bath, for $75–135. Open year-round, mostly weekends in the off-season.

FOOD

Old Orchard is synonymous with fast food, most of it the order-at-the-counter, carry-it-away variety. For a once-a-year cholesterol pig-out, try **Lisa's Pizza** or **Pier French Fries.** To compound your sins, you can always have fried dough for dessert. You can find all this on Old Orchard St., and that's only the beginning.

Joseph's By the Sea, 55 W. Grand Ave., Old Orchard Beach 04064, 207/934-5044, www.josephsbythesea.com, should be named Joseph's Oasis—a quiet, dignified shorefront restaurant amid all the hoopla. Request a table on the screened patio. The menu—continental with a catch of the day, and lobster cooked three ways—has entrées in the $17–29 range. Try the specialty Saco Bay stew, Maine-

accented bouillabaisse. Desserts are exceptional, from strawberry Pavlova to banana praline crepe. Reservations advisable in midsummer. Open for dinner Thurs.–Sat. at 5 PM, for breakfast Sat. 7 AM–11 AM, Sun. 7 AM–noon.

With its tables set with flickering candles, the porch is inviting at **The Landmark Restaurant,** 28 E. Grand Ave., Old Orchard Beach 04064, 207/934-0156. Located in a restored Victorian home (with a small parking lot—walk if you're staying nearby), it has an imaginative menu, from scallion pancakes to duck to dessert wines. Entrées are in the $18–20 range, but there are often early-bird and other specials. Open early March for dinner Thurs.–Sun. 5 PM, with expanded summer hours.

INFORMATION

The staff at the **Old Orchard Beach Chamber of Commerce,** First St., P.O. Box 600, Old Orchard Beach 04064, 207/934-2500, www.oldorchardbeachmaine.com, is especially helpful.

Greater Portland

Maine visitors often come hungry only for lobsters, lighthouses, and the great outdoors. As a result, the state's cities tend not to show up on the itinerary. Big mistake. Portland is a must-see, a human-level place offering—among other features—lobsters, lighthouses, and the great outdoors (this is, after all, known as "Forest City").

With about 64,300 souls (and its bedroom satellites, which almost quadruple that head count to 243,000), Portland is as big as Maine cities get. This makes for a stimulating, cosmopolitan blend in a most manageable environment—a year-round destination, not just a summer place.

Portland's assets merely start with a striking art museum with a world-class permanent collection; a thriving, handsomely restored downtown crammed with shops, galleries, and restaurants of every persuasion and flavor; a cultural agenda that can keep you going

all day and out all night; a brand-new, public market modeled on Seattle's Pike Place; several professional sports teams; and countless miles of hikeable, bikeable urban and suburban turf. Meanwhile, down along the working waterfront, there's serious business—commercial fishing vessels, long-distance passenger boats, and ferries lugging freight, commuters, and visitors to the islands of Casco Bay.

Greater Portland includes the communities of Westbrook and Gorham to the west; South Portland, Cape Elizabeth, and Scarborough to the south; Falmouth and Cumberland to the north, and the Casco Bay Islands, offshore to the east.

HISTORY

Portland's downtown, a crooked-finger peninsula projecting into Casco Bay and today defined vaguely by I-295 at its "knuckle," was named Machigonne (Great Neck) by the Wabanaki, the Native Americans who held sway when English settlers first arrived in 1632. Characteristically, the Brits renamed the region Falmouth (it included present-day Falmouth, Portland, South Portland, Westbrook, and Cape Elizabeth) and the peninsula Falmouth Neck, but it was some 130 years before they secured real control of the area. Anglo-French squabbles, spurred by the governments' conflicts in Europe, drew in the Wabanaki from Massachusetts to Nova Scotia. Falmouth was only one of the battlegrounds, and a fairly minor one. Relative calm resumed in the 1760s, only to be broken by the stirrings of rebellion centered on Boston. When Falmouth's citizens expressed support for the incipient revolution, the punishment was a 1775 naval onslaught that wiped out 75 percent of the houses—a debacle that created a decade-long setback. In 1786, Falmouth Neck became Portland, a thriving trading community where shipping flourished until the 1807 imposition of the Embargo Act. Severing trade and effectively shutting down Portland Harbor for a year and a half, the legislation did more harm to America's fledgling colonies than to the French and British it was designed to punish.

In 1820, when Maine became a state, Portland was named its capital. The city became a crucial transportation hub with the arrival of the railroad. The Civil War was barely a blip in Portland's history, but the year after it ended, the city suffered a devastating blow: exuberant July Fourth festivities in 1866 sparked a conflagration that virtually leveled the city. The Great Fire spared only the Portland Observatory and a chunk of the West End. Evidence of the city's Victorian rebirth remains today in many downtown neighborhoods.

Following World War II, Portland slipped into decline for several years, but that is over. The city's waterfront revival began in the 1970s and continues today, despite commercial competition from South Portland's Maine Mall; Congress Street has blossomed as an arts and retail district; public green space is increasing; and an influx of immigrants is changing the city's cultural makeup. With the new century, Portland is on a roll.

PORTLAND NEIGHBORHOODS

The best way to appreciate the character of Portland's neighborhoods is on foot. Like any city, Portland also has a few problem spots (particularly the larger parks), places you need to avoid after dark, but, compared to major cities in other states, dangers are relatively few.

The Old Port

Tony shops, cobblestone sidewalks, replica streetlights, and a casual, upmarket crowd (most of the time) set the scene for a district once filled with derelict buildings. The 1970s revival of the Old Port has infused funds, foot traffic, and flair into this part of town. Scores of unusual shops, ethnic restaurants, and spontaneous street-corner music make it a fun area to visit year-round. Nightlife centers on the Old Port, where about two dozen bars keep everyone hopping until after midnight. Police keep a close eye on the district, but it can get a bit dicey after 11 PM on weekends. Caveat emptor—or maybe caveat peregrinator!

Congress Street/ Downtown Arts District

Bit by bit, once-declining Congress Street is becoming revitalized, showcasing the best of the city's culture. Artists, starving and otherwise, spend much of their time here, thanks largely to encouragement from the energetic grassroots Downtown Arts District Association (DADA). Galleries, artists' studios, coffeehouses, cafés, craft shops, two libraries, the State Theatre, the Merrill Auditorium (in City Hall), the Portland Museum of Art, the Maine College of Art, and even L.L. Bean and the new Portland Public Market are all part of the renaissance, with no end in sight.

West End

Probably the most diverse of the city's downtown neighborhoods, and one that largely escaped the Great Fire of 1866, the West End includes the historically and architecturally splendid Western Promenade, Maine Medical Center (the state's largest hospital), the city's best B&Bs, a gay-friendly community with a laissez-faire attitude, a host of cafés and restaurants, as well as a few niches harboring the homeless and forlorn.

Munjoy Hill

A slightly down-at-the-heels neighborhood enclave with a pull-'em-up-by-the-bootstraps attitude, Munjoy Hill is probably best known for the distinctive wooden tower that adorns its summit.

Named for George Munjoy, a wealthy 17th-century resident, the hill has a host of architectural and historic landmarks—well worth a walking tour. Fortunately, Greater Portland Landmarks, 165 State St., Portland 04101, 207/774-5561, has produced a 24-page booklet, *Munjoy Hill Historic Guide* ($3), which documents more than 60 notable sites, including the National Historic Register Eastern Cemetery and, with spectacular harbor views, the Eastern Promenade and Fort Allen Park.

West Bayside and Parkside

A Babel of languages reverberates in these pockets just east of Portland City Hall. West Bayside and Parkside have experienced the arrival of refugees—Cambodian, Laotian, Vietnamese, Central European, and Afghan families—from war-torn lands during the 1980s and 1990s. Nowadays, you'll hear references to Somali Town, an area named for all the resettled refugees from that shattered country. Others have come from Sudan and Ethiopia. All have been assisted by Portland's active **Refugee Resettlement Program.** Many have found employment with **Barber Foods,** a fantastically conscientious firm that hires many new immigrants in its processing plant and provides opportunities for employees to learn English and obtain social services.

Beyond the Peninsula

At the western edge of Portland, close to the Portland Jetport, is the historic area known as **Stroudwater,** once an essential link in Maine water transport. The 20-mile-long **Cumberland and Oxford Canal,** hand-dug in 1828, ran through here as part of the timber-shipping route linking Portland Harbor, the Fore and Presumpscot Rivers, and Sebago Lake. Twenty-eight wooden locks allowed vessels to rise the 265 feet between sea level and the lake. By 1870, trains took over the route, condemning the canal to oblivion. Centerpiece of the Stroudwater area today is the historic 18th-century Tate House.

SIGHTS

Portland Museum of Art

Maine's oldest and finest art museum, the Portland Museum of Art (PMA), 7 Congress Sq., Portland 04101, 207/775-6148, fax 773-7324, www.portlandmuseum.org; recorded info: 207/773-2787 or 800/639-4067, earns its renown thanks to a topflight collection of American and impressionist masters and an award-winning I. M. Pei building. The museum is the cornerstone of the Maine Art Museum Trail, which highlights the state's seven major museums. Free gallery tours occur at 2 PM daily; galleries are wheelchair-accessible. The museum also has a pleasant café, a well-stocked gift shop, and special activities for children. The café is open for lunch daily, and for dinner Thursday and Friday. From Memorial Day to Columbus Day, the PMA is open Mon.–Sat. 10 AM–5 PM (to 9 PM Fri.) and Sun. noon–5 PM From Columbus Day to Memorial Day, it's closed Mon. Admission is $8 adults, $6 seniors and students, $2 children 6–12. Children under six are free. Free admission 5–9 PM every Fri. Next door, conveniently, is the Children's Museum of Maine (see below).

The Longfellow Connection

A few blocks down Congress Street from the PMA, you'll step back in time to the era of

Portland-born poet Henry Wadsworth Longfellow, who lived in the **Wadsworth-Longfellow House,** 485 Congress St., Portland 04101, 207/774-1822, as a child in the early 1800s—long before the brick mansion was dwarfed by surrounding high-rises. Wadsworth and Longfellow family furnishings fill the three-story house (owned by the Maine Historical Society), and savvy guides provide insight into Portland's 19th-century life. Even little kids respond to the guides' enthusiasm during the hour-long tours. Purchase tickets next door (489 Congress St.) at the Maine Historical Society Museum, 207/879-0427, where you can take in the society's current exhibits and patronize the gift shop. The Wadsworth-Longfellow House is open May–Oct. Mon.–Sat. 10 AM–4 PM, Sun. noon–4 PM. Admission is $7 adults, $3 children 5–17, children under 5 free. Admission includes entrance to the museum. Don't miss the urban oasis—a wonderfully peaceful garden—behind the house. The Maine Historical Society Museum is open Mon.–Sat. 10 AM–5 PM, Sun. noon–5 PM. Closed on Sun. Nov. 1–Apr. 30. Admission is $4 adults, $2 children 5–17, free for children under 5.

Portland Observatory, built in 1807

Victoria Mansion

The Italianate Victoria Mansion (also called the Morse-Libby Mansion), 109 Danforth St., Portland 04101, 207/772-4841, is rife with Victoriana—carved marble fireplaces, elaborate porcelain and paneling, and plenty of trompe l'oeil touches. It's even more spectacular at Christmas, with yards of roping, festooned trees, and carolers. (This is the best time to bring kids, as they may not be particularly intrigued by the house itself.) The mansion was built in the late 1850s by Ruggles Sylvester Morse, a Maine-born entrepreneur whose New Orleans–based fortune enabled him to hire 93 craftsmen to complete the house. Today the house is maintained by the nonprofit Victoria Society (originally the Victoria Society of Women). Guided, 45-minute tours begin every half hour (on the quarter-hour). Open May–Oct., Tues.–Sat. 10 AM–4 PM and Sun. 1–

5 PM. Also open during December for tours and holiday events. Admission is $7 adults, $3 children 6–17.

Portland Observatory

Providing a head-swiveling view of Portland (and the White Mountains on a clear day), the octagonal red-painted Portland Observatory, 138 Congress St., Portland 04101, 774-5561, is the only remaining marine signal tower on the eastern seaboard. Closed in 1994, when inspectors found powderpost beetles dining on its timbers, the 86-foot wooden tower underwent a $1.2-million restoration and reopened in June 2000. Built in 1807 at a cost of $5,000 by Capt. Lemuel Moody to keep track of the port's shipping activity, the tower has 122 tons of rock ballast in its base. Admission in those days (only men were allowed to climb the 103 interior steps) was 12.5 cents; today it's $5 adults, $3 children (6–16). The city-owned tower, managed by Greater Portland Landmarks, is open Mon.–Sun. Memorial Day–Columbus Day, 10 AM–5 PM. Guided tours available, the last tour begins at 4:40 PM.

Riding the Narrow-Gauge Rails

A three-mile ride along Portland's waterfront comes with admission to the **Maine Narrow Gauge Railroad Company and Museum,** 58 Fore St., Portland 04101, 207/828-0814. The museum owns more than three dozen train cars and has others on long-term loan—most from Maine's five historic narrow-gauge railroads (the last one closed down in 1943). A two-car train takes riders along the two-foot-wide track from the museum's building in the Portland Company complex to Fish Point, below the Eastern Promenade—a short but enjoyable excursion. Years ago, hundreds of steam engines were built here. Trains operate daily early June–mid-Oct., 11 AM–4 PM on the hour. The museum opens at 10 AM daily. Trains run on weekends Mar.–May and mid-Oct.–early Nov. Tickets are $8 adults, $7 for seniors (except for special events), $5 children 3–12. At the eastern end of Fore St., turn at the railroad-crossing sign on the water side; the museum is at the back of the complex.

Art from Africa

Founded in 1998, the **Museum of African Tribal Art,** 122 Spring St., Portland 04101, 207/871-7188, fax 773-1197, is the brainchild of Oscar Mokeme (the director) and Arthur Aleshire. Among the 500 treasures in the fledgling museum—not all on display at once—are Nigerian tribal masks and Beninese lost-wax bronzes. The museum also has an ambitious outreach program, educating the community about African art and culture. Admission is free. Open Tues.–Sat. 10:30 AM–4 PM.

BEYOND THE DOWNTOWN PENINSULA

Seeing Stars

Under a 30-foot dome with comfy theater seats and a state-of-the-art laser system, the **Southworth Planetarium,** 96 Falmouth St., Science Building, lower level, University of Southern Maine, Portland 04103, 207/780-4249, fax 780-4051, presents a changing schedule of astronomy shows (Fri.–Sat. 7 and 8:30 PM), and family matinees (Sat. 3 PM; also Sun. at 3 PM during the school year). If your kids tend to be squirmy, take them to a matinee, not to an evening show. No reservations are needed. Computer-savvy kids will head for the interactive computers in the exhibit area; the gift shop stocks astronaut ice cream and other science-type stuff. Adult admission is $5. Kids and seniors pay $4. For recorded information on moon and planet positions, eclipses, and other astronomical happenings, call the **Skywatch Hotline:** 207/780-4719. Take Exit 6B off I-295 and go west on Forest Ave. to Falmouth St. (left turn). The Science Building is on the left, after the parking lot.

Tate House

Just down the street from the Portland International Jetport, in the Stroudwater district, is the 1755 Tate House, 1270 Westbrook St., P.O. Box 8800, 207/774-6177, a National Historic Landmark owned by the Colonial Dames of America. Built by Capt. George Tate, a prominent shipbuilder, the house has superb period furnishings and a lovely 18th-century herb garden overlooking the Stroudwater River. Open for 40-minute guided tours June 15–Oct. 15, Tues.–Sat. 10 AM–4 PM, Sun. 1–4 PM. Admission is $7 adults, $5 seniors, $2 children 6–12, under 6 are free. Wednesdays in July and August are "summer garden days," when tea and goodies follow tours of the garden. Architectural tours on Tuesdays. There is no extra charge for these special tours. From downtown Portland, it's 3.2 miles; take Congress St. West (Rte. 22) to a left turn at Westbrook Street. If you have spare time at the Portland Jetport, Tate House is an easy walk. Ask for directions at the airport information desk.

Portland Harbor Museum

The maritime history of Casco Bay and Maine is the focus at the small Portland Harbor Museum, Fort Rd., South Portland 04106, 207/799-6337, on the waterfront campus of Southern Maine Community College (SMCC). To reach the museum, head over the Casco Bay Bridge from downtown

Portland (Rte. 77) and continue onto Broadway. Watch for SMCC signs. A permanent exhibit features a section of the 19th-century clipper *Snow Squall,* retrieved from its graveyard in the Falkland Islands and returned to its Maine birthplace. The museum now holds the title to the nearby Spring Point Ledge lighthouse, which is open for tours periodically during the summer. Call to check. Also nearby are the remains of Fort Preble and the Spring Point Shoreline Walkway leading to Willard Beach. The museum is open Apr. 15–Memorial Day Fri.–Sun. 10 AM–4:30 PM. Memorial Day–Columbus Day open daily from 10 AM–4:30 PM. Columbus Day–Nov. 27 open daily 10 AM–4 PM. Admission is $4 adults, $2 children (6–16), and free for kids under six.

Prouts Neck

About 12 miles south of downtown Portland, at the junction of Rtes. 77 and 207, is Black Point Rd., leading to the exclusive community of Prouts Neck—and the year-round and summer residents want to keep it that way. No Parking and Private Way signs are posted everywhere. Respect private property, but you can visit the **Winslow Homer Studio,** the famed 19th-century artist's haunt for the last 27 years of his life and recently acquired by the Portland Museum of Art.

The lack of parking thwarts many visitors; unless you get lucky, or you're staying at the Black Point Inn, it's best to walk or bike to the studio from Scarborough Beach Park.

After you pass the sprawling, gray-shingled Black Point Inn Resort, stop at the seasonal **Prouts Neck Post Office,** 207/883-4058, where Postmaster Roger Snelling cheerfully greets everyone under a ceiling strung with colorful, toy-size aluminum airplanes—all made from soda cans. Continue along the Marginal Way, past the yacht club, to Winslow Homer Rd., marked by a Positively No Passing sign. There's no parking here, either, but you can walk to Homer's small studio, just beyond the gate

on the right. It's generally open July–Aug. 10 AM–4 PM, but you may want to call 207/883-2249 to be sure. To the right of the Positively No Passing sign is the beginning of the 1.5-mile **Cliff Walk,** a pathway with spectacular views along the southern and eastern edges of the neck.

PARKS, PRESERVES, AND BEACHES

Greater Portland is blessed with green space, thanks largely to the efforts of 19th-century mayor James Phinney Baxter, who foresightedly hired the famed Olmsted Brothers' firm to develop an ambitious plan to ring the city with public parks and promenades. Not all the elements fell into place, but the result is what makes Portland such a livable city. When heading for the beaches, keep in mind that even on a hot day, Atlantic water is not bathtub-warm; you'll need to adjust—make sure you don't go hypothermic by staying in too long. And don't forget the sunblock.

Portland Peninsula

Probably the most visible of the city's parks, 51-acre **Deering Oaks,** Park and Forest Aves. and Deering St., may be best known for the quaint little duck condo in the middle of the pond. Other facilities and highlights here are tennis courts, playground, horseshoes, rental paddleboats, a snack bar, outstanding rose gardens, a Saturday farmers market (7 AM–noon), and, in winter, ice skating. (Winter scenes in the film *The Preacher's Wife,* starring Denzel Washington and Whitney Houston and a slew of Portland extras, were shot here.) After dark, steer clear of the park.

At one end of the Eastern Promenade, where it meets Fore St., **Fort Allen Park** overlooks offshore **Fort Gorges** (coin-operated telescopes bring it closer). A central gazebo is flanked by an assortment of military souvenirs dating as far back as the War of 1812. All along the Eastern Prom are walking paths, benches, play areas, even an ill-maintained fitness trail—all with that terrific view. Down by the water is

Fort Gorges, in Portland Harbor

East End Beach, with parking, token sand, and the area's best launching ramp for sea kayaks or powerboats.

West of Downtown
Just beyond I-295, along Baxter Blvd. (Rte. 1) and tidal **Back Cove,** is a skinny green strip with a 3.5-mile paved trail for walking, jogging, or just watching the sailboards and the skyline. Along the way, you can cross Baxter and spend time picnicking, playing tennis, or flying a kite in 48-acre **Payson Park.**

Talk about an urban oasis. The 85-acre **Fore River Sanctuary,** owned by the Maine Audubon Society, has two miles of blue-blazed trails that wind through a salt marsh, link up with the historic Cumberland and Oxford Canal towpath, and pass near **Jewell Falls,** Portland's only waterfall, protected by Portland Trails. From downtown Portland, take Congress St. West (Rte. 22), past I-295. From here there are two access routes: Either turn right onto Stevens Ave. (Rte. 9), continue to Brighton Ave. (Rte. 25), turn left and go a little over a mile to Rowe Ave.,

turn left and park at the end of the road; or continue past Stevens Ave., about half a mile to Frost Ave., take a hard right, then left into the Maine Orthopaedic Center parking lot. Portland Trails raised the funds for the handsome, 90-foot pedestrian bridge at this entrance to the sanctuary. Open daily, sunup to sundown. No pets, free admission.

South of Portland
The Maine Lighthouse Bicycle Tour, a well-planned bike route, takes in several of the following sites; for a handy map guide to the route ($2), stop at the Visitor Information Center or contact the Bicycle Coalition of Maine, P.O. Box 5275, Augusta 04332, www.BikeMaine.org.

Just over the Casco Bay Bridge (formerly the "Million-Dollar Bridge") from downtown Portland (Rte. 77), take a left onto Broadway and continue to the end at **Southern Maine Community College** (SMCC), overlooking the bay. The best time to come here is evenings and weekends, when there's ample parking. Unless it's foggy (when the signal is deafening) or thundering (when you'll expose yourself to lightning), walk out along the 1,000-foot granite breakwater to the **Spring Point Ledge Light,** with fabulous views in every direction. Also here are picnic benches, the remains of Fort Preble, the Peter A. McKernan Hospitality Center, and the Portland Harbor Museum. At the southern edge of the SMCC campus is the **Spring Point Shoreline Walkway,** a scenic three-mile pathway with views off to Casco Bay and House, Peaks, and Cushings Islands. At the end of the shoreway, you'll reach crescent-shaped **Willard Beach,** a neighborhoody sort of place with lifeguards, a changing building, a snack bar, and those same marvelous views. If you're headed directly to Willard Beach from downtown Portland, follow the same directions as above, but instead of entering the SMCC campus, turn right onto Preble St. Continue to Willow St. (near Willard Square), then go left to the beach. Park in the designated lot, not on the street.

Built in 1791—during George Washington's administration—the stunningly sited **Portland Head Light,** 1000 Shore Rd., Fort Williams Park, Cape Elizabeth 04107, 207/799-2661, has been immortalized in poetry, photography, and philately. The surf here is awesome. There's no access to the 58-foot automated light tower, but the superbly restored keeper's house has become the **Museum at Portland Head Light,** filled with local history and lighthouse memorabilia. Museum admission is $2 adults, $1 children 6–18. It's open daily 10 AM–4 PM, Memorial Day–mid-Oct., open some weekends before Memorial Day. Call to check.

In the 94-acre municipally owned **Fort Williams Park,** surrounding the lighthouse, there's lots of manicured space for kids to run and play. Bring a picnic, binoculars, and kites. The park has tennis courts and a beach and is open sunup to sundown all year. The **Portland Symphony Orchestra,** 207/773-8191, performs a pops concerts in the park bandshell to celebrate the Fourth of July. From downtown Portland, take Rte. 77, then Broadway, Cottage Rd., and Shore Rd.—a total of four miles to the south and east.

Almost a vest-pocket park, 40-acre **Two Lights State Park,** Two Lights Rd., off Rte. 77, Cape Elizabeth 04107, 207/799-5871, has picnicking and restroom facilities, plus a bike rack in the parking area; its biggest asset is the panoramic ocean view from atop a onetime gun battery. Open all year. Summer admission is $3 adults, $1 kids 5–11, seniors 65 and older and children under five are free. Before or after visiting the park, take a left just before the park entrance (continuation of Two Lights Rd.—the sign says Lighthouses). Continue to the parking lot at the end, where you'll see the signal towers for which Two Lights is named. (There's no access to either one; only one still works.) If you haven't brought a picnic for the state park, enjoy the food and the view at **The Lobster Shack,** 222 Two Lights Rd., next to the parking area, Cape Elizabeth, 207/799-1677; it's open daily 11 AM–8 PM, mid-Apr.–mid-Oct. (to 8:30 in July and Aug.).

If you don't mind company, **Crescent Beach State Park,** Rte. 77, Cape Elizabeth 04107, 207/767-3625, has Greater Portland's largest, most attractive beach—a 243-acre park with changing rooms, lifeguard, restrooms, picnic tables, and a snack bar. It's officially open Memorial Day weekend to September 30, but the beach is accessible all year (off season, expect to meet plenty of dog walkers). Admission is $3.50 adults, $1 children 5–11, free for kids under five and seniors over 65. Directly offshore is Saco Bay's **Richmond Island**—a 200-acre private preserve with a checkered past dating to the 17th century.

Scarborough's major neighborhood beach is **Higgins Beach,** at the mouth of the Spurwink River. There's plenty of access via local roads to the huge beach—with dunes and tidal pools—but parking is nonexistent. Best option is to book a room or rent a cottage nearby. Turn onto Ocean Ave. from Rte. 77 (Spurwink Rd.).

Scarborough Beach Park, Black Point Rd., Rte. 207, Scarborough 04074, 207/883-2416, is open all year for swimming, surfing, beachcombing, and ice skating. Between the parking area and the lovely stretch of beach, you'll pass Massacre Pond, named for a 1703 skirmish between resident Indians and resident wannabes. (Score: Indians 19, wannabes 0.) You might want to leave your car here and walk down Black Point Road to visit Prouts Neck. The park is open May 1–Oct. 1, the entry fee is $3.50 adults, $2 seniors, $1.50 kids, under 5 free.

At 3,100 acres, **Scarborough Marsh,** Pine Point Rd., Rte. 9, Scarborough 04074, 207/883-5100, Maine's largest salt marsh, is prime territory for birding while walking the self-guided nature trails or canoeing. Rent a canoe ($12 an hour/members, $15 an hour/non-members) at the small nature center, operated by Maine Audubon Society (www.maineaudubon.org), and explore on your own. Or join one of the daily 90-minute guided tours at 10 AM (also Sun. at 1 PM). Cost is $11 adults, $9 children (subtract $1.50 pp if you have your own canoe). June–Sept., guided full-moon tours ($12 per adult, $10 per child) are particularly exciting; dress warmly and bring a flashlight. Other special programs, some geared primarily for children (nature art, pet tales, tiny-tot tours and pottery class) include wildflower walks, edible and medicinal plants, and early-morning birding trips. All require reservations and fees. Call or write for a schedule: **Maine Audubon Society,** 20 Gilsland Farm Rd., Falmouth 04105, 207/781-2330. Located on Rte. 9, 0.8 mile east of the junction with Rte. 1, the Scarborough center is open daily 9:30 AM–5:30 PM, mid-June–Labor Day. Open weekends after Memorial Day through end of Sept.

Falmouth (North of Portland)

Nearly a dozen of Falmouth's parks, trails, and preserves, official and unofficial, are described and mapped in the *Falmouth Trail Guide,* a handy little booklet published by the Falmouth Conservation Commission. Copies are available at Gilsland Farm, Falmouth Town Hall, and local bookstores. Two of the best options are described below.

A 60-acre wildlife sanctuary and environmental center on the banks of the Presumpscot estuary, **Gilsland Farm** is state headquarters for the Maine Audubon Society. More than two miles of easy, well-marked trails wind through the grounds, taking in salt marshes, rolling meadows, woodlands, and views of the estuary. Observation blinds allow inconspicuous spying during bird-migration season. In the education center are hands-on exhibits, a nature store, and classrooms and offices. Open daily, all year (except major holidays). Closed Sun. Jan.–Feb. Fees are charged for special events, but otherwise it's all free. The visitors center is 0.25 mile off Rte. 1. For more info contact the Maine Audubon Society, 20 Gilsland Farm Rd., Falmouth 04105, 207/781-2330, www.maineaudubon.org.

Once the summer compound of the prominent Baxter family, Falmouth's 100-acre **Mackworth Island,** reached via a causeway, is now the site of the Governor Baxter School for the Deaf. Limited parking is available just beyond the security booth on the island. On the 1.5-mile, vehicle-free perimeter path, you'll meet bikers, hikers, and dog-walkers. Just off the trail on the north side of the island is the late Governor Percival Baxter's stone-circled pet cemetery, maintained by the state at the behest of Baxter, who donated this island as well as Baxter State Park to the people of Maine. From downtown Portland, take Rte. 1 across the Presumpscot River to Falmouth Foreside. Andrews Ave. (third street on the right) leads to the island. Open sunup to sundown, all year.

If you have a sea kayak (even a rented one), consider a little picnicking excursion to **Basket Island,** a nine-acre island best reached from the Falmouth town landing (Town Landing Rd., just off Rte. 88 in Falmouth Foreside; or take Johnson Rd., southeasterly from Rte. 1 in Falmouth, to connect with Town Landing Rd.). Owned by the Cumberland Mainland & Island Trust (207/829-3201), the island has gravel beaches, a salt marsh, rugosa roses, and the foundation of an old lighthouse. Be forewarned: It also has prolific poison ivy. No camping or fires are allowed. Visitors are asked to stay off Basket Island between mid-May and the end of June to protect nesting eider ducks. The island is popular with boaters on weekends, so plan to arrive on a weekday. For further information, contact Jonathan Larabee at 207/729-7366.

RECREATION

Hiking and Walking

So much of Portland can (and should) be covered on foot that it would take a book to list all the possibilities, but several dedicated volunteer groups have produced guides to facilitate the process.

Greater Portland Landmarks, 165 State St., Portland 04101, 207/774-5561, www.portlandlandmarks.org, is the doyenne, founded in 1964 to preserve Portland's historic architecture and promote responsible construction. The organization has published more than a dozen books and booklets, including *Discover Historic Portland on Foot,* a packet of four well-researched walking-tour guides to architecturally historic sections of Portland's peninsula: Old Port, Western Promenade, State Street, and Congress Street. It's available for $5.95 at local bookstores, some gift shops, and the Visitor Information Center, 245 Commercial St., Portland 04101, 207/772-5800, fax 874-9043.

Greater Portland Landmarks sponsors a series of **summer tour programs** mid-June–Columbus Day Mon.–Sat. at 10:30 A.M. Knowledgeable landmarks guides lead fascinating 90-minute walking tours—**Historic Portland on Foot**—in downtown Portland. No reservations are needed. Buy tickets at the Visitor Information Center, 245 Commercial St., where the tours begin and end. The tour "Homes of Portland's Golden Age" (1800–1860) begins Fridays at noon at the Portland Museum of Art. The Historic Eastern Cemetery (dating from 1668) tour begins Thursday at noon at the Portland Observatory. All tours are $8; children under 16 and with an adult are free.

Portland Trails, 305 Commercial St., Portland 04101, 207/775-2411, fax 871-1184, www.trails.org, a dynamic membership conservation organization incorporated in 1991, continuously adds to the mileage it has mapped out

for hiking and biking around Portland. The group's recent accomplishments include the 2.1-mile **Eastern Promenade Trail,** a pathway circling the base of Munjoy Hill and linking East End Beach to the Old Port, a continuing trail connecting the Eastern Prom with the 3.5-mile Back Cove Trail, and a two-mile trail along the Presumpscot River. The goal for the 21st century? A 30-mile network of Greater Portland multiuse recreational trails. Count on it. Contact Portland Trails for a colorful foldout map ($4.95) of Portland's entire trail and park system—including some proposed routes—a joint effort of Portland Trails and the Greater Portland Council of Governments' Kids and Transportation Program. Better still, join Portland Trails ($35 a year) and support their ambitious efforts.

The newest walking-tour project, in downtown Portland, is the **Portland Women's History Trail,** sponsored by the Women's Studies Program at the University of Southern Maine and the Maine Humanities Council and spearheaded by history professor Polly Kaufman. Four loops cover Congress Street, Munjoy Hill, State Street, and the West End, with about 20 stops on each loop. Among the sites: a long-gone chewing-gum factory where teenage girls worked 10-hour days, a girls' orphan asylum, and City Hall, site of Portland's first women's suffrage meeting in 1870. The trail guide, "Working Women of the Old Port," is available for $8.95 at the **Maine Historical Society Museum** gift shop, 489 Congress St., Portland 04101, 207/879-0427.

The **Southern Maine Volkssport Association** P.O. Box 722, Westbrook 04098, 929-4047, affiliated with the American Volkssport Association, has several hundred members and annually sponsors a half-dozen *Volksmarsch* events (noncompetitive family-oriented walks) that you can do at your own pace. Most last 2–4 hours and are around 10 kilometers long.

Bicycling

A mandatory stop for anyone planning to get around on two wheels in Greater Portland is **Back Bay Bicycle,** 333 Forest Ave., Portland

04101, 207/773-6906, where you can get a tune-up, a repair, or just talk bikes. Helpful with rentals (road bikes $30, hybrids $20 a day) and repairs is **Cycle Mania,** 59 Federal St., Portland 04101, 207/774-2933. **Allspeed Bicycle & Ski,** 1041 Washington Ave., Portland 04103, 207/878-8741, sells a huge variety of bikes (and skis), and does repairs.

Excellent **bike-route maps** of the islands and the lighthouse trail just south of Portland have been produced by the Bicycle Coalition of Maine, www.BikeMaine.org. Copies of *Two Casco Bay Island Bicycle Tours* (variable mileage) and *Maine Lighthouse Bicycle Tour* (21 miles) are sold at the Visitor Information Center.

The best locales for island bicycling—fun for families and beginners but not especially challenging for diehards—are Peaks and Great Chebeague Islands.

Golf

You'll have no problem finding a place to tee off in Greater Portland. Some of the best courses are private, so if you have an "in," so much the better, but there are still plenty of public and semiprivate courses for every skill level. If you're planning to play a lot of golf, consider buying an American Lung Association **Golf Privilege Card,** covering greens fees for 200 rounds of golf for $70. You can choose among more than 85 courses. Besides, it's a great cause. Many courses on the list require reservations 24–48 hours in advance, and some require player's fees. Write or call American Lung Association of Maine, 122 State St., Augusta 04330, 207/622-6394 or 800/499-5864, fax 207/626-2919.

Let's just consider Greater Portland's 18-hole courses. **Sable Oaks Golf Club,** 505 Country Club Dr., South Portland, 207/775-6257, is considered one of the toughest and best of Maine's public courses. Tee times are always required. Since 1998, **Nonesuch River Golf Club,** 304 Gorham Rd., Rte. 114, Scarborough 04074, 207/883-0007, has been drawing raves for the challenges of its par-70 course and praise from environmentalists for preserving wildlife habitat. Tee times are essential. Gor-

ham **Country Club,** 134 McLellan Rd., Gorham, 207/839-3490, has a par-71 course with plenty of challenging terrain. Call for tee times weekends and holidays. At **Val Halla Golf and Recreation Center,** 1 Val Halla Rd., off Rte. 9, Cumberland Center, 207/829-2226, tee times are always required. **Willowdale Golf Club,** 52 Willowdale Rd., Scarborough, 207/883-9351 is opposite Scarborough Downs race track. Scarborough's salt marsh is visible from a couple of the holes. The City of Portland's **Riverside Municipal Golf Course,** 1158 Riverside St., Portland, 207/797-3524, has an 18-hole par-72 course (Riverside North) and a nine-hole par-35 course (Riverside South). Opt for the 18-hole course. The clubhouse is just west of I-95, between exits 848 and 52. Call for tee times on weekends.

When lousy weather sets in, the local alternative is **Fore Season Golf,** 110 US Route #1 Falmouth, 04105 207/797-8835, where you can play virtual golf at more than a dozen famous courses with regulation clubs and balls, thanks to computerized simulators. A snack bar keeps you going, and beer and wine are available.

Tennis

Portland's 31 free municipal tennis courts, open dawn to dusk, first-come, first-served, are scattered all over the city. Best ones are in Deering Oaks, Payson Park, and on the Eastern Promenade. The **City of Portland Recreation Division,** 389 Congress St., Portland 04101, 207/874-8793, manages them all; call for other locations.

Swimming

Besides the saltwater beaches listed above, Portland has two municipal pools open to the public: **Reiche Pool,** 166 Brackett St., in the West End, 207/874-8874; and **Riverton Pool,** 1600 Forest Ave., Rte. 302, west of I-295, 207/874-8456. Both are part of community center/school complexes. **South Portland's municipal pool** is at 21 Nelson Rd., 207/767-7655. Hours for open swimming vary, so call for schedules.

Climbing

With 24-foot-high walls and 20 major sections covering 5,000 square feet of surface, the **Maine Rock Gym,** 127 Marginal Way, Portland 04101, 207/780-6370, has become hugely popular since it opened in 1994. Angled walls and molded handholds simulate the real thing, and the gym management rearranges the handholds regularly to maintain variety. During the summer, you can also scale a 40-foot monster outdoor climbing wall. (It's air-conditioned inside.) Cost for the introductory package—including mandatory instructions and gear—is $25. If you've climbed elsewhere, a climbing pass is $14, but you'll still need to pass a belay test ($5) before being allowed to climb. Rules are enforced and you'll have to sign a liability release. Parents or guardians have to sign for anyone under 18. Vending machines have good-for-you snacks, such as Gatorade and granola bars. Summer hours (May–Oct.) are Tues. 2–10 PM, Fri 2–8 PM, Sat.–Sun. noon–6 PM. Winter hours are Mon.–Thurs. 2–10 PM, Fri. 2–8 PM, Sat.–Sun. 11 AM–6 PM. (During school vacations, they're open daily at noon.)

Spectator Sports

A pseudo-fierce mascot named Slugger stirs up the crowds at baseball games played by the **Portland Sea Dogs,** Hadlock Field, 271 Park Ave., Portland 04102, 207/879-9500 or 800/936-3647, fax 207/780-0310, a AA farm team for the Boston Red Sox. Ever since the team arrived, in 1994, loyal local fans have made tickets scarce, so it's essential to reserve well ahead (you'll pay a minimal reservation surcharge) with a major credit card. The season schedule (early Apr.–early Sept.) is available after January 1. General-admission tickets are $6 adults, $3 seniors (62 and over), and $3 kids 3–16; kids age two and under are free in parent's lap. Reserved seats are $7 adults, $6 all others. For hassle-free parking, leave your car at the Maine Medical Center parking ramp on Congress Street or behind the Portland Expo. There's a $5 charge at both locations.

For ice-hockey action, the **Portland Pirates,** a farm team for the American Hockey League Washington Capitals, plays winter and spring home games at the 8,700-seat Cumberland County Civic Center, 1 Civic Center Sq., Portland 04101, 207/775-3458. The civic center is also the locale for year-round special sporting events and exhibition games, as well as ice shows, concerts, and college hockey games. Check the *Portland Press Herald* for schedules or call the center.

Sea Kayaking

With all the islands scattered throughout Casco Bay, Greater Portland has become a hotbed of sea-kayaking activity in the past few years. The best place to start is out on Peaks Island, 15 minutes offshore via Casco Bay Lines ferry. **Maine Island Kayak Company** (MIKCO), 70 Luther St., Peaks Island 04108, 207/766-2373 or 800/796-2373, www.maineisland-kayak.com, is a successful tour operation that organizes half-day, day-long, and multi-day local kayaking trips as well as national and international adventures. An introductory half-day tour in Casco Bay starts at $60 pp; a full day starts at $95, including lunch. Reservations are essential. MIKCO also does private lessons and group courses and clinics (some require previous experience). MIKCO's owner, Tom Bergh, has a flawless reputation for safety and skill. Send for their extensive trip schedule. In early October (usually Columbus Day weekend), there's a day-long sale of used boats and gear—lots of real bargains.

KIDS STUFF

The **City of Portland Recreation Division,** 389 Congress St., Portland 04101, 207/874-8793 or 874-8300, supervises playgrounds and parks throughout the city and sponsors a huge list of summer activities for youngsters, including a "Summer in the Parks" teen program. Call in spring to get the summer schedule.

Portland's best in-town playground is at the **Reiche Elementary School,** 166 Brackett St., 207/874-8175, about five blocks west of the Children's Museum. No cement here, just wood chips to break the falls.

Children's Museum of Maine

Here's the answer to parents' prayers—a whole museum in downtown Portland catering to kids. At the Children's Museum of Maine, P.O. Box 4041, 142 Free St., next to the Portland Museum of Art, Portland 04101, 207/828-1234, lots of hands-on displays encourage interaction and guarantee involvement for a couple of hours. What's here? A submarine, computer lab, supermarket, bank, lobster boat, an incredible camera obscura, and more than a dozen other activities. Call to check on the special-events schedule. Admission is $6 for anyone over a year old. Open daily, Memorial Day weekend to Labor Day, 10 AM–5 PM Mon.–Sat. and noon–5 PM Sun. Labor Day–Memorial Day, the museum is open Tues.–Sat. 10 AM–5 PM, Sun. noon–5 PM, plus the first Fri. of each month 5–8 PM (free admission that night).

Smiling Hill Farm

Six miles west of downtown Portland is 450-acre Smiling Hill Farm, 781 County Rd., Rte. 22, Westbrook 04092, 207/775-4818. Here you'll find a dairy market showcasing the full range of Smiling Hill's milks and ice creams. Open 11 AM–7 PM seven days a week. In winter there are about 13 kilometers of beautifully groomed cross-country-skiing trails—weather permitting, of course. Full-day weekend, holiday, and school vacation rate is $10. Ski rentals are also $10.

GETTING AFLOAT

Casco Bay Lines Cruises

Casco Bay Lines, Commercial and Franklin Sts., Old Port, Portland 04101, 207/774-7871, www.cascobaylines.com, the nation's oldest continuously operating ferry system (since the 1920s), is the lifeline between Portland and six inhabited Casco Bay islands. Some 650,000 people patronize the service annually. What better way to sample the islands than to go along for the three-hour ride with mail, groceries, and island residents? The Casco Bay Lines mailboat stops—briefly—at **Long Island,** **Chebeague, Cliff,** and **Little and Great Diamond Islands.** Daily departures are 10 AM and 2:15 PM mid-June–Labor Day (plus 7:45 AM weekdays), 10 AM and 2:45 PM other months. Fares are $12.50 adults, $11 seniors, and $6 children 5–9. Children under five are free. Longest cruise on the Casco Bay Lines schedule is the five-hour, 45-minute narrated summertime trip (late June–Labor Day) to **Bailey Island,** with a two-hour stopover, departing from Portland at 10 AM daily ($18 adults, $16 seniors, $8 children). Adult one-way tickets are $12. No smoking, and dogs (on leashes) and bicycles need separate tickets.

Sailboat and Powerboat Excursions

If boats make you queasy, take the easy way out with lunch or dinner at **DiMillo's Floating Restaurant,** a converted car ferry on Portland's waterfront. Seafood is always the specialty du jour and you can't beat the view.

Down on the Old Port wharves are several excursion-boat businesses. Each has carved out a niche, so choose according to your interest and your schedule. Dress warmly and wear rubber-soled shoes. Remember that all cruises are weather-dependent.

Bay View Cruises operates the *Bay View Lady,* 184 Commercial St., Fisherman's Wharf, Old Port, 207/761-0496, every day mid-June–early Sept. Call for spring and fall schedule and for rates. Lobsterbakes are available on short notice and are available for private charters.

The **Olde Port Mariner Fleet,** with three vessels, is based at Long Wharf on Commercial St. (207/775-0727 or 774-2022 or 800/437-3270 outside Maine; mailing address 634 Cape Rd., Standish 04084). Six-hour whale-watching trips are a specialty, departing from Long Wharf aboard the *Odyssey* at 10 AM daily late June–Labor Day, plus weekends early June–Sept. (Don't overload on breakfast that day, and take preventive measures if you're motion-sensitive.) Tickets are $30–40 per person. Credit cards for reservations only; payment in cash or travelers checks. (There's an ATM on the wharf.) Olde Port also offers half-day and full-day deep-sea-fishing excursions.

Also based at Long Wharf is the **Coast Watch & Guiding Light Navigation Company,** Long Wharf, Old Port, 207/774-6498, offering several excursion options, but the best is the four-hour trip (departing 10 AM daily) to 17-acre **Eagle Island,** where arctic explorer Adm. Robert Peary built his summer home. Now the state-owned house is open daily, late June–Labor Day, plus September weekends. The cruise allows time on the island to visit the house and wander the grounds. Pack a picnic. Cost is $24 adults, $22 seniors, $13 children.

Or how about a day-sail in an elegant classic yacht? The 58-foot *Palawan,* P.O. Box 9715-240, Portland 04104, 207/773-2163, www.sailpalawan.us, makes several trips daily in summer from Long Wharf. The 10:30 AM (two hours) cruise is $20 adults, $10 children; the three-hour afternoon cruise (2 PM) is $40 adults, $20 children. A two-hour evening cruise (5:30 PM) is $30 adults, $15 children.

ENTERTAINMENT AND NIGHTLIFE

The best place to find out what's playing at area theaters, cinemas, concert halls, and nightclubs is the *Go* supplement in the Thursday edition of the *Portland Press Herald*. It is available at bookstores and supermarkets. Also check www.portland.com/go.

Free are the **Summer Performance Series** presentations, every summer weekday, late June–Aug., in the downtown pocket parks. Sponsored by Portland's Downtown District (PDD), 207/772-6826, the action rotates among Monument Square, Congress Square, Tommy's Park, and Post Office Park.

Center for Cultural Exchange

In the heart of the Downtown Arts District, the Center for Cultural Exchange, One Longfellow Square, Portland 04101, 207/761-0591 (box office: 761-1545), exposes Portlanders to multicultural arts—music and dance performers from throughout the world, as well as Portland's own ethnic community. Lectures, classes, and other special events are also on the

agenda; the center acts as a clearinghouse for an impressive array of activities. Check newspapers for their programs or call the office for a schedule.

State Theater

After an astonishing renovation that produced a stunning gilded, painted performance space, the 1929 State Theatre, 609 Congress St., Portland 04101, 207/780-8265, has had financial ups and downs. Nonetheless, it's the focal point of Congress Street's Downtown Arts District; the city and private citizens have worked hard to keep it afloat. Plays, big-name rock concerts, and classical performances have all contributed to the theater's renown. Call for current schedule.

Classical Music, Pops, Opera

The **Portland Symphony Orchestra** (207/842-0800) and **PCA Great Performances** (207/773-3150) share use of the stage at the magnificently restored Merrill Auditorium, 20 Myrtle St., Portland 04101, 207/874-8200, a 1,900-seat theater inside Portland City Hall (on Congress St.) with two balconies and one of the country's only municipally owned pipe organs. Both the PSO and PCA have extensive, well-patronized fall and winter schedules; the PSO, under longtime conductor Toshiyuki Shimada, presents summer pops concerts in Cape Elizabeth and other locales around the state.

The **Portland String Quartet,** one of the nation's most enduring chamber-music ensembles, performs in various locations around the state on a schedule arranged by the Lark Society. Call 207/761-1522 for information.

Founded in 1995, **Port Opera Repertory Theatre,** 207/879-7678, has a short season, a relatively short history, and an impressive reputation. It performs each summer in City Hall's Merrill Auditorium. Tickets are $15–100. Artistic Director is Dona D. Vaughan, with the New York City Metropolitan Opera.

Drama

Innovative staging and controversial contemporary dramas are typical of the **Portland Stage Company,** Portland Performing Arts Center, 25A Forest Ave., P.O. Box 1458, Portland 04101, 207/774-0465, established in 1974 and going strong ever since. Equity pros present a half-dozen plays each winter season in a 290-seat performance space. Other theater groups are **Acorn Productions, Mad Horse Theatre,** and **Portland Players.** Check local papers for schedules. Also check out the **St. Lawrence Arts and Community Center,** 76 Congress St., 207/775-5568. The center operates the Parish Hall Theater with regular performances by the resident theater company—the Good Theater. The center also showcases the Stone Pinheads, Two Lights Theater Ensemble, Acorn Theater, and Winter Harbor Theater Company. Call or check newspapers for schedules.

Cinemas

Downtown Portland's two movie theaters aren't quite highest-tech, but they'll do just fine, especially since ticket prices are reasonable. At the six-screen **Nickelodeon,** Temple and Middle Sts., 207/772-9751, the seats are comfy. **The Movies,** 10 Exchange St., 207/772-9600, screens esoterica such as *The Sexual Life of the Belgians,* and its seats are guaranteed to keep you awake, but tickets and popcorn are cheap and there are weekend matinees.

Beyond downtown are two garden-variety multiplexes: **Regal Cinema's Clarks Pond 8,** 888 Clarks Pond Pkwy., behind Maine Mall, South Portland, 207/879-1511; and **Hoyts Falmouth Cinemas,** 206 Rte. 1, Falmouth, 207/781-5616. Both of these biggies have daily matinees that are cheaper than evening screenings.

Brewpubs and Bars

By the time you read this, several more brewpubs will have surfaced; the phenomenon has mushroomed since the early 1990s.

Not only is **Gritty McDuff's** ("Gritty's"), 396 Fore St., Old Port, Portland, 207/772-2739, one of Maine's most popular breweries, its brewpub was the state's first to open, in 1988. The pub is heavy into burgers and pizza. Among the six or seven Gritty's beers and ales on tap are Sebago Light and Black Fly Stout. Gritty's also books live entertainment fairly regularly. There's another branch in Freeport.

In 1995, a longtime favorite pub, **Three Dollar Dewey's,** 241 Commercial St., Old Port, 207/772-3310, moved into its current bigger location, not missing a beat with a loyal crew of regulars. Visiting Brits, Kiwis, and Aussies head here to assuage their homesickness. The menu changes nightly, and it's predictably good. Friday and Saturday nights, it's SRO. With darts, an eclectic jukebox, and something of a behavior code, the **Fifties Pub,** 225 Congress St., Portland, 207/772-6398, keeps its ferociously loyal clientele coming back for more.

Of all Portland's neighborhood hangouts, **Ruski's,** 212 Danforth St., 207/774-7604, is most authentic—a small, usually crowded onetime speakeasy that rates just as high for breakfast as for nighttime schmoozing. Basic, homemade fare can be had for well under $10. There are darts and a big-screen TV, too. Dress down or you'll feel out of place. Open Mon.–Sat. 7 AM–12:45 AM, Sun. 9 AM–12:45 AM.

West of I-295, the **Great Lost Bear,** 540 Forest Ave., 207/772-0300, has no brewery, but it does have Portland's hugest inventory of designer beers, with 53 on tap. The bear motif and the punny menus are a bit much, but the 15-or-so varieties of burgers are not bad; the "Bear" has been here since 1979. Open Mon.–Sat. 11:30 AM–11:30 PM, Sun. noon–11:30 PM.

For more upscale tippling, head for **Top of the East,** the lounge at the Eastland Park Hotel, 157 High St., near Congress Sq., Portland 04101, 207/775-5411, where all of Portland's at your feet and the Sunday jazz brunch is terrific (reservations necessary). A few blocks away, down toward the Old Port, is the elegant Armory Lounge at the **Portland Regency Hotel,** 20 Milk St., Portland 04101, 207/774-4200.

Comedy

Portland's forum for stand-up comedy is the

Comedy Connection, 6 Custom House Wharf, next to Boone's, in the Old Port, Portland 04101, 207/774-5554, a crowded, smoky space that draws nationally known pros. Avoid the front tables unless you're inclined to be the fall guy/guinea pig, and don't bring anyone squeamish about the F-word. Bring your sense of humor, enjoy the show, and be kind to the wait staff; they have a tough job. Tickets are $6–12; reservations are advisable on weekends. Shows Wed.–Sun. at 8:30 PM, Sat. at 7:30 and 9:30 PM.

Live Music

There are so many possibilities in this category, but not a lot of veterans. The Portland club scene is a volatile one, tough on investors and reporters. The best advice is to scope out the scene when you arrive; the *Go* section of Thursday's *Portland Press Herald* has the best listings. Most clubs have cover charges. A couple of options are **Brian Boru,** 57 Center St., Portland, 207/780-1506, which often (but not always) has Celtic music; and the **Free Street Taverna,** 128 Free St., Portland, 207/774-1114, which offers eclectic venues.

FESTIVALS AND EVENTS

Pick up a copy of the *Portland Visitor and Convention Bureau's schedule of Festival and Special Events* (updated monthly) or check www.portland.com/go.

Henry Wadsworth Longfellow, born in Portland on February 27, 1807, merits his own public event, **Longfellow's Birthday Party,** at the Maine Historical Society, 489 Congress St., Portland.

June brings a host of events: the **Old Port Festival** (one of Portland's largest festivals), with entertainment, food and crafts booths, and impromptu fun in Portland's Old Port; **Back Cove Family Fun Day,** with live music, food and crafts, a cardboard canoe race, and games at Payson Park; the **Greek Heritage Festival,** featuring Greek food, dancing, and crafts at Holy Trinity Church, 133 Pleasant St., Portland; and the **Summer Performance**

Series, sponsored by Portland's Downtown District, which runs through early September and offers free weekday noon concerts, dramas, and mime, rotating among several downtown parks.

In August, the **Italian Street Festival** showcases music, Italian food, and games at St. Peter's Catholic Church, 72 Federal St., Portland.

The **Maine Brewers' Festival,** the first weekend in November at the Portland Exposition Building, is a big event that expands every year, thanks to the explosion of Maine microbreweries. It includes samples galore. And from Thanksgiving weekend to Christmas Eve, **Victorian Holiday Portland,** in downtown Portland, harks back with caroling, special sales, concerts, tree lighting, horse-drawn wagons, and Victoria Mansion tours and festivities.

On December 31, **New Year's/Portland** is an annual family festival and extravaganza featuring 50 free events 10 AM–8 PM including children's activities, concerts, great food, public skating, and indoor swimming. It's sponsored by the Portland Downtown District.

SHOPPING

The Portland peninsula—primarily Congress St. and the Old Port waterfront district—is thick with non-cookie-cutter shops and galleries. This is just a taste to spur your explorations.

Antiquarian Bookstores

Carlson-Turner Books, 241 Congress St., Portland 04101, 207/773-4200 or 800/540-7323, based on Munjoy Hill, seems to have Portland's largest used-book inventory. Look for unusual titles and travel narratives. Open all year, Mon.–Sat. 10 AM–5 PM, Sun. noon–5 PM.

Antique maps and atlases are the specialty at the Old Port's **Emerson Booksellers,** 18 Exchange St., Portland 04101, 207/874-2665, but there's an excellent used-book selection as well. Open year-round, daily in summer.

Antiques

Dating back to the early 19th century, **F.O. Bailey Antiquarians,** 35 Depot Rd., Falmouth 04105, 207/781-8001, fax 781-8009, has a solid reputation for its inventory of fine antiques. Most fun is to attend one of their auctions, watch the action, and maybe pick up a bauble or two. Open all year, 9 AM–5 PM Mon.–Fri., 10 AM–4 PM Sat.

A newish entry in this category is **The Clown,** 123 Middle St., Portland 04101, 207/756-7399, which carries an unusual mix of European antiques, art, and a huge wine selection (specializing in Italian). The owners also have a seasonal shop in Stonington, on Deer Isle. The Clown is open Mon.–Wed. 10 AM–6 PM, Thurs.–Sat. 10 AM–7 PM.

Polly Peters Antiques, 26 Brackett St., Portland 04101, 207/774-6981, is Polly Blake's funky, fusty West End shop specializing in eccentric furniture, architectural fragments, and other exotica. Theoretically open Mon.–Wed. 10 AM–5 PM, but call ahead to be sure.

Art Galleries

Davidson and Daughters Contemporary Art, 148 High St., 207/780-0766; **Greenhut Galleries,** 146 Middle St., 207/772-2693; the **Hay Gallery,** 594 Congress St., 207/773-2513; and **June Fitzpatrick Gallery,** 112 High St., 207/772-1961, are the area's best art galleries. Call for hours or stop in when you're exploring the area.

Crafts and Gifts

More than 15 Maine potters—with a wide variety of styles and items—market their wares at the **Maine Potters Market,** 376 Fore St., Portland 04101, 207/774-1633, an attractive shop in the heart of the Old Port. Established in 1980, the cooperative remains a consistently reliable outlet for some of Maine's best ceramic artisans. Open daily 10 AM–6 PM (to 9 PM in midsummer and Dec.).

For the kid in all of us, there's **Northern Sky Toyz,** 388 Fore St., Portland 04101, 207/828-0911, probably the best kite shop you've ever seen. Price range is vast—$10 to several hundreds—and owners Bob and Nancy Ray can recommend the best places to try out your purchase(s). Open all year.

Just around the corner is **Abacus,** 44 Exchange St., Portland 04101, 207/772-4880, where craft rises to a high art. Whimsy is the byword here; if you don't arrive smiling, you'll leave that way. Open all year. Abacus has branches in Kennebunkport and Freeport, and a seasonal shop in Boothbay Harbor.

Gourmet Food and Gadgets

Maine's hands-down best all-round gourmet-cooking resource shop is **LeRoux Kitchens,** 161 Commercial St., Old Port, Portland 04101, 207/553-7665—a grownup toy store. Food processors, whisks, tea strainers, and esoteric single-purpose whatsits—you'll find them all here, plus specialty foods, beer-making supplies, cookbooks, exotic coffees, wines, and a very attentive staff willing to demonstrate any gadget that confounds you. Cooking classes are held in spring and fall.

Newest entry in the "gourmet goodies" category is **Browne Trading Market,** Merrill's Wharf, 262 Commercial St., Portland 04101, 775-7560. Owner Rod Mitchell became the Caviar King of Portland by wholesaling Caspian caviar, and he's now letting the rest of us in on it. Ultimately fresh fish and shellfish fill the cases next to the caviar and cheeses. The mezzanine is wall-to-wall (literally) wine, specializing in French. Order a sandwich, pick up some wine, and you're ready to go. The shop is open Mon.–Sat. 10 AM–6:30 PM.

Offbeat Shopping

Trustmi, you have to see **Suitsmi,** 35 Pleasant St., Portland 04101, 207/772-8285, which carries wearables (including jewelry) perfect for rock concerts, funky cafés, and, if you're dying to make a statement, your class reunion.

Shipwreck and Cargo, 207 Commercial St., Old Port, Portland 04101, 207/775-3057, stocks a wide assortment of marine-related items—boat models, barometers, navy surplus stuff, and more. Open daily all year.

L.L. Bean

In late 1996, the giant Freeport-based sports outfitter established a major presence with a factory store in a vacant building in the Downtown Arts District. Other shops have raced to cash in on the clientele. L.L. Bean Factory Store, 542 Congress St., Portland 04101, 207/772-5100, is open 10 AM–6 PM daily.

Maine Mall

With more than 140 stores and restaurants, the Maine Mall, 364 Maine Mall Rd., South Portland 04106, 207/774-0303 or 828-2060, is the state's largest shopping complex, and several offshoot mini-malls have moved into the neighborhood to take advantage of the traffic. The mall is just off I-95 exit 7. Major stores in or near the Maine Mall are **Macy's, The Gap, Sears, Filene's, Brookstone, Eastern Mountain Sports, Victoria's Secret, Radio Shack, Borders Books, Williams Sonoma, Eddie Bauer,** and a huge **food court** serving up juices, gyros, Mrs. Field's cookies, chocolates, pretzels, coffee, ice cream, and cheeses. **Services** available at the mall include ATMs, restrooms, phones, ear piercing, engraving, shoe dying, film developing, car repair, and stroller and wheelchair rental. Mall management has made a major commitment to recycling, so bins are placed throughout the complex. Hours are Mon.–Sat. 9:30 AM–9 PM, Sun. 11 AM–6 PM. Many national fast-food chains have eateries within the mall or within walking distance outside.

ACCOMMODATIONS

Downtown Portland

Portland's peninsula has many new and seasoned hotels and great B&Bs. All are open year-round.

B&Bs: The biggest plus of Portland's downtown B&Bs is that they're all in West End buildings loaded with history. Each has a fascinating story to tell; all are open year-round.

Sue and Phil Cox are especially hospitable hosts at **The Inn on Carleton,** 46 Carleton St., Portland 04102, 207/775-1910 or 800/639-1779, fax 207/761-2160, a 17-room National Historic Register mansion. Breakfast is a feast. Six attractively decorated second- and third-floor guest rooms have private baths. No smoking, no pets. Rooms are $159–199 in summer, lower other months.

The Danforth, 163 Danforth St. at Winter St., Portland 04102, 207/879-8755 or 800/991-6557, fax 207/879-8754, is a beautifully restored, 21-room Federal-style mansion. Nine guest rooms have such state-of-the-art amenities as fax service and dataports, as well as cable TV, air-conditioning, phones, and working fireplaces. Climb to the cupola for a great view of the Portland Harbor sunrise, and don't miss the gardens. Pets and children are welcome; no smoking. Rooms are $135–285 d in summer, lower other months.

Built in 1877, the **West End Inn,** 146 Pine St. at Neal St., Portland 04102, 207/772-1377 or 800/338-1377, has six second- and third-floor guest rooms with private baths and TV.

Staying at **The Pomegranate Inn,** 49 Neal St. at Carroll St., Portland 04102, 207/772-1006 or 800/356-0408, fax 207/773-4426, is an adventure in itself, with faux painting, classical statuary, and whimsical touches everywhere. The elegant 1884 Italianate mansion has seven guest rooms and a suite, all with private baths and phones. A two-night minimum is required during summer weekends and holidays. No pets, no smoking, no children under 12. Rooms are $175–265 in summer, lower other months.

Inns: The Inn at St. John, 939 Congress St., Portland 04102, 207/773-6481 or 800/636-9127, fax 207/756-7629, is a clean, comfortable, moderately priced 40-room hostelry. Cable TV, air-conditioning, free local calls and continental breakfast are all included. All rooms have private baths (some are detached). Pets and children are welcome, and they'll pick you up at the Jetport. It's a healthy walk to the Old Port but close to the Downtown Arts District. No smoking. Summer rates are $55–175. Open all year.

Beyond Downtown

Island accommodations are described under *Casco Bay Islands,* below.

B&Bs: Here's a sleeper, west of I-295 but an easy drive into town. Elizabeth and Doug Andrews have carefully restored the 18th-century **Andrews Lodging Bed & Breakfast,** 417 Auburn St., Rte. 26, Portland 04103, 207/797-9157, fax 797-9040, which has welcomed guests since the 1920s. All five guest rooms have private baths. Rates run $90–165 d in summer. Big pluses are a lovely solarium, a fully equipped second-floor guest kitchen, and Elizabeth's exquisite gardens. Three kinds of berries grow on the 1.5-acre grounds. No smoking, no small children. Pets are $10 extra on first visit, free thereafter. Open all year.

Inns: If your wallet and your wardrobe are up to it, you can splurge at a couple of upper-level inns south of Portland. Or you can opt for the third one in the less-stratospheric category. Seven miles south of downtown Portland, **Inn by the Sea,** 40 Bowery Beach Rd., Rte. 77, Cape Elizabeth 04107, 207/799-3134 or 800/888-4287, fax 207/799-4779, is a well-managed modern complex with the stylishly casual feel of an upscale summer house. Forty-three one- and two-bedroom suites and cottages have kitchen facilities and spectacular water views. Best of all, a boardwalk winds down through the salt marsh to the southern end of Crescent Beach State Park. Facilities at the inn, built in 1986, include a tennis court, outdoor pool, croquet lawn, and bicycles. By prior reservation, pets are honored guests. The suites and cottages go for $149–549 d, not counting breakfast, depending on the season. Make your reservations early; the inn is incredibly popular. Priceless Audubon prints cover the walls in the appropriately named **Audubon Room,** 207/767-0888, where moderate-to-expensive breakfasts and excellent lunch and dinners are served daily to guests—and to the public by reservation. (Try the crab cakes.) Open all year.

You'll get a sense of the **Black Point Inn Resort,** 510 Black Point Rd., Prouts Neck, Scarborough 04074, 207/883-2500 or 800/258-0003, fax 207/883-9976, as soon as you notice the honeymooners, yuppies, dowagers, and sedate film stars rubbing shoulders here. Many guests are repeats. Many also never leave Prouts Neck during their stay—everything's here for a real getaway, including tennis courts, 18-hole golf course, indoor and outdoor pools, bicycles, fitness room, wicker chairs on the glassed-in veranda, sand beach, local library, gift shop, and walking paths. The inn's superb dining room is open to the public by reservation only; don't show up without a jacket. There are 85 rooms and suites in the inn and cottages, most with water views. A two-night minimum is required over weekends. No pets. Rates are $400–570 d, MAP, in midsummer. Open all year, the inn is 12 miles south of downtown Portland.

The **Peter A. McKernan Hospitality Center,** Southern Maine Community College, Fort Rd., South Portland 04106, 207/741-5672, provides a different twist on the inn experience. In fact, it's the proving ground for students in the Hotel, Motel, and Restaurant Program at Southern Maine Technical College. The center, a turn-of-the-20th-century brick building that once served as officers' quarters, has spectacular views of Casco Bay and the offshore islands. Eight rooms with private baths go for $175 a night (for four at a time, the price is $125 per room). Students staff the inn, and they all aim to please. The inn is open year round. Call for availability during school vacations. The inn's restaurant serves lunch two days a week.

Campgrounds

If camping is more in your budget and interest, two spots are within relatively easy access to downtown Portland. Closest is **Wassamki Springs,** 855 Saco St., Westbrook 04092, 207/839-4276, a family-run Good Sampark campground on a private lake with a mile of sandy beachfront. It features 170 wooded and shorefront sites on 35 acres. Peak-season sites are $19–27 a night (two adults and two kids under 12); discounts for seniors. Recreational opportunities include canoe and paddleboat rentals, a playground, and lots of games, which are also open to noncampers. There are

© KATHLEEN M. BRANDES

Portland Public Market

planned events on weekends. Noise rules are strictly enforced. Five miles west of I-95, via exits 7 or 8. Open May–mid-Oct.

Established in 1970, **Bayley's Camping Resort,** 275 Pine Point Rd., Scarborough 04074, 207/883-6043, is the Disney World of campgrounds, with 500 well-kept sites, well-organized day and night entertainment, and a free local trolley service for trips to area beaches. You certainly won't be lonely; facilities include three swimming pools, a rec hall, laundry, playground, horseshoe pits, Jacuzzis, general store, restaurant, mini-golf, and nightly entertainment. From Memorial Day weekend to Labor Day, sites are $37–55 (two persons); kids under three are free. Limited access for pets. Reservations are advisable mid-June–Aug.; full prepayment is required for one- to four-night reservations. Open May–Columbus Day, with reduced rates early and late in the season.

FOOD

Downtown Portland alone has more than a hundred restaurants, so it's impossible to list even all the great ones. Below is a choice selection.

In addition to the many restaurant options listed here, check the *Go* supplement in each Thursday's *Portland Press Herald.* Under "Potluck," you'll find listings of **public meals,** usually benefiting nonprofit organizations. Prices are always quite low (under $10 for adults, $2–4 for children), meal times quite early (5 or 6 PM), and the flavor quite local.

Downtown Portland

Portland Public Market: Opened with great fanfare in October 1998, the L-shaped 37,000-square-foot **Portland Public Market,** Cumberland and Preble Sts., 207/228-2000, has almost-fairytale origins. Maine philanthropist Elizabeth Noyce donated the funds to develop and build the $6 million brick, glass, and wood structure modeled on Seattle's Pike Place Market, but unfortunately she didn't live to see the stunning results. About two dozen Maine vendors display and sell a broad variety of intriguing wares (even flowers). Show up here any day (Mon.–Sat. 9 AM–6 PM, Sun. 10 AM–5 PM) and graze through the samples—shellfish pâté, fresh bread, home-grown bison, bottled milk, exotic coffees, farm-made cheeses, organic produce, and on and on. It's a foodie's paradise. Also in the market are restrooms and an ATM. An across-the-street parking garage connects to the third floor of the market; get your ticket stamped for two free hours of parking.

Breakfast: Portland is a breakfast kind of place. Best known for its earliest and most filling breakfast, **Becky's Diner,** 390 Commercial St., Old Port, 207/773-7070, now serves dinner. How can you beat a haddock dinner for $5.95? Becky's is famous; don't miss it. Open daily 4 AM–9 PM. Also noted for breakfast—well, brunch—is **Bintliff's American Café,** 98 Portland St., Portland, 774-0005. Even though the café serves dinner (5:30–9 PM; entrées $15–20) every night but Sunday, it's best known for daily brunch, 7 AM–2 PM. Look for the main post office; it's across the street. Open all year.

"In" Grills: Chef Sam Hayward, who's made a name for himself in Maine foodland for more than two decades, has struck gold at **Fore Street,** 288 Fore St., Old Port, 207/775-2717. Even though the copper-topped tables and the industrial decor create a din in this ex-warehouse, no one seems to mind much. A joint project with Street & Company owner Dana Street, the restaurant is extremely popular, and reservations are essential. Entrées are in the $13–23 range. Game is roasted on a spit, seafood is grilled over apple wood or roasted in the wood oven. Appetizers are particularly imaginative.

Back Bay Grill, 65 Portland St., near the main post office, 207/772-8833, in 1988 was the first Portland restaurant to go the grill route—and it's maintained high standards ever since. The decor is colorful (especially the mural), the ambience is serene, the wine list is astonishing (about 12 pages), and the menu ranks among the best in the city. Entrée range is $17–33. Despite all the new restaurants in the area, reservations are still needed here on weekends. Open for dinner Mon.–Sat., all year.

It's especially hard to resist ordering Atlantic salmon at **Rachel's Wood Grill,** 496 Woodford Street, 207/774-1192—it's done so well.

But they also do a fine job with everything else. Entrées are $15–22 and come with wine or beer only. Open all year for dinner, Wed.–Sat. after 5 PM.

Ethnic Fare: If you like sushi, beat a path to the sushi bar at **Benkay Sushi Bar and Japanese Restaurant,** 2 India St., Old Port, 207/773-5555, Maine's best Japanese eatery. Reservations are not accepted, so you may have to wait. Parking is free. Open for lunch (11:30 AM–2 PM) weekdays, Sunday brunch (at noon), and dinner daily (from 5 PM). Running a close second is **Sapporo,** 230 Commercial St., Union Wharf, Old Port, 207/772-1233, Maine's most enduring Japanese restaurant. Kids gravitate to the tempura and teriyaki—and of course they're entranced by the in-your-face, table-side preparation. Reservations are advisable on weekends. Open for lunch weekdays 11:45 AM–2 PM and dinner daily at 5 PM; no lunch Sat.–Sun.

If Italian cuisine is on your agenda, a family-oriented restaurant, and one that's endured since 1936, is the Reali family's **Village Café,** 112 Newbury St., east of Franklin St., 207/772-5320. The huge place has a moderate menu of respectable Italian food (dinner entrées $7–25), healthful specials, and free crayons for the kids. Open Mon.–Thurs. 11 AM–10 PM (to 11 PM Fri.–Sat.) and Sun. 11:30 AM–8 PM (to 9:30 July–Aug.).

Primo rustic Italian fare is the rule at **Ribollita,** 41 Middle St., Old Port, 207/774-2972. You'll want reservations at this small, casual, very popular spot. Beer and wine only. Open for dinner Tues.–Sat.

Determinedly Eclectic: Whimsy is the hallmark at **Katahdin,** 106 High St., corner of Spring St., near the civic center, 207/774-1740, named after Maine's highest mountain. Decor is definitely offbeat here. Countless loyal regulars gasped when Katahdin changed hands in early 2000, but fortunately the spirit of the decor stayed. Owner Becky Lee Simmons added her West Coast influence to the menu, bringing a pleasing, unexpected twist to what seem, at first glance, to be standards. No reservations are accepted, so expect to wait on

Saturday night. Open Tues.–Thurs. 5–9 PM, Fri.–Sat. 5–10 PM.

Be sure to have a reservation if you're going, pre-theater, to **BiBo's Madd Apple Café,** 23 Forest Ave., 207/774-9698—it's right next to the Portland Performing Arts Center. On the other hand, it's popular any time—thanks to Bill Boutwell (BiBo), who created Portland's first "chef's table" at the Café Stroudwater. No chef's table here—just an incredibly creative menu in brightly, cheery surroundings. There's no way of predicting what will be on the bistro-fusion menu. Bibo's is open for lunch Wed.–Fri. 11:30 AM–2 PM; dinner Wed.–Sun. 5:30–9:30 PM; and brunch Sun.

Five Fifty-Five, 555 Congress St., 207/761-0555, www.fivefifty-five.com, is the latest inhabitant of what long-time Portlanders will remember as Raffles. Culinary imagination is at work here. Small plates go from $6.95 for minted pea soup up to $15.95 for lobster risotto. Entrées go for $17–26, except for the black angus burger ($12.95) and mixed-grill paella for two ($36.95). There are distinctive cheese and sweet plates, a delightful Sunday brunch, and the service is exceptionally attentive.

Seafood: Ask around (even on the Internet) and everyone will tell you the best seafood in town is at **Street & Company,** 33 Wharf St., Old Port, 207/775-0887. Fresh, beautifully prepared fish is what you get, often with a Mediterranean flair—in an informal, brick-walled environment that's been here since 1989. A local newspaper called this "the best place for dinner if money's no object—or even if it is." Prices are moderate to expensive (entrées $14–25). Don't show up without a reservation. Beer and wine only; no smoking. Owner Dana Street is also behind the Fore Street Restaurant (see above). Open for dinner daily, 5:30 PM–9:30 PM (to 10 PM Fri. and Sat.).

Pasta, Vegetarian Fare: You never know what'll be on the menu (Indonesian chicken, North African stuffed peppers, Caribbean shrimp cakes?) at funky **Pepperclub,** 78 Middle St., east of Franklin St., 207/772-0531, but take the risk. Vegetarian and vegan specials are always available, as are organic meats. If your

kids are even vaguely adventuresome, they'll find food to like here—and prices to match (entrées $10–15). If you have to wait, you can hang out in the lounge with a microbrew or chardonnay. Open daily at 5 PM.

On the Waterfront: It's tough to top the prime waterfront location of **DiMillo's Floating Restaurant,** 25 Long Wharf, Commercial St., Old Port, 207/772-2216. The 206-foot converted ferryboat has been tied up here since 1982. Best spots for lunch or a light meal are the outdoor decks. Dinner entrées run $15–21. The menu isn't extraordinary, but the view is—Portland Harbor is everywhere you look. No reservations, but you shouldn't have to wait long for one of the 600(!) seats. Free parking. Open daily 11 AM–11 PM.

The color's a lot more local just down the street at **The Porthole,** 20 Custom House Wharf, Commercial St., Old Port, 207/780-6533, a bit of a dive where the all-you-can-eat Friday fish fry pulls in *real* fisherfolk, in-the-know locals, and fearless tourists. In good weather, hang out on the deck for breakfast, lunch, or dinner. Sunday brunch is 8 AM–3 PM. Under second-generation ownership since 1995, the Porthole has had a bit of refurbishing, but it's still the Porthole. Open daily 6 AM–9 PM.

Street Food: Portland has maybe a dozen street vendors on a regular basis, but the prize for longevity goes to Mark Gatti, of **Mark's Hot Dogs,** usually set up at the corner of Exchange and Middle Sts., in the Old Port, since 1983. He gets going about 8:30 AM weekdays (plus Sat. in summer) and by noon looks up at a long line of faithful regulars. Hot dogs, sausages, sauerkraut, condiments—he's got the works.

Coffee: You'll never run out of places to overload on caffeine in downtown Portland; coffeehouses seem to have sprung up everywhere. **Coffee by Design,** 620 Congress St., Portland 04101, 207/772-5533, is almost more art gallery than coffeehouse, and it's one of the "hippest" hangouts. The wall art is a big deal here, and you're welcome to buy it. Open from 7 AM weekdays, 8 AM weekends. A branch coffeehouse/espresso bar, **Coffee by Design Monument Square,** 207/761-2424, is at 24 Monument Square. **Java Joe's,** 13 Exchange St., Portland 04101, 207/761-5637, conscientiously buys coffee from Equal Exchange, supporting fair prices and labor practices. Across from The Movies, it's a locale for everything from checkers matches to jazz concerts.

South Portland

Ricetta's Brick Oven Pizzeria, 29 Western Ave., Rte. 9, between Maine Mall and Portland Jetport, South Portland 04106, 207/775-7400, is regularly voted Greater Portland's best pizza palace. Not surprising when you see the lunchtime-only pizza smorgasbord—all the pizza you can eat, plus salad and soup. Specialty pizzas are outstanding, or you can invent your own combo. Also on the menu are antipasti, calzones, giant salads, soups, pasta dishes, and high-calorie desserts. Open for lunch and dinner Sun.–Thurs. 11:30 AM–10 PM, Fri.–Sat. 11 AM–11 PM. The north-of-Portland crowd celebrated when Ricetta's announced its new branch on Rte. 1 in Falmouth. Ricetta's has the magic touch.

One of Greater Portland's best Chinese restaurants is tucked away in a mini-mall near the Maine Mall. **Imperial China,** 220 Maine Mall Rd., South Portland, 207/774-4292, produces high-quality Hunan and Szechuan cuisine in an attractive setting. Prices are very reasonable. Open daily for lunch and dinner.

How about a three-course lunch, with a matchless view, on the cheap? The students in the hospitality program at Southern Maine Community College need practice for their cooking and service skills, so their "labs" are two restaurants. The **Peter McKernan Hospitality Center** on the college's Spring Point campus, Fort Rd., South Portland, 207/741-5622, serves lunch, with reservations. Call for availability. The Culinary Dining restaurant serves a well-prepared lunch Wed.–Thurs., plus Fri. during the academic year only. Reservations required. While at the center, be sure to stroll the grounds and follow the Spring Point

Shoreline Walkway down to Willard Beach. (The center also has rooms; see *Accommodations,* above.)

Cape Elizabeth

Besides the restaurants described here, a sure bet for a splurge is the handsome **Audubon Room** at Inn by the Sea on Rte. 77 in Cape Elizabeth (see *Accommodations,* above).

The Good Table, 527 Ocean House Rd., Rte. 77, Cape Elizabeth, 207/799-4663, a small, casual place near the entrance to Two Lights State Park, has Mediterranean touches, courtesy of the Greek-American owners. Entrées are $4–15. Funky old photos cover the walls (even in the restrooms), and the tables have jars of crayons for kids (or wannabe kids). Sunday brunch is jammed. Open Tues.–Fri. 11 AM–9 PM, Sat. 8 AM–9 PM, Sun. 8 AM–3 PM.

Every Mainer has a favorite lobster eatery (besides home), but **The Lobster Shack,** 222 Two Lights Rd., Cape Elizabeth, 207/799-1677, tops an awful lot of lists. Seniority helps—it's been here since the 1920s. Scenery, too—a panoramic vista in the shadow of Cape Elizabeth Light. Plus the menu—seafood galore (and hot dogs for those who'd rather). Choose a lobster from the tank; indulge in the lobster stew; grab a table on the rocks and watch the world go by. Opt for a sunny day; the lighthouse's foghorn can kill your conversation when the fog rolls in. Open daily 11 AM–8 PM, mid-Apr.–mid-Oct. (to 8:30 July–Aug.).

Falmouth

Most new restaurants need warm-up time, but not **Ricetta's,** 240 Rte. 1, Falmouth 04105, 207/781-3100, the clone of South Portland's best pizza palace. This branch opened in the fall of 2000 and it was immediately tough to get in the door. The pizza buffet lets you try everything—you'll get the picture. Open daily all year for lunch and dinner.

Up the road a piece, north of the Falmouth shopping centers, heading toward Yarmouth, is one of Falmouth's treasures, the **European Bakery, Inc. and Tea Room,**

395 Rte. 1, Falmouth 04105, 207/781-3541. Proprietors Helen and Emil Budri present an array of beautifully produced pastries; try the cheese Danish with sliced almonds and light, sweet glaze. In addition to the takeout bakery counter, there are tables where you can have your coffee and pastry; the coffee cups are delicate, and there is a nice view of the planted island outside.

INFORMATION AND SERVICES

The **Convention and Visitors Bureau of Greater Portland,** 245 Commercial St., Portland 04101, 207/772-5800, www.visitportland .com, is open all year. Hours are Mon.–Fri. 8 AM– 5 PM, Sat. and holidays 10 AM–5 PM, mid-May– mid-Oct. This changes to Mon.–Fri. 8 AM–5 PM, Sat. and holidays 10 AM–3 PM, mid-Oct.–mid-May. The office has tons of brochures, plenty of restaurant menus, and public restrooms.

The Portland Downtown District, an independent merchants' association, instituted a very successful **Downtown Guides** program in the summer of 1996. Early June–Oct. 15, a handful of young, enthusiastic guides patrols the Old Port District and the Portland Arts District. Carrying maps, brochures, and cell phones, they're on the streets Mon.–Sat. 11:30 AM–8 PM, Sun. 9:30 AM–5 PM. Ask them anything; they love the challenge, and, as one visitor noted, they're "relentlessly friendly."

The **Portland Public Library,** 5 Monument Sq., Portland 04101, 207/871-1700 (events info: 871-1710), www.portlandlibrary.com, has an extremely helpful staff, a bright reading room, and a fine children's room. You can even check your email on their computers. Open Mon., Wed., and Fri. 9 AM–6 PM; Tues. and Thurs. noon–9 PM; Sat. 9 AM–5 PM. Smaller branch libraries include **Munjoy Hill,** 44 Moody St., 207/772-4581; **Reiche,** 166 Brackett St., in the West End, 207/774-6871; and **Riverton,** 1600 Forest Ave., west of I-295, 207/797-2915. Smaller branch libraries include **Munjoy Hill,** 44 Moody St., 207/772-4581; **Reiche,** 166 Brackett St., in the West End, 207/774-

6871; **Riverton,** 1600 Forest Ave., west of I-295, 207/797-2915; and **Burbank,** 377 Stevens Ave., 207/774-4229. Reiche and Riverton are part of school/community center complexes. There's also a branch on **Peaks Island,** 129 Island Ave., 207/766-5540.

For **time and temperature information,** call 207/775-4321; for the current **weather report,** call 207/688-3210. For **winter parking-ban information,** call 207/879-0300.

Emergencies

In Portland, call 911 for **fire, police, or ambulance.**

The state's largest hospital, **Maine Medical Center,** 22 Bramhall St., Portland 04101, emergency 207/662-2381, offers round-the-clock emergency-room care and a cafeteria that can turn out cheap and tasty made-to-order omelets any hour of the day or night. Also in downtown Portland is Catholic **Mercy Hospital,** 144 State St., Portland 04101, emergency 207/879-3266.

Media

Portland's (and Maine's) major daily newspaper is the *Portland Press Herald,* published six mornings a week. The *Maine Sunday Telegram* is under the same ownership. The *Press Herald's* Thursday edition carries a special entertainment supplement—*Go*—listing the week's cultural and recreational activities throughout Greater Portland.

A crusading bent and an irreverent attitude mark the free *Portland Phoenix,* which is part of a national chain. It's also published weekly (Wed.).

Special Discounts

The **Portland Dine Around Club,** 477 Congress St., Portland 04101, 207/775-4711 or 877/732-2582, www.dineportland.com, gets you two-for-the-price-of-one meals (usually dinner entrées) at 170 or so restaurants with a wide variety of menus, decor, and price ranges. Membership, good for a year, is $30. Some limitations apply, but it's still a bargain.

Those intent on spending a lot of time on the links should consider purchasing an American Lung Association **Golf Privilege Card,** covering greens fees for 200 rounds of golf in Maine, New Hampshire, and the Canadian Maritimes for $70. It's a great cause. Many courses on the list require reservations 24–48 hours in advance, and some require player's fees. Write or call American Lung Association of Maine, 122 State St., Augusta 04330, 207/622-6394 or 800/586-4872.

Postal Service

Portland is the home of Maine's first **postal store,** 400 Congress St., Portland 04101, 207/871-8464, a glitzy, 6,500-square-foot emporium where you can select your own stamps, buy collectors' packets and books, make photocopies, and send faxes. Lines are short, and self-service machines speed things along. Open Mon.–Fri. 8 AM–7 PM.

Public Restrooms

In the **Old Port** area, you'll find restrooms at the Convention and Visitors Bureau Visitor Information Center (245 Commercial St.), the Spring Street parking garage (45 Spring St.), the seasonal Fore Street Parking Garage (419 Fore St.), and the Casco Bay Lines ferry terminal (Commercial and Franklin Sts.).

On **Congress Street,** you can use the facilities at Portland City Hall (389 Congress St.) and the Portland Public Library (5 Monument Sq.). In the **West End,** use Maine Medical Center. Of course, if you're in a big hurry, be creative and look for restrooms in hotel lobbies, department stores, and police stations.

GETTING THERE

By Air

Delta and Delta Connection, 800/221-1212, Continental, 800/523-3273, Northwest, 800/225-2525, USAirways, 800/428-4322, and United, 800/241-6522, all serve Portland at the **Portland International Jetport.**

The three-story terminal underwent a multimillion-dollar facelift in 1996 and contains all the amenities—including offices of Avis, Budget, Hertz, Alamo, and National car-rental agencies (Enterprise has an office off the premises). Visitor information is available at a desk (not always staffed; 207/775-5809) between the gates and the baggage-claim area. Baggage-handling offices surround the luggage carousels. If you have an emergency, contact Jetport Administration office at 207/772-0690.

By Bus

Concord Trailways, 800/639-3317, departs downtown Boston (South Station Transportation Center) and Logan Airport for the hundred-mile trip to Portland about 10 times daily, making pickups at all Logan airline terminals (lower level). Rates are very reasonable. The bright, modern Trailways Transportation Terminal is at 100 Sewall St., about two blocks off I-295, behind the Doubletree Inn. It's not particularly convenient to downtown for pedestrians, but if you need to leave a car, there's a large parking lot, with unlimited free parking. Three daily nonexpress buses continue from Portland along the coast, ending at the Trailways terminal in Bangor.

Vermont Transit Lines, 950 Congress St., Portland, 207/772-6587 or 800/537-3330, a division of Greyhound Bus Lines, serves Maine, the rest of New England, and beyond, connecting with Greyhound routes. The schedule is slightly less convenient than that of Concord Trailways, but rates are lower.

Van Service

Mermaid Transportation in Portland, 207/883-5630 or 800/696-2463, operates the best van service between Boston and Portland (and vice versa). Pick-up and drop-off, five times daily, are at Portland Jetport and Logan Airport, by reservation only. Cost is $55 one-way; kids under six are free, caged pets are $15 extra. Home pick-up can be arranged. By prior arrangement, Mermaid also will pick up and drop off customers at Maine Turnpike park-and-ride lots from Auburn to Wells. There is also daily van service between the Manchester, New Hampshire, airport, and the Portland Jetport.

Highway Access

The major highway access to Portland is the **Maine Turnpike,** which links up with I-95 at the New Hampshire border. I-295, a spur of I-95, runs through Portland, providing easy access to the Old Port district.

GETTING AROUND

Parking garages and lots are strategically located all over downtown Portland, particularly in the Old Port and near the civic center. Unless you're lucky, you'll probably waste a lot of time looking for on-street parking (meters start at $0.25 a half-hour), so a garage or lot is the best option. If you land in a garage or lot with a Park & Shop sticker, you can collect free-parking stamps, each good for an hour, from participating shops and restaurants. You could even end up parking for free. The **Casco Bay Line**s website, www.cascobaylines.com, has a very useful parking map, regularly updated, listing parking lots and garages and their hourly and daily rates. It's good for comparison shopping.

Portland's bus network, **Metro,** 114 Valley St., P.O. Box 1097, Portland 04104, 207/774-0351, is well planned and often underutilized. Metro produces a colorful, easy-to-read route map and schedule that facilitates getting around—including a loop (Mon.–Sat. only) linking the Portland International Jetport and the Maine Mall (both in South Portland) with downtown Portland. Buses have wheelchair lifts and bike racks (room for two of each). Free transfers are available between routes. Cost per ride is $1 adults, $0.75 18 and under, free for kids under five—up to two children per paying adult. Sunday bus service is very limited, and there's no service on major national holidays.

For a 1.5-hour **narrated sightseeing tour** of Portland in a trolley-bus, check with your hotel or contact **Mainely Tours,** 5½ Moulton St., Old Port, Portland 04101, 207/774-0808. Tours start at their office, the Portland Museum of Art, the Portland Public Market, and include Portland Head Light. Since 1995, Kathy and John Jenkins have been heading out on this route five or six times daily, beginning at 9:30 AM, late May–mid-Oct. Cost is $13 adults, $12 seniors, $7 children 6–12. Reservations are suggested. A three-hour lighthouse tour ($25 adults, $15 kids), mid-June–mid-Oct., visits four lighthouses, including Portland Head and Spring Point Ledge.

Portland and South Portland have a dozen **taxi** fleets, most radio-operated. You won't have much luck trying to flag one down on the street. Reliable services in Portland are **ABC Taxi,** 207/772-8685, **Airport Limo & Taxi,** 207/773-3433, and **Town Taxi,** 207/773-1711. In South Portland, call **South Portland Taxi,** 207/767-5200.

For details on **Casco Bay Lines ferry service** to local islands, see *Getting Afloat,* above. **Great Chebeague Island** is on the Casco Bay Lines route, but you can also get there via Chebeague Transportation Company (CTC) from nearby Cousins Island, in Yarmouth. All Casco Bay Lines tickets are round-trip, and they're collected when you board in Portland, so if you manage to get to one of the islands by some other means, such as via the CTC, there's no charge for going from island to island or returning to Portland on a Casco Bay Lines vessel.

CASCO BAY ISLANDS

Of the six year-round islands, Peaks, Great Diamond, Little Diamond, and Cliff fall within Portland's jurisdiction. Long Island seceded from Portland in 1993 to become a separate municipality; Chebeague belongs to the town of Cumberland. Access to the islands described here is via Casco Bay Lines and, in the case of Chebeague, Chebeague Transportation Company.

Peaks Island

With frequent ferry service to and from downtown Portland, at $6.25 pp (less in winter), Peaks Island is eminently convenient for commuters and visitors alike. The best way to see it is to take a bike ($5.25 extra on the ferry) and pedal around clockwise to the back (east) side, where there are great views and no hint that the island's within spitting distance of downtown Portland. It can take less than an hour to do the five-mile island circuit, which has its hilly moments, but don't rush. Bring a picnic and stay the day. (You can walk the circuit in three or four hours.) In summer, you can stop in at the **Fifth Maine Regiment Center,** 45 Seashore Ave., P.O. Box 41, Peaks Island 04108, 207/766-3330, fax 766-3083, a Queen Anne–style Civil War museum built in 1888 on the southern side of the island. Inside are historical displays and a small gift shop. If the center is closed, sit on the veranda and enjoy the view. July–Aug. it's open 11 AM–4 PM daily. June–Sept. it's only open 11 AM–4 PM weekends. Admission is free, but donations are welcomed. Rental bikes are available on the island from Brad Burkholder at **Brad's ReCycled Bike Shop,** 115 Island Ave., Peaks Island 04108, 207/766-5631. (If Brad isn't there, it's the honor system—choose a bike, sign a release, and leave the correct rental amount in the box.)

The best **sea kayaking** operation in Greater Portland is on Peaks Island.

Most people walk or bike the perimeter road on Peaks; for a change of pace, head inland through the woods. To read the trailhead for the Indian Trail, go up Welch St. from the wharf; go left on Island Ave. and right on Brackett St. On the right, watch for the Trail sign; the path is red-blazed.

Great Diamond Island

Here's a totally different scene. In 1891, the U.S. government began building an Army post on Great Diamond Island, a quick ferryboat ride from the Portland harbor front. Completed in 1907, **Fort McKinley** (named after President William McKinley) became part of Portland Harbor's five-fort defense system during World Wars I and II. When peace descended, the fort's red-brick structures were left to crumble for nearly five decades. In 1984, developers stepped in, purchased the derelicts, and began restoration—albeit not without financial setbacks and opposition from environmental organizations.

Today, the 193-acre **Diamond Cove** enclave boasts stunning barracks-turned-town homes, single-family houses, a general store (open daily late May–Labor Day), outdoor theater, a beach bar (open mid-June–mid-Sept.), an art gallery, outdoor pool, health club, no cars (only bikes and golf carts), a supervised children's program, and the first-rate **Diamond's Edge Restaurant,** 207/766-5850, serving lunch and dinner daily, mid-May–early Oct. The restaurant's Sunday brunches (mid-June–Labor Day) are incredibly popular, as is the Wednesday-night lobster clambake on the beach. Casco Bay Lines ferries serve the island about every two hours daily. Staying overnight on the island is a big splurge, but a worthwhile one; buying property is another matter altogether. Minimum stay, mid-June–Labor Day, is seven nights; a town home booking begins at $2,000 per week and rises to $4,000. Minimum stay off-season is two nights at $225–500 per night. No pets, no smoking. Contact Great Diamond Rentals, 207/766-3005, www.greatislandrentals.com.

Great Chebeague Island

Everyone calls Great Chebeague just "Chebeague" (shuh-BIG). Yes, there's a Little Chebeague, but it's a state-owned park, and no one lives there. The fourth regular stop on the Casco Bay Lines ferry route, Chebeague is also accessible via Cousins Island in Yarmouth. It's an hour from Portland (docking at **Chandler's Cove,** on the island's west end) and 15 minutes if you go via Yarmouth (arriving at the **Stone Pier,** closer to the east end).

Settled in the mid-18th century by Europeans (and eons earlier by Native Americans), Chebeague is perhaps best known as the source of wooden "stone sloops" that carried granite from

Maine quarries to markets all along the eastern seaboard. Ambrose Hamilton, the Scotsman who started the stone-sloop business, still has many descendants on the island.

Chebeague is the largest of the bay's islands—4.5 miles long, 1.5 miles wide, and home to 325 or so year-rounders (swelling to around 2,500 in summer)—and the relatively level terrain makes it easy to get around. Don't bring a car; it's too complicated to arrange.

The best way to get a sense of the place is to bring a bike, which requires a small fee on the ferry. There's no bike-rental place near Chebeague's Casco Bay Lines dock, but **Great Island Bike Rentals,** 207/846-6568, is based at Sunset House Bed & Breakfast, just up the road from the Chebeague Transportation Company dock. You can do a leisurely 10-mile circuit of the island in a couple of hours, but don't rush. The terrain is almost entirely level, so there's no challenge here for big-time cyclists. Pick up an island map at the Portland terminal or on the ferry; all the high points are listed, including two beach-access points off North Road.

If the tide is right, you can pack a picnic lunch, cross the sand spit from The Hook, and explore **Little Chebeague.** Start out about two hours before low tide (preferably around new moon or full moon, when the most water drains away) and plan to be back on Chebeague no later than two hours after low tide.

Just east of Little Chebeague is state-owned **Crow Island,** beginning of the **Maine Island Trail,** an island-to-island boating route. If you have a sea kayak, it's a lovely little island to explore, and there's even a cabin ashore.

Back on Great Chebeague, when you're ready for a swim, head for **Hamilton Beach,** a beautiful small stretch of sand lined with dune grass, not far from the Chebeague Island Inn. (There's a potty in the little beach

shack, known locally as "Phil's Camp.") Also on this part of the island is **East End Point,** with a spectacular panoramic view of Halfway Rock and the bay. In winter, you can cross-country ski on island trails and the beach, or ice-skate on Sanford Doughty's well-maintained pond.

About 0.75 mile from the Stone Pier is the **Chebeague Orchard Inn,** 453 North Rd., Chebeague Island 04017, and fax 207/846-9488, Vickie and Neil Taliento's comfortable, antiques-filled home. Seven rooms have handmade quilts (three have private baths and two share a bath); some have water views. Rates are $130–175 Memorial Day–mid-Oct., lower other months. The congenial Talientos are big supporters of the Maine Island Trail Association, which begins near Chebeague, so you'll get a discount if you arrive by kayak. Coffee's ready at 7 AM; breakfast is a feast, overlooking the backyard's bird feeders and apple orchard. There are bikes for guests, a fireplace in the common room, and tons of helpful advice about the island. No smoking, no pets; children are welcome. Open all year.

Overlooking the Stone Pier and the golf course, the **Chebeague Island Inn,** Chebeague Island 04017, 207/846-5155, is an imposing three-story hotel with a spectacular sunset-view veranda. The inn's been here for decades. It's open May 1–Oct. 30 and includes 21 second- and third-floor guest rooms (16 with private bath) for $165–315 (during the July–August high season), including full breakfast. Rates are lower off-season. Higher-priced rooms have water views. The dining room, with moderate-to-expensive continental fare and great homemade desserts, serves three meals daily. Dress is informal. The massive first-floor Great Room, with a huge stone fireplace, is a great place to gather. No pets, no minimum stay.

Freeport

Freeport has a special claim to historic fame—it's the place where Maine parted company from Massachusetts in 1820. The documents were signed on March 15, probably in the Jameson Tavern (now a restaurant), making Maine its own separate state.

At the height of the local mackerel-packing industry here, countless tons of the bony fish were shipped out of South Freeport, often in ships built on the shores of the Harraseeket River. Splendid relics of the shipbuilders' era still line the streets of South Freeport, and no architecture buff should miss a walk, cycle, or drive through the village. Even downtown Freeport still reflects the shipbuilder's craft, with contemporary shops tucked in and around handsome historic houses. Some have been converted to B&Bs, others are boutiques, and one even disguises the local McDonald's franchise.

Today, Freeport is best known as the mecca for the shop-till-you-drop set. Ground zero, of course, is sportswear giant L.L. Bean, which has been here since 1912, when founder Leon Leonwood Bean began making his trademark hunting boots (and also unselfishly handed out hot tips on where the fish were biting). More than 120 retail operations now fan out from that epicenter, and you can find almost anything in Freeport (pop. about 7,300)—except maybe a parking spot in midsummer.

When (or if) you tire of shopping, you can always find quiet refuge in the town's preserves and parks—Mast Landing Sanctuary, Wolf Neck Woods State Park, and Winslow Memorial Park—as well as plenty of local color at the Town Wharf in the still honest-to-goodness fishing village of South Freeport.

An orientation note: Don't be surprised to receive directions (particularly for South Freeport) relative to "the Big Indian"—a 40-foot-tall landmark at the junction of Rte. 1 and South Freeport Rd. If you stop at the Maine Visitor Information Center in Yarmouth and continue on Rte. 1 toward Freeport, you can't miss it, just north of the Freeport Inn and the Casco Bay Inn.

SHOPPING

Logically, this category must come first in any discussion of Freeport, since shopping's the biggest game in town. It's pretty much a given that anyone who visits Freeport intends to darken the door of at least one shop. If it's *only* one, it's likely to be "Bean's."

The whole world beats a path to **L.L. Bean,** 95 Main St., Rte. 1, Freeport 04033, 207/865-4761 or 877-552-3268, www.llbean.com—or so it seems in July, August, and December. Open 24 hours a day, 365 days a year.

A block south of L.L. Bean, the **Freeport Historical Society** operates the restored **1830 Enoch Harrington House,** 45 Main St., Rte. 1, Freeport 04032, 207/865-0477. It's a great place to check out Freeport's local-history

L.L. BEAN

Established as a hunting and fishing supply shop, this giant sports outfitter now draws about 3.5 million shoppers and takes in close to $1 billion annually. After Acadia National Park, it's the most-visited Maine site.

Until the 1970s, Bean's remained a rustic store with a creaky staircase and a closet-size women's department. Then a few other merchants began arriving, Bean's expanded, and a feeding frenzy followed. The Bean reputation rests on a savvy staff, high quality, an admirable environmental consciousness, and a no-questions-asked return policy. Bring the kids—for the indoor trout pond, the clean restrooms, and the "real deal" bargain department. The store's open-round-the-clock policy has become its signature, and if you show up at 2 AM, you'll have much of the store to yourself!

displays. It's open 10 AM–6 PM Tues., Thurs., and Fri., 10 AM–9 PM Wed.

After this, it's up to your whims and your wallet. The stores stretch for several miles up and down Main Street and along many side streets. Pick up a copy of the *Official Map & Visitor Guide* at any of the shops and restaurants, at one of the visitor kiosks, or at the Hose Tower Information Center, 23 Depot St., two blocks east of L.L. Bean. Among Freeport's **big-name outlets** are Banana Republic, Brooks Brothers, Coach, Cole-Haan, Crabtree & Evelyn, Lennox, Burberry, Gap, J. Crew, North Face, Patagonia, Ralph Lauren, and J.L. Coombs.

SIGHTS AND RECREATION
Winslow Memorial Park
Owned by the town of Freeport, Winslow Memorial Park, Staples Pt., South Freeport, 207/865-4198, is a spectacular 90-plus-acre seaside park, overlooking the islands of upper Casco Bay. Swim off the beach (changing house, restrooms, but no lifeguards), picnic on the shore, walk the short nature trail and perch on the point, launch a canoe or kayak, or reserve one of the 100 campsites (about two dozen are on the shore). The boat landing and beach area are tidal, so boaters and swimmers should plan to be here two hours before and two hours after high tide; otherwise, you're dealing with mudflats. The park opens Memorial Day weekend and closes the last Sunday in September; admission is $1.50 pp ages 6–62, payable at the gatehouse. (Off season, there's no fee.) Inland and waterfront campsites are $19–22 for nonresidents; no hookups, but some sites can take RVs. From the "Big Indian" on Rte. 1, take South Freeport Rd. one mile to Staples Point Rd. and continue to the end.

Mast Landing Sanctuary
More than two miles of easy, yellow-blazed trails wind through the 140-acre Mast Landing Sanctuary, an area that once was the source of masts for the Royal Navy. Pick up a trail map at the parking area and start watching for

birds. The best (and longest) route is the 1.6-mile Loop Trail, which passes fruit trees, hardwoods, and an old milldam. (Keep the kids off the dam.) The sanctuary is owned by Maine Audubon Society, 20 Gilsland Farm Rd., Falmouth 04105, 207/781-2330. Each summer, late June–mid-Aug., the society operates a very popular nature day camp here; call for a schedule. The sanctuary is open sunrise to sunset, year-round, and is popular in winter with cross-country skiers. Admission is free. From downtown Freeport (Rte. 1), take Bow St. (opposite L.L. Bean) one mile east to Upper Mast Landing Road. Turn left (north) and go 500 feet to the parking area.

Wolf Neck Woods State Park
Five miles of easy to moderate trails meander through 233-acre Wolf Neck Woods State Park, Wolf Neck Rd., Freeport 04032, 207/865-4465, just a few minutes' cycle or drive from downtown Freeport. You'll need a trail map, available near the parking area. The easiest route (partially wheelchair-accessible) is the Shoreline Walk, about 0.75 mile, starting near the salt marsh and skirting Casco Bay. Sprinkled along the trails are helpful interpretive panels explaining various points of natural history—bog life, osprey nesting, glaciation, erosion, and tree decay. Leashed pets are allowed. Adjacent **Googins Island,** an osprey sanctuary, is off-limits. The park sponsors year-round educational programs and guided hikes. Admission Memorial Day–Labor Day: $3 pp ages 12–64, $1 pp ages 5–11. Admission May 1–31 and Labor Day–Oct. 31: $1.50 pp ages 12–64. The park is accessible in winter for cross-country skiing. From downtown Freeport, follow Bow St. (across from L.L. Bean) for 2.25 miles; turn right onto Wolf Neck Rd. and go another 2.25 miles.

Wolfe's Neck Farm
Visitors are invited at Wolfe's Neck Farm, 10 Burnett Rd., Freeport 04032, 207/865-4469, fax 865-6927. Sustainable agriculture and environmental sensitivity are the overriding philosophies at this working farm, known

for its organic beef, chicken, turkeys, and pigs. It's owned and operated by the non-profit Wolfe's Neck Farm Foundation. The farm's products can be purchased in local Hannaford supermarkets.

Also part of the farm is **Recompence Shore Campsites,** 184 Burnett Rd., Freeport 04032, 207/865-9307, fax 865-0367—an ecosensitive campground with 100 wooded tent sites (a few hookups are available), many on the farm's three-mile-long Casco Bay shorefront. For anyone seeking peace, quiet, and low-tech camping (outhouses and hot showers) in a spectacular setting, this is it. Ice, firewood, and snacks are available at the camp store. Quiet time begins at 9 PM. As with Winslow Memorial Park, swimming depends on the tides; check the tide calendar in a local newspaper. Rates are $14–24 per night, depending on location, mid-May–mid-Oct. A few cabins are $60–80 a night. Take Bow St. (across from L.L. Bean) to Wolf Neck Rd., turn right and go 1.6 miles to Burnett Rd. (on the left).

L.L. Bean Outdoor Discovery Schools

Since the early 1980s, the sports outfitter's Outdoor Discovery Schools have trained thousands of outdoors enthusiasts to improve their skills in fly-fishing, archery, hiking, canoeing, sea kayaking, winter camping, cross-country skiing, orienteering, and cycling. Some of the lectures, seminars, and demonstrations held in Freeport are free, and a regular newsletter lists the schedule. All of the fee programs, plus canoeing and camping trips, require registration well in advance because of their popularity. Some are held in the mountains of western Maine. For information, or to get on the mailing list, contact the program at 800/341-4341, ext. 26666, or www.llbean.com.

Pownal and Gray

Inland, in the two adjoining communities of Pownal and Gray, you'll find an underutilized state park and the state's home for orphaned wildlife.

Bradbury Mountain State Park

Six miles from the hubbub of Freeport and you're in tranquil, wooded, 590-acre Bradbury Mountain State Park, Rte. 9, Pownal 04069, 207/688-4712, with facilities for picnicking, hiking, and rustic camping, but no swimming. (Sleep here and save your funds for shopping.) Pick up a trail map at the gate and take the easy, 0.4-mile (round-trip) Mountain Trail to the 485-foot summit, with superb views east to the ocean and southeast to Portland. In fall, it's gorgeous. Or take the Tote Road Trail, on the western side of the park, where the ghost of Samuel Bradbury occasionally brings a chill to hikers in a hemlock grove. A playground keeps the littlest tykes happy. Admission is $3 adults, $1 children 5–11; kids under five and seniors are free. The nonresident camping fee is $15 per site per night. The park season is May 15–Oct. 15, but there's winter access for cross-country skiing. From Rte. 1, cross over I-95 at exit 20 and continue west on Pownal Rd. to Rte. 9.

Where the Wild Things Are

The **Maine Wildlife Park,** Shaker Rd., Rte. 26, Gray 04039, 207/657-4977,www.mainewildlifepark.com, run by the state's Department of Inland Fisheries and Wildlife, is a hospital and nursing home for Maine's wild animals when they've been injured, orphaned, or otherwise traumatized. State staffers rehabilitate them and, when possible, release them. You'll see moose, pheasants, owls, turtles, bear, deer, bobcats, and whatever other creatures wardens and private citizens happen to have rescued. Other features here are a wildlife garden, interactive displays in the visitors center, an attractive picnic area, and nature trails winding through the farm. There is a gift shop with lots of conservation-oriented books and gifts. Wildlife experts present programs each summer-Saturday afternoon; in summer and fall, there are "night walks" 8–10 PM (6–8 PM in Oct.). Bring a flashlight covered with red cellophane, or buy one when you arrive. No alcohol is allowed on the premises, and no pets are permitted beyond the parking area. Admission is $5 adults, $4 seniors, $3.25 children

(4–12), free for kids three and under. Open daily 9:30 AM–6 PM, mid-Apr.–Veterans' Day; no entry after 4:30 PM. The park is 3.5 miles north of downtown Gray and Maine Turnpike exit 63. From the coast, take Rte. 115 from Main St. in downtown Yarmouth, continuing through North Yarmouth (with stunning old houses) to Gray.

ENTERTAINMENT

Shopping seems to be more than enough entertainment for most of Freeport's visitors, but don't miss the **L.L. Bean Summer Concert Series.** From early July to Labor Day weekend, at 7:30 PM each Saturday, Bean's hosts free big-name, family-oriented events in Discovery Park. Arrive early (these concerts are *very* popular) and bring a blanket or folding chairs.

ACCOMMODATIONS

If you'd prefer to drop where you shop, Freeport has a large country inn, several motels, and more than two dozen B&Bs, so finding a pillow is seldom a problem, but it's still wise to have reservations.

For camping, see Winslow Memorial Park, Wolfe's Neck Farm, and Bradbury Mountain State Park, above.

Downtown

One of Freeport's pioneering B&Bs is on the main drag yet away from much of the traffic, in a restored house where Arctic explorer Adm. Donald MacMillan once lived. The 19th-century **White Cedar Inn,** 178 Main St., Freeport 04032, 207/865-9099 or 800/853-1269, has six attractive guest rooms with air-conditioning and private baths. Doubles are $85–165, depending on the season. No smoking, no pets. Open all year.

In the same part of town, but off Main St., is the early-19th-century **Maple Hill Bed & Breakfast,** 18 Maple Ave., Freeport 04032, 207/865-3730 or 800/867-0478, (www.maplehillbedandbreakfast.com), an easy stroll from the center of town—unless you're laden

with packages. Chip and Janet Lawrence have three rooms with private baths, air-conditioning, and TV. A dataport is available. Children and pets are welcome; no smoking. Don't miss the gardens. Rates are $85–160, depending on the season. Open all year.

Two blocks north of L.L. Bean, near I-95 exit 20 (close to the two B&Bs above), the **Harraseeket Inn,** 162 Main St., Freeport 04032, 207/865-9377 or 800/342-6423, fax 207/865-1684, is a well-run 84-room country inn with an indoor pool, cable TV, air-conditioning, phones, and dataports; some rooms have fireplaces and Jacuzzis. Decor is colonial reproduction in the two antique buildings and a modern addition. Rooms are $215–350 d, mid-July–Oct., including breakfast and afternoon tea; they're $119–285 d other months. Special packages and MAP rates are available, including the "serious shopper" package. The cloth-and-candles **Maine Dining Room,** 207/865-1085, justifiably popular for its excellent service, creative cuisine, and Sunday brunch, is open to the public daily; buffet breakfast is served 7–10:30 AM, dinner 5:30–9 PM (to 9:30 PM Fri.–Sat.). Dinner entrées are $25–40. No smoking. Reservations are advisable. The informal **Broad Arrow Tavern** serves microbrews and moderately priced brick-oven specialties daily, 11:30 AM–10:30 or 11 PM.

Three blocks south of L.L. Bean, on a quiet side street shared with a couple of other B&Bs, is **The James Place Inn,** 11 Holbrook St., Freeport 04032, 207/865-4486 or 800/964-9086. Darcy and Bill James and their two dogs are immediately welcoming, sharing their enthusiasm for all the area's activities. They'll even organize a free round of golf at the local club. Seven comfortable rooms have private baths, air-conditioning, and TV; four have Jacuzzis. Rates are $135–155 d in summer, $125–145 d other months. No smoking, no pets (no competition needed!), no children under eight. Open all year.

Beyond Downtown

In South Freeport you'll find the **Atlantic Seal**

Bed & Breakfast, 25 Main St., South Freeport 04078, 207/865-6112 or 877/285-7325, a mid-19th-century Cape-style house with stupendous harbor views and lots of fascinating maritime collectibles. The suite and one room have private baths; another room has a shared bath. Doubles are $125–200, depending on the season. No smoking, no pets. Open all year. Late May–late Oct., owner Tom Ring operates **Atlantic Seal Cruises** (same phone)—two or three 2.5-hour cruises daily from the nearby Freeport Town Wharf (located in South Freeport) to 17-acre **Eagle Island,** a State Historic Site once owned by Adm. Robert Peary of North Pole fame. The trip includes a lobstering demonstration (except Sun., when lobstering is banned) and seal watching. Capt. Ring also does excursions Thurs. 10 AM–4 PM to Seguin Island, off the Phippsburg Peninsula, where you can climb the light tower. To get there, take Bow St., then right onto South St. continuing to Porter's Landing; travel along South Freeport Rd. to Main St. (left turn).

Six miles north of I-95 exit 20, in Durham, is the National Historic Register **Royalsborough Inn at Bagley House,** 1290 Royalsborough Rd., Rte. 136, Durham 04222, 207/865-6566 or 800/765-1772, fax 207/353-5878, filled with antiques and superbly run by Sue Backhouse and Sue O'Connor—both ex-nurses—since 1993. Only a 10-minute drive from downtown Freeport, the 1772 house, the oldest in Durham, sits amid six acres of woods and fields. No smoking; children are welcome. Five guest rooms (private baths) in the main house go for $125–135 d in summer, $105–125 d in winter. Two rooms and a suite in the next-door Bliss Barn are $115–135 d. The converted barn has a comfortable first-floor common room, a great place to relax after a day of pounding Freeport's pavement. Open all year.

One of the town's most enduring hostelries, the **Freeport Inn,** 335 Rte. 1, Freeport 04032, 207/865-3106 or 800/998-2583, fax 207/865-6364, www.freeportinn.com, overlooks the Cousins River estuary, on the Freeport-Yarmouth boundary three miles south of downtown Freeport. The 80 motel-style

rooms go for $120–160 d late May–late Oct., $75 and up other months. Escape traffic noise by requesting a rear-facing room. Cable TV, air-conditioning, phones, and canoes are free for guests. There's an outdoor pool and a playground, which helps keep kids happy, and there are 16 pet-friendly rooms. The inn's café, open 6 AM–8 PM, has good, reasonably priced meals. A short walk away, along Rte. 1 and actually in Yarmouth, is the inn's bright, modern **Muddy Rudder Restaurant,** 207/846-3082, an extremely popular spot for lunch, dinner, and weekend entertainment (open until midnight). The inn, café, and restaurant are open all year.

FOOD

Lunch and Lobsters

Two blocks south of L.L. Bean is the **Lobster Cooker,** 39 Main St., Freeport 04032, 207/865-4349. Lobster rolls are predictably good and not overpriced for the neighborhood; try the award-winning chowder. It's a popular place where you order at the counter, so expect to stand in line. Beer and wine are available, but no credit cards are accepted.

Don't laugh. **McDonald's,** 155 Main St., at Mallett Drive, Freeport 04032, 207/865-9566, is almost incognito—in a historic downtown home two blocks north of L.L. Bean and across from the Harraseeket Inn. No giant golden arches here—only discreet ones at the entrances and exits. Residents allowed capitalism to run rampant in their town, but the idea of a fast-food chain terrified them. Hence this compromise. Lobster sandwiches are available. Open all year.

Freeport's original brewpub, **Gritty McDuff's,** 187 Rte. 1 So., Freeport 04032, 207/865-4321, is open daily 11:30 AM–1 AM, year-round. You'll find good pub grub, fine pizza, designer brews (try Black Fly Stout or McDuff's Best Bitter), and short, on-demand brewery tours.

When you head toward South Freeport (which you must), stop in at **The Village Store,** 97 South Freeport Rd., next to the post office, South

Freeport 04078, 207/865-4230, for breakfast, lunch, dinner, or a snack. Find a table, sit on the deck, or do takeout. This upscale convenience store produces homemade soups, giant muffins, great pizza, hearty sandwiches, even cappuccino—all at reasonable prices. No smoking, no credit cards. Open daily 6:30 AM–7 PM, year-round.

Once you get to South Freeport, order lobster-in-the-rough at **Harraseeket Lunch & Lobster Company,** Main St., Town Wharf, South Freeport 04078, 207/865-3535. Grab a waterfront picnic table, place your order, and go at it. (There's also inside dining.) Be prepared for a wait on midsummer weekends. Fried clams are particularly good here. Another option: If you're camping nearby, call ahead and order boiled lobsters to go. BYOL; no credit cards but ATM machine is available. Open daily 11 AM–7:45 PM, May 1–mid-June; 11 AM–8:45 PM, mid-June–mid-Oct.

Moderate to Expensive

Consider springing for the buffet brunch at the Harraseeket Inn's **Maine Dining Room,** 162 Main St., 207/865-1085—how can you resist sampling cured Pacific flying-fish roe? Or chilled poached salmon? Or Maine Coast bouillabaisse? Plus chocolate marble cashew tart for dessert. Be sure to make a reservation, and check your arteries at the door.

Believe it or not, one of Maine's best Chinese restaurants is right around the corner from L.L. Bean. Aficionados beat a path to **China Rose,** 10 School St., Freeport, 207/865-6886, for Hunan, Mandarin, and Sichuan dishes. The ambience is elegant, the service first-rate. Open for lunch and dinner daily, 11 AM–9:30 PM (to 10 PM Fri.–Sat.). The creative "chef's special" entrées run $11–14 (but Peking duck is $24); typical veggie, seafood, and meat dishes are less.

Allegedly (and still a matter of dispute), Maine was born at the 18th-century **Jameson Tavern,** 115 Main St., just north of L.L. Bean, Freeport 04032, 207/865-4196, where statehood documents were signed in 1820. Now you can steep yourself in history over lunch or dinner every day, year-round. The ambitious bistro-type dinner menu is huge. In good weather, try for the outside patio. Dining rooms are small and casually elegant; the informal Tap Room has lighter fare and tends to be noisy. Dinner reservations are advisable on weekends, when service can be a bit slow. Open all year, 11:30 AM–10 PM.

INFORMATION AND SERVICES

With shopping being Freeport's occupation and preoccupation, the best source of information is the **Freeport Merchants Association,** P.O. Box 452, Freeport 04032, 207/865-1212 or 800/865-1994, www.freeportusa.com. Its **Hose Tower Information Center** (including restrooms and ATM), at 23 Depot St., two blocks east of L.L. Bean, is open all year. Summer hours are Mon.–Sat. 9 AM–5 PM. The association annually produces the invaluable *Official Map & Visitor Guide,* showing locations of all the shops, plus sites of lodgings, restaurants, visitor kiosks, pay phones, restrooms, and car and bike parking. If you're serious about "doing" Freeport, send for a guide before you arrive so you can plan your attack and hit the ground running.

Emergencies

Freeport has no hospital or first-aid center; **Maine Medical Center** is a 20-minute drive to the south, in Portland, 207/871-0111. The local **ambulance** can be reached at 207/865-4211; contact the **fire department** at the same number and the **police department** at 207/865-4213.

Getting There and Getting Around

See *Getting There,* under *Greater Portland,* for information on flying to the Portland area.

Some of the larger hotels and motels in Portland and South Portland will arrange shopping trips to Freeport for their guests. Inquire when booking reservations.

If you have a car, park downtown in Freeport and walk to the shops; then drive to the outlying shopping areas. If you need a ride to outlying shopping areas, or even beyond Freeport, contact **Yarmouth Taxi,** 846-9336.

Yarmouth

Between Freeport to the north and Greater Portland to the south, Yarmouth seldom gets the respect it deserves for its classic architecture, unusual shops, and splendidly scenic Royal River winding through town.

Settled in 1680 and named Old North Yarmouth, the town was twice leveled by Indians (who'd recognized its attractions far earlier) before a third settlement took root in 1727. Yarmouth separated from North Yarmouth in 1849. During the 1800s, more than 300 sailing vessels were built along the Cousins and Royal Rivers. Two energetic volunteer organizations, the **Yarmouth Historical Society** and the **Village Improvement Society,** have managed to encourage historic preservation and stir up curiosity and enthusiasm about the ghosts of Yarmouth's past.

RECREATION
Getting Afloat
Locally, the best-known canoeing (and kayaking) route is along the meandering Royal River. For a leisurely day's outing, you can first canoe the river before stopping for a picnic and walk in **Royal River Park.**

To reach the put-in from Main St. (Rte. 88) in Yarmouth, head west on West Main St. (Rte. 115) to Rte. 9. Turn right onto Rte. 9 and go about three miles, crossing railroad tracks and the river; park in the grassy clearing on your right.

The six-mile downstream paddle is no big challenge—all quiet water, with little current—and you won't be alone, but it's totally relaxing. Allow 2–4 hours. Toward the end, after you've paddled under a railroad trestle, continue about another 20 minutes, under another trestle, and take out at municipal Royal River Park, just before the river plunges over a dam.

The park has a lovely half-mile walkway bordering the southern shore of the river, roughly between East Elm and Bridge Streets. Near the

parking lot and downstream are two fish ladders (to assist fish upstream for spawning), plus you'll see remnants of old mills. To skip the paddling and just visit the park, go west on Main St. (Rte. 88) in downtown Yarmouth, then turn right onto East Elm, cross the railroad tracks, and park in the small lot on your right.

FESTIVALS AND EVENTS

The **Yarmouth Clam Festival,** the third weekend in July, is an enormous town-wide extravaganza and the highlight of Yarmouth's summer, with events everywhere you look: a parade, balloon rides, an art show, live music, food booths, pancake breakfasts, a carnival, a clam-shucking contest, and more clams than anyone can eat. If you want to join in, be sure to make lodging reservations well in advance.

SHOPPING

"Eartha," a 42-foot rotating globe, exactly one-millionth the size of the earth and weighing 6,000 pounds, dominates the three-story-high, glass-walled lobby of the **DeLorme Mapping Company,** Two DeLorme Dr., Yarmouth 04096, 207/846-7000, fax 846-7051, www.delorme.com. Internationally known as the source of charts, maps, software, CD-ROMs, and the essential *Maine Atlas and Gazetteer,* DeLorme has a fantastic map store here, with a bank of try-out computers, books for adults and kids, and almost every map you could possibly want. The store is open all year, Mon.–Sat. 8:30 AM–6 PM, Sun. 9:30 AM–5 PM.

The third generation now runs the show at **A.E. Runge, Jr.,** 139 Main St., Yarmouth 04096, 207/846-9000, purveyors of Oriental rugs. Tad Runge's selection is particularly interesting, and if high-quality Turkish, Persian, and Caucasian carpets intrigue you, it's well worth a visit. Open all year, Tues.–Fri. 10 AM–5 PM, Sat. 10 AM–3 PM. If you're making a special detour, be sure to call ahead in case he's out hunting down old carpets.

Handworks of Yarmouth, 298 Main St., Yarmouth 04096, 207/846-5513, a cooperative, has an extremely fine selection of Maine crafts. The shop is open Tues.–Sat. 10 AM–5 PM.

For antiques, don't miss **W.M. Schwind, Jr., Antiques,** 51 E. Main St., Rte. 88, Yarmouth 04096, 207/846-9458, in a splendid 1810 house. Look for country and formal furniture and accessories, including antique glass. Open weekdays 10 AM–5 PM, year-round, other times by appointment.

FOOD

Freeport, very nearby, offers several other convenient choices.

Pat's Pizza, 43 Rte. 1, Yarmouth 04096, 207/846-3701, part of a statewide chain, is predictably good, open for lunch and dinner daily, all year. Best times to go are Sunday and Monday 5–9 PM, to graze the all-you-can-eat pizza buffet. Open until midnight Fri.–Sat.

Housed in a retrofitted theater, **Clayton's,** 189 Main St., Yarmouth 04096, 207/846-1117, creates imaginative grilled, wrap, and deli sandwiches, plus salads and soups that'll keep you going all day. Commandeer one of the dozen tables, pick up picnic fare, or just browse the gourmet shop and stock up from the excellent selection of exotic condiments, cheeses, and other goodies. You can't go wrong here, and the service is speedy. There's even peanut butter and jelly for the kids. The lunch menu is available weekdays 11 AM–6 PM, Sat. 11 AM–3 PM; the shop is open Mon.–Fri. 8 AM–6 PM, Sat. 9 AM–5 PM.

Just north (toward Freeport) of the Visitor Information Center and across the road is the roadside stand of **Day's Crabmeat & Lobster,** Rte. 1, Yarmouth 04096, 207/846-3436—the area's best source for lobster and fresh crabmeat. Eat at one of the few tables here—or maybe order cooked lobsters to go. They'll also pack crabmeat and live lobsters for travel. During the summer, it's open daily, 11 AM–7 PM (to 8 PM Fri.–Sat.).

INFORMATION AND SERVICES

The **Maine Visitor Information Center,** Rte. 1, at I-95 exit 17, Yarmouth 04096, 207/846-0833, is part of the statewide tourism-information network. Staffers are particularly attuned to Freeport and Yarmouth, but the center has brochures and maps for the entire state. Also here are restrooms, phones, picnic tables, vending machines, and a dog-walking area.

The **Yarmouth Chamber of Commerce,** 158 Main St., Yarmouth 04096, 207/846-3984, www.yarmouthmaine.org, is a small office open weekdays only.

Photo Services

Photo 59, 438 Rte. 1, Yarmouth Marketplace, Yarmouth 04096, 207/846-1556, does enlargements while you wait and one-hour photo processing. It's open Mon.–Fri. 10 AM–5:30 PM, Sat. 10 AM–2 PM.

Getting Around

The Yarmouth/Cumberland town line is the closest jumping-off point for getting to Casco Bay's Great Chebeague Island via the **Chebeague Transportation Company (CTC);** you can also take a longer boat ride from downtown Portland via Casco Bay Lines. The logistics of the CTC operation make it sound complicated, but it really isn't; chalk it up as an adventure. Plans are afoot to simplify the procedure (it used to be even more complicated), but don't hold your breath.

Year-round, the CTC operates a 15-minute passenger ferry to the island, carrying more than 100,000 people annually, and also makes special arrangements for car and freight transport. The *Islander* makes the summer runs; the smaller *Big Squaw* does the winter trips.

Mid-Apr.–late Oct., as well as during winter holidays, if you're staying overnight on Chebeague, you'll need to drive to the CTC Parking Lot on Rte. 1, between Tuttle Rd. and I-95 exit 16. You'll park your car ($10 per day) and board a van or bus for the 20-minute ride to the Cousins Island dock at the southeastern edge of Yarmouth. The bus departs Cumberland *precisely*

30 minutes before boat time. The boat makes 8–10 roundtrips daily, beginning at 6:40 AM on Chebeague and 7 AM in Yarmouth. Last boat from Chebeague departs at 10:30 PM on summer weekends, but you'll need to return earlier on other days. Tickets are available on the bus and on the boat. Roundtrip fares: $12 adults, $3 kids under 12, $3 dogs, $6 bikes. No charge for infants. Reservations are not required.

Nov.–Apr., or if you're only going to Chebeague for a weekday, you can drive straight to Cousins Island and hope to find a parking space. From Main St., Yarmouth, take Lafayette St. under I-95, then left onto Princes Point Rd., then left to Gilman Rd. Cross the causeway onto the island and continue to Wharf Rd. Go left and look for the Blanchard Parking Lot on the left. Parking is $10 a day, but space is not always available.

Best solution of all is to cycle to Cousins Island from downtown Yarmouth (the back roads have bike lanes) and take your bike on the boat to Chebeague.

For a boat schedule and a copy of *A User's Guide to the Chebeague Transportation Company,* call 207/846-3700; write the CTC, P.O. Box 27, Chebeague Island 04017; or visit www.chebeaguetrans.com.

Mid-Coast Region

In contrast to the South Coast's gorgeous sandy beaches, the Mid-Coast region features a deeply indented shoreline with snug harbors and long, gnarled fingers of land. Even though these fingers are inconvenient for driving (but wonderful for sailing), this is where you'll find picture-book Maine—drive to the tips of the peninsulas and find lighthouses, fishing villages, country inns, and lobster wharves.

Admittedly, I'm biased about this area, where I put down roots in the early 1970s, but at times I almost wish it weren't quite so popular. Problem is, what's not to like? Above all, it's hard to resist championing the scenery.

The Mid-Coast stretches roughly (you'll find disagreement on the boundaries) from Brunswick (in the northeastern corner of Cumberland County) on the Androscoggin River to Stockton Springs on the Penobscot—roughly 95 miles by road, traversing Sagadahoc, Lincoln, Knox, and Waldo Counties.

After York County, the Mid-Coast sees midsummer's greatest population explosion. (Obviously, I'm not the only one promoting the area.) On or near Rte. 1, visitors come for Brunswick's Bowdoin College, Wiscasset's antique shops, Rockland's art galleries,

© KATHLEEN M. BRANDES

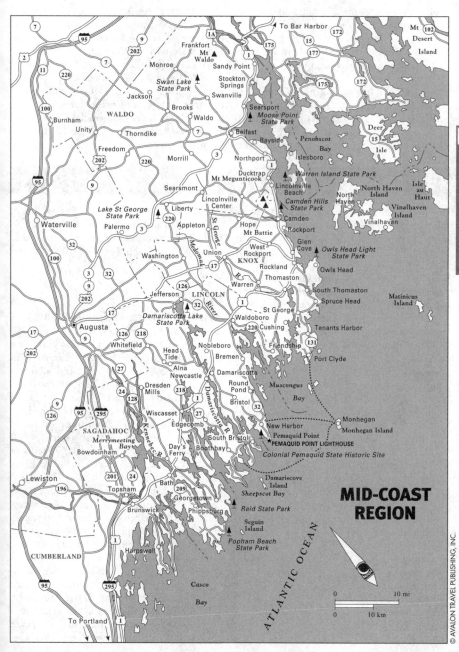

Mid-Coast Region

MID-COAST REGION

0   10 mi
0   10 km

© AVALON TRAVEL PUBLISHING, INC.

Camden's picturesque mountainside harbor, Lincolnville's pocket beach, and Searsport's sea captains' homes.

From Port Clyde, Rockland, and Lincolnville Beach, car and passenger ferries head offshore to the islands of Monhegan, Vinalhaven, North Haven, Matinicus, and Islesboro—all occupied year-round by hardy souls and joined in summer by less-hardy ones. Except for Matinicus, they're great day-trip destinations. If what appeals to you about a ferry trip is traveling on the water, you can get a taste of the great age of sail by booking a three- or six-day cruise on one of the classic windjammer schooners berthed in Rockland, Rockport, and Camden.

In July and August, try to avoid arriving without a reservation. Helpful chamber of commerce staffers in prime locations often can work last-minute miracles, but special events and festivals can fill up all the beds for miles around.

Brunswick Area

Brunswick (pop. 20,520), straddling Rte. 1, relies partly on modern defense dollars—but it was incorporated in 1738 and is steeped in history. The town is home to both prestigious Bowdoin College and the sprawling Brunswick Naval Air Station—an unusual and sometimes conflicting juxtaposition that makes this a college town with a difference. You'll find lots of classic homes and churches, several respected museums, year-round cultural attractions—plus aerobatic extravaganzas at the naval base.

Brunswick and Topsham face each other across roiling waterfalls on the Androscoggin River. The falls, which Native Americans knew by the tongue-twisting name of Ahmelahcogneturcook ("place abundant with fish, birds, and other animals"), were a source of hydropower for 18th-century sawmills and 19th- and 20th-century textile mills. Franco-Americans arrived in droves to beef up the textile industry in the late 19th century (but lost their jobs eventually in the Depression).

Brunswick is also the gateway to the stunning Harpswells, a peninsula/archipelago complex linked by causeways, several bridges, and one unique granite cribstone bridge. Scenic back roads on Harpswell Neck inspire detours to the fishing hamlets of Cundy's Harbor, Orr's Island, and Bailey Island.

In summer 2004, the Maine Eastern Railroad, 207/797-9228, www.merail.com, began running weekend trips between Brunswick (the stop's at Cedar St., in back of the chamber of commerce office) and Rockland, with a stop in Bath. The train runs the midcoast route into fall; there's one round-trip on Saturday, and one on Sunday.

SIGHTS

Bowdoin College and Its Museums

Bowdoin College got its start here nearly 150 years before the Naval Air Station landed on the nearby Brunswick Plains. Founded in 1794 as a men's college with a handful of students, Bowdoin (coed since 1969) now has 1,625 students from all 50 states and many foreign countries. The college has turned out such noted graduates as authors Nathaniel Hawthorne and Henry Wadsworth Longfellow, sex pioneer Alfred Kinsey, U.S. President Franklin Pierce, Arctic explorers Robert Peary and Donald MacMillan, former U.S. Senator George Mitchell and former Secretary of Defense William Cohen, American Express Chairman Ken Chenault, a dozen Maine governors, and thousands of others. Massachusetts Hall, oldest building on the 200-acre campus, dates from 1802, predating the ancient-seeming Bowdoin pines on the northeast boundary. Campus additions in the past decade include the striking David Saul Smith Union, Druckenmiller Hall, several new dormitories and renovated fraternity houses, a renovated theater and a new "black box" the-

JOSHUA L. CHAMBERLAIN—MAINE'S CIVIL WAR HERO

When the American Civil War began in 1861, Joshua Chamberlain was a 33-year-old logic instructor at Bowdoin College in Brunswick; when it ended, in 1865, Chamberlain had distinguished himself in the Battle of Gettysburg at Little Round Top, earned the Congressional Medal of Honor for the Battle of Petersburg, and had been the man to formally accept the official surrender of Robert E. Lee at Appomattox Court House. He later became governor of Maine and president of Bowdoin College, but Chamberlain's greatest renown, ironically, came more than a century later—when 1990s PBS filmmakers focused on the Civil War and highlighted his strategic military role.

Joshua Lawrence Chamberlain was born in 1828 in Brewer, Maine, son and grandson of soldiers. After graduating from Bowdoin in 1852, he studied for the ministry at Bangor Theological Seminary, then returned to his alma mater as an instructor.

With the nation in turmoil in the early 1860s, Chamberlain signed on to help, receiving a commission as a lieutenant colonel in the Twentieth Maine Volunteers in 1862. After surviving 24 encounters and six battle wounds and having been promoted to general (brigadier, then major), Chamberlain was elected Republican governor of Maine in 1866—by the largest margin in the state's history—only to suffer through four one-year terms of partisan politics. In 1871, Chamberlain became president of Bowdoin College, where he remained until 1883. He then dove into speechmaking and writing, his best-known work being *The Passing of the Armies,* a memoir of the Civil War's final campaigns. From 1900–1914, Chamberlain was surveyor of the Port of Portland, a presidential appointment that ended only when complications from a wartime abdominal wound finally did him in. He died at the grand old age of 86.

Brunswick's Joshua L. Chamberlain Museum, located in his onetime home at 226 Maine St., commemorates this illustrious Mainer, and thousands of Civil War buffs annually stream through the door in search of Chamberlain "stuff." To make it easier, the Pejepscot Historical Society has produced a helpful map entitled *Joshua Chamberlain's Brunswick,* highlighting town and college ties to the man—his dorm rooms, his presidential office, his portraits, even his church pew (number 64 at First Parish Church). Chamberlain's gravesite is in Brunswick's Pine Grove Cemetery, just east of the Bowdoin campus.

ater, the Schwartz Outdoor Leadership Center, the Lubin Family Squash Center, and the Coastal Studies Center in nearby Harpswell, with more planned. For admissions and campus-tour information, call 207/725-3100, write to Bowdoin College, Brunswick 04011, or visit www.bowdoin.edu. (The main switchboard number is 207/725-3000.)

Photos and artifacts bring Arctic expeditions to life at the **Peary-MacMillan Arctic Museum,** Hubbard Hall, Bowdoin College, Brunswick 04011, 207/725-3416. Among the specimens are stuffed animals, a skin kayak, fur clothing, snow goggles, and Inuit carvings—most collected by Arctic pioneers Robert E. Peary and Donald B. Macmillan. The small gift shop specializes in Inuit books and artifacts. Admission is free, but donations are welcome. Open Tues.–Sat. 10 AM–5 PM, Sun. 2–5 PM.

An astonishing array of Greek and Roman artifacts is only one of the high points at the **Bowdoin College Museum of Art,** Walker Art Building, Bowdoin College, Brunswick 04011, 207/725-3275. The building alone is worth a look. Designed in the 1890s by Charles McKim of the famed McKim, Mead & White firm, it's a stunning neoclassical edifice with an interior rotunda and stone lions flanking the entry. Also here is an impressive permanent collection of 19th- and 20th-century American art. Admission is free, but donations are welcome. Normally open Tues.–Sat. 10 AM–5 PM, Sun. 2–5 PM, the museum closed for a major renovation project in June of 2005, projected for conclusion at the end of 2006. The museum is one of the seven top museums featured in the **Maine Art Museum Trail,** a cultural-heritage itinerary.

Pejepscot Historical Society Museums

Side by side in an unusual, cupola-topped duplex facing Brunswick's Mall (village green), the **Pejepscot Museum,** 159 Park Row, and the **Skolfield-Whittier House,** 161 Park Row, are both operated by the Pejepscot Historical Society, 207/729-6606, www.curtis-library.com/pejepscot.htm, founded in 1888 and headquartered at the museum. Focusing on local history, the museum, in the left-hand section, has a collection of more than 50,000 artifacts and mounts always-interesting special exhibits throughout the year. Admission is free; there's a small gift shop. Open year-round Tues.–Fri. 9 AM–5 PM (to 8 PM Thurs.), Sat. hours vary seasonally. The 17-room Skolfield-Whittier House, on the right-hand side of the building, looks as though the owners just stepped out for the afternoon, though it was last occupied in 1925. The onetime sea captain's house has elegant Victorian furnishings and lots of exotic artifacts collected on global seafaring stints. Hour-long guided tours are available at 10 and 11:30 AM, 1 and 2:30 PM. Admission is $5 adults, $2.50 children 6–16. Open late May–Columbus Day, Tues.–Sat.

Also operated by the Pejepscot Historical Society, the **Joshua L. Chamberlain Museum,** 226 Maine St., Brunswick (207/729-6606), across from First Parish Church, commemorates the Union Army hero of the Civil War's Battle of Gettysburg, who's now gaining long-overdue respect. The mostly restored house where Chamberlain lived in the late 19th century (and Henry Wadsworth Longfellow lived 30 years earlier) has seven rooms containing Chamberlain memorabilia, much of it Civil War-related. A gift shop stocks lots of Civil War publications, especially ones covering the

Twentieth Maine Volunteers. Guided tours (45 minutes) occur on the hour and the half-hour. Tickets are $5 adults, $2.50 children 6–16. Open May 1–Oct., Tues.–Sat. 10 AM–5 PM. A combination ticket for both historic houses is $8 adults, $4 children. Also of note: a guided walking tour of Brunswick is offered at predetermined times throughout the summer. For $5 a person, participants can learn what the town looked like at the turn of the century.

Uncle Tom's Church

Across the street from the Chamberlain museum is the historic 1846 **First Parish Church,** 9 Cleaveland St. at Bath Rd., Brunswick 04011, 207/729-7331, www.firstparish.net, a Gothic Revival (or carpenter Gothic) board-and-batten structure crowning the rise at the head of Maine St. Scores of celebrity preachers have ascended this pulpit, and Harriet Beecher Stowe was inspired to write *Uncle Tom's Cabin* while listening to her husband deliver an antislavery sermon here. If you're a fan of organ music, arrive here before noon any Tuesday, early July to early August (or call ahead for details), when guest organists present 40-minute lunchtime concerts (12:10–12:50 PM) on the 1883 Hutchings-Plaisted tracker organ. Admission is free, but a small donation is requested. Stick around for the post-concert church tour. At other times, the church is open by appointment.

Brunswick's Noted Women

With more than 20 points of interest, the **Brunswick Women's History Trail** covers such national notables as authors Harriet Beecher Stowe and Kate Douglas Wiggin and lesser-known lights including naturalist Kate Furbish, pioneering Maine pediatrician Dr. Alice Whittier, and the Franco-American women who slaved away in the textile mills at the turn of the 20th century. Pick up the walking-tour booklet at the Pejepscot Museum gift shop for $2. Then set out to follow the fascinating story. Or take the guided tour in summer, at $5 per person; contact the museum for a schedule.

Go, Fish!

If you're in town mid-May–late June, plan to visit FPL Energy's **Brunswick Hydro** generating station, straddling the falls on the Androscoggin River, Lower Maine St., next to Fort Andross, Brunswick-Topsham town line. A glass-walled viewing room lets you play voyeur during the annual ritual of anadromous fish heading upstream to spawn. Amazingly undaunted by the obstacles, such species as alewives (herring), salmon, and smallmouth bass make their way from salt water to fresh via a 40-foot-high, 570-foot-long manmade fish ladder. The viewing room, which maxes out at about 20 people, is open Wed.–Sun. 1–5 PM, during the brief spawning season.

Touring Topsham

Just across the Androscoggin River, the Topsham Historic Commission has produced a handy illustrated guide, *Topsham, Maine, Historical Walking Tour,* with photos and descriptions of 35 significant architectural and historical landmarks—mostly 18th- and 19th-century Federal and Greek Revival residences. Topsham, incorporated in 1764, is a sleeper of a town; this walking tour proves it. The free booklet is available from the Town of Topsham Planning Office, 22 Elm St., Topsham 04086, 207/725-1724.

Historic consciousness is behind a joint effort by Topsham (town clerk, 207/725-1719) and Brunswick (town clerk, 207/725-6658) to save the swinging pedestrian bridge, over 100 years old, that connects the two towns. Also working on the effort (www.saveourbridge.org) is the Brunswick Rotary Club.

RECREATION

Hiking and Walking

Besides the hikes listed below, be sure to consider the **Androscoggin River Bicycle Path,** which also has a lane for walkers.

In the village of Bailey Island, there's a mini-walk to the **Giant Stairs,** a waterfront stone stairway of mammoth proportions. To get there, take Rte. 24 from Cooks Corner toward Bailey Island and Land's End, keeping an eye out for Washington Ave., on the left about 1.5 miles after the cribstone bridge. (Or drive to Land's End, park the car with the rest of the crowds, survey the panorama, and walk 0.8 mile back along Rte. 24 to Washington Ave. from there.) Turn onto Washington Ave., go 0.1 mile, and park at the Episcopal Church (corner of Ocean St.). Walk along Ocean St. to the shorefront path. Watch for a tiny sign. Don't let small kids get close to the slippery rocks on the surf-tossed shoreline. (The same advice, by the way, holds for Land's End, where the rocks can be treacherous.)

Thanks to the **Brunswick-Topsham Land Trust,** founded in 1985, two nature preserves (one on Harpswell Neck, one in Topsham) are open to the public for hiking, birding, and cross-country skiing. Both are free and accessible from sunrise to sunset; no bikes or pets are allowed. Be a conscientious trail-keeper and carry a litter bag when you go. The 11-acre **Captain Alfred Skolfield Nature Preserve** has two blue-blazed nature-trail loops; one skirts a salt marsh, where you're apt to see egrets, herons, and osprey in summer. Adjacent to the preserve is an ancient Indian portage site that linked Middle Bay and Harpswell Coves when Native Americans spent their vacations here. (No dopes, they!) Dr. Alice Whittier donated the preserve in memory of her seafaring grandfather. Take Rte. 123 (Harpswell Rd.) south from Brunswick about three miles; when you reach the Middle Bay Rd. intersection (on right), continue on Rte. 123 for 1.1 miles. Watch for a small sign, and a small parking area, on your right.

In Topsham, the 163-acre **Bradley Pond Farm Preserve** has two well-laid-out nature loops (a total of 2.5 miles) that let you sample marshes, woodlands, fields, and the pond—all astonishingly close to civilization. Farm owners Florence and Fred Call have generously agreed to share their special turf, so heed the rules and stay on the trails. From Maine St. in Brunswick, cross the river to Topsham's Main St. At the junction of Rtes. 196 and 201, take

201 four miles to Bradley Pond Rd. (on the left). Turn in and park (or leave your bike) in the designated parking areas on the left. For further info on these and other reserved lands, or even to volunteer some trail-maintenance time, contact the Brunswick-Topsham Land Trust, 108 Maine St., Brunswick 04011, 207/729-7694.

In the communities to the north (Bath) and south (Freeport) are several more nature preserves well worth visiting.

Bicycling

The safest and most attractive place for biking in the Brunswick area is the new 2.6 mile **Androscoggin River Bicycle Path** running between downtown Brunswick and Cooks Corner, meandering along the scenic Androscoggin River and paralleling Rte. 1. The landscaped asphalt path, also popular with joggers, strollers, and inline skaters, deserves to be a model for many other Maine communities where biking is likely to be hazardous to your health, like the twisting, narrow roads of the Harpswells, where the beauty must be weighed against the serious risks. To reach the path from the lower end of Maine St. in downtown Brunswick, take Mason St. and then the next left onto Water St. Continue about two blocks to the parking area (often very crowded) next to the boat-launching site. There's no loop to the path yet, so you'll need to return the way you came.

Center Street Bicycles, 11 Center St., just off Maine St., Brunswick 04011, 207/729-5309, www.centerstreetbicycles.com, a local institution since 1981, does repairs and sells bikes and a good range of accessories.

Swimming

Thomas Point Beach, 29 Meadow Rd., Brunswick 04011, 207/725-6009 or 877/872-4321, www.thomaspointbeach.com, is actually 85 acres of privately owned parkland with facilities for swimming (lifeguard on duty; bathhouses), fishing, field sports, picnicking (500 tables), and camping (80 tent and RV sites at $20; no water hookups). No pets are allowed. The sandy beach is tidal, so the swimming

"window" is about two hours before high tide until two hours afterward; otherwise, you're wallowing in mudflats. (The same rule holds for kayakers or canoeists.) There's a big playground with lots of room to run that's perfect for toddlers. Teenagers gravitate to the arcade and the ice cream parlor; for adults, there's a gift shop (which also carries paper plates and such). The park is also the site of several annual events: the Maine Highland Games, the Saltwater Music Festival, and the Bluegrass Festival. Parking is ample. At Cooks Corner, where Bath Rd. meets Rte. 24 south, take the Thomas Point Rd. southwestward about two miles to the park. Open mid-May–Sept., 9 AM–sunset. Admission to the park is $3.50 adults, $2 children under 12.

If the tide is low and freshwater swimming appeals, head to town-owned **Coffin Pond,** River Rd., Brunswick, 207/725-6656, www.brunswickme.org/parkrec, a manmade swimming hole with a sandy beach, lifeguards, water slide, picnic tables, playground, changing rooms, and snack bar. Kids' swimming lessons (ages 5–14) are held in August. It's a popular spot, so expect plenty of company. Open mid-June–Labor Day, 10 AM–7 PM. Admission is charged. Heading west on Rte. 1 (Pleasant St.), turn right onto River Rd. and go about 0.5 mile to the parking area (on the right).

Another terrific spot for freshwater swimming is **White's Beach,** White's Beach and Campground, Durham Rd., Brunswick 04011, 207/729-0415. The sandy-bottomed pond maxes out at nine feet, so it's particularly good for small kids. Admission is $3 for adults, $2 for children under 12. There are also 45 campsites to rent, at $15–25. Open mid-May–mid-Oct. From Rte. 1 just south of the I-95 exit into Brunswick, take Durham Rd. 2.2 miles northwest.

Golf

Established in 1888 primarily for Bowdoin College students, the **Brunswick Golf Club,** River Rd., Brunswick 04011, 207/725-8224, is now an especially popular 18-hole public course, so you'll need to call for a starting time.

Heading west on Rte. 1 (Pleasant St.), turn right onto River Rd. and go 0.5 mile. Open Apr.–mid-Nov. If you can stand the runway backdraft challenging your swing, the nine-hole **Brunswick Naval Air Station Golf Club,** Bath Rd., Brunswick, 207/721-9995, is open to the public. You'll have access to the pro shop, snack bar, and driving range. Call for tee times; greens fees are $15 for nine holes, $20 for 18.

Getting Afloat

Departing at noon from the Cook's Lobster House Wharf in Bailey Island (end of Rte. 24), a large, sturdy **Casco Bay Lines ferry** does a 1.75-hour nature-watch circuit of nearby islands, including Eagle Island, the onetime home of Adm. Robert Peary (there are no stopovers on these circuits). The nature-watch cruise operates daily, late June–Labor Day. Reservations aren't needed. Cost is $12 adults, $10 seniors, $5.50 children 5–9; under five are free. To confirm the schedule when weather is iffy, call Casco Bay Lines, 207/774-7871, or Cook's, 207/833-2818.

For a more intimate excursion in a smaller boat, Capt. Les McNelly, owner of **Sea Escape Charters,** Box 7, Bailey Island 04003, 207/833-5531, www.seaescapecottages.com, operates two-hour on-demand sightseeing cruises throughout the summer (weather permitting) for $70 pp (two persons), $50 pp (three persons), or $40 pp (four–six persons). Or he'll take you out to Eagle Island for $130 a couple ($55 pp for three or more passengers), or on a private two- to four-hour fishing charter. Call to schedule a trip; full price list on web.

The Captain's Watch, 926 Cundy's Harbor Rd., Cundy's Harbor, Harpswell 04079, 207/725-0979, offers sailing excursions but is far enough off the beaten track that most of their customers tend to be their guests.

Sea Kayaking: Contact **H2Outfitters**, P.O. Box 72, Orr's Island 04066, 207/833-5257 or 800/205-2925, www.H2Outfitters.com, a thriving operation since 1982. Based in a red-painted wood building on the Orr's Island side of the famed cribstone bridge, this experienced

company offers instructional programs, day trips, multi-day trips including island camping, bed-and-breakfast programs (beginning at $595 pp for a Maine weekend), kids and family programs, and international adventures. Overnight trips include all food and gear. There's also a retail shop.

If you're an experienced sea kayaker, consider exploring Harpswell Sound from the boat launch on the west side of the cribstone bridge; kayaks can also put in at Mackerel Cove, near Cook's Lobster House.

ENTERTAINMENT

There's no lack of classical music in Brunswick each summer, but for lighter fare, the **Maine State Music Theatre,** Pickard Theater, Bowdoin College, mailing address 22 Elm St., Brunswick 04011, 207/725-8769, www.msmt.org, has been a summer tradition since 1959. The state-of-the-art, air-conditioned theater brings real pros to its stage for four musicals (early June–late Aug.). Loyal subscribers book the same seats year after year, and performances tend to sell out, so make reservations as soon as you can. (Single tickets go on sale in early May.) Performances are at 8 PM Tues.–Sat., with a family Sunday night scheduled once during each run, at 7:30 PM; matinees are staged at 2 PM on a rotating schedule—each week is different. No children under four. Ticket range is $27–47. Budget hints: Two preview performances, with discount seats, precede each opening; and student-rush price (valid student I.D. required) is $10, half an hour before curtain.

Largest performing arts center in the region, and a source of community pride, **The Orion Performing Arts Center,** 50 Republic Ave., Topsham, a 900-seat auditorium next to Mt. Ararat High School, brings nationally known concert performers to town.

The Theatre Project, 14 School St., Brunswick 04011, 207/729-8584 or 207/729-0866, www.theaterproject.com, is a nonprofit community-based theater with a pay-what-you-can policy for its three acting companies: $15 for

Mid-Coast Region

the Professional Company, $10 for the Young Company, and $6 for the Young People's Theater. There's an outreach touring program for schools and communities, extensive residencies, year-round classes, a summer festival, and community festivals, as well as vibrant and compelling theater.

First-run films, and at least one kids' flick, are on offer at **Regal Cinemas Brunswick 10,** 19 Gurnet Rd., Cooks Corner, 207/798-4505, a multiplex that opens about 11:30 AM and closes about 12 hours later. Call for a schedule or check Brunswick's *Times Record* or the *Portland Press Herald.*

Eveningstar Cinema, Tontine Mall, Brunswick, 207/729-5486, www.eveningstarcinema .com, screens "only the best in high content motion pictures." Rentals are available for student activities-call office, 207/729-6796. Open all year.

FESTIVALS AND EVENTS

Late June–early Aug., the **Bowdoin International Music Festival,** www.bowdoinfestival. org, is a showcase for virtuoso musicians from five continents. Guest artists and faculty perform classical and contemporary concerts Wednesday and Friday evenings. Friday MusicFest concerts (8 PM, $25) and Wednesday Upbeat! concerts (7:30 PM, $20) are in the state-of-the-art Crooker Theater at Brunswick High School. The Artists of Tomorrow student series (Sun., Tues., Thur., 7:30 PM, free) and Gamper Festival of Contemporary Music (free) are in Kresge Auditorium at Bowdoin College. For more information, check with the festival office, 207/373-1400.

Wednesday evenings (Thurs. if it rains) July–Aug., **Music on the Mall** presents family band concerts at 7 PM on the Brunswick Mall (the lovely park in the center of town).

The first full week of August, the **Topsham Fair** is a week-long agricultural festival with exhibits, demonstrations, live music, ox pulls, contests, harness racing, and fireworks at the Topsham Fairgrounds. The third Saturday of

Aug., the **Maine Highland Games** mark the annual wearing of the plaids—but you needn't be Scottish to join in the games or watch the highland dancing or browse the arts and crafts booths. (Only a Scot, however, can appreciate that unique concoction called haggis.) If you're seeking your clan roots, this is the place; lots of genealogical networking goes on here. It all happens at Thomas Point Beach; tickets at the gate are $10 adults, $5 kids 6–12.

Also at Thomas Point, September's **Annual Bluegrass Festival** is a four-day event which includes big-name artists. A full pass at the gate is $120, but various daily combinations and prepayment options are available.

The networking arts organization **Midcoast REACH,** 108 Maine St., Brunswick 04011, 207/729-6964, www.baaca.org, is a great resource for finding out about cultural and arts resources and events. It has put together a Bath/Brunswick Region Arts & Cultural Map and Guide, produces a monthly events calendar, and also sponsors some arts events.

SHOPPING

About a dozen small shops, including unique clothing and confection retailers, are part of the **Tontine Mall,** 149 Maine St., Brunswick; the mall entrance is right in the middle of downtown.

Gifts and Gourmet

Wyler, 100 Maine St., Brunswick 04011, 207/729-5599 (furniture and home), and 150 Maine St., Brunswick 04011, 207/729-1321 (crafts, clothes, and games), carries well-chosen items in both locations. Both stores are open Mon.–Sat., 10 AM–6 PM, Sun. 11 AM–4 PM, summer Fri–Sat. till 8 PM.

And then there's gourmet heaven—masquerading under the name of **Provisions,** 148 Maine St., Brunswick 04011, 207/729-9288. There are fine wines and cheeses, specialty foods, gift baskets, and gourmet accessories. Open Mon.–Sat. 10 AM–6 PM.

Art, Craft, and Antiques Galleries

The **Bayview Gallery,** 58 Maine St., Brunswick 04011, 207/729-5500, www.bayviewgallery.com, specializes in contemporary American paintings, with an emphasis on local land- and seascapes. A spacious gallery, suited to the work, it's open Tues.–Sat., 10 AM–5 PM.

The **Window Tree Gallery & Frame Shop,** 44 Maine St., Brunswick 04011, 207/729-4366, www.thewindowtree.com, owned and operated by David and Heather Whiting, shows oil, pastels, and watercolors in the fine-arts vein, with a regional focus. Open Tues.–Fri. 10 AM–6 PM, Sat. 10 AM–4 PM.

Facing the Mall, **Day's Antiques,** 153 Park Row, Brunswick 04011, 207/725-6959, occupies five rooms and the basement of the handsome historic building known as the Pumpkin House. Quality is high at David Day's shop; prices are fair. Open all year, Mon.–Sat. 10 AM–5 PM.

On the first floor of Fort Andross, on the Androscoggin, the multi-dealer **Cabot Mill Antiques,** 14 Maine St., Brunswick 04011, 207/725-2855, www.cabotiques.com, has over 140 displays in its 15,000-square-foot showroom. Open 10 AM–5 PM Mon.–Sat., Sun. by chance or appointment.   Along Rte. 123 in South Harpswell, south of Mountain Rd., watch for distinctive blue-heron signs that mark the studios of **Harpswell Art and Craft Guild** members— nearly a dozen artisans who welcome visitors to see (and buy) their pottery, sculpture, and jewelry. Appointments are necessary for some studios. Membership varies from year to year, so call 207/833-6081 (Gallery at Widgeon Cove, www.widgeoncove.com) for details.

Bookstores

Bet you can't leave Brunswick without buying a book! Bookstores are plentiful. In addition to the ones described below, there's also the Bowdoin College Bookstore, located in the campus's David Saul Smith Student Union.

With an eclectic new-book inventory that includes lots of esoterica, **Gulf of Maine Books,** 134 Maine St., Brunswick 04011, 207/729-5083, "an independent and alternative bookseller," has held the competition at bay since the early 1980s. The selections evidence intelligence at work, happy thought for a bookstore. Co-owners Beth Leonard and Gary Lawless oversee everything. Open all year.

Brunswick Bookland & Cafe, Cooks Corner Shopping Center, corner of Bath Rd. and Rte. 24 south, Brunswick 04011, 207/725-2313 (store) or 207/725-7033 (café), www.booklandcafe.com, is a terrific store with an especially helpful staff. Inside the 20,000-square-foot emporium are a zillion books (plus CDs and cards) as well as the very popular Hardcover Cafe. At *least* try one of their desserts. Open Mon.–Sat. 9 AM–9 PM, Sun. 9 AM–6 PM.

Natural Foods and Farmers Markets

Morning Glory Natural Foods, 64 Maine St., Brunswick 04011, 207/729-0546, stocks natural and bulk foods, an awesome array of body products, supplements, fresh produce, fresh bread, and happy-making muffins. Unusual candles, incense, healthy gifts, and yoga equipment round out the abundant-feeling store. Open weekdays 9 AM–7 PM, Sat. 9 AM–6 PM, Sun. 11 AM–5 PM.

One of Maine's best farmers markets is the **Brunswick Farmers Market,** which sets up, rain or shine, on the Mall (village green) Tues. and Fri. 8 AM–3 PM, May–Nov. Produce, cheeses, crafts, condiments, live lobsters, and serendipitous surprises—depending on the season. There's also a Saturday Market at Crystal Spring Farm on the Pleasant Hill Rd., 207/729-7694, 8:30 AM–1:30 PM, May–Oct. (you'll see a big sign and lots of cars). Crystal Spring Farm is part of the Brunswick-Topsham Land Trust, and the Community Supported Agriculture network (CSA), where people buy pre-season shares of a farm in order to receive produce throughout the growing season.

Mid-Coast Region

ACCOMMODATIONS

Hotels, Motels, Inns

Combining an 1819 Federal-style manse with a new hotel wing, **The Captain Daniel Stone Inn,** 10 Water St., Brunswick 04011, 207/725-9898 or 877/573-5151, www.someplacesdifferent.com, has 34 guest rooms and suites with reproduction furnishings and a country-hotel feel. Private baths, air-conditioning, phones, cable TV, wireless Internet throughout; no pets. In summer, doubles are $153–240, including continental breakfast; rates are lower other months, and special packages are available. The inn's casually elegant **Narcissa Stone Restaurant,** open daily year-round for dinner (and weekdays for lunch), serves a mean Sunday brunch 10 AM–2 PM. Dinner entrées are $12–24. There are function facilities for smaller business meetings and weddings up to 125 persons.

With Maine's increased tourism and retirement destination popularity has come a building boom, making many reliable national chains available in Brunswick, including the **Comfort Inn,** 199 Pleasant St., Rte. 1, Brunswick 04011, 207/729-1129 or 800/228-5150; **The Atrium Inn,** 21 Gurnet Rd., Rte. 24, Cooks Corner, Brunswick 04011, 207/729-5555, www.brunswickatrium.com; **Econo Lodge,** 215 Pleasant St., Rte. 1, Brunswick 04011, 207/729-9991 or 800/654-9991; **Fairfield Inn & Suites,** 36 Old Portland Rd., Brunswick 04011, 207/721-0300 or 800/228-2800, www.marriott.com/pwmbw; **Super 8 Motel,** 224 Bath Rd., Brunswick 04011, 207/725-8883 or 800/800-8000, www.super8.com; and **Travelers Inn,** 130 Pleasant St., Brunswick 04011, 207/729-3364 or 800/457-3364, www.travelersinnme.com.

A dozen miles down Rte. 24 from Cooks Corner is the turnoff for the **Little Island Motel,** 44 Little Island Rd., Box 15, Orr's Island 04066, 207/833-2392 or 207/833-7362 guest phone, www.littleislandmotel.com, an eight-unit complex on its own spit of land with deck views you won't believe. Basic rooms have

cable TV and small fridge. Doubles go for $136 July–Sept. ($116–120 May, June, Oct.), including buffet breakfast (homemade muffins) and use of bikes, boats, and a little beach. No pets, no smoking, no credit cards. Open mid-May–mid-Oct.

Continue another mile down Rte. 24, cross the cribstone bridge, and you'll come to the **Bailey Island Motel,** Rte. 24, P.O. Box 4, Bailey Island 04003, 207/833-2886, www.baileyislandmotel.com, a congenial, clean, no-frills waterfront spot with 11 rooms that go for $90–120 d, depending on the month. Kids under 10 are free, continental breakfast is included, and rooms have cable TV. No pets. Open May–late Oct.

Bed-and-Breakfasts

Right downtown, facing the tree-shaded Mall, is Mercie and Steve Normand's **Brunswick Bed & Breakfast,** 165 Park Row, Brunswick 04011, 207/729-4914 or 800/299-4914, www.brunswickbnb.com, an 1849 Greek Revival mansion. There are 15 guest rooms, all with private baths, in three buildings: Main Inn, Garden Cottage, and Carriage House. Special touches are the twin parlors (with fireplaces), lots of antiques, and the Normands' extensive collection of antique and modern quilts and local artists' work. A full breakfast is served by a crackling fire in the cool months or on the garden deck in warmer weather. There's a library, kitchenettes, guest gathering spaces, and wireless Internet. Children are welcome, no smoking, no pets. Doubles are $115–225. Open the end of Jan.–Dec.

At the 1761 **Harpswell Inn,** 108 Lookout Point Rd., South Harpswell 04079, 207/833-5509 or 800/843-5509 (reservations only), www.harpswellinn.com, hospitable hosts Dick and Ann Moseley have created a comfortable, welcoming, antiques-filled oasis on 2.5 secluded acres. It's tough to break away from the glass-walled great room, but Middle Bay sunsets from the porch can do it. And just down the hill is Allen's Seafood, where you can watch lobstermen unload their catch in a gorgeous cove. In fall, the foliage on two little islets in the cove turns brilliant red. The B&B has nine lovely rooms (most with private baths; $89–150 d) and three suites ($175–230 d). Cottages available $750–1200 per week. Two-night minimum for all rooms July, Aug., and Oct. weekends. No children under 10, no pets, no smoking. However, children and pets welcome in cottages. From Bath Rd., in Brunswick, take Rte. 123 eight miles to Lookout Point Rd. (on right). Open all year.

Another bed-and-breakfast-cum-boat operation is a mouthful: **The Captain's Watch at Cundy's Harbor B&B and Sail Charter,** 926 Cundy's Harbor Rd., Cundy's Harbor, Harpswell 04079, 207/725-0979. Based in the National Historic Register Cupola House—an inn since Civil War days—the B&B has four guest rooms, including a suite, all with private baths and unusual features (two share access to the head-swiveling octagonal cupola). Energetic hosts Donna Dillman and Ken Brigham, innkeepers since 1986, took the reins here in 1996. Ken captains the 37-foot sloop *Symbion* for day-sails and overnights (up to six persons; cost depends on the time and itinerary); Donna produces the gourmet breakfasts and goes sailing off-season. Doubles are $125–175. No smoking, no pets, no children under 10. Credit cards are accepted but cash and checks are preferred. The Captain's Watch serves as the lodging for several multiday kayaking trips run by H2Outfitters in Orr's Island, across Quahog Bay. There is a second building in Card Cove available for a variety of accommodation options, and the former B&B, the 1770s Captain Drummond house is available to rent. The Captain's Watch is open all year, by reservation off-season. From Cooks Corner, go 4.5 miles on Rte. 24, turn left and go another 4.4 miles to Cundy's Harbor, near the "fingertips" of Great Island's easternmost "arm."

Thirteen miles south of Cooks Corner, **The Log Cabin,** Rte. 24, P.O. Box 41, Bailey Island 04003, 207/833-5546, www.logcabin-maine.com, has eight rooms, all with private baths, phones, TV/VCR, and private decks facing the bay and, weather permitting, splendid sunsets over the White Mountains. Four rooms have kitchen facilities. Rates are $99–299 d in midsummer, lower early and late in the season. Full breakfast is included. No smoking; pets are allowed for $10 extra. Dinner, featuring first-rate regional specialties, is available to guests only. Open Apr.–Oct.

Across the Androscoggin in Topsham is the **Black Lantern Bed & Breakfast,** 6 Pleasant St., Topsham 04086, 207/725-4165 or 888/306-4165, www.blacklanternbandb.com. Judy and Tom Connelie spent a year restoring this handsome Federal home first started in 1810 and expanded in 1839. Three second-floor rooms have private baths (one detached) and quilts and Oriental rugs (Judy's an avid quilter.) Rooms are $90 year-round. The Connelies light a fire each night in the cozy parlor, where the *New York Times* appears every morning (coffee is ready for early risers). An unusual touch is the "book exchange"—a handy swap service where you leave one and take one. No smoking, no pets (small hypo-allergenic dog in residence), no children under 10. Open all year.

Seasonal Rentals and Campgrounds

For weekly and monthly rentals in Great, Orr's, and Bailey Islands, contact Becky-Sue Betts at **Your Island Connection, LLC**, P.O. Box 300, one mile past the cribstone bridge, on the left, Bailey Island 04003, 207/833-7779, www.mainerentals.com. Extremely knowledgeable and helpful about her turf, she manages more than 65 homes, cottages, and apartments ($500–3,000 a week). **Harpswell Property Management,** Bailey Island, 207/833-5078, www.baileyisland.com, has been in the business for more than 20 years and has a wide range of summer and year-round rentals. The chamber of commerce also keeps a list of seasonal cottage rentals.

Cottages on Harpswell Neck are available through the Harpswell Inn. On Bailey Island, the McNellys rent cottages in addition to their charters.

Campsites are available at Thomas Point Beach and White's Beach.

FOOD

Brunswick and Topsham

Breakfast and Lunch: Wild Oats Bakery and Café, 149 Maine St., Tontine Mall, Brunswick 04011, 207/725-6287, turns out terrific made-from-scratch breads and pastries in its comfortable cafeteria-style place. (Just so you know, the name stands for Original And Tasty Stuff.) Outside tables, moderate prices, good-for-you salads, and great sandwiches (try one of a trio of best-sellers: turkey BLT, chutney chicken salad, oven-roasted turkey). Other special touches here are breakfast muesli, Maine-roasted Carrabassett coffee, and an array of pies—in addition to the standard chocolate, there's pumpkin, vanilla, and peanut butter. You can even have your wedding cake made by the bakery. Open Mon.–Sat. 7:30 AM–5 PM, Sun. 8 AM–3 PM.

The toasted Borealis cranberry nut bread is doggone good at **The Little Dog Coffee Shop,** 87 Maine St., Brunswick 04011, 207/721-9500, a spacious and comfortable place for man, woman, and his or her best friend to take their ease while enjoying coffee—plain or in latte, espressso, and other concoctions—tea, chai, homemade pastries and desserts, accompanied by wi-fi and music. Also offering a coffee and computer blend, **Bohemian Coffee House,** 4 Railroad Ave., Brunswick 04011, 207/725-9095, is open 7 AM–7 PM Mon.–Sat., 8 AM–2 PM Sun.

Great sandwiches are also the rule at **The Humble Gourmet,** 103 Pleasant St., Rte. 1, Brunswick 04011, 207/721-8100. The wraps are especially well-filled for an average $5, and counter service is swift. Almost hidden along the Brunswick "strip" at the southern end of town, the Humble Gourmet is worth finding—on the east side of the street just before Rte. 1 takes a 90-degree turn. It's open all year.

For food-on-the-run—no-frills hot dogs straight from the cart—head for Brunswick's Mall, the village green where **Danny's On the Mall** (no telephone) has been cooking up dirt-cheap tube steaks since the early 1980s.

Inexpensive: At the upper end of the downtown drag is Doug and Colleen Lavallee's **Scarlet Begonias,** 212B Maine St., Brunswick 04011, 207/721-0403, an especially cheerful place with a bistro-type pizza-and-pasta menu. Order at the counter and look for a table. How could anyone resist an $9.95 pasta puttanesca dubbed Scarlet Harlot? You can't go wrong here; everything's a winner. No credit cards. BYOL. Open Mon.–Fri. 11 AM–8:30 PM (to 9:30 PM Fri.), Sat. noon–9:30 PM.

If Chinese appeals, head for **China Rose,** 42 Bath Rd., Brunswick 04011, 207/725-8813, a clone of the superb Freeport restaurant of the same name. Sichuan, Hunan, Cantonese, and Mandarin are all on the extensive lunch and dinner buffets. Buffet hours are limited (11 AM–2:30 PM and 4:30–8:30 PM), which keeps the food fresher, but the restaurant is open daily 11 AM–9 PM (to 9:30 PM Fri.–Sat.).

If you'd rather go a bit more ethnic, try **Rosita's Mexican Food,** 212 Maine St., Brunswick 04011, 207/729-7118—Tex-Mex with a veggie slant. Order at the counter and grab a table. Prices are incredibly reasonable: cheese nachos ($4.75) are topped with homemade guacamole, a grilled portabello quesadilla is $5.75, and beans are lard- and oil-free. No credit cards; beer license only. Open daily, Mon.–Thurs. 11 AM–8 PM (to 8:30 PM Fri.), Sat. noon–8:30 PM, Sun. noon–7 PM.

You can also choose from two Indian restaurants, **Bombay Mahal,** 99 Maine St., 207/729-5260, open 7 days, 11 AM–10 PM, with a full-course buffet Sat.–Sun., 11 AM–3 PM; and **Shere Punjab,** 46 Maine St., 207/373-0422, open 7 days, lunch 11 AM–3 PM, dinner 4:30 PM–10 PM, with a Sat.–Sun. lunch buffet 11 AM–2:45 PM. On the ground floor of Fort Andross, headquarters for a number of environmental groups, with terrific views from the upper stories, is a Thai restaurant, **Bangkok Garden,** 14 Maine St., 207/725-9714, www .bangkokgardenrestaurant.com, open Mon.– Thurs. 11:30 AM–9 PM, Fri. 11:30 AM–10 PM, Sat. 4–10 PM.

Generous portions, moderate prices, efficient service, and narrow aisles are the story at **The Great Impasta,** 42 Maine St., Brunswick 04011, 207/729-5858, www.thegreatimpasta.com, a cheerful, informal eatery where the garlic meets you at the door. No reservations, so expect to wait, although you can call ahead and add your name to the waiting list. Dinner entrées are $10–15.50. Small but varied wine list; "bambino menu" for the kids. Open Mon.–Sat. for lunch 11 AM–4 PM; for dinner 4 PM–9 PM Mon.–Thurs. (to 10 PM Fri.–Sat.).

Fat Boy Drive-In, Bath Rd., Old Rte. 1, Brunswick 04011, 207/729-9431 is a genuine throwback—a landmark since 1955 boasting carhops, window trays, $1.45 cheeseburgers, and a menu guaranteed to clog your arteries. Fries and frappes are specialties. If you insist, there are five booths indoors. No credit cards. Open—get this—the third Thursday in March to the second Sunday in October, daily 10:55 AM–8:25 PM (to 8:55 PM weekends). The second Saturday in August, about 500 people show up, many in 1950s get-ups, for the annual sock hop. Tickets are $7. Only pre-1970 cars can park in the lot that night (if you have one, stop in ahead of time for a pass).

The **Back Street Bistro,** 11 Town Hall Place, (next to the Fire Station), Brunswick 04011, 207/725-4060, is true to its name, with blackboard specials and a changing weekly menu of fresh seafood, steaks, vegetarian entrées, and pasta, in the $14–20 range. There is an upstairs wine bar with lighter fare, open 9–11 PM, as well as a downstairs bar in the bistro. Open 5–9 PM daily; reservations are advisable, especially on weekends. Outdoor dining in summer.

El Camino Cantina, 15 Cushing St., Brunswick 04011, 207/725-8228, serves fresh, organic, California Mexican food. Soft tacos might contain Wolfe Neck Farm meat or antibiotic-free Maine chicken. Daily specials,

soups, and vegan offerings. Dinner prices range from $10–15. Full bar, great margaritas. No reservations taken. Open Tues.–Sat. 4 PM–9 PM.

Moderate: A whiff of Bavaria drifts over Topsham from the **Old Munich Restaurant,** 6 First St., Topsham 04086, 207/729-1688, www.oldmunich.us. Yearning for some Wienerschnitzel or Nuernberger wurst? Or maybe some stollen around Christmastime? Be here. Plenty of pork, veal, and authentic sausages. Traditional German tortes and strudel made on the premises. Entrée range is $7.95–21.95. The bistro-type ambience extends to the pleasant beer garden outside, where you can order from a sampling of 19 German beers. Reservations are advisable, especially on weekends; this has become a popular spot. Old Munich is open Tues.–Thurs. 5–9 PM, Fri.–Sun. 11 AM–9 PM.

Informality is definitely the rule at **Henry and Marty,** 61 Maine St., P.O. Box 147, Brunswick 04011, 207/721-9141, owned by Henry D'Allesandris and Martin Perry, but there's nothing casual about the culinary skill here. Head chef Dana Robicheaw concentrates on preparing the best local meat, fish, produce, and vegetarian specialties; lots of loyal customers show up here. Entrées run $11–32. The restaurant does several special events, and serves Cuban-inspired foods during Brunswick's spring Cuba Week. There's a good wine list, or you can choose from a full selection of spirits at the Blue Dog bar. Open all year for dinner Tues.–Sun at 5 PM. Reservations recommended.

Expensive: Seafood is king at the **Star Fish Grill,** 100 Pleasant St., Rte. 1, Brunswick 04011, 207/725-7828, www.starfishgrill.com, where you feel like a submarine when you walk in the door. Everything carries out the marine theme. No starfish on the menu, but everything else is, depending on what's fresh and in season—including a fabulous lobster paella, and locally harvested, nationally acclaimed oysters. Entrées are $16 and up; the paella is $45, supposedly for two, but you'd better be hungry. For carnivores and vegetarians, there are several standing options, plus a few specials every day. The restaurant (and a cozy bar) is open all year at 5 PM Tues.–Sun. for dinner (reservations strongly encouraged). Lunch is served Tues.–Sat. 11 AM–3 PM. Finding it can be a bit tricky, even though it's on the main road. Coming from the south, watch for the road sign on your left, across the street from the Miss Brunswick Diner, at the southern end of Brunswick just before Rte. 1 takes a 90-degree left turn.

Joshua's Restaurant & Tavern, 123 Maine St., Brunswick 04011, 207/725-7981, www.joshuastavern.com, named after the local-turned-national hero, overlooks Brunswick's main drag. Lack of choice is not a problem here; there are four basic menus, plus a beer and wine list. Between the 20th Maine Regiment Original Chili and the finishing dessert coffee lies many a possibility. Entrées generally range $14.95–18.95; steak, lobster, and scallops are prominent. Open daily, hours vary seasonally.

The Harpswells

Inexpensive to Moderate: Arguments rage endlessly about who makes the best chowder in Maine, but **The Dolphin Restaurant,** Dolphin Marina, Basin Point, South Harpswell, 207/833-6000, heads lots of lists for its fish chowder. Plus you can't beat the scenic 13-mile drive south from Brunswick and the spectacular water views at the tip of Harpswell Neck. This popular spot is open daily 11 AM–8 PM, May 1–Oct. 31.

Moderate: A Bailey Island landmark since the 1950s, the sprawling **Cook's Lobster House,** Garrison Cove Rd., Rte. 24, Bailey Island 04003, 207/833-2818, www.cookslobster .com, is one of the most reliable of several seafood places near the peninsula's tip. The fish is predictably fresh, service is efficient, and the view is unbeatable. Besides, meat freaks can even order a steak. The restaurant overlooks the hamlet's unique cribstone bridge—a massive latticelike structure that's been allowing tides to ebb and flow since 1928. Open all year, daily 11:30 AM–9 PM in summer, reduced hours in winter. No reservations, so you may have to wait. The Casco Bay Lines summertime nature cruise departs from the restaurant's dock.

INFORMATION AND SERVICES

Contact the **Southern Midcoast Maine Chamber of Commerce,** 59 Pleasant St., corner of Spring St., Brunswick 04011, 207/725-8797, for info on lodgings, restaurants, and area activities. The Chamber represents 16 communities: Arrowsic, Bath, Bowdoin, Bowdoinham, Brunswick, Dresden, Edgecomb, Georgetwon, Harpswell, Phippsbrg, Richmond, Topsham, West Bath, Westport Island, Wiscasset, and Woolwich. The staff is particularly helpful. The useful *Bath Brunswick Region Map and Guide* is $2.50. The information center is open weekdays 8:30 AM–5 PM year-round. On weekends, local innkeepers maintain a lodging referral service to make sure every visitor finds a bed.

The **Curtis Memorial Library,** 23 Pleasant St., Brunswick 04011, 207/725-5242, one of the state's best public libraries, also has an especially friendly children's department. Open Mon.–Thurs. 9:30 AM–8 PM (to 6 PM Fri.), Sat. 9:30 AM–5 PM. The all-volunteer Friends of the Curtis Memorial Library has produced the *Children's Resource Handbook,* a periodically updated booklet containing dozens of well-organized ideas for entertaining the under-14 set. Copies are available free at the library and on the library's website: www.curtis-library.com/crh.

Newspapers

Brunswick's *Times Record,* 207/729-3311, www.timesrecord.com, published weekdays, runs extensive arts and entertainment listings in its Thurs. edition. The paper also produces a summer vacation supplement available free at the chamber of commerce and at restaurants and lodgings. The weekly *Coastal Journal,* 207/443-6241, a free tabloid available throughout the Brunswick/Bath area and beyond, has extensive calendar listings and special *Summer in Maine* supplements. It is also inserted into the Thursday edition of *Portland Press Herald,* published daily and covering most of southern Maine, and there is a monthly Sunday edition that appears on the second Sunday of the month in the *Maine Sunday Telegram.*

Emergencies

Mid Coast Hospital, 123 Medical Center Dr., Brunswick 04011, 207/729-0181, has a 24-hour emergency department. Also maintaining round-the-clock emergency service is **Parkview Adventist Medical Center,** 329 Maine St., a mile south of Bowdoin College, Brunswick, 207/373-2000, a Seventh Day Adventist facility. Parkview's emergency room has "levels" of care—persons with minor injuries or illnesses are welcome to use it. For **police, fire, and ambulance,** dial 911.

Veterinarians and Kennels

The **Bath-Brunswick Veterinary Associates,** 257 Bath Rd., Brunswick 04011, 207/729-4164, kennel 207/729-4188, 0.25 mile east of Cooks Corner, is an especially well-run full-service facility with a boarding kennel. Rates are $13–17 a night for cats or dogs. There's also grooming and a pet daycare service. Open Mon.–Fri. 8 AM–6 PM, Sat. 9 AM–1 PM.

Getting Around

Call **Brunswick Taxi,** 1 Simpson's Point Rd., Brunswick, 207/729-3688. Six taxis and an oversized van provide local and airport service.

Laundry

Sunshine Center has a coin-operated laundry at each end of Brunswick: 87-A Pleasant St., Rte. 1, 207/729-1564, and 200 Bath Rd., Rte. 24, 207/729-6072. Both are open daily 24 hours, with attendants on site until 7 PM, all year.

Bath Area

One of the smallest in area of Maine's cities, Bath—with a population of about 9,920 in only nine square miles—has many similarities to Brunswick. It sits astride Rte. 1 and a river, counts on modern military dollars, yet has centuries of tradition. The defense part is impossible to ignore, since giant cranes dominate the riverfront cityscape at the huge Bath Iron Works complex—source of state-of-the-art warships. Less evident (but not far away) is the link to the past: just south of Bath, in Popham on the Phippsburg Peninsula, is a poorly marked site where a trouble-plagued English settlement predated the Plymouth Colony by 13 years. (Of course, Champlain arrived before that, and Norsemen left calling cards even earlier.) In 1607 and 1608, settlers in the Popham Colony managed to build a 30-ton pinnace, *Virginia of Sagadahoc,* designed for transatlantic trade, but they lost heart during a bitter winter and abandoned the site.

Bath is the jumping-off point for two peninsulas to the south—Phippsburg (of Popham Colony fame) and Georgetown. Both are dramatically scenic, with glacier-carved farms and fishing villages. Drive or cycle a dozen miles down any of these fingers and you're in different worlds, ones where artists and photographers, hikers and historians go crazy with all the possibilities.

Across the soaring Sagahadoc Bridge from Bath is Woolwich, from which you can continue northeastward along the coast or detour northward on Rte. 128 to the hamlet of Day's Ferry. Named after 18th-century resident Joseph Day, who shuttled back and forth in a gondola-type boat across the Kennebec here, the picturesque village has a cluster of 18th- and 19th-century homes and churches—all part of the Day's Ferry Historic District. And the village's Old Stage Rd. saw many an old stage in its day; passengers would ferry from Bath and pick up the stage here to continue onward.

In 2005, Bath was one of a dozen places recognized as America's Distinctive Destinations

Mid-Coast Region

by the National Trust for Historic Preservation. Trust President Richard Moe called Bath "a jewel hidden in plain sight," and the Trust described the little city as "a New England oil painting come to life."

SIGHTS

Bath Iron Works

Only during one of its relatively infrequent launchings is Bath Iron Works (BIW) open to the public, and then it's a mob scene, with hordes of politicos, townsfolk, and military poohbahs in their scrambled eggs and brass. But the launchings are exciting occasions, with flags flying everywhere. BIW, under the umbrella of giant defense contractor General Dynamics, employs thousands in its Bath and smaller Brunswick sites. When BIW talks, everyone listens. And when BIW's afternoon shift changes, everyone within 10 miles suffers from the gridlock. In fact, anyone who shows up in Bath on a weekday between 3:25 and 4 PM lives to rue it. Be forewarned and plan your schedule around the witching hour. Despite the construction of the brand-new Sagadahoc Bridge, traffic still backs up at shift-change time.

Maine Maritime Museum

Spread over 20 acres on the Kennebec River is the state's premier marine museum, the Maine Maritime Museum, 243 Washington St., Bath 04530, 207/443-1316, www.mainemaritime-museum.org.

Explore the relics of the 19th-century Percy & Small Shipyard (1897–1920), historic William T. Donnell House, and a hands-on lobstering exhibit. See the architecturally dramatic Maritime History Building, locale for permanent and temporary displays of marine art and artifacts and a shop stocked with nautical books and gifts.

Bring a picnic and let the toddlers loose in the children's play area. Then join up with one of the twice-daily, hour-long guided shipyard tours. In summer, weather permitting, the museum sponsors a variety of special river cruises; call for info.

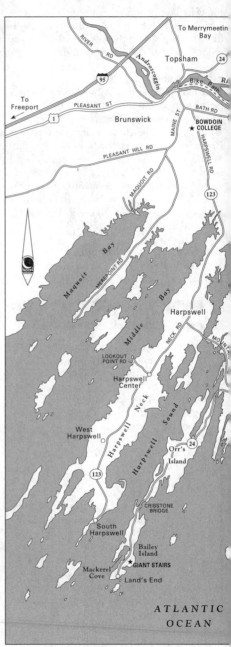

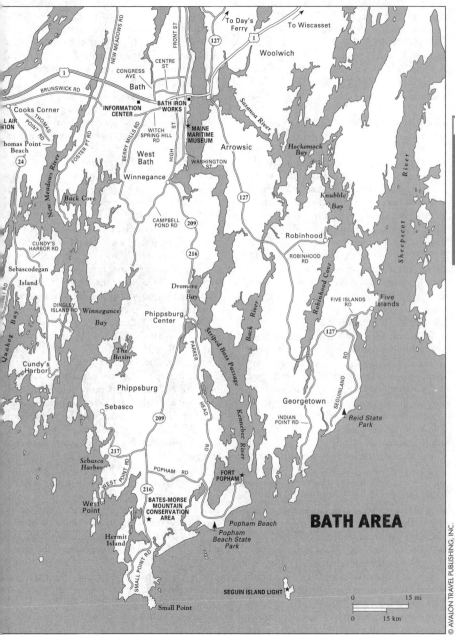

Mid-Coast Region

BATH AREA

© AVALON TRAVEL PUBLISHING, INC.

Open 9:30 AM–5 PM daily, year-round; Percy & Small Shipyard is open all year as long as the weather holds. Admission is $9.75 adults, seniors $8.75, $6.75 children 6–17, and free for kids under six. Family rate (two adults, two kids) is $28. The museum, an important stop on the state's Maritime Heritage Trail, is 1.2 miles south of Rte. 1.

Bath History Preserved

Sagadahoc Preservation Inc. (SPI), www.sagadahocpreservation.org, founded in 1971 to rescue the city's architectural heritage, has produced *Architectural Tours: Self-Guided Walking and Driving Tours of the City of Bath,* a terrific foldout brochure (with maps) to guide you—via car, ankle express, or bicycle—around Bath. Pick up a copy at the chamber of commerce or contact SPI, Box 322, 880 Washington St., Bath 04530, 207/443-2174, open Mon.–Thurs. 10 AM–3 PM. SPI also sponsors tours like "Open Houses/Hidden Gardens."

Phippsburg Peninsula

You can spend a whole day—or, better still, several days—exploring the peninsula that drops down from Bath. Along the way are campgrounds, B&Bs, a resort, restaurants, a unique state park, hiking trails, secluded coves, spectacular scenery, and tons of history.

About two miles south of Bath is a causeway known as **Winnegance,** an Abnaki name usually translated as "short carry" or "little portage." Native Americans crossed here from the Kennebec to the New Meadows River. Early settlers erected nearly a dozen tide-powered mills to serve the shipbuilding industry, but they're long gone. Just before the causeway, on the Bath-Phippsburg boundary, is the **Winnegance General Store,** 36 High St., Bath 04530, 207/443-9805, a local favorite for the miscellanea that general stores offer. About 1.5 miles farther is a left turn onto Fiddler's Reach Rd., leading to the **Morse Cove Public Launching Facility,** one of the state's most scenic boat-launch sites. If you have a kayak, plan to go downriver on the ebb tide and return

on the flow (otherwise, you'll be battling the strong Kennebec River current). There's plenty of paved parking here, plus a restroom.

Back on Rte. 209, it's another 1.3 miles to the **Dromore Burying Ground** (on the right), with great old headstones; the earliest is dated 1743. The next mile opens up with terrific easterly views of Dromore Bay. Right in the line of sight is 117-acre Lee Island (which the owners sold to the state in 1995). From May–mid-July, the island is off-limits to protect nesting eagles and waterfowl.

Next you're in **Phippsburg Center,** alive with shipbuilding from Colonial days to the early 20th century. Hang a left onto Parker Head Rd. (but avoid this detour if you're on a bicycle; it's too narrow and winding). After the Phippsburg Historical Museum (in an 1859 schoolhouse) and the Alfred Totman Library, turn left onto Church Lane to see the **Phippsburg Congregational Church,** built in 1802. Out front is the "Constitution Tree," a huge English linden allegedly planted in 1775.

Parker Head Rd. continues southward and meets up with Rte. 209, which takes you to **Popham Beach State Park.** Continue to the end of Rte. 209 for **Fort Popham Historic Site,** where parking is woefully inadequate in summer. The fort is accessible Memorial Day–Sept. Youngsters love this place—they can fish from the rocks, climb to the third level of the 1865 stone fortress (though the chicken-wire fencing ruins photos), picnic on the grounds, and create sand castles on the tiny beach next to the fort. Resist the urge to swim, though; the current is dangerous, and there's no lifeguard. Across the river is Bay Point, a lobstering village at the tip of the Georgetown Peninsula. **Percy's Store,** 207/389-2010, by the way, with a handful of tables, is the best place down here for pizza, lobster rolls, fried clams, 17 flavors of Gifford's Maine-made ice cream, and fishing tackle. On weekends, if your arteries can tolerate it, sample their fried dough.

Across the cove from the fort is a narrow, winding road leading to the poorly marked

Mid-Coast Region

shorefront site of the 1607 Popham Colony. Climb the path up Sabino Hill to World War I–era **Fort Baldwin,** the best vantage point for panoramic photos.

Backtrack about four miles on Rte. 209, turn left onto Rte. 216, and head toward **Small Point.** On the left, watch for the sign marking the tiny (eight cars) parking area for the **Bates-Morse Mountain Preserve.** Farther south are Head Beach and Hermit Island.

Returning northward on Rte. 216, you'll hook up with Rte. 209 and then see a left turn (Rte. 217) to Sebasco Harbor Resort. Take the time to go beyond the Sebasco resort area. When the paved road goes left (to the Water's Edge Restaurant), turn right at a tiny cemetery and continue northward on the Old Meadowbrook Rd., which meanders for about four miles along the west side of the peninsula. About midway along is **the Basin,** regarded by sailors as one of the Maine coast's best "hurricane holes" (refuges in high winds). As you skirt the Basin and come to a fork, bear right to return to Rte. 209; turn left and return northward to Bath.

Woolwich Historical Society Museum

Next to a Rte. 1 flashing caution light, 2.5 miles north of Bath, the two-story Woolwich Historical Society 19th Century Rural Life Museum, Rte. 1 at Nequasset Rd., P.O. Box 98, Woolwich 04579, 207/443-4833, www.woolwichhistory.org, admirably well organized, has rooms full of early 19th- to early 20th-century quilts, clothing, tools, and tradesmen's wares. The oldest part of the building dates from the early 19th century. Open Tues.–Sat. 10:30 AM–2:30 PM, July–Aug. Admission is $3 adults, $1 children over six, $2.50 senior or AAA, $10 maximum family rate.

PARKS AND RECREATION

In-Town Parks

An old-fashioned gazebo, just right for hanging out with a book (bring a cushion), is the centerpiece of **Library Park,** the manicured space fronting the Patten Free Library, Summer and Washington Sts. In summer, the park is the site of weddings, concerts, art exhibits, and children's story hours.

Waterfront Park, bordering the Kennebec on Commercial St., has covered picnic tables and restrooms. The waterfront area is undergoing a long-overdue renaissance, with shops, restaurants, and even more green space.

For the kids, there's a particularly creative playground at **Fischer-Mitchell Elementary School,** 597 High St., across from the Hyde School.

Hamilton Sanctuary

Owned by Maine Audubon Society, Hamilton Sanctuary, Foster Point Rd., West Bath, is a peaceful site for walking and nature study on the New Meadows River, with 1.5 miles of trails winding through meadows and forests and along the Back Cove shoreline. From Rte. 1 between Bath and Brunswick, take the New Meadows Rd. exit. Head south on New Meadows. When it becomes Foster Point Rd., go 3.3 miles to the sanctuary entrance. Open all year, sunrise to sunset; free admission. For more information, contact **Maine Audubon Society,** 20 Gilsland Farm Rd., Falmouth 04105, 207/781-2330.

Popham Beach State Park

On hot July and Aug. weekends, the parking lot at Popham Beach State Park, Rte. 209, Phippsburg 04562, 14 miles south of Bath, 207/389-1335, fills up by 10 AM, so plan to arrive early at this huge crescent of sand backed by sea grass, beach roses, and dunes. Facilities include changing rooms, outside showers, restrooms, seasonal lifeguards. Admission is $3 adults, $1 children 5–11, free for seniors and kids under five. Officially open Apr. 15–Oct. 30, but the beach is accessible all year (no winter contact number).

A mile down the road, at the end of Rte. 209, is the four-acre **Fort Popham Historic Site,** where kids of all ages can explore the waterfront tower and bunkers of a 19th-century granite fort. No swimming here—the current is dangerous—but there's fun fishing from the rocks (no license needed), plus picnic tables and restrooms.

Bates-Morse Mountain Conservation Area

Consider visiting the lovely, 600-acre Bates-Morse Mountain Conservation Area, Rtes. 209 and 216, Small Point, Phippsburg Peninsula, *only* if you are willing to be extra-conscientious about the rules for this private preserve. A relatively easy four-mile round-trip hike takes you through marshland (you'll need insect repellent) and to the top of 210-foot Morse Mountain, with panoramic views, then down to privately owned Seawall Beach. On a clear day, you can see New Hampshire's Mt. Washington from the summit. No dogs or vehicles; no recreational facilities; stay on the preserve road and the beach path at all times (side roads are private). Least terns and piping plovers—both endangered species—nest in the dunes, so avoid this area, especially mid-May–mid-Aug. Birding hint: Morse Mountain is a great locale for spotting hawks during their annual September migration southward. Pick up a map (and the rules) from the box in the parking lot about 300 feet from Rte. 209, up Morse Mt. Rd.(no parking on Morse Mt. Rd. or Rte. 209—your car will be ticketed or towed). No admission fee; open sunrise to sunset.

Head Beach

Just off Rte. 216, about two miles south of the Rte. 209 turnoff to Popham Beach, is Head Beach, a sandy crescent that's open until 10 PM. A minimal day-use fee is payable at the small gatehouse; there's a restroom on the path to the beach.

Reid State Park

Reid State Park, on the Georgetown Peninsula, 375 Seguinland Rd., Georgetown 04548, 207/371-2303, is no secret, so plan to arrive early on summer weekends, when parking is woefully inadequate. Highlights of the 765-acre park are 1.5 miles of splendid beach (in three distinct sections), marshlands, sand dunes, and tide pools. Kids love the tide pools, treasure troves left by the receding tide. Facilities include changing rooms (with showers), picnic tables, restrooms, and snack bars. Test the water before racing in; even in midsummer, it's breathtakingly cold. In winter, bring cross-country skis and glide along the shoreline. The park—14 miles south of Rte. 1 (Woolwich) and two miles off Rte. 127—is open daily all year. Admission is $4.50 adults, $1 children 5–11, free for kids under five and seniors over 65.

Just half a mile beyond the Reid State Park entrance is **Charles Pond,** where the setting is unsurpassed for freshwater swimming in the long, skinny pond. You'll wish this were a secret, too, but it isn't. No facilities.

Josephine Newman Sanctuary

A must-see for any nature lover, the 119-acre Josephine Newman Sanctuary, Rte. 127, Georgetown, has 2.5 miles of blazed loop trails winding through 110 wooded acres and along Robinhood Cove's tidal shoreline. Josephine Oliver Newman (1878-1968), a respected naturalist, bequeathed her family's splendid property to the Maine Audubon Society, which maintains it today. The 0.6-mile Self-Guiding Trail is moderately difficult, but the rewards are 20 informative markers highlighting special features: glacial erratics, reversing falls, mosses, and marshes. Easiest route is the 0.75-mile Horseshoe Trail, which you can extend for another mile or so by linking into the Rocky End Trail. The sanctuary is open daily, all year, sunrise to sunset; free admission. No pets or bikes. The best way to appreciate it is to buy *Forests, Fields, and Estuaries,* a 60-page sanctuary guide ($3.50), with lots of natural-history info useful for other preserves. Contact the Maine Audubon Society, 20 Gilsland Farm Rd., Falmouth 04105, 207/781-2330, or stop in at the society's environmental center in Falmouth. To reach the Newman sanctuary, take Rte. 127 from Rte. 1 in Woolwich (the road to Reid State Park) for 9.1 miles. Turn right at the sanctuary sign and continue to the small parking lot. A map of the trail system is posted at the marsh's edge.

Montsweag Preserve

Owned by The Chewonki Foundation since 1993, and directly opposite Chewonki Neck in the town of Woolwich, 45-acre Montsweag Preserve, Montsweag Rd., Woolwich, is a peaceful estuarine microcosm on the shore of tidal Montsweag Brook. Though called a brook, it's 100 yards across. A 1.5-mile, blue-blazed loop trail meanders through woods, tidal frontage, and salt marsh. Wear long pants and waterproof shoes or boots. Open all year, sunrise to sunset. From Bath, take Rte. 1 northwest about 6.5 miles, to Montsweag Rd. (not well marked). Turn right and go 1.2 miles to the preserve, on the left (also not well marked). Park alongside the road and do the trail clockwise. For more information, contact the Chewonki Foundation, 207/882-7323.

Golf

The 18-hole **Bath Country Club,** 387 Whiskeag Rd., Bath, 207/442-8411, www.harrisgolfshop.com, has moderate greens fees, a particularly well-stocked pro shop, and a restaurant serving lunch and dinner. Starting times are needed. Open early Apr.–Oct. From Rte. 1 in West Bath, take New Meadows Rd., then Ridge Rd., north 0.8 miles to Whiskeag Rd. and the club.

The Sebasco Harbor Resort has a nine-hole course open to nonguests on a space-available basis; call the resort's pro shop (207/389-9060) to inquire. The course is open late Apr.–early Nov.

Bicycling

Bath-area headquarters for anything to do with bikes is **Bath Cycle and Ski,** Rte. 1, opposite Rte. 127 north, Woolwich 04579, 207/442-7002 or 800/245-3626, www.bikeman.com. Open Mon.–Fri. 9 AM–6 PM (to 8 PM Thurs.), Sat. 9 AM–5 PM.

A relatively easy nine-mile loop begins at the downtown Bath post office (750 Washington St.; parking available). Go north on Washington St. to North St., turn left and go 0.5 mile to Oak Grove Ave. Turn sharp right (five-way intersection) and continue about one mile to Whiskeag Rd.; turn left. Go another 0.7 mile and turn right, continuing for 1.6 miles. Turn left at Hawkes Farm and go about two miles (part unpaved) to Old Brunswick Rd.; turn left. Continue 2.3 miles back toward town (Old Brunswick becomes Lincoln St.) to Centre St.; turn left and continue down the hill to Washington St. Turn right to return to the post office.

Canoeing

Close to civilization, yet amazingly undeveloped, 392-acre **Nequasset Lake** is a great place to canoe. You'll see a few anglers, a handful of houses, and near-wilderness along the shoreline. Personal watercraft (Jet Skis) and motors over 10 horse power are banned. Take Rte. 1 from Bath across the bridge to Woolwich. Continue to the flashing caution light at Nequasset Rd.; turn left and continue to Rte. 127. Turn right and go about 1.5 miles to Old Stage Rd. Turn right and go about 0.5 mile to the Nequasset Brook bridge. The hand-carry launch is west of the bridge, the trailer launch is east of the bridge; parking is limited. Canoe the lake itself and/or paddle upstream along Nequasset Brook for a mile or so until you reach a small waterfall.

In 1996, town fathers in their wisdom established an even more convenient launch site, close to Rte. 1. At the flashing caution light described above, turn *right* and go 0.1 mile. Turn left, and left again, into the parking area for the Nequasset Stream Waterfront Park. Launch your canoe and head upstream, under Rte. 1, to the lake.

Excursion Boats

The 50-foot *Yankee* operates out of Small Point's Hermit Island Campground Mon.–Sat. throughout the summer. You can go on nature cruises, enjoy the sunset, or visit Eagle Island; the schedule is different each day. It's $8–22 adults, $6–16 kids. For reservations, call 207/389-1788. The *Yankee* also has scheduled trips to Seguin Island (see below).

The M/V *Ruth,* a 38-foot excursion boat,

runs cruises out of Sebasco Harbor Resort late June–Sept. You don't need to be a Sebasco guest to take the trips, but reservations are essential. The schedule changes weekly, but the most popular cruise goes out several times a week; it's a scenic nature cruise along some of Maine's prettiest coast where seabirds and marine life are abundant and often spotted. Price is $11 for adult guests (nonguests $12), $6 child guests 3–12 (nonguest child $7). Call the Sebasco Harbor Resort, 207/389-1161, for the schedule; other trips include lunch, lobstering, sunset, and deep-sea fishing.

Based in Bath, *Long Reach Cruises,* 870 Washington St., Bath 04530, 207/442-0092 or 888/538-6786, www.LongReachCruises.com, covers the waters of the midcoast with charter, fishing, whale-watching, and scenic cruises, ranging from a Harbor Lights and Shipbuilding Cruise, with lunch available for purchase onboard, at $17.75 adults, $9.75 children, and $12.75 for Maritime Museum members, to a Seguin Island exploration cruise for $52.75, $19.75, and $47.75. Latest addition is a pirate ship at the Wiscasset town dock, offering family expeditions, birthday parties, and evening adult pirate parties.

For charter trips to Seguin Island and its two-century-old lighthouse, about 20 minutes from Fort Popham, check with the nonprofit **Friends of Seguin Island Inc**., P.O. Box 866, Bath 04530, 207/443-4808, www.seguinisland.org, or see the website. There's also an office, with limited hours, at 72 Front St, #3, in Bath. Many of the hundreds of annual visitors come on their own boat, so Seguin offers five "at your own risk" guest moorings. There's no dock; a dinghy and good balance are usually required. All trips are weather-dependent, the island lying two miles out from the mouth of the Kennebec. Once on the 64-acre island, you can climb the hill to the lighthouse, then climb the 53-foot light tower for a fabulous view from the deck. Seguin is Maine's most powerful light and the only operating first order light in New England. Afterward, visit the three-room **Seguin Museum,** loaded with lighthouse memora-

bilia. The Friends of Seguin maintains the island's five historic structures and arranges for the summertime caretakers, in residence from Memorial Day to Labor Day. The Coast Guard maintains the automated light, which has a 20-mile range.

The Maine Maritime Museum also runs excursion boats to Seguin in summer, weather permitting, allowing you about three hours to explore the island. *Atlantic Seal Cruises,* South Freeport, 207/865-6112, offers Thursday trips in summer, 10 AM–4 PM.

ENTERTAINMENT

Bath's most diversified entertainment setting is the **Chocolate Church Arts Center,** 870 Washington St., Bath 04530, 207/442-8455, www.chocolatechurcharts.org. It's a chocolate-brown board-and-batten structure built in 1846 as the Central Congregational Church, and put to adaptive reuse. Year-round activities at the arts center include music and dance concerts, dramas, exhibits, and children's programs. Check local papers for listings or call ahead for a schedule. The art gallery is open Tues.–Sat. noon–4 PM.

Throughout the summer, the **Maine Maritime Museum,** 207/443-1316, schedules special events, often hinging on visits by tall ships and other vessels. Some of the visiting boats are open to the public for an extra fee. Call the museum to check.

FESTIVALS AND EVENTS

Happenings in Boothbay Peninsula and the Brunswick area are also nearby.

Every Friday, June–Labor Day, the **Bath Gazebo Concerts** are held at 7 PM in Library Park. The week of the Fourth of July, **Bath Heritage Days** fills three or four days with art exhibits, a carnival, a parade, and fireworks.

SHOPPING

Antiques

Three antiques shops lined up along Front

St. are all worth a visit (and several others are in this area as well). At **Front Street Antiques and Books,** 191 Front St., Bath 04530, 207/443-8098, a group shop, Limoges, ironstone, and Staffordshire are a specialty, as well as early paint, country furniture and books. Open daily 10 AM–5 PM. **Pollyanna's Antiques,** 182 Front St., Bath, 207/443-4909, is a good bet for Civil War items, vintage clothing, and old tools. Open daily 10 AM–5 PM. **Brick Store Antiques,** 143 Front St., Bath, 207/443-2790, also open daily 10 AM–5 PM, has a particularly wide variety of country and formal pieces.

Books

Here's yet another good independent bookstore successfully bucking the mega-store trend. The **Bath Book Shop,** 96 Front St., Bath 04530, 207/443-9338, has friendly, hometown service and a discerning taste in books. The shop is open all year, 9:30 AM–5 PM Mon.–Sat.

Gifts, Crafts, and Clothing

Right in the shadow of the Rte. 1 overpass is an incredible resource for knitters and weavers. **Halcyon Yarn,** 12 School St., Bath 04530, 207/442-7909 or 800/341-0282, a huge warehouse of a place, carries domestic and imported yarns, looms, spinning wheels, kits, rug-making supplies, and a large selection of how-to videos and pattern books. Open year-round, Mon.–Sat. 10 AM–4 PM (to 8 PM Wed.).

And, while you're in town, there's the well-stocked, marine-oriented gift shop at the Maine Maritime Museum.

For adult and kids' sportswear bargains, check out **Goodwill Industries Retail Store,** 1 Chandler Dr., Bath Shopping Center, Rte. 1, Bath 04530, 207/443-4668. A big-name sports outfitter distributes its overstocks to Goodwill stores, whose proceeds benefit people with disabilities. Open all year, Mon.–Sat. 9 AM–8 PM, Sun. 10 AM–6 PM.

About nine miles down Rte. 127, you'll come to **Georgetown Pottery,** Rte. 127, 755 Five Isles Rd., Georgetown 04548, 207/371-2801, www.georgetownpottery.com, a top-quality ceramics studio/shop. Open daily year-round.

North on Rte. 1, next to a teepee in a field, is **Native Arts,** Rte.1, Woolwich 04579, 207/442-8399, www.nativeartsonline.com, featuring Native American arts, jewelry, herbs, and gifts. Drum and other workshops and talks by elders, authors, and musicians are also on the program. Open daily 10 AM–6 PM.

Flea Market

One of Maine's biggest and most-enduring flea markets is right on Rte. 1 north of Bath, often creating near-accidents as rubbernecking motorists slam to a halt. **Montsweag Flea Market,** Rte. 1 at Mountain Rd., P.O. Box 252, Woolwich 04579, 207/443-2809, is a genuine treasure trove, located about five miles northeast of the Bath bridge. Open weekends and Wed., May–Oct., plus Fri. June–Aug., 6:30 AM–3 PM.

Another way to find treasure is at one of the area's many auctions. **Kennebec River Auctions,** 207/443-1197, take place at 5:30 PM on bimonthly Saturday evenings at the Knights of Columbus Hall. Check local newspapers for other regular and occasional auctions, some specialized.

Farmers Market

In Waterfront Park, Commercial St., the **Bath Farmers Market** operates every Thurs. and Sat., 8:30 AM–12:30 PM, May–Oct., featuring crafts, plants, condiments, baked goods, and cheeses in addition to seasonal produce.

The **Bath Natural Market,** 36 Centre St., Bath 04530, 207/442-8012, is filled with organic foods and natural products. Hours are Mon.–Fri. 9 AM–6 PM, Sat. 9 AM–5 PM, Sun. noon–4 PM.

ACCOMMODATIONS

Most of Bath's inns and B&Bs are located in historic residences built by shipping magnates and their families, giving you a chance to appreciate the quality of craftsmanship they

Mid-Coast Region

demanded in their ships and their homes alike. Most of the Bath inns have a two-day minimum requirement.

Bath

The Galen C. Moses House, 1009 Washington St., Bath 04530, 207/442-8771 or 888/442-8771, www.galenmoses.com, is an elaborate Italianate Victorian located in Bath's recently-honored Historic District. It has six rooms, two of which can be used together as a suite. Rates are $99–199 d, mid-May–Oct. 31, $99–129 d rest of the year. Check for exceptions to their two-day minimum requirement. No smoking, no pets, no children under 13.

The Fairhaven Inn, 118 No. Bath Rd., Bath 04530, 207/443-4391 or 888/443-4391, www.mainecoast.com/fairhaven inn, near Bath Country Club, is an 18th-century colonial on 16 acres. Rates are $80–140 d in season; call for off-season rates. There are eight rooms, most with private baths. No smoking, no pets; children welcome.

The Inn at Bath, 969 Washington St., 207/443-4294 or 800/423-0964, www.innat-bath.com, is an outstanding 1810 Greek Revival in the Historic District with rooms for $150–185, May 27–Oct. 31; lower rates off-season. There are eight rooms. Some rooms can be joined as suites, and all include private baths, air-conditioning, phones, and TV. There are also fireplaces and some rooms have Jacuzzis. No smoking or children under four; dogs are welcome on a case-by-case basis. There's one wheelchair-accessible room.

The Pryor House B&B, 360 Front St., 207/443-1146 or 866/977-7967, www.pryorhouse.com, has three rooms, all with private baths. The Elizabeth Room is $95 d; the Captain's Room $105 d; and the Tall Chimney Room, with two-person Jacuzzi, $130. Exceptions to the no-pet policy can be made for well-traveled pets. There is no smoking, and children over 12 are welcome.

Phippsburg Peninsula

Sebasco Harbor Resort, Rte. 217, P.O. Box 75, Sebasco Estates 04565, 207/389-1161 or 800/225-3819, www.sebasco.com, on the saltwater New Meadows River, is a self-contained seaside resort on close to 600 acres 12 miles south of Bath. Families have come here year after year—since 1930, when Sebasco opened. Many guests stay for a week. Sebasco changed hands in 1997, and the enthusiastic new owners began a major overhaul, with astonishing speed and success. Scattered around the property are 118 rooms in about two dozen buildings—23 widely varying cottages, some multi-room structures (condo construction is underway around the golf course). All have private baths, phones, and cable TV; many have water views. Most intriguing (and most expensive; $229–319 d in summer) is the Lighthouse, a four-story, multisided, cupola-topped building right on the harbor. July–Aug., room rates are $179–279; cottage rates vary widely, depending on type and location. MAP rates also exist, and special packages (and lower rates) are available spring and fall. The resort's **Pilot House** restaurant, with a dramatic water view, is also open to the public; dinner $18 and up. Below it, the patio at the casual Ledges Pub is a late-day magnet. Recreational facilities include a kayaking center, spa services, tennis courts, golf course (extra fee) and golf clinic and putting contest (free), an outdoor saltwater pool, a playground, a free Tuesday walking tour, evening entertainment, a weekly barbecue and family dance, and as much or as little organized activity as you want. There is also an extensive children's program, called Camp Merritt. Pets are welcome in certain cottages. See *Excursion Boats,* above, for info on cruises in the M/V *Ruth.* Sebasco Harbor Resort is open mid-May–mid-Oct.

Located right on the beach, in a restored 1883 Coast Guard station, the **Popham Beach Bed & Breakfast,** 4 Ocean View Ln., Popham Beach, Phippsburg 04562, 207/389-2409, www.pophambeachbandb.com, has three rooms and a suite, $175 and $215 d in midsummer, lower other seasons; request the Library if it's in your budget. A two- to three-course breakfast is served in the dining room each morning, and guests can hang out in the large oceanfront living room. No pets, no smoking, no children under 15. Open all year.

Just south of the turnoff to Popham Beach, and close to the access for Morse Mountain, is **Edgewater Farm Bed & Breakfast,** 71 Small Point Rd., Rte. 216, Phippsburg 04562, 207/389-1322 or 877/389-1322, www.edgewaterfarmbedandbreakfast.com, Carol and Bill Emerson's restored 19th-century farmhouse. Six rooms and two suites with private baths start at $95 for one person and go to $180 for five in a suite. A brunch-size breakfast served in the many-windowed solarium benefits from lots of organic produce grown on the four-acre grounds. (The Emersons always plant extra to donate to the Bath soup kitchen each summer.) And then there's the four-foot-deep *indoor lap pool,* and a hot tub outside on the deck. A fine reward after a day of hiking, biking, or kayaking. No smoking. Pets are allowed for a $25 fee; children are welcome. Open year-round.

Georgetown Peninsula

Staying at **The Grey Havens Inn,** Seguinland Rd., P.O. Box 308, Georgetown 04548, 207/371-2616 or 800/431-2316, www.greyhavens.com, is like holing up at a classic seacoast summer home: National Historic Register Shingle-style building, huge wraparound porch, tongue-and-groove paneling, lounge decorated in a very comfortable coastal cottage style. Marcus and Cathy Headley and their children keep everything up and running. There are 14 rooms; views are particularly spectacular from the turret rooms and oceanfront suite. Rates are $140–255 d. Two-night minimum summer weekends. No pets, no smoking, no children under 12. The inn adjoins Reid State Park and is 0.25 mile off Rte. 127. Open mid-May–mid-Oct.

Campgrounds

Plan to book a site in January if you want a waterfront campsite in midsummer at the Phippsburg Peninsula's **Hermit Island Campground,** Small Point 04567, 207/443-2101, winter mailing address 42 Front St., Bath 04530, www.her-

mitisland.com. With 275 campsites (no vehicles larger than pickup campers; no hookups) spread over a 255-acre causeway-linked island, this is oceanfront camping at its best. Prime sites surround Sunset Lagoon. The well-managed operation has a store, snack bar, boat rentals, boat excursions, trails, and seven private beaches. Rules are strictly enforced (no pets, no visitors allowed in the camping area). Open and wooded sites run $32–53 mid-June–Labor Day, $30 early and late in the season. No credit cards. Open mid-May–mid-Oct., but full operation is really late June–Labor Day. The campground is at the tip of the Phippsburg Peninsula.

At **Ocean View Park Campground,** Rte. 209, (adjacent to Popham Beach State Park), Phippsburg 04562, 207/389-2564, winter address P.O. Box 129, Phippsburg 04562, the 48 sites are quite small, but many are right next to the sandy beach. Hookups are available. Sites are $30–38. Open mid-May–Sept.

FOOD

Casual

Bath's best pizza comes from **The Cabin,** 552 Washington St., Bath 04530, 207/443-6224—a local landmark since 1973. The white garlic sauce is outstanding, and the cheese steak is about the best outside of Philly. Order food to go or eat in at this decidedly casual place across from Bath Iron Works. Beer and wine license only. Reservations are wise Fri.–Sat. evenings. Open all year, Sun.–Wed. 10 AM–10 PM, Thurs.–Sat. 10 AM–11PM.

Moderate to Expensive

J.R. Maxwell & Co., 122 Front St., Bath 04530, 207/443-2014, fits right in with Bath's maritime tradition—there's lots of nautical stuff everywhere you look. Thanks to a loyal clientele, dinner reservations are advisable. The basic meat-and-seafood menu ($13.95–14.95 for many dinner entrées) is well prepared. Prime rib Fri.–Sat. Open all year, Mon.–Sat. lunch 11:30 AM–2:30 PM, light lunch 2:30–5 PM, dinner 5–9 PM (to 10 PM Fri.–Sat.); Sun. noon–9 PM, serving lunch and dinner all day.

Mae's Cafe, 160 Centre St., at High St., Bath, 207/442-8577, has replaced Kristina's, but regulars are fine with the change, as there is still the laden bakery counter, and the same creative approach to the menu, with numerous choices-sandwiches, salads, pizzas, and entrées. Be sure to make reservations for weekend brunches and summer weekends. Breakfasts are the best in the area. Omelettes are huge and famous; breakfast and brunch choices run $4–13, for the lobster omelette. Lunch ranges from a cup of soup at $3.75–14, and the lunch menu is available at dinner, too. The crab cakes and stuffed haddock are highlights of the dinner menu, which ranges up to $21. There is a full bar and a children's menu, as well as dog-friendly dining on the outside deck when the weather's right. Rotating art exhibits and performances by local musicians add to the imaginative ambience here. Wheelchair accessible. Open Tues.–Sun. 8 AM–9 PM (to 3 PM Sun.) during summer. Call for seasonal hours.

Worthwhile Wallet-Cruncher

The building alone is worth a visit to the **Robinhood Free Meetinghouse,** 210 Robinhood Rd., Georgetown 04548, 207/371-2188, www.robinhood-meetinghouse.com, a five-star restaurant and catering facility in a beautifully restored 1855 building on the Georgetown Peninsula. Most tables are on the main floor; several are available in the second-floor chapel, where many of the original pews remain. The high-quality menu makes it even more enticing. Noted chef Michael Gagné presides over the kitchen. Creativity is the menu byword for Gagné, who gained fame during eight years as the innovative chef of Robinhood's nearby Osprey Restaurant. Entrées are in the $18–28 range, and portions are large. Reservations are recommended. Open daily 5:30–9 PM, Memorial Day weekend–mid-Oct., and Thurs.–Sat. 5:30–8 PM mid-Oct.–late May. The restaurant is on the left, about a mile east of Rte. 127.

Lobster-in-the-Rough

Phippsburg Peninsula: Overlooking the New Meadows River, **Anna's Water's Edge Restaurant,** 75 Black's Landing Rd., off Rte. 217, Sebasco Estates 04565, 207/389-1803, www.thewatersedgerestaurant.com, is aptly named—and well worth the effort to find it. The unassuming red-shingled place has indoor and deck dining, plus waterside picnic tables. Mahogany quahogs are a specialty, and desserts are great. Unlike many lobster places, Water's Edge has a full liquor license and takes credit cards. Dining-room reservations are wise on weekends. Open daily 11 AM–9 PM, mid-May– Labor Day. Take Rte. 209 south from Bath 11 miles, then turn right on Rte. 217. Continue beyond Sebasco Harbor Resort and make two left turns to the restaurant.

Back on Rte. 209, continue south and pick up Rte. 216. About 2.5 miles south of the Rte. 217 turnoff stands the rustic, buoy-draped **Lobster House,** 395 Small Point Rd., Rte. 216, Small Point, 207/389-1596 or 207/389-2178. The windowed eating area, with open beams, overlooks a scenic tidal cove; the view is best when the tide's in. Open Tues.–Sat. 5– 9 PM, Sun. noon–8:30 PM, Memorial Day– Labor Day.

INFORMATION AND SERVICES

The Bath office of the **Southern Midcoast Maine Chamber of Commerce,** 45 Front St., Bath 04530, 207/443-9751, www.midcoastmaine.com, is open weekdays, 8:30 AM–5 PM, with occasional Saturday hours in summer. The chamber's seasonal **information center** on Rte. 1 at Witch Spring Hill (right side northbound from Brunswick to Bath, about a mile south of Bath) is open seasonally. Request copies of the *City of Bath Downtown Map and Guide* and the *Bath-Brunswick Region Arts & Cultural Map & Guide.*

Bath's **Patten Free Library,** 33 Summer St., Bath 04530, 207/443-5141, www.patten.lib.me.us, has one of the state's most comfortable and elegant library reading rooms. It's entirely too easy to spend a rainy day hanging out here with the huge supply of newspapers and magazines. The library's outstanding Sagadahoc History and Genealogy Room draws genealogists from all over (open Mon.–Thurs. and Sat. noon–4 PM, closed Fri.), and the Children's Room is especially kid-friendly. The library is open Mon.–Sat. 10 AM–5 PM (to 8 PM Tues.–Thurs.).

Newspapers

Brunswick's *Times Record,* 207/729-3311, published weekdays, runs extensive arts and entertainment listings in its Thursday edition. The paper also produces a summer vacation supplement available free at the chamber of commerce and at restaurants and lodgings. The weekly *Coastal Journal,* 207/443-6241, a free tabloid available throughout the Brunswick/Bath area and beyond, has extensive calendar listings and special *Summer in Maine* supplements. It is also inserted into the Thursday edition of *Portland Press Herald,* published daily and covering most of southern Maine, and there is a monthly Sunday edition that appears on the second Sunday of the month in the *Maine Sunday Telegram.*

Emergencies

The nearest hospital with 24-hour emergency-room care is 10 miles south of Bath, at **Mid Coast Hospital,** 123 Medical Center Dr., Brunswick 04011, 207/729-0181. Emergency care is also available at **Parkview Adventist Medical Center,** 329 Maine St., a mile south of Bowdoin College, Brunswick, 207/373-2000, a Seventh Day Adventist facility. For **police, fire, and ambulance,** dial 911.

Public Restrooms

Public restrooms are at **Bath City Hall,** 55 Front St.; **Patten Free Library,** 33 Summer St.; **Sagadahoc County Courthouse,** 752 High St.; and (summer only) **Waterfront Park,** Commercial St.

Photo Services

With an excellent reputation, **Kennebec**

Camera & Darkroom, 1 Elm St. (corner of Front and Elm Sts.), Bath 04530, 207/442-8628, does professional color and black-and-white work, and sells cameras and darkroom supplies.

Laundry

There's cable TV and always an attendant on the premises at the **Garden Island Cleaners-Laundromat and Dry Cleaners,** 3 Congress Ave., off Rte. 1, Bath 04530, 207/442-7054, open daily, hours vary.

Special Courses

In 1974, enterprising entrepreneurs Pat and Patsy Hennin jumped on the do-it-yourself bandwagon and established the **Shelter Institute** in downtown Bath, to train neophytes in energy-efficient home design and construction techniques. Since then, more than 25,000 students have taken courses here, and enthusiastic alumni (and their building projects) span the globe. Students range in age from late teens to early 80s. A one-week post-and-beam course, for instance, is $750 per person. Expansion of the program led to a move in the spring of 2000 to a 68-acre campus in Woolwich, five miles north of Bath: 873 Rte. 1, Woolwich 04579, 207/442-7938, fax 442-7939, www.shelterinstitute.com. Visitors are welcome any time during business hours, and anyone who appreciates fine-woodworking tools *has* to visit the institute's **Woodbutcher Tools** retail shop and bookstore, open Mon.–Sat.

Getting Around

Platinum Plus Taxi, 207/443-9166 provides airport and local service. Thurs.–Sat. they run round-the-clock; otherwise they're off-line briefly in the dead of night. Bath has a summer trolley, which makes a loop around town, and there is a City of Bath shuttle bus, 207/443-8363, for 60 cents per trip, operating Mon.–Fri.

Wiscasset Area

Billing itself as "The Prettiest Village in Maine," Wiscasset (pop. 3,500) works hard to live up to its slogan, with quaint street signs, well-maintained homes, and an air of attentive elegance. Behind the scenes, however, it's actually a rather workaday community—not overrun with deep-pocketed retirees. The interesting mix includes artists, antiques dealers, worm diggers, and blue-collar types. And it seems to work.

Wiscasset (meeting place of three rivers), incorporated as part of Pownalborough in 1760, has had its current name since 1802. In the late 18th century, it became the shire town of Lincoln County and the largest seaport north of Boston. Countless tall-masted ships sailed the 12 miles up the Sheepscot River to tie up here, and shipyards flourished, turning out vessels for domestic and foreign trade. The 1807 Embargo Act and the War of 1812 delivered a one-two punch that shut down trade and temporarily squelched the town's aspirations, but Wiscasset yards soon were back at it, producing vessels for the pre–Civil War clipper-ship era—only to face a more lasting decline with the arrival of the railroads and the onset of the Industrial Revolution.

From the 1930s to the mid-1990s, two derelict four-masted wooden ships, the *Hesper* and the *Luther Little,* reminders of the town's heyday, languished in Wiscasset Harbor, providing a distinctive landmark and photo ops for locals and visitors. But years of storms, and even a fire, took their toll, eventually reducing the schooners to little more than piles of toothpicks, finally demolished in 1998, to the dismay of sentimentalists.

Just east of Wiscasset, across the Donald Davey Bridge, is Edgecomb, a tiny town that primarily serves as a funnel to the Boothbay Peninsula.

The Donald Davey Bridge, built in 1983, is the most recent span over the Sheepscot. The earliest, finished in 1847, was a toll bridge that charged a horse-and-wagon $0.15 to cross, pe-

destrians $0.03 each, and pigs $0.01 apiece. Prior to that, ferries carried passengers, animals, and vehicles between Wiscasset and Edgecomb's Davis Island (then named Folly Island).

North and a bit east of Wiscasset are the lovely rural communities of Sheepscot and Alna, definitely worth a detour.

Wiscasset was long known as the site of the controversial Maine Yankee nuclear-power plant, built in 1973 on Montsweag Bay, six miles south of town. Maine's first and only nuclear facility, plagued by problems and protesters, suspended operations in 1997 to begin the long-term process of decommissioning. During its lifetime, Maine Yankee was a cash cow, allowing Wiscasset to have all the civic benefits of a huge tax base. The plant's closure has been a major blow to the town's economy, but Wiscasset will survive.

Whether it will survive its notoriety for midsummer gridlock is another matter. Especially on weekends, traffic backs up on Rte. 1 for miles in both directions—to the frustration of drivers, passengers, and Wiscasset merchants. (When you stop in town, try to park pointed in the direction you're going; it's impossible to make turns across oncoming traffic.)

SIGHTS

In 1973, a large chunk of downtown Wiscasset was added to the National Register of Historic Places, and a walking tour is the best way to appreciate the Federal, classical revival, and even pre-Revolutionary homes and commercial buildings in the Historic District. Below are a few of the prime examples. If you do nothing else, be sure to swing by the homes on High St.

Castle Tucker

Once known as the Lee-Tucker House, Castle Tucker, Lee and High Sts., Wiscasset 04578, 207/882-7169, is a must-see. Built in 1807 by

Judge Silas Lee, and bought by sea captain Richard Tucker in 1858, the imposing mansion has Victorian wallpaper and furnishings, Palladian windows, an amazing elliptical staircase, and a dramatic view over the Sheepscot River. In early 1997, Jane Tucker, Richard's granddaughter, magnanimously deeded the house to the Society for the Preservation of New England Antiquities (SPNEA). Same dates, hours, tour times, and admission as Nickels-Sortwell, below.

Nickels-Sortwell House

Also owned by SPNEA, the three-story Nickels-Sortwell House, Main St., Rte. 1, Wiscasset 04578, 207/882-6218, looms over Rte. 1, yet it's so close to the road many motorists miss it. Don't. Sea captain William Nickels commissioned the mansion in 1807 but died soon after its completion. For 70 or so years, it became the Belle Haven Hotel, prior to Alvin and Frances Sortwell's meticulous colonial revival restoration in the early 20th century. Today, the house is open June 1–Oct. 15, Fri.–Sun.; tours begin on the hour, 11 AM–4 PM. Admission is $5; Historic New England/SPNEA members and Wiscasset residents free.

Lincoln County Jail and Museum

Wiscasset's Old Jail, completed in 1811, was the first prison in the District of Maine (then part of Massachusetts). Amazingly, it remained a jail—mostly for short-termers—until 1953. Two years after that, the Lincoln County Historical Association took over, so each summer you can check out the 40-inch-thick granite walls, floors, and ceilings; the 12 tiny cells; and historic graffiti penned by the prisoners. Attached to the prison is the 1839 jailer's house, now the Lincoln County Museum, containing antique tools, the original kitchen, and various temporary exhibits. The complex is open Sat. 10 AM–4 PM and Sun. noon–4 PM in June and Sept., then Tues.–Sat. 10 AM–4 PM, and Sun. noon–4 PM, July–Aug. Admission is $4 adults, $2 children under 13. A Victorian gazebo, overlooking the Sheepscot River, is a great spot for a picnic. From Rte. 1 (Main St.) in downtown Wiscasset, take Federal St. (Rte. 218) 1.2 miles. For more information, contact **Lincoln County Historical Association,** Federal St., P.O. Box 61, Wiscasset 04578, 207/882-6817, www.lincolncountyhistory.org.

Musical Wonder House

The treasures in the Musical Wonder House, 18 High St., P.O. Box 604, Wiscasset 04578, 207/882-7163, www.musicalwonderhouse.com, an 1852 sea captain's mansion, are indeed astonishing, and eccentric Austrian-born museum founder Danilo Konvalinka delights in sharing them—for a price. The best way to appreciate the collection of hundreds of 19th-century European music boxes, player pianos, and musical rarities is to take a guided tour (call ahead for an appointment), including two dozen player-piano and music-box demonstrations. A 45-minute tour is $10; a 1.5-hour tour, $18; a four-hour tour, $40. Admission to the building and gift shop is $2 adults—providing access only to about 20 coin-operated music boxes, but credited on any purchases over $20. The museum and the Merry Music Box Gift Shop are open daily 10 AM–5 PM, May 25–Oct. 31.; guided tours are limited after Labor Day (11 AM and 1 and 3 PM daily). There is a second shop in downtown Freeport, and a mail-order sideline on the website, offering music-boxes and music of the past in various formats, continues year-round.

Head Tide Village

Follow Rte. 218 north from Wiscasset for about eight miles to Head Tide Village, an eminently picturesque hamlet at the farthest reach of Sheepscot River tides. From the late 18th century to the early 20th, Head Tide (now part of the town of Alna) was a thriving mill town, a source of hydropower for the textile and lumber industries. All that's long gone, but hints of that era come from the handful of well-maintained 18th- and 19th-century homes in the village center.

Up the hill, the stunning 1838 **Head Tide Church,** another fine example of local prosperity, is open Sat. 2–4 PM in July (or by appointment; contact Honora Jordan, 207/586-5484). Volunteer tour guides point out the original pulpit, a trompe l'oeil window, a kerosene chandelier, and walls lined with historic Alna photographs. The church was the subject of a number of paintings by Marsden Hartley, two of which are in the Colby College art museum.

Head Tide's most famous citizen was the poet **Edwin Arlington Robinson,** born here in 1869. His family home, at the bend in Rte. 194 and marked by a plaque, is not open to the public. Perhaps his Maine roots inspired these lines from his poem *New England:* "Here where the wind is always north-north-east/And children learn to walk on frozen toes."

Just upriver from the bend in the road is a favorite swimming hole, a millpond where you can join the locals on a hot summer day. Not much else goes on here, and there are no restaurants or lodgings, so Head Tide can't be termed a destination, but it's a village frozen in time—and an unbeatable opportunity for history buffs and shutterbugs.

Pownalborough Court House

Prepare to enter a pre-Revolutionary riverfront courthouse where President John Adams once handled a trial—in a mid-18th-century frontier community (named Pownalborough) established by French and German settlers. During the 30-minute tour of the three-story Pownalborough Court House, River Rd., Rte. 128, Dresden 04342, guides delight in pointing out the restored beams, paneling, and fireplaces, as well as the on-site tavern that catered to judges, lawyers, and travelers. Walk a few hundred feet south of the dramatically sited courthouse and you'll find a cemetery with Revolution-era graves. Along the river is a nature trail developed by local Eagle Scouts. The complex is open Sat. 10 AM–4 PM and Sun. noon–4 PM in June and Sept., then Tues.–Sat. 10 AM–4 PM and Sun. noon–4 PM July–Aug. Admission is $4 adults, $2 children under 13. For more information, call or write **Lincoln County Historical Association,** Federal St., P.O. Box 61, Wiscasset 04578, 207/882-6817, www.lincoln-

countyhistory.org. From Rte. 1 in Wiscasset, take Rte. 27 about nine miles north to the junction with Rte. 128. Turn left (south) and go 2.5 miles to the courthouse sign. The courthouse is also an easy drive from Bath or Augusta.

PARKS AND RECREATION

Across Federal St. from the Nickels-Sortwell House in downtown Wiscasset is the lovely **Sunken Garden,** an almost-unnoticed pocket park created around the cellar hole of a long-gone inn. Bring a book or a picnic (or buy one across the street at Treat's) and ignore the traffic streaming by on Main St.

Inland from Rte. 1, just beyond the Morris Farm, the **Wiscasset Community Center,** 242 Gardiner Rd., Rte. 27, Wiscasset 04578, 207/882-8230, has a fitness center and a six-lane pool open to the public. Changing rooms and showers are available. May–Oct. the center is open 5 AM–8 PM Mon.–Fri. (to 6 PM Fri.), 8 AM–noon Sat., and 1–4 PM Sun. (Hours are longer in winter.) Nonresident daily fee is $8 adults, $5 children, $18 for a family.

Morris Farm

In 1995, a group of civic-minded citizens managed to stave off developers and buy the Morris Farm, Rte. 27, 156 Gardiner Rd., P.O. Box 136, Wiscasset 04578, 207/882-4080, www.morrisfarm.org. Thanks to the energy of Morris Farm Trust members and the resident caretakers, the 60-acre working farm has become a community center for agriculture-related education and recreation, including after school programs, school vacation and summer day-camps, and year-round lectures, events and demonstrations for both children and adults. Farm products including certified organic, unpasteurized, nonhomogenized milk, eggs, beef, chicken, turkey, pork, and raspberries are available for purchase seasonally at the farm.

Arrive here any day at 4:30 PM and you can watch the milking of the predominantly Jersey herd. In winter, there are workshops, events, and lecture series in the farm's Learning Center and adjacent pasture and woods. In spring, there's an Easter egg hunt ($5 per child), including egg-coloring with natural dyes, visiting all the spring newborns in the barn, and the hunt itself. In summer, there's a pick-your-own raspberry patch. Always, dawn to dusk, the farm is open for walking, hiking, and picnicking. A popular annual event is the **Tour de Farms,** which attracts dozens of bike riders for several different routes. Along the way are stops at various local farms, followed by a wrap-up barbecue at the Morris Farm. The ride takes place mid- to late August. Other current and upcoming events are available on the Farm's website. The Morris Farm is 0.75 mile from Rte. 1 (turn onto Rte. 27 next to the Wiscasset Municipal Building).

If you're traveling with kids, continue along Rte. 27, about 0.25 mile farther, to the creative playground run by the Wiscasset Recreation Department.

Winters Gone Farm
Follow Rte. 218 (Federal St., opposite the Wiscasset post office) north from Wiscasset for 2.5 miles to **Winters Gone Farm and Alpaca Store,** 245 Alna Rd. (Rte. 218), Wiscasset 04578, 207/882-9191 or 800/645-0188, the "Softest Farm in Maine," where you can learn about alpacas, buy clothes and gifts, walk the grounds and trails, and picnic. Open year-round, 10 AM–6 PM.

Sherman Lake Rest Area
About four miles east of Wiscasset (in the town of Newcastle) is the state-operated Sherman Lake Rest Area, a scenic spot along Rte. 1 with picnic tables, outhouses, and a dog-walking area. Bring a kayak or canoe and paddle around the mile-long lake. Birders should have good luck spotting waterfowl. Open all year.

FESTIVALS AND EVENTS
Wiscasset's day-long **Annual Strawberry Festival and Country Fair** celebrates with tons of strawberries, plus crafts and an auction at St. Philip's Episcopal Church, 12 Hodge St., 207/882-7184, from 10 AM–2 PM the last Sat. in June.

St. Philip's Episcopal Church on Hodge St. is the site of **Monday-night fish-chowder suppers** for six Mondays beginning early–mid-July. Reservations are advised (207/882-7184) for these very popular 5:30 PM suppers.

SHOPPING
Antiques and Collectibles
It's certainly fitting that a town filled end-to-end with antique homes should have over 20 solo and group antiques shops. The majority are located all along downtown Main St., but take a peek down side streets for open flags or sidewalk displays. Most do cooperative advertising, so newspapers and shops have ads and brochures listing them all.

Right downtown, the **Marston House,** Main and Middle Sts., Wiscasset 04578, 207/882-6010, specializes in 18th- and 19th-century antiques—homespun textiles, high country furniture, and accessories of the period—from America, France, Sweden, and England, and caters to serious dealers and collectors. Hours are noon–5 PM daily, May–Dec. Call for an appointment off-season.

High-quality American antiques are also the specialty at **Priscilla Hutchinson,** 62 Pleasant St., Wiscasset 04578, 207/882-4200, located in an attractive carriage house half a block from Rte. 1. Open daily, 10 AM–5 PM, June–Sept., other months by appointment or chance.

Art Galleries
European and American 19th- and 20th-century painters are the broad focus at **Wiscasset Bay Gallery,** 67 Main St. (Rte. 1), P.O. Box 309, Wiscasset 04578, 207/882-7682 or 888/622-9445, which schedules high-quality rotating shows throughout its season. Open daily 10:30 AM–5 PM Apr.–Dec., Thurs.–Sat. Jan.–Mar.

Located in the handsome open spaces of an early-19th-century brick schoolhouse, the **Maine Art Gallery,** Warren St., P.O. Box 315, Wiscasset 04578, 207/882-7511, www.maineartgallery.org, was founded in 1957 as a nonprofit corporation to showcase

Mid-Coast Region

contemporary Maine artists. Rotating exhibits occur throughout the season, May–Nov. Late May to early Oct., the gallery is open Tues.–Sat. 10 AM–4 PM, Sun. 1–4 PM. In spring and fall, it's open Thurs.–Sat. 10 AM–4 PM and Sun. 1–4 PM.

Gifts and Crafts

The oldest commercial building in town is the **Wiscasset Old General Store,** aka Wiscasset Hardware, 49 Water St., P.O. Box 289, Wiscasset 04578, 207/882-6622, built in 1797 as a ship chandlery on the east side of Water St. Since 1949, the Stetson family has run this hardware-plus business, next to Red's. Request a free town map and check out the great view from the riverview deck, where you can buy sandwiches from the deli, hot dogs, ice cream, and coffee. While you're at it, do your Wiscasset gift shopping here, too, or pick up a bottle from the wine cellar; there's plenty of variety. The store is open all year except Jan.–Feb., Mon.–Sat. 8 AM–5 PM and Sun. 11 AM–4 PM, sometimes later in summer.

Erika Soule is the friendly proprietor at the stylish **Rock Paper Scissors,** 78 Main St., P.O. Box 120, Wiscasset 04578, 207/882-9930, presiding over a collection of fashionable papers, an extensive card selection, games for kids, and gift items you won't see everywhere else. Open 10 AM–5 PM Tues.–Sat. in winter, daily in summer.

You can have your wedding done by Andrée Baston, the agreeable proprietress of **Flowers by Pepée,** P.O. Box 758, Main St., Wiscasset 04578, 207/882-9901 or 888/889-9901, and you can buy plants or décor for home or garden, or opt for a piece of high-quality chocolate to relieve the stress of selecting your bouquet or décor. Open year-round, 9 AM–5 PM Mon.–Sat.

The Butterstamp Workshop, 55 Middle St., Wiscasset 04578, 207/882-7825, http://butterstampworkshop.tripod.com, not only creates and sells designs copied from antique molds, but is also a source of hard-to-find gravestone-rubbing supplies. Plus sometimes you can watch the workshop operation, which

produces butter and cookie molds, beeswax ornaments, even magnets. Open daily 10 AM–5 PM, Memorial Day weekend–mid-Oct.

Sinks, tiles, dinnerware, accessory pieces, vases, and lamps are among the hand painted and glazed pottery pieces available at **Sheepscot River Pottery,** 34 Rte. 1, Edgecomb 04556, 207/882-9410, www.sheepscot.com, just across the bridge from Wiscasset. The Maine Island pattern is especially striking. Located in a handsome modern roadside building (opposite the Sheepscot River Inn's restaurant), the shop also accepts commissions. Open daily 9 AM–6 PM in summer, 9 AM–5 PM the rest of the year.

Discount Shopping

Carving out its own unique niche is **Big Al's Super Values,** Rte. 1, Wiscasset 04578, 207/882-6423, a catchall emporium specializing in odd lots, closeouts, funky souvenirs, and half-price birthday cards. Bargains galore, plus free coffee. Lots of tourism brochures are also available here. Three miles south of Wiscasset, across from the Sea Basket Restaurant, Big Al's is open Apr.–Christmas Eve, Mon.–Sat. 9 AM–8 PM and Sun. 9 AM–6 PM.

ACCOMMODATIONS
Bed-and-Breakfasts

Wiscasset isn't loaded with B&Bs, but the choices are intriguing. One is downtown and two are within easy walking distance of antiques shops and the waterfront. Two others are out of town—farm B&Bs with their own special charm.

Named after a famous Maine clipper ship, the gracious **Snow Squall B&B,** 5 Bradford Rd. at Rte. 1, Wiscasset 04578, 207/882-6892 or 800/775-7245, www.snowsquallinn.com, is a renovated mid-19th-century house with four lovely rooms ($100–150 d) and three suites (ranging from $150–220, depending on number of occupants). Nov. 1–Apr. 30, rates are about 15 percent lower. Rooms are named for clipper ships, and all have private baths. There are four working fireplaces, a breakfast room with a selection of tables, and a porch full of rocking chairs. Open all year, but only by reservation Nov.–Apr. No smoking, no pets; children are welcome in the suites.

On the other side of Rte. 1, **Highnote Bed & Breakfast,** 26 Lee St., Wiscasset 04578, 207/882-9628, is a handsome Victorian on a quiet side street. John and Marie Reinhardt (he's an opera singer, hence the name) serve a European-style breakfast, including Marie's world-class scones. Three rooms (shared bath) are $80 d the entire year. No smoking, no pets, no credit cards.

Attached to the Marston House antiques shop, the **Marston House B&B,** Main and Middle Sts., Wiscasset 04578, 207/882-6010, www.marstonhouse.com, has two good-size rooms, each with a queen-size bed, for $90 d in the carriage house out back (away from Rte. 1 traffic noise). Each has a fireplace, private bath, and private garden entrance. No smoking, no pets. Open May–Oct.

Then there's a major getaway—**The Squire Tarbox Inn,** 1181 Main Rd., Westport Island, Wiscasset 04578, 207/882-7693 or 800/888-0626, www.squiretarboxinn.com, Roni and Mario De Pietro's elegantly casual B&B/inn. Eleven lovely rooms (all private baths) are divided between the early-19th-century main house and the late-18th-century carriage house. The property's 13 acres include a marsh where guests can go boating. Rate range for a couple is $99–170 Apr. 1–June 30 and Oct. 31–Dec. 31, except holidays; and $130–190 July 1–Oct. 30. Minimum two-night stay some Saturdays and selected dates. Mario's four-course dinners, open to the public by reservation, are memorable, and may include vegetables from the organic garden (breakfasts might include eggs from inn chickens). Smoking outdoors only. Open Apr. 1–Jan. 1. From downtown Wiscasset, head southwest to Birch Point Rd. (on left—you'll see an Inn sign) until you join Rte. 144 south (another left). Coming from the south, take Rte. 144 all the way. From either side it is about 8.5 scenic miles to the inn from Rte. 1. An appealing extra is the presence of Westport Island Pottery, potter Nancy

W. Shaul, 207/882-7783, in the inn's former chicken coop.

Motels

One Wiscasset-area motel is on the southwestern outskirts of town; two others are in Edgecomb, just over the bridge northward from Wiscasset, making it convenient to the Boothbay Peninsula as well.

Fairly close to Rte. 1 but buffered a bit by century-old hemlocks, the **Wiscasset Motor Lodge,** 596 Bath Rd., (Rte. 1), Wiscasset 04578, 207/882-7137 or 800/732-8168, www.wiscassetmotorlodge.com, is a comfortable, well-maintained motel. The 10-acre complex, open Apr.–Nov., has 26 motel rooms for $48–95, depending on the month. Cable TV and air-conditioning in all units; free breakfast buffet mid-June–Labor Day, coffee and donuts other months. No pets.

The Sheepscot River Inn, and **Bintliff's Ocean Grill,** are right on the river, *just* over the bridge from Wiscasset (beware of bridge speeders behind you), Rte. 1, Edgecomb 04556, 207/882-6343 or 800/437-5503, www.sheepscotriverinn.com. In fact, the athletically-inclined can abandon their cars at the inn and walk over the half-mile-long Donald Davey bridge into town. There's a fenced sidewalk on the bridge, and views are gorgeous, especially at sunset. Enjoy river breezes and those from the traffic speeding past you. The inn has a variety of accommodations in two buildings, plus shore cottages. There's a free continental breakfast, cookies and coffee for afternoon and evening snacking, and a solarium to lounge in. Terraces and kitchenette rooms are available. Rates are $66–160 depending on season. No smoking, pets an additional $10/night in suites and cottages. Open all year.

Newest, spiffiest motel in the area is the gray-shingled **Cod Cove Inn,** 22 Cross Rd., Rtes. 1 and 27, Edgecomb 04556, 207/882-9586 or 800/882-9586, www.codcoveinn.com, perched high on a hill overlooking Cod Cove and Wiscasset harbor beyond. Thirty rooms have balcony or patio, air-conditioning, cable TV, and telephones. The heated outdoor pool is a big hit with kids. Rates from June 16–Oct. 16, Sun.–Thurs., are $130 queen bed/$140 two queen beds/$150 king bed, including continental breakfast; weekend rates higher, off-season lower. No pets, no smoking. The inn is a mile east of Wiscasset, at the turnoff to the Boothbay Peninsula. Open late Apr.–Nov.

Campgrounds

Geared toward RV and seasonal campers, well-managed **Chewonki Campgrounds,** P.O. Box 261, Wiscasset 04578, 207/882-7426 or 800/465-7747, www.chewonkicampground .com, has 48 sites that go for $28–45 mid-June–Labor Day, less early and late in the season. Many sites are close to tidal Montsweag Bay. Facilities include a pool, rec hall, small store, games, and canoe and boat rentals. Leashed pets are welcome. Open mid-May–mid-Oct. From downtown Wiscasset, head southwest four miles on Rte. 1 to Rte. 144. Turn left, then turn right onto Chewonki Neck Rd., go one mile to campground entrance on right.

FOOD

Lunch

Red's Eats, Main and Water Sts., Wiscasset 04578, 207/882-6128, is a takeout stand, but don't let that dissuade you. It's been here for decades (formerly Al's Eats), and there's always a line for hot dogs, lobster rolls, shrimp, crabmeat, and, says a spokeswoman, "the whole nine yards." The few tables on the sidewalk and behind the building, overlooking the river, are seldom empty (except in bad weather), but it's only a two-block walk across Main St. to picnic tables (and a public restroom) on the Town Wharf. Open daily, mid-Apr.–mid-Oct. 11 AM–11 PM in summer. Mid-Apr.–mid-June and after Labor Day, hours are Mon.–Thurs. 11 AM–5 PM, Fri.–Sat. 11 AM–9 PM, and Sun. noon–6 PM. No credit cards.

The luncheon quiche is scrumptious and satisfying at **Treat's,** Main St., Box 156, Wiscasset 04578, 207/882-6192, www.treatsofmaine .com, where other luncheon offerings include two soups, sandwiches, and possibly a fantastic

fruit pie. The antique counter is much-coveted, but not that big. Get here early in summer. Treats is also a source for gourmet picnic fixings: wine, cheese, condiments, goodies, and homemade bread. Open all year, Mon.–Sat. 10 AM–6 PM, Sun. noon–5 PM.

Two miles southwest of downtown Wiscasset, **The Sea Basket Restaurant,** Rte. 1, Wiscasset 04578, 207/882-6581, www.seabasket .com, has been serving up hearty bowls of lobster stew and good-size baskets of eminently fresh seafood since 1981. Frying is done convection style with canola oil and without trans fats. Three hundred pounds of scallops get devoured here each week, and the lobster stew is so popular it's available by mail order. There's always a crowd—locals eat here, too—so expect to wait. Picnic tables are outside, lots of tables inside. Best plan is to order lunch to go, wait for your number to be called, and head for the picnic tables on the Wiscasset waterfront. (If traffic looks heavy, though, stay here; it could take ages to get to the waterfront.) Open daily Tues.–Sat. 11 AM–8 PM, late Feb.–mid-Dec.

Inexpensive to Moderate

Two waterfront restaurants get high marks for their views.

Across Rte. 1 from Red's Eats, **Sarah's Cafe,** Main and Water Sts., Rte. 1, Wiscasset 04578, 207/882-7504, www.sarahscafe.com, is the home of huge "whaleboat" and "dory" sandwiches, popular homemade soups, pizza, and an array of salads. Lobster meat shows up in quesadillas, croissants, and much more. The deck has front-row seats on the Sheepscot River. Full-service bar. Open all year for lunch and dinner, breakfast on weekends.

Also overlooking the water is **Le Garage,** 15 Water St., Wiscasset 04578, 207/882-5409, which has upper and lower enclosed porch/decks. Request a porch/deck table, and dine by candlelight. Lamb is a specialty, as is finnan haddie (entrée range is $8–22); omelettes and light suppers are thrifty choices. Reservations are wise on weekends. The restaurant is two blocks off Rte. 1. Open Feb. 2–Dec. 28 for lunch (11:30 AM–2:30 PM) and dinner (5:30–8:30 PM), closed Mon.

Moderate to Expensive

A relative of the popular Bintliff's Restaurants in Portland and Ogunquit, **Bintliff's Ocean Grill,** Rte. 1, Edgecomb 04556, 207/882-9401, www.bintliffs.com, at the Sheepscot River Inn, opened in spring 2005, serving brunch 8 AM–3 PM, and dinner 5 PM–10 PM. Live entertainment Wed.–Thurs. nights, deejay Fri.–Sat.

INFORMATION AND SERVICES

Since there's no official information center, the best place to find the annual WRBA booklet is the display rack at Big Al's Super Values, three miles southwest of downtown. Once you get into town, stop at Wiscasset Hardware for a free walking map of the downtown area. Another resource is the Wiscasset Town Hall, Rte. 1, Wiscasset 04578, 207/882-8205, in the brick municipal building at the western end of town. It's open weekdays.

The brick **Wiscasset Public Library,** 21 High St., P.O. Box 367, Wiscasset 04578, 207/882-7161, built as a bank in 1805, is a lively year-round operation, with book-discussion groups, children's story hours, a small art collection, and an annual used-book sale. Hours are Tues.–Fri. 10 AM–5 PM (to 7 PM Wed.), Sat. 9 AM–2 PM. Closed Sat. July 1–Labor Day.

Newspapers

The best coverage of local news and events appears in the *Wiscasset Newspaper,* 207/882-6355, under the same ownership as the *Boothbay Register.* It's published each Thursday. The daily *Portland Press Herald* includes Wiscasset in its coverage, particularly the Thursday *Go* entertainment supplement.

Emergencies

The nearest full-service hospital is **St. Andrews** Hospital and Healthcare Center, 3 St. Andrews Ln., Boothbay Harbor 04538, 207/633-2121, with 24-hour emergency care.

For **police, fire, and ambulance** in Wiscasset, Alna, or Edgecomb, dial 911.

Public Restrooms

The **Town Wharf,** Water St. (seasonal), and the **Lincoln County Court House,** on Rte. 1 next to the sharp curve as you come down the hill from the south, have public facilities.

Special Courses

The Chewonki Foundation, 485 Chewonki Neck Rd., Wiscasset 04578, 207/882-7323, www.chewonki.org, is the umbrella group for an impressive nonprofit educational organization begun as a summer boys' camp in 1915. The late birding guru Roger Tory Peterson, a Chewonki counselor in the 1920s, wrote the first edition of his *Field Guide to the Birds* here and dedicated it to Clarence Allen, Chewonki's founder. The philosophy of Chewonki (which predates Outward Bound) emphasizes personal growth, group interaction, and sensitivity to the natural world. Summer programs include boys' camp ($3,800 for 3.5 weeks, $5,600 for the full seven-week session) and co-ed wilderness expeditions (3.5–5 weeks; $3,800–5,200). Scholarship funds are available. There is also a one-week Adventure Camp in August ($525). Other programs run during the school year, such as the Maine Coast Semester (for 11th graders), Elderhostel, residential environmental education programs, and traveling natural science lessons. The foundation is very active in the biofuels area, is doing a demonstration hydrogen project, and is constructing a trail for muscle-powered activities that will eventually run into the town of Wiscasset.

Boothbay Peninsula

East of Wiscasset, en route to Damariscotta, only a flurry of signs along Rte. 1 in Edgecomb (pop. 1,000) hints at what's down the peninsula bisected by Rte. 27. Drive southward down the Boothbay Peninsula between Memorial Day and Labor Day and you'll find yourself in one of Maine's longest-running summer playgrounds.

The three peninsula towns of Boothbay (pop. 3,200), Boothbay Harbor (pop. 2,280), and, connected by a bridge, Southport Island (pop. 650) have sightseeing and whale-watching excursions, a first-rate small aquarium, an antique-railway museum, wall-to-wall shops, scads of restaurants and beds, and quiet preserves for escaping the inevitable midsummer crowds.

When Rte. 27 arrives at the water, having passed through Boothbay Center, you're at the hub, Boothbay Harbor ("the Harbor"), scene of most of the action. The harbor itself is a boat fan's dream, loaded with working craft and pleasure yachts. Ashore, you'll face one-way streets, traffic congestion, and pedestrians everywhere. But there's plenty in this area to appreciate. Parking areas are noted on the Boothbay Harbor Region Chamber of Commerce's walking map.

Try to save time for quieter spots: East Boothbay, Ocean Point, Southport Island, or even just over the thousand-foot-long footbridge stretching across one corner of the harbor. Cross the bridge and walk down Atlantic Ave. to the Fishermen's Memorial, a bronze fishing dory commemorating the loss of hardy souls who've earned a rugged living here by their wits and the sea. Across the street is Our Lady Queen of Peace Catholic Church, with shipwright-quality woodwork and its own fishing icon—a lobster trap next to the altar.

Peak season in the Boothbay Region kicks off each year with Windjammer Days, a two-day midweek celebration around the third week in June, when more than a dozen antique and replica windjammer schooners parade into the harbor under full sail, followed by concerts, fireworks, and a big, old-fashioned street parade.

Despite Boothbay Harbor's distinctly contemporary, tourist-oriented veneer, plenty of history lies below the surface. The English productively worked fishing grounds around Damariscove Island, just offshore, as far back as the early 17th century, when settlers established a fishing entrepôt on Cape Newagen. Conflicts between settlers and Indians scattered the newcomers, and 40 years passed before the next wave of settlers put down roots around present-day Boothbay Harbor. Established as Townsend in 1730, it was incorporated as the town of Boothbay in 1764. Southport spun off into a separate town in 1842, and Boothbay Harbor in 1889.

During the War of 1812, the area gained some renown for the capture of the Royal Navy brig *Boxer* by the U.S. Navy brig *Enterprise* offshore between Damariscove and Monhegan Islands. Damariscove's residents had front-row seats.

In the 1870s, when many scenic coastal areas experienced an influx of steamboat-borne rusticators from the Boston area and beyond, the Boothbay region entered its tourism phase—an era that shows no indication of coming to a close.

In fact, a pioneering summer colony chartered in 1871, 130-acre Squirrel Island, at the mouth of the harbor, remains an exclusive yet low-key enclave with about one hundred sizable Victorian cottages, no cars or bikes, no private phones, and a wonderfully relaxed pace. The squirrel motif is everywhere, though you won't see many examples of the real thing. Still controlled by the members-only Squirrel Island Village Corporation, message center 207/633-4715, the island is officially part of the town of Southport. The island has no interest in tourism, and there are no public facilities, but visitors are permitted on the island's paved perimeter path; allow at least an hour for the circuit, taking in open ocean, a sandy beach, rugged cliffs, and dense woods. It's a window on another era. Balmy Days Cruises operates the seasonal Squirrel Island ferry from Boothbay Harbor, 207/633-2284, landing on the northwest corner of the island.

SIGHTS

Before turning off Rte. 1 for the Boothbay Peninsula, make a quick, interesting detour in Edgecomb, immediately east of the Wiscasset bridge, to historic Fort Edgecomb—perfect for a riverfront picnic. Afterward, back roads can connect you to Rte. 27 for Boothbay and Boothbay Harbor, but it's less confusing to return to Rte. 1, continue a bit east, and turn onto Rte. 27. (Stock up on picnic fodder at Sarah's or Treat's or Red's Eats, in Wiscasset.)

Fort Edgecomb

Built in 1808 to protect the Sheepscot River port of Wiscasset, the Fort Edgecomb State Historic Site, Eddy Rd., RR 1, Box 89, Edgecomb 04556, 207/882-7777, occupies a splendid, three-acre riverfront spread ideal for picnicking and fishing (no swimming; admission is $2 adults, $1 children 5–11, free for seniors and kids under five). The fort officially is open daily 9 AM–5 PM, Memorial Day weekend to Labor Day, but the grounds are easily accessible all year. From Rte. 1 at the Sheepscot River Inn, take Eddy Rd. and go half a mile to Fort Rd.

Ride the Rails

Boothbay Railway Village, Rte. 27, P.O. Box 123, Boothbay 04537,

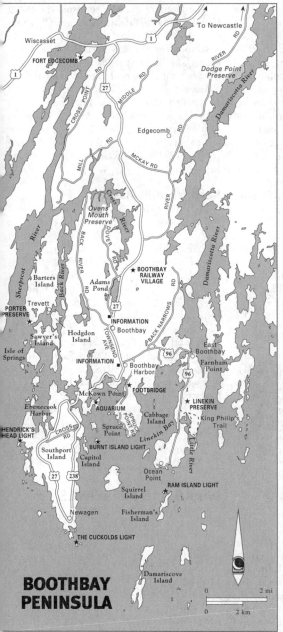

BOOTHBAY
PENINSULA

© AVALON TRAVEL PUBLISHING, INC.

Mid-Coast Region

207/633-4727, www.railwayvillage.org, feels like a life-size train set. More than two dozen old and new buildings have been assembled here since the museum was founded, in 1964, and a restored narrow-gauge steam train makes a 1.5-mile, 20-minute circuit throughout the day. Among the structures are a toy shop, a one-room schoolhouse, a chapel, a barbershop, a 19th-century town hall, a homestead, two railroad stations, and a firehouse. You'll also find more than four dozen antique cars and trucks. The museum store stocks train-oriented items. During the summer, special events include an antique auto meet (third weekend in July), Children's Day (third Sunday in August), and the Columbus Day weekend fall foliage festival. The village is open daily 9:30 AM–5 PM, mid-June–Columbus Day; train rides also operate on Memorial Day weekend, early-June weekends, and the last weekend in October (a ghostly Halloween ride). Admission is $8 adults, $4 children 3–16. The village is 3.5 miles north of downtown Boothbay Harbor, 7.5 miles south of Rte. 1.

Feel the Fish, See the Light

A 20-foot touch tank, with slimy but pettable specimens, is a major kid magnet at the **Marine Resources Aquarium,** McKown Point Rd., West Boothbay Harbor 04538, 207/633-9000, www.state.me.us/dmr, operated by the state Department of Marine Resources. Exhibits in the hexagonal aquarium include rare lobsters (oversize, albino, and blue) and other Gulf of Maine creatures, and new residents arrive periodically. Self-guiding leaflets are available. Admission is $5 adults, $3 seniors and children 5–18, free for children under five. July–Aug., marine scientists present free daily programs at 11 AM and 2 PM. The aquarium is open Memorial Day weekend–Sept., daily 10 AM–5 PM. Consider bringing a picnic—it's a great setting. At the height of summer, parking is limited, and it's a longish walk from downtown around the west side of the harbor, so plan to take the free local trolley-bus, departing on the half-hour from the Meadow Mall, or from one of the downtown trolley-bus stops.

The Department also sponsors the Burnt Island Living Lighthouse Museum, 207/633-9559, www.maine.gov/dmr, a program where costumed interpreters portray a lighthouse keeper and his family. There is also a natural history walk. The tour is two hours and includes a climb up to the lantern room, as well as a chance to fish and picnic for those who wish to stay on the island. A scenic cruise on the *Novelty,* at 12:15 PM or 2:15 PM, takes visitors to this "national treasure." The fee is $20 adults, $12 children. Tours run Mon.–Fri. late June–early Sept.

Hendricks Hill Museum

A historic 1810 Cape-style building, carefully restored, is the home of the Hendricks Hill Museum, Rte. 27, P.O. Box 3, Southport 04576, 207/633-1102, www.hendrickshill .org, a community attic filled with all kinds of workaday tools and utensils and fascinating maritime memorabilia. The 11-room museum is open Tues., Thurs., and Sat. 11 AM–3 PM, July–Labor Day. Admission is free, but donations are welcome. The museum is about two miles south of the Southport Island bridge, on the right, in the center of West Southport.

Continuing down Rte. 27 toward Cape Newagen, stop at the **Southport Memorial Library,** 207/633-2741. Here's a rare, surprising treat: a huge collection of beautifully mounted butterflies once owned by Dr. and Mrs. Stanley Marr. The library is open all year, Tues. and Thurs. 9 AM–4 PM and 7–9 PM, plus Sat. 9 AM–4 PM.

PARKS AND PRESERVES

Courtesy of the very active **Boothbay Region Land Trust** (BRLT), 924 acres on the peninsula and nearby islands have been preserved for wildlife, residents, and visitors. About 25 miles of trails are open to the public in its 11 preserves and parks. Preserve trail maps are available at the property kiosks or at the BRLT office, 1 Oak St., P.O. Box 183, Boothbay Harbor 04538, 207/633-4818, www.bbrlt .org. (Inquire at the office about guided walks in the various preserves.) In return for your use of the lands, carry a litterbag and help the BRLT and everyone who follows you. To do even more, make a cash donation to the BRLT (any amount is welcome), or volunteer your time. Another way to contribute is to buy the 25th-anniversary cookbook, *Fiddleheads and Lobster Tails,* now available from the trust for $15.

In East Boothbay, on the way to Ocean Point, is the 94.6-acre **Linekin Preserve,** located between Rte. 96 and the Damariscotta River. The 2.3-mile, white-blazed River Loop (best done clockwise) takes in an old sawmill site, a beaver dam, and great riverfront views. You'll meet a couple of quite steep sections on the eastern side, near the river, but otherwise it's relatively easy.

On the west side of the peninsula, at the southern end of Barters Island, is the wooded, 19-acre **Porter Preserve,** with two loop trails that get you to great views over the Back and Sheepscot Rivers. From the trailhead, you can do a clockwise half-mile loop (red- and white-blazed) or stop midway for an added 0.4-mile (yellow-blazed) trail that rejoins the first loop. Next to the trail is a tiny sandy beach.

Other BRLT holdings open to the public are the 146-acre **Ovens Mouth Preserve,** almost five miles of trails on two peninsulas linked by a bridge (wear insect repellent), 12-acre **Colby Wildlife Preserve** off the River Rd., 22.5-acre **Marshall E. Saunders Memorial Park** in Boothbay, and 16-acre **Singing Meadows.**

Besides the BRLT preserves on the Boothbay Peninsula, see *Damariscotta/Newcastle* for info on the 506-acre Dodge Point Preserve, on River Rd. in Newcastle (geographically on Boothbay's peninsula, but maintained by the Damariscotta River Association), and several other special locales on the Pemaquid Peninsula.

Still in its early stages but growing quickly is **Coastal Maine Botanical Gardens,** Barters Island Rd., P.O. Box 234, 207/633-4333, www.mainegardens.org, a nonprofit project designed to preserve 128 acres of woodlands. There are two miles of trails, walks, and drives, and landscaped pocket gardens. Occasional special tours are led by horticulturists and other experts, and there are walks, including a Fern Foray, and workshops, as well. Entrance to the preserve (watch for two stone pillars and a sign) is on Barters Island Rd., about 1.3 miles west of Boothbay center. Open daily to the public, no charge, dawn to dusk. The garden offices are on Rte. 27, in the Old Fire Station, 400 feet past the Civil War monument in Boothbay's town center, open weekdays, 8:30 AM–4:30 PM.

Damariscove Island

Summering Wabanakis knew it as Aquahega, but Damerill's Cove was the first European name attributed to the secure, fjordlike harbor at the southern tip of 209-acre Damariscove Island in 1614, when Capt. John Smith of the Jamestown Colony explored the neighborhood. By 1622, Damerill's Cove fishermen were sharing their considerable codfish catch with starving Plimoth Plantation colonists desperate for food. Fishing and farming sustained resident Damariscovers during their up-and-down history, and archaeologists have found rich deposits for tracing the story of this early island settlement about five miles south of Boothbay Harbor.

Rumors persist that the ghost of Capt. Richard Pattishall, decapitated and tossed overboard by Indians in 1689, still roams the island, accompanied by the spectre of his dog. The fog that often overhangs the low-slung, bleak, almost-treeless island makes it easy to fall for the many ghost stories about Pattishall and other onetime residents. In summer, the island is awash with wildflowers, bayberries, raspberries, blackberries, and Rugosa roses.

The Nature Conservancy, which owned the 210-acre island for 39 years, transferred ownership to the Boothbay Region Land Trust in March 2005. Day-use visitors are welcome on the island anytime, but the northern section (called Wood End) is off limits Apr.–Aug. 15,

Mid-Coast Region

to protect the state's largest nesting colony of eiders—nearly 700 nests. Damariscove Island became a National Historic Landmark in 1978. Dogs are not allowed.

Access to the island is most convenient if you have your own boat. Enter the cove at the southern end of the island and disembark at the dock on the west side of the harbor. Summertime caretakers live in the small cabin above the dock, where a trail map is available. Stay on the trail (watch out for poison ivy) or on the shore and away from any abandoned structures; the former Coast Guard station is privately owned.

For information about Damariscove Island, contact **The Boothbay Region Land Trust.** The Boothbay Harbor Region Chamber of Commerce can provide info on getting to the island.

RECREATION

The **Boothbay Region YMCA,** Rte. 27, Boothbay Harbor 04538, 207/633-2855, www.brymca.com, an impressive new complex, has an Olympic pool, fitness center, sauna, racquetball and tennis courts, indoor jogging track, and aerobics classes. Scuba certification classes are held in June and July, and the summer sports camps for kids (preregistration required) are terrific. Call the Y for racquetball reservations. Daily Y memberships are available for visiting adults ($10 pp, $8 seniors) and families ($15). The Y is open Mon.–Fri. 5:30 AM–8:30 PM and Saturday 7 AM–5:30 PM It's also open Sun. 1–5:30 PM, early Sept.–June. Stop in at the Y, or call, to check on the pool schedule.

To unwind toddlers, or even the primary-school set, take them to the marvelously creative **Harold B. Clifford Community Playground** on Back River Rd., just north of Rte. 27 near Boothbay Center; turn right at the monument. Pack a picnic and eat it here; kids love it.

Cycling, Etc.

If you haven't brought your own bike, the local rental source is **Tidal Transit Co.,** Chowder House Bldg., Boothbay Harbor 04538,

207/633-7140, near the footbridge. Cost is $25 a day, $15 a half-day; $10 for each additional day.

When you're ready to take your bike on the road, get some direction at the chamber's information office about trying the 31-mile Barters Island/Southport loop (also a fine driving itinerary). Pack a picnic. Allow a full day to bike it, including stops and detours. The terrain is mostly easy and relatively level, but many stretches are narrow and winding, with poor shoulders, so it's *essential* to follow biking rules and exercise caution.

An alternate loop route, about 15 miles long, follows only the Southport Island section, from downtown Boothbay Harbor. If you're biking with kids, opt for this itinerary—but make sure they know the rules of the road, too. Again, take a picnic, or plan to stop at the **Southport General Store,** Rte. 27, 207/633-6666, about two miles south of the bridge. Also check out the nearby historic cemetery, the Hendricks Hill Museum, and the Hendricks Head Light (go west on Beach Rd. from the general store; the light is privately owned, so don't trespass).

When crossing the swing bridge that spans Townsend Gut, between West Boothbay Harbor and Southport Island, be especially cautious. The surface can be a bear trap for bike tires.

Another good biking (and driving) route begins at the junction of Rtes. 27 and 96, going through East Boothbay, then on down to **Ocean Point,** where the Shore Rd. loop skirts the rocky shoreline. (Ocean Point is about six miles from the Rte. 27/96 crossroads.) About halfway down Linekin Neck toward Ocean Point, hang a left onto King Philip's Trail, then left onto the loop road, clockwise, through the hamlet of Little River, returning to Rte. 96. Like the Southport Island route, the roads are narrow and winding along Linekin Neck, and traffic can be heavy at the height of summer. Early morning is a great time to bike here; park your car in the Shop 'n Save supermarket lot, the Small Mall (Meadow Mall), or the YMCA, back on Rte. 27 at the entrance to Boothbay Harbor.

Getting Afloat

The Boothbay Harbor region is prime territory for getting out on the water; don't miss an opportunity, whether it's a harbor cruise, sunset cruise, whale-watching or sportfishing trip, or Monhegan Island excursion.

Cabbage Island Clambakes, Pier 6, Fisherman's Wharf, Boothbay Harbor, 207/633-7200, mailing address P.O. Box 21, East Boothbay 04544, www.cabbageislandclambakes.com, deserves a category all its own. Touristy, sure, but it's a delicious adventure. You board the 126-passenger excursion boat *Argo* at Pier 6 in Boothbay Harbor; cruise for about an hour past islands, boats, and lighthouses; and disembark at 5.5-acre Cabbage Island. Watch the clambake in progress, if you like, explore the island, or play volleyball. When the feast is ready, pick up your platter, find a picnic table, and dig in. A cash bar is available in the lodge, as are restrooms. When the weather's iffy, the lodge and covered patio have seats for a hundred. For $44.95 pp, you'll get two lobsters (or half a chicken), chowder, clams, corn, potatoes, dessert, beverage, and the boat ride. For children under 12, a boat-ride-plus-hot-dog option goes for $19.20. No credit cards. Clambake season is late June–Labor Day. The 3.5-hour trips depart Mon.–Fri. at 12:30; Sat. trips depart at 12:30 and 5 PM, Sun. trips are 11:30 AM and 1:30 PM.

Excursions

Boothbay Harbor's veteran excursion fleet is **Cap'n Fish's Cruises,** Pier 1, Wharf St., Boothbay Harbor 04538, 207/633-3244 or 633-2626 or 800/636-3244, www.capnfishsboats.com. In addition to whale-watching trips, Cap'n Fish's 150-passenger boats do two-hour **nature cruises** ($18 adults/$9 children) and three-hour **puffin-watching trips** ($20 adults/$10 children; mid-June–mid-Aug.), plus **seal-watching trips, lighthouse cruises,** and **Kennebec River cruises.** Pick up a schedule at one of the information centers and call for reservations.

The harbor's other big fleet is **Balmy Days Cruises,** Pier 8, 42 Commercial St., P.O. Box 535, Boothbay Harbor 04538, 207/633-2284 or 800/298-2284, www.balmydayscruises.com, operating three vessels on a variety of excursions. The *Novelty* does about seven daily one-hour **harbor tours** on a varying schedule, 7 AM–8:30 PM, late June–Labor Day, reduced schedule off-season; cost is $10 adults, $5 children. (The boat stops at Squirrel Island for drop-offs and pickups.) Reservations usually are unnecessary. The 31-foot Friendship sloop *Bay Lady* does five 90-minute **sailing trips** daily in summer. Cost is $18 pp. Reservations are wise for the *Bay Lady* as well as for the fleet's most popular cruise, a day-long trip to Monhegan Island on the *Balmy Days II,* departing daily at 9:30 AM and returning at 4:15 PM, early June–early Oct., plus weekends in late May and mid-Oct. The three-hour round-trip allows about 3.5 hours ashore on idyllic Monhegan Island. Cost is $30 adults, $18 children 3–11. You're headed 12 miles offshore on this trip, so be sure to dress warmly, wear sturdy walking/hiking shoes, and take a camera and binoculars.

Whale-watching

Variations in Gulf of Maine whale-migration patterns have added whale-watching to the list of Boothbay Harbor boating options as the massive mammals travel northeastward within reasonable boating distance. **Cap'n Fish's,** Pier 1, Wharf St., Boothbay Harbor 04538, 207/633-3244 or 207/633-2626, or 800/636-3244, www.mainewhales.com, is the best choice. Three- to four-hour trips depart daily, mid-June–mid-Oct. Cost is $33 for adults, $20 for children, with a raincheck if the whales don't show up. Reservations are advisable, especially early and late in the season and on summer weekends. No matter what the weather on shore, dress warmly and carry more clothing than you think you'll need. Motion-sensitive children and adults need to plan ahead with appropriate medication.

Daysailing

The 65-foot windjammer *Eastwind,* 207/633-6598, www.fishermanswharf.com, skippered by noted sailors Herb and Doris Smith, sails daily to the Outer Islands and Seal Rocks May–Oct., four times a day early July–early Sept., varies other times. The 2.5-hour cruise is $22 pp.

Or take a two-hour sail on the Schooner *Lazy Jack,* 207/975-2628 or 207/236-9761, www.sailschoonerlazyjack.com. The Lazy Jack leaves from Pier 7 four times a day on weekends May–June, weekdays July 1–mid-Sept., three times on May–June weekdays and mid-Sept.–mid-Oct. The trip costs $25.

Sea Kayaking

From Memorial Day weekend–September, **Tidal Transit,** 18 Granary Way, Boothbay Harbor 04538, 207/633-7140, www.kayak-boothbay.com will get you afloat with rentals or guided **wildlife, lighthouse,** or **sunset tours** for $35 pp. for two- to three-hour lighthouse and wildlife tours, and $65 pp. for a sunset tour with lobster bake. No experience is necessary, but you'll need a reservation. Tidal Transit also rents bikes in the Chowder House Building, near the Footbridge.

Walking Tours

Boothbay Harbor is one of the locales for five-day, easy-to-moderate walks organized by **Country Walkers,** P.O. Box 180,Waterbury, VT, 802/244-1387 or 800/464-9255, www.countrywalkers.com, a well-managed firm started in 1980. Lodging is at country inns. Cost, excluding airfare, is about $2,000.

ENTERTAINMENT

For nightlife, **Gray's Wharf,** Pier 1, Boothbay Harbor 04538, 207/633-5629, is a casual, fun hot spot, with live entertainment and dancing most weekends all year, and most weeknights during the summer. The deck is almost *in* the harbor. Pool tables and giant TVs enhance the din inside. Open to 1 AM.

Across from Hannaford's, the **Harbor Theatre,** Meadow Mall, Rte. 27, Boothbay Harbor 04538, 207/633-0438, screens first-run films.

FESTIVALS AND EVENTS

The **Fishermen's Festival** is a locally colorful early-season celebration, held in late April, beginning with a Friday Miss Shrimp Princess pageant. Saturday brings a lobster crate race, and contests such as trap hauling and a tug of war. There's an arts-and-crafts show, and a Fishermen's Festival supper at the Congregational church. Sunday, the blessing of the fleet and boat parade remind everyone of the significance of Maine's fishing industry and hopes for a good and safe season.

June is the month for **Windjammer Days,** two days of festivities centering on traditional windjammer schooners. Highlights are the Windjammer Parade, harborfront concerts, plenty of food, parades, and a fireworks extravaganza. The **Lincoln Arts Festival,** which celebrated its 25th anniversary in 2005, presents concerts—classical, pops, choral, and jazz—at various locations on the Boothbay Peninsula from mid-June–mid-Sept. All events are free to those 12 and under; some are free to adults, and tickets for others range from $2–25. Many events are at the Congregational Church, and there is a series of Bath Municipal Jazz Band Outdoor Concerts on the Boothbay Common every Tuesday night at 7, beginning mid-July, when Jazz Week events also take place at the Opera House.

Early July–Aug. is a great time for music in Boothbay Harbor. In addition to Lincoln Arts concerts, free Thursday night **band concerts** at 8 PM are performed by the Hallowell Band on the Memorial Library lawn, Boothbay Harbor. Bring a blanket or folding chair.

Columbus Day weekend marks the **Fall Foliage Festival,** featuring craft and food booths, entertainment, train rides, and more at Boothbay Railway Village.

SHOPPING
Art Galleries

A handsome 19th-century restored farmhouse is the home of **Gleason Fine Art,** 31 Townsend Ave. Boothbay Harbor 04538, 207/633-6849 www.gleasonfineart.com, one of Maine's top retail venues for 19th- through 21st-century paintings and sculpture. The gallery is open Tues.–Sat. 10 AM–5 PM, Apr.–Dec., winter hours by chance or appointment.

The nonprofit **Boothbay Region Art Foundation,** 7 Townsend Ave., P.O. Box 124, Boothbay Harbor 04538, 207/633-2703, www.boothbayartists.org, founded in the 1960s, has been at its present location since 1993. Mid-May–mid-Oct., the gallery mounts five juried shows of members' work, plus a student art show. Open daily 10 AM–5 PM.

Books, Etc.
You're bound to find something at the two-story **Sherman's Books & Stationery Store,** 5 Commercial St., Boothbay Harbor 04538, 207/633-7262 or 800/371-8128, www.shermans.com. Cards, games and gifts, books and more books, kitchenware and kitsch. The shop is open all year, daily 9 AM–10 PM in summer, daily to 6 PM in winter.

Gifts and Crafts
If pottery is high on your shopping list, plan an attack on the Edgecomb/Boothbay Peninsula area. Several talented ceramicists have long-established reputations, and there's enough variety to cover every interest.

A veteran area craft shop is **Abacus,** 12 McKown St., Boothbay Harbor 04538, 207/633-2166, www.abacusgallery.com, which has expanded from the original 1971 Boothbay Harbor store (seasonal) to include year-round stores in Freeport, Portland, and Kennebunkport. Great stuff—functional items, wearable art, and charming doodads—high-end American crafts from several hundred artisans.

Another veteran craft shop (since 1952) is **Andersen Studio,** One Andersen Rd., P.O. Box 246, East Boothbay 04544, 207/633-4397 or 800/640-4397, www.andersenstudio.com. Their slipcast birds are famous; ceramic vases, animals, sculpture, and seconds make this a worthwhile stop. Open daily 9 AM–5 PM in season. Call ahead off-season.

Also downtown is the **Gold/Smith Gallery,** 41 Commercial St., Boothbay Harbor 04538, 207/633-6252, featuring intriguing gold jewelry and contemporary paintings. The gallery is open Mon.–Sat. 10 AM–6 PM and Sun. by chance or appointment, mid-May–Oct. Off-season, owners John Vander and Karen Swartsberg regroup at their home in the Tuscan hills—a recurring theme in some of their exhibits.

General Store
At the blinking light in East Boothbay, stop in at the **East Boothbay General Store,** Rte. 96, Ocean Point Rd., East Boothbay 04544, 207/633-4503, www.eastboothbaygeneralstore.com, source of lobster rolls, take-out sandwiches, snacks, beer, fine wine, baked goods, pies, pizza, fresh salads, and scooped ice cream, with an emphasis on Maine-made products. Summer hours are 7 AM–7 PM Mon.–Wed. (to 8 PM Thurs.–Sat.), 7 AM–5 PM Sun.

Farmers Market
Lots of variety is the key at the excellent Boothbay Farmers Market, operating early June–early Sept., each Thurs. 9 AM–noon. Set up at the Common at Boothbay Center (across from the town office), a dozen vendors have goat cheese, breads, dim sum, poultry, flowers, and fresh produce.

ACCOMMODATIONS
Boothbay Harbor's longevity as a holiday destination means beds galore—more than anyone cares to count. Even so, late June–mid-Aug., you'll meet a blur of No Vacancy signs. If that's when you decide to show up here, make reservations ahead. There are also several lodging choices in nearby Wiscasset.

Inns with Restaurants
To get away from it all, book in at the **Newagen Seaside Inn,** Rte. 27S, P.O. Box 29, Cape Newagen, 04576, 207/633-5242 or 800/654-5242, www.newagenseasideinn.com, a full-service, unstuffy inn with casual fine dining and views that go on forever from the 85-acre

grounds. Plus there's a mile-long rocky shore, a nature trail, tennis courts, oceanfront saltwater pool, guest rowboats, lawn games, and bikes. Honeymooners and seniors head the guest list, but it's also a great spot for a family vacation. Twenty-six rooms and suites (private baths) are $215–250 d in peak season, $110–200 other times, including full breakfast. Several cottages are available by the week. The dining room, the Cape Harbor Grill, is open to the public, reservations requested, for dinner, 5:30–9 PM. The pub, with a lighter menu, opens at 4:30 PM. Open mid-May–early Oct. The inn is six miles south of downtown Boothbay Harbor.

Another getaway, on a private, 100-acre peninsula jutting into the harbor, is the **Spruce Point Inn Resort & Spa,** Atlantic Ave., P.O. Box 237, Boothbay Harbor 04538, 207/633-4152 or 800/553-0289, www.sprucepointinn .com, which has expanded dramatically in recent years, adding modern condos to its already extensive complex of traditional inn rooms and cottages. Decor and prices vary widely. Last count was 93 rooms/suites/cottages/condos (all with private baths, phones, and cable TV). Attentive staffers, creative cuisine, a homey lounge, and a knockout setting create a big demand for rooms at Spruce Point. Reserve well ahead, and if you can swing it, request a water-view room. The inn holds big weddings on many midsummer weekends, so try for midweek or shoulder seasons. Rooms, suites, and cottages are $170–550 d, mid-July–early Sept., minimum stays apply; off-season rates vary by season: spring, early summer, and fall. Special packages are also available, and there is a Children's Program for young visitors. Amenities at the 15-acre resort include freshwater and saltwater pools with whirlpool spas, clay tennis courts, fitness center, massage services, rocky shorefront, and a shuttle bus to downtown (about two miles, although it seems farther). The **harbor-view dining rooms** are open to the public; dress casual attire is required for dinner in the main dining room, 83 Grandview; casual dress is fine in Bogie's Hideaway. There are lobsterbakes on occasion. The inn is open mid-May–early Oct.

Across the harbor from Spruce Point, the **Lawnmere Inn,** Rte. 27, P.O. Box 29, Southport 04576, 207/633-2544 or 800/633-7645, www.lawnmereinn.com, is only two miles from downtown Boothbay Harbor. Built in 1898 on Southport Island, overlooking Townsend Gut, the Lawnmere has 34 comfortable rooms—31 with water views—and was renovated by new owners in 2004. There are two buildings, a traditional inn and a separate modern motel building. All have private baths. Late June–Labor Day, rooms are $145–185 d; other months, $90–165 d, including breakfast or brunch. Children are welcome. Pets are a steep $20 per night. The inn's multi-star restaurant is open to the public for dinner. Seafood is predominant on the extensive menu, which is imaginative and well prepared; entrées run $18–25. Dessert specialty is Key lime pie. Dinner reservations are essential; with its water view, the restaurant is a popular spot. The inn is open late May–Columbus Day.

On a private cove in Linekin Bay, **Smugglers Cove Inn & 1820 House Restaurant,** 727 Ocean Point Rd., East Boothbay 04564, 800/633-3008, www.smugglerscovemotel.com, has been newly renovated, with new decks, furniture, and other improvements. Ocean views, a small private sandy beach, an outdoor heated pool, fishing off the Inn's deck, rowboats, and sailboat trips right from the Inn's pier on the *S/V Tribute,* 207/882-1020, make it clear you're on vacation on the coast. Limited pet accommodations. The 1820 House Restaurant, run by Chris Gistis, has lovely views. Rates are $79–189 d., July 1–Sept. 4 and Sept. 30–Oct. 15, $59–159 the rest of the year.

Bed-and-Breakfasts

All 15 rooms have Linekin Bay views and private baths (five have fireplaces) at the **Five Gables Inn B&B,** Murray Hill Rd., P.O. Box 335, East Boothbay 04544, 207/633-4551 or 800/451-5048, www.fivegablesinn.com, which began life as a no-frills summer hotel in the late 19th century. She's gone steadily upmarket since then, and well-traveled innkeepers De and Mike Kennedy, owners since 1995, have added their own unique touches. The living room is congenial, the gardens are gorgeous, and the porch goes on forever. Rates are $135–200 d, depending on the season, including Mike's gourmet buffet breakfast. No smoking, no pets, no children under 12. Book well ahead at this popular spot. The inn, on a side road off Rte. 96 in the traditional boatbuilding hamlet of East Boothbay, is 3.5 miles from downtown Boothbay Harbor. Two moorings are available for guests. Open mid-May–Oct.

Square in the middle of downtown, overlooking the harbor and close to everything, the **1830 Admiral's Quarters Inn,** 71 Commercial St., Boothbay Harbor 04538, 207/633-2474 or 800/644-1878, www.admiralsquartersinn.com, is an antique sea captain's home renovated by personable innkeepers Les and Deb Hallstrom, who work hard to put everyone at ease. Two rooms and five two-room suites have private baths, cable TV, air-conditioning, phones, water views, fireplaces, and private decks and entrances. Forget about lunch after the killer breakfast. Rates are $165–195 d mid-June–mid-Oct; $95–145 d mid-Oct.–mid-June. No pets or smoking, no children under 12. Open all year except December.

Across the street from the Admiral's Quarters is **The Greenleaf Inn,** 65 Commercial St., Boothbay Harbor 04538, 207/633-7346 or 888/950-7724, www.greenleafinn.com, Jeff Teel's mid-19th-century home. Seven brightly decorated rooms all have harbor views, fireplaces, fans, private baths, TV/VCR, Internet, even small refrigerators; five also have private balconies. There's comfort throughout the inn, with library, Internet station, sunroom, porch, and outdoor hot tub overlooking the ocean. Rates are $135–195 d mid-May–Oct. 31, $115–145 d other months. No smoking, no pets, no children under 12. Open year-round.

Just up the hill is **The Welch House,** 56 McKown St., Boothbay Harbor 04538, 207/633-3431 or 800/279-7313, www.welchhouseinn.com, with stunning 180-degree views from the upper deck (and not-shabby ones from the lower deck). Owners Susan Hodder and Michael Feldmann have transformed this cen-

tury-old shipbuilder's home into an elegant getaway. Watch the boats sail by as you enjoy a gourmet breakfast from the deck or the glass-front dining room. (If the views won't bring you back, the breakfasts certainly will!) Most of the 14 uniquely furnished guestrooms have spectacular water views, many have gas fireplaces, and some have whirlpool tubs. All rooms have private baths, cable TV, and VCR. Other amenities include a video library, wireless Internet, and a large collection of books and games. Kids are welcome "if they understand 'no.'" No smoking. Rates are $85–195 d. Open all year.

Ask around town; Lucy Barter's breakfasts are legendary at **Lion d'Or B&B,** 106 Townsend Ave., Boothbay Harbor 04538, 207/633-7367 or 800/887-7367, www.liondorboothbay.com. A few blocks from the harbor, her Victorian house is in the thick of things, yet it quiets down at night. Five comfortably decorated rooms have queen beds, private baths, gas fireplaces, air-conditioning, and TV ($70–135 d, depending on season). And then there's the breakfast—not to mention the homemade cookies in the afternoon. No smoking, no pets. Open year-round.

Staying at Sherri and Steve Matte's **Hodgdon Island Inn,** 374 Barters Island Rd., P.O. Box 603, Boothbay 04537, 207/633-7474 or 800/314-5160, www.hodgdonislandinn.com, puts you in a lobstering community just five minutes from Boothbay Harbor. Nine beautifully decorated rooms on three floors of this sea captain's home have views of a small cove, and some have fireplaces. There's a heated outdoor pool. Rates range from $105–175 d depending on room and time of year. Open all year. No smoking, no pets.

Campgrounds

With 150 well-maintained wooded and open sites on 45 acres, **Shore Hills Campground,** 523 Wiscasset Rd. (Rte. 27), Boothbay 04537, 207/633-4782, www.shorehills.com, is a popular destination where reservations are essential in midsummer. Rates are $25–35 per family. Be sure to request a wooded site away from the biggest RVs. Leashed pets are allowed. Facilities include coin-operated showers and laundry, free use of canoes. Located on the tidal Cross River, 7.5 miles south of Rte. 1 and across the road from the Boothbay Railway Village, Shore Hills is open mid-Apr.–mid-Oct.

Seasonal Rentals

For a long-term rental, start with the **Cottage Connection of Maine,** P.O. Box 662, Boothbay Harbor 04538, 207/633-6545 or 800/823-9501, www.cottageconnection.com, which has a free catalog of more than 150 rental properties. The annual tourism booklet published by the Boothbay Harbor Region Chamber of Commerce includes three pages of cottage-rental listings.

FOOD

No one starves in the Boothbay area, thanks to food emporia ranging from sandwich shops to pizza palaces to tearooms, lobster wharves, and upscale dining rooms. This is merely a sampling.

Watch local papers and bulletin boards for notices of **public suppers** and **chowder suppers,** great opportunities for sampling local home cooking and local color. Most start relatively early, do not include liquor, and usually cost $8 for all you can eat. Such a deal.

Miscellanea

A foot-long overstuffed lobster roll ($13.95) is the summertime best-seller at **Hungry Dan's,** Rte. 27, Boothbay 04537, 207/633-3063, a deservedly popular spot across from Adams Pond, about 8.5 miles south of Rte. 1. Superb meatball or sausage subs, with tasty sauce, are also in demand; sandwiches are in the $2–5.50 range. Eat at one of the picnic tables or get it to go. No credit cards. It's open all year, Mon.–Fri. 6 AM–2 PM.

Breakfast and Beyond

Jump-start the day with a moon muffin ($2.95) or a breakfast burrito ($3.95) from the **Blue Moon Café,** 54 Commercial St.,

Boothbay Harbor 04538, 207/633-2349, or lunch on the harborview deck with homemade soups and salads, great sandwiches, and sinful pastries. If you're headed out for a picnic, the fixings are all here. "The Moon" is open daily Apr.–Oct. In-season (mid-June–Labor Day) hours are 7:30 AM–2:30 PM, off-season 8 AM–2 PM.

Another breakfast-and-beyond choice is **Andrews' Harborside Restaurant,** 12 Bridge St., Boothbay Harbor 04538, 207/633-4074, where chef Craig Andrews concentrates on hearty starter-uppers in the morning then turn out pasta, chowder, steak, and fish specialties (as well as Friday- and Saturday-night prime rib). Open daily 7:30–11 AM for breakfast, 11:30 AM–8:30 PM (to 9 PM Fri.–Sat.) for lunch and dinner, May–mid-Oct.

Moderate to Expensive

The Boat House Bistro, 12 The By-Way, Boothbay Harbor 04538, 207/633-7300, serves the same bistro-style, New American cuisine on all three floors, but reservations are requested for the more intimate first floor. Five kinds of fish daily-there's a raw bar, too—and homemade pasta with marinara or pesto sauce over a choice of seafood are entrée (range $13–29) highlights, but there's pizza and burgers, too. Open year-round, 11 AM–11 PM from May–Oct. Other months open daily for dinner from 4 PM, and lunch Sat. and Sun., at 11 AM.

Tearoom

The Boothbay region even has a Scottish tearoom. *Tea: A Magazine* gives a thumbs-up to **MacNab's Tea Room,** Back River Rd., P.O. Box 206, Boothbay 04537, 207/633-7222 or 800/884-7222, www.macnabstea.com, near the center of Boothbay (not the harbor). Tartans and terriers are the dominant motifs in this informal, folksy place, where Frances Browne inquires about your tea choice as soon as you settle in. Homemade soups, Highland pie, open-faced scone sandwiches, and typically Scottish sweets are all on the lunch menu. There's also a Tea Bar to sample international teas and get an education about them at the same time. Even if you can't get here, send for the entertaining mail-order catalog. Located 0.4 mile off Rte. 27, MacNab's is open Tues.–Sat. 10 AM–4 PM (to 5 PM in July– Aug.). Afternoon and high tea are available by reservation.

Lobster-in-the-Rough

Boothbay Harbor and East Boothbay seem to have more eat-on-the-dock lobster shacks per square inch than almost anywhere else on the coast. If you're a lobster fanatic, you've reached nirvana, heaven, ground zero, whatever. Two excellent choices are Robinson's Wharf and Lobsterman's Wharf. On the Southport Island side of the harbor, overlooking Townsend Gut next to the swing bridge, **Robinson's Wharf,** Rte. 27, Southport Island, 207/633-3830, mailing address P.O. Box 544, West Boothbay Harbor 04575, is a sprawling place with tons of indoor and outdoor seating. Lobster dinners, lobster stew, fried seafood, steamed clams, mussels—it's all here. Plus burgers, dogs, fries, pasta salad, even BLTs and grilled cheese sandwiches. Save room for homemade pie with Round Top ice cream. Beer and wine are available. The restaurant is open daily 11:30 AM–8:45 PM, mid-June–Labor Day, the store from 9 AM–5 PM daily.

Around the other side of the harbor, facing the Damariscotta River in East Boothbay, is the **Lobsterman's Wharf,** Rte. 96, East Boothbay 04544, 207/633-5481 or 633-3443. Everything from ties to T-shirts adorns the clientele, usually a mix of locals and flatlanders. The lobsters are great; so are the steaks and fries; dinner entrées are $14.95–28.95 (lazy lobster is $23.95). Nearly 200 seats inside and out. There's a unique bar—the former pilothouse of a locally built minesweeper. Midsummer hours are daily 11:30 AM–10 PM; in spring and fall, it closes at 9 PM and all day Mon. From the junction of Rtes. 27 and 96 in Boothbay Harbor, take Rte. 96 three miles to the wharf, on the left.

INFORMATION AND SERVICES

The **Boothbay Harbor Region Chamber of Commerce,** Rte. 27, P.O. Box 356, Boothbay Harbor 04538, 207/633-2353, www.boothbayharbor.com, maintains one seasonal and one year-round information center. The seasonal center (Memorial Day–Columbus Day) is on Rte. 1, across from the Cod Cove Inn, at the Rte. 27 junction. Seasonal hours on weekends are Sat. 10 AM–5 PM, Sun. 11 AM–4 PM. Daily operation begins in mid-June and continues through Columbus Day. It is open noon–6 PM Fri.–Sat. Memorial Day–June, and also from Columbus Day–Oct. Down Rte. 27, 10.8 miles from Rte. 1, is the chamber's main office, across from the Meadow Mall and just south of the Carousel Music Theatre. It's open Mon.–Fri. 8 AM–5 PM, all year. From Memorial Day to Columbus Day, the Chamber main office is also open weekends, Sat. 10 AM–5 PM, Sun. 10 AM–4 PM.

About eight miles south of Rte. 1, in between the two centers above, is the **Boothbay Information Center,** Rte. 27, Boothbay Center 04537, 207/633-4743. It's open daily throughout the summer, as well as from Labor Day to Columbus Day.

All three centers stock brochures for the entire peninsula; wherever you stop, be sure to request the handy annual *Boothbay Harbor walking map,* and the *Boothbay Harbor Region Guide,* published by the Boothbay Harbor Region Chamber of Commerce, covering the whole peninsula.

The handsome Greek Revival **Boothbay Harbor Memorial Library,** 4 Oak St., Boothbay Harbor 04538, 207/633-3112, www.bmpl.lib.me.us, holds Friday-morning (10 AM) story hours for kids, and the library's "used bookstore" is a magnet for everyone else; it's open seven days a week in July– Aug. "World Famous Porch Books" are available 24/7 for a dime in the door slot. Summer library hours are Tues.–Sat. 10 AM–4:30 PM (to 7 PM Wed.). Thursday evenings in July and August, there are band concerts on the lawn.

Mid-Coast Region

Newspapers

Best local news and feature coverage is provided by the **Boothbay Register,** 207/633-4620, www.boothbayregister.com, published every Thursday since 1876. The *Portland Press Herald,* published daily, includes the Boothbay region in its news and cultural sections.

Each summer, the *Boothbay Register* publishes a free tabloid, *Summertime,* filled with features, touring suggestions, ads, and calendar listings. It's available at all information centers as well as local shops, lodgings, and restaurants.

Emergencies

For fire, police, and ambulance services, dial 911 in Boothbay, Boothbay Harbor, Edgecomb, and Southport.

Round-the-clock emergency care is available at **St. Andrews Hospital and Healthcare Center,** 3 St. Andrews Lane, Boothbay Harbor 04538, 207/633-2121, which has great views over Mill Cove.

Public Restrooms

At the municipal parking lot on Commercial St. (next to Pier 1), and at the municipal lot on Howard St., are public restrooms. St. Andrews Hospital and the Marine Resources Aquarium also have restrooms. There are also restrooms located near the Footbridge, by Granary Way.

Getting Around

The Rocktide Inn operates a free trolley on continuous scheduled routes mid-June–Labor Day. Approaching Boothbay Harbor on Rte. 27, you can pick up a trolley-bus at the Flagship Inn or at the Harbor Village Shopping Plaza, across from the Boothbay Harbor Region Chamber of Commerce. The Rocktide trolley-bus makes special hourly trips (on the half-hour) to the Marine Resources Aquarium, alleviating the parking problem there. Check at any of the information centers to confirm the trolley schedule, usually mid-June–Labor Day, 10 AM–5 PM (aquarium runs are 10:30 AM–2:30 PM).

Special Courses

Watershed Center for the Ceramic Arts, 19 Brick Hill Rd., Newcastle 04553, 207/882-6075, www.watershedcenterceramicarts.org, is a nationally known summer residency/retreat for ceramic artists, from Maine, elsewhere in the United States, and abroad, providing them with time and space to create in clay. Watershed's Mudmobile is a traveling ceramics resource center that brings clay art education to diverse sites and populations throughout Maine. Though technically in Newcastle, turnoff for Watershed is just after the turnoff for Boothbay, on the opposite side of Rte. 1 (Cochran Rd.) right before the Citgo Gas Station.

Damariscotta/Newcastle

At the head of the Pemaquid Peninsula, the two riverfront towns of Damariscotta (pop. 2,100) and her Siamese twin, Newcastle (pop. 1,800), serve as the gateway to New Harbor (probably Maine's most photographed fishing village), Pemaquid Point (site of one of Maine's most photographed lighthouses), and historic ports reputedly used by Capt. John Smith, Capt. Kidd, and assorted less-notorious types. Here, too, are a restored fortress, Native American historic sites, craft shops galore, a thriving cultural center, boat excursions to off-shore Monhegan, and one of the best pocket-size sand beaches in Mid-Coast Maine.

On Christmas Day 1614, famed explorer Capt. John Smith anchored on Rutherford Island, at the tip of the peninsula, and promptly named the spot Christmas Cove. And thus it remains today. Christmas Cove is one of three villages belonging to the town of South Bristol, the southwestern finger of the Pemaquid Peninsula. South Bristol and Bristol (covering eight villages on the bottom half of the peninsula) were named after the British city.

As early as 1625, settler John Brown received title to some of this territory from the Abnaki sachem (chief) Samoset, an agreeable fellow who learned snippets of English from British codfishermen. Damariscotta (dam-uh-riss-COT-ta), in fact, is Abnaki for "plenty of alewives [herring]." The settlement here was named Walpole but was incorporated, in 1847, under its current name.

Newcastle, incorporated in 1763, earned fame and fortune from shipbuilding and brickmaking—which explains the extraordinary number of brick homes and office buildings throughout the town. In the 19th century, Newcastle's shipyards sent clippers, Downeasters, and full-rigged ships down the ways and around the world.

SIGHTS

Pemaquid Light and Fishermen's Museum

There's something irresistible about lighthouses, and the setting here makes it even more so.

Commissioned in 1827, **Pemaquid Light**—the lighthouse pictured on the Maine state quarter—stands sentinel over some of Maine's nastiest shoreline—rocks and surf that can reduce any wooden boat to kindling. Now automated, the light tower, 207/677-3266, is open to the public from Memorial Day to Columbus Day, Sat.–Sun. 10 AM–5 PM, and Mon.–Fri. 11 AM–5 PM, depending on volunteer availability. The tower is managed and staffed by an all-volunteer group called the Friends of Pemaquid Point Lighthouse (FPPL), a division of the American Lighthouse Foundation (ALF). Volunteers give a history of the tower to visitors before they ascend (five people at a time). The charge paid at the gate—$2 for adults—is for admission to Lighthouse Park, owned by the town of Bristol. Admission to the tower is free, but maintenance and operation depend totally on donations. The adjacent Fishermen's Museum, in the former lightkeeper's house, 207/677-2494, points up the pleasures and perils of the lobstering industry. Admission to the museum is also free, and it is open daily, Memorial Day weekend–mid-Oct. Bring a picnic and lounge on the rocks below the light tower, but don't plan to snooze. You'll be busy protecting your food from the dive-bombing gulls and your kids from the treacherous surf. The lighthouse grounds are accessible all year, even after the museum and tower close for the season, when admission is free. The point is 15 miles south of Rte. 1, via winding, two-lane Rte. 130.

Colonial Pemaquid and Fort William Henry

Four national flags fly over the ramparts of Fort William Henry, a replica of a fort dating from 1692. From the tower, you'll have fantastic views of John's Bay and John's Island, named for none other than Capt. John Smith; inside are artifacts retrieved from archaeological excavations of the 17th-century trading outpost. Also part of this eight-acre Colonial Pemaquid complex, end of Huddle Rd.,

207/677-2423, are a 1695 burying ground and the small **Colonial Pemaquid Museum,** 207/677-2423, displaying European and Native American archaeological discoveries. Admission is $2 adults, free for children. The museum and fort are open daily, Memorial Day weekend to Labor Day. The surrounding park, sloping down to John's Bay, is a great picnic spot, accessible all year. (During blackfly season, a reliable sea breeze keeps the insects away.) Colonial Pemaquid is 14 miles south of Rte. 1 and one mile west of Rte. 130.

Chapman-Hall House

Damariscotta's oldest surviving building is the Cape-style Chapman-Hall House, Main St., no telephone, built in 1754 by Nathaniel Chapman, whose family tree includes the legendary John Chapman, aka Johnny Appleseed. Highlights are a 1754 kitchen and displays of local shipbuilding memorabilia. The National Historic Register house, meticulously restored by the Chapman-Hall House Preservation Society in the styles of three different eras, has 18th Century roses in the back garden. Tours available in summer for a minimal admission charge.

Historic Houses of Worship

One of the oldest houses of worship in Maine that still holds services, **The Old Walpole Meeting House,** Rte. 129, Bristol Rd., Walpole, 207/563-5554, built in 1772, remains remarkably unchanged, with the original box pews, hand-shaved shingles and handmade nails and hinges. The balcony—where indentured servants once were relegated—is paneled with boards more than two feet wide. A nondenominational service is held Sunday afternoons in August (call for dates and times), but better still is the annual candlelight concert, a dramatic occasion in this building with no electricity and splendid acoustics. It's at 7 PM the Sunday after Labor Day; tickets are $18, call for reservations. It's always a sell-out, but the acoustics are so good that attendees outside can hear every note. The meeting house is 3.5 miles south of Damar-

iscotta and 0.25 mile south of where Rtes. 129 and 130 fork.

The **Harrington Meeting House,** Old Harrington Rd., off Rte. 130, begun in 1772 and completed in 1775, now serves as Bristol's local-history museum—town-owned and run by the Pemaquid Historical Association. The museum is open Mon., Wed., Fri., and Sat. 2–4:30 PM, July– Aug. No admission fee, but donations are welcome. An annual nondenominational service, with guest speaker, occurs the third Sunday in August.

Built in 1808, **St. Patrick's Catholic Church,** Academy Hill Rd., Damariscotta Mills, Newcastle 04553, 207/563-3240, a solid brick structure with 1.5-foot-thick walls and a Paul Revere bell, is New England's oldest surviving Catholic church, and the first in the United States north of Boston. Open daily 9 AM to sundown. Academy Hill Rd. starts at Newcastle Square, downtown Newcastle; the church is 2.25 miles from there, and one mile beyond Lincoln Academy.

St. Andrew's Episcopal Church, Glidden St., Newcastle 04553, 207/563-3533, built in 1883, is nothing short of exquisite, with carved-oak beams, stenciled ceiling, and, for the cognoscenti, a spectacular Hutchings organ.

Darling Marine Research Center

Not far beyond the Old Walpole Meeting House is the turnoff to the Ira C. Darling Marine Center, 193 Clark's Cove Rd., off Rte. 129, Walpole 04573, 207/563-3146, part of the University of Maine System. Generally known as the Darling Center, it's the state-of-the-art laboratory for the university's marine biology and oceanography students. Mid-July–late Aug., the Gulf of Maine Foundation (a local nonprofit organization) sponsors several summer programs at the Center including a summer seminar series and campus tours during July–Aug. Call extension 252 for program information. From downtown Damariscotta, take Rte. 130 three miles to Rte. 129. Continue three miles on Rte. 129 to Clark's Cove Rd.; turn right and go about one mile to the campus.

Return of the Alewives

If you're in the Damariscotta area in May and early June, don't miss a chance to go to Damariscotta Mills to see the annual Alewife Run. More than 250,000 alewives (*Alosa pseudoharengus,* a kind of herring) make their way during this time from Great Salt Bay to their spawning grounds in freshwater Damariscotta Lake, 42 feet higher. Waiting eagerly at the top are ospreys, gulls, cormorants, and sometimes eagles, ready to feast on the weary fish. Connecting the bay and the lake is a manmade stone-and-masonry "fish ladder," a zigzagging channel where you can watch the foot-long fish wriggle their way onward and upward. The ladder was built in 1807 and restored in the 1990s. A walkway runs alongside the route, and informative display panels explain the event. It's a fascinating historical ecology lesson. To reach the fishway, take Rte. 215 for 1.5 miles west of Rte. 1. When you reach a small bridge, cross it and take a sharp left down a slight incline to a small parking area. Walk behind the barn to follow the path to the fish ladder. Try to go on a sunny day—the fish are more active and their silvery sides glisten as they go. To volunteer time, energy, or money to the alewives restoration effort, contact the Damariscotta River Asociation, 207/563-1393, or the Damariscotta Lake Watershed Association, 207/549-3836.

The Iceman Cometh

On a late-January or February Sunday morning (weather and ice permitting), several hundred helpers and onlookers gather at Thompson Pond, next to **The Thompson Ice House,** Rte. 129, South Bristol 04568, 207/644-8551 or 644-8120, for the annual ice harvest. Festivity prevails as a crew of robust fellows marks out a grid and saws out 12-inch-thick ice cakes, which are pushed up a ramp to the ice-storage house. More than 60 tons of ice are harvested

Mid-Coast Region

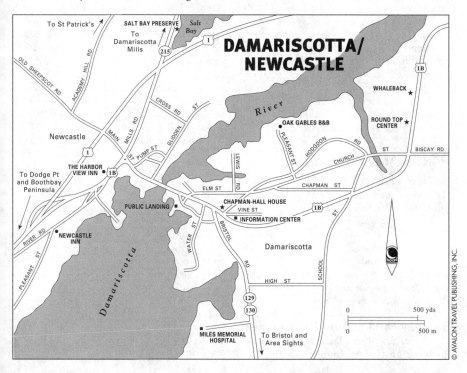

each year. Sawdust-insulated 10-inch-thick walls keep the ice from melting in this National Historic Register building first used in 1826. In 1990, the house became part of a working museum. The grounds are accessible free all year, including a photographic display board depicting a 1964 harvest. The museum (with ice tools and a window view of the stored ice cakes) is open Wed., Fri., and Sat. 1–4 PM, July–Aug. Suggested donation is $1 adults, $0.50 kids. The site is on Rte. 129, 12 miles south of Damariscotta. Roadside parking is allowed. On the Sunday of Fourth of July weekend, there's an ice-cream social 1–4 PM; the ice cream is made using Ice House ice.

The Gut

At the foot of a hill on Rte. 129 is the tiny community of **South Bristol,** the heart of the town that stretches along the western edge of the Pemaquid Peninsula. In the village center is a green-painted swing bridge (swinging sideways) spanning a narrow waterway quaintly named the Gut. Separating the mainland from Rutherford Island, The Gut is a busy thoroughfare for local lobsterboat traffic, so the bridge opens and closes (a 10-minute procedure) often. No one is in much of a hurry in this sleepy hamlet, so the frequent stoppages never seem to bother anyone, and the scenery is worth it all. So be patient.

PARKS AND PRESERVES

Residents of the Pemaquid Peninsula are incredibly fortunate to have several foresighted local conservation organizations, each with its own niche and mission: Damariscotta River Association, Pemaquid Watershed Association, and Damariscotta Lake Watershed Association. In addition, The Nature Conservancy, Maine Audubon Society, and National Audubon Society all have holdings on the peninsula, a natural-resource bonanza.

Salt Bay Farm and Heritage Center

Headquarters of the **Damariscotta River Association** (DRA), founded in 1973, is a late-18th-century farmhouse on 110-acre DRA Salt Bay Farm and Heritage Center, 110 Belvedere Rd., P.O. Box 333, Damariscotta 04543, 207/563-1393, www.draclt .org. Here you can pick up maps, brochures, and other info on the over 2,000 acres of land protected and managed by the DRA—notably the Dodge Point Preserve, Menigawum (Stratton Island) Preserve, and the Salt Bay Preserve. Salt Bay Farm's fields, saltmarsh, and shore frontage are open to the public daily, year-round, from sunrise to sunset; the office is open weekdays, usually 8 AM–5 PM. No camping or fires. To reach the farm from downtown Newcastle, take Mills Rd. (Rte. 215) to Rte. 1. Turn right (north) and go 1.4 miles to the blinking light (Belvedere Rd.). Turn left and go 0.4 mile; park in the grassy area on the right.

Salt Bay Preserve Heritage Trail

Across Salt Bay from the DRA Salt Bay Farm is the trailhead for the Salt Bay Preserve Heritage Trail, a relatively easy three-mile loop around Newcastle's Glidden Point that touches on a variety of habitat and also includes several areas of major historical interest going back 2,500 years. Part of the trail is protected by the feds; do *not* disturb or remove anything. Better still, carry a litterbag and help maintain the path.

This is a super family hike, and leashed dogs are allowed. Along the trail, watch for eagles, osprey, herons, several stands of rare white oaks, and open views of Great Salt Bay. Best time to come is close to low tide, as some parts of the trail require slight detours at high tide—especially during the new or full moon. In any case, rubberized shoes or boots are a good idea. To reach the preserve from Newcastle Square, take Mills Rd. (Rte. 215) about two miles to the offices of the *Lincoln County News* (just after the post office). Go inside and request permission to park in their lot (park to the right, as far away from the buildings as possible). Walk across Rte. 215 to the trailhead, and pick up a brochure/map.

Dodge Point Preserve

In 1989, the state of Maine acquired the 506-acre Dodge Point Preserve—one of the stars in its crown—as part of a $35 million bond issue. The Damariscotta River Association (DRA), which initiated its protection, helps manage and maintain the property. To sample what the Dodge Point Preserve has to offer, pick up a map at the entrance and follow the Old Farm Rd. counterclockwise to an interpretive section, then hook into the Shore Trail, heading clockwise. Consider stopping for a riverside picnic and swim at Sand or Pebble Beach before continuing back to the parking lot. Hunting is permitted in the preserve, so November isn't the best time for hiking here (unless you hike on Sunday, when hunting is banned). Winter brings out ice-skaters and cross-country skiers. The Dodge Point parking area is on River Rd., 2.6 miles southwest of Rte. 1 and 3.5 miles southwest of downtown Newcastle. Open all year for day use only, closing at sunset. Admission is free. For more information, contact the Maine Bureau of Parks and Lands, 207/287-3821.

Menigawum Preserve (Stratton Island)

Owned by the Damariscotta River Association (DRA), 30-acre Stratton Island is also known locally as Hodgdon's Island. Unless you're a DRA member, you'll need your own small boat, canoe, or kayak to get here—it's at the entrance to Seal Cove on the west side of the South Bristol peninsula. If you are a DRA member—a worthwhile $25—you can use an Association canoe at the nearby Plummer Point Preserve. Closest public boat launch is at the Gut, about four miles downriver—a trip better done *with* (in the same direction as) the tide. Best place to land is in the northeast corner—also a great spot for shelling. Pick up a map in the small box at the north end of the island and follow the perimeter trail. At the northern end, you'll see eagle nests (stay at least 100 yards away from the nests); at the southern tip are Native American shell middens—discards from hundreds of years of marathon summer

lunches. (Do *not* disturb or remove anything.) You can picnic in the pasture, but camping and fires are not allowed. Stay clear of the abandoned homesite on the island's west side. The preserve is accessible from sunrise to sunset.

Witch Island Preserve

Named for a 19th-century local woman dubbed "The Witch of Wall Street" for her financial wizardry, Witch Island Preserve is owned by the Maine Audubon Society. The wooded, 18-acre island has two beaches, a perimeter trail, and the ruins of the "witch's" house. Located a quarter of mile offshore, it's accessible by canoe or kayak from the South Bristol town landing, just to the right after the swing bridge over The Gut. Put in, paddle under the swing bridge, and go north to the island. For more information, contact Maine Audubon Society, 20 Gilsland Farm Rd., Falmouth 04105, 207/781-2330.

Rachel Carson Salt Pond

If you've never spent time studying the variety of sea life in a tidal pool, the Rachel Carson Salt Pond is a great place to start. Named after the famed author of *Silent Spring* and *The Edge of the Sea,* who summered in this part of Maine, the salt pond was a favorite haunt of hers. The whole point of visiting a tidal pool is to see what the tide leaves behind, so check the tide calendar (in local newspapers, or ask at your lodging) and head out a few hours after high tide. Wear rubber boots and beware of slippery rocks and rockweed. Among the many creatures you'll see in this quarter-acre pond are mussels, green crabs, periwinkles, and starfish. Owned by The Nature Conservancy, the salt pond is on Rte. 32 in the village of **Chamberlain,** about a mile north of New Harbor. Parking is limited. Across the road is a trail into a 78-acre inland section of the preserve, most of it wooded. Brochures are available in the registration box. For additional information about the preserve, accessible from sunrise to sunset year-round, contact The Nature Conservancy, Maine Chapter, 14 Maine St., Fort Andross, Brunswick 04011, 207/729-5181.

Todd Wildlife Sanctuary

The mainland section of a 345-acre Audubon Society property, the Todd Wildlife Sanctuary, 11 Audubon Rd., Bremen 04551, includes a visitors center and gift shop (open daily 10 AM–4 PM, June–Aug., 207/529-5148), and the **Hockomock Nature Trail,** winding through the woods and down to the shore (open year-round). Pick up a trail guide at the center and follow the informative signs. Allow about an hour. Don't forget a picnic so you can have lunch on the beach. Just offshore is 333-acre **Hog Island,** site of the summertime **Audubon Ecology Camp** for youth and adults. If you have your own boat, you can walk the island's beautiful perimeter trail (no camping). However, the nearest public boat launch is in Round Pond, about 15 minutes south, may be crowded in summer, and charges a small fee. Allow about three hours for the hike. Just check in beforehand at the office near the dock at the north end of the island.

RECREATION

For the kids, there's a great creative playground—the **Lonna Bunting Playground,** built by local volunteers—on Business Rte. 1 next to the **Central Lincoln County YMCA,** 207/563-3477, www.clcymca.com, which has day-guest prices for short-term access to facilities.

Golf

The nine-hole **Wawenock Country Club,** Rte. 129, Walpole, 207/563-3938, established in the 1920s, is a challenging and very popular public course about midway down the Pemaquid Peninsula from Damariscotta. The par-three eighth hole features a treacherous bunker named Big Bertha. Starting times are required on summer weekends.

Bicycling

As with so many other parts of Maine, bike lanes on the Pemaquid Peninsula are poor to nonexistent, so exercise the utmost caution. Roads are narrow, winding, and poorly shouldered.

Swimming

Best bet (but also most crowded) on the peninsula for saltwater swimming is town-owned **Pemaquid Beach Park,** 207/677-2754, a lovely, tree-lined sandy crescent. No lifeguard, but there are showers (cold water) and bathrooms, and the snack bar serves decent food. No alcohol is allowed on the beach. There is an admission fee for anyone over 12 years old., and the beach closes at about 5 or 6 PM, depending on the weather. The beach is just off Snowball Hill Rd., west of Rte. 130.

A much smaller beach is the pocket-size sandy area in Christmas Cove, on Rutherford Island. Take Rte. 129 around the cove and turn to the right, then right again down the hill.

One of the area's most popular freshwater swimming holes is **Biscay Pond,** a long, skinny body of water in the peninsula's center. From Business Rte. 1 at the northern edge of Damariscotta, take Biscay Rd. (turn at McDonald's) three miles to the pond (on the right, heading east). On hot days, this area sees plenty of cars; pull off the road as far as possible.

Farther down the peninsula, on Rte. 130 in **Bristol Mills,** is another roadside swimming hole, between the dam and the bridge.

GETTING AFLOAT

Boat Excursions

At 9 AM each day mid-May–mid-Oct., the 60-foot powerboat *Hardy III* departs for **Monhegan,** a Brigadoon-like island a dozen miles offshore, where passengers can spend the day hiking the woods, picnicking on the rocks, birding, and inhaling the salt air. At 3:15 PM, everyone re-boards, arriving in New Harbor just over an hour later. The boat has toilets and a snack bar. Dress warmly and wear rubber-soled shoes. Cost is $28 adults, $16 children under 12. Reservations are strongly recommended, and they're held until 20 minutes before departure. Trips operate rain or shine, but heavy seas can affect the schedule.

Go light on breakfast before boarding. From mid-June through the beginning of October, and Sat.–Mon. of Memorial and Columbus Day weekends, there's also a second Monhegan trip—used primarily for overnighters—departing New Harbor at 2 PM daily. The *Hardy III* also operates 1.5-hour puffin watches (Wed. and Sat.–Sun. mid-May–mid-June; daily, mid-June–Aug., 5:30 PM; $20 adults, $12 children), special Monhegan puffin watches, one-hour seal-watching tours (daily, late June–Labor Day, noon, $10 adults, $8 children, then Sat.–Sun. through Sept.), and one-hour lighthouse cruises (Tues.–Sat., late June–Aug., 7:30 PM, $12 adults, $8 children). Fall Coastal Cruises begin in early Sept., are 1.5 hours, beginning at 4:45 PM, and cost $15 adults, $10 children. **Hardy Boat Cruises** is 19 miles south of Rte. 1, based at Shaw's Fish and Lobster Wharf, Rte. 32, New Harbor 04554, 207/677-2026 or 800/278-3346, www.hardyboat.com. Parking is $2 per day.

Sea Kayaking

The Pemaquid Peninsula's only sea-kayaking operation is **Sea Spirit Adventures,** 1140 Rte. 32, Round Pond 04564, (mailing address: 56 Greenland Cove Rd, Bremen, Maine 04551), 207/529-4732, www.seaspiritadventures.com, about 13 miles seaward from Rte. 1. A half-day kayak tour is $75 pp, including an island stop and a gourmet lunch. Other tours include a three-hour introduction to kayaking, with two hours on Muscongus Bay or the Damariscotta River, for $35. Beginners age five and up are welcome, and tours include all gear and instruction. Group and private lessons are available. Rentals and sales of kayaks and gear are also available. There is a demonstration center at Schooner Landing in Damariscotta, 207/563-5732.

Canoeing

Experienced canoeists may want to take the **Damariscotta-Pemaquid River Canoe Trail,** a 40-mile clockwise loop that begins in Damariscotta and follows some of the region's traditional Indian canoe routes. Although few portages are required, one, fairly close to the beginning, is about a mile long over private land. For a route map, contact Mike Krepner at **Native Trails,** P.O. Box 240, Waldoboro 04572, 207/832-5255.

If you have your own canoe, or just want to paddle the three-mile length of **Biscay Pond,** you can park at the beach area and put in there. Another good launching site is right next to Rte. 1 in **Nobleboro,** at the head of eight-mile-long **Lake Pemaquid.**

ENTERTAINMENT

The hub of culture on the Pemaquid Peninsula is the **Round Top Center for the Arts,** 3 Round Top La. (off Business Rte. 1), P.O. Box 1316, Damariscotta 04543, 207/563-1507, www.roundtoparts.org. This energetic association, staffed largely by volunteers, seems to have no limits. Classes, concerts, workshops, and exhibits go on throughout the year; call, check local papers, or see website for the schedule. Once a 19th century dairy farm, the grounds are picnic-friendly, and you can walk down to the river.

First-run films are shown at the **Lincoln Theater,** Main St., Damariscotta 04543, 207/563-3424, www.lcct.org, at 7 PM Fri., Sat. Sun., and Wed. Admission is $6 adults, $4 children under 12.

FESTIVALS AND EVENTS

In early July, the Miles Memorial Hospital League sponsors a **House and Gardens Tour.** The second weekend in August, **Olde Bristol Days** features a crafts show, a parade, road and boat races, live entertainment, and fireworks. At Fort William Henry, in Pemaquid, it's a summer highlight on the peninsula.

SHOPPING

Since many of the shops listed below are downtown, a parking advisory is in order. Downtown parking in summer is a major headache; the municipal lot, behind the storefronts, has

Mid-Coast Region

a three-hour limit, and it's almost always full. (On weekends, head just up the hill to the Bath Savings Institution, on Church St., opposite Bristol Rd.; the bank is closed after noon on Saturday, and all day Sunday, so there's ample space in its parking lot, plus Church St. itself often has open spaces. The bank advises that it is not responsible for theft, damages, or injuries to anyone using its lot.)

Antiquarian Books

Based in a screen-fronted antique carriage house just south of Round Pond village, **Jean Gillespie Books,** 1172 Rte. 32, Round Pond 04564, 207/529-5555, has separate rooms and alcoves, all very user-friendly. Specialties are cookbooks, nautical and Maine titles, and illustrated children's books; the "Royalty" category fills six shelves. Open daily noon–5 PM, July–Aug.; other months, open by appointment or chance.

Art Galleries

Worth a visit for the building alone, the **Stable Gallery,** 26 Water St., P.O. Box 1060, just off Main St., Damariscotta 04543, 207/563-1991, was built in the 19th-century clipper-ship era and still has original black-walnut stalls—providing a great foil for the work of dozens of Maine artists and craftsmen. Director Jackson Ferry displays paintings, prints, and crafts from the gallery's large "stable" of artists. Open June–Oct., Mon.–Sat. 10 AM–5 PM.

In his **River Gallery,** 79 Main St., P.O. Box 805, Damariscotta 04543, 207/563-6330, www.rivergalleryfineart.com, dealer Geoff Robinson specializes in 19th- and early-20th-century European and American fine art—a connoisseur's inventory. Open Mon.–Sat. 10 AM–3 PM; call ahead off-season.

Showing a high profile ever since it opened, **The Firehouse Gallery,** One Bristol Rd., P.O. Box 1478, Damariscotta 04543, 207/563-7299, www.thefirehousegallery.com, has a tasteful, well-displayed selection of paintings, sculpture, ceramics, and jewelry. Penn and Helen Frost Way spent a year renovating the two-story antique fire station, and their efforts

are evident. The gallery mounts half a dozen shows during its season (May–Dec.); it's open by appointment Jan.–Apr. as well as Tues.–Sat. 10 AM–5 PM May–June. Hours in season are 10 AM–5 PM Mon.–Sat., 11 AM–4 PM Sun.

Books, Gifts, Crafts, and Clothing

The Pemaquid Peninsula is fertile ground for crafts and gifts, and many of the shop locations provide opportunities for exploring off the beaten path.

One of the state's best independent bookstores is in downtown Damariscotta. The inventory at the **Maine Coast Book Shop and Café,** 158 Main St., P.O. Box 309, Damariscotta 04543, 207/563-3207, café 207/563-3370, always seems to anticipate customers' wishes, so you're unlikely to walk out empty-handed. Superb children's section; large magazine selection; helpful staff.

Even non-knitters enjoy **Pine Tree Yarns,** Main St., P.O. Box 506, Damariscotta 04543, 207/563-8909, www.pinetreeyarns.com, located in the 1832 Nathaniel Austin House—with all the beautiful colors around, it's a gallery experience. Expert owner, Elaine Eskesen, author of *Dyeing to Knit,* has been hand-dyeing and painting yarn for two decades, and her artistry makes it hard to resist stocking up for the next couple years' worth of projects. Classes and knitting cruises are also available. The dye studio is on-premises, so knitters can match or dye their own yarns. You can revel in your purchases or figure out your next move in the store's sunny courtyard amidst blueberries, raspberries, roses, and a peach tree.

If you'd rather purchase beautiful things than make them, facing the courtyard is **Salt Bay Trading Co.** Main St., P.O. Box 972, Damariscotta 04543, 207/563-6611, filled with Turkish, Afghan, Tibetan, and Central Asian carpets and kilims (all for sale—and at reasonable prices). Open all year, Mon.–Fri. 9 AM–5 PM, Sat. 9 AM–4 PM.

Two Fish Boutique, 133 Main St., Damariscotta, 207/563-2220, offers clothing, gifts, and home accessories. Open Mon.–Sat. 10 AM–5 PM.

Known for its whimsy, and with an intriguingly similar name, is **Tin Fish Etc.,** Elm St., Box 1254, Damariscotta 04543, 207/563-8204, fax 633-2723. Located above Weatherbird (see below), Dana Moses's shop features brilliantly handpainted tin *objets* made from recycled roofing metal. She also accepts commissions. The shop is open Mon.–Sat. 9:30 AM–5 PM mid-May–mid-Dec.; off-season, Dana revs up her creative juices in the Caribbean.

Just off Main St. (turn at Reny's), is **Weatherbird,** 72 Courtyard St., P.O. Box 1168, Damariscotta, 207/563-8993, a terrifically eclectic shop with an inventory that defies description. Housewares, wines, toys, cards, gourmet specialties, and intriguing women's clothing are all part of the mix. Weatherbird is open Mon.–Sat. 8:30 AM–5:30 PM, year-round.

Brambles, Inc., Main St., P.O. Box 1089, Damariscotta 04543, 207/563-2800, has six rooms filled with wonderful wares. Unusual birdhouses, whimsical garden ornaments, wind chimes, great garden tools, plus books and cards, make all those upscale home-and-garden catalogs come to life. Open daily, all year.

The **Round Top Center for the Arts,** 3 Round Top Ln. (off Business Rte. 1), P.O. Box 1316, Damariscotta 04543, 207/563-1507, www.roundtoparts.org, in addition to putting on all kinds of cultural activities, has a gift shop with especially unusual arts and crafts—distinguished local artists display and sell their wares here. It's open all year, Mon.–Fri. 10 AM–4 PM, Sat. 9 AM–1 PM.

Down the peninsula, there's no question that the **Granite Hall Store,** 9 Backshore Rd., just off Rte. 32, Round Pond 04564, 207/529-5864, is unique. Eric and Sarah Herndon's eclectic inventory is tough to describe. The first floor of this mid-19th-century emporium carries pottery, CDs, paper dolls, fudge, baskets, even catnip mice and cookie cutters. The "penny" candy, grab bags, and the old-fashioned peanut-roasting machine capture the kids. Upstairs, their parents usually succumb to books, toiletries, T-shirts, house and kitchen wares, or British Isles sweaters and hats. Adding to the flavor are old ship models, hardwood

floors, and a ship's bell that tolls the time. Kids and parents will both be interested in the Giffords ice-cream stand. Open daily 10 AM–8:30 PM, May–Labor Day; 10 AM–5 PM Labor Day–Christmas Eve; closed Mon. in May and Nov. The shop is in "downtown" Round Pond, 11 miles south of Rte. 1.

Also in Round Pond, on Rte. 32, is the **Scottish Lion Blacksmith,** 1486 SR 32, Round Pond 04564, 207/529-5523, www.scottish-wroughtiron.com, where skilled smith Andrew Leck turns out all kinds of attractive wrought-iron accessories: wall brackets, fireplace tools, and more. His wife, Phyllis, the "Village Weaver," makes hand-loomed fabric, and textiles for the home. Open all year, 9 AM–5 PM Mon.–Fri., 10 AM–5 PM Sat., and 1–5 PM Sun.

Natural Foods and Farmers Markets

Rising Tide Natural Foods Market, Business Rte. 1, 15 Coastal Market Place, Damariscotta 04543, 207/563-5556, has been a thriving co-op organization since 1978, and it keeps on growing. Bulk items are available, plus books, cosmetics, and all kinds of preservative-free organic food. A self-service deli section has soups, sandwiches, salads, and entrées; you may be lucky enough to snag one of the four tables in the dining area. Located at the northern end of town, the market is open all year, Mon.–Sun. 8 AM–7 PM.

Mid-May–Oct., 9 AM–noon Fri., the **Damariscotta Farmers Market** sets up at the Assembly of God Church parking lot on the corner of Business Rte. 1 and the Belvedere Rd., Damariscotta. Late June–Aug., the market is also held the same hours on Mondays. You can find baked goods, pies, breads, vegetables, cheeses, mushrooms, chicken, fresh eggs, jams and jellies, flowers, seedlings, and more.

ACCOMMODATIONS
Inns with Restaurants

Within easy walking distance of Pemaquid Light and 16 miles south of Rte. 1, **The Bradley Inn,** 3063 Bristol Rd., Rte. 130, Pemaquid

Mid-Coast Region

Point, New Harbor 04554, 207/677-2105 or 800/942-5560, www.bradleyinn.com, is a well-maintained, century-old building with 15 guest rooms (private baths and phones), a cottage, and lovely gardens—a great location for a quiet weekend getaway. The inn's restaurant, overlooking the gardens and open to the public, has an ambitious, mostly seafood menu (entrées $20–30). Check out the granite bar in the adjoining pub. Rooms (with full breakfast and afternoon tea) are $135–235 d mid-May–Oct., $105–160 d other months. No smoking; no pets. The inn is closed Jan.–Mar.

On Rutherford Island, just off the end of the South Bristol peninsula, **Coveside Inn & Marina,** Christmas Cove, South Bristol 04568, 207/644-8282, http://lincoln.midcoast.com/ ~coveside, has been in the Mitchell family since 1969. The red-clapboard main building, built in the 1880s, is a Victorian inn. Across the lawn is the motel-style Shorefront building, with skylights, private decks, and unbeatable views of the cove. Coveside caters to yachtsmen, providing guest moorings, dock space, and fuel; the pennant-draped Dory Bar and the 84-seat restaurant attract a steady stream of boaters and summer vacationers during the cruising season. Shorefront is open late May–early Oct.; rooms are $95–110 d, depending on the season. The restaurant is open mid-June–Sept.

Along a scenic road is **The Newcastle Inn,** River Rd., Newcastle 04553, 207/563-5685 or 800/832-8669, www.newcastleinn.com, with its award-winning restaurant, **Lupines.** The inn has a variety of accommodations-main inn, cottage, and carriage house-summer rates (late May–Oct.) are $155–295, winter rates (Nov. 1–late May) are lower.

Inns without Restaurants

Almost on top of Pemaquid Light is the rambling **Hotel Pemaquid,** Rte. 130, 3098 Bristol Rd., New Harbor 04554, 207/677-2312, www .hotelpemaquid.com. Fourteen miles south of Rte. 1 but just 450 feet from the lighthouse, the hotel has been welcoming guests since 1888; it's fun to peruse the old guest registers. Hang out in the large, comfortable parlor or the wrap-around veranda. The inn building has seven rooms (four share two baths) costing $70–85 d. in Aug., less other months, and four suites ($145 d. in Aug.). Other buildings have five smaller motel-style units with private baths ($85–90 d. in Aug.) and eight larger Bungalow rooms ($107 d. in Aug.). Some kitchen facilities. For the Victorian flavor of the place, request an inn room or suite. No smoking, no pets, no credit cards, no small children in the inn building. There's no restaurant, but the Bradley Inn and the Sea Gull Shop are nearby. Open mid-May–Oct.

Up the eastern side of the peninsula, in the middle of New Harbor, **The Gosnold Arms,** 146 Rte. 32, New Harbor 04554, 207/677-3727, off-season 561/575-9549, www.gosnold .com, has been here since 1925 and remains deliberately old-fashioned, with pine-paneled rooms and a country-cottage common room. Customers return year after year. The family-owned operation includes the inn building and a wide variety of other buildings, so there's choice in layout, location, and decor. Many of the inn rooms (private baths) include water views, but the loudspeaker at the lobster wharf across the street (Shaw's) can preclude an afternoon nap in front rooms. Cottage units are $99–230 d. Inn rooms are $99–120 d, including breakfast, July 1–Labor Day, lower off-season. No pets. Open mid-May–mid-Oct.

Bed-and-Breakfasts

Commemorating the legendary, mid-19th-century globe-circling clipper ship, **The Flying Cloud Bed-and-Breakfast,** River Rd., P.O. Box 549, Newcastle 04553, 207/563-2484, www.theflyingcloud.com, is an exquisitely restored home with five gracious guest rooms, four of which offer harbor and Damariscotta river views. All rooms have private baths. Innkeepers Karen and Dave Bragg have added special touches like laptop Internet connections and puffin packages. A full gourmet breakfast is served—the inn has two recipes in the latest *New England Bed and Breakfast Cookbook*. Rates are $100–190 d; lower rates off-season. No smoking, no pets, no small children. Open all year.

You have an unusual option at Richard and Cheryl Munson's **The Unique Yankee Bed-and-Breakfast,** 53 Coveside Rd., South Bristol 04568, 866/644-1502, www.uniqueyankeeof-maine.com. You can sleep ashore at the B&B's four rooms, or stay a week and upgrade to an overnight stay on the yacht *Timeless* (all guests have the option of scheduling day cruises). Inn rooms are $130 d May 1–Oct. 31, 20 percent less Nov. 1–Mar. 31 (includes buffet breakfast). Children and pets welcome in the private entrance room, but prior notice is required (there are two "Golden Girls," retrievers, on the premises). Room amenities include media center, two-person tub, and fireplaces, and the inn has an ocean observatory, with great hilltop views of Christmas Cove.

Run by the friendly Sue and Bill Morton, **The Inn at Round Pond,** 1442 State Rte. 32, Round Pond 04564, 207/529-2004, www.the-innatroundpond.com, is an especially welcoming B&B in a minuscule Pemaquid Peninsula village gaining fame for its unique parade. Three suites are $140–170 d Memorial Day weekend to Columbus Day weekend (two-night weekend minimum during this high season). Off-season rates are $95–125 d., and there are winter specials Jan.–Feb. Amenities include a full hot breakfast, "served in style," original artwork, gardens to stroll through, and breakfast on the porch in summer. The inn is just across the road from the water, and there's lots to do within walking distance, including visiting art galleries and studios, antique shops, and neighborhood church concerts. Eleven miles south of Rte. 1, and just five miles from the Monhegan boat. Open all year.

A lovely water-view living room with piano and harp sets the tone for **The Harbor View Inn,** Business Rte. 1, P.O. Box 791, Newcastle 04553, 207/563-2900, www.theharborview .com. Joe McEntee's family antiques fill the three beautifully decorated first- and second-floor suites ($135–195 d—$20 less for single occupancy—July–Oct., less Nov.–June). All rooms have phones, cable TV, comfortable

chairs; two have fireplaces and private decks Breakfast is an extravaganza reflecting one of Joe's former careers as an executive chef (he was also a publishing executive). No smoking, no pets. Open all year.

Joe Hovance, innkeeper at the historic **Brannon-Bunker Inn,** Rte. 129, Walpole 04573, 207/563-5941 or 800/563-9225, is an avid collector/dealer in political and military memorabilia, and the inn's upper halls are a virtual gallery of World War I posters, medals, and photos. Lots of character and informality here; Jeanne Hovance makes the breakfast muffins. Five rooms with homemade quilts and stenciling on the walls (private and shared baths; $80–90 d) and a three-room suite ($100–160 d, depending on the crowd). No smoking, no pets. Kids are welcome, and the well-equipped kitchen even has a lobster pot for guests' eat-in convenience. Open Apr.–Nov.

Martha Scudder provides a warm welcome for her guests at **Oak Gables Bed-and-Breakfast,** 36 Pleasant St., P.O. Box 276, Damariscotta 04543, 207/563-1476 or 800/335-7748, www.oakgablesbb.com. At the end of a pretty lane, this 11-acre hilltop estate overlooks the Damariscotta River. Despite a rather imposing setting, everything's homey, informal, and hospitable. Four second-floor rooms ($95 d) share a bath; a guest wing ($150 d) has a private bath and separate entrance. The heated swimming pool is a huge plus, and guests can harvest blackberries from scads of bushes. Also on the grounds are a three-bedroom cottage ($1200 a week) and two attractive riverfront apartments ($875 and $980 a week, off-season rented by assorted time periods), usually booked up well ahead. No pets, no smoking. Open all year.

Motels

Families gravitate to **The Oyster Shell Motel,** 574 Main St. (Business Rte. 1), P.O. Box 1296, Damariscotta 04543, 207/563-3747 or 800/874-3747 outside Maine, www.oystershellmotel.com, at the northern edge of Damariscotta. Twenty one- and two-bedroom motel/condo-type units have

Mid-Coast Region

air-conditioning, cooking facilities, and free HBO. There's a new heated pool, and free lodging for kids. Rates are $135–159 d in summer, $89–115 d the rest of the year. Open all year.

Campgrounds

The area's best-run campground is 150-acre **Lake Pemaquid Camping,** off Biscay Rd., P.O. Box 967, Damariscotta 04543, 207/563-5202, www.lakepemaquid.com, with over 200 tent and RV sites, many right on the seven-mile-long lake. It's a lively operation, well managed, with tennis, pool and lake swimming, fishing (licenses available), playground, game room, store (lobsters available), laundry, sauna, and canoe and motorboat rentals. July–Aug., lakeside sites are available by the week only. Sites (two adults, four children) are $22–42, late June–Labor Day; lower off-season. Rustic cabins and cottages are available by the week. The campground is open Memorial Day weekend to the end of September.

FOOD

Lunch

In a barn-style building at the northern edge of Damariscotta is the area's best homemade ice cream—about four dozen flavors, including some unusual ones you'd never dream up. **Round Top Ice Cream,** Business Rte. 1, Damariscotta 04543, 207/563-5307, in business since 1924, is open daily, first weekend in Apr.–Columbus Day. Summer hours are 11:30 AM–10 PM (8 PM Apr.–Memorial Day, 9 PM to about mid-June).

A New Harbor landmark since 1928, **C.E. Reilly & Son,** Village Center, New Harbor 04554, 207/677-2321, is one of those local markets that has nearly everything: pizza, sandwiches, meat, first-rate produce, roast chicken, baked goods, liquor, lottery tickets, video rentals, upscale goodies, a few hardware items, and daily New York and Boston newspapers. Open daily, 8 AM–6 PM (to 8 PM Fri.–Sat.).

Right next to Pemaquid Light (and with free parking) is **The Sea Gull Shop,** Pemaquid Point, 207/677-2374, an oceanfront place serving breakfast (7:30 AM–noon), lunch (11:30 AM–3 PM), and dinner (5–7:30 PM) in season. There are two sizes of lobster rolls, one for $10, one for $15. Off-season, dinner is served Fri.–Sat. only.

Inexpensive to Moderate

A reliable standby in downtown Damariscotta, next to the Damariscotta Bank & Trust, the **Salt Bay Café,** Main St., Damariscotta 04543, 207/563-3302, has a loyal following—thanks to its imaginative, reasonably priced menu and cheerful, plant-filled setting. Dinner entrées are $10–20. Liquor license. Open for breakfast (at 7:30 AM), lunch, and dinner Mon.–Sat.

Just down the street, family-run **King Eider's Pub,** 2 Elm St., Damariscotta 04543, 207/563-6008, www.kingeiderspub.com, acquired the status of local hangout soon after it opened. Chalk that up to host Todd Maurer. The first-floor pub, all wood and brick, serves up designer beers; food is available there, but it can be noisy. The bright restaurant has a small oyster bar with Damariscotta River Oysters. There's a moderately priced menu ($11–16) focusing on local produce and seafood (crab cakes are a specialty). Late in the evening, there's "after-theater fare" (appetizers and sandwiches). Closed Tues. Jan.–May, open seven days the rest of the year, 11 AM–close.

Behind Main St. and right on the Damariscotta River, **Backstreet Restaurant,** 17 Back Elm St., Damariscotta, 207/563-5666, has a far better view than Salt Bay and King Eider's (which have none) and a creative menu as well. Chef Stephen Richards leans toward world fusion, with a classical base. Entrées $13–20. Open Mon.–Sat. 11:30 AM–8:30 PM (to 9 PM Fri.–Sat.), in summer. Off-season, to 8 PM weeknights, 8:30 PM Fri.–Sat.

Opposite the post office in New Harbor is the unfussy **Samoset Restaurant,** Rte. 130, New Harbor 04554, 207/677-2788, a longtime favorite among families and seniors. In 1996, they added a pub to tempt a younger crowd. The restaurant is open all year, daily 4–8:30 PM (8 PM on Sun.); Fri.–Sun., lunch is served beginning at 11:30 AM.

One of the best meal deals in the area is the **Anchor Inn,** Harbor Rd., Round Pond 04564, 207/529-5584, tucked away on the picturesque harbor in Round Pond, on the eastern side of the peninsula. Informal and rustic, with a menu that'll surprise you (entrées $13–25), the place always attracts a crowd. Lobster is available, but why eat it here when the Anchor Inn has so many more interesting choices? If lobster's your obsession, go to one of Round Pond's lobsteries. Reservations are advisable any time July–Aug. Open for lunch and dinner mid-May–mid-Oct. (After Labor Day, the schedule can be a bit erratic; call to confirm.)

Moderate to Expensive

Most of the restaurants in this category are eateries located in lodgings. The Bradley Inn, Coveside, and The Newcastle Inn are all good options.

Lobster-in-the-Rough

The Pemaquid Peninsula must have more lobster-in-the-rough places per capita than anyplace in Maine. Some are basic, no-frills operations, others are big-time commercial concerns. Each has a loyal following.

The biggest and best-known lobster wharf is **Shaw's Fish and Lobster Wharf,** Rte. 32, New Harbor, 207/677-2200, where you place your order, take a number, and wait for it to come booming back at you over the loudspeaker. (You can also order steak here. And margaritas. And oysters on the wharf raw bar.) Open mid-May–mid-Oct. Summer hours are 11 AM–9 PM daily; in spring and fall, Shaw's closes at 8 PM Sun.–Thurs. and 9 PM weekends.

Facing each other across the dock in the hamlet of Round Pond are the **Round Pond Lobster,** 207/529-5725, open till 7 PM; and **Muscongus Bay Lobster,** 207/529-5528, hours 11 AM–8 PM. Hard to say which is better; both are good. If you're in a rush, look for the smallest crowd.

Other seasonal lobster wharves on the peninsula are the **New Harbor Co-Op,** Rte. 32, New Harbor, 207/677-2791; **Pemaquid Fishermen's Co-Op,** Pemaquid Harbor Rd., Pemaquid Harbor, 207/677-2801; **South Bristol Fishermen's Co-Op,** Thompson Inn Rd., South Bristol, 207/644-8224 or 644-8246; and **Broad Cove Marine Services,** off Rte. 32, Medomak, 207/529-5186.

INFORMATION AND SERVICES

The **Damariscotta Information Bureau,** 276 Main St., P.O. Box 217, Damariscotta 04543, a private organization established in 1935, has a seasonal office in downtown Damariscotta, Business Rte. 1 at Church St., 207/563-3175. Hours are 10 AM–4 PM Tues.–Fri., and 10 AM–1 PM on Mon. and Sat., early June–Labor Day. Hours Labor Day–Columbus Day are 10 AM–1 PM Mon.–Sat.

The **Damariscotta Region Chamber of Commerce,** P.O. Box 13, Damariscotta 04543, 207/563-8340, www.damariscottaregion.com, publishes a free annual information booklet about the area; its office, just off Main St., is open weekdays, 8 AM–4 PM. The **Pemaquid Area Association,** Chamberlain 04541, no telephone, produces a very useful annotated map covering the lower half of the Pemaquid Peninsula. Both publications are available by mail and at the information bureaus. Also ask for a copy of *The Upper River Region Field Guide,* a foldout map/brochure produced by the Damariscotta River Association and containing excellent information about the area's preserves and natural history.

The best local library is the **Skidompha Library,** 184 Main St., P.O. Box 70, Damariscotta, 207/563-5513, www.skidompha.org. Wonder *where* they get that name? It's an acronym. The library sponsors a number of activities and events, including Jazz in June, Breakfast of Champions, and a reading club. The library's gem of a secondhand-book shop has lots of bargain books for sale, all to benefit library projects. The library is open Tues.–Fri. 9 AM–5 PM (Thurs. to 7 PM), Sat. 9 AM–1 PM.

Newspapers

Rival newspapers, both published every

Thursday, cover the territory and include lots of local listings. They are the *Lincoln County News,* 207/563-3171, www.mainelincolncountynews.com, and the *Lincoln County Weekly,* 207/563-5006, www.courierpub.com/lincolncountyweekly.

The largest daily paper serving the area is the *Portland Press Herald,* 800/442-6036, which includes the Damariscotta/Newcastle area in the *Go* supplement of its Thursday edition.

Emergencies

Just south of downtown Damariscotta, the respected **Miles Memorial Hospital,** 35 Miles St., off Rtes. 129/130, just down the road from Main St., Damariscotta 04543, 207/563-1234, has 24-hour emergency-room services. For **police, fire, and ambulance,** dial 911.

Getting Around

Based in Newcastle, **Salt Bay Taxi,** 207/563-7331, serves the midcoast to New Hampshire. Regular hours are 8 AM–6 PM off-season; in summer, Mon.–Thurs. 8 AM–9 PM, Fri.–Sat. 8 AM–1:30 AM. Sun. by appointment only. Off-hours trips by reservation.

Waldoboro Area

Just east of the Pemaquid Peninsula and the Damariscotta/Newcastle area, Rte. 1 cuts a commercial swath through Waldoboro without revealing the attractive downtown—or the lovely Friendship Peninsula, south of the highway. Duck into Waldoboro, then follow Rte. 220 south 10 miles to Friendship.

Waldoboro's heritage is something of an anomaly in Maine—predominantly German, thanks to 18th-century Teutons who swallowed the blandishments of Gen. Samuel Waldo, holder of a million-acre "patent" stretching as far as the Penobscot River. In the cemetery at the Old German Church, on Rte. 32, is a 19th-century marker whose inscription sums up the town's early history: "This town was settled in 1748, by Germans who emigrated to this place with the promise and expectation of finding a populous city, instead of which they found nothing but a wilderness; for the first few years they suffered to a great extent by Indian wars and starvation. By perseverance and self-denial, they succeeded in clearing lands and erecting mills. At this time [1855] a large proportion of the inhabitants are descendants of the first settlers." (Makes you wonder why Waldo's name stuck to the town.)

After the mill era, the settlers went into ship-building in a big way, establishing six shipyards and producing more than 300 wooden vessels, including the first five-masted schooner, the 265-foot *Governor Ames,* launched in 1888. Although the *Ames's* ill-supported masts collapsed on her maiden voyage, repairs allowed her to serve as a coal hauler for more than 20 years, and many more five-masters followed in her wake. It's hard to believe today, but Waldoboro once was America's sixth-busiest port. At the Town Landing, alongside the Medomak River, a marker describes the town's shipyards and shipbuilding heritage.

With a population of about 4,900, Waldoboro's major draws now are the world headquarters of the *Maine Antique Digest,* a clutch of unusual shops, the handsomely restored Waldo Theatre, and the spring-time alewife fishery in the Medomak River. Commercial clamming is a thriving industry. Most of the time, it's a quiet place with a lot of character (and characters—one admirer described it as a "Down East Lake Wobegon").

Down Rte. 220 from Waldoboro, the town of **Friendship** (pop. 1,100) is best known as the birthplace of the Friendship sloop, a distinctive traditional sailing vessel formerly used as a fishing workhorse and now dedicated to recreational purposes. Lobstering is the major industry here these days; beyond the busy workboat harbor, everything's mighty quiet—a picturesque place to relax and watch the world go by.

Back up the peninsula and across Rte. 1, Rte. 32 leads north and a bit west to Jefferson, a pastoral community settled in the late 18th century, and the site of Damariscotta Lake State Park.

SIGHTS
Historic Sites
The **Waldoborough Historical Society Museum,** 1164 Main St., Waldoboro 04572, 207/832-7552, is a three-building roadside complex just 0.1-mile south of Rte. 1, at the eastern end of town. On the grounds are the one-room 1857 **Boggs Schoolhouse,** the 1819 **Town Pound** (to detain stray livestock), and two buildings filled with antique tools, toys, and utensils, plus period costumes, antique fire engines, and artifacts from the shipbuilding era. There is also a collection of antique quilts, some predating the Civil War, and some sculptured, hooked "Waldoborough Rugs." The museum is open daily 1–4:30 PM, from Waldoboro Day in June through Labor Day, as well as weekends in September. While you're here, ask about the nature trail out back.

A remnant of the German connection is the **Old German Church** and its cemetery, Rte. 32, Waldoboro 04572, 207/832-5369 or 832-7742. The Lutheran church, built in 1772 on the opposite side of the Medomak River, was moved across the ice in the winter of 1794. Inside are box pews and a huge hanging pulpit. One of the three oldest churches in Maine, it lost its flock in the mid-19th century, when new generations no longer spoke German. The church is open daily 1–3 PM July–Aug.

Maine Antique Digest
Believe it or not, the home of the nationally renowned *Maine Antique Digest,* 911 Main St., P.O. Box 1429, Waldoboro 04572, 207/832-7534 or 800/752-8521, www.maineantique-digest.com, is a modern, partially solar-heated structure just off the main drag in downtown Waldoboro. Founded by Sam and Sally Pen-nington, it's a busy operation, not geared up for squads of visitors, but you can stop in on a weekday, admire the William Zorach sculpture, and buy a copy of the fat monthly tabloid.

PARKS AND RECREATION
Damariscotta Lake State Park
As opposed to the chilly ocean, the water here is warmer. You'll also find a lovely sand beach, a lifeguard, changing rooms, and picnic tables with hibachis. The only problem is that 17-acre Damariscotta Lake State Park, Rte. 32, Jefferson 04348, 207/549-7600, is no secret to area residents, so arrive early on hot summer days; the parking lot fills up quickly. Officially open Memorial Day weekend to Labor Day, the park is accessible in winter for ice-skating, snowmobiling, and cross-country skiing. Admission in season is $4 adults, $1 kids 5–11, and free for kids under five and seniors over 65. From Rte. 1, take Rte. 32 north about eight miles to the park entrance.

Osborn Finch Preserve
Even if you can't squeeze in a visit to the Osborn Finch Preserve, Dutch Neck Rd., Waldoboro, at least allow time for a drive down **Dutch Neck.** If you can hike the 11-acre preserve, so much the better, as you'll end up on the shores of the Medomak River (bring a picnic and enjoy it on the rocks). Terrain is easy, through fields and woods. To reach the preserve—owned by the Pemaquid Watershed Association (207/563-2196, www.pemaquidwatershed.org)—from Rte. 1, go 2.7 miles south on Rte. 32 and turn left onto Dutch Neck Rd. Continue 2.5 miles to the small preserve sign (on left). Park along the road, pulling off as far as possible.

About 500 feet before you reach the preserve, you'll see a public boat landing, a fine place to launch a sea kayak or other small boat. Check the tide calendar in a local newspaper and ride with the tide.

Nelson Nature Preserve

Owned by the Mid-Coast Audubon Society, the 95-acre Nelson Nature Preserve, Rte. 97, Friendship 04547, is a rectangular property between Rte. 97 and the Goose River. A network of seven short trails totals about four miles. Much of the terrain is marshy, so wear rubberized boots and insect repellent. The trailhead is just off Rte. 97, a mile north of Friendship's village center.

Massage

Students come from all over New England to attend the year-long courses at the **Downeast School of Massage,** 99 Moose Meadow Lane, Rte. 220, P.O. Box 24, Waldoboro 04572, 207/832-5531, www.downeastschoolofmassage.net, and the school's graduates are much in demand for their skill and professionalism.

ENTERTAINMENT

The center of local entertainment is the neoclassic **Waldo Theatre,** 916 Main St., Waldoboro 04572, 207/832-6060, www.waldotheatre.org, built as a cinema in 1936. Restored in the mid-1980s, it now operates as a nonprofit organization, presenting first-rate concerts, plays, films, workshops, and other year-round community events.

FESTIVALS AND EVENTS

The big event is **Waldoboro Day,** about the middle of June, when the town center is closed to traffic and open for celebration. There's a pancake breakfast, BBQ, church supper, ice cream sundaes, arts and crafts, horse-drawn wagon rides, concerts, kayaking at the Town Landing, a parade, and fireworks—among other diversions.

SHOPPING

Gifts and Miscellanea

On the western outskirts of Waldoboro, **The Well-Tempered Kitchen,** 122 Atlantic Hwy., Rte. 1, Waldoboro 04572, 207/563-5762, can furnish your kitchen with gourmet gadgets, coffees and teas, pots and pans, cards and cookbooks. The shop, based in a renovated barn at the end of a long driveway, is open all year, Mon.–Sat. 9 AM–5 PM, Sun. noon–5 PM. It's closed Sun. Jan.–Mar. Look for a large Open pennant on the north side of Rte. 1.

Fernald's 5&10, 17 Friendship St., Waldoboro 04572, 207/832-4624, is one of those old-fashioned, little-of-everything variety stores that disappeared ages ago. Check this one out while it's still here, in the middle of downtown, and you'll probably spot something you need. They also have Round Top ice cream and excellent sandwiches. Open all year, Mon.–Fri. 8 AM–5:30 PM, Sat. 9 AM–4 PM.

If you're in the market for really good fabric gear, custom made, you'll want to get in touch with Mike Krepner at **Igas Island,** P.O. Box 240, Waldoboro 04572, 207/832-5255. Working in a solar-powered shop (when he's not trekking or canoeing or testing gear in Siberia, Belize, or northern Maine), Mike makes backpacks, all kinds of luggage, canoe packs, raingear, and a handy carryall for your *Maine Atlas and Gazetteer.* His gym bag even has an outside mesh pocket for wet towels and stinky socks. He'll do custom work and mail order (the flyer/catalog is entertaining itself), and you can visit his shop by appointment. Mike is also founder of **Native Trails,** a national organization working to revive and map trails used by our Native American forerunners.

ACCOMMODATIONS

The lodgings in Waldoboro, Friendship (10 miles south), and Jefferson (10 miles north) are all bed-and-breakfasts or weekly-rate cottages.

Waldoboro

Globetrotters Robin and Bill Branigan have made the in-town Victorian **Roaring Lion Bed and Breakfast,** 995 Main St., 207/832-4038, www.roaringlion.com, an informal home away from home for their many guests. The Rose Room, with queen bed and private bath, goes for $100 d. The other three rooms, two with double beds, and one with twin beds, have shared baths, and are $90 d. Single rate is $25 less. Bill's hearty breakfasts (often lion eggs—a secret recipe) are served in the tin-walled, tin-ceilinged dining room; he's a whiz with vegetarian/macrobiotic diets. Maine crafts, paintings, and Bill's superb photos are sold in the screened-porch "gallery." No smoking, no pets; children are welcome. Open all year.

Just up the hill from the Waldo Theatre, hospitable Libby Hopkins has been running the **Broad Bay Inn and Gallery,** 1014 Main St., P.O. Box 607, 207/832-6668 or 800/736-6769, www.broadbayinn.com, since 1984, and she's an energetic breakfast chef, with many new recipes from her latest sojourn in France. Five antiques-filled rooms share three baths—$75–95 d. Guests can play the piano, browse through the huge art-book collection, or watch old films. No smoking, no pets, no kids under 10. Two-night minimum August weekends. In 2005, Libby began an association with Parisian chef M. Jean Paul Doyen to collaborate on by-reservation candlelight dinners. The B&B is open all year; call ahead off-season.

Friendship and Jefferson

The Outsiders' Inn Bed-and-Breakfast, 4 Main St., Rtes. 97 and 220, Friendship 04547, 207/832-5197, is a prime destination for sea kayakers. Bill and Debbie Michaud have converted an 1830 home (once a doctor's office) into a comfortable village-based getaway about 10 miles south of Rte. 1. Tin ceilings, stenciled walls, flower-filled vases, and a woodstove all add to the cozy ambience. Two rooms share a bath; the elegant Chamberlain Room has a private bath. Rooms with shared bath are $65 d., the Chamberlain Room is $80; an efficiency cottage is $350 a week, $385 with breakfast. Breakfast is always special. No smoking, no pets. Children are welcome, but there's no TV. Open all year. Bill, a Professional Maine Guide, rents kayaks (single or double), gives instructions, and leads tours—but you'll need to make arrangements in advance.

Delicious Scandinavian breakfasts, lovely gardens, and a harbor-view terrace are the special features at Liga and Len Jahnke's **Harbor Hill Bed-and-Breakfast,** 5 Harbor Hill Lane, Friendship 04547, 207/832-6646. Three comfortable rooms with private baths go for $100–110 d; a separate cottage is $575 a week. No smoking, no credit cards; pets by arrangement in the apartment; children are welcome. Open May 1–Oct. and in winter by arrangement.

Less than half a mile northeast of Jefferson, **The Jefferson House Farm Bed-and-Breakfast,** Rte. 126, Jefferson 04348, 207/549-5768, gets you away from it all on 12 acres bordering Davis Stream. Since 1987, Jim and Barbara O'Halloran have welcomed guests to their mid-19th-century farmhouse with three second-floor rooms (sharing one bath). Rates are $50 d. Settle on the deck overlooking a mill-pond and waterfall, or walk the farm's nature trail, or launch one of their canoes and paddle down to Damariscotta Lake. In winter, bring cross-country skis. No smoking, no credit cards; well-behaved pets are welcome. Open all year, but call ahead off-season.

FOOD

Truck drivers, tourists, locals, and notables have been flocking to **Moody's Diner,** Rtes. 1 and 220, Waldoboro 04572, 207/832-7785, moodysdiner.com, since 1934, when the Moody family established this classic diner on a Waldoboro hilltop. The antique neon sign has long been a Rte. 1 beacon, especially on a foggy night, and the crowds continue, with new generations of Moodys and considerable expansion of the premises. Expect hearty, no-frills fare and such calorific desserts as peanut-butter or walnut pie. Most of breakfast is on all day (a few items excluded, specials not offered), and coffee is only $0.85. After eating, you can buy the cookbook. No smoking, air-conditioning. Open 4:30 AM–10 PM weekdays, 5 AM–10 PM Sat., and 6 AM–10 PM Sun.

Specialty Foods

Each fall, around mid-September, a tiny cryptic ad appears in local newspapers: "Kraut's

Ready." Savvy readers recognize this as announcing the first batch of the new season's **Fresh Morse's Sauerkraut**—an annual ritual since 1918. The handmade kraut is served fresh out of the wooden barrel it fermented in, sans heat treatment or preservatives. The crisp, tangy kraut's available in stores and by mail-order, but it's more fun (and cheaper) to visit the **Kraut Haus** store and small daytime restaurant, Rte. 220, North Waldoboro, 866/832-5569, about 10 miles north on Rte. 220 from Rte. 1 at Moody's Diner, or 2.5 miles south on Rte. 220 from Rte. 17. At the red-brick farm store you can pick up a 2 lb. bucket of kraut for under $5, along with a variety of other Morse-made products like Aunt Lydia's Beet Relish, Sour Mustard Pickles, and Brown Bread. There are also "Rat" and other specialty cheeses, salamis, six kinds of liverwurst, 20 sausages, smoked pork chops, country ham and bacon, fresh breads, pastries, babka, and rugeluch, plus an array of German products (Schinken, headcheese, teawurst, pantry goods, and chocolates). The store and restaurant are open daily all year.

At the corner of Rtes. 1 and 220, opposite Moody's Diner, is the warehousey, yellow building that turns out superb **Borealis Breads,** 1860 Atlantic Hwy., Rte. 1, Waldoboro 04572, 207/832-0655, www.borealisbreads.com. Using sourdough starters (and no sweeteners, eggs, or dairy products), owner Jim Amaral and his crew produce baguettes, olive bread, rosemary bread, apple cranberry bread, and about a dozen other inventive flavors. Many of the breads are made using locally grown organic wheat. Borealis bakes and delivers fresh bread daily to retail outlets and sandwich shops from Kittery to Bangor, Maine, but why not patronize the source? (There's also another bakery/retail store on Rte. 1 in Wells.) A refrigerated case holds a small selection of picnic fixings (sandwich spreads, juices). Great soups and salads, and excellent sandwiches ($5.25) are available to go. Open Mon.–Fri. 8:30 AM–5:30 PM, Sat.–Sun. 9 AM–4 PM.

INFORMATION AND SERVICES

Unfortunately, Waldoboro has no active chamber of commerce, hence no centralized information source. Once you get here, the best resource is Waldoboro Town Clerk Linda Perry. She's in the Waldoboro Town Office, Rte. 1, P.O. Box J, Waldoboro 04572, 207/832-5369. It's staffed weekdays 8:30 AM–5 PM, all year.

In Friendship, the best source of local info (besides B&B proprietors) is **Wallace's Market,** right in the village, 207/832-2200. While you're at it, they also have pizza and all kinds of sandwiches. Open all year, Mon.–Sat. 5 AM–8 PM, Sun. 6 AM–8 PM.

Next door to the Waldo Theatre is the similarly imposing **Waldoboro Public Library,** 908 Main St., Waldoboro 04572, 207/832-4484, www.waldoborolibrary.org, an 1855 Italianate building that once was a thriving customs house. It's open Mon. 9:30 AM–8 PM, Wed.–Fri. 9:30 AM–4:30 PM, and Saturday 9:30 AM–noon.; closed Tues. and Sun.

Emergencies

The closest **hospital** with a round-the-clock emergency room is **Miles Memorial Hospital,** down Rte. 1 in Damariscotta. For **police, fire, and ambulance,** dial 911.

Thomaston Area

Thomaston is a little gem of a town, and it has become even more attractive since the closing of the maximum-security prison that long greeted everyone arriving from the south on Rte. 1. (A new prison was built in Warren, well off the main highway.) Thomaston is also the gateway to two lovely fingers of land bordering the St. George River and jutting into the Gulf of Maine—the Cushing and St. George Peninsulas.

In 1605, British adventurer Capt. George Waymouth sailed up the river now named after him (it was originally called the Georges River). A way station for Plymouth traders as early as 1630, Thomaston was incorporated in 1777 and officially named after Gen. John Thomas, a Revolutionary War hero.

Industry began with the production of lime, which was used for plaster. A growing demand for plaster, and the frequency with which the wooden boats were destroyed by fire while carrying loads of extremely flammable lime, spurred the growth of shipbuilding and all its related infrastructure. Thomaston's slogan became "the town that went to sea."

Seeing the sleepy harborfront today, it's hard to visualize the booming era when dozens of tall-masted wooden ships slid down the ways. But the town's architecture is a testament and tribute to the prosperous past—all those splendid homes on Main and Knox Sts. were funded by wealthy ship-owners and shipmasters who well understood how to occupy the idle hands of off-duty carpenters.

SIGHTS
Montpelier
As you head out of Thomaston on Rte. 1, toward Rockland, you'll come face to face with an imposing Colonial hilltop mansion at the junction with Rte. 131 South. (Behind it, unfortunately, is the ugly outline of the huge Dragon Cement plant.) Dedicated to the memory of Gen. Henry Knox, President George Wash-

ington's secretary of war, Montpelier, Rtes. 1 and 131, Thomaston 04861, 207/354-8062, www.generalknoxmuseum.org, is a 1930s replica of Knox's original Thomaston home. The mansion today contains Knox family furnishings and other period antiques—all described with great enthusiasm during guided tours. A gift shop run by the Friends of Montpelier carries books and other relevant items. Concerts and other special events occur here periodically throughout the summer; General Knox's birthday is celebrated with considerable fanfare on the weekend closest to his July 25 birthday. Open Tues.–Sat. 10 AM–4 PM, Memorial Day weekend to Columbus Day. Admission is $6 adults, $5 seniors, $3 children 5–13, $15 per family.

Down near Thomaston's waterfront is the site of Gen. Knox's original Montpelier. The complex of eight or nine buildings, in decrepit condition, was razed in 1871 when the railroad came through. Only a late-18th-century brick farmhouse remains—today the headquarters of the **Thomaston Historical Society,** 80 Knox St., Thomaston 04861, 207/354-2295, www.thomastonhistoricalsociety.com. Special local-interest exhibits are held here each summer; open Tues.–Thurs. 2–4 PM, June–Aug. Free admission.

National Historic District
Montpelier is the starting point for a walking, cycling, or (if you must) driving tour (about three miles) of nearly 70 sites in Thomaston's National Historic District. Pick up a copy of the tour brochure at one of the local businesses. Included are lots of stories behind the facades of the handsome 19th-century homes that line Main and Knox Sts.; the architecture here is nothing short of spectacular.

Thomaston also has its own **"Museum in the Streets,"** with 25 attractively designed, numbered historical signposts (in both English and French) at locations throughout town. The do-it-yourself walking tour begins at the

Mid-Coast Region

corner of Main (Rte. 1) and Pine Sts. (at the northern end of town); most of the markers are on Main and Knox Sts.

If you're in the area in December, another treat's in store: Thomaston's holiday decorations are stunning. All over town, but especially in the Historic District, huge wreaths, tiny white lights, and (usually) a blanket of snow create a scene lifted right out of a Currier & Ives print.

RECREATION

The nearest **golf courses** are in Rockland and Rockport. For **bicycling, sea kayaking,** and **tennis,** try the St. George Peninsula. Best nearby **hiking** is in the Camden-Rockport area.

ENTERTAINMENT

The multiplex **Flagship Cinema,** 9 Moody Dr. (Rte. 1), Thomaston 04861, 207/594-2100, www.flagshipcinemas.com, draws customers from a wide area; the only competition is downtown Rockland's beautifully revamped Strand Theatre (see *Rockland Area*).

FESTIVALS AND EVENTS

Thomaston's **Fourth of July,** an old-fashioned hometown celebration reminiscent of a Norman Rockwell painting, draws huge crowds. A spiffy parade—with bands, veterans, kids, and pets—starts off the morning (11 AM), followed by races, craft and food booths, and lots more. If you need to get *through* Thomaston on July Fourth, do it well before the parade or well after noon, as the marchers go right down Main St. (Rte. 1), and gridlock forces a detour.

SHOPPING

Thomaston has a block-long shopping street (on Rte. 1), with ample free parking out back behind the stores. No big businesses here, but you'll find book, antiques, and gift shops.

Books

If you arrive at Marti Reed's **Personal Book Shop,** 144 Main St., Thomaston 04861, 207/354-8058, on the right Monday morning, you'll run into a gaggle of local writers gathered to swap tips and gossip. That's just the kind of place this is—an independent bookstore with a warm, nurturing feel. Not to mention a dog named Platero in residence. Lots of unusual titles, too—you won't leave empty-handed. Open Mon.–Sat. 10 AM–5:30 PM, year-round, and occasional Sundays in summer.

Gifts—From Behind Bars

The **Maine State Prison Showroom,** 385 Main St. (Rte. 1), corner of Wadsworth St., Thomaston 04861, 207/354-9237, markets the handiwork of inmate craftsmen. Some of the souvenirs verge on kitsch; the bargains are wooden bar stools, toys (including dollhouses), and chopping boards. You'll need to carry your purchases with you; prison-made goods cannot be shipped. Open daily 9 AM–5 PM, all year.

Antiques

High-end 17th- and 18th-century American furniture and accessories are the stock-in-trade of **David C. Morey American Antiques,** 161 Main St., Thomaston 04861, 207/354-6033. Don't miss this shop. Open Wed.–Sat. 10 AM–5 PM.

At the southern end of Thomaston, in a renovated chicken barn, is **Thomaston Place Auction Galleries,** 51 Atlantic Highway (Rte. 1), Thomaston 04861, 207/354-8141 or 888/834-5538, www.thomastonauction.com, the home of Kaja Veilleux Antiques, a longtime dealer, appraiser, and auction house. Auctions occur frequently throughout the summer (also in winter), with previews beforehand. The auctions are catered; call to reserve a place. You never know what you'll find. Check *Maine Antique Digest* for the current schedule.

ACCOMMODATIONS

For other nearby lodgings, see the sections for *Rockland Area* and *St. George Peninsula*.

The best local camping is at **Saltwater Farm Campground,** 47 Kalloch Lane (off Wadsworth St./Cushing Rd.), Cushing, mailing address P.O. Box 165, Thomaston 04861, 207/354-6735, a 35-acre Good Sampark 1.5 miles south of Rte. 1. Forty open and wooded tent and RV sites ($27–34, for four) overlook the St. George River. Facilities include a bathhouse, heated outdoor pool, hot tub, laundry facilities, Internet access, store, and a play area. The river is tidal, so swimming there is best near high tide; otherwise, you're dealing with mudflats. Open mid-May–mid-Oct.

FOOD

Often overlooked by visitors (but certainly not by locals) is casual **Thomaston Café & Bakery,** 154 Main St. (Rte. 1), Thomaston 04861, 207/354-8589, www.thomastoncafe.com. German-born chef Herb Peters is one of the region's best-known culinary pros. He and his wife, Eleanor, produce superb pastries, breads, and desserts (eat here or takeout). Everything's homemade, there are children's options, the café uses only organic poultry, and prices are very reasonable. Try the incredible wild mushroom hash. Beer and wine only. Open all year, Mon.–Sat. 7 AM–2 PM, and Sun. for brunch (8:30 AM–1:30 PM); in summer, the café serves dinner (entrées $13–22) Fri.–Sat.

Hidden away on Thomaston's waterfront is the **Harbor View Restaurant,** Public Landing, Water St., Thomaston 04861, 207/354-8173. Try for a table in the back, where you'll have a front-row seat on the harbor. The ambience is informal and seafood is the specialty here (entrées $14–22). From Rte. 1 in Thomaston, take Knox St. to Water St. The restaurant is a half mile off Rte. 1. Open daily 11:30 AM–2:30 PM and 5–9 PM, year-round; call ahead off-season.

INFORMATION AND SERVICES

Thomaston and its two peninsulas come under the umbrella of the **Rockland-Thomaston Area Chamber of Commerce,** based in downtown Rockland at the Gateway Center, One Park Dr., Rockland 04841, 207/596-0376 or 800/562-2529, www.therealmaine.com.

The **Thomaston Public Library,** 60 Main St., Thomaston 04861, 207/354-2453, www.thomaston.lib.me.us/, occupies part of the Greek Revival Thomaston Academy, once the town's elementary school (until 1982). Now the library shares the space with the Thomaston branch of the University of Maine's Thomaston Center; college classes are held here throughout the school year. The library is open Mon. and Wed. 2–8 PM, Tues. and Sat. 10 AM–2 PM, and Thurs. and Fri. 10 AM–5 PM.

Emergencies

For anyone in Thomaston, or on the Cushing and St. George Peninsulas, the nearest hospital is **Penobscot Bay Medical Center** in Rockport, Rte. 1, 207/596-8000, where there is 24-hour emergency-room care. For **police, fire, and ambulance,** dial 911.

Cushing Peninsula

Mid-Coast Region

Cushing's recorded history goes back at least as far as 1605, when someone named "Abr [maybe Abraham] King"—presumably a member of explorer George Waymouth's crew—inscribed his name on a ledge (now private property) here. Since 1789, settlers' saltwater farms have sustained many generations, and the active Cushing Historical Society keeps the memories and memorabilia from fading away. But the outside world knows little of this. Cushing is better known as "Wyeth country," the terrain depicted by the famous artistic dynasty of N. C. Andrew, and Jamie Wyeth (and assorted talented other relatives).

Even though several Wyeths still spend time here, you're not likely to meet any members of the family (unless you hang out near Fales's Store for days on end). However, if you're an Andrew Wyeth fan, visiting Cushing will give you the feeling of walking through his paintings. The flavor of Maine is here—rolling fields, wildflower meadows, rocky tidal coves, broad vistas, character—filled farmhouses, and some well-hidden summer enclaves. The only retail businesses are a general store, a few farmstands, and a seasonal takeout—plus a campground on the Cushing/Thomaston town line.

SIGHTS

Cushing's town boundary begins 1.3 miles south of Rte. 1 (take Wadsworth St. at the Maine State Prison Showroom). Two miles farther, you'll pass giant wooden sculptures in the yard of the late artist **Bernard Langlais,** who died in 1977.

Six miles from Rte. 1 is the **A.S. Fales & Son Store** (locally, just "Fales's Store"), Cushing's heart and soul-source of fuel, film, gossip, and groceries. Built in 1889, the store has been in the Fales family ever since. Just beyond the store, take the left fork, continuing down the peninsula toward the Broad Cove Church and the Olson House.

Broad Cove Church

Wyeth aficionados will recognize the Broad Cove Church as one of his subjects-alongside River Rd. en route to the Olson House. Most days, it's open, so step inside and admire the classic New England architecture. The church is also well known as the site of one of the region's best beanhole bean suppers, held on a mid-July Saturday and attracting several hundred appreciative diners. Bear left at the fork after Fales's Store; the church is 0.4 mile farther, on the right.

The Olson House

Many an art lover makes the pilgrimage to the Olson House, a famous icon near the end of Hathorn Point Rd. The early-19th-century farmhouse appears in Andrew Wyeth's 1948 painting *Christina's World* (which hangs in New York's Museum of Modern Art), his best-known image of the disabled Christina Olson, who died in 1968. In 1991, two philanthropists donated the Olson House to the Farnsworth Art Museum (www.farnsworthmuseum.org), which has retained the house's sparse, lonely, and rather mystical ambience. The clapboards outside remain unpainted, the interior walls bear only a few Wyeth prints (hung close to the settings they depict), and it is easy to sense Wyeth's inspiration for chronicling this place. The house is open daily 11 AM–4 PM, Memorial Day weekend through Columbus Day; 207/354-0102. Admission is $4 adults and seniors, free for anyone under 18. From Rte. 1 in Thomaston, at the Maine State Prison Showroom, turn onto Wadsworth St. and go six miles to Fales's Store. Take the left fork after the store, go 1.5 miles, and turn left onto Hathorn Point Rd. Go another 1.9 miles to the house.

The Georges River Bikeways

The Cushing Peninsula is the endpoint for The Georges River Bikeways, 111 miles of bicycle routes (including some loops) meandering through three sections of the St. George River watershed, beginning in North Searsmont (west of Belfast). Organized and signposted by the Georges River Land Trust (GRLT), based in Rockland, the routes follow mostly side roads (some unpaved) rather than major roads, reaching salt water near the tip of the Cushing Peninsula. A mountain bike is your best choice—for the hilly terrain and unpaved roads in the upper regions and the shoulderless roads along the whole route. You'll need a GRLT map (call the land trust office in Rockland at 207/594-5166, or visit www.grlt.org) as well as a copy of the DeLorme *Maine Atlas and Gazetteer.*

St. George Peninsula

Even though the Cushing and St. George Peninsulas face each other across the St. George River, they differ dramatically. Cushing is far more rural, seemingly less approachable—with little access to the surrounding waters; St. George has a whole string of things to do and see, and places to sleep and eat—plus shore access in various spots along the peninsula.

The St. George Peninsula is actually better known by some of the villages scattered along its length: Tenants Harbor, Port Clyde, Wiley's Corner, Spruce Head—plus the smaller neighborhoods of Martinsville, Smalleytown, Glenmere, Long Cove, Hart's Neck, and Clark Island. Each has a distinct personality, determined partly by the different ethnic groups-primarily Brits, Swedes, and Finns—who arrived to work the granite quarries in the 19th century. Wander through the Seaview Cemetery in Tenants Harbor (also called "T. Harbor") and you'll see the story: row after row of gravestones with names from across the sea.

A more famous former visitor was 19th-century novelist Sarah Orne Jewett, who holed up in an old schoolhouse in Martinsville, paid a weekly rental of $0.50, and penned *The Country of the Pointed Firs,* a tale about "Dunnet's Landing" (Tenants Harbor).

Today the picturesque peninsula has saltwater farms, tidy hamlets, a striking lighthouse, spruce-edged tidal coves, an active yachting harbor, and, at the tip, a tiny fishing village (Port Clyde), which serves as the springboard to offshore Monhegan Island.

Port Clyde, in fact, may be the best-known community here. (Fortunately, it's no longer called by its unappealing 18th-century name—Herring Gut.) George Waymouth explored Port Clyde's nearby islands in 1605, but you'd never suspect its long tradition. It's a sleepy place, with a general store, an inn, a couple of galleries, and expensive parking. (Enterprising locals charge $4 a day, mostly to capture visitors heading to car-free Monhegan.)

SIGHTS

Lighthouse Museum

Not many settings can compare with the spectacular locale of the **Marshall Point**

Marshall Point Lighthouse

© KATHLEEN M. BRANDES

Lighthouse Museum, Marshall Point Rd., P.O. Box 247, Port Clyde 04855, 207/372-6450, www.marshallpoint.org, a distinctive nineteenth-century lighthouse and park overlooking Port Clyde, the harbor islands, and the passing lobsterboat fleet. Bring a picnic and let the kids run on the lawn (but keep them well back from the shoreline). The tiny museum, in the 1895 keeper's house, displays local memorabilia. Admission is free, but donations are welcomed. Open Sun.–Fri. 1–5 PM, Sat. 10 AM–5 PM, Memorial Day weekend to Columbus Day, and weekend afternoons in May. The grounds are accessible year-round. The museum is 15.2 miles from the junction of Rtes. 1 and 131 in Thomaston. Take Rte. 131 South toward Port Clyde and watch for signs to the museum.

Georges River Scenic Byway

The brainchild of energetic members of the Georges River Land Trust, the Georges River Scenic Byway is a 50-mile auto route along the St. George River (aka Georges River) from its inland headwaters to the sea in Port Clyde. You can follow the trail in either direction, or pick it up anywhere along the way, but first obtain a map/brochure at a chamber of commerce or other information locale. You can also contact **The Georges River Land Trust** (GRLT), 328 Main St., Rockland 04841, 207/594-5166, www.grlt.org. Better still, support the GRLT and become a member; the basic rate is $35 a year. The land trust also maintains local hiking routes (the Georges Highland Path) as well as bicycle routes through the St. George River watershed to Cushing (Georges River Bikeways). Following mostly side roads (some unpaved) rather than major highways, the routes reach salt water near the tip of the Cushing Peninsula. A mountain or hybrid bike is your best choice—for the hilly terrain and unpaved roads in the upper regions and the shoulderless roads along the whole route.

RECREATION
Swimming and Beachcombing
Drift Inn Beach, on Drift Inn Beach Rd. (also called Candy's Cove Rd.), isn't a big deal as beaches go, but it's the best public one on the peninsula, so it gets busy on hot days. The name comes from the Drift Inn, a summer hotel located here early in the twentieth century. Drift Inn Beach Rd. parallels Rte. 131, and the parking lot is accessible from both roads. Heading south on the peninsula, about 3.5 miles after the junction with Rte. 73, turn left at Drift Inn Beach Rd. The sign frequently disappears; watch for an imposing square granite house and a red farm on your left. Go 0.2 mile from the turn.

Bicycling
A popular local bicycling route follows Rte. 131 south from Thomaston (Rte. 1) to Port Clyde (14 miles)—with a side trip along Rte. 73 to Spruce Head for the ambitious. Another option—a 35-mile loop—is to take Rte. 131 south from Thomaston, then turn left at Rte. 73, continue on Rte. 73 through Spruce Head and South Thomaston to Rockland, where Rte. 1 loops back to Thomaston. Be forewarned, however, that these roads are narrow and at times rather heavily traveled, especially July–Aug., and shoulders are poor-to-nonexistent. Rte. 1 has some shoulders (breakdown lanes) but a great deal of traffic. If you need a rental bike, contact **Bikesenjava,** 481 Main St., Rockland 04841, 207/596-1004, www.hay-bikesenjava.com, or **Maine Sport Outfitters,** Rte. 1, Rockport 04856, 207/236-7120, www.mainesport.com. (There are no rental bikes on the St. George Peninsula or in Thomaston.)

Tennis
Public courts, available on a first-come, first-served basis, are located behind the municipal building in **South Thomaston,** Rte. 73, about 0.75 mile south of the Keag Store, Rte. 73, Village Center, South Thomaston.

Getting Afloat
If you have your own sailboat or motorboat, there are moorings in Tenants Harbor (near the East Wind Inn), Port Clyde (near the Port Clyde General Store), and Spruce Head (at Merchants Landing).

The St. George Peninsula is especially popular for **sea kayaking,** with plenty of islands to add interest and shelter. If you need a rental kayak, contact **Maine Sport Outfitters,** Rte. 1, Rockport, 207/236-7120, www.mainesport.com, about 10 miles north of Thomaston. They'll supply you with charts and all necessary gear. If you're a novice, they offer lessons and beginner tours. Maine Sport also does multi-day kayaking trips. If you've had experience, you can launch on the ramp just before the causeway that links the mainland with Spruce Head Island, in Spruce Head (Island Rd., off Rte. 73). Parking is very limited. A great paddle goes clockwise around Spruce Head Island and nearby Whitehead (there's a lighthouse on its southeastern shore) and Norton Islands. Duck in for lunch at Waterman's Beach Lobster. Around new moon and full moon, plan your schedule to avoid low tide near the Spruce Head causeway, or you may become mired in mudflats. Spruce Head's postmaster, Dana Winchenbach, is a kayaking pro. Contact him weekdays 10 AM–1 PM and 2–4 PM, 207/594-7647, if you need advice; at lunchtime, he's out on the water.

The best boating experience on this peninsula is a passenger-ferry trip to offshore **Monhegan Island**—for a day, overnight, or longer. Perhaps because the private ferry company has a monopoly on this harbor, the trip isn't cheap, and parking adds to the cost, but it's a "must" excursion, so try to factor it into the budget. Port Clyde is the nearest mainland harbor to Monhegan; this service operates all year (summer-only boats depart from New Harbor and Boothbay Harbor). **Monhegan Boat Line,** P.O. Box 238, Port Clyde 04855, 207/372-8848, www.monheganboat .com, uses two boats: the *Laura B.,* 70 minutes each way; and the newer *Elizabeth Ann,* 55 minutes. Round-trip tickets are $27 adults, $14 kids 2–12, $2 pets. (Leave your bicycle in Port Clyde; you won't need it on the island.) Reservations are essential in summer, especially for the 10:30 AM boat; a $5 pp fee holds the reservation until an hour before departure, so you have to get to the dock early. No deposit is needed for other boats, but it's best to show up 30 minutes before departure. Parking near the dock in Port Clyde is $4 a day. If a summer day-trip is all you can manage, aim for the first or second boat and return on the last one; don't go just for the boat ride.

In May, before Memorial Day weekend, there's only one daily boat, so you'll need to stay overnight unless you just do the round-trip boat ride. There are three boats daily (except Sun.) in June, then three trips every day July–Labor Day. From Labor Day to Columbus Day, there are three daily (except Sun.) trips, then one trip the rest of October. Nov.–Apr., the boats depart Port Clyde at 9:30 AM Mon., Wed., and Fri. (except postal holidays), and return immediately.

SHOPPING
Art Galleries

The St. George Peninsula has been attracting artists for decades, so it's no surprise that galleries seem to be everywhere you look. Some have been here for years, others started yesterday; most are worth a stop, so keep an eye out for their signs.

The Drawing Room Gallery, 864 River Rd. (Rte. 131), St. George 04860, 207/372-6242, mounts several theme-based group shows each summer. Philip and Barbara Anderson's gallery is just north of the junction with Rte. 73, about five miles south of Rte. 1. Open summers only.

Overlooking the reversing falls in "downtown" South Thomaston, **Art of the Sea at the Old Post Office Gallery,** 5 Spruce Head Rd. (Rte. 73), South Thomaston 04858, 207/594-9396, www.artofthesea.com, focuses on marine art and antiques: ship models, prints, paintings, sculpture, scrimshaw, and jewelry. The selection is first-rate and the price range is broad. Open Tues.–Sat. 10 AM–4 PM, sometimes Sun. in summer.

Pottery

Since 1972, Tony Oliveri has been the inspiration and the artisan behind **Keag River**

Pottery, Westbrook St., P.O. Box 227, South Thomaston 04858, 207/594-7915, a small shop attached to his home just 0.1 mile off Rte. 73 (or 2.2 miles east of Rte. 131). He produces brilliantly glazed functional wares, such as bowls, dishes, and lamps, and readily accepts commissions. Open July–Labor Day on a rather unpredictable schedule, the rest of the year by appointment.

Used Books

Drive up to the small parking area at **Lobster Lane Book Shop,** Island Rd., Spruce Head 04859, 207/594-7520, and you'll see license plates from everywhere. Owner Vivian York's tiny shop, a crammed but well-organized shed that's been here since the 1960s, has 50,000 or so treasures for used-book fans. For a few dollars, you can stock up on a summer's worth of reading. Open Thurs.–Sun. afternoons, June–Sept. The shop is just under a mile east of Rte. 73, with eye-catching vistas in several directions (except, of course, when Spruce Head's infamous fog sets in).

General Store

Despite periodic ownership changes, **Port Clyde General Store,** Rte. 131, Port Clyde 04855, 207/372-6543, remains a character-ful destination, a two-century-old country store with a few yuppie touches. Stock up on groceries, pick up a newspaper, order a pizza, or buy a sweatshirt (you may need it on the Monhegan boat). Open daily 6 AM–9 PM in summer, shorter hours the rest of the year. Out back is the Dip Net Restaurant, a great place to eat on the dock.

ACCOMMODATIONS

Inns

The East Wind Inn, Mechanic St., Rte. 131, P.O. Box 149, Tenants Harbor 04860, 207/372-6366 or 800/241-8439, www.eastwindinn.com, is the perfect rendition of an old-fashioned country inn. Built in 1860 and originally used as a sail loft, it has a huge veranda, a cozy parlor, harbor-view rooms, and a quiet dining room with a creditable menu. Of the 16 traditional rooms in the main inn building, nine have private baths; the others share four baths. Rates are $129–159 d mid-June–Labor Day, $89–139 d other months (lowest Nov.–Apr.). Next door, the inn's spiffed-up 19th-century Meeting House, a former sea captain's home, has 10 modern rooms and suites, all with great views and private baths ($189 d in midsummer, $149–169 d other months). Also on the premises, the Wheeler Cottage has three superb lodging options—$219–299 d in midsummer, $179–279 d other months. Full breakfast is included; two-night minimum summer weekends. Children are welcome; pets are $15 per visit (make arrangements in advance). Apr.–Nov., the water-view dining room is open to the public daily for breakfast (7:30–9:30 AM, to 10 AM July–Aug.) and dinner (5:30–8:30 PM, to 9 PM July–Aug.). Dinner entrées are $16–26. Reservations are wise. Lunch is available in summer at the inn's dockside Chandlery. Inquire at the inn about tugboat cruises ($34–41 pp), May–Oct., aboard the restored tugboat *Seanaghi.* Located 9.5 miles south of Rte. 1, the inn is open Apr.–Nov.; other months it's open for groups by special arrangement.

If you stay at the **The Ocean House,** Rte. 131, P.O. Box 66, Port Clyde 04855, 207/372-6691 or 800/269-6691, www.oceanhousehotel.com, you can plan to roll out of bed, eat breakfast, and roll down the hill to the Monhegan boat. It's ultraconvenient, and you can leave your car here (free). Several of the 10 unpretentious inn rooms (seven with private bath) have great harbor views (especially number 11). Doubles at the Ocean House are $75–93, plus $5 for a single-night stay; no credit cards. Open mid-May–Oct. Breakfast, served 7 AM–noon, is a big deal. Before the boat, try the Monhegan quickie, a great egg sandwich.

Bed-and-Breakfasts

The **Blue Lupin Bed-and-Breakfast,** 372 Waterman's Beach Rd., South Thomaston 04848, 207/594-2673, www.bluelupinbandb.com, has an out-of-this-world view in an off-the-beaten-track locale. Three rooms and a suite, all with private bath and TV/VCR, go for $85–155 d, mid-May–Oct., less off-season. Breakfast is a feast. You're right on the water, so bring a sea kayak and launch it from the beach. Or bring a bicycle to explore the area. Next door is Waterman's Beach Lobster. No smoking, no pets, no children under five. Open all year, but call ahead off-season. The B&B is seven miles from Rockland, slightly farther from Thomaston.

In the center of South Thomaston village and overlooking the reversing falls on the tidal Wessaweskeag River, the 1830 **Weskeag Inn,** 14 Elm St. (Rte. 73), South Thomaston 04858, 207/596-6676 or 800/596-5576, www.weskeag.com, has four rooms with private baths, two with detached baths, for $120–155 d in summer (lower rates off-season). This place is especially relaxing; guests have access to games, puzzles, books, a huge video library, a great deck, and a lawn stretching to the river. Bring your sea kayak and bicycles. It's 1.5 miles from the Owls Head Transportation Museum (owner Gray Smith loves vintage cars) and a few more miles from the restaurants of downtown Rockland. No smoking, no pets; kids are welcome. Credit cards accepted, but cash or check is preferred. Open all year.

Seasonal Rentals

Lots of **rental cottages** are tucked into secluded coves throughout the St. George Peninsula. Many of the owners advertise in the classified pages of *Down East* magazine, usually the March and April issues. In addition, the Rockland-Thomaston Area Chamber of Commerce, based in downtown Rockland, Gateway Center, One Park Drive, P.O. Box 508, Rockland 04841, 207/596-0376, www.therealmaine.com, maintains a listing of cottage-rental opportunities in the area—especially in **Tenants Harbor, Port Clyde, Spruce Head,** and **Owls Head.**

FOOD

Besides the places described below (and the dining room of the East Wind Inn, above), the wide range of interesting restaurants in the

Rockland area is close enough to the St. George Peninsula to sample conveniently.

Lunch

Don't be surprised to see the handful of tables occupied at the **Keag Store,** Rte. 73, Village Center, South Thomaston, 207/596-6810, one of the most popular lunch stops in the area. (Keag, by the way, is pronounced "gig"—short for "Wessaweskeag.") Overstuffed lobster rolls are a major draw, as is the pizza, which verges on the greasy but compensates with its flavor—no designer toppings, just good pizza. Order it all to go and head across the street to the public landing, where you can hang out and observe all the comings and goings. Open all year, 6 AM–9 PM Mon.–Sat. and 7 AM–8 PM Sun.

Other good spots for picnic fare are the **Port Clyde General Store** Rte. 131, Port Clyde 04855, 207/372-6543; the **Schoolhouse Bakery,** Rte. 131, Tenants Harbor, 207/372-9608; and the **Off Island Store,** Island Rd., Spruce Head, 207/594-7475.

Inexpensive to Moderate

Farmer's Restaurant, Main St., Rte. 131, P.O. Box 240, Tenants Harbor 04860, 207/372-6111, a longtime neighborhoody place, has undergone ownership changes in the past several years, but it always has a loyal following for all three meals. The dinner menu is simple but solid, with fresh seafood, steaks, and such. Open daily 7 AM–8 PM (to 9 PM Fri.–Sat.) in summer, fewer hours off-season. The restaurant is in Tenants Harbor.

Seafood is everything at **The Harpoon,** Drift Inn and Marshall Point Rds., Port Clyde 04855, 207/372-6304, and it's about as fresh as it gets. Steaks are also on the menu, along with Cajun dishes. Lobster's available, but save that for an outdoor deck. Rebuilt from the ashes of an early-1990s fire, the informal restaurant is just over a low hill from the center of Port Clyde. Open Wed.–Sat. 5–9 PM (to 10 PM Fri.–Sat.), mid-May–mid-Oct.

The peninsula's newest restaurant is **Sul Mare,** 13 River Rd. (Rt. 131), Tenants Harbor 04860, 207/372-9995, www.sulmarerestaurant.com, a popular trattoria created from—no kidding—the town's former laundry. (Some faux effects help the camouflage.) The chef pulls off an ambitious regional Italian menu (entrées $11–22), so reservations are essential. Open for dinner 5–10 PM daily in summer, shorter hours off-season.

Lobster-in-the-Rough

These open-air lobster wharves are the best places in the area to get down and dirty and manhandle a steamed or boiled lobster.

With outside picnic tables overlooking the harbor, **Cod End,** Commercial St., next to the town dock, Tenants Harbor 04860, 207/372-6782, www.codend.com, is the right kind of rustic. Dig into lobster, fried clams, chowders, and delicious homemade pies; beer and wine available. Lobster-dinner discount (10 percent) for seniors. Open daily 11 AM–8:30 PM, July–Aug., shorter hours June and Sept.–Oct. Take Rte. 131 south 9.5 miles from Rte. 1 in Thomaston; turn left about 30 yards beyond Hall's Market.

Out back behind the Port Clyde General Store, and overlooking the Port Clyde lobsterboat fleet and the Monhegan Boat dock, are the picnic tables of the **Dip Net,** Rte. 131, Port Clyde 04855, 207/372-6543, www.dipnetrestaurant.com. It's been heading rather upmarket in recent years—besides the typical lobster-wharf fare, the menu features local oysters, scallop ceviche, and even bouillabaisse. Beer and wine are available. Open mid-May–mid-Sept., 11 AM–10 PM.

Poking right out into Wheeler's Bay, **Miller's Lobster Co.,** Eagle Quarry Rd., off Rte. 73, Spruce Head 04859, 594-7406, is the quintessential lobster pound, a well-run operation that draws crowds all summer long. Lobster rolls, steamed clams, crabmeat rolls, homemade pies—the works. Even hot dogs if you need them. Several picnic tables are under cover for chilly or rainy or buggy weather. BYOL. Open daily mid-June–Labor Day, 11 AM–7 PM.

A broad view of islands in the Mussel Ridge Channel is the bonanza at **Waterman's Beach Lobster,** 359 Waterman's Beach Rd., South Thomaston 04858, 207/596-7819. This tiny operation turns out well-stuffed lobster and crabmeat rolls and superb pies. Step up to the window and place your order. BYOL; no credit cards. Open Thurs.–Sun. 11 AM–7 PM, mid-June–Labor Day. Located next door to the **Blue Lupin Bed-and-Breakfast,** the wharf is on a side road off Rte. 73 between Spruce Head Village and South Thomaston; watch for signs on Rte. 73.

Monhegan Island

Eleven or so miles from the mainland lies a unique island community with gritty lobstermen (most women also prefer to be called lobstermen), close-knit families, a can-do spirit, a longstanding summertime artists' colony, no cars, astonishingly beautiful scenery, and some of the best birding on the eastern seaboard. Until the 1980s, the island only had radiophones and generator power. With the arrival of electricity and real phones, the pace has quickened a bit—but not much. Welcome to Monhegan Island.

But first a cautionary note: Monhegan has remained idyllic largely because generations of residents, part-timers, and visitors have been ultrasensitive to its fragility. When you buy your ferry ticket, you'll receive a copy of the regulations, all very reasonable, and the captain of your ferry will reiterate them. *If you're not inclined to heed them, please don't go to the island.*

Many of the regulations have been developed by The Monhegan Associates, an island land trust founded in 1954 by Theodore ("Ted") Edison, son of Thomas Alva Edison. Firmly committed to preservation of the island in as natural a state as possible, the group maintains and marks the trails, sponsors natural-history

TEN RULES FOR MONHEGAN VISITORS

1. Smoking is banned everywhere except in the village.
2. Rock climbing is not allowed on the wild headlands on the back side of the island.
3. Preserve the island's wild state—do not remove flowers or lichens.
4. Bicycles and strollers are not allowed on island trails.
5. Camping and campfires are forbidden.
6. Swim only at Swim Beach, just south of the ferry landing—if your innards can stand the shock. Wait for the incoming tide, when the water is warmest (and this warmth is relative). It's wise not to swim alone.
7. Dogs must be leashed; carry a pooper-scooper to remove waste.
8. Be respectful of private property; stay on the trails. (As the island visitor's guide puts it, "Monhegan is a village, not a theme park.")
9. If you're staying overnight, bring a flashlight; the village paths are very dark.
10. Carry the island trail map when you go exploring; you'll need it.

A strong suggestion: Carry a trash bag, use it, and take it off the island when you leave.

talks, and insists that no construction be allowed beyond the village limits.

The origin of the name *Monhegan* remains up in the air; it's either a Maliseet or Micmac name meaning "out-to-sea island" or an adaptation of the name of a French explorer's daughter. In any case, Monhegan caught the attention of Europeans after English explorer John Smith stopped by in 1614, but the island had already been noticed by earlier adventurers including John Cabot, Giovanni da Verrazzano, and George Waymouth. Legend even has it that Monhegan fishermen sent dried fish to Plimoth Plantation during the Pilgrims' first winter on Cape Cod. Captain Smith returned home and carried on about Monhegan, snagging the attention of intrepid souls who established a fishing/trading outpost here in 1625. Monhegan has been settled continuously since 1674, with fishing as the economic base.

In the 1880s, lured by the spectacular setting and artist Robert Henri's enthusiastic reports, gangs of artists began arriving, lugging their easels here and there to capture the surf, the light, the tidy cottages, the magnificent headlands, fishing boats, even the islanders' craggy features. American, German, French, and British artists have long (and continue to) come here; well-known signatures associated with

Monhegan include Rockwell Kent, George Bellows, Edward Hopper, James Fitzgerald, Andrew Winter, Alice Kent Stoddard, Reuben Tam, William Kienbusch, and Jamie Wyeth.

Officially called Monhegan Plantation (part of Lincoln County), the island has about 75 year-rounders (as of the 2000 census). Several hundred others summer here. A handful of students attend the tiny school through eighth grade; high-schoolers have to pack up and move "inshore" to the mainland during the school year.

At the schoolhouse, the biggest social event of the year is the Christmas party, when everyone brings casseroles, salads, and desserts to complement a big beef roast. Kids perform their Christmas play, Santa shows up with presents, and dozens of adults look on approvingly. The islanders turn out en masse for almost every special event at the school, and the adults treat the island kids almost like common property, feeling free to praise or chastise them any time it seems appropriate—a phenomenon prevalent in isolated island communities.

As if the isolation weren't rigorous enough, Monhegan's lobster-fishing season—a legislatively sanctioned period—perversely begins on December 1 (locally known as Trap Day). An air of nervous anticipation surrounds the dozen or more lobstermen after midnight the day before, as they prepare to steam out to set their traps on the ocean floor. Of course, with the lack of competition from mainland anglers that time of year, and a supply of lobsters fattening up since the previous May, there's a ready market for their catch. But success still depends on a smooth "setting." Meetings are held daily during the month beforehand to make sure everyone will be ready to "set" together. The season ends on May 25.

March brings the annual town meeting, an important community event that draws every able-bodied soul and then some. The island's entire annual budget is less than $200,000.

Almost within spitting distance of Monhegan's dock (but you'll still need a boat) is **Manana Island,** once the home of an ex–New Yorker named Ray Phillips. Known as the Hermit of Manana, Phillips lived a solitary sheepherding existence on this barren island for more than half a century, until his death in 1975. His story had spread so far afield that even *The New York Times* ran a front-page obituary when he died. (Photos and clippings are displayed in the Monhegan Museum.) In summer, youngsters with skiffs often hang around the harbor, particularly Fish Beach and Swim Beach, and you can usually talk one of them into taking you over, for a fee. (Don't try to talk them down too much or they may not return to pick you up.) Some curious inscriptions on Manana (marked with a yellow X near the boat landing) have led archaeologists to claim that Vikings even made it here, but cooler heads attribute the markings to Mother Nature.

WHEN TO GO

If a day-trip is all your schedule will allow, visit Monhegan between Memorial Day weekend and mid-October, when ferries from Port Clyde, New Harbor, and Boothbay Harbor operate daily, allowing 5–9 hours on the island—time enough to do an extensive trail loop, visit the museum and handful of shops, and picnic on the rocks. Other months, there's only one ferry a day from Port Clyde (only three a week

Nov.–Apr.), so you'll need to spend the night—not a hardship, but it definitely requires advance planning.

Almost any time of year, but especially in spring, fog can blanket the island, curtailing photography and swimming (although usually not the ferries). A spectacular sunny day can't be beat, but the fog lends an air of mystery you won't forget, so don't be deterred. Rain, of course, is another matter; some island trails can be perilous even in a drizzle.

Other Points to Consider

Monhegan has no bank, but there's an ATM in The Barnacle. Credit cards are not universally accepted. Personal checks, travelers checks, or cash will do. The few **public telephones** in the village require phone cards.

The only **public restroom** unconnected to a restaurant or lodging is on Horn Hill, at the southern end of the village (near the Monhegan House), and it will cost you $1 to use it. It may sound pricey, but the restroom was installed to protect the woods and trails and deter day-trippers from bothering innkeepers. Unfortunately, the fee inspires some people to spurn these facilities and head for the woods. Do spend the dollar and help preserve the island.

If you're staying overnight, be sure to bring a flashlight for negotiating the unlighted island walkways, even in the village. Whitetail deer used to overrun the island, leading to a relatively high incidence of Lyme disease (transmitted by deer ticks), but deliberate thinning of the herd (don't ask how) in recent years seems to have alleviated the situation. Nonetheless, birders and hikers should err on the side of caution and wear long pants rather than shorts and tuck pant legs into socks. Check for ticks after hiking.

SIGHTS AND RECREATION

Monhegan is a getaway destination, a relaxing place for self-starters, so don't anticipate entertainment beyond the occasional lecture or narrated nature tour. Bring sturdy shoes (maybe even an extra pair in case trails are wet), a windbreaker, binoculars, a camera, and a journal. If you're staying overnight, bring a book. (If you forget, there's an amazingly good library.) In winter, bring ice skates for use on the Ice Pond.

Museum, Galleries, and Shopping

The National Historic Register **Monhegan Lighthouse**—activated in July 1824 and automated in 1959—stands at the island's highest point, Lighthouse Hill, an exposed summit that's also home to the **Monhegan Museum,** 207/596-7003, www.monheganmuseum.org, in the former keeper's house and adjacent buildings. Overseen by the **Monhegan Historical and Cultural Museum Association,** Monhegan 04852, the museum contains an antique kitchen, lobstering exhibits, and a fine collection of paintings by noted and not-so-noted artists. Two outbuildings have tools and gear connected with fishing and ice-cutting, traditional island industries. A replica of the assistant lightkeeper's house—built from the original blueprints—serves as a handsome art gallery with a climate-controlled environment for the museum's impressive art collection. A volunteer usually is on hand to answer questions. Museum hours, coordinated with the ferry schedule, are 11:30 AM–3:30 PM July–Aug., 12:30–2:30 PM in Sept. Admission is technically free, but donations are encouraged.

About 20 **artists' studios** are open to the public during the summer (usually July–Aug.), but not all at once. At least five are open most days—most in the afternoon. Wednesday and Saturday tend to have the most choices. Sometimes it's tight time-wise for day-trippers who also want to hike the trails, but most of the studios are relatively close to the ferry landing. An annually updated map/schedule details locations, days, and times. It's posted on bulletin boards and is available at lodgings and shops.

Galleries and shops in the village include **Winter Works** (craft co-op), **Lupine Gallery,** 207/594-8131, www.lupinegallery.com (art, some crafts), **Black Duck** (gifts), and the

Carina Shop (bread, produce, coffee, wine, newspapers, gourmet specialties).

Hiking and Walking

Just over half a mile wide and 1.7 miles long, barely a square mile in area, Monhegan has 18 numbered hiking trails, most easy to moderate, covering about 17 miles. All are described in the *Monhegan Associates Trail Map,* available at mainland ferry offices and island shops and lodgings—or print it out from www.monheganassociates.org/trails/map.htm. (The map is not to scale, so the hikes can take longer than you think.)

Dress in layers, including long pants, and wear hiking boots or sturdy walking shoes. Even if you're warm in the village, you'll feel the wind on the island's backside and up at the lighthouse.

The footing is uneven everywhere, so Monhegan can present major obstacles to the physically challenged, even on the well-worn but unpaved village roads. Maintain an especially healthy respect for the ocean here, and don't venture too close; over the years, rogue waves on the island's backside have claimed victims young and old.

A relatively easy **day-tripper loop** (with a couple of moderate sections along the backside of the island) that takes in several of Monhegan's finest features starts at the southern end of the village, opposite the church. To appreciate it, allow at least three hours. From the Main Rd., go up Horn Hill, following signs for the **Burnthead Trail** (#4). Cross the island to the **Cliff Trail** (#1). Turn north on the Cliff Trail, following the dramatic headlands on the island's backside. Lots of great picnic rocks in this area. Continue to Squeaker Cove, where the surf is the wildest, but be cautious. Then watch for signs to the **Cathedral Woods Trail** (#11), carpeted with pine needles and leading back to the village.

When you get back to Main Rd., detour up the **Whitehead Trail** (#7) to the museum. If you're spending the night and feeling energetic, consider circumnavigating the island via the

Cliff Trail (#s 1 and 1-A). Allow at least five or six hours for this route; don't rush it.

Birding

One of the East Coast's best birding sites during spring and fall migrations, Monhegan is a migrant trap for exhausted creatures winging their way north or south. (The Ice Pond area is a favorite site.) Avid birders come here to add rare and unusual species to their life lists, and some devotees return year after year.

Predicting exact bird-migration dates can be dicey, since wind and weather aberrations can skew the schedule. Generally, the best times are mid- to late May and most of September, into early October. If you plan to spend a night (or more) on the island during migration seasons, don't try to wing it—reserve a room well in advance.

ACCOMMODATIONS

The island has a variety of lodgings from rustic to comfortable; none qualify in the multistar category. Pickup trucks of dubious vintage meet all the ferries and transport luggage gratis to the lodgings. For cottage renters, Monhegan Trucking charges a fee for each piece of luggage.

Best lodging is the **Island Inn,** Box 128, Monhegan 04852, 207/596-0371, www.island-innmonhegan.com, an imposing three-story mid-19th-century building with an expansive veranda and lawns overlooking the ferry landing. Thirty-two harbor- and meadow-view rooms and suites (eight rooms have shared baths) are $135–325 d, including full breakfast, July–Labor Day. Early and late in the season, doubles are $110–280. (There's a $5 pp charge for a one-night stay.) The inn's restaurant, open to the public for breakfast, lunch, and dinner, has developed an excellent dinner menu with creative entrées (BYOL). Children are welcome (under five are free). No pets. Cash or check preferred, but credit cards are accepted. Open late May–early Oct.

In the heart of the village, **Monhegan House,** Monhegan 04852, 207/594-7983, www.monheganhouse.com, built in 1870, is a large four-story building with 33 rooms (shared baths, not always on the same floor as your room), which go for $123–134 d July–Labor Day, plus a $5 fee for a one-night stay. Doubles are $99 d early and late in the season. Full breakfast is included. Don't miss the loose-leaf notebook in the lobby. Labeled *A Monhegan Novel,* it's the ultimate in shaggy-dog sagas, created by a long string of guests since 1992. No smoking, no pets; credit cards accepted. Children are welcome (age three and under are free). Islanders and visitors flock to the inn's airy dining room, overlooking the village, for breakfast and dinner (BYOL); the menu has gone upscale in recent years—lobster spring rolls would have been unheard-of not so long ago on Monhegan! They'll pack a picnic if you want to hit the trails. Open late May to Columbus Day.

John and Winnie Murdock's **Shining Sails Bed-and-Breakfast,** P.O. Box 346, Monhegan 04852, 207/596-0041, www.shiningsails.com, has been thoroughly updated, has all private baths, is convenient to the dock, and stays open all year. Five efficiency apartments and two rooms (some with water views) go for $95–185 d, May–early Oct. (highest July–Aug.); two-night minimum often required. Rates are lower for multiple nights and off-season stays. A generous continental breakfast is included May–Columbus Day. No pets; no smoking; credit cards accepted. "Well-supervised" children are welcome.

Funkiest lodging, and not for everyone, is **The Trailing Yew,** 8 Lobster Cove Rd., P.O. Box 98, Monhegan 04852, 207/596-0440, owned for eons by colorful islander Josephine Davis Day, who remained omnipresent until 1996, when she died at the age of 99. Now it's managed by Marian Chioffi. Spread among five rustic buildings south of the village on the road to Lobster Cove, the 35 rooms are $62 a person (shared baths, not always in the same building), including breakfast and dinner. The old-fashioned, low-key, 50-seat dining room is also open to the public for dinner (about $18 pp) at 5:45 PM, served family-style by reservation, and for breakfast at 7:45 AM. Bring a sleeping bag in spring or fall; rooms are unheated. Only the main building has electricity. No credit cards; no pets. Open late May–early Oct.

Seasonal Rentals

More than two dozen weekly-rental cottages and apartments—categorized as very rustic, fair, very good, and excellent—are well managed by **Shining Sails Real Estate,** P.O. Box 346, Monhegan 04852, 207/596-0041, www .shiningsails.com/rentals.html. About half have electricity; the others have gas lights and appliances. Kids, pets, and smoking may be limited. Peak-season (July–Aug.) weekly rates are $685–2,370 (sleeping 2–12). Rates are lower during the rest of the season ($620–1,685). A few are available by the night, space permitting, especially off-season. To rent the most desirable places at the height of the season, you may have to make a minimum commitment (usually two weeks). If you can plan ahead, try to reserve as early as January 1, when John and Winnie Murdock begin taking reservations for the summer.

FOOD

Most visitors don't arrive on Monhegan expecting gourmet cuisine. Everything is quite casual, and food is hearty and ample, with touches of culinary creativity here and there. None of the eateries have liquor licenses, so purchase beer or wine at the Carina Shop, North End Market, or The Barnacle or bring it from the mainland. All of the restaurants and food sources are in or close to the village.

As you disembark from the ferry, you'll see the **The Barnacle,** 207/596-0371, www.island-innmonhegan.com/barnacle.html, under the same ownership as the nearby Island Inn. Mid-May–mid-Oct., this casually upscale operation is open daily 8 AM–5 PM, offering picnic-ready sandwiches and salads, plus croissants, scones, and designer coffees. There's also an ATM, and you can buy wine and beer.

North End Market, 207/594-5546, dishes up pizza (whole or by the slice), sandwiches, salads, and soups. It's a favorite of islanders, as well as a popular day-trippers' lunch spot, so beat the crowd by making this your first stop after getting off the ferry. Go up the hill from the wharf and turn right; it's ahead on your left. You can always backtrack to the galleries afterward. It's open daily.

Also a popular spot is **Murdocks' Fish and Maine,** 207/596-0041, doing seafood wraps, homemade soups and chowders. There's also an ice-cream takeout window. It's open for lunch 11 AM–3 PM weekdays and for dinner on weekends.

Behind the Monhegan House is **The Novelty,** a good location for picking up lunch (sandwiches, pizza, pastries, etc.) just before hitting the Burnthead Trail leading to the far side of the island. If you've never had a whoopie! pie, try one here.

GETTING THERE AND AROUND

See *Getting Afloat* under *Recreation* in the *St. George Peninsula* section, above, for details on cost and schedule of the only year-round Monhegan passenger ferries, which depart from Port Clyde (www.monheganboat.com). Seasonal service to the island is provided from **New Harbor** by Hardy Boat Cruises, www.hardyboat.com; and from **Boothbay Harbor** by Balmy Days Cruises, www.balmydayscruises.com.

Part of the daily routine for many islanders and summer folk is a stroll to the harbor when a ferry comes in, so don't be surprised to see a good-size welcoming party when you arrive. You're the live entertainment.

Monhegan's only vehicles are the small trucks used by **Monhegan Trucking.** If you're staying a night or longer and your luggage is too heavy to carry, they'll be waiting when you arrive at the island wharf.

The latest wrinkle in island transport is a handful of shiny golf carts, adding a different "feel" to the well-trod village paths. At least it eases the access for long-termers who, despite increasing infirmity, want to continue to return annually to the island. The carts are not available for the casual visitor; a doctor's certificate is required to use a cart on the island.

INFORMATION

Several free brochures and booklets, revised annually, will answer most questions about planning a day-trip or overnight visit to Monhegan. At the ferry ticket office in Port Clyde, pick up Clare Durst's *Visitor's Guide to Monhegan Island* (or download it ahead of time from www.briegull.com/MonheganWelcome) as well as the *Monhegan Associates Trail Map* (also available at www.monheganassociates. org/trails/map.htm). Both are also available at Monhegan shops, galleries, and lodgings, as well as at the New Harbor and Boothbay Harbor ferry offices. To obtain a copy of the latest ferry schedule, contact **Monhegan Boat Line,** P.O. Box 238, Port Clyde 04855, 207/372-8848, or print out the schedule from www.monheganboat.com/schedule.html.

The **Rockland-Thomaston Area Chamber of Commerce,** Gateway Center, One Park Drive, Rockland 04841, 207/596-0376 or 800/562-2529, www.therealmaine.com, also has information about Monhegan.

Monhegan's pleasant little library, the **Monhegan Memorial Library** (also known as the Jackie and Edward Library, after two children who drowned in the surf in the 1920s) has an especially extensive fiction collection as well as fascinating histories of Monhegan Island. It's open to everyone—and a particularly popular spot on rainy days. At the head of Wharf Hill, it's usually open Tues., Thurs., and Sat. 1–4 PM, plus two or three evenings a week; check when you arrive.

Also check the **Rope Shed,** the community bulletin board next to the meadow, right in the village. Monhegan's version of a bush telegraph, it's where everyone posts flyers and notices about nature walks, lectures, excursions, and other special events. You'll also see the current map of **Monhegan Artists Studio Locations.** Nowadays, there's also the virtual Rope Shed, an online message board where you can get a sense of Monhegan's "island culture" even before you reach the island. Log on to Monhegan Commons at www.monhegan.com, then click on the link for Rope Shed Message Board.

EMERGENCIES

Monhegan has an all-volunteer **emergency rescue squad,** 911, but the island has no doctor or medical facility, so watch your step while hiking—broken bones can make the boat ride to the mainland excruciating. Locations of several **fire boxes** are noted on the island's trail map.

Rockland Area

A "Share the Pride" campaign—kicked off in the 1980s to boost sagging civic self-esteem and the local economy—was the first step in the transformation of Rockland. Once a run-down county seat best known for the aroma of its fish-packing plants, the city has undergone a sea change—most of it for the better. Benches and plants line Main St. (Rte. 1), stores offer appealing wares, coffeehouses and more than a dozen art galleries attract a diverse clientele, and Rockland Harbor boasts more windjammer cruise schooners than neighboring Camden (which had long claimed the title "Windjammer Capital"). If you haven't been to Rockland in the last decade, prepare to be astonished.

Foresighted entrepreneurs had seen the potential of the bayside location in the late 1700s and established a tiny settlement here called "Shore Village" (or "the Shore"). Today's commercial-fishing fleet is one of the few reminders of Rockland's past, when multimasted schooners lined the wharves, some to load volatile cargoes of lime destined to become building material for cities all along the eastern seaboard, others to head northeast—toward the storm-racked Grand Banks and the lucrative cod fishery there. Such hazardous pursuits meant an early demise for many a local seafarer, but Rockland's 5,000 or so residents were enjoying their prosperity in the late 1840s. The settlement was home to more than two dozen shipyards and dozens of lime kilns, was enjoying a construction boom, and boasted a newspaper and regular steamship service. By 1854, Rockland had become a city.

Today, Rockland remains a commercial hub—with Knox County's only shopping plazas (not quite malls, but Wal-Mart has arrived), a fishing fleet that heads far offshore, and car and passenger ferries to nearby islands. Rockland also claims the title of "Lobster Capital of the World"—thanks to Knox County's shipment nationally and internationally of some 10 million pounds of lobster each year.

Present-day entrepreneurs, carried along on a whole new wave of enthusiasm, are quickly making Rockland an interesting place to live, work, and play. And, with roughly 8,000 souls, Rockland remains more year-round community than tourist town. But visitors pour in during two big summer festivals—the North Atlantic Blues Festival, in early July, and the Maine Lobster Festival, in early August. Highlight of the Lobster Festival is King Neptune's coronation of the Maine Sea Goddess—carefully selected from a bevy of local young women—who then sails off with him to his watery domain.

SIGHTS
The Farnsworth Art Museum and Wyeth Center
Anchoring downtown Rockland is the nationally respected Farnsworth Art Museum, 16 Museum St., P.O. Box 466, Rockland 04841, 207/596-6457, www.farnsworthmuseum.org, established in 1948 through a trust fund set up by Rocklander Lucy Farnsworth. With an ample checkbook, the first curator, Robert Bellows, toured the country, accumulating a splendid collection of 19th- and 20th-century Maine-related American art—the basis for the permanent *Maine in America* exhibition. The Farnsworth is a major highlight of the seven-site **Maine Art Museum Trail.**

The 10,000-piece collection today includes work by Fitz Hugh Lane, Gilbert Stuart, Eastman Johnson, Childe Hassam, John Marin, Maurice Prendergast, Rockwell Kent, George Bellows, and Marsden Hartley. Best known are the paintings by three generations of the Wyeth family (local summer residents) and sculpture by Louise Nevelson, who grew up in Rockland. Sculpture, jewelry, and paintings by Nevelson form the core of the third-floor Nevelson-Berliawsky Gallery for 20th Century Art. (The only larger Nevelson collection is in New York's Whitney Museum of American Art.)

The **Wyeth Center,** across Union St. in a former church, contains the work of Andrew, N. C., and Jamie Wyeth. The 6,000-square-foot **Jamien Morehouse Wing,** part of the main museum building, is an elegant venue for rotating exhibits.

In the Farnsworth's library—a grand, high-ceilinged oasis akin to an English gentleman's reading room—browsers and researchers can explore an extensive collection of art books and magazines. The museum's hyperactive education department annually sponsors dozens of lectures, concerts, art classes for adults and children, poetry readings, and field trips. Most are open to nonmembers; some require an extra fee. A glitzy gift shop stocks posters, prints, note cards, imported gift items, and art games for children.

Next door to the museum is the mid-19th-century Greek Revival **Farnsworth Homestead,** with original high-Victorian furnishings. Looking as though William Farnsworth's family just took off for the day, the house has been preserved rather than restored.

The Farnsworth also owns the Olson House, 14 miles away in nearby Cushing, where the whole landscape looks like a Wyeth diorama. Pick up a map at the museum to help you find the house—definitely worth the side trip.

The Farnsworth is open all year, including summer holidays; the Homestead and the Olson House are open Memorial Day weekend to Columbus Day, 11 AM–4 PM daily. Summer museum hours: every day, 10 AM–5 PM (to 7 PM Wed.–Fri.). Winter museum hours: Tues.–Sun. 10 AM–4 PM. Admission to the museum and the homestead is $10 adults, $8 seniors, $8 students 18 and older, free for kids under 18.

Main Street Historic District

Rocklanders are justly proud of their Main Street Historic District, lined with 19th- and early-20th-century Greek and Colonial Revival structures, as well as examples of mansard and Italianate architecture. Most now house retail shops on the ground floor; upper floors have offices, artists' studios, and apartments. The district starts at the corner of Winter and Main Sts. and runs north to the alley just after Kelsey's Appliance Village. The chamber of commerce has a map and details.

Lighthouse Museum

Overlooking the harbor just off Main St. (Rte. 1), the **Maine Lighthouse Museum,** One Park Drive, Rockland 04841, 207/594-3301, www.mainelighthousemuseum.com, claims to have the nation's largest collection of lighthouse and Coast Guard memorabilia: foghorns, ships' bells, nautical books and photographs, marine instruments, ship models, scrimshaw, even a giant lens built for Maine's tallest lighthouse. The eclectic flavor makes it fun for children, especially since lights and noisemakers still work. In the gift shop, the lighthouse motif adorns almost everything—postcards and T-shirts, buttons and bookends. The museum is open daily July–Labor Day weekend, Mon.–Sat. in the fall, and weekdays the rest of the year. Admission is $3 for everyone over 11.

Owls Head Transportation Museum

Don't miss this place, even if you're not an old-vehicle buff. A generous endowment has made the Owls Head Transportation Museum, Rte. 73, P.O. Box 277, Owls Head 04854, 207/594-4418, www.owlshead.org, a premier facility for celebrating wings and wheels; it draws more than 75,000 visitors a year. Scads of eager volunteers help restore the vehicles and keep them running. On weekends, May–Oct., the museum sponsors air shows (including aerobatic displays) and car and truck meets for hundreds of enthusiasts. Season highlight is the annual Wings and Wheels Spectacular (late July), when nearly 300 classic vehicles gather for two days of festivities. Want your own vintage vehicle? Attend the antique, classic, and special-interest auto auction (third weekend in August). The gift shop carries transportation-related items. If the kids get bored (unlikely), there's a play area outside, with picnic tables. In winter, groomed cross-country-skiing trails wind through the museum's 60-acre site. (Ask for a map at the information desk.) The museum, two miles south of Rockland, is open daily all year: 10 AM–5 PM (to 4 PM Nov.–Mar.). Admission is $7 adults, $5 ages 5–11, $18 for a family of four. (Special events are extra.)

PARKS AND RECREATION

Rockland Breakwater

Protecting the harbor from wind-driven waves, the 4,346-foot-long Rockland Breakwater took 18 years to build, with 697,000 tons of locally quarried granite. In the late 19th century, it was piled up, chunk by chunk, from a base 175 feet wide on the harbor floor (60 feet below the surface) to the 43-foot-wide cap. The Breakwater Light—now automated and maintained by the U.S. Coast Guard—was built in 1902 and added to the National Historic Register in 1981. The city of Rockland has leased the keeper's house to the Friends of the Rockland Breakwater (www.rocklandlighthouse.com), which opens the house on weekends from late May–mid-Oct. The breakwater provides unique vantage points for photographers, and a place to picnic or catch sea breezes or fish on a hot day, but it is extremely dangerous during storms. Anyone on the breakwater risks being washed into the sea or struck by lightning (ask the local hospital staff: it *has* happened!). Do not take chances when the weather is iffy.

To reach the breakwater, take Rte. 1 north to Waldo Ave. and turn right. Take the next right onto Samoset Rd. and drive to the end, to **Marie Reed Memorial Park** (tiny beach, benches, limited parking). Or go to the Samoset Resort and take the path to the breakwater from there.

Harbor Park

If you're looking for a municipal park with more commotion than quiet green space, spend some time at Harbor Park. Boats, cars, and delivery vehicles come and go, and you can corner a picnic table or a bench or a patch of grass and watch all the action. Public restrooms (open late May–mid-Oct.) are in the harbormaster's office. The park is just off Main St., below the Gateway Center, home of the Maine Lighthouse Museum and the chamber of commerce.

Creative Play

Kids have a great time at the **Rockland Community Playground** in Merritt Park, just behind the Rockland Recreation Center, Union and Limerock Sts. (enter on Limerock). The layout is especially imaginative, with castles, swings, and even a boat. Parents can watch from convenient benches; two-hour parking. Open sunrise to sunset.

Owls Head Light State Park

On Rte. 73, about 1.5 miles past the junction of Rtes. 1 and 73, you'll reach North Shore Rd., in the town of Owls Head. Turn left, toward Owls Head Light State Park. Located 3.6 miles from this turn, Owls Head Light occupies a dramatic promontory with panoramic views over Rockland Harbor and Penobscot Bay. Don't miss it. The keeper's house and the light tower are off limits, but the park surrounding the tower has easy walking paths, picnic tables, and a pebbly beach where you can sunbathe or check out Rockland Harbor's boating traffic. (If it's foggy or rainy, don't climb the steps toward the light tower: the view evaporates in the fog, the access ramp can be slippery, and the foghorn is dangerously deafening.) Follow signs to reach the park. From North Shore Rd., turn left onto Main St., then left onto Lighthouse Rd., and continue along Owls Head Harbor to the parking area. This is also a particularly pleasant bike route—about 10 miles round-trip from downtown Rockland—although the roadside shoulders are poor along the Owls Head stretch.

Swimming

Lucia Beach is the local name for **Birch Point Beach State Park,** one of the best-kept secrets in the area. Located in Owls Head, just south of Rockland—and about two miles from Owls Head Light—the spruce-lined sand crescent (free; outhouses but no other facilities) has rocks, shells, tidepools, and very chilly water. There's ample room for a moderate-size crowd, although parking and turnaround space can get a bit tight on the access road. From downtown Rockland, take Rte. 73 one mile to North

Shore Dr. (on your left). Take the next right, Ash Point Dr., and continue past Knox County Regional Airport to Dublin Rd. Turn right, go 0.8 mile, then turn left onto Ballyhac Rd. (opposite airport landing lights). Go another 0.8 mile, fork left onto an unpaved road, and continue 0.4 mile to the parking area.

If frigid ocean water doesn't appeal, head for freshwater **Chickawaukee Lake,** on Rte. 17, two miles inland from downtown Rockland. Don't expect to be alone, though; on hot days, **Johnson Memorial Park**'s pocket-size sand patch is a major attraction. A lifeguard holds forth; there are restrooms, picnic tables, a snack bar, and a boat-launch ramp. (In winter, iceboats, snowmobiles, and ice-fishing shacks take over the lake.) A signposted bicycle path runs alongside the busy highway, making the park an easy pedal from town.

Golf

The **Rockland Golf Club,** 606 Old County Rd., 0.2 mile northeast of Rte. 17, Rockland 04841, 207/594-9322, ranks high on many a Maine golfer's list. Established in 1932, the 18-hole public course is open Apr.–Oct. In July–Aug., you'll need to reserve a starting time a day or so in advance if you plan to tee off anytime after 7 AM The modern clubhouse—rebuilt after a disastrous fire in the late 1980s—has a full bar and serves breakfast and lunch at reasonable prices. Parking is plentiful.

For an 18-hole course in an unsurpassed waterfront setting (but steeper rental and greens fees), check out the links at the **Samoset Resort,** technically in Rockport but most often reached via Rockland. Resort guests receive golf discounts, and the course often has a longer season than others in the area.

(See *Golf* in the Camden-Rockport Area for another nearby public course.)

Bike and Sea-Kayak Rentals

The go-to place for bike sales and rentals is **Bikesenjava,** 481 Main St., Rockland 04841, 207/596-1004, www.haybikesenjava.com, which rents adult hybrid or mountain bikes for $16 a day (including a map). The shop sponsors

group rides and other activities—and you can fill your Thermos at the coffee bar with Red Bull or an iced latte before you head out. Bikesenjava is open weekdays 8 AM–5 PM, weekends 9 AM–4 PM.

Maine Sport Outfitters, Rte. 1, Rockport 04856, 207/236-8797, 888/236-8797 (store), 800/722-0826 (rentals, tours), www.mainesport.com, just north of Rockland, is the best full-service source for renting bikes and kayaks and buying gear. For suggested cycling and sea kayaking routes, see the Thomaston Area and Camden-Rockport Area sections.

GETTING AFLOAT

Rockland has a variety of ways to get afloat: windjammer cruises, excursion boats, and the Maine State Ferry Service. Plus the yachting fraternity has discovered Rockland Harbor, and mooring space has mushroomed. If you're arriving aboard your own boat, the Rockland harbormaster, operating out of the white building in Harbor Park, 207/594-0314, can provide details on guest moorings. Inside the building are pay showers and restrooms.

Other nearby anchorages with facilities for boaters are Spruce Head, Tenants Harbor, and Port Clyde to the south; Camden and Rockport to the north.

Windjammer Cruises

Nine traditional windjammer schooners call Rockland home; all but one head out for 3–14 days, late May–mid-Oct, tucking into coves and harbors around Penobscot Bay and its islands. The mostly engineless craft set their itineraries by the wind, propelled by stiff breezes to Bucks Harbor, North Haven, and Deer Isle where passengers can hike, shop, and sightsee. Then it's back to the boat for chow—windjammer cooks are legendary for creating three hearty, all-you-can-eat meals daily, including at least one lobster feast! Everything's totally informal, geared for relaxing.

Down below, cabins typically are small and basic, with paper-thin walls—sort of a campground afloat (earplugs are available for light sleepers). Romantic it isn't, although some captains keep track of post-cruise marriages. Most boats have shared showers and toilets. If you're Type-A, given to pacing, don't inflict yourself on the cruising crowd. If you're flexible, ready for whatever, sign on. You can help with the sails, eat, curl up with a book, inhale salt air, shoot photos, eat, sunbathe, birdwatch, eat, chat up fellow passengers, sleep, eat, or just settle back and enjoy spectacular sailing you'll never forget.

The best-known boats in Rockland's fleet are two schooners based at North End Shipyard, P.O. Box 482, Rockland 04841, 207/594-8007 or 800/648-4544, www.schooneramericaneagle.com and www.schoonerheritage.com. Capt. John Foss skippers the 92-foot, 26-passenger *American Eagle* (three, four, six, or fourteen days; no kids under 12; $450–1,995 pp), Capts. Doug and Linda Lee operate the 95-foot, 30-passenger *Heritage* (four or six days; no kids under 12; $575–865 pp). Also based at the North End Shipyard is the 65-foot, 22-passenger *Isaac H. Evans,* P.O. Box 791, Rockland 04841, 877/238-1325, www.isaacevans.com, skippered by Capt. Brenda Walker (three, four, or six days; no kids under six; $475–850 pp). The *Eagle* and the *Evans* are National Historic Landmarks.

Built in 1900, and largest in the fleet, is the three-masted, 132-foot, 35-passenger *Victory Chimes* (three, four, five, or seven days; kids welcome; $450–850 pp), skippered by Capt. Kip Files, P.O. Box 1401, Rockland 04841, 207/594-0755 or 800/745-5651, www.victorychimes.com. The *Chimes,* an especially elegant vessel with all sails set, is also a National Historic Landmark.

Other schooners sailing out of Rockland are the 22-passenger *Stephen Taber,* P.O. Box 1050, Rockland 04841, 207/236-3520 or 800/999-7352, www.stephentaber.com (three, four, or six days; $445–915 pp); the 24-passenger *Nathaniel Bowditch,* 4 Gay St. Pl., Rockland 04841, 207/596-0401 or 800/288-4098, www.windjammervacation.com (three, four, five, or six days; $450–825 pp); the 24-passenger *J. & E. Riggin,* 136 Holmes St., Rockland 04841, 207/594-1875 or 800/869-0604, www.mainewindjammer.com (three, four, or six days; no kids under 6; $495–875 pp); and the seven-passenger *Summertime,* 115 S. Main St., Rockland 04841, 800/562-8290 (three or six days; no kids under 14; $395–635 pp). The *Riggin* and the *Taber* are also National Historic Landmarks.

If you can't spare three days or, ideally, a week, the 67-foot, 14-passenger schooner-yacht *Wendameen,* P.O. Box 252, Rockland 04841, 207/594-1751, www.schooneryacht.com, does one-night sails (2 PM–9 AM) out of Rockland's North End Shipyard. Cost is $180 pp, including dinner and breakfast. No children under three.

On the summer cruising schedule, several weeks are particularly popular because they coincide with special windjammer events, so you'll need to book a berth far in advance for these: mid-June (Windjammer Days in Boothbay Harbor), first week in August (Swans Island Sweet Chariot Music Festival), Labor Day weekend (Windjammer Weekend in Camden), second week in September (WoodenBoat Sail-In).

Seven of Rockland's schooners *(Eagle, Heritage, Evans, Riggin, Bowditch, Taber, Chimes)* and seven of Camden and Rockport's are members of **The Maine Windjammer Association,** P.O. Box 1144, Blue Hill 04614, 800/807-9463, www.sailmainecoast.com, an excellent one-stop resource for vessel and schedule information.

Daysailing

Based at Rockland's Harbor Park is the classic 55-foot ketch *A Morning in Maine,* designed by noted naval architect R. D. (Pete) Culler, built by Concordia Yachts, and owned by Captain Bob Pratt (207/691-7245, www.amorninginmaine.com). Between late May and mid-Oct., *Morning* departs from the Middle Pier at the Rockland Public Landing at 10 AM and 1 and 4 PM for two-hour daysails, with knowledgeable commentary from Captain Pratt. (Weather permitting, sunset cruises are also on the schedule in July–Aug.) Maximum

21 passengers ($30 pp). Inquire about special boat-and-breakfast overnights ($375 a couple), which include a two-hour sail.

Sea Kayaking

Veteran Maine Guide and naturalist Mark Di-Girolamo is the sparkplug behind **Breakwater Kayak,** Landings Restaurant dock, Rockland 04841, 207/596-6895 or 877/559-8800, www.breakwaterkayak.com, which has a full range of tours, even multiday ones. A three-hour Rockland Harbor tour is $60 pp, and a four-hour Owls Head Light tour is $75 pp, including a picnic lunch. Reservations are advisable. This outfit is particularly eco-sensitive, definitely worth supporting. Maine Audubon often taps Mark to lead natural-history field trips. Dress warmly for these tours, and be sure to bring your own water bottle (filled).

Maine State Ferry Service

In 1996, a fancy new ferry terminal opened on Rockland's waterfront, serving regular car and passenger ferries headed for the islands of Vinalhaven, North Haven, and Matinicus. (See the On the Road chapter for ferry schedules.) The Vinalhaven and North Haven routes make fantastic day-trips (especially with a bike), or you can spend the night; the Matinicus ferry is much less predictable.

ENTERTAINMENT

Rockland's downtown movie house, built in 1923, underwent an upmarket rehabbing in 2004, reopening in mid-2005 under a handsome retro marquee as **The Strand Theatre,** 345 Main St., Rockland 04841, 207/594-0070, www.rocklandstrand.com. The Strand offers films as well as live concerts, with cinema tickets going for $8 adults, $6.50 seniors and teens, and $6 kids under 12. Open all year.

The Strand's competition—but without its artistic flair—is the Flagship Cinema multiplex, out on Rte. 1, just over the Rockland line in Thomaston. (See the Thomaston Area section.)

Prime locales for live entertainment are **Waterworks Pub** and **Second Read Books &** **Coffee,** the **Time Out Pub,** and the **Breakwater Lounge** at the Samoset Resort.

FESTIVALS AND EVENTS

In early July (usually the second weekend), the **North Atlantic Blues Festival** (www .northatlanticbluesfestival.com) has become a huge summer event since it began in 1994. (More than 16,000 enthusiasts showed up in 2004.) More than a dozen blues stars take the stage in Rockland's Harbor Park for two days, and the Saturday-night "club crawl" brings nonstop blues to more than a dozen downtown venues. August's **Maine Lobster Festival** is a five-day lobster extravaganza, with live entertainment, the Maine Sea Goddess pageant, a lobster-crate race, craft booths, boat rides, a parade, countless lobster dinners, and mega-crowds (the hotels are full for miles in either direction). Tons of lobsters bite the dust during the weekend—despite occasional protests by the People for the Ethical Treatment of Animals. (The protests seem to increase the crowds.)

SHOPPING

Art Galleries

Piggybacking on the fame of the Farnsworth Museum, or at least working symbiotically, more than a dozen art galleries have opened in Rockland since 1990, with more likely to come. Ask around and look around. During the summer, many of them coordinate monthly openings (usually a Wednesday evening), so you can meander and munch (and sip) from one gallery to another.

Across from the Farnsworth's side entrance, the **Caldbeck Gallery,** 12 Elm St., Rockland 04841, 207/594-5935, www.caldbeck.com, has gained a topnotch reputation as a "must-see" (and "must-be-seen") space. Featuring the work of contemporary Maine artists, the gallery mounts more than half a dozen solo and group shows each year, May–Sept. Open Mon.–Sat. 11 AM–5 PM, Sun. 1–5 PM.

In a boutique-y building next to the Caldbeck is **Elan Fine Arts,** 8 Elm St., 207/596-9933, www.ElanFineArts.com, which features an eclectic range of group shows throughout the summer.

Also gaining a high profile is **The Gallery at 357 Main,** 357 Main St., 207/596-0084. It's open Mon.–Sat. 10 AM–5 PM, Sun. 1–5 PM, May–late Dec.

Other eminently browse-worthy downtown-Rockland galleries are **Harbor Square Gallery,** 374 Main St., 207/594-8700 or 877/594-8700, www.harborsquaregallery.com; **Nan Mulford Gallery,** 313 Main St., 207/594-8481, www.nanmulfordgallery.com; **ART SPACE,** 342 Main St., 207/594-8784, www.LincolnStreet-Center.org, a cooperative gallery showing the works of more than two dozen members; and **Gallery One,** 365 Main St., 207/594-5441, above Huston-Tuttle.

Books, Crafts, Gifts, and Clothing

An independent bookstore with inventories of best-sellers, cookbooks, kids' books, remainders, magazines, and CDs, **The Reading Corner,** 408 Main St., Rockland 04841, 207/596-6651, occupies two full rooms in downtown Rockland. Open all year, Mon.–Sat.

Left (south) of The Reading Corner is **The Grasshopper Shop,** 400 Main St., Rockland 04841, 207/596-6156, an eclectic emporium filled with jewelry, clothing, shoes, accessories, cards, toys, and unusual gifts, all tastefully displayed beneath a handsome antique tin ceiling. An updated version of a Camden shop that closed in the mid-1990s, The Grasshopper is open all year, including Sundays in summer.

Again walking south, you'll come to the **Island Institute,** 386 Main St., Rockland 04841, 207/594-9209, fax 594-9314, a nonprofit steward of Maine's 4,617 offshore islands. The ground floor is occupied by **Archipelago,** 207/596-0701 or 800/339-9209, www.thearchipelago.net, an attractive retail outlet for talented craftspeople from 14 local islands (as well as some from the mainland). The shop also carries island-related books. Summer hours are 9 AM–7 PM Mon.–Sat. and

11 AM–5 PM Sun.; winter hours are 10 AM–5 PM Mon.–Sat.

Appropriately labeling its wares "elegant necessities and practical indulgences," **Meander,** 373 Main St., Rockland 04841, 207/596-6781, www.meanderofmaine.com, has all those splurge items you'd love to own but can't quite bring yourself to buy. Lamps, ties, leather items, jewelry, even furniture—it's all here. The shop is open Mon.–Sat. 10 AM–5:30 PM (Sun. noon–5 PM in summer).

Discount Shopping

Rockland has several outlets for real bargains on new and used clothing and footwear. **Puddleduck's** 150 Union St., Rockland 04841, 207/596-0791, is a consignment shop for used infants' and children's clothing and maternity wear. Open all year, Tues.–Sat. 10 AM–4 PM, **Ravishing Recalls,** 389 Main St., Rockland 04841, 207/596-6164, is a high-quality consignment shop. **Goodwill Industries Retail Store,** Harbor Plaza, 235 Camden St., Rockland 04841, 207/594-2419, carries hand-me-downs plus overstocks from a big-name sportswear outfitter; proceeds benefit people with disabilities. And—unsurprisingly—Rockland has both Wal-Mart and T.J. Maxx.

In Rockport, less than a mile north of Rockland's city limits, you'll find the **Super Shoes,** 1070 Commercial St. (Rte. 1), Glen Cove 04846, 207/594-2001, where you can buy many brand-named casual and dress shoes at reduced rates. The store is open daily most of the year.

Natural Foods and Farmers Markets

An old-fashioned cooperative where members "do time" in return for reduced prices, the **Good Tern Natural Foods,** 750 Main St., Rockland 04841, 207/594-8822, carries lots of bulk grains and nuts, plus organic produce and frozen foods. Nonmembers pay slightly higher prices. Open Mon.–Sat. 9:30 AM–6 PM (to 5 PM Sat.). Several other good sources of natural foods and vitamins are a few miles up Rte. 1 in Rockport and Camden.

The **Rockland Farmers Market** gets

underway each Thursday 9 AM–1 PM, June–early Oct. at Harbor Park, on Rockland's Public Landing. Wares include home-grown produce, crafts, syrup, free-range poultry, mushrooms, baked goods, and artisan cheeses. Most weeks, there's a special event—music, dancers, lectures, special giveaways, and occasionally a llama or goat for the kids to pet.

ACCOMMODATIONS

If you're planning an overnight stay in the Rockland area the first weekend in August—during the Maine Lobster Festival—*be sure* to make reservations well in advance. Festival attendance runs close to 100,000, No Vacancy signs extend from Waldoboro to Belfast, and there just aren't enough beds or campsites to go around.

Samoset Resort

The 221-acre waterfront Samoset Resort, 220 Warrenton St., Rockport 04856, 207/594-2511 or 800/341-1650, www.samosetresort .com, straddles the boundary between Rockland and Rockport, the next town to the north. Most guests get to it via Rockland, from the south. Built on the ashes of a classic, 19th-century summer hotel, the Samoset is a top-of-the-line modern resort with knockout ocean views from most of its 178 rooms and suites, plus 72 separate condos. (Plans are afoot for a major expansion.) Conferences go on here throughout the year, but it's also a great family place, particularly off-season—with special package rates, indoor and outdoor swimming pools, fitness center, lighted tennis courts, cross-country skiing, kids' programs, and a fabulous 18-hole waterfront golf course. The elegant, bay-view Marcel's Restaurant has an ambitious, pricey menu (entrées $19–34); jackets are suggested for dinner, and reservations are a good idea. It's open for breakfast and dinner. The best deal is Sunday brunch—a huge, all-you-can-eat buffet. Marcel's is open daily, 7–10:30 AM and 6–9 PM; Sunday brunch is available 10 AM–2 PM. More casual is the Breakwater Lounge, with light fare, live entertainment, and a fabulous

water-view patio area (weather permitting). The lounge is open 11:30 AM–9:30 PM for lunch and dinner, to midnight for drinks.

Peak-season (early July–Labor Day) doubles go for $199–389; $129–249 other months. One-bedroom condos year-round range $215–499 per night, with weekly rates available. Rooms, suites, and condos have phones, cable TV, air-conditioning, and lots of other amenities; no pets.

Motels

Directly opposite the state terminal for passenger and car ferries serving the islands of Vinalhaven, North Haven, and Matinicus, the 81-room **Navigator Motor Inn,** 520 Main St., Rockland 04841, 207/594-2131 or 800/545-8026, www.navigatorinn.com, is a five-story shingled place with cable TV, air-conditioning, phones, and laundry facilities. Upper-floor rooms have plenty of space and great views of the harbor, but be prepared for traffic noise from the parking lot and street. Rates are $59–139 d, depending on the view and the season (two-night minimum during the lobster festival, three-night minimum during the blues festival). The bright, modern Portside Restaurant and Lounge serves reasonably priced food, 6:30 AM–9:30 PM. Open all year.

Rockland abuts Rockport, and several Rockport motels are close to Rockland's city limits.

Bed-and-Breakfasts

Newest of Rockland's bed-and-breakfasts is **The Berry Manor Inn,** 81 Talbot Ave., P.O. Box 1117, Rockland 04841, 207/596-7696 or 800/774-5692, www.berrymanorinn.com, on a quiet side street a few blocks from downtown. Cheryl Michaelsen and Michael LaPosta have totally restored the manse built in 1898 by wealthy Rocklander Charles Berry as a wedding gift for his wife (thoughtful fellow!). High ceilings and wonderful Victorian architectural touches are everywhere, especially in the enormous front hall and two parlors. Twelve Victorian-decor rooms (eight in the main house, four in the carriage house) have private baths, gas fireplaces, air-conditioning, hair dryers, dataports, journals, and more. A guest pantry is stocked with free soda and juices. Rates are $245–235 d, mid-June–mid-Oct.; $95–155 the rest of the year. In a quirky twist, Groundhog Day is a big deal here, with special packages at $125–185. No smoking, no pets, no children under 12. Open all year.

Opened in 1996, the three-story **Captain Lindsey House Inn,** 5 Lindsey St., P.O. Box 864, Rockland 04841, 207/596-7950 or 800/523-2145, www.lindseyhouse.com, dates back to 1837. Ken and Ellen Barnes (former owners of the Rockland-based windjammer *Stephen Taber*) gutted the handsome brick structure and restored it dramatically, adding such modern touches as phones, air-conditioning, wireless Internet access, and TV. The library has a desk and dataport. Don't miss the 1926 safe in the front hall—not to mention the antiques that fill the nine comfortable rooms. Rates are $85–190 d, including continental breakfast, depending on the season. No smoking, no pets, no children under 12. Open all year.

Filled with reproduction furnishings and unusual touches, the **Limerock Inn,** 96 Limerock St., Rockland 04841, 207/594-2257 or 800/546-3762, www.LimeRockInn.com, is an 1890s National Historic Register mansion on a quiet street. Each of the eight rooms has its own distinctive flavor–such as the Turret Room with a wedding canopy bed and the Island Cottage Room with a private deck overlooking the back gardens. No pets, no smoking; children are welcome. Rooms are $100–195 d, including breakfast in the Victorian dining room. Open year-round, but call ahead in midwinter.

Across the street from the ferry terminal (and next door to the Navigator Motor Inn), the turn-of-the-19th-century **Old Granite Inn,** 546 Main St., Rockland 04841, 207/594-9036 or 800/386-9036, www.oldgraniteinn.com, couldn't be more convenient for island-goers. Innkeepers Ragan and John Cary will get you started with a hearty breakfast. Nine rooms with private baths have homey touches and several are wheelchair-accessible. The three-story

inn is on Rte. 1, but thick granite walls subdue traffic noise, so most rooms are quiet. (Request a back or side room if you're particularly noise-sensitive.) No smoking; three-day minimum during the Maine Lobster Festival. Rates are $140–170 d, June–Oct. Open all year, but call ahead off-season.

Graciously run by the mother-and-daughter team of Judy and Melissa Waterman, the **Waterman House & Gardens,** 33 Grove St., Rockland 04841, 207/596-0093, www.watermanhouse.com, has two Victorian-style rooms with queen beds at $90 d, including Judy's more-than-generous breakfasts. (Rates are higher during summer festival weekends.) Located in a quiet residential area (across from the Lincoln Street Center for Arts and Education), the Waterman House is a five-minute walk from the waterfront. No smoking, no pets, no credit cards. Open all year.

FOOD
Breakfast and Lunch

It used to be tough to find anything more than run-of-the-mill lunch fare in Rockland; now it's tough to make a decision. The prize for most-creative breakfasts and lunches goes to the **Brown Bag,** 606 Main St., Rockland 04841, 207/596-6372 or 800/287-6372, bakery 207/596-6392, which has grown from a single room in 1987 to two rooms and a bakery. The Brown Bag is *the* place for breakfast, especially weekends, with fantastic baked goods and a full blackboard of other options. Lunches include a half-dozen veggie choices and imaginative salads. This is a great place to assemble a picnic. Order at the counter; no table service. Open Mon.–Sat. 6:30 AM–4 PM, the Brown Bag is at the junction of Rte. 1 and N. Main St.

Backed up against an outside wall of the Brown Bag is a longstanding Rockland lunch landmark—**Wasses Hot Dogs,** 2 N. Main St., Rockland 04841, 207/594-7472, source of great chili dogs and creative ice cream (in waffle cones). This onetime lunch wagon is now a permanent modular building—only for takeout, though. It's open all year, Mon.–Sat. 10:30 AM–6 PM and Sun. 11 AM–4 PM. Branch "wagons" carry on the tradition in Belfast and the south end of Rockland.

Probably the most popular "lunch bunch" locale is **Market on Main,** 315 Main St., Rockland 04841, 207/594-0015, www.marketonmain.com. Owned by the energetic entrepreneurs of Café Miranda (see below), "MOM's" has homemade soups, ethnic munchies and salads, chili, burgers, and super sandwiches made with hot-from-the-oven focaccia. Sunday brunch includes such creativity as Thai eggs and Italian French toast; dinner entrées are similarly imaginative. (The kids' menu includes PB&J as well as "Evan's—nothing, $0.00.") Open all year, 11 AM–7 PM (to 8 PM in summer).

Lots of Rockland-watchers credit **Second Read Books & Coffee,** 328 Main St., Rockland 04841, 207/594-4123, with sparking the designer-food renaissance in town. In 1995, it outgrew its original space and moved into this high-ceilinged room in a historic downtown block. Order soup, sandwiches, coffee, or pastries at the counter, then peruse the shelves of "pre-read books" while you wait. Second Read has become an institution. Open all year, Mon.–Sat. 7:30 AM–5:30 PM (to 10 PM Fri.–Sat.), Sunday noon–5 PM. Check local papers (or call) for a schedule of live entertainment, including Irish music, acoustic acts, and poetry readings.

If you're craving a decent breakfast (or lunch or snack) and up for a little foray "down the peninsula," head for the **Owls Head General Store,** 2 S. Shore Dr., Owls Head 04854, 207/596-6038, where the atmosphere is friendly and definitely contagious. The lobster rolls (on homemade bread) are among the best in the area, and the helpful staff will even take your photograph in front of the store. Summer hours are 5:30 AM–7 PM Mon.–Sat. (to 8 PM Fri.–Sat.) and 7 AM–3 PM Sun. In winter, they're open 6:30 AM–6 PM Mon.–Sat. (to 7 PM Fri.–Sat.) and 7 AM–3 PM Sun. The store is quite close to Owls Head Light.

Inexpensive to Moderate

The surest sign of Rockland's gentrification was the 2004 opening of **In Good Company,** 415 Main St., Rockland 04841, 207/593-9110, an eclectically decorated two-room wine bar with antique ceilings and a decommissioned bank vault overflowing (not quite literally) with wine bottles. Best of all, owner Melody Wolfertz, a skilled chef, turns out a changing weekly selection of unusual and very reasonably priced appetizers and entrées to accompany the 50 or 60 wine choices (by the bottle or the glass; boutique beers are also available). No reservations, so you take your chances getting into this popular spot. Open all year, beginning at 4 PM, but not every day in winter.

When you're *really* famished, head for **Conte's Fish Market & Restaurant,** Harbor Park, off Main St., Rockland 04841, 207/596-5579, where portions are humongous and prices are not. John Conte moved here from New York in 1995, bringing his family's century-old restaurant tradition. Specialties are pasta and seafood—Italian all the way, loaded with garlic. The decor is wildly funky—fishnets, marine relics, old books, even stacks of canned plum tomatoes—all with a terrific view of Rockland Harbor. Menus are handwritten and in-your-face at the door (order before you sit down), table coverings are yesterday's newspapers, and Edith Piaf *chansons* or operatic arias might be playing in the background. Bring your sense of humor and don't be put off by the exterior or the attitude; there's life behind the doors. No credit cards. Open daily for dinner, all year.

Moderate

Café Miranda, 15 Oak St., Rockland 04841, 207/594-2034, www.cafemiranda.com, is summed up in one of its many hilarious slogans, "We do not serve the food of cowards." This popular, casual place is terrific—and moderately priced—with a huge and eminently adventurous menu that changes daily. Lots of pastas, smoked items, veggies, olive oil, greens, and way-out combinations. Entrées are $16–22, but many of the appetizers ($4–9) are enough for a meal—or order two appetizers.

Fresh-from-the-brick-oven focaccia comes with everything. Sit at the counter and watch chef/co-owner Kerry Altiero orchestrate his creations. Beer and wine only. Reservations are essential in summer, on weekends, and whenever a good flick is playing at the local cinemas. Open daily, early Feb.–Dec., 5:30–9 PM.

Amalfi, 421 Main St., Rockland 04841, 207/596-0012, www.amalfi-tonight.com, is a Mediterranean oasis in the middle of downtown. The three dozen seats fill up quickly, but occasionally they'll set up a handful of tables in the brick-walled basement. Reservations are essential, especially on weekends. Entrées are in the $14–21 range; appetizers are $6–13. Excellent wine list and hard-to-resist desserts. Open for dinner at 5 PM Tues.–Sun. all year.

Southwest fare dominates the menu at the **Park Street Grille,** 279 Main St. at Park St., Rte. 1, Rockland 04841, 207/594-4944. Steaks and seafood are also specialties at this casual, bright spot at the southern end of the main drag. Local TV chef Royce Wright oversees everything, and service is efficient. The nacho platter could make a whole meal. Entrée range is $5–15. Open 11:30 AM–2:30 PM Tues.–Sat., and 5:30–9 PM daily.

Ethnic Options

East meets West at **Oh! Bento,** 10 Leland St., Rockland 04841, 207/593-9216, where the Japanese owners have created a local destination for Japanese cuisine. Named after the traditional Japanese box lunches, the restaurant fills small rooms and niches on the first floor of a backstreet house. Japanese family treasures are everywhere, and some handcrafts are for sale. Service is excellent. Entrées average $14 on the extensive menu; it's hard to resist the appetizers and great sushi choices ($4–6). Oh! Bento is a block off Rte. 1, on the street behind the Brown Bag (see above). It's open Tues.–Sat. 11 AM–2:30 PM and 5:30–8:30 PM.

Worthwhile Wallet-Cruncher

Arriving in Rockland trailing an award-winning reputation, chef Melissa Kelly opened **Primo,** 2 S. Main St. (Rte. 73), Rockland 04841, 207/596-0770, www.primorestaurant.com, in the spring of 2000 and hasn't had time to breathe. With six rooms in an air-conditioned Victorian home, the aptly named Primo has first-rate cuisine (and presentation) and attentive service. Fresh local ingredients are a high priority (note the greenhouses out back), and unusual fish specials appear every day. Appetizers are especially imaginative; entrée range is $24–34. Co-owner and pastry chef Price Kushner produces an impressive range of breads and desserts. Reservations are essential, typically a few weeks ahead on mid-summer weekends—and you still may have to wait when you get there. Open 5:30–10 PM daily in summer; reduced days and hours off-season. The restaurant is at the southern end of Rockland, on the Owls Head boundary.

Lobster-in-the-Rough

Although several Rockland restaurants serve lobster dinners, the best, closest alfresco spots for pigging out on the delicious crustaceans are several wharves on the St. George Peninsula.

INFORMATION AND SERVICES

The **Rockland-Thomaston Area Chamber of Commerce,** Gateway Center, One Park Dr., Rockland 04841, 207/596-0376 or 800/562-2529, www.therealmaine.com, with a very welcoming staff, occupies the newly created Gateway Center, overlooking Rockland's waterfront. Sharing the newly rehabbed building with the Maine Lighthouse Museum, the chamber is open daily in summer, weekdays off-season.

The handsome stone **Rockland Public Library,** Union St., Rockland 04841, 207/594-0310, www.rocklandlibrary.org, has been a local landmark since 1904, when townsfolk received a $20,000 Carnegie grant to jump-start its construction. Recently enhanced by a multimillion-dollar renovation, with state-of-the-art facilities, the library is open Mon., Tues., and Thurs. 9 AM–8 PM; Wed., Fri., and

Mid-Coast Region

Sat. 9 AM–5 PM. The Book Stop, where you can buy secondhand books, is open Mon.–Tues. afternoons and Sat. morning.

Newspapers

Local news, features, and calendar listings appear in the weekly *VillageSoup Times* (which also has an online version: http://knox.villagesoup.com) and in Rockland's *Courier-Gazette,* published three times weekly. *The Free Press,* a weekly, 207/596-0055, has feature articles, excellent opinion pieces, and the area's most extensive calendar listings. It also produces a helpful *Summer Dining Guide,* available at shops, supermarkets, and other locales throughout the area.

Emergencies

The closest hospital is on the Rockland/Rockport boundary. **Penobscot Bay Medical Center,** 6 Glen Cove Dr., Rockport 04856, 207/596-8000, www.nehealth.org/pbmc.asp, has round-the-clock emergency-room care and all private rooms. For **police, fire, and ambulance,** dial 911.

Public Restrooms

You'll find public restrooms at the **Gateway Center;** the **Knox County Court House,** Union and Masonic Sts.; the **Rockland Recreation Center,** across from the court house, next to the playground, Union and Limerock Sts.; the **Rockland Public Library;** and the **Maine State Ferry Service terminal.**

Special Courses

Part of the international Outward Bound network, **Hurricane Island Outward Bound School,** 75 Mechanic St., Rockland 04841, 207/594-5548 or 866/746-9771, www.hurricaneisland.org, was founded in 1964 as a maritime adjunct to the national program. Maine sea courses take place in Penobscot Bay; land-based courses are held around Newry, in western Maine's mountains. An extensive course catalog is available.

Begun in 1986 to provide language classes for adults, **Penobscot School,** 28 Gay St.,

Rockland 04841, 207/594-1084, www.languagelearning.org, has become a multicultural clearinghouse with ties around the globe. The school, always alert to new networking opportunities, has managed to heighten cultural awareness among statewide corporations, state government, and local service organizations. The school offers day and evening courses in nearly a dozen languages, sponsors ethnic dinners and festivals, organizes language-immersion weekends, and puts on international study programs in local schools. During July and August, international students (ages 18–65) arrive at the school for intensive three-week English-language courses. So many alumni have talked up the summer program that there is often a waiting list. On summer weekdays, visitors are often invited for lunch at the school to interact with students practicing their English. Call for information.

Bay Island Sailing School, 117 Tillson Ave., Rockland 04841, 207/596-7550 or 800/421-2492, www.sailme.com, is an American Sailing Association–approved summer program that has weekday, weekend, and live-aboard learn-to-sail classes. Contact the school for details. (Bay Island also charters bareboats for experienced skippers.)

Photo Services

Whatever photo service you need, it's available at **P.D.Q. Photo** (Prints Done Quickly), 491 Main St., Rockland 04841, 207/594-5010, close to the Maine State Ferry Service terminal. Debbie and Steve Morrison sell film, provide one-hour photo services (regular or digital), and take passport photos.

Laundry

Across from the fire station, **Park St. Laundromat & Dry Cleaners,** 117 Park St., Rockland 04841, 207/594-9393, lets you do your own laundry—or they'll do it if you bring it in before 10 AM. Open daily 7 AM–9 PM. Across from McDonald's, **Garden Island Cleaners and Laundry,** 44 Maverick St., Rockland 04841, 207/596-0001, with plenty of self-service machines, is open daily 7 AM–9 PM (to 7 PM Sun.).

Getting Around

Coastal Trans, 207/596-6605 or 800/289-6605, a nonprofit organization, operates a weekday, wheelchair-accessible van service throughout Rockland, 8:15 AM–3:30 PM, with a dozen regular stops (signposted Rockland Shuttle). One-way fare is $1.50; round-trip (good for unlimited rides all day) is $3 (exact change required). Other special in-town services are available, as well as transport to and from outlying communities. Call for a schedule.

Between Memorial Day and Labor Day, **All Aboard Trolley Company,** 207/594-9300 or 866/594-9300, www.aatrolley.com, provides daily service (9 AM–5 PM) along a scheduled route between Snow Marine Park (south end of Rockland) and the Samoset Resort (next to the Rockland Breakwater). The 15 stops along the way (blue signposts) include the Public Landing, the Maine State Ferry Service terminal, the shopping plazas, the library, and the Farnsworth Art Museum.

An efficient **taxi** service is active in Rockland and the surrounding areas. Telephone for a pickup. **Schooner Bay Limo and Taxi,** 207/594-5000, www.alldirections.net, provides round-the-clock service. Taxis usually are waiting at the Maine State Ferry Service terminal (where Concord Trailways buses from Boston and Portland stop), and there's a pay phone outside when the terminal is closed. The Rockland taxis are accustomed to making runs to Port Clyde for the ferry to Monhegan.

Camden-based **Mid-Coast Limo,** 207/236-2424 or 800/937-2424, www.midcoastlimo.com, provides van service, by reservation, between Rockland and Portland International Jetport.

Besides connecting Rockland with Vinalhaven, North Haven, and Matinicus, the **Maine State Ferry Service** has car ferries from other Maine coastal locations to Islesboro, Swans Island, and Frenchboro. Passenger-ferry trips to Monhegan depart from New Harbor and Boothbay Harbor.

Mid-Coast Region

Rockland's Ferry-Linked Islands

Penobscot Bay's three major year-round islands are Vinalhaven, North Haven, and Matinicus. Each has its own distinct personality. To generalize, Vinalhaven is the largest and busiest, while North Haven is sedate and exclusive. Matinicus might best be described as frontier-like. The Rockland terminal of the Maine State Ferry Service serves all three of the islands, although service to Matinicus operates only a few times a month in summer. Charter air service (not inexpensive) is available to the islands via **Penobscot Island Air** (207/596-7500, www.penobscotislandair.com) from Knox County Regional Airport in Owls Head, just south of Rockland. PIA carries the mail to both of these islands every day but Sundays and holidays; any available extra seats go for about $44 pp (one way).

VINALHAVEN

Five miles wide, 7.5 miles long, and covering some 10,000 acres, Vinalhaven is 13 miles off the coast of Rockland—a 75-minute ferry trip. The shoreline has so many zigs and zags that no place on the island is more than a mile from water.

With a full-time population of about 1,235 souls, Vinalhaven is a serious working community, not primarily a playground. Nearly 200 anglers bring in lobsters, shrimp, and scallops; shopkeepers cater to locals as well as visitors; and increasing numbers of artists and artisans work away in their studios. For day-trippers, there's plenty to do—shopping, picnicking, hiking, biking, swimming—but an overnight stay provides a chance to sense the unique rhythm of life on a year-round island.

The Maine State Ferry Service, 207/596-2202, www.state.me.us/mdot/opt/ferry/ferry.htm, operates six round-trips daily from Rockland to Vinalhaven in summer ($12 adults, $5.25 kids 5–11, round-trip), fewer runs in winter. The ferry takes cars ($34.50 round-trip

VINALHAVEN

for car and driver), but a bicycle ($11.50 round-trip per adult bike, $5.75 for a child's bike) will do fine unless you have the time or inclination to see every corner of the island. Rental cars and bikes are available at the Tidewater Motel. Getting car space on the ferry during high season can be a frustrating—and complicated—experience, so *avoid taking a car to the island for a day trip at the height of summer.* If you're not spending the night on the island, watch the clock while you're there so you don't miss the last boat back to Rockland.

There's no official ferry service between Vinalhaven and North Haven, even though the two islands are almost within spitting distance. Fortunately, the J. O. Brown & Sons boat shop on North Haven (207/867-4621) will send a boat—for a small fee—most days from 7 AM on. Call the boat shop to arrange a pickup on the Vinalhaven side—at the north end of Vinalhaven (North Haven Rd.). (There's even a handy outdoor pay phone.) Don't let anyone convince you to return to Rockland for the ferry to the other island.

History

Vinalhaven and neighboring North Haven have been known as the Fox Islands ever since

1603, when English explorer Martin Pring sailed these waters and allegedly spotted gray foxes in his search for sustenance. Nowadays, you'll find reference to that name only on nautical charts, identifying the passage between the two islands as the Fox Islands Thorofare—and there's nary a fox in sight.

Vinalhaven's earliest known resident was one David Wooster, in 1762, but the first permanent non-Indian settlement here seems to have sprung up around 1765. The Thaddeus Carver family—for whom Carver's Harbor is named—arrived a few years later, and as the population increased, lumbering became the major industry. In 1789, the town was incorporated, and soon thereafter, residents were collecting taxes, subsidizing the indigent, and hiring a minister and a schoolteacher.

Vinalhaven granite first headed for Boston around 1826, and within a few decades, quarrymen arrived from as far away as Britain and Finland to wrestle out and shape the incredibly resistant stone. Schooners, barges, and "stone sloops" left Carver's Harbor carrying mighty cargoes of granite destined for government and commercial buildings in Boston, New York, and Washington, D.C. In the 1880s, nearly 4,000 people lived on Vinalhaven, North Haven, and Hurricane Island. After World War I, demand declined, granite gave way to concrete and steel, and the industry petered out and died. But Vinalhaven has left its mark—ornate columns, paving blocks, and curbstones in communities as far west as Kansas City.

Sights

One Main St. landmark that's hard to miss is the three-story, cupola-topped **Odd Fellows Hall,** a Victorian behemoth with assorted gewgaws in the streetfront display windows. Artist Robert Indiana, who first arrived as a visitor in 1969, owns the structure, built in 1885 for the IOOF Star of Hope Lodge.

At the top of the hill just beyond Main St. (corner of School and East Main Sts.) is a greenish-blue replica **galamander,** a massive reminder of Vinalhaven's late-19th-century

granite-quarrying era. Galamanders, hitched to oxen or horses, carried the stone from island quarries to the finishing shops. (By the way, the origin of the name remains unexplained.) Next to the galamander is a colorful wooden bandstand, site of very popular evening band concerts held sporadically during the summer.

The unusually energetic **Vinalhaven Historical Society,** P.O. Box 339, Vinalhaven 04863, 207/863-4410, www.midcoast.com/ ~vhhissoc/, operates a museum in the onetime town hall on High St., just east of Carver's Cemetery. The building itself has a tale, having been floated across the bay from Rockland, where it served as a Universalist church. The museum's documents and artifacts on the granite industry are particularly intriguing, and special summer exhibits add to the interest. Open Wed.–Sun. 11 AM–3 PM, early June–mid-Sept. Admission is free, but donations are welcome. At the museum, request a copy of *A Self-Guided Walking Tour of the Town of Vinalhaven and Its Granite-Quarrying History,* a handy little brochure that details 17 in-town locations related to the late-19th and early-20th-century industry.

Built in 1832 and now owned by the town of Vinalhaven, **Brown's Head Light** guards the southern entrance to the Fox Islands Thorofare. To reach the grounds (no access to the light itself; the keeper's house is a private residence for the town manager), take the North Haven Rd. about six miles, at which point you'll see a left-side view of the Camden Hills. Continue to the second road on the left, Crockett River Rd. Turn and take the second road on the right, continuing past the Brown's Head Cemetery to the hill overlooking the lighthouse.

Parks and Preserves

No, you're not on the moors of Devon, but you could be fooled in the 45-acre **Lane's Island Preserve.** Masses of low-lying ferns, Rugosa roses, and berry bushes cover the granite outcrops of this sanctuary—and a foggy day makes it even more moorlike and mystical, a Brontë novel setting. Best (albeit busiest) time to come is early August, when you can compete

Mid-Coast Region

with the birds for blackberries, raspberries, and blueberries. Easy trails wind past old stone walls, an aged cemetery, and along the surf-pounded shore. The preserve is a 20-minute walk (or five-minute bike ride) from Vinalhaven's ferry landing. Set off to the right on Main St., through the village. Turn right onto Water St., then right on Atlantic Ave. Continue across the causeway on Lane's Island Rd. and left over a salt marsh to the preserve. The large white house on the harbor side of Lane's Island, formerly an inn, is privately owned.

Next to the ferry landing in Carver's Harbor is **Grimes Park,** a wooded, vest-pocket retreat with a splendid view of the harbor. Owned by the American Legion, the 2.5-acre park is perfect for picnics or for hanging out (especially in good weather) between boats.

Just behind the Islands Community Medical Center, close to downtown, is 30-acre **Armbrust Hill Town Park,** once the site of granite-quarrying operations. Still pockmarked with quarry pits, the park has beautifully landscaped walking paths and native flowers, shrubs, and trees—much of it thanks to late island resident Betty Roberts, who made this a lifelong endeavor. From the back of the medical center, follow the trail to the summit for a southerly view of Matinicus and other offshore islands. If you're with children, be especially careful about straying onto side paths, which go perilously close to old quarry holes. Before the walk, lower the children's energy level at the large playground off to the left of the trail. The creative climbing structure is bound to wear them down.

Recreation

Vinalhaven is loaded with wonderful hikes and walks, some deliberately unpublicized. Since 1986, the foresighted **Vinalhaven Land Trust,** P.O. Box 268, Vinalhaven 04863, 207/863-2543, has expanded the opportunities. The land trust has protected more than 1,400 acres, including 12 outlying islands. When you reach the island, inquire at the land trust's seasonal office at Skoog Memorial Park, Sands Cove Rd., west of the ferry terminal, or at the town

office or the Paper Store. Some hiking options are the Perry Creek Preserve (terrific loop trail), Middle Mountain Town Park, Tip-Toe Mountain, Polly Cove Preserve, Isle au Haut Mountain, Huber Preserve, Arey's Neck Woods, and Sunset Rock Park.

The Maine chapter of **The Nature Conservancy,** 14 Maine St., Fort Andross, Brunswick 04011, 207/729-5181, owns or manages several islands and island clusters near Vinalhaven. **Big Garden** (formerly owned by Charles and Anne Morrow Lindbergh) and **Big White Islands** are easily accessible and great for shoreline picnics if you have your own boat. Other Conservancy holdings in this area are fragile environments, mostly nesting islands off-limits mid-Mar.–mid-Aug. Contact the Conservancy for specifics.

Swimming: Abandoned quarries are all over the island, and most are on private property, but two town-owned ones are easy to reach from the ferry landing. **Lawson's Quarry,** on the North Haven Rd., is about a mile from downtown; **Booth's Quarry** is on Pequot Rd., 1.5 miles from downtown. Both are signposted. You'll see plenty of swimmers and sunbathers-on-the-rocks on a hot day, but there are no lifeguards, so swimming is at your own risk. There are no restrooms or changing rooms. *Note:* Pets and soap are not allowed in the water; camping, fires, and alcohol are not allowed in the quarry areas.

Down the side road beyond Booth's Quarry is **Narrows Park,** a town-owned space looking out toward Narrows Island, Isle au Haut, and, on a clear day, Mount Desert Island.

For saltwater swimming, continue along Pequot Rd. about 1.5 miles beyond Booth's Quarry. At the crossroads, you'll see a whimsical bit of local folk art—the Coke lady sculpture. Turn right (east) and go 0.5 mile to **Geary's Beach** (also called **State Beach**), where you can picnic and scour the shoreline for shells and sea glass.

Bicycling: Even though Vinalhaven's 40 or so miles of public roads are narrow, winding, and poorly shouldered, they're relatively level, so a bicycle is a fine way to tour the island.

Bring your own, preferably a hybrid or mountain bike ($11.50 round-trip on the ferry), or rent one at the **Tidewater Motel,** on Main St. near the ferry landing, 207/863-4618. You'll need to supply your own helmet. For repairs, track down **Pete Gasperini,** 207/863-4837. (He also does boat tours on demand; islanders are versatile folk.) Rental bikes are available on the mainland in Rockland at **Bikesenjava,** 481 Main St., Rockland 04841, 207/596-1004, www.haybikesenjava.com, which rents adult hybrid or mountain bikes for $16 a day (including a map). Or, just up Rte. 1 from there, in Rockport, is **Maine Sport Outfitters** Rte. 1, Rockport 04856, 207/236-8797 or 888/236-8796, www.mainesport.com, with a wide selection of rental bikes and other gear.

A 10-mile, 2.5-hour bicycle route begins on Main St. and goes clockwise out the North Haven Rd., past Lawson's Quarry, to Round the Island Rd., then Poor Farm Rd. to Geary's Beach and back to Main St. via Pequot Rd. and School St. Carry a picnic and enjoy it on Lane's Island; stop for a swim in one of the quarries; or detour down to Brown's Head Light. If you're here for the day, keep track of the time so you don't miss the ferry.

Sea Kayaking: Based at Harbor Wharf (not far from the ferry landing), **SeaEscape Kayak,** W. Main St., 207/863-9343, www.seaescape-kayak.com, offers a beginner-level harbor tour for $45 pp and a more ambitious island tour (with gourmet picnic) for $85. This enterprising operation also arranges biking/hiking tours (with lunch) for $65–85 pp. Reservations are essential, at least 24 hours in advance.

Shopping, Galleries

The Paper Store (Vinal's News Stand), Main St., 207/863-4826, www.foxislands.net/~paperstr, carries newspapers, gifts, film, maps, Vinalhaven T-shirts, and odds and ends. **Carver's Harbor Market,** Main St., 207/863-4319, is a full-service supermarket. Takeout sandwiches are available in summer. Both stores are open all year.

Here's a chance to support a great cause. On Main St. you'll find the most unusual

Second-Hand Prose, an amazing outgrowth of the local library's annual August book sale. The all-volunteer Friends of the Vinalhaven Public Library staff the shop, which is loaded with pre-owned books donated by island residents, summer people, and former visitors from around the country. More book donations are always welcome, although duplicates are sold off twice a year at bargain-basement prices. Surplus children's books are sent to a school in Kenya; other remainders are given to the veterans' hospital and to the Swap Shop at Vinalhaven's recycling center. The shop is open all year, Mon.–Sat. 9 AM–4:30 PM.

An interesting year-round shop is **Island Home and Crafts,** 207/863-2020, carrying garden gear, vegetables, antiques, beautiful sweaters, and plenty of yarn for knitters.

Across the street from the Tidewater Motel is the **New Era Gallery,** Main St., P.O. Box 546, 207/863-9351, where artist Elaine Crossman (co-owner of the Tidewater) shows her own impressive artwork as well as paintings, photography, sculpture, and pottery by a range of artists. Open Wed.–Sat. 11 AM–5 PM May–Dec.

Midway between the ferry landing and the downtown area is the **Harbor Wharf** complex (in a rehabbed fish factory), an eclectic handful of low-key shops and eateries.

Accommodations

Vinalhaven isn't overflowing with spare beds, so if you plan to spend the night (or stay longer), especially between mid-July–mid-Aug., be sure to make a reservation. If you're going for the day, pay attention to the ferry schedule and allow enough time to get back to the boat. Islanders may be able to find you a bed in a pinch, but don't count on it. There are no campsites on the island.

Seasonal bed-and-breakfasts, both convenient to downtown, are **The Libby House,** Water St., Vinalhaven 04863, 207/863-4696; $70–150 d, open summer only; and Donna Payne's grand Victorian **Payne Homestead at the Moses Webster House,** Atlantic Ave., P.O. Box 216, Vinalhaven 04863, 207/863-9963 or 888/863-9963, www.paynehomestead.com;

$90–165 d (two-night minimum; shared baths); open May–Oct.; no credit cards.

Your feet practically touch the water when you spend the night at the **Tidewater Motel,** 12 Main St., Carver's Harbor, P.O. Box 29, Vinalhaven 04863, 207/863-4618, www.tidewatermotel.com, a well-maintained, modernized building cantilevered over the harbor. Owned by Phil and Elaine Crossman, the 15-room motel (with private baths) was built by Phil's parents in 1970. It's the perfect place to sit on the deck and watch the lobsterboats do their thing. Be aware, though, that commercial fisherfolk are early risers, and lobsterboat engines can rev up as early as 4:30 on a summer morning—all part of the pace of Vinalhaven. Doubles are $115–256 mid-June to Labor Day, $85–198 other months; kids 10 and under are free; seven units are efficiencies. No smoking, no pets. Open all year. Single-speed rental bikes are available; you'll need your own helmet. A few rental cars are available at the Tidewater (or they'll meet you at the ferry landing). Call well ahead to reserve—it's *the* place to stay.

Seasonal Rentals: The best resource for weekly and monthly "camp," cottage, and village-house rentals is Lorraine Walker at **Vinalhaven Realty,** Main St., Vinalhaven 04863, 207/863-4474, www.vinalhavenrealty.com.

Food

The island's best summertime dinner spot is the harborside room at **The Haven,** Main St., 207/863-4969, with a great view and a creative menu that changes nightly in summer, and two seatings—at 6 and 8:15 PM by reservation, Tues.–Sat. The restaurant's streetside room, serving Tues.–Sat. 6–9 PM, is more casual and less creative (they call it "pub style"), but the walls are lined with rotating artwork. There are no reservations, so you may need to wait, especially on summer weekends.

Opposite the municipal parking lot, the **Harbor Gawker,** "At the Mill Race," Main St., 207/863-9365, has been a local landmark since 1975. On the menu are burgers, lobster rolls, seafood baskets, terrific fish chowder (by

the cup, pint, or quart), and soft ice cream. Open Mon.–Sat. 10:30 AM–8 PM (to 9 PM July–Aug.), early May–Oct.

The **Pizza Pit,** Harbor Wharf, 207/863-4311, serves pizza-with-a-view Wed.–Sun. 4–9 PM. (Calzones, pasta, and quesadillas are also on the menu.) Also at Harbor Wharf is **Surfside,** 207/863-2767, known for its hearty breakfasts but also serving lunch in summer.

If you're up for a picnic (or perhaps a late-afternoon wine-and-cheese break), be sure to stop in at **Island Spirits,** Main St. at the Tidewater Motel, 207/863-4618, for cheese, wine, beer, designer breads, and a variety of go-withs. Open daily, 11 AM–6 PM.

Each year, one or two takeout wagons also set up shop and dish out food-on-the-run between the ferry landing and Main St.

Information and Services

The **Vinalhaven Chamber of Commerce,** P.O. Box 703, Vinalhaven 04863, fax 207/863-4866, www.vinalhaven.org, produces a helpful little flyer/map showing locations in the Carver's Harbor area. For a copy, contact the chamber or call the **Vinalhaven Town Office,** 207/863-4471. It's also available at the Rockland-Thomaston Area Chamber of Commerce on the mainland in Rockland (www.therealmaine.com).

Even more useful is the *Vinalhaven Visitor's Guide,* published annually by Phil Crossman, co-owner of the Tidewater Motel. It's available for $3.50—part of which supports the island's Eldercare program.

Vinalhaven's weekly newsletter, *The Wind,* P.O. Box 194, Vinalhaven 04863, 207/863-2158, named after the island's original newspaper, first published in 1884, is loaded with island flavor: news items, public-supper announcements, editorials, and ads. A year's subscription is $35; single copies are available free at most downtown locales.

The **Vinalhaven Public Library,** E. Main and Chestnut Sts., 207/863-4401, a distinctive, Carnegie-funded granite building built in 1906, is open Tues. and Thurs. 1–5 PM and 6–8 PM, Wed. and Fri. 9 AM–noon and 1–5 PM,

Sat. 9 AM–1 PM. (There's a children's story hour Tues. and Sat. at 10 AM.)

The **Maine State Ferry Service** office on Vinalhaven is at the Carver's Harbor ferry landing, 207/863-4421, or call the Rockland terminal, 207/596-2202.

Public restrooms are at the ferry landing and the town office, but the town office is only open weekdays.

Emergencies

The **Islands Community Medical Center,** Armbrust Hill, Vinalhaven 04863, 207/863-4341, on the hill just beyond the downtown area, coordinates medical facilities on the island and has a full-time doctor. Critical cases are ferried or airlifted from the island's tiny airstrip to Rockland or Portland. To report a **fire** or summon an **ambulance,** call 911.

NORTH HAVEN

Eight miles long by three miles wide, North Haven is 12 miles off the coast of Rockland—an hour by ferry. The island boasts sedate summer homes, open fields where hundreds of sheep once grazed, 381 year-round residents (in the 2000 census), a yacht club called the Casino, and a village gift shop that's been here since 1954.

Originally called North Island, North Haven had much the same settlement history as Vinalhaven, but, being smaller (about 5,280 acres) and more fertile, it has developed—or not developed—differently. It was one of the landforms dubbed the Fox Islands by explorer Martin Pring in 1603. David Wooster, considered Vinalhaven's earliest white settler, is accorded the same distinction for North Haven. But carbon dating of shell middens (mounds) piled up by Native Americans has shown that Pring's and Wooster's precursors were here as early as 3300 BC.

In 1846, North Haven was incorporated and severed politically from Vinalhaven, and by the late 1800s, the Boston summer crowd began buying up traditional island homes, building tastefully unpretentious new ones, and settling

in for a whole season of sailing and socializing. Several generations later, "summer folk" now come for weeks rather than months, often rotating the schedules among slews of siblings. Informality remains the key, though—now more than ever.

The island has two distinct hamlets, North Haven Village, on the Fox Islands Thorofare, where the state ferry arrives, and Pulpit Harbor, particularly popular with the yachting set.

North Haven Village

Fanning out from the ferry landing is a delightful cluster of substantial, year-round clapboard homes—a marked contrast to the weathered-shingle cottages typical of so many island communities. It won't take long to stroll Main St., but you'll want a camera.

Anchoring the cluster of shops "downtown" is the **North Haven Gift Shop,** Main St., 207/867-4444, a rabbit warren of rooms that June Hopkins has been running since 1954. No problem spending money here—everything's tastefully selected, from the pottery to the note cards to the books, jewelry, and gourmet condiments. One room is a gallery, with work by Maine artists. The shop is open mid-May–mid-Oct. Summer hours are 9 AM–5 PM Mon.–Sat. After Labor Day, the schedule becomes less predictable.

Next door (connected via an elevated corridor) is the **Eric Hopkins Gallery,** Main St., 207/867-2229, www.erichopkins.com, owned by June Hopkins's son, a talented painter who's gained repute far beyond Maine. If you can't spring for an original (figure on several thousand dollars), his distinctive work—luminous bird's-eye views of island, sea, and forest—now appears also on note cards, postcards, T-shirts, and one-of-a-kind sweaters. Open mostly by appointment, but you may get lucky and find it open.

Just down the street is the four-story, early-20th-century **Calderwood Hall,** Main St., 207/867-2265, artist Herb Parsons' eclectic gift shop/art gallery/entertainment center. It's open May–Columbus Day, Mon.–Sat. 10 AM–5 PM, and evenings when concerts, slide shows, poetry readings, and other events are on the agenda.

The hub of island cultural/social activity is **Waterman's Community Center,** Main St., 207/867-2100, www.watermans.org, which arose in 2002 from the demolition debris of the former Waterman's Store. The center is the locale for concerts, films, plays, lectures, a preschool program, and even a coffee shop (open daily).

Bicycling

North Haven has about 25 miles of paved roads, but, just as on most other islands, they are narrow, winding, and nearly shoulderless. Starting near the ferry landing in North Haven Village, take South Shore Rd. eastward, perhaps stopping en route for a picnic at town-owned Mullin's Head Park (also spelled Mullen Head) on the southeast corner of the island. Then follow the road around, counterclockwise, to North Shore Rd. and Pulpit Harbor.

Sailing

If you have your own boat, this area is a sailor's nirvana. Be sure to have on board an up-to-date copy of *A Cruising Guide to the Maine Coast.*

Boat fanatics will enjoy peeking into the **J. O. Brown & Sons** boatshop, 207/867-4621, on the Thorofare in North Haven Village. It's a remnant of a bygone era, with the scents and feel of traditional craftsmanship. The fifth generation now works here. In the late 19th century, Brown's built the first **North Haven Dinghy,** a 14.5-foot wooden sailboat, and followed it with dozens more. The fleet has had a summer racing season here since the 1880s. The boatyard, by the way, has a laundromat and showers and also rents moorings. If you need boat transportation across the Thorofare to Vinalhaven, someone at the shop may be able to help you out. It's open all year.

Accommodations and Food

Guest beds are scarce on North Haven; other than the longtime summer folk and seasonal renters, most visitors are day-trippers.

Food choices are also slim. For a sit-down lunch (or breakfast or dinner), head for the **Coal Wharf Restaurant,** Main St., 207/867-4739, next to Brown's Boatshop. A rustic seasonal eatery that can serve 60 or so, it's open Tues.–Sun. 6 AM–9 PM July–Aug., weekends in June, Sept., and early Oct. Reservations are wise.

Information and Services

The best source of information is the **North Haven Town Office,** Upper Main St., North Haven 04853, 207/867-4433, fax 867-2207. It's open weekdays, all year. The shops closest to the ferry landing are accustomed to fielding questions, so try them for answers.

The **Maine State Ferry Service** office on North Haven is at the North Haven Village ferry landing, 207/867-4441, or call the Rockland terminal, 207/596-2202.

Emergencies

To reach the island's **doctor or physician's assistant,** call 207/867-2021, or dial 911. Critical cases are airlifted from the island airstrip to a hospital in Rockland or Portland. To contact the sheriff or report a fire, dial 911.

Getting There

The **Maine State Ferry Service,** 207/596-2202, www.state.me.us/mdot/opt/ferry/ferry.htm, operates three round-trip car ferries a day, year-round, between Rockland and North Haven Village. Round-trip tickets are $12 adults, $5.25 kids, $11.50 adult bicycles. Even though the ferry carries cars ($34.50 round-trip for car and driver), it can be tough to get space at peak times (midsummer and holiday weekends), so consider taking a bike instead. No rental bikes are available on the island. If you're not spending the night, watch the clock so you don't miss the last boat back to Rockland.

North Haven is also accessible via **Penobscot Island Air,** 207/596-7500, www .penobscotislandair.com, operating out of the Knox County Regional Airport in Owls Head, near Rockland. The service operates all year, but weather can cancel a trip; check the website for details.

Camden-Rockport Area

Driven apart by a local squabble in 1891, Camden and Rockport have been separate towns for a century, but they're inextricably linked. They share school and sewer systems and an often-hyphenated partnership. On Union St., just off Rte. 1, a white wooden arch reads Camden on one side and Rockport on the other. These days, this area is one of the Mid-Coast's—even Maine's—prime destinations.

Camden, the better known of the two, has a year-round population of just over 5,000, but that triples during the summer months; Rockport, with a much lower profile, doubles in summer from about 3,000 year-round. While Rockport's harbor is relatively peaceful—with yachts, lobsterboats, and a single windjammer schooner—Camden Harbor is a summer-long madhouse, jammed with dinghies, kayaks, windjammers, yachts, and a handful of fishing craft.

Much of Camden's appeal is its drop-dead-gorgeous setting—a deeply indented harbor with parks, a waterfall, and a dramatic backdrop of low mountains. It is views of Camden that typify Maine nationwide, even worldwide, on calendars, postcards, and photo books. This is one of those places seemingly created for summer tourism, but it's far more than that. An influx of well-situated retirees has tipped the median age balance in recent years. The recent departure of credit-card giant MBNA, when its Maine-oriented founder retired, left behind some community improvements and some mixed feelings.

HISTORY

Not very long ago—as recently as the 1970s, in fact—Camden was a sleepy mill town still reminiscing about its shipbuilding heyday at the turn of the century. The Holly M. Bean Shipyard had turned out stoutly crafted multimasted vessels, including the nation's first six-masted schooner, the 300-foot *George W. Wells*, which weighed nearly 3,000 tons when she was launched here, in 1900. During World War II, the Camden Shipbuilding yard was a hive of production for military tugs and minesweepers. Nowadays, Wayfarer Marine, a giant yachting enterprise, sprawls along the prime harborfront real estate.

In the late 1880s, Camden's proximity to steamer transport made it a destination of choice for urban industrialists scouting for summer retreats. Camden became a fair-weather colony for families with names such as Watson, Curtis, Bok, and Dillingham. Their handsome shingled summer "cottages" still line the outer harbor and the outer reaches of Chestnut and Bay View Sts.; many are now occupied year-round.

Rockport has its own workaday heritage as the site of 19th-century kilns used to burn lime for the construction industry. Ship after ship took on the volatile powder and carried it off to cities all along the eastern seaboard. With the death of wooden ships and the decline of the lime industry, Rockport saw the birth of a summer music colony—prominent musicians who have left their considerable mark on the town. The Bay Chamber Concerts organization, founded in the 1960s, and Camden's Salzedo Harp Colony are impressive legacies of this tradition.

SIGHTS

Self-Guided Historical Tour

The **Camden-Rockport Historical Society,** supported by a group of B&Bs, has produced a handy little flyer, *A Walking Tour and Bicycle or Car Tour,* detailing more than 50 significant historic sites (mostly private residences) in downtown Camden, Camden's High Street and Chestnut Street Historic Districts, and downtown Rockport. To cover it all, you'll want a car or bike; to cover segments, and really appreciate the architecture, don your walking shoes. Pick up a copy of the flyer at the chamber of commerce or at the historical society.

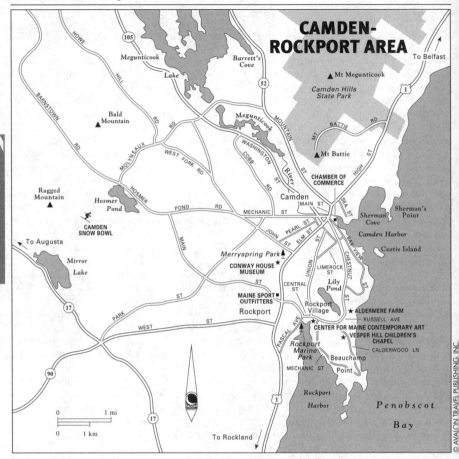

CAMDEN-
ROCKPORT AREA

To Belfast

Megunticook
Lake

Barrett's
Cove

HOWE
HILL

105

52

Mt Megunticook

Camden Hills
State Park

1

Meguntícook

Bald
Mountain

MOUNTAIN

BATTIE

RD

BARNSTOWN RD

MOLYNEAUX RD

WEST FORK RD

WASHINGTON ST

COBB
RD

River

MT

Mt Battie

HIGH ST

Ragged
Mountain

HOSMER

Hosmer
Pond

POND
RD

RD

MECHANIC ST

CHAMBER OF
COMMERCE

Camden

MAIN ST

SEA ST

Sherman
Cove

Sherman's
Point

CAMDEN
SNOW BOWL

Camden Harbor

BAY VIEW ST

To Augusta

Mirror
Lake

17

ST

MAIN

PARK ST

WEST ST

90

17

JOHN ST

PEARL ST

ELM ST

UNION ST

Merryspring Park
CONWAY HOUSE
MUSEUM

CENTRAL ST

MAINE SPORT
OUTFITTERS

Rockport

PASCAL AVE

Rockport
Marine
Park

MECHANIC ST

LIMEROCK
ST

Lily
Pond

Rockport
Village

Curtis Island

CHESTNUT ST

ALDERMERE FARM
RUSSELL AVE
CENTER FOR MAINE CONTEMPORARY ART
VESPER HILL CHILDREN'S
CHAPEL
CALDERWOOD LN

Beauchamp
Point

Rockport
Harbor

Penobscot
Bay

0   1 mi
0   1 km

MOON

To Rockland

© AVALON TRAVEL PUBLISHING, INC.

Old Conway Homestead and Museum

Just inside the Camden town line from Rockport, the Old Conway Homestead and Museum, Conway Rd., Camden, mailing address P.O. Box 747, Rockport 04856, 207/236-2257, www.crmuseum.org, is a five-building complex owned and run by the Camden-Rockport Historical Society. The 18th-century Cape-style **Conway House,** on the National Register of Historic Places, contains fascinating construction details and period furnishings; in the barn are carriages and farm tools. Two other buildings—a blacksmith

shop and a 19th-century sap house used for making maple syrup—have been moved to the grounds and restored. In the contemporary **Mary Meeker Cramer Museum** (named for the prime benefactor) are displays from the historical society's collection of ship models, old documents, and period clothing. For local color, don't miss the Victorian outhouse. The complex is open early July–Aug., Mon.–Thurs. 10 AM–4 PM, and Sun. 1–4 PM. Admission is $5 adults, $2 children. The museum and sap house are also open for maple-syrup demonstrations on Maine Maple Sunday (fourth Sunday in March).

Vesper Hill

Built and donated to the community by a local benefactor, the rustic, open-air **Vesper Hill Children's Chapel** is dedicated to the world's children. Overlooking Penobscot Bay and surrounded by gardens and lawns, the nondenominational chapel is an almost mystical oasis in a busy tourist region. Except during weddings or memorial services, there's seldom a crowd, and if you're lucky, you might have the place to yourself. From Central St. in downtown Rockport, take Russell Ave. east to Calderwood Ln. (fourth street on right). On Calderwood, take the second right (Chapel St.) after the (private) golf course. If the sign is down, look for a boulder with Vesper Hill carved in it. From downtown Camden, take Chestnut St. to just past Aldermere Farm; turn left at Calderwood Ln. and take the second right after the golf course.

Aldermere Farm, by the way, is the home of America's original herd of Belted Galloway cattle—Angus-like beef cattle with a wide white midriff. First imported from Scotland in 1953, the breed now shows up in pastures all over the United States. The animals' startling "Oreo-cookie" hide pattern never fails to halt passersby—especially in spring and early summer, when the calves join their mothers in the pastures. The 136-acre farm is owned by the Maine Coast Heritage Trust, a state conservation organization based in Topsham.

Center for Maine Contemporary Art

Once a local firehouse, this attractive building has been totally rehabbed to provide display space for the work of Maine's best contemporary artists. The nonprofit Center for Maine Contemporary Art, 162 Russell Ave., P.O. Box 147, Rockport 04856, 207/236-2875, www.artsmaine.org, mounts as many as 25 shows each year; has an active educational program, including lectures, gallery talks, and workshops; has a wildly popular art auction (early August); an annual juried art exhibition featuring more than 100 selections; and an annual juried craft show (mid-October) spotlighting about 50 Maine craftspersons. An

exceptional gift shop carries high-end crafts. Open all year, Tues.–Sat. 10 AM–5 PM, Sun. 1–5 PM. Admission is $5.

PARKS AND PRESERVES

For more than a century, the Camden-Rockport area has benefited from the providence of conscientious year-round and summertime conservationists. Thanks to their benevolence, countless acres of fragile habitat, woodlands, and scenic viewpoints have been preserved. Nowadays, the most active organization is the **Coastal Mountains Land Trust,** 101 Mount Battie St., Camden 04856, 207/236-7091, www.coastalmountains.org, founded in 1986. For a full schedule of outdoor events, see the website, check local papers, or contact trust offices.

A Rockland-based group, **The Georges River Land Trust,** www.grlt.org, whose territory covers the Georges (St. George) River watershed, is the steward for **The Georges Highland Path,** a low-impact hiking trail that reaches Rockport and Camden from the back side of the surrounding hills.

Camden Hills State Park

A five-minute drive and a $3 pp fee gets you to the top of **Mount Battie,** centerpiece of 5,650-acre Camden Hills State Park, Belfast Rd., Rte. 1, 207/236-3109, and the best place to understand why Camden is "where the mountains meet the sea." The summit panorama is, well, breathtaking, and reputedly the inspiration for Edna St. Vincent Millay's poem "Renascence" (a bronze plaque marks the spot); information boards identify the offshore islands. Climb the summit's stone tower for an even better view. The 25 miles of hiking trails (some for every ability) include two popular routes up Mt. Battie—an easy, hour-long hike from the base parking lot (Nature Trail) and a more strenuous 45-minute one from the top of Mt. Battie St. in Camden (Mount Battie Trail). Or drive up the paved Mount Battie Auto Rd. The park has plenty of space for picnics, and the 107-site camping area (no

© MARY LYONS

antique steam engine, Marine Park, Rockport

hookups) is wheelchair-accessible. In winter, ice climbers use a rock wall near the Maiden's Cliff Trail, reached via Rte. 52 (Mountain St.). The park entrance is 1.5 miles north of downtown Camden. Day-use admission is $3 adults, $1 children 5–11, free for children four and under and seniors over 65. The nonresident camping fee is $20 per site per night; two-night minimum. Request a free trail map. The park is open May 1–Oct. 30. Hiking trails are accessible all year, weather permitting.

Merryspring Park

Straddling the Camden-Rockport boundary, 66-acre Merryspring Park, Conway Rd., P.O. Box 893, Camden 04843, 207/236-2239, www.merryspring.org, is a magnet for nature lovers. More than a dozen well-marked trails wind through woodlands, berry thickets, and wildflowers; near the preserve's parking area are hosta, rose, and herb gardens. Admission is free, but donations are welcome. Special programs (fee charged) include lectures, demonstrations, and a summer Ecology Camp for youngsters. Most programs are held in the park's modern new Ross Center, named for Merryspring founders Mary Ellen and Ervin Ross. The entrance is on Conway Rd., 0.3 mile off Rte. 1, at the southern end of Camden. Open dawn to dusk, year-round.

Parks in Town

Just east of the Camden Public Library is the **Camden Amphitheatre** (also called the Bok Amphitheatre, after a local benefactor), a sylvan spot resembling a set for *A Midsummer Night's Dream* (which, yes, has been performed here). Concerts, weddings, and all kinds of other events take place in the park. Across Atlantic Avenue, sloping to the harbor, is **Harbor Park,** with benches, a couple of monuments, and some of the best waterfront views in town. The noted landscape firm of Frederick Law Olmsted designed the park. The park and amphitheater are listed on the National Register of Historic Places and were restored and rehabilitated in 2004 with funds from Camden taxpayers and contributions to the Conservancy for Camden Harbor Park and Amphitheatre.

Rockport's intown parks include **Marine Park,** off Pascal Ave., at the head of the harbor; **Walker Park,** on Sea St., west side of the harbor; **Mary-Lea Park,** overlooking the harbor next to the Rockport Opera House; and **Cramer Park,** alongside the Goose River just west of Pascal Avenue. At Marine Park are the remnants of 19th-century lime kilns, an antique steam engine, picnic tables, a boat-launching ramp, and a polished granite sculpture of André, a harbor seal adopted by a local family in the early 1960s. André had been honorary harbormaster, ring-bearer at weddings, and the subject of several books and a film—and even did the honors at the unveiling of his statue—before he was fatally wounded in a mating skirmish in 1986, at the age of 25.

Curtis Island

Marking the entrance to Camden Harbor is town-owned Curtis Island, with a 26-foot automated light tower (and adjoining keeper's house) facing out into the bay. Once known as Negro Island, it's a sight (and site) made for photo ops; the views are stunning in every direction. A kayak or dinghy will get you out to the island, where you can picnic (take water; there are no facilities), wander around, gather berries, or just watch the passing fleet. Land on the Camden (west) end of the island, allowing for tide change when you beach your boat. Respect the privacy of the keeper's house in summer; it's occupied by volunteer caretakers.

G.W. Hodson Park

Another good picnic spot is a tiny little town park just outside of Camden, overlooking the Megunticook River outlet from Megunticook Lake. G.W. Hodson Park is a serene, pine-needled space with a riverfront picnic table. It's open daily 6 AM–10 PM. From downtown Camden, take Rte. 105 (Washington St.) 2.6 miles to Molyneaux Rd. Turn right and go 0.5 mile to the park, on the right. Alternatively, take

Rte. 52 (Mountain St.) 1.8 miles to Beaucaire Rd.; turn left and go 0.6 mile to the park.

Fernald's Neck Preserve

Three miles of Megunticook Lake shoreline, groves of conifers, and a large swamp ("the Great Bog") are features of 315-acre Fernald's Neck Preserve, on the Camden-Lincolnville line (and the Knox-Waldo County line). Shoreline and mountain views are stupendous, even more so during fall-foliage season. Easiest trail is the Blue Loop, at the northern end of the preserve; the longer Orange Loop begins at the same point, goes past the Great Bog, and loops around the southern end of the preserve. Yellow Trails connect the loops. While on the Blue Loop, take the offshoot for a great view of the lake and hills. Some sections can be wet; wear boots or rubberized shoes, and use insect repellent. From Rte. 1 in Camden, take Rte. 52 (Mountain St.) about 4.5 miles to Fernald's Neck Rd., about 0.2 mile beyond the Youngtown Inn. Turn left, then bear left at next fork. Continue past the gray farmhouse at the road's end, continue into the hayfield, and park near the woods. Head into the woods (look for signs bearing The Nature Conservancy oak leaf) and pick up a map/brochure at the trailhead register.

RECREATION

Local entrepreneurs Stuart and Marianne Smith have made **Maine Sport Outfitters,** Rte. 1, Rockport 04856, 207/236-7120 or 888/236-8797, www.mainesport.com, a major destination for anyone interested in outdoor recreation. The knowledgeable staff can lend a hand and steer you in almost any direction, for almost any summer or winter sport. Nothing seems to stump them.

Kudos to the town of Rockport for establishing a first-rate recreation area, with ballfields, a playground, picnic tables, basketball court, horseshoe pits, and tennis courts. Open sunrise to sunset, the **Rockport Recreation Park** is on Rte. 90, 1 mile west of Rte. 1 (watch for the sign on right).

You can't ski in summer at the Camden Snow Bowl's **Ragged Mountain Recreation**

Area, but you can enjoy a ball field, lake access, tennis courts, lots of woods and ski trails for hiking and dog walking, and several miles of mountain bike trails. Sunday mornings Sept.–Oct., the Ragged Mountain Ski and Snowboard Club holds a pancake breakfast at the Snow Bowl, with the chair lift running for wonderful fall foliage viewing. Call the Snow Bowl office, 207/236-3438, for details.

Bicycling

Despite a scarcity of designated bike routes, cycling is popular in the Camden-Rockport area. (Plans are afoot to create off-road bike routes; check when you arrive.) It's partly the scenery, partly exercise, and partly a solution to summer auto gridlock. At the chamber of commerce, pick up a bike-route map, which has lots of suggestions for short and long rides. Here's an easy option for a start. A short, mostly level, **eight-mile loop** begins in downtown Camden on the Bay View St. side of Camden National Bank (a busy, five-way intersection). Continue along Bay View until it dead-ends at Upper Chestnut St. (next to the cemetery). Turn left (the street becomes Russell Ave. and you're in Rockport), continue past Aldermere Farm, then turn left onto Calderwood Lane. At a cluster of mailboxes in the middle of the road, leave the unpaved road and bear right, pedaling around Beauchamp Point (unpaved) to Mechanic St. (paved). Turn left onto Russell Ave. and continue to the Rockport Public Library. Bear right onto Union St., returning to Camden.

Maine Sport Outfitters Rte. 1, Rockport 04856, 800/722-0826, www.mainesport.com, rents bikes for $12–18 a day and provides info on biking routes. **Ragged Mountain Sports,** 46 Elm St., Camden 04843, 207/236-6664, www.raggedmountainsports.com, is another cycling source.

Hiking

There's enough hiking in **Camden Hills State Park**—including the spectacular Maiden Cliff Trail—to fill any vacation, but many other options exist as well. For instance, there's **Bald Mountain,** northwest of downtown Camden, for magnificent views of Penobscot Bay. From Rte. 1 at the center of town, take Mechanic St. until it forks at the edge of town; bear right onto Melvin Heights Rd. (left goes to the Snow Bowl). Continue to the next fork and bear left onto West Fork Rd. (right is East Fork Rd.). Continue to Molyneaux Rd., take a quick left then an immediate right onto Howe Hill Rd. Drive uphill 0.8 mile, at which point you'll see a tiny gravel clearing at the beginning of a woods road on the left. Park as far off the road as possible. The blue-blazed trail is moderate, requiring about 1.5 hours on the ascent; the summit views are well worth the trek, especially in fall. Avoid it in late May and early June, when the blackflies take command. Depending on the season, you may encounter squishy areas, so wear rubberized shoes or waterproof boots.

Eventually, **The Georges Highland Path** will wind about 35 miles through the Georges (St. George) River watershed from the source in Liberty to Thomaston. Thus far, more than eleven miles of trails have been cleared and blazed (blue) in the so-called Bald-Ragged Section. Developed by members of the Georges River Land Trust, this section of the trail currently has four access points in Camden, Rockport, and West Rockport. Contact the Rockland-based land trust (207/594-5166, www.grlt.org) for up-to-date maps, or pick it up the box at each trailhead. The easiest access point is on Rte. 17, about 10 miles from downtown Rockland. Just past Mirror Lake (on your right) is a small, well-signposted parking area. The Ragged Mountain direction (north) is more strenuous than the Spruce Mountain/Mt. Pleasant section (south and west, starting across Rte. 17). The latter is a great three-hour round-trip. Views are spectacular in either direction; Ragged Mountain gets you closer to the ocean panorama.

Swimming

The Camden area is blessed with several locales for freshwater swimming—a real boon, since Penobscot Bay can be mighty chilly, even at summer's peak. **Shirttail Point,** with limited parking, is a small sandy area on the Megunticook River. It's shallow enough for young kids and has picnic tables and a play area. From Rte. 1 in Camden, take Rte. 105 (Washington St.) 1.4 miles; watch for a small sign on the right. **Barrett's Cove,** on Megunticook Lake, has more parking space, usually more swimmers, and restrooms, picnic tables and grills, as well as a play area. Diagonally opposite the Camden Public Library, take Rte. 52 (Mountain St.) about three miles; watch for the sign on the left, and make the left turn onto Beaucaire Avenue. To cope with the parking crunch on hot summer days, bike to the beaches. You'll be ready for a swim after the uphill stretches, and it's all downhill on the way back. Also, Barrett's Cove is only 0.25 mile from the Maiden's Cliff trailhead.

Camden and Rockport both have saltwater swimming but no major sandy beaches. In Camden, it's **Laite Beach Park,** on Bay View St. about 1.5 miles from downtown Camden. Right on Camden Harbor, the park has great views, a strip of sand, picnic tables, a playground, and children's musical events every Wed. (1–3 PM) in July–Aug. Check the local papers or contact Camden Parks & Recreation, 236-3438, for the schedule. Rockport has **Walker Park,** tucked away on the west side of the harbor. From Pascal Ave., take Elm St., which becomes Sea St. Walker Park is on the left, with picnic tables, a play area, and a small, pebbly beach.

Indoor-pool options are the **Camden YMCA,** 116 Union St., Camden, 207/236-3375; and the **Samoset Resort,** on the Rockport-Rockland boundary.

Golf

On a back road straddling the Camden-Rockport line, the **Goose River Golf Course,** 50 Park St., P.O. Box 1230, Rockport 04856, 207/236-8488, competes with the best for outstanding scenery. A second set of tees in the nine-hole layout makes the course virtually an 18-holer. Starting times are needed on weekends and holidays. Snack bar; cart and

club rentals; moderate greens fees. Open mid-Apr.–Oct. Simonton Rd. is roughly parallel to Rte. 1, and you can reach it several ways. Easiest is to take John St. from Rte. 1 in Camden. Continue to Simonton Rd. and turn left. The clubhouse is about two miles from downtown Camden or Rockport.

Playgrounds

Two creative playgrounds will give the kids a chance to defuse some excess energy. In Camden, head for the Elm Street School, a big old wooden building at the corner of Rte. 1 (Elm St.) and Union St. In Rockport, an even more elaborate playground is at the Rockport Elementary School, corner of Rtes. 1 and 90.

Winter Sports

With the Gulf Stream not far offshore, winters can be unpredictable in the Camden-Rockport area—as well as in many other Maine coastal communities. Still, the snow gods often do cooperate. The town-owned **Camden Snow Bowl,** P.O. Box 1207, Camden 04843, 207/236-3438, snow phone 207/236-4418, is a family-oriented ski area that has provided a jump-start for many a budding alpine standout. Besides, where else can you begin a downhill run with a panoramic view of ocean and islands?

On Ragged Mountain, the Snow Bowl has nine trails (easy to difficult), two T-bars, a double chairlift, and snowmaking and floodlights for night skiing (Tues.–Fri.) on major runs. Best of all, the lift tickets are incredibly reasonable compared to prices at the major ski areas. Vertical drop is 950 feet. The Ragged Mountain Ski School offers lessons for every age and skill level; equipment rentals are available; and the cozy A-frame lodge has a snack bar. There's skating on adjacent Hosmer Pond in winter. When the pond is frozen, the unique **toboggan chute** also is open—weekends and holidays 9 AM–4 PM. Cost is $1 a run on a Snow Bowl toboggan, $0.50 if you bring your own. The Snow Bowl is three miles west of Camden; turn off Rte. 1 at John St. and follow signs.

The Snow Bowl is the home of the annual

U.S. National Toboggan Championships during the first weekend of February, attracting over 1000 "sliders" to this Mardi-Gras-comes-to-winter-Maine family event.

You'll find **cross-country ski trails** in nearby Lincolnville, at the Owls Head Transportation Museum and in the Thomaston area. The Camden Snow Bowl is in the process of re-developing cross-country and snowshoe trails.

GETTING AFLOAT

There's no excuse for staying ashore in Camden and Rockport. Take your pick from week-long windjammer cruises, windjammer daysails, powerboat excursions, and sea kayak rentals.

The yachting crowd is drawn here by the Camden Yacht Club (private) as well as **Wayfarer Marine,** 207/236-4378, www.wayfarermarine.com, (primarily sailing yachts); and **P.G. Willey,** 207/236-3256 (primarily luxury power yachts). If you're aboard your own boat and looking for a mooring, Camden has more than 400 of them—albeit not always available. Camden's harbormaster, operating out of a small signposted building near the head of the harbor, 207/236-7969, can provide details.

Rockport Marine, 207/236-9651, specializing in wooden boats, is the draw in that harbor; the private Rockport Boat Club is a deliberately laid-back version of the tony Camden Yacht Club.

Other nearby anchorages with facilities for boaters are Rockland, Spruce Head, Tenants Harbor, and Port Clyde. Offshore options are in North Haven and Vinalhaven.

If you have your own canoe, kayak, rowboat, or whatever, there are a number of boat-launching sites, both saltwater (Eaton Point, at the end of Sea St., in Camden; and, even better, Marine Park, in Rockport) and freshwater (Megunticook Lake, west and east sides; Bog Bridge, on Rte. 105, about 3.5 miles from downtown Camden; and Barrett's Cove, on Rte. 52, also about 3.5 miles from Camden).

Windjammer Cruises

In 1936, Camden became the home of the "cruise schooner" trade when Capt. Frank Swift restored a creaky wooden vessel and offered sailing vacations to paying passengers. He kept at it for 25 years, gradually adding other boats to the fleet—and the rest, as they say, is history. Windjammers have become big business on the Maine coast, with Camden and Rockland sparring for the title of Windjammer Capital. Rockland wrested it from Camden in the mid-1990s.

Six traditional windjammer schooners homeported in Camden, and one in Rockport, head out for three- to six-day cruises, late May–mid-Oct. Relax and do nothing or pitch in and help—the choice is yours. The camaraderie is tangible and contagious, the food is extraordinarily satisfying, and the sailing is unsurpassed. Accommodations are not elegant, but no one seems to mind. Costs depend on accommodation type, cruise length, and time of year.

Heir to Frank Swift's original Camden fleet is the three-vessel **Maine Windjammer Cruises,** P.O. Box 617, Camden 04843, 207/236-2938 or 888/692-7245, which includes the 29-passenger *Grace Bailey* (five days or weekends; no children under 12; $325–695 pp); 29-passenger *Mercantile* (three or four days; no kids under 12; $425–595 pp); and the six-passenger *Mistress* (three, four, or five days or weekends; kids welcome; the vessel is usually chartered by a group; $375–820 pp).

Others sailing out of Camden are the 22-passenger *Lewis R. French,* P.O. Box 992, Camden 04843, 207/785-2883 or 800/469-4635 (three, four, or six days; no kids under 16; $395–775 pp); the 30-passenger *Mary Day,* P.O. Box 798, Camden 04843, 207/785-5670 or 800/992-2218 (four or six days; no kids under 16; $399–775 pp); and the 29-passenger gaff-topsail steel ketch *Angelique,* P.O. Box 736, Camden 04843, 207/785-3020 or 800/282-9989 (three, four, six, or 10 days; no kids under 14; $450–1,595 pp).

Rockport is home to the 20-passenger *Timberwind,* P.O. Box 247, Rockport 04856,

207/236-0801 or 800/759-9250 (three or six days; no kids under six; $295–659 pp).

All of the above windjammers are members of the **Maine Windjammer Association,** P.O. Box 1144, Blue Hill 04614, 800/807-9463, www.sailmainecoast.com, a helpful one-stop resource for vessel and schedule information.

On the summer cruising schedule, several weeks coincide with special windjammer events, so you'll need to book a berth far in advance for these: mid-June (Boothbay Harbor's Windjammer Days), July Fourth week (Great Schooner Race), first week in August (Swans Island Sweet Chariot Music Festival), Labor Day weekend (Camden's Windjammer Weekend), and second week in September (WoodenBoat Sail-In).

Daysails and Excursions

You can't compare a two-hour daysail to a week-long cruise, but at least you get a hint of what could be—and it's a far better choice for most kids, who aren't allowed on most windjammer cruises. Several excursion boats operate out of Camden in summer. Most weekdays, you can just show up at the dock and find a space, but on weekends, better call for a reservation. Several are based at Bay View Landing, formerly known as Sharp's Wharf.

The classic wooden schooner *Olad* does several two-hour sails daily from Camden's public landing, weather permitting, late May–mid-Oct. There are sunset sails mid-June–mid-Aug. Call 207/236-2323 or go to www.maineschooner.com to check on the sailing schedule and/or make reservations. *Olad* tickets are $27 adults, $15 for kids under 12.

Another historic Camden daysailer is the 57-foot schooner *Surprise,* built in 1918 and skippered by congenial educator Jack Moore. He and his wife, Barbara, do four two-hour sails daily in season, departing from Camden's public landing. Cost is $25–30, including snacks. No kids under 12. For info, call 207/236-4687 or go to www.camdenmainesailing.com.

The 49-passenger *Appledore,* www.appledore2.com, built in 1978 for round-the-world cruising, sails from Bay View Landing

three or four times daily, June–Oct., beginning around 10 AM. Cruises last two hours and cost $25 pp. Beer, wine, and sodas are available. Call 207/236-8353 for information or reservations.

Over in Rockport, the schooner yacht *Heron* has superseded the *Shantih II.* The *Heron* goes out for lunch, lighthouse, and gourmet sunset cruises, May–Oct. Cost is $38–65 pp (includes lunch on lunch cruise or hors d'oeuvres on sunset cruise.) Call 207/236-8605 or 800/599-8605, www.woodenboatco.com.

For a one- or two-hour cruise ($10 or $20 adults/$5 or $10 children under 12), or a three-hour combo—a great way to see Camden and Rockport, their lighthouses and shorelines—head down to the Camden public landing and buy a ticket for the 30-passenger converted lobsterboat *Betselma.* Reservations usually aren't needed. Retired schooner captain Les Bex knows these waters, the wildlife, and the history. He does about eight hour-long trips daily, beginning at 10:30 AM, June–Sept. Last trip is at 7:30 PM. Pets and children under three are free. For information, call 207/236-4446 or go to www.betselma.com.

If the kids are bombarding you with FAQs about lobsters, here's the solution. Take a two-hour trip aboard Capt. Alan Philbrick's *Lively Lady Too,* berthed at Camden's Bay View Landing, 207/236-6672, winter 418/839-7933, www.sympatico.ca/lively.lady. He hauls in a trap, takes out a lobster, explains all its parts, and generally provides all the answers. As a former biology teacher, he's a whiz at natural history, so there's also information about seabirds, seals, and lots more. Trips depart two or three times a day, June–Sept. No lobstering trips on Sundays; it's illegal to haul traps Sundays June 1–Aug. 31. Cost is $20 adults, $5 kids under 14.

Sea Kayaking

Sea kayaking mushroomed throughout the 1990s, and many businesses have surfaced to fill the demand. If you've brought your own craft, head for the boat-launching ramps listed above. Otherwise, stop in or call **Maine Sport**

Outfitters Rte. 1, Rockport 04856, 800/722-0826, www.mainesport.com, which rents (and sells) kayaks and organizes lessons and guided day and overnight tours. Kayak rentals require previous paddling experience.

Another contact for guided tours is **Mount Pleasant Canoe & Kayak,** P.O. Box 86, West Rockport 04865, 207/785-4309. Owner Don Peckham leads a variety of trips on Megunticook Lake, and also organizes overnight sea-kayaking tours, Spruce Head to Rockland.

Harbor tours of Camden or Rockport put on by **Riverdance Outfitters,** 207/763-3139 or 800/770-3139, www.riverdanceoutfitters.com, stop at an island lighthouse for refreshments ($60–85 pp.) The company also takes freshwater paddlers out on Megunticook Lake in Camden, with swim and lesson included, and packages hiking, fly-fishing, and multisport adventures.

ENTERTAINMENT

Wednesday, Thursday, and Friday evenings July–Aug., and once a month the rest of the year, **Bay Chamber Concerts** draw sell-out audiences to the beautifully restored (and air-conditioned) Rockport Opera House, the Camden Opera House, the Strand Theatre in Rockland, and the Strom Auditorium in Rockport. Founded in the 1960s as a classical series, the summer concerts feature a resident quartet, prominent guest artists, and outstanding programs. Two "Next Generation Week"(s)—the second and third weeks in August—are devoted to classes and concerts for and by young Maine musicians, plus regular programming continues. All seats are reserved (adult tickets from $18–34); winter tickets are less expensive, and programs vary from classical to pops to jazz. (Season tickets and flex passes are available.) For information, or an advance copy of the schedule, call or write Bay Chamber Concerts, P.O. Box 228, Rockport 04856, 207/236-2823 or 800/707-2770, www.baychamberconcerts.org.

Fans of art flicks would scream if **The Bayview Street Cinema,** 10 Bay View St., Camden, 207/236-8722, www.bayviewcinema.com, ever closed its doors (it's been a tradition since 1975), but there's seldom a mob at this second-floor movie house in downtown Camden. The management screens all sorts of esoterica, as well as films already available at the local video store. Biggest turnouts are for movies filmed in the area—*Peyton Place, Man Without a Face, Thinner.* Screenings nightly at 7, also at "9ish" on Fri.–Sat.; Sun. matinees are at 3 PM. Tickets are $6.50 adults, $5.50 seniors, $4.50 children. The sound is particularly good, but headphones are available for the hearing impaired. Nearest cinemas for first-run films are in Rockland, Thomaston, and Belfast.

Founded in the 1970s, the **Camden Civic Theatre** presents impressively creditable performances, thanks to lots of fine local talent. Musicals and dramas are mounted primarily in summer at the Camden Opera House at 7:30 PM. Call 207/236-2281 for schedule info.

Maritime Music

Area resident Gordon Bok was awarded an honorary doctorate by Maine Maritime Academy in 1997 in recognition of his contributions to Maine's seafaring heritage. A Maine folksinger, with a focus on songs, ballads, and legends of the sea, he has written and sung some of the most beautiful and haunting songs about Maine seafaring in existence. His music is available in stores and on his website, www.gordonbok.com. His concert schedule varies, but if you have an opportunity to see him locally, take it.

FESTIVALS AND EVENTS

One weekend in February is given over to the **Camden Conference,** an annual three-day foreign-affairs conference with nationally and internationally known speakers. The first weekend in February marks the **National Toboggan Championships,** two days of races and fun at the nation's only wooden toboggan chute—Camden Snow Bowl.

Classical **Bay Chamber Concerts** are offered Wed.–Fri. evenings early July–late Aug. in the Camden Opera House, and Rockport's Opera House and Strom Auditorium. The third Thursday of July is **House and Garden Day,** when you can take a self-guided tour (10 AM–4:30 PM) of significant homes and gardens in Camden and Rockport. Proceeds benefit the Camden Garden Club. And the **Annual Arts and Crafts Show,** on the third weekend in July, draws dozens of artists and craftspeople displaying and selling their wares at the Camden Amphitheatre, Harbor Park, and along Atlantic Avenue. (It coincides with the Camden Public Library's annual book sale.)

The week-long **Union Fair** is a country fair with a carnival, agricultural exhibits, harness racing, food booths, and a focus on blueberries. At the Union Fairgrounds, Union (Rte. 17, west of Camden-Rockport), the third week of August.

Labor Day weekend is also known as **Windjammer Weekend** here, with cruises, windjammer open houses, fireworks, and live entertainment in and around Camden Harbor.

Dozens of artists and craftspeople display and sell their wares at the **Fall Festival and Arts and Crafts Show,** the first weekend in October in Harbor Park.

Christmas by the Sea is a family-oriented weekend—first weekend of December—featuring open houses, special sales, concerts, and a visit from Santa Claus, using a lobsterboat for a sleigh.

SHOPPING

Downtown Camden is a tough place to find socks or thread, but it's a boutique-shopper's paradise if gifts are your goal. Rockport has a handful of unusual gift and antiques shops and galleries.

Antiques

Located in an upscale Rte. 1 carriage house, **Ten High Street Art and Antiques,** 10 High St., Camden 04843, 207/236-2770, off-season 617/429-0008, has been the site of one of Camden's finest antiques shops since the mid-1940s.

Specialties are country and eclectic furniture and accessories. Open Mon.–Sat. 9 AM–5 PM, Sun. noon–4 PM.

Fine English antiques are the specialties at **Suffolk Gallery,** 47 Bay View St., Camden 04843, 207/236-8868. Owner Madge Jones has unusual treasures here, especially English paintings, plus china and silver. Open daily, 10 AM–5 PM, in summer; call ahead the rest of the year.

Books

The Owl and Turtle Bookshop, 32 Washington St., Camden 04843, 207/236-4769 or 800/876-4769, www.owlandturtle.com, has books and cards, plus a convenient special-order service. Specialties? Marine and children's books. Summer hours are 9 AM–5:30 PM daily; extended hours in summer.

At the Camden branch of the small down home group of bookstores, **Sherman's Books & Stationery,** 8 Bay View St., Camden 04843, 207/236-2223, www.shermans.com, you will find the same varied inventory and attentive service as at the other stores, but you'll also find a comfortable fireplace seating area and enjoyable view. A snug port in winter. Open year-round, seven days a week, 9 AM–6 PM (to 9 PM Memorial Day–mid-June, to 10 PM mid-June–mid-Oct.)

Gifts and Crafts

You'll need to wander the streets to take in all the gift and craft shops, particularly in Camden—some are obvious, others are tucked away on side streets and back alleys. Explore.

Planet Emporium, 31 Main St., Camden 04843, 207/236-9022, and **Planet Kids,** 10 Main St., face each other across Main St. in downtown Camden. The former features eco-sensitive gifts, books, and clothing; the latter is a gold mine of educational toys, including books and software. Guard your wallet—lots of tempting stuff here. Open all year, daily to 10 PM in summer.

A downtown-Camden landmark since 1940, **The Smiling Cow,** 41 Main St., Camden, 207/236-3351 or 800/646-6169, is as good a

Mid-Coast Region

place as any to pick up Maine souvenirs—a few slightly kitschy, but most reasonably tasteful. Before or after shopping here, head for the rear balcony for free coffee and a knockout view of the harbor and the Megunticook River waterfall. Open daily 9 AM–9 PM Apr.–Oct.

The name tells it all at **Once a Tree,** 46 Bay View St., Camden, 207/236-3995 or 800/236-0440. Wood is everywhere: cutting boards, clock faces, vases, game boards, spoons, furniture. It's an education in the versatility of wood. The shop is open all year, daily in summer.

At the intersection of Rtes. 90 and 17, about 2.5 miles from Rockport Village, is **Danica Candleworks,** Rte. 90, West Rockport 04865, 207/236-3060, www.danicacandles.com, producers of the loveliest candle colors you've ever seen. Owner Erik Laustsen learned the hand-dipping trade from his Danish relatives, and Danica now ships its work all over the country. The Scandinavian-style shop, which carries other gift items, is open all year, Mon.–Fri. 10 AM–5 PM, Sat. 10 AM–4 PM.

Clothing and Sporting Gear

Established in 1976, **The Admiral's Buttons,** 36 Bay View St., Camden 04843, 207/236-2617, stocks a carefully selected line of classic, high-end men's and women's clothing and accessories (bowties, foul-weather gear, great sweaters), plus Maine-created Shard pottery. Open mid-Apr.–Jan., 10 AM–5:30 PM Mon.–Sat., and Sun. in summer.

Sturdy, well-designed, homemade (by knitting machine) wool and cotton sweaters are the specialty at **Unique One,** 2 Bay View St., Camden 04843, 207/236-8717. Or you can pick out yarn and make your own. Open daily 9 AM–7 PM in summer, shorter hours the rest of the year.

A manageable microcosm of giant outfitter L.L. Bean, **Maine Sport Outfitters,** Rte. 1, Rockport 04856, 207/236-7120 or 888/236-8797, www.mainesport.com, sells canoes, kayaks, bikes, skis, and tents, plus all the relevant clothing and accessories. The savvy staff is especially helpful, willing to demonstrate everything—even skating and kayaking on the tiny

pond outside the modern multi-level building. **Maine Sport Outdoor School,** same address, 800/722-0826, has a full schedule of canoeing, kayaking, and camping trips, and rents equipment. The store is 0.5 mile north of the junction of Rtes. 1 and 90. Open all year, daily 9 AM–8 PM Mon.–Sat., to 6 PM Sun., mid-June–Aug., then 9 AM–6 PM daily till winter, when Sun. hours are 10 AM–5 PM.

Discount Shopping

With a name like **Heavenly Threads,** 57 Elm St., Rte. 1, Camden 04843, 207/236-3203, how can anyone resist this thrift shop? Established by Camden's community-oriented First Congregational Church (next door to the shop), Heavenly Threads carries high-quality pre-owned clothing, books, and jewelry. Staffed by volunteers, with proceeds going to such local ecumenical causes as Meals-on-Wheels, the shop is open all year, Tues.–Fri. 10 AM–4 PM and Sat. 10 AM–1 PM. Also open on Mondays June–Aug.

Natural Foods and Farmers Markets

The best source for health foods, homeopathic remedies, and fresh, seasonal produce is **Fresh Off the Farm,** Rte. 1, Rockport 04856, 207/236-3260, an inconspicuous red-painted roadside place that looks like an overgrown farmstand (it is). Watch for one of those permanent/temporary signs highlighting latest arrivals (Native Blueberries, Native Corn, etc.). The shop is 1.3 miles south of the junction of Rtes. 1 and 90. Open daily year-round.

The **Camden Farmers Market,** 207/273-2809, www,camdenfarmersmarket.org, one of the best in the state, holds forth in a parking lot on Colcord Avenue. Temporary signs are posted on Rte. 1 on market days— Wed. 4:30–6:30 PM and Sat. 9 AM–noon, mid-May–Oct. The market goes on, rain or shine. Besides an unusually good selection of produce, you'll find jams, cheeses, plants, crafts, and sometimes even a petting zoo. The winter market is at the State of Maine Cheese Company.

Maine-Made Products Center

At the southern entrance to Rockport, a sprawling red building is the home of **The State of Maine Cheese Company,** 461 Commercial St., Rte. 1, Rockport 04856, 207/236-8895 or 800/762-8895, www.cheese-me.com, makers of a dozen varieties of cows'-milk hard cheeses, all named after Maine locations (Aroostook Jack, St. Croix Black Pepper, and so on). Under the cheese company's umbrella (and roof) is the Maine-Made Products Center, covering 9,500 square feet. Blueberry chutneys, maple syrup, designer breads, great jams—a one-stop-shopping site. The shop is open Mon.–Sat all year.

ACCOMMODATIONS

The Camden-Rockport area (including Lincolnville) is loaded with lodgings—from basic motels to cottage complexes to elegant inns and B&Bs. Many of Camden's most attractive accommodations (especially B&Bs) are located on Rte. 1 (variously disguised as Elm St., Main St., and High St.), heavily trafficked in summer. If you're unusually sensitive to nighttime noises, request a room facing away from the street.

The chamber of commerce is very helpful with lodging information and also maintains a lengthy list of **seasonal rentals.** A private firm, **Camden Accommodations,** 43 Elm St., Rte. 1, Camden 04843, 207/236-6090 or 800/344-4830, www.camdenac.com, arranges reservations at all kinds of lodgings in Camden and surrounding communities—for a week or all summer. The office is open Mon.–Sat. June–Aug., weekdays the rest of the year. July–Aug., it's best to reserve far in advance. The toughest time to find a last-minute bed is the first week in August, when the Maine Lobster Festival is underway in next-door Rockland.

Camden

Thirteen of Camden's finest B&Bs have banded together in the **Camden Bed and Breakfast Association,** P.O. Box 553, Camden 04843, www.camdeninns.com, with an attractive website. Many of them are described below.

One of Maine's most unusual (and priciest) B&Bs, **Norumbega,** 63 High St., Rte. 1, 207/236-4646, www.norumbegainn.com, is an 1886 turreted stone castle overlooking Camden's outer harbor. Provided your wallet can stand the crunch, splurge for a night (or two) here—if only to feel like temporary royalty. Honeymooners are frequent guests. Twelve strikingly decorated rooms and suites (with private baths) are $160–475 d in summer, including gourmet breakfast and evening hors d'oeuvres; lower rates and special packages off-season. No pets, no smoking. Open all year.

Opened for guests in 1901 and operated since the 1970s by the Dewing family, the **Whitehall Inn,** 52 High St., Rte. 1, 207/236-3391 or 800/789-6565, www.whitehall-inn.com, retains its century-old genteel air. Lovely gardens, rockers on the veranda, a tennis court, and attentive service all add to the appeal of this historic country inn. The inn has a special link with famed poet Edna St. Vincent Millay, who graduated from Camden High School and first recited her poem "Renascence" to Whitehall guests in 1912. Forty comfortable, unpretentious rooms in the inn and two separate buildings (Maine House and Wicker House). Doubles are $135–175. Rates include full breakfast and light afternoon tea. No pets; children are welcome. The dining room is open to the public for dinner (6–8:30 PM); dinner entrées are $16.50–26. Open late May–late Oct.

Bob and Juanita Topper—the knowledgeable, hospitable hosts at **Maine Stay,** 22 High St., Rte. 1, 207/236-9636, www.camdenmainestay.com—do everything right, from the elegant decor to the delicious breakfasts to the welcoming window candles. The stunning residence, built in 1802 and known as the Bass-Huse House, faces busy Rte. 1 and is just a bit uphill from downtown, but inside and out back, behind the carriage house and barn, you'll feel worlds away. (Request a rear room if you're worried about traffic noise.) Eight doubles (all with private bath) are $125 and $205 Memorial Day–Oct., $100 and $150 other months. No smoking, no pets, no children under 10. Open all year.

Just off busy Rte. 1 and two blocks from downtown Camden, in the National Historic District, **The Nathaniel Hosmer Inn,** 4 Pleasant St., 207/236-4012 or 800/423-4012, www.nathanielhosmerinn.com, built in the early 1800s, earns high marks for comfort, convenience, and quiet ambience. Seven guest rooms (private baths) go for $125–165 d June–Oct., $95–135 off-season; four rooms have air-conditioning. Breakfast is a feast. Innkeepers are Glenn and Deborah Eichel; Deborah shares her gourmet breakfast recipes on the Inn's website. No smoking, no pets. Two- and three-night minimum weekends, holidays, and special events. Open all year, the inn is a participant in the early-November Knit-Inn.

A block away from the Hosmer Inn is the **Hartstone Inn,** 41 Elm St., Camden 04843, 207/236-4259 or 800/788-4823, www.hartstoneinn.com, Michael and and Mary Jo Salmon's imposing mansard-roofed Victorian close to the heart of downtown. Although some rooms face on the street, most do not, and all have air-conditioning. Once inside, you're away from it all. Eight rooms and six suites are $145–235 d June–Oct., $100–175 d the rest of the year. No smoking, no children under 12; pets can be accommodated by special arrangement. There's wireless internet throughout. Be *sure* to reserve one of the 20 seats for dinner: Michael, named Caribbean chef of the year when they lived in Aruba, produces five-course prix-fixe extravaganzas for $42.50 a person. The menu changes daily in order to use the freshest ingredients. Dinner is at 7 PM, Wed.–Sun. mid-May–Oct.; the rest of the year, it's at 7 PM Thurs.–Sun. And then, next morning, there's the incredible breakfast. If you get hooked, the Salmons organize culinary classes during the winter. Or buy their magnificent cookbook, to drool over or cook from.

Southward on Main St. are the two **Inns at Blackberry Common,** www.innsatblackberry-common.com, where guests can really pick

blackberries and raspberries, consisting of **The Blackberry Inn,** 82 Elm St., 207/236-6060 or 800/388-6000, and **The Elms,** 84 Elm St., Camden 04843, 207/236-6250 or 800/755-3567, where innkeepers Cyndi and Jim Ostrowski work to help guests plan a personalized vacation itinerary, with an emphasis on lighthouse cruises in cooperation with Capt. Alan Philbrick of the *Lively Lady Too,* as well as the schooners *Heron* and *Surprise.* The B&Bs both offer delicious breakfasts, and some accommodations have fireplaces and whirlpools. The Victorian Blackberry, open all year, has seven rooms in the main inn, and a suite and three rooms in the adjoining carriage house. Rates in high season are $119–249, off-season, $89–175. The Elms, open late May–late Oct., has seven rooms with private baths, $129–199 d in summer, $105–165 d the rest of the year. No smoking, no pets.

Almost the same vintage as The Elms (1810), but slightly closer to downtown is the eye-grabbing **Captain Swift Inn,** 72 Elm St., Camden 04843, 207/236-8113 or 800/251-0865, www.swiftinn.com, named after Frank Swift, who launched Penobscot Bay's windjammer trade. Norm, Linda, and Alex Henthorn are the innkeeping family; the atmosphere is informal, and there is wireless internet. Three of the four rooms have four-poster beds, two are good for a family, having a queen and a twin; two have fireplaces; all have private baths and air-conditioning. Rates are $99–159 d mid-June–mid-Oct., $85–159 other months. Hearty breakfasts are served in the antique keeping room, and there's tea and a snack in the afternoon. No smoking, no pets, no children under five. Open all year.

About midway between two clusters of B&Bs, **The Lord Camden Inn,** 24 Main St., Rte. 1, 207/236-4325 or 800/336-4325, www.lordcamdeninn.com, is a hotel alternative in a historic, four-story downtown building (with elevator). Decor is reproduction Colonial with exposed brick walls and scads of old framed photos in rooms and hallways, plus The M. W. Smith Gallery. (The brick moderates the noise level.) Rooms are pricey ($179–269 d, late June–Aug., lower rates other months), but kids under 16 stay free, and buffet breakfast is included. All 36 rooms and suites have phones, air-conditioning, wi-fi, and cable TV, some have fireplaces. Top-floor rooms have harbor-view balconies. No smoking, well-behaved pets permitted. Open all year.

A fine choice for families is **The Lodge at Camden Hills,** Rte. 1, P.O. Box 794, 207/236-8478 or 800/832-7058, www.thelodgeatcamdenhills.com, with 14 modern suites and cottages in an especially attractive modern enclave a mile uphill from downtown Camden. Doubles are $99–225, depending on the season; children under 12 stay free. Facilities include air-conditioning, phones, cable TV, some kitchens. No pets, no smoking. Open all year.

A hybrid of an inn, B&B, motel, and cottage three miles north of town, **The High Tide Inn,** Rte. 1, 207/236-3724 or 800/778-7068, www.hightideinn.com, has enough variety for every budget—all in an outstanding, seven-acre oceanfront setting with a private pebbly beach and fabulous panoramic views of Penobscot Bay and its islands. The two-story, eight-unit "Oceanfront" motel unit is closest to the water and farthest from Rte. 1. Thirty rooms (with private bath) are $75–195. Rates include a continental breakfast on the water-view porch—there's always a choice of homemade muffins or popovers. Pets can be accommodated in some rooms. Open spring through fall.

In a town full of high-end lodgings, **The Good Guest House,** 50 Elm St., Rte. 1, 207/236-2139, may be the biggest bargain. Two no-frills rooms (private baths, air-conditioning) are $65–75 d, including continental breakfast. Children are welcome, one per room. No pets, no smoking. Located right downtown, it's open all year.

Additionally, there are many other excellent Camden B&Bs, including the Belmont Inn, Hawthorn Inn, A Little Dream, Windward House, and Abigail's Bed-and-Breakfast.

Rockport

Although the elegant, award-winning **Samoset Resort** is technically in Rockport, most guests reach it from the south, via Rockland.

One of the area's spiffiest motels also has terrific Penobscot Bay views. In the Glen Cove section of Rockport (three miles south of downtown Rockport, three miles north of downtown Rockland; next door to Penobscot Bay Medical Center), the **Glen Cove Inn,** Rte. 1, P.O. Box 35, Glen Cove 04846, 207/594-4062 or 800/453-6268, sits on a 17-acre bluff with a lovely trail leading to the rocky shore. Many of the 35 units boast water views; all have air-conditioning, phones, cable TV. There's also a heated pool. No pets. Request a room set back from Rte. 1. Doubles are $79–149 mid-June–Aug., lower other months; open all year.

Megunticook Campground by the Sea, Rte. 1, P.O. Box 375, Rockport 04856, 207/594-2428 or 800/884-2428, www.campgroundbythesea.com, is the area's best-run commercial campground, a 17-acre facility with 87 wooded sites. Amenities include hot showers, playground, snack bar, heated pool, laundry, and kayak rentals. Noise rules are strictly enforced; pets are allowed. Sites are $33–44 a night (four persons), lower early and late in the season; there are also ten camping cabins. Lobsterbakes take place in season on Saturday nights; inquire about off-season weekend vacation packages. Open mid-May–mid-Oct. The campground is three miles south of Camden, five miles north of Rockland.

FOOD
Breakfast and Lunch

The **Camden Bagel Cafe,** Brewster Mill, Mechanic St., Camden, 207/236-2661, has a hugely loyal clientele, drawn by *real* coffee, fresh bagels, fast service, daily newspapers, and a casual air. No credit cards. Open all year, Mon.–Sat. 6:30 AM–2 PM, Sun. 7:30 AM–2 PM.

Good coffee is also a draw at the **Camden Deli,** 37 Main St., Camden, 207/236-8343, in the heart of downtown, but its biggest asset is the windowed seating area overlooking the Megunticook River waterfall. The view doesn't get much better than this. Made-to-order sandwiches, homemade soups, veggie burgers, and subs (try the Deli Lama) all add to the mix. Beer and wine only for takeout. Open all year, 6 AM–9 PM, to 10 PM in season, beginning in June.

Just down the street, **The Village Restaurant,** 7 Main St., Camden, 207/236-3232, gets raves for an equally fine view and, say aficionados, the town's best chowder. At lunchtime, locals throng to this longtime standby, along with the tour-bus crowd. Try to hold out for a window table. Open all year for lunch and dinner.

Since the early 1970s, **Scott's Place,** 85 Elm St., Rte. 1, Camden, 207/236-8751, a roadside lunch stand near Harbor Audio-Video, has been dishing up inexpensive burgers and dogs, nowadays adding veggie burgers ($3.99). Call ahead and it'll be ready. Open Mon.–Sat. 10 AM–4 PM, except in winter when there are shorter hours.

Peek behind the old-fashioned façade at **Boynton-McKay Food Co.,** 30 Main St., Camden 04843, 207/236-2465, and you'll see an espresso bar, eight booths, antique pharmacy accessories, and a thoroughly modern café menu. Restored and rehabbed in 1997, Boynton-McKay had been *the* local drugstore for more than a century. The new incarnation features bagels, creative salads, homemade soups, a superb lunch menu, and an espresso bar. Most affordable item on the menu is a veggie fajita wrap for $4.75, most expensive a $6.95 Thai chicken on skewers, with soba noodles and stir-fried vegetables. Open daily except Mondays for breakfast and lunch.

Zaddik's Pizza, Pasta & Mex, 20 Washington St., Rte. 105, Camden, 207/236-6540, a kid-friendly place, has one foot in Mexico and one in Italy—an extensive menu with pizza, burritos, fajitas, calzones, and quesadillas. Beer, wine, and Margaritas available. Open Tues.–Sun. 5–10 PM in summer; Tues.–Sat. 5–9 PM in winter.

Facing downtown Camden's five-way inter-section, **French & Brawn,** 1 Elm St., Camden, 207/236-3361, www.frenchandbrawn.com, is an independent market that earns the description *super*. It's gourmet heaven—exotic produce, oven-ready takeout meals, high-cal frozen desserts, esoteric meats, and a staff with a can-do attitude. A specialty is yacht provisioning. Loyal longtime customers even have charge accounts. Open all year, Mon.–Sat. 6 AM–7 PM, Sun. 8 AM–7 PM.

The **Rockport Corner Shop,** Main and Central Sts., Rockport, 207/236-8361, a bright, clean, airy place, is the ultimate local hangout, so seats can be hard to come by. Lunch menu is basic American, always reliable—sandwiches, burgers, soups, salads. No credit cards. Open all year, Mon.–Fri. 6:30 AM–2 PM, Sat. 7 AM–2 PM, and Sun. 7 AM–1 PM.

The barn at the junction of Rtes. 1 and 90 is the home of the **Market Basket,** Rte. 1, Rockport 04856, 207/236-4371, takeout source for creative sandwiches, homemade soups, cheeses, exotic condiments, pastries, wine, beer, and entrées-to-go. In winter, the Market Basket sponsors cooking classes. The shop is open all year.

Inexpensive to Moderate

In the heart of Camden, **Cappy's,** 1 Main St., 207/236-2254, is small, a bit cramped, reliably good, and very popular with locals and out-of-towners alike. In summer, ask for a table in the second-floor Crow's Nest. Burger-and-sandwich menu; seafood chowder is a specialty. Stop by the lower-level bakery for croissants, bread, and lots of other goodies. Open daily 11 AM–10 PM, most of the year except midwinter, when it's apt to close earlier.

Overtaken by an urge for pasta or other Italian cuisine? **Sonny G's,** 32 Elm St., Camden 04843, 207/236-4477, www.sonnygs.com, serves scampi, cacciatore, parmesans, manicotti, and the rest of the traditional Italian menu. Open daily for dinner, 5–9 PM.

Upstairs from Sonny G's is **Mikado,** 207/236-4477, serving sushi and other Japanese dishes. Meals are under $20, and sushi and sashimi can be had by numbers of pieces or as samplers.

Moderate to Expensive

Since 1974, **Peter Ott's,** 16 Bay View St., Camden 04843, 207/236-4032, has been a mainstay of the Camden restaurant scene—an informal spot where you can count on excellent steaks, seafood, heart-healthy entrées, and heart-unhealthy (but award-winning) desserts. Reservations for large groups only, so expect to wait in July–Aug., but the comfortable lounge eases the anxiety. The bar is also a local watering hole for the after-work crowd. Open daily, 5:30–9 PM, (9:30 PM on weekends, 10 PM in summer), early May–Nov.; closing earlier, usually 8:30 PM the rest of the year, call or check days in winter.

At the former site of the Frogwater Café, the **Bouchée Bistro,** 31 Elm St., Rte. 1, Camden, 207/236-8998, serves American and regional cuisine with a French influence. Entrée range is $18–25. Open all year, Serving lunch 11:30 AM–2:30 PM, except Tues. and Sun; dinner 5:30–9 PM Wed.–Mon., Fri.–Sat. until 10 PM.

The Waterfront Restaurant, Bay View St., Camden, 207/236-3747, has the best waterside dining in town, but arrive early for a table on the deck. Lunches are the most fun, overlooking lots of harbor action; at high tide, you're eye-to-eye with the boats. The restaurant is open daily in summer for lunch 11:30 AM–2:30 PM and dinner 5–10 PM (entrées $12–19). The lounge and oyster bar are open 11:30 AM–midnight. Winter hours can be unpredictable; call ahead.

Natalie's at the Mill, 46 Mechanic St., Ste. 200, Camden 04843, 207/236-7008, overlooks the falls of the Megunticook River, a little right-in-town surprise, because this restaurant serving American cuisine with a French and Asian twist is located in the former Knox Woolen mill. Natalie's is part of the organic trend, uses organic vegetables, local when possible, and all local seafood. The talented chef creates such entrées as Crispy Duck Breast with wilted baby greens, potato pancetta gratin, fennel puree juniper pepper red wine emulsion; range is $23–33. Open Tues.–Sat. for dinner 5:30–9 PM, and on Sun. early July–Oct.

Originally a gallery representing one hundred high-end glass artists, **PrismGlass,** 297 Commercial St. (Rte. 1), Rockport 04856, 207/230-0061, www.prismglassgallery.com, has been getting great reviews for its gallery café, where artful presentation of an imaginative menu is key. Typical dishes are Soft and Crispy Crab ($22) and Vegetarian Risotto ($16). The gallery is still there, along with a glass-blowing studio. The restaurant is open Wed.–Sun. for dinner 5–9 PM (Sun. 4 PM–7 PM), Wed.–Sat. for lunch 11 AM–3 PM, and 10 AM–3 PM for Sun. brunch.

What to watch at **Atlantica,** 1 Bayview Landing, Camden 04843, 207/236-6011 or 888/507-8514, www.atlanticarestaurant.com, could be a problem. Should you keep an eye on the open kitchen, where chefs are preparing French-inspired world cuisine, or on the harbor, where some of the yachts are cruising the world? It's a dilemma you need to make reservations to enjoy, along with a seafood-oriented menu. Entrées like Butter Poached Maine Lobster Tail and Oven Roasted Monkfish do have some carnivore-friendly company like Bistro Steak and Lamb Rack, costing $20–26. Atlantica serves lunch and dinner daily except Tuesdays.

At **Francine,** 55 Chestnut St., Camden 04843, 207/230-0083, the bread is made on the premises, and most of the meal's ingredients don't come from much farther away, reflecting the growing local consciousness of sophisticated restaurants. Fresh and local are Francine's bywords, resulting in a menu high in creative improvisation. The idea works. Entrées are $18–26, and reservations are recommended. Open Tues.–Sat. 5:30–10 PM all year.

In summer, another option in this category is the sedate dining room at the elegantly old-fashioned **Whitehall Inn.** Year-round, another inn with a dining room open to the public is the **Youngtown Inn.**

INFORMATION AND SERVICES

One of Maine's busiest local tourism offices is the **Camden-Rockport-Lincolnville**

Mid-Coast Region

Chamber of Commerce, Public Landing, P.O. Box 919, Camden 04843, 207/236-4404 or 800/223-5459, www.visitcamden.com. They've heard every possible question by now, so don't hesitate to ask. The chamber sponsors a number of special events each year, so it's a lively operation. Request a copy of their map of area streets and businesses, as well as the official chamber guide. The gray building, facing the parking lot and the harbor at Camden's public landing, is open daily in summer, Mon.–Fri. the rest of the year.

The community website—with news as well as links to businesses in the area—is http://Camden.k2Bh.com.

Both Camden and Rockport have undertook major expansions of their libraries in the 90s—and the results are worth a visit. A $2.3 million expansion at the **Camden Public Library,** Main St., Rte. 1, Camden 04843, 207/236-3440, created a state-of-the-art facility with a subterranean lecture room and community Internet access. Don't miss the wonderful children's garden, with stone bench supports made to look like books (all classic Maine children's titles). Open Mon.–Sat. 9:30 AM–5 PM (to 8 PM Tues. and Thurs.), Sun. 1–5 PM. The **Rockport Public Library,** 1 Limerock St., Rockport 04856, 207/236-3642, is a smaller but very user-friendly oasis at the head of Rockport's main drag. Even the gardens are conducive to a good read. Open Mon.–Sat. 9 AM–5:30 PM (to 8 PM Wed.).

Newspapers

The beat for the *Camden Herald,* 207/236-8511, is Camden, Rockport, Lincolnville, Appleton, and Hope. Published every Thursday, the paper carries calendar listings and, in summer, a waterfront info section. The weekly *Free Press,* 207/596-0055, based in Rockland, has the area's most extensive calendar listings. In a case of the tail wagging the dog, the folksy *VillageSoup Times,* went to print from its popular web presence, which it retains and promotes: www.villagesoup.com, 207/236-8468. The only statewide daily newspaper paying attention to this part of the Mid-Coast is the *Bangor Daily News,* 461 Commercial St., Rockport, 207/236-3575.

Emergencies

The closest hospital is on the Rockport/Rockland boundary. **Penobscot Bay Medical Center,** Rte. 1, Rockport 04856, 207/596-8000, has 24-hour emergency-room care and all private rooms. For police, fire, and ambulance in Camden, Rockport, and Lincolnville, call 911.

Public Restrooms

With the number of visitors who arrive in Camden each summer, merchants and restaurateurs tend to be reluctant to allow use of their restrooms to noncustomers. Fortunately, the town provides public facilities—in the gray building across the parking lot from the chamber of commerce on Camden's public landing.

Photo Services

Maine Coast Photo, 23 Elm St., Camden, 207/236-1010, does three-hour slide processing, overnight and rush print processing, and stocks an extensive array of slide and print film. In summer, it's open daily except Sunday.

Laundry

Bishop's Laundry and Carpet Service, 96 Washington St., Rte. 105, Camden, 207/236-3339, is 0.6 mile off Rte. 1; it's open daily 5:30 AM–9 PM. Two-day dry-cleaning service. Do your own laundry or drop it off early and they'll do it for you the same day.

Special Courses

Students come from all over the world to the prestigious **Maine Photographic Workshops,** P.O. Box 200, Rockport 04856, 207/236-8581, www.theworkshops.com, where international photo luminaries teach one- and two-week courses, summer and fall, to neophytes and professionals. A degree-granting program, called **Rockport College,** continues during the winter. Courses are fairly pricey; evening slide lectures are open to the public.

Alumni of the one-, two-, and 12-week workshops at the **Center for Furniture Craftsmanship,** 25 Mill St., Rockport 04856, 207/594-5611, established in 1993, can't say enough about their experiences. Courses are for various skill levels, from beginner to pro. There is also a nine-month comprehensive program, as well as studio fellowships. About 250 attend each year; a 12-week session is $5,400. The center can help arrange for lodging and meals. The Messler Gallery, a fine woodworking gallery, is on-site.

Getting Around
Downtown Camden, at the height of summer, is a traffic nightmare. Rte. 1 bisects the village, and getting across it on foot or by car can be perilous. It's not Boston or Rome, but it's still aggravating. The scarcity of parking creates a musical-cars situation with drivers circling endlessly to find a space. At the chamber of commerce, be sure to request local maps, which show locations of two-hour and all-day parking areas.

Better still, bring or rent a bike and use that to get around. There are few bike lanes, so safety is an extra concern, but bike enthusiasts have placed racks at strategic locations around town. Take advantage of them.

Lincolnville

Since the early 1990s, the town of Lincolnville, just north of Camden, has outpaced all the surrounding communities in population growth. An influx of new residents has pushed the census over the 2,000 mark. Two distinct enclaves make up the town—oceanfront Lincolnville Beach ("the Beach") and, about five miles inland, Lincolnville Center ("the Center"). Lincolnville is laid-back and mostly rural; the major activity center is a short strip of shops and restaurants at the Beach, and few visitors realize there's anything else.

About a mile north of Lincolnville Beach is a part of town with the quaint name of Ducktrap. Near the mouth of the Ducktrap River, where shoreline trees screen the water, ducks used to gather as ducks do. During molting season, when the ducks shed their feathers and were unable to fly, foraging Native Americans would sneak up on them and capture them for dinner. Or so the story goes.

Directly offshore from Lincolnville Beach, almost within spitting distance, is the island of Islesboro, a fine day-trip destination from Lincolnville and the Camden-Rockport areas. The car ferry departs from the southern end of Lincolnville Beach.

SIGHTS
Lincolnville's Microbrewery
A ride into rural country inland from Camden ends up at Andrew Hazen's farm-cum-brewery, **Andrew's Brewery,** 353 High St., Lincolnville 04849, 207/763-3305. Except for major national holidays, Andrew will give a free tour—by appointment only—any time of year. While you tour the operation, the kids can visit the donkey in the barn. Brewery specialties are Andrew's Old English Ale, Andrew's Brown Ale, St. Nick Porter, and Summer Golden Ale. From Camden, take Washington St. (Rte. 105) to Rte. 235. Go 0.6 mile and turn left onto Moody Mountain Rd. Continue 1.6 miles and turn right onto High St. The brewery is one mile ahead, on the left.

RECREATION
Swimming
Penobscot Bay flirts with Rte. 1 at **Lincolnville Beach,** a sandy stretch of shorefront in the congested hamlet of Lincolnville Beach. This is about as close as the road gets to the ocean. On a hot day, the sand is wall-to-wall people; during one of the coast's legendary northeasters, it's quite a wild place. There's **freshwater swimming** at several area ponds (most people would call them lakes). On Rte. 52 in Lincolnville Center, there's a small town-owned swimming/picnic area on **Norton Pond.** Other swimming ponds are **Coleman Pond, Pitcher Pond,** and **Knight's Pond.**

Sea Kayaking and Canoeing

Ducktrap Sea Kayak Tours, 2175 Atlantic Highway (Rte. 1), Lincolnville Beach 04849, 207/236-8608, owned by Lorraine Davis and Daniel Henry, rents kayaks, gives lessons, and runs two-hour coastal tours and half-day guided tours (reservations necessary, experience not; tours start at $30/pp.). Ducktrap specializes in private and small group lessons, and Davis says they have "some incredible teachers." If you decide you need your own kayak, they'll even sell you one, beginning at $279. If you're around in Oct., inquire about the date for the annual fall clearance sale—a good chance to pick up an affordable kayak.

Best places to canoe are Norton Pond and Megunticook Lake, and you can even canoe (or kayak) all the way from the head of Norton Pond to the foot of Megunticook Lake. The only tricky part is navigating the drainage culvert between the pond and the lake.

Hiking

The boundaries of both Camden Hills State Park and Fernald's Neck extend into Lincolnville, where the major state-park hike follows the **Ski Shelter Trail** to the **Bald Rock Trail.** From Rte. 1 in Lincolnville Beach, take Rte. 173 west about 2.5 miles to the marked parking area just beyond the junction of Youngtown Rd. The 1,200-foot summit—with great views of Penobscot Bay (weather permitting)—is about two miles one way, easy to moderate hiking. The route links up with the rest of the state-park trail network, but unless you've arranged for a shuttle, it's best to do Bald Rock as a round-trip hike.

Cross-Country Skiing

Tanglewood 4-H Camp and Learning Center, Lincolnville, 207/789-5868, www.tanglewood4h.org, spreads out over close to 1,000 acres. In winter, Tanglewood has more than 10 miles of cross-country trails, the best network in this part of the Mid-Coast. Some winters, Mother Nature provides scanty snow cover here, but when she obliges, the trails are superb. Some trails are also used by snowmo-

biles. No pets. To reach Tanglewood from Rte. 1, continue 1 mile north of the ferry terminal at Lincolnville Beach and turn left at the Tanglewood sign, onto Ducktrap Rd; go 0.7 mile and turn right onto an unpaved road; continue 0.8 mile to the camp and park on the right side. At the gate, pick up a trail map.

SHOPPING

Art, craft, and souvenir shops are clustered along the Rte. 1 strip at Lincolnville Beach; just north of town are a couple of unusual shops and galleries worth a visit.

Handsome, dark wood buildings 0.2 mile north of the Beach are home to **Windsor Chairmakers,** Rte. 1, P.O. Box 120, Lincolnville 04849, 207/789-5188 or 800/789-5188, www.windsorchair.com. You can observe the operation, browse the display area, or order some of their well-made chairs, cabinets, and tables. Open daily 9 AM–5 PM, June–Oct.; open weekdays Nov.–May.

Professional boat-builder Walt Simmons has branched out into decoys and wildlife carvings, and they're just as outstanding as his boats. Walt and his wife, Karen, run **Duck Trap Decoys,** Duck Trap Rd., P.O. Box 88, Lincolnville 04849, 207/789-5363, www.ducktrap.com, a gallery/shop that also features the work of nearly five dozen other woodcarvers. Jan.–Memorial Day, open by chance or appointment; Memorial Day–Christmas, open Mon.–Sat. 9 AM–5 PM.

ACCOMMODATIONS

Bed-and-Breakfasts

About four miles north of Camden and a mile south of Lincolnville, **The Victorian by the Sea,** Seaview Dr., Lincolnville Beach 04849, 207/236-3785 or 800/382-9817, www.victorianbythesea.com, mailing address P.O. Box 1385, Camden 04843, overlooks the bay at the end of a winding lane from Rte. 1. Seven Victorian-style rooms with private baths—some with fireplaces and water views—are $160–235 d in summer, lower off-season. Access is through Abbington's Motel. No smoking, no pets, no children under 12. Open all year.

Tim and Joan Porta, owners of Migis Lodge on Sebago Lake, acquired the **Inn at Ocean's Edge,** Rte. 1, Lincolnville Beach, mailing address P.O. Box 704, Camden 04843, 207/236-0945, www.innatoceansedge.com in 2005. Already located as close to the shore as is legally allowed, the inn now features a horizon-edge heated pool, spa facilities, and elegant waterfront dining at The Edge. Most of the 32 accommodations ($159–295 d) feature ocean view, a king bed, Jacuzzi for two, fireplace, and cable TV. Rates include a full gourmet breakfast overlooking Penobscot Bay, and use of an exercise room, plus wi-fi. No pets, no smoking, not recommended for children under 12. Open Apr.–Dec.

About midway between Camden and Lincolnville, down an oceanward lane, **The Inn at Sunrise Point,** Rte. 1, Lincolnville, mailing address P.O. Box 1344, Camden 04843, 207/236-7716, www.sunrisepoint.com, has three handsome rooms in the main lodge, four separate cottages, a suite, and the Wyeth loft. Rates run $225–495 d. Decor is tastefully elegant; breakfast in the conservatory is spectacularly good. Each cottage has a double Jacuzzi, phone, fireplace, TV/VCR, mini-bar, and private bay-view deck. No smoking, no pets, children 12 and over only. Two-night minimum Memorial Day–Columbus Day. Open mid-Apr.–Oct.

Motels and Cottages

Motels and cottage complexes are strung all along Rte. 1 between Camden and Lincolnville Beach. Rates vary widely, depending on amenities.

Pine Grove Cottages, Rte. 1, Lincolnville 04849, 207/236-2929 or 800/530-5265, is a neat, comfortable, no-frills cottage complex with bay views. Nine one- and two-bedroom cottages are $60–150 d, including kitchen, phone, and cable TV. No smoking. Children and pets are welcome. Pine Grove is four miles north of Camden, set back from the highway. Open mid-Apr.–mid-Oct.

The **Mount Battie Motel,** 2158 Atlantic Highway, Rte. 1, Lincolnville 04849, 207/236-3870 or 800/224-3870, www,mountbattie.com, a particular favorite of Islesboro residents, charges $75–120 d in summer ($59 May–June) for its 22 motel-style rooms with air-conditioning, TV, phones, and generous buffet-style continental breakfast. No smoking, no pets. Four miles north of Camden, and fairly close to the highway, it's open May–Oct.

Snow Hill Lodge, 2298 Atlantic Highway, Rte. 1, Lincolnville Beach 04849, 207/236-3452 or 800/476-4775, www.midcoast.com/~theview, is an unpretentious, well-maintained motel with a splendid view of Penobscot Bay. Hospitable hosts Sitki and Marie Kocak have 30 rooms with TV, phones, and free continental breakfast. Rates are $60–80 d (lower off-season). No pets, no smoking. It's 4.5 miles north of Camden, less than a mile south of Lincolnville Beach, fairly near the highway, and open all year. Mid-May–mid-Oct., breakfast can be purchased at the Café at Snow Hill Lodge.

FOOD

Moderate to Expensive

Chef Manuel Mercier gives his French cuisine a Maine twist at the **Youngtown Inn,** Rte. 52 and Youngtown Rd., Box 4246, Lincolnville 04849, 207/763-4290 or 800/291-8438, an early-19th-century restaurant and inn 4.5 miles northwest of Camden. Ambience is low-key yet elegant. Specialties include rack of lamb and Coquille St. Jacques (entrées $22–27). Reservations advised. Open for dinner Tues.–Sun. year-round, but call ahead in winter. Upstairs are six country-French guest rooms with private baths for $110–175 d, including breakfast. Children are welcome; no smoking, no pets.

Lobster-in-the-Rough

Lincolnville's best-known landmark is **The Lobster Pound Restaurant,** Rte. 1, P.O. Box 118, Lincolnville Beach 04849, 207/789-5550. About 300 people—some days, it looks like more than that—can pile into the main restaurant, an enclosed patio, and a separate oceanfront eating area, so be sure to make reservations on summer weekends.

Despite the crowds, food and service are reliably good. Lobster, of course, is king, and unless you're allergic, it's crazy not to order it here. Poultry and steaks are also available. Entrées are $8–23. Request a patio table. Open late Apr.–Oct. for lunch and dinner, 11:30 AM–8 PM (to 9 PM July–Aug.).

Lincolnville is part of the **Camden-Rockport-Lincolnville Chamber of Commerce,** and most of its visitor info is channeled through the chamber office in Camden (Public Landing, P.O. Box 919, Camden 04843, 207/236-4040).

Islesboro

Lying three miles offshore from Lincolnville Beach, via 20-minute car ferry, is 12-mile-long Islesboro, a year-round community with a population of about 655—beefed up annually by a sedate summer colony. Time was when islanders and summer rusticators barely intermingled—except that many islanders served as caretakers, kitchen staff, and general gofers for wealthy visitors in their grand mansions, primarily in the enclave of Dark Harbor. The summer social scene remains exhaustingly active, and many islanders still have jobs as caterers and property managers, but apartheid has diminished. Year-rounders and summer folk roll up their sleeves and work together for worthy island causes—land trust, churches, school, library, and historical society—and there's even gentle joshing about the island culture. A 1996 talent show, for example, featured the song "I Wanna Go Back to My 40-Room Shack in Dark Harbor."

Islesboro's first white settlers put down their roots in the late 1760s, taking up fishing and farming, then some shipbuilding, including boats for the giant Pendleton fleet sailing out of Searsport, across the bay. The town—covering about 6,000 acres on this and adjacent islands—was incorporated in 1788. In the 1860s, population peaked at about 1,200; grand estates and resort hotels began sprouting in the 1890s.

Nowadays, besides the service industry, the major employment options are construction and maritime trades. There are three boatyards, and more than 30 lobsterboats are homeported here. A 1990s phenomenon is an expanding crop of high-tech freelancers living here and commuting to work via the information highway.

Car ferries are frequent enough to make Islesboro an ideal day-trip destination—and that's the choice of most visitors, partly because lodging is pretty scarce. The only camping is on nearby Warren Island State Park—and you have to have your own boat to get there. If you're not spending the night, keep an eye on the time so you don't miss the last ferry (4:30 PM) back to the mainland.

SIGHTS
Views from the Road
The best way to get an island overview (besides flying into the tiny airstrip) is to do an end-to-end auto tour. You won't see all the huge "cottages" tucked down long driveways, and you won't absorb island life and its rhythms (that requires a longer stay), but you'll scratch the surface of what Islesboro is about. Drive off the ferry, which docks about a third of the way down the island, and go one mile to a stop sign. Turn right and go 1.2 miles to another stop sign. Turn right, onto Main Rd., and go 4.3 miles south to Town Beach at the bottom of the island. Then backtrack on Main Rd., past the turnoff to the ferry dock, heading "up island" (as it's known locally) and covering 12 miles to northernmost Pripet and Turtle Head. En route, you'll pass exclusive summer estates, workaday homes, spectacular seaside vistas, and a smattering of shops for crafts, books, and takeout food. On the up-island circuit, watch for a tiny marker on the west side of the road. It commemorates the 1780 total eclipse witnessed here—the first recorded in North America. At the time, British loyalists still held Islesboro, but they temporarily suspended hostilities, allowing Harvard

astronomers to lug their instruments to the island and document the eclipse.

Sailors' Memorial Museum

As the ferry glides into the western side of Gilkey Harbor, you can't miss the squat little **Grindle Point Light,** 207/734-2253, built in 1850, rebuilt in 1875, and now automated. Next to it, in the former keeper's house, is the town-owned Sailors' Memorial Museum, filled with seafaring memorabilia acquired in the 1970s. The volunteer-staffed museum is open late June–Labor Day; call for hours and admission.

Islesboro Historical Society

Right about the center of the island, 3.8 miles from the ferry and just south of the aptly named Narrows, stands the two-story Islesboro Historical Society, corner of Main and West Side Rds., 207/734-6733, in the former town hall. On the first floor are rotating temporary exhibits, throughout the summer, while the second-floor museum contains the permanent collection of island memorabilia. The society also sponsors program/meetings with guest lecturers at 8 PM the last Wednesday of the month. The building generally is open July–Labor Day. Schedule varies, call ahead for info. Or call for an appointment; volunteers often are in the building even when it's closed.

PARKS AND RECREATION

Warren Island State Park

Why is 70-acre Warren Island State Park the most underutilized of Maine's state parks? There's no organized transportation to the island. If you want to hike, camp, or picnic on Warren, you'll need a boat—but it's well worth the effort. Besides, it'll give you a chance to see some of Islesboro's shorefront homes. A painless way to do this, and avoid mainland parking fees, is to lash a kayak, canoe, or skiff atop your vehicle, take the ferry from Lincolnville Beach, park at the Islesboro ferry landing, and paddle the protected quarter mile to the east side of the island. (There is also water-taxi ser-

vice from Lincolnville.) There is a group picnic site, and seven well-spaced, wooded family campsites—two are shelters—with picnic tables and firewood; water comes from a solar spigot. Make reservations at 800/332-1501 (in-state) or 207/287-3824 (out-of-state). For information, contact the Camden Hills State Park manager, 207/236-3109. Camping is $19 per site per night for nonresidents. The park is open Memorial Day weekend to September 15, and the manager will find space for visitors even when the official camping sites are full.

Town Beach

At Pendleton Point, Islesboro's southern tip, the Town Beach has two sandy pockets, tidepools, unique rock formations, wooded paths, well-spaced picnic tables, blackberry bushes (in season), and great views. The beach is 2.5 miles south of Dark Harbor Village.

Kids Programs

Summer programs for children are organized by the Islesboro Islands Trust and the Islesboro Recreation Committee.

Bicycling and Hiking

Islesboro is fairly level, and walking end to end is unrealistic for a day-trip, so a bicycle would seem to be the perfect solution. Not exactly. Bicycles are very controversial here—hardly surprising, since the shoulderless roads are narrow and too many cyclists have failed to heed commonsense rules. A safer solution is to take leisurely drives to both ends of the island, then park the car (in summer, there's room near the handsome stone Islesboro Central School, which also has two creative playgrounds) and walk along the road through Dark Harbor Village to the Town Beach at the southern end of the island.

ENTERTAINMENT

Churches, the library, and the historical society manage to organize impressive schedules of concerts, lectures, crafts fairs, public suppers, and other events in July and August—when the population is at its height and fundraising is most successful. Check the *Islesboro Island News* for listings. The **Performing Arts Series** of the Society for the Preservation of the Free Will Baptist Church might include classical, jazz, bluegrass, traditional, a barbershop quartet, and/or the Portland Brass. Concerts are at 8 PM—the first two on Saturdays, the second two on Thursdays—at the church (also known as the Up Island Church). Tickets are $15 adults, $5 youth. The **Islesboro Forum** brings guest speakers to the church on summer Sundays at 5:30 PM. Topics range widely, usually thanks to noted experts summering on or visiting the island. One year, for instance, the series included experts on dressage, social change, environmental law, and astronomy. If you're coming from the mainland, be cognizant of ferry schedules; sometimes it's possible to hitch a ride on a special water taxi with the musicians returning home.

SHOPPING

Galleries and Books

There's a different art show every week at Paula McNamara and Jack McConnell's **Seven Knots Gallery,** 300 Main Rd., 207/734-8877, www.sevenknotsgallery, open early July–mid-Sept., Tues.–Sat., for morning workshops, afternoon gallery visits, evening music, and receptions. The gallery is in the former Pendleton Schoolhouse.

Artisan Books & Bindery, 113 Derby Rd., 207/734-6852, www.abebooks.com/home/artisan84, is a rare and new book store, and a full-service working bindery, begun in 2001 by former museum director Craig Olson.

Island **gift shops** worth a look-see are **Apples,** 207/734-9727; the **Islesboro Trader,** 207/734-9788; **Islesboro Artisans,** 207/734-6944; and **Sundry Scents,** 207/734-9704.

ACCOMMODATIONS AND FOOD

Unless you have island pals, a seasonal rental, or a boat anchored in the harbor, Islesboro has only three places to stay. The only public campsites are on Warren Island, accessible only by boat. For rentals, talk to Don Pendleton at **Islesboro Realty,** 270 West Bay Rd., 207/734-6488.

Hospitable Bonnie St. Peter is the innkeeper at **Dark Harbor Bed and Breakfast,** 119 Derby Rd., Islesboro 04848, 207/734-9772. In her turn-of-the-19th-century farmhouse, not far from the Dark Harbor Shop, she serves a full breakfast that includes homemade pie. Four warmly decorated rooms with private baths are $125 d (less for additional nights) between Memorial Day and Labor Day. Other months, they're $75 d. As with other island accommodations, the cancellation policy is strict, so be sure of your plans before making reservations. No smoking, no pets, no children under 12. Open all year. The inn's restaurant is open to the public for lunch and dinner.

Elegant seasonal accommodations are available at the bright yellow **Dark Harbor House,** P.O. Box 185, Dark Harbor, Islesboro 04848, 207/734-6669, www.darkharborhouse.com—and what a place it is. Built in the late 19th century by a Philadelphia banker, the Georgian Revival mansion (on the National Historic Register) has 11 rooms, all with private baths, some with fireplaces and balconies. Despite the pomp, the ambience is casual. Rooms are $115–185 d (the penthouse suite is $275 d), including full breakfast—worth the splurge if you can swing it. A two-night minimum is required on holiday weekends. Dinner, open to the public, is available in the inn dining room 6–8:30 PM. Smoking only on outdoor porch areas, no pets, no children under 12. The inn has bikes for guests to use, and they'll arrange access to the island's private golf club. Open Apr.–Oct.

The Dark Harbor Shop, Dark Harbor, 207/734-8878, is the hub for local gossip over breakfast, lunch, snacks, sandwiches, or just an ice-cream cone. Kids love the penny candy, and there's a selection of gifts. When the late Sen. Margaret Chase Smith cruised to Islesboro on her namesake ferry, she lunched at the counter here. Open daily 8 AM–5 PM (to 7 PM July–Aug.). Bill Warren, the Dark Harbor Shop's owner, also operates **Warren Realty,** 207/734-8857; if you're interested in a **seasonal rental,** check with him.

Islesboro's two markets sell sandwiches and other picnic fare in summer—much easier than packing lunch ahead of time. **Durkee's General Store,** Main Rd., corner of Ryder's Rd., 207/734-2201, sells a full line of groceries, plus burgers, pizza, sandwiches, hardware, fuel, newspapers, T-shirts, and liquor. Open Mon.–Sat. 8 AM–6 PM, Sun. 10 AM–2 PM. Near the post office and the municipal building, **The Island Market,** 207/734-6672, run by Shake and Loony Mahan, carries a similar inventory (beer and wine, but no liquor), plus Loony's terrific baked goods, and is open Mon.–Fri. 7 AM–5:30 PM, Sat. 8 AM–5:30 PM.

INFORMATION AND SERVICES

There's no chamber of commerce on the island, so the best source of information is a free annual map/brochure called *The Island of Islesboro,* available at the ferry landings in Lincolnville Beach and Islesboro; and the **Town Office,** Municipal Building, Main Rd., P.O. Box 76, Islesboro 04848, 207/734-2253, which is open weekdays 8:30 AM–4:30 PM.

The handsome stone **Alice L. Pendleton Memorial Library,** 309 Main Rd., 207/734-2218, is open all year, Mon. and Wed. 10 AM–noon and 1:30–4:30 PM, Sat.–Sun. 1:30–4:30 PM, plus Wed. 7–9 PM in July–Aug. The library also has a "port-o-call" branch at the ferry terminal on Gilkey Harbor. Inside the waiting room is a carousel of paperbacks available for the borrowing. A long wait for the ferry? No problem—borrow a book to pass the time. Or take it away and return it (or something else) next time. It's all on the honor system—and it *works.*

The local newspaper is the chatty *Islesboro Island News,* P.O. Box 104, Islesboro 04848, 207/734-6921, an ad- and news-filled tabloid published six times a year.

For **fire, police, and ambulance** call 911. There are three physician's assistants based at the **Islesboro Health Center** in the munici-

pal building, 207/734-2213, and one of them is always available by pager for emergencies. Health Center hours are 9 AM–4:30 PM weekdays, during which they handle minor and chronic medical conditions and minor acute emergencies. Critical cases are ferried or airlifted to mainland hospitals. Under the best conditions, though, it can take up to two hours to get to the nearest emergency room.

There are **public toilets** at the ferry terminal in Gilkey Harbor during ferry operational hours and at the Town Beach.

GETTING THERE

The car ferry *Margaret Chase Smith* departs Lincolnville Beach almost every hour on the hour, 8 or 9 AM–5 PM, and Islesboro on the half hour, 7:30 AM–4:30 PM. Round-trip fares are $17.50 for car and driver, $6 adults, $2.50 children, $5.75 adult bicycles, and $3 kids' bikes. There is a fee for reservations. A slightly reduced schedule prevails mid-Oct.–mid-Apr. The 20-minute trip crosses a stunning three-mile stretch of Penobscot Bay, with views of islands and the Camden Hills. In summer, avoid the biggest bottlenecks: Friday afternoon (to Islesboro) and Sunday afternoon and Monday holiday afternoons (from Islesboro). The *Smith* remains on Islesboro overnight, so don't miss the last run to Lincolnville Beach. For more information contact **Maine State Ferry Service,** P.O. Box 214, Lincolnville 04849, 207/789-5611, Islesboro 207/734-6935 or 800/491-4883, www.state.me.us/mdot/opt/ferry.

Since ferry service ends in the late afternoon, a water-taxi service helps islanders and mainlanders attend evening programs, meetings, and social events. The 28-passenger *Quicksilver,* 207/734-8379, operates Thurs. and Sat., departing Islesboro at 9:40 PM and returning to the island from Lincolnville Beach at 10 PM. There are also two weekday runs, before the ferry starts running, leaving the island at 5:55 AM and 6:30 AM. Cost is $6 pp; the service operates all year, weather permitting. No credit cards. Owners Tom Daley and Sandy Alexander also do special charter runs for $190 an hour.

Belfast Area

With a population of 7,008, Belfast is relatively small as cities go, but changes have been occurring at lightning speed—courtesy of gigantic credit-card company MBNA (the nation's largest in affinity cards), which established a major presence here in 1996. Even before MBNA arrived, Belfast was becoming one of those off-the-beaten-track destinations popular with tuned-in visitors. Chalk that up to its status as a magnet for leftover back-to-the-landers and enough artistic types to earn the city a nod for cultural cool. Belfast boasts a curling club, meditation centers, a clutch of art galleries and boutiques, theater companies, the oldest shoe store in America, and half a dozen different 12-step self-help groups.

This eclectic city is a work in progress, a study in Maine-style diversity. It's also a gold mine of Federal, Greek Revival, Italianate, and Victorian architecture—some of it occasionally came on the market for only a tad more than the proverbial song but that has changed as Maine's real estate market has become superheated. Take the time to stroll the well-planned back streets, explore the shops, and hang out at the newly gussied-up waterfront.

Separating Belfast from East Belfast, the Passagassawaukeag River is pronounced "Puh-sag-gus-uh-WAH-keg," but fortunately it is known more familiarly as "the Passy." The Indian name has been translated as both "place of many ghosts" and the rather different "place for spearing sturgeon by torchlight." You choose.

Native Americans, of course, were here long before the first Scotch-Irish settlers, who put down roots in 1765 and soon named their village for the Irish city. After the Revolutionary War, development began in earnest, with shipbuilding remaining the major enterprise well into the 20th century. Most of the workers lived along Bay View St., a district leveled by fire in 1873; the prosperous ship owners and other entrepreneurs built grand mansions on Church St., High St., and Primrose Hill.

Following World War II, the economy shifted, and poultry eclipsed shipbuilding. At one point, Belfast was the largest chicken processor in the world. The annual July Broiler Festival celebrated the industry with a marathon chicken barbecue (although the chickens have flown the coop, the barbecue is still a highlight of the successor Belfast Bay Festival, 207/338-5719, www.belfastbayfestival.com).

As the hub of 724-square-mile Waldo County, which has a population of about 35,000, Belfast draws its traffic and talent from many surrounding communities—Northport, Searsmont, Liberty, Freedom, Thorndike, Unity, Brooks, Waldo, Swanville, and Monroe.

SIGHTS

Historic Walking Tour

No question, the best way to appreciate Belfast's fantastic architecture is to tour by ankle express. Amazing for a community of this size, the city actually has three distinct National Historic Districts: Commercial District (47 downtown buildings), Church Street District (residential), and Primrose Hill District (also residential). Pick up the three walking tours of these districts at the Belfast Area Chamber of Commerce. There are also panels with vintage photographs and text in the downtown and waterfront known as the **Museum In The Streets,** providing a self-guided tour, helping pedestrians learn history in place. Map panels are located at the Chamber of Commerce Information on Lower Main St. and at the Opera House building, corner of Church and Main Sts. Free map brochures are available at the Belfast Museum and the Chamber of Commerce. For more information contact the Belfast Historical Society, 207/338-9229, www.belfast-maine.org/historywalk. The Belfast Historical Society has a conventional museum, the **Belfast Museum,** 10 Market St., displaying maritime and historical exhibits and Percy Sanborn paintings. Summer hours are 11 AM to 4 PM

Thurs.–Mon. or by appointment. Admission is free.

Bayside

Continuing the focus on architecture, just south of Belfast, in Northport, is the Victorian enclave of Bayside, a neighborhoody sort of place with small, well-kept, gingerbreaded cottages cheek by jowl on pint-size lots. Formerly known as the Northport Wesleyan Grove Campground, the village took shape in the mid-1800s as a summer retreat for Methodists. In the 1930s, the retreat was disbanded and the main meeting hall was razed, creating the waterfront park at the heart of the village. Today, many of the colorfully painted homes are rented by the week, month, or summer, and their tenants now indulge in athletic rather than religious pursuits. The camaraderie remains, though, and a stroll (or cycle or drive) through Bayside is like a visit to another era. Bayside is four miles south of Belfast, just east of Rte. 1.

Temple Heights

Continue south on Shore Rd. from Bayside to **Temple Heights Spiritualist Camp,** Shore Rd., Northport, 207/338-3029 (June–Sept.), the rest of the year 207/338-1355 or 207/582-6745, mailing address c/o Secretary Sue Jalbert, 66 Martin Heights, Raymond 04071, www.templeheightscamp.org, yet another religious enclave—this one still going. Founded in 1882, Temple Heights has become a shadow of its former self, reduced to the funky, 12-room Nikawa Lodge on Shore Rd., but the summer program continues, thanks to prominent mediums from all over the country. Even a temporary setback in 1996—when the camp president was suspended for allegedly putting a hex on Northport's town clerk—failed to derail the operation. Camp programs, late June–Labor Day, are open to the public. Spiritualist services and group healing sessions are free; Saturday-morning workshops are $20. Better yet, sign up for a 1.5-hour **group message circle,** when you'll sit in a circle with a medium and a dozen or so others and receive

insights—often uncannily on-target—from departed relatives or friends. Message circles occur Monday, Wednesday, and Saturday at 7:30 PM (arrive a half-hour early). Cost is $10 pp and reservations are necessary. Private readings can be arranged for $30 for half an hour. Rooms are also available; rooms, readings, workshops, and circles should be reserved at the seasonal number.

A Little-of-Everything Museum

Only three miles southeast of Unity, **Bryant Stove and Music Museum,** Rtes. 139 and 220, Rich Rd., 11 Stovepipe Alley, Thorndike 04986, 207/568-3665, www.bryantstove.com, the creation of Joe and Bea Bryant, started out as a woodstove business. Now it's an eclectic collection of antique woodstoves, player pianos, nickelodeons, and cars, plus an incredible doll circus. Bring the old folks, bring the kids—everyone finds this barn of a place (and its owners) fascinating. Open Mon.–Sat. 8 AM–4:30 PM, all year. Admission is $5. The museum is 30 miles northwest of Belfast.

PARKS AND RECREATION

One of the state's best municipal parks is just on the outskirts of downtown. Established in 1904, **Belfast City Park,** 87 Northport Ave., has lighted tennis courts, an outdoor pool (207/338-1661), a pebbly beach, plenty of picnic tables, an unusually creative playground, lots of green space for the kids, and fantastic views of Islesboro, Blue Hill, and Penobscot Bay. The park is the site of the annual Belfast Bay Festival in July. For more action, right in the heart of Belfast, head for **Heritage Park,** at the bottom of Main St., with front-row seats on waterfront happenings. Bring a picnic, grab a table, and watch the yachts, tugs, and lobsterboats.

Lake St. George State Park

Along the lake's western shore, 360-acre Lake St. George State Park, Rte. 3, Liberty 04949, 207/589-4255, is another of Maine's secret treasures—known best to local residents. The

Mid-Coast Region

spring-fed lake tends to be cool, but not as cold as the ocean, so a warm day brings out the crowds. Wooded picnic sites border the lake, as do some of the 38 campsites, which go for $20 for nonresidents. (Try for a waterfront site; those nearer the highway can be noisy.) Pack your fishing gear and a small boat—or rent one here for $3/hr. Across Rte. 3 is a strenuous hiking trail, "straight up the mountain." Admission is $4 adults, $1 kids 5–11, kids under 5 and seniors over 65 free. Open May 15–Sept. 30 for camping, but since the park is alongside Rte. 3, it's accessible and open all year. The park entrance is two miles west of downtown Liberty, 19 miles west of Belfast.

Swan Lake State Park

Lovely name, this one—and a lovely 66-acre park for a picnic and swim: Swan Lake State Park, Frankfort Rd., Swanville 04915, 207/525-4404. Admission is $4 adults, $1 kids 5–11, seniors over 65 and kids under five free. Open Memorial Day weekend to Labor Day, but accessible all year. Swanville is six miles north of Belfast. On Rte. 141 in downtown Swanville is the **Swan Lake Grocery,** 207/338-4029, where you can pick up picnic fixings and wine before heading to the park. To reach the park, take Rte. 141 about three miles north of Swanville and turn right (signposted) onto Frankfort Rd. Continue to the park access road (on the right).

Hiking

Belfast and the rest of Waldo County have some fine hiking spots, but for serious hikes, drive to Camden Hills State Park. An excellent hiking resource for the entire state, but especially for Waldo County, is *Hiking Maine,* by Tom Seymour, who lives in the Belfast area. He describes hikes along the two B&ML excursion railbeds, plus **Frye Mountain** (with an abandoned fire tower), Mt. Waldo and Howard Mendall Marsh (near Frankfort), Halfmoon Pond (near Brooks), and Lake St. George State Park.

Golf

Just south of Belfast is the nine-hole **Northport Golf Club,** 581 Bluff Rd., Northport,

207/338-2270, established in 1916. Operating out of a classic shingled clubhouse, the club is open mid-Apr.–Oct. Snacks and carts are available; starting times only necessary on holiday weekends.

Much newer (opened in 1963) and less fussy is the aptly named **Country View Golf Club,** Rte. 7, Brooks 04921, 207/722-3161. No starting times are needed at this well-maintained, family-run club. Rural vistas are fabulous on the nine-hole course, especially in spring and fall. Snacks and carts are available. Open mid-Apr.–Oct. The club is a mile north of Brooks, 12 miles northwest of Belfast.

Georges River Scenic Byway

Seventeen miles west of Belfast, in Liberty, is the beginning of the Georges River Scenic Byway, a 50-mile auto route along the St. George River (aka Georges River) from its inland headwaters to the sea in Port Clyde. The official start is at the junction of Rtes. 3 and 173 in Liberty, but you can follow the trail in either direction, or pick it up anywhere along the way. Road signs are posted, but it's far better to obtain a map/brochure at a chamber of commerce or other information locale. Or contact the architects of the route: **The Georges River Land Trust** (GRLT), 328 Main St., Rockland 04841, 207/594-5166.

Cyclists can follow the Georges River Bikeways, one of which also goes through this headwaters area east and north of Liberty. Two other routes begin around Searsmont and include Union, Warren, and Thomaston. To follow these routes, you'll need a mountain bike, the GRLT map, and a copy of the DeLorme *Maine Atlas and Gazetteer.* Contact the GRLT for its bikeways map.

Getting Afloat

Until the early 1990s, pleasure boats were scarce in Belfast Harbor. Tugboats, however, were abundant—sturdy workhorses based here and used for heavy-duty towing all along the coast. But, as with Rockland to the south, polluting industry has declined in Belfast, the waterfronts have been upgraded, and yachts have moved in.

If you've brought your own kayak or canoe, several lakes and ponds inland from Belfast are prime destinations (with boat-launching sites): Freedom Pond (officially, Sandy Pond), Unity Pond, Quantabacook Lake, Levenseller Pond, and the lakes at the two state parks.

Searsmont, southwest of Belfast, is the starting point for the annual St. George River Canoe Race, one of the earliest spring whitewater races. Once summer arrives, there's great canoeing on this river, a real pastoral experience. The *AMC River Guide: Maine* has details.

Winter Sports

Nearest downhill ski area is the Camden Snow Bowl, and the best cross-country skiing is at Tanglewood 4-H Camp and Learning Center in Lincolnville. In Belfast itself there's **ice-skating** at "The Muck," a pond at the edge of town (corner of Lincolnville Ave. and Miller St.), east of the Rte. 1 bypass.

The Scottish national sport of curling has dozens of enthusiastic supporters at Maine's only curling rink, the **Belfast Curling Club,** Belmont Ave., Rte. 3, Belfast 04915, 207/338-9851, www.belfastcurlingclub.com, an institution here since the late 1950s. Leagues play regularly on weeknights, and the club holds tournaments *(bonspiels)* and open houses several times during the season, which runs early Nov.–late March for on-ice activities. The Awards Banquet and Annual Meeting take place in April.

ENTERTAINMENT

It's relatively easy to find nightlife in Belfast—not only are there theaters and a cinema, but there usually are a couple of bars open at least until midnight, and sometimes later. Some spots also feature live music, particularly on weekends.

If you don't feel like searching out a newspaper to check the entertainment listings, just go to the Belfast Co-op Store, 123 High St., 207/338-2532, and study the bulletin board. You'll find notices for more activities than you could ever squeeze into your schedule.

An old-fashioned downtown cinema—recently restored to its art deco splendor—shows first-run films for moderate ticket prices. The **Colonial Theatre,** 163 High St., Belfast, 207/338-1930, www.colonialtheatre.com, has three screens, each with one or two showings a night and matinees Sat.–Sun. Open all year.

Check local papers for the schedule of the **Belfast Maskers,** a community theater group that never fails to win raves for its interpretations of contemporary and classical dramas. Performances are held throughout the year in the funky waterfront Railroad Theater, 43 Front St., Belfast, 207/338-9668, www.belfast-maskerstheater.com. In winter, wear an extra pair of socks; the floor is drafty.

Just south of Belfast, the funky **Blue Goose Dance Hall,** Rte. 1, Northport, 207/338-3003, has to be seen to be believed. This low-slung roadside establishment is the site of folk concerts, contra dances, auctions, and more. Most events occur Saturday nights. Check local papers or the Belfast Co-op Store bulletin board.

FESTIVALS AND EVENTS

Belfast is a hive of activity, but lots of the surrounding Waldo County communities also put on some ambitious fairs, festivals, and public suppers. Check the newspapers for schedules.

In early July, soon after July Fourth, the **Arts in the Park** festival gets underway at Heritage Park, on the Belfast waterfront. It's a weekend event, two days of music, children's activities, and lots of food booths. The **Annual Garden Tour,** usually the second or third weekend of July, offers two days (10 AM–4 PM) of self-guided access to some of Belfast's loveliest horticulture. Proceeds benefit Waldo County General Hospital. Tickets are $12 on the day of the tour. The third week in July, the **Belfast Bay Festival** is the highlight of the summer—five days of fun including a seniors' day, a children's day, carnival, live music, kids' games, bingo, fireworks, a parade, craft booths, and a chicken barbecue in Belfast City Park. **Belfast Summer Nights** offers music most Thurs.

Mid-Coast Region

evenings from late June–Aug., 5:30–7:30 PM at different venues around town.

Labor Day weekend brings the **Annual Maine Healing Arts Festival** to Lake Cobbosseecontee in Winthrop. The four-day New Age get-together includes workshops, meditations, sweat-lodge ceremonies, gourmet vegetarian meals, fire-walking, and a full program for children. Lodging is in cabins, or you can bring a tent. Advance registration is required; call 207/336-2065. A brochure is available. No alcohol is allowed. Cost is $245 adults, $95 children 6–14, under 5 free. The third weekend in September is the unique **Common Ground Country Fair** in Unity, featuring hayrides, ethnic- and wholesome-food booths, country dancing, folk arts and crafts demonstrations, exotic animals, world music, books, and alternative-lifestyle booths. Sponsored by Maine Organic Farmers and Gardeners Association.

Downtown Belfast comes alive in October with the **Church Street Festival** and its food booths, art and craft exhibits and sales, unique parade, and kids' events. The second weekend in October, Festivo honors the muse during the **Belfast Poetry Festival** at various locations includng the Hutchinson Center, Colonial Theatre, and the streets of Belfast. Big- and little-name poets are in attendance.

SHOPPING

Antiques

Searsport, just east on Rte. 1, holds the Mid-Coast "antiques capital" title, but Belfast has several fine antiques sources. Outlying **Liberty** gets the prize for being the best area source of antique tools.

It's a store! It's a museum! It's amazing! More than 20,000 "useful" tools—plus used books and prints and other tidbits—fill the three-story **Liberty Tool Company,** Main St., Liberty 04949, 207/589-4771, www.jonesportwood.com. Drawn by nostalgia and a compulsion for handmade adzes and chisels, thousands of vintage-tool buffs arrive at this eclectic emporium each year; few leave empty-handed. June–mid-Oct., it's open 9 AM–5 PM Mon.–

Fri. and Sun.; 8 AM–5 PM Sat. Other months, it's open 9 AM–5 PM Wed.–Sun. From the Rte. 1 bypass in Belfast, take Rte. 3 west, 17 miles, then turn left at the signs for Liberty village.

Across the street is Liberty Graphics, and just down Main St. is the old **Liberty Post Office,** a unique octagonal structure that looks like an oversized box. Built in 1867 as a harness-maker's shop and later used as the town's post office, it's now the headquarters/museum of the Liberty Historical Society, 207/589-4393.

Art Galleries

Exactly midway between Lincolnville Beach and Belfast (five miles in each direction), **The Studio at Saturday Cove,** 608 Atlantic Hwy., Rte. 1, Northport, 207/338-3654, www.saturdaycove.com, is a retired post office/gas station transformed into a dramatically cheerful gallery. Featuring Maine artists in excellent rotating exhibits, the gallery is open Mon.–Sat. 10 AM–5 PM and Sun. noon–5 PM in summer, shorter hours off-season.

Ten of Belfast's downtown galleries, all but one on Main St., have banded together to produce a fun "Gallery Trail" map and descriptions of the individual galleries. Says the brochure: "The short trip is easy on Degas, so Wyeth not make your van Gogh to BelfastArt real soon?" For a brochure, contact Art Alliance, 207/338-9994; Bay River Gallery & Restaurant, 207/338-5888; Belfast Framer & Gallery, 207/338-6465; Engraven Images, 207/338-4396; Indigo Gallery, 207/338-6448; M. H. Jacobs Gallery, 207/338-3324; Parent Gallery,207/338-1553; Shamrock, Thistle & Rose, 207/338-1864; THE CLOWN, 207/338-4344; The Working Art Gallery, 207/338-4820. Or just drop into one or all when you're making a day of it downtown.

Books

Belfast's independent bookstore celebrated its 25th anniversary in 2005, a considerable achievement for an independent bookstore. The quaintly named **Fertile Mind Bookshop,** 105 Main St., Belfast 04915, 207/338-2498, has a particularly good children's section. It's open daily all year.

The Booklover's Attic, 30 Searsport Ave., Rte. 1, Belfast, 207/338-2450, is a treasure trove. The store carries inventory in the areas of Americana, aviation, military, hunting and fishing, music, children's books, science fiction, art, photography, nautical, and American first editions. Plus old LP recordings encompass jazz, Broadway and movie soundtracks, classical vocals and pop, opera, and Big Bands; open May–Oct., Mon.–Sat. 10 AM–5 PM, Sun. 11 AM–4 PM.

Clothing, Gifts, and Crafts

With historic brick buildings, eclectic boutiques, cafés, and even a couple of Joe-Sixpack stores, downtown Belfast is a fun place to shop and window-shop.

Even if shoes aren't on your shopping list, stop in at "the oldest shoe store in America." Founded in the 1830s, **Colburn Shoe Store,** 79 Main St., Belfast 04915, 207/338-1934 or 877/338-1934, www.downtownme.com/colburnshoe, may be old, but it isn't old-fashioned—all the latest brands and styles are here. Open all year, Mon.–Sat. 9 AM–5 PM (to 7 PM Thurs.–Fri.) and Sun. 10 AM–3 PM.

Coyote Moon, 54 Main St., Belfast, 207/338-5659, is an especially attractive New Age-y boutique carrying natural-fiber clothing, jewelry, recycled-paper items, and, of course, incense. Open all year. Summer hours are Mon.–Thurs. 9 AM–6 PM, Fri.–Sat. 9 AM–7 PM, and Sun. 10:30 AM–6 PM. Off-season, it's open daily, but with shorter hours.

If you're seeking a cap or cloak, a gem or glass, or anything else from the British Isles, wend your way to **Shamrock Thistle & Rose,** 48 Main St., Belfast, 207/338-1864 or 866/624-6438, www.shamrockthistlerose.com. Summer hours, July 1–Dec. 24, are 10 AM–6 PM Mon.–Sat. (till 9 PM on Fri., and Sun. 11 AM–4 PM in July–Aug.). Winter hours, Dec. 26–June 30, are 10 AM–6 PM Tues.–Sat.

Foodies should just head straight for **The Good Table,** 68 Main St., Belfast, 207/338-4880 or 800/588-7591, source of cookbooks galore and almost any kitchen tools and gadgets you can think of. Open all year, Mon.– Sat. 10 AM–5:30 PM. Between Thanksgiving and Christmas, and also in summer, The Good Table is open Sun. 11–4 PM.

About two miles east of Belfast's bridge, on the right, is the small roadside shop of **Mainely Pottery,** 181 Searsport Ave., Rte. 1, Belfast, 207/338-1108, www.mainelypottery.com. Since 1988, Jeannette Faunce and Jamie Oates have been marketing the work of 30 Maine potters, each with different techniques, glazes, and styles. It's the perfect place to select from a wide range of reasonably priced work, and careful shipping is available. Peek into the adjacent studio and you'll find Jamie, who specializes in lamps, and is happy to answer questions. Don't miss Jeannette's garden out back. The shop is open daily, 9 AM–7 PM, July–Aug.; 10 AM–5 PM May–June and Sept.–Dec.

Natural Foods and Farmers Markets

The **Belfast Co-op Store,** 123 High St., Belfast 04915, 207/338-2532, www.belfast.coop, is an experience in itself. Don't miss it. You'll have a good impression of Belfast after one glance at the clientele and the bulletin board. Open to members and nonmembers alike (with lower prices for members), the co-op store has local organic produce, fresh and frozen pesto, baked goods, bulk grains and nuts, a great deli, meat and fish, dozens of cheeses, camping foods, wine and beer, and a café. Hours are 7:30 AM–8 PM daily. Lunch is available in the café all day until 7 PM, and there's a grab-and-go case of fresh items daily; Sat.–Sun. brunches are 9 AM–2 PM.

The popular **Belfast Farmers Market** www.belfastfarmersmarket.org, sets up, rain or shine, in downtown Belfast, in the parking lot across from Coyote Moon, Tues. 3–6 PM (June 21–mid-Oct.) and Fri. 9 AM–1 PM (Mother's Day weekend–mid-Nov.). The market celebrated its 25th anniversary in 2005, with a birthday party and a huge chocolate cake for its customers. Among the goodies are honey, body potions, prepared foods, eggs, crafts, baked goods, flowers, locally raised poultry, berries, veggies, goat- and sheep-milk products, goat-milk fudge, apples, cider, blankets, jams, and even more.

If you're in the area in mid-September, head out to **Schartner's Farm,** Rte. 220, Thorndike 04986, 207/568-3668, when their acres of pick-your-own apple trees are ready, Schartner's is open Fri.–Sun. 10 AM–5 PM in season. On fall weekends, there are horse-drawn hayrides, 10 AM–3 PM. Thorndike is about 30 miles from Belfast and is a fun detour.

Discount Shopping

Bargains are here to be had, but caveat emptor—check items carefully before you plunk down your cash.

Across the street from the Liberty Tool Company is the **Liberty Graphics Outlet Store,** 1 Main St., P.O. Box 5, Liberty 04949, 207/589-4035, www.lgtees.com, selling the ecosensitive company's overstocks, seconds, and discontinued-design T-shirts, as well as first-quality goods. Outstanding silkscreened designs are done with water-based inks, and many of the shirts are organic cotton. Also available here are Maine-made craft items and good-for-you snacks. It's open daily 9 AM–5 PM Memorial Day–Columbus Day; 9 AM–5 PM Thurs.–Sun. Columbus Day–Dec. and Mar.–Memorial Day. The store is closed Jan.–Feb., but if you find yourself here then and you're warm enough to think about t-shirts, call the shop at 207/589-4596 to see if someone might be around. Liberty is 17 miles west of Belfast.

ACCOMMODATIONS

Bed-and-Breakfasts

Located on a quiet side street, **The Jeweled Turret,** 40 Pearl St., Belfast 04915, 207/338-2304 or 800/696-2304, www.jeweledturret.com, is one of Belfast's pioneer B&Bs, located just a block from the Bay and within a short stroll to town. Carl and Cathy Heffentrager understand the business and go out of their way to make guests comfortable. They serve a gourmet breakfast, plus afternoon refreshments; crackers and cheese and sherry are served in the dining room from 5:30–6:30 PM. The 1898 Victorian inn is loaded with handsome woodwork and Victorian antiques—plus an astonishing stone fireplace. Carl can even fix your bike, if necessary, and he's up on all the local byways. Seven rooms (with private baths) are $105–155 d—some have turrets, some fireplaces or a whirlpool tub. No smoking, no pets; the accommodations are not set up for very young children. Open all year.

The White House, 1 Church St., Belfast, 207/338-1901 or 888/290-1901, www.mainebb.com, the handsomest manse in Belfast, is the star of the Church Street Historic District. Built in the mid-19th century, the Greek Revival building is elegant inside and out—parlors, library, guest rooms, and gardens dominated by a giant copper beech tree (holding the Maine state record). The original gazebo is the only gazebo on the National Register of Historic Places in the United States and is often the site of wedding ceremonies. Hosts Terry Prescott and Robert Hansen will pack you a picnic lunch, or make dinner reservations—more than the comforts of home. And breakfasts in the formal dining room are to die for. Six good-size rooms and suites are $115–175 d (one room is in the carriage house, with a private entrance). No smoking, no pets, no children under 12. Open all year.

Marble fireplaces, tin ceilings, antiques, and ornate woodwork fill the public and guest rooms of the 1840 **Alden House Bed-and-Breakfast,** 63 Church St., Belfast, 207/338-2151 or 877/337-8151, www.aldenhouse.com, in the Church Street Historic District. Sue and Bruce Madara, enthusiastic innkeepers, have seven rooms (five with private baths) for $99–135 d, including full breakfast. Some rooms have VCRs, and the inn has wireless Internet service. No smoking, no pets. Open all year.

Motels

Most of the Belfast-area motels are on the Rte. 1 stretch just to the east of town, toward Searsport. Some have been here for decades, others are brand new; prices and quality vary widely. Below are two good choices. Both are rather close to the highway, so request a room facing the bay.

Belfast's flagship motel, opened in 1996, is

the **Comfort Inn Ocean's Edge,** Searsport Ave., Rte. 1, Belfast 04915, 207/338-2090 or 800/303-5098, www.comfortinnbelfast.com, with 83 ocean-view rooms and suites. All have air-conditioning, cable TV, and phones. The motel has an indoor pool, sauna, wheelchair access, and free continental breakfast. Doubles are $100–170 in summer, $80–100 off-season. Pets can be accommodated on a limited basis; children are welcome. On the road to Searsport, east of Belfast, the motel is open all year.

Not far from the Comfort Inn is the 61-room **Belfast Harbor Inn,** 91 Seaersport Ave., Rte. 1, Belfast 04915, 207/338-2740 or 800/545-8576, www.belfastharborinn.com, not quite as fancy but certainly comfortable. Rooms have cable TV, air-conditioning, and phones; there's an outdoor pool. Pets and children are welcome; there is a $10 pet fee. Doubles are $79–149 in summer, $59–129 in fall, $49–89 spring, winter $49–69. A complimentary continental-breakfast buffet is offered. Open all year.

Campgrounds

About 2.5 miles east of Belfast, **The Moorings,** 191 Searsport Ave., Rte. 1, Belfast 04915, 207/338-6860, www.mooringscamp.com, has been a campground since the 1930s and has 44 sites, all with hookups. Views are fabulous, and the rocky beach has a pocket of sand; swimming is only for the hardy. Sites in midsummer are $36–44 (two adults plus three kids under 17), less early and late in the season. Facilities include laundry, modem access and wireless internet, kayak launch, playground area, on-site restaurant, and special events like lobster shore dinners and complimentary happy hours by the sea. Extra fees for extra persons and pets. Open early May–late Oct.

Seasonal Rentals

Most of the Belfast area's seasonal rentals are in Northport, specifically the charming Victorian enclave of Bayside, where the **Blair Agency,** Bayside, mailing address P.O. Box 368, Belfast 04915, 207/338-2257, www.blairagency.com, has cornered the market in sales and rentals.

FOOD

Lunch

Wraps are fast food at **Bay Wrap,** 20 Beaver St., Belfast 04915, 207/338-9757. There's no limit to what they'll stuff into various flavors of tortillas. Go for the adventure. Wraps are in the $7 range. Eat here or get them to go. Open Mon.–Sat. 11 AM–7:30 PM.

Old-fashioned general stores are always an adventure, and one of the best is the red-clapboard **Fraternity Village General Store,** Rte. 173, Searsmont 04973, 207/342-5866, near the beginning of two Georges River Bikeway routes, southwest of Belfast. Early-20th-century author Ben Ames Williams set some of his short stories in Searsmont, dubbing it Fraternity Village; the store trades on the connection. Inventory is all the usual country-store hodgepodge—apples to zippers. Load up on snacks here before heading out on your bike. It's open all year, Mon.–Thurs. and Sun. 6 AM–8 PM (Fri.–Sat. to 9 PM).

Downtown, in a wonderful Victorian Gothic building with tin ceilings and unusual wainscoting, **The Gothic Café and Coffeehouse,** 108 Main St., Belfast, 207/338-4933, serves fabulous ice cream, pastries, and cakes. Open Mon.–Fri., 7:30 AM–5 PM, Sat.–Sun. 8:30 AM–5 PM in summer. Closed Jan.–Mar. and Sun. off-season.

Inexpensive to Moderate

A longtime standby for creative (including vegetarian) cuisine, **Darby's Restaurant & Pub,** 155 High St., Belfast, 207/338-2339, had tofu before tofu was cool. This place has been serving food and drink since just after the Civil War; the tin ceilings and antique bar are reminders of that. Reservations are wise on weekends and Belfast Maskers performance nights. Open daily, year-round, for lunch (11:30 AM–3:30 PM) and dinner (5–9 PM; entrées $12–20).

Maine seafood, including lobster, homemade chowder, and scallops, is the specialty at the **Maine Chowder House,** Rte. 1, East Belfast, 207/338-5225, www.mainechowderhouse.com, a modern eatery with spectacular panoramic views of Penobscot Bay. Entrées are $6.50–30; there's also a fixed-price ($7.95) children's menu. Dine on the deck or even order takeout and eat at picnic tables. The Chowder House is about two miles from downtown Belfast (1.5 miles east of the bridge), en route to Searsport. Open all year, 11 AM–9 PM daily; shorter hours in winter.

Thai cuisine has finally come to Belfast at **Seng Thai,** Rte. 1, RR5, Box 5383, Belfast 04915, 207/338-0010, in a small, low building across from the Comfort Inn. Pad Thai and curries are $8.50 here. The ambience is pleasant and everything's available for takeout if you prefer. Seng Thai is open all year, Tues.–Sun.

Maine seafood, in all its forms, is also most of the menu at **Weathervane Seafoods,** 3 Main St., Belfast, 207/338-1774, www .weathervaneseafoods.com. The casual restaurant is right at the Public Landing, the views are just right for consuming watery denizens. Open daily at 11 AM.

Who'd expect big crowds at an unpretentious, brightly painted building advertising south-of-the-border cuisine alongside Rte. 1? **Dos Amigos' Mexican Restaurant and Cantina,** Rte. 1, 144 Bayside Rd., Northport, 207/338-5775, has earned its reputation as purveyor of the area's best Tex-Mex cuisine for over 15 years. Or is it the ambience? Margaritas are jumbo; nachos are loaded. Thirteen miles north of Camden, about three miles south of Belfast; open daily, mid-March to sometime in December. Hours are 4:30–9 PM (later on weekends); the restaurant also opens at noon for lunch Sat.–Sun. in season.

Moderate to Expensive

No one talks about dining in Belfast without mentioning the upscale **Twilight Cafe,** 39 Main St., Belfast 04915, 207/338-0937, open Thurs.–Sat. for dinner at 5:30 PM.

Lobster-in-the-Rough

Young's Lobster Pound, Mitchell Ave., Box 4, East Belfast, 207/338-1160, is a classic eat-on-the-dock lobster place overlooking the bay.

Dress down, relax, and pile into the crustaceans. BYOL. No credit cards. From downtown, cross the bridge to East Belfast and turn right at Jed's Restaurant. Continue to the end of Mitchell St. Open summer 8 AM–8 PM, 7 AM–4 PM the rest of the year.

INFORMATION AND SERVICES

The information center of the **Belfast Area Chamber of Commerce,** 17 Main St., P.O. Box 58, Belfast 04915, 207/338-5900, www .belfastmaine.org, is conveniently located near the public landing and Heritage Park and close to the municipal parking lot. Open Memorial Day–mid-Oct., 10 AM–6 PM daily. The chamber's annual visitors' booklet is a useful compendium, with lodging and dining directories.

Founded in 1888, the **Belfast Free Library,** 106 High St., Belfast 04915, 207/338-3884, www.belfastlibrary.org, in addition to normal library activities, has Internet access and an active community-service program with terrific lectures and films in the Abbott Room. On Tuesdays, there are children's story hours, and on Thursdays, Infant Time; there's extra children's programming in summer. The library is open Mon. 9:30 AM–8 PM, Tues. and Thurs.–Fri. 9:30 AM–6 PM, Wed. noon–8 PM, Sat. 10 AM–2 PM.

Newspapers

Belfast's dueling weekly newspapers keep residents acutely attuned to local happenings. The grande dame is *The Republican Journal,* 207/338-3333, since 1829, "on the streets" Wednesday, with subscribers receiving it on Thursday. The scrappy, widely read upstart, speaking right up since 1985, is *The Waldo Independent,* 207/338-5100, with a Thursday pub date, but on newsstands Wednesday. Both papers have extensive calendar listings.

Emergencies

A round-the-clock emergency room (207/338-9324) is only one of the convenient features at the first-rate **Waldo County General Hospital,** 118 Northport Ave., P.O. Box 287, Belfast 04915, 207/338-2500 or 800/649-2536, a community-oriented private (despite its name) institution with Maine's first inpatient hospice beds. For **police, fire, and ambulance** in Belfast and throughout Waldo County, dial 911.

Public Restrooms
You won't have much trouble finding public restrooms in Belfast. Facilities are at the waterfront **public landing** and at the **Waldo County General Hospital.**

Sauna
The **Belfast Dance Studio,** 109 High St., Belfast 04915, 207/338-5380, opens its sauna (and showers) to the public. The sauna schedule is erratic, so you'll need to call for details. The studio also offers classes in all kinds of movement (African dance to yoga) and gives periodic performances and recitals (check local papers).

Special Courses
Linked to the National Audubon Society and Lesley University, the **Audubon Expedition Institute** (AEI), P.O. Box 365, Belfast 04915, 207/338-5859, www.getonthebus.org, is an extraordinary traveling environmental-education program that just happens to be headquartered in Belfast. Ranging in age from 18–40, students board buses for semester-long, hands-on experiences in various parts of the United States. Overseas programs are now being added.

Founded in 1978, AEI offers college credit and MS (environmental education) degrees in partnership with Lesley University.

In the fall of 2000, the University of Maine opened its sprawling, 20,000-square-foot **Hutchinson Center,** 80 Belmont Ave., Rte. 3, Belfast 04915, 207/338-8000 or 800/753-9044, www.hutchinsoncenter.umaine.edu. Designed to bring undergraduate and graduate-level classroom and distance-learning courses to this part of the Mid-Coast, the center has state-of-the-art facilities and a 105-seat auditorium.

Getting Around
Downtown Belfast parking is limited to two hours, so if you're hanging around longer, head for the municipal parking lot on lower Main St., convenient to the waterfront and the chamber of commerce.

For taxis, contact the **Belfast Taxi Company,** 207/338-2943.

Waldo County Transportation, 207/338-4769 or 800/439-7865, a nonprofit bus/van service designed primarily for seniors and other nondrivers, is open to anyone who needs a ride. Except for the Belfast Shopper, which follows a set in-town route on Monday, Wednesday, and Friday, you'll need to reserve a seat at least two business days in advance; most trips operate only one or two days a week (no weekends). One-way fares are $1–2.50. Routes go to communities all over Waldo County, as well as to Augusta, Bangor, Waterville, and Rockland.

Searsport Area

Five miles northeast of downtown Belfast, you're in the heart of Searsport, a name synonymous with the sea, thanks to an enduring seafaring tradition that's appropriately commemorated here in the state's oldest maritime museum. The seafaring heyday occurred in the mid-19th century, but white settlers from the Massachusetts Colony had already made inroads here 200 years earlier. By the 1750s, Fort Pownall, in nearby Stockton Springs, was a strategic site during the French and Indian War (the American phase of Europe's Seven Years' War).

Ship-building was underway by 1791, reaching a crescendo between 1845 and 1866, with six year-round shipyards and nearly a dozen more seasonal ones. Incredibly, by 1885, 10 percent of all full-rigged American-flag ships on the high seas were under the command of Searsport and Stockton Springs captains—many bearing the name of Pendleton, Nichols, or Carver. Many of these were involved in the perilous China trade, rounding notorious Cape Horn with great regularity.

All this global contact shaped Searsport's culture, adding a veneer of cosmopolitan sophistication. Imposing mansions of seafaring families were filled with fabulous Oriental treasures, many of which eventually made their way to the Penobscot Marine Museum. Brick-lined Main St. is more evidence of the mid-19th-century wealth, and local churches reaped the benefits of residents' generosity. The Second Congregational Church, known as the Harbor Church and patronized by captains and ship-builders (most ordinary seamen attended the Methodist church), boasts recently restored Tiffany-style windows and a Christopher Wren steeple.

Another inkling of this area's oceangoing superiority comes from visits to local burial grounds: check out the headstones at Gordon, Bowditch, and Sandy Point cemeteries. Many have fascinating tales to tell.

Near the peak of its prosperity, Searsport incorporated in 1845, deriving its name from David Sears, a summer resident and wealthy Boston merchant active in the China trade.

In the late 19th and early 20th centuries, when summering in Maine became "in," the Eastern Steamship Line brought passengers from Boston to Searsport (Maine's second-largest deep-water port) for the princely sum of $5.70. All that ceased in the 1920s, with the advent of the automobile and the Great Depression.

Today, with a population of 2,749, the Searsport area's major draws are the Penobscot Marine Museum, the still-handsome brick Historic District, several B&Bs, a couple of special state parks, and wall-to-wall antiques shops and flea markets.

SIGHTS

Penobscot Marine Museum

Exquisite marine paintings, ship models, and unusual China-trade *objets* are just a few of the 10,000 treasures at the Penobscot Marine Museum, 5 Church St., at Rte. 1, P.O. Box 498, Searsport 04974, 207/548-2529, www.penobscotmarinemuseum.org, Maine's oldest maritime museum—founded in 1936. The museum is a significant stop on the state's Maritime Heritage Trail. Allow several hours to explore the 12 old and new buildings just east of downtown. For a start, you'll see one of the nation's largest collections of paintings by marine artists James and Thomas Buttersworth. And the 1830s Fowler-True-Ross House is filled with exotic artifacts from foreign lands. Check out the exhibits, have a picnic, then visit the unusual museum store on Main St. (Rte. 1). Pick up tickets at the Museum Store on Main St. Call or write for the schedule of lectures, concerts, and temporary exhibits. Admission is $8 adults, $6 seniors, $3 children 7–15, free for kids six and under. Family rate is $18. Open Memorial Day weekend–mid-Oct., Mon.–Sat. 10 AM–

5 PM, Sun. noon–5 PM (no tickets are sold after 4:30 PM).

Historic District
The Maine Historic Preservation Commission considers the buildings in Searsport's Main Street Historic District the best examples of their type outside of Portland—a frozen-in-time, mid-19th-century cluster of brick and granite structures. The ground floors of most of the buildings are shops or restaurants; make time to stop in and admire their interiors.

Lupine Landscape
If you happen to be here in late June and early July, take a quickie detour onto **Prospect St.,** off Rte. 1 at the southern end of Searsport (turn at the Victorian Inn). Just after the inn, off to the east, the landscape is a blanket of purple lupines—with a few pink and white ones thrown in for good measure. In the distance, the distinctive white spire of the First Congregational Church pokes up from the center of town—all in all, a perfect Kodak moment.

PARKS AND RECREATION
Moose Point State Park
Here's a smallish park with a biggish view—183 acres wedged between Rte. 1 and a dramatic Penobscot Bay panorama. Moose Point State Park, Rte. 1, Searsport, 207/548-2882, is 1.5 miles south of downtown Searsport. Bring a picnic, let the kids hang out and play (there's no swimming), walk through the woods. Moose-crossing signs are posted on the highway, but don't count on seeing one. Open Memorial Day weekend to October 1, 9 AM to just before sunset, but since it's alongside the highway, the park is accessible, weather permitting, all year. Admission is $2 adults, $1 children 5–11, free for kids under five.

Mosman Park
Southeast of busy Rte. 1, four-acre Mosman Park, a town-owned facility, has picnic tables, a traditional playground, lots of grassy space, a pocket-size pebbly beach, seasonal toilets, and

fabulous views of the bay. Turn off Rte. 1 at Water St. and continue to the end.

Sears Island
After almost two decades of heavy-duty squabbling over a proposed cargo port on Searsport's 940-acre Sears Island, the state purchased the island for $4 million in November 1997. Discussions are ongoing about the establishment of visitor facilities, but for now, the only improvement on this lovely, causeway-linked island is a road. It's a fine place for biking, picnicking, walking, fishing, and cross-country skiing. From downtown Searsport, continue northeast on Rte. 1 two miles to Sears Island Rd. (on your right). Turn and go 1.2 miles to the beginning of the island, where you can pull off and park before a gate (cars aren't allowed on the island). An easy 1.5-mile walk will take you to the other side of the island, overlooking Mack Point (site of a rather unattractive cargo port) and hills off to the left. Bring a picnic and binoculars—and a swimsuit if you're hardy enough to brave the water.

Fort Point State Park
Continuing northeast on Rte. 1 from Sears Island will get you to the turnoff for Fort Point State Park, Fort Point Rd., Stockton Springs 04981, 207/567-3356, on Cape Jellison's eastern tip. Within the 154-acre park are the earthworks of 18th-century **Fort Pownall** (a British fortress built in the French and Indian War), **Fort Point Light** (a square, 26-foot, 19th-century tower guarding the mouth of the Penobscot River), shoreline trails, and a 200-foot pier where you can fish, or bird- or boat-watch. (Birders can spot waterfowl—especially ruddy ducks, but also eagles and osprey.) Bring picnic fixings, but stay clear of the keeper's house—it's private. At the Rte. 1 fork for Stockton Springs, bear right onto Main St. and continue to Mill Rd., in the village center. Turn right and then left onto East Cape Rd., then another left onto Fort Point Rd., leading to the parking area. Officially, the park is open Memorial Day weekend through Labor Day, but it's accessible all year, weather permitting.

Admission is $2 adults, $1 children 5–11, free for kids under five.

Bicycling

One of the state's most hyperactive bicycle shops is about a mile north of downtown Searsport. **Birgfeld's Bicycle Shop,** 184 E. Main St., Rte. 1, Searsport 04974, 207/548-2916 or 800/206-2916, fax 207/548-0372, in business since the 1970s, is a mandatory stop for any cyclist, novice or pro. Local info on about 100 biking loops, supplies, maps, weekly group rides, sales (also skateboards—a huge selection—and scooters), and excellent repair services are all part of the Birgfeld's mix. There's free parking behind the shop, which is headquarters for the Waldo County International Cycling and Dining Society—an informal group that gets together for rides and follow-up food. Inquire about its schedule. Group rides usually are at 6 PM Tues. and Wed. The bike shop is open 9 AM–5 PM Tues.–Sat., Apr.–mid-Oct.

An especially good ride in this area is the **Cape Jellison** loop, in Stockton Springs, even though it means biking from Birgfeld's about four miles along congested Rte. 1. If you have your own bike or care to transport the rental, park at Stockton Springs Elementary School and do the loop from there. Including a detour to Fort Point, the ride totals less than 10 miles from downtown Stockton Springs.

FESTIVALS AND EVENTS

The fourth Saturday in August, a day-long series of **lobsterboat races,** with a dozen classes, is the last event on the annual Maine lobsterboat racing circuit. Races take place in Searsport Harbor, starting off Mack Point. The best place to watch is from Mosman Park, where there's a chicken barbecue and live entertainment.

SHOPPING

The word shopping in Searsport usually applies to antiques—from 25-cent flea-market collectibles to tools to high-end china, furniture, and glassware. The town has more than a dozen separate businesses—and some of *those* are group shops with multiple dealers. Searsport is definitely Maine's "Antiques Capital."

More than two dozen dealers supply the juried inventory for the **Pumpkin Patch,** 15 W. Main St., Searsport 04974, 207/548-6047—with a heavy emphasis on Maine antiques. Specialties, priced reasonably, include quilts, silver, American country furniture, Victoriana, and nautical items. Open daily except Mon., 9:30 AM–5 PM, Apr.–Nov.

Maine's mother lode of antique tools is **Liberty Tool Company,** west of Belfast. But you can sample the wares at the company's sister shop, **Captain Tinkham's Emporium,** 34 Main St., Searsport 04974, 207/548-6465. It's open all year, Sat. 9 AM–5 PM, by chance other times.

Crafts and Gifts

Close to the highway in a farmstand-style building about a mile east of downtown Searsport, the **Waldo County Craft Co-op,** 307 E. Main St., Rte. 1, Searsport 04974, 207/548-6686, features the work of more than two dozen Mainers: quilts, jams, jewelry, baskets, pottery, and lots else. Open daily 9 AM–5 PM, mid-May–mid-Oct.

If you're into Victorian and country gifts and crafts, stop at **Silkweeds,** 191 E. Main St., Rte. 1, Searsport, 207/548-6501, in the midst of antiques shops and flea markets at the eastern end of town. Open daily 9 AM–5 PM May–Dec., 10 AM–5 PM Jan.–Apr.

Marine Hardware

You may not *think* you're in the market for marine gewgaws, but wait till you get a load of this shop. Almost everyone who walks into **Hamilton Marine,** 155 E. Main St., Rte. 1, P.O. Box 227, Searsport 04974, 207/548-6302 or 800/639-2715, walks out with a purchase—and often lots of them. Filling 8,000 feet in a former trucking warehouse, Hamilton Marine is the largest ship chandlery north of Boston—a candy store for boat-builders and recreational and commercial nautical types. (There are branches in Rockland and in Portland's Old Port, and you can send for a 250-page catalogue.) Costs are especially moderate, virtually discount prices. The store is less than a mile east (actually northeast) of downtown Searsport, close to the Searsport Antique Mall. Open Mon.–Sat. 8 AM–5 PM, all year; also open 9 AM–4 PM Sun., Apr.–June.

Books

A local fixture in Stockton Springs since 1960, **Victorian House Books/Book Barn,** E. Main St., P.O. Box 397, Stockton Springs 04981, 207/567-3351, is an especially welcoming shop with well-organized shelves. Open daily in summer, 8 AM–6 PM, sometimes to 8 PM; shorter hours off-season. Call ahead to check.

In an adorable old bank building, **Left Bank Books,** 21 E. Main St., Searsport, 207/548-6400, www.leftbankbookshop.com, has a selection of the basics and best-sellers you would expect, but also books and some trinkets and goodies you won't find just anywhere, making it worthwhile to stop in and be surprised. Open year-round, usually 9:30 AM–5:30 PM Mon.–Sat., 11 AM–4 PM Sun.; shorter hours in winter.

ACCOMMODATIONS
Bed-and-Breakfasts
The veteran B&B in town is **The Homeport Inn,** 121 E. Main St., Rte. 1, P.O. Box 647, Searsport 04974, 207/548-2259 or 800/742-5814, www.homeportbnb.com, a fabulous 1861 sea captain's mansion presided over since 1978 by genial Edith Johnson. Her fascination with antiques and British royalty is evident everywhere, creating an unstuffy, user-friendly museum of a place: four-poster and canopied beds, fireplaces, Spode pottery, Oriental carpets, even wallpaper copied from Queen Victoria's bedroom. Breakfast is served on the glassed-in porch overlooking gardens beautifully landscaped by Edith's husband, George. Guests can play darts or do puzzles in the pub-style family room on the lower level. Ten rooms, seven with private baths, eight with an ocean view, run $75–125. There are also three Victorian cottages (pets welcome) for $800–900/wk. No children under two, but bear in mind that unruly kids of any age could threaten the treasures. Open all year.

Another of Searsport's magnificent old mansions, this one second empire, is now the **Carriage House Inn,** 120 E. Main St., Searsport 04974, 207/548-2167 or 800/578-2167, www.carriagehouseinmaine.com, set on two acres and overlooking the bay. Visited by Ernest Hemingway when his friend, painter Waldo Peirce, owned it, the inn has three rooms with large private baths in the main building, $85–115 high season, $59–89 in winter, including a full breakfast. There is a loft in Waldo Peirce's former studio, accommodating families. It sleeps 6–8, $125 d, $25 each additional person. Open all year.

Waving pennants mark the entrance to **1794 Watchtide… by the Sea!,** 190 W. Main St., Rte. 1, Searsport 04974, 207/548-6575 or 800/698-6575, www.watchtide.com, in a sprawling late-18th-century sea captain's home formerly known as the College Club Inn. Each of the three rooms and two suites (all with private baths) has a historic-name connection; the Eleanor Roosevelt Suite acknowledges visits by former First Ladies in decades past. Amenities are endless, from white-noise clock radios (the inn is on a busy highway) to hot and cold drinks to unusual snacks. Nancy-Linn Nellis was a designer/decorator in a previous life; it's evident here. (She and husband Jack Elliott are innkeeping experts, and the inn has been featured in numerous publications.) Collapse on the 60-foot sun porch, overlooking the bay, and you may never want to leave. But when you must, the bill will be $157–225 d in summer; lower winter rates and a passel of interesting specials are available at various times during the year. No pets, no smoking, no children under 12. In the barn is an antiques and gift shop with lots of great treasures. The inn is open all year, and the shop is open as long as the weather holds out.

Campgrounds
How can you beat 1,200 feet of tidal oceanfront and unobstructed views of Islesboro, Castine, and Penobscot Bay? **Searsport Shores Camping Resort,** 216 W. Main St., Rte. 1, Searsport 04974, 207/548-6059, gets high marks for its fabulous 40-acre setting. A hundred good-size sites (including a wilderness camping area) go for $33–48 a day. Facilities include a private beach, small

store, free showers, laundry, play areas, recreation hall, nature trails, and volleyball court. Request a site away from organized-activity areas. Bring a sea kayak and launch it here. Leashed pets are allowed. The campground is slightly more than a mile southwest of downtown Searsport, about four miles east of downtown Belfast. Open mid-May–Columbus Day.

FOOD

Whether you're up for a splurge or hunting for a bargain, restaurants in Searsport and Stockton Springs run the gamut. A couple of the low-end places are notably unpretentious (almost off-putting, in fact), but don't be fooled. They'll fix you up with hearty New England cooking, hefty portions, local color, no frills, and a bill that won't dent your wallet.

Inexpensive

Etiquette (and preparation time) requires that you order your chocolate soufflé or other chocolate goodie before dinner at the **Chocolate Grille,** 1 E. Main St., Rte. 1, Searsport, 207/548-2555, www .chocolategrille.com. Once that's accomplished you can indulge in entrées like sirloin or pan-seared duckling for dinner. A wide range of entrées, including pasta, go for $10–19. The restaurant also serves lunch and a late-night put menu. Open daily at 11 AM, to 11 PM Mon.–Thurs., 12:30 AM Fri.–Sat., 10 PM Sun.

The **Anglers Restaurant,** 215 E. Main St., Rte. 1, Searsport, 207/548-2405, is probably the least assuming and one of the most popular. Big favorites are fish chowder and lobster rolls. Dinner entrées are $7–14, although lobsters are higher. The "minnow menu" for smaller appetites runs $6–10. It's open year-round, 11 AM–8 PM daily. **Just Barb's,** Main St., Rte. 1, Stockton Springs, 207/567-3886, at the Rte. 1 turnoff to Stockton Springs, is a funky, nondescript place with a daily, all-you-can-eat fish fry for $5.99. Open every day, all year, 6 AM–8 PM (to 9 PM Fri.–Sat.).

Inexpensive to Moderate

Screened from the highway behind bushes, **The Rhumb Line,** 200 E. Main St., Rte. 1, Searsport

04974, 207/548-2600, www.therhumblinerestau-rant.com, occupies two rooms on the first floor of an imposing Victorian house. Chef/owners Charles and Diana Evans have created an excellent "new American" menu with such entrées as sautéed filet of haddock and grilled rack of lamb (entrées are $21–28). The dessert menu includes dishes like cinnamon ice cream with chocolate and caramel and a selection of dessert wines. Reservations are suggested, especially on weekends, at this popular place. Open all year for dinner, seven nights in summer; call for seasonal days and times. Watch for the sign across from the Irving gas station.

INFORMATION AND SERVICES

It's not always easy to get information about Searsport, so you may need to ask around a bit to get questions answered. Or check with the hosts at your B&B. A small, volunteer-run information center is open on an unpredictable schedule—it's in a shedlike building on Rte. 1 (at Norris St.), across from the Pumpkin Patch antiques shop. On weekdays, you can check at the **Searsport Town Office,** on Reservoir St. (just after the Penobscot Marine Museum), 207/548-6372. A good place to ask questions, and the one likeliest to be open at odd hours, comes up after you've been through town—the **Steamboat** gas station on Rte. 1, 207/548-2728. While you're at it, you can stock up on snacks and use the restrooms and the ATM. It's across Rte. 1 from a gray-shingled lighthouse shop.

The handsome fieldstone **Carver Memorial Library,** 12 Union St., Searsport 04974, 207/548-2303, was built in 1910. Children's story hour is Fri. at 10 AM; library hours are Mon.–Fri. 11 AM–5 PM (to 7 PM Tues. and Thurs.) and Sat. 9 AM–noon. The library is a block off Rte. 1.

Emergencies

The nearest hospital is **Waldo County General Hospital,** 118 Northport Ave., Belfast 04915, 207/338-2500, a community facility with round-the-clock emergency-room care. For **police, ambulance, and fire,** dial 911 in Searsport and Stockton Springs.

Acadia Region

Stretching from the banks of the Penobscot River to the eastern border of Hancock County, and inland to Bangor, this region takes its appellation from Acadia National Park, a gem of a natural resource that dangles like a pendant just south of the mainland.

Surrounding the national park on Mount Desert Island are Bar Harbor (the area's commercial center), Northeast Harbor, Southwest Harbor, Bass Harbor, and a couple of smaller enclaves. Offshore are the Cranberry Isles and Swans Island, accessible by ferry.

Stringing the region together is slow-moving Rte. 1; the prime locales for exploring are handsome historic towns and villages lying seaward from the highway. The vital coastal artery is only two lanes wide, and summertime traffic creates frustrating delays (hardly surprising,

given that some three million visitors descend on Acadia each year), often doubling the off-season travel time. But a widening of the highway could spoil this area forever.

Most of this region will never be spoiled—maybe over-appreciated, but not spoiled. There's beauty enough to go around. Consider the Acadia region a transition zone—a place where you begin to decompress as you edge slowly Down East from the more congested South Coast and Mid-Coast regions. You can watch the sun set from atop Blue Hill Mountain, or the sun *rise* from Cadillac Mountain; join kayakers surfing through Blue Hill Falls; stroll through the village of Castine (charming verging on precious), whose streets are lined with dowager-like homes; discover America's largest yellow-birch tree (on Deer Isle); visit

©KATHLEEN M. BRANDES

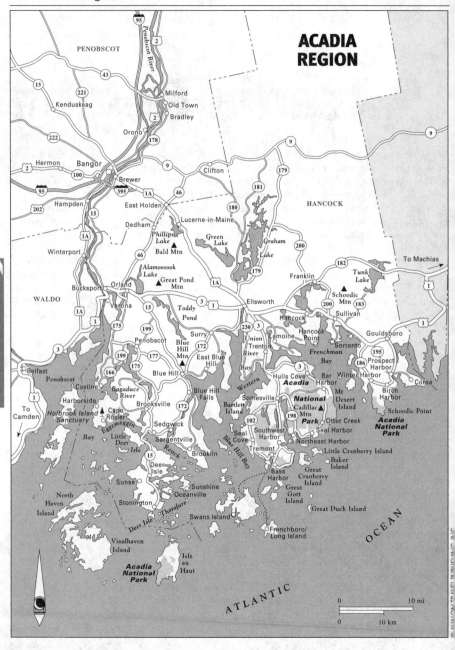

ACADIA
REGION

WoodenBoat magazine's world headquarters in tiny Brooklin; stretch out on the beach at Lamoine State Park, across the bay from Acadia's mountains; show up at tony Northeast Harbor's May azalea extravaganza; surf-watch from the rocks at Schoodic Point; or hang out on the fishermen's wharves in Stonington or Corea.

An essential key to understanding this special region is its islands—each, like people, with a distinct personality. Some are linked to the mainland by causeways or bridges, others are reachable only by ferry. Mount Desert Island heads almost anyone's list, but it's so eminently accessible that it almost doesn't qualify as an "island." Farther south is Deer Isle, a unique agglomeration of craftspeople and fisherfolk; offshore is Isle au Haut—part hamlet, part national park.

During the replacement of the landmark 2,040-foot-long, bright green Waldo-Hancock Bridge, built in 1931 at a cost of $850,000, the Maine Department of Transportation invited community involvement via the website www.waldohancockbridge.com, where MDOT responded to public comments and questions, sponsored a bridge-naming contest, and used webcams to show the construction of the bridge and observatory. The high span links Waldo and Hancock Counties and introduces you to the Bucksport area—it remains to be seen whether the old bridge's resident osprey will nest on the new bridge. Working hard and well to gentrify its longtime rough-and-ready river-port image, Bucksport changes even as you watch.

From Bucksport, Rte. 1 makes a 20-mile run, flanked by blueberry fields that flame red in the fall, to Ellsworth. Off to the south is the smattering of very attractive communities that make up the Blue Hill Peninsula.

In the northeastern corner of the region, up the mighty Penobscot, a dose of reality intrudes in the form of metropolitan bustle in Bangor, a city shifting in the late 20th century from a frontier-style scrappiness to a newfound sophistication (we're still not talking Big Apple trendiness, but rather a greater openness to the world beyond). Bangor is the state's third-largest city and the commercial hub for all of northern and eastern Maine. The antique brick and wooden buildings provide a serious sense of history, and the stream bisecting the streets downtown lends an aura of surprising calm.

On the peaceful eastern fringe of Hancock County, at the tip of the Schoodic Peninsula, a stunning pocket of Acadia National Park sees only a fraction of the visitors who descend on the main part of the park. And towns lining the eastern shore of Frenchman Bay have some of the best views of all: front-row seats facing the peaks of Mount Desert Island.

Acadia Region

Bucksport to Ellsworth

When Bar Harbor is filled to overflowing, especially in July and early August, this area provides a buffer on the fringes, still conveniently close to Acadia National Park and the Blue Hill Peninsula. Between Bucksport and Ellsworth you can explore a fort, hike a mountain, visit a fish hatchery and a bird sanctuary, tour an elegant mansion, and do some shopping.

Anchoring Rte. 1 at the western edge of Hancock County and dominated by the giant International Paper mill, Bucksport has in recent years striven to become more than a mill town—and it's succeeding. New businesses have arrived, a marina has been built, and the local newspaper has improved communications and sparked community spirit. With a population of 5,065, it's the county's second-largest town (edged out only by Ellsworth, with 6,271).

Bucksport is no upstart. Native Americans first gravitated to these Penobscot River shores in summers, finding here a rich source of salmon for food and grasses for basket-making. In 1764, it was officially settled by Col. Jonathan Buck, a Massachusetts Bay Colony surveyor who modestly named it Buckstown and organized a booming shipping business here. His remains are interred in a local cemetery, where his tombstone bears the distinct outline of a woman's leg; this is allegedly the result of a curse by a witch Buck ordered executed, but in fact it's probably a flaw in the granite. Most townsfolk prefer not to discuss the matter, but the myth refuses to die—and it has immortalized a man whose name might otherwise have been consigned to musty history books. (The monument is across Rte. 1 from the Shop 'n Save supermarket; a sign tells the tale, and a new sidewalk has made access easier.)

By the 1840s, steamships were already carrying vacationers between Boston and Bangor, via Bucksport. The town is still a major port, receiving large tankers bringing in heating oil for the region and jet fuel for Bangor International Airport.

Papermaking came to Bucksport in 1930, and about 1,000 employees now staff the International Paper mill on Indian Point.

Just south of Bucksport, at the bend in the Penobscot River, Verona Island (pop. 560) is best known as the mile-long link between Prospect and Bucksport. Just before you cross the bridge from Verona to Bucksport, hang a left, then a quick right to a small municipal park with a boat launch and broad views of Bucksport Harbor (and the paper mill). In the Buck Memorial Library is a scale model of Adm. Robert Peary's arctic exploration vessel, the *Roosevelt,* built on this site.

Rte. 1 east of Bucksport leads to Orland, whose idyllic setting on the banks of the Narramissic River makes it a magnet for shutterbugs. It's also the site of a unique service organization called h.o.m.e. (Homeworkers Organized for More Employment). East Orland (officially part of Orland) claims the Craig Brook National Fish Hatchery and Great Pond Mountain (you can't miss it, jutting up from the landscape on the left as you drive east on Rte. 1).

Twenty miles east of Bucksport on Rte. 1, Ellsworth-Hancock County's shire town unfortunately has earned a reputation as the summertime bottleneck to Bar Harbor. In fact, there's much more here, including handsome architectural remnants of the city's 19th-century lumbering heyday (which began shortly after its incorporation in 1800). Brigs, barks, and full-rigged ships, built in Ellsworth and captained by local fellows, loaded lumber here and carried it round the globe. Despite a ruinous 1855 fire that swept through downtown, the lumber trade thrived until late in the 19th century, along with factories and mills turning out shoes, bricks, boxes, and butter.

SIGHTS
The Other Fort Knox
Looming over Bucksport Harbor is **Fort Knox,** Rte. 174, Prospect, mailing address RR1, Box 1316, Stockton Springs 04981, 207/469-7719; for tour and special events information call the Friends of Fort Knox, 207/469-6553, fortknox. maineguide.com. A 125-acre state historic site, the fort actually is in Waldo County, though only a few hundred feet from the altitudinous Rte. 1 span linking Prospect, Verona Island, and Bucksport.

Stage two of the new state-of-the-art cable-stay bridge, whose 440-foot towers resemble the Washington Monument, enables visitors to enter Fort Knox and ride an elevator to the top of one of the towers, to an observation platform. Visitors will be treated to expansive vistas atop the tower, the only one of its kind in the United States.

Named for Maj. Gen. Henry Knox, George Washington's first secretary of war, the sprawling granite Fort Knox was begun in 1844. Built to protect the upper Penobscot River from attack, it was never finished, never saw battle, but was manned for defensive purposes during the Civil War. To explore the underground passages, wear rubberized shoes and bring a flashlight; you can set the kids loose. Bring a picnic.

The site is open May 1–Oct. 31 8:30 AM–dusk. Tours are available every day during peak season, June–Sept. A variety of Friends of Fort Knox special events take place throughout the season including: Civil War reenactments, blacksmith demonstrations, cannon

© KATHLEEN M. BRANDES

Fort Knox, overlooking Bucksport Harbor

Acadia Region

firings, Scottish Bagpiping, a Medieval Tournament, and a Halloween Fright at the Fort. The grounds are accessible all year. Admission is $3 adults, $1 children 5–11. Children under five and seniors are free.

Old-Time Flicks

Phoenix-like, the 1916 **Alamo Theatre,** 85 Main St., P.O. Box 900, Bucksport 04416, 207/469-0924 or 800/639-1636, (event line: 207/469-6910), www.alamotheatre.org, has been retrofitted for a new life—focusing on films about New England produced and/or revived by unique **Northeast Historic Film** (NHF), which is headquartered here. Stop in, survey the restoration, visit the displays (free), and purchase reasonably priced videos on ice harvesting, lumberjacks, maple sugaring, and other traditional New England topics. Located half a mile west of Rte. 1, it's open weekdays 9 AM–4 PM all year. The Alamo has also become an active cinema, screening classic and current films on a regular basis in the 120-seat theater, usually weekends. Tickets are $6. Each summer there's also a silent-film festival, with $12 tickets. Continue the fun by joining NHF

($25 annual membership; $15 for students and teachers), so you can borrow by mail from the NHF video collection.

Historical Museums

Two small, volunteer-staffed local-history museums in Bucksport and Orland are open briefly in summer. No admission fees, but donations are welcomed. A preserved 1874 Maine Central Railroad station is home to the **Bucksport Historical Society Museum,** Main St., P.O. Box 798, Bucksport 04416, 207/469-2464, open Wed.–Fri. 1–4 PM July–Aug. The one-time depot is slightly below street level, adjoining Bucksport's waterfront walkway. **Orland Historical Society Museum,** Main St., Rte. 175, P.O. Box 97, Orland 04472, 207/469-2476, containing collections of minerals, Native American artifacts, antique photos, and military uniforms, is open Wed. and Sat. 2–4 PM July–Aug.

h.o.m.e.

Located adjacent to the flashing light on Rte. 1 in Orland, h.o.m.e. is tough to categorize. Linked with the international Emmaus

Movement founded by a French priest, h.o.m.e. (Homeworkers Organized for More Employment) was started in 1970 by Lucy Poulin, still the guiding force, and two nuns at a nearby convent. The quasi-religious organization has a small museum and a church on the property, shelters the homeless, operates a soup kitchen and a clinic, runs a day-care center, and teaches work skills in a variety of hands-on cooperative programs. Much of its income comes from sales of crafts, produce, and services. At the Rte. 1 store (corner of Upper Falls Rd.; open daily 9 AM–5 PM), you can buy handmade quilts, jams, syrup, and other crafts from over 200 Mainers—and support a worthwhile effort. Good eating at the October Harvest Fair includes a blueberry pancake breakfast and a fish fry; entertainment and children's games round out the day. To volunteer time in the sawmill, store, or learning center, write P.O. Box 10, Orland 04472, or call 207/469-7961, www.homecoop.net.

Woodlawn Museum (The Black House)

Very little has changed at Woodlawn, the Colonel Black Mansion in Ellsworth, West Main St./Surry Rd., Rte. 172, Ellsworth 04605, 207/667-8671, www.woodlawnmuseum.com, since George Nixon Black donated it to the town in 1928. Completed in 1828, the Georgian house is a marvel of preservation, one of Maine's best, filled with Black-family antiques and artifacts. Enthusiastic docents lead 45-minute tours ($7.50 adults, $3 children 5–12), beginning on the hour, to point out the circular staircase, rare books and artifacts, canopied beds, a barrel organ, and lots more. Even kids appreciate all the unusual stuff. Afterward, plan to picnic on the manicured grounds, then explore two carriage- and sleigh-filled barns, the Memorial Garden, and the two miles of mostly level trails in the woods up beyond the house. Restrooms are next to the parking area. On most Wednesday afternoons (3 PM) July–Aug., there are elegant teas in the garden (or the carriage house if it's raining). China, silver, linens, special-blend tea, sandwiches, pastries, and live music—for $15 a person. Call

for information, reservations are necessary for tea. The house is open May 1–Oct. 31, closed Mondays. In May and October, hours are 1–4 PM Tues.–Sun., tours at 1, 2, and 3 PM. June 1–Sept. 30, from Tues.–Sat., hours are 10 AM–5 PM, with the last tour at 4 PM; Sun. it's open 1–4 PM, with the last tour at 3 PM. In winter, there's cross-country skiing on the trails. On Rte. 172, a quarter of a mile southwest of Rte. 1, watch for the sign and turn into the winding uphill driveway.

Telephone Museum

A "hands-on" museum, where you can learn how to run a switchboard, and experience nostalgia or amazement, depending on your birth date, by operating a dial phone, The Telephone Museum, 166 Winkumpaugh Rd., Ellsworth 04605, 207/667-9491, www.thetelephonemuseum.org, has so much equipment that its two barns (big and bigger) are not large enough for its collection. In August there's a free Telephone Fair. Open July–Sept., 1–4 PM Thurs.–Sun. It's about 10 miles north of Ellsworth on Rte. 1A.

For the Birds

Just beyond Ellsworth, en route to Bar Harbor, watch carefully on the right for the sign that marks **Birdsacre,** 289 High St., Rte. 3, Bar Harbor Rd., P.O. Box 485, Ellsworth 04605, 207/667-8460, a 200-acre urban sanctuary. Picnic, wander the trails, or contemplate the pond in this peaceful preserve—spotting wildflowers, birds, and well-labeled shrubs and trees—and you'll have trouble believing you're surrounded by prime tourist territory. The sanctuary is open all year, sunrise to sunset; admission is free, but donations are welcome. At the sanctuary entrance is the 1850 **Stanwood Homestead Museum,** with period furnishings and wildlife exhibits. Once owned by noted ornithologist Cordelia Stanwood, the museum is open for tours daily, 10 AM–4 PM, May–Oct. Admission is free, but donations are appreciated. Birdsacre is also a wildlife rehab center, so expect to see all kinds of winged creatures in various stages of rescue from oblivion. Some will be returned to the wild. The nature center and its grounds are open year-round.

PARKS AND RECREATION

For a day of hiking, picnicking, swimming, canoeing, and a bit of natural history, pack a lunch and head for 135-acre **Craig Brook National Fish Hatchery,** 306 Hatchery Rd., East Orland 04431, 207/469-2803, on Alamoosook Lake. Turn off Rte. 1 six miles east of Bucksport and continue 1.4 miles north to the parking area just above the new visitors center (open 7:30 AM–3:30 PM weekdays; no charge; maps and restroom). Except on special open-house occasions, you won't be allowed to see the hatchery's raceways. The grounds are accessible all year, daily 6 AM–sunset. Established in 1871, the U.S. Fish and Wildlife Service hatchery raises sea-run Atlantic salmon for stocking seven Maine rivers, and each river has a different subspecies, so they're kept separate. The birch-lined shorefront has picnic tables and grills, a boat-launching ramp, Atlantic salmon display pool, additional parking, and a spectacular cross-lake view. Watch for eagles, osprey, and loons. Hiking options include a mile-long nature trail loop partly bordering Craig Brook, a two-mile (round-trip) walking path to scenic, swimmable Craig Pond, and an easy-to-moderate two-hour (round-trip) hike up Great Pond Mountain. You can pick up a trails brochure at the hatchery visitors center.

Great Pond Mountain's biggest asset is its 1,038-foot summit, with 360-degree views and lots of space for panoramic picnics. On a clear day, Baxter State Park's Katahdin is visible from Great Pond Mountain's north side. In fall, watch for migrating hawks. Access to the mountain is via gated private property beginning about a mile north of the hatchery parking area. Roadside parking is available near the trailhead, but during fall-foliage season, you may need to park at the hatchery. Stay on the trail, and respect the surrounding

private property. The **Great Pond Mountain Conservation Trust,** P.O. Box 266, Orland 04472, acts as conscientious local steward for Great Pond Mountain and other wild lands in the Alamoosook watershed, and has spearheaded the acquisition of 4,200 acres around the mountain for preservation.

In addition to Craig Brook, there is one other federal fish hatchery in Maine—**Green Lake National Fish Hatchery,** Rte. 180, 207/667-9531, also dedicated to the restoration of the Atlantic salmon. It's free, hours are 7:30 AM–4 PM, and there are group tours by arrangement. It's located seven miles north of Ellsworth.

Contact the **Bucksport Parks and Recreation Department,** 207/469-3518, weekdays 8 AM–5 PM, for year-round information on facilities they supervise. The Community Recreational Center includes an outdoor pool, ball fields, lighted tennis courts, basketball and volleyball courts, and a skating rink. Parks and Rec also maintains the half-mile walkway along the restored Bucksport waterfront—a great place to relax on a bench and enjoy the expansive view of the harbor, Fort Knox, and the impressive new bridge.

Take a break at the **Ellsworth Harbor Park,** Water St., on the Union River, where you'll find parking, a boat launch, and a place to sit and enjoy a picnic. Water St. turns into Bayside Rd., Rte. 230, a back way to Trenton, avoiding High St. and part of Rte. 3, which is infamous for summer congestion. The **Union River Watershed Coalition,** c/o Hancock Extension Office, 66 Boggy Brook Rd., 207/667-8212, works for a healthy watershed, sampling for quality and sponsoring the Union River Spoken History Project and an annual canoe trip.

Bike Rentals

In Ellsworth, on the way to Mount Desert Island, **Bar Harbor Bicycle Shop,** 193 Main St., Ellsworth 04605, 207/667-6886, is a branch of the Bar Harbor firm, providing sales, service, and repair, but no rentals. Open all year, Tues.–Sat. 10 AM–5:30 PM.

Acadia Region

Golf

Bucksport Golf Club, 397 State Rte. 46, 1.5 miles north of Rte. 1, 207/469-7612, prides itself on having Maine's longest nine-hole course. It also has a pro shop, snack bar, driving range, and carts. It's open from mid-April "until it snows." On Rte. 1, 1.5 miles east of Ellsworth, the **White Birches** motel complex, 207/667-0015, has a nine-hole course (discount with lodging), carts, and a restaurant. Open Apr.–Oct. Tee times are not required.

Kids Stuff

If the kids need some unwinding, the answer to parents' prayers is the creative playground on Elm Street in Bucksport, across from the Jewett School (make sure they see the dragon).

If you're in the area as long as a week, contact the **Down East Family YMCA,** Rte. 1A, Upper State St., Ellsworth 04605, 207/667-3086, www.defymca.org, for its schedule of fitness, swim, and outdoor programs for kids, teens, adults, and families. Most popular is the activity-filled day camp, mid-June–mid-Aug., for kids in grades 1 through 8 ($115 a week for nonresidents); reserve well ahead if you plan to take advantage of it.

One of the kid-friendliest libraries around, the **Ellsworth Public Library,** 46 State St., Ellsworth 04405, 207/667-6363, completely renovated its juvenile fiction room, lowering the shelves so little people could reach them easily; two internet-access computers are dedicated for children's use only. Open Mon.–Fri. 9 AM–5 PM (to 8 PM Wed.–Thurs.), Sat. 9 AM–2 PM. Don't miss the River Walk, the pathway park behind the library on the banks of the Union River.

Along Rte. 3 (Bar Harbor Rd.), en route from Ellsworth to Mount Desert Island, is a whole string of commercial attractions to keep kids entertained (and your wallet drained).

ENTERTAINMENT

The carefully restored art deco **Grand Auditorium of Hancock County,** 100 Main St., Ellsworth 04405, 207/667-9500, grandonline.org, is the year-round site of films, concerts, plays, and art exhibits. Most films are at 7:30 PM. Call, check local publications, or see website for schedule.

First-run films, usually showing twice a night, plus bargain matinees in midsummer, are on the docket at **Hoyts Maine Coast Mall Cinemas 2,** High St., Rte. 1, Ellsworth 04405, 207/667-3251, where adult tickets are $5 before 6 PM, $8 after; children and seniors are $5 anytime. Bucksport residents also patronize the **Colonial Theatre** in Belfast.

A summer highlight is the **Ellsworth Concert Band** concert series, held Wednesday evenings July–Aug. in the plaza outside Ellsworth City Hall (an imposing building just north of Main St.). If it rains, it's held inside City Hall. Practice begins at 6:30 PM, concerts start at 8 PM, and the 50-member community band even welcomes visitors with talent and instruments. Just show up at practice time. The repertoire is mostly marches and show music; a prize goes to the person who correctly identifies a mystery tune.

FESTIVALS AND EVENTS

Ellsworth is home to the **Annual Rotary Club All-You-Can-Eat Blueberry Pancake Breakfast,** 6–10:30 AM the second Saturday in August at City Hall. Also in Ellsworth, on a late-September weekend, a Chowder Fest and Auto Show are two of the events at **Autumn Gold Days.** The early July **Orland River Days** include a Huck Finn Raft Regatta. Entry qualification is "if it floats or you think it will," and entrants "normally stop before the dam." One of the recent winning entries was made of gallon milk jugs held together with Liquid Nails. There's music all day long.

Also see the Castine and Blue Hill sections for other nearby events.

SHOPPING

Antiques, Books, Art Galleries

You're unlikely to meet a single soul who has left the **Big Chicken Barn Books and**

Antiques, Rte. 1, 1768 Bucksport Rd., Ellsworth 04605, 207/667-7308, www.bigchickenbarn.com, without buying *something*. You'll find every kind of collectible on the vast first floor, courtesy of more than four dozen dealers. Climb the stairs for books, magazines, old music, and more. With 21,000 square feet, this place is addictive. Free coffee, hassle-free browsing. Open daily, all year. Big Chicken is 11 miles east of Bucksport, 8.5 miles west of Ellsworth.

BookStacks, 333 Main St., P.O. Box 1879, Bucksport 04416, 207/469-8992 or 888/295-0123, is an especially bright and welcoming community-oriented independent bookstore run by personable Andy Lacher, who calls himself "owner at large." It's open Mon.–Sat. 9 AM–8 PM, Sun. 9 AM–5 PM.

In downtown Ellsworth, the **Union River Gallery,** 17 School St., Ellsworth 04605, 207/667-7700, www.maineartgallery.com, showcasing a dozen or so artists, plus posters, photos, and antique prints, is open all year. Summer hours are Mon.–Sat. 10 AM–5 PM (to 3 PM Sat.).

Clothing, Gifts, Gourmet Goodies

In Bucksport, check out **The Vineyard,** Main St. at Third St., Bucksport 04416, 207/469-7844, based in three rooms of a yellow house. Since 1989, owner Barbara Vittum has carried an eclectic mix of wine, beer, cheese, and gourmet goodies, plus high-quality local crafts and paintings. Somehow the combination works. She also teaches an adult-ed wine-appreciation course and holds monthly tastings in her shop. Open all year, Mon.–Fri. 2–6 PM, Sat. 9 AM–1 PM.

Don't miss **Rooster Brother,** 29 Main St., Rte. 1, Ellsworth 04605, 207/667-8675 or 800/866-0054, for gourmet cookware, cards, and books on the main floor; coffee, tea, candy, cheeses, a huge array of exotic condiments, and fresh breads in the basement. Open all year, 9:30 AM–5:30 PM Mon.–Sat. (2nd-floor sale area 10 AM–5 PM), the shop is in a handsome old riverside building on busy Rte. 1. Access can be tricky at times, so be cautious and patient.

The Grasshopper Shop, 124 Main St., Ellsworth 04605, 207/667-5816, appeals primarily to those under 40, with eclectic clothes, unusual gifts, and great cards. The two-story emporium is open daily year-round and evenings in summer. Other Grasshopper Shops are in Searsport, Rockland, and Bangor, with a minishop at the Bangor airport. Distinctive, Maine-themed pottery is the focus at **Monroe Salt Works,** 150 High St., 207/667-3349, www.monroesaltworks.com; there are branches in Lincolnville Beach and Belfast, too. The store also carries Maine books and New England-related items.

For an extensive sporting-gear inventory, plus advice on outdoors activities, stop in at **Cadillac Mountain Sports,** 34 High St., Rte. 1, Ellsworth 04605, 207/667-7819. Open daily year-round, 9 AM–9 PM.

An Unusual Nursery

Surry Gardens, Rte. 172, Surry 04684, 207/667-4493, www.surrygardens.com, is a flower fan's paradise, with knowledgeable staff and hundreds of plant varieties—many geared for northern climes. Open all year; summer hours are Mon.–Sat. 8 AM–5 PM, Sun. 9 AM–5 PM.

Discount Shopping

You can certainly find bargains at the **L.L. Bean Factory Store and Ellsworth Clearance Center** 150 High St., Rte. 1, Ellsworth 04605, 207/667-7753, but this is an outlet, so scrutinize the goods for flaws and blemishes before buying. Open all year, with summer hours 9 AM–9 PM daily. They're only closed on Christmas and Easter.

Across the road is **Reny's Department Store,** Ellsworth Shopping Center, High St., Rte. 1, Ellsworth 04605, 207/667-5166, a Maine-based discount operation with a you-never-know-what-you'll-find philosophy. Summer hours are Mon.–Sat. 9 AM–8 PM, Sun. 9 AM–5 PM.

Maine Coast Mall, 225 High St., Rte. 1, Ellsworth, 207/667-9905, has several outlet stores, in addition to fast-food meccas, retail shops, a bank, a cinema, and the Holiday Inn. All stores are open daily. Also in the mall is a branch of Marden's, the Maine-wide discounter, www.mardenssurplus.com; other outlets can be found along this commercial strip. Across from the mall, Rte. 1 bears off toward Eastport and Calais, while Rte. 3 continues on to Mount Desert Island.

Natural Foods and Farmers Markets

Down East Maine's biggest selection of health foods is at **John Edward's Market,** 158 Main St., Ellsworth 04605, 207/667-9377. Organic produce, fresh breads, wines, and self-help books are also in the inventory. Stop in for a cup of coffee or tea and some healthful go-withs. There's always interesting art on the walls. No credit cards. It's open all year, Mon.–Thurs. 9 AM–5:30 PM, Fri. 9 AM–8 PM, Sat. 9 AM–5 PM, and Sun. noon–5 PM.

The **Bucksport Riverfront Farmers Market,** in the town office parking lot on lower Main St., operates Sat. 9 AM–3 PM, July–Oct. Vendors have goat cheese, lots of fine produce, maple syrup, and breads.

Even larger, the **Ellsworth Farmers' Market** gets underway at 245 Main St., next to Larry's Pastry, mid-June–Oct., Mon. and Thurs. 2–5:30 PM and Sat. 9:30 AM–12:30 PM. There's also a farmers market in nearby Blue Hill.

ACCOMMODATIONS

Bed-and-Breakfasts

An attractive B&B in this area is **The Sign of the Amiable Pig,** 74 Castine Rd., Rte. 175, P.O. Box 232, Orland 04472, 207/469-2561, www.acadiavacations.com, once a hideout on the Underground Railroad. Three rooms (one with a private bath) are $60 and $75 d, without breakfast. A separate guest house, sleeping five, goes for $550 a week. Guests have the run of Charlotte and Wes Pipher's very comfortable home with parlor, keeping room, and lots of fireplaces. The oldest house section dates from 1765. Oriental carpets and fresh flowers are everywhere. No pets, credit cards, or smoking; children are welcome. The Amiable Pig (named

for the weathervane atop the barn) is open all year, but be sure to call ahead and reserve space off season. It's located two miles east of Bucksport and 0.3 mile east of Rte. 1.

Sitting atop a knoll just off Rte. 1, the 1820 Greek Revival **Orland House,** 10 Narramissic Dr., P.O. Box 306, Orland 04472, 207/469-1144, www.orlandhousebb.com. Three rooms with full breakfast range from $65–105 d. Innkeepers Cindi and Alvion Kimball say they combine Yankee charm with Hoosier hospitality. (She's the Yankee, he's the Hoosier.) Amenities include use of hot tub and sauna, and a canoe and kayak ready to put in the Narramissic River right in front of the house. No pets. A cottage across the street is rented by the week, or used as an extension of the B&B. The Orland House is less than a quarter mile off Rte. 1, between Rte. 1 and the Castine Rd., in the village of Orland.

Motels

In downtown Bucksport, the award for best view goes to the **Jed Prouty Motor Inn,** 52 Main St., P.O. Box 826, Bucksport 04416, 207/469-3113 or 800/528-1234, a four-story Best Western motel nudged right up to the harbor's edge. Forty-one modern rooms have phones, air-conditioning, and cable TV. Be sure to request a water view, or you'll be facing a parking lot. Doubles are $79–149, varying with season and room.

National chain and independent motels line High St. (Rtes. 1 and 3), a densely commercial stretch in Ellsworth, and continue southward toward Mount Desert Island. (Bar Harbor is 20 miles from downtown Ellsworth.) If you can handle sleeping in the middle of a shopping mall, the best of these is the **Holiday Inn,** 215 High St., Rte. 1, Ellsworth 04605, 207/667-9341 or 800/401-9341, www.holiday-inn .com. Request a room facing the mall, not the highway. The 103-room facility has air-conditioning, phones (and dataports), cable TV, laundry, serious fitness center, indoor tennis courts, restaurant, and heated indoor pool. A king double is $145 in July, $165

July 31–Aug. 27, $120 Aug. 29–Oct. 15, and $75 Oct. 16–Apr. 30. Kids and pets are welcome. Open all year.

About a mile north of the Holiday Inn, heading Down East, **White Birches,** Rte. 1, P.O. Box 236, Ellsworth 04605, 207/667-3621 or 800/435-1287, is a clean, generic motel with 67 rooms ($90–200 d July 1–Aug. 20, $70–160 June 18–30, lower other months), popular with tour groups. A big plus for golfing guests: discounted use of the nine-hole course. Request a room overlooking the course. The motel's restaurant does a breakfast buffet on weekends for $5.95, as well as lunch and dinner. Rooms have phones, cable TV, and air-conditioning. Pets and kids are welcome. Open all year. About 1.5 miles from the Holiday Inn.

Campgrounds

The rivers, lakes, and ponds in the area between Bucksport and Ellsworth make it especially appealing for camping, and sites tend to be cheaper than in the Bar Harbor area. July–Aug., especially weekends, reservations are wise.

Six miles east of Bucksport, across from Craig Pond Rd., is Back Ridge Rd., leading to **Balsam Cove Campground,** P.O. Box C, East Orland 04431, 207/469-7771 or 800/469-7771 in Maine, www.balsamcove.com. From Rte. 1, take Back Ridge Rd. 1.5 miles to the left turn for the campground, on the shores of 10-mile-long Toddy Pond. Facilities include 60 wooded and waterfront tent and RV sites ($18–25 in season for two adults with their children under 18, 20 percent less off season, pet fee $2 per day), dump station, store, laundry, hot showers, boat rentals, and freshwater swimming. Dock slips, a log cabin and on-site trailers are for rent. Open late May–late Sept. The same season holds for 10-acre **Whispering Pines Campground,** Rte. 1, P.O. Box 91, East Orland 04431, 207/469-3443, www.campmaine.com/whisperingpines, also on Toddy Pond but accessed directly from Rte. 1. Facilities include 50 tent and RV sites (request one close to the lake), canoes and rowboats,

freshwater swimming, playground, free showers, and rec hall. Cost is $25–29 for two persons. Whispering Pines is 6.5 miles east of Bucksport.

Seasonal Rentals

For cottages and homes available by the week, month, or season, contact **Coastal Cottage Rental Company,** 1 Music Library Ln., P.O. Box 835, Blue Hill 04614, 207/374-3500, www.vacationcottages.com.

FOOD

Breakfast and Lunch

Order breakfast anytime at **The Riverside Café,** 151 Main St., Ellsworth 04605, 207/667-7220. Juices are fresh (if a bit pricey), buckwheat pancakes are outstanding, but try the veggie benedict, with spinach and tomato ($6.95). Lunch menu includes homemade soups, salads, sandwiches, grilled sandwiches, and high-cal desserts; skip the fried-seafood platters. Sunday brunches (summer and fall only) are legendary. And the café's name? It used to be down the street, overlooking the Union River. Open all year, Mon.–Fri. 6 AM–3 PM, Sat. 7 AM–3 PM, Sun. 7 AM–2 PM.

On the Main S. spur heading east from Ellsworth (also called Washington Junction Rd.), **Larry's Pastry Shop,** 241 Main St., Ellsworth 04605, 207/667-2557, may look unassuming, but *everyone* goes there for bread, rolls, pies, and Saturday night's baked beans. No preservatives are used. Open all year, Mon.–Sat. 5 AM–5 PM.

Moderate

All of the restaurants in this category are likely to please both palate and wallet. However, if you're looking for more elegance and creativity (and higher prices), drive a bit farther to Blue Hill, Castine, Deer Isle, or even Mount Desert Island.

MacLeod's, Main St., Bucksport 04416, 207/469-3963, is Bucksport's most popular restaurant. The menu is varied, children are

Acadia Region

welcome, it has a liquor license, and it's air-conditioned. French chocolate silk pie is a specialty. Reservations are wise for Saturday dinner. Open all year for dinner, daily at 4 PM.

In Ellsworth, go to **Frankie's Café & Good Stuff,** 40 High St., Rte. 1, in the Cadillac Mountain Sports building, 207/667-7701, for excellent Mediterranean/vegetarian specialties ($4–5)—veggie-rice pie, spanakopita, brie pasta pie, sesame-butter-topped bagels. Pâté and meat sandwiches are available. Everything's very casual. Only a handful of tables, so order food to go if it's crowded (which it often is). Open 8 AM–8 PM weekdays, 9 AM–3 PM Sat.

The Mex, 185 Main St., Ellsworth, 207/667-4494, has been a popular local eatery since 1979. The menu is punnily entertaining ("Juan-derful Beginnings"), service is good, and you won't go hungry. Lots of vegetarian choices. Entrée range is $7–14. Take home a bottle of their fiery hot sauce. Open all year, daily 11 AM–9 PM.

"We thank the farmers, growers, fishermen, and cheese makers of Maine, without whom we would have nothing to cook," says the terrific **Cleonice,** 112 Main St., Ellsworth, 207/664-7554, www.cleonice.com, and they mean it. The Mediterranean bistro—and only tapas bar north of Portland—uses fresh local ingredients to create meals like Grilled sushi grade tuna steak with Sugo di Pomodori Fresca, Bistecca alla Fiorentina, and Turkish Vegetarian Kofte. The menu changes regularly, entrée range is $19–23. Open for lunch Mon.–Sat. 11:30 AM–2:30 PM, 2:30–5:30 for tapas (Oysters Rockefeller and spanakopita might be among the choices) and desserts, and from 5 PM for dinner seven nights.

There's even a Thai restaurant in Ellsworth, and it's a good one. **The Bangkok Restaurant,** 321 High St., Rte. 3, Ellsworth, 207/667-1324, does a creditable job, and the always-popular pad Thai is a winner. No smoking, no MSG. Open all year, Mon.–Sat. 11 AM–3 PM and 4–9 PM, Sun. 4–9 PM.

INFORMATION AND SERVICES

The **Bucksport Bay Area Chamber of Commerce,** 52 Main St., P.O. Box 1880, Bucksport 04416, 207/469-6818, www.bucksportchamber.org, is right next to the municipal office in downtown Bucksport. Office hours are Mon.–Fri. 10 AM–5 PM. The local *Enterprise* newspaper and the Bucksport Chamber of Commerce produce an annual *Sourcebook* at Christmas time, covering Bucksport, Orland, and Verona Island. Be sure to request a copy.

It can be hard to spot the **Ellsworth Area Chamber of Commerce,** 163 High St., P.O. Box 267, Ellsworth 04605, 207/667-5584, www.ellsworthchamber.org, amid the malls and fast-food places lining High St. (Rte. 1). Watch for a small gray building topped by an Information Center sign (on the right, close to the road, when heading toward Bar Harbor). Open daily mid-June–mid-Sept., weekdays the rest of the year.

Don't miss a chance to visit one of the state's loveliest libraries, the **Ellsworth Public Library,** 46 State St., Ellsworth, 207/667-6363, www.ellsworth.lib.me.us. The National Historic Register Federalist building was donated to the city in 1897 by George Nixon Black, grandson of the builder of Woodlawn. Services include photocopies, computer and Internet access, lectures, art exhibits, and a popular paperback exchange (take one and leave one). Open Mon.–Fri. 9 AM–5 PM (Wed.–Thurs. to 8 PM), Sat. 9 AM–2 PM.

The **Buck Memorial Library,** 47 Main St., P.O. Box DD, Bucksport 04416, 207/469-2650, established in 1887, has Wednesday-morning story hours and free Internet access. The library is open Mon.–Fri. 10 AM–5 PM and Sat. 10 AM–noon.

Newspapers

The *Bangor Daily News,* is Down East Maine's daily resource, presenting some local news but also state, national, and international stories. Bucksport's community-spirited local

Acadia Region

paper, *The Enterprise,* 346 Main St., P.O. Box 829, Bucksport 04416, 207/469-6722, appears every Thursday, with news, features, calendar info, and local ads. The respected *Ellsworth American,* 207/667-2576, also published weekly, has been around since the mid-19th century. The *Ellsworth Weekly,* a newcomer, appears every Thursday, 207/667-5514. In summer and fall, the *Ellsworth American* publishes *Out & About in Downeast Maine,* a very helpful free monthly vacation supplement in tabloid format.

Community Radio

Founded in 1985, **WERU 89.9 FM,** Maine's only community radio station, in 1997 moved its headquarters from a converted henhouse in East Blue Hill to a converted restaurant in East Orland, Rte. 1, P.O. Box 170, East Orland 04431, 207/469-6600, www.weru.org. Tune in for an eclectic array of contemporary music, as well as liberal commentary and interviews. The station's major fundraiser is the annual **Full Circle Fair,** an extraordinary cultural festival held on a mid-July weekend at the Blue Hill Fairgrounds.

Emergencies

In **Bucksport, Verona Island, Ellsworth,** and **Orland,** call 911 for emergencies.

Maine Coast Memorial Hospital, 50 Union St., Ellsworth 04605, 207/664-5311, the largest hospital in the area, has 24-hour emergency-room service. Walk-in care is available at the Med Now Clinic, 226 High St., 207/667-4655.

Area residents also patronize Blue Hill Memorial Hospital in Blue Hill and the giant Eastern Maine Medical Center in Bangor.

Veterinarians and Kennels

Bucksport Veterinary Hospital, 11 Gross Point Rd., Orland 04472, 207/469-3614, provides medical care as well as cat and dog boarding facilities year-round. Drop-off hours are liberal, and rates are especially reasonable.

Laundry

Hanf Laundromat, 151 High St., Ellsworth 04605, 207/667-4428, has self-service machines and is open 24 hours.

Public Restrooms

In Bucksport, public restrooms next to the **town dock** (behind the Bucksport Historical Society) are open spring, summer, and fall. There are year-round restrooms in the **Bucksport Irving gas station** (Lower Main St.), and in the **Bucksport Municipal Office** (weekdays) on Main St.

Getting Around

Downeast Transportation, 207/667-5796, offers limited fixed-route transportation between Ellsworth and area towns.

Getting There

One bus a day, originating out of state, stops in Ellsworth on its way to Bar Harbor. It's run by **Vermont Transit,** 800/451-3292, www.vermonttransit.com.

Acadia Region

Bangor Area

Lumber Capital of the World in the 19th century, Bangor (BANG-gore), with a population of 31,500, is still northern Maine's magnet for commerce and culture—the big city for the northern three-quarters of the state. Chief draws now in this region are the epic Bangor Mall (and surrounding shops and mini-malls), Bangor International Airport, and the academic, athletic, and artistic activities of the flagship University of Maine campus, in Orono, a few miles northeast.

The county seat for Penobscot County, downtown Bangor is awakening from a 1960s slump typical of many urban areas, and today you can stroll alongside Kenduskeag Stream, duck into shops and restaurants, and spend a comfortable night in the city's heart. The 2002–2004 waterfront National Folk Festivals brought excitement and major crowds to the city, and dusted off its sense of possibility, and Bangor has continued the two-day, late-August event as the American Folk Festival.

Bangor incorporated in 1791, but when explorer Samuel de Champlain landed here in 1604 (an event commemorated by a plaque downtown, next to Kenduskeag Stream), the Queen City bore the Native American name of Kenduskeag, meaning "eel-catching place."

In the late 19th century, when the lumber trade moved westward, smaller industries moved into greater Bangor to take up the slack, but a disastrous fire on April 30, 1911, leveled 55 acres of Bangor's commercial and residential neighborhoods, retarding progress for several decades.

Plenty of elegant architecture from Bangor's lumbering heyday escaped incineration, so you can still appreciate it by wandering around with a Bangor Region Visitors Guide available at the Bangor Region Chamber of Commerce. Or get oriented at the Historical Society's Bangor Museum and Center for History. Bangor highlights include giant statue of legendary lumberjack Paul Bunyan, and fine specimens of Victorian, Italianate, Queen Anne, and Greek Revival architecture—and who knows, you might see legendary author Stephen King in your travels. Part of what King enjoys about Bangor is that locals are used to him, and accord him "normal-person" treatment.

You can also take one of several interesting Bangor Historical Society (207/942-1900) tours: a Mt. Hope Cemetery tour; the autumn "Midday in the Garden of Good and Evil" bike or van tour of Bangor cemeteries; there's also a "Tommyknockers and More" tour of Bangor as seen through the books of Stephen King.

SIGHTS
Walk the Walk
Downtown Bangor lends itself to walking, especially if hills don't intimidate you. A distinctive west-side landmark is the National Historic Register **Thomas Hill Standpipe,** a squat 1897 water tower on one of the city's highest points. It's seldom open to the public, unfortunately—there's a great view from the observation platform. For tour information, call the Bangor Water District, 207/947-4516.

Paul Bunyan, Native Son?
On Main Street, next to the chamber of commerce office and across from the Holiday Inn, stands a 31-foot-high statue of the mythical lumberjack Paul Bunyan, allegedly born in Bangor on February 12, 1834. Weighing 3,200 pounds, the colorful statue was erected in 1959, during the city's 125th anniversary. Inside the base is a time capsule due to be opened in 2084. Kids can run and play in adjacent **Paul Bunyan Park.**

Stephen Kingdom
Maine native and naturalized hometown boy, horror honcho Stephen King is anything but a myth. Born in Portland, he's lived in Bangor since 1980, and you may spot him around town (especially at base-

ball and basketball games). His rambling mansion on West Broadway looks like a set from one of the movies based on his novels and stories—complete with a wrought-iron front gate and fence festooned with iron bats and cobwebs. Heed the No Trespassing sign; the best-selling author has had his share of odd encounters with off-the-wall devotees—not to mention his 1999 encounter with an out-of-control minivan. These days, even though he's back at work, it's best to keep up with him via his website, www.stephenking.com.

Bangor Museum and Center for History

In downtown Bangor, near the Museum of Art and the Discovery Museum, the **Bangor Historical Society,** 6 State St., Bangor 04401, 207/942-1900, www.bangorhistorical.org, offers a full schedule of tours, lectures, concerts, special events, and exhibits. The collection includes over 10,000 images, historic clothing, and Civil War artifacts. Admission is free. Hours are Tues.–Fri. 10 AM–4 PM, Sat. noon–4 PM. Maine arts and crafts can be purchased in the museum's Golden Fleece Shop, as well

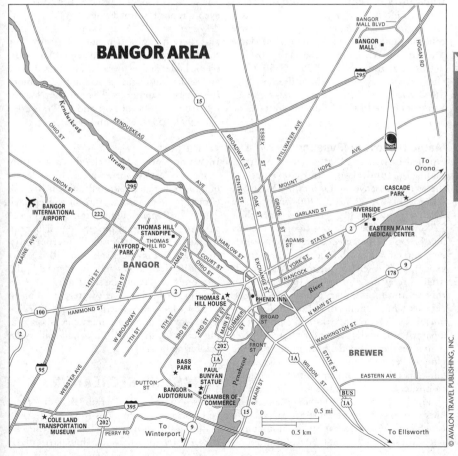

BANGOR AREA

Acadia Region

© AVALON TRAVEL PUBLISHING, INC.

Acadia Region

as books from a very comprehensive about-Bangor collection. The Society also owns and manages the Greek Revival **Thomas A. Hill House,** 159 Union St., Bangor 04401, 207/942-1900. Built by a wealthy attorney in 1836, and listed on the National Register of Historic Places, the handsome brick building on the corner of High Street has been restored to Victorian elegance, with period furnishings, Maine paintings, and special exhibits. Admission is $5 adults, $4 seniors, free for children. Tours are available Tues.–Fri. noon–3 PM, by appointment only.

University of Maine Museum of Art

Winslow Homer, Goya, Kollwitz, and Picasso are just four of the painters in the impressive collection at the downtown University of Maine Museum of Art, Norumbega Hall, 40 Harlow St., Bangor 04401, 207/561-3350. Contemporary exhibits are on the walls, too. Open Tues.–Sat. 9 AM–5 PM, Sun. 11 AM–5 PM; $3 admission; free to USM students with Maine Card.

Maine Discovery Museum

Opened in Jan. 2001, after several years of planning, fundraising, and construction, the Maine Discovery Museum, 74 Main St., Bangor 04401, 207/262-7200, www.maine discoverymuseum.org, occupies more than 22,000 square feet on three floors of the former Freese's Department Store. Seven permanent interactive exhibit areas feature nature, geography, art, science, anatomy, Maine children's literature, and music. It all awaits in this multimillion-dollar facility—the largest children's museum north of Boston. Kids can operate pulleys, open locks and dams, create a painting or sculpture, and explore a beaver dam from the underside. Most exciting are the global adventures in a Peruvian classroom, a Ghanaian market, and an Australian outback campsite. Special programs are scheduled for children and families throughout the year, and kids will like the museum store, called "Too Much Fun!" Admission is $6. The museum is open Tues.–Sat. 9:30 AM–5 PM, Sun. noon–

5 PM. It's also open Monday during school holidays. Summer hours are extended, and there is a summer camp program.

Cole Land Transportation Museum

On the other hand, children *love* the **Cole Land Transportation Museum,** 405 Perry Rd., P.O. Box 1166, Bangor 04401, 207/990-3600, www.colemuseum.org, a sprawling facility founded by Bangor trucking magnate Galen Cole. More than 200 19th- and 20th-century vehicles—just about anything that has ever rolled across Maine's landscape—fill the museum. Besides vintage cars, there are fire engines, tractors, logging vehicles, baby carriages, even a replica railroad station. You can walk down Snow Plow Alley or Fire Engine Lane, and there is a WWII memorial. A gift shop stocks transportation-related items. Outside are picnic tables and a covered bridge to walk over and under. Admission is $6 adults, $4 seniors, free for those under 19. The museum, located near the junction of I-95 and I-395, is open daily 9 AM–5 PM, May–mid-Nov.

Winterport

In Waldo County, 12 miles downriver from Bangor, is Winterport, a pretty little sleeper of a town, perched on the Penobscot River. It earned its name as the limit of winter navigation for Bangor's lumber trade; ice blocked shipping traffic from proceeding farther upriver. The National Register **Winterport Historic District** includes splendid 19th-century Greek Revival homes and commercial buildings on Rte. 1A and the short side streets descending to the river. The **Winterport Winery,** 279 So. Main St., Winterport 04496, 207/223-4500, www.winterportwinery.com, has a tasting room for its fruit wines and a gallery for exhibiting local artists.

PARKS AND RECREATION

Parks pop up everywhere in Bangor—from vest-pocket oases to a downtown pedestrian mall to a sprawling garden cemetery. Beyond the city in all directions (but particularly north) lie preserves and countless recreational opportunities.

In a state where burial grounds usually command views to die for, the standout is **Mount Hope Cemetery,** www.mthopebgr.com, 207/945-6589, consecrated in 1836 and easily the state's loveliest. Among the prominent Mainers interred here is Civil War-era U.S. Vice President Hannibal Hamlin. Inspired by the design of Mt. Auburn Cemetery in Cambridge, Massachusetts, 264-acre Mount Hope is more park than cemetery—with gardens, ponds, bridges, paved paths, lots of greenery, a few picnic tables, and wandering deer. Inline skaters consider it paradise. Open 7:30 AM–7:30 PM daily, Apr. 1–Nov. 1, then 7:30 AM–4 PM, Nov. 1–Apr. 1. The Bangor Historical Society sponsors tours of the cemetery. The entrance to the green-fenced cemetery is at 1048 State St. (Rte. 2), about 0.25 mile east of Hogan Rd.

Built over the meandering Kenduskeag Stream, right downtown, are two block-long parks: **Norumbega Parkway,** with a war memorial and benches, and **Hamlin Mall,** with cannons, the Champlain landing plaque, and a statue of Hannibal Hamlin.

A waterfall and a fountain are the focus at **Cascade Park,** State St., Rte. 2, an oasis 0.3 mile east of Eastern Maine Medical Center, where you can collapse on a bench or grab a picnic table and chill out.

The best kid place is **Hayford Park,** 115 13th St., off Union St., northwest of downtown, where the Gothic-looking **Bangor Creative Playground,** with two structures appropriate to two different age groups—one for two- to five-year-olds, the other for the 5–12 age group. The park is also home to the Beth Pancoe Maine Aquatic Center, a 7,000 sq. ft. pool with, among other features, a lap area and two water slides. The Center is open daily from the end of June–mid-Aug. 1–5 PM, and for family swims 6–8 PM Mon.–Fri. Nonresident fee is $4 adults, $2 children under 16. Next to it is the state-of-the-art, 1,500-seat Shawn T. Mansfield baseball stadium, locally dubbed the Field of Screams, since it was underwritten by

baseball super-enthusiast Stephen King (who annually abandons his computer to attend Boston Red Sox opening day).

With parks and recreation sites spotted all over the city, the best way to check on locations and opening times for municipal swimming pools, tennis courts, and skating rinks is to contact the **Bangor Parks and Recreation Department,** 207/992-4490.

Golf

Considered a standout among public courses, the **Bangor Municipal Golf Course,** 280 Webster Ave., Bangor 04401, 207/941-0232, has 18 holes dating from 1964 and a newer (and tougher) nine holes. Stretching over both sides of Webster Ave., the course is also on the Bangor Airport flight path; don't flinch when a jet screams overhead. Tee times are needed for the newer nine, and on weekends for the 18, but plan to arrive early in midsummer (the course opens at 7 AM). Open mid-Apr.–mid-Nov. The clubhouse (with pro shop and snack bar) is 0.4 mile south of Hammond St. (Rte. 2), on the southwest side of town.

Twelve miles southeast of Bangor, across from the Lucerne Inn, the nine-hole **Lucerne-in-Maine Golf Course,** Rte. 1A, Dedham 04429, 207/843-6282, is worth a visit just for the spectacular view. The course is open May–Oct., the fall foliage is fabulous, and greens fees are moderate. A tunnel taking golfers under Rte. 1A has eliminated the dodgem game of attempting to cross that speedway to get from the inn to the course.

Bicycling

Three Bangor-area bike shops spearhead the bicycling activity in this part of Maine. They sponsor road and off-road group rides, most briskly paced. For the most up-to-date schedule of bicycling events, check out the website of the Bicycle Coalition of Maine, www.BikeMaine.org.

A good place to rent a bike is **Ski Rack Sports,** 24 Longview Dr., Bangor, 207/945-6474, with a huge selection of mountain bikes and fast repair service. Cost is $15–20 a day.

The shop is open all year, Mon.–Sat. 10 AM–6 PM (to 8 PM Fri.) and Sun. 11 AM–4 PM. There's a road ride on Thurs. at 6 PM.

Across the Penobscot River is well-stocked **Pat's Bike Shop,** 373 Wilson St., Rte. 1A, Brewer 04412, 207/989-2900, for sales and service, but no rentals. Pat's has a Monday and Wednesday road ride. It's open Mon.–Fri. 9 AM–6 PM and Sat. 9 AM–5 PM.

Upriver is **Rose Bicycle,** 9 Pine St., Orono 04473, 207/866-3525 or 800/656-3525 in Maine, www.rosebike.com, catering to the university crowd with sales and service. Hours are Mon.–Sat. 9 AM–5 PM, (Wed.–Fri. to 6 PM). On Thurs. at 5 PM there's a women's ride and a mountain ride.

Spectator Sports

Most spectator sports are affiliated with the University of Maine at Orono (see *Orono and Vicinity*).

Downtown at Bass Park, the **Bangor Auditorium,** 100 Dutton St., Bangor 04401, 207/947-5555, is the site of other sporting events, with high-school basketball taking the lead in winter. Call for a schedule or check the website, basspark.com.

Hiking

After you've done the walking tour of Bangor, and cruised the Bangor Mall (if you're so inclined), you'll need to get out of town for anything in the way of hiking. In Dedham, 12 miles southeast of Bangor, a favorite hike goes up **Bald Mountain** (sometimes called Dedham Bald Mountain) to the disused fire tower on the bald summit. On a clear day, climb the tower for panoramic views to both Katahdin and Cadillac Mountain. Allow about two hours round-trip if you plan to picnic and climb the tower. To reach the trailhead from downtown Bangor, take Rte. 1A (Wilson St.) about 8.5 miles from the Penobscot River bridge to the Rte. 46 junction. Just beyond the junction, turn right onto Upper Dedham Rd. Go about 2.5 miles and, just after a stream, bear left onto Dedham Rd. Continue about 3.5 miles to the parking area (on left). The trail leads up from here, over a few steep, ledgy spots. It's well worth the climb, especially during fall-foliage season.

Audubon Center

South of Bangor/Brewer (although it feels like you're heading east) is the Maine Audubon Society's **Fields Pond Audubon Center,** 216 Fields Pond Rd., Holden 04429, 207/989-2591. About four miles of footpaths wind through 192 acres of woods, fields, marshes, and lakeshore—all open daily, year-round, sunrise to sunset. (Wear waterproof shoes or boots; parts of the trail can be wet.) Headquarters is the L. Robert Rolde Nature Center building, where you can pick up brochures and maps. A full schedule of programs occurs here throughout the year, including lectures, nature walks, slide talks, even a nature-book discussion group. Cost averages $4–5 per person. A nature store carries books, cards, and gifts. Most of the year, the Rolde building is open 10 AM–5 PM Thurs.–Sat. and 1–5 PM Sun.; in winter it closes at 4 PM.

ENTERTAINMENT

More than a century ago, when cabin-feverish lumberjacks roared into Bangor for R&R, they were apt to patronize Fan Jones's "establishment" on Harlow Street. Adult entertainment is still available in the city, but so is higher-brow stuff. The **Bangor Symphony Orchestra,** founded in 1896, has an enviable reputation as one of the country's oldest and best community orchestras. Call 207/942-5555 or 800/639-3221 for a schedule, or see website, www.bangorsymphony.com. During the regular season, Sept.–May, monthly concerts are presented weekends at the Maine Center for the Arts, in Orono. *The Nutcracker* is often the December offering, and there are some summer concerts.

The professional **Penobscot Theatre Company,** 183 Main St., P.O. Box 1188, Bangor 04401, 207/942-3333, www.penobscottheatre.org, performs six classic and contemporary comedies and dramas Sept.–May. The sixth show is always *A Christmas Carol,* in December. Ticket range is $12–24. There is a summer camp for children and young adults ages 7–22.

Every Thursday evening in June and July, free outdoor concerts are held on the waterfront.

The biggest local film multiplex is **Bangor Cinemas 10,** 557 Stillwater Ave., Bangor 04401, next to the Bangor Mall, 207/942-1303, with substantially lower prices before 6 PM.

In summer, the Arcady Music Society presents the **Arcady Summer Music Festival,** 207/288-2141, www.arcady.org, mid-July–late Aug., with an intriguing concert schedule. Flex passes save on the $13 admission if you attend all six. Venues for the concerts—each is given several times—include Bangor, Bucksport, Bar Harbor, Orono, and Dover-Foxcroft.

FESTIVALS AND EVENTS

In April (usually the third Saturday), the **Kenduskeag Stream Canoe Race** is an annual (since 1969) 16.5-mile spring-runoff race sponsored by Bangor Parks and Recreation, 207/992-4490. It draws upwards of 700 canoes and thousands of spectators and finishes in downtown Bangor. The best location for spotting action is Six Mile Falls—take Broadway (Rte. 15) about six miles northwest of downtown.

June is the month for the **Orland River Day** festivities, including a hometown parade, and raft race. The day celebrates the Narramissic River, because, among other reasons, alewives caught in weirs in the river generated revenue to build the town's consolidated school.

Late July into early August, the **Bangor State Fair,** held in Bass Park, is a huge 10-day affair with agricultural and crafts exhibits, a carnival, fireworks, sinful food, and big-name live music. This is a big deal and attracts thousands from all over northern Maine.

Admission to the late-August, three-day weekend **American Folk Festival,** on the Bangor waterfront, is free. Traditional music

and other entertainment features more than 20 performing groups on five stages. Call 207/992-2630 or see their website, www.americanfolkfestival.com.

Six concerts are held during the **Arcady Summer Music Festival,** mid-July–late Aug., with performances at several locales in the area.

SHOPPING
Art Gallery

A handsome brick wall serves as a backdrop for the work of prominent Maine and American realistic and abstract painters at the **Clark House Gallery,** 128 Hammond St., Bangor 04401, 207/942-9162, a sure sign of Bangor's cultural promise. Gallery director Susan Maasch's discerning taste has mounted respected shows here about once a month since she opened in 1996. A specialty is the photography of Berenice Abbott, Ansel Adams, and August Sander. Hours are Tues.–Fri. 11 AM–4 PM, and by appointment.

New and Used Books

Two independent bookstores in downtown Bangor have carved out their own niches, helping them compete with Borders and the like.

At the welcoming **BookMarc's Bookstore and Café,** 78 Harlow St., Bangor 04401, 207/942-3206, northern Maine's largest independent bookstore, with an impressive selection of Maine and Maine-related books, including Maine native American and forest-themed works. You can read your purchases in the adjoining café, Java Joe's. BookMarc's, located opposite Bangor City Hall, is open all year, weekdays 9:30 AM–5:30 PM and Sat. 10 AM–4 PM.

Just around the corner from BookMarc's is **Lippincott Books,** 36 Central St., Bangor 04401, 207/942-4398, a longtime antiquarian-book resource, with more than 30,000 old and rare books. Specialties are Maine titles and nonfiction volumes on Native Americans and Canada, but you'll find lots of surprises. The eclectic shop is open all year, Mon.–Fri. 10 AM–5:30 PM (to 5 PM Sat., 3 PM Sun.)

Also in downtown Bangor is **Pro Libris,** 10 Third St., Bangor 04401, 207/942-3019, billing itself as a "readers' paradise." With 30,000 used paperbacks and hardcovers, that's just about right. Hours are Tues.–Sat., 10 AM– 6 PM.

Betts Bookstore, 584 Hammond St., Bangor 04401, 207/947-7052, www.bettsbooks.com, in business since 1938, specializes in Stephen King. All of his books are here (and available by mail), including autographed copies and limited editions with an average value of $2,000, plus King posters, T-shirts, magazines, and stickers. King groupies will love this place. The store is open Mon.–Fri. 9 AM–4 PM, Sat. 9 AM–3 PM.

The stock is mostly out-of-print hardcovers at **Sarah's Used and Rare Books,** 32 Central St., Bangor 04401, 207/992-2080. Hours are generally 11 AM–5 PM except Sundays and some Thursdays, but if you're making a special trip, call ahead.

Gifts and Clothing

Believe it when **The Grasshopper Shop** claims to be the state's largest boutique—it sprawls over two floors in downtown Bangor, 1 W. Market Sq., Bangor 04401, 207/945-3132. Steer kids toward the T-shirts, music, and toys. Adults will find unstodgy imported clothing, housewares, jewelry, gifts, and cards. The Grasshopper Shop, under different owners, has popped up in different incarnations at varied, mostly mid-coastal, locations. The Bangor shop is open daily, all year, 9 AM–7 PM weekdays, 9 AM–6 PM Sat., and 10 AM–5 PM Sun.

Bangor Mall

The largest mall north of Portland is the 80-store Bangor Mall, Hogan Rd. and Stillwater Ave., just north of I-95 exit 49, with such household names as J.C. Penney, Porteous, and Sears. The mall is open Mon.–Sat. 9 AM–9 PM, Sun. 11 AM–6 PM. When the mall closes, at 9 PM, lots of shoppers head to the nearby giant **Borders** bookstore, 116 Bangor Mall Blvd., Bangor, 207/990-3300, which has live entertainment, coffee, and night-owl hours on Fri.–Sat.

ACCOMMODATIONS

Downtown

The **Charles Inn at West Market Square,** 20 Broad St., Bangor 04401, 207/992-2820, www.thecharlesinn.com, is a National Historic Register hostelry in downtown Bangor, as well as an art gallery showing over 150 works of art on its walls. Built in 1873, the four-story hotel underwent extensive restoration in the 1980s. Walls are thick, furnishings are tasteful replicas, and the lobby feels like an English gentlemen's reading room. Request a room overlooking Kenduskeag Stream. Thirty-two doubles (private baths, air-conditioning) go for $79–139 Apr.1–Sept. 30, $65–119 off season, including a continental breakfast, served at the Inn's Noni Village Café. The café also serves coffee, tea, beer, and wine. Children under 12 stay free. Pets are allowed. Open all year.

Many of the guests at the **Riverside Inn,** 495 State St., Bangor 04401, 207/973-4100 or 800/252-4044, www.riversidebangor.org, have business at Eastern Maine Medical Center, next door, but the inn is open to everyone (as is the hospital's 24-hour cafeteria). Inn rooms—56 total, including 15 suites—are several notches above generic motel decor. Request one overlooking the Penobscot River; avoid rooms overlooking the hospital parking lot. Prices are moderate (beginning at $79 d in summer, lower other times) and special discounts are available; no charge for an under-18 child who doesn't need a cot. Phones, air-conditioning, and cable TV are all included. Arrangements can be made for pets. Continental breakfast is included with the room. Open all year.

Bangor Airport and Mall Area

Your choice of airport-area motel may depend on your frequent-flyer memberships. There are lots of options. Linked to the terminal by a skyway, the **Sheraton Four Points Hotel,** 308 Godfrey Blvd., Bangor 04401, 207/947-6721 or 800/228-4609, www.fourpoints .com, at ground zero, has 102 rooms, an average restaurant, and an outdoor pool. Next closest (two miles) to the airport are Marriott's

153-room **Fairfield Inn,** 300 Odlin Rd., Bangor 04401, 207/990-0001 or 800/228-2800, with an indoor pool, a fitness center, and reasonable family rates; **Ramada Inn,** 357 Odlin Rd., Bangor 04401, 207/947-6961 or 800/445-7787, www.bangorramada.com, with 115 rooms, an indoor pool, and free shuttle service; and the 207-room **Holiday Inn,** 404 Odlin Rd., Bangor 04401, 207/947-0101 or 800/914-0101, with a terrific fitness center and pools indoors and out. The 96-room **Comfort Inn,** 750 Hogan Rd., Bangor 04401, 207/942-7899 or 800/338-9966, www.comfortinn.com, has a fitness center, outdoor pool, and free shuttle service. **Motel 6,** 1100 Hammond St., Bangor 04401, 207/947-6921 or 800/466-8356, www.motel6.com, and the **Super 8 Motel,** 462 Odlin Rd., Bangor 04401, 207/945-5681 or 800/800-8000, www.super8.com, free shuttle, are also on this side of the city. Pets are allowed at many of the motels.

South and Southeast of Bangor
Route 1A runs between Winterport and Bangor, then turns southeast and goes back down to the coast. Twelve miles southeast of Bangor (and 25 miles northwest of Ellsworth) is **The Lucerne Inn,** Bar Harbor Rd., Rte. 1A, RR 3, Box 540, Dedham 04429, 207/843-5123 or 800/325-5123, www.lucerneinn.com, a retrofitted early-19th-century stagecoach hostelry on a 10-acre hilltop overlooking Phillips Lake and the hills beyond. The fall panorama is spectacular. Thanks to a 1920s tourism scheme, the area is known, with a bit of stretching, as Little Switzerland—hence the Lucerne designation. Despite the highway out front, noise is no problem in the antiques-filled, rear-facing rooms. Twenty-one rooms and four suites ($139–199 d July–mid-Oct., $99–159 other months) have air-conditioning, phones, cable TV, and working fireplaces. Outside there's a pool. No pets. The Sunday-brunch buffet (9 AM–1 PM) in the inn's dining room is a big draw, as is the adjacent golf course. Dinner is from 5–9 PM nightly; choices are extensive, including scampi, rack of lamb, and prime rib. Entrées range from $16–29. It's a popular wedding spot.

Campgrounds
On Bangor's western perimeter are two clean, well-managed campgrounds convenient to I-95 and Bangor. Closest to the city is the 52-site **Paul Bunyan Campground,** 1862 Union St., Rte. 222, Bangor 04401, 207/941-1177, about three miles northwest of I-95 exit 184. Facilities at this attractive Good Sampark include a rec hall and huge outdoor pool; activities are offered most weekends. Leashed pets are welcome and noise rules are strictly enforced. Sites (for two adults, two children) are $17 with no hookup, $25.50 with full hookup, $21.50 for water and electric option. Open mid-Apr.–Oct.

About two miles farther out on Rte. 222, **Pleasant Hill Campground,** 45 Mansell Rd., Hermon 04401, 207/848-5127, also a Good Sampark, has 105 sites on 60 acres. Facilities include mini-golf, heated pool, cable TV, laundry, play areas, rec room, free showers, and a small store. Pets are welcome. Rates are $20–29.50, and the campground is open May–mid-Oct.

FOOD
Breakfast Bites
A downtown landmark since 1978, but with a new name and a new location nearby, **Bagel Central,** 33 Central St., Bangor 04401, 207/947-1654, is a cheerful spot to meet, greet, and grab some really good handmade bagels (try the blueberry), great deli sandwiches, soups, and more. It's closed Sat. but open Mon.–Thurs. 6 AM–6 PM, Fri. 6 AM–5:30 PM, and Sun. 6 AM–2 PM.

Downtown
Reservations are also essential at **Thistle's,** 175 Exchange St., Bangor 04401, 207/945-5480. Creative, moderately priced continental entrées ($16–25) with a Latin flair, plus excellent homemade breads and desserts, have drawn the crowds, especially at lunchtime. Paella is a specialty. A pianist plays quietly in the background Thurs. and Sat. evenings, and most lunchtimes. Open all year, Mon.–Sat. 11 AM–2:30 PM and 4:30–9 PM.

A prime spot for view-and-brew is the riverfront **Sea Dog Brewing Co.,** 26 Front St., Bangor 04401, 207/947-8004, www.seadogbrewing.com, where you can dine on the deck in summer. The menu can be uneven, but the award-winning lagers and ales are superb. Attractively decorated with tongue-and-groove pine on the inside, the brewpub serves lunch and dinner daily 11:30 AM–12:30 AM.

Neighborhood chic describes the atmosphere of **Café Nouveau,** 84 Hammond St., Bangor 04401, 207/942-3336, but what distinguishes it is attentive, friendly service, and imaginative, well-plated dishes. Among the appetizers are a fromage plate and lobster brioche. A vegetarian torte at $10 and lavender duck breast or tournedos of beef at $15 are among the entrées. Wine choices are extensive. Tues.–Sat, lunch is served 11 AM–3 PM, dinner 5–9 PM The wine bar is open till 11 PM Fri.–Sat.

Adjoining BookMarc's is **Java Joe's,** 98 Central St., Bangor 04401, 207/990-0500, serving Carrabassett Valley coffee, fruit smoothies, wraps, and salads 7:30 AM–3:30PM weekdays, 8 AM–2 PM Sat.

On the same block as Bagel Central **Friars Bakehouse,** 21 Central St., Bangor 04401, 207/947-3770, has an Express Lunch during the off-season. Year-round, they have baked goods at breakfast time—everything is made on the premises—sandwiches for lunch, with daily specials, like Wednesday's chicken salad. Open Wed.–Fri. 7 AM–3 PM, Sat. 8 AM–2 PM.

Behind City Hall, the stylish **New Moon Café,** 47 Park St., Bangor 04401, 207/990-2233, has been voted the best fine-dining restaurant in Bangor. Salads like a beet and spinach combo with candied walnuts (candied on premises) are $5–7. Appetizers are $7–11. Exemplifying the entrées ($16–28) are pistachio-crusted lamb kebabs, herb-crusted haddock, and orange and blackberry lacquered duck breast. Dessert could be a vanilla bean crème brûlée, or from-scratch ice cream ($5–8) with Coffee by Design coffee. There's an open kitchen, so you can watch fresh ingredients—organic and from local producers in-season—being transformed into your dinner.

There are more than 200 wines on the wine list, and over 20 scotches to choose from. The bar has an appetizer/tapas menu ($4–14), too. Open in summer Tues.–Sat. for dinner 5 PM–9 PM, with later bar hours. Open seven days the rest of the year, beginning in fall.

Bangor Airport

Across from the airport, **Captain Nick's,** 1165 Union St., Rte. 222, Bangor 04401, 207/942-6444, is best known for seafood, including a triple-lobster special, but it also serves up steak, chicken, and pasta. Reservations are a good idea on summer weekends. Open all year, daily 11 AM–10 PM (closing at 9 PM on Sun. in winter).

Ethnic Restaurants

Amazingly, the Bangor area supports more than half a dozen Chinese restaurants, of which the best known is **Oriental Jade,** Bangor Mall Blvd., Bangor 04401, 207/947-6969, next to the Hoyts Bangor Cinemas in the Bangor Mall area. Established in the late 1970s, Oriental Jade has developed a loyal year-round clientele. No reservations are needed, and it's open 11 AM–10:30 PM.

Noodles and Company, at 492 Wilson Street (Rte. 1A) across the river in Brewer, 207/989-9898, with a full Chinese menu. Cantonese and Szechuan noodles, lo mein, curries, and combos range from $2.95 for pork fried rice to $9.75 for Thai-style stir-fried shrimp. Open daily 11 AM–10 PM (to 10:30 Fri.–Sat.)

Maine's relative scarcity of ethnic restaurants makes cheerful, family-owned **Bahaar Pakistani Restaurant,** 23 Hammond St., Bangor 04401, 207/945-5979, especially welcome. Vegetarians find lots of options among the 70-plus reasonably priced appetizers, biryanis, and curries, which you can order hot, hotter, and hottest. Takeout available; full liquor license. Reservations are advisable Fri.–Sat. Open Mon.–Fri. 11:30 AM–2:30 PM and 5–10 PM; open Sat. 11:30–3 PM and 5–10 PM.

Three blocks from Bahaar, another downtown ethnic option is **Taste of India,** 68 Main St., Bangor 04401, 207/945-6865, an enduring South Asian favorite. It's open Mon.–Sat. 11 AM–10 PM and Sun. 2–9 PM. Beer and wine only.

For a good attitude, large menu,, and superb sushi, try **Ichiban,** 226 Union St. (at Third St.), Bangor 04401, 207/262-9308, disguised as part of a little shopping center. Mon.–Wed. it's open 11 AM–2:30 PM and 4:30–9 PM; Thurs.–Sat., it's open 11 AM–2:30 PM and 4:30–10 PM; Sun. 1–9 PM, serving dinner only.

Brewer
Just over the bridge from Bangor, the **Muddy Rudder,** 5 S. Main St., Brewer 04412, 207/989-5389, is a sister restaurant to Yarmouth's Muddy Rudder. Casual fine dining features fresh sea-food and local produce. In strawberry season, sample the homemade shortcake topped with fresh strawberries. A variety of menus—lunch specials, matinee menu with entrée and beverage for $9.99, happy hour appetizer menu—to suit your mood (and pocketbook). Open daily 11 AM–10 PM (to midnight Fri.–Sat.).

Local Color
Convenient to I-95 exit 180, **Dysart's,** Cold-brook Rd., Hermon 04401, 207/942-4878, is a truckers' destination resort—you can grab some grub, shower, shop, phone home, play video games, fuel up, and even sneak a bit of shut-eye. For real flavor, opt for the truckers' dining room, where the music is country and dozens of bleary-eyed drivers have reached the end of their transcontinental treks. If you're here with a carload, order an 18-Wheeler—18 scoops of ice cream with a collection of top-pings. No question, Dysart's is unique, and it's open 24 hours, every day, all year.

INFORMATION AND SERVICES
The **Bangor Region Chamber of Commerce,** 519 Main St., P.O. Box 1443, Bangor 04401, 207/947-0307, www.bangorregion.com, is an especially active outfit. Located next to the Paul Bunyan statue, the office is open week-days 8 AM–5 PM, all year, and usually on Sat. July 5 –Labor Day.

Two **Maine Visitor Information Centers** are located just south of Bangor on I-95, one on each side of the highway. The modern gray-clapboard buildings have racks of state-wide information, agreeable staffers, clean rest-rooms, vending machines, and covered picnic tables. Northbound, the center is at mile 175, 207/862-6628; southbound, it's at mile 179, 207/862-6638. They're open 8 AM–6 PM all year, unless the summer heat index goes into the danger zone.

If you plan ahead, the **Greater Bangor Convention & Visitors Bureau,** PO Box 1938, Bangor, ME 04401, 207/947-5205 or 800/91-MOOSE, www.bangorcvb.org, will send you information packets tailored to your needs, by priority mail.

Claiming one of the state's best reference sections, with a staff of librarians fielding about 30,000 questions a year, the **Bangor Public Library,** 145 Harlow St., Bangor 04401, 207/947-8336, www.bpl.lib.me.us, also pro-vides interlibrary loans throughout the state and has one of the highest per-capita circula-tion rates in the United States. A large, metered parking lot is just across the street. The hand-some 1912 structure, built after the 1911 fire and renovated at a cost of $8.5 million in the mid-1990s, is open Mon.–Thurs. 9 AM–7 PM, Fri. 9 AM–5 PM in summer (mid-June–Labor Day); in winter, open Mon.–Thurs. 9 AM–9 PM, Fri.–Sat. 9 AM–5 PM.

Newspapers
The *Bangor Daily News,* 207/990-8000 or 800/432-7964, carries the densest coverage of Bangor and northern Maine, plus national and international news. The Thursday edition has extensive calendar listings. *Bangor Metro,* 207/941-1300, has morphed into a magazine of business, lifestyle, and opinion; it's a good read and a great introduction to the flavor of the region.

Emergencies
Maine's second-largest medical center is **Eastern Maine Medical Center,** 489 State St., P.O. Box 404, Bangor 04402, 207/973-7000.

Round-the-clock emergency-room service (207/973-8000), a walk-in clinic (207/973-8030), and a state-of-the-art children's wing are among the first-rate features here. **St. Joseph Hospital,** 360 Broadway, Bangor, 207/262-1000, a Catholic facility, also has a 24-hour emergency department (207/262-5000).

For **police, fire, and ambulance** in Bangor, Orono, and Old Town, dial 911.

Photo Services

Bangor Photo, 559 Union St., Bangor 04401, 207/942-6728, in business since 1976, has a wide range of services, including passport photos, film, one-hour prints, E-6 slide processing, printing from digital media, and new and used gear. The shop is open all year, Mon.–Fri. 9 AM–5:30 PM and Sat. 9 AM–1 PM.

Getting There and Getting Around

If you're headed for Maine's North Woods, Bar Harbor and Acadia National Park, or the Down East counties of Washington and Hancock, Bangor is the handiest large airport. Incredibly, nearly half a million passengers annually move through **Bangor International Airport** (BIA), 207/992-4600, a user-friendly facility on the outskirts of the city. Major scheduled airlines with frequent service are **Delta, US Airways, Continental, American Eagle,** and **Northwest.** International charter planes regularly refuel here, and passengers often clear customs before heading on to points south and west. Bad weather in Portland or Boston also creates unexpected arrivals at Bangor's less-foggy airfield.

Concord Trailways, 1039 Union St., Rte. 222, Bangor 04401, 207/945-4000 or 800/639-3317, www.concordtrailways.com, operates three **express buses** daily to and from Boston's Logan Airport, with a stop in Portland. Concord's coastal route operates twice daily between Brunswick and Bangor, making nine stops and connecting with buses to Portland and Boston. The Concord Trailways stop is near I-95 exit 184.

Vermont Transit Co., 158 Main St., Bangor 04401, 207/945-3000 or 800/552-8737, www.vermonttransit.com, stopping in downtown Bangor, operates daily and connects with **Greyhound bus** routes. There's a daily express bus to Boston and New York, and five a day with fairly direct, more inland, routing, some buses topping in Waterville, Augusta, and Lewiston. Vermont Transit connects with Greyhounds' summer Bar Harbor route.

Avis, Budget, Hertz, and **National** car rental companies all have desks at Bangor Airport, **Enterprise** is about five miles away.

In downtown Bangor, the inexpensive **Pickering Square Parking Garage,** 207/941-1654, alongside Kenduskeag Stream, is especially convenient for downtown shopping and dining. Many of the merchants will stamp your parking ticket to void the fee. Parking is free on Saturday.; the garage is closed Sunday.

Round-the-clock **taxi service** is provided by Airport/River City Taxi, 207/947-8294.

Orono and Vicinity

Home of the University of Maine's flagship campus, Orono is part college town, part generic Maine village—and a fine example of the tail wagging the dog. Over 11,000 university students converge on this Bangor suburb every year, fairly overwhelming the 8,600 year-round residents.

Called Stillwater when it was settled by Europeans in the 1770s, the town adopted the name of Penobscot Indian chief Joseph Orono and incorporated in 1806. By 1840-as with Bangor, eight miles to the southwest—prosperity descended, thanks to the huge Penobscot River log drives spurring the lumber industry's heyday. A stroll along Orono's Main Street Historic District, especially between Maplewood Avenue and Pine Street, attests to the timber magnates' success; the gorgeous homes are a veritable catalog of au courant architectural styles: Italianate, Greek Revival, Queen Anne, Federal, and Colonial Revival. Contact Orono's municipal office for a free copy of *Orono Tree Walk,* describing the trees of the town.

Old Town (pop. 8,000) gained its own identity in 1840, after separating from Orono. ("Old Town" is the English translation of the settlement's Abnaki name.) In those days, sawmills lined the shores of the town's Marsh Island, between the Stillwater and Penobscot Rivers—the end-of-the-line for the log drives and the backbone of Old Town's economy. That all crumbled in 1856, though, when a devastating fire swept through the area. Occurring as residents exited from memorial services for Abraham Lincoln, it was called the "Lincoln Fire." Several decades later, Old Town finally regained its economic footing, thanks to factories making shoes, canoes, and paper products.

Under separate tribal administration and linked to Old Town by a bridge built in 1951, Indian Island Reservation is home to about 400 Penobscot Indians. Since the 1980 resolution of an enormous land-claims case, providing Maine's Indians with reparations, many of the island village's residents have managed to broaden their horizons and improve their living conditions. A new school and a health clinic have been built, most houses have been rehabbed, and dozens of island residents are pursuing college degrees. But controversy surfaces periodically over Indian Island's state-sanctioned high-stakes bingo operation, bringing in gamblers by the busload, and social-welfare problems still need resolution. It's been no easy road, and more bumps lie ahead.

SIGHTS

Orono's major sights are on the 660-acre campus of the **University of Maine** (UMO), www.umaine.edu, a venerable institution founded in 1868 as the State College of Agriculture and Mechanical Arts. It received its current designation in 1897 and now awards bachelor's, master's, and doctoral degrees. Oldest building on campus is North Hall, an updated version of the original Frost family farmhouse.

One of the newest buildings, built in 1986, is the architecturally dramatic **Maine Center for the Arts,** scene of year-round activity. Cleverly occupying part of the center is the small **Hudson Museum,** 5746 Maine Center for the Arts, Belgrade and Beddington Rds., University of Maine, Orono 04469, 207/581-1901, spotlighting traditional and contemporary world cultures in a series of well-designed galleries on three floors. Frequent special exhibits augment an eclectic ethnographic collection that includes Peruvian silver stickpins, African fetish dolls, Navajo looms, and the superlative Palmer Gallery of Pre-Hispanic Mexican and Central American Culture. An interactive corner lets visitors learn a few words in the Penobscot (Native American) language, and a small shop, 207/581-1903, stocks unusual global gifts. Admission is free. The museum is open Tues.–Fri. 9 AM–4 PM and Sat. 11 AM–4 PM. It's also open about an hour prior to performances in the adjoining Hutchins Concert Hall.

Acadia Region

The Maine sky takes center stage at the **Maynard F. Jordan Planetarium,** 5781 Wingate Hall, Munson Rd., University of Maine, Orono 04469, 207/581-1341, www.umainesky.com, on the second floor of Wingate Hall. Multimedia presentations help explain the workings of our universe and bring astronomy to life. Comet collisions and rocketing asteroids keep the kids transfixed. Program scheduling is variable, so you'll need to call ahead to confirm the schedule and reserve space in the 45-seat auditorium. Admission to scheduled events is $3 across-the-board. The public is invited to view the sky though a telescope at the Jordan Observatory on clear Friday evenings. Call 207/581-1348 for more information.

At the eastern edge of the campus, the seven-acre **Lyle E. Littlefield Ornamental Trial Garden,** Rangeley Rd., University of Maine, Orono 04469, contains more than 3,500 plant species, many being tested for winter durability. Best time to come is early June, when crabapples and lilacs put on their perennial show. The garden is open daily; bring a picnic. Horticulture fans will also enjoy the 10-acre riverside **Fay Hyland Arboretum,** on the western edge of campus.

In the last agricultural building on campus (the barn predating UMO), the **Page Farm and Home Museum,** 207/581-4100, houses a collection of farm implements and home items; on-site are a one-room schoolhouse and heritage gardens. The Museum presents an annual community picnic lunch at the end of July. Blacksmithing, old-fashioned games, and ice cream-making are part of the festivities. The lunch goes 11 AM–3 PM; the museum's hours are 9 AM–4 PM daily, May 15–Sept. 15; the rest of the year Tues.–Sat. 9 AM–4 PM, except holidays.

Campus **parking** is a major sticking point at UMO, so you'll need a parking permit for most areas except the Main Center for the Arts and the sports complex when events are taking place. For other times and lots, you can obtain a free one-day permit either from campus security or the parking office. For more information call 207/581-4053.

Old Town Museum

Located in the former St. Mary's Catholic Church, the Old Town Museum, 353 S. Main St., P.O. Box 375, Old Town 04468, 207/827-7256, www.old-town.org, has well-organized exhibit areas focusing primarily on Old Town's pivotal role in the 19th-century lumbering industry. Other displays feature woodcarvings by sculptor Bernard Langlais, an Old Town native, and an excellent collection of Native American sweetgrass baskets. Each year, temporary exhibits add to the mix. Try to attend one of the regular Sunday-afternoon (2 PM) programs—anything from carving, weaving, beadwork, and quilting demonstrations to hand-bell concerts and historical lectures. Admission is free. Hours vary.

Penobscot Nation Museum

Indian Island's Penobscot Nation Museum, 5 Downstreet St., Indian Island 04468, 207/827-4153, has exhibits of baskets, beadwork, tribal dress, antique tools, and birch-bark canoes. Curator James Nepture is welcoming and knowledgeable and will show videos of Penobscot life, including "Penobscot: The People and Their River." Jewelry, dream catchers, and other handcrafted items are for sale in the small store. The museum is open Mon., Wed., Thurs. 10 AM–4 PM, and Tues. 10 AM–1 PM, other times by appointment, but be sure to call ahead.

In the island's Protestant cemetery is the grave of **Louis Sockalexis,** the best Native American baseball player at the turn of the 20th century. Allegedly, his acceptance onto Cleveland's baseball team spurred management to dub them the Indians—a name that has stuck.

Leonard's Mills

Officially known as the **Maine Forest and Logging Museum,** 400-acre Leonard's Mills re-creates a late-18th-century logging village, with a sawmill, blacksmith shop, covered bridge, a log cabin, and other buildings. The site is accessible late Apr.–Oct., sunrise to sunset, but the best times to visit are during the museum's special-events days—variable schedule—when dozens of museum volunteers don period dress and bring the village to life. Demonstrations, beanhole bean dinners, hayrides, antique games, and kids dipping candles or making cider, are all part of the mix. The season's biggest events are **Living History Days,** a two-day festival held in mid-July and the first weekend in October. Admission to special programs is $5 adults, $2 children 2–12 and under. For more info write to the Office of the Maine Forest and Logging Museum, Inc., 5768 South Annex A, Room 100, University of Maine, Orono 04469,04469 207/581-2871, www.leonardsmills.com. An ongoing museum project is the restoration to working condition of one of the old Lombard Haulers, an important part of the North Woods story. The museum is on Penobscot Experimental Forest Rd., in Bradley, 1.3 miles southeast of Rte. 178. It's directly across the river from Orono, but the only bridges are north (Old Town/Milford) and south (Bangor/Brewer).

PARKS AND PRESERVES
Sunkhaze Meadows
The best time to visit **Sunkhaze Meadows National Wildlife Refuge,** Milford, mailing address 1168 Main St., Old Town 04468, 207/827-6138, www.fws.gov/refuge, is during the fall waterfowl migration, but hunting is allowed then, so wear a hunter-orange hat and/or vest. More than 200 bird species have been spotted here; moose and beaver are common. Best way to see them is to paddle the five-mile stretch of Sunkhaze Stream that bisects the refuge. Allow about six hours for this expedition, putting in on Stud Mill Road (park in the lot at the Ash Landing trailhead; do not park on the Stud Mill Road) and taking out on Rte. 2. (You'll need two vehicles for this.) Don't forget insect repellent. Access is via the unpaved Stud Mill Rd. or County Rd., north of Milford. No staff or facilities are available at the 11,672-acre refuge; visit or call the Old Town office for information and a map. The office is open Mon.–Fri. 7:30 AM–4 PM. In winter, the refuge trails are open for cross-country skiing.

Accessed through the Bangor City Forest, the **Orono Bog Boardwalk,** 207/581-2850, www.oronobogwalk.com, is handicapped-accessible, has a restroom, benches every 200 feet, and signs with flora and fauna descriptions. Almost all the guided Saturday nature walks are free, and take place from 9 AM–11 AM, early June–late Sept. Summer hours through Aug. are 7 AM–7 PM; Sept.–Nov., hours are 8 AM–5 PM.

RECREATION
At the University of Maine's **MaineBound Outdoor Equipment Rental Center,** 5748 Memorial Union, Orono 04469, 207/581-1794, www.umaine.edu/campusrecreation, you can rent camping gear, touring and telemark skis, snowshoes, mountaineering and ice-climbing equipment, canoes, kayaks, and all kinds of accessories. Very reasonable rates are charged by the day, weekend, or week. Summer hours are Mon.–Fri. 8 AM–4:30 PM, but all hours are subject to change, so be sure to call ahead—not a bad idea in any case, to be sure the equipment you need is on hand. A 10 percent reservation fee will hold your stuff.

Canoeing
Besides canoeing at Sunkhaze, paddlers can join the area's annual rite of spring, the 16.5-mile **Kenduskeag Stream Canoe Race,** a chilly challenge held in late April (usually the third Saturday) with a downtown-Bangor finish line.

Savvy canoeists will want to stop in at the visitor center/outlet store of the **Old Town Canoe Company,** 239 Main St., Old Town 04468, 207/827-1530. There are real bargains to be had.

Spectator Sports
Operating from an impressive athletic complex, the University of Maine has turned out national champions in several sports, including women's basketball. To check on current schedules and ticket availability, call 207/581-2327.

Acadia Region

EVENTS

Learn how to blacksmith (durable product) or make ice cream (ephemeral) at **Page Farm and Home Museum annual community picnic lunch** at the end of July. Call 207/581-4100 for information.

Orono Bog Boardwalk Nature Walks 207/581-2850, take place throughout the summer season, and come with lots of information, chances to see unusual birds, and amenities.

In early December, at the Hudson Museum on the Orono campus of the University of Maine, the Maine Indian Basketmakers Sale includes Maine Indian baskets, carvings, jewelry, and traditional arts. Demonstrations, drumming, and singing are all on the agenda. There's an admission fee for early-bird shopping from 9–10 AM. Free admission is 10 AM–3 PM. For more information, contact the Hudson Museum at 207/581-1904.

ENTERTAINMENT

On the UMO campus, the **Maine Center for the Arts** is the year-round site of concerts, dramas, and other events with big-name performers. The box office for the 1,600-seat Hutchins Concert Hall is open weekdays 9 AM–4 PM, 207/581-1755 or 800/622-8499 (ticket orders), www.mainecenterforthearts .org. Call for schedule information. There's a seating chart on the website.

Catering to the college audience is the six-screen **Spotlight Cinemas,** 6 Stillwater Ave., Orono 04473, 207/827-7411, www .spotlightcinemas.com. Stadium-style seating was added in a recent renovation. Ticket price is $4.50 Mon.–Thurs., for 12 and under at all times, and for matinees before 6 PM Fri.–Sun.; after 6 PM on those days, adults pay $7. Spotlight is in University Mall, near I-95 exit 193.

Anything happening in the Bangor area is also close enough to Orono to attend conveniently.

SHOPPING

Carrying a superbly selective line of gifts, wine, and gourmet goodies, **The Store-Ampersand,** 22 Mill St., Orono 04473, 207/866-4110, just off Main St., is a very easy place to drop a few bucks, but you won't have to spend many of them on the cappuccino—an eight-ounce cup is $1. Open all year, Mon.–Sat. 7 AM–7 PM, Sun. 9 AM–4 PM.

Shopping at the **Wabanaki Arts Center Gallery,** 240 Main St., P.O. Box 3253, Old Town 04468, 207/827-0391, www.maineindianbaskets.org, is an artful experience. The gallery exhibits and sells the work of over six dozen tribal artisans. Delicate jewelry, some made from quills, the magnificent baskets of the Maine Indian Basketmakers Alliance, photography, carving, and more, is displayed and sold from Mon.–Sat., 10 AM–5 PM.

Next door to the Arts Center is a traveler's delight, **The Map Store,** 240 Main St., Unit 5, Old Town 04468, 207/827-4511, chock full of maps, aerials, nautical charts, and GPS systems. If they don't have it, they can special-order it for you. Open Mon.–Fri. 9 AM–5 PM, 9 AM–3 PM Sat.

On the UMO campus, on the north side of the Memorial Union, ground floor, the **University Bookstore,** 207/581-1700, besides handling routine textbook business, is the source of logo-printed gifts and clothing, plus cards and a good general-book selection. Open all year, with reduced hours during the summer.

Native American art, jewelry, and musical instruments are the focus at **Penobscot Indian Art,** 276 Main St., Old Town 04468, 207/827-4725, open daily 10 AM–6 PM.

The **Orono Farmers' Market** has a particularly fine reputation for selection and quality. You'll find everything from organic produce to free-range chickens, seasonal berries, cider, sheepskins, cheeses, baked goods, and unusual condiments. Open Sat. 8 AM–1 PM May 7–Nov. 19, and Tues. 2–5:30 PM June 28–Nov. 1. The market is set up at the university heating-plant parking lot, (the Steam Plant Parking lot) College Ave., Rte. 2A, at the western edge of the UMO campus.

The world's oldest continuously operating canoe manufacturer, **Old Town Canoe Company,** still has its big old factory on Middle St., close to the Penobscot River in downtown Old Town. Incorporated in 1904, the company was turning out as many as 400 boats a month two years later. In 1915, the list of dealers included Harrod's in London and the Hudson's Bay Company in far northern Canada, and Old Town had supplied canoes to expeditions in Egypt and the Arctic. Quality is high at Old Town, so their boats are pricey, but you can visit the **Old Town Canoe Factory Outlet Store,** 130 N. Main St., Old Town 04468, 207/827-1530, www.oldtowncanoe.com, and look over the supply of "factory-blemished" canoe and kayak models. You may end up with a real bargain. There's also a full line of paddles, jackets, compasses, and other accessories. The shop and visitors center is open all year: Summer 9 AM–6 PM Mon.–Sat. and 10 AM–3 PM Sun. In winter, it's open 9 AM–5 PM Mon.–Sat. and 10 AM–3 PM Sun.

ACCOMMODATIONS

Six columns frame the entrance to the **High Lawn Bed-and-Breakfast,** 193 Main St., Orono 04473, 207/866-2272 or 800/297-2272, an elegant early-19th-century mansion set back from the street on four acres. An early-20th-century classics professor, yearning for a Greek facade, added the columns. Convenient to the University of Maine campus, High Lawn has attracted an international clientele since 1984. Six antiques-filled rooms (private baths) are $55–70 d. Guests relax by the fireplace in the living room, or in the den, and innkeeper Betty Lee Comstock prepares an impressive breakfast. No smoking, no pets, no children under 12. Two-night minimum on special university weekends. The B&B is 0.8 mile from I-95 exit 50 (Kelly Rd.). Open all year.

Even closer to the university is the three-story **Best Western Black Bear Inn,** 4 Godfrey Dr., Orono 04473, 207/866-7120 or 800/528-1234, fax 207/866-7433. Opened in 1990, it has 68 motel-style rooms with private baths and cable TV. Rates are $99 d, including continental breakfast, July–Oct., and $55 d other months. Concertgoers, sports fans, and university visitors fill up the rooms during the school year, so book well ahead to get in here then. Open all year.

FOOD

Catering to the notoriously slim budgets of college students, eating establishments in Orono all range from inexpensive to moderate. Three of the most popular spots are on Mill St., just off Rte. 2 (Main St.).

Orono's veteran restaurant is **Pat's Pizza,** 11 Mill St., Orono 04473, 207/866-2111, a statewide family-owned chain founded in Orono in July 1931 by C.D. "Pat" Farnsworth. Then known as Farnsworth's Café, it became Pat's Pizza in 1953. Pizza toppings are endless, even pineapple, sauerkraut, and capers. Subs, calzones, burgers, and "tomato Italian" entrées are also on the menu. Open all year, Sun.–Thurs. 7 AM–midnight (Fri.–Sat. to 1 AM).

Tex-Mex is the rule at **Margarita's,** 15 Mill St., Orono 04473, 207/866-4863, sibling of four other Maine restaurants turning out some of the state's best—you guessed it—margaritas. This popular student hangout is open all year, 4 PM–1 AM daily, the dining room is open till 10 PM, 11 PM Fri.–Sat. Busiest time is happy hour, weekdays 4–7 PM Dinner reservations are advisable on weekends during the school year.

Even though the drinking age is 21, every college town manages to have a variation on the pub theme. At the **Bear Brewpub,** 36 Main St., Orono 04473, 207/866-2739, try a mug of Crow Valley Blonde, Midnight Stout, or I'll Be Darned Amber Ale. Brews are seasonal, made on premises, there can be as many as seven on tap. Menu specials change daily, four at lunch, four at dinner; try the ribs.

Wednesday is "All You Can Eat Rib Night." The Bear is open all year, daily 11:30 AM–1 PM, dinner to 10 PM.

Like its Searsport spot, the **Chocolate Grille,** 301 North Main St. Old Town 04468, 207/827-8971, www.chocolategrille .com, wants you to plan your chocolate dessert before your dinner, since the chocolate soufflé and the chocolate-cookie sensation take a little time to prepare so that they will turn out swoon-inducing. While you wait, you can choose non-chocolate entrées from sandwiches and burgers to pastas, tuna steak, or filet mignon at prices from $6–19. Or have a signature cocktail, like the "university intellectual." Hours: Mon.–Sat. 11 AM–12:30 AM (Sun. to 10 PM).

INFORMATION AND SERVICES

The best source of information on Orono and Old Town is the **Bangor Region Chamber of Commerce,** 519 Main St., P.O. Box 1443, Bangor 04402, 207/947-0307, www.bangorregion.com. Also helpful is the **Orono Town Office,** 59 Main St., P.O. Box 130, Orono 04473, 207/866-2556, www.orono.org. The office is open all year, Mon.–Fri. 8:30 AM–4:30 PM.

Information about the University of Maine campus, including guided tours, is available from the **visitors center,** Buchanan Alumni House, University of Maine, 207/581-3740. The center is open Mon.–Fri. 8 AM–4:30 PM. Guided campus tours occur Mon.–Sat. at 9:15 and 11:15 AM and 1:15 PM.

Blue Hill Peninsula

Acadia Region

When a 1995 magazine article dubbed the Blue Hill Peninsula "The Fertile Crescent," local residents winced—they'd been discovered. Few other Maine locales harbor such a high concentration of artisans, musicians, and on-their-feet retirees juxtaposed with top-flight wooden boat builders, lobstermen, and umpteenth-generation Mainers. Perhaps surprisingly, the mix seems to work.

The peninsula comprises several enclaves with markedly distinctive personalities: Blue Hill, Castine, Deer Isle and Isle au Haut, and Brooklin, Brooksville, and Sedgwick.

BLUE HILL

Twelve miles south of Rte. 1 is the hub of the peninsula, Blue Hill (pop. 2,076), exuding charm from its handsome old homes to its waterfront setting to the shops, restaurants, and galleries that boost its appeal.

Eons back, Native American summer folk gave the name Awanadjo ("small, hazy mountain") to the mini-mountain that looms over the town and draws the eye for miles around. The first permanent settlers arrived after the French and Indian War, in the late 18th century, and established mills and shipyards. More than a hundred ships were built here between Blue Hill's incorporation, in 1789, and 1882—bringing prosperity to the entire peninsula.

Critical to the town's early expansion was its first clergyman, Jonathan Fisher, a remarkable fellow who's been likened to Leonardo da Vinci. In 1803, Fisher founded Blue Hill Academy (predecessor of today's George Stevens Academy), then built his home (now a museum), and eventually left an immense legacy of inventions, paintings, engravings, and poetry.

Throughout the 19th century and into the 20th, Blue Hill's granite industry boomed, reaching its peak in the 1880s. Scratch the Brooklyn Bridge and the New York Stock Exchange and you'll find granite from Blue Hill's quarries. Around 1879, the discovery of gold and silver brought a flurry of interest, but little came of it. Copper was also found here, but quantities of it, too, were limited.

At the height of industrial prosperity, tourism took hold, attracting steamboat-borne summer boarders. Many succumbed to the scenery, bought land, and built waterfront summer homes. Thank these summer folk and their offspring for the fact that music has long been a big deal in Blue Hill. The Kneisel Hall Chamber Music School, established in the late 19th century, continues to rank high among the nation's summer music colonies. New York City's Blue Hill Troupe, devoted to Gilbert and Sullivan operettas, was named for the longtime summer home of the troupe's founders.

Sights

A few of Blue Hill's elegant houses have been converted to museums, inns, restaurants, even some offices and shops, so you can see them from the inside out. To appreciate the private residences, you'll want to walk, bike, or drive around town.

Named for a brilliant Renaissance man who arrived in Blue Hill in 1794, the 1814 **Parson Fisher House** immerses visitors in period furnishings and Jonathan Fisher lore. And Fisher's feats are breathtaking: a Harvard-educated preacher who also managed to be an accomplished painter, poet, mathematician, naturalist, linguist, inventor, cabinetmaker, farmer, architect, and printmaker. In his spare time,

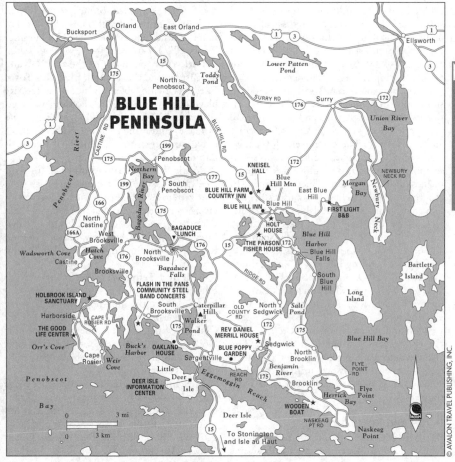

© AVALON TRAVEL PUBLISHING, INC.

Acadia Region

he fathered nine children. Fisher also pitched in to help build the yellow house on Tenney Hill, Rte. 15/176, 44 Mines Rd., Blue Hill 04614, 207/374-2459, www.jonathanfisherhouse.org, which served as the Congregational Church parsonage. Now it contains intriguing items created by Fisher, memorabilia that volunteer tour guides delight in explaining. Don't miss it. Open July–mid-Sept., Tues.–Fri. 1–4 PM, Sat. 11 AM–2 PM. Admission is $3.

In downtown Blue Hill, a few steps off Main St., stands the **Holt House,** Water St., Blue Hill 04614, 207/374-5590, home of the Blue Hill Historical Society. Built in 1815, the Federal-style building contains restored stenciling, period decor, and masses of memorabilia contributed by local residents. Open July–mid-Sept., Tues. and Fri. 1–4 PM and Sat. 11 AM–2 PM. Small admission charge for adults, free for kids 12 and under.

At the foot of Greene's Hill in Blue Hill stands one of Maine's more unusual institutions, a library where you can borrow by mail or in person from a collection of 625,000 scores and sheet music. There are over 7000 choral works in multiple copies. Somehow this seems so appropriate for a community that's a magnet for music lovers. Annual membership is $10 ($5 for students); the library publishes 10 catalogs of its holdings, also available on its website; fees range from $1 and up per piece—and you can keep it for up to three months, chorales and organizations for four months. The **Bagaduce Music Lending Library,** 3 Music Library Ln., Rte. 172, P.O. Box 829, Blue Hill 04614, 207/374-5454, www.bagaducemusic.org, is open all year, Mon.–Fri. 10 AM–3 PM, or by appointment.

Walk or drive up Union St. (Rte. 177), past George Stevens Academy, and wander **The Old Cemetery,** established in 1794. If gnarled trees and ancient headstones intrigue you, there aren't many good-size Maine cemeteries older than this one.

Parks and Recreation

Blue Hill Mountain: Mountain seems a fancy label for a 943-footer, yet Blue Hill stands alone, visible from Camden and even beyond. On a clear day, head for the summit and take in the wraparound view. Climb the fire tower if it's open and you'll see even more. In fall, the colors are spectacular—with reddened blueberry barrens added to the variegated foliage. Go early in the day; it's a popular easy-to-moderate hike, 1.5–2 hours round-trip. The trailhead is on Mountain Rd., just north of town off Rte. 15. Watch for the Firetower sign on the north side of the road, about 0.4 mile east of Rte. 15. Parking is allowed along Mountain Rd., but you can also walk (uphill) the mile from the village. The trail can be squishy, especially in the wooded sections, so you'll want rubberized or waterproof shoes or boots. For more information, contact Blue Hill Heritage Trust, 207/374-5118.

Parks/Playgrounds: At the end of Water St., just beyond the hospital, **Blue Hill Town Park** has picnic tables, an incredibly creative playground (including little houses), and a terrific view. Pick up picnic fixings at Merrill and Hinckley and bring it all here. There's also a playground next to the **Blue Hill Consolidated School** (off High St.).

Scenic Routes: Parker Point Rd. (turn off Rte. 15 at the Blue Hill Library) takes you from Blue Hill to Blue Hill Falls the back way, with vistas en route toward Acadia National Park. For other great views, drive the length of **Newbury Neck,** in nearby Surry, or head west on Rte. 15/176 toward Sedgwick, Brooksville, and beyond.

Golf and Tennis: The golf course at the Blue Hill Country Club is private; nearest public courses are the nine-hole Island Country Club (Deer Isle), the nine-hole Castine Golf Club (Castine), and the nine-hole Bucksport Golf Club (Bucksport). Both Castine Golf Club and Island Country Club also have public tennis courts.

Bicycling: Again, most of Maine's side roads are not bike-friendly, so be super-cautious, alert to traffic, and wary of soft shoulders. You can rent mountain bikes at Rocky Coast outfitters, 207/374-8866. **Summerfeet Maine Coast Cycling Adventures,** P.O. Box 10822, Portland

04104, 866/857-9544, www.summerfeet.net, offers six-day bike tours of the Blue Hill Peninsula and Mount Desert Island, staying at top-flight inns, and scheduled five times during the season, for about $2,000, excluding your travel.

Winter Sports: There's **cross-country skiing** on the Blue Hill Country Club golf course (Parker Point Rd.), also on the relatively level trails at Holbrook Island Sanctuary and on the carriage roads in Acadia National Park. For winter **sleigh rides,** as well as summer hayrides, contact Horsepower Farm, just north of Blue Hill on Rte. 15 in North Penobscot, 207/374-5038. There's no schedule; it's all "on demand," so don't count on a ride unless you make arrangements in advance.

Getting Afloat

Kayaking: Daily and weekly canoe and single and tandem kayak rentals at **The Activity Shop,** 61 Ellsworth Rd., (Rte. 172), Blue Hill, 04614, 207/374-3600, www.theactivityshop.com, can be delivered for you. Rentals begin at $25.

Daily and weekly sea kayak and canoe rentals can also be found at **Rocky Coast Outfitters,** P.O. Box 351, Grindleville Rd., Blue Hill 04614, 207/374-8866. Rental fishing poles and back packs will complete your outfit.

A favorite spot for experienced kayakers and canoeists is **Blue Hill Falls,** which churns with whitewater when the tide turns. Check for times of high and low tide. Roadside parking is illegal, but the law is too often ignored. The Rte. 175 bridge is narrow, and cars often stop suddenly as they come over the hill, so be particularly cautious here.

Native Trails, Inc., based in Waldoboro, Box 240, Waldoboro 04572, 207/832-5255, is currently working to increase awareness of the ancient **Minnewokun Canoe Trail,** a 25-mile circuit of the southeast corner of the Blue Hill Peninsula—including the Bagaduce River and Eggemoggin Reach—used by Native Americans to tap the fisheries of the Bagaduce Estuary.

MERI, Marine Environmental Research Institute, 55 Main St., P.O. Box 1652, Blue Hill 04614, 207/374-2135, www.meriresearch.org, has eco-cruise programs, late June through Labor Day, for families and for children and teens, exploring the aquatic life of Blue Hill Bay with the naturalist on board. Other programs include an ocean story hour on Fridays at 10 AM, year-round. MERI has an aquarium room with a touch tank, and does educational programs at their location or at schools and other sites.

Sailing: Unless you own a boat or know a member of the Kollegewidgwok Yacht Club, in East Blue Hill, 207/374-5581, there's no sailing out of Blue Hill. If you're trailing a boat, there's a public boat launch down on the harbor. Kollegewidgwok, incidentally, is a Penobscot Indian word meaning "blue hill on shining green water."

Entertainment and Events

Variety and serendipity are the keys here. Check local calendar listings and tune in to radio station **WERU** (89.9 FM), the peninsula's own community radio; there might be announcements of concerts by local resident Noel Paul Stookey or the Bagaduce Chorale, or maybe a contra dance or a tropical treat from Carl Chase's Atlantic Clarion Steel Band or Flash-in-the-Pans Community Band. WERU's program guide, *Salt Air,* is available free in shops, restaurants, and lodgings. In 1997, after nearly 10 years in a converted henhouse in East Blue Hill, the station moved its headquarters to East Orland.

Check out the **Kneisel Hall Chamber Music Festival.** Since 1922, chamber-music students have been spending summers perfecting their skills and demonstrating their prowess at the **Kneisel Hall Chamber Music School** on Rte. 15, P.O. Box 648, Blue Hill 04614, 207/374-2811, www.kneisel.org. Faculty concerts run Friday evening (8:15 PM) and Sunday afternoon (4 PM), late June–mid-Aug. All seats, except those in the tent, are reserved; the schedule is published in the spring, and tickets ($30 inside, $20 on the veranda outside, $10 in the tent; nonrefundable) can be ordered by phone or on the website. A

Acadia Region

less-expensive option is a $10 unreserved ticket for one of the FanFare events: eight Young Artist concerts (four in July and four in August, most at 7:30 PM), open rehearsals on Friday morning for faculty concerts, and six evening master classes. The Young Artist Concerts are "chamber music marathons," with 27 pieces performed during the two hours. Season Fanfare tickets are $30.

The **Blue Hill Fair,** is held at the Blue Hill Fairgrounds, Rte. 172, Blue Hill, 207/374-3701, during the extended Labor Day weekend (first weekend in September), the Blue Hill Fair is one of the state's best agricultural fairs. Besides the food booths (good-for-you fare competes with fried dough), a carnival, fireworks, sheepdog trials, and live musical entertainment, you can check out the blue-ribbon winners for finest quilt, beefiest bull, or largest squash.

Shopping

Antiques and Art Galleries: Blue Hill Antiques, 8 Water St., Blue Hill 04614, 207/374-8825, specializing in 18th- and 19th-century French and American furniture—attracts a high-end clientele. Open Mon.–Sat. 10 AM–5 PM, otherwise by appointment. The same patrons seek out Brad Emerson's **Emerson Antiques,** Main St., Blue Hill 04614, 207/374-5140, concentrating on early Americana, such as hooked rugs and ship models.

It's pretty tough not to find something at **Belcher's Antiques and Gifts,** 232 Ellsworth Rd., Rte. 172, Blue Hill 04614, 207/374-3751, where the emphasis is on the antiques. The shop seems to have cornered the market on Victorian twig furniture reproductions. Open daily, 10 AM–5 PM, June–mid-Oct.

The **Liros Gallery,** Parker Point Rd., P.O. Box 14, Blue Hill 04614, 207/374-5370 or 800/287-5370 in Maine, has been dealing in Russian icons since the mid-1960s. Prices are high, but the icons are fascinating. The gallery also carries Currier & Ives prints, antique maps, and 19th-century British and American paintings. Open Mon.–Fri. 9 AM–5 PM July–Aug., weekend hours are Sat. 10 AM–5 PM,

Sun. noon–5 PM. Otherwise, Liros is closed Sun. and open Sat. 10 AM–1 PM. The gallery is open mid-Apr.–Christmas.

If bronze sculpture appeals, the **Jud Hartmann Gallery,** Main St. at Rte. 15, P.O. Box 753, Blue Hill 04614, 207/374-9917 or 359-2544, carries Hartmann's figures—many of Native Americans—as well as paintings by Maine and non-Maine artists. The well-lighted gallery is open Mon.–Sat. 10:30 AM–5 PM, early June–late Sept.

Count on seeing outstanding contemporary art at the **Leighton Gallery,** Parker Point Rd., Blue Hill 04614, 207/374-5001. Owner Judith Leighton has built a reputation as one of Maine's best art connoisseur/dealers. Don't miss the sculpture garden out back. Open Memorial Day weekend–mid-Oct., Mon.–Sat. 10:30 AM–5 PM, Sun. noon–5 PM.

Books: Blue Hill's literate population manages to support two full-service, year-round, independent bookstores. Best selection is at **Blue Hill Books,** 2 Pleasant St., Rte. 15, Blue Hill 04614, 207/374-5632, thanks to owners Nick Sichterman and Mariah Hughs. Open all year, Mon.–Sat. 9:30 AM–5:30 PM; also Sun. 11 AM–4 PM July–Aug. Around the corner, **North Light Books,** Main St., Blue Hill 04614, 207/374-5422, carrying a healthy inventory of Maine and children's books, is open Mon.–Sat. 9:30 AM–5:30 PM and Sun. 10 AM–4 PM in summer, and some winter Sundays, too.

Gifts and Crafts: Blue Hill also has two noted, year-round pottery workshops, both turning out wheel-thrown ware with distinctive lead-free glazes—not surprising, since one evolved from the other. First came **Rowantrees Pottery,** Union St., Rte. 177, Blue Hill 04614, 207/374-5535, then **Rackliffe Pottery,** 132 Ellsworth Rd., Rte. 172, Box 393, Blue Hill 04614, 207/374-2297 or 888/631-3321. Rowantrees is open weekdays 8 AM–5 PM and Sat. 9 AM–5 PM. Winter hours are weekdays 8 AM–3:30 PM. Rackliffe is open Mon.–Sat. 8 AM–5 PM, plus Sun. noon–4 PM July–Aug and 8 AM–4 PM Mon.–Sat. in winter.

On Tenney Hill, two miles south of town on Rte. 15, is a "don't miss." **Mark Bell Pottery,**

Rte. 15, Blue Hill 04614, 207/374-5881, in a tiny building signaled only by a small roadside sign, is the home of exquisite, award-winning porcelain by the eponymous artist. The delicacy of each vase, bowl, whatever, is astonishing, and the glazes are gorgeous. Open daily, all year (he and his family live on the premises).

On Main St. in Blue Hill, **North Country Textiles,** Levy House, 207/374-2715, and **Handworks Gallery,** P.O. Box 918, 207/374-5613, are seasonal (May–Dec.) crafts galleries featuring high-quality work by Maine artisans. Handworks is open May 15–Dec. 31, in winter 10 AM–5 PM Mon.–Sat.; July–Aug. Mon.–Sat. 10 AM–6 PM, noon–5 PM on Sun. North Country is open Mon.–Sat. 10 AM–5 PM, Sun. noon–4 PM in summer, shorter hours the rest of the year.

The Himalayas meet Blue Hill at Jeff Kaley's **Asian World Imports,** Pleasant St., Rte. 15, P.O. Box 1234, Blue Hill 04614, 207/374-2284, www.asianworldimports.com. A Nepal Peace Corps veteran who has lived in Asia for seven years and traveled there for 39, Kaley seeks out ecosensitive suppliers using fair-trade practices, bringing back custom-made Nepalese, Tibetan, Indian, and Thai clothing, jewelry, and artifacts, as well as hand-carved buttons and over 350 different papers. The shop is loaded with treasures, old as well as new. Open late May–Christmas, Mon.–Sat. 10 AM–6 PM, other months by chance or appointment. Call for directions or holiday hours.

Blue Hill Wine Shop, Main St., P.O. Box 71, Blue Hill 04614, 207/374-2161, fax 374-3828, tucked into a converted horse barn, carries a huge selection of wines, plus teas, coffees, and blended tobaccos and unusual pipes for diehard, upscale smokers. Periodic wine tastings are always an adventure. Open all year, Mon.–Sat. 10 AM–5:30 PM.

Natural Foods and Farmers Markets: Local gardeners, farmers, and craftspeople peddle their wares at the **Blue Hill Farmers Market,** set up Sat. 9–11:30 AM in two different locales, depending on the month. It's a particularly enduring market, well worth a visit. The major effort is Memorial Day to Labor Day weekend at the Blue Hill Fairgrounds (Rte. 172, just north of downtown), From Labor Day weekend into October, it's in the Union Trust parking lot on Main St. in the center of town.

The **Blue Hill Co-Op,** Greene's Hill, Rte. 172, Blue Hill 04614, 207/374-2165, café, 207/374-8999, sells organic and hydroponic produce and grains, cheeses, organic coffee, and more. Breads are terrific here; sandwiches, salads, soups, and pastries are also available. Summer hours are Mon.–Fri. 8 AM–7 PM, Sat. 8 AM–6 PM, Sun. 10 AM–5 PM; co-op members receive a discount.

Accommodations

Don't visit Blue Hill for cheap sleeps or eats; visit for the handful of select inns and B&Bs. Remember, though, that rooms are scarce July–Aug., as well as on summer and fall holiday weekends (Memorial Day, Labor Day, Columbus Day). Reserve ahead or show up during quieter times.

Two miles north of town, at the **Blue Hill Farm Country Inn,** Rte. 15, P.O. Box 437, Blue Hill 04614, 207/374-5126, a huge refurbished barn serves as the gathering spot for guests. If the weather is lousy, you can plop down in front of the oversize woodstove and start in on cribbage or other games. Antique sleigh-runner banisters lead to the barn's seven second-floor rooms—all with private baths, skylights, hooked rugs, and quilts ($110 d, $90 off-season). Breakfast is generous continental. During the summer, visiting jazz or classical musicians sometimes entertain in the barn, but it all eases off early. A wing of the farmhouse has seven more rooms with shared baths and more quilts ($90 d, lower off-season; a cozy single is $80, lower off-season). On the inn's 48 acres are well-cleared nature trails, an 18th-century cellar hole, and a duck pond. Limited accommodations for kids under 12. No minimum stay, no TV, no smoking, no pets. Open all year.

On a quiet side street close to town, **The Blue Hill Inn,** Union St., Rte. 177, P.O. Box 403, Blue Hill 04614, 207/374-2844 or

800/826-7415, www.bluehillinn.com, has been welcoming guests since 1840. If you're trying to imagine a classic country inn, this would be it. Hosts Mary and Don Hartley do everything right. Stay here if you enjoy antiques, warm hospitality, and classic New England inns; don't stay if you're on a tight budget or have small children. Nine rooms and two suites, all with private baths, boast real chandeliers, four-posters, down comforters, fancy linens, working fireplaces, braided and Oriental rugs. The third-floor garret suite is ideal for families with well-behaved children. Rear rooms overlook the extensive cutting garden, with chairs and a hammock. The library, dominated by a Persian chandelier, has masses of local information on an old country-store counter. Nonalcoholic refreshments are available all day; superb complimentary hors d'oeuvres are served 6–7 PM in two elegant parlors or the garden. Doubles are $138–195, depending on accommodation and season. An adjacent suite in the elegant Cape House—the ground floor of a tiny dwelling—is $225–285 d in season, $175 in winter. Special packages—May and October wine dinners, inn/schooner overnights, kayaking or concert weekends, cooking classes, even day trips with the innkeepers—are bargains. The inn will arrange for Kneisel Hall tickets, kayak rentals, cruises, massages, and more. Two-day minimum on summer weekends; no TV, no pets, no children under 10. Open mid-May–Oct.; the Cape House is open year-round.

Blue Hill's only motel is the **Heritage Motor Inn,** Rte. 172, P.O. Box 453, Blue Hill 04614, 207/374-5646, www.bhheritagemotorinn.com, a clean, no-frills, 22-room year-round place on Greene's Hill. Rooms have cable TV, air-conditioning, coffeemakers, phones, and great views of Blue Hill Bay. Doubles are $95–122 d July–Aug., assorted lower rate levels other seasons. No pets. Open May 1–mid-Oct.

The nearest **campgrounds** are in East Orland and Surry, not far away.

Seasonal Rentals: Weekly rentals (or longer) can pay off if you have a large family or are doing a group vacation. The Blue Hill Peninsula has lots of rental cottages, camps, and houses, but the trick is to plan ahead: This is a popular area in summer, and many renters sign up for the following year before they leave town. For information, contact **Peninsula Property Rentals,** Main St., P.O. Box 611, Blue Hill 04614, 207/374-2428, www.peninsulapropertyrentals.com, or **Coastal Cottage Rental Company,** 1 Music Library Ln., P.O. Box 835, Blue Hill 04614, 207/374-3500, www.vacationcottages.com, which has more than 150 listings.

Food

Lunch: Picnic fare and pizza are available at **Merrill & Hinckley,** a quirky, 150-year-old, family-owned grocery/general store, Union St., Blue Hill 04614, 207/374-2821; open Mon.–Sat. 7 AM–9 PM, Sun. 8 AM–9 PM. M&H carries liquor and wine and has a **photo-developing** service.

When you develop a lust for open-air fish and chips, or scallops, clams, or mussels, head for the **Fish Net,** 162 Main St., Blue Hill 04614, 207/374-5240, open late Apr.–Columbus Day, summer hours 10:30 AM–9 PM daily.

Appealing lunch and supper menu choices at **The Vinery,** Main St., Blue Hill 04614, 207/374-2441, next door to Arborvine, make the decision difficult. This piano bar and light-filled eatery with a tree-shaded patio serves lunch Wed.–Sat. noon–2 PM, and supper Wed.–Sun. 5–9 PM. It's open for summer season into early September.

Moderate to Expensive: Save your pennies and splurge on dinner at **Arborvine,** Main St., Blue Hill 04614, 207/374-2119, www.arborvine.com, but don't plan to show up without a reservation. Chef/owner John Hikade and his wife, Beth, finally have their own restaurant, after working at various locales (and a catering business) in the area. A conscientiously renovated two-century-old Cape-style house is the setting for what one innkeeper calls "the best food in a 100-mile radius." Four rooms with fireplaces, candlelight, and antiques provide a variety of dining atmospheres. Entrées, which might include crispy roast duckling or tournedos bordelaise, are in the $22–29 range; the dessert menu always includes something with chocolate, perhaps Grand Marnier chocolate mousse, and something with fruit, perhaps pear crisp with whipped cream. The wine list is well-selected. Open Tues.–Sun. 5:30–9 PM in summer; Fri.–Sun. 5:30–8:30 PM in winter.

Drop by the **Blue Moose at Jonathan's,** 50 Main St., Blue Hill 04614, 207/374-3274, for the occasional belly dancing or for breakfast, lunch, and dinner. Enjoy the basket of breakfast pastry or the morning glory parfait; have a completely vegetarian mushroom burger, or a sandwich like the Main Street club, for lunch—sandwiches run $5–6; for dinner try the shrimp Athens with onions, bell peppers, ouzo, and orzo (large is $17, small $12). Moroccan tagine is $14, and can be made in chicken or vegetarian versions. Appetizers could include Belgian mussels or a flaming cheese. Open for breakfast Mon.–Sat. at 7 AM, Sun. at 9 AM; stops serving dinner Mon.–Fri. at 9 PM, weekends at 9:30 PM. From 3 PM–5:30 PM, tea, coffee, afternoon drinks, and dessert are served.

Farther down the main drag is **Wescott Forge,** 66 Main St., Blue Hill 04614, 207/374-9909, occupying the space once filled by the legendary Firepond. The two-story wooden building huddled almost unobtrusively next to the millstream in the village center has an upstairs bar/lounge with large deck, where light bar food, including terrines, pates, and cheese plates are served from 3:30 PM. Lunch is served Tues.–Sat. 11:30 AM–2:30 PM. Dinner is served 5:30–9:30 or 10 PM, beginning with appetizers like fresh lobster salad with jicama and mango curry. Entrée range on the menu, which changes biweekly, is $15–25 for dishes like seared seaweed-crusted yellowfin tuna with wasabi coulee and sticky rice or Moroccan spiced chickpea stew with coriander mint *raita.* One of the restaurant's strengths is its wine-pairing program; all wines are served by the glass, so patrons can sample unfamiliar vintages.

Information and Services

the **Blue Hill Peninsula Chamber of Commerce,** 28 Water St., P.O. Box 520, Blue Hill 04614, 207/374-3242, www.bluehillpeninsula.org, is open June 1 to the second week of September: Mon.–Fri. 9:30 AM–4:30 PM; Sat. 9:30 AM–1:30 PM; and Sun. 11:30 AM–1:30 PM. Off-season, chamber members reply to phone inquiries, and North Light Books is prepared to help with information. Staffers at the **Blue Hill Town Hall,** 18 Union St., Blue Hill 04614, 207/374-2281, open weekdays, also can help. Don't hesitate to ask shopkeepers for information—they're a helpful bunch. The **Blue Hill Public Library,** Main St., 207/374-5515, www.bluehill.lib.me.us, is open Mon.–Fri. 10 AM–6 PM (to 8 PM Thurs.), Sat. 10 AM–2 PM, maintaining an active schedule of ongoing arts shows, film series, lectures, and a mid-day concert series, once a month on Mondays, more often during the summer. Check with the library or on the web for schedule.

Newspapers: Useful local publications are Blue Hill's *Weekly Packet,* and the *Ellsworth American,* published every Thursday. The *Packet* carries extensive events listings and lots of local ads. The *Bangor Daily News,* published daily, covers some local news but also carries state, national, and international stories.

Emergencies: For emergencies in the **Blue Hill** area, call 911. The respected **Blue Hill Memorial Hospital,** Water St., Blue Hill 04614, 207/374-2836, has 24-hour emergency-room service.

Laundry: The **Blue Hill Laundry,** Main St., Blue Hill, 207/374-2777, is open all year, daily 7 AM–6 PM (to 8 PM Sun. and Tues.).

Public Restrooms: There are no public restrooms, and restaurant owners don't appreciate noncustomers asking to use their facilities. Public buildings that have restrooms are the Blue Hill Town Hall (Main St.), Blue Hill Public Library (Main St.), and Blue Hill Memorial Hospital (Water St.).

Getting There and Away

There is no public transportation, nor are there taxis, within Blue Hill; the nearest transportation hub is Ellsworth, 14 miles away. Major car-rental agencies have offices at Bar Harbor Airport and Bangor International Airport.

© KATHLEEN M. BRANDES

WoodenBoat School, Brooklin

BROOKLIN, BROOKSVILLE, AND SEDGWICK

Nestled near the bottom of the Blue Hill Peninsula and surrounded by Castine, Blue Hill, and Deer Isle, this often-missed area offers superb hiking, kayaking, and sailing, plus historic homes and unique shops, studios, lodgings, and personalities.

Best-known town is Brooklin (pop. 797), thanks to two magazines: *The New Yorker* and *WoodenBoat*. Wordsmiths extraordinaire E. B. and Katharine White "dropped out" to Brooklin in the 1930s and forever afterward dispatched their splendid material for *The New Yorker* from here. (The Whites' former home, a handsome Colonial not open to the public, is on Rte. 175 in North Brooklin, 6.5 miles from the Blue Hill Falls bridge.) In 1977, *WoodenBoat* magazine moved its headquarters to Brooklin, where its 60-acre shoreside estate attracts builders and dreamers from all over the globe. Nearby Brooksville (pop. 779) drew the late Helen and Scott Nearing, whose *Living the Good Life* made them role models for back-to-the-landers. Buck's Harbor, a section

of Brooksville, is the setting for *One Morning in Maine,* one of Robert McCloskey's beloved children's books. Oldest of the three towns is Sedgwick (pop. 931, incorporated in 1789), which once included all of Brooklin and part of Brooksville. Now wedged between Brooklin and Brooksville, it includes the hamlet of Sargentville, the Caterpillar Hill scenic overlook, and a well-preserved complex of historic buildings. The flow of pilgrims continues in this area—many of them artist wannabes bent on capturing the spirit that has proved so enticing to creative types.

Sights

On Naskeag Pt. Rd., 1.2 miles from downtown Brooklin (Rte. 175), a small sign marks the turn to the world headquarters of the **WoodenBoat** empire. Buy magazines and books at the new bookstore, stroll the grounds, or sign up for one of the dozens of one- and two-week spring, summer, and fall courses in seamanship, navigation, boatbuilding, marine carving, and more. Special courses are geared to women, pros, and all-thumbs neophytes; the camaraderie is legendary. One-week tuition runs $550–

1,000, plus materials in some courses. Room and board is $400. Courses are popular, and 45 percent of students are returnees. School visiting hours are Mon.–Fri. 8 AM–5 PM, June–Oct. For more info, contact WoodenBoat School, 86 Great Cove Dr., Naskeag Pt. Rd., P.O. Box 78, Brooklin 04616, 207/359-4651, www.woodenboat.com.

Now used as the museum/headquarters of the Sedgwick-Brooklin Historical Society, the 1795 **Rev. Daniel Merrill House,** Rte. 172, P.O. Box 171, Sedgwick 04676, 207/359-8958, was the parsonage for Sedgwick's first permanent minister. Inside the house are period furnishings, old photos, toys, and tools; a few steps away are a restored 1874 schoolhouse, an 1821 cattle pound (for corralling wandering bovines), and a hearse barn. The complex, a mile north of the junction with Rte. 175, is open Sun. 2–4 PM July–Aug., or by appointment. Admission is free but donations are welcomed. The **Sedgwick Historic District,** crowning Town House Hill, comprises the Merrill House and its outbuildings plus the imposing 1794 Town House and the 23-acre Rural Cemetery (oldest headstone dates from 1798) across Rte. 172.

About 2500 people a year come to see Forest Farm, home of the late Helen and Scott Nearing, now the site of **The Good Life Center,** 372 Harborside Rd., Harborside 04642, 207/326-8211, www.goodlife.org. Advocates of simple living and authors of 10 books on the subject, the Nearings created a trust to perpetuate their farm and philosophy. Resident stewards lead tours Thurs.–Tues. 1–5 PM, July–Aug., and copies of Nearing books, as well as books on ecology and politics, are available for sale. The center is also open Thurs.–Mon. 1–5 PM Sept.–June. Mid-June–mid-Sept., Monday Night Meetings (7 PM) at the farm feature free programs by gardeners, philosophers, musicians, and other guest speakers. Occasional work parties (Outward Bound has sailed into the cove with 24 people to work on the center) and conferences are also on the center's schedule. Of interest as oil prices rocket through the stratosphere: The house is heated and run by a six-solar-panel system. The farm is on an unpaved road on Orr's Cove in Harborside—not the easiest place to find. Call for directions. If you're hiking in Holbrook Island Sanctuary, relatively close to the farm, ask there for directions.

Parks and Recreation

In the early 1970s, foresighted benefactor Anita Harris donated to the state 1,230 acres in Brooksville that would become the **Holbrook Island Sanctuary,** Box 35, Brooksville 04617, 207/326-4012. From Rte. 176, between West Brooksville and South Brooksville, head west on Cape Rosier Rd., following brown-and-white signs for the sanctuary. Maps are available at trailheads. Park across the dirt road (next to the outhouse). The easy Backshore Trail (about 30 minutes) starts here, or go back a mile and climb the steep trail to **Backwoods Mountain,** for the best vistas. Also in the park are shorefront picnic tables and grills, four old cemeteries, a beaver flowage, and super birding during spring and fall migrations. Leashed pets are allowed; no bikes on the trails; no camping. Admission is free. Officially open May 15–Oct. 15, but the access road and parking areas are plowed for cross-country skiers.

Or you can take a picnic to the **Bagaduce Ferry Landing,** in West Brooksville, off Rte. 176, where there are picnic tables and cross-river vistas toward Castine.

A small, relatively little-known beach is Brooklin's **Pooduck Beach.** From the Brooklin General Store (Rte. 175), take Naskeag Pt. Rd. about half a mile, watching for the Pooduck Rd. sign on the right. Drive to the end. You can also launch a sea kayak into Eggemoggin Reach here.

For both **golf** and **tennis,** the best and closest choice is the Island Country Club, on Deer Isle.

Bicycling: Roads here are particularly narrow and winding, with poor shoulders, so be especially attentive; mountain bikes are a wise idea. Bring your own bike if you can; rentals are hard to find here. If you're up to a 40-plus-mile

Acadia Region

circuit of low-to-moderate difficulty, start in Blue Hill (check with the town hall or the hospital about parking) and go counterclockwise, following Rtes. 15, 176, and 175 through West and South Brooksville (Buck's Harbor), Brooksville, Sargentville, Sedgwick, Brooklin, and back to Blue Hill. The same circuit makes a good day trip by car from Blue Hill, or a variation from Castine. See below for food and lodging possibilities en route. Carry a water bottle and arm yourself with a picnic lunch.

Scenic Routes: No one seems to know how **Caterpillar Hill** got its name, but its reputation comes from a panoramic vista of water, hills, and blueberry barrens—with a couple of convenient picnic tables where you can stop for lunch, photos, or a ringside view of sunset and fall foliage. The signposted rest area is on Rte. 175/15, between Brooksville and Sargentville; watch out for the blind curve when you pull off the road. Between Sargentville and Sedgwick, Rte. 175 offers nonstop views of Eggemoggin Reach, with shore access to the Benjamin River just before you reach Sedgwick village. The 40-mile cycling circuit described above includes both Caterpillar Hill (the only really tough section) and the Sedgwick area.

Two other scenic routes, via car or bike, are **Naskeag Point,** in Brooklin, and **Cape Rosier,** westernmost arm of the town of Brooksville. Naskeag Pt. Rd. begins off Rte. 175 in "downtown" Brooklin, heads down the peninsula for 3.7 miles past the entrance to WoodenBoat Publications, past Amen Farm (home of the late author Roy Barrette), to a small shingle beach (limited parking) on Eggemoggin Reach where you'll find picnic tables, a boat launch, a seasonal toilet, and a marker commemorating the 1778 Battle of Naskeag, when British sailors came ashore from the sloop *Gage,* burned several buildings, and were run off by a ragtag band of local settlers. Cape Rosier's roads are poorly marked, perhaps deliberately, so keep your DeLorme atlas handy. The Cape Rosier loop takes in Holbrook Island Sanctuary, Goose Falls, the hamlet of Harborside, and plenty of water and island views.

Getting Afloat

See the Blue Hill and Castine and Deer Isle sections for information on sea kayaking.

Native Trails, Inc., Box 240, Waldoboro 04572, 207/832-5255, and headed by Mike Krepner, is working to increase consciousness of the ancient Minnewokun Canoe Trail, a 25-mile circuit of the southeast corner of the Blue Hill Peninsula—including the Bagaduce River and Eggemoggin Reach—used by Native Americans to tap the fisheries of the Bagaduce Estuary. The name allegedly means "many-angled route," and that it is. The 15-mile section between Castine and Walker Pond is already a popular (mostly flat-water) paddling route. Contact Native Trails for a map and an update on the project's status.

Entertainment and Events

Nightlife is mostly catch-as-catch-can in this area (it's not why most people are here). Head for Blue Hill or Castine if you feel the urge for live music—or Bar Harbor if you want even more choices. But if you're a fan of steel-band music, arrange to hear the **Flash in the Pans Community Steelband,** www.peninsulapan .org, at the Bucks Harbor Community Building, Blue Hill Town Park, or other area locales. The musicians aren't professionals, but you'd never know it. Local papers carry the summer schedule for the band, or check the website. The steel-band phenomenon is big on the Blue Hill peninsula; classes, community involvement, and street dances are part of it.

Wooden boats are big attractions hereabouts, so when a huge fleet sails in for the **Eggemoggin Reach Regatta** (usually the first Saturday in August, but the schedule can change), crowds gather. Don't miss the parade of wooden boats. Best locale for watching the regatta itself is on or near the bridge to Deer Isle, or near the Eggemoggin Landing grounds on Little Deer Isle. Contact *WoodenBoat* magazine, P.O. Box 78, Brooklin 04616, 207/359-4651, www.woodenboat.com. (The race ends there with a barbecue, awards, and entertainment.)

Nearest cinemas are the Grand Auditorium

in Ellsworth and the Criterion in Bar Harbor; the Alamo Theatre in Bucksport also draws from this area.

Shopping

Antiques: When you need a slate sink, a claw-foot tub, brass fixtures, or a Palladian window, **Architectural Antiquities,** Harborside 04642, 207/326-4938, on Cape Rosier, is just the ticket—a restorer's delight. Prices are reasonable for what you get, and they'll ship your purchases. Open all year by appointment; ask for directions. Country and formal furniture, decoys, and nautical items are specialties at Peg and Olney Grindall's **Old Cove Antiques,** Rte. 15, Sargentville 04673, 207/359-2031 or 359-8585. The weathered-gray shop, across from the Eggemoggin Country Store, is open most days 10 AM–5 PM, but be sure to call ahead.

Gifts, Crafts, Art Galleries: If you like folk art, check out the Noah's Arks at George, Georgene, and Kathy Allen's **Creeping Thyme Farm,** 39 Thyme Farm Lane, North Brooklin 04616, 207/359-2067. Hours vary; call if you're making a special trip.

On Rte. 175 (Reach Rd.) in Sedgwick, watch for a small sign for **Mermaid Woolens,** Reach Rd., Sedgwick 04676, 207/359-2747, source of Elizabeth Coakley's wildly colorful hand-knits—vests, socks, and sweaters. They're pricey but worth every nickel.

Three varieties of English-style hard cider are specialties at **The Sow's Ear Winery,** 303 Coastal Rd. (Rte. 176 at Herrick Rd.), Brooksville 04617, 207/326-4649, a minuscule operation in a funky, gray-shingled building. Winemaker Tom Hoey also produces sulfite-free blueberry, best-selling wildberry, and rhubarb wines; he'll let you sample it all. Ask to see his cellar, where everything happens. No credit cards. Open mid-May–mid-Oct., Tues.–Sat. 10 AM–5 PM, other days by appointment; it's best to call ahead in any case.

Nautical books, T-shirts, gifts, snacks, and boat gear line the walls of the tiny shop at **Buck's Harbor Marine,** on the dock, South Brooksville 04617, 207/326-8839. Owned by boating author Jerry Kirschenbaum and his

wife, Lois, the marina is open daily 9 AM–5 PM (8 AM–7 PM in Aug.), Memorial Day–Columbus Day.

Upstairs via the outside stairway is **Larson Fine Art,** Box 176, Penobscot, 207/326-8222, David Larson's studio and gallery. Open June–Sept., daily 10 AM–5 PM. Rumor has it that Duncan Hines Blueberry Muffin Mix was invented in this building.

Accommodations

Cottages: The two operations in this category feel much like informal family compounds—where you quickly become an adoptee. Don't even think about dropping in, however; successive generations of hosts have catered to successive generations of visitors, and far-in-advance reservations are essential July–Aug. Many guests book for the following year before they leave. We're not talking fancy; cottages are old-shoe rustic, of varying sizes and decor. Most of the cottages have cooking facilities, although both colonies offer MAP July–Aug. Both also have hiking trails, playgrounds, rowboats, and East Penobscot Bay on the doorstep.

Jim and Sally Littlefield are the enthusiastic fourth-generation hosts at **Oakland House Seaside Inn and Cottages,** 435 Herrick Rd., Brooksville 04617, 207/359-8521 or 800/359-7352, www.oaklandhouse.com, a sprawling complex of 15 wooded and waterfront cottages, as well as Shore Oaks Seaside Inn. Much of this land, now threaded with hiking trails, was part of the original king's grant to Jim's ancestors. Cottages range from $475/week without meals in the off-season to $5,500/week with meals (MAP) for a family of four (with teenagers—children are less) in high season. Thursday, mid-July–Labor Day, is lobster-picnic night, on the beach. Biggest bargains are early May–mid-June and Sept.–Oct. The Lone Pine cottage has an astonishing toaster collection; another cottage has a stuffed owl bequeathed by a departed guest. Lots of tradition here! Rowboats are free for guests, and the staff organizes boat excursions on request. Two cottages (Lone Pine and

Boathouse) are winterized and available all year; the other cottages are closed in winter.

The fourth generation also manages the **Hiram Blake Camp,** 220 Weir Cove Rd., Harborside 04642, 207/326-4951, hiramblake.com, but with a difference: the second and third generations still pitch in and help with gardening, lobstering, maintenance, and kibitzing. Fourteen cottages line the shore of this 100-acre complex. Don't bother bringing reading matter: the dining room has ingenious ceiling niches lined with countless books. Open mid-May–mid-Oct. One-week minimum (beginning Sat. or Sun.) July–Aug., when cottages go for $1,300–2,400 a week (MAP). Off-season rates (no meals, but cottages have cooking facilities) are $575–775 per week; during the off-season, you'll need to bring your own linens or rent them here. Best chances for getting a reservation are in June and September. Pets are allowed. Open mid-May–mid-Oct.

Bed-and-Breakfasts: A few steps up from the half-mile-long shorefront at the Oakland House cottage colony is **Shore Oaks Seaside Inn** (same address and phone as Oakland House), a handsome green-trimmed stone mansion carefully restored to its Arts and Crafts heritage. Hang out for too long in the common rooms or the veranda rockers and you might never leave; this place is magical. Ten first-, second-, and third-floor rooms (seven with private baths) go for $185–385 d, MAP (a bargain with gourmet dinners and the weekly summer lobster feast), Memorial Day–mid-Oct.; two-night minimum on weekends. Shoulder-season rates (May and late Oct.) are $85–129 d, without dinner. No pets, no children under 14. Open May–Oct.

The Brass Fox, Southern Bay Rd., RR1, Box 218, Rt. 175, Penobscot 04476, 207/326-0575, about seven miles from Blue Hill, is a retirement project for former art teacher Gerry Freeman and his wife, Dawn. Their 1830s farmhouse has three second-floor rooms (private baths) furnished with family antiques and opening onto a sunset-view balcony overlooking the Bagaduce River. After breakfast in the tin-ceilinged dining room, you won't go hungry. Rates are $85–110 d June–Oct., $75–100 the rest of the year. No smoking, no small children. Well-behaved pets are allowed, only in the off-season, for a fee of $10, which the Freemans donate to the greyhound rescue fund. Open all year.

Seasonal Rentals: For information on one-week or longer cottage rentals, contact **Peninsula Property Rentals,** Main St., Blue Hill, 207/374-2428.

Food

Breakfast, Lunch, and Tea: Competition is stiff for lunchtime seats at the **Morning Moon Café,** in the center of Brooklin, junction of Rte. 175 and Naskeag Pt. Rd., Brooklin 04616, 207/359-2373, mostly because *WoodenBoat* staffers consider it an annex to their offices. "The Moon" is a friendly hangout for coffee, pizza, or great sandwiches and salads—or order it to go. Open all year, Tues.–Sun. 7 AM–2 PM.

In North Brooksville, where Rte. 175/176 crosses the Bagaduce River, stands the **Bagaduce Lunch,** a popular takeout stand (outdoor tables only) open daily 11 AM–7 PM (to 8 PM Thurs.–Sat.), mid-May–mid-Sept. Check the tide calendar and go when the tide is changing; order an $8.25 crab roll, settle in at a picnic table, and watch the reversing falls. The food is so-so, the setting is tops.

Country (Everything-and-More) Stores: Across the street from the Morning Moon Café, the **Brooklin General Store,** junction of Rte. 175 and Naskeag Pt. Rd., Brooklin 04616, 207/359-8817, vintage 1872, carries groceries, beer and wine, newspapers, takeout sandwiches, and local chatter. It's open Mon.–Sat. 5 AM–8 PM and Sun. 7 AM–7 PM.

Sargentville's center has the well-stocked **Eggemoggin Country Store,** Rte. 15, Sedgwick 04676, 207/359-2125, source of everything from meat and muffins to beer, wine, liquor, fresh breads, lobster pizza, spit-grilled chicken—and public restrooms. The warehouse-like place is open all year, Mon.–Sat. 6 AM–9 PM and Sun. 7 AM–9 PM (to 8 PM off-season).

Box lunches and boat lunches are specialties at the **Buck's Harbor Market,** Rte. 176, South Brooksville 04617, 207/326-8683, fax 326-9577, a low-key, marginally yuppified general store popular with yachties in summer. It serves breakfast and, for lunch, above-average pizza, quiche, exotic condiments, and freshly baked foccacia. The market is open all year, Mon.–Sat. 7 AM–8 PM, Sun. 8 AM–6 PM. With the café here at the market and summertime steel-band street concerts outside, this is a busy corner.

In South Penobscot village, the **Northern Bay Market,** 207/326-8606, is another little-of-everything country store that's open daily 6:30 AM–8:30 PM. Lobsters and pizza are specialties.

Inexpensive to Moderate: If elegant (read "expensive") dining is on your mind, head for Blue Hill, Deer Isle, or Castine. For easier-on-the-budget prices in off-the-beaten-track locales, try one (or all) of the following. Behind the Buck's Harbor Market is the **Bread & Water Cafe,** Rte. 176, South Brooksville 04617, 207/326-0655, serving a wide range of dinner choices, from clam chowder to grilled quail. Salads are of fresh greens from Eliot Coleman's famous farm, entrées can be haddock or salmon variations, or a burger or rib steak, and are $7.50–19, and there are daily specials. Desserts change nightly. The congenial café—including a full bar seating an extra 18—is open all year, Thurs.–Mon. 5–9:30 PM. No reservations for parties of less than eight.

The dining room at **Oakland House Seaside Inn & Cottages,** Herrick Rd., Brooksville, 207/359-8521, is open to the public by reservation from Memorial Day–mid-Oct. for Sun. brunch (9–11 AM), breakfast buffet (8–9:30 AM), Thurs. night shorefront lobster-bake (6 PM), and dinner all other nights (6–7:45 PM). Entrée range is $16–20.

Owners Gail and Chip Angell see a steady stream of enthusiastic patrons at the **Brooklin Inn,** P.O. Box 25, Rte. 175, Brooklin 04616, 207/359-2777, www.brooklininn.com. Boat nuts to the core, the Angells are certainly in the right place—about midway between *Wood-*

enBoat magazine and the noted Brooklin Boatyard. The menu is elegant—lobster and smoked fish pâté appetizer and a Gulf of Maine halibut filet potato rusted with mahogany clams entrée are examples—and says "We try to know who raised, grew, picked or caught all the food you eat here. All our fish are wild and free swimming and caught in our waters," and producers are listed by name. There is a section of children's choices. Dinner entrées are in the $20–24 range. Dinner served daily, pub open daily. Open all year, but call ahead off-season. Inquire about lodging upstairs—five rooms share two baths.

Also in Brooklin, at the tip of Flye Point, **The Lookout** restaurant, 455 Flye Point Rd., off Rte. 175, North Brooklin, 207/359-2188, www.acadia.net, has a knockout view of Herrick Bay. Dinner is served 5:30–8:30 PM, Memorial Day–Oct. 15. Days vary—call first. Quality can be inconsistent, but you can't beat the scenery.

Information and Services

Finding tourism information about this area can be frustrating, but area residents are usually very helpful in orienting you and making suggestions. Since most visitors in this area start in Blue Hill, see that section for more advice—as well as for information on coping with any **medical emergencies.**

The public libraries in this area are small and welcoming, but hours are limited. The **Friend Memorial Library,** Rte. 175, Brooklin 04616, 207/359-2276, is open Tues.–Sat. 10 AM–4 PM (to 8 PM Wed. and 6 PM Thurs.), closed Wed. in winter. The library's lovely Circle of Friends Garden, with benches and brick patio, is dedicated to the memory of longtime Brooklin residents E.B. and Katharine White. Other area libraries are the **Brooksville Library,** 1 Town House Rd., Rte. 176, Brooksville 04617, 207/326-4560, open Mon. and Wed. 9 AM–5 PM, Thurs. 6–8 PM, and Sat. 9 AM–noon; and **Sedgwick Village Library,** Main St., Sedgwick Village 04676, 207/359-2177, open Wed. 5–7 PM, Thurs. 3–5 PM, and Sat. 9 AM–noon in summer. Winter hours are Thurs. 3–5 PM and

Sat. 10 AM–noon. The all-volunteer library delivers books to the elderly.

CASTINE

Castine (pop. 1,198) is a gem of a place—a serene New England village with a tumultuous past. Once beset by geopolitical squabbles, saluting the flags of three different nations (France, Britain, and Holland), its only crises now are local political skirmishes. This is an unusual community, a National Historic Register enclave that many people never find. The town celebrated its bicentennial in 1996. If you're staying in Blue Hill or even Bar Harbor, spend a day here. Or bunk here and use Castine as a base for exploring here and beyond. Either way, you won't regret it.

Originally known as Fort Pentagoet, Castine received its current name courtesy of Jean-Vincent d'Abbadie, Baron de St.-Castin. A young French nobleman manqué who married a Wabanaki princess named Pidiwamiska, d'Abbadie ran the town in the second half of the 17th century, and eventually returned to France.

A century later, in 1779, occupying British troops and their reinforcements scared off potential American seaborne attackers (including Col. Paul Revere), who turned tail up the Penobscot River and ended up scuttling their more than 40-vessel fleet—a humiliation known as the Penobscot Expedition and still regarded as one of America's worst naval defeats.

During the 19th century, peace and prosperity became the bywords for Castine—with lively commerce in fish and salt—but it all collapsed during the California Gold Rush and the Civil War trade embargo, leaving the town down on its luck.

Today a major presence is Maine Maritime Academy, yet Castine remains the quietest imaginable college town. Students in search of a party school won't find it here; naval engineering is serious business.

What visitors discover is a year-round community with a busy waterfront, an easy-to-conquer layout, a handful of hostelries and boutiques, wooded trails on the outskirts of town, and an astonishing collection of splendid Georgian and Federalist architecture.

Of the many historical landmarks scattered around town, one of the most intriguing must be the sign on "Wind Mill Hill," at the junction of Rte. 166 and State St.: "On Hatch's Hill there stands a mill. Old Higgins he doth tend it. And every time he grinds a grist, he has to stop and mend it." In smaller print, just below the rhyme, comes the drama: "Here two British soldiers were shot for desertion." Castine indeed has quite a history.

Sights

To appreciate Castine fully, you need to arm yourself with the Castine Merchants Association's visitors' brochure/map (all businesses and lodgings in town have copies) and follow the numbers on bike or on foot. With no stops, walking the route takes less than an hour, but you'll want to read dozens of historical plaques, peek into public buildings, shoot some photos, and perhaps even do some shopping.

A highlight of the tour is the **The Wilson Museum,** Perkins St., 207/326-9247, a five-building complex: the museum itself, the blacksmith shop, the Hearse House, the Doudiet house, and the Perkins House. The late-18th-century **John Perkins House** was moved to Perkins St. from Court St. in 1969 and restored with period furnishings. It's now open July–Aug. for guided tours Sun. and Wed. 2–4:45 PM; admission is $5. The Wilson Museum itself, founded in 1921, contains an intriguingly eclectic two-story collection of prehistoric artifacts, ship models, dioramas, baskets, tools, and minerals assembled over a lifetime by John Howard Wilson, a geologist/anthropologist who first visited Castine in 1891 (and died in 1936). Among the exhibits are Balinese masks, cuneiform tablets, Zulu artifacts, pre-Inca pottery, and assorted local findings. Don't miss this. (The only comparable Maine institutions are the Nylander Museum, in Caribou, and the L.C. Bates Museum, in Hinckley.) Open late May–late Sept., Tues.–Sun. 2–5 PM;

free admission. Next door, and open the same hours (free admission), are the **Blacksmith Shop,** where a smith does demonstrations on Wed. and Sun. afternoons from 2–4:45 PM, and the **Hearse House,** containing Castine's 19th-century winter and summer funeral vehicles. The nonprofit **Castine Scientific Society,** P.O. Box 196, Castine 04421, operates the complex. A 1779 **windmill** on Madockawando St., now a private residence, once was a six-gun battery.

At the end of Battle Ave. stands the 19th-century **Dyce's Head Lighthouse,** no longer operating; the keeper's house is owned by the town. Alongside it is a public path (signposted) leading via a wooden staircase to a tiny patch of rocky shoreline and the beacon that has replaced the lighthouse.

Maine Maritime Academy, on Pleasant St., www.mainemaritime.edu, the state's only merchant-marine college (and one of only seven in the nation), founded in 1941, offers undergraduate and graduate degrees in such areas as marine engineering technology, marine transportation operations, international business and logistics, maritime management, and the marine sciences, preparing about 825 men and women for careers as licensed ship's officers, professional engineers, international logisticians, and marine biologists. The academy owns a fleet of 60 vessels, including the historic research schooner *Bowdoin,* flagship of Arctic explorer Adm. Donald Macmillan, and the 500-foot training ship, *State of Maine,* berthed down the hill at the college's waterfront campus. In 1996–97, the T/S *State of Maine,* formerly the U.S. Navy hydrographic survey ship *USNS Tanner,* underwent a $12 million conversion for use as a hands-on training platform at the academy. Midshipmen conduct free 30-minute tours of the vessel on weekdays in summer (about mid-July–late Aug.).The schedule is posted at the dock, or call 207/326-4311 to check. The college's Corning School of Ocean Studies sponsors a free summer Marine Science Interpretive and Information Center in Dirigo House, an historic yellow brick building at the base of Castine's Main St. The center in-

cludes hands-on and visual exhibits of marine life common to the local area, regional seashore ecology, and physical characteristics of Maine's coastal environment. Free guided field excursions are also offered during the summer by student naturalists. Hours and field-excursion dates are posted online during the season at http://oceans.mma.ed, or call 207/326-0706. Campus highlights include three-story Nutting Memorial Library, in Platz Hall (open daily during the school year, weekdays in summer and during vacations, 207/326-2263); the Henry A. Scheel Room, a cozy oasis in Leavitt Hall containing memorabilia from late naval architect Henry Scheel and his wife, Jeanne; and the well-stocked bookstore, 207/326-2430, in Curtis Hall, open year-round weekdays 8 AM–3 PM, excluding campus and national holidays.

Highest point in town is **Fort George State Park,** site of a 1779 British fortification. Nowadays, little remains except grassy earthworks, but there are interpretive displays and picnic tables.

Main Street, descending toward the water, is a feast for historic-architecture fans. Artist Fitz Hugh Lane and author Mary McCarthy once lived in elegant houses along the elm-lined street (neither building is open to the public). On Court St. between Main and Green stands turn-of-the-20th-century **Emerson Hall,** site of Castine's municipal offices. Since Castine has no official information booth, you may need to duck in here (it's open weekdays) for answers to questions.

Across Court St., **Witherle Memorial Library,** a handsome early-19th-century building on the site of the 18th-century town jail, looks out on the Town Common. Also facing the Common are the Adams and Abbott Schools, the former still an elementary school. The **Abbott School,** built in 1859, has been carefully restored for use as a museum/headquarters for the **Castine Historical Society,** P.O. Box 238, Castine 04421, www.castinehistoricalsociety.org. A big draw at the volunteer-run museum, 207/326-4118, is the 24-foot-long Bicentennial Quilt, assembled for Castine's 200th anniversary in 1996. The museum is open July–Labor Day, Tues.–Sat. 10 AM–4 PM and Sun. 1–4 PM. Admission is free, but donations are welcome. The historical society, founded in 1966, organizes lectures, exhibits, and special events (some free) in various locations around town.

Across the narrow neck between Wadsworth Cove and Hatch's Cove stretches a rather overgrown canal scooped out by the occupying British during the War of 1812. Effectively severing land access to the town of Castine, the Brits thus raised havoc, collected local revenues for eight months, then departed for Halifax with enough funds to establish Dalhousie College (now Dalhousie University). Wear waterproof boots to walk the canal route; best time to go is at low tide.

Parks and Recreation

Witherle Woods, a 96-acre preserve owned by Maine Coast Heritage Trust and managed by the Conservation Trust of Brooksville, Castine, and Penobscot, is a popular walking and bicycling area with a maze of numbered trails, formerly British artillery trails. Adjacent property is privately owned, so carry a trail map and stick to it. Access is via a shaded path, signposted Hatch Natural Area, from Battle Ave. Several lodgings keep a supply of maps, or contact (by phone or mail) the **Conservation Trust of Brooksville, Castine, and Penobscot** (CCT), Court St., Box 421, Castine 04421, 207/326-9711. The CCT has been protecting the natural resources of Castine, Penobscot, and Brooksville since the early 1980s. Also ask locally about the **Henderson Natural Area** and other public-access preserves, some of which are accessible only by boat.

If a waterfront picnic sounds appealing, purchase the fixings at Bah's Bakehouse or T & C Market and settle in on the grassy earthworks along the harborfront at **Fort Madison,** site of an 1808 garrison (then Fort Porter) near the corner of Perkins and Madockawando Sts. The views from here are fabulous, and it's accessible all year.

Golf and Tennis: The **Castine Golf Club,**

Battle Ave. and Wadsworth Cove Rd., Castine 04421, 207/326-8844, dates back to 1897, when the first tee required a drive from a 30-step-high mound. Redesigned in 1921 by Willie Park, Jr., the nine-hole course is open May 15–Oct. 15. Starting times are seldom required, and greens fees are reasonable. The club also has four clay tennis courts. Call to schedule a court time.

Bicycling: You can rent a bike at **Dennett's Wharf,** next to the Town Dock, 207/326-9045, for $24 full day, $15 half.

Swimming: Backshore Beach, a crescent of sand and gravel on Wadsworth Cove Rd. (turn off Battle Ave. at the Castine Golf Club), is a favorite saltwater swimming spot, with views across the bay to Stockton Springs. Be forewarned, though, that ocean swimming in this part of Maine is not for the timid. Best time to try it is on the incoming tide, after the sun has had time to heat up the mud. At mid- to high tide, it's also the best place to put in a sea kayak. Park along the road.

If a pool sounds more attractive, the Cary W. Bok indoor pool at Maine Maritime Academy has a limited summer schedule; call 207/326-4311, ext. 451, to confirm.

Getting Afloat

Based at Dennett's Wharf is **Castine Kayak Adventures,** 207/326-9045, www.castinekayak.com. Master Maine Sea Kayak Guide Karen Francoeur, known locally as "Kayak Karen," is particularly adept with beginners, delivering wise advice from beginning to end. All skill levels are accommodated by Karen and her staff. Full-day tours are $105 pp, including an island lunch and usually lots of bird and seal sightings. Half-day tours are 9 AM–noon and 1–4 PM. Cost is $55 pp. Two-hour **sunset tours** are $40 pp; the **sunrise tour** includes breakfast for $45 pp. Friday nights, there are special **phosphorescence tours** under the stars (weather permitting), for $45 pp.

Eaton's Boatyard, Sea St., P.O. Box 123, Castine 04421, 207/326-8579, is a full-service marina renting moorings by the day or week.

You can also buy live lobsters May–Oct. or order them shipped anywhere year-round.

Festivals and Events

Castine's **Fourth of July** celebration is a big one, starting off with a walk/run race, moving to a children's costume parade and tug of war and sack races on the common. Lunch is a pig roast, supper a porch barbecue followed by a concert on the common.

The Maine Maritime Academy's Smith Gym is the site of a **used-book sale** benefiting Witherle Memorial Library the first Saturday of August.

Shopping

Antiques and Galleries: Tucked into the back of the 1796 Parson Mason House, one of Castine's oldest residences, **Leila Day Antiques & Gallery,** 53 Main St., Box 200, 207/326-8786, www.leiladayantiques.com, is a must for anyone in the market for folk art, period furniture, quilts, and 19th-century and contemporary oil paintings. Access is via a lovely, flower-lined walkway. The shop, established in 1978, is open daily 10 AM–5 PM, Memorial Day weekend to Labor Day, by chance or appointment the rest of the year.

McGrath Dunham Gallery, 9 Main St., 207/326-9175, www.mcgrathdunhamgallery.com, a well-lighted, two-story space, shows work by painter Greg Dunham and over three dozen other artists. Open May–mid-Oct., Mon.–Sat. 10 AM–5 PM.

Books: Driving toward Castine on Rte. 166, watch on your right for a small sign for **Dolphin Books and Prints,** 314 Castine Rd., P.O. Box 225, Castine 04421, 207/326-0888, www.dolphin-book.com, where Pete and Liz Ballou have set up their antiquarian business after a dozen years in Camden and decades in the publishing world. Specialties are botanical prints, first editions, biographies, and maritime books. Open June–Sept. 11 AM–5 PM Wed.–Sat., but it's best to call ahead.

In downtown Castine, a block up from the waterfront, **The Compass Rose,** 3 Main St., 207/326-9366, carries an ever-expanding selection of new books, cards, games, and prints chosen by owners Sharon Biggie. In the back of the shop is the well-named **Linger Longer Café,** serving hot and cold drinks (espresso, too), soup, and tasty baked goods. Open all year. Summer hours are 10 AM–5 PM Mon.–Sat. Closed Wed. in fall and winter; winter hours are 10 AM–4 PM.

Gifts and Crafts: Water Witch, Main St., P.O. Box 329, Castine 04421, 207/326-4884, specializes in Indonesian batik and Liberty fabric, clothing, and accessories. Buy off the rack or choose a fabric and a style and Jean de Raat will have it made up flawlessly within a few days. Don't expect a bargain—but it's a lot less than flying to London or Jakarta. Just down the street, close to the harbor, **Four Flags,** 1 Main St., P.O. Box 232, 207/326-8526, carries high-quality Maine and nautical gifts, plus an excellent card selection. Open daily 9:30 AM–5 PM, Apr.–Dec., reduced schedule Jan.–Mar.

Accommodations

Inns and Bed-and-Breakfasts: The three-story **Castine Inn,** Main St., P.O. Box 41, Castine 04421, 207/326-4365, www.castine-inn.com, earns a stellar rating for its stunning semiformal gardens, extremely helpful staff, and mural-lined dining room where the inn is offering a special private-dinner arrangement. The 19 rooms are simply furnished, gradually being updated from their 1890s origins, with twin or queen beds, private baths, and good lighting ($105–275 d, with full breakfast). Two-night minimum July–Labor Day. There's a very simpatico and unpretentious air, encouraged by enthusiastic young innkeepers Amy and Tom Gutow. In the small, English-style pub, hikers, bicyclists, kayakers, and less energetic guests mingle with a loyal local clientele. No pets, no kids under eight. Open late Apr.–late Oct.

Just across the street is the three-story **Pentagoet Inn,** Main St., P.O. Box 4, Castine 04421, 207/326-8616 or 800/845-1701, www.pentagoet.com. Innkeepers Jack Burke and Julie Van de Graaf took over the century-old inn in 2000 and are making a name for it

Acadia Region

in discerning travel circles, with both romantic hideaway and dining awards. Decor is Victorian in the 16 rooms, with luscious antique headboards and lots of gentle pastels. Doubles (all with private baths) are $95–225 in high season, including breakfast, afternoon refreshments, and guest bikes, lower off-season. During the summer, the inn's dining room and the atmospheric Passports Pub is open to guests and the public. Typical dining-room entrées are whole grilled lobster and wild mushroom cannelloni. Baking is done by Van de Graaf, former owner of the acclaimed Pink Rose Pastry Shop in Philadelphia. Reservations are required. Limited pet accommodations; appropriate for older children.

Once the summer "cottage" of a New York Yacht Club commodore, **The Manor Inn,** Battle Ave., P.O. Box 873, Castine 04421, 207/326-4861 or 800/464-7599, www.manor-inn.com, overlooks town and harbor from five mostly wooded acres elevated above Battle Ave. Though the atmosphere is informal, there are lots of elegant architectural touches. Nancy Watson and Tom Ehrman took over in 1998, upgrading beds, linens, and furniture, and expanding the dining room to cater to conferences, weddings, and other events. The 14 second- and third-floor rooms are an eclectic mix—some with canopied beds and fireplaces, all with private baths. Rates are $110–210 d July–Aug., $95–165 d other months, including a full breakfast. Two-night minimum in peak season. Well-behaved kids and pets are allowed. The guest lounge has TV and games, and Nancy has a yoga studio, where guests are welcome to join her classes (for a fee). The trailhead for Witherle Woods is close by. Open all year.

Castine's least-fancy (and least-expensive) rooms are at the **Village Inn,** set back from Main and Water Sts., P.O. Box 183, Castine 04421, 207/326-9510, where summer rates are $85 d (shared bath) to $125 d (private bath and water view). A full breakfast is included. The four-room inn is above Bah's Bakehouse, but noise doesn't seem to be a problem. Open May–Oct.

Seasonal Rentals: Perched in a field along the edge of Hatch's Cove, with terrific views, are the six two-bedroom log cabins of **Castine Cottages,** 33 Snapp's Way, Rte. 166, Castine 04421, 207/326-8003, www.castinecottages.com, operated by Alan and Diana Snapp. Weekly rates are $625 late June–late Sept., $500 early and late in the season. Open all year. You'll need to provide your own sheets and towels. Several Castine realtors have listings for summer cottage rentals; start with **Castine Realty,** Main St., P.O. Box 234, Castine 04421, 207/326-9392, www.castinerealty.com.

Food

Lunch: On lower Main St. is a tiny sign for the creative **Bah's Bakehouse,** Water St., Castine 04421, 207/326-9510, a higgledy-piggledy eatery of three rooms and a deck at the end of an alleyway beneath the Village Inn. Stop here for morning coffee, cold juices, interesting snacks and salads, homemade soups, wine or beer, and the best sandwiches in town ($2.95-7.50; eat in or take out). They'll pack a picnic basket for you or deliver a pre-arranged order dockside. Open Mon.–Sun. 7 AM–5 PM.

T & C Market, corner of Main and Water Sts., 207/326-4818, is the second-best picnic source, and they'll deliver your order if you're aboard a boat or just don't feel like budging. Open all year. Summer hours: Sun.–Wed. 7 AM–8 PM, Thurs.–Sat. 7 AM–9 PM.

Inexpensive to Moderate: Dennett's Wharf, Sea St., next to the Town Dock, P.O. Box 459, 207/326-9045, is a colorful barn of a place with outside deck and front-row windjammer-watching seats in summer. The service is particularly cheerful, and kids are welcome—a kids' menu is available. The varied menu has Black Angus steak as well as vegetarian and seafood selections. Try attaching a dollar bill to the soaring ceiling; countless others have. Open daily 11 AM–midnight, May–Columbus Day. Castine Kayak Adventures is based here.

Expensive: You can arrange for a private dinner at the **Castine Inn,** Main St., Castine 04421, 207/326-4365, with chef/co-owner Tom Gutow as your private chef. Gutow has won acclaim for his culinary ability and will prepare a seven-course dinner, with a fixed menu arranged well in advance, for $90 pp, a wine-pairing menu is additional. The inn's dining room is no longer open on a nightly basis, but the pub still has regular hours.

Dinner at **The Manor Inn,** Battle Ave., Castine 04421, 207/326-4861, is served from an extensive menu, including vegetarian choices (entrées $18–30), 6–8:30 PM Wed.–Mon. in summer. Reservations are advisable on weekends. The inn's cozy pub serves pub-type fare like fish and chips, hamburgers, and chicken pot pie.

Information and Services

Castine has no local information office, but all businesses and lodgings in town have copies of the Castine Merchants Association's visitors' brochure/map. For additional info, go to the **Castine Town Office,** Emerson Hall, Court St., Castine 04421, 207/326-4502. It's open Mon.–Fri. 8 AM–3:30 PM.

Witherle Memorial Library, 41 School St., Box 202, 207/326-4375, www.witherle .lib.me.us, is open Mon. 4–8 PM, Tues.–Fri. 11 AM–5 PM, Sat. 11 AM–2 PM. Also accessible to the public is the **Nutting Memorial Library,** in Platz Hall on the Maine Maritime Academy campus. It's open Mon.–Fri. 8 AM–4:30 PM during summer, longer hours during the school year.

Newspapers: The *Castine Patriot,* published every Thursday, has the best local coverage, including calendar listings. The *Bangor Daily News,* published daily, carries local, state, and a smidgen of international news. The *Ellsworth American* is published every Thurs. June–Sept. The *American* publishes *Out & About in Downeast Maine,* a free monthly vacation supplement in tabloid format.

Emergencies: For emergencies in **Castine,** call 911. **Castine Community Health Services,** Court and Dyer Sts., 207/326-4348. The nearest acute-care hospital is Blue Hill Memorial Hospital.

Veterinarians/Kennels: Boarding facilities are available in Bucksport, Ellsworth, and Surry. For animal emergencies, most Castine residents rely on the Bucksport Veterinary Hospital in Orland, which also has kennels.

Other Services: The Castine **post office,** Main St., between Court and Perkins Sts., Castine 04421, 207/326-8551, reportedly is the nation's oldest continuously used post office, dating from 1815. A ham-handed government attempt to relocate it several years ago resulted in an unholy outcry. It worked. The building has since been upgraded, expanded to the rear, and left in its prominent downtown location. There are **public restrooms** on the town dock, at the foot of Main St.

Getting Around

There is no public transportation within Castine, but the village itself is easily walkable or bikeable.

DEER ISLE

"Deer Isle is like Avalon," wrote John Steinbeck in *Travels with Charley*—"it must disappear when you are not there." Deer Isle (the name of both the island and its midpoint town) has been romancing authors and artisans for decades, but it's unmistakably real to the quarry and fisherfolk who've been here for centuries. These longtimers are a sturdy lot—as even Steinbeck recognized: "I would hate to try to force them to do anything they didn't want to do."

Early-18th-century maps show no name for the island, but by the late 1800s, nearly a hundred families lived here, supporting themselves first by farming, then by fishing. In 1789, when Deer Isle was incorporated, some 80 local sailing vessels were scouring the Gulf of Maine in pursuit of mackerel and cod, and Deer Isle men were circling the globe as yachting skippers and merchant seamen. At the same time, in the once-quiet village of Green's Landing (now called Stonington), the shipbuilding and granite industries boomed, spurring development, prosperity, and the kinds of rough hijinks typical of commercial ports the world over.

Green's Landing became the "big city" for

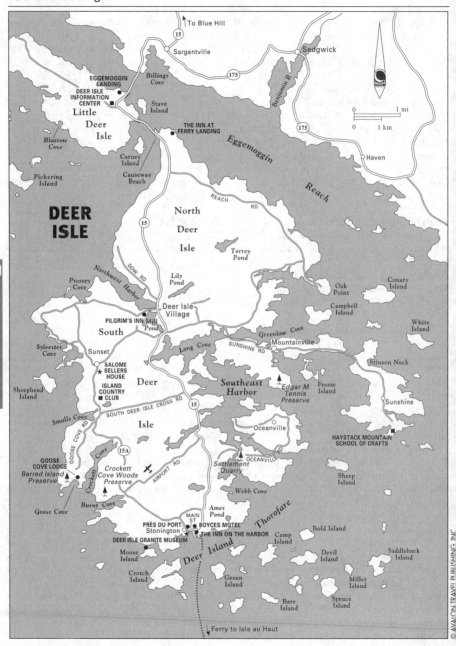

To Blue Hill
15
Sargentville
175
Sedgwick

EGGEMOGGIN
LANDING
DEER ISLE
INFORMATION
CENTER
Billings
Cove
Stave
Island

Little
Deer
Isle

Blastow
Cove

Carney
Island

Causeway
Beach

THE INN AT
FERRY LANDING

Eggemoggin

Haven

Benjamin R.

175

Pickering
Island

REACH
RD

North
Deer
Isle

REACH

Reach

15

DOW RD

Northwest Harbor

Pressey
Cove

Lily
Pond

Torrey
Pond

Oak
Point

Conary
Island

Campbell
Island

White
Island

Deer Isle
Village

DEER
ISLE

PILGRIM'S INN
Mill
Pond

South

Greenlaw Cove

SUNSHINE RD

Mountainville

Stinson Neck

Sylvester
Cove

Sunset

Long Cove

SALOME
SELLERS
HOUSE

ISLAND
COUNTRY
CLUB

Deer

Southeast
Harbor

Edgar M
Tennis
Preserve

Freese
Island

Sunshine

Sheephead
Island

SOUTH DEER ISLE CROSS RD

Isle

15

Smalls Cove

GOOSE COVE RD

15A

Crockett Cove

Crockett
Cove Woods
Preserve

AIRPORT RD

Oceanville

HAYSTACK MOUNTAIN
SCHOOL OF CRAFTS

GOOSE
COVE LODGE
Barred Island
Preserve

OCEANVILLE RD

Settlement
Quarry

Sheep
Island

Goose Cove

Burnt Cove

Webb Cove

Ames
Pond

MAIN
ST

PRÈS DU PORT
Stonington

BOYCES MOTEL
THE INN ON THE HARBOR

Thorofare

Camp
Island

Bold Island

DEER ISLE GRANITE MUSEUM

Deer Island

Moose
Island

Devil
Island

Saddleback
Island

Crotch
Island

Green
Island

Millet
Island

Bare
Island

Spruce
Island

Ferry to Isle au Haut

0   1 mi
0   1 km

MOON

Acadia Region

© AVALON TRAVEL PUBLISHING, INC.

an international crowd of quarrymen carving out the terrain on Deer Isle and nearby Crotch Island, source of high-quality granite for Boston's Museum of Fine Arts, the Smithsonian Institution, a humongous fountain for John D. Rockefeller's New York estate, and less showy projects all along the eastern seaboard. The heyday is long past, but the industry did extend into the 20th century (including a contract for the pink granite at President John F. Kennedy's Arlington National Cemetery gravesite). Today, Crotch Island is the site of Maine's only operating island granite quarry.

Measuring about nine miles north to south (plus another three miles for Little Deer Isle), the island of Deer Isle today has a handful of hamlets (including Sunshine, Sunset, Mountainville, and Oceanville) and two towns—Stonington and Deer Isle—with a population just under 3,200. Road access is via Rte. 15 on the Blue Hill Peninsula. A huge suspension bridge, built in 1939 over Eggemoggin Reach, links the Sargentville section of Sedgwick with Little Deer Isle; from there,

a sinuous, 0.4-mile causeway connects to the northern tip of Deer Isle.

Eight miles off Stonington lies 4,700-acre Isle au Haut, roughly half of which belongs to Acadia National Park. Pronounced variously as "I'll-a-HO" or "I'LL-a-ho," the island has nearly 20 miles of hiking trails, excellent birding, a tiny village, and one rustic, romantic, and pricey inn.

Sights

Sightseeing on Deer Isle means exploring back roads, browsing the galleries, walking the trails, hanging out on the docks, soaking in the ambience.

The 1830 **Salome Sellers House,** Rte. 15A, Sunset Village, 207/348-2897, a repository of local memorabilia, is the headquarters of the **Deer Isle-Stonington Historical Society.** Volunteer guides love to provide tidbits about various items; seafarers' logs and ship models are particularly intriguing. Located just north of the Island Country Club and across from Eaton's Plumbing, the house is open Wed. and Fri. 1–4 PM, mid-June–late Sept.

Settlement Quarry, Deer Isle

: KATHLEEN M. BRANDES

Acadia Region

Close to the Stonington waterfront, the **Deer Isle Granite Museum,** Main St., P.O. Box 469, Stonington 04681, 207/367-6331, was established to commemorate the centennial of the quarrying business hereabouts. Best feature of the small museum is an is a 15-foot-long working model of Crotch Island, center of the industry, as it appeared at the turn of the 20th century. Flatcars roll, boats glide, and derricks move—it all looks very real. The museum is July to Labor Day, 9 AM–5 PM daily. Admission is free, but donations are accepted.

Another downtown-Stonington attraction is a Lilliputian complex known hereabouts as the "Miniature Village." Some years ago, the late Everett Knowlton created a dozen and a half replicas of local buildings and displayed them on granite blocks in his yard. Since his death, they've been restored and put on display each summer in town—along with a donation box to support the upkeep. The village is set up on E. Main St. (Rte. 15).

Parks and Preserves

Foresighted benefactors have managed to set aside precious acreage for respectful public use on Deer Isle. The Nature Conservancy owns two properties, **Crockett Cove Woods Preserve** and **Barred Island Preserve.** For information, contact the Conservancy, 14 Maine St., Fort Andross, Brunswick 04011, 207/729-5181. The conscientious steward of other local properties is the **Island Heritage Trust** (IHT), Main St., at Rte. 15, P.O. Box 42, Deer Isle 04627, 207/348-2455. When the office is open (9 AM–5 PM weekdays, year-round), you can pick up note cards, photos, T-shirts, and maps and information on hiking trails and nature preserves. Proceeds benefit the IHT's efforts to protect land in the Deer Isle are that has natural and cultural value, including Settlement Quarry.

Settlement Quarry has one of the easiest, shortest hikes (a stroll, really) in the area, leading to an impressive vista. From the parking lot on Oceanville Rd. (just under a mile off Rte. 15), marked by a carved granite sign, it's about five minutes to the top of the old quarry, where the viewing platform takes in the panorama—all the way to Isle au Haut on a good day. Three short loop trails lead into the surrounding woods from there. A map is available in the trailhead box. Other IHT preserves include **Shore Acres,** in the Fish Creek area of Deer Isle, and **Causeway Beach,** a swimming beach (for those with Viking genes) on the Deer Isle end of the causeway.

Inquire locally about the **Holt Mill Pond** and the **Edgar M. Tennis Preserves.** The 120-acre Tennis Preserve, in particular, off the Sunshine Rd., has very limited parking, so don't try to squeeze in if there isn't room; schedule it for another hour or day. When you go, allow at least 90 minutes to enjoy the 1.5-mile yellow-blazed trail. Part of the trail skirts Pickering Cove, with convenient rocky outcrops for a picnic (carry in, carry out, though). The preserve is open sunrise to sunset.

Crockett Cove Woods Preserve: Donated to The Nature Conservancy by benevolent, eco-conscious local artist Emily Muir, 98-acre Crockett Cove Woods Preserve is Deer Isle's natural gem—a coastal fog forest laden with lichens and mosses. There are trails throughout the entire preserve, starting with a short nature trail. Pick up the helpful map/brochure at the registration box. Wear rubberized shoes or boots and respect adjacent private property. The preserve is open daily, sunrise to sunset, all year. Admission is free; no camping. From Deer Isle Village, take Rte. 15A to Sunset Village. Go 2.5 miles to Whitman Rd., then to Fire Lane 88.

Ames Pond: There's excellent birding at Ames Pond, which is neither park nor preserve, but it might as well be. On a back road close to Stonington, it's a mandatory stop July–Aug., when the pond wears a blanket of pink and white water lilies. From downtown Stonington, take Indian Point Rd. east, just under a mile, to the pond. There's no official parking, so if you're shooting photos, pull off the road as far as possible, respecting private property.

Recreation

Bicycling: As with so many other parts of

Maine, the roads on Deer Isle are narrow and winding, with inadequate shoulders for bikes, so be particularly cautious. In general, Deer Isle is fairly level, so we're not talking rigorous. Rte. 15, the major north-south artery, has the heaviest traffic, so plan to cycle on the less-busy side routes.

Some lodgings provide bicycles for guests, or you can bring your own. Rental bikes—for adults, no booster seats—are available from **Old Quarry Ocean Adventures** for $18 a day (Apr.–Oct.). Old Quarry Ocean Adventures also offers the opportunity to bike to the Acadia's Isle au Haut Campground, with an Acadia Hike & Bike Adventure & Ferry Service to Isle Au Haut—their lobster boat ferries you to the island (you take your own bike or rent a bike from them and ride to park hiking trails), making it possible to see the park in a reasonable amount of time without camping. You need to be in good shape. The boat trip is $32 round-trip adult, $15 under 12. Trip leaves Stonington at 9 AM and Isle au Haut at 5 PM, arriving back in Stonington at 6 PM.

The same folks who run the restaurant, run **Finest Kind Bike Rentals,** Center District Crossroad, (halfway between Rte. 15 and 15A), Deer Isle, 207/348-7714, www. finestkindenterprises.com, renting adult and children's mountain bikes for $15 a day adult, $10 children, and $10/5 half-day. An easy, five-mile round-trip starts at the Chamber of Commerce information booth on Little Deer Isle. Park your car there and head northwest along Eggemoggin Rd. to the tip of Little Deer Isle. From the turnaround at road's end, there's a splendid view of **Pumpkin Island Light** and Cape Rosier (Brooksville) in the distance. If you plan this spin for late afternoon, you can backtrack on Eggemoggin Rd. and detour down Blastow's Cove Rd. to Eaton's Lobster Pool for dinner and a sunset.

From Deer Isle village, a seven-mile route goes east along the Sunshine Rd., through Mountainville, to Sunshine and south to the Haystack Mountain School of Crafts. On the way, stop at Nervous Nellie's. If you're staying at the Sunshine Campground, you can do the route in reverse.

Swimming: The island's only major freshwater swimming hole is the **Lily Pond,** northeast of Deer Isle village. Just north of the Shakespeare School, turn into the Deer Run Apartments complex. Park and take the path to the pond, which has a shallow area for small children.

Golf and Tennis: About two miles south of Deer Isle village, watch for the large sign (on the left) for the **Island Country Club,** Rte. 15A, Sunset, 207/348-2379, a nine-hole public course that's been here since 1928. Starting times aren't needed, and greens fees are moderate. Open late May–late Sept. Also at the club are three beautifully maintained tennis courts. Or just commandeer a rocking chair and watch the action from one of the porches. The club's cheeseburgers are among the island's best bargain lunches.

Getting Afloat

Sea Kayaking: With lots of islets and protected coves in the waters around Deer Isle, especially off Stonington, sea kayaking has come up fast in the recreation department. The biggest kayaking operation is **Old Quarry Ocean Adventures,** 130 Settlement Rd., Stonington 04681, 207/367-8977, www.oldquarry.com, with a broad range of outdoor-adventure choices. Bill Baker's ever-expanding enterprise rents canoes, kayaks, sailboats, bikes, moorings, and tent, RV, and platform sites. All-day guided tours in single kayaks are $105; tandems are $175. Half-day tours are $55 and $110, respectively. Rental rates are $55 per day for a single, $65 for a tandem. Half-day rates are $40 and $50, respectively. If you bring your own kayak, park your car and launch from here ($5 per boat for launching, $6 per night for parking). Filing a float plan, being monitored, and, if necessary and has happened, being rescued, accompany the launch charge.

Another way to get afloat with Old Quarry is their Afternoon Sight-Seeing & Natural History Cruise, a three-hour trip through the Stonington Archipelago, home to seabirds,

Acadia Region

eagles, osprey, harbor seals, and porpoises. Kids like the lobster trap hauling; everyone enjoys passing a lighthouse, coastal schooners, and an active granite quarry. Take a swim suit and a towel for a dip in an island quarry. $35 pp, $20 under 12. Old Quarry is off the Oceanville Rd., less than a mile from Rte. 15, just before you reach the Settlement Quarry preserve. It's well signposted.

A smaller kayaking outfitter is in the village of Sunset—not surprisingly, located on the western side of the island. **Granite Island Guide Service,** 66 Dunham Point Rd., Deer Isle 04627, 207/348-2668, www.graniteisland-guide.com, is owned by Dana Douglass and his wife, Anne, both registered Maine Guides. June–Sept., all-day guided trips, including lunch, are $90 adults, $60 children under 12. Half-day trips are $50 adults, $40 children. They also lead canoe trips on the St. John River in May, the Allagash Wilderness Waterway, the Penobscot River's West Branch, and Chesuncook Lake at various times in spring and fall.

You get a good deal at **Finest Kind Canoe & Kayak Rentals,** Center District Crossroad, (halfway between Rtes. 15 and 15A), Deer Isle, 207/348-7714, www.finestkindenterprises.com, renting kayaks with no-extra-charge pickup and delivery for $35 a day, $45 for tandem.

If you sign up with the **Maine Island Trail Association,** (P.O. Box C, Rockland 04841, www.mita.org, 207/596-6456; $45 a year), you'll receive a handy manual that steers you to more than a dozen islands in the Deer Isle archipelago where you can camp, hike, and picnic—ecosensitively. Boat traffic can be a bit heavy at the height of summer, so to best appreciate the tranquility of this area, try this in September, after the Labor Day holiday. Nights can be cool, but days are likely to be brilliant.

If you're not up for self-propulsion, from mid-June through Labor Day, the excursion boat *Miss Lizzie* departs at 2 PM daily from the Isle au Haut Boat Company dock on Sea Breeze Ave. in Stonington for a narrated trip among the islands. Cost of the memorable hour-long trip is $14 adults, $6 kids under 12. Reser-

vations are advisable. Reservations: 207/367-5193 or 367-6516. *Miss Lizzie* is owned by the same company that operates the regular mail boat/passenger-ferry service to offshore Isle au Haut.

Festivals and Events

From early June to late Aug., on varying weeknights, evening slide programs, lectures, demonstrations, and concerts are open to the public at **Haystack Mountain School of Crafts,** in Sunshine.

In mid-June, when lupines color the hillsides, Deer Isle's **Lupine Festival** brings visitors to follow the Lupine Loop Map, browse a craft fair, take a boat excursion or garden tour, and see an art-and-sculpture show.

July brings the **Stonington Lobsterboat Races,** very popular competitions held in the harbor, with lots of possible vantage points. Stonington is one of the major locales in the lobsterboat race circuit.

Shopping

Antiques and Antiquarian Books: When you head south, toward Deer Isle village, you'll come to **Old Deer Isle Parish House Antiques,** 7 Church St., Rte. 15, P.O. Box 445, Deer Isle 04627, 207/348-9964 or 367-2455, a funky shop heavy into vintage clothing and linens, antique kitchen utensils, and other collectibles. No credit cards. Open mid-June–Oct., Mon.–Fri. 11 AM–6 PM and Sat.–Sun. 2–6 PM.

Anyone on the trail of rare books should also be sure to stop en route to Deer Isle at **Wayward Books,** in Sargentville, just the other side of the Deer Isle bridge.

When you get to the bottom of the island, **The Clown,** Main St., Stonington 04681, 207/367-6348, awaits. The imaginative owners came up with this combination of art, antiques, and. . . food and wine. Look, it works. In fact, it has worked so well that there's now a larger branch in Portland's Old Port district, and one in downtown Belfast. Part of the key is the owners' farm in Tuscany, source of olive oil, wines, unusual furnishings, and other "necessities." Art openings are also wine tastings—a fine idea. Open June–Oct., Tues.–Sat. 10 AM– 6 PM (also Mon. July–Aug.).

Art and Crafts Galleries: Thanks to the presence and influence of Haystack Mountain School of Crafts, super-talented artists and artisans lurk in every corner of the island. Most are tucked away on back roads, and many have studios open to the public, so watch for roadside signs and pick up a free copy (available in shops and galleries statewide) of the Maine Crafts Association's annual *Maine Guide to Craft Artists and Culture.* The MCA, formerly headquartered here on the island, is now based in Portland, 207/780-1807.

Name a craft and Mary Nyburg probably has an example in her high-ceilinged barn, the **Blue Heron Gallery & Studio,** Church St., Deer Isle 04627, 207/348-6051, www.blueherondeerisle.com. Formerly a Haystack board member and still an honorary trustee, her gallery provides a retail outlet for the work of the school's internationally renowned faculty—printmakers, blacksmiths, potters, weavers, papermakers, glassworkers, and more. Prices are reasonable. The gallery is open Mon.–Sat. 10 AM–5:30 PM and Sun. 1–5:30 PM, early June–mid-Oct., but hours are less predictable after Labor Day, so call ahead.

The **Deer Isle Artists Association** (DIAA) is headquartered less than a mile northwest of Deer Isle village at 6 Dow Rd., P.O. Box 634, Deer Isle 04627, 207/348-2330, www.deerisleartists.com. The DIAA's co-op gallery features two-week exhibits of paintings, prints, drawings, and photos by local pros. Open daily, 11 AM–5 PM, mid-June–mid-Sept.

One of the island's premier galleries gained a larger home in 1996. Elena Kubler moved **The Turtle Gallery,** Rte. 15, P.O. Box 219, Deer Isle 04627, 207/348-9977, www.turtlegallery.com, to a handsome space formerly known as the Old Centennial House Barn (owned by retired Haystack director Francis Merritt). Group and solo shows of contemporary paintings, prints, and crafts are hung upstairs and down, and there's a Sculpture Court.

Just north of Deer Isle village—across from the Shakespeare School, oldest on the island—the gallery is open May–Oct., Mon.–Sat. 10 AM–5:30 PM and Sun. 2–6 PM, the rest of the year by appointment.

You will find some old rugs, most new, at **William Mor Oriental Rugs,** 663 Reach Rd., Deer Isle 04627, 207/348-2822, www.williammororientalrugs.com. The rugs may be new, but they are handwoven in traditional ways of vegetable-dyed yarns. The select stock includes Afghan and Tibetan rugs via the nonprofit Cultural Survival organization—stunning work for a worthy cause. Mor is also a potter, and sells his work, too. The shop is open daily 10 AM–5 PM, May–Oct., other times by appointment. Reach Rd. is a mile south of the Rte. 15 Little Deer Isle-Deer Isle causeway; the shop is 3.5 miles down the road.

Gifts: If you're looking for pottery, "wooden things," jewelry, any type of tiles, or walking sticks, go directly to **Harbor Farm,** Rte. 15, P.O. Box 64, Little Deer Isle 04650, 207/348-7737 or 800/342-8003, www.harborfarm.com, one of the state's best gift shops, and source for imported and U.S. tiles. Based in a mid-19th-century schoolhouse a mile south of the Deer Isle suspension bridge, the Lee and Richard McWilliams carry thousands of very unusual, high-quality items, and it's all available by mail as well. They also sell evergreens and wreaths. Hours are Mon.–Sat. 10 AM–5 PM.

Also well stocked with Maine-made gifts and crafts is **The Rugosa Rose,** Main St., Deer Isle 04627, 888/778-7505, on the grounds of The Pilgrim's Inn. It's all very tasteful, so you can't go wrong; over 20 local artists have their work here. The small, two-story shop is open daily 8 AM–8 PM, mid-May–mid-Oct.

Deer Isle may be the unlikeliest spot in all of Maine for an African gift shop, but it's here. **Deepest Africa Imports,** 171 Dow Rd., Deer Isle 04627, 207/348-6624, www.deepestafrica.com, is the creation of South African-born Jackie Pelletier, who has stocked her small shop with carvings, baskets, hand-printed fabrics, traditional jewelry, and more, from over two dozen African countries.

Several of her sources are cottage industries supporting women and the disadvantaged, she practices fair trade, and gives 10 percent of profits to an AIDS hospice in South Africa. The shop is open throughout the summer, 1–5 PM Tues.–Sat.

Now for a bit of whimsy. From Rte. 15 in Deer Isle village, take the Sunshine Rd. east 2.9 miles to **Nervous Nellie's Jams and Jellies,** 598 Sunshine Rd., Deer Isle 04627, 207/348-6182 or 800/777-6845, www.nervousnellies .com, to visit the jam kitchen, where jam is poured Mon.–Thurs. Outstandingly creative condiments are the rule here; sample the hot-pepper jelly or blackberry-peach conserve or cranberry-peach chutney. The promotional brochures are hilarious. Best time to come is May–Oct., when the shop operates the ultra-casual **Mountainville Café,** serving tea, coffee, and delicious scones, brownies, and linzertorte—with, of course, Nervous Nellie's products. While you're at it, the surrounding meadow teems with whimsical wood and metal sculptures (all for sale) by Nellie's owner Peter Beerits. Kids are welcome to play in the sand-box under the apple tree. The condiments are available by mail, but that's missing half the fun. The shop is open daily 9 AM–5 PM, May–Christmas, and often daily during the off-season, but call ahead to check off-season.

In downtown Stonington, below the Opera House, **Dockside Books & Gifts,** 62 W. Main St., P.O. Box 205, Stonington 04681, 207/367-2652, carries just what its name promises, with a specialty in marine and Maine books. Nautical gifts, charts, and fabulous locally hand-knit sweaters for children and adults can also be found here. The rustic two-room shop owned by Elmer Webber is open mid-May–mid-Oct.

Clothing: Be careful going into **The Dry Dock,** 24 Main St., P.O. Box 485, Stonington 04681, 207/367-5528—the merchandise sells itself. Women's clothing by young American designers, and imported from Nigerian, Tibetan, and Indian cottage industries, unique jewelry, great crafts from Haystack artists, and unusual note cards are just some of the options

in one large room and a smaller back room. The shop is open May–Christmas, 9 AM–5 PM daily.

Farmers Market: The **Deer Isle/Stonington Farmers Market** is held from Mother's Day–Oct. Fri. 10 AM–noon in the Congregational Church parking lot in Deer Isle village. A broad array of stands offer smoked meats, fresh herbs and hydroponic lettuce, organic produce, honey and spices, cheese and breads, and more.

Accommodations

Inns and Bed-and-Breakfasts: The most elegant place to sleep on Deer Isle is in one of the antiques-filled rooms at the **Pilgrim's Inn,** 20 Main St., P.O. Box 69, Deer Isle 04627, 207/348-6615 or 888/778-7505, www.pil-grimsinn.com, a beautifully restored Colonial building overlooking the peaceful Mill Pond. Rates, including breakfast, are $99 d for a small room off-season to $229 d for a supreme room for one or two nights at the height of the season (there are four rate seasons.) Two water-view units at "Ginny's," the building next door, are $179–249 in season with breakfast, or $100 off-season (no breakfast). Ginny's units are open all year. The Rugosa Rose cottage runs $199–259 d. The National Historic Register inn began life in 1793 as a boardinghouse named the Ark; be sure to check out the fascinating guestbook, with names dating to 1901. The inn has sloping lawns, bikes for guests, an adjacent gift shop, and a fine dining room, the Whale's Rib Tavern, serving dinner to guests and the public at 5 PM by reservation. No pets, no children under 10 in the inn; families are welcome in cottages, which permit pets, for a $50 fee. Open early May–late Oct.

Just when you're convinced you're lost, and the paved road has turned to dirt, you arrive at **Goose Cove Lodge,** Goose Cove Rd., P.O. Box 40, Sunset 04683, 207/348-2508 or 800/728-1963 outside Maine, www.goosecovelodge.com, a 20-acre hillside complex of rustic and modern cottages/cabins and main-lodge rooms and suites—all with private baths, most with fireplaces, and many with stunning views of secluded Goose Cove. Request one of the seven older "secluded cabins," with cove-facing decks. Rates vary widely here, and so does the decor; the cost can add up (service and lodging taxes are 22 percent on top of the quoted rate). Some cabins/cottages require a three-person-minimum rate July–Labor Day. B&B rates in the high season are $185–525 d; don't forget to add the cost of dinner per day for two (dining room closed Mon. nights). Late-fall B&B rates are $130–200 d, but not all services are open. The inn organizes nature walks and astronomy talks and provides maps and descriptions of local trails, including Barred Island Preserve, close to the lodge property. Bikes, kayaks, and games are available for guests. The dining room, open to the public by reservation for breakfast and dinner, has a reputation well beyond Deer Isle. No pets. Children are welcome at this family-oriented spot; there's a no-extra-charge children's program, Kids Camp, July–Aug., and children eat together on midsummer evenings, in Toad Hall. The inn is open mid-May–mid-Oct. The lodge is 4.5 miles from Rte. 15, via Deer Isle village.

In 1995, a longtime downtown-Stonington landmark known as the Captain's Quarters changed hands, became the **Inn on the Harbor,** Main St., P.O. Box 69, Stonington 04681, 207/367-2420 or 800/942-2420, www.innontheharbor.com, and headed a bit upscale. But not totally; the updated 1880s complex still has an air of unpretentiousness. Most of the 13 rooms and suites have fantastic harbor views, some have private decks and wood-burning fireplaces, and you can keep an eye on lobsterboats, small ferries, windjammers, and pleasure craft from the inn's deck, which extends into the harbor. An espresso bar is open 11 AM–4:30 PM daily in season. Nearby are antiques, gift, and craft shops; guest moorings are available. Rates are $119–144 d in season, including extensive homemade continental breakfast. The American Eagle, a two-bedroom apt., is $199. No pets, no children under 12; smoking only on decks. Open all year, but call ahead off-season.

Eggemoggin Reach is almost on the doorstep at **The Inn at Ferry Landing,** 77 Old Ferry Rd., Deer Isle 04627, 207/348-7760, www.ferrylanding.com, overlooking the abandoned Sargentville–Deer Isle ferry wharf. The view is wide open from the inn's "great room," where guests gather to read, play games, talk, and watch passing windjammers. Professional musician Gerald Wheeler has installed two grand pianos in the room; it's a treat when he plays. His wife, Jean, is the hospitable innkeeper. Three water-view guest rooms and a private-entrance suite go for $120–175 d, full breakfast included. A harpsichord and a great view are big pluses in the suite. The Mooring, an annex that sleeps five, is rented by the week (no breakfast) July–Aug. ($1,400 weekly), for three nights (minimum) other months. No pets, no children under 10 in the main building; kids are welcome in the annex. The inn is open all year except Thanksgiving and Christmas.

In downtown Stonington, convenient for walking to everything (even a small sandy beach a mile away), is **Prés du Port,** W. Main St. and Highland Ave., P.O. Box 319, Stonington 04681, 207/367-5007, www.presduport.com, a bright B&B run by amiable innkeeper Charlotte Casgrain. After many summers at a Deer Isle French summer camp, and a career as a Connecticut French teacher, she's settled here. Two rooms have detached baths, one has a private bath; vanity sinks in the rooms ($125 d). Amenities include a Jacuzzi and in-room refrigerators; full buffet breakfast is included in the rate. Children are welcome; there's even a toy cupboard to entertain them; grownups might be entertained by "Charlotte's Folly," a crow's nest on the roof—on a clear day you can see forever. No credit cards. Open May 1–Oct. When Deer Isle beds are scarce at the height of summer, Charlotte is the best resource for dozens of last-minute overnight rooms in local homes. This location is ideal if you're en route to or returning from Isle au Haut.

Geared to sea kayakers and the low-key boating set is **Oceanville Seaside Bed-and-Breakfast,** Oceanville Rd., RR 1, Box 890,

Stonington 04681, 207/367-2226, Tim and Kathy Emerson's mid-19th-century Cape-style home at 44°11' N, 68°37' W. It's tough to find a more idyllic setting for a paddling or sailing rest stop—a secluded, pink-granite-lined cove overlooking ocean and islands. The kitchen and living room in this informal spot have tin ceilings and great views. Nearby are miles of trails. A first-floor room (shared bath) is $80 d; the second-floor suite (private bath), sleeping five, is $90 d ($25 per extra person). Kathy's fabulous breakfasts are included; she'll prepare dinner (extra charge; BYOL) by prior arrangement. No smoking, no credit cards, no children under five. A mooring is available for guests; kayakers can paddle in and paddle out on any tide. As if all that isn't enough, the Emersons can send you off to spruce-covered Sheep Island, owned by their family, for hiking, birding, and picnicking. The B&B, east of Stonington in the hamlet of Oceanville, is open all year by reservation.

Seasonal Rentals: For house and cottage rentals by the week, month, or season, contact **Island Vacation Rentals,** 50 Main St., P.O. Box 446, Stonington 04681, 207/367-5095, www .deerisleproperties.com. Plan well ahead, as the best properties get snapped up as much as a year in advance. Or contact Jean Ford at **Sargent's Rentals,** P.O. Box 115, Stonington 04681, 207/367-5156, www.sargentsrentalsinc.com.

Campgrounds: There are only two camp-grounds on Deer Isle, so plan ahead if you're thinking about camping. Offshore, on Isle au Haut, are a few sought-after lean-tos managed by Acadia National Park and available only by reservation.

Sunshine Campground, RR1, Box 521D, Deer Isle 04627, 207/348-2663, www.sunshine-campground.com, has 24 wooded RV (maximum 40 feet) and tent sites for $24–28 (for one or two people, per-night fees for additional). Facilities include firewood, horseshoe area, and a small store. Leashed pets are allowed. The campground is associated with Old Quarry Ocean Adventures. Open late May to the beginning of October. From Deer Isle village, the campground is on the Sunshine Rd., 5.7 miles east of Rte. 15.

Food

Stonington is a dry town, so you'll want to plan ahead for beer or wine with dinner. Burnt Cove Market can fix you up; buy fine wines at the Clown.

You'll find a creative menu at **Lily's Café,** Rte. 15, P.O. Box 653, Stonington 04681, 207/367-5936, in a cute house at the corner of Airport Rd., just over two miles from down-town. It's all very casual; order at the counter and find a table. (Some of the tables have fun windowpane shadowboxes.) Eat here—full breakfast and lunch served—or assemble a *haut gourmet* picnic: veggie and meat sand-wiches, Mediterranean salads, cheeses, and homemade soups and breads. BYOL. In summer (from Memorial Day), Lily's is open week-days 7 AM–5 PM.

Best pizza on the island? Head for **Burnt Cove Market,** Rte. 15, Stonington, 207/367-2681. Besides pizza, you can get fried chicken and sandwiches, plus beer and wine. The store is open all year, Mon.–Sat. 6 AM–8 PM (to 9 PM Fri.–Sat.) and Sun. 9 AM–8 PM.

Inexpensive to Moderate: July–Aug., don't show up at **Finest Kind Dining,** Center District Cross Rd., P.O. Box 388, Deer Isle 04627, 207/348-7714, www.finestkindenter-prises.com, without a dinner reservation. This log-cabin family restaurant is no longer a se-cret. Nothing fancy—just good, homemade all-American food served conscientiously in a come-as-you-are setting. Pizza, pasta, prime rib, seafood. And save room for dessert. Wheel-chair access; liquor license. Open May–Oct., 5–9 PM daily. The restaurant is halfway be-tween Rte. 15 and Sunset Rd. (Rte. 15A). Ad-jacent is **Round the Island Mini Golf** (same phone, open the same months). Finest Kind also rents canoes, kayaks, and bikes.

The Fisherman's Friend Restaurant, Main St., Stonington 04681, 207/367-2442, gets high marks for respectable food, gener-ous portions, fresh seafood, and outstanding desserts. It's all very casual—pine paneling, booths, and reasonable prices. A local favor-ite for years. BYOL. Open daily 11 AM–8 PM (to 9 PM summer), Apr.–late Oct. Another respectable choice, open all year, is **Connie's Restaurant,** School St., Rte. 15A, Stonington, 207/367-2742, where you'll find daily specials and local flavor. Mon.–Thurs. 7 AM–2 PM, Fri.–Sun. 7 AM–7:30 PM. No credit cards.

Moderate to Expensive: Both restaurants in this category are conveniently linked to lodgings. If you have the time, and your wallet and waistline will stand it, be sure to try them both. (They also both have full liquor licenses, so no need to BYOL.)

At the **Pilgrim's Inn,** Main St., Sunset Rd., Deer Isle Village 04627, 207/348-5222 (dining room), www.pilgrimsinn.com, dinner is an elegantly casual affair, in the restored barn and adjacent small dining room. The huge menu has lobster, pasta, many seafood choices, plus chicken, beef, and pork entrées; entrées average about $15. This is a grown-up kind of place, so don't bring children unless they qualify as angelic. Open mid-May–mid-Oct., serving 4:30–9:30 PM.

Running head-to-head with the Pilgrim's Inn in the culinary department is **Goose Cove Lodge,** Goose Cove Rd., P.O. Box 40, Sunset 04683, 207/348-2508, www.goosecovelodge .com, where creative dinners are served to guests and the public in the attractive main lodge restaurant, called The Point Dining Room, by reservation every night except Monday, mid-June–mid-Oct. The lodge also serves breakfast daily. Dinner menu changes biweekly, vegetarians are accommodated. Full bar. Call well ahead to make reservations; Goose Cove may be remote, but it's no secret.

Lobster-in-the-Rough: **Eaton's Lobster Pool,** Blastow's Cove, Little Deer Isle, 207/348-2383, qualifies in this category because you can order your crustaceans by the pound, but it's a bit more gussied up than the eat-on-the-dock places. (There are a few tables on the outdoor deck, and some shorefront picnic tables for takeout customers.) You'll find more interesting food and faster service at other island restaurants, but you'd be hard put to find a better view than here on Blastow's Cove. Dramatic sunsets can even subdue the usual din in the rustic dining room. BYOL; no credit

cards; smoking only outside. Reservations are advisable, especially on weekends. Open Mon.–Fri. 5–9 PM, Sat.–Sun. noon–9 PM, mid-June–mid-Sept.; open Fri.–Sun., mid-May–mid-June and mid-Sept.–early Oct. Look for signs across from the Chamber of Commerce information booth.

In downtown Stonington, a good bet for fresh-out-of-the-water seafood is **The Lobster Deck,** Sea Breeze Ave., Stonington, 207/367-6526, in the heart of the fishing docks. Burgers are also available, and there's indoor seating. This casual spot is open Mon.–Tues. 6 AM–2 PM, Wed.–Sat. 6 AM–7 PM, and Sun. 6 AM–noon.

Information and Services
The **Deer Isle–Stonington Chamber of Commerce,** P.O. Box 490, Stonington 04681, 207/348-6124, www.deerislemaine.com, has a summer information booth on a grassy triangle on Rte. 15 in Little Deer Isle, a quarter of a mile after crossing the bridge from Sargentville (Sedgwick). Staffed by volunteers, the office is open weekdays 10 AM–4 PM and Sunday 11 AM–5 PM.

Across from the Pilgrim's Inn, is the **Chase Emerson Memorial Library,** Main St., Deer Isle Village 04627, 207/348-2899. The **Stonington Public Library,** Main St., Stonington 04681, 207/367-5926, is open Tues. 12:30–5:30 PM, Fri. 12:30–4:30 PM, and Sat. 10 AM–noon.

Emergencies: The **Island Medical Center,** Airport Rd., South Deer Isle, 207/367-2311, a division of Blue Hill Memorial Hospital, handles minor medical problems. The nearest round-the-clock emergency room is at Blue Hill Memorial Hospital, Water St., Blue Hill 04614, 207/374-2836. Throughout Deer Isle, in emergencies requiring police, fire, or ambulance services, call 911.

Newspapers: *Island Ad-Vantages,* 207/367-2200, published every Thursday, includes the *Compass* supplement, listing area events and activities. The same publisher also owns the *Castine Patriot* and Blue Hill's *Weekly Packet.*

The Ellsworth American, 63 Main St.,

Ellsworth 04605, 207/667-2576, published every Thursday, produces a monthly summer tabloid supplement, *Out and About in Downeast Maine,* with feature articles, maps, ads, and calendar listings that include Deer Isle. The supplement is available free at shops, lodgings, and restaurants throughout the area.

Public Restrooms: There are public restrooms on Atlantic Ave. behind the firehouse and at the Stonington Town Hall, Main St. (open Mon.–Fri. 8 AM–4 PM), as well as at the Chase Emerson Library in Deer Isle village.

Special Courses: Internationally famed artisans—sculptors and papermakers, weavers and jewelers, potters and printmakers—become the faculty each summer for the unique **Haystack Mountain School of Crafts,** Sunshine Rd., P.O. Box 518, Deer Isle 04627, 207/348-2306, www.haystack-mtn.org. Chartered in 1950, the school has weekday classes and round-the-clock studio access for the adult students, ranging from beginners to advanced professionals. Portfolio review is required for advanced courses. Two or three evenings a week (8 PM), early June–late Aug., faculty and visiting artists present slide/lecture programs open to the public. An hour-long Wednesday (1 PM) tour of the architecturally and scenically dramatic 40-acre shorefront campus usually includes visits to some of the studios. None of the work is for sale. Haystack is seven miles east of Deer Isle village.

ISLE AU HAUT

Just over half a hundred souls call 5,800-acre Isle au Haut home year-round, most of them eking out a living from the sea. Each summer, the population temporarily swells with day-trippers, campers, and cottagers—then settles back in fall to the measured pace of life on an island six miles offshore.

Samuel de Champlain, threading his way through this archipelago in 1605 and noting the island's prominent central ridge, came up with the name of Isle au Haut—High Island. Appropriately, the tallest peak (543 feet) is now named Mt. Champlain. Incorporated in 1868, Isle au Haut became, courtesy of political horse-trading, part of Knox County, whose shire town (Rockland) is nearly four hours away by boat and car.

Most of the southern half of the six-mile-long island belongs to Acadia National Park, thanks to the wealthy summer visitors who began arriving in the 1880s. It was their heirs who, in the 1940s, donated valuable acreage to the federal government. Today, this offshore division of the national park has a well-managed 20-mile network of trails, a few lean-tos, several miles of unpaved road, and summertime passenger-ferry service to the park entrance.

In the island's northern half are the private residences of fisherfolk and summer folk, a minuscule village (including a market and post office), a four-mile paved road, and the only inn. The only vehicles on the island are owned by residents.

If spending the night on Isle au Haut sounds appealing (it is), you'll need to plan well ahead; it's no place for spur-of-the-moment sleepovers. (Even spontaneous day-trips aren't always possible.)

The most exotic and priciest overnight option is **The Keeper's House,** P.O. Box 26, Robinson Point Lighthouse Station, Isle au Haut 04645, 207/460-0257, www.keepershouse.com, Maine's only light-station inn. Attached to Robinson's Point Light (automated) and within night sight of three other lighthouses, the five-room inn gets booked up months ahead. Judi Burke, daughter of a Cape Cod lightkeeper, bought the 1907 National Historic Register building with her husband, Jeff, in 1986. (Jeff later wrote a book about their experiences.) The top-floor Garret Room has the only private bath. Three other rooms share two baths. Best view is from The Keeper's Room, overlooking the light tower and Isle au Haut Thorofare. Detached from the main house is the rustic Oil House, with a deck, solar shower and private outhouse. Rooms are $310–385 d, covering three meals, tea and snacks, eco-tours, and bicycles. BYOL and pack light. A two-night minimum July–mid-Sept. (and all weekends) escalates the tab. The ferry operates

Mon.–Sat. all year, and Sundays and holidays late June–Labor Day. If you're going hiking or biking, the Burkes will pack you a lunch. No electricity, no phones, no smoking, no credit cards, no pets, no stress. Nirvana. Open late May–late Oct.

Another peaceful island choice is the **Inn at Isle au Haut,** P.O. Box 78, Isle au Haut 04645, 207/335-5141, www.innatisleauhaut.com, near the Park entrance and the town landing. One room has a private bath, bathrobes are provided for the three second-floor rooms sharing a bath; rates, beginning at $250 d, include gourmet breakfast, picnic lunch, and dinner. BYOL. The inn is a classic Maine coast cottage with polished wood floors, curtains lifting in the sea breeze, and a look-out-to-sea-and-reverie porch. Open late May–early Oct.

Getting There

You could take your own vessel or go on Old Quarry Ocean Adventures' Isle au Haut hike and bike excursion. Otherwise, access to Isle au Haut's town landing is via the private boat owned by the **Isle au Haut Company,** Sea Breeze Ave., P.O. Box 709, Stonington 04681, 207/367-6516, www.isleauhaut.com, which generally operates four daily trips Mon.–Sat., and one on Sun., plus a few extras at special times, mid-June–Labor Day. Best advice is to call for a copy of the current schedule, or check the website, covering dates, variables, fares, and extras.

Apr. to mid-Oct. Isle au Haut Company round-trips are $32 adults, $16 kids under 12 (two bags or parcels each). Round-trip surcharges: bikes ($16), kayaks/canoes ($30 minimum), pets ($8). A season special, subject to availability, permits you to ride the same boat to the island and back for half-price. Weather seldom affects the schedule, but be aware that ultra-heavy seas could cancel a trip.

Mid-June–early Sept., Mon.–Sat., there is twice-daily ferry service from Stonington to Duck Harbor, at the edge of Isle au Haut's Acadia National Park campground. For a day-trip, the schedule allows you six-and-one-half hours on the island. No boats or bikes are allowed

on this route, and no dogs are allowed in the campground. A ranger boards the boat at the town landing and goes along to Duck Harbor to answer questions and distribute maps. Before mid-June and after mid-September, you'll be offloaded at the Isle au Haut town landing, about five miles from Duck Harbor. The six-mile passage from Stonington to the Isle au Haut town landing takes 45 minutes; the trip to Duck Harbor tacks on 30 minutes more.

Ferries depart from the Isle au Haut Company Dock, Sea Breeze Ave., off E. Main St. in downtown Stonington. Parking (daily fee $9 indoor, $7 out, subject to high season surcharge) is available next to the ferry landing. Arrive at least an hour early to get all this settled so you don't miss the boat. Better yet, spend the night on Deer Isle before heading to Isle au Haut.

A note on the weather: Fog is no stranger to Isle au Haut (or, for that matter, many other Maine islands and coastal areas), so keep in mind that even though it doesn't halt boat service, it can affect what you see. Fog shouldn't faze hikers or walkers, but it certainly affects photographers. Then again, moody fog shots have their own special appeal. There's nothing you can do about fog, so make the best of it.

Recreation

Hiking on national park trails is the major recreation on Isle au Haut, and even in the densest fog, you'll see valiant hikers going for it. **Biking** is a bit iffier, limited to the 12 or so miles of paved and unpaved roads. If you're staying at The Keeper's House, they're handy around the village and for going swimming. Mountain bikes are not allowed on the park's hiking trails, and rangers try to discourage park visitors from bringing them to the island. The mail boat carries bikes only to the town landing, not to the park's Duck Harbor Landing.

For **freshwater swimming,** head for Long Pond, a skinny, 1.5-mile-long swimming hole running north-south on the east side of the island. You can bike over there, clockwise along the road, almost five miles, from the town landing. Or bum a ride from an island resident.

If you're only here for the day, though, there's not enough time to do this *and* get in any hiking. Opt for the hiking.

Acadia National Park

Mention Acadia National Park and most people think of Bar Harbor and Mount Desert Island, where more than three million visitors arrive each year. The Isle au Haut section of the park sees maybe 5,000 visitors a year—partly because only a limited number of people a day (not counting campers) are allowed to land here. But the remoteness of the island and the scarcity of beds and campsites also contribute to the low count.

Near the town landing, where the year-round mail boat docks, is the **Park Ranger Station,** where you can pick up trail maps and park information—and use the island's only public facilities (outhouses).

A loop road circles the whole island; an unpaved section goes through the park, connecting with the paved nonpark section. Walking is easy. Beyond the road, none of the park's 20 miles of trails could be labeled "easy"; the footing is rocky, rooty, and often squishy. But the trails *are* well marked, and the views—of islets, distant hills, and ocean—maximize the effort.

The most-used park trail is the four- to five-mile (one way) **Duck Harbor Trail,** connecting the town landing with Duck Harbor. Figure about two hours each way. (You can use this route or follow the road to get to the campground when the summer ferry ends its Duck Harbor run.) Toughest trail is probably **Duck Harbor Mountain,** about 1.2 miles (one way) that'll take you about three hours round-trip. For terrific shoreline scenery, take the **Western Head** and **Cliff Trails,** at the island's southwestern corner. If the tide is out (and *only* if it's out), you can walk across the tidal flats to the quaintly named Western Ear for views back

toward the island. Western Ear is private, so don't linger. The **Goat Trail** adds another four miles (round-trip) of moderate hiking east of the Cliff Trail; views are fabulous and birding is good, but you'll need to decide whether there's time to catch the return mail boat.

Of course, there's much less pressure if you're camping, but you'll need to get your bid in early to reserve one of the five six-person lean-tos at **Duck Harbor Campground,** open May 15–Oct. 15. Before April 1, contact the park for a reservation request form. Write to Acadia National Park, P.O. Box 177, Bar Harbor, 04609. Anytime from April 1 on *(not before, or they'll send it back to you),* return the completed form, along with a check for $25, covering camping for up to six persons for a maximum of five nights May 15–June 15, three nights June 15–Sept. 15, and five nights again Sept. 15–Oct. 15. Competition is stiff in the height of summer, so list alternate dates. The park refunds the check if there's no space; otherwise, they'll send you a "special-use permit" (don't forget to bring it along). There's no additional camping fee.

Unless you don't mind backpacking nearly five miles to reach the campground, try to plan your visit between mid-June and early September, when the mail boat stops in Duck Harbor. It's wise to call the Isle au Haut Company for the current ferry schedule before choosing dates for a lean-to reservation.

Trash policy is carry-in/carry-out, so pack a trash bag or two with your gear. Also bring a container for carting water from the campground pump, since it's 0.3 mile from the lean-tos. It's a longish walk to the general store for food—when you could be off hiking the island's trails—so bring enough to cover your stay.

The best part about staying overnight on Isle au Haut is that you'll have so much more than seven hours to enjoy this idyllic island.

Mount Desert Island

Summer folk have been visiting Mount Desert Island (MDI) for millennia. The earliest Native Americans discovered fabulous fishing and clamming, good hunting and camping, and invigorating salt air here; today's arrivals find variations on the same theme: thousands of lodgings and campsites, hundreds of restaurant seats, dozens of shops, plus 30,000 acres of Acadia National Park.

It's no coincidence that artists were a large part of the 19th-century vanguard here: the dramatic landscape, with both bare and wooded mountains descending to the sea, still inspires everyone who sees it. Once the word got out, painterly images began confirming the reports, and the surge began. Even today, no saltwater locale on the entire eastern seaboard can compete with the variety of scenery on Mount Desert Island.

Those pioneering artists brilliantly portrayed this area, adding romanticized touches to landscapes that really need no enhancement. From the 1,530-foot summit of Cadillac Mountain, preferably at an off hour, you'll sense the grandeur of it all—the slopes careening toward the bay and the handful of islands below looking like the last footholds between Bar Harbor and Bordeaux.

For nearly four centuries, controversy has raged about the pronunciation of the island's name, and we won't resolve it here. French explorer Samuel de Champlain apparently gets credit for naming it l'Ile des Monts Déserts, "island of bare mountains," when he sailed by in 1604. The accent in French would be on the second syllable, but today "Mount DeSERT" and "Mount DES-ert" both have their advocates, although the former seems to get the most use.

However, either way, the island is anything but deserted today. Even as you approach the island, via Trenton on Rte. 3, you'll run the gauntlet of a minor-league Disneyland, with water slides, bumper cars, and enough high-cholesterol eateries to stun the surgeon general.

Don't panic. Acadia National Park lies ahead. My own first instinct is to head straight for the park, for the less-commercial air and the incredible vistas.

As you drive or bike around the island—vaguely shaped like a lobster claw and indented by Somes Sound (the only fjord on the United States' east coast)-you'll cross and re-cross the national-park boundaries, reminders that Acadia National Park, covering a third of the island, is indeed the major presence here. It affects traffic, indoor and outdoor pursuits, and, in a way, even the climate.

The other major presence is Bar Harbor, largest and best-known of the island's communities. It's the source of just about anything you could want (if not need), from T-shirts to tacos, books to bike rentals. The contrast with Acadia is astonishing, as the park struggles to maintain its image and character.

Bar Harbor shares the island with Southwest Harbor, Tremont, and a number of small villages: Bass Harbor, Bernard, Northeast Harbor, Seal Harbor, Otter Creek, Somesville, and Hall Quarry. From Bass, Northeast, and Southwest Harbors, private and state ferries shuttle bike and foot traffic to offshore Swans Island, Frenchboro (Long Island), and the Cranberry Isles (and cars to Swans Island).

If time permits, spend a week on the island (longer would be even better) and squeeze in as much hiking, biking, kayaking, whale-watching, bird-watching, pub-crawling, and grub-grazing as you can manage.

TRENTON: GATEWAY TO MOUNT DESERT ISLAND

Unless you're arriving by boat, you can't get to Mount Desert Island without first going through Trenton, straddling Rte. 3 from Ellsworth southward. Restaurants, motels, amusements, and gift shops line the congested six-mile strip, and some are worth at least a genuflect. If you're traveling with children, count on being begged to stop.

Before or after visiting Mount Desert Island, if you're headed farther Down East—to Lamoine, the eastern side of Hancock County, and beyond—there's a good shortcut from Trenton. About five miles south of Ellsworth on Rte. 3, just north of the Acadia Zoo, turn east onto Rte. 204.

Sights

What kid doesn't like water slides, mini-golf, and go-karts? Indulgent parents can join in the fun at **Seacoast Fun Park,** Bar Harbor Rd., Rte. 3, Trenton, 207/667-3573, www.seacoast-funparks.com, or settle in at one of the picnic tables overlooking the monstrous blue water slides. Good thing here is the range of activities for various ages—even a video arcade. Home to Pursuit Park Paintball, Maine's only tented paintball arena. A snack bar serves just what you'd expect. A pass admission system is multi-leveled; the max pass ($22 pp) covers all day on the water slide, all-day golf, and one ride. Separate fees are available for individual activities. The park, 2.8 miles south of downtown Ellsworth, is open 10 AM–9 PM Thurs.–Sun. (to 10 PM Fri.–Sat.), Memorial Day–Labor Day. Evening hours are weather permitting, call to verify.

Roaming 15 acres at the **Acadia Zoo,** 446 Bar Harbor Rd., Trenton 04605, 207/667-3244, www.acadiazoo.org, a nonprofit educational facility, are more than 100 exotic and not-so-exotic creatures—reindeer, wolves, moose, and more. Enter the barn and-voilâ—you're in a simulated rain forest populated with monkeys, Amazon fishes, and tropical birds and reptiles. There's a small petting area, and regular daily shows. Admission is $7.50 adults and $6 seniors and children 3–12; no charge for children under three. The zoo is open daily at 9:30 AM, early May–Christmas.

For an overview of the area, take flight in a Cessna 182 with **Bar Harbor Aviation,** at the Hancock County-Bar Harbor Airport, Bar Harbor Rd., Rte. 3, Trenton 04605, 207/667-6527, www.barharboraviation.com, in either their 25-minute flight around Mount Desert Island and Somes Sound ($55 pp) or the 45-minute flight

over seven area lighthouses ($85 pp). The appeal to small children depends on parents, kids, and their relevant experience. Some kids love these flights, others would be terrified. The airport is just north of Mount Desert Island and 12 miles north of downtown Bar Harbor. Reservations are preferred, but not necessary. Planes operate daily, weather permitting, Memorial Day–mid-Oct. (fall foliage flights are fabulous). If that's not enough excitement, look into their motorless glider rides.

Lodgings and Lobster

As you make your way from Ellsworth to Mount Desert Island along Rte. 3 (Bar Harbor Rd.), you'll pass plenty of **motels and cabins.** If you're sensitive to highway noise and/or want to be closer to Bar Harbor and Acadia National Park, keep going. If your budget is tight, you may want to stop along here; at the height of summer, when No Vacancy signs sprout all around Bar Harbor, these lodgings sometimes have the only remaining beds for travelers who haven't planned ahead.

Rte. 3 (Bar Harbor Rd.) is lined with eateries, including several lobster "pounds" that deserve a stop. One of the best-known and longest-running (since 1956) is **Trenton Bridge Lobster Pound,** Rte. 3, 1237 Bar Harbor Rd., Trenton 04605, 207/667-2977, www.trentonbridgelobster.com, on the right, next to the bridge leading to Mount Desert Island. Watch for the "smoke signals"—steam billowing from the huge vats; this lobster will knock your socks off, it's so fresh it's sweet. The pound is open 10:30 AM–8 PM, last order cooked at 7:30 PM, Mon.–Sat., Memorial Day–Columbus Day. Closed Sun., except on holiday weekends. They also accept mail orders throughout the year, and sell gift certificates and lobsters packed to travel.

MOUNT DESERT ISLAND INFORMATION

Trenton is home to two information centers designed to orient you to Mount Desert Island.

A for-profit operation that sounds like it's

connected to Acadia National Park but isn't, the **Acadia Information Center,** Rte. 3, Bar Harbor Rd., Trenton 04605, 207/667-8550 or 800/358-8550, www.acadiainfo.com, is the first info center you'll encounter along the way. Clean restrooms, a new building, telephones, some high-tech interactive gadgetry, and racks of brochures and maps make it worth stopping. The center is associated with southwestern Nova Scotia and can book passage on the CAT for you. It's on the right, only a thousand feet before the bridge to Thompson Island. The center is open May–Oct., 9 AM–7 PM.

The best independent resource for all the communities of Mount Desert Island is the **Mount Desert Island Information Center,** 207/288-3411, a joint project of four chambers of commerce and the National Park Service. There's information here on the park and its campground vacancies (but be sure to stop also at the park's visitors center). The modern building, on bridge-linked Thompson Island in Mount Desert Narrows, has restrooms, pay phones, scads of brochures and maps, and particularly congenial staffers who will help you find a bed or campsite and plan your visit. You can buy National Park passes here. The center is open mid-May–mid-Oct. 8 AM–6 PM daily, later if traffic warrants.

Acadia Weekly Magazine, 207/288-9025, publishes an issue in May, then publishes weekly from June to Columbus Day; it's a useful 60-page booklet emphasizing Acadia National Park but also carrying ads and features for other parts of the island. It's available free, almost everywhere you look on the island. The same publisher also produces a free annual menu guide, primarily for Bar Harbor restaurants.

FESTIVALS AND EVENTS

This list only skims the surface of the busy schedule on Mount Desert Island; check with the information centers for up-to-date lists of other happenings. Also check the weekly *Bar Harbor Times.*

The **Fourth of July** is always a big deal in Bar Harbor, celebrated with a blueberry-pancake breakfast (6 AM), a parade (10 AM), a seafood festival (11 AM on), a band concert, and fireworks. A highlight is the Lobster Race, a crustacean competition drawing contestants such as Lobzilla and Larry the Lobster to compete at the Bar Harbor Athletic Field. And Independence Day celebrations in the island's smaller villages evoke a bygone era.

The Abbe Museum, the College of the Atlantic, and the Maine Indian Basketmakers Alliance sponsor the annual **Native American Festival and Maine Indian Basketmakes Festival,** 10 AM–4 PM, in early July. Baskets, beadwork, and other handcrafts for sale; Indian drumming and dancing. Free admission. College of the Atlantic, Bar Harbor, www .abbemuseum.org.

The **Arcady Music Festival,** which celebrated its 25th anniversary in 2005, presents evening concerts, mid-July–late Aug., at various locations on and off the island (off-island sites are Dover-Foxcroft, Bangor, and Bucksport). Bar Harbor concerts usually are Thurs. evening. The array of music is broad, from ragtime to classical. For information: 207/288-3151, www.arcady.org.

The **Bar Harbor Music Festival,** a summer tradition since 1967, emphasizes up-and-coming musical talent in a series of classical, jazz, and pops concerts, usually Saturdays and Sundays, at various island locations early July to early August. Reservations are wise: 212/222-1026 (pre-season), 207/288-5744 (after July 1), www.barharbormusicfestival.org. One of the festival's big draws (about 1,000 attendees) is the Acadia National Park Outdoor Concert at the Blackwoods Campground Ampitheater in late July. Shuttle service is available from the parking lot at Jackson Lab.

In even-numbered years, the **Mount Desert Garden Club Tour** presents a rare chance to visit some of Maine's most spectacular private gardens the second or third Saturday in July (confirm the date in advance with the Bar Harbor Chamber of Commerce).

For more music, the **Bar Harbor Town Band** performs free Monday and Thursday

Acadia Region

evening (8 PM) on the Village Green, Main and Mt. Desert Sts., Bar Harbor, throughout July and August.

The **Sweet Chariot Music Festival,** 207/359-2127, is a unique midweek festival of folk singing and traditional sea music, held Tues.–Thurs. the first week of August. Windjammers and other traditional and modern vessels converge on the Swans Island area from all over the Gulf of Maine for jam-packed concerts ashore at various locations including Burnt Coat Harbor, www.sweetchariotfestival .com. The **Directions Craft Show** fills the last weekend of July with extraordinary displays and sales of crafts by over 80 members of Directions. You'll find it at Mount Desert Island High School, Rte. 233, Eagle Lake Rd. Hours are 5–9 PM Fri., 10 AM–5 PM Sat.–Sun.

EMERGENCIES

Mount Desert Island's only full-service hospital is **Mt. Desert Island Hospital,** 10 Wayman Ln., Bar Harbor 04609, 207/288-5081, with a 24-hour emergency room, 207/288-8439. The next-closest facility is in Ellsworth, and the nearest major medical center is Eastern Maine Medical Center, in Bangor.

For ambulance service, and police and fire emergencies, call 911 in Bar Harbor, Northeast Harbor, Southwest Harbor and Mount Desert.

GETTING THERE AND AWAY

The **Hancock County/Bar Harbor Airport,** 143 Caruso Dr., Rte. 3, Bar Harbor Rd., Trenton 04605, 207/667-7329, 12 miles from downtown Bar Harbor, is centrally located for anyone headed for Mount Desert Island. **USAirways Express/Colgan Air,** 800/428-4322, www.colganair.com, operates daily commuter-plane service from Boston to Bar Harbor Airport. Flight time is about 50 minutes, unless there is a scheduled stop in Rockland (usually one flight a day, adding about half an hour.) In summer, there are five flights on weekdays, six or seven on weekend days. Larger jets (usually less expensive) arrive at Bangor International Airport, 50 miles away. Avis, National, Hertz and Budget have rental-car offices at the Bar Harbor Airport; in summer, be sure to reserve a car well in advance. By car, Bar Harbor is 268 miles from Boston.

Bar Harbor is the starting point for the summertime car-and-passenger ferry to Yarmouth, Nova Scotia, which shaves more than 600 miles off the driving route. Late May–mid-Oct., the high-speed 900-passenger catamaran called *The Cat,* owned by Bay Ferries, zips to Yarmouth in 165 minutes, departing Bar Harbor daily at 8 AM (and 4 PM six days a week in high season, variable days other times). (Yarmouth is on Atlantic time.) Not without controversy, *The Cat* has been criticized for creating harbor wakes, and has even received speeding tickets. Fares vary according to type of vehicle and season. There are a number of discounts and packages. Fuel surcharges are in place, and security surcharges may apply. Car reservations are wise. For a current schedule and other fare information, contact Bay Ferries, 888/249-7245 or 207/288-3395, www.catferry.com. Mid-May–mid-Oct., there is a **Nova Scotia Visitor Information Center,** 207/288-9432 or 207/288-9401, at the ferry terminal (121 Eden St., Rte. 3, Bar Harbor 04609); hours are 6:30–8 AM and 11 AM–5 PM.

GETTING AROUND

The best thing that ever happened to Mount Desert Island, traffic-wise, was the establishment in 1999 of the *free* **Island Explorer** bus network, 207/667-5796, www.exploreacadia.com, which operates late June–early Oct. (reduced service on July 4). Eight routes cover all but the westernmost side of the island; the schedules are available at all information centers, most lodgings, and many shops and restaurants. Although there are scheduled stops, the bus drivers are very amenable to stopping almost anywhere it's safe. The propane-powered buses connect with the Swans Island ferry, the Cranberry Isles mail boat, and the Nova Scotia ferry. The downtown route (#2) begins at 6:45 AM and continues frequently until 10:45 PM. Other routes begin at 6:45, 7:10, 8, 8:15, and 9 AM. It's amazingly well organized.

ROUTE 3 TOWARD BAR HARBOR

Just after the Thompson Island information center, you're faced with a choice—Rte. 3 toward the Acadia National Park Visitor Center and Bar Harbor *or* Rte. 102/198 toward Southwest Harbor and lesser-known parts of the island's "quiet side." If you head toward the Bar Harbor side, here's what you'll first encounter (aside from a portion of the 19,999 other vehicles using the Rte. 3 the same day you are).

Accommodations: Staying in the northern end of the island means informality, less hubbub than in Bar Harbor, and relatively lower prices. **The Cove Farm Inn Bed & Breakfast,** 25 Crooked Rd., Bar Harbor 04609, 207/288-5355, run by the Keene family, is a great place to bring the kids and let down your hair. It's not for introverts. Everyone mixes in. You'll find a guest refrigerator and a guest vegetable patch, and you can even use the kitchen to pack picnics. The farm has resident roosters, ducks, and geese. Jerry Keene, an island expert, loves sharing his local knowledge. Pets allowed. Eleven basic rooms (some private baths, some shared) go for $50–150 d July–mid-Oct., lower rates off-season. Full breakfast is served. The Keenes also have housekeeping cottages available by the week in summer. Open May–Feb. Cove Farm is 0.25 mile west of Rte. 3, near Hulls Cove and the Acadia National Park Visitor Center.

Within two miles of Thompson Island are two well-sited **campgrounds,** both large and well maintained and both on an Island Explorer bus route. Next to the causeway, and 10 miles northwest of Bar Harbor, the **Bar Harbor KOA,** 136 County Rd., Bar Harbor 04609, 207/288-3520, www.barharborkoa.com, occupies 40 acres with 200 open and wooded tent and RV sites. Views are terrific. Facilities include free showers and laundry, playground, beach, game areas, and a small shop. Pets are al-

lowed. Rates are $45–75 a night (four persons) late June–Labor Day, $32–52 (two persons) other months. Open mid-May–mid-Oct.

Mt. Desert Narrows Camping Resort, 1219 State Hwy. 3, Bar Harbor 04609, 207/288-4782 or 866/780-4782, www.narrowscamping.com, 1.5 miles east of the causeway, has a fantastic view over Thomas Bay and the Narrows. The 40-acre campground has 239 wooded and open tent and RV sites, heated pool, convenience store, canoe and kayak rentals, playground, coin laundry, and live entertainment mid-June–Labor Day. Pets are allowed. Sites are $30–65 per night (two persons) mid-June–Labor Day, lower early and late in the season. Open mid-May–late Oct.

ACADIA NATIONAL PARK

America's first national park east of the Mississippi River, and the only national park in the northeastern United States, Acadia National Park covers more than 40,000 acres on Mount Desert Island, the neighboring Schoodic Peninsula, and several islands close by and farther offshore. Within the boundaries of this splendid space are mountains, lakes, ponds, trails, fabulous vistas, and several campgrounds. Each year, over two million visitors bike, hike, and drive into and through the park. Yet even at the height of summer, when the whole world seems to have arrived here, it's possible to find peaceful niches and less-trodden paths.

The most comprehensive guide to the park and surrounding area is *Moon Handbooks Acadia National Park.*

History

Thanks to the incredible drive and determination of a handful of astute environmentalists, Acadia National Park became reality on January 19, 1929, after previous incarnations as Sieur de Monts National Monument (1916) and Lafayette National Park (1919). Inspired and prodded by dedicated conservationist George B. Dorr, benevolent summer and year-round citizens donated land and campaigned for federal recognition of the park. Starting as

ACADIA NATIONAL PARK HIGHLIGHTS

The highlights listed here are all within the park territory on Mount Desert Island. The park also occupies territory on the Schoodic Peninsula and Isle au Haut, as well as on several islands in the bay. Many of the locations mentioned below are accessible from various parts of the island via the very convenient **Island Explorer** bus. Take advantage of this cost-free, hassle-free service, operating late June–Labor Day.

Cadillac Mountain: Acadia's prime feature is the tallest point on the eastern seaboard, allegedly where the sun's first rays land. You can drive, bike, or hike to the 1,530-foot summit for head-swiveling vistas, as well as a gift shop and restrooms. Be sure to walk the paved 0.5-mile Summit Trail loop for the full effect.

Carriage Roads: On the eastern side of Mount Desert Island, some 57 miles of meandering, crushed-stone paths, crossing 17 handsome stone bridges, welcome walkers, bikers, horseback riders, snowshoers, and cross-country skiers.

Hiking Trails: Besides the carriage roads, the park has more than 120 miles of easy, moderate, and rugged trails just for hikers.

Naturalist Programs: Park rangers present lectures and lead walks and hikes throughout the summer season. Most are free, some require reservations; many are specially geared to children and families. For reservations, call 207/288-8832. Park rangers also accompany several natural and cultural history cruises, all requiring reservations and fees.

Park Loop Road: If you have only a few hours for exploring Acadia, the best capsule experience is the paved, 20-mile Park Loop Road, followed clockwise. The road to the Cadillac Mountain summit adds another seven miles, roundtrip, to this total. One of the Island Explorer bus routes covers a large section of this loop.

Bass Harbor Head Light: This cliffside lighthouse within park boundaries at the southern tip of Mount Desert Island is a prime photo-op site.

the Hancock County Trustees of Public Reservations, the group acquired land parcel by parcel, eventually turning it over to federal jurisdiction. Corporate giant John D. Rockefeller, Jr., owner of a sprawling summer estate on Mount Desert Island, was responsible for securing nearly a third of the park's prime acreage, as well as building the unique 57-mile carriage-road system (44 miles of carriage roads belong to the park; another 13 miles are privately owned but open to the public). In 1935, his contribution was valued at $4 million. Even today, the park continues to expand as philanthropic individuals donate more land to benefit future generations.

National Park Visitors Center

To plan a park visit, contact: Information, Acadia National Park, Eagle Lake Rd., P.O. Box 177, Bar Harbor, ME 04609, 207/288-3338, www.nps.gov/acad. Be sure to request a park map, a carriage-road map, a hiking-trail list, and camping information. The park also publishes an access guide, detailing wheelchair accessibility of information centers, campgrounds, shops, cruises, museums, and trails. Other flyers worth requesting cover geology, plants, birds, mammals, and the park's history. You can request information by email, too, but the park requests you first check the website, which is dense with information.

Once you arrive on the island and head toward Bar Harbor, make your first stop the modern **Hulls Cove Visitor Center,** 207/288-3338, on Rte. 3 in Hulls Cove, eight miles southeast of the causeway to the island. Here you can rendezvous with pals, make reservations for natural and cultural history programs, watch *The Gift of Acadia,* a short park presentation, rent or buy cassette guides, admire the view of Frenchman Bay, and use the restrooms. Pick up a copy of the summertime *Beaver Log,* a tabloid listing the schedule of park activities, plus tide calendars and the entire schedule for the marvelous **Island Explorer** shuttle bus. The Island Explorer is supported by park entrance fees; purchase a pass while you're here at the center.

Parking is ample at the visitors center, although the lot gets mighty full in midsummer, when as many as 9,000 people a day visit the center. Ascend a stairway from the parking lot to the center, which is open Mid-Apr.–June, and Oct., 8 AM–4:30 PM daily; July–Aug., 8 AM to 6 PM daily; Sept., 8 AM–4:30 PM daily. Closed Nov. 1–mid-Apr. Nov.–mid-Apr., information is available daily 8 AM–4:30 PM at **Winter Visitor Center/Acadia National Park Headquarters,** Rte. 233, about 3.5 miles west of downtown Bar Harbor. The office is closed Thanksgiving, Christmas Eve, Christmas, and New Year's Day. The headquarters is also open mid-Apr.–Oct., weekdays 8 AM–4:30 PM.

See *Suggested Reading,* for a selection of books that will prove very helpful if you're spending any amount of time in the national park. The park sells *The Complete Map & Guide—Acadia National Park* for $4.50.

Friends of Acadia

One of the park's greatest assets today is an energetic membership organization called Friends of Acadia (FOA), founded in 1986 to preserve and protect the park for resource-sensitive tourism and myriad recreational uses. You can join FOA and support the cause for $35 a year (43 Cottage St., P.O. Box 45, Bar Harbor 04609, 207/288-3340 or 800/625-0321, www.friendsofacadia.org), or just lend a hand while you're here. The three-thousand-member FOA organizes volunteer work parties for Acadia trail and carriage-road maintenance three times weekly June–Nov.: Tues., Thurs., and Sat., 8:30 AM–12:30 PM. In one recent year, over 1,500 FOA volunteers gave 7,600 hours to park maintenance. Call the recorded information line (207/288-3934) for the work locations. This is a terrific way to give something back to the park, and the camaraderie is contagious. Be sure to take your own water, lunch, and bug repellent. Dress in layers.

If you happen to be in the area on the first Saturday in November, call the office to register for the annual fall Take Pride in Acadia Day, which requires several hundred volunteers. Bring water and gloves; there's a free hot meal and t-shirts for participants. In the spring, you can join the Earth Day roadside cleanup.

Even if you don't have time to join a work party, be a conscientious trail-keeper as you hike, and carry a trash bag.

Park Loop Road

The best way to fully appreciate Acadia is to hike the trails, bike the carriage roads, canoe and swim the ponds, and camp overnight. But if your time is limited, the 20-mile Park Loop Rd. covers scenic highlights, including access to the summit of Cadillac Mountain. (Going to the summit and back adds another seven miles.) A drive-it-yourself tour booklet ($2) is available at the Thompson Island center as well as the park's visitor center. Start at the parking lot below the visitor center and follow the signs pointing in a clockwise direction; part of the loop is one-way. Traffic gets heavy at midday in midsummer, so aim for an early morning start. Maximum speed is 35 mph, but be alert for gawkers and photographers stopping without warning. Along the route are lots of trailheads, scenic overlooks, Sand Beach, Thunder Hole, Otter Cliffs, Jordan Pond House, and Eagle Lake, plus the Cadillac summit. North of Sand Beach is the park's entrance station. The park admission fee is $20 per vehicle (valid for a week), or $40 for an annual pass. To drive up Cadillac without doing the rest of Park Loop Rd., take the Cadillac Mountain access road off Rte. 233, west of Bar Harbor. It's 3.5 miles to the top.

The road is also open to bicyclists (as are the carriage roads, unlike the hiking trails, where bikes are banned). While the carriage roads are more scenic (and don't permit cars), Park Loop

Acadia Region

Rd. provides a workout and a sightseeing opportunity for mountain bikers. (But don't do this in the middle of the day; get an early start or go late in the day to minimize breathing automobile exhaust fumes.)

Recreation

The Carriage-Road System: In 1913, John D. Rockefeller, Jr., began laying out what eventually became a 57-mile carriage-road system, overseeing the project through the 1940s. Motorized vehicles have never been allowed on these lovely graded byways, making them real escapes from the auto world. Devoted now to multiple uses, the "Rockefeller roads" see hikers, bikers, baby strollers, horse-drawn carriages, even wheelchairs. Busiest times are 10 AM–2 PM.

Pick up a free copy of the carriage-road map at the visitor center. Fortunately, a $6 million restoration campaign, undertaken during the 1990s, has done a remarkable job of upgrading surfaces, opening overgrown panoramas, and returning the roads to their original 16-foot width.

The most crowded carriage roads are those closest to the visitor center—the Witch Hole Pond Loop, Duck Brook, and Eagle Lake. Avoid these, opting instead for roads west of Jordan Pond, or go early in the morning or late in the day. Better still, go off-season, when you can enjoy the fall foliage (late September/early October) or winter's cross-country skiing.

If you need a bicycle to explore the carriage roads, see the Bar Harbor and Southwest Harbor sections for rental information. Be forewarned that hikers are allowed on the carriage roads that spill over onto private property south of the Jordan Pond House, but they are off limits to bicyclists. The carriage-road map clearly indicates the biking/no-biking areas: *Bicyclists must be especially speed-sensitive on the carriage roads, keeping an eye out for hikers, horseback riders, small children, and the hearing impaired.*

To recapture the early carriage-roads era, take one of the horse-drawn open-carriage tours run by Ed Winterberg's **Wildwood Stables,** a mile south of the Jordan Pond House,

on the Park Loop Rd., P.O. Box 241, Seal Harbor 04675, 207/276-3622. Six one- and two-hour trips start at 9:30 AM daily, mid-June–Columbus Day. Reservations are not required, but they're encouraged, especially in midsummer. Best outing is the two-hour **Sunset at the Summit** to the top of Day Mountain, departing at 6:30 PM in June, 6:15 PM in July, and 6 PM in August. Cost is $22 adults, $6 for children 2–5, and $9 for children 6–12. Other routes are $16–18 per adult. (Besides the horse-carriage tours based in the park itself and ranger-accompanied cruises, a couple of bus-tour firms operate out of Bar Harbor. See the Bar Harbor section for information on boat, bus, and trolley-bus tours.)

Hikes: If you're spending more than a day on Mount Desert Island, plan to buy a copy of *A Walk in the Park: Acadia's Hiking Guide,* by Tom St. Germain, which details more than 60 hikes, including some outside the park. Remember that pets are allowed on park trails, but only on leashes no longer than six feet. Four of the Island Explorer bus routes are particularly useful for hikers, alleviating the problems of backtracking and car-jammed parking lots. Here's a handful of personal favorite Acadia hikes, ranging from easy to rugged.

Jordan Pond Nature Trail: Start at the Jordan Pond parking area; easy, one-mile wooded loop trail; pick up a brochure for a nominal fee. Include Jordan Pond House (for tea and popovers) in your schedule.

Ship Harbor Nature Trail: Start at the Ship Harbor parking area, on Rte. 102A between Bass Harbor and Seawall Campground, in the southwestern corner of the island; easy, 1.3-mile loop trail leading to the shore; pick up a brochure at the trailhead. Ship Harbor is particularly popular among birders seeking warblers, and you just might spot an eagle while you picnic on the rocks. An even easier trail, with its parking area just east of the Ship Harbor parking area, is **Wonderland.** It's a mile round-trip. Across Rte. 102A from Wonderland is **Seawall Bog,** attractive primarily to birders. Be sure to stay on the trails (worn but not marked); the peat underfoot is especially fragile.

Great Head Trail: A moderate, 1.7-mile loop trail starts at the eastern end of Sand Beach, off the Park Loop Rd. Park in the Sand Beach parking area and cross the beach to the trailhead. Or take Schooner Head Rd. from downtown Bar Harbor and park in the small area where the road dead-ends. There are actually two trail loops here, both of which have enough elevation to provide terrific views.

Beech Mountain: Also a moderate hike, Beech Mountain's summit has an abandoned fire tower, from which you can look out toward Long Pond and the Blue Hill Peninsula. Round-trip on the wooded route is about 1.2 miles, although a couple of side trails can extend it. You'll have less competition here, in a quieter part of the park. Take Rte. 102 south from Somesville, heading toward Pretty Marsh. Turn left onto Beech Hill Rd. and follow it to the parking area at the end.

Beehive Trail and **Precipice Trail:** These two are the park's toughest routes, with sheer faces and iron ladders; Precipice often is closed (usually mid-Apr.–Aug.) to protect nesting peregrine falcons. If challenges are your thing, you have no problem with heights, and these trails are open (check beforehand at the visitor center), go ahead. But a fine alternative in the difficult category is the **Beachcroft Trail** on Huguenot Head. Also called the Beachcroft Path, the trail is best known for its 1,500 beautifully engineered granite steps. Round-trip is 1.6 miles, or you can continue a loop at the top, taking in the Bear Brook Trail on Champlain Mt., for 3.6 miles. The parking area is just north of Rte. 3, near the Abbe Museum and Sieur de Monts Spring, and just west of the Park Loop Rd., near the Jackson Memorial Laboratory.

Rock Climbing: The main climbing areas are Otter Cliffs and the south wall of Champlain Mountain; other cliffs are also used. Sadly, rope friction and overuse have led to receding vegetation on Otter Cliffs. Inquire at the visitors center, and follow all requirements. Unless you're a pro, the best advice is to contact an outfitter in Bar Harbor and sign on for a half-, full-, or multi-day climbing experience, including professional lessons and at least one rappel. Accredited by the American Mountain Guides Association, **Acadia Mountain Guides Climbing School,** 92 Main St., P.O. Box 121, Orono 04473, 207/866-7562 or 888/232-9559, www.acadiamountainguides.com, offers all levels of instruction and guided climbs for individuals and families in Acadia as well as in Camden, Clifton, and Baxter State Park. All gear is provided. Costs vary widely, depending on site, number of climbers, and session length. The school runs climbs year-round.

Swimming: Sand Beach, next to Park Loop Rd. and near the park entrance station, is the park's only sandy beach on salt water. Lifeguards are on duty during the summer, and even then, the biggest threat can be hypothermia. The water is terminally glacial, and even though kids seem not to notice, they can become chilled quickly. The best solution is to walk to the far end of the beach, where a warmer, shallow stream meets the ocean. On a hot August day, arrive early; the parking lot fills up. Bring a picnic.

A less-crowded saltwater beach, not in the park, is at the head of the appealing harbor in chic Seal Harbor, a few miles east of Northeast Harbor.

Don't assume you can swim in any freshwater pond or lake you encounter. Six island locations—Upper and Lower Hadlock Ponds, Bubble and Jordan Ponds, Eagle Lake, and the southern half of Long Pond—are drinking-water reservoirs where swimming and windsurfing are banned (but boating is allowed). Don't let your dog swim in these ponds, either.

The most popular freshwater swimming site, staffed with a lifeguard and inevitably crowded on hot days, is **Echo Lake,** south of Somesville on Rte. 102. If you have a canoe, kayak, or rowboat, you can reach swimming holes in **Round, Seal Cove,** or **Somes Pond** (all on the western side of Mount Desert). The eastern shore of **Hodgdon Pond** (also on the western side of the island) is accessible by car (via Hodgdon Rd. and Long Pond Fire Rd.).

Lake Wood (at the northern end of Mount Desert) has a small beach and auto access. To get to Lake Wood from Rte. 3, head west on Crooked Rd. to unpaved Park Rd. Turn left and continue to the parking area. Arrive early.

Accommodations and Food

The only accommodations within Acadia National Park are two **campgrounds,** Seawall and Blackwoods, neither of which has RV hookups. In addition, the park operates a handful of lean-to campsites, at its Duck Harbor location on Isle au Haut. Commercial campgrounds and a variety of other lodgings are located all over Mount Desert Island.

Both of the Acadia National Park campgrounds have seasonal restrooms (no showers) and dumping stations. Both also have amphitheaters, where park rangers present free, hour-long evening programs (usually at 9 PM) during the summer on a variety of natural- and cultural-history topics. Noncampers are also welcome at these events.

With more than 300 campsites, **Blackwoods Campground,** just off Rte. 3, five miles south of Bar Harbor, is open all year. Reservations are suggested May 1–Oct. 31, 800/365-2267; have your credit card handy. Cost is $20 per site per night. Off-season camping is first come, first served, and (limited) facilities include pit toilets, fire rings, and a hand-operated water pump. When bathrooms are open off-season, there is a minimal camping fee.

No reservations are required or accepted at **Seawall Campground,** on Rte. 102A, four miles south of Southwest Harbor, but you'll need to arrive as early as 8 AM in midsummer to secure one of the 200 or so sites. Seawall is open late May–late Sept. Cost is $20 per night for drive-up sites and $14 per night for walk-in sites.

The only full-service restaurant within the park is the **Jordan Pond House,** Park Loop Rd., P.O. Box 24, Acadia National Park, Bar Harbor 04609, 207/276-3316, www.jordan-pond.com, a modern facility in a spectacular waterside setting. Jordan Pond House is a destination—an oasis for indulging in tea, popovers, and extraordinary strawberry jam, served on the lawn or daily, 11:30 AM–5:30 PM, in summer, weather permitting; or, you can have lunch on the lawn. During the same hours, you can also enjoy lunch or tea inside. Dinner is served beginning at 5:30 PM, inside or on the porch, according to weather conditions. No bargains here, but the menu is varied, featuring the excellent popover in many places, and it's convenient, pretty, and part of the park experience. There is a gift shop. However, Jordan Pond is far from a secret, so expect to wait for seats at the height of summer. Reservations will help cut waiting time—as much as an hour and a half in summer for tea—to about 10 minutes. Make a reservation, and then check in when you arrive. Jordan Pond House is on the Island Explorer bus route. *A health note:* Perhaps because of all the sweet drinks and jam served outdoors, patrons at the lawn tables sometimes find themselves pestered by bees. They don't usually sting unless you pester them back, but if you're hyperallergic to bee stings, or with anyone who is, be alert.

Jordan Pond House began life as a rustic 19th-century teahouse; wonderful old photos still line the walls of the current incarnation, which went up following a disastrous fire in 1979. The restaurant is open daily; luncheon and tea are served 11:30 AM–5:30 PM, dinner after 5:30 PM, May–Oct.

Emergencies

If you have an emergency while in the park, call 207/288-3338, during business hours; otherwise, dial 911. The nearest hospital is in Bar Harbor. The nearest major medical center is in Bangor, via a congested route that can take well over an hour at the height of summer. Best advice for averting emergencies: Be cautious and sensible in everything you undertake in the park. Don't hike alone or go off the trails—people are seriously injured or killed falling from the cliffs nearly every year.

BAR HARBOR AND VICINITY

In 1996, Bar Harbor celebrated the bicentennial of its founding (as Eden). In the late 19th century and well into the 20th, the town grew to become one of the east coast's fanciest summer watering holes.

In those days, steamboats arrived from points south, large and small resort hotels sprang up, and exclusive mansions (quaintly dubbed "cottages") were the venues of parties thrown by resident Drexels, DuPonts, Vanderbilts, and prominent academics, journalists, and lawyers. The "rusticators" came for the season, with huge entourages of servants, children, pets, and horses. The area's renown was such that by the 1890s, even the staffs of the British, Austrian, and Ottoman embassies retreated here from summers in Washington, DC.

The establishment of the national park, in 1919, and the arrival of the motorcar changed the character of Bar Harbor and Mount Desert Island; two world wars and the Great Depression took an additional toll in myriad ways; but the coup de grâce for Bar Harbor's era of elegance came in 1947.

Nothing in the history of Bar Harbor and Mount Desert Island stands out like the Great Fire of 1947, a wind-whipped conflagration that devastated more than 17,000 acres on the eastern half of the island and leveled gorgeous mansions, humble homes, and more trees than anyone could ever count. Only three people died, but property damage was estimated at $2 million. Whole books have been written about the October inferno; fascinating scrapbooks in Bar Harbor's Jesup Memorial Library dramatically relate the gripping details of the story. Even though some of the elegant cottages have survived, the fire altered life here forever.

Bar Harbor Today

Land in Bar Harbor in mid-July and you'll find it tough to believe that the year-round population is only about 4,700. Bar Harbor is liveliest (in both positive and negative senses) July–Aug., but the season keeps stretching. Many clued-in travelers try to take advantage of September's prime weather, relative quiet, and spectacular foliage, although even September activity has stepped up in recent years. In the dead of winter, the town is close to moribund, kept alive by devoted year-rounders; the students and faculty of the College of the Atlantic, a unique four-year liberal-arts college geared to environmental studies; and the staff of the internationally recognized Jackson Laboratory for Mammalian Research.

If you're traveling with children, Bar Harbor can be a very convenient base of operations, comprising a smallish downtown area where kids can walk around, play in the parks, hang out at the waterfront, buy ice cream, and hit the movies. It's also a source for sporting-gear rentals and the starting point for boat, bus, kayaking, and walking tours. Staying downtown can be a real plus, but the high cost of even ordinary lodging is a minus—especially for families. Bar Harbor Chamber of Commerce staffers are particularly adept at rounding up rooms, but don't abuse their helpfulness; contact them early and plan well ahead for a height-of-summer holiday.

Sights

Acadia National Park comes right up to the edge of town, providing enough sights and activities to fill weeks, but the Bar Harbor area has attractions of its own.

World renowned in genetic research, **The Jackson Laboratory,** 600 Main St., Rte. 3, Bar Harbor 04609, 207/288-6000, or 207/288-6051 (public information) www.jax.org, breeds special mice used to study cancer, diabetes, muscular dystrophy, and other diseases—with considerable success. More than two million mice are shipped out of here each year. August Wednesdays from 3–4 PM, a lively audio-visual program explains the lab's impressive work; three of the programs, for adults, feature scientists describing their work, while two are geared to kids. The lab is 1.5 miles south of downtown Bar Harbor.

St. Saviour's Episcopal Church, 41 Mt. Desert St., Bar Harbor 04609, 207/288-4215, http://ellsworthme.org/ssaviour, close to

BAR HARBOR

Shore Path

Grant Park

TOWN PIER

Agamont Park

ULLIKANA B&B

BAR HARBOR INN

SHERMAN'S BOOK STORE

BASS COTTAGE

GEORGE'S

SEACROFT INN

Village Green

MAIN ST

BIRDSNEST GALLERY

ABBE MUSEUM

BAR HARBOR MDI HOSTEL

ISLAND ARTISANS

CRITERION THEATRE

SONG OF THE SEA

HARBORSIDE HOTEL & MARINA

Bar Harbor

To Bar Island

Passable by Foot at Low Tide

BRIDGE

CHAMBER OF COMMERCE

MIRA MONTE INN

HIGHBROOK MOTEL

EDENBROOK MOTEL

To International Ferry Terminal

Frenchman Bay

Cromwell Cove

Acadia National Park

Bar Island

COLLEGE OF THE ATLANTIC

MAP AREA

0.1 mi

0.1 km

© AVALON TRAVEL PUBLISHING, INC.

downtown Bar Harbor, boasts Maine's largest collection of Tiffany stained-glass windows. Ten originals are here; an 11th was stolen in 1988 and replaced by a locally made window. Of the 32 non-Tiffany windows, the most intriguing is a memorial to Clarence Little, founder of the Jackson Laboratory and a descendant of Paul Revere. Images in the window include the laboratory, DNA, and mice. July–Aug., volunteers conduct free tours of the Victorian-era (completed in 1878) church. The church is open daily, 8 AM–dusk. Off-season, call to arrange a tour. If you're intrigued by old cemeteries, spend time wandering the 18th-century town graveyard next to the church. St. Saviour's is also the site of concerts in summer, including performances of the Arcady Musical Festival.

At the northern edge of Mount Desert Island, 8.5 miles northwest of downtown Bar Harbor, is the Bar Harbor part of the **Mt. Desert Oceanarium,** Rte. 3, Bar Harbor 04609, 207/288-5005, www.theoceanarium.com, one of the island's two related aquariums. As with its sister site (in Southwest Harbor), this low-tech, high-interest operation awes the kids—with a tank full of live harbor seals, a marsh walk to check out tidal creatures and vegetation, and a lobsterman who answers all their questions and explains lobstering life and lore. At the aquarium's adjacent lobster hatchery, visitors can view thousands of tiny lobster hatchlings. The Oceanarium and the hatchery building are open Mon.–Sat. 9 AM–5 PM, mid-May–late Oct. Oceanarium tickets are $10 adults, $6 children 4–12 for lobster museum and lobster hatchery. With salt-marsh tour added, tickets are $12 adult, $7 child. This gets rather pricey for a family, but combination tickets, covering both Bar Harbor and Southwest Harbor locations, are $15 adults, $9.75 children 4–12. The Island Explorer makes several stops at both oceanarium locations.

Located on the College of the Atlantic (COA) campus in a handsome renovated building (the original headquarters of Acadia National Park), the **George B. Dorr Museum of Natural History,** 105 Eden St., Rte. 3, Bar

Harbor 04609, 207/288-5395 or 288-5015, www.coamuseum.org, showcases regional birds and mammals in realistic dioramas made by COA students. Biggest attraction for children is the please-touch philosophy; kids can pick up the indoor tide pool's live animals. Tickets are $3.50 adults, $2.50 seniors, $1.50 teenagers, and $1 children (3–12). The museum is open Mon.–Sat. 10 AM–5 PM, mid-June–Labor Day, off-season by appointment. In summer, a daily interpretive program focuses on the museum collection, and there is a weekly lecture series. The museum also sponsors an excellent **Summer Field Studies** day camp program for children grades 1–9, and other educational programs for children and adults throughout the summer. Off-season, there are school and group programs. The museum gift shop has a particularly good collection of books and gifts for budding naturalists. The college and its museum are located 0.5 mile northwest of downtown Bar Harbor.

About 2.3 miles south of Bar Harbor, at Sieur de Monts Spring, where Rte. 3 meets Park Loop Rd., is the **Abbe Museum,** Rte. 3, P.O. Box 286, Bar Harbor 04609, 207/288-3519, a superb place to introduce children (and adults) to prehistoric and historic Native American tools, crafts, and other cultural artifacts. Everything about this privately funded museum, established in 1927, is tasteful, including the park setting, a handsome National Historic Register building, and displays from a 50,000-item collection. Just as tasteful is the newish, 17,000-square-foot year-round Abbe Museum downtown, 26 Mt. Desert St. (Rte. 3), across from the Village Green in downtown Bar Harbor, incorporating the former YMCA. "Wabanaki: People of the Dawn," the permanent exhibition, is an excellent introduction to Maine's original peoples. A unique gallery, Circle of the Four Directions, reflects the cultural significance of the circle to Native Americans. Museum-sponsored summer events include Fantastic Fridays family programs, which are free or low-cost on Friday mornings July–Aug., craft workshops, and the **Native American Festival** (held at the College of the Atlantic the first Saturday in July). The museum at Sieur de Monts is open mid-May–late Oct., 9 AM–4 PM daily (9 AM–5 PM July–Aug.). Tickets are $2 adults, $1 kids 5–16. However, access is limited, so call ahead. Abbe downtown is open year-round, with the exception of Jan.–Feb. and major holidays. Open daily July–Aug., 9 AM–5 PM; in spring and fall, 9 AM–5 PM Thurs.–Sat. Admission is $6 adults, $2 children 6–15. Both museums have primo gift shops, and are wheelchair-accessible.

While you're at the Abbe Museum, take the time to wander the paths in the adjacent **Wild Gardens of Acadia,** an incredible 0.75-acre microcosm of more than 400 plant species native to Mount Desert Island. Twelve separate display areas, carefully maintained and labeled by the Bar Harbor Garden Club, represent native plant habitats; pick up the map/brochure that explains each.

Historical Walking Tours

How are bikes and kayaks related to a walking tour? Good question. The answer's at **Acadia Bike and Coastal Kayaking Tours,** 48 Cottage St., Bar Harbor 04609, 207/288-9605, headquarters for "A Step Back in Time," a one-hour walking tour of downtown Bar Harbor. The costumed guide (he or she, depending on the schedule) leads you up one street and down the other, all the while staying in Victorian character and sharing the secrets of the rich and famous (and often outrageous) of the 19th century. Sounds kitschy, but it's most entertaining, primarily for adults. The tours occur daily at 4 PM, mid-June–Oct. Additional tours are added from time to time. Reservations aren't required, but they're wise. Cost is $12 per person.

Bar Harbor Historical Society

The Bar Harbor Historical Society, 33 Ledgelawn Ave., Bar Harbor 04609, 207/288-0000, www.barharborhistorical.org, has fascinating displays, stereopticon images, and a scrapbook about the 1947 fire that devastated the island. The photographs alone are worth the visit. The museum is open June–

Oct., Mon.–Sat. 1–4 PM In winter, it's open by appointment. Admission is free, but donations are welcome.

Bar Harbor and Park Tours

The veteran of the Bar Harbor-based bus tours is **Acadia National Park Tours** 207/288-0300, www.acadiatours.com, operating May–Oct. A 2.5-hour, naturalist-led tour of Acadia departs at 10 AM and 2 PM daily from downtown Bar Harbor (look for the green-and-white bus across from Testa's). Reservations are wise in midsummer and during fall-foliage season (late Sept.–early Oct.); pick up reserved tickets 30 minutes before departure. Cost is $25 adults, $10 children under 12.

Get an old-fashioned glimpse of Bar Harbor and the Park by riding **Oli's Trolley,** 1 West St., P.O. Box 794, 207/288-9899 or 288-5443 in summer or 866/987-6553, www.acadiaislandtours.com. In July and Aug., daily one-hour tours ($15) leave at 10 AM, 11:30 AM, 2 PM, 3:30 PM, and 6 PM May–Oct., 2.5-hour tours ($25) leave at 10 AM and 2 PM. Reservations strongly recommended; picking up tickets half an hour pre-departure guarantees a reservation. Buy tickets at One Harbor Place, 1 West St. (next to Town Pier on the waterfront), aboard the trolley, and one hour before departure at Oli's Trolley ice-cream stop (Cottage St., across from the Post Office).

For private tours of the park and other parts of the island, contact Michael Good at **Down East Nature Tours,** P.O. Box 521, Knox Rd., Town Hill, Bar Harbor 04609, 207/288-8128. A biologist with a special interest in birds, he'll take neophyte birders on a tour they won't forget. Michael can also do custom eco-tours. Call for information.

Recreation

Although Acadia steals the limelight for much of the island's recreation, Bar Harbor has its own pursuits—plus several outfitters for anyone headed to the park.

A real treat is a stroll along downtown Bar Harbor's **Shore Path,** a well-trodden, granite-edged byway built around 1880. Along the craggy shoreline are granite-and-wood benches, town-owned **Grant Park** (great for picnics), birch trees, and several handsome mansions that escaped the 1947 fire. Offshore are the four Porcupine Islands. The path is open 6:30 AM–dusk, and leashed pets are okay. Allow about 30 minutes for the mile loop beginning next to the Town Pier and the Bar Harbor Inn and returning via Wayman Lane. There's also access to the path next to the Balance Rock Inn.

Check the *Bar Harbor Times* or with the Bar Harbor Chamber of Commerce for the times of low tide, then walk across the gravel bar (wear hiking boots or rubberized shoes) to wooded **Bar Island** (formerly Rodick's Island) from the foot of Bridge St. in downtown Bar Harbor. Shell heaps recorded on the eastern end of the island indicate that Native Americans enjoyed this turf in the distant past. You'll have the most time to explore the island during new-moon or full-moon low tides, but no more than four hours—about two hours before and two hours after low tide. Be sure to wear a watch so you don't get trapped (for up to 10 hours). The foot of Bridge St. is also an excellent kayak launching site.

Golf: Duffers first teed off in 1891 at **Kebo Valley Golf Club,** 100 Eagle Lake Rd., Rte. 233, Bar Harbor 04609, 207/288-5000, www.kebovalleyclub.com, Maine's oldest club. The 17th hole is legendary; it took President William Howard Taft 27 tries to sink the ball in 1911. Kebo is very popular, with a gorgeous setting, an attractive clubhouse, and decent food service, so tee times (six-day advance) are essential; greens fees are high. Open daily, May–Oct., the 18-hole course is a mile west of downtown Bar Harbor.

Bike Rentals: With all the great biking options, including 44 miles of carriage roads (13 miles of carriage roads are off limits to bicycles) and some of the best roadside bike routes in Maine, you'll want to bring a bike or rent one here. Two firms are based in downtown Bar Harbor, and both handle repairs as well as rentals. **Acadia Bike & Coastal Kayaking Tours,** 48 Cottage St., Bar Harbor 04609, 207/288-

9605 or 800/526-8615 outside Maine, rents adult mountain bikes for $18 a day with reservations, $20 without, kids' bikes for $12; reserve with a credit card, preferably at least a day ahead. Helmet, lock, and map are included. The shop opens at 8 AM daily in spring, summer, and fall. Down the street, at the National Park Outdoor Activities Center, the **Bar Harbor Bicycle Shop,** www.barharborbike.com, 141 Cottage St., Bar Harbor 04609, 207/288-3886, has earned a reputation for well-maintained bikes, renting for $19 a day, $14 for half-day up to four hours. Price includes a helmet, map, bungee cord, and lock. There are other styles of bike for rent at higher prices, and lots of rental carrying and accessory gear. Hours are 8 AM–6 PM daily, open all year except Jan.–Feb. On Sun. morning an informal group gathers for a ride.

Getting Afloat

Bar Harbor has so many ways for you to get out on the water that it would be a shame not to do it at least once. In addition to the whale-watching, lobster-fishing, sailing, and kayaking options, see *Getting There and Away* in the Mount Desert Island introduction for information on the car-and-passenger ferry service between Bar Harbor and Yarmouth, Nova Scotia.

Whale-watching Excursions: Whale-watching boats go as much as 20 miles offshore, so no matter what the weather in Bar Harbor, dress warmly and bring more clothing than you think you'll need—even gloves, if you're especially sensitive to cold. Motion-sensitive children and adults should plan ahead with appropriate medication.

Humpback, finback, and minke whales are prime targets of the **Bar Harbor Whale Watch Co.,** 1 West St., Bar Harbor 04609, 207/288-2386 or 800/942-5374, www.barharborwhales.com, sailing from the dock at 1 West St. in downtown Bar Harbor. Their 112-foot, 200-passenger catamaran *Friendship V* tends to remain more stable than other boats—a big advantage when (not if) you meet offshore swells. Downside is there isn't quite as much open deck space as on other boats. An onboard

Acadia Region

snack bar has sandwiches and cold drinks, and breakfast on the earliest trip. Trips last two to three hours. Late June–Labor Day, there is a whale- and puffin-watching trip at 8:30 AM, and whale-watches at 1 PM and 4:30 PM. Tickets are $46, adults, $25 children 6–14, $8 children five and under. A second catamaran, **Bay King III,** offers viewing decks with 360-degree railing. The company also has lobstering and sightseeing cruises. Between the four boats, there are 15 trips a day in season.

Undersea Exploring: You don't have to go diving in these frigid waters; others will do it for you. After the kids have touched the slimy sea cucumbers and starfish at the Oceanarium, they're likely to be primed for Diver Ed's **Dive-In Theater,** operating from the Harborside Hotel & Marina, 55 West St., 207/288-3483, www.divered.com. Former Bar Harbor harbormaster Ed Monat heads the crew aboard the 46-passenger *Seal,* which heads a mile or two offshore and sends down two professional divers (including Ed) with video cameras. You stay on deck, all warm and dry, and watch the action on a TV screen. There's communication back and forth, so the kids can ask questions as the divers pick up urchins, starfish, crabs, lobsters, and other sea life. When the divers surface, they bring a bag of touchable specimens—another chance to pet some slimy creatures. Great concept, and it's a big hit. During the summer, the tours depart at 9:30 AM (Mon.–Sat.), 1:30 PM, and 5:30 PM (Mon.–Fri.), and last approximately two hours. Cost is $30 adults, $25 seniors, $20 children 5–12, $5 under 5. Reservations are required. Two tours (three hours, $5 extra) weekly feature a National Park Service ranger/naturalist.

Sailboat Cruises: Captain Stephen Pagels, under the umbrella of **Downeast Windjammer Cruises,** 207/288-4585 or 288-2373 or 207/546-2927 in winter; mailing address P.O. Box 28, Cherryfield 04622, www.downeastwindjammer.com, offers two-hour day-sails on the 151-foot steel-hulled *Margaret Todd,* a gorgeous four-masted schooner built in 1997. Three or four daily trips, beginning around 8 AM, mid-May–mid-Oct. (weather permit-

ting), depart from the Bar Harbor Inn pier, just east of the Town Pier in downtown Bar Harbor. Buy tickets either at the pier or at 27 Main St. A sunset cruise often includes live music; bring a picnic supper. Cost is $29.50 adults, $27.50 seniors, $19.50 children under 12. Buy tickets over the phone, online, or at the office, 27 Main St. Bar Harbor. Downeast Windjammer also runs the Bar Harbor Ferry and the Cranberry Cove Ferry. Round-trip tickets on the Bar Harbor ferry to Winter Harbor are $27.50 adult, $17.50 child, and $6.50 for bikes. June 15–Oct. 10, the ferry's first trip from Winter Harbor is at 7 AM, from Bar Harbor at 8 AM. Boats run daily every two hours, with hourly boats added according to demand. Last boat from Winter Harbor is 5 PM; Bar Harbor's is at 6 PM.

Sea Kayaking: Sea kayaking is wildly popular along the Maine coast, and Bar Harbor has become a major kayaking destination. No experience is necessary to join tours operated by either of the firms in Bar Harbor. Half-day ($45 pp for four hours, $59 for five), full-day ($69 pp, 7 hours), and multi-day ($249–375) sea-kayak tours are on the schedule organized by **Coastal Kayaking Tours,** 48 Cottage St., P.O. Box 405, Bar Harbor 04609, 207/288-9605 or 800/526-8615, www.acadiafun.com, a spirited operation. Best option for beginners is the 2.5-hour harbor tour, beginning at 8:30 AM ($37 pp). Special half-day family tours, departing at 1:30 PM, can handle kids eight and over ($45 pp). A 2.5-hour sunset cruise begins around 5 PM (depending on season), at $35 pp. Other kayak trips are offered mid-May–late Sept. All trips are weather-dependent, and reservations are essential. If you want to go it alone, solo kayaks rent for $45 a day.

National Park Sea Kayak Tours, 39 Cottage St., P.O. Box 705, Bar Harbor 04609, 207/288-0342 or 800/347-0940, www.acadiakayak.com, runs half-day (four-hour) ecological coastal trips in tandem kayaks (six-boat maximum). Cost is $45 pp. The skilled guides (equipped with cell phones) hug the shoreline to point out birds, seals, and other wildlife. Each trip includes an island or beach stopover to stretch your legs (bring a snack). All trips are weather-dependent, and reservations are advised, but the shop opens at 8 AM in summer if you want to take a chance. Even if you've brought your own kayak, stop in here for local advice. The season runs late May–late Sept. The shop is next to the Criterion Movie Theatre. Beginners are welcome.

Entertainment
At the height of the summer season, there's plenty of live entertainment, ranging from pub music to films to classical concerts.

Above Rupununi's restaurant, **Carmen Verandah,** 119 Main St., Bar Harbor 04609, 207/288-2766, www.carmenveranda.com, is the weekend place to be and be seen. Everything gets rolling about 9:30 PM—blues, rock, salsa, funk, jazz, you-name-it—and there's lots of square footage for dancing. Cover is $3–4 if there's a live band—a bargain. Other nights (lower or no cover) there's a DJ, and Miss Hylies Tuesday Show. Darts and pool round out the picture. Open daily, 11 AM–1 AM, May 1– Nov. 1.

Cinema: At the beautifully refurbished National Historic Landmark **Criterion Theater,** 35 Cottage St., Bar Harbor 04609, 207/288-3441 or 288-5829, www.criteriontheater.com, built in 1932, adults soak up the nostalgia of this art deco classic; kids just call it "awesome." Light food and drinks are offered on the floating balcony. Films, live music, and drama are on the entertainment menu.

You can take the Island Explorer right to the door, then enjoy gourmet pizza and beer or wine with your classic or first-run film at the two cinemas comprising **Reel Pizza Cinerama,** 33 Kennebec Pl., on the Village Green, Bar Harbor 04609, film 207/288-3811, food 207/288-3828. There are two screenings nightly in each theater, which open at 4:30 PM.

Shopping
Bar Harbor's boutiques are indisputably visitor-oriented; many shut down for the winter, even removing or covering their signs and blanketing the windows. Fortunately, the island has enough of a year-round community to support the cluster of loyal shopkeepers determined to stay open all year, but shop-till-you-droppers will be happy here only between Memorial Day weekend and Columbus Day. (Remember, too, that Bar Harbor isn't MDI's only shopping area.)

Galleries and Crafts: Birdsnest Gallery, 12 Mt. Desert St., Bar Harbor 04609, 207/288-4054, has a well-earned reputation for a fine selection of paintings, sculpture, and prints. Prices match the quality. Open Mon.– Sat. 10 AM–9 PM, Sun. noon–9 PM in summer, shorter hours other months, mid-May–mid-Oct.

Downtown Bar Harbor's best craft gallery is **Island Artisans,** 99 Main St., Bar Harbor 04609, 207/288-4214, www.islandartisans.com. More than 75 Maine artists are represented here, and the quality is outstanding. Don't miss it. You'll find basketwork, handmade paper, wood carvings, blown glass, jewelry, weaving, metalwork, ceramics, and more. Open May–Dec. Summer hours are 10 AM–10 PM daily. Winter hours and days vary; call to be sure. (Island Artisans has a summertime branch at 119 Main St. in Northeast Harbor, 207/276-4045.)

Books: Toys, cards, and newspapers blend in with the new-book inventory at **Sherman's Book Store,** 56 Main St., Bar Harbor 04609, 207/288-3161. There's even some fusty clutter here, but it's all user-friendly. Sherman's is just the place to pick up maps and trail guides for fine days and puzzles for foggy days. Open daily 9 AM–5:30 PM (to 10:30 PM in summer), all year.

Souvenir Gifts and Crafts: Souvenir shops are *everywhere* on Mount Desert Island, so why single out the Acadia Shops? If you need Maine-made mementos for Uncle Harry and Aunt Mary, if the kids need trinkets for friends back home, the Acadia Corporation has several shops in downtown Bar Harbor that can cover it all. Price range is broad, quality is fairly high, and clerks are especially friendly at **The Acadia Shop,** 85 Main St., Bar Harbor, 207/288-5600. It's open daily 8 AM–11 PM in midsummer, 9 AM–5 PM off-season. At 45 Main St., another branch, **Acadia Outdoors,** 207/288-2422, features sportswear.

Musical Instruments: Most vacationers don't expect to shop for musical instruments, but everyone with an affinity for folkloric music gravitates toward **Song of the Sea,** 47 West St., Bar Harbor 04609, 207/288-5653, www.songsea.com, a unique, jam-packed harborfront shop where you can find guitars, banjos, harmonicas, and tin whistles—but also such esoterica as hammered dulcimers, bagpipes, and psalteries. Ed and Anne Damm are incredibly knowledgeable and helpful, even to the point of playing instruments over the phone for call-in orders. Summer hours are Mon.–Sat. 10 AM–5:30 PM, Sun. noon–5 PM. More limited hours off-season. Open all year.

Farmers Market: Between Mother's Day and late October, the **Eden Farmers' Market** operates out of the YMCA parking lot off lower Main St. each Sun., 10 AM–1 PM.

Accommodations

Bar Harbor alone has thousands of beds in hotels, motels, inns, B&Bs, and cottages, not to mention campsites—and the rest of the island adds to the total. Nonetheless, lodgings can be scarce at the height of summer (particularly the first two weeks in August), also the outrageous peak period for room rates. Off-season, there's plenty of choice, even after the seasonal places shut down, and rates are always lower, often dramatically so.

Hotels and Motels: One of the town's best-known, most-visible, and best-located hotels is the **Bar Harbor Inn,** Newport Drive, Box 7, Bar Harbor 04609, 207/288-3351 or 800/248-3351, www.barharborinn.com, a sprawling complex on eight acres overlooking the harbor and Bar Island. The 153 rooms vary considerably in style, from traditional inn to motel, in three different buildings; rates are $199–369 d late June–Labor Day; there are six other rate seasons. Continental breakfast is included and special packages are available—an advantage if you have children. The kids also will appreciate the heated outdoor pool. There are three

rooms for pets. Service is attentive. Open mid-June–late Dec.

At the opposite end of the budgetary scale is the **Aurora Motel,** 51 Holland Ave., Bar Harbor 04609, 207/288-3771 or 800/841-8925, a clean, no-frills, family-run motel from which you can walk everywhere. Nine first-floor rooms ($109–149 d June–Oct., $59–99 Nov.–May) have private baths, phones, air-conditioning, and cable TV. No pets. Open all year.

Inns and B&Bs: Even the address is appealing at **Ullikana Bed & Breakfast,** 16 The Field, Bar Harbor 04609, 207/288-9552, www.ullikana.com, a Victorian Tudor house close to Bar Harbor's Shore Path. Everything blends beautifully here, even the modern-art collection. Ten comfortable rooms, all with private baths and some with water views, are $165–310 d in season, $125–275 d other months. The Yellow House, next door, has six rooms at $175–245 d. An incredible breakfast is served on the water-view patio. Reserve well ahead for this popular bed-and-breakfast. Open May–Oct.

Energetic Marian Burns, a former math/science teacher and former president of the Maine Innkeepers Association, is the reason everything runs smoothly at **Mira Monte Inn,** 69 Mt. Desert St., Bar Harbor 04609, 207/288-4263 or 800/553-5109, www.miramonte.com, close (but not too close) to downtown. Born and raised here, and an avid gardener, Marian's a terrific resource for island exploring. Ask about her experience during the 1947 Bar Harbor fire during hors d'oeuvres from 5–7 PM. And don't miss her collection of antique Bar Harbor hotel photos. The Victorian-style rooms have air-conditioning, cable TV, and other welcome touches ($150–230 d mid-June–Labor Day); three suites ($235–290 in peak season) in a separate building are ideal for families. Rates include buffet breakfast. No pets. Open early May–Oct. (the suites are open all year).

Innkeeper Jeffrey Anderholm, who runs the inn with wife Teri, calls it the "Un-Victorian:" **The Bass Cottage Inn,** 14 the Field, P.O. Box 242, Bar Harbor 04609, 207/288-

1234 or 888/782-9924, www.basscottage.com, has been garnering perfect travel review scores for its ultra-luxurious accommodations. Many rooms have whirlpool tubs and fireplaces. Rates from $185 d off-season to $240 d high season, including full gourmet breakfast, hors d'oeuvres, turndown and concierge service. Open early May–mid-Oct.

Three gorgeous water-view suites (and one smaller room) on a quiet side street are big draws at **The Bar Harbor Tides,** 119 West St., Bar Harbor 04609, 207/288-4968, www.bar-harbortides.com, a handsome Greek Revival manse on 1.5 acres overlooking the bay. Settle onto the veranda overlooking the water, and you might never want to leave. Access to Bar Island is right around the corner, restaurants a stroll away. Peak-season rates are $375–395 d for the two-room (with fireplace) suites, $225 d for the smaller room, including a full gourmet breakfast. Off-season packages available. No pets. Open all year.

Hostel: The **Mount Desert Island Youth Hostel,** 321 Main St., P.O. Box 1025, Bar Harbor 04609, 207/288-5587, www.barharborhostel.com, has just undergone a two-and-one-half year restoration, which Director Ron Gamble terms "quite spectacular." The seasonal (Apr. 1–Nov. 1) accommodation has a new shower room, an organic garden, maid service, and a Weber grill, among other luxuries. Rates are $24–27 per person per night, prepaid credit card reservations accepted Reservations are essential, as this is a popular location.

Campgrounds: There are no campsites within Bar Harbor's town limits, but there are plenty nearby; for a selection, see the sections on Mount Desert Island, Southwest Harbor and Vicinity, and Acadia National Park.

Seasonal Rentals: Contact Maine Island Properties, P.O. Box 1025, Mount Desert 04660, 207/244-4348, www.maineisland-properties.com, for listings of cottages available by the week or month. In high season (June–Labor Day), rates are also high.

Food

You won't go hungry in Bar Harbor, and you won't find chain fast-food places. The summer tourism trade and the College of the Atlantic students have created a demand for pizzerias, vegetarian bistros, brewpubs, and a handful of creative restaurants. But of course almost every restaurant has some variant of lobster. And even if you're using Bar Harbor as a base of operations, don't miss opportunities to explore restaurants elsewhere on the island.

Miscellanea: An unscientific but reliable local survey gives the best-pizza ribbon to **Rosalie's Pizza & Italian Restaurant,** 46 Cottage St., Bar Harbor 04609, 207/288-5666, where the Wurlitzer jukebox churns out tunes from the 1950s. This family-owned standard gets high marks for consistency with its homemade pizza (in four sizes or by the slice), calzones, and subs—lots of vegetarian options. Rosalie's is open daily from 11:30 AM, all year. Beer and wine are available.

Combine a pizza with a first-run or art flick at **Reel Pizza Cinerama,** 33 Kennebec Pl., on the Village Green, Bar Harbor 04609, film 207/288-3811, food 207/288-3828, where you order your pizza, grab an easy chair, and watch for your number to come up on the Bingo board. There are two screenings a night in each cinema. Pizzas ($10–18.25) have cinematic names—Zorba the Greek, The Godfather, Manchurian Candidate. Then there's Mussel Beach Party—broccoli, tomatoes, goat cheese, and smoked mussels. You get the idea. Film tickets are $6. Reel Pizza opens daily at 4:30 PM and has occasional Sat. matinees; open seven days a week year-round. Be sure to arrive early; the best chairs go quickly.

Efficient, friendly, cafeteria-style service makes **EPI Sub and Pizza Shop,** 8 Cottage St., Bar Harbor 04609, 207/288-5853 or 800/981-5853, an excellent choice for picnics or a quick break from sightseeing. The dozen-plus sub-sandwich choices at EPI's (short for epicurean) are bargains (try the Cadillac), and the pizza is right up there. If the weather closes in, there are always the pinball machines in the back room. No credit cards. Open daily 10 AM–8 PM July–Aug., evening hours curtailed in winter.

Brewpubs and Microbreweries: Bar

Harbor's longest-lived brewpub is the **Lompoc Café & Bocce Garden,** 36 Rodick St., Bar Harbor 04609, 207/288-9392, www .lompoccafe.com, serving creative lunches and dinners daily 11:30 AM–1 AM in season. Thin-crust pizza, wine by the glass, local ale (including Bar Harbor Blueberry Ale), grilled entrées, vegetarian choices. Dinner sandwiches and pizza in the $8–10 range, entrées $12–19. The congenial café has a heated outdoor dining room, a garden, a bocce court, and live entertainment (blues, bluegrass, and jazz) every weekend. During the summer, Thursdays are open-mic nights.

The pub's Blueberry Ale, plus five or six others, including Bar Harbor Real Ale, are brewed by the **Atlantic Brewing Company's Estate Brewery,** 15 Knox Rd., Town Hill (in the upper section of the island), Bar Harbor 04609, 207/288-2337 or 800/475-5417, www.atlanticbrewing.com, designed after the country wineries and beer gardens of Europe. Free brewery tours, including tasting of beers and Old Soaker Root Beer, are given daily at 2, 3, and 4 PM, in summer. The brewery also operates a tavern/café, 10 AM–6 PM daily, grill hours till 8 PM Each Saturday the tavern puts on an all-you-can-eat "brewer's BBQ," with live music, for $15, starting at 11 AM. The brewery sponsors the Town Hill Garlic Festival in late September.

Bar Harbor Brewing Company & Soda Works, 135 Otter Creek Dr., Bar Harbor 04609, 207/288-4592, www.barharborbrewing.com, begun in 1990 by Tod and Suzi Foster as a mom-and-pop operation, remains a small but select, friendly, hands-on microbrewery producing five kinds of beer and ale. Start off at the log-cabin tasting room/gift shop, where kids can sample Homemade Bar Harbor Root Beer or Blueberry Soda. Free 20-minute tours are given frequently between 3:30 and 5 PM Tues.–Fri., late June–late Aug. Tours and tastings every 20 minutes 3:30–5 PM. The brewery is 4.5 miles south of downtown Bar Harbor.

Inexpensive to Moderate: Once a Victorian boarding house and later a 1920s speakeasy, **Galyn's Galley,** 17 Main St., Bar Harbor 04609,

207/288-9706, www.galynsbarharbor.com, has been a popular eatery since 1986. Lots of plants, modern decor, reliable service, a great downtown location, and several indoor and outdoor dining areas contribute to the loyal clientele. The cuisine is consistently good if not outstandingly creative (dinner entrées $15–18). Reservations advisable in midsummer. The upstairs Galley Lounge has a mahogany bar. Open daily for lunch (11:30 AM–3 PM), dinner (4–10 PM in season), except major national holidays, and closed Dec.–Feb.

Just down the street from Galyn's, **Rupununi,** 119 Main St., Bar Harbor 04609, 207/288-2886, www.rupununi.com, gets its name from a river in Guyana. Billed as "an American bar and grill," Rupununi draws a lively, fun crowd for great burgers (even veggie and ostrich burgers), pasta, seafood, and meat dinner entrées ($10–23), and about two dozen beers on draft. Patio, children's menu. Open daily 11 AM–1 AM, mid-Apr.–Nov. Upstairs is **Carmen Verandah**.

Around the corner from Rupununi, in a funky side-street building with higgledy-piggledy decor (well, maroon paint, a wall lined with books, and a refrigerator door loaded with poetry magnets), is a not-very-well-kept secret, **Cafe This Way,** 14½ Mt. Desert St., Bar Harbor 04609, 207/288-4483. The café has been a hit since it opened in 1997, serving such eclectic items as crab cakes with tequila/lime sauce, on a menu that changes seasonally. The breakfast menu is a genuine wake-up call. Dinner entrées are in the $12–25 range; the wine list is very selective and the desserts are outstanding. Cafe This Way is open 7–11 AM Mon.–Sat., 8 AM–1 PM Sun., and 5:30–9 PM daily May–Oct.

Garlic shrimp and A-plus margaritas are specialties at **Miguel's Mexican Restaurant,** 51 Rodick St., Bar Harbor 04609, 207/288-5117, home of "The Picasso of Picante" and the island's most authentic traditional Mexican food. In midsummer, try for the patio (there's no air-conditioning, but there are ceiling fans). Expect to wait on weekends; this is a popular spot. Open daily for dinner 5 to close (usually 9 PM or a bit later); open daily, May–mid-Nov.

Southeast Asian cuisine has arrived with **Nakorn Thai,** 30 Rodick St., Bar Harbor 04609, 207/288-4060. A few super-spicy entrées appear on the huge menu with lots of the Thai usuals—pad thai ($7 at lunch, $9 at dinner), coconut soup, spicy duck, green curry. Entrée range is $8.50–13. Plenty of choices for vegetarians. Check on MSG when ordering. Beer and wine only. Open Mon.–Fri. for lunch and dinner, Sat.–Sun. for dinner only (from 4 PM). Open all year.

Moderate to Expensive: One of Bar Harbor's fine longtime reliables, **George's,** 7 Stephens Ln., Bar Harbor 04609, 207/288-4505, www.georgesbarharbor.com, occupies three attractively laid-out rooms in a restored home on a downtown side street. Mediterranean accented cuisine culminates in outrageous desserts. Appetizer grazers are approved here; it's recommended that one could make a meal of dishes like pungent steamed mussels, Spinney Creek oyster on the half shell, and lobster consommé. Lobster is treated in a unique way—it comes in a strudel, or char-grilled. Also on order might be char-grilled beef and vegetarian tandoori tempeh. Reservations are essential July–Aug. In addition to a well-chosen wine list, there are about a dozen wines by the glass. There's patio dining when weather permits. Open 6–9 PM daily, from mid-June, usually through fall. Six nights early and late in the season.

Cuban-esque cuisine is the hottest new entry on Bar Harbor's restaurant scene. With its bright orange walls and white tablecloths, and a jazz duo providing the background, **Havana,** 318 Main St., Bar Harbor 04609, 207/288-CUBA (2822), www.havanamaine.com, is a hit. Billing its cuisine as "American with a Latin flair," the café ends up with its own kind of fusion—as in chile and cinnamon seared scallops, black bean and Dijon crusted rack of lamb. Entrée range is $16–34; for $6.50, you get *mojito* cheesecake, based on the flavors of the Cuban national drink. Menu changes weekly to take advantage of seasonal produce.

Reservations are essential on weekends. Havana is open daily 5–10 PM, year-round.

The simply-lettered sign design, the windows with flower boxes, and the slate specials board on a chair—it must be a bistro—and it is. It's **Mache Bistro,** 135 Cottage St., Bar Harbor 04609, 207/288-0447, www.machebistro.com, where staples like coq au vin come with an accent of caramelized fennel and parsnips, and the chicken's organic, like much of the restaurant's food. There's pan-roasted salmon, and panko-crusted tofu, on an interesting menu where entrées go from $13–25. Mache Bistro, with an "eclectic" wine list and full bar, serves dinner nightly from 5 PM.

The view's the thing at the Bar Harbor Inn's **Reading Room Restaurant,** Newport Dr., Bar Harbor, 207/288-3351; request a window seat. Once the stuffy Bar Harbor Reading Room, a gentlemen's club, the dining room still has an incredible sweeping curve of windows overlooking Bar Island and Frenchman Bay. Dinner entrées, emphasizing meat and seafood, are commendably creative ($21–31), the wine list is good. On the dessert list are flourless chocolate cake, mango sorbet, pistachio and white chocolate mousse, and blueberry pie. Despite the elegant setting, dress is informal, and there's a children's menu. The Sunday brunch buffet (11:30 AM–2:30 PM; $25 adults, $12.50 kids) is extremely popular, eggs benedict are a favorite. Reservations are essential. Breakfast (mid-Apr.–Oct.) is 7–10:30 AM, dinner is 5:30–9:30 PM. At both meals, there is a harpist and pianist. Lighter fare is served at the **Terrace Grille,** for lunch and dinner, 11:30 AM on. The Grille also has lobsterbakes. It's a pretty picture with yellow umbrellas and a fabulous view of Frenchman's Bay from the terrace.

Five miles south of Bar Harbor is the nondescript-looking **Burning Tree,** Rte. 3, Otter Creek 04665, 207/288-9331, which is anything but nondescript inside. Bright and airy, with about 20 tables in three areas, it's one of Mount Desert Island's best restaurants, serving a casually chic crowd. Reservations are essential in summer. Specialties are imaginative seafood entrées, but there are organic chicken entrées, too. Pan sautéed monkfish glazed with a sweet chile sauce and served with Thai-style eggplant and coconut rice is a good bet on the huge menu of local seafoods. As are the cioppino, Maryland (yes!) crab cakes—and vegetarian dishes made from organic produce. The specialty crab cakes are 90 percent crabmeat, and edible flowers garnish the entrées ($18.50–23). The homemade breads and desserts are incredible. At the height of summer, service can be a bit rushed and the kitchen runs out of popular entrées. Solution: Plan to eat early; it's worth it. The Burning Tree is open for dinner, 5–10 PM, June–mid-Oct.; June–Labor Day, Wed.–Mon., after Labor Day. Wed.–Sun.

Ice Cream: Only a masochist could bypass **Ben and Bill's Chocolate Emporium,** 66 Main St., Bar Harbor 04609, 207/288-3281 or 800/806-3281, www.benandbills.com, a long-running taste-treat-cum-experience in downtown Bar Harbor. Candies and ice cream (including the dubious lobster flavor) are made fresh daily, and nothing short of outrageous; the whole place smells like the inside of a chocolate truffle. The shop, a cousin of three Massachusetts ice-cream parlors, is open daily.

Information and Services

The **Bar Harbor Chamber of Commerce,** 93 Cottage St., Bar Harbor 04609, 207/288-5103 or 888/540-9990, recorded message 207/288-3393, www.barharbormaine.com, close to the downtown action, has an especially helpful staff accustomed to a steady stream of summer traffic. The office is open Mon.–Fri. 8 AM–5 PM. A second Chamber office, in 1 Harbor Place on the Town pier, is open daily 9 AM–5 PM. The only drawback is a certain myopia: There's little information here on other parts of the island, so you'll need to remedy that by stopping at one of the information centers near the bridge from the mainland. Bar Harbor's annual visitor information booklet usually is off the presses in January, so you can plan ahead for a summer vacation. If you've managed to bestir yourself early enough to catch sunrise on the Cadillac summit, stop in at the chamber of commerce office and request an official membership card for the **Cadillac Mountain Sunrise Club** (they'll take your word for it).

Jesup Memorial Library, 34 Mt. Desert St., Bar Harbor 04609, 207/288-4245, is open all year, Tues.–Sat. 10 AM–5 PM (to 7 PM Wed.).

Newspapers: The *Bar Harbor Times,* 76 Cottage St., Bar Harbor 04609, 207/288-3311, founded in 1914, is published each Thursday, with extensive calendar listings. The paper also produces four summer issues of *The Acadia Visitor,* a free newsprint booklet containing features, ads, events listings, and other helpful touring tidbits for Acadia National Park and the rest of Mount Desert Island.

Public Restrooms: Downtown Bar Harbor has public restrooms at the town pier, in the municipal lot near the Village Green, and on the School St. side of the athletic field, where there is RV parking. There are also restrooms at the Mount Desert Island Hospital and the International Ferry Terminal.

Photo Services: Across from the Village Green, **First Exposure USA,** 156 Main St., P.O. Box 6, Bar Harbor 04609, 207/288-5868, provides one-hour photo service and rents cameras and camcorders. Open daily, 9 AM–8 PM, May–Oct., shorter hours off-season.

Getting Around

In the summer, driving and parking used to be hellacious in Bar Harbor, and it still can get congested if you're at the wheel, but the Island Explorer buses have been hugely successful in alleviating the gridlock.

On weekends, be creative: use bank parking lots on Main St. if you don't see signs prohibiting it, and the town-office lot on Cottage St. RVs are not allowed to park near the town pier; designated RV parking is alongside the athletic field, Lower Main and Park Sts., about eight blocks from the center of town.

NORTHEAST HARBOR AND VICINITY

Some sort of Northeast Harbor bush telegraph must have been operating in the Philadelphia area in the late 19th century, because Main

Liners from the City of Brotherly Love have been summering in and around this village since then. Sure, they also show up in other parts of Maine, but it's hard not to notice the preponderance of Pennsylvania license plates surrounding Northeast Harbor's elegant "cottages" from mid-July–mid-Aug. (In the last decade, the Pennsylvania plates have been joined by growing numbers from the District of Columbia, New York, and Texas.)

Actually, even though Northeast Harbor is a well-known name with special cachet, it isn't even an official township; it's a zip-coded village within the town of Mount Desert.

The small downtown area's attractive boutiques and eateries cater to a casually posh clientele, while the well-protected harbor attracts a tony crowd of yachties. For their convenience, a palm-size annual directory, *The Redbook,* discreetly lists owners' summer residences and winter addresses—but no phone numbers. The directory also includes listings for the village of Seal Harbor—an even more exclusive village a few miles east of Northeast Harbor where style maven Martha Stewart purchased a palatial estate in 1997, much to the chagrin of long-timers.

Except for two spectacular public gardens and two unusual museums, not much here is geared to budget-sensitive visitors—but there's no charge for admiring the scenery.

Sights

As you head toward Northeast Harbor on Rte. 198 from the northern end of Mount Desert Island, you'll begin seeing cliff-lined **Somes Sound** on your right. This glacier-sculpted fjord juts five miles into the interior of Mount Desert Island from its mouth, between Northeast and Southwest Harbors. Watch for the right-hand turn for Sargent Drive (no RVs allowed), and follow the lovely, granite-lined route along the east side of the sound. Halfway along, a marker explains the geology of this natural fjord, the only one on the eastern seaboard. There aren't many pullouts en route, and traffic can be fairly steady in midsummer, but don't miss it. An ideal way to appreciate Somes Sound is from the water—sign up for an excursion out of Northeast or Southwest Harbor.

If you have the slightest interest in gardens (even if you don't, for that matter), allow time for Northeast Harbor's two marvelous public gardens, **Asticou and Thuya Gardens.** Information about both is available from the local chamber of commerce. If gardens are extra-high on your priority list, inquire also about visiting the private Rockefeller garden, accessible on a very limited basis.

Maine's best spring showcase is the **Asticou Azalea Garden,** a 2.3-acre pocket where about 70 varieties of azaleas, rhododendrons, and laurels—many from the classic Reef Point garden of famed landscape designer Beatrix Farrand—burst into bloom. When Charles K. Savage, beloved former innkeeper of the Asticou Inn, learned the Reef Point garden was being undone in 1956, he went into high gear to find funding and managed to rescue the azaleas and provide them with the gorgeous setting they have today, across the road and around the corner from the inn. Oriental serenity is the key—with a Japanese sand garden, stone lanterns, granite outcrops, pink-gravel paths, and a tranquil pond—so try to visit early in the season, early in the morning, to savor the effect. The garden is on Rte. 198, at the northern edge of Northeast Harbor, immediately north of the junction with Peabody Dr. (Rte. 3). Watch for a tiny sign on the right, marking access to the parking area. Although Asticou is open daily, all year, prime time for azaleas is mid-May–mid-June.

Behind a carved wooden gate on a forested hillside not far from Asticou lies an enchanted garden also designed by Charles K. Savage, and inspired by Beatrix Farrand. Special features of **Thuya Garden** are perennial borders, sculpted shrubbery, and Oriental touches. On a misty summer day, when few visitors appear, the colors are brilliant. Adjacent to the garden is **Thuya Lodge,** 207/276-5130, former summer cottage of Joseph Curtis, donor of this awesome municipal park. The lodge, with an extensive botanical library and quiet rooms for reading, is open daily 10 AM–4:30 PM, late June–Labor Day. The garden is open 7 AM–7 PM, July–Sept. A collection box next to the front gate requests a small donation. To reach Thuya, continue on Rte. 3 beyond Asticou Garden and watch for the Asticou Terraces parking area (no RVs, two-hour limit) on the right. Cross the road and climb the Asticou Terraces Trail (0.4 mile) to the garden. Or drive 0.2 mile beyond the Rte. 3 parking area, watching for a minuscule Thuya Garden sign on the left. Go half a mile up the driveway to the parking area.

After you've visited Thuya Garden, go outside the back gate, where you'll see a sign for the **Eliot Mountain Trail,** a 1.4-mile moderately difficult (lots of exposed roots) round-trip. Near the summit, Northeast Harbor spreads out before you. If you're here in August, sample the wild blueberries. Eliot Mountain is not an Acadia National Park trail, and much of it is on private land, so stay on the path and be respectful of private property.

On Northeast Harbor's quiet South Shore Rd., **Petite Plaisance** is a museum commemorating noted Belgian-born author and college professor Marguerite Yourcenar (pen name of Marguerite de Crayencour), first woman elected to the prestigious Académie Française. From the early 1950s to 1987, Petite Plaisance was her home, and it's hard to believe she's no longer here; her intriguing possessions and presence fill the two-story house. Free, hour-long tours of the first floor are given in French or English, depending on visitors' preferences. French-speaking visitors often make pilgrimages here. The house is open daily, June 15–Aug. 31. No children under 12. Call 207/276-3940 at least a day ahead, 9 AM–4 PM, for an appointment and directions, or write: Petite Plaisance Trust, P.O. Box 403, Northeast Harbor 04662. Yourcenar devotees should request directions to Brookside Cemetery in Somesville, seven miles away, where she is buried.

Nautical buffs and kids of all ages will thrill to the model ships, small boats, historic naval equipment (including a 1908 gasoline engine six feet long and four feet tall), and exhibits on the maritime history of the Mount Desert Is-land area in the small, eclectic **Great Harbor Maritime Museum,** 125 Main St., P.O. Box 145, Northeast Harbor 04662, 207/276-5262, housed in the old village fire station and municipal building. ("Great Harbor" refers to the Somes Sound area—Northeast, Southwest, and Seal Harbors, as well as the Cranberry Isles.) Yachting, coastal trade, and fishing receive special emphasis. What else is here? Antique photos and tools, furniture and clothing—even a working player piano. Special programs and exhibits are held during the summer. The museum is open Tues.–Sat. 10 AM–5 PM, June–Columbus Day, plus weekends Sept.–Oct.

Getting Afloat

Northeast Harbor is the starting point for most of the boats headed for the **Cranberry Isles.** The vessels depart from the commercial floats at the end of the concrete Municipal Pier on Sea St.

Captain James and Andy Allen's 75-foot *Sea Princess,* 207/276-5352, carries visitors as well as an Acadia National Park naturalist on a three-hour morning trip around the mouth of Somes Sound and out to Little Cranberry Island (Islesford) for a 50-minute stopover. The boat leaves Northeast Harbor daily at 10 AM, mid-May–mid-Oct. Cost is $24 adults, $23 seniors, $15 children under 12. An afternoon trip, departing at 1 PM on the same route, spends less time on Islesford and visits Southwest Harbor instead. The *Sea Princess* also does a scenic 1.5-hour Somes Sound cruise, departing daily at 3:45 PM, late June–early Sept. The same months, there's also a three-hour sunset/dinner cruise, departing 5:15 PM for the Islesford Dock Restaurant on Little Cranberry (Islesford), and a 1.5-hour sunset Somes Sound cruise at 7 PM. Tickets for all but the 10 AM cruise are $20 adults, $19 seniors, and $15 children (does not include dinner). Reservations are advisable for all trips.

Shopping

Gifts and Clothing: Two upscale shops here are worth a visit (if you have the money) and maybe even a major splurge.

Early and late in the season, the summer crowd shops at **The Kimball Shop & Boutique,** 135 Main St., P.O. Box 468, Northeast Harbor 04662, 207/276-3300, www.kimballshop.com, to stock up on wedding and Christmas gifts. It's all very tasteful. Open all year on Thursdays, 9:30 AM–5 PM. From the July Fourth weekend to Labor Day, it's open Mon.–Sat. 9 AM–6 PM, Sun. 11 AM–4 PM. Other times, no Sun. hours, open 9 AM–5 PM Mon.–Sat.

At **Local Color,** 147 Main St., Northeast Harbor 04662, 207/276-5544, you'll find stunning silk and chenille sweaters and blouses, and exquisite jewelry. Most of the clothing is designed by talented owner Jayn Thomas and locally made from incredible imported fabrics. Quality is high, and so are prices. The shop is open Mon.–Sat. 10 AM–5 PM, 10 AM–4 PM Sun., May–Sept.

Luxuries: Consider it a yuppie adventure to visit the **Pine Tree Market,** Main St., Northeast Harbor 04662, 207/276-3335, where you'll find gourmet goodies, a huge wine selection, resident butcher, fresh fish, deli, and homemade breads and pastries. A landmark here since 1921, the market is open Mon.–Sat. 7 AM–7 PM, Sun. 8 AM–6 PM; delivery to your yacht is extra.

Farmers Market: Late June–Aug., the Northeast Harbor Farmers Market is set up each Thurs., 9 AM–noon, on Huntington Rd., across from the Kimball Terrace Inn. Look for cheeses, cider, poultry, pork, milk, eggs, breads and cookies, berries, and vegetables.

Accommodations

Unless you're celebrating a landmark occasion, Northeast Harbor's lodgings may be a little too pricey, but if money's no object and a haute ambience appeals, spring for the **Asticou Inn,** Rte. 3, Northeast Harbor 04662, 207/276-3344 or 800/258-3373, www.asticou.com. Built in 1883 and refurbished periodically, the classic inn has 48 accommodations, both rooms and suites, many ocean-view, plus several modern cottages. August is the priciest month, with rooms ranging from $235–325, including breakfast. A MAP plan is also offered July–Aug. Facilities include clay tennis courts and an outdoor pool. The elegant, mural-lined dining room, open to the public for Sunday brunch (July–Aug., 11:30 AM–2 PM) and dinner (6–9 PM, all season) by reservation, has fabulous views of the harbor. No jeans; collared shirts required at dinner. Lunch is also open to the public, served 11:30 AM–2 PM (July–Aug.); reservations aren't needed. The inn is open mid-May–mid-Oct. Plan a late-May or early-June visit; you're practically on top of the Asticou Azalea Garden, and Thuya Garden is a short walk away.

Food

Lobster-in-the-Rough: At the edge of Somes Sound, five miles north of downtown Northeast Harbor, **Abel's Lobster Pound,** Rte. 198, Mount Desert 04660, 207/276-5827, prides itself on its knockout view and sometimes rests on those laurels. Outdoor or indoor dining; liquor license. You can also order crustaceans cooked to go. Abel's is open late May–Columbus Day. Open noon–9 daily July–Aug. Reservations are taken for 6, 6:30, 8, and 8:30 PM.

Inexpensive: Real Local Color and crab cakes ($20.95) and crab sandwiches are *the best* at the **Docksider,** 14 Sea St., Northeast Harbor 04662, 276-3965, a low-key, family-friendly, unassuming, hole-in-the-wall place inevitably jammed with devoted locals and summer folk. Located just up the hill from the chamber office, the Docksider has an outside deck, plus a couple of veteran (since forever) waitresses, no view, and a reputation far and wide. At $27.95, the shore dinner (chowder, clams, lobster, salad) is one of the best bargains in the state. Wine and beer only. If you're smitten, buy one of their T-shirts, featuring an upright lobster announcing, "Frankly, I don't give a clam." Open for lunch and dinner in summer, 11 AM–9 PM (early-bird specials 4:30–6 PM). Closed off-season.

Moderate to Expensive: Using as much locally grown, produced, and humanely raised foodstuffs as possible, **151 Main Street,** 151 Main St., Northeast Harbor 04662,

207/276-9898, www.151mainst.com, puts it all together in a casual bistro where locals rub elbows with Rockefellers. Gourmet thin-crust pizzas cost about $10. The café is famous for its crab cakes, meatloaf, and warm, inviting atmosphere. Entrées range $17–24. Dinner Tues.–Sat. 5:30 PM till close. Open May into late October, early November, or "when people stop coming."

Information

The harborfront Chamber Information Bureau (also called the Yachtsmen's Building) of the **Mount Desert Chamber of Commerce,** 18 Harbor Rd., P.O. Box 675, Northeast Harbor 04662, 207/276-5040, www.mountde-sertchamber.org, is open daily, 8 AM–5 PM, Memorial Day–Sept. The chamber covers the villages of Somesville, Northeast Harbor, Seal Harbor, Otter Creek, Pretty Marsh, Hall Quarry, and Beech Hill. The extremely cordial staff can provide information on Northeast Harbor's gardens, museums, and trails, in addition to food and lodging. They even monitor two tennis courts and rental tennis rackets are available. Coin-operated ($2, quarters only) hot showers, intended primarily but not exclusively for the boating crowd, are available here round the clock. Hair dryers are rentable, too. There's free coffee and tea, too. Request a free copy of the annual *Port Directory* for Northeast Harbor and other villages. To obtain a copy early in the year, call 207/244-5040.

ROUTE 102/198 TOWARD THE ISLAND'S WESTERN SIDE

Now let's back up to the head of the island. Just after the Thompson Island information center, if you don't take Rte. 3 toward the Acadia National Park Visitors Center and Bar Harbor, your other choice is Rte. 102/198, toward Southwest Harbor and lesser-known parts of the island's "quiet side." Here's what you'll encounter if you bear right at the fork.

Indian Point/Blagden Preserve: It's an easy side trip from the fork to a lovely preserve owned by The Nature Conservancy. From the junction of Rtes. 3 and 102/198, continue 1.8 miles to Indian Point Rd. and turn right. Go 1.7 miles to a fork and turn right. Watch for the preserve entrance on the right, marked by a Nature Conservancy oak leaf.

Five trails wind through forested, 110-acre Indian Point/Blagden Preserve, a rectangular Nature Conservancy parcel with island, hill, and bay vistas. Seal-watching and birding are popular—harbor seals on offshore rocks and woodpeckers (plus 130 other species) in blow-down areas. To spot the seals, plan your hike around low tide, when they'll be sprawled on the rocks close to shore. Wear rubberized shoes. Bring binoculars or use the telescope installed here for the purpose. To keep from disturbing the seals, watch quietly and avoid jerky movements. Park near the preserve entrance and follow the Big Woods Trail, running the length of the preserve. There's a second parking area farther in, but then you'll miss much of the preserve. When you reach the second parking area, just past an old field, bear left along the Shore Trail to see the seals. Register at the caretakers' house (just beyond the first parking lot, where you can pick up bird and flora checklists), and respect private property on either side of the preserve. Open daily, dawn–6 PM, all year.

SOUTHWEST HARBOR AND VICINITY

From Town Hill drive south toward Somesville and then on to Southwest Harbor, which considers itself the hub of Mount Desert Island's quiet side. In fact, in summer, Southwest Harbor's tiny downtown district is probably the busiest spot on the whole western side of the island (west of Somes Sound), but that's not saying a great deal. It has the feel of a settled community, a year-round flavor that Bar Harbor sometimes lacks. And it competes with the best in the scenery department. The Southwest Harbor area deserves the nod as a very convenient base for exploring Acadia National Park, the island's less-crowded villages, and offshore Swans Island.

Officially, the town of Southwest Harbor only includes the village of Bass Harbor, but the island's lovely western-side village of Somesville is nearby, as is the neighboring town of Tremont, which includes the villages of Bernard and Seal Cove.

Be sure to drive or bike around the smaller villages, especially Somesville, Bass Harbor, and Bernard. Views are fabulous, the pace is slow, and you'll feel you've stumbled upon "the real Maine." The Somesville Historic District, with its distinctive arched white footbridge, is especially appealing, but traffic gets congested here along Rte. 102, so rather than just rubbernecking, plan to stop and walk around.

A broad swath of Acadia National Park cuts right through the center of this side of the island, and many of its hiking trails are far less congested than elsewhere in the park.

Sights

Museums: In the center of Southwest Harbor, the **Wendell Gilley Museum,** 41 Herrick Rd., corner of Rte. 102, P.O. Box 254, Southwest Harbor 04679, 207/244-7555, was established in 1981 to display the life's work of local woodcarver Wendell Gilley (1904-83). The modern, energy-efficient museum houses more than 200 of his astonishingly realistic bird specimens. Don't miss it. Special summer exhibits feature other wildlife artists. Many days, a local artist gives woodcarving demonstrations, and the gift shop carries an ornithological potpourri—books to binoculars to carving tools. Kids over eight appreciate this more than younger ones. Wheelchair access. Tickets are $5 adults, $2 children 5–12. Open Tues.–Sun. 10 AM–4 PM, June–Oct. (to 5 PM July–Aug.), Fri.–Sun. in May and Nov.–Dec.

Touching a sea cucumber or a starfish may not be every adult's idea of fun, but kids sure enjoy the hands-on experience at the **Southwest Harbor Oceanarium,** Clark Point Rd., Southwest Harbor 04679, 207/244-7330, sister-site to the Bar Harbor Oceanarium. A knowledgeable naturalist introduces creatures from a watery touch tank during a tour of the facility. Twenty other exhibits line the walls of this intriguing, low-tech museum located next

to the Coast Guard station. It's open Mon.–Sat. 9 AM–5 PM, mid-May–late Oct. Oceanarium tickets are $8 adults, $6 children 4–12; combination tickets, covering this and the Oceanarium, are $15 and $9.75.

On the westernmost side of the island, a nondescript blue building camouflages **The Seal Cove Auto Museum,** Pretty Marsh Rd., Rte. 102, Seal Cove 04674, 207/244-9242, a fantastic collection of more than 100 antique autos and several dozen antique motorcycles—many from the turn of the 20th century. It's easy for kids of any age to spend an hour here, reminiscing and/or fantasizing. Tickets are $5 adults, $2 children under 12. Open daily 10 AM–5 PM, June 1–Sept. 15, the museum is about six miles southwest of Somesville. Or, if you're coming from Southwest Harbor, take the Seal Cove Rd. (partly unpaved) west to Rte. 102 and go north about 1.5 miles.

Bass Harbor Head Light: At the southern end of Mount Desert's western "claw," follow Rte. 102A to the turnoff toward Bass Harbor Head. Drive or bike to the end of Lighthouse Rd., walk down a steep wooden stairway, and look up and to the right. Bass Harbor Head Light—its red glow automated since 1974—stands sentinel at the eastern entrance to Blue Hill Bay. Built in 1858, the 26-foot tower and lightkeeper's house are privately owned, but the dramatic setting is a photographer's dream. Winter access to the parking lot may be limited, but otherwise the area is open all year. Not far from the light (east along Rte. 102A) are the trailheads for the easy Ship Harbor and Wonderland nature trails, part of Acadia National Park.

Recreation

Acadia National Park is the recreational focus throughout Mount Desert Island; on the island's western side, the main nonpark recreational activities are bike-, boat-, and picnic-related.

At the Southwest Harbor/Tremont Chamber of Commerce office, or at any of the area's stores, lodgings, and restaurants, pick up a free copy of the *Trail Map/Hiking Guide,* a

Acadia Region

very handy foldout map showing more than 20 hikes on the west side of Mount Desert Island. Trail descriptions include distance, time required, and skill levels (easy to strenuous).

Picnic spots are everywhere on this side of the island, but an Acadia National Park site that many people miss is the **Pretty Marsh Picnic Area,** overlooking Pretty Marsh Harbor. Dense woods shelter grills and tables, and you can walk down to the shoreline and even launch a sea kayak. Kids love this place, but be prepared with insect repellent. The picnic area is just west of Rte. 102, on the westernmost side of Mount Desert Island.

Bicycling: Southwest Cycle, Main St., Southwest Harbor 04679, 207/244-5856 or 800/649-5856, a veteran business with a first-rate reputation, rents bikes by the day ($19 adults, $12 children) and week and is open all year. July–Aug., hours are Mon.–Sat. 8:30 AM–5:30 PM and Sun. 10 AM–4 PM. See *Islands near Mount Desert,* below, for planning a biking day-trip from Bass Harbor to Swans Island or from Southwest Harbor to the Cranberry Isles. The staff at Southwest Cycle will fix you up with maps and lots of good advice for three loops (10-30 miles) on the western side of Mount Desert. They also rent every imaginable accessory, from baby seats to jogging strollers. Open Mar.–Christmas; call for hours off-season.

Getting Afloat

Southwest Harbor is the home of one of the nation's premier boat-builders, **The Hinckley Company,** 130 Shore Rd., P.O. Box 699, Southwest Harbor 04679, 207/244-5531, a name with stellar repute since the 1930s. There are no tours of the Hinckley complex, but most yachtsmen can't resist the urge to look in at the yard. Plus you can stop in at the **Hinckley Ship's Store,** 207/244-7100 or 800/446-2553, and pick up books, charts, and all sorts of Hinckley-logo gear. The shop is open all year, Mon.–Fri. 8 AM–5 PM, Sat.–Sun., 9–2:30 PM.

Canoeing/Kayaking: Across the road from Long Pond, the largest lake on Mount Desert Island, **National Park Canoe Rental,** 145 Pretty Marsh Rd., Rte. 102, Box 120, Mount Desert 04660, 207/244-5854, makes canoeing or kayaking a snap; it's even easier if you're staying at the adjoining Long Pond Inn. Just rent the boat, carry it across to Pond's End, and launch it. Be sure to pack a picnic. Half-day (July–Aug. 8–11 AM, 11 AM–2 PM, 2–5 PM) rate for a canoe is $25, tandem kayak $27, solo kayak $24; off-season (May, June, Sept., and Oct., 8:30 AM–12:30 PM and 1–5 PM) rates are $25 for a canoe; $27 for a tandem kayak, $25 for a solo; full-day rate (in-season) is $45 canoe, $52 tandem kayak, $40 solo. Reservations are advisable, and essential July–Aug. Open mid-May–mid-Oct.

If you've brought your own canoe (or kayak), launch it here at Pond's End and head off. It's four miles to the southern end of the lake. If the wind kicks up, skirt the shore; if it *really* kicks up from the north, don't paddle too far down the lake, as you'll have a devil of a time getting back.

You can swim at Pond's End, and in the upper half of the lake, but swimming is banned in the lower half, as it's used for drinking water. Almost the entire west side of Long Pond is national park property, so plan to picnic and swim along there; tuck into the sheltered area west of Southern Neck, a crooked finger of land that points northward from the western shore. Stay clear of private property on the east side of the lake.

Entertainment

It's not too far to drive from Southwest Harbor to Bar Harbor for evening dinner and entertainment, but Southwest has a cabaret theater that even draws customers in the reverse direction—**The Deck House Restaurant and Cabaret Theater** 11 Apple Lane, Southwest Harbor 04679, 207/244-5044, www.thedeckhouse.com. For dinner, served daily, try to arrive by 6:30 PM to enjoy the spectacular harbor view and order your meal (entrées are $21.95; appetizers and salads are à la carte, and there is a house entertainment charge of $7). The table is yours for the evening (reservations are essential in midsummer). About 8:15 PM, the young waitstaff, chameleonlike, unveils its other talents—singing, dancing, even storytelling and puppetry. After hearing the dozen or so numbers, you won't be surprised to learn that many Deck House staff have moved on to Broadway and beyond. The Deck House is open nightly, early June–mid-Sept.

Since the early 1970s, the **Acadia Repertory Theatre,** Rte. 102, Somesville, mailing address P.O. Box 106, Mount Desert 04660, 207/244-7260, www.acadiarep.com, has been providing first-rate professional thespian repertory on the stage of Somesville's antique Masonic Hall. Classic plays by Wilde, Goldsmith, even Molière, have been staples, as has the annual Agatha Christie mystery. Performances run early July–early Sept., Tues.–Sun. at 8:15 PM, with 2 PM matinees on the last Sunday of each play. Tickets are $20 adults; $15 seniors, students, and military; $10 children 16 and under. Special children's programs, such as *Charlotte's Web,* or *Beauty and the Beast,* occur Wed. and Sat. at 10:30 AM; tickets are $7 adults, $5 children.

Events

The towns on Mount Desert which are *not* Bar Harbor are claiming their communal identity with the **Quietside Festival** in July. Highlight is always a pink flamingo event. It's highly creative, and a lot of fun.

Shopping

The best shopping locales on this side of the island are Southwest Harbor and the villages of Somesville and Bernard. Mind you, there aren't *lots* of shops, but the small selection is interesting. Somesville, Southwest Harbor, and Bernard are all on Rte. 7 of the free Island Explorer bus service.

Antiques: It's hard to label **Nancy Neale Typecraft,** Steamboat Wharf Rd., Bernard 04612, 207/244-5192, fax 244-5090. Museum? Shop? Gallery? Right on Bernard Harbor, Nancy and Irving Silverman have assembled the nation's largest collection (three million pieces) of wooden printing type. Stop in, browse through the goodies (some not for sale), and create your own type art (at no

charge). The shop theoretically is open June–mid-Oct., but if you're making a special detour, it's best to call ahead for an appointment; the hours are unpredictable. From downtown Southwest Harbor, it's four miles. Take Rte. 102, through the center of Tremont, and turn left onto Bernard Rd. Continue to Steamboat Wharf Rd. and turn right. You can't miss the shop, covered with a wall of lobster buoys and next to the Silvermans' private lighthouse. It's a shutterbug's delight. And while you're at it, have lunch or dinner here at Thurston's Lobster Pound.

Stop in at **E.L. Higgins,** Bernard Rd., P.O. Box 69, Bernard 04612, 207/244-3983, www.antiquewicker.com. Located in two one-time classrooms in an 1890s schoolhouse, Edward Higgins has the state's best collection of antique wicker furniture—about 400 pieces at any given time. Three generations work in the shop, open mid-Apr.–Oct., usually daily 10 AM–5 PM, but since this is a bit out of the way, call ahead to be sure.

Books: The two-story **Port in a Storm Bookstore,** Main St., Rte. 102, Somesville, Mount Desert 04660, 207/244-4114 or 800/694-4114, www.portinastormbookstore.com. This book store is totally seductive, guaranteed to lighten your wallet. High ceilings, comfortable chairs, whimsical floor sculptures, open space, and Somes Cove views all contribute to the ambience. Inventory is not huge, but it's well selected—especially nature and children's books—and the staff is very knowledgeable. Especially in summer, noted authors often appear to lecture or sign their books. The shop is open during the summer Mon.–Sat. 9:30 AM–6:30 PM, and Sun. noon–6:30 PM. Off-season hours are Mon.–Sat. 10 AM–5:30 PM, Sun. 1–5 PM.

Accommodations

As the Asticou Inn is to Northeast Harbor, so is the Claremont to Southwest Harbor. On the other end of the lodging scale, there are several commercial campgrounds in this part of the island, plus an Acadia National Park campground.

Acadia Region

When you're ready to splurge, **The Claremont,** P.O. Box 137, Southwest Harbor 04679, 207/244-5036 or 800/244-5036, (theclaremonthotel.com) may well be your choice, but you'll have to plan a year ahead to land a room in July or August. Most popular time is the first week in August, during the annual Claremont Croquet Classic. This yellow-clapboard grande dame, dominating a six-acre hilltop overlooking Somes Sound, caters to honeymooners, yuppies, and gentrified folk. Service is impeccable; enjoy it.

The Claremont Dining Room, with a view from every table, is open to the public for breakfast and dinner (jackets and ties requested for dinner). Dining-room reservations are wise in midsummer. In July and Aug., informal lunches and cocktails are served in the shorefront Boat House, also open to the public. Dating from 1884, the main building has 26 rooms (with bath and phones), most of them recently refurbished. Other accommodations are in two other buildings (six-room Phillips House and one-suite Clark House) and 14 cottages, with a wide range of daily and weekly rates. Cottages can go as high as $3,200 a week in midsummer. Main-building and Phillips House rooms are $305 d, MAP, mid-July–Labor Day, plus a hefty 22 percent service and lodging tax. (Rooms without water views can be rented at a B&B rate, $185 d). Rates are lower in shoulder seasons. No pets, no credit cards, no smoking in rooms. Children are welcome. The hotel and dining room are open early June–mid-Oct.; cottages are open late May–mid-Oct.

The Birches is on Fernald Point Rd., P.O. Box 178, Southwest Harbor 04679, 207/244 5182, www.thebirchesb&b.com, Dick and Rocky Homer's waterfront home on five acres 0.4 mile east of Rte. 102. Outside are gardens and a croquet court. Three lovely rooms (two with water views) have private baths; $115–125 d. Two-night minimum. From the last week in October through the third week in May rate is $90. No pets.

In downtown Southwest Harbor, the following two B&Bs stand cheek-by-jowl—hard to choose between them.

The only amenity not provided at the tasteful **Inn at Southwest,** 371 Main St., Rte. 102, Box 593, Southwest Harbor 04679, 207/244-3835, www.innatsouthwest.com, is a TV, but no one misses it. Guests gather for games, reading, conversation, and afternoon tea in a huge living room with fireplace and comfortable couches. Built in 1884 as the Freeman Cottage, the elegant building has 13 dormers and a wraparound veranda. Seven second- and third-floor guest rooms—named for Maine lighthouses and full of character—are fitted out with wicker furniture, ceiling fans, down comforters, and lots more. All have private baths. It's hard to choose, but the Cape Elizabeth Room is a winner. Rates are $125–175 d mid-June–mid-Oct., $95–135 other months. Two-night minimum on holiday weekends. No pets, no small children; smoking only on the veranda. Open May–Oct.

Across the lane, the **Kingsleigh Inn 1904,** 373 Main St., P.O. Box 1426, Southwest Harbor 04679, 207/244-5302, www.kingsleighinn.com, is a very attractive Queen Anne manse with eight well-thought-out rooms (private baths) on three floors. If you're sensitive to street noise, request a back-facing (harbor-view) room, although air-conditioners muffle the sound in summer. There's a separate guest phone, and innkeepers Dana and Greg Moos provide afternoon tea with delicious baked treats. Rates are $135–265 d mid-June–mid-Oct., $110–175 d other months. Be sure to check out the huge turret suite, with fireplace, TV, telescope, large bathroom, and lots of comfortable wicker furniture. No smoking, no pets, no small children. Open all year.

Ann and Charlie Bradford's **Island House,** 36 Freeman Ridge Rd., Box 1006, Southwest Harbor 04679, 207/244-5180, www.islandhousebb.com, has recently been reborn in a brand new B&B on a hill surrounded by fragrant pine and fir. Though their location has changed, the Bradford's hospitality and breakfast are as memorable as ever. Two easily accessible rooms rent for $110 per night July–Oct. Off-season rates are $75. They also offer a loft efficiency over their garage which has 2 sleeping rooms, and full kitchenette. It rents for $150 per night including breakfast ($10 surcharge for a one-night stay) July–Aug. No smoking, no pets, no children except in the loft efficiency. The Bradfords also rent Wood-Sea, a comfortable two-bedroom summer cottage, (June–Oct.) for $650–875 a week. It's near Bass Harbor Head Light, about five miles from Southwest Harbor.

At the **Lindenwood Inn,** 118 Clark Point Rd., Box 1328, Southwest Harbor 04679, 207/244-5335 or 800/307-5335, (lindenwood-inn.com) the linden-blossom fragrance is incredible if you're here in summer. Jim King, the Australian owner, has imaginatively decorated the main house's eight second- and third-floor rooms (private baths) with artifacts from everywhere. After hiking Acadia's trails, the heated pool is especially welcome. Rates are $115–295 d mid-June–mid-Oct., $95–245 d may–mid-June. Separate cottages are $215 in high season, $185 other months. No pets; smoking only on decks and porches.

Campgrounds: A smallish, low-key campground in an outstanding setting, **Somes Sound View Campground,** 86 Hall Quarry Rd., Mount Desert 04660, 207/244-3890 (off-season: 723-7965), has 60 large tent and RV (max 32 feet) sites on the edge of the eponymous quarry. Facilities include hot showers; nearest store is two miles. Tent sites are $25–40 July–Aug., (RV's $30) less early and late in the season. No credit cards. Open late May–mid-Oct. The campground is two miles south and east of Somesville and a mile east of Rte. 102.

On the eastern edge of Somesville, just off Rte. 198 at the head of Somes Sound, the **Mount Desert Campground,** Rte. 198, Somesville, mailing address P.O. Box 181, Mount Desert 04660, 207/244-3710, www .mountdesertcampground.com, is especially centrally located for visiting Bar Harbor, Acadia, and the whole western side of Mount Desert Island. The campground has 148 wooded tent sites, about 45 on the water. Reservations are advisable for this popular and low-key campground, which gets high marks for maintenance, noise control, and convenient

tent platforms. Rates are $33–45 a night. No pets July–Aug. or Labor Day weekend. No trailers over 20 feet. Kayak rentals are available. Open mid-June–Sept.

Seasonal Rentals: Contact **L.S. Robinson Real Estate,** 337 Main St., Southwest Harbor 04679, 207/244-5563, www.lsrobinson.com, which commands an inventory of 500 seasonal (and year-round) rentals, covering all of Mount Desert Island.

Food

Thurston's Lobster Pound, Steamboat Wharf Rd., Bernard 04612, 207/244-7600, is probably the best lobster-alfresco deal on the island. Family-oriented Thurston's also has chowders, sandwiches, and terrific desserts. The screened dining room practically sits in the water. Beer and wine available. Open Memorial Day weekend to Columbus Day, daily 11 am–8:30 pm. Closed Labor Day.

Inexpensive to Moderate: Some of the island's most creative sandwiches and pizza toppings emerge from Arthur and Kate Jacobs's **Little Notch Pizzeria**, 340 Main St., P.O. Box 1295, Southwest Harbor 04679, 207/244-3357, next to the library in Southwest Harbor's downtown. How about a small broccoli, sausage, and black-olive pizza? Freshly baked breads, outrageous desserts, a couple of dinner entrées, and homemade soups, stews, and chowders make the Little Notch a winner. Open all year, Mon.–Sat. 11 am–8 pm mid-May–mid-Oct.; open 11 am–7 pm weekdays mid-Oct.–mid-May.

With a spectacular harbor view and outrageous decor (even a lava light behind the bar), **Restaurant XYZ**, 80 Sewall Rd., Southwest Harbor 04679, 207/244-5221, specializes in "classical food of the Mexican interior"—unusual entrées from Xalapa, Yucatán, and Zacatecas. Most popular dish? Cochinitas—citrus-marinated pork rubbed with achiote paste. The margaritas are classic—requiring, allegedly, 1,800 pounds of fresh limes each year. For dessert, try the exquisite XYZ pie. Open for dinner daily July–Aug. (reserve ahead), Thurs.–Sat. in shoulder seasons. XYZ is an easy 10-minute walk from the Town Dock.

Information and Services

At the corner of Rte. 103 and Seal Cove Rd., in the Southwest Harbor Shoppes mini-mall, **Southwest Harbor/Tremont Chamber of Commerce,** 204 Main St., P.O. Box 1143, Southwest Harbor 04679, 207/244-9264 or 800/423-9264, www.acadiachamber.com, is open on an erratic schedule, but you can usually find someone here weekdays in summer.

The information center at Thompson Island has longer and more predictable hours.

Recently renovated to double its size, the **Southwest Harbor Public Library,** 338 Main St., Southwest Harbor 04679, 207/244-7065, is open Mon.–Fri. 9 AM–5 PM (to 8 PM Wed.), and Sat. 9 AM–noon.

Public Restrooms: In downtown Southwest Harbor, public restrooms are located at the southern end of the parking lot behind Carroll's Drug Store (Main St.). The Swans Island ferry terminal in Bass Harbor also has public facilities.

Islands Near Mount Desert

The most popular island day-trip destinations from Mount Desert Island are the Cranberry Isles and Swans Island. Most commercial and mail boats for the Cranberries depart from Northeast Harbor, although one line originates in Southwest Harbor (both carry bikes but no cars); state car ferries for Swans Island depart from Bass Harbor, south of Southwest Harbor.

The Maine State Ferry Service also operates a ferry to Long Island (referred to as Frenchboro, the name of the village on the island) from Bass Harbor, but the schedule requires careful planning for day-trips.

CRANBERRY ISLES

The Cranberry Isles, south of Northeast and Seal Harbors, comprise Great Cranberry, Little Cranberry (called Islesford), Sutton, Baker, and Bear Islands. Islesford and Baker include property belonging to Acadia National Park. Bring a bike and explore the narrow, mostly level roads on the two largest islands (Great Cranberry and Islesford), but *remember to respect private property.* Unless you've asked permission, don't cut across private land to reach the shore.

The Cranberry name has been attributed to 18th-century loyalist governor Francis Bernard, who received these islands (along with all of Mount Desert) as a king's grant in 1762.

Cranberry bogs (now long gone) on the two largest islands evidently caught his attention. Permanent European settlers were here in the 1760s, and there was even steamboat service by the 1820s.

Lobstering and other fishing industries are the commercial mainstay, boosted in summer by the various visitor-related pursuits. Artists and writers come for a week, a month, or longer; day-trippers spend time on Great Cranberry and Islesford.

Largest of the islands is **Great Cranberry,** first stop on the mailboat route. Here you'll find the island's only store, **Cranberry General Store,** near the dock, 207/244-5336, for picnic fixings, and the **Whale's Rib Gift Shop,** about midway along the main road, 207/244-5153.

The second-largest island is **Little Cranberry,** locally known as **Islesford.** Close to the dock is **The Islesford Historical Museum,** operated by the National Park Service, 207/288-3338. The exhibits focus on local history, much of it maritime, so displays include ship models, household goods, fishing gear, and other memorabilia. The museum is open Mon.–Sat. 9 AM–noon and 12:30–3:30 PM, and Sun. 10:45–noon and 12:30–3:30 PM, mid-June–Labor Day. Free admission.

Islesford Artists, 207/244-3145, is a small but excellent gallery specializing in local artists' depictions of local sites (lots of landscapes, naturally). Run by Danny and Katy Fernald, the gallery is open daily 10 AM–6 PM July–Aug.; weekdays "by chance or appointment" the rest of the season, closed in winter.

At dockside is **The Islesford Dock,** 207/244-7494, serving lunch and dinner Tues.–Sun. 11 AM–3 PM and 5–9 PM, June–Labor Day. Sunday brunch is 10 AM–2 PM. Prices are moderate, food is home-cooked, and views across to Acadia's mountains are incredible. If the weather's good, eat on the deck. Reservations are wise, for dinners, in midsummer. Ferries are available for returning to Northeast Harbor after dinner. Also on the dock is **Islesford Pottery,** Islesford 04646, 207/244-9108, Marian Baker's summertime ceramic studio. Her functional pieces are particularly attractive. The shop is open daily 10 AM–4 PM, June–Labor Day.

Islesford's imaginative postmaster, Joy Sprague, brought the island a bit of postal fame by creating Maine's busiest stamps-by-mail operation. Many of the other year-round islands' postmasters have now followed suit, aided by the Rockland-based Island Institute, which publishes an order form and address list in each issue of its monthly tabloid newspaper. The goal is to support a dozen island post offices and their local economies.

Getting to the Cranberries

Decades-old, family-run **Beal & Bunker Mail Boat & Ferry Service,** P.O. Box 33, Cranberry Isles 04625, 207/244-3575, provides year-round mail boat/passenger service to the Cranberries from Northeast Harbor. The ferries don't carry cars, but you can take a bike. Or just plan to explore on foot. The summer season runs mid-June–Labor Day. The boats depart Northeast Harbor's Municipal Pier every two hours, from 10 AM–6 PM, seven days a week. (There's a 7:30 AM mail boat for early birds, excluding Sundays.) The last boat for Northeast Harbor leaves Islesford at 6:30 PM and (Great) Cranberry at 6:45 PM. The boats do a bit of to-ing and fro-ing on the three-island route (including Sutton in summer), so be patient as they make the circuit. It's a people-watching treat. If you just did a round-trip and stayed aboard, the loop would take about 1.5 hours. Round-trip tickets (covering the whole loop, including intra-island if you want to visit both Great Cranberry and Islesford) are $15 adults, $10 kids under 12 (free for kids under three). Bicycles are $5 round-trip. The off-season schedule operates early May–mid-June and early Sept.–late Oct.; the winter schedule runs late Oct.–early May.

Cranberry Cove Boating Company, Upper Town Dock, Clark Point Rd., Southwest Harbor 04679, 207/244-5882, operates a summertime ferry service to the Cranberries, mid-June–Labor Day, aboard Capt. Pagel's 47-passenger *Island Queen.* Departures from Southwest Harbor are every two hours, 7 AM–5 PM. Departures from Islesford are every two hours from 8 AM–6 PM. Round-trip fares are $20 adults, $12 children under 12 (free for kids under three), bikes $6. Leashed dogs are welcome. Off-season, call to check on the schedule.

Ferry service to the beautiful, uninhabited **Baker Island,** part of Acadia National Park, was offered by Islesford Ferry Co., in conjunction with the National Park Service (tel. 207/288-3338). These tours are no longer available, but the National Park Service hopes to offer cruises in the future.

Capt. John Dwelley, 207/244-5724, operates a water-taxi service to the Cranberries. His six-passenger *Delight* makes the run from Northeast or Southwest Harbor for $50 a trip, 6 AM–5 PM; $55 a trip 5–11 PM.

Capt. Storey King, 207/460-5200, operates *Private Charters Water Taxi,* 8 AM–8 PM, for $50 a trip. Group rates are available.

SWANS ISLAND

Six miles off Mount Desert Island lies scenic, 6,000-acre Swans Island (pop. about 360), named after Col. James Swan, who purchased it and two dozen other islands as an investment in 1786. As with the Cranberries, fishing—especially lobstering—is the year-round way of life here; summer sees the arrival of artists, writers, and other seasonal visitors.

With plenty of relatively level terrain (but narrow roads), and a not-impossible amount of real estate to cover, Swans is ideal for a bicycling day-trip. The island has no campsites, no public restrooms, a tiny "motel," and a tiny B&B. Visitors who want to spend more than a day tend to rent cottages by the week.

If you can be flexible, wait for a clear day, then catch the first ferry (7:30 AM) from Bass Harbor. At the ferry office in Bass Harbor, request a Swans Island map (and take advantage of the restroom). Keep an eye on your watch so you don't miss the last ferry (4:30 PM) back to Bass Harbor.

Pack a picnic (and a bike), then pedal around to the west side of the harbor and down the peninsula to **Hockamock Head Light** (officially, Burnt Coat Harbor Light). From the ferry landing, Hockamock Head is about five miles, but it's not difficult.

The distinctive square lighthouse, built in 1872 and now automated, sits on a rocky promontory overlooking Burnt Coat Harbor, Harbor Island, lobsterboat traffic, and crashing surf. The keeper's house is unoccupied; the grounds are great for picnics.

If it's hot, ask for directions to one of two prime island swimming spots **Fine Sand Beach** (salt water) or **Quarry Pond** (fresh water). Fine Sand Beach is on the west side of Toothacher Cove; you'll have to navigate a short stretch of unpaved road to get there, but it's worth the trouble. Be prepared for chilly water, however. Quarry Pond is in Minturn, not far from the post office.

Formerly an island attraction, **Swans Island Blankets** has relocated to 231 Atlantic Hwy, Northport 04849, 207/338-9691. New owners, Jody and Bill Laurita, invite visitors to their farmhouse studio and to their website at www.swanislandblankets.com.

A Swans Island summer highlight is the **Sweet Chariot Music Festival,** a three-night midweek extravaganza in early August. Windjammers arrive from Camden and Rockland, enthusiasts show up on their private boats, and the island's Oddfellows Hall is SRO for three evenings of folk singing, storytelling, and impromptu hijinks. In midafternoon of the first two days (about 3:30 PM), musicians go from boat to boat in Burnt Coat Harbor, entertaining with sea chanteys. Tickets for evening concerts (7:30 PM) are $20. Along the route from harbor to concert, enterprising local kids peddle lemonade, homemade brownies, and kitschy craft items. It's all very festive, but definitely a "boat thing," not very convenient for anyone without waterborne transport.

Getting to Swans Island

Swans Island is a six-mile, 40-minute trip on the car ferry *Captain Henry Lee*. Between mid-Apr. and late Oct., the ferry makes five or six round-trips a day, the first from Bass Harbor at 7:30 AM (9 AM. Sun.) and the last from Swans Island at 4:30 PM Other months, the first and last runs are the same, but there are only four or five trips. For more information, contact **Maine State Ferry Service**, P.O. Box 114, Bass Harbor 04653, 207/244-3254; 303 Atlantic Rd., Swans Island 04685, 207/526-4273. Round-trip fares are $12 adults, $5.25 children 5–11. Bikes are $11.50 round-trip per adult, $ 5.75 per child. Parking across the road from the Bass Harbor ferry terminal is $7 a day. Round-trip ticket for vehicle and driver is $34.50. Reservations are accepted only for vehicles.

To reach the Bass Harbor ferry terminal on Mount Desert Island, follow the distinctive blue signs, marked Swans Island Ferry, along Rtes. 102 and 102A.

Southwest Cycle, Main St., Southwest Harbor 04679, 207/244-5856 or 800/649-5856, rents bikes by the day ($19 adults, $12 children) and week. Hours are Mon.–Sun. 8:30 AM–5:30 PM July–Aug. They are open late Mar.–Dec., with less hours during off-peak times. They have ferry schedules and

Swans Island maps. (For the early-morning ferry, you'll need to pick up bikes the day before; reserve them in advance if you're doing this in July or August.)

FRENCHBORO (LONG ISLAND)

Since Maine has more Long Islands than anyone cares to count, most of them have other labels for easy distinction. Here's a case in point—a Long Island known universally just as Frenchboro, the name of its harbor village. With a year-round population hovering around 50, Frenchboro has only had ferry service since 1960. Since then, the island has acquired phone service, electricity, and satellite TV, but don't expect to notice much of that when you get there. It's an incredibly quiet place where islanders live as islanders always have—making a living from the sea and proud of it. In 1999, when more than half the island (967 acres, including 5.5 miles of shorefront) went up for sale by a private owner, an incredible fundraising effort collected nearly $3 million, allowing purchase of the land in January 2000 by the Maine Coast Heritage Trust. Among their projects, the Trust has restored the village church and one-room schoolhouse. Islanders and visitors have full access to all the acreage. The island has a seasonal restaurant and museum, a B&B, two public restrooms, and a full-time post office. There is no general store.

A good way to get a sense of the place is to take the 3.5-hour lunch cruise run by Capt. Kim Strauss of **Island Cruises,** Little Island Marine, Shore Rd., Bass Harbor 04653, 207/244-5785. The 49-passenger *R.L. Gott* departs daily during the summer at 11 AM and 3 PM. On these narrated nature cruises, there's time for a picnic and a village stroll on Frenchboro, then a return through the sprinkling of islands along the 8.3-mile route. Cost is $25 adults, $15 children, age 11 and under. Be sure to reserve, and double-check if the weather looks iffy. Most of the trip is in sheltered water, but rough seas can put the kibosh on it. You'll find the Island Cruises dock by following signs to the Swans Island Ferry and turning off at the sign shortly before the ferry dock.

For an even longer stay on Frenchboro, plan to take the ***R.L. Gott*** during her weekly run for the Maine State Ferry Service. Each Friday, Apr.–Nov., the *Gott* departs Bass Harbor at 8 AM, arriving in Frenchboro at 8:40 AM and 9 AM. The return trip to Bass Harbor is at 5 PM, allowing eight hours on the island. Round-trip cost is $6 adults, $2.50 children. Take a picnic with you, or stop at David Lunt's Dockside Deli, open July–Aug. The island has a network of maintained trails through the woods and along the shore, easy and not-so-easy; some can be squishy and some are along bouldery beachfront. In the center of the island is a beaver pond. The Frenchboro Historical Society, just up from the dock, has interesting old tools and other local artifacts.

Acadia Region

Eastern Hancock County

Sneak around to the eastern side of Frenchman Bay and you'll see this region from a whole new perspective. One hour from the Acadia National Park visitor center, you'll find Acadia's mountains silhouetted against the sunset, the surf slamming onto Schoodic Point, the peace of a calmer lifestyle.

If you're coming from Trenton—the funnel to Mount Desert—duck east via Rte. 204 toward Lamoine and its state park. From Ellsworth, follow Rte. 1 toward Hancock, Sullivan, Sorrento, Gouldsboro, and Winter Harbor.

Winter Harbor (pop. 1,240), on the Gouldsboro Peninsula, is known best as the gateway to the Schoodic Peninsula, Acadia National Park's only mainland acreage. The old-money, Philadelphia-linked summer colony on exclusive Grindstone Neck keeps a low profile, as once did a highly classified U.S. Navy communications operation (officially, Naval Security Group Activity, NSGA). In 2002, after 67 years, the navy left Winter Harbor, and deeded its 100-acre property (dormitory, apartment complex, cafeteria, clinic, fire station, commissary, gymnasium, day care center, maintenance and recreational facilities, partly eligible for listing in the National Register of Historic Places), to the National Park Service. Plans are afoot to convert the property to the "Schoodic Education and Research Center" (SERC), one of 12 such centers operated by the National Park Service as part of its Natural Resource Challenge program.

Winter Harbor's summer highlight is the annual Lobster Festival, second Saturday in August. The gala day-long event includes a parade, live entertainment, games, and more crustaceans than you could ever consume.

Gouldsboro (pop. 2,037)—including the not-to-be-missed villages of Birch Harbor, Corea, and Prospect Harbor—earned its own minor fame from Louise Dickinson Rich's 1958 book *The Peninsula,* a tribute to her summers on Corea's Cranberry Point—"a place that has stood still in time." Since 1958, change has crept into Corea, but not so's you'd notice. It's still the same quintessential lobster-fishing community, perfect for photo ops.

SIGHTS

The biggest attractions in Eastern Hancock County are the spectacular vignettes and vistas—of offshore lighthouses, distant mountains, close-in islands, and unchanged villages. Check out each finger of land: Lamoine, Hancock Point, Sorrento, and Winter Harbor's Grindstone Neck. Loop around the Schoodic Peninsula, circle the Gouldsboro Peninsula, and detour to Corea. Then head inland and follow Rte. 182, a designated Scenic Highway, from Hancock to Cherryfield. Accomplish all this and you'll have a fine sense of place. (Make sure to stock up on film, and remember that a wide-angle lens or a panoramic camera is a major asset.)

Bartlett's Winery

German and Italian presses, Portuguese corks, and Maine fruit all go into the creation of Bob and Kathe Bartlett's award-winning dinner and dessert wines made from locally grown fruit. Founded in 1982, Bartlett Maine Estate Winery, 175 Chicken Mill Pond Rd., Gouldsboro 04607, 207/546-2408, www.bartlettwinery.com, produces over 15,000 gallons annually in a handsome wood-and-stone building designed by the Bartletts. They no longer give tours or Maine's first winery, but you're welcome to sample the wines, and you can buy single bottles and gift packages. Bartlett's, 0.5 mile south of Rte. 1 in Gouldsboro, is open Memorial Day weekend to Columbus Day, Mon.–Sat. 10 AM–5 PM, except major holidays, or by appointment off-season.

PARKS, PRESERVES, AND RECREATION

Acadia National Park

Slightly more than 2,000 of Acadia National Park's acres are on the mainland, and they're all here on the **Schoodic Peninsula,** visited by about a quarter-million people annually, yet you can often find yourself alone, or at least it will seem that way. It might be named Acadia, but the hustle and bustle of Acadia on Mount Desert is not at all present here. Along the six-mile one-way (counterclockwise) road that loops through the park are picnic spots, a few hiking trailheads, an offshore lighthouse, and scenic turnouts. There's no camping in the park, but Ocean Wood Campground, 207/963-7194, on the Schoodic Peninsula, is convenient and beautiful. The world-class scenery, free admission, and the general lack of congestion make Schoodic the preferred Acadia destination of many a savvy visitor. Note: If you're driving and see a viewpoint you like, stop; it's a long way around to return.

To reach the park boundary from Rte. 1 in Gouldsboro, take Rte. 186 south to Winter Harbor. Continue through town, heading east, then turn right and continue to the park-entrance sign, just before the bridge over Mosquito Harbor.

Just after the bridge, the first landmark is **Frazer Point Picnic Area,** with lovely vistas, picnic tables, and convenient outhouses. Other spots are fine for picnics, but this is the only official one. If you've brought bikes, leave your car here and do a counterclockwise 12.2-mile loop through the park and back to your car via Birch Harbor and Rte. 186. It's a fine day-trip.

From the picnic area, the **Park Loop Road** becomes one-way. Go about 2.5 miles and watch for a narrow, unpaved road on the left, leading a mile up to the open ledges on 440-foot Schoodic Head. (Don't confuse it with Schoodic Mountain, which is well north of here.) For exercise, hike up, although you'll need to keep an eye out for cars.

Continue on the Park Loop Rd., past the former U.S. Navy base, and hang a right onto a short, two-way spur to **Schoodic Point,** where the parking lot, amazingly, seldom fills up. Check local newspapers for the time of high tide and try to arrive here then; the word "awesome" is overused, but it sure fits Schoodic

Point's surf performance on the rugged pink granite. **Caution:** If you've brought children, keep them well back from the water; a rogue wave can sweep them off the rocks all too easily. Picnics are great here (make sure you bring a litter bag), and so are the tide pools at mid- to low tide. Birding is spectacular during spring and fall migrations.

Return to Park Loop Rd. and go about a mile to the Blueberry Hill parking area. Across the road is the trailhead to the 180-foot-high **Anvil** headland, and then on up to Schoodic Head. Allow 2–3 hours for the clockwise Schoodic Head-Anvil loop back to your car.

From Blueberry Hill, continue another two miles to the park exit, just before Birch Harbor.

Lamoine State Park

July–Aug., when every single campsite on Mount Desert Island is booked solid, those in the know go eight miles southeast of Ellsworth to the wooded, no-frills campground at 55-acre Lamoine State Park, Rte. 184, Lamoine 04605, 207/667-4778. Park facilities include a pebble beach and picnic area with a spectacular view, a boat-launch ramp, saltwater fishing pier, and a children's play area. Day-use admission is $3 adults, $1 children 5–11. Camping (61 sites) is $20 per site per night for nonresidents ($13 for Maine residents); no hookups; two-night minimum. The park is open daily, mid-May–mid-Oct., and accessible off-season for daytime activities.

Donnell Pond Public Reserved Land

More than 14,000 acres have been preserved for public access in a huge mountain-and-lake area north and east of Sullivan. Developers had their eyes on this gorgeous real estate in the 1980s, but preservationists fortunately rallied to the cause. Outright purchase of 7,316 of the acres, in the Spring River Lake area, came through the foresighted Land for Maine's Future program. Rte. 182, an official Scenic Highway, cuts right through the Donnell Pond preserve.

Major water bodies here are **Donnell Pond**

(big enough by most gauges to be called a lake) and **Tunk** and **Spring River Lakes;** all are accessible for boats (even, alas, powerboats). Tunk Lake has a few campsites in its southwestern corner. The eastern and southern shores of Donnell Pond have primitive, first-come, first-served sites (no charge), which are snapped up quickly on midsummer weekends. Schoodic Beach, the prime swimming area, is in the southeastern corner of Donnell Pond.

By boat, trailheads at Schoodic Beach as well as Black Beach provide access to **Caribou, Black,** and **Schoodic Mountains,** all tied together by connector trails. None are easy but it's great hiking—and there's a tower on 1,069-foot Schoodic. The Caribou-Black Mountain Loop, clockwise, is about a seven-mile round-trip from the Black Beach boat-access trailhead.

To reach the boat-launching area for Donnell Pond from Rte. 1 in Sullivan, take Rte. 200 north to Rte. 182. Turn right and go about 1.5 miles to a right turn just before Swan Brook. Turn and go not quite two miles to the put-in; the road is poor in spots but adequate for a regular vehicle. The Narrows, where you'll put in, is lined with summer cottages ("camps" in the Maine vernacular); keep paddling eastward to the more open part of the lake.

To reach the vehicle-access trailhead for Schoodic Mountain from Rte. 1 in East Sullivan, drive just over four miles northeast on Rte. 183 (Lake Rd.). Cross the Maine Central Railroad tracks and turn left onto an unpaved road (marked as a jeep track on the USGS map). Continue to the parking area and trailhead. Follow the Schoodic Mountain Loop clockwise, heading westward first. To make a day of it, pack a picnic and take a swimsuit (and don't forget a camera and binoculars for the summit views). On a brilliantly clear day, you'll see Baxter State Park's Katahdin, the peaks of Acadia National Park, and the ocean beyond. For such rewards, this is a popular hike, so don't expect to be alone on summer and fall weekends.

Still within the preserve boundaries, but farther east, you can put in a canoe at the northern end of Long Pond and paddle southward into adjoining Round Pond. In early August, Round Mountain, rising a few hundred feet from Long Pond's eastern shore, is a great spot for gathering blueberries and huckleberries. The put-in for Long Pond is on the south side of Rte. 182 (park well off the road), about two miles east of Tunk Lake.

Golf

Play a nine-hole round at the **Grindstone Neck Golf Course,** Grindstone Ave., Winter Harbor 04693, 207/963-7760, just for the dynamite scenery, and for a glimpse of this exclusive, late-19th-century summer enclave. Established in 1895, the public course attracts a tony crowd; 150-yard markers are cute little birdhouses. Tee times usually aren't needed, but call to make sure. The course is open early June–Sept.

ENTERTAINMENT

The **Pierre Monteux School for Conductors and Orchestra Musicians,** Rte. 1, Hancock 04640, 207/422-3931, www.monteuxschool.org, a prestigious summer program founded in 1943, presents two well-attended concert series starting in late June and running through July. Known also as the Domaine School, it has an internationally renowned faculty and has trained dozens of national and international classical musicians. Five Wednesday concerts (7:30 PM) feature chamber music (general admission $7); six Sunday concerts (5 PM) feature symphonies. Concerts are held in the School Hall on Rte. 1. Tickets are $12 adults, $5 students.

Nearest cinemas are in Ellsworth and Bar Harbor, as are lots of other entertainment possibilities.

SHOPPING

Zero in on Eastern Hancock County to shop for everyone on your list who appreciates unusual crafts and gifts. Hancock, Sullivan, and Gouldsboro are loaded with great gallery-shops.

Art and Craft Galleries

Bet you can't keep from smiling at the whimsical animal sculptures of talented sculptor/painter Philip Barter. His work is the cornerstone of the eclectic, two-room **Barter Family Gallery,** Shore Rd., Box 102, Sullivan 04664, 207/422-3190, www.barterfamilygallery.com, on a back road in Sullivan. But there's more: Barter's wife and seven children have put their considerable skills to work producing braided rugs, jewelry, and other craft items sold here at moderate prices. No credit cards. Located 2.5 miles northwest of Rte. 1, the gallery is sign-posted soon after you cross the bridge from Hancock. It's open May 15–Oct. 15, Mon.–Sat. 10 AM–5 PM; other times by chance or appt.; call at least 2–3 hours ahead.

Artist Paul Breeden, best known for the remarkable illustrations, calligraphy, and maps he's done for *National Geographic,* Time-Life Books, and other national and international publications, displays and sells his paintings at the **Spring Woods Gallery,** 40A Willowbrook Lane, Rte. 200, Sullivan 04664, 207/422-3007, www.springwoodsgallery.com. Also filling the handsome modern gallery space are paintings by Ann Breeden. The beautifully landscaped gallery, 0.2 mile north of Rte. 1, is open Mon.–Sat. 9 AM–5 PM, May–Oct.

Gifts and More Crafts

Lunaform, Cedar Lane, P.O. Box 189, W. Sullivan 04664, 207/422-0923, www.lunaform.com, is in a class by itself. First there's the setting—the beautifully landscaped grounds surrounding an abandoned granite quarry. Then there's the realization that many of the wonderfully aesthetic garden ornaments created here look like hand-turned *pottery,* when in fact they're hand turned, but made of steel-reinforced concrete. Buy an urn or pot or fountain and dazzle your friends, even your enemies. It takes a bit of zigging and zagging to get here. After you cross the bridge into Sullivan, go left

onto Hog Bay Rd., then take the next right (Track Rd.) After 0.5 mile, go left into Cedar Lane. Lunaform is open Mon.–Fri. 9:30–11:30 AM and 1–4:30 PM, Sat. by appt.

Blue-and-white Japanese-style motifs predominate at **Gull Rock Pottery,** 103 Gull Rock Rd., Hancock 04640, 207/422-3990, Torj and Kurt Wray and daughter-in-law Akemi's studio and shop 1.5 miles south of Rte. 1 (the driveway is another half mile). They'll also do special orders of their wheel-thrown, hand-painted, dishwasher-safe pottery. No credit cards. The shop is open all year, Mon.–Sat. 9 AM–5 PM.

Overlooking Hog Bay, 3.6 miles north of Rte. 1, Charles and Susanne Grosjean have been the key players at **Hog Bay Pottery,** 245 Hog Bay Rd., Rte. 200, Franklin 04634, 207/565-2282, www.hogbay.com, since 1974. Inside the casual, laid-back showroom are Charles's functional, nature-themed pottery and Susanne's stunning hand-woven rugs. They often fill custom orders. The shop, next to their house, is open May–Oct.; call ahead other months.

Chickadee Creek Stillroom, Rte. 186, P.O. Box 220, W. Gouldsboro 04607, 207/963-7283 or 800/969-4372, www.chickadeecreek.com, is the Toys R Us of herb fanciers. Jeanie and Fred Cook seem to have thought of everything—potpourri, teas, wreaths, fresh herbs for cooking. The barn-shop, 1.7 miles south of Rte. 1, is open Tues.–Sun. 10 AM–4 PM, May–mid-Oct., variable hours other months.

Visiting the **U.S. Bells & Watering Cove Pottery,** 56 West Bay Rd., Rte. 186, P.O. Box 73, Prospect Harbor 04669, 207/963-7184, is a treat for the ears, as browsers try out the many varieties of cast-bronze bells made in the adjacent foundry by Richard Fisher. If you're lucky, he may have time to explain the process—particularly intriguing for children, and a distraction from their instinctive urge to test every bell in the shop. The store also carries a tasteful selection of crafts, and Liza Fisher's woodfired stoneware and porcelain. It's open all year, Mon.–Fri. 9 AM–5 PM and Sat. 9 AM–2 PM. U.S. Bells is a quarter mile up the hill from Prospect Harbor's post office.

Just up the road (toward Rte. 1) from U.S. Bells, Cindy and Bill Thayer's enthusiasm is contagious as they explain their incredibly prolific 133-acre restored saltwater organic farm—home to hairy Scotch Highland cattle, turkeys, sheep, pigs, chickens, and border collies. At **Darthia Farm,** 51 Darthia Farm Rd., Rte. 186, Box 520, Gouldsboro 04607, 207/963-7771, www.darthiafarm.com, kids love the farm atmosphere; parents can check out Hattie's Shed for Cindy's outstanding ikat weavings and work by half a dozen other craftspeople. The farm stand is open Mon.–Fri. 8 AM–5 PM, Sat. 8 AM–noon. If you can't visit Hattie's Shed, request a mail-order catalog. In winter, group sleigh rides are followed by cocoa, $50 for 6–8 people, higher maximum if some of them are little people. Cynthia Thayer is the author of *Strong for Potatoes,* and *A Certain Slant of Light*. The farm is 1.7 miles south of Rte. 1.

ACCOMMODATIONS
Country Inns with Restaurants
Buffered from the highway by a tall hedge, **Le Domaine,** Rte. 1, Box 519, Hancock 04640, 207/422-3395 or 800/554-8498, www.ledomaine.com, has gained a five-star reputation for its restaurant, founded by the mother of longtime owner/chef Nicole Purslow in 1946—long before fine dining had cachet here. Purslow, who termed Le Domaine her "life's work," sold it after a life-threatening illness, and turned the kitchen over to her protégé, Christopher Meynell, who also has done training in Provence. No major changes were planned, in the Maine spirit of not fixing what isn't broken. But that's only part of the story. Above the restaurant is a charming, five-room, country-French inn, updated in the spring of 2000. The lush inn property, nine miles east of Ellsworth, is virtual Down East Provence, an oasis transplanted magically to Maine. On the garden-view balconies, or on the lawn out back, you're oblivious to the traffic whizzing by. Better yet, follow the lovely wooded trail to a quiet pond. Three guest rooms ($200 d, breakfast only) and two suites ($285 d B&B)

all are named after locales in Provence. Continental breakfast, usually including croissants, can be served in your room or in the dining room. Alert the inn if you'll be arriving after 5:30 PM, when the staff has to focus on dinner. The ultra-French restaurant, with a 5,000-bottle wine cellar and lovely Provençal decor, is open to the public Tues.–Sun. 6–9 PM. Reservations are essential, especially July–Aug. The tab may dent your budget—this is not a "local restaurant"—but stack it up against plane fare to France. Le Domaine's season is early June–mid-Oct.

Follow Hancock Point Rd. 4.8 miles south of Rte. 1 to the three-story, gray-blue **Crocker House Country Inn,** 967 Point Rd., HC 77, Box 171, Hancock 04640, 207/422-6806, www.crockerhouse.com, Rich and Liz Malaby's antidote to Bar Harbor's summer traffic. Built as a summer hotel in 1884, the inn underwent rehabbing a century later, but it retains an old-fashioned air. Eleven rooms (private baths) are $110–155 d mid-June–mid-Oct.; $85–110 d other months. Breakfast is included. Guests can hang out in the comfortable common room or use the guest kayak, bikes, or hi-speed Internet. Nearby are clay tennis courts, quiet walking routes past Hancock Point's elegant seaside "cottages," and a unique octagonal public library. If you're arriving by boat, request a mooring. The restaurant, focusing on fresh, local, and elegant food, is open to the public daily for dinner May 1–Oct. 31, and Thurs.–Sun. in Apr. and Nov.–Dec. Reservations are requested.

Bed-and-Breakfasts
Just down the road is the **Island View Inn,** 12 Miramar Ave., Rte. 1, Sullivan 04664, 207/422-3031, its name the height of understatement. Out front are the peaks of Mount Desert, a remarkable panorama. Four of the seven rooms (all private baths) capture the view from this updated turn-of-the-20th-century summer home run by Evelyn Joost and her daughter Sarah. Rooms are $100–140 d July–mid-Sept., $95–120 d other times, including full breakfast. The Island View has its

own private beach, but the water is terminally chilly. Experienced sailors can rent an 18-foot Rhodes sailboat for the day (with advance reservation). Guests have free use of a canoe and a dinghy. There are tennis courts nearby. Children over five and pets are welcome. Open Memorial Day weekend–mid-Oct.

Sorrento is such a low-key place that lots of people don't realize it has a B&B. **Bass Cove Farm Bed & Breakfast,** 312 Eastside Rd., Rte. 185, Sorrento 04677, 207/422-3564, www.basscovefarm.com, was opened in 1992 by spinner/weaver/gardener/editor Mary Ann Solet and her husband Michael Tansey, a group-home supervisor whose resume also includes the Harry S. Truman Manure Pitchoff Championship at the annual Common Ground Country Fair. Mary Ann can rattle off dozens of ideas for exploring the area, particularly in the craft department, and she raids her extensive vegetable garden daily to produce a hearty, healthful breakfast. Two first-floor rooms (one with private bath) and a second-floor suite have quilt-covered beds and other homey touches. Summer and holiday rates $65–100 d. Well-behaved children are welcome, pets are considered on an individual basis. The B&B is open all year, but be sure to call ahead off-season.

Aptly named, **The Sunset House Bed & Breakfast,** Rte. 186, HC 60, Box 62, Gouldsboro 04607, 207/963-7156 or 800/233-7156, www.sunsethousebnb.com, overlooks the setting sun off to the west and water from more than one direction. Most of the six rooms (three with private baths) in Carl and Kathy Johnson's charming three-story Victorian home have water views. Jones Pond, Gouldsboro's swimming hole, borders the property; bring a canoe and launch it here—but not before launching into award-winning chef Carl's generous breakfast. Kathy's homemade goat cheese is often on the menu. May–Oct. rates are $89 d with shared bath, $129 d with private bath; two-night minimum on weekends July–Oct. Children and pets welcome. Open all year; lower rates off-season. In winter, there's ice-skating and cross-country skiing. Sunset House is a quarter mile south of Rte. 1, in the village of West Gouldsboro. The Johnsons also own Grindstone Neck of Maine Smoked Seafood, and The Fisherman's Inn in Winter Harbor, a convenient place to head for dinner.

Overlooking the Gouldsboro Peninsula's only sandy saltwater beach, **Oceanside Meadows Inn,** Rte. 195, Corea Rd., P.O. Box 90, Prospect Harbor 04669, 207/963-5557, www.oceaninn.com, is a jewel of a place on 200 acres with fabulous gardens, wildlife habitat, and walking trails. The elegant 1860s Captain's House has seven attractive rooms and the 1820 Shaw farmhouse next door has another seven; all have private baths ($138–198 d in high season, lower other months). Breakfast is an impressive three-or-four-course event, staged by the energetic husband-and-wife team of Sonja Sundaram and Ben Walter, who seem to have thought of everything that could make a guest happy. Well-behaved children are welcome. Open May–mid-Oct. As if all that weren't enough, Sonja and Ben have totally restored the 1820 timber-frame barn out back—creating the **Oceanside Meadows Institute for the Arts and Sciences,** which sponsors a summer series of lectures and concerts. They have also created a preserve to protect the various flora and fauna—including eagle—habitats on the property. There are two walking trails. Oceanside Meadows is six miles off Rte. 1.

Even more of a detour, and definitely worthwhile, is Bob Travers and Barry Canner's **Black Duck Inn on Corea Harbor,** Crowley Island Rd., P.O. Box 39, Corea 04624, 207/963-2689, www.blackduck.com, literally the end of the line on the Gouldsboro Peninsula. Set on 12 acres in this timeless fishing village, the B&B has four handsomely decorated rooms (two are private, the suite shares a bath) for $120–180 d (the latter for the small suite with three or four people), depending on the season. Across the way are two little seasonal cottages, one rented by the week, one with a three-day minimum. The inn and Corea are geared to wanderers, readers, and anyone seeking serenity (who isn't?). Rocky outcrops dot the property and a nature trail meanders to a mill pond; in early August, the blueberries are ready. If the fog socks in, the large parlor has comfortable chairs and loads of books. No pets, pretoddlers and children over eight are accepted. Open May–mid-Oct.

Something of a categorical anomaly, **The Bluff House Inn,** Rte. 186, P.O. Box 249, Gouldsboro 04607, 207/963-7805, www.bluffinn.com, is part motel, part hotel, part B&B—a seemingly successful mix in a contemporary building overlooking Frenchman Bay on the west side of the Gouldsboro Peninsula. Verandas wrap around the first and second floors, so bring binoculars for osprey and bald eagle sightings. The eight second-floor rooms (private baths; $95–130 d in summer) are decorated "country" fashion, with quilts on the very comfortable beds. (In hot weather, request a corner room.) Breakfast is generous continental, including excellent baked goodies. In summer, walk the steep path to the pink granite shore or launch your kayak there; in winter, you can cross-country ski. Open all year.

Cottages

Set back from the highway 12 miles east of Ellsworth, **Sullivan Harbor Farms,** Rte. 1, P.O. Box 96, Sullivan 04664, 207/422-3735 or 800/422-4014, is a beautifully sited 19th-century farmhouse with spectacular sea and mountain views. Across the road from a quiet cove, the driveway curves through two giant outcrops higher than a car—great lookout points for watching the passing scene. Three self-catering cottages are available by the week for $775–1450. Ask innkeepers Joel Frantzman and Leslie Harlow to steer you toward their favorite ponds and hiking trails—they'll even lend you a canoe. Or grab a book from their eclectic library and hang out in the peaceful backyard. Or visit their spotless **Sullivan Harbor Smokehouse** and ship your pals some fantastic cold-smoked salmon (they also do hot-smoked salmon, not to mention fabulous salmon pâté). Sullivan Harbor's product has become the salmon *du jour* for some of the biggest-name restaurants and high-end provisioners in New England and beyond.

Campgrounds

On a wooded finger of land projecting eastward from the Schoodic Peninsula, **Ocean Wood Campground,** P.O. Box 111, Birch Harbor 04613, 207/963-7194, gets kudos for eco-sensitivity, noise control, and a portion dedicated to a fantastic walk-in wilderness camping area, with some sites right on the ocean. There are two seawalls and spacious campsites. Don't expect frills; nature provides the entertainment. The 70 campsites (some with hookups) are $20–35, depending on location, time of year, and services. There is an extra-person fee. Leashed and well-behaved pets permitted under rules. No credit cards; free hot showers round-the-clock. Dumping station. Open early May–late Oct., the campground is a terrific base for exploring the Schoodic section of Acadia National Park.

Seasonal Rentals

Next to their Black Duck Inn, Barry Canner and Bob Travers operate **Black Duck Properties,** Crowley Island Rd., P.O. Box 39, Corea 04624, 207/963-2689, www.blackduck.com, handling both home sales and seasonal rentals. Corea is the primary focus, with harborfront cottages a specialty, but they can suggest suitable spots in Winter Harbor, Gouldsboro, and Prospect Harbor. Most of the rentals forbid smoking. Weekly-rental range is $775–1,800, with $950 being a fairly typical rate.

FOOD

Make a point to attend one of the many **public suppers** held throughout the summer in this area and so many other rural corners of Maine. Typically benefiting a worthy cause, these usually feature beans or spaghetti and the serendipity of plain potluck. Everyone saves room for the homemade pies.

General Stores

By definition, old-fashioned country stores are eclectic sources of local color, last-minute items, and plenty of answers for which you probably have questions. Three good examples are right in this area.

Lots of people stop at **Dunbar's Store,** Rte. 1, Sullivan 04664, 207/422-6844, just to admire the view. Then they go inside the old-fashioned market and almost always manage to make a purchase—maybe compensation of sorts for the scenery. Some even offer to buy the place. More of a grocery store than a fast-food source, Dunbar's is open all year, Mon.–Sat. 8 AM–9 PM and Sun. 9 AM–6 PM.

Farther east on Rte. 1, in a new building that replaced a half-century-old country store, **Young's Market,** 130 Rte. 1, Gouldsboro 04607, 207/963-7774, also has a fabulous view—along with pizza, gasoline, ATM, fishing gear, auto parts, and more. It's open all year, daily 4 AM–9 PM (Sun. 5 AM–9 PM).

Ice cream from the traditional soda fountain is the specialty at **Gerrish's Store,** 352 Main St., Winter Harbor 04693, 207/963-2727, officially J.M. Gerrish Provisions. Only hitch is that it's seasonal, usually open mid-May–mid-Oct. And it's become a bit yuppified, so penny candy and postcards coexist with gourmet goodies and designer coffee. But no matter; it's fun.

In "downtown" Prospect Harbor is the best picnic solution in the area. The **Downeast Deli,** Rtes. 186 and 195, Prospect Harbor 04669, 207/963-2700, will fix you right up with a foot-long hoagie for $4.75–9.35. There are a dozen other sandwich choices, plus hot hoagies, hot dogs, reubens, and pizza. The hot baked beans are scrumptious. The deli is open Sun.–Thurs. 10:30 AM–7:30 PM (to 8 PM Fri.–Sat.).

Inexpensive

Don't be put off by the lobster "sculpture" outside **Ruth & Wimpy's Kitchen,** Rte. 1, Hancock 04640, 207/422-3723; you'll probably see a crowd as well. This family-fare standby serves a wide range of food very affordably: there's twin lobster, lazy tail, and surf and turf, in addition to $3.95 soup-and-sandwich dinners and $2.25 sandwiches, plus exotic cocktails, all served with a sense of humor. The pasta and potato salads on the salad bar are homemade, as are 20 desserts in season. When raspberries are in, you can smell the pies baking. Bring the kids. Located five miles east of Ellsworth, close to the Hancock Point turnoff, Ruth & Wimpy's is open all year except Jan., Feb., and Mar. for lunch and dinner, 11 AM–9 PM.

Best place for grub and gossip in Winter Harbor is **Chase's Restaurant,** 193 Main St., Winter Harbor 04693, 207/963-7171, a seasoned, no-frills booth-and-counter operation that turns out first-rate fish chowder, fries, and onion rings. It's open all year for breakfast, lunch, and dinner, 6 AM–8:30 PM daily in summer.

Moderate to Expensive

Opened in 1947, **The Fisherman's Inn,** 7 Newman St., Winter Harbor 04693, 207/963-5585, is owned by Kathy Johnson and her chef/husband Carl of Sunset House (see *Accommodations*). Seafood is a specialty here, and it's all carefully prepared. Carl's won several awards for his clam chowder. Entrée range is $15–28. Open for lunch and dinner daily, Memorial Day–mid-Oct.

INFORMATION AND SERVICES

For advance information, contact the **Schoodic Peninsula Chamber of Commerce,** P.O. Box 381, Winter Harbor 04693, 207/963-7658, www.acadia-schoodic.org, and request its handy map/brochure, revised annually. The nearest convenient **information center** is run by the Ellsworth Area Chamber of Commerce, 163 High St., Ellsworth 04605, 207/667-5584, on the Rte. 1/3 commercial strip, close to where the highway forks toward Mount Desert Island and Eastern Hancock County.

Acadia Region

The Sunrise Coast

"Down East," people say, is the direction the wind blows—the prevailing southwest wind that powered 19th-century sailing vessels along this rugged coastline. But to be truly Down East, in the minds of most Mainers, you have to be physically here, in Washington County—a stunning landscape of waterways, forests, blueberry barrens, rocky shoreline, and independent, pocket-size communities.

At one time, *most* of the Maine coast used to be as underdeveloped as this portion of it. You can set your clock back a generation or two while you're here, but don't bet on time's standing still for much longer.

When eastern Hancock County flows into western Washington County, you're on the Sunrise Coast. From Steuben eastward to Jonesport, Machias, and Lubec, then "around the corner"—inland to Eastport, Calais, and Grand Lake Stream—Washington County is twice the size of Rhode Island, covers 2,528 square miles, has about 35,000 residents, and stakes a claim as the first U.S. real estate to see the morning sun. The Sunrise Coast also includes handfuls of offshore islands—some accessible by ferry, charter boat, or private vessels. (Some, with sensitive bird-nesting grounds, are off limits.) At the uppermost point of the coast, and conveniently linked to Lubec by a bridge, New Brunswick's Campobello Island is a popular day-trip destination—the locale of Franklin D. Roosevelt's summer retreat. Other attractions in this area include festivals, concert series, art and antique galleries, lighthouses,

© KATHLEEN M. BRANDES

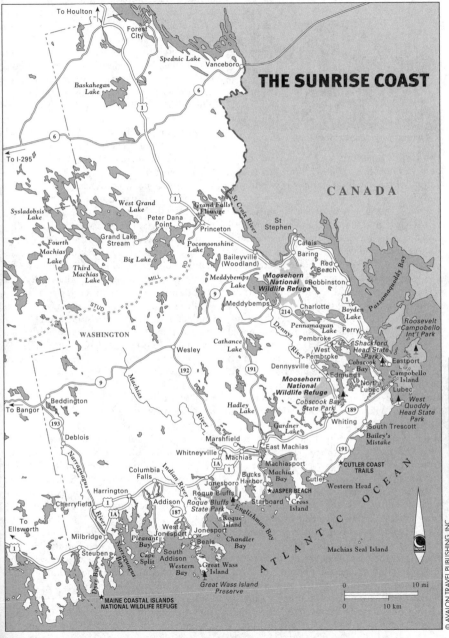

THE SUNRISE COAST

To Houlton
Forest City
Spednic Lake
Vanceboro
Baskahegan Lake
6

6
To I-295

CANADA

Sysladobsis Lake
West Grand Lake
Peter Dana Point
Grand Falls Flowage
St Croix River
St Stephen
Calais
Fourth Machias Lake
Grand Lake Stream
Pocomoonshine Lake
Princeton
Baring
Red Beach
Third Machias Lake
Big Lake
Baileyville (Woodland)
Meddybemps Lake
Moosehorn National Wildlife Refuge
Robbinston
MILL RD.
Meddybemps
Charlotte
Boyden Lake
Perry
Roosevelt Campobello Int'l Park
STUD
9
214
Pennamaquan Lake
Dennys River
WASHINGTON
Cathance Lake
Wesley
Pembroke
West Pembroke
Shackford Head State Park
Eastport
192
191
Dennysville
Edmunds
Cobscook Bay
Campobello Island
Machias River
Moosehorn National Wildlife Refuge
Cobscook Bay State Park
North Lubec
Lubec
West Quoddy Head State Park
Passamaquoddy Bay
To Bangor
Beddington
9
Hadley Lake
Whiting
189
193
Gardner Lake
South Trescott
Deblois
Marshfield
East Machias
Bailey's Mistake
191
Whitneyville
Machias
Machiasport
Machias Bay
Cutler
CUTLER COAST TRAILS
Columbia Falls
1A
1
Bucks Harbor
JASPER BEACH
Western Head
Harrington
Jonesboro Harbor
Roque Bluffs
Starboard
Cross Island
Cherryfield
1
Addison
Roque Bluffs State Park
Roque Island
ATLANTIC OCEAN
To Ellsworth
1A
187
Englishman Bay
Jonesport
1
Milbridge
West Jonesport
Beals
Chandler Bay
Steuben
Pleasant Bay
South Addison
Cape Split
Western Bay
Great Wass Island
Machias Seal Island
Great Wass Island Preserve
MAINE COASTAL ISLANDS NATIONAL WILDLIFE REFUGE

0   10 mi
0   10 km

MOON

The Sunrise Coast

The Sunrise Coast

© AVALON TRAVEL PUBLISHING, INC.

It's a long way down at low tide.

© KATHLEEN M. BRANDES

The Sunrise Coast

two Native American reservations, and all the outdoors for hiking, biking, birding, sea kayaking, whale-watching, camping, swimming, and fishing.

One of the Sunrise Coast's millennial buzz-words has been ecotourism, and local conservation organizations and chambers of commerce have targeted and welcomed visitors willing to be careful of the fragile ecosystems here—visitors who will contribute to the economy while respecting the natural resources and leaving them untrammeled, visitors who know how not to cross the fine line between light use and overuse. Low-impact tourism is essential for this area.

One natural phenomenon no visitor can affect is the tide—the inexorable ebb and flow, predictably in and predictably out. If you're not used to it, even the 6- to 10-foot tidal ranges of southern Maine may surprise you. But here, along the Sunrise Coast, they're astonishing—as much as 26 feet of difference in water level within six hours. Old-timers tell stories of big money lost betting on horses racing the fast-moving tides.

Another compelling natural feature of Washington County is its 200 square miles of blueberry barrens (fields), created by the action of the glaciers. Depending on the time of year, the fields will be black (torched by growers to jump-start the crop), blue (ready for harvest), or maroon (fall foliage, fabulous for photography). In early summer, a million rented bees set to work pollinating the blossoms. By August, when a blue haze forms over the knee-high shrubs, bent-over bodies use old-fashioned

wooden rakes to harvest the ripe berries. It's backbreaking work, but the employment lines form quickly when newspaper ads announce the advent of the annual harvest.

Although most Down East barren barons harvest their blueberries for the lucrative whole-sale market—averaging 65 million pounds annually—a few growers advertise pick-your-own blueberries in mid-August. Watch the local newspapers and go for it. Or, as you hike the county's public-access trails, just help yourself to any wild blueberries you find (Moosehorn National Wildlife Refuge, near Calais, is prime blueberrying turf).

Whenever possible, venture off Rte. 1. In part, this is so you don't miss the scenery. Also, though, it's wise in summer to avoid this major (albeit two-lane) artery, which can become congested, although nowhere near as static as farther south. Taking this into account, you'll find that local residents often estimate distances in time rather than miles. The only thing that makes travel slower in winter than in summer is blizzard conditions. I once conducted an unscientific survey and quizzed five separate Machias residents on how long it would take to reach Jonesport; four differed by as much as 45 minutes, and the fifth refused to play the game.

Visitor Information (and Two Caveats)

For general information about Washington County, contact the **Sunrise County Economic Council,** 1 Stackpole Rd., P.O. Box 679, Machias 04654, 207/255-0983, www.sunrisecounty.org. The council has an informative web page, part of its mission to stimulate the economic growth of Washington County. Another good source for general (and some specific) Washington County information is the Quoddy Loop Tour Guide website, www.quoddyloop.com, which covers both Washington County and the adjoining Canadian province of New Brunswick.

One bit of advice you might not receive from the tourism people is that warm clothing is essential in this corner of Maine. It may be named the Sunrise Coast, but it also gets plenty of fog, rain, and cool temperatures. Temperatures tend to be warmer, and the fog diminishes, as you head toward the inland parts of the county, but you can *never* count on that—Mother Nature is an accomplished curveball pitcher, and el Niño and la Niña periodically provide an assist.

Note, too, that Maine has tough drunk-driving laws, and enforcement seems to be especially rigid in Washington County, where police and county sheriffs patrol major roads diligently—particularly on weekends—and hand out frequent citations for operating under the influence. You can find much better souvenirs.

Western Washington County

The pace begins to slow a bit by the time you reach western Washington County, the beginning of the Sunrise Coast. In this little pocket are the towns of Steuben, Milbridge, Cherryfield, and Harrington.

Life can be tough here nowadays, where once great wooden ships slid down the ways and brought prosperity and trade to shippers, builders, and barons of the timber industry. Cherryfield's stunning houses are evidence enough. The barons now control the blueberry fields, covering much of the inland area of western Washington County and annually shipping millions of pounds of blueberries out of headquarters in Milbridge (pop. 1,310) and Cherryfield (pop. 1,200). The big names here are Jasper Wyman & Sons and Cherryfield Foods.

Milbridge straddles Rte. 1, as well as the Narraguagus River (Nar-ra-GWAY-gus, a Native American name meaning "above the boggy place"), once the state's premier source of Atlantic salmon. Cherryfield is at the tidal limit of the Narraguagus. Even though Rte. 1A trims maybe three miles off the trip from Milbridge to Harrington (pop. 900), resist the urge to take it. Take Rte. 1 from Milbridge to Cherryfield—the Narraguagus Highway—and then continue on to Harrington. You just shouldn't miss Cherryfield.

SIGHTS

Local History

A group of energetic residents worked tirelessly to establish the **Milbridge Historical Soci-**

ety Museum, 83 Main St., P.O. Box 194, Milbridge 04658, 207/546-4471, which opened its Rte. 1 building in 1996. Displays in the large exhibit room focus on Milbridge's essential role in the shipbuilding trade. The volunteer-staffed museum, in the center of town, is open June–Sept. In July and Aug., hours are Tues., Sat., and Sun. 1–4 PM; other months, Sat. and Sun. 1–4 PM. Admission is free but donations are welcome.

Scenic Fall-Foliage Routes

In fall—roughly early Sept. to early October in this part of Maine—the post-harvest blueberry fields take on brilliant scarlet hues, then maroon. They're gorgeous. The best barren-viewing road is **Rte. 193** between Cherryfield and Beddington, via Deblois, the link between Rtes. 1 and 9—a 21-mile stretch of granite outcrops, pine windscreens, and fiery-red fields.

Also in fall, consider taking a lovely alternate route from Hancock County into western Washington County. A few miles east of Ellsworth, Rte. 182 veers northeast off Rte. 1 to Franklin and on to Cherryfield, a 25-mile stretch of sparkling ponds, brilliant colors, and no civilization. Schoodic Mountain, Donnell Pond, and Tunk Lake are just three of the natural treasures along the way. As you enter Washington County and land in Cherryfield, you're brought gently back to civilization by a whole town full of architectural treasures.

Cherryfield Historic District

Imagine a little town this far Down East having a 75-acre National Register Historic District

The Sunrise Coast

with 52 architecturally significant buildings. If architecture appeals, don't miss Cherryfield. The **Cherryfield-Narraguagus Historical Society,** P.O. Box 96, Cherryfield 04622, has produced a free brochure/map, *Guide to the Cherryfield Historic District,* which you can obtain in advance or pick up once you get here. Architectural styles included on the route are Greek Revival, Italianate, Queen Anne, Colonial Revival, Second Empire, Federal, and Gothic Revival—dating from 1803–1940, with most being late 19th century. The society, displaying artifacts of the mid-1800s and mid-1900s, including the sawmill era, is open July–Aug., Wed. and Fri. 1–4 PM, otherwise by appointment. Call Margery Brown, Town Historian, 207/546-7979, for appointments at other times. She also can help you with genealogy and historic records.

PARKS, PRESERVES, AND RECREATION
Maine Coastal Islands
Occupying a 2,195-acre peninsula in Steuben with 10 miles of rocky shoreline (and three offshore islands), outstandingly scenic Maine Coastal Islands National Wildlife Refuge, Point Division, formerly known as Petit Manan National Wildlife Refuge, Pigeon Hill Rd., Steuben, mailing address P.O. Box 279, Milbridge 04658, 207/546-2124, www.fws.gov/northeast/petitmanan, sees only about 15,000 visitors a year coming to enjoy its many seabirds and bald eagle population. The moderately easy, four-mile-round-trip Birch Point Trail and easy, 1.5-mile-round-trip Hollingsworth Trail (formerly the Shore Trail) provide splendid views and opportunities to spot wildlife alongshore and in the fields, forests, and marshland. Best is the Hollingsworth, taking you to the shoreline. This is foggy territory, but on clear days, you can see the 123-foot lighthouse on Petit Manan Island, 2.5 miles offshore. From Rte. 1, on the east side of Steuben, take Pigeon Hill Rd. Almost six miles down is the first parking lot, for the Birch Point Trail; another 0.5 mile takes you to the

parking area for the Hollingsworth Trail; space is limited. If you arrive in August, help yourself to blueberries. The refuge is open daily all year, sunrise to sunset; cross-country skiing is permitted in winter. The refuge headquarters are in Milbridge in the center of town on Rte. 1, open weekdays 8 AM–4:30 PM, but printed materials available 24 hours daily.

Milbridge's McClellan Park
As you enter Milbridge on Rte. 1 from the west and south, turn right onto Wyman Rd. and drive four miles down the peninsula to McClellan Park, an outstanding 10-acre town-owned park on Narraguagus Bay with picnic tables, restrooms, hiking trails, and even a handful of campsites with fire rings. Be sure you have film; it's a lovely park.

ENTERTAINMENT
The only cinema in western Washington County is the updated, air-conditioned **Milbridge Theatre,** Main St., Rte. 1, Milbridge 04658, 207/546-2038, a classic movie house that's been here since 1937. First-run films, with a good sound system, go on at 7:30 PM; all seats are $4.50. It's open daily, Memorial Day weekend–Dec.; weekends (Fri.–Sun.) Apr.–May; closed Jan.–Mar. Occasionally there are Sat. or Sun. matinees of family films at 2 PM.

FESTIVALS AND EVENTS
The biggest event in this end of Washington County, and even beyond, is **Milbridge Days,** a celebration of the town's anniversary, held the last weekend in July, drawing hundreds of visitors. The Saturday-afternoon highlight is the codfish relay race—hilarious enough to have been featured in *Sports Illustrated* and on national television. The four-member teams, clad in slickers and hip boots, *really do* hand off a greased cod instead of the usual baton. Race rules specify that runners must be "reasonably sober" and not carry the codfish between their teeth or legs. Also on the schedule are a blueberry pancake breakfast, a fun parade, kids'

games, auction, dance, cribbage tournament, craft booths, music, fireworks, lobster and clam cookout, and a real Maine baked bean supper. You have to be there. The relay race has been going since the mid-1980s; the festival has been going for a century and a half.

SHOPPING
Antiques
On the outskirts of town, in lots and nooks and crannies of a rambling farmhouse signposted **The Dusty Rose,** 297 Blackwoods Rd., (Rte. 182), mailing address 577 Sprague Falls Rd., Cherryfield 04622, 207/546-8997, www.the-dustyrose.com, veteran dealer Mary Weston seems to have assembled just about anything you could ever want in the collectibles vein: toys, old utensils, pottery, tinware, quilts—everything but dusty roses. Browsing is fun here, and so is buying. Mary is also ready with answers to touring questions. The shop, about 1.5 miles off Rte. 1, is open 10 A.M.–5 P.M. Mon.–Tues. in summer, other days by appointment.

Gifts and Crafts
In downtown Milbridge is this town's answer to Camden's Smiling Cow. The **Sea Witch,** 1 Main St., Rte. 1, Milbridge 04658, 207/546-7495, has three rooms of just about anything you could want in the inexpensive gift and souvenir category; blueberry and lobster themes dominate. It's open mid-May–mid-Oct., Mon.–Sat. 9 A.M.–5 P.M., Sun. noon–5 P.M.

ACCOMMODATIONS
Bed-and-Breakfasts
One of Cherryfield's 52 Historic Register buildings, the 1803 **Ricker House,** 49 Park St., Cherryfield 04622, 207/546-2780, borders the Narraguagus River and makes a superb base for exploring inland and Down East Maine. Jean and Bill Conway keep coming up with unending lists of things to do—*after* a huge breakfast, maybe a loll on the lovely sun porch, then a stroll to the river. Bill is an enthusiastic proponent of this region, the spark-

plug for several local organizations and events. Three second-floor bedrooms ($65 d) share a bath; two have a view of the river. Bicycles are available for guests; tennis courts are across the street. No pets, no smoking, no credit cards. Open mid-May–Nov. Ricker House is a block off Rte. 1, near the center of town.

Campgrounds
Covering seven acres on the tidal Harrington River, small, low-key **Sunset Point Campground,** 102 Marshville Rd., Harrington 04643, 207/483-4412, has 30 open sites ($18–22 for two), a playground, and saltwater swimming. Leashed pets are allowed. Open mid-May–mid-Oct. Heading north on Rte. 1, east of Harrington, go right on the Marshville road—the campground is three miles, on the right.

Town-owned **McClellan Park,** in Milbridge, has 11 campsites, costing $10 each (four persons) on a first-come, first-served basis. Make inquiries and arrangements at the Milbridge Town Office, School St., Milbridge 04658, 207/546-2422.

FOOD
Inexpensive to Moderate
In the heart of Milbridge is the aptly named **Red Barn Restaurant,** 3 Main St., Milbridge 04658, 207/546-7721, a locally popular spot for breakfast, lunch, and dinner, featuring ample portions of down-home clam chowder, lobster stew, fried seafood, and steaks. From the lowest sandwich to the highest dinner, you'll be out $2.50–20.99. Open all year. In-season hours are daily, 7 A.M.–8 P.M. (to 9 P.M. Fri.–Sat.) The restaurant is set back a bit from Main St., easiest to access from Bridge St. (just off Rte. 1).

INFORMATION AND SERVICES
To reach the **Milbridge Town Office,** School St., Milbridge 04658, 207/546-2422, from the south, turn right onto Bridge St. from Rte. 1, then turn right onto School St. The office is open weekdays 8 A.M.–4 P.M., all year.

Jonesport and Beals Area

Between western Washington County and the Machias Bay area is the molar-shaped Jonesport Peninsula, reached from the west via the attractive little town of Columbia Falls, bordering Rte. 1. Down the peninsula are the picturesque towns of Addison, Jonesport, and Beals Island. First settled around 1762, Columbia Falls (pop. about 600) still has eight intriguing historical buildings, but its best-known structure is the early-19th-century Ruggles House. For history or architecture fans, the town is a must-see, a pretty pocket of the past.

On the banks of the Pleasant River, just south of Columbia Falls, Addison (pop. 1,215) once had four huge shipyards cranking out wooden cargo vessels that circled the world. Since that 19th-century heyday, little seems to have changed, and the town today may be best known as the haunt of painter John Marin, who first came to Maine in 1914. His onetime home and studio, on outstandingly scenic Cape Split, at the bottom of Addison's peninsula, are not open to the public, but it's worth driving there to understand his inspiration.

Jonesport and Beals Island, with a combined population of about 2,230, are traditional hardworking fishing communities—old-fashioned, friendly, and incredibly photogenic. Beals, connected to Jonesport via an arched bridge over Moosabec Reach, is named for Manwarren Beal, Jr., and his wife, Lydia, who arrived around 1773 and quickly threw themselves into the Revolutionary War effort. But that's not all they did—the current phone book covering Jonesport and Beals Island lists dozens of Beal descendants (as well as dozens of Alleys and Carvers, other early names).

Even more memorable than Manwarren Beal was his six-foot, seven-inch son Barnabas, dubbed "Tall Barney" for obvious reasons. The larger-than-life fellow became the stuff of legend all along the Maine coast—and a popular Jonesport restaurant preserves his name.

Also legendary here is the lobsterboat design known as the Jonesport hull. People from away won't recognize its distinctive shape, but count on the fishing pros to know it. The harbor here is jam-packed with Jonesport lobsterboats, and souped-up versions are consistent winners in the summertime lobsterboat-race series, www.lobsterboatracing.com, held in Jonesport, Stonington, Searsport, Winter Harbor, and other coastal towns.

The finest natural treasure in this part of Maine, a must-see, is the Great Wass Archipelago, partly owned by The Nature Conservancy. Some areas are open to the public, notably the Great Wass Island preserve and Mistake Island.

SIGHTS

Ruggles House

Behind a picket fence on a quiet street in Columbia Falls stands the remarkable Ruggles House, 146 Main St., P.O. Box 116, Columbia Falls 04623, 207/483-4637. Built in 1818 for Judge Thomas Ruggles—lumber baron, militia captain, even postmaster—the tiny house on a grand scale boasts a famous flying (unsupported) staircase, intricately carved moldings, Palladian window, and unusual period furnishings. Rescued in the mid-20th century and maintained by the Ruggles House Society, this gem has become a magnet for savvy preservationists. Located a quarter of a mile east of Rte. 1, it's open for hour-long guided tours

Ruggles House, Columbia Falls

June 1–Oct. 15, Mon.–Sat. 9:30 AM–4:30 PM, Sun. 11 AM–4:30 PM. Suggested donation is $5 adults, $2 children.

At the house, pick up a copy of the Columbia Falls **walking-tour brochure,** which details the intriguing history of other houses in this hamlet.

Maine Central Model Railroad

Here's Nirvana for model-train enthusiasts. Harold ("Buz") Beal and his wife, Helen, have created a fantastic model railroad layout—the Maine Central Model Railroad—covering about 900 square feet in a building next to their house. There are 4,000 trees, 417 freight cars, 20 diesel engines, 3,000 feet of track, 11 bridges and trestles, 200 switches.... Buz Beal, a 26-year Coast Guard veteran, figures railroading is in his blood; his grandfather was a Canadian Pacific engineer. Visitors are welcome any day of the year, but it's best to call ahead (207/497-2255) to be sure someone's home. On Rte. 187, about four miles northeast of downtown Jonesport, watch for the Church Enterprises sign on the right, then take the next left to the Beals' house. A railroad crossing sign marks the driveway. (Rte. 187 makes a loop through the peninsula; the Beals are on the easternmost side of the loop—7.7 miles south of Rte. 1.) There's no charge, but donations are welcomed.

The Downeast Institute

Welcome to the world's only soft-shell clam hatchery. The Downeast Institute, Beals Island 04611, 207/497-5769 or 255-1314 off season, www.downeastinstitute.org, is also Maine's only public shellfish hatchery, and visitors are welcome daily 9 AM–4 PM, June–Sept. The annual aquaculture process begins in mid-March; by November millions of tiny soft-shell clams *(Mya arenaria)* are transplanted into Maine coastal clam flats from Kittery to Eastport. A staff member will answer questions and guide you through the hatchery. Admission is free. To reach the hatchery, take Rte. 187 from Rte. 1, continuing through Jonesport and across the arched bridge to Beals Island. Turn left, go straight through a stop sign, at the next stop sign, take a right, then go straight for about 5 miles, then go down Wildflower Lane on the right-hand side. You will be able to recognize the building by its size—large—and the red lobster on the roof.

PRESERVES AND RECREATION

Great Wass Island

Allow a whole day to explore 1,579-acre Great Wass Island, an extraordinary preserve, even when it's drenched in fog—a not-infrequent event. Owned by The Nature Conservancy, the preserve is at the tip of Jonesport's peninsula. Hiking routes are the wooded, two-mile Little Cape Point and 1.5-mile Mud Hole Trails; the Conservancy warns they may be harder than you would think, or even "dangerous in bad weather, like fog." You retrace your path for each. (Making a loop by connecting the two along the rocky shoreline adds considerably to the time and difficulty, but do it if you have time; allow about six hours, wear sturdy waterproof footwear, carry clothing suitable to all weathers.) Expect to see beach-head iris (like blue flag) and orchids (like dragon's mouth), jack pine, a peat bog, seals, pink granite, pitcher plants, lots of warblers, osprey, and eagles. Carry water and a picnic; wear bug repellent. No camping, fires, or pets; no toilet facilities. Daytime access only. To reach the preserve from Rte. 1, take Rte. 187 to Jonesport (12 miles), then cross the arched bridge to Beals Island. Continue across Beals to the Great Wass causeway (locally called "the Flying Place"), then go three miles on Black Duck Cove Rd. to the parking area (on the left). Watch for The Nature Conservancy oak-leaf symbol. At the parking area, pick up a trail map and a bird checklist.

Also owned by The Nature Conservancy is 21-acre **Mistake Island,** accessible only by boat. Low and shrubby, Mistake has a Coast Guard-built boardwalk from the landing at the northwest corner to **Moose Peak Light,** standing 72 feet above the water at the eastern end of the island. The only negative on this lovely

The Sunrise Coast

island is rubble left behind when the government leveled the keeper's house.

For more information about the Great Wass Archipelago, contact **The Nature Conservancy, Maine Chapter,** Fort Andross, 14 Maine St., Brunswick 04011, 207/729-5181.

Golf and Swimming

You can play golf and swim (in salt or fresh water) on the adjoining **Roque Bluffs Peninsula.** On the east side of the Jonesport peninsula, there's saltwater swimming at **Sandy River Beach,** but be prepared for glacial temperatures. Bring a picnic—it's a lovely spot—but respect private property here. From Rte. 187, take Beach Ln. (signposted Church Enterprises), about four miles northeast of downtown Jonesport.

GETTING AFLOAT

A great-grandson of legendary local "Tall Barney" Beal, Capt. Barna Norton began offering puffin-watching trips to Machias Seal Island (MSI) in 1940 in a 33-foot boat incautiously named *If.* Now his son, Capt. John, has taken over the helm, in *The Chief,* heated and specially built for the trip and for safety. The boat takes those in search of the puffin—and the original "Puffin Patch"—20 miles offshore to an island with a colorful history. To preserve the fragile nesting sites of Atlantic puffins and arctic terns, access to the 15-or-so acre island is restricted. Passengers are offloaded into small boats, but sea swells sometimes prevent landing. The trip is not appropriate for small children or unsteady adults. The boat departs Jonesport around 7 AM, allowing two or three hours on MSI before returning about 1 PM. Departure time is affected by the weather, call the previous evening for information. Cost is $65 pp; reservations are necessary. Wear waterproof hiking boots and pack some munchies. The Nortons have very casual accommodations available in their **Puffin House Hostel.** They also rent two cottages—Tern and Sea View—by the week or day. Trips begin Me-

morial Day weekend and end by Labor Day. For information and reservations, contact **Norton of Jonesport,** 118 Main St., Box 330, Jonesport 04649, 207/497-5933 or 207/497-2560, www.machiassealisland.com.

Captain Laura Fish, 14 Kelley Strand, Jonesport 04649, 207/497-3064, does daily (weather permitting) three-hour Moosabec Reach cruises in her 23-foot powerboat *Aaron Thomas.* Among the sights are Great Wass Island and Mistake Island. Call for reservations and information. Trips depart from Jonesport and operate June–mid-Sept.

FESTIVALS AND EVENTS

The biggest annual event hereabouts is the wingding Jonesport **Fourth of July** celebration, with several days of special activities, including barbecues, beauty pageant, kids' games, fireworks, parade, and the famed **Jonesport Lobsterboat Races** in Moosabec Reach.

The August **Maine Wild Blueberry Festival,** in neighboring Machias, is an easy jaunt from the Jonesport/Beals area.

SHOPPING
Gifts and Crafts

Lupine is a popular motif on the hand-thrown earthenware pottery at **Columbia Falls Pottery,** 150 Main St., P.O. Box 235, Columbia Falls 04623, 207/483-4075 or 800/235-2512, www.columbiafallspottery.com, an appealing shop in a rehabbed country store next to the Ruggles House. Veteran potter April Adams keeps the inventory fresh, and the company does a hefty mail-order business. The shop, 0.5 mile east of Rte. 1, is open Mon.–Sat. 10 AM–5 PM, 11 AM–4 PM Sun., from Memorial Day–Columbus Day; late Oct.–Dec., Tues.–Sat. 10 AM–5 PM; Mar.–May, Thurs.–Sat. 10 AM–5 PM. The two-bedroom suite above the store is available for weekly or monthly rentals, depending on the season.

Barbara Doak specializes in oil paintings at the **1789 Gallery,** 204 Main St., Columbia

Falls 04623, 207/483-2031, and also runs "Art by Barbara," an illustration business. Owner Stephanie Gertz shows the work of various fine artists, and sells pottery and jewelry, in her 1836 **Crandon House Gallery,** 141 Main St., P.O. Box 245, Columbia Falls 04623, 207/483-3871.

Church's True Value, Main St., Rte. 187, Jonesport 04649, 207/497-2778, carries all the usual hardware items, plus gifts, souvenirs, and sportswear. Helpful owners John and Sharon Church can also answer any question about the area and solve most any problem. The store is open all year, Mon.–Sat. 7 AM–5 PM.

Farmers Market

The **Milbridge Farmers Market** sells fresh farm goods, plants, strawberries, blueberries, apples, and veggies at the Milbridge Market parking lot on Rte. 1 in downtown Milbridge, Sat. 9 AM–noon, early June–Oct.

ACCOMMODATIONS
Bed-and-Breakfasts

How about staying in a beautiful, modern farmhouse overlooking the water—with deer and llamas llolling outside? At **Pleasant Bay Bed & Breakfast and Llama Keep,** 386 West Side Rd., Box 222, Addison 04606, 207/483-4490, www.pleasantbay.com, Joan and Lee Yeaton manage to pamper about 30 llama and 50 red deer as well as their two-legged guests. Over two miles of trails on the farm, and two miles of shoreline are there for the walking. Three lovely rooms (private and shared baths) are $50–135 d, including a delicious breakfast. No pets, no smoking. Well-behaved children are welcome; arrange in advance for a (weather-dependent) llama walk at $15 per llama. Open all year. The farm borders tidal Pleasant River, 4.5 miles southeast of Rte. 1.

Ireland meets Alaska on the outskirts of Columbia Falls, where Jack and Maureen Murphy opened **The Dream Catcher,** Rte. 1, P.O. Box 157, Columbia Falls 04623, 207/483-0937, home.midmaine.com/~catcher, in an 1885 house and filled it with Alaskan and Irish artifacts and plenty of quilts. The Irish part is obvious; the Alaska comes from their years working there as nurses. Two rooms (private baths; $80 d) are named County Limerick and County Cork; the latter has a four-poster bed and a fireplace. There's also a two-room suite good for family stays. Guests have the use of two parlors, one with a TV. Breakfast is breathtaking—even including dessert; forget about lunch. Make advance arrangements for children and pets. Open all year. Even though the house is on Rte. 1, it's elevated and buffered a bit from the road; there's a peaceful deck out back. The B&B sign is very small; watch carefully for it.

The fanciest digs in Jonesport are at **Harbor House on Sawyer Cove,** P.O. Box 468, 27 Sawyer Sq., Jonesport 04649, 207/497-5417, www.harborhs.com, hospitably run by Maureen and Gene Hart—she an ex-nurse, he an ex-engineer—who enjoy sharing the Jonesport area with Harbor House guests. Two very comfortable second-floor suites (private baths)—named Beach Rose and Lupine and decorated to fit—have incredible views of Moosabec Reach. Binoculars are provided so you can watch the action, including passengers embarking on the Norton puffin trip. The Harts operate an antiques shop, too, selling what they call "curiosities," on the first floor of this fascinating old building, once Jonesport's telegraph office and ship chandlery. Harbor House is open all year, and equipped with high-speed Internet. Rates are $110 d Memorial Day–Labor Day, $95 d other months, including a wonderful gourmet breakfast on the porch. No pets, no smoking, no children under 10.

Seasonal Rentals

Close to the best sandy beach on the peninsula, **Church's Ocean Front Cottages,** Rte. 187, 49 Sandy River Beach Rd., Jonesport 04649, 207/497-2829, www.oceancottages-maine.com, are three rustic, well-maintained cottages available seasonally by the week. The best view is from Sandpiper, which sleeps six

The Sunrise Coast

and rents for $1,000 a week; the others (Linnet and Lemon Drop) are $700 a week. No pets. Bring your own sheets and towels. The cottages are seven miles south of Rte. 1 and four miles northeast of downtown Jonesport. A fourth cottage, Harbor View ($700 per week), is an eccentric little place with a spectacular panoramic view, on Main St. in downtown Jonesport.

The seasonal-rental information produced by the Machias Bay Area Chamber of Commerce sometimes includes Jonesport-area cottages.

FOOD

Lunch

For local color, start at **Tall Barney's,** Main St., Rte. 187, Jonesport 04649, 207/497-2403, where you'll find homemade baked beans and chowders, pizza, seafood platter, and more—and you won't break the bank. Sit back and watch the servers chat up the lobstermen regulars camped out at the "liars' table." Open all year, 5 AM–8 PM Mon.–Sat., Sun. from 6 AM, changes in winter. The restaurant is just before the bridge to Beals Island; watch for the statue of Barney.

If you're anywhere near Jonesport in August, head for Lois Hubbard's farm stand and bakery, called **Mason Bay Berry & Egg Farm, home of the Farm Bakery,** 1561 Mason's Bay Rd., Rte. 187, Jonesport 04649, 207/497-5949, a popular produce source. Time your trip for August, when you can acquire the blueberry whoopee pies, made only during that month. Located 3.3 miles south of the Jonesboro end of Rte. 1, Mason Bay is open 10 AM–4 PM Mon. and Wed.–Fri., as well as Sat. by appointment only.

Inexpensive

About midway between Harrington and Columbia Falls, near the turnoff for Addison, **Judy Ann's,** Rte. 1, Columbia 04623, 207/483-2045, is your basic no-frills roadside seafood restaurant with everything fresh and homemade. Steaks are also available, as are great onion rings, if that's your

thing. It's open daily 6 AM–8 PM (to 9 PM Fri.–Sat.).

Also inexpensive is the **Ol' Salt Restaurant.**

Moderate

The food is family-style and all homemade at the **Snare Creek Grill,** Rte. 187, Jonesport 04649, 207/497-5903. Steaks, seafood, and pasta entrées range from $9.95–13.95. It's open daily 5 AM–8 PM.

INFORMATION AND SERVICES

The **Machias Bay Area Chamber of Commerce** handles inquiries for the Jonesport/Beals Area, which has no official information center. In downtown Jonesport, the best source of local information is **Church's True Value,** Main St., Rte. 187, Jonesport 04649, 207/497-2778, open every day but Sunday.

Newspapers

Newspapers that cover the Jonesport/Beals Area are the competing *Machias Valley News Observer,* 207/255-6561, published every Wednesday, and the Cutler-based *Downeast Coastal Press,* 207/259-7751, published every Tuesday. The daily of choice is the *Bangor Daily News.*

Emergencies

For emergencies requiring fire, police, and/or ambulance in **Addison, Columbia, and Columbia Falls, and Jonesport,** call 911.

The nearest hospital is **Down East Community Hospital** in Machias.

Public Restrooms

There are restrooms at the CITGO station at the Four Corners Shopping Center, Rte. 1 in **Columbia,** midway between Harrington and Columbia Falls. This mini-mall also has an ATM, supermarket (picnic fare available), clothing shop, furniture store, hardware store, and rod-and-gun shop. Also sold here are computers, videos, and, for those who want a permanent souvenir, a tattoo and piercing establishment.

The Sunrise Coast

Machias Bay Area

The only negative thing about Machias (Muh-CHY-us; pop. 2,626) is its Micmac Indian name, meaning "bad little falls" (even though that's accurate—the midtown waterfall here *is* treacherous, but it's fun to watch from a bench on the overlook). A contagious local esprit pervades this shire town of Washington County, thanks to antique homes, a splendid river-valley setting, Revolutionary War monuments, and a small but busy university campus.

If you regard crowds as fun, an ideal time to land here is during the renowned annual Machias Wild Blueberry Festival, www.machiasblueberry.com, third weekend in August, when harvesting is underway in Washington County's blueberry fields and you can stuff your face with blueberry-everything—muffins, jam, pancakes, ice cream, pies. You can also collect blueberry-logo napkins, T-shirts, magnets, pottery, and jewelry. The menu at the local McDonald's even lists blueberry pancakes and shakes that weekend. Among the other summer draws are a chamber-music series, art shows, and semiprofessional theater performances. Within a few miles are day-trips galore—options for hiking, biking, golfing, swimming, and sea kayaking.

English settlers, uprooted from communities farther west on the Maine coast, put down permanent roots here in 1763, harvesting timber to ensure their survival. Stirrings of revolutionary discontent surfaced even at this remote outpost, and when British loyalists in Boston began usurping some of the valuable harvest, Machias patriots plotted revenge. By 1775, when the armed British schooner *Margaretta* arrived as a cargo escort, local residents aboard the sloop *Unity,* in a real David-and-Goliath episode, chased down and captured the *Margaretta.* On June 12, 1775, two months after the famed Battles of Lexington and Concord (and five days before the Battle of Bunker Hill), Machias Bay was the site of what author James Fenimore Cooper called "The Lexington of the Sea"—the first naval battle of the American

Revolution. The name of patriot leader Jeremiah O'Brien today appears throughout Machias—on a school, a street, a cemetery, and a state park. In 1784, Machias was incorporated; it became the shire town in 1790.

Timber remained a valuable resource for this area well into the 20th century. Fed with timber headed downriver by courageous log drivers, sawmills lined the banks of the Machias River in the 19th century, and trains hauled timber from mills to harbors as early as 1842. The locomotive Lion, a Machias-area workhorse from 1846 to 1883, now greets visitors to the Maine State Museum in Augusta. The last log drive on the Machias River occurred as recently as the 1970s.

Also included within the Machias sphere are the towns of Roque Bluffs, Jonesboro, Whitneyville, Marshfield, East Machias, and Machiasport. Just to the east, between Machias and Lubec, are the towns of Whiting and Cutler.

SIGHTS

History is a big deal in this area, and since Machias was the first settled Maine town east of the Penobscot River, lots of enthusiastic amateur historians have helped rescue homes and sites dating from as far back as the Revolutionary era.

Museums

One-hour guided tours vividly convey the atmosphere of the 1770 **Burnham Tavern,** Main St., just off Rte. 1 on Rte. 192, Machias 04654, 207/255-4432, where upstart local patriots met here in 1775 to plot revolution against the British. Job and Mary Burnham's tavern/home next served as an infirmary for casualties from the Revolution's first naval battle, just offshore. Lots of fascinating history in this National Historic Site maintained by the Daughters of the American Revolution. Hanging outside is a sign reading, "Drink for the thirsty, food for the hungry, lodging for the weary, and good keeping for horses, by Job Burnham." Admission is $5 adults, $0.25 for kids under 12. It's open Mon.–Fri. 9 AM–5 PM, last tour at 4:30 PM, mid-June–Sept., and by appointment off season. If you're here on the first Tuesday in August, you can join in the museum's annual **lawn party,** including lunch, tours, and handicraft sales.

Headquarters for the Machiasport Historical Society and one of the area's three oldest residences, the 1810 **Gates House,** 344 Port Rd., Rte. 92, P.O. Box 301, Machiasport 04655, 207/255-8461, was snatched from ruin and restored in 1966. The National Historic Register building overlooking Machias Bay contains fascinating period furnishings and artifacts— many related to the lumbering and shipbuilding era. The museum, four miles southeast of Rte. 1, is open Tues.–Sat. 12:30–4:30 PM July–Aug. Admission is free, but donations are appreciated. The nearby Cooper House dates from 1850. Limited parking on a hazardous curve.

Centre Street Congregational Church

Machias's most distinctive landmark is the steeple of the 1836 Gothic Revival Centre Street Congregational Church, Center St., Machias 04654, 207/255-6665. The community-oriented parishioners spearhead the annual Maine Wild Blueberry Festival, and the church is the site of the festival's annual Blueberry Musical. The musical, a sellout for which reservations are wise, always includes the piece "Blueberry Blues." Past musicals were "My Blue Hero" and "It's a Wonderful Blueberry."

The July–Aug. Machias Bay Chamber Concerts are also held in this church.

O'Brien Cemetery

Old-cemetery buffs will want to stop at O'Brien Cemetery, resting place of the town's earliest settlers. It's next to Bad Little Falls Park, close to downtown, off Rte. 92 toward Machiasport. A big plus here is the view, especially in autumn, of blueberry barrens, the waterfall, and the bay.

University of Maine at Machias

Founded in 1909 as Washington State Normal School, University of Maine at Machias (UMM), 9 O'Brien Ave., Machias 04654, 207/255-1200, www.umm.maine.edu, is part of the state university system, and was recently named 5th among public comprehensive colleges in the north by a national magazine. UMM has about 1,000 students, eastern Maine's biggest gym, and impressive degree programs in marine biology, recreation management, and teacher education. During the summer, the **UMM Art Galleries,** in Powers Hall, feature works from the university's expanding permanent collection of Maine painters—including John Marin, William Zorach, Lyonel Feininger, and Reuben Tam. Rotating exhibits occur throughout the school year. Hours are Mon.–Fri. noon–4 PM, or by appointment.

In 1999 and 2000, UMM opened two sections of its $3 million **Center for Lifelong Learning,** with a state-of-the-art fitness center, six-lane heated pool, and the George Simpson Murdock Bookstore. The pool and fitness room are open to the public daily (for a fee), as is the bookstore. Summer bookstore hours are 9 AM–4 PM. Pool hours are 5:30 AM–1:30 PM, and 3–9 PM weekdays; 8 AM–4 PM Sat. and 10 AM–4 PM Sun. Cost of a one-day pass to use the pool and fitness facilities is $6; a three-day pass is $15. For additional information, call 207/255-1403.

SCENIC ROUTES

The drives described below can also be bike routes (easy to moderately difficult), but be forewarned that the roads are narrow and shoulderless, so caution is essential. Heed biking etiquette.

Route 191, The Cutler Road

Never mind that Rte. 191 between East Machias and West Lubec is one of Maine's most stunning coastal drives, you can still follow the entire 27-mile stretch and meet only a handful of cars. **East Machias** even has its own historic district, with architectural gems dating from the late 18th century along High and Water Streets. Farther along Rte. 191, you'll find fishing wharves, low moorlands, a hamlet or two, and islands popping over the horizon. The only peculiarly jarring note is the 26-tower forest of North Cutler's Naval Computer and Telecommunications Station, nearly a thousand feet high—monitoring global communications—but you see this only briefly. (At night, the sky-scraping red lights are really eerie.) Off Rte. 191 are minor roads and hiking trails worth exploring, especially the coastal trails. About three miles south of the Rte. 191 terminus, you can also check out **Bailey's Mistake,** a hamlet with a black-sand (volcanic) beach. And the name? Allegedly it stems from one Capt. Bailey who, misplotting his course and thinking he was in Lubec, drove his vessel ashore here one night in the late 19th century. Unwilling to face the consequences of his lapse, he and his crew offloaded their cargo of lumber and built themselves dwellings. Whether true or not, it makes a great saga. Even though it's in the town of **Trescott,** and the hamlet is really South Trescott, everyone knows this section as Bailey's Mistake.

Route 92, Starboard Peninsula

Pack a picnic and set out on Rte. 92 (beginning at Elm St. in downtown Machias) down the 10-mile length of the Starboard Peninsula to a stunning spot known as the Point of Maine. Along the way are the villages of Larrabee, Bucks Harbor, and Starboard, all part of the town of Machiasport. In Bucks Harbor is the turnoff (a short detour to the right) to **Yoho Head,** a controversial upscale development overlooking Little Kennebec Bay.

South of the Yoho Head turnoff is the sign for **Jasper Beach.** From here, continue 1.4 miles to two red buildings (the old Starboard School House and the volunteer fire department). Turn left onto a dirt road, continue to a sign reading Driveway, go around the right side of a shed, and park on the beach. (Keep track of the tide level, though.) You're at **Point of Maine,** a quintessential Down East pan-

orama of sea and islands. On a clear day, you can see offshore **Libby Island Light,** the focus of Philmore Wass' entertaining narrative *Lighthouse in My Life.*

PARKS, PRESERVES, AND RECREATION

Just as dedicated as the historical preservationists are the hikers, birders, and other eco-sensitive outdoors enthusiasts who've helped preserve thousands of acres in this part of Maine for public access and appreciation.

An especially active local organization in eastern Washington County is the **Quoddy Regional Land Trust** (QRLT), Rte. 1, P.O. Box 49, Whiting 04691, 207/733-5509, www.qrlt.org, which has secured conservation easements on more than 900 acres and more than eight miles of shoreline. The QRLT publishes the *Cobscook Trails* hiking guide, and it's actively involved in a variety of other projects. If you'd like to support their efforts, individual memberships are $10 a year.

Bad Little Falls Park

At Bad Little Falls Park, alongside the Machias River, stop to catch the view from the footbridge overlooking the roiling falls (especially in spring). Bring a picnic and enjoy this mid-town oasis tucked between Rtes. 1 and 92.

Mill Memorial Park

On the east bank of the East Machias River, at the edge of the East Machias Historic District, Mill Memorial Park is a great, grassy place for the kids to let off steam. A large sign here shows the locations of 13 grist and sawmills once powered by the river.

Fort O'Brien State Memorial

The American Revolution's first naval battle was fought just offshore from Fort O'Brien in June 1775. Now a State Historic Site, the fort was built and rebuilt several times—originally to guard Machias during the Revolutionary War. Only Civil War–era earthworks now remain, plus well-maintained lawns overlooking the Machias River. Steep banks lead down to the water; keep small children well back from the edge. No restrooms or other facilities, but there's a playground at the Fort O'Brien School, next door. Officially, the park is open Memorial Day weekend to Labor Day, but it's easily accessible all year. Admission is free. Take Rte. 92 from Machias about five miles toward Machiasport; the parking area is on the left.

Jasper Beach

Thanks to a handful of incredibly foresighted year-round and summer residents, spectacular, crescent-shaped Jasper Beach—piled high with ocean-polished jasper and other rocks— has been preserved by the town of Machiasport. No sand here, just stones, in intriguing shapes and colors. Resist the urge to fill your pockets with souvenirs, maybe settling for just a single special rock. Parking is limited; no facilities. From Rte. 1 in downtown Machias, take Rte. 92 (Machias Rd.) 9.5 miles southeast, past the village of Bucks Harbor. Watch for a large sign on your left. The beach is on Howard's Cove, 0.2 mile off the road, and accessible all year.

Roque Bluffs State Park

Southwest of Machias, six miles south of Rte. 1, is 275-acre Roque Bluffs State Park, Roque Bluffs Rd., Roque Bluffs 04648, 207/255-3475. Saltwater swimming this far north is for the young and brave, but this park also has a 60-acre freshwater pond warm and shallow enough for toddlers and the old and timid. Facilities include primitive changing rooms, outhouses, a play area, and picnic tables (no food or lifeguards); views go on forever from the wide-open, mile-long sweep of sand beach. Admission is $2 adults, $1 children 5–11. The fee box relies on the honor system. The park is open daily May 15–Sept. 15, but the beach is accessible all year.

Cutler Coast

On Rte. 191, about 4.5 miles northeast of the center of Cutler, watch for the parking area (on the right) for the **Cutler Coast Unit,** a 12,000-acre preserve with nearly a dozen miles of beautifully engineered hiking trails on the seaward side of Rte. 191. Allow 5–6 hours to do the shorter, 5.8-mile **Black Point Brook Loop,** providing an easy start for about 1.5 miles, partly on a narrow trail through cedar bog, before getting to the Coastal Trail, a stretch of moderately rugged hiking southward along dramatic, tree-fringed shoreline cliffs. Log ladders allow beach access. Then head back via the Black Point Brook cutoff and connect with the Inland Trail to return to your car (or bicycle). Bring binoculars and plenty of film; the views from this wild coastline are fabulous, and whale sighting possibilities exist. Also bring insect repellent—inland boggy stretches are buggy. Carry a picnic and commandeer a granite ledge overlooking the surf. Precipitous cliffs and narrow stretches can make the shoreline section of this trail perilous for small children or insecure adults, so use extreme caution. There are no facilities in the preserve, but there are owls, falcons, and eagles. If you're here July–Aug., you can stock up on blueberries, and even some wild raspberries. Another option, the 9.8-mile **Fairy Head Loop,** starts the same way as the Black Point Brook Loop but continues on southward along the coast, leading to three primitive campsites (stoves only, no fires), available on a first-come, first-served basis. There's no way to reserve these, so you take your chances. Unless you have gazelle genes, the longer loop almost demands an overnight. Information on the preserve, including a helpful map, is available from the **Maine Bureau of Parks and Lands,** 22 State House Station, Augusta 04333, 207/287-3821, www.parksandlands.com.

Originally about 2,100 acres, this incredible preserve was quintupled in 1997, when several donors, primarily the Richard King Mellon Foundation, deeded to the state 10,055 acres of fields and forests across Rte. 191 from the trail area, creating a phenomenal tract that now runs from the ocean all the way back to Rte. 1. Located mostly in Cutler but also in Whiting, it was Maine's second-largest public-land gift—after Baxter State Park.

Golf

With lovely water views, and tidal inlets serving as obstacles, the nine-hole **Great Cove Golf Course,** 387 Great Cove Rd., Jonesboro 04648, 207/434-7200, is a good challenge. You'll find reasonable greens fees, carts, and a snack bar; you can also rent clubs. From Jonesboro (Rte. 1), go 3.5 miles east and south on Roque Bluffs Rd. Open May–Oct.

GETTING AFLOAT

If you've brought your own **sea kayak,** there are public launching ramps in Bucks Harbor (east of the main Machias Rd.) and at Roque Bluffs State Park. You can also put in at Sanborn Cove, beyond the O'Brien School on Rte. 92, about five miles south of Machias, where there's a small parking area. Before setting out, be sure to check the tide calendar and plan your strategy so you don't have to slog through acres of muck when you return. Or contact Machias Bay Boat Tours and Sea Kayaking.

Bold Coast Charter Company

Andrew Patterson, skipper of the 40-foot *Barbara Frost,* operates the Bold Coast Charter Company, P.O. Box 364, Cutler 04626, 207/259-4484, www.boldcoast.com, homeported in Cutler Harbor. Andy provides knowledgeable narration, answers questions in depth, and shares his considerable enthusiasm for this pristine corner of Maine. His two-hour Bold Coast cruises usually depart in early afternoon, mid-May–Oct., swing around Little River Light (invisible from the mainland), and move in close to Cutler's fish-farming pens, where Andy explains the fascinating aquaculture process. Cost is $35 per person.

Andy is best known for his five-hour **puffin-sighting trips** to Machias Seal Island (mid-May–Aug.), departure times vary, as early as 7 AM) All trips are dependent on weather and tide conditions. Reservations are recommended; reserve early for the very popular Machias Seal Island (MSI) trip; seats are easiest to come by in May or mid- to late Aug. Cost for the MSI trip is $65 adults, $40 kids (small

children not recommended). Daily access to the island is restricted, and swells can roll in, so passengers occasionally cannot disembark, but the curious puffins often surround the boat, providing plenty of photo opportunities. No matter what the air temperature on the mainland, be sure to dress warmly, and wear good gripping shoes. The *Barbara Frost* departs from the town boat ramp on Wharf Rd, just off Rte. 191 in Cutler Harbor.

Sea Kayaking Excursions

Jen and Rob Scribner—he's a Maine guide—run **Sunrise County Canoe and Kayak,** RR 1, Box 344A, Machias 04654, 207/255-3375 or 877/980-2300, www.sunrisecanoeandkayak .com, where they rent kayaks and canoes, and guide sea-kayaking trips. On the most popular excursion, in Machias Bay, you'll see Indian petroglyphs estimated at 1,700 years old. Native Americans evidently came to this area in summer to harvest fish and shellfish, leaving behind these mysterious spirit symbols carved into island slate. (The Machias area has at least five island and mainland petroglyph sites; the Maine State Museum is assembling a full-scale inventory of the carvings.) A four-hour trip is $48 per person.

Canoeing

The spectacular **Machias River,** one of Maine's most technically demanding canoeing rivers, is a dynamite trip mid-May–mid-June, but no beginner should attempt it. Best advice is to sign on with an outfitter/guide who will get you through. The run lasts 3–8 days, the latter if you start from Fifth Machias Lake. Expect to see such wildlife as osprey, eagles, ducks, loons, moose, deer, beaver, and snapping turtles. Be aware, though, that the Machias is probably the buggiest river in the state, and blackflies will form a welcoming party. Bring khaki duds; the bugs are attracted to colors. The major portage is at Upper Holmes Falls; trying to run the half-mile-long rips would buy you a ticket to the morgue. Two companies experienced on the Machias are **Sunrise Expeditions,** 4 Union Plaza, Ste. 2, Bangor 04401, 207/942-9300 or

800/748-3730, www.sunrise-exp.com, with a base camp in Cathance Lake; and **Wilds of Maine Guide Service,** 192 Congress St., Belfast 04915, 207/338-3932, www.wildsofmaine.com. All-inclusive cost is around $200 per day.

ENTERTAINMENT, FESTIVALS, AND EVENTS

The University of Maine at Machias is the cultural focus in this area, particularly during the school year.

The **Downriver Theatre Company** P.O. Box 75, Machias, 207/255-4997, puts on one production a year at the University's Performing Arts Center, in late June and early- to mid-July, for a total of 9 performances. They've performed *Annie, Anne of Green Gables*, and *Carousel* (adult tickets $10). A more casual group, the **Magnificent Liars,** with no fixed base of operations, has performed in Eastport, Pembroke, Lubec, UMM, and even in local bars.

Six Tuesday-evening **Machias Bay Chamber Concerts** occur early July–mid-Aug. at 7 PM at the Centre Street Congregational Church.

The **Maine Wild Blueberry Festival** is the summer highlight, running Fri.–Sun. the third weekend in August, featuring a pancake breakfast, road races, concerts, a craft show, a baked-bean supper, and more. The blueberry motif is everywhere. Organized by Centre Street Congregational Church, in downtown Machias.

SHOPPING
Gifts, Crafts, Clothing
Maine-made crafts and clothing, a select book inventory, ecosensitive toys, and unusual greeting cards fill the two rooms at **The Sow's Ear,** 7 Water St., Machias 04654, 207/255-4066, the oddest-named but nicest shop in Machias. The Sow's Ear also carries intriguing "things from away" (also known as "imports"), and the staff is especially helpful. Open Mon.–Sat. Feb.–Dec.

Influenced by traditional Japanese designs, Connie Harter-Bagley markets her large selection of dramatic ceramics at **Connie's Clay of Fundy,** Rte. 1, East Machias 04630, 207/255-4574 or 888/255-8131, www.clayoffundy.com, on the East Machias River. If your timing is right, you can tour the studio, watch Connie and apprentices at work, and possibly see a raku firing. The shop, four miles east of downtown Machias, is open all year, usually 8 AM–6 PM daily, but call if you are making a special trip.

Natural Foods and Farmers Markets
"The dike," a low causeway next to the Machias River, is the setting for pro tem vendors throughout the year, but each Wed., Fri., Sat., 8 AM–noon, May–Oct., it's also the site for the **Machias Valley Farmers Market,** source of great produce and blueberries late July–Aug. When the growing season peaks, vendors are there most days. There aren't many farmers markets in this part of Maine, so this is a good one to patronize.

It's not quite Alice's Restaurant, but you can find just about anything you want, organically speaking, at the **Whole Life Natural Market,** 80 Main St., Machias 04630, 207/255-8855, even organic candy bars. In a welcoming, light-filled space, you'll find organic produce, prepared soup and foods, body products from Kiss My Face to Burt's Bees, a library, CDs, and gift baskets. Open all year, Mon.–Sat. 9 AM–6 PM, Sun. 10 AM–3 PM.

ACCOMMODATIONS
Bed-and-Breakfasts
Victoriana rules at the **Riverside Inn,** Rte. 1, P.O. Box 373, East Machias 04630, 207/255-4134, www.riversideinn-maine.com, a restored early-19th-century sea captain's home. Relax on the deck overlooking the East Machias River and you'll forget you're a few steps from a busy highway. Sit in the lovely terraced perennial gardens and you'll feel the same way. Four rooms (all with private baths), as well as a popular dining room, are on the river—a hangout for osprey and eagles. Rates are $95–130

d, June–Oct., less Nov.–May. No smoking, no pets. The inn is four miles northeast of downtown Machias.

Six months of renovation preceded the opening of the 1850s **Captain Cates House B&B,** Rte. 92, P.O. Box 314, Machiasport 04655, 207/255-8812, www.captaincates.com, located about four miles south of Machias. Kay and Lise Duckworth (he a retired banker, she a former travel consultant) have loaded their comfortable house with interesting antiques and delved into the family history of Captain J. W. Cates, who sailed the world and bought this house in 1865. It includes six rooms with shared baths. (The third-floor Starboard room has an awkward mid-room chimney.) Rates June–Sept. are $95 ($60 for the single room); Oct.–May $75 ($60), including a full breakfast. No smoking, no pets. The inn is 3.6 miles from downtown Machias on Rte. 92.

Motels

The second generation now runs **The Bluebird Motel,** Rte. 1, Box 45, Machias 04654, 207/255-3332, a clean, upgraded, 1950s-style motel, and Peter and Sharon Stackpole are especially knowledgeable about the area. Forty rooms (13 are smoking) have cable TV, phones, air-conditioning, and large baths. The motel is set back from Rte. 1 enough to keep down noise, but request a room in the rear section if you're a light sleeper. The motel, a mile south of downtown, has two handicapped-accessible rooms. Children are welcome; pets are allowed in some units. Rooms are $65–70 d mid-June–mid-Sept., $60–65 d other months.

The best feature of the two-story **Machias Motor Inn,** 26 E. Main St., Rte. 1, Machias 04654, 207/255-4861, www.machiasmotorinn.com, is its location overlooking the tidal Machias River. Sliding doors open onto decks-with-a-view. Thirty-five units, $72 d., have extra-long beds, cable TV, air-conditioning, and phones with dataports. Next door is Helen's Restaurant—famed for seasonal fruit pies and winner of an award for the #1 blueberry pie in the United States. Pets are welcome at the motel for a fee of $5 per day; kids under 12 are free. The motel is within easy walking distance of downtown. Open all year.

Campgrounds and Seasonal Rentals

Campgrounds close to Machias are near Lubec and at Cobscook Bay State Park. The Machias Bay Area Chamber of Commerce lists some rentals on its website and also stocks individual brochures from owners at the chamber office.

FOOD

Watch the local papers for listings of **public suppers, spaghetti suppers,** or **baked bean suppers,** a terrific way to sample the culinary talents of local cooks. Most begin at 5 PM, and it's worth arriving early to get near the head of the line. The suppers often benefit needy individuals or struggling nonprofits—always worth supporting—and where else can you eat nonstop for under $10?

Breakfast and Lunch

Murphy's Shiretown Pizza, 50 Main St., Machias, 207/255-3733, also makes grinders (or hoagies or subs or whatever you prefer to call them). This place is popular with the college crowd and open daily 11 AM–11 PM (until 2 AM Fri.–Sat.).

Inexpensive to Moderate

Family-owned, and very popular all day long, is **The Blue Bird Ranch,** 3 E. Main St., Rte. 1, Machias 04654, 207/255-3351, named for the Prout family's other enterprise, Blue Bird Ranch Trucking Company. Service is efficient, food is hearty, portions are ample in the three dining rooms. The restaurant has a liquor license and is open all year, Mon.–Sat. 5 AM–8:30 PM (until 9 PM Fri.–Sat.) and Sun. 6 AM–8:30 PM.

Moderate to Expensive

The **Artist's Café,** 3 Hill St., Machias 04654, 207/255-8900, occupies two rooms in a small house across the street from the university. Machias lucked out with chef/owner Susan Ferro, a former Boston designer, working magic with her quasi-fusion menu here. (She claims she got her start garnishing mud pies as a kid.) Luncheon sandwiches—named The Realist, Garden of Eden, The Rococo, etc.—are always reasonably priced adventures ($5–9). Dinner entrées, which change frequently and often include Thai influences and a vegetarian option, are $22–30. Beer and wine are available. The café is open Mon.–Fri. for lunch (11 AM–2 PM) and Mon.–Sat. for dinner (5–8 PM). Be sure to reserve for dinner, especially on weekends.

Patterned hardwood floors add to the warm atmosphere at the **Riverside Inn,** overlooking the East Machias River on Rte. 1 in East Machias (207/255-4134). Gourmet dinners include entrées such as Riverside Wellington. Reservations are essential. Open for dinner Tues.–Sun. June–Oct., Thurs.–Sun. Nov.–Dec. 31.

INFORMATION AND SERVICES

Stock up on area brochures, hiking, biking, and snowmobiling informaton at the **Machias Bay Area Chamber of Commerce,** Main St. next to the Irving Station, Machias 04654, 207/255-4402, www.machiaschamber.org. The office is generally open Mon.–Fri. 10 AM–3 PM. It's in the midst of a fund-raising drive to move to improved quarters—restrooms, trails, museum—by restoring the old train station, built in 1898, when the 104-mile Ellsworth-to-Calais line came to town.

Summer hours at the handsome stone **Porter Memorial Library,** 52 Court St., Machias 04654, 207/255-3933, www.porter.lib.me.us, built in 1892, are Tues.–Fri. noon–6 PM, Sat. 10 AM–2 PM.

Summer hours at the University of Maine's **Merrill Library,** on the UMM campus, 207/255-1284, www.umm.maine.edu/library, which is open to the public, are Mon., Tues., Thurs. 8 AM–6 PM, Wed. 8 AM–8 PM, Fri. 8 AM–4:30 PM.

Newspapers
Two dueling weeklies cover coastal Washington County, with a wide range of local news, features, ads, and calendar listings. *Machias Valley News Observer,* 207/255-6561, based in Machias, is published every Wednesday; the *Downeast Coastal Press,* 207/259-7751, in Cutler, comes out every Tuesday. Since Washington County's major shopping hub is Bangor, the *Bangor Daily News* has a grip on readership in this part of Maine.

Emergencies
To reach police, fire, or ambulance in an emergency, call 911 in Machias, East Machias, Machiasport, and Jonesboro.

Down East Community Hospital, Upper Court St., Rte. 1A, Machias 04654, 207/255-3356, www.dech.org, has a 24-hour emergency room. Machias residents also patronize hospitals in Ellsworth, Bangor, and Calais.

Laundry
Machias Cleaners and Laundry Inc., 9 Water St., Machias 04654, 207/255-3833, with coin-operated machines, is open all year, 8 AM–8 PM.

Getting There and Getting Around
The nearest major airport is Bangor International Airport (see *Bangor Area*).

Lubec and Vicinity

Literally the beginning of America—at the nation's easternmost point—Lubec (pop. 1,800) can serve as a base for exploring New Brunswick's Campobello Island, the Cutler coastline, and territory to the west. With a couple of appealing B&Bs, more than 90 miles of meandering waterfront, and a marina, Lubec conveys the aura of realness: a hardscrabble fishing community that extends a welcome to visitors.

Settled in 1780 and originally part of Eastport, Lubec was split off in 1811 and named for the German port of Lübeck (for convoluted reasons still not totally clear). The town's most famous resident was Hopley Yeaton, first captain in the U.S. Revenue-Marine (now the U.S. Coast Guard), who retired here in 1809.

Along the main drag (Water St.), a row of shuttered buildings reflects the town's roller-coaster history. Once the world's sardine capital, Lubec today has only one plant, processing sea cucumbers and sea urchins, and new businesses are slowly arriving.

In summer, the free **Mary Potterton Memorial Piano Concerts** take place at 7:30 PM Wed., late June–Aug., at the Congregational Christian Church. They're part of the schedule for SummerKeys, www.summerkeys.com, 6 Bayview St., Lubec 04652, 207/733-2316, an unusual music school founded in 1992 by Bruce Potterton, a New York music teacher in his other life. Limited to adults, the school can handle any skill level from rank beginner to rusty professional. Practice studios in the former Masonic Hall are all soundproofed. Originally set up for piano students, the school now has classes in flute, clarinet, violin, guitar, cello, voice, and composition. The camaraderie and enthusiasm are contagious. Tuition is $415–465 a week, depending on the course.

SIGHTS AND RECREATION

If walking and hiking are on your Lubec (and Washington County) agenda, be sure to send for a copy of *Cobscook Trails,* published by the Quoddy Regional Land Trust. The parks and preserves described below, and many others in eastern Washington County, are included in the QRLT booklet.

And if time allows, tag along with Lubec's **Pathfinders Walking Group,** 207/733-4984—enthusiastic area residents who go exploring every Sun., year-round, 2–4 PM. Nonmembers are welcome, there's no fee, and you'll see a Lubec (and more) that most visitors never encounter.

Even the humongous tides and dramatic sunsets over Johnson Bay can get your attention if you hang out at the **Lubec breakwater.** Across the channel, on Campobello Island, is red-capped **Mulholland Point Lighthouse,** an abandoned beacon built in 1885. As the tide goes out—18 or so feet of it—you'll also see hungry harbor seals dunking for dinner. And if you're lucky, you might spot the eagle pair that nests on Pope's Folly, an island in the channel (bring binoculars).

Quoddy Head State Park

Beachcombing, hiking, picnicking, and an up-close look at Maine's only red-and-white-striped lighthouse are the big draws at 481-acre Quoddy Head State Park, W. Quoddy Head Rd., Lubec 04652, 207/733-0911, www.parksandlands.com, the easternmost point of U.S. land. The cliffs of Canada's Grand Manan Island are visible from the grounds of West Quoddy Head Light, located just outside the park boundary. A 1.75-mile, moderately difficult trail follows the 90-foot cliffs to Carrying Place Cove, and an easy, mile-long boardwalk winds through a unique moss and heath bog designated as a National Natural Landmark. The park opens daily at 9 AM, mid-May–mid-Oct. Be forewarned that the park gate is locked at sunset. Admission is $2 adults, $1 children 5–11. In winter, the park is accessible for snowshoeing. From Rte. 189 on the outskirts of Lubec, take S. Lubec Rd. (well signposted) to

W. Quoddy Head Rd. Turn left and continue to the parking area.

West Quoddy Head Light, towering 83 feet above mean high water, was built in 1808. (Its counterpart, East Quoddy Head Light, is on New Brunswick's Campobello Island.) Views from the lighthouse grounds are fabulous, and whale sightings are common in summer. Located in the former keepers' house is the West Quoddy Head Light Keepers' Association & Visitor Center, open 10 AM–5 PM, Memorial Day weekend–mid-Oct.

SHOPPING

Flower fans and inquisitive nature lovers should definitely make the short detour, 4.5 miles north of Rte. 189, to the **Cottage Garden,** and **Shoreline Nature Center,** 934 N. Lubec Rd., Lubec 04652, 207/733-2902, www.quoddyloop.com/gardens, a lovely oasis of old-fashioned roses and delphiniums. Bring a picnic and stroll through the perennial, herb, stream-side, and alpine gardens, or learn about local flora and fauna in the nature center via exhibits, films, trail guides, and fun. There's no charge for wandering, but you'll probably be tempted by the small print, craft, and gift shop on the premises. Artists are welcome to set up their easels, and photographers their cameras. Cottage Garden is open dawn to dusk all week.

Handmade gourmet chocolates are the *raison d'etre* at **Seaside Chocolates,** 72 Water St., Lubec 04652, 207/733-2575, or 800/282-7220, www.seasidechocolates.gourmetfoodmall.com. You can pick up your needhams, sea turtles, truffles, cremes, bonbons, and other delights in person, or mail-order them. Open all year.

ACCOMMODATIONS

Many visitors use Lubec as a base for day-trips to Campobello Island or Machias Seal Island, so it's essential to reserve rooms ahead at the height of summer. Several lodgings are also available on Campobello.

Bed-and-Breakfasts

At **The Peacock House B&B,** 27 Summer St., Lubec 04652, 207/733-2403 or 888/305-0036, www.peacockhouse.com, innkeepers Sue and Dennis Baker provide a friendly and relaxing atmosphere. Overlooking the Bay of Fundy, The Peacock House was built in 1860 by English Sea Captain William Trott. Five generations of the Peacock Family have lived here, in one of Lubec's most prestigious addresses. Seven rooms, all with private baths, are $85–125 d., including a full breakfast. Open May 1–Oct. 31. No pets, no smoking. The Peacock House is best suited for children 7 or older. Special-access accommodations are available on the first floor.

The 19th-century **Home Port Inn,** 45 Main St., P.O. Box 50, Lubec 04652, 207/733-2077 or 800/457-2077 outside Maine, www.homeportinn.com, ensconced on a Lubec hilltop, has seven rooms (private baths) for $90–105 d, including generous continental breakfast. No smoking and no pets, but well-behaved children welcome. Reservations are advisable for the inn's very popular restaurant—a sunken dining room with seafood as a specialty; creative entrées run $12–24. It's open daily 5–8 PM.

Motel

If you're traveling with small children, the **Eastland Motel,** County Rd., Rte. 189, RR1, Box 6915, Lubec 04652, 207/733-5501, www.eastlandmotel.com, is Lubec's best bet. The motel has 20 clean rooms at $65–75 d May–Oct., lower rates other months. Small pets are $5. Rooms have cable TV and air-conditioning. Request one of the 12 rooms in the newer section. Free fresh-ground morning coffee, juice, tea, and rolls. The motel is open Apr.–Dec.

Campground

The 80-acre **South Bay Campground,** 591 County Rd., Rte. 189, Lubec 04652, 207/733-1037 or 877/733-1037, has 74 tent and full-service RV sites, a third on the shore of beautiful South Bay. A private island site (accessible on foot at low tide) is also available. There's a pool. Rates are $17–28 (family of four); check on minimum stays. Leashed pets are allowed, limit two dogs per site. Open mid-May–mid-Oct., the campground is about seven miles from Rte. 1.

FOOD

The **Atlantic House Coffee Shop,** 52 Water St., Lubec 04652, 207/733-0906, www .atlantichouse.net, is one of the brightest spots on a rather forlorn street. You'll find breakfast pastries, tasty sandwiches, great desserts, and decent coffee—load up before you head out for a hike. Atlantic House is open daily 7 AM–7 PM.

Depending on your source, **Uncle Kippy's,** County Rd., Rte. 189, Lubec 04652, 207/733-2400, www.unclekippys.com, gets high and higher marks in Lubec for wholesome cooking. A sign out front announces, "Stop in or we'll both starve." Steak and seafood are specialties—at unfancy prices—and the pizza is the area's best. Beer and nonvintage wine are available. Located 0.5 mile southwest of downtown Lubec, it's open daily 11 AM–8 PM, (to 9 PM Fri.–Sat.) all year.

INFORMATION AND SERVICES

Lubec is one of the area towns in the **Cobscook Bay Area Chamber of Commerce,** P.O. Box 42, Whiting 04691, or call 207/733-2201, www.cobscookbay.com. Once you're here,

stop on the outskirts of town at the **Eastland Motel,** County Rd., Rte. 189, for brochures and advice.

The **Lubec Memorial Library,** 55 Water St., Lubec 04652, 207/733-2491, is open all year, Mon., Tues., and Fri. 10 AM–4 PM, Wed. 10 AM–8 PM, and Sat. 10–2 PM.

Newspapers
Local coverage appears in the twice-monthly Eastport-based *Quoddy Tides,* 207/853-4806, www.quoddytides.com, the monthly *The Lubec Light Newspaper,* 207/733-2939, and the weekly Cutler-based *Downeast Coastal Press,*/fax 207/259-7751. Check for tide tables—critical information in this part of Maine. The only daily paper covering this area is the *Bangor Daily News.*

Emergencies
For **police, fire, and ambulance** in Lubec, call 911. The **Regional Medical Center at Lubec** (RMCL), S. Lubec Rd., Lubec 04652, 207/733-5541, can handle minor medical and dental emergencies weekdays 8 AM–5 PM, and a doctor is on call for emergencies around the clock, but the nearest 24-hour emergency room is at Machias's Down East Community Hospital.

Getting There
Lubec is about 2.5 hours by car from Bangor International Airport, the nearest major airport.

Campobello Island

Just over the Franklin D. Roosevelt Memorial Bridge from Lubec lies 10-mile-long Campobello Island, in Canada's New Brunswick province. Since 1964, 2,800 acres of the island have been under joint United States and Canadian jurisdiction as **Roosevelt Campobello International Park,** commemorating U.S. President Franklin D. Roosevelt. FDR summered here as a youth, and it was here that he contracted infantile paralysis (polio) in 1921. The park, covering most of the island's southern end, has well-maintained trails, picnic sites, and dramatic vistas, but its centerpiece is the imposing Roosevelt Cottage, a mile northeast of the bridge.

Roosevelt Cottage

Little seems to have changed in the 34-room red-shingled Roosevelt "Cottage" overlooking Passamaquoddy Bay since President Roosevelt last visited in 1939. The grounds are beautifully landscaped, and the many family mementos—especially those in the late president's den—bring history alive. It all feels very personal, far less stuffy than most presidential memorials.

Stop first at the park's Visitor Centre, where you can acquire literature and souvenirs, use the restrooms, and see a short video setting the stage for the cottage visit. Then walk across to the house/museum, which is open daily, Memorial Day weekend to Columbus Day (Canadian Thanksgiving). Hours are 10 AM–6 PM Atlantic daylight time (9 AM–5 PM eastern daylight time). Last tour is at 5:45 PM. Admission is free, but donations are accepted. The visitors center is open through Oct. For more information, contact **Executive Secretary, Roosevelt Campobello International Park,** P.O. Box 129, Lubec 04652, or 459 Rte. 774, Welshpool, Campobello, NB, Canada E5E 1A4. Seasonal phone (in Canada) is 506/752-2922, www.fdr.net.

The Park by Car

If time is short, or you're unable to hike, at least take some of the park's driving routes—**Cranberry Point Drive,** 5.4 miles round-trip from the visitors center; **Liberty Point Drive,** 12.4 miles round-trip, via Glensevern Rd., from the visitors center; and **Fox Hill Drive,** a 2.2-mile link between the other two main routes. Even with the car, you'll have access to beaches, picnic sites, spruce and fir forests, and incredible views of lighthouses, islands, and the Bay of Fundy.

Just west of the main access road from the bridge is the **Mulholland Point Picnic Area,** where you can spread out your lunch next to the distinctive red-capped lighthouse overlooking the Lubec Narrows.

Hiking and Picnicking

Within the international park are 10 miles of walking/hiking trails, ranging from dead easy to moderately difficult. Easiest is the 1.2-mile (round-trip) walk from the visitors center to **Friar's Head Picnic Area,** named for its distinctive promontory jutting into the bay. For the best angle, climb up to the observation deck on the "head." Grills and tables are here for picnickers. (If you haven't packed a picnic, the nearest source for the makings is the town of Welshpool.)

The most difficult—and most dramatic—trail is a 2.4-mile stretch from **Liberty Point to Raccoon Beach,** along the southeastern shore of the island. Precipitous cliffs can make parts of this trail chancy for small children or insecure adults, so use caution. Liberty Point is incredibly rugged, but observation platforms make it easy to see the tortured rocks and wide-open Bay of Fundy. At broad Raccoon Beach, you can walk the sands, have a picnic, and watch for whales, porpoises, and osprey. To avoid returning via the same route, park at Liberty Point and walk back along Liberty Point Drive from Raccoon Beach. If you're traveling with nonhikers, arrange for them to meet you with a vehicle at Con Robinson's Point.

You can also walk the park's perimeter,

including just over six miles of shoreline, but only if you're in good shape, have waterproof hiking boots, and can spend an entire day on the trails. Before attempting this, however, inquire at the visitors center about trail conditions and tide levels.

CAMPOBELLO BEYOND THE INTERNATIONAL PARK

Take a day or two and explore Campobello beyond the park; overnighters have several lodging and food options. You can also continue on by ferry from here to New Brunswick's Deer Island.

Herring Cove Provincial Park

New Brunswick's provincial government does a conscientious job of running Herring Cove Provincial Park, 506/752-7010, with picnic areas, 76 campsites, 40 with electrical hookups, a four-mile trail system, a mile-long sandy beach, freshwater Glensevern Lake, and the nine-hole championship-level **Herring Cove Golf Course.** The club restaurant, overlooking the cove and open to the public, has the same phone as the park; it's open 11 AM–9 PM (Atlantic time). The golf course is open daily 8:30 AM–9 PM (Atlantic time). The park is open late May–early Oct.

East Quoddy Head Light

Consult the tide calendar before planning your assault on East Quoddy Head Light (also known as Head Harbour Light), at Campobello's northernmost tip. It's on an islet accessible only at low tide. The distinctive lighthouse has a huge red cross painted on its white tower. (You're likely to pass near it on whale-watching trips out of Eastport.) From the Roosevelt cottage, follow Rte. 774 through the village of Wilson's Beach and continue on an unpaved road to the parking area. A stern Canadian Coast Guard warning sign tells the story: *Extreme Hazard. Beach exposed only at low tide. Incoming tide rises five feet per hour and may leave you stranded for eight hours. Wading or swimming are extremely dangerous due to swift currents and cold water. Proceed at your own risk.* It's definitely worth the effort for the bay and island views from the lighthouse grounds, often including whales and eagles. Allow about an hour before and after dead low tide (be sure your watch coincides with the Atlantic-time tide calendar).

ACCOMMODATIONS AND FOOD

In midsummer, if you'd like to overnight on the island, be sure to reserve lodgings well in advance; Campobello is a popular destination. Nearest backup beds are in Lubec, and those fill up, too.

Bed-and-Breakfasts

The Owen House, 11 Welshpool St., Welshpool, Campobello Island, NB, Canada E5E 1G3, 506/752-2977, www.owenhouse.ca, is the island's best address, an elegant early-19th-century inn on 10 acres overlooking Passamaquoddy Bay and Eastport in the distance. Nine guest rooms (private and shared baths) are about US$75–138 per double. Just north of the inn is the Deer Island ferry landing. Open late May–mid-Oct.

The Lupine Lodge, 610 Rte. 774, Welshpool, Campobello Island, NB, Canada E5E 1A5, 506/752-2555, www.lupinelodge.com, an updated summer estate of Roosevelt kin, is only 0.25 mile from the Roosevelt cottage, with terrific bay views. Eleven rooms in two buildings (private baths, some fireplaces) go for about US$60–110 d. No smoking in rooms, no pets. The adjacent restaurant serves breakfast, lunch, and dinner, 8 AM–9 PM. Elderhostel groups sometimes book in here for week-long stays. Open late May–mid-Oct.

Don't expect culinary creativity on Campobello, but you won't starve—at least during the summer season. Best choice is the **Herring Cove Restaurant,** on the east side of the island. Another option is **Friar's Bay Restaurant,** in Welshpool, 506/752-2056, owned by the Friar's Bay Motor Lodge and emphasizing seafood. Take the time to explore Friar's Bay beach while you're here. For a good takeout lobster roll or fish-and-chips, head for **Family Fisheries,** Wilson's Beach, 506/752-2470, toward the northern end of the island. The kids can use the playground while you wait for your order. Open daily in summer.

INFORMATION AND SERVICES

The local information source is **Campobello Island Tourism Association,** 506/752-7010, www.campobello.com.

To visit Campobello, you'll have to pass Customs checkpoints on the Lubec, U.S., 207/733-4331, and Campobello, Canada, 506/752-2091, ends of the Franklin D. Roosevelt Memorial Bridge. **U.S. citizens** need some form of identification, typically a driver's license, although you may not even need to show it. You'll be asked your purpose in going to the island, and the length of your stay. Most clearances are perfunctory, but be sure you are not carrying any live plant material; it will be confiscated. If you're traveling with a dog, carry documentation of its rabies vaccination; a rabies tag is not always accepted.

Even for a day trip to Campobello, **non-U.S. citizens** need to show a valid passport; citizens of most non-European countries must also have a Canadian visa, obtained in advance. **U.S. resident aliens** must be prepared to show a valid green card. With the Homeland Security Act, border crossing requirements change regularly. Check the requirements before making your trip.

Be aware that crossing this short little bridge takes an hour, because there's a one-hour time difference between Lubec and Campobello. Lubec (like the rest of Maine) is on eastern

standard time; Campobello, like the rest of Canada's Maritime Provinces, is on Atlantic time, an hour later. As soon as you reach the island, set your clock ahead an hour.

There is no need to convert U.S. currency to Canadian for use on Campobello; U.S. dollars are accepted everywhere on the island, but prices everywhere tend to be quoted in Canadian dollars. The exchange rate has fluctuated drastically in recent years, creating major hardships for Canadians and bargains for Americans.

Just after Canadian Customs waves you through from Lubec, stop at the **Tourist Information Centre,** 506/752-2997, on your right. The staff can fix you up with trail maps of the international park and New Brunswick propaganda, then steer you toward the Roosevelt property.

Getting Away

A funky, bargelike car ferry, "The Road of the Isles," runs between Welshpool on Campobello and lovely **Deer Island,** where you can explore, picnic, or camp (even without a car). You can also board another ferry from Deer Island to Eastport (every hour on the hour, beginning at 9 AM Atlantic time, 8 AM EDT). Operated by **East Coast Ferries Ltd.,** 506/747-2159, www.eastcoastferries.nb.ca, the ferry does 10–11 daily round-trips to Deer Island from Welshpool, late June–mid-Sept., beginning at 9 AM Atlantic time (8 AM EDT). The Welshpool dock is on North Rd., near Owen House. The cost of a one-way ticket for car and driver is about US$12; passengers are $2.50 and children under 12 are free.

Eastport and Vicinity

Settled in 1772, the city (yes, it's officially a city) of Eastport (pop. 1,911) has had its ups and downs. Now it's mostly up, with only an occasional sideslip, thanks to an influx of commercial development and a tangible optimism among natives and newcomers. Aquaculture is big business; the commercial port has expanded; and new restaurants, galleries, and B&Bs have opened. But no one goes to Eastport for bright lights and nightlife; it's more to explore a Down East community with a genuine history and a can-do attitude.

In 1780, the first European settlement here was named Freetown; 19 years later, it became incorporated as Eastport. Until 1811, the town also included Lubec, which is about 2.5 miles across the water in a boat, but 40 or so in a car.

Eastport is on Moose Island, connected by causeway to the mainland at Pleasant Point. Views are terrific on both sides, especially at sunset, as you hopscotch from one blob of land to another and finally reach this mini-city, where the sardine industry was introduced as long ago as 1875. Five sardine canneries once operated here, employing hundreds of local residents who snipped the heads off herring and stuffed them into cans—one of those skills not easily translatable to other tasks. The focus now is on fish farming; many of hilly Eastport's vantage points overlook the salmon nurseries floating in the bay. Aquaculture has brought jobs and money to Eastport.

Also bringing jobs and money is the deepwater port for oceangoing vessels. Not everyone appreciates the large, noisy trucks that descend Washington St. to the harbor early in the morning when cargo carriers are in port, but no one complains about their benefit to the local economy.

Periodically, a plan surfaces to establish a ferry linking Eastport and Lubec, but for now most everyone approaches Eastport from the southwest, via coastal Rte. 1, curving inland east of Machias. Along the way are the towns of Whiting, Edmunds Township, Dennysville, and Pembroke.

Edmunds Township's claims to fame are its splendid public lands—Cobscook Bay State Park and a unit of Moosehorn National Wildlife Refuge. Just past the state park, loop along the scenic shoreline before returning to Rte. 1.

Pembroke, once part of adjoining Dennysville, claims Reversing Falls Park, where you can watch (and hear) ebbing and flowing tides draining and filling Cobscook Bay.

If time allows a short scenic detour, especially in fall, turn left (northwest) on Rte. 214 and drive 10 miles to quaintly named Meddybemps, allegedly a Passamaquoddy word meaning "plenty of alewives [herring]." Views over Meddybemps Lake, on the north side of the road, are spectacular, and you can launch a canoe or kayak into the lake here, less than a mile beyond the junction with Rte. 191 (take the dead-end unpaved road toward the water).

Backtracking to Rte. 1, heading east from Pembroke, you'll come to Perry, best known for the Pleasant Point Indian Reservation, a Passamaquoddy settlement, two miles east of Rte. 1, that's been here since 1822. If there's time, stop at the small Waponahki Museum. Or plan a visit around the reservation's August Indian Days celebration.

SIGHTS
City Stroll
The best way to appreciate Eastport's history is just to stroll the city, taking in its 18th-, 19th-, and early-20th-century homes, businesses, and monuments, many now on the National Register of Historic Places. Among the highlights are historic homes converted to B&Bs, two museums, and a large chunk of downtown Water St., with many handsome brick buildings erected after a disastrous fire swept through in 1886.

The Sunrise Coast

TIDES

Nowhere in Maine is the adage "Time and tide wait for no man" more true than along the Sunrise Coast. (They don't wait for women or kids, either.) The nation's most extreme tidal ranges occur in this area, so the hundreds of miles of tidal shore frontage between Steuben and Calais provide countless opportunities for observing tidal phenomena. Every six hours or so, the tide begins either ebbing or flowing. The farther Down East you go, the higher (and lower) the tides. Although tides in Canada's Bay of Fundy are far higher, the highest tides in New England occur along the St. Croix River, at Calais.

Tides govern coastal life—particularly Down East, where average tidal ranges may be 10–20 feet and extremes approach 28 feet. Everyone is a slave to the tide calendar, which coastal-community newspapers diligently publish. Boats tie up with extra-long lines; clammers and worm-diggers schedule their days by the tides; hikers have to plan ahead for shoreline exploring; and kayakers need to plan their routes to avoid getting stuck in the muck.

Tides, as we all learned in elementary school, are lunar phenomena, created by the gravitational pull of the moon; the tidal range depends on the lunar phase. Tides are most extreme at new and full moons—when the sun, moon, and Earth are all aligned. These are **spring tides,** supposedly because the water springs upward (the term has nothing to do with the season). And tides are smallest during the moon's first and third quarters—when the sun, Earth, and moon have a right-angle configuration. These are **neap tides** ("neap" comes from an Old English word meaning "scanty"). Other lunar/solar phenomena, such as the equinoxes and solstices, can also affect tidal ranges.

The best time for shoreline exploration is on a new-moon or full-moon day, when low tide exposes mussels, sea urchins, sea cucumbers, starfish, periwinkles, hermit crabs, rockweed, and assorted nonbiodegradable trash. Rubber boots or waterproof, treaded shoes are essential on the wet, slippery terrain.

Caution is also essential in tidal areas. Unless you've carefully plotted tide times and heights, don't park a car or bike or boat trailer on a beach; make sure a sea kayak is lashed securely to a tree or bollard; don't take a long nap on shoreline granite; and don't cross a low-tide land spit without an eye on your watch.

A perhaps-apocryphal but almost believable story goes that one flatlander stormed up to a ranger at Cobscook Bay State Park one bright summer morning and demanded indignantly to know why they had had the nerve to drain the water from her shorefront campsite during the night.

Tide charts for the entire state can be found at www.maineharbors.com and www.saltwatertides.com.

Raye's Mustard Mill Museum

How often do you have a chance to watch mustard being made in a turn-of-the-20th-century mustard mill? Drive by J.W. Raye & Co., Outer Washington St., Rte. 190, P.O. Box 2, Eastport 04631, 207/853-4451 or 800/853-1903, www.rayesmustard.com, at the edge of Eastport, and stop in for a free 15-minute tour, on the hour 10 AM–3 PM, weekdays and some Saturdays. You'll get to see the granite millstones, the mustard seeds being winnowed, and enormous vats of future mustard. Raye's sells mustard under its own label and produces it for major customers under their labels. The shop stocks all of Raye's mustard varieties, other Maine-made food and gift items, and sells store items mail order at the online Pantry or by phone. You can sit down and have a scone with blueberry (or another) coffee, or get takeout sandwiches, salads, cheese, and beverages from the Mustard Shed Takeout. In summer, the shop is open 9 AM–4 PM Mon.–Fri., earlier and later in the busy season. From spring until after Christmas it's also open 10 AM–4 PM.

Maine's Native Americans
Baskets, tools, beadwork, a birch-bark canoe, and photo-lined walls are all part of the **Waponahki Museum,** Pleasant Point Reservation, Rte. 190, Perry 04667, 207/853-4001, a small collection dedicated to preserving the history and culture of Maine's Passamaquoddy Indians. The museum spurred a revival of the Passamaquoddy language. The most interesting time to visit is in August, during Pleasant Point Reservation's annual **Indian Ceremonial Days.** The museum—two miles east of Rte. 1 and seven miles north of Eastport—is open all year, Mon.–Fri. 8–11 AM and 1–3 PM, but the schedule can be erratic, so call ahead to be sure. Admission is free, but donations are welcomed.

Barracks Museum
Located in the officers quarters of the original (1809) Fort Sullivan, the **Barracks Museum,** 74 Washington St., Eastport 04631, 207/853-6630, is operated by members of the Border Historical Society, and has a Fort Sullivan model and artifacts, plus other historical and maritime exhibits. The Society can help with genealogical research. Open mid-June–Labor Day, Wed.–Sat. 1–4 PM. In the Quoddy Craft Shop on Water St., across from Overlook Park, the Society exhibits the Quoddy Dam model, Memorial Day–Sept., 10 AM–6 PM daily, staffed by community volunteers.

Tides Institute
An ambitious project of two former Salt Institute staffers, the **Tides Institute,** 43 Water St., Eastport 04631, 207/853-4047, www.tidesinstitute.org, is interested in exploring the art and culture of the international region of Passmaquoddy Bay and connecting it to broader trends. In pursuit of their mission, they mount fine arts exhib-

its, have a collection of art and objets, and are committed to making new work. Housed in an attractive 1887 brick building, formerly a bank, they have a printmaking letterpress facility where workshops are given. Open all year, call for schedule.

PARKS, PRESERVES, AND RECREATION
If walking and hiking are on your agenda here—and they should be—send for a copy of *Cobscook Trails,* published by the Quoddy Regional Land Trust. The parks and preserves described below, and many others in eastern Washington County, are included in the QRLT booklet.

One section of Moosehorn National Wildlife Refuge adjoins Cobscook Bay State Park, but the headquarters and major recreational tracts are located near Calais.

Shackford Head
The highlight of 90-acre Shackford Head, Deep Cove Rd., Eastport, is an easy, half-mile-long wooded trail leading to a headland with wide-open views of Eastport, salmon aquaculture pens, and, depending on weather, Campobello Island, Lubec, and Pembroke. This state preserve is a particularly good family hike. Use bug repellent and carry binoculars and a camera. There's a toilet near the parking area, but no other facilities. Even in winter, trail access is not difficult. The trailhead and parking area are at the southern end of town.

Cobscook Bay State Park
A 2.5-mile network of nature trails, picnic spots, great birding and berry-picking, usually hot showers, and wooded shorefront campsites make 888-acre Cobscook Bay State Park, Rte. 1, Edmunds Township, P.O. Box 127, Dennysville 04628, 207/726-4412, www.parksandlands.com, one of Maine's most spectacular state parks. It's even entertaining just to watch the 24-foot tides surging in and out of this area at five or so feet

an hour; there's no swimming because of the undertow. And get in the shower line early; the hot water tends to run out when the park is busiest. The park used to be underutilized, and you could usually find a site even at the height of summer, but that's changed. The word has gotten out. Reserve well ahead to get a place on the shore. To guarantee a site in July and August, using a credit card, call 207/287-3824 or reserve online at www .CampwithMe.com; reservation fee is $2 per site per night; two-night minimum. The park is open daily, mid-May–mid-Oct.; trails are groomed in winter for cross-country skiing, and one section goes right along the shore. Summer day-use fees are $3 adults, $1 children 5–11; children under five are free. Nonresident camping fees are $19 per site per night; the fee for Maine residents is $14. The park entrance is just off Rte. 1, four miles south of Dennysville.

Reversing Falls Park

There's plenty of room for adults to relax and kids to play at the 140-acre Reversing Falls Park in West Pembroke—plus picnic tables, restrooms, shorefront ledges, and a front-row seat overlooking a fascinating tidal phenomenon. Pack a picnic, then check newspapers or information offices for the tide times, so you can watch the saltwater surging through a 300-yard-wide passage at about 25 knots, creating a whirlpool and churning "falls." The park is at Mahar Point in West Pembroke, 7.2 miles south of Rte. 1. Coming from the south (Dennysville), leave Rte. 1 in West Pembroke when you see the Triangle Grocery Store. Turn right and go 0.3 mile to Leighton Point Rd., where you'll see a sign saying, Shore Access 5.5 Miles. Turn right and go 3.8 miles, past gorgeous meadows, low shrubs, and views of Cobscook Bay. Turn right at a very tiny Reversing Falls sign. After about 1.5 miles, turn left onto a gravel road and continue two miles to the park. The zigzagging is worth it. The park is open all year, except when snow blocks car access.

GETTING AFLOAT

Schooner Trips

The 84-foot, red-sailed, 50-passenger *Sylvina W. Beal* departs from the Eastport Pier daily, 207/853-2500 or 207/853-4303, www.eastportwindjammers.com, and heads out into the prime whale-feeding grounds of Passamaquoddy Bay—passing the Old Sow whirlpool (largest tidal whirlpool in the Northern Hemisphere), salmon aquaculture pens, and Campobello Island. En route, you'll see bald eagles, porpoises, and more. Best months to spot whales are July–Aug. Dress warmly and wear sunscreen. Three-hour whale-watching cruises depart at 1:30 PM; cost is $35 adults, $18 children 12 and under. Additionally, there are sunset (7 PM, $25/15); Quoddy Dam fishing (8 AM, $25/15), and lobster ($35/18) trips.

Ferries to Deer and Campobello Islands

In July and Aug, **East Coast Ferries Ltd.,** Deer Island, New Brunswick, 506/747-2159, operates flatbed car ferries between Eastport and Deer Island, and then on to Campobello Island—and vice versa.

The ferry schedule lists both eastern daylight time and Atlantic time, since Eastport is on the former and the two Canadian islands are on the latter. Eastport departures are on the half-hour, beginning at 8:30 AM EDT (9:30 AM Atlantic time). Check the schedule carefully to avoid missing the last boat back to Eastport. (If you take a car, you can drive back to Eastport from Campobello. It's 1.5 miles by water and almost 50 miles by road.) The ferry landing in Eastport is just at the end of Water St., next to the Eastport Chowder House. Cost for car and driver is about US$12. It all seems very informal, and the trip is an adventure, but remember that you're crossing the Canadian border. U.S. citizens need valid identification (such as a driver's license); non–U.S. citizens need a passport. Most non-Europeans also need a Canadian visa.

ENTERTAINMENT

An enthusiastic local theater group, **Stage East,** mounts three or four productions between April and Christmas at the **Eastport Arts Center,** the renovated c. 1850 Washington St. Baptist church in downtown Eastport. Most performances are at 7 PM, but there are occasional matinees. Check newspapers for schedule information, or call the box office at the Motel East, 207/853-4747.

The **Eastport Arts Center,** 34 Washington St., P.O. Box 153, Eastport 04631, 207/853-2358, is also the locale for concerts, films, summer art classes and workshops, and other cultural events throughout the year.

FESTIVALS AND EVENTS

For a small community, Eastport manages to pull together and put on plenty of successful events during the year. Besides the celebrations listed below, popular nearby events are the Calais International Festival, the first week in August, and the Maine Wild Blueberry Festival, held in Machias the third weekend in August.

Eastport's annual four-day **Fourth of July–Old Home Week** extravaganza includes a parade, food, crafts, contests, music, and fireworks. This is one of Maine's best July Fourth celebrations and attracts a crowd of thousands. Lodgings are booked months in advance, so plan ahead.

Indian Ceremonial Days, a three-day Native American celebration, includes children's games, bonfire, crafts demos, fireworks, and traditional food and dancing at the Pleasant Point Indian Reservation, in Perry, the second weekend in August.

The **Eastport Salmon Festival** celebrates the area's aquaculture industry. If you like salmon, you'll *love* this event, which combines a salmon barbecue, craft booths, live entertainment, and boat trips at the Eastport breakwater 11 AM–4 PM the Sunday after Labor Day.

SHOPPING

Art, Crafts, and Antiques

Eastport has long been a magnet for artists and craftspeople yearning to work in a supportive environment, and the influx has increased in recent years, so you can find studios and art for sale throughout the area. Among local shops is **Earth Forms,** 5 Dana St., Eastport 04631, 207/853-2430, above La Sardina Loca, featuring ceramicist Donald Sutherland's intriguing (and sometimes whimsical) wheel-thrown work—self-described as "functional, nonfunctional, and dysfunctional" pottery. It's tough to walk out without buying one of these special pieces. The shop/studio is open most of the year, daily 9 AM–5 PM (and some evenings in summer), but he's a solo show, so call ahead to be sure.

Gifts and a Whole Lot More

Describing **45th Parallel,** Rte. 1 (or "Halfway between the North Pole & the Equator"), Perry 04667, 207/853-9500, www.fortyfifthparallel.com, is a tough assignment. You really have to *go there* and see for yourself. The aesthetic displays are worth the trip to this eclectic emporium. Housed in an old schoolhouse a mile (in the Calais direction) from the junction of Rtes. 190 and 1, the 45th Parallel is part antiques shop, part gift shop, part global marketplace—and entirely seductive. Tiny white lights glimmer here and there, antique architectural remnants hang from the ceiling, and every little niche holds yet another fascinating treasure. Shop owners are Britani and Philip Holloway-Pascarella. It's open daily May–Oct., weekends Nov.–Dec.

Farmers Market

The **Sunrise County Farmers Market** sets up its tables next to Raye's Mustard Mill, Washington St., Eastport, every Thurs. 11 AM–2 PM, late June–mid-Oct., selling strawberries, corn, eggs, herbs, dried flower bouquets, seedlings, flowers, potatoes, and fresh garden veggies, some of which are organic.

The Sunrise Coast

ACCOMMODATIONS

Lodgings in Eastport can fill up in summer, and since it's literally the end of the road, it's wise to reserve ahead. Fortunately, choices include an excellent selection of B&Bs, plus a fine motel, so it's a great place to spend the night.

Bed-and-Breakfasts

In 1833, renowned artist John James Audubon stayed at the elegant **Weston House,** 26 Boynton St., Eastport 04631, 207/853-2907 or 800/853-2907, www.westonhouse-maine.com, so one of the three second-floor guest rooms bears his name—and walls lined with Audubon bird prints. Rates are $70–85 d (2.5 shared baths). Jett and John Peterson's family antiques and interesting art and crafts fill the beautifully decorated house, which is on a quiet side street two blocks above the waterfront. Breakfast is outstanding, accompanied by a candelabra and classical music. Outside are croquet and badminton facilities, plus lovely gardens with a gazebo, chairs, and table. Tea and sherry are available in the afternoon. No smoking, no pets (cute Scotties in residence); well-behaved children welcome. Open all year.

Tasteful antiques are everywhere at Bill and Mary Williams' **The Milliken House Bed & Breakfast,** 29 Washington St., Eastport 04631, 207/853-2955, where flower fans will enjoy the gardens. Breakfast is served in the elegant dining room. Six attractive rooms are $75–85 d. Traffic sometimes begins early on Washington St., so request a side or back room if you're noise-conscious. Children and pets are welcome. Open all year.

At the 1775 **Todd House,** Todd's Head, Eastport 04631, 207/853-2328, Eastport native Ruth McInnis converts guests into instant history buffs. The National Historic Register Cape-style house has character, from the book and arrowhead collections to the beautiful quilts. Six first- and second-floor rooms (two with private baths) are $55–95 d. A generous continental breakfast is served in the lovely common room. Guests can grill dinner in the backyard fireplace. Well-behaved pets and children are welcome. Open all year.

Motel

Here's a motel with the spirit of a B&B. Enthusiastic about their adopted community, host Owen Lawlor and manager Deb Moore at **The Motel East,** 23A Water St., Eastport 04631, 207/853-4747, www.eastportme.info/moteleast.html, provide all kinds of advice and guarantee you'll enjoy the area. Got a problem or question? Owen or Deb can solve it or answer it. Guests at the modern, three-story hostelry have front-row seats on Passamaquoddy Bay, overlooking Campobello Island, and you can walk to everything downtown. A total of 14 rooms, some extra-large, most with fully-equipped kitchenettes, all with refrigerator, microwave, hair dryers, and iron and ironing board ($90–110 d). Request a balcony room. No pets; children welcome. Free coffee in the lobby. Open all year. The separate Friar Roads Cottage is available for $150 d a day.

Campground

On the outskirts of town is the quiet, well-maintained **Seaview Campground,** 16 Norwood Rd., Eastport 04631, 207/853-4471, eastport-maine.com/lodging.html, just off Rte. 190, with tent and RV open and semi-wooded sites, nine cabins, and a small motel. Shorefront sites on Harrington Cove have great views, but they're snapped up quickly. Cabins have excellent vistas. There's a camp store and a full-service restaurant with live lobster. Sites are $20–37 July–Aug., lower other months. Cabins are $475–700 per week July–Aug.; motel rooms are $80–90 d per day. Open mid-May–mid-Oct.

FOOD

Lunch

The best pizza in Eastport comes from **Bank Square Pizzaria and Deli,** 34 Water St., Eastport 04631, 207/853-2709, where you can also get calzones, pasta, and deli sandwiches. There are only a dozen seats, so grab your stuff and eat it elsewhere. Bank Square is open all year, 11 AM–8 PM in summer, 11 AM–6:30 PM winter. No credit cards.

When you're wandering around the Eastport breakwater, you'll notice the line at **Rosie's Hot Dogs,** municipal pier, Eastport, a veteran takeout stand open only in summer. Rosie's tube steaks are the best around.

Inexpensive to Moderate

A popular roadside eatery with a well-deserved reputation, the aptly named **New Friendly Restaurant,** Rte. 1 at Shore Rd., Perry 04667, 207/853-6610, lays on "dinnah" (a Maine-ism meaning lunch), beginning at 11 AM daily. The restaurant, specializing in steak and seafood, closes at 8 PM. Don't be surprised to find it crowded. The New Friendly is just north of the Rte. 190 turnoff to Eastport.

A downtown-Eastport institution since 1924, and the oldest year-round restaurant in Maine, the **Wa-Co Diner and Dining Room** (WHACK-o, short for Washington County *or,* the story goes, for Nelson Watts and Ralph Colwell), at Bank Square on Water St., 207/853-4046, is a must-do local-color stop. Nancy Bishop, a native Eastporter, returned after 35 years and spruced up the place in 1997, changing the image a bit with a bright dining room and bay-view deck added to the diner-style booths and counter—but the service remains friendly and the food inexpensive and filling. A lobster roll, for instance, is $12.95. The Wa-Co is open all year 6 AM–9 PM, with shorter hours in winter.

And there's another funky place almost across the street. How many restaurants keep Christmas lights going year-round—and on a Christmas tree that's upside-down, no less? How many places open for dinner and serve breakfast fare as well? In downtown Eastport, **La Sardina Loca** ("the crazy sardine"), 32 Water St., 207/853-2739, bills itself as the easternmost Mexican restaurant in the United States. It's not totally authentic Tex-Mex, but it's good enough—and the place will keep you entertained. Enchiladas are $6–9. Open all year, seven days a week, starting with (an American) breakfast at 7 AM.

Close to the Deer Island ferry landing, the **Eastport Chowder House,** 169 Water St., Eastport 04631, 207/853-4700, serves traditional Down East lunches and dinners. In warm weather, you can eat right on the working wharf. Takeout and box lunches are available. Open daily from 11 AM.

INFORMATION AND SERVICES

The volunteer-run **Eastport Area Chamber of Commerce,** P.O. Box 254, Eastport 04631, 207/853-4644, www.eastport.net, produces *The Eastport Area Business Guide,* a useful directory/ map of places to sleep, eat, shop, and play. It's available at various locations around town.

If you haven't planned ahead, stop in at the conveniently located **Motel East,** 23A Water St., 207/853-4747. They'll set you up and steer you in the right direction. They also handle advance ticket purchases for performances by Stage East.

The handsome stone **Peavey Memorial Library,** 26 Water St., Eastport 04631, 207/853-4021, built in 1893, is named after the inventor of the Peavey grain elevator. Open Mon. noon–8 PM, Tues. and Thurs. noon–5 PM, Wed. and Fri. 10 AM–5 PM, Sat. 10 AM–3 PM.

Newspapers

The best coverage of Eastport news appears in the twice-monthly *Quoddy Tides,* 123 Water St., Eastport 04631, 207/853-4806, billing itself as the "most easterly newspaper published in the United States." Check the paper for tide tables and be sure to note which time zone is being used. The paper also carries ads and features on Canada's Campobello and Grand Manan Islands.

The only statewide daily newspaper covering Washington County is the *Bangor Daily News,* but it's used mostly by Eastporters headed for shopping or movies in Bangor.

Emergencies

In Eastport, for police, fire, and ambulance, call 911.

The nearest 24-hour emergency room is 27 miles away at **Calais Regional Hospital,** 207/454-7521, Washington County's largest hospital.

Public Restrooms

The public library has restrooms, and in summer, there are portable toilets on Eastport's breakwater.

The Sunrise Coast

Calais and Vicinity

Europeans showed up in the Calais area (CAL-us) as early as 1604, when French adventurers established an ill-fated colony on St. Croix Island in the St. Croix River—16 whole years before the Pilgrims even thought about Massachusetts. After a winter-long debacle, all became relatively quiet until 1779, when the first permanent settler arrived. By 1851, Calais was incorporated as a city, and shipping was the biggest industry in this head-of-tide port. In August 1870, a fire devastated Calais, sparking the construction of today's Main Street Historic District.

Today, the city is quiet again, almost dormant, and dependent on a single industry. The lifeblood of the Calais area is pulp and paper giant Georgia-Pacific Corporation (G-P), whose forest and mill jobs, headquartered in nearby Baileyville (Woodland), prop up the economy. Any hint of instability at G-P sends immediate shivers down the local spine.

The 400th anniversary of the St. Croix Colony in 2004 was the impetus for a celebration, as well as the construction of the $6.6 million Downeast Heritage Museum, a bilingual, interactive museum with great views across the St. Croix to Canada. The museum is a concrete expression of the town's interest in increasing visitors.

The most interesting time to show up in Calais (pop. 4,000) is during the nine-day International Festival, the first or second week in August, when the city and neighboring St. Stephen, New Brunswick, go all out with pageants, concerts, parades, tours, races, golf and dart tournaments, and fireworks—reinforcing the trans-border cooperation that has long benefited both communities. Races include the Great Ducky Race on the St. Croix.

After that, head north and west to Princeton, then 10 miles into the woods west of Rte. 1, where the tiny town of Grand Lake Stream has long beckoned visitors for legendary sportfishing and hunting, plus family-oriented canoeing, swimming, and birding vacations.

Southeast of Calais is tiny Robbinston, a booming shipbuilding community in the 19th century but today little more than a 500-person blip on the map. Highlights nowadays are a great B&B, a wonderful chocolate shop, and the Calais-Robbinston "milestones."

Calais is the eastern terminus for a 98-mile section of Maine Rte. 9 quaintly known as "The Airline." Connecting Bangor and Calais (actually, Eddington and Baring), it's this area's major inland artery, a two-lane highway used by a colorful array of commuters, visitors, sportsmen, and logging-truck drivers. Mostly it's a convenient shortcut, and sometimes not even that, since there's just a smattering of restaurants, shops, or lodgings along the way—a well-known magnet is the Airline Snack Bar, in Beddington. And then come the winter perils of Dunker Hill, Day Hill, Hardwood Hill, and Breakneck Hill. In the fall, though, it's a delight, with gorgeous colors as far as you can see, especially in the elevated blueberry barrens closer to Bangor. The road, built for postal stagecoaches in the mid-19th-century, trimmed nearly 60 miles off the longer coastal Rte. 1. Hazards in those days were bad weather, wolves, and marauding bandits; today, they are bad weather, moose, drivers attempting airborne speeds, and go-for-broke fuel and lumber trucks.

SIGHTS
Downeast Heritage Museum
Incorporating the old train station, the Downeast Heritage Museum, 39 Union St., P.O. Box 696, Calais 04619, 207/454-7878 or 877/454-2500, www.downeastheritage.org, is a bilingual introduction to the history and attractions of the area. The building is sparklingly modern, with expansive views of the St. Croix. Displays are often interactive—there's a startling holographic exhibit, convincing enough to make you believe in ghosts. The gift shop is high-end, with work from Passmaquoddy

artisans and local craftspeople. Next to the museum is the northern end of the East Coast Greenway, a walking and biking trail projected to link Calais, Maine, and Key West, Florida. It's a good place to begin a local visit. Open 10 AM–6 PM daily in season.

St. Croix Island

Unless you have your own boat, you can't get over to 6.5-acre St. Croix Island, an International Historic Site under joint U.S. and Canadian jurisdiction. The current in the St. Croix River is strong, and tidal ranges can be as high as 28 feet, so neophyte boaters shouldn't even attempt a crossing, but local residents often picnic and swim off the island's sandy beach on the southern end. You can see the island from an attractive 16-acre roadside rest area on Rte. 1 at **Red Beach Cove,** eight miles southeast of Calais. Here you'll find picnic tables, restrooms, a gravel beach, a boat launch, and a small parking lot. It's a great place to stop for a picnic. You can also stop at St. Croix Island International Park, across from the island.

The island is the site of the pioneering colony established by French explorers Samuel de Champlain and Pierre du Gua (Sieur de Monts) in 1604. Doomed by disease, mosquitoes, lack of food, and a grueling winter, 35 settlers died; in spring, the emaciated survivors abandoned their effort and moved on to Nova Scotia. In 1969, archaeologists found graves of 23 victims, but the only monument on the island is a commemorative plaque dating from 1904.

Whitlock Mill Lighthouse

From the lovely Pikewoods Rest Area, beside Rte. 1, about four miles southeast of Calais, there's a prime view of 32-foot-high Whitlock Mill Lighthouse, on the southern shore of the St. Croix River. Built in 1892, the northernmost lighthouse in the United States, with a green flashing light, is only accessible over private land, so check it out from this vantage point. Besides, you can also have a picnic break here.

Calais-Robbinston Milestones

A quirky little local feature, the Calais–Robbinston milestones are a dozen red-granite chunks marking each of the 12 miles between Robbinston and Calais. Presaging today's highway mileage markers, late-19th-century entrepreneur and journalist James S. Pike had the stones installed on the north side of Rte. 1 to keep track of the distance while training his pacing horses.

PARKS, PRESERVES, AND RECREATION

Moosehorn National Wildlife Refuge

More than 50 miles of trails and disused roads wind through the approximately 20-acre Baring Unit of the Moosehorn National Wildlife Refuge, 103 Headquarters Rd., Suite 1, Baring 04694, 207/454-7161, on the outskirts of Calais. Start with the 1.2-mile **nature trail** near the refuge headquarters, and get ready for major-league wildlife-watching: 35 mammal and 220 bird species have been spotted in the refuge's fields, forests, ponds, and marshes, including pairs of nesting eagles. Wear waterproof shoes and insect repellent. In August, help yourself to wild blueberries. During hunting seasons, either avoid the refuge Mon.–Sat. or wear a hunter-orange hat and vest. The refuge is open daily, all year, sunrise to sunset; trails are accessible by snowshoe, snowmobile, or cross-country skiing in winter. There's biking on 50 miles of logging trails. Some lakes and ponds are open for fishing, motorized boats, canoes, and kayaks. Admission is free. To reach refuge headquarters, take Rte. 1 west and south from downtown Calais (it's called Rte. 1 north because eventually it goes that way) about three miles. Turn left onto the Charlotte Rd. and go 2.4 miles to the headquarters sign. The office is open Mon.–Fri. 7:30 AM–4 PM, all year (except major national holidays); you can pick up free trail maps, bird checklists, and other informative brochures.

If you don't have time to walk the trails, watch for the elevated manmade nesting platforms, avian high-rises for bald eagles, outside of Calais alongside Rte. 1 north (near the junction with the Charlotte Rd.). Depending on the season, you may spot a nesting pair or even a fledgling. The chicks (usually twins but occasionally triplets) hatch around mid-May and try their wings by early August. A 400-square-foot observation deck across Rte. 1 is the best place for eagle-watching. It's handicapped-accessible and has binoculars.

Continuing on the Charlotte Rd. past the Moosehorn refuge headquarters, you'll come to **Round Lake** (locally called Round Pond), a lovely spot where you can picnic, swim, or put in a kayak or canoe. Across the road, with a great lake view, is the interesting old Round Pond Cemetery, dating from the early 19th century. (Why do graveyards always have the best views?) Just after the cemetery, a left turn puts you on Pennamaquam Lake Rd. (or Charlotte Rd.) toward Perry; a right turn takes you to Rte. 214, near Pembroke.

St. Croix Island International Historic Site

At Calais' Red Beach, on the water across from the island, is a scenic park and historical site, St. Croix Island International Historic Site, with larger-than-life bronze sculptures of indigenous and French people of old, set in a park landscape and accompanied by informational plagues. A ranger interprets (207/454-3871) in season. Administration is out of Acadia National Park.

Golf

At the nine-hole **St. Croix Country Club,** 48 River Rd., Rte. 1, P.O. Box 294, Calais 04619, 207/454-8875, the toughest and most scenic hole is the seventh, one of five holes on the river side of Rte. 1. Starting times usually aren't needed for the course, located on the southeastern outskirts of Calais. It's open late Apr.–late Oct.

Bicycling

If you've brought your own bike, shoulders are wide enough along most of Rte. 1 in this area for comfortable cycling. You'll need to figure on 26–28 miles each way between Eastport and Calais, perhaps a bit long for a one-day round-trip. If you're staying in Robbinston, figure on a 25-mile round-trip to pedal to Calais and cross over to St. Stephen. Robbinston is also a good base for biking to Eastport—about 30 miles round-trip, slightly longer if you take the more scenic **Shore Rd.,** east of and parallel to Rte. 1, between Perry and North Perry.

Getting Afloat

On a back road (Rte. 191), about midway between Calais and Machias, **Sunrise Expeditions,** with a base camp at Cathance Lake, and an office in Bangor, is one of the state's premier canoeing outfitters—and the local expert on the St. Croix River, the boundary between Maine and New Brunswick. ESPN even covered the company on the river, designated a Canadian Heritage River, and Sunrise has received a Governor's Award for Tourism. Company director Martin Brown says the St. Croix is the best option for Maine visitors with different levels of experience, since the water is interesting enough for skilled paddlers, but navigable for novices. He should know, as his company has run 2,000 trips on the St. Croix. Memorial Day–mid-Oct., Sunrise Expeditions does guided four-day trips every week on the St. Croix, typically putting in below the dam at Vanceboro and taking out 33 miles later at Grand Falls Flowage (longer trips are also possible). Along the way, with continuous Class I and II water, you'll see bald eagles, loons, and moose. You can canoe the dam-controlled river from spring through fall, but the best time to go is Sept.–Oct., for the fantastic fall foliage. Cost for four days is $845 adults, $495 for children, including everything but transportation to base camp on Cathance Lake (there's an option to start the trip in Bangor). Six-day trips run $1,175 for one, $2,195 for two, and $695 for children. Sunrise has trips on the Machias and St. John Rivers as well—these start in early to mid-May and end by mid-June.

Sunrise Expeditions also offers canoe rentals and shuttle service if you want to use the Appalachian Mountain Club's *AMC River Guide* and do it yourself. Sunrise was established in 1973 and now does rivers in Iceland, Scotland, Portugal, Australia, Costa Rica, Mongolia, France, all of Canada, including the Canadian Arctic, and the U.S. Southwest. Their headquarters is Sunrise Expeditions, 4 Union Plaza, Bangor 04401, 207/942-9300 or 800/748-3730, www.sunrise-exp.com.

Canoe rentals are also available at Long Lake Camps. From the Calais area, the nearest **whale-watching** excursions depart from Eastport.

ENTERTAINMENT, FESTIVALS, AND EVENTS

Nearby Eastport and the Machias Bay area are good locales for additional sources of entertainment and summertime celebrations.

First-run films show at **State Cinemas,** 79 Main St., Calais, 207/454-8830, at 7 PM. Open all year; Sat. and Sun. matinees, if scheduled, are usually at 1:30 PM.

The two-day **Grand Lake Stream Folk Art Festival,** the last weekend in July, features a juried craft show, Native American basket-making, canoe-building demonstrations, live entertainment, sporting-camp open houses, and dinner at Grand Lake Stream, 207/796-8199.

For nearly two weeks in late July–early Aug., Calais, Maine, and St. Stephen, New Brunswick, collaborate on an **International Festival** of dinners, concerts, dances, a craft fair, ball games, and cross-border parade and road race. Newspapers carry schedules (just be sure to note which events are on eastern time and which are on Atlantic time).

In the Cobscook area, you could conceivably add 230 different kinds of birds to your life list. So it only makes send to have a four-day, late May **Down East Spring Birding Festival,** www.downeastbirdfest.org, including guided and self-guided tours of wildlife refuges and other habitat, a boat trip to Machias Seal Island, and further birder delights around Eastport, Trescott, Lubec, and Campobello.

SHOPPING

Gifts

If you stop in at **Katie's on the Cove,** 9 Katie Lane, Robbinston 04671, 207/454-3297, do it at your own risk. Chocoholics may need a restraining order. Joseph and Lea Sullivan's family operation, begun in 1982, has become a great success story. They now produce about four dozen varieties of homemade fudge, truffles, caramels, and peanut brittle. The Oxygen Network did a piece on Katie's mustard truffle, made with mustard from Raye's in Eastport. Quality and prices are high. The candies are available in Washington County gift shops, and elsewhere in Maine, and the Sullivans do mail orders, but the aroma alone is worth a trip to the source. The shop, 12 miles southeast of Calais and about 15 miles west of Eastport, is open Memorial Day weekend to Columbus Day, Mon.–Sat. 10 AM–4 PM, closed Sun. This is no place for unruly or demanding kids—space is limited and the candy is pricey.

The name alone is a clue that you will not see a collection of crafts, gifts, and home accents like that of **The Urban Moose,** 345 Main St., Calais 04619, 207/454-8277, in other shops. The owner has a fine eye for what you don't need but must have. Open daily May–Oct., long weekends till Christmas, when you can justify a buying frenzy even better than in summer.

Farmers Market

The **Sunrise County Farmers Market** sets up its tables on Union St. in Calais (the same market that's at Raye's in Eastport on Thursdays) on Tuesdays, 11 AM–3 PM, selling many of the same products plus jams, soaps, and jellies, mid-June–mid-Oct.

ACCOMMODATIONS

Bed-and-Breakfasts

An 1828 National Register Greek Revival sea captain's mansion, **Brewer House B&B,** Rte. 1, P.O. Box 88, Robbinston 04671, 207/454-2385, has become something of an arts center, and centerpiece for a chamber music festival. Five rooms, most with water views, and an apartment with a separate entrance and kitchen—great for travelers with pets—go for $75–155 d. There is a gourmet breakfast in the water-view breakfast room, and special dietary needs can be accommodated with notice.

Open all year, but be sure to call ahead in winter. Innkeeper Joan Siem is a painter and shows her works in the **J. B. Siem Gallery,** where violinist husband and fellow innkeeper Trond Saeverud plays in some of the festival concerts, also held at the Downeast Heritage Museum and the Robbinston Historical Society's headquarters in the restored Grace Church, across from the B&B. Brewer House is 12 miles southeast of Calais, and was once a stop on the Underground Railroad.

If Brewer House is filled, the nearest B&Bs are about 15 miles back down the road in Eastport.

Motels and Cottages

At the gingerbread-trimmed **Redclyffe Shore Motel & Dining Room,** Rte. 1, P.O. Box 53, Robbinston 04671, 207/454-3270, www.redclyffeshoremotorinn.com, motel units begin at $75 d (cable TVs and sunset-facing river views). Redclyffe is locally popular for its dining room, serving moderately priced entrées daily 5–9 PM. Dinner reservations are a good idea July–Aug., especially during the International Festival. It's located 12 miles south of Calais. The motel is open mid-May–Oct.

Continuing toward Calais, you'll soon come to **Brooks Bluff Cottages,** Rte. 1, Box 393, Robbinston 04671, 207/454-7795, on 25 acres with superb river views. Sixteen rustic cottages, half with kitchens and most with heat, are $350–450 a week. No pets, but smoking is allowed. The complex is open late June–mid-Sept

About 5.5 miles southeast of Calais, family-run **Heslin's Motel and Cottages,** Rte. 1, 26 Brogan Rd., Calais 04619, 207/454-3762, www.mainerec.com/heslins1.shtml, has 11 clean, basic rooms and nine rustic cottages on 60 acres alongside the St. Croix River. Room rates are $62–70 d (air-conditioning but no phones); cottages are $48–125 d. No pets. In the motel's informal river-view restaurant, seafood, steaks, and chicken, plus lobster and haddock chowders, precede homemade cheesecakes and pies (entrées $10–23), served daily 5–9 PM, June–Oct. Vegetarian

and pasta selections and small senior and child portions are options, as are lunch picnic baskets. The cocktail lounge draws a loyal local clientele.

Sporting Camps

Thirteen American Plan (three meals daily) or housekeeping log cabins are part of the lakeside complex at **Long Lake Camps,** West St., P.O. Box 817, Princeton 04668, 207/796-2051, www.longlakecamps.com, built on a lovely 40-acre private wooded peninsula in the 1940s. AP is $95 pp for adults, $50 for kids 3–13 (less by the week); pets are $10 extra per pet per night; no charge for kids two and under. Cabins have electricity and showers. This is a great family locale, with facilities for fishing (especially smallmouth bass; catch-and-release preferred), canoeing, and swimming. Boat-and-motor rentals are $55 a day; a canoe is $15 a day. No credit cards.

Long Lake Camps serves hearty, home-cooked meals to its guests in **The Lodge.** It's open mid-May–Oct. and will pack picnic lunches and shoreside dinners for an extra charge. From Rte. 1 in Princeton (25 miles northwest of Calais), go one mile southwest on West St. then hang a right onto the unpaved Long Lakes Camp Rd. Or charter a float plane at Bangor International Airport from KT Aviation, 207/945-5087.

Campgrounds

High enough for a great view of the St. Croix River, **Hilltop Campground,** 317 Ridge Rd., Robbinston 04671, 207/454-3985, has 84 tent and RV sites on 100 wooded and open acres, plus a pool, a pond, a small store, and laundry facilities. Sites are $22–28 a night. Open mid-May–Columbus Day, the campground is on Ridge Rd., a mile west of Rte. 1 (turn at Mill Cove).

FOOD

If you're near downtown Calais, order picnic sandwiches to go at **The Sandwich Man,** 382 North St., Rte. 1, Calais 04619,

207/454-2460, a reliable local favorite with lots of choices. It's open all year, Mon.–Sat. 9 AM–9 PM, closed Sun.

A touch of Italia Down East: **Bernardini's,** 89 Main St., Calais 04619, 207/454-2237, has earned its repute with always-reliable Italian cuisine; entrées are $9–15. Save room for the tiramisu. Open all year for lunch and dinner, 11 AM–8 PM Mon.–Sat.

INFORMATION AND SERVICES

The **Maine Visitor Information Center,** 39 Union St., Ste. B, Calais 04619, 207/454-2211, is now located in the Downeast Heritage Museum building, as is the **St. Croix Valley Chamber of Commerce,** 207/454-2308. The Information Center is open daily 8 AM–6 PM, and can supply you with information for all of Maine and some of Canada.

Next door to the Information Center is the imposing stone **Calais Free Library,** 3 Union St., Calais 04619, 207/454-2758, www.calais.lib.me.us, summer hours Mon. and Tues. noon–8 PM, Wed. and Fri. 9 AM–5 PM, Thurs. 9 AM–6 PM. Closed Sat.

Newspapers
The Calais Advertiser, 207/454-3561, published every Wednesday, carries features, ads, and local events listings. The *Downeast Times,* 207/454-2884, also published weekly in Calais, comes out late Monday afternoon. The statewide daily for this area is the *Bangor Daily News.*

Emergencies
In Calais, contact the **police, fire department, and ambulance** at 911. **Calais Regional Hospital,** 22 Hospital Lane, Calais 04619, 207/454-7521, has round-the-clock emergency-room care.

Public Restrooms
The **Downeast Heritage Museum,** 39 Union St., Calais, has restrooms, as does the headquarters of the **Moosehorn National Wildlife Refuge** (across from the office).

Crossing into Canada
If you plan to cross into Canada, you'll have to pass Customs checkpoints on both the Calais (U.S., 207/454-3621) and St. Stephen (Canada, 506/466-2363) ends of the bridges. Requirements for U.S. citizens, once minimal, are changing with provisions of the Homeland Security Act. Check when planning your trip. You'll be asked your purpose in going to Canada, and the length of your stay. Most clearances are perfunctory, but if you are carrying any live plant material, Canadian Customs will confiscate it.

Even for a day trip to St. Stephen, non-U.S. citizens need to show a valid passport; citizens of most non-European countries must also have a Canadian visa (which must be obtained in advance). U.S. resident aliens must be prepared to show a valid green card.

Pay attention to your watch, too—Calais is on eastern time, St. Stephen (as well as the rest of Canada's Maritime Provinces) is on Atlantic time.

The Sunrise Coast

Grand Lake Stream

For a tiny community of about 160 year-rounders, Grand Lake Stream has a well-deserved, larger-than-life reputation. It's the center of a vast area of rivers and lakes, ponds and streams—a recreational paradise.

The famous stream is a narrow, three-mile neck of prime scenic and sportfishing water connecting West Grand Lake and Big Lake. A dam spans the bottom of West Grand, and just downstream is a state-run salmon hatchery. Since the mid-19th century, the stream and its lakes have been drawing fishing fans to trout and landlocked-salmon spawning grounds, and fourth and fifth generations now return here each year.

Fly anglers arrive in May and June for landlocked salmon and smallmouth bass (the stream itself is fly-fishing only); families show up in July and Aug. for canoeing, birding, swimming, fishing, and hiking; hunters arrive in late October for game birds and deer; and snowmobilers, snowshoers, and cross-country skiers descend as the snow piles up.

A great time to visit the village is the last weekend in July, for the annual Grand Lake Stream Folk Art Festival. Traditional crafts, such as canoe-building and basket-making, are the focus. Other activities are hatchery tours, lodge open houses, and dinners. For more info, contact Grand Lake Stream Festival Committee, P.O. Box 1, Grand Lake Stream 04637, 207/796-8199.

Canoe-building, in fact, has contributed to the area's mystique. The distinctive Grand Lake canoe (or "Grand Laker"), a lightweight, square-sterned, motorized 20-footer, was developed in the 1920s specifically for sportfishing in these waters. In the off season, several villagers still hunker down in their workshops and turn out these stable cedar beauties.

In the early 1990s, the specter of development galvanized lodge owners, guides, and the environmental community to preserve most of the land bordering Grand Lake Stream itself; their efforts permanently preserved four miles of stream frontage and 271 acres, now managed by the Maine Department of Inland Fisheries and Wildlife.

RECREATION

If you're only in Grand Lake Stream for the day, head for the **public landing,** just north of the main road into town, where you'll find a big parking area, a dock, beach, restrooms, and a boat launch. A small takeout stand may or may not be open. You can also walk the path on the western shore of the stream.

If you're here longer, think about reserving a date with a Maine Guide. About a fourth of Grand Lake Stream's residents are Maine Professional Guides and some are Master Maine Guides, most specializing in leading fishing and hunting outings. You can find them, and guides for different types of outings, at the Grand Lake Stream Guides Association, Grand Lake Stream 04637, with an online guide directory at www.grandlakestream.com.

ACCOMMODATIONS AND FOOD

Cabin accommodations, with or without meals, are the lodgings of choice in Grand Lake Stream, and there's enough variety for every taste and budget. Few guests stay one night; most stay several days or a week. Rates quoted below are for two; many cabins can sleep more than that, and rates may be lower for extra persons. Some housekeeping cabins require your own sheets and/or towels. Most camps have boat rentals for about $25 a day (motor brings the total to about $50).

American Plan or Housekeeping

Ken and Jo-Anne Cannell's **Indian Rock Camps,** P.O. Box 117, Grand Lake Stream 04637, 207/796-2822 or 800/498-2821, has five rustic two-bedroom log cabins, plus a lodge where everyone gathers for Jo-Anne's fine home cooking. Rates are $70 pp AP, $30 pp without meals. The dining room is open to the public for dinner Tues.–Sun. by reservation ($19.95). In summer, the Cannells organize pontoon-boat lake tours, with lunch back at the lodge. Open all year; snowmobilers are welcome.

Almost 12 miles west of Grand Lake Stream, via an unpaved road, **The Pines,** P.O. Box 158, Grand Lake Stream 04637, 207/557-7463 or 825-4431 off season, is a special gem, a family-oriented oasis on the shore of Sysladobsis (Sis-la-DOB-sis) Lake. Nancy and Steve Norris come from a Norris family tradition of sporting-camp ownership. They know how it's done. Five log cabins and five second-floor rooms in the main lodge; two remote island housekeeping cabins. The log cabins have cold water, gas lights, and Port-a-Pottis; a clean bathhouse has hot showers. Rate at the lodge and in the log cabins is $75 pp, AP, per day, but of course no one stays only a day in a place this peaceful. Children 3–10 are $55 a day; children under three are free. Canoe rental is $25 a day. No credit cards. Open early May–Sept., closing before hunting season.

Modified American Plan Only
Leen's Lodge, Box 40, Grand Lake Stream 04637, 207/796-2929 or 800/995-3367, www.leenslodge.com, on a spacious wooded shore and peninsula of West Grand Lake, has 10 small and large rustic cabins with baths. MAP daily rate (two-day minimum) is $115–145 pp. Children 12 and under are half-price, and kids five and under are free. Dinners are probably more than you can eat. Leashed pets are welcome. BYOL. Canoe and motor boat rentals should be arranged in advance. Open May–Oct.

Housekeeping Only
Grand Lake Lodge, P.O. Box 8, Grand Lake Stream 04637, 207/796-5584, www.grandlakelodgemaine.com, on the shore of West Grand Lake and two blocks from the village center, is a particularly good choice for families, with a safe swimming area. Daily rates are $32–41 pp; there are special family rates July–Aug. Open ice out through Oct. No credit cards.

Food
If you opt for housekeeping arrangements, you'll want to provision before you get here, but you can pick up pretty much anything at Kurt and Kathy Cressey's **Pine Tree Store,** 3 Water St., P.O. Box 129, Grand Lake Stream 04637, 207/796-5027, in the heart of the village. This mom-'n'-pop emporium is open daily. People have been getting their gas and groceries here for over 60 years.

INFORMATION
The **Grand Lake Stream Chamber of Commerce,** P.O. Box 124, Grand Lake Stream 04637, has a well-done website, with extensive area information; see www.grandlakestream.com. The **Pine Tree Store,** Water St., P.O. Box 129, Grand Lake Stream 04637, 207/796-5027, is also a good source of local information, since it is open long hours. Another option is the **Grand Lake Stream Town Office,** 4 Water St., Grand Lake Stream 04637, 207/796-2001, which is open weekdays.

Getting There
On Rte. 1 north, about two miles northwest of Princeton, turn left (west) onto Grand Lake Stream Rd. (also called Princeton Rd.). Continue about 10 miles to the village.

The Sunrise Coast

Aroostook County

This is the Crown of Maine—at 6,500 square miles, Maine's largest county. When Mainers refer to "the County," this is the one they mean. Although Aroostook (a Micmac Indian word meaning "bright" or "shining") has plenty of wide-open space for its 82,000 residents, fully a fourth of them live in only two smallish cities, Presque Isle and Caribou.

Neat farmhouses and huge, half-buried potato-storage barns anchor vast, undulating patches of potatoes, broccoli, and barley. The sky seems to go on forever. Potato fields define the County—bright green in spring, pink and white in summer, dirt-brown and gold just before the autumn harvest.Native to South America, the potato is king here, where 90 percent of Maine's spuds grow on over 60,000 acres—Maine is America's fifth- to eighth-largest producer (depending on the harvest).

Annual festivals in Fort Fairfield and Houlton celebrate the blossoms and the harvest; potatoes appear on every restaurant menu and family table; countless roadside stands peddle them by the bag; and high schools still close for two or three weeks in September so students (and teachers) can assist with the harvest. Even

© KATHLEEN

grade-schoolers used to fan out over the fields, though these days you'll find more teachers than students in the fields, since federal regulations require students to be over 16 to operate harvesting machines (tedious hand-digging is rare nowadays). No matter, though—to the younger kids, it still means school's out.

Now if you don't get enough of this potato business while you're here in the County, there's always a membership in the **Maine Potato Sampler of the Month Club.** Eight months a year, Wood Prairie Farm in Bridgewater sends its members a 10-pound gift box of three different kinds of organic potatoes. The package comes with postcards and recipes, so you're all set. The base price for the eight-month club is $269; two months $34.95. Send inquiries/orders to Wood Prairie Farm, 49 Kinney Rd., Bridgewater, ME 04735, 800/829-9765 (weekdays) www.woodprairie.com.

Aroostook County, like the rest of Maine, has its share of hills, forests, and waterways, but the most significant hills here—Quaggy Jo, Mars, Debouillie, Haystack, Number Nine—are startling. Almost accidental, they appear out of nowhere—chunks the glaciers seem to have overlooked. Thanks to them, you'll find authentic vertical hiking, although Aroostook's trails are more often horizontal, through marshlands and woodlands, and along abandoned railbeds.

Snowmobiling is a big deal here (one national magazine ranked the County's snowmobile trails second best in the country), and a huge boost to the local economy. Legions of snowmobilers (often called "sledders" locally) crisscross the County every winter, exploring hundreds of miles of the incredible Interconnecting Trail System (ITS). Lodgings and restaurants fill up and the fields and woods hum with horsepower. The region is enough to tempt almost anyone onto a snowmobile—for the chance to see and perhaps capture on film the beauty of a rural winter. Time was when snowmobilers had less-than-attractive reputations and accidents were rampant. Today, sledders span the social strata, and safety holds high priority (although serious accidents do still occur). For me, the primary

drawback is still the engine noise, an inevitably irritating whine.

The County's agricultural preeminence sets it apart from the rest of Maine, but so does the Acadian culture of the northernmost St. John Valley, where the French dialect is unlike anything you'll ever hear in language classes (or even in France). It leads to some wonderfully whimsical street and road names—for instance, Brise Culotte Road, roughly translated as "Torn Trousers Road." Islands of Acadian or French culture exist in other parts of Maine, but it's in "the Valley" that you'll be tempted to pile on the pounds with such Acadian specialties as *poutine* (French fries smothered with cheese and gravy), *tourtière* (pork pie), and *tarte au saumon* (salmon tart). Rituals are important here, especially Saturday afternoon Mass—often followed by a visit to a neighborhood "cook shop" to pick up baked beans for Saturday night supper.

Another unique ethnic enclave is Aroostook's pocket of Swedish culture, centered about eight miles northwest of Caribou, in New Sweden, and dating from the late 19th century. If you didn't realize you were driving out of Caribou, you'd certainly know that you'd landed in New Sweden—the homes have a distinctly Scandinavian look, mailboxes carry Swedish names, and if you've traveled in Nordic countries, you'll feel instantly at home. But most visitors don't arrive here by accident. The last time I visited the historical museum, I encountered two Swedish descendants of local settlers. In the midst of a pilgrimage they'd been planning for years, they were excitedly poring over town documents for mention of their relatives.

Aroostook County's major brush with historic notoriety occurred in 1839, with the skirmish known as the Aroostook War. Always described by the adjective "bloodless"—since there were no casualties (other than a farmer accidentally downed by friendly fire)—the war was essentially a boundary dispute between Maine and New Brunswick that had simmered since 1784, when New Brunswick was established. The 1783 Treaty of Paris had set the St. Croix River as the Washington County line, but loopholes left the northernmost border ill-defined. Maine feared losing timber-rich real estate to Canada, and matters heated up when 200 burly militiamen descended on the region in early 1839 to defend the young state's territory. Some 3,000 troops ended up supporting the Maine cause, and legendary war hero Gen. Winfield ("Old Fuss and Feathers") Scott was sent to Augusta for three weeks in March 1839 to negotiate the successful truce. Following the "war," Aroostook was incorporated as a county, and by 1842 the Webster-Ashburton Treaty (sometimes also called the Treaty of Washington), negotiated by Daniel Webster and Lord Ashburton, brought a long-awaited peace that opened the area for stepped-up settlement. Among the remnants of the Aroostook War is a wooden blockhouse, now a National Historic Site, on the banks of the St. John River in Fort Kent.

As often occurs with remote rural areas, the County sometimes gets a bum rap (never from the snowmobiling crowd) among downstaters and others who've never been here. But it deserves notice—for the scenery if nothing else. Admittedly, it's a long haul—it's about as far as you can get from the rockbound coast—but you're guaranteed a totally different Maine experience.

FESTIVALS AND EVENTS

As with other parts of Maine, Aroostook County has frequent **public suppers** throughout the summer. Visitors are welcome, even encouraged (most suppers benefit a good cause), so check the papers, line up early, and enjoy the local food and color.

Fort Kent hosts a Maine-style **Mardi Gras,** usually the first week of February, with several days of pre-Lenten festivities. Spectators crowd the snowy streets to watch Fort Kent's five-day March **Can Am Crown International Sled Dog Races.** Special locations offer vantage points for watching teams competing in 30-, 60- and 250-mile races. A mushers' award ceremony is the finale.

Spring runoff generates the thrills for Houlton's

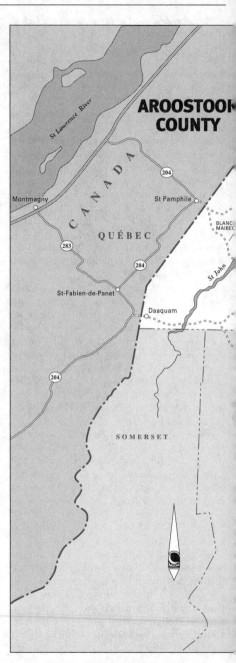

Aroostook County

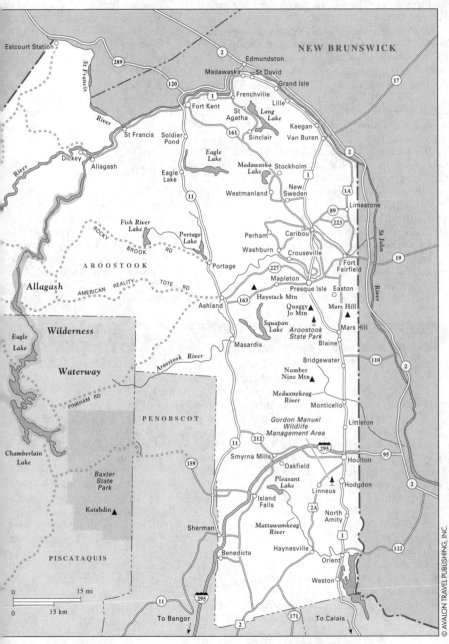

© AVALON TRAVEL PUBLISHING, INC.

Aroostook County

Meduxnekeag River Race, usually the last Saturday in April.

New Sweden's Scandinavian **Midsommar** festival features music and dancing, Swedish food, and other Nordic events on the weekend closest to June 21. And Madawaska hosts the Franco-American **Acadian Festival,** with a historical re-enactment, tournaments, fishing derby, Acadian food, music, and dancing, a parade, and a featured family reunion late in June.

The four-day **Houlton Fair** includes a carnival, a pig scramble, truck pulling, entertainment, baking contests, and craft and agricultural exhibits right around the Fourth of July. For 10 days from early to mid-July, Fort Fairfield's **Potato Blossom Festival** puts on well over 100 events—pageants, tournaments, fireworks, a pie social, races—all celebrating the surrounding fields carpeted with potato blossoms.

Agriculture exhibits, harness racing, live entertainment, and fireworks are all part of Presque Isle's **Northern Maine Fair,** the biggest country fair in this part of Maine, the first full week of August.

Sherman celebrates **Olde Home Days** on Labor Day weekend with an old-fashioned celebration including a parade, lobster dinner, a variety show, and games Another celebration of the spud is Houlton's **Potato Feast Days,** the weekend after Labor Day, featuring a potato feast supper, entertainment, a classic car show, and arts and crafts.

INFORMATION

Besides individual chambers of commerce in half a dozen towns and cities, Aroostook County maintains a central information resource: **Aroostook County Tourism (ACT),** 888/216-2463, www.visitaroostook.com.

Information on the potato industry is available from the **Maine Potato Board,** 744 Main St., Room 1, Presque Isle 04769, 207/764-4148, www.mainepotatoes.com.

Southern Aroostook County

Driving north on I-95, you find the interstate petering out at Houlton, about 120 miles northeast of Bangor. That sometimes makes this feel like the end of the earth, but it's actually just the beginning of Aroostook County.

Southern Aroostook, centered on Houlton, is a narrow north-south corridor, roughly straddling Rte. 1 from Danforth to Presque Isle. Among its communities are Island Falls, Oakfield, Bridgewater, and Mars Hill.

Hard by the New Brunswick border, Houlton (pop. about 6,420) has carved out its own niche as the shire town—and, according to the local historical society, "history's hiding place." Some of it is well hidden indeed, but not the Market Square Historic District, with its 28 turn-of-the-20th-century National Historic Register buildings. Incorporated in 1834, Houlton is quiet and not often considered a "destination," but the county courts and other government offices are all located here,

so there's a fair amount of activity—at least during the week.

North, south, and west of Houlton, you can canoe, swim, and fish in lakes, ponds, streams, and rivers; you can go golfing, birding, or camping; and you can visit small museums, shops, and the state's northernmost (and easternmost) covered bridge.

Less than 30 miles north of Houlton, Mars Hill is a strategic link in the International Appalachian Trail (IAT), www.internationalat.org, a planned 600-mile extension of the Appalachian Trail from Katahdin in Baxter State Park to Mt. Carleton in New Brunswick and on to 4,160-foot Mt. Jacques Cartier, highest peak in Quebec province, ending at Cap Gaspé, on the Gulf of St. Lawrence. Parts of the trail have already been cut and blazed; much remains to be done, including approval of rights-of-way.

From Houlton, you can traverse Southern

Aroostook, via Rtes. 2 and 212, to reach north-south Rte. 11, but the best way to "do" Rte. 11 is to wait until you've reached Fort Kent. Start in Fort Kent and head south.

SIGHTS

Historic Houlton

Pick up the *Walking Guide to Market Square Historic District* at the Houlton chamber, 207/532-4216 and wander the downtown, being sure to expand the route to include **Pierce Park.**

At the edge of the district is the 1903 White Memorial Building, a Colonial Revival residence that now houses Houlton's chamber of commerce and the **Aroostook County Historical and Art Museum,** 109 Main St., Houlton 04730. The museum—containing photos, books, vintage clothing, antique tools and housewares—is open mid-May–Labor Day, daily Tues.–Fri. 1–4 pm, Sat 10–2 pm or by appointment. Contact the chamber office, 207/532-4216, for an appointment.

Watson Settlement Bridge

About six miles north of Houlton, amid typical Aroostook farmland, stands Maine's northernmost (yes, and easternmost) covered bridge, the Watson Settlement Bridge, Carson Rd., Littleton 04730, built in the early 20th century and last used in 1985. The wood-truss bridge, straddling a branch of the Meduxnekeag River, feels quite forlorn, a remnant of the past just sitting here unused. Maine once had 120 or so covered bridges; only nine remain. To reach the bridge, take Foxcroft Rd. from Rte. 2 and continue 6.1 miles; turn left onto Carson Rd. If you're on your way north to Presque Isle, continue westward on Carson Rd. after the bridge to meet up with Rte. 1.

Flightseeing

Since 1966, **Beal's Aircraft,** Houlton International Airport, 19 Industrial Road Houlton 04730, 207/532-9489 or 532-9079. Beal's is on call 24 hours a day and regular hours are 7 am to 5 pm daily. Beal's offers flight instruc-

tion and scenic rides. Scenic rides offer some of the best viewing of this area. Off to the west, you'll see Katahdin. Headphones allow passengers to hear his commentary over the noisy engine. Flights are weather-dependent and on demand. Foliage trips usually start in late September and continue two to three weeks. The office is open weekdays 8 am–5 pm, plus weekends during fall-foliage season. Cost is $80 an hour per planeload for regular charters; 20-minute foliage flights are $15 pp; three-person minimum preferred. Parents will have to make a judgment call on this; most kids love it, some don't.

During World War II, Houlton's airport was the site of Maine's largest German POW camp—4,000 prisoners lived here in barracks while doing forced labor in lumber camps, canneries, potato farms, and paper mills.

On your way to or from the airport, notice the pond near the U.S. Customs office—linger here a bit, especially early or late in the day, and you may spot a moose.

Oakfield Railroad Museum

Seventeen miles west of Houlton, off I-95 Exit 60, is the Oakfield Railroad Museum, Station St., Oakfield 04743, 207/757-8575. Housed in a 1910 Bangor and Aroostook Railroad station and run by the Oakfield Historical Society, the museum contains an impressive collection of iron-horse memorabilia—guaranteed to fascinate kids of any age. Wheelchair-accessible. It's easy to get caught up in the enthusiasm of the railroad buffs who staff the museum. The gift shop carries all kinds of railroad-logo items. The museum, next to the fire station in Oakfield, is open Memorial Day weekend to Labor Day, weekends only 1 pm–4 pm. Admission is free, but donations are welcomed.

The Height of Fashion

Nostalgia reigns at the **John E. and Walter D. Webb Museum of Vintage Fashion,** Sherman St., Rte. 2, Island Falls 04747, 207/463-2404, off season P.O. Box 18, Hampden 04444, 207/862-3797, an unlikely hamlet where Frances Webb Stratton exhibits her lifetime accumulation of antique clothing and accessories—including 700 hats!—in a 14-room Victorian house. This museum is a sleeper, worth a detour. Docents (sometimes Mrs. Stratton) lead hour-long tours pitched to seniors and children. Kids love the "dress-up" children's clothes, antique toys, and military uniforms. Call ahead to reserve for afternoon tea and crumpets (extra charge). The museum is open June–early Oct., Mon.–Thurs. 10 AM– 4 PM, or weekends by appointment. Suggested donation is $3 adults, $2 seniors, $1 children under 12. Island Falls is about 25 miles southwest of Houlton.

PARKS, PRESERVES, AND RECREATION

For canoeists and kayakers, the year's biggest event is the eight-mile spring-runoff **Meduxnekeag River Race,** held on a Saturday in late April or early May. Beginning in New Limerick, west of town, the route includes a short stretch of Class III rapids. Registration is $10; fees benefit local Boy Scouts. For more information contact the Houlton Chamber of Competence, 207/532-4216.

Pierce Park

Near downtown Houlton, mystery surrounds the origins of Pierce Park's quaint fountain with a centerpiece statue usually called "The Boy with the Leaking Boot." Donated to the town in 1916, it's one of two dozen or so similar statues in the United States and Europe. Legends have it coming from Germany or Belgium or Italy, but no record exists. Benches surround the fountain, and lower- and upper-level troughs provide fresh water for pets and their owners. The Houlton Garden Club maintains the flowers in the park—a popular local spot for photographs, picnics, and coffee breaks.

Community Park

Also close to Houlton's downtown, Community Park has a great playground, tennis courts, picnic tables, and plenty of space for kids to run. The park is the venue for major

outdoor concerts and the July Fourth fireworks extravaganza.

Garrison Park

Another picnic location is Garrison Park, off Upper Military St., Houlton, a reminder of the troops garrisoned here at the time of the 1838–39 Aroostook War. Only a few rundown buildings remain, but it's a fine place for a picnic. Take Rte. 2 toward the airport and turn left onto Garrison Rd., across from Drake's Dairy Bar.

Art Howell's Wildlife Refuge

At the **A.E. Howell Wildlife Conservation Center and Spruce Acres Refuge,** Lycette Rd., HC 61, Box 6, North Amity 04471, 207/532-6880, www.houlton.com/howell.htm. Art and Dot Howell and their family have dedicated their land (64 acres) and their lives to conservation and wildlife rehabilitation, and their enthusiasm is contagious. Most creatures in the nonprofit refuge will be cared for and released, but permanent residents include a great horned owl, two bald eagles, and a bobcat. The refuge layout is a bit higgledy-piggledy, but that adds to its charm. Kids under 12 can fish in stocked trout ponds, and families can explore 5.5 miles of trails; nearly 70 bird species have been spotted here. If you have time, volunteer to lend a hand; there's always a need, and it's a rewarding experience. Membership in the organization is $25 a year, providing free admission and a quarterly newsletter. A gift shop carries T-shirts and posters. Suggested donation is $5 adults, $2 seniors, $2 kids 13–18, and free for kids under 12. The season is mid-May–Oct., Tues.–Fri. 10 AM–4 PM, to 3 PM Sat., but trails are open all year for hiking or cross-country skiing. Do *not* bring pets. The refuge is just west of Rte. 1, 14 miles south of Houlton.

Gordon Manuel Wildlife Management Area

Just south of Houlton, the Gordon Manuel Wildlife Management Area, Hodgdon, no tel., covers 5,592 acres of fields, woods, and marshland along the Meduxnekeag River. From Rte.

1, turn right (west) onto Hodgdon Rd. and watch for Layton's Dairy Bar. Take the first left after Layton's onto the unpaved Horseback Road. Continue 1.7 miles and turn left at a narrow dirt road. Wind through the trees, about 0.2 mile, to a small parking area on the Meduxnekeag River. Watch for osprey, green herons, even bald eagles. You can launch a canoe or kayak (no motors allowed) and explore the area. The setting is particularly gorgeous during the fall-foliage season, but be forewarned that hunting is allowed here, so wear a hunter-orange vest and/or hat mid-Oct.–Nov.

If you don't have a canoe or kayak, and just want to do some birding, this is a particularly relaxing bike ride, even from Houlton. If you haven't packed a picnic, **T & S Market,** 207/532-6672, on Main St. in Hodgdon, has the best pizza in the whole area.

Golf

On a clear day, Baxter State Park's Katahdin is visible from **Va-Jo-Wa Golf Club,** 142-A Walker Settlement Rd., Island Falls 04747, 207/463-2128, a scenic 18-hole, par-72 course named after Vaughn, John, and Warren Walker. Call for a starting time; this course is popular. Greens fees are moderate. Facilities include a restaurant and bar, plus a driving range. Open May–Oct., Va-Jo-Wa is five miles north of I-95, off Rte. 2, between Pleasant and Upper Mattawamkeag Lakes.

Southwest of Houlton is the nine-hole **Houlton Community Golf Club,** Drew's Lake Rd., New Limerick 04761, 207/532-2662, built on onetime potato fields in 1921. The setting is lovely, on the shores of Nickerson Lake; the lakefront clubhouse has a snack bar. Bring a swimsuit; a dip in the lake feels great after a round of golf. Credit cards accepted. The course is open mid-May–mid-Oct. Take Rte. 2A (Bangor Rd.) west and south of Houlton about three miles to Drew's Lake Rd. (also known as Nickerson Lake Rd.), continuing 2.5 miles to the club.

A much newer 18-hole course is in Mars Hill, 28 miles north of Houlton, near the Bigrock ski area. The **Mars Hill Country Club,** York Rd., Mars Hill 04758, 207/425-4802, built in 1991, has a restaurant and is open June–mid-Oct. From Rte. 1A in Mars Hill, take Boynton Rd. east to York Rd.

Winter Sports

Houlton is at the fringe of prime **snowmobiling** country. The crowds tend to head up the road to Presque Isle, Caribou, and the St. John Valley, but there are plenty of trails here, as well. For information on snowmobiling in the Houlton area, contact the chamber of commerce or the **Maine Snowmobile Association,** 207/622-6983, www.mesnow.com, which can put you in touch with local snowmobile clubs.

When snowmobiling in the Houlton area, you'll notice on trail maps that some routes cross into Canada. Be sure you are carrying valid identification when you are anywhere near the border. The Houlton border crossing is open 24 hours.

On Mars Hill Mountain, about 28 miles north of Houlton, **Bigrock,** P.O. Box 518, Mars Hill 04758, 207/425-6711 in Maine, is a small, family-oriented ski area with one double chairlift, three Poma lifts, and 14 trails with a maximum elevation of 980 feet. Rentals, lessons, and lift tickets are a fraction of the prices in western Maine; nothing fancy here, but a fun place to play. Night skiing is available, and access to 3.6 miles of cross-country trails is $4 a day. Bigrock is signposted off Rte. 1, but you can't miss the mountain—a giant eruption on an otherwise-flat landscape.

SHOPPING

About 22 miles north of Houlton, a small showroom piled high with variations on the barrel theme is the retail shop for the **Bradbury Barrel Company,** 100 Main St., Rte. 1, Bridgewater 04735, 207/429-8141 or 800/332-6021, a decades-old firm with an international clientele. The hand-built white-cedar products make great planters, storage bins, toy buckets, or catchalls. The showroom is open all year, Mon.–Fri. 8 a m–5 p m.

Antiques and Collectibles

Across the road from the Bradbury Barrel Company is **Milliken's Old Stuff,** Main St., P.O. Box 220, Bridgewater 04735, and fax 207/429-9000. Leon Milliken and his wife Carolle run the shop in the former general store operated by Leon's father, Ralph for 30 years. Plenty of potential collectible treasures here—pots, paintings, linens, china, hats, and more. The shop is open 10 AM–5 PM Mon.–Sat., 1–5 PM Sun.

Books

At the heart of downtown, **York's Bookstore,** 19 Market Sq., Houlton 04730, 207/532-3354, carries a respectable selection of new hardcover and paperback titles as well as Hallmark cards and magazines. It's open all year, Mon.–Sat. 8:30 AM–5 PM (to 6 PM Thurs.–Fri.).

Just north of the Shiretown Motor Inn is **Volumes,** North Rd., Rte. 1, Houlton 04730, 207/532-7727, an especially user-friendly used-paperback emporium in a nondescript building. Besides the 40,000 or so books, well categorized, you'll find Maine-made everything: jewelry, wooden items, T-shirts, wind chimes, condiments, and even music. Volumes is open daily all year, Mon.–Sat. 9:30 AM–5 PM (to 8 PM Fri.), Sun. noon–5 PM.

Farmers Market

Most of Maine's farmers markets operate one or maybe two days a week; the **Houlton Farmers Market** sets up shop daily, early May–mid-Oct., next to McDonald's on Rte. 1, just south of I-95 exit 62.

ACCOMMODATIONS

Lodgings are not Houlton's strong suit, but at least there are a couple of choices. Close to downtown Houlton, the 50-room **Shiretown Motor Inn,** North Rd., Rte. 1, RR3, Box 30, Houlton 04730, 207/532-9421 or 800/441-9421 lacks atmosphere, but it's convenient to I-95, Rte. 1, and the Trans-Canada Highway. Health-club facilities, including an indoor pool, are free for guests and open

10 AM–9:45 PM. Rooms have phones, cable TV, and air-conditioning; $72–92 d. No pets. Request a back-facing room if you're particularly noise-sensitive. The adjoining **Govenor's Restaurant,** 207/521-0035, serving reasonably priced continental fare (entrées $12–19) amid lots of greenery, is open Sun.–Wed 6:20 AM–8, Thurs.–Sat 6:30 AM–9 PM. Dinner reservations are a good idea, as this is Houlton's best all-around restaurant. The complex is open all year.

A smaller, less expensive operation on the same stretch of Rte. 1 is **Ivey's Motor Lodge,** Rte. 1, P.O. Box 241, Houlton 04730, 800/244-4206 in Maine, with 24 good-size rooms ($48–68 d) and cable TV. It's open all year.

FOOD

Inexpensive to Moderate

For large portions, home cooking, good service, and local color, the **Elm Tree Diner,** 146 Bangor St., Rte. 2A, Houlton 04730, 207/532-3181, is Houlton's place to go. Nothing fancy, mind you, and not a diner in the strict sense—a sprawling, one-story, modern building—but this is a good spot to fill up the kids. It's been here since 1947. Save room for dessert. Located 1.5 miles south of I-95 exit 62, the Elm Tree is open all year, Mon.–Sat. 6 AM–8 PM and Sun. 6 AM–9 PM, Apr.–Oct.

The best choice for *interesting* food is Joyce Transue's **The Courtyard Café,** 61 Main St., Houlton 04730, 207/532-0787. It's in the Main St. Emporium, formerly known as the Fishman Mall. This location has seen cafés come and go; pray that this incarnation lasts, because they're doing a fine job. Best are the sandwiches, with such floral names as Bittersweet and Tiger Lily. Sweet Pea turns out to be good ol' PB&J. For dinner, try the apple-glazed salmon. The café is open for lunch 11 AM–2 PM Mon.–Fri. and for dinner 5 PM–8 PM Tue.–Thurs., till 9 PM Fri. and Sat., closed Sun.

Where can you find a grilled-cheese sandwich on homemade bread for just over $2 or a nine-inch cheese pizza for $3.50? In Mars Hill, 28 miles north of Houlton. For a guaranteed dose of local color—and decent food besides—pull up at the antique neon sign outside **Al's Diner,** 87 Main St., Rte. 1, Mars Hill 04758, 207/429-8186, a friendly village eatery. Started as an ice-cream shop in 1937, it has booths, a counter, a back room, and air-conditioning. The third generation is now running the place. Visa and MasterCard accepted. Open all year, Mon.–Thurs. 5 am–8 pm, Fri., Sat., and Sun. 5 am–9 pm.

York's Dairy Bar, North Rd., Rte. 1, Houlton 04730, 207/532-6079, owned by Marlynn London, is open late Apr.–Aug., serving great ice cream from Houlton Farms Dairy. Hours are 10:30 am–8 pm daily.

INFORMATION AND SERVICES

The **Greater Houlton Chamber of Commerce,** 109 Main St., Houlton 04730, 207/532-4216, www. Houlton.com, in the same 1903 Colonial Revival building as the Aroostook Historical and Art Museum, is open weekdays all year, 9 am–5 pm. Be sure to request the *Walking Guide to Market Square Historic District.* A helpful website covering the local area is http://houlton.com.

Next door is the handsome **Cary Memorial Library,** 107 Main St., Houlton 04730, 207/532-1302, www.careylib.me.us, another early-20th-century legacy from Andrew Carnegie. In winter, it's open Mon.–Thurs. 9 am–6 pm (to 8 pm Tues.), Fri. 9 am–5 pm, and Sat. 9 am–1 pm.

The **Maine Visitor Information Center,** 28 Ludlow Rd., Houlton 04730, 207/532-6346, with brochures and maps covering the entire state, is open weekdays 9 am–5 pm, all year, with weekend and extended weekday hours in summer. The staff is helpful here, and there are restrooms.

A helpful guide to the cultural pulse of this part of Maine is the new *Southern Aroostook Cultural Arts Directory,* produced by the Southern Aroostook Cultural Arts Project with assistance from the Maine Arts Commission. The directory lists individuals and organizations across a broad spectrum—bands to belly-dancers, poets to painters, and the occasional metalsmith and harp-maker. Copies are available at the Cary Memorial Library, the Greater Houlton Chamber of Commerce, and other locations in the area.

Newspapers

The best source for calendar listings is the *Houlton Pioneer Times,* 207/532-2281, published every Wed. under the endearing slogan, "The only newspaper in the world interested in Houlton, Maine." The *Bangor Daily News* covers the rest of the world.

Emergencies

In an emergency, for fire, police, or ambulance in Houlton call 911. To reach the state-police barracks in Houlton, call 207/532-2261 or 800/924-2261.

Houlton Regional Hospital, 20 Hartford St., Houlton 04730, 207/532-9471, has round-the-clock emergency-room coverage.

Photo Services

Right downtown, **Houlton Photo Labs,** 1 Kendall St., Union Sq., Houlton 04730, 207/532-3631, provides efficient, reliable one-hour photo service. Open Mon.–Fri. 9 am–5:30 pm and Sat. 9 am–3 pm; closed Sat. in Jan.

Laundry

The **Military Street Laundromat,** 35 Military St., Rte. 2, Houlton 04730, 207/532-2898, with coin-operated machines, is open daily 8 am–8 pm. It also has air-conditioning, so the dryer heat won't fry you.

Getting Around

Houlton has two competing taxi services: **Houlton Cab,** 207/532-6116, and **Shiretown Taxi,** 207/532-7173.

Central Aroostook County

At the heart of central Aroostook are the cities of Presque Isle and Caribou, their downtowns separated by 13 miles of Rte. 1. The cities have long enjoyed a friendly rivalry—and distinct personalities. Both are at the hub of the County's potato industry and miles of snowmobile trails; each has a weekly newspaper; both are less than 15 miles from the Canadian border.

Presque Isle (pop. 9,700) boasts a University of Maine branch, a 577-acre state park, the Aroostook Centre Mall, a six-mile multiuse trail (and access to a larger network), TV and radio stations, and the County's largest hospital. Caribou (pop. 8,840) has a unique natural-history museum, a respected performing-arts center, an energetic recreation department, and a sleepy downtown.

Maine Senator Susan Collins comes from Caribou, and legions of Aroostook County supporters turned out to help send her to Washington in 1996. No wonder—several generations of her family have been prominent local and state leaders.

Northwest of Caribou are the Swedish-American communities of New Sweden, Stockholm, and Westmanland. Off to the east and west—creating a sort of geographical diamond shape—are the towns of Fort Fairfield (pop. almost 4,000) and Washburn (pop. 1,830). I'm massaging the geometry a bit here: three of these communities—Presque Isle, Caribou, and Fort Fairfield—usually are known collectively as the Potato Triangle.

Presque Isle, incorporated in 1859, received electricity in 1887, welcomed the Bangor and Aroostook Railroad in 1895, and became the County's first city in 1940.

Caribou, incorporated in 1859 as Lyndon, received its present name in 1877. Agriculture, mainly potatoes, has always been the mainstay of the local economy. Caribou has the dubious distinction of being the third-coldest and fifth-snowiest city in the United States, with an average annual temperature of 39°F and an average annual snowfall (cross-country skiers and snowmobilers, take note) of 110.4 inches.

Scenic Routes

With so much open space in the County, particularly in the Potato Triangle, drivers and bicyclists can enjoy great long vistas. One route, a favorite of Sen. Susan Collins, who ought to know, is **Route 164** between Caribou and Presque Isle, half of it along the Aroostook River. (Locals call it the Back Presque Isle Rd.; it's also the Washburn Rd. and the Caribou Rd.—just to make things totally confusing.) On the way, you can check out the museums in Washburn, detour on the multiuse trail, and visit the Woods Edge Gallery in Perham.

Another scenic drive is **Route 167,** between Presque Isle and Fort Fairfield; the 12-mile stretch is especially dramatic in mid-July, when the rolling fields are draped with pink and white potato blossoms and Fort Fairfield puts on its annual Potato Blossom Festival.

PRESQUE ISLE AREA SIGHTS

University of Maine at Presque Isle

Established in 1903 as the Aroostook State Normal School, for training teachers, the University of Maine at Presque Isle (UMPI), 181 Main St., Rte. 1, Presque Isle 04769, 207/768-9400, has more than 1,500 two- and four-year students on its 150-acre campus at the southern end of the city. The school is noted for its training in physical education and recreation. In the Campus Center is the **Reed Art Gallery,** where rotating exhibits spotlight Maine and Canadian artists. During the school year, the gallery is open Mon.–Fri. 10 AM–5 PM, Sat. 1–5 PM; the summer schedule tends to be less predictable.

Salmon Brook Historical Society Museums

Here's a worthwhile two-for-one deal, with lots of charm and character: In tiny, downtown Washburn, across from the First Baptist Church, the **Salmon Brook Historical Society,** P.O. Box 71, Washburn, 04786,

207/455-4339, operates the **Benjamin C. Wilder Homestead,** an 1852 National Historic Register farmhouse, and the **Aroostook Agricultural Museum** in the adjacent red barn. The well-restored 10-room house has period furnishings and displays; the barn contains old tools and antique cookware and pottery. The museums, on 2.5 acres at 17 Main St. (Rte. 164), are open Wed. 8–11 AM and Sun. 1–4 PM, mid-June–mid-Sept., other times by appointment. Admission is free, but donations are welcomed. Washburn is 11 miles northwest of Presque Isle and 10 miles southwest of Caribou.

Also in Washburn (next to Perham Rd., Rte. 228) is a convenient parking lot for access to the region's multiuse trail network.

CARIBOU AREA SIGHTS

Nylander Museum

If you were an eccentric, self-educated geologist and needed a place to display and store everything you'd accumulated, you'd create a place like the **Nylander Museum,** 393 Main St., P.O. Box 1062, Caribou 04736, 207/493-4209, www.nylandermuseum.com. Swedish-born Olof Olssen Nylander traveled the world collecting specimens, settled in Caribou, and bequeathed his work—including 6,000 fossils and 40,000 shells—to the city. Since his 1943 death, the museum has acquired other collections: butterflies, mounted birds, and additional geological specimens. The dinosaur displays particularly appeal to kids. A small gift shop has nature-related items. The museum is open Tues.–Sat. 12:30–4:30 PM. Admission is free, but donations are welcomed.

PARKS AND RECREATION

Presque Isle

Parks: Hiking, picnicking, swimming, fishing, and camping are among the options at 577-acre **Aroostook State Park,** State Park Rd., Presque Isle 04769, 207/768-8341, on the shores of Echo Lake. Twin-peaked **Quaggy Jo Mountain,** accessible via park trails beginning

in the camping area, juts from the landscape and provides superb views from the summit, especially North Peak. A three-mile easy-to-moderate clockwise loop starts next to campsite 18 and goes first to South Peak. Allow two or three hours. Quaggy Jo comes from the Micmac word *quaquajo,* meaning either "boundary mountain" or "twin-peaked." Canoe rentals are available; check with the ranger. Park admission is $1 adults, $0.50 children 5–11. Campsites are $12 per site per night; facilities are basic, but sites are wooded, close to Echo Lake. Canoe rentals are $2.50 an hour. To be sure of a campsite on summer weekends, call 207/287-3824 (MasterCard or Visa needed), at least two weeks ahead; two-night minimum for reservations. The park is open daily, mid-May–mid-Oct. In winter, nine miles of trails are accessible for cross-country skiing and snowmobiling. A tiny, rustic day-use lodge is open weekends in winter. The gate is 1.5 miles west of Rte. 1, five miles south of downtown Presque Isle.

Double Eagle Park, Spragueville Rd., Presque Isle 04769, featuring a replica of the helium balloon *Double Eagle II,* was the launch site of the first transatlantic balloon flight in August 1978. A three-man crew made the Presque Isle-to-France passage in less than a week. There's room here for kids to run, and the state park is nearby. The access road is the same as for the state park: just off Rte. 1, five miles south of downtown Presque Isle. (The first *solo* transatlantic balloon flight, six years later, took off from Caribou.)

Bike Rentals: Aroostook Bicycle and Sport, 690 Main St., Presque Isle 04769, 207/764-0206, rents bikes by the half-day and full day. The shop also can handle almost any bike repair. It's open all year, Mon.–Sat. 9 AM–5 PM.

Golf: The 18-hole **Presque Isle Country Club,** Parkhurst Siding Rd., P.O. Box 742, Presque Isle 04769, 207/764-0430 or 769-7431, established in 1958, was the County's first 18-hole course. Tee times usually aren't necessary. Facilities include a restaurant, driving range, cart and club rentals, and lessons. The course is open May–Oct. From downtown Presque Isle, take Rte. 163/167, Fort Fairfield Rd., east to Rte. 205, Parkhurst Siding Rd. Turn left and go about a mile to the club, on the right.

Caribou Recreation

The **Caribou Recreation Department,** 59 Bennett Dr., Caribou 04736, 207/493-4224, www.caribou.org, is an especially dynamic municipal operation with a huge variety of programs open to Caribou residents (free) and nonresidents (small charge). The office is open weekdays 8 AM–5 PM. Among the offerings are ski rentals and groomed cross-country trails at the Caribou Country Club; fitness classes; indoor walking; pickup basketball; outdoor community pool (at Teague Park, across the street from the office); children's arts and crafts classes. Many of the programs require preregistration. The department also supervises development and maintenance of the huge network of multiuse trails for biking and hiking. Pick up a free trail map and a recreation schedule at the office. (Or call in advance if you want to plan ahead.)

The prettiest and most rural section of this impressive **rails-to-trails network** begins in Washburn and ends in Stockholm, including a short stretch through the Woodland Bog. Park in downtown Washburn. Be sure to carry plenty of water. Other trails go from Caribou to Van Buren, 25 miles (about 2.5 hours one-way), and Washburn to New Sweden.

Woodland Bog Preserve: About six miles west of Caribou, Woodland Bog Preserve, a 265-acre Nature Conservancy property, is home to several rare orchid species and dozens of bird species (nearly 90 have been banded here). Mid-May–mid-July, Perham resident Richard Clark—the Conservancy's on-site steward—leads fascinating free walks through this bog (technically, a calcareous fen surrounded by a cedar swamp) as well as the 200-acre **Perham Bog Preserve.** Clark also leads walks in **Salmon Brook Lake Bog,** 1,850 acres purchased by the state under the Land for Maine's Future program. To set up a time, call him at 207/455-8359 days or 207/455-8060 evenings. Wear waterproof shoes and insect re-

pellent. Dedicated environmentalists, Richard and his wife, Susan, have donated an easement on a 135-acre parcel that connects two sections of the state's land. **Note:** These preserves have extremely fragile ecosystems, so don't even consider visiting them on your own.

Multiuse Trails: Spearheaded by the Caribou Recreation Department, several volunteer groups have worked to open up more than 70 miles of abandoned railroad beds for year-round use by bikers, hikers, snowmobilers, and cross-country skiers. The trails are mostly packed gravel, so you'll want a mountain bike. ATVs (all-terrain vehicles) also use the trails, creating a certain amount of racket, but otherwise they're great. From Caribou, you can go to Stockholm and on to Van Buren (29 miles one-way). Or start in Washburn and go to Stockholm and Van Buren (40 miles one-way). Or begin in Carson (just west of Caribou) and go to New Sweden (nine miles one-way).

Almost qualifying as an amusement park, **Goughan's Berry Farm,** Rte. 161, 872 Fort Fairfield Rd., Caribou 04736, 207/498-6565, has a bit of everything, depending on when you show up. Open March–mid-Dec., 8 AM–5 PM daily, Goughan's (pronounced GAWNS) has maple syrup in spring; pick-your-own strawberries, raspberries, and veggies (string beans and peas) in summer; buy apples and choose-your-own pumpkins in fall; and Christmas wreaths and trees in winter. Kids can feed and pet the farm animals, ride the carousel, and get delicious homemade ice cream at the dairy bar in the granary. Also in the granary is a gift shop with Maine-made goodies. The farm is three miles southeast of Caribou, on the Fort Fairfield Road (Rte. 161).

Snowmobile **rentals** are also available at **The Sled Shop,** 108 Main St., Presque Isle 04769, 207/764-2900, next to the Presque Isle Inn.

ENTERTAINMENT

Caribou and Presque Isle have plenty of movie screens. The **Hoyts Cinemas,** Aroostook Centre Mall, 830 Main St., Presque Isle 04769, 207/764-8506, have eight screens showing

Aroostook County

first-run flicks day and night, usually including at least one child-approved film. Reduced prices before 6 PM. Open all year. The **Caribou Cinema Center,** 66 Sweden St., Rte. 161, Caribou 04736, 207/493-3013, www.caribou .k12.me.us/pac/pac,html has four screens and cheaper tickets, but only evening shows. It's also open all year.

Throughout the year, concerts, plays, and other live events occur at the 800-seat **Caribou Performing Arts Center,** Caribou High School, 410 Sweden St., Rte. 161, Caribou 04736, 207/493-4278. Check the newspapers or ask at the Caribou Chamber of Commerce.

SHOPPING

The major shopping destination in the Presque Isle-Caribou area is Presque Isle's Aroostook Centre Mall, but both cities have other shops worth patronizing.

Presque Isle

On the banks of the Aroostook River, the 40-store **Aroostook Centre Mall,** 830 Main St., Rte. 1, Presque Isle 04769, 207/764-2616, has several of the usual suspects: Sears, J.C. Penney, Porteous; plus book and card shops, shoe stores, a food court with a good restaurant, and an eight-screen cineplex. Amenities include an ATM machine, public restrooms, and free use of strollers and wheelchairs. This largest mall north of Bangor is open Mon.–Sat. 9:30 AM–9 PM, Sun. noon–5 PM.

The Aroostook Centre Mall is also the location of the **Presque Isle Farmers Market,** biggest farmers market in the County. A good-size crowd of vendors sets up shop every Sat., 9 AM–2 PM, mid-May–mid-Oct.

Caribou Area

Tucked away in downtown Caribou, **Quickprint,** 112 Sweden St., Caribou 04736, 207/493-4430, exhibits and sells the work of a broad spectrum of Northern Maine artists—paintings, photographs, pottery, and prints. The shop also offers T-shirt printing and other

graphic-design services. Located in a building called the Sweden Street Mall, it's open all year, Mon.–Fri. 8 AM–5 PM. There's also a branch on Main St. in Presque Isle.

About 11 miles west of Caribou, the **Woods Edge Gallery,** High Meadow Rd., P.O. Box 77, Perham 04766, 207/455-8359 or 455-8060, devotes almost a thousand feet of exhibit space to watercolor and acrylic landscapes, plus photography—most by Aroostook County artists. Located 1.25 miles west of Rte. 228, the gallery is open all year, Tues.–Sat. 1–5 PM. Gallery owner Richard Clark, steward for The Nature Conservancy's nearby Woodland Bog, also leads seasonal nature tours there.

ACCOMMODATIONS
Hotels and Motels

University professors, snowmobilers, and traveling salespeople all gravitate to the 151-room **Presque Isle Inn and Convention Center,** Rte. 1, P.O. Box 270, Presque Isle 04769, 207/764-3321 or 800/533-3971, www.presqueisleinn.com, atop a hill overlooking Presque Isle and beyond. Decor is motel-modern. Amenities include a health club, indoor pool, on-site coin laundry, and cable TV. The bar is a popular local rendezvous spot, and there's live entertainment weekends in the lounge. The motel, under the same ownership as the Caribou Inn and Convention Center, www.caribouinn.com, is close to the University of Maine's Presque Isle campus. In winter, when the parking lot has more snowmobiles than cars, don't even think about arriving sans reservation. Pets are welcome.

Patronized primarily for its convenient downtown site, **The Northeastland Hotel,** 436 Main St., Presque Isle 04769, 207/768-5321 or 800/244-5321 in Maine, www.mainerec.com/eastland.shtml., caters to business travelers but also offers good value for families, with inexpensive meals available on the premises. Fifty large, modern rooms with air-conditioning, TVs, and phones, are $58–85 d. No pets; children 12 and under stay free. Open all year. Located here since 1934, the two-story Northeastland is a central Aroostook tradition; the informal restaurant is a popular local breakfast and lunch spot.

The best all-around lodging in the area, the two-story **Caribou Inn and Convention Center,** Rte. 1, RFD 3, Box 25, Caribou 04736, 207/498-3733, fax 498-3149, has 73 large, comfortable rooms and suites with air-conditioning, cable TV, and refrigerators (suites have kitchenettes). Pool and health-club facilities, free to guests, are open 17 hours daily. (Request a room away from the pool area.) Rooms are $64–118 d; children 12 and under stay free. The attractive **Greenhouse Restaurant** serves breakfast, lunch, and dinner daily; dinner entrées are $11–16. Turkey with all the trimmings is served every Sunday. As with their sister inn in Presque Isle, snowmobilers end up here, so be sure to reserve well in advance in winter. The Caribou Inn is three miles south of downtown Caribou, junction of Rtes. 1 and 164.

Bed-and-Breakfasts

Art professor Clifton Boudman and his wife Judith put out an unforgettable spread—a Scottish breakfast—when you stay at the **Rum Rapids Inn,** Rte. 164, Rum Rapids Dr., Crouseville 04738, 207/455-8096, www.rumrapidsinn.com, a beautifully furnished 1839 house. By prior arrangement, he'll also produce an elegant multicourse candlelight dinner (extra charge; BYOL), served at 7 PM. Specialties include baked trout Italiano, grilled and limed steak, and penne Medici. In summer, relax on the deck overlooking Rum Rapids; in winter, cross-country ski on the Boudmans' 15 acres. Guests have free use of bikes, cross-country skis, and tennis rackets. Two rooms (private baths) are $89 d. No smoking, no pets; one room suits children. Open all year. The inn is five miles northwest of Presque Isle; watch for a tiny sign on the left.

Close to downtown Caribou, the **Old Iron Inn B&B,** 155 High St., Caribou 04736, 207/492-4766, www.oldironinn.com, comes by its name honestly. Hundreds of antique irons are displayed through this turn-of-the-20th-century house, and geology professor

Kevin McCartney can recount the background of each one. Four rooms ($45–59 d; two rooms have private baths) are comfortably furnished with quilts and antiques. Guests can use the office and fax machine or browse through the McCartneys' book and magazine collection. No smoking, no small children, no pets. Known for her culinary talent, Kate McCartney serves a delicious breakfast in the Victorian dining room. Open all year.

Campgrounds

Camping can be found at Aroostook State Park. For details see *Presque Isle* under *Parks and Recreation,* above.

FOOD

Presque Isle

Where can you get an $18 bowl of gourmet lobster stew in February? At **Winnie's Restaurant and Dairy Bar,** 79 Parsons St., Presque Isle 04769, 207/769-4971. The restaurant's delicious lobster stew became so famous for being "the real thing" (no fillers) that owner Patty Leblanc made it into a business of its own in 1999 (Winnie was the first owner, in the 1940s), but the stew is still served here. Also known for its Winnie's burgers, this is a super-casual, call-your-number kind of place, with food served in plastic containers. It's always thronged with locals; in winter, snowmobilers arrive en masse, so be prepared to wait. Winnie's is open all year, 10:30 AM–9 PM daily.

Also popular is the **Riverside Inn Restaurant,** 399 Main St., Presque Isle 04769, 207/764-1447, a small place with zero ambience but reliable, inexpensive food. Located in downtown Presque Isle, close to Riverside Park and set back from the street, the restaurant is open all year, Mon.–Sat. 5 AM–10 PM, Sun. 6 AM–10 PM.

For a taste of the Southwest, go directly to **Ruby Tuesday,** 830 Main St., Aroostook Centre Mall, Presque Isle 04769, 207/764-2874, where specialties are steaks, ribs, fajitas, and more ($7–15). As the name (after a Rolling Stones song) suggests, it's a popular spot. Reservations are advisable on weekends. Open all year, Sun.–Thurs. 11 AM–10 PM, Fri.–Sat. 11 AM–11 PM. Ruby Tuesday is near the Kmart-and cinema-end of the mall.

Caribou

An extremely loyal clientele makes unpretentious **Frederick's Southside,** 217 S. Main St., Caribou 04736, 207/498-3464, busy most of the time. Inexpensive home cooking is the draw. It's open all year, Mon.–Sat. 5 AM–8 PM, Sun. 6:30 AM–8 PM.

(See *Accommodations* for a description of the Greenhouse Restaurant at the Caribou Motor Inn.)

INFORMATION AND SERVICES

Presque Isle, Caribou, and Fort Fairfield all have their own chambers of commerce. The **Presque Isle Area Chamber of Commerce,** 3 Houlton Rd., Rte. 1, P.O. Box 672, Presque Isle 04769, 207/764-6561 or 800/764-7420, www .pichamber.com, on the southern outskirts of the city, is open Mon.–Fri. 8 AM–5 PM; it may be closed 12:30–1:30 PM for lunch. On weekends and after hours, brochures and maps are available at the Aroostook Centre Mall, 830 Main St., Rte. 1, Presque Isle. The **Caribou Chamber of Commerce,** 111 High St., P.O. Box 357, Caribou 04736, 207/498-6156 or 800/722-7648, www.caribouchamber.com, with an especially helpful staff, is open Mon.–Fri. 8:30 AM–4:30 PM. The office is close to downtown Caribou. Hardest to find is the **Fort Fairfield Chamber of Commerce** 121 Main St., P.O. Box 607, Fort Fairfield 04742, 207/472-3802, in a poorly signposted second-floor office in the municipal complex along the main drag. It's open weekdays 8 AM–5 PM, all year. The **Caribou Public Library,** 30 High St., Caribou 04736, 207/493-4214, is open Mon.–Fri. noon–6 PM, Sat. 10 AM–4 PM in winter; summer hours (June–Aug.) are Mon.–Fri. noon–8 PM.

Emergencies

In **Presque Isle** and **Caribou,** call 911 for emergency police, fire, and ambulance services. The nearest state police barracks is in Houlton (800/924-2261).

Aroostook County's largest hospital is **A.R. Gould Memorial Hospital,** a division of The Aroostook Medical Center, 140 Academy St., Rte. 10, Presque Isle 04769, emergency room 207/768-4100, with round-the-clock emergency-room care. The **Cary Medical Center,** 163 Van Buren Rd., Caribou 04736, 207/498-1234, has medical staff on call round the clock and a daily walk-in clinic.

Newspapers

Presque Isle's hometown paper is *The Star-Herald,* 207/768-5431, published every Wednesday; Caribou's paper, under the same ownership, is the *Aroostook Republican and News,* 207/496-3251, also published Wednesday. Both carry local calendar listings. The *Bangor Daily News* is the daily paper for local residents.

GETTING THERE

After losing its Pine State Airlines commuter service in early 1998, Presque Isle picked up a new service later that year. **US Airways Express/US Airways,** operates half a dozen daily nonstop flights between Boston's Logan Airport and Northern Maine Regional Airport in Presque Isle. The commuter planes have overhead storage bins, standing headroom, and complimentary beer and wine service.

New Sweden

On July 23, 1870, a determined and dynamic fellow named William Widgery Thomas, Jr., a Portland native and Bowdoin College graduate, arrived in the wilds of Aroostook County with 50 sturdy Swedish farmers and their families. This was the first wave of "a noble experiment," which grew to 600 Swedes within three years and to 1,400 in 25 years. By 1895, the New Sweden area had 689 buildings on more than 7,500 productive acres.

The inspiration for the settlement came from Thomas, who had been trained as a diplomat. After posts in Constantinople (now Istanbul) and Moldavia (present-day Moldova), he went to Sweden, where he fell right in, learning the language and marrying a Swedish woman. Returning to Maine in the late 1860s, he was asked to help reverse the state's tide of emigration, so he devised a unique plan to encourage Swedish farmers to come to a wilderness not unlike their own land. After three or four years of wheedling, Thomas won approval, cornered enough acreage, and sailed for Sweden to deliver his sales pitch. Within only six weeks, he had assembled his core group, and the adventure began.

It wasn't easy, and Aroostook was no paradise on earth. The families cleared the land, built log houses and churches, spun wool for clothing, and kept on keeping on, apparently undaunted by subzero temperatures, sickness, and unpredictable crops. After this feat, William Widgery Thomas became U.S. Minister to Sweden and Norway in 1883, serving for more than a dozen years. He died in 1927, but residents still honor "Father Thomas," who called those early settlers "my children in the woods."

One of the little-recognized contributions made by New Sweden's settlers was the introduction of skiing to Maine during that first winter. Nordic skiing, of course, was as natural as breathing for the Swedes, and the town even had something of a ski jump on Ringdahl Hill.

Today, Swedish culture survives among the thousand or so residents of the towns of New Sweden and Stockholm and the hamlet of Westmanland. The phone book lists dozens of Thomases, plus plenty of Soderbergs, Nelsons, Carlsons, Petersons, and Andersons—all blended in among the Franco-Americans and Yankees who earlier had settled this area.

Sights

New Sweden is eight miles northwest of downtown Caribou, via Rte. 161. At the **New Sweden Historical Museum,** Capitol Hill and Station Rds., New Sweden 04762, 207/896-3018, www.geocities.com/maineswedishcolony, three floors of memorabilia reflect the rugged life in this frontier community. An exact replica of the colony's "Kapitoleum" (capitol), the museum was built in 1971 after fire leveled the original structure. Check out the museum's guestbook: Visitors have come from all over Scandinavia to see this cultural enclave. The museum, 0.5 mile north and east of Rte. 161, is open Memorial Day weekend–mid-Sept., daily 1–4 PM, Admission is free, but donations are welcome. Next door, in the **Capitol Hill School,** a gift shop carries Swedish items. Out back is a monument with the list of the original settlers.

Continuing east on Station Road, you'll pass **W.W. Thomas Memorial Park** on the left, a great spot for a picnic, with a play area for kids and a dramatic vista over the rolling countryside. Concerts occur periodically in the bandshell. About 0.2 mile farther, also on the left, is the shingled **Lars Noak Blacksmith and Woodworking Shop,** another remnant of the early settlers.

A fun time to visit New Sweden is during the **Midsommar** festival, on the closest weekend to Midsummer Day (June 21), when residents don traditional Swedish costumes and celebrate the year's longest day. Activities include decoration of a Maypole, Swedish dancing, a smorgasbord, concerts, and a prayer service.

Non-Scandinavians are welcome to join in, but you'll need to plan way ahead; the smorgasbord (two seatings, 4:30 and 6 PM) is usually sold out by mid-May. New Sweden has no accommodations, but Caribou is only eight miles away. Information on the festival is available from the Caribou Chamber of Commerce or the New Sweden Town Office, 207/869-3306, www.caribou.net.

Continuing on Rte. 161 will get you to Fort Kent and the rest of the St. John Valley, but unless time demands the shortcut, you'll see more of "the Valley" by taking Rte. 1 north to Van Buren from Caribou.

So turn back toward New Sweden and make a 1.5-mile detour to Stockholm, where you'll find **Eureka Hall Restaurant,** School and Main Sts., 207/896-3196, in an old Grange Hall–type building. The place has real character—old signs, tons of kitschy collectibles, padded metal chairs, metal tables, a counter and room for about two dozen diners. Then comes the menu—entrées such as shrimp linguini, chicken marsala, char-broiled Atlantic salmon, and the excellent Stockholm Skewer (shrimp-and-scallop kebabs). They claim to serve "home-style cooking," but it's better than most homes we know. Entrée price range is $10–14, and there's even Linzertorte ($2) for dessert. The restaurant has a full liquor license. Reservations are essential on weekends; the secret is out. Eureka Hall is open Thurs.–Sat., 4:30–8 PM, 9 AM–2 PM, breakfast only Sun. Be sure to call ahead to confirm in any case, as there's not much else around here.

Information

The best place in town for general information is the museum, Capitol Hill and Station Rds., New Sweden, where you can pick up a map and a New Sweden brochure. Or try the New Sweden Town Office on Station Rd.

The St. John Valley

Plan to visit The Upper St. John River Valley from east to west, counterclockwise, from Van Buren to Fort Kent, and perhaps on to Allagash, giving yourself a buildup to this unique cultural region settled by Acadians in 1785.

Van Buren calls itself "The Gateway to the St. John River Valley," and you begin to notice here the change of cultural pace. Valley hallmarks are huge Roman Catholic churches, small riverside communities, unfancy but tidy homes, an eclectic French patois, and a handful of unique culinary specialties—all thanks to a twist of fate.

Henry Wadsworth Longfellow's immortal epic poem *Evangeline* relates a saga of *le grand dérangement,* when more than 10,000 French-speaking Acadians tragically lost their lease on Nova Scotia after the British expelled them for disloyalty in 1755—a date engraved ever since in the minds of their thousands of descendants now living on the American and Canadian sides of the St. John River. (Thousands more of their kin ended up in Louisi-ana, where Acadian—Cajun—traditions also remain strong.)

In this part of Maine, Smiths and Joneses are few- countless residents bear such names as Cyr, Daigle, Gagnon, Michaud, Ouellette, Pelletier, Sirois, and Thibodeau. In Van Buren, Grand Isle, Madawaska, St. Agatha, and Frenchville, French is the mother tongue for 97 percent of the residents, who refer to the Upper St. John Valley as *chez nous* ("our house"), their homeland. Many roadside and shop signs are bilingual—even the nameboard for the University of Maine branch in Fort Kent.

Religion is as pervasive an influence as language. When a Madawaska beauty represented Maine in the Miss America contest in 1995, the local *St. John Valley Times* admonished its readers: "Keep your fingers crossed and your rosaries hot."

Since the 1970s, renewed local interest in and appreciation for Acadian culture has spurred cultural projects, celebrations, and genealogical research throughout the valley,

Aroostook County

with the eventual goal of a National Park Service Acadian culture center. "Valley French," a unique, archaic patois long stigmatized in Maine schools, has undergone a revival. Since the 1970s, several valley schools have established bilingual programs, and a 1991 survey estimated that 40 percent of valley schoolchildren speak both English and French.

Controversy erupts periodically over whose lineage is "true" Acadian (as opposed to Quebecois—although many Acadians also fled to Quebec), but Valley residents all turn out en masse for the summer highlight: Madawaska's multiday Acadian Festival, centered on Acadian Day, June 28. It's a local festival unlike any other in Maine.

Between Madawaska and Fort Kent, detour off Rte. 1 into the lovely lake district—locally known as the "back settlements"—through the town of St. Agatha and the village of Sinclair, on Rte. 162, entering Fort Kent on Rte. 161 from the southeast. Better still, after reaching the end of Rte. 162, turn northwest onto Rte. 161 and meander through the back roads off to the east and north before landing in Fort Kent. (Use Map 68 in the DeLorme *Maine Atlas and Gazetteer*.)

West of Fort Kent are the tiny and tinier riverside communities of St. John, St. Francis, Allagash, and Dickey, the latter two serving as endpoints for two of Maine's most popular long-distance canoe routes: the St. John River and the Allagash Wilderness Waterway.

Heading out of Aroostook County, via Rte. 11 south from Fort Kent, be prepared for stunning scenery and lakes, ponds, and rivers off to the right and left.

VAN BUREN

Twenty-five miles north of Caribou, Van Buren, www.vanburenmaine.com, town hall 207/868-2222, isn't the end of Rte. 1; the highway takes a sharp turn and follows the St. John River to Fort Kent, terminus of the long, long road running from Florida to Maine. Named after President Martin Van Buren, the town of Van Buren (pop. about 2,660) has lovely,

long views but a not-too-promising short-term outlook. Unemployment is high, and many youngsters escape soon after high school (if not before). Life isn't easy on this frontier.

In the hamlet of Keegan, about two miles northwest of downtown Van Buren, is a prominent reminder of the heritage in this valley—Acadian settlement in 1785. Begun as a small-scale bicentennial project in 1976, the **Acadian Village,** Rte. 1, Van Buren 04785, 207/868-5042, www.themainelink.com/Acadian village, is a 2.5-acre open-air museum comprising 16 antique and replica buildings in an A-shaped layout. Included are a country store, forge, schoolhouse, chapel, and several residences. Tours by attentive guides vividly convey the daily struggles for 18th- and 19th-century Acadians in the valley. Kids particularly enjoy the schoolhouse and the barbershop; outside, there's plenty of letting-off-steam room. Admission is $3.50 adults, $1.50 children. The museum is open daily noon–5 PM, mid-June–mid-Sept.

GRAND ISLE AND LILLE

As with the other religion-dominated communities in the valley, the most prominent landmark in Grand Isle (pop. 569), is the Catholic church, a twin-towered building undergoing long-term restoration as a nonprofit bilingual museum/cultural center: **Le Musée et Centre Culturel du Mont-Carmel.** Built in 1909 in the section of town known as Lille, Our Lady of Mount Carmel Church had its first Mass in 1910 and its last in 1978. Since historian/preservationist/Renaissance man Don Cyr took over the wooden church in 1984, he's organized concerts and other events under the aegis of l'Association Culturelle et Historique du Mont-Carmel. Each Labor Day weekend, the center sponsors the **Lille Classical Impressionist Music Festival.** The church is open early June–mid-Sept., noon–4 PM. Sun.–Fri. For information on the project, or the festival, contact Cyr, 207/895-3339, or the **Greater Madawaska Chamber of Commerce,** 378 Main St., Rte. 1, Madawaska 04756, 207/728-7000.

About four miles farther northwest on Rte. 1, on the Grand Isle-Madawaska town line, you'll come to the state-run **Mount Carmel Rest Area,** with picnic tables and an outhouse. If you've brought the fixings, it's a good spot for a picnic. Across the road is a monument to Acadian pioneers.

MADAWASKA

Bounced back and forth in a U.S.–Canada border dispute, Madawaska (pop. 4,565) finally was incorporated with its present boundaries in 1869. The name allegedly is Micmac, "where one river runs into another"; the Madawaska and St. John Rivers meet here.

Fort Kent may be the head of the valley, the site of the official Acadian Archives, but Madawaska is its heart. You'll understand why if you arrive for the annual **Acadian Festival.** Each year, Maine's governor recognizes June 28 as **Acadian Day,** so the heritage celebration always wraps around this date, generally for a week. The festival includes mountain bike races, a pageant, entertainment, boat rides, pie bake-off, wagon rides, barbecue, parade, and fireworks. Acadian specialties like *ployes* (buckwheat cakes) are a highlight. Most of the events occur on Main St., Rte. 1. Plan ahead if you want to be there, though; the festival fills lodgings throughout the valley.

As you reach the eastern edge of Madawaska, you can't help but notice the bell tower of the imposing brick **St. David Catholic Church,** established in 1871 and still holding services in French. The National Historic Register building, usually open, has a high arched ceiling, a domed altar, and stained-glass windows.

Just to the right (east) of St. David's is the one-room **Tante Blanche Museum,** Rte. 1, St. David Parish, Madawaska 04756, 207/728-4518, containing Acadian artifacts. Run by the **Madawaska Historical Society,** P.O. Box 258, Madawaska 04756, the log museum commemorates **Marguerite Blanche Thibodeau Cyr** ("Tante Blanche"), an Acadian heroine during a 1797 famine. The museum usually is open June 10–Aug. 10, Mon.–Fri. 10 AM–3 PM,

Sun. 1–3 PM. Next door to the museum, kids enjoy the hands-on exhibits in **School House #1.** Beside the museum (to the right), take the 0.5-mile gravel road leading down to the shore, where a 14-foot-high marble cross marks the reputed 1785 landing spot of Acadians expelled by the British from Nova Scotia and New Brunswick. An Acadian flag flies here, near memorials to the original settlers.

In downtown Madawaska, **Fraser Paper Ltd.,** 25 Bridge St., Madawaska 04756, 207/728-8200, is the only American plant in Canada's Fraser Paper network. French is as common as English among the 1,100 or so employees, who each day produce 1,200 tons of paper. Knowledgeable staff members conduct free, hour-long factory tours. You have to don a hard hat and earplugs, so the machinery noise can drown out the narrative, but it's worth it to see the operation. No children under 12, no open-toed shoes. Tour hours are weekdays 9 AM–4 PM, all year, but avoid arriving near the end of the day. You don't need a reservation, but you might have to wait a few minutes.

Madawaska is a major border crossing to New Brunswick—one of only three in the St. John Valley—so the two-lane bridge to Edmundston (on Bridge St., of course) gets incredibly backed up, especially during papermill shift changes. If you go across, be sure to carry proper identification (photo ID for U.S. citizens, passport and Canadian visa for non–U.S. citizens). The **U.S. Customs office** in Madawaska, 207/728-4376, is open round-the-clock. Remember, also, that New Brunswick is on Atlantic time, an hour later than eastern time.

Fine dining isn't Madawaska's strong suit, but you won't starve. A good café, plus four pizzerias and several fast-food outlets will take care of that. Michael Corbin's **Café de la Place,** 594 Main St., Madawaska 04756, 207/728-0944, is a cheerful little place open for breakfast (homemade muffins) and lunch (superb homemade soups, salads, and sandwiches) Mon.–Fri. 4:30 AM–2 PM. Prices are all under $10. If the weather's good, sit at one of the deck's umbrella-topped tables. If only they served dinner.

The **Greater Madawaska Chamber of Commerce,** 378 Main St., Rte. 1, Madawaska 04756, 207/728-7000, between N. 6th and N. 7th Aves., is open weekdays 9 AM–5 PM. The *St. John Valley Times,* 207/728-3336, published every Wed. in Madawaska, provides local coverage for the area.

FRENCHVILLE

Eleven miles roughly west of Madawaska, on Rte. 1 North, you'll find Frenchville (pop. about 1,300). If you arrive in time for lunch or dinner, stop in at **Rosette's Restaurant,** 240 Main St., Rte. 1, Frenchville 04745, 207/543-7759, a Valley favorite. Everything's homemade, prices are very reasonable, and the color is local. Rosette's is open Tues.–Sun. 7 AM–9 PM, all year.

Headquartered at Frenchville's Northern Aroostook Regional Airport is **Valley Air** 74 Airport Ave., P.O. Box 88, Frenchville 04745, 207/543-6300 operates on-demand **sightseeing flights.** Fall-foliage flights are the most spectacular, but summer trips run a close second, and they'll even do night flights over the valley. The one-hour **Fish River Chain** flight makes a clockwise circuit over Long Lake, Square Lake, and Eagle Lake; watch for moose on this route. The **Valley and Allagash Run,** lasting about 70 minutes, follows the St. John from east to west, Madawaska to Allagash and back. A 20-minute fall-foliage flight is $12 pp (minimum three people). Valley Air is open 8:30 AM–5 PM Mon.–Fri., weekends 10 AM–4 PM. The airport is about three miles east of Rte. 1.

ST. AGATHA

From Rte. 1 in Frenchville, instead of continuing directly to Fort Kent, take the long, scenic route by detouring first down Rte. 162 to the town of St. Agatha (often pronounced the French way—"Saint a-GAHT"), on Long Lake, about 4.5 miles from Rte. 1. T-shaped **Long Lake** is the northernmost of the Fish River Chain of Lakes, extending southwest to Eagle Lake.

Across the lake is an overnight option, the **Long Lake Motor Inn,** Rte. 162, St. Agatha 04772, 207/543-5006, Ken and Arlene Lerman's clean, modern motel. All 18 rooms have phones and cable TV; 11 rooms have lake views (and great sunrises). Continental breakfast is included. Rates run $54 d in winter, less in summer. If you're here in winter, reserve well ahead or the snowmobilers will beat you to it. Open all year.

When it's time for a meal, head up the hill for the best panorama in town, at **The Lakeview Restaurant,** 7 Lakeview Dr., St. Agatha 04772, 207/543-6331. An awning-covered deck overlooks Long Lake; indoor booths and tables have plenty of visibility. Reasonably priced steak and seafood ($8–19) are dinner specialties. The restaurant is open all year, daily 11 AM–1 AM. A big surge occurs on Saturday after 5 PM mass lets out, so don't plan to eat early; Lakeview doesn't take reservations. They've now added an 80-site campground to their empire; most guests are in RVs. Sites are $17–22; open mid-May–Sept. To reach the Lakeview, take Rte. 162 to Flat Mountain Rd., then to Lakeview Dr. It's well signposted.

For something a little different, the best view in the village of **Sinclair,** about six miles down the road from St. Agatha, is at the **Long Lake Sporting Club Resort,** Rte. 162, Sinclair 04779, 207/543-7584 or 800/431-7584. In the middle of nowhere, this informal place is almost always crowded. In summer, guests come by boat or car, occasionally by floatplane; in winter, they arrive by snowmobile. The deck has a fabulous view over Long Lake. Huge steaks and giant lobsters are specialties, and all meals come with *ployes,* Acadian buckwheat pancakes typically served with an artery-clogging paté called *creton.* Settle in the lounge, choose from six entrées ($10–19, except lobster), and they'll usher you to your table when it's all ready. Open Mon.–Sat. 5–9 PM, Sun. noon–8 PM July–Aug.; Tues.–Sat. 5–9 PM, Sun. noon–8 PM the rest of the year. If you're ready to party, there's live music Saturday night, but be prepared for plenty of noise.

For **picnicking, swimming, and canoeing** in the St. Agatha area, head for **Birch Point Beach,** Chapel Rd., St. David, on the east side of Long Lake. The turnoff to the beach (at St. Michael's Chapel), is 1.3 miles south of the Auberge du Lac B&B. There's a small grassy area, plus picnic tables, and the lake views are fantastic.

Less than a mile south of the Birch Point Beach turnoff is the nine-hole **Birch Point Country Club,** Birch Point Rd., St. David 04773, 207/895-6957. Ultra-casual, it's a perfect place for amateur golfers out for exercise and fun; no starting times are needed. The ninth hole has the distinction of being New England's northernmost golfing hole. The clubhouse has a bar and basic menu; cart rentals are available. The course is open May–mid-Oct.

On the western shore of Long Lake, Rte. 162 in St. Agatha, is a lovely picnic and recreation area, plus a boat launch.

Fort Kent

In the middle of downtown Fort Kent, close to the bridge to Canada, is an almost offhand roadside sign with an impressive message: This Site Marks the Northern Terminus of Historic U.S. Rte. 1 Originating in Key West, Florida. You're 318 miles north of Portland, 368 miles north of the New Hampshire border at Kittery, and 2,209 miles north of Key West.

Fort Kent (pop. 4,120) was incorporated in 1869, after the dust settled from the 1839 Aroostook War. Named for Edward Kent, Maine governor at the time of the border skirmish, the town is the largest in the St. John Valley, occupying a strategic and attractive site on the southern banks of the St. John River, just across from Clair, New Brunswick.

SIGHTS
Fort Kent Blockhouse
Built in 1839 during the decades-long U.S.–Canada border dispute known as the Aroostook War, the National Historic Register Fort Kent Blockhouse, Blockhouse Rd., Fort Kent 04743, is the only remnant of a complex that once included barracks, a hospital, and an ammunition hoard. On the second floor are historic artifacts—unfortunately, not well labeled—plus information about the curious "bloodless" border skirmish over timber rights. Bring a picnic and commandeer a table in the pretty little riverside park just below the fort. Early in the summer, before the river dwindles,

© KATHLEEN M. BRANDES

Fort Kent Blockhouse

you can also launch a canoe or kayak here. The Fort Kent Boy Scouts, 207/834-3866, maintain and staff the blockhouse and the nearby log-cabin gift shop, which are open daily 9 AM to 7 PM, Memorial Day weekend to Labor Day. Admission is free.

Fish River Falls
Getting to Fish River Falls is an adventure in itself. Not a sign in sight—perhaps deliberately.

Aroostook County

The optimum situation is having a local person lead you there. Otherwise, check with the chamber of commerce office. It's very near Bouchard Farm (where they grow acres of buckwheat for *ploys*), and you can also ask for directions there. The falls are a 10-minute stroll slightly downhill once you get to the parking area. Carry a picnic and sit on the rocks, which have great wells formed by the grinding of boulders. It's a lovely setting, worth seeking out.

University of Maine at Fort Kent

Founded in 1878 as a teacher-training school, the University of Maine at Fort Kent (UMFK) 25 Pleasant St., Fort Kent 04743, 207/834-

7500, still prides itself on the quality of its teacher-education program. Because of its location in the Upper St. John Valley, UMFK also offers a B.S. degree in bilingual/bicultural studies, and the school's **Acadian Archives,** 207/834-7535, are the state's best resource on Maine's Acadian heritage. The campus, just off Rte. 1, has a bucolic feel.

RECREATION

The Bangor & Aroostook Railroad line runs right through the first and ninth holes at the **Fort Kent Golf Club,** St. John Rd., Rte. 161, Fort Kent 04743, 207/834-3149, but that never seems to bother anyone. The meticulously groomed, hilly course has dynamite views of the St. John River. Call for a tee time on weekends; cart rentals are available. The attractive clubhouse has a bar and light meals. The club, three miles west of town (toward Allagash), is open May–Oct.

Fort Kent's chamber of commerce can dispense information on guided or do-it-yourself **fishing and canoeing** trips, as well as offer **snowmobiling** advice in winter. **Cross-country skiing** has picked up in recent years; the chamber office has information on trails in the area.

FOOD

The best place to eat in Fort Kent is **River House Restaurant,** 315 W. Main St., Rte. 1, Fort Kent 04743, 207/834-5266, a bright, friendly, family-run operation with creative nightly specials, steaks, pizzas, burgers, a handful of Italian entrées, and first-rate prime ribs ($9–18). The only Acadian menu item is *poutine,* a cholesterol-loaded pile of French fries topped with gravy and cheese. It has a limited wine list but a full liquor license. On weekends, reservations are a good idea. Open all year, Tues.–Fri. 11 AM–9 PM, Sat. 3–10 PM, and Sun. 9 AM–9 PM.

MAINE'S IDITAROD

The **Can Am Crown International Sled Dog Races,** www.can-am.sjv.net, are a multi-sight, multi-sound experience for spectators as well as participants. Maine's version of the Iditarod, the Can Am 30, Can Am 60, and Can Am 250 (two or three days, 250 miles) races are held in late February or early March. Several dozen teams sign on for the three different races, which start on Fort Kent's Main St. (The Can Am 250 also ends there.) Thousands of people line Main St. for the race starts. The Greater Fort Kent Area Chamber of Commerce provides maps showing a half-dozen spectator vantage points. Nonparticipants are welcome at the two mushers' awards banquets.

Children, in particular, are not allowed near the sled dogs, but race organizers set aside a special petting area with kid-friendly huskies and mushing gear.

As with Madawaska's Acadian Festival, you'll have to book lodgings well ahead if you want to get in on the action. In March, you're competing for beds with snowmobilers, so don't wait till the last minute. And don't forget to bring far more warm clothing than you think you'll ever need.

INFORMATION AND SERVICES

The **Greater Fort Kent Area Chamber of Commerce,** 76 W. Main St., Rte. 1, P.O. Box 430, Fort Kent 04743, 207/834-5354 or 800/733-3563, www.fortkentchamber.com, serves as a clearinghouse for much of the Upper St. John Valley. The downtown office is open weekdays 9 AM–5 PM. On weekends, stop in at the log cabin near the Fort Kent Blockhouse, where area brochures and maps are available.

Customs note: Carry proper identification (passport or photo ID) if you plan to cross into Canada at Fort Kent. The **U.S. Customs** office here, 207/834-5255, is open round-the-clock. Remember that New Brunswick is on Atlantic time, an hour later than eastern time.

The **Northern Maine Medical Center,** 143 E. Main St., Rte. 1, Fort Kent 04743, 207/834-3155, has round-the-clock emergency-room care.

South from the Peak of the Crown

FORT KENT TO ALLAGASH

It's 30 miles from Fort Kent southwest to Dickey (just west of Allagash)—a scenic riverside drive or pedal on Rte. 161. The first 20-mile stretch is comfortably level; beyond St. Francis, it becomes more winding and hilly. Pack up a picnic, allow a couple of hours, and head out. In mid-September, one of the best times to be here, the hills on your left are a riot of color, all the way to Allagash. On your right, the river usually dribbles along this time of year, exposing gravel bars much of the way. A far cry from late winter and spring, when ice jams and spring runoff are the rule.

St. Francis (pop. 636) is a good spot for a lunch break; the rest area here, overlooking the river, has covered picnic tables, grills, a pit toilet, and a boat-launching ramp. If you're up for an easy, 40-mile bike ride, pedal here from Fort Kent, stop for lunch, and return.

Twenty-three miles from Fort Kent, you'll see the **Welcome to Allagash** sign, announcing a tiny town (about 315 residents) and a legendary waterway (the 92-mile Allagash Wilderness Waterway). Just before the sign is a minuscule riverview rest area with a picnic table and limited parking (a steep bank prevents river access).

The town of **Allagash,** curiously enough, was settled by Irish and English immigrants, so it's not unusual to find lots of Irish surnames in this part of the valley. Contemporary author

Cathie Pelletier grew up in Allagash, called "Mattagash" in her entertaining novels of life in northern Maine. Townspeople love identifying each of the characters.

Rte. 161 ends in the hamlet of **Dickey,** best known for the frontier-style **Dickey Trading Post,** 207/398-3157, source of odds and ends, basic lunch fare, and just enough groceries to keep you going.

Allagash and St. John Canoeing

Shuttles, pickups, food, and very basic lodgings are all available in Allagash and Dickey, the endpoints for many Allagash and St. John paddlers. Information on outfitters, guides, and access appears in the *Katahdin/Moosehead Region* chapter, where these trips begin.

SOUTH ON ROUTE 11

If you took a poll among those who know, especially photographers, Rte. 11 southbound from Fort Kent to Portage probably would rank near the top as a favorite fall-foliage drive. What's so appealing along this 37-mile Scenic Highway? Brilliant colors, rolling hills, open vistas, and a smattering of lakes and ponds. It's really stunning, either by car or bike.

Eagle Lake

A good stopping point is Eagle Lake (pop. 810) www.eaglelaketown.org, about 18 miles south of Fort Kent. The official rest area, overlooking the lake, has picnic tables and plenty of parking. Many a photo has been snapped here. If it's a typically bright fall day, you'll see why: a prime hilltop with a pristine lake surrounded by multicolored foliage. Eighteen-mile-long, L-shaped Eagle Lake is a key link in the Fish River Chain of Lakes, starting at Long Lake in St. Agatha. In winter, the lake supports wall-to-wall ice-fishing shacks.

Eagle Lake's **town park,** down at lake level, has shorefront picnic tables and grills. The wind kicks up wildly at times, but on a calm day, this is a fine place to launch a canoe. From Rte. 11, turn at Old Main St. and go 0.6 mile; there's plenty of parking.

If you'd like to overnight along Route 11, opt for the immaculately maintained **Overlook Motel,** N. Main St., Rte. 11, Eagle Lake 04739, 207/444-4535, www.overlookmotel.com, with the same dramatic view as the official rest area. Opened in 1995, it's become one of Rte. 11's most popular lodgings. Rooms include three singles ($53 s), two doubles ($62 d), four efficiencies ($68), two hot-tub suites ($92 d, including free champagne). Amenities include phones, air-conditioning, cableTV, and free continental breakfast. Children 10 and under are free; pets are allowed. Even the singles have a microwave and refrigerator. In winter, snowmobilers pile in here.

Over the years, Eagle Lake has benefited heavily from being the hometown of John Martin, one of Maine's most influential politicians, who served an unprecedented ten terms as Speaker of Maine's House of Representatives. The town just really looks as though someone has been paying attention.

About eight miles south of Eagle Lake is the wooded **Hedgehog Mountain Rest Area,** trailhead for Hedgehog Mountain. It's not your most exciting climb, and the summit view is so-so, but it's easy exercise for an hour or so. The trail is just over a mile round-trip.

Portage

The end of the officially designated Scenic Highway, but not the end of the scenery, Por-

tage (pop. 422) is particularly popular as a summer playground, and many County residents have built or rented camps on the shores of Portage Lake.

Golfers may want to play a round at nine-hole **Portage Hills Country Club,** Portage 04768, 207/435-8221, where the challenges come with the rolling terrain. Starting times aren't needed; the course is open Memorial Day weekend through Labor Day.

Need a bite to eat? The dining room at **Dean's Motor Lodge,** Rte. 11, Portage 04768, 207/435-3701 or 207/435-6840, www.mainerec.com/deans, specializing in steaks and seafood, is open all year for breakfast, lunch, and dinner.

From Rte. 11, turn west at W. Cottage Rd. and go 0.5 mile to reach the Portage **town beach.** The view is fabulous and parking is ample; there are picnic tables, a grill, and a grassy "beach."

Rte. 11 in Portage provides access to **Moose Point Camps,** Fish River Lake, P.O. Box 170, Portage 04768, 207/435-6156, an idyllic spot with 10 rustic cabins on the shore of five-mile-long Fish River Lake (aka Fish Lake). Rates are $350 a week pp, AP (all meals), $75 a week for children under 12. BYOL. Motorboat rentals are $40 a day, canoes are $15 a day. In the main lodge are games, books, and a huge fireplace. Open early May–Nov. Watch for the sign on Rte. 11 and turn west. About four miles from Portage, you'll reach the Fish River Checkpoint, the toll booth for entering the logging area. Round-trip fee is $14 for non-Maine residents; seniors and kids under 15 are free. **Note:** Don't expect to be alone with the moose and other wildlife out here; logging trucks legally own the road, and they know it, so give them a wide berth.

Ashland

Considered the "Gateway to the North Maine Woods," Ashland (pop. 1,535) is the home of **North Maine Woods,** P.O. Box 421, Ashland 04732, 207/435-6213, www.northmainewoods.org, a private organization charged with managing recreational use of more than three million acres of northern Maine's working timberlands. North Maine Woods publishes maps, newsletters, and serves as an information resource for camping, fishing, hunting, hiking trails, and logging roads. Call (weekdays only) for a free packet of regulations and list of outfitters, plus an order form for maps and other publications.

The open-air **Ashland Logging Museum,** Garfield Rd., Ashland 04732, 207/435-6679, www.townofashland, has six buildings containing a blacksmith shop, old woods rigs, and other gear—a taste of what the timber industry was like. The museum is currently closed but may reopen. Just before Ashland, when Rte. 11 takes a sharp left, turn right onto Garfield Rd. and go a little less than a mile. (You'll get an even better taste of the trade at the Patten Lumberman's Museum in Patten, east of Baxter State Park.)

About 10 miles east of Ashland on Rte. 163 (Presque Isle Rd.) is the trailhead (on the left) for **Haystack Mountain,** a short, steep climb—easy to moderate—to a fairly bald summit. Pack a picnic so you can enjoy the almost-360-degree view.

Roughly midway between Ashland and Masardis, in the town of Masardis, is an access road to the boat landing for **Squa Pan Lake,** probably the oddest-shaped lake in the state. One wag alleges the name comes from a squaw who married a French man named Pan, but if you believe that, there's this bridge…

Rte. 11 continues southward and out of Aroostook County, to Patten, Medway, and Millinocket.

Aroostook County

Katahdin and Moosehead Region

Named for Maine's highest mountain and largest lake, the Katahdin/Moosehead region—covering all of Piscataquis County and the northern two-thirds of Penobscot County—typifies Maine's rugged North Woods. Within Piscataquis County are 40-mile-long Moosehead Lake, the appealing frontier town of Greenville, the headwaters of the Allagash Wilderness Waterway, and the controlled wilds of Baxter State Park.

Sport hunters and anglers have always frequented the North Woods, and they still do. But hunters, sport fishers, and back-to-the-landers increasingly have to share their untamed turf with a new generation of visitor. Sporting camps originally built for rugged anglers and hunters now welcome photographers, birders, and families; white-water rafting, canoeing, kayaking, and snowmobiling are all big business; and hikers have found nirvana in a vast network of trails—particularly the huge, carefully monitored trail system in Baxter State Park, my own favorite destination for peace, renewal, and old-fashioned vertical exercise.

In the 1970s, paper companies were forced by environmental concerns to halt the perilous river-run log drives that took their products to market. This cessation not only cleaned up the rivers, but also spared the lives of the hardy breed of men who once made a living unjamming the logs in roiling waters. The alternative now is roads, lots of them, mostly unpaved—a huge network that has opened up the area to more and more outdoors enthusiasts. (Fortunately, despite some resentment and grumbling among outdoorsfolk about user fees, the paper companies allow public recreation on their roads and lands.) These timber-company throughways are there for all to use, but never forget that the logging trucks *own* them—in more ways than one. As they barrel along, give them room—and some slack as well; you may even be glad they're there. I've been lost on some of these roads and wound up eternally grateful to loggers who have stopped to help. The *DeLorme Atlas* is essential for exploring the area, but every time the loggers begin working a new patch, they open new roads, so the cartographers can barely keep up.

The area is rich in aquatic possibilities, too. Maine's best-known, classic canoe trips follow the Allagash and St. John Rivers northward, but no one can even begin to count the other lakes, rivers, and streams that have wonderful canoeing. Among the best are Lobster, Allagash, Caucomgomoc, Ambajejus, and Chesuncook Lakes; Seboeis and Pleasant Rivers, plus the East and (upper) West Branches of the Penobscot River.

The largest town in this region is Millinocket, home to fewer than 7,000 souls (almost outnumbered by lumber trucks). Stay at one of this region's primitive forest campsites and you'll really sense the wilderness—owls hoot, loons cry, frogs croak. . . and, oh yes, insects annoy.

No matter how much civilization intrudes, it's still remote and wild. As one writer put it, "Trees grow, die, fall, and rot, never having been seen by anyone. They litter the shores of lakes, form temporary islands, block streams, and quickly eradicate paths." Don't underesti-

mate the North Woods: bring versatile clothing (more than you think you'll need), don't strike out alone without telling anyone, stock up on insect repellent and water, use a decent vehicle (4WD if possible), and carry a flashlight, maps, and a compass. Perhaps most important, be a conscientious, ecosensitive visitor.

SPORTING CAMPS

Although dozens of traditional sporting camps exist all over Maine, most of the veterans are in the Katahdin/Moosehead Region, with the Kennebec Valley and Western Mountains running a close second. Almost all are north of Bangor.

Sporting camps are unique, and so varied that it's impossible to paint them with one broad brush. They're so much more than a place to stay—they're an experience, often a throwback to the 19th century, or at least to the earlier 20th. All but a few are accessible by road, but the "road" might be a rutted, muddy tank trap, making passengers yearn for a floatplane. All are rustic, no-frills operations, some much more so than others. (If you're a frill-seeker, forget it; seek elsewhere.) Some have electricity and flush toilets; others have kerosene lanterns and private or shared outhouses. All are on or close to fresh water, meant to be convenient for fishing. Some offer American Plan rates, serving three meals a day, usually family-style; others have housekeeping facilities, where you're on your own; some let you choose.

About a third of the camps are open all year to capture the snowmobile trade, but most are open only May–Nov., opening for fishing season and closing after deer-hunting season. All but a few sporting camps sell resident and nonresident fishing and hunting licenses.

With all the logging roads crisscrossing the region, there are only a few sporting camps now inaccessible by road, but most guests opt to fly in and out. As one guide put it, "People prefer flying over dying; those

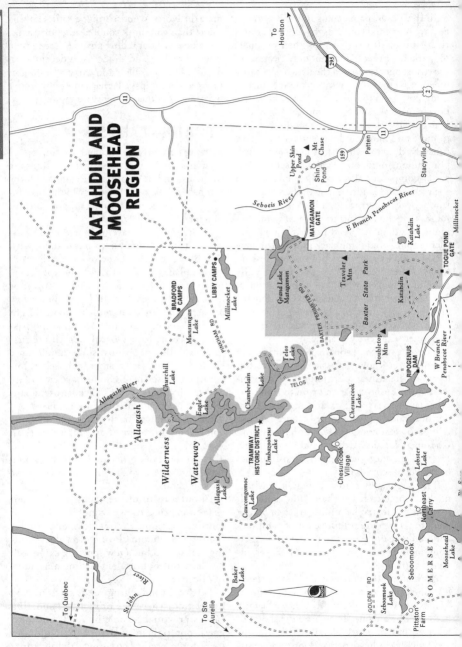

Katahdin/Moosehead

KATAHDIN AND
MOOSEHEAD
REGION

To Houlton

295

2

11

159 Patten

Stacyville

Upper Shin Pond

Mt Chase

Shin Pond

Seboeis River

MATAGAMON GATE

E Branch Penobscot River

Katahdin Lake

Millinocket

TOGUE POND GATE

BRADFORD CAMPS

LIBBY CAMPS

Munsungan Lake

Millinocket Lake

PINKHAM RD

Grand Lake Matagamon

BAXTER PERIMETER RD

Traveler Mtn

Katahdin

Baxter State Park

Doubletop Mtn

W Branch Penobscot River

RIPOGENUS DAM

Telos Lake

Churchill Lake

Allagash River

Eagle Lake

Chamberlain Lake

TELOS RD

Chesuncook Lake

Lobster Lake

Allagash

Wilderness

Waterway

TRAMWAY HISTORIC DISTRICT

Umbazooksus Lake

Chesuncook Village

Caucomgomoc Lake

Allagash Lake

Northeast Carry

Seboomook

Moosehead Lake

GOLDEN RD

SOMERSET

To Québec

St John River

Baker Lake

To Ste Aurelie

Seboomook Lake

Pittston Farm

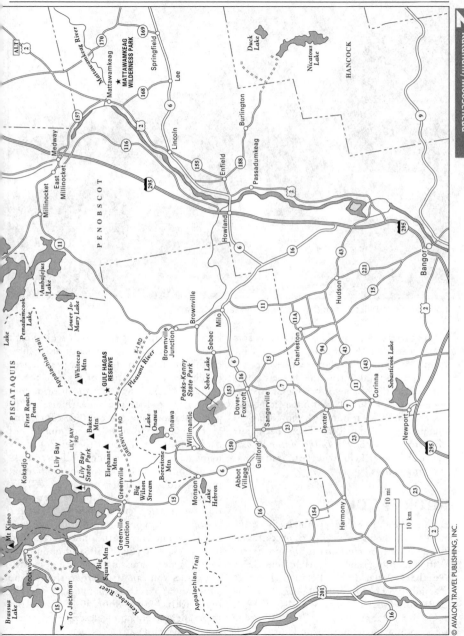

© AVALON TRAVEL PUBLISHING, INC.

Katahdin/Moosehead

© KATHLEEN M. BRANDES

Katahdin from Daicey Pond Campground, Baxter State Park

logging trucks run up and over a coupla cars every year." (See *Flightseeing,* below, for information about floatplane service.)

If all this sounds intriguing, request a brochure from the **Maine Sporting Camp Association,** P.O. Box 119, Millinocket 04462, 207/723-6622, a group with more than 50 members founded in 1987. Then check your bookstore for a copy of *In the Maine Woods,* by Alice Arlen, a helpful guide to traditional sporting camps.

INFORMATION

Besides the chambers of commerce in Millinocket, Greenville, and Dover-Foxcroft, and Baxter State Park Headquarters, regional recreational information is available from **Great Northern Paper,** Public Relations Dept., 1 Katahdin Ave., Millinocket 04462, 207/723-2229, and **North Maine Woods** (NMW), P.O. Box 425, Ashland 04732, 207/435-6213, www.northmainewoods.org. Both

have very helpful maps (small fee). North Maine Woods will send you an order form listing publications for sale as well as free brochures covering use of logging roads, campsites, and other relevant information. They also produce an eminently useful 20-page informational tabloid ($3) containing all the regulations you'll need, plus lots of useful information about the territory they manage. It lists emergency numbers, checkpoint hours, and fees for various activities. NMW also sells a hunter-orange hat ($7), required gear in the woods during deer-hunting season (late Oct.–late Nov.).

You, too, can be an information source—extra eyes and ears for the understaffed warden service. If you're out and about and spot poachers harassing, wounding, or killing game, you can assist **Operation Game Thief** and report them anonymously by calling (within Maine) 800/253-7887. Do not intervene; merely supply descriptions or any other relevant details.

Millinocket and Vicinity

Crucial to the timber industry, Millinocket (pop. 6,221) is not exactly a hot vacation spot, but since it's the closest civilization to Baxter State Park's southern entrance, most Baxter visitors find themselves here at some time or other. Food, lodging, books, auto fuel, and other essentials are all available in Millinocket, so don't be surprised to see ruddy-cheeked families chowing down at McDonald's here before heading for Baxter's wilderness.

Giant, smoke-belching stacks owned by Great Northern Paper dominate the skyline in Millinocket and adjoining East Millinocket (pop. 2,000), providing the major support for the local economy. Nearly 20 percent of the nation's newsprint comes out of these plants, built at the turn of the 20th century.

The town of Medway links I-95 with the two mill towns; just to the north on Rte. 11 are the communities of Sherman, Sherman Station, Patten, and Shin Pond, providing access to the less-used northeast entrance (Matagamon Gate) of Baxter State Park.

SIGHTS

Besides the sights described below, try to squeeze in a visit to the Webb Museum of Vintage Fashion in Island Falls, about 48 miles northeast of Millinocket—just over the border in Aroostook County. One of Maine's unique museums, it's an easy drive from Millinocket, partly via I-95.

Patten Lumbermen's Museum

About 40 miles northeast of Millinocket, 0.5 mile west of downtown Patten, and about 25 miles southeast of Baxter State Park's Matagamon Gate, is a family-oriented museum commemorating the lumberman's grueling life. The nine buildings at the open-air Patten Lumbermen's Museum, Waters Rd., Rte. 159, P.O. Box 300, Patten 04765, 207/528-2650, tell the tale of timber in the 19th and early 20th centuries: cramped quarters, hazardous equipment,

rugged terrain, nasty weather. Lots of working gear and colorful dioramas appeal to children, and there are picnic tables, a snack bar, and room to roam. The reception center has a crafts shop and restrooms. Summer highlight is the annual **beanhole bean dinner** (beans baked underground overnight), held the second Saturday in August. The museum is open Memorial Day to Columbus Day, 10 AM–4 PM: Fri.–Sun. Memorial Day–June and Sept. to closing; Tues.–Sun. in July and Aug. Admission is $7 adults, $2 kids 6–11, free for kids under six, 10 percent AAA discount.

Ambajejus Boom House

You'll need either a boat or a snowmobile to get to the Ambajejus Boom House, Ambajejus Lake, eight miles northwest of Millinocket (no), but once you get there, it's always open, and filled with incredible lumbering-era artifacts. Sign the register and jot down the weather conditions. The boom house, erected here in 1906, was used as a rest stop for 65 years by rugged river drivers, lumbermen who "boomed out" (collected with immense chains) and actually rode logs downstream to the sawmills. As many as 14 could sleep and eat here. Listed on the National Historic Register, the boom house is owned by Great Northern Paper, but the meticulous restoration of the once-derelict house has been done as a personal project by Chuck Harris, a onetime river driver. Launch your boat in Spencer Cove, near Katahdin Air Service, on the west side of the Golden Road, and paddle or motor out and around to the right, to the head of the lake. Stay close to shore, as the wind can pick up unexpectedly. (If you need a canoe, you can rent one across the road at the Big Moose Inn.)

The Golden Road

On the outskirts of Millinocket is the eastern end of The Golden Road, best-maintained logging route in the North Woods and the lifeline for the Great Northern Paper Company.

Running 96 mostly unpaved miles from here, across the top of Moosehead Lake to the Quebec border, the private wilderness road reputedly earned its name from the mega-cost ($3.2 million) of construction, completed in 1975. Red-and-white mile markers tick off the distance. Logging trucks have the right-of-way, moose frequently stray onto the road, and the scenery is captivating, and you'll need to sign in and out at paper-company checkpoints en route—not a big deal. The nonresident user fee is $8 a day per person, plus $6 a day if you're planning to camp. Bicycles, motorcycles, ATV's and horses are *not* allowed on the road. (Besides the Golden Road checkpoints, there are checkpoints at all entrances and exits for North Maine Woods territory.)

The Golden Road has seen a huge surge in use in recent years, particularly the section that leads from Baxter State Park toward Moosehead Lake. It's also the major access route for the beginning of the Allagash Wilderness Waterway as well as white-water-rafting trips on the West Branch of the Penobscot River. Even though you'll never see a traffic jam (unless a moose creates it), and the road has no visitor facilities, one driver sighted a *Bangor Daily News* vending box along the roadside. What next?

The Golden Road is the most scenic link between Millinocket and Greenville, a 71-mile trip, two-thirds unpaved. You'll exit the Golden Road after about 48 miles, then drive along Moosehead Lake's east shore to Greenville.

Flightseeing

Based at Ambajejus Lake, about eight miles northwest of Millinocket, on the road to Baxter State Park, Jimmy Strang's **Katahdin Air Service** (KAS), P.O. Box 171, Millinocket 04462, 207/723-8378 or 888/742-5527, www. katahdinair.com; email fly@katahdinair.com, provides access to wilderness locations in every direction, but even if you have no particular destination, the scenic floatplane flights are fabulous. Fall-foliage trips are beyond fabulous. Three short options, 15–30 minutes each, cost $25–40 pp (two-person minimum). You'll fly over Katahdin and the Penobscot River's West Branch, perhaps spotting moose en route. The best flight, though, is an hour-long one over Baxter State Park to the Allagash Wilderness Waterway and back along the West Branch. Cost is $75 pp (two-person minimum). Flights operate daily, late May–Oct., weather permitting.

Katahdin Air Service is also a major link in the sporting-camp network, flying guests into and out of the remote camps via floatplane. When you contact a sporting camp for rate information, be sure to request the rates for floatplane access. It won't be cheap, but it's safe and fun. For a token sporting-camp experience without an overnight, sign up for one of KAS's "fly 'n' dine" trips. For $70 pp (two-person minimum, covering meals and transport), they'll fly you into a sporting camp for dinner and take you back afterward. A delicious adventure.

PARKS AND RECREATION

Besides the recreational opportunities in the Millinocket area, the town is also the site of **Baxter State Park Headquarters,** 64 Balsam Dr., Millinocket 04462, 207/723-5140, just off Central St., Rte. 157. Day-use park visitors don't need to stop at the headquarters, since there are information centers at both park gates, but it's a convenient meeting place, close to food and shopping sites, and you'll have to come here if you're planning to drive up in January for summer camping reservations.

Mattawamkeag Wilderness Park

Talk about a well-kept secret that shouldn't be! Check out 1,000-acre, town-owned Mattawamkeag Wilderness Park, Rte. 2, P.O. Box 5, Mattawamkeag 04459, 207/736-4881 or 888/724-2465, www,mwpark.com, about an hour's drive southeast of Baxter State Park's southern gate. The park's well-managed facilities include 15 miles of trails, picnic tables, restrooms, free hot showers, recreation hall, playground, sand beach (on the Mattawamkeag River), and fishing for bass, salmon, and trout. There's also access to fine canoeing, including flat water and Class V white water, on one of northern Maine's most underutilized rivers. And you can stay the night at one of the 50 wooded campsites and 11 lean-tos. Entrance is about eight miles east of Rte. 2, on an unpaved logging road locally called "the park road"; it's signposted on Rte. 2. Admission is $2 pp, maximum $5 per car for day use. Camping fees are $11–15 per site per night; seven sites have hookups. No credit cards. The park is open daily, late May–mid-Sept.

New England Outdoor Center

Maine's biggest white-water-rafting area is around the Forks, where the Kennebec and Dead Rivers meet, in the Kennebec Valley Region, but the second-largest area is along the West Branch of the Penobscot River, near Millinocket. Class IV and V rapids named Exterminator, Bone Cruncher, and Cribwork make the Penobscot River trip a real challenge and a terrific adventure.

The primary rafting outfitter here, as well as a major player in The Forks, is the New England Outdoor Center (NEOC), Old Medway Rd., P.O. Box 669, Millinocket 04462, 207/723-5438 or 800/766-7238, www.neoc.com, based in a huge new complex on the eastern outskirts of Millinocket. NEOC's Rice Farm headquarters organizes white-water rafting on the West Branch ($79–124 pp, depending on day and month); canoeing and kayaking courses; clinics and rescue courses. No children under 16 on Penobscot trips. For lodging, NEOC has 40 campsites ($10–12 pp) and cabin tents ($24–28 pp) at its Rice Farm location and traditional sporting-camp log cabins ($155–321 per cabin) at its Twin Pine Camps on Millinocket Lake, eight miles northwest of Millinocket. Twin Pines also has a sauna and a heated indoor pool. No pets at either Rice Farm or Twin Pines. Lots of special packages are available, covering lodging, breakfasts, and dinners. The River Drivers' Restaurant at Rice Farm has a great deck overlooking the Penobscot. In winter, snowmobiling is on the agenda, with sled rentals ranging from $160–210 a day.

To reach the Rice Farm from I-95, take exit 56 and head west on Rte. 157 toward Millinocket for eight miles. After the causeway over Dolby Pond, turn left (south) and go 1.2 miles to the NEOC.

Canoeing and Kayaking

This part of Maine is a canoeist's paradise, well known as the springboard for Allagash Wilderness Waterway and St. John River trips.

Close to Millinocket, experienced canoeists and kayakers may want to attempt sections of the **East and West Branches of the Penobscot River,** but no neophyte should try them. We're talking Big Water. Refer to the *AMC River Guide* for details, or contact one of the local outfitters, such as New England Outdoor Center or Penobscot River Outfitters at Katahdin Shadows Campground.

For recorded information on the **water flow** on the West Branch of the Penobscot River, regulated by Great Lakes Hydro American, call 207/723-4341, ext. 163, Apr.–mid-Oct. The message is updated daily at 5:30 and 8 AM. The flow also affects white-water rafters, but all the rafting outfitters are tied into this communications network and already will have the latest info.

A relatively gentle, early-summer canoe trip ideal for less-experienced paddlers is on the **Seboeis River,** between the Shin Pond/Grand Lake Rd. and Whetstone Falls, about 24 miles. Even easier, and a good family trip, is the flatwater run putting in below Whetstone Falls (west of Stacyville) and taking out before Grindstone Falls. Shuttle service is available from Penobscot River Outfitters at Katahdin Shadows Campground. During the summer, try to figure out your shuttle needs a day or two in advance, as the campground is a multifaceted operation with lots of demands.

If you launch your canoe early in the day on **Sawtelle Deadwater,** near Shin Pond, west of Patten, you're bound to see moose. From Shin Pond, head northwest, crossing the Seboeis River at about six miles, then turn right onto the next unpaved road and continue less than two miles to the water. You can also reach the Deadwater off the parallel, paved Huber Road. Canoe rentals are also available at Shin Pond Village.

Hiking

The area's best hiking, hands down, is in Baxter State Park, but experienced hikers should also consider the Gulf Hagas Reserve and Borestone Mountain Sanctuary, both described in the *Dover-Foxcroft Area* section, below.

WINTER SPORTS

The north country gets socked with snow more often than not, so winter recreation provides a major boost for the local economy. Among the winter sports in the Millinocket area are snowmobiling, snowshoeing, cross-country skiing, and ice fishing. To accommodate winter-sports enthusiasts, several sporting camps in the area remain open all year.

Snowmobiling

Motels in Millinocket fill up fast in snow season, so you'll need to plan ahead to try this sport. More than 350 miles of the Interconnecting Trail System (ITS) crisscross the Millinocket area, including some that run right through town. Local snowmobile clubs produce excellent trail maps available from the Katahdin Area Chamber of Commerce.

Snowmobile rentals are available from **Sport Shop Express,** 23 Katahdin Ave. Ext., Millinocket 04462, 207/723-5333, starting at $150 a day. The shop is open 24 hours a day, seven days a week. The New England Outdoor Center, based near ITS-86 in Millinocket, rents snowmobiles and also offers guided all-day snowmobile trips.

If you've never tried snowmobiling, a one-day guided trip is the safest, sanest way to begin, even if it's not the cheapest.

FESTIVALS AND EVENTS

Millinocket is widely known for its week-long **Fourth of July** celebration (the fireworks display is outstanding). Every fifth year, there's

also a giant homecoming celebration, bringing several thousand former residents back to their roots.

Patten's **Annual Bean-Hole Bean Dinner** is a great celebration featuring good food (and a fascinating culinary tradition) at the Patten Lumberman's Museum the second Saturday in August.

Labor Day weekend marks the **Olde Home Days Celebration** in Sherman with a parade, chicken barbecue, food booths, children's games, and lobster boil. Email info@katahdinmaine.com for information on local festivals and events.

ACCOMMODATIONS

Lodgings in Millinocket itself cater primarily to pre- and post-Baxter visitors, Appalachian Trail through-hikers, and paper-industry executives in town for meetings—a rather disparate clientele.

Millinocket is also the springboard for a number of wilderness sporting camps, some of which are inaccessible, or nearly so, by road. Small planes equipped with skis or pontoons ferry clients to the remote sites—not an inexpensive undertaking, but a great adventure.

Bed-and-Breakfasts

Ultra-casual, congenial, and inexpensive, the **Katahdin Area B&B,** 94–96 Oxford St., Millinocket 04462, 207/723-5220, www.katahdinoutdoors.com/katahdinbb/, occupies an unpretentious green house with a view of Katahdin down Oxford Street from the front steps. Two suites and a single are $50–70 d, including the proprietors' legendary breakfast, and outdoor hot tub. Recreational Guide Services available with Rodney Corriueau, a Registered Maine Guide. No smoking, no pets, no credit cards; children are welcome.

Motels and Inns

Seventy-two rooms and 10 suites at the three-story **Katahdin Inn,** 740 Central St., Rte. 157, Millinocket 04462, 207/723-4555 or 877/902-4555, www.katahdininn.com, wrap around an enclosed space—partly occupied by a heated pool, wading pool, and hot tub. Don't be put off by the warehouselike exterior; it's cheerier inside. Kids love this place, and pool noise usually quiets down early. The only drawback is a slight aroma of chlorine. Amenities include fitness center, coin-operated laundry, and bar. Rates are $74–100 d except mid-Oct.–mid-May, when rates are lower. Pets are allowed. The free continental breakfast is more than ample. The motel is set back from the highway, a bit hard to spot, next to the Northern Plaza shopping center at the eastern edge of Millinocket, 10 miles west of I-95. Open all year.

The two-story, 48-room **Heritage Motor Inn,** 935 Central St., Rte. 157, Millinocket 04462, 207/723-9777, www.heritageinnmaine.com, part of the Best Western chain, sees steady business in winter from snowmobilers. The motel is unpretentious, on a busy highway; request a back-facing room. Rates are $89–109 d Jan.–Mar. and July–mid-Oct., $69–79 other months. There's free continental breakfast and cable TV. Pets are allowed for a fee. Open all year.

Close to I-95, exit 56, is the **Gateway Inn,** Rte. 157, P.O. Box 637, Medway 04460, 207/746-3193, www.medwaygateway.com, a 38-room/suite motel opened in 1995. Rooms on the west side have decks, great views of Katahdin (weather permitting), and higher rates. Rooms are $55–100 d July–Aug.; eight suites are $80–100 d. Special rates are available for snowmobilers; pets are welcome. Free continental breakfast, air-conditioning, phones, cable TV, and an indoor pool are all available. Open all year.

Hardest to characterize is the **Big Moose Inn,** Millinocket Lake, P.O. Box 98, Millinocket 04462, 207/723-8391, www.bigmoose-cabins.com, midway between Millinocket and Baxter State Park's southern boundary. It's part inn, part sporting camp, part campground. And two white-water rafting companies are based here—North Country Rivers and Magic Falls Rafting. In the main lodge are 11 basic rooms ($40–44 d; three shared baths). Guests hang out in the common room, with a huge

fireplace. On the grounds are 36 tent sites ($10 pp) and screened lean-tos ($13 pp), plus 11 good-size cabins ($38–42 pp; bring your own towels). Canoe rental is $15 per day. The dining room is open to the public by reservation, Wed.–Sat. June–Columbus Day; food is first-rate and moderately priced. Breakfast is available on weekends. No smoking, no pets. The lodge, cabins, and campground are open May–Columbus Day.

Sporting Camps by Road

At the eastern side of Baxter State Park, in the Patten area, are two road-accessible sporting camps: Mt. Chase Lodge and Bowlin Camps. Roughly midway between Patten and the northeast gate of Baxter State Park, **Mt. Chase Lodge,** 1517 Shin Pond Rd., Patten 04765, 207/528-2183, is an especially congenial operation thanks to owners Rick and Sara Hill. Old-timers and globetrotters hang out together in the huge, wood-paneled common room overlooking Mt. Chase and the thoroughfare between Upper and Lower Shin Ponds. Eight second-floor rooms (one with private bath) in the main lodge are $50–60 d in summer, lower off season; MAP rates are also available. Five cabins ($69–85) vary in size and quality; request a newer one. Sara's cooking earns raves; in summer, the dining room is open to the public for dinner by reservation. Rick guides canoe trips ($100 for two) on Sawtelle Deadwater, a premier moose-watching site. Canoes, boats, snowmobiles, and cross-country skis are available for rent. Mt. Chase is open all year except December and April.

Closer to Baxter is **Bowlin Camps,** P.O. Box 251, Patten 04765, 207/528-2022, www.bowlincamps.com, a traditional fishing/hunting camp on the shore of the Penobscot's East Branch. It now also welcomes family groups, especially July–Aug. Kids love the suspension bridge across the river, and there are trails to ponds and two waterfalls. An easy, 16-mile canoe run starts here (rentals are available), and someone will meet you at the other end. Cabins are rustic, heated with woodstoves; two have bathrooms and six share the clean

Katahdin/Moosehead

bathhouse. Summer rates in cabins are about $475 pp a week for adults, $400 a week for a child under 16, AP; family-style meals are served in the main lodge. There are three good-size housekeeping cabins (no meals provided, unless AP selected). Snowmobiling is huge here, and there are 12 miles of cross-country trails; Bowlin is open all year. From Patten, take Rte. 159, then the Shin Pond/Grand Lake Rd. about 10 miles west of Shin Pond. At Hay Lake (on the right), turn south and continue eight miles to Bowlin Camps.

Sporting Camps via Floatplane

Two excellent sporting camps off to the north, with longstanding reputations, are Libby Camps and Bradford Camps. Both require 60- to 90-minute drives on unpaved roads, so plan to arrive by floatplane. July and August are the best times for families—when fishing is slow and hunting hasn't started.

About 150 miles north of Bangor, **Libby Camps,** Millinocket Lake, Township 8, Range 9, mailing address P.O. Box 810, Ashland 04732, 207/435-8274, www.libbycamps.com (on the east shore of a different Millinocket Lake than the one near Millinocket), is flanked by Baxter State Park and the Allagash Wilderness Waterway. Matt and Ellen Libby are the third generation to run this fishing and hunting camp, built in 1890, and it's a serious business. If you catch a trophy salmon or brook trout, they'll even ready it for the taxidermist. Eight comfortable cabins have flush toilets, propane lights, and quilt-topped beds. The basic daily rate—including three meals, boat, and cabin—is $145 per person, double occupancy; weekly rates are lower and special family rates are available. Pets are allowed. Hearty meals are served in the handsome log-beamed lodge, close to an enormous stone fireplace. (Pray that Ellen will make her peanut-butter squares for dessert.) Canoes, kayaks, and motorboats are available for guests, and there's a sandy beach. The Libbys also own 10 "outpost cabins" on wildly remote ponds. (Even more remote is their Riverkeep Lodge on the Atikonak River in Labrador.) Libby Camps is open May–

Nov.; most convenient air service (20-minute flight, for example, from the *other* Millinocket Lake) is via Katahdin Air Service.

The only sporting camp on a pristine, 1,500-acre lake, **The Bradford Camps,** Munsungan Lake, P.O. Box 729, Ashland 04732, 207/746-7777, in winter P.O. Box 778, Kittery 03904, 207/439-6364, www.bradfordcamps.com, is leased from the Seven Islands Land Company by Igor and Karen Sikorsky. The scenery and sunsets are magnificent, the loons are mystical, and moose sightings are frequent. This is a special place. Eight good-size log cabins (with bathrooms and propane lamps), lined up along the lakefront, are $124 a day pp, AP, less for children; excellent meals are served family-style in the lake-view lodge. Family rates are available. Most fascinating is the antique ice house, containing brilliantly clear ice cut arduously from the lake the previous winter. Canoes and kayaks are available for guests, and hiking trails await. A guide ($200 a day, less for multiple days) is essential for fishing these waters—noted for rare blueback trout—and veteran Dick Mosher has the magic touch, whether working with neophytes or pros. He's in residence here from May–Oct. Open May–Nov. (Oct.–Nov. most guests are hunters seeking deer, moose, and grouse). The round-trip flight from Millinocket (about 15 minutes one way) via Katahdin Air Service runs about $125 a person, but check current rates. From Bangor, contact KT Aviation, www.ktaviation.com, for charter rates.

One of the most remote sporting camps is Al and Suzan Cooper's **Katahdin Lake Wilderness Camps,** P.O. Box 398, Millinocket 04462, 207/723-4050 or 207/723-9867, just east of Baxter State Park. Why remote? Access is *only* via floatplane ($65 round-trip), pack horses, ankle express, snowshoes, or cross-country skis. Most guests opt for the plane. As you might suspect, the place is utterly simple, a quiet outpost on the shores of 4.5-square-mile Katahdin Lake. The view of Katahdin is so dramatic here that painter Marsden Hartley once captured it on canvas. Ten rustic cabins have woodstoves, kerosene lamps, linens, and outhouses. Several rate options are available, depending on length of stay, meal plan, and season. Check www.katahdinlake camps .com for current rates. The daily AP rate (three meals, served in the main lodge) for five days or more is $100 pp. Canoe rentals are available. The camp is open all year. Trail access is south of Roaring Brook Campground in Baxter State Park.

Campgrounds and Campsites

Hundreds of wilderness campsites sprinkled throughout Maine's North Woods—many accessible from Millinocket—are part of the recreational-management program overseen by North Maine Woods (NMW), the umbrella organization based in Ashland.

The best-run commercial campground in the Millinocket area is 32-acre **Katahdin Shadows Campground,** Rte. 157, P.O. Box 606, Medway 04460, 207/746-9349 or 800/794-5267, www.katahdinshadows.com, a Good Sampark where owner Rick LeVasseur works like an octopus to keep tabs on cabins, campsites, canoeing expeditions, and more pet rabbits than you could ever count. Kids are never bored here, with such features as basketball, horseshoes, heated pool, playground, arcade, pool table, and all those bunnies to feed (bring your own carrots). Parents get free morning coffee and hot showers. Tent and RV sites are $20–25 a day (two adults). Wooden "hutniks," cabins, and a 10-unit motel are other options. Kids 17 and under are free; leashed pets are allowed. Canoe rentals are available, as are pontoon boats and motorboats. The campground, 1.7 miles west of I-95 exit 56, is open all year except April and December. Even though there are 125 sites, this place is so popular you'll need to reserve well in advance for any holiday weekend. Also based here is **Penobscot River Outfitters,** providing guided canoe trips, Old Town canoe rentals and sales, and shuttle service.

Between Upper and Lower Shin Ponds, 100-acre **Shin Pond Village,** Shin Pond Rd., Rte. 159, RR1, Box 280, Patten 04765, 207/528-2900, www.shinpond.com is much more than a campground. It's a multifaceted operation with 30 campsites ($16–23 a site), six one- and two-

bedroom cottages starting at $69, a lunch counter (open daily 7:30 AM–9 PM), and other facilities such as laundry room, public restrooms, gift shop, canoe and boat rentals, and a swimming hole in the nearby brook. In winter, there are snowmobile rentals. Most RV sites are ample but provide little privacy; the dozen tent sites are nicely wooded. Shin Pond Village is 10 miles northwest of Patten and 15 miles east of Baxter State Park's northeast (Matagamon) entrance. Cabins are open all year; laundry facilities and restrooms are only open May–Nov.

FOOD

Lunch

Millinocket House of Pizza, Northern Plaza, 782 Central St., Millinocket 04462, 207/723-4528, always busy, includes Greek salad, gyro sandwiches, and Greek pizza on its menu. Order at the stand-up counter and grab a Formica-topped table. Or get it all to go. It's open daily 11 AM–10 PM, all year; free delivery until 9 PM if you're staying nearby.

Plenty of local color is your reward at the **Patten General Store & Sporting Goods,** Rte. 11, P.O. Box 479, Patten 04765, 207/528-2549, one of those old-fashioned, little-of-everything emporia. Ammo, bait, hunter-orange hats, newspapers, and, if you hang around long enough, plenty of local gossip. The store is open daily 10 AM–10 PM, all year.

Next door is **Downtown Deli,** 207/528-2012, open 4 AM–9 PM.

Inexpensive to Moderate

A huge stone fireplace dominates the dining room of **The Hotel Terrace,** 52 Medway Rd., Millinocket 04462, 207/723-4525, Millinocket's most congenial restaurant. It's hard to beat a prime-rib dinner, with all the extras, for under $15. The wine list is small but adequate; the lounge is a local watering hole. No problem bringing kids to this informal spot. Located just off Rte. 157, on a hill above downtown, it's open all year, daily 5:30 AM–2 PM and 4–9 PM. Reservations are only accepted for groups. Also here are 11 motel rooms at $40–55 d, including air-conditioning, phones, and cable TV. No pets.

Steaks, pizza, calzones, and seafood are the specialties at the **Scootic In,** 70 Penobscot Ave., Millinocket 04462, 207/723-4566, along with big-screen TV and a good-size local crowd. A more sedate group patronizes the adjoining **Penobscot Room,** where the menu is more creative and prices are marginally higher. Kids' entrées run $4–6. Save room for homemade desserts. The Scootic In is open Mon.–Sat. at 11 AM, Sun. at noon, and closes daily at 1 AM (sometimes earlier in the shoulder seasons). The Penobscot Room is open for lunch weekdays only, open for dinner at 4 PM daily. No reservations in either room.

INFORMATION AND SERVICES

The **Katahdin Area Chamber of Commerce,** 1029 Central St., Rte. 157, Millinocket 04462, 207/723-4443, www.KatahdinMaine.com, based in a small prefab building at the eastern edge of Millinocket, is open daily 9 AM–4 PM Memorial Day weekend through Labor Day; the rest of the year, it's open weekdays 9 AM–2 PM.

The **Millinocket Memorial Library,** 5 Maine Ave., Millinocket 04462, 207/723-7020, is open all year, Mon. and Thurs. 9 AM–8 PM, Tues.–Wed. 1–8 PM, and Fri.–Sat. 1–5 PM (closed Sat. in summer).

Newspapers

For thorough coverage of local information and events listings, the *Katahdin Times,* 207/723-8118, fax 723-4434, is published every Tuesday. The daily newspaper covering the Millinocket area is the *Bangor Daily News,* 800/432-7964.

Emergencies

For police, fire, and ambulance service in **Millinocket, East Millinocket, Medway,** and **Patten,** call 911.

The 50-bed **Millinocket Regional Hospital,** 200 Somerset St., Millinocket 04462, 207/723-5161, has 24-hour emergency care. The nearest major medical facility is **Eastern Maine Medical Center,** in Bangor, nearly 70 miles to the south via I-95.

Public Restrooms

Just east of Northern Plaza in Millinocket, **Baxter State Park Headquarters,** open weekdays, has public restrooms, as does Millinocket's **municipal building,** 197 Penobscot Avenue.

Laundry

In a region where backpackers abound, laundries are popular spots. The **Downtown Laundromat,** 55 Penobscot Ave., Millinocket 04462, 207/723-5825, is open all year, Mon.–Fri. 8 AM–6 PM, and Sat.–Sun. 9 AM–4 PM. At **Shin Pond Village,** Shin Pond Rd., Rte. 159, Patten 04765, 207/528-2900, close to Baxter State Park's northeast gate, you can use the laundry room even if you aren't spending the night. The machines are accessible 7:30 AM–8 PM.

Kennels

If you're headed with your pet for Baxter State Park, you'll need a kennel, as pets are not allowed in the park. For $7–9 a day, Joyce Landry's **North Ridge Boarding Kennel,** Jones Rd., Medway 04460, 207/746-9537, takes superb care of dogs, cats, and whatever else you consider a pet. Capacity here is 15, and they walk dogs three times a day, so call at least two weeks in advance for a reservation—farther ahead for July–Aug. weekends. To avoid disrupting the animals, kennel hours are limited to Mon.–Sat. 9–10 AM and 6–7 PM, all year. No credit cards. The kennel is on Rte. 116, four miles south of Rte. 157.

Getting Around

Two firms beyond Millinocket's town lines provide **floatplane** and **skiplane** access to remote campsites and sporting camps. **Katahdin Air Service (KAS),** P.O. Box 171, Millinocket 04462, 207/723-8378 or 888/742-5527, www.katahdinair.com, has an excellent half-century reputation, offering charter floatplane flights to remote campsites and sporting camps May–Nov. KAS also does a variety of flightseeing trips.

Taxi service in the Millinocket area is provided by Minuteman Taxi, 207/723-2000. They're on call 6 AM–1 AM, all year.

Baxter State Park

Consider the foresight of Maine Governor Percival Proctor Baxter. After years of battling the state legislature to protect the area around Katahdin, Maine's highest mountain, he bade good-bye to state government in 1925 and proceeded on his own to make his dream happen. Determined to preserve this chunk of real estate for Maine residents and posterity, he pleaded the cause with landowners and managed to accumulate an initial 5,960-acre parcel—the nucleus of today's 204,733-acre Baxter State Park-and donated it to the state in 1931. From then on, he acquired and donated more and more bits and pieces (adding his last 7,764-acre parcel in 1962, just seven years before his death at the age of 90). The governor's prescience went far beyond mere purchases of land; his deed of gift carried stiff restrictions that have been little altered since then. And interest from his final bequest has allowed park authorities to add even more acreage since his death.

Today this fantastic recreational wilderness has 46 mountain peaks and more than 180 miles of trails. One rough, unpaved road (20 mph limit) circles the park; no pets, radios, or cellular phones are allowed; no gasoline or drinking water is available; camping is carry-in, carry-out.

Camping, in fact, is the only way to sleep in Baxter—at tentsites, lean-tos, bunkhouses, or rustic log—cabins. Competition for sleeping space is fierce on midsummer weekends; it's pure luck to find an opening, so you need to plan ahead. Guaranteeing a spot, particularly one of the coveted 22 cabins, means reserving in January (no refunds). The rewards are rare alpine flowers, unique rock formations, pristine ponds, waterfalls, wildlife sightings (especially moose), dramatic vistas, and, in late September, spectacular fall foliage.

The hiking here is incomparable. Peak-baggers accustomed to 8,000-footers (or more) may be unimpressed by the altitudes, but no one should underestimate the ruggedness of Baxter's terrain.

Percival Baxter was by no means the first to discover this wilderness. His best-known predecessor was author Henry David Thoreau, who climbed Katahdin in 1846 from what's now Abol Campground but never reached the summit. He didn't even reach Thoreau Spring (4,636 feet), named in his honor, but he *did* wax eloquent about the experience: "This was that Earth of which we have heard, made out of Chaos and Old Night. . . It was the fresh and natural surface of the planet Earth, as it was made forever and ever. . . so Nature made it, and man may use it if he can."

Locked in what he called "a cloud factory," Thoreau declined to approach the summit: "Pomola [Pamola, the Penobscot Indians' malevolent spirit of Katahdin] is always angry with those who climb to the summit of Ktaadn." And Native Americans traditionally stayed below treeline, fearing the resident evil spirits. They all had a point. The current trail system didn't exist in the Native Americans' or Thoreau's days, of course (the first recorded summiteer was Charles Turner, Jr., in 1804), so fatalities were probably more frequent, but in this century climbers have died on Katahdin, and difficult rescues occur every year.

Regulations

The list of rules is long at Baxter (www.baxterstateparkauthority.com / rules / index.html)—and enough park rangers make the rounds to ensure enforcement. In the end, the rules are what make Baxter so splendid. It's not unusual to hear complaints that there's too much regimentation here, but longtime Park Director Irvin ("Buzz") Caverly, who retired in 2005, was often seen as a kind of one-man Supreme Court, interpreting Governor Baxter's stipulations. As one of the few surviving persons who had known Baxter, Caverly had a leg up, with support from the Baxter State Park Authority, an autonomous

Katahdin/Moosehead

THE UNGAINLY, BELOVED MOOSE

Everyone loves Maine's state animal, *Alces alces americana*. The ungainly moose, bulbous-nosed and top-heavy, stops traffic and brings out the cameras. It also stops cars literally, usually creating a lose-lose situation. The moose's long legs put its head and shoulders about windshield level, and a collision can propel the animal head-first through the glass. Human and animal fatalities are common.

State biologists estimate that Maine has nearly 30,000 moose, most in the North Woods, so it's pretty hard not to encounter one if you're driving the roads or hiking the trails in the Katahdin/Moosehead region.

Moose pay no heed to those yellow-and-black, diamond-shaped moose-crossing signs, but officials post them near typical moose hangouts, so *slow down* when you see them. During daylight hours, especially early and late in the day, keep your binoculars and camera handy. In late spring and early summer, pesky flies and midges drive the moose from the deepest woods, so you're more likely to see them close to the roadside. At night, be even more careful, as moose don't tend to focus in on headlights (as deer do), and their eyes don't reflect at an angle that drivers can see.

Moose are vegetarians, preferring new shoots and twigs in aquatic settings, so the best places to see them are wetlands and ponds fringed with grass and shrubs. These spots are likely to be buggy, too, so slather yourself with insect repellent.

Moose hunting, officially sanctioned, is somewhat controversial—partly because the creatures seem to present little sporting challenge. But they are a challenge—not because of wile or speed but because of heft. Imagine dragging one of these fellows out of the woods to a waiting truck; it's no mean feat. In Maine's annual Moose Lottery—a herd-thinning scheme concocted by the Department of Inland Fisheries and Wildlife—nearly 3,000 hunters receive permits to shoot moose in 19 specific zones in late September and early to mid-October. At official state weighing stations, the hapless moose are strung up, weighed, tested for parasites, and often butchered on the spot by freelance meat packagers. Moose meat is actually tasty—especially if you try not to think about where it came from.

Moose Trivia

• Typical height for an adult bull moose is seven feet at the shoulders; typical weight is about 1,000 pounds, with 1,400-pounders also recorded. Cow moose run about 800 pounds.

• Moose usually lumber along, seemingly in no hurry, but they've been known to run as fast as 35 mph.

• The bull moose's rack of antlers can measure six feet across; the largest recorded was a hair under seven feet.

• Moose give birth in late May or early June, after a 35-week pregnancy; singles are normal, twins are less common, triplets are very rare. A newborn calf weighs 20–30 pounds, occasionally 35 pounds.

• Moose have extremely acute senses of hearing and smell, but their eyesight is pitiable. If you're utterly quiet and stay downwind of them, they probably won't spot you.

• Moose have no history of harming humans, but stay out of their way during "the rut," when they're charging around and out of the woods looking for females in heat. This usually occurs between mid-September and mid-October, when the foliage is at its peak, hikers are out and about, and moose-lottery winners are in hot pursuit.

board comprising three state officials who have ultimate park power.

• Mid-May–mid-Oct., the park's **entrance gates** are staffed 6 AM–9 PM (Matagamon Gate) and 6 AM–10 PM (Togue Pond Gate); campers must arrive with their reservation forms at one of these two gates by 8:30 PM. Rangers ask that campers adhere to the seven outdoor-ethics principles of the national **Leave No Trace** organization (www.lnt.org). gallon of water). A small-pore filter (three microns or smaller) will also work.

• **No motorcycles, motorbikes, or ATVs** are allowed in the park; **bicycles** are allowed only on maintained roads, not on trails, but the narrow, rough Perimeter Road is not particularly bike-friendly. When weather has been especially dry, bicyclists end up with mouthfuls of dust. **Snowmobiles** are restricted to certain areas; check with park rangers.

• As mentioned above, the park bans operation of **cell phones, TVs, radios, and CD or cassette players.** Noise levels in the park are strictly monitored by the rangers. There are no pay phones in the park, but all park rangers have radiophones.

Baxter in Winter

The roads aren't plowed, campgrounds are closed, and the lakes and ponds are frozen solid, but Baxter authorities allow winter use of the park—with a multi-page list of rigid restrictions. If this sounds appealing, contact the Baxter State Park Authority for winter information.

DAY USE

Most day-use visitors are here to hike; on summer and fall weekends, you'll need to arrive early—even if you're not climbing Katahdin—because the day-use parking areas fill up. (There are only 224 day-use parking spots in the park.) On weekends, a long line forms before dawn at the Togue Pond gatehouse. A notice board at each gatehouse specifies which day-use parking areas are closed and which are

open; there's almost always someplace to park (though *never* alongside the Perimeter Road or campground access roads), and zillions of trails to hike, but it may not be what you had in mind. So plan ahead and arrive early (no later than 7 AM to hike Katahdin) or be prepared to be totally flexible about your hiking choice.

The northern end of the park is much less utilized than the southern end, so consider entering via the northern Matagamon Gate and hiking the wonderful trails in that part of Baxter. From I-95 exit 56 (Medway; the exit for Millinocket and the southern park entrance), it's 19 miles to exit 58 (Sherman), then another 33 miles west to Matagamon Gate, via Patten and Shin Pond.

Picnicking

Picnic areas, some with only a single table, are spotted throughout the park; most of the vehicle-accessible campgrounds (except Kidney Pond and Daicey Pond) also have picnic areas where noncampers are welcome. At the campgrounds, park in the day-use parking area, not the campers' area.

HIKING

Baxter's 180-plus miles of trails can occupy hikers for their entire lives. There's no such thing as "best" hikes, but some are indeed better (for various reasons) than others. Below is a range of options; consult Stephen Clark's *Katahdin* guide for details and more suggestions.

Trails originating at campgrounds all have registration clipboards; sign-in is *required* for Katahdin hikes and encouraged for all other hikes. All trails are blue-blazed, except for white-blazed ones that are part of the Appalachian Trail. Carved brown signs appear at all major trail junctions. All hikers are required to carry a flashlight—which any hiker should know enough to do anyway.

Wear Polartec, polypropylene, Gore-tex, or wool clothing, not cotton. Jeans can be a real drag (literally) if you get soaked in a stream or rainstorm. If you're planning to hike Katahdin, bring more layers than you think you'll need.

Bring plenty of insect repellent, especially in June, when the blackflies are on the rampage. In June, you'll probably be best off with 100 percent DEET bug dope, although the eco-friendly Buzz-Off insect repellent is very effective, and some outfitters (such as L.L. Bean) are now featuring clothing impregnated with Buzz-Off. Wear light-colored long pants and a long-sleeved shirt/sweater with tight-fitting wrists and a snug collar.

Nature Trails and Family Hikes

Baxter has three easy nature trails that make ideal hikes for families with a range of age and skill levels. Nature-trail maps are available at park headquarters, the park entrance gates, and the nearest ranger stations to the trailheads. The 1.8-mile **Daicey Pond Nature Trail,** beginning at Daicey Pond Campground, circumnavigates the pond counterclockwise, taking about an hour. In August, help yourself to the raspberries near the end of the circuit. Best of all, you can extend the hike at the end by renting a canoe ($1 an hour) at the campground's ranger station, in the shadow of Katahdin's west flank. After that, take the easy 1.2-mile round-trip hike from the campground to Big Niagara Falls.

The other nature trails are the **South Branch Nature Trail,** a 0.7-mile walk starting at South Branch Campground, in the northern part of the park, and **Roaring Brook Nature Trail,** a 0.75-mile walk starting near Roaring Brook Campground, in the southeastern corner of the park, with dramatic views of Katahdin's eastern flank.

Other good family hikes, easy to moderate, are Trout Brook Mountain, Burnt Mountain, and Howe Brook Trail—all in the northern section of the park. Burnt Mountain has a fire tower at the top, and you'll need to climb it to see the view; the summit itself is quite overgrown. In the southern end of the park, a short, easy trail leads from Upper Togue Pond to **Cranberry Pond.** An easy, 5.2-mile round-trip from Daicey Pond Campground goes to **Lily Pad Pond,** then via canoe to **Windy Pitch Ponds.** Plan to picnic en route alongside Big

MOOSE-WATCHING

Moose-watching Hot Spots (Katahdin/Moosehead Region)

- Sandy Stream Pond, Baxter State Park
- Grassy Pond, Baxter State Park
- Russell Pond, Baxter State Park
- Sawtelle Deadwater, off Shin Pond Road, about seven miles northwest of Shin Pond
- Lazy Tom Bog, off Lily Bay Road, about 19 miles north of Greenville
- Route 6/15, between Greenville Junction and Rockwood, on the west side of Moosehead Lake
- The Golden Road, between Ripogenus Dam and Pittston Farm

Niagara Falls. (Before departing, stop at the Daicey Pond office and pick up the keys for the canoe locks.)

Howe Brook Trail, departing from South Branch Campground, requires fording the brook several times in summer, so wear waterproof footgear. The reward, higher up, is a series of waterfalls and little pools where the kids can swim (the water is frigid)—and flat boulders where you can picnic and sunbathe. In the fall, the foliage on this hike is especially gorgeous. For this six-mile hike, allow about four hours round-trip for lunch, a swim, and dawdling. Afterward, rent a canoe at the campground ($1 an hour) and paddle around scenic Lower South Branch Pond, in the shadow of North Traveler Mountain.

Moderate Hikes

Good hikes generally classified as moderate are Doubletop Mountain, Sentinel Mountain, and the Owl. If you decide to hike **Doubletop Mountain,** start at the Nesowadnehunk (Ne-SOWD-na-hunk) Field trailhead and go south to Kidney Pond Campground, an eight-mile one-way trek, up and over and down. It's much less strenuous this way. Allow about six hours.

Allow about six hours also for the **Sentinel Mountain Trail** from Daicey Pond

Campground (6.6 miles round-trip) or Kidney Pond Campground (four miles round-trip). It's not difficult; the only moderate part involves a boulder field about midway up. Take a picnic and hang out at the top; the view across to Katahdin, the Owl, and Mt. OJI is splendid. With binoculars, you'll probably spot moose in the ponds below. Keep one eye on your lunch, however; a resident Canada jay at the summit has an acquisitive streak.

If weather has been rainy, *do not* hike the Owl. It verges on being strenuous even under normal conditions.

Katahdin

Mile-high Katahdin, northern terminus of the Appalachian Trail, is the Holy Grail for most Baxter State Park hikers—and certainly for Appalachian Trail thru-hikers, who have walked 2,158 miles from Springer Mountain, Georgia, to get here. Thousands of hikers scale Katahdin annually via several different routes. The climb is strenuous, requires a full day, and is not suitable for small children; kids under six are banned above tree line. You'll be a lot happier and a lot less exhausted if you plan to camp in the park before and after the Katahdin hike.

Katahdin, by the way, is a Native American word meaning "greatest mountain"—hence there's no need to refer to it as *Mount* Katahdin. The Katahdin massif actually comprises a single high point (Baxter Peak, 5,267 feet) and several neighboring peaks (Pamola Peak, 4,902 feet; Hamlin Peak, 4,756 feet; and the three Howe Peaks, 4,734–4,612 feet).

Even though Thoreau never made it to Katahdin's summit (Baxter Peak), countless others have, and the mountain sees a virtual traffic jam in summer and fall, particularly late in the season, when most of the thru-hikers tend to show up. Some hikers make the summit an annual ritual; others consider it a onetime rite of passage, then opt for less-trodden paths and less-strenuous climbs.

Weather reports are posted at 7 AM daily at all the campgrounds. Katahdin has its own biome, and weather on the summit can be dramatically different from that down below. At times, especially in high-wind and blowing-snow conditions, park officials close trails to the summit. They don't do it frivolously; Katahdin is a killer, literally.

Besides the requisite photo next to the Baxter Peak summit sign, Katahdin's other "been there, done that" experience is a traverse of the aptly named **Knife Edge,** a treacherous, 1.1-mile-long granite spine (minimum width three feet) between Baxter and Pamola Peaks. If you can stand the experience, hanging on for all you're worth, next to a 1,500-foot drop, go for it; the views are incredible. But don't push beyond your personal limits; you're hours from the nearest hospital.

The most-used route to Baxter Peak is the **Hunt Trail,** a 10-mile round-trip that coincides with the Appalachian Trail from Katahdin Stream Campground; allow at least eight hours round-trip. Other routes start from Russell Pond, Chimney Pond, Roaring Brook, and Abol Campgrounds. See Stephen Clark's *Katahdin* guide for specific route information.

CAMPING

Facilities at 10 campgrounds range from cabins to tent sites, lean-tos, and bunkhouses; there are also several wilderness campsites supervised by the nearest campground rangers.

All the campgrounds close October 15; they open at various times, beginning May 15. Two hike-in campgrounds open June 1. Fees range from $9 per person per night in lean-tos (two-person minimum) to $25 per person in cabins (minimums depend on cabin size). Fees must be prepaid and are not refundable.

The 22 cabins are at **Daicey Pond Campground** and **Kidney Pond Campground,** in the park's southwest corner. Daicey Pond has the best views-Katahdin from every cabin, and the sunrises are matchless. With two exceptions, Kidney Pond cabins overlook the pond and surrounding woods, but not the mountains; Doubletop Mountain is in back of the campground. All cabins have woodstoves (for heating only), propane lanterns, outhouses, outside fireplaces, and beds; bring your own linens, water, food, and everything else.

Chimney Pond and Russell Pond Campgrounds are hike-in campgrounds. Distance from the Roaring Brook parking area to Chimney Pond is 3.3 miles; to Russell Pond is seven miles. Chimney Pond has a bunkhouse and nine four-person lean-tos. Russell Pond has a bunkhouse, four lean-tos, and three tent sites—all arranged around the pond, where you can also rent canoes ($1 an hour).

South Branch Pond Campground, close to Matagamon Gate, has a bunkhouse, 12 lean-tos, and 21 tent sites in an especially idyllic setting; seven of the lean-tos are right next to the pond.

From June through Aug., bring fabric screening if you're staying in a lean-to; a tarp may foil the blackflies, mosquitoes, and no-see-ums, but you don't want to suffocate.

Getting Reservations

Camping reservations must be made by mail or in person; no phone reservations (except at the last minute). July gets booked up first, then August; weekends are more crowded than weekdays.

In 2005, Baxter officials established a new reservation system in hopes of providing a more equitable allocation of space in the park's cabins, bunkhouses, tent sites, and lean-tos. Under this "rolling reservation system," campers can make reservations any time beginning four months before the desired camping start date. For instance, to request a site or sites for July 14, you'll need to mail your reservation to arrive no earlier than March 14 (see www.baxterstateparkauthority.com/camping/chart.htm for the reservation schedule). Maximum length of stay is seven nights per campground, 14 nights total in the park.

Download the application form from the park website and mail it along with payment and a self-addressed, stamped legal-size envelope to Baxter State Park Reservations, 64 Balsam Drive, Millinocket, ME 04462. (If you'd prefer to hand-deliver it, the office is open weekdays 8 AM–4 PM in spring, daily between Memorial Day and Columbus Day. Do not send the reservation via email, as the website is not secure.) Reservations are processed each day the office is open—applications from Maine residents are handled first.

If you can't plan that far ahead but can be fairly flexible, send in your request close to when you want to camp, or even take a chance on showing up at the last minute. Phone requests (207/723-5140; have your Visa or MasterCard handy) are accepted within 10 days of your visit—but there are no guarantees. Except on weekends July–mid-Aug., however, a tent site can usually be found. But be sure to have a fallback plan. (It might have to be in Millinocket.)

In previous years, several hundred diehard campers, especially ones hoping for midsummer cabin reservations, drove to park headquarters in Millinocket in early January in order to have the pick of the sites. Some even spent the night in tents or motels to be there when the door opened at 7 AM on January 2; since Millinocket is deep in Maine's snow belt, the trek became something of an adventure. The absence of computers and a convoluted system made this a lengthy but oddly enjoyable process.

A few members of the hardest core showed up for the mid-January opening in 2005, but the number is expected to dwindle each year because only a limited number of sites can be reserved that day under the current system.

If you make a reservation and can't keep it, be considerate and call or email the park headquarters to cancel, even though you won't receive a refund. It will give someone else a chance to enjoy the beauty of Baxter.

PARK ACCESS, INFORMATION, AND SERVICES

Unless you're hiking the Appalachian Trail (AT), the only way to enter the park is via one of two gates. **Togue Pond Gate,** at the southern end of the park, is the choice for visitors from Greenville or Millinocket and the most-used gate. At the northeast corner of the park is **Matagamon Gate,** accessed via I-95, Patten, and Shin Pond Rd. Togue Pond Gate is open weekdays 6 AM–10 PM May 15–Oct. 15; Matagamon Gate is open 6 AM–9 PM the same months. Sat.–Sun. the gates open at 5 AM, a change designed to alleviate the morning pressure, allow Katahdin hikers to get an earlier start, and to distribute hikers throughout the park.

Note: Before you enter the park, check your fuel gauge and fill up your tank; there are no fuel facilities in the park.

If you have camping reservations, be sure that you do not arrive at the park with more people than your receipt indicates; the rangers at the gate check this, and the campground rangers even do body counts to be sure you haven't stuffed extra people into cabins or lean-tos.

Appalachian Trail thru-hikers are required to register at the Abol Stream kiosk, as well as at Katahdin Stream Campground, before ascending Katahdin.

Maine residents have free daytime use of the park—one of Governor Baxter's stipulations. At the gates, **nonresidents** pay $12 per vehicle for a day pass; a nonresident season pass is $37. (A rental car with Maine plates qualifies in the resident category.) Everyone must pay for camping.

There is no public transportation to or within Baxter State Park, so you'll need a car, truck, or bicycle. (The park's website lists a couple of enterprises that offer shuttle service.) RVs are also allowed, but maximum size is nine feet high, seven feet wide, and 22 feet long (or 44 feet for car-and-trailer). Baxter is not a drive-through park. The park's 43-mile unpaved **Perimeter Road,** connecting Togue Pond and Matagamon Gates, is narrow and corrugated, evidently deliberately so; it's designed for access, not joyriding.

A few trail loops include the Perimeter Road, but avoid walking on it if possible. In wet weather, you'll be splashed by cars navigating the potholes; in hot weather, the gritty dust gets in your teeth. Hitchhiking is discouraged, but you can usually get a ride if you need it.

Information

Books, maps, and information are available at **Baxter State Park Headquarters,** 64 Balsam Dr., Millinocket 04462, 207/723-5140, www .baxterstateparkauthority.com, open Mon.–Fri. 9 AM–5 PM, all year, at campground ranger stations, and at the Togue Pond Visitor Center. (Camping reservations must be made by mail or in person.)

Pick up a *Day Use Hiking Guide* ($1) at the visitors center or at park headquarters. The foldout map, quite sketchy, also has basic info on major park trails.

Helping Hands

The Boston-based **Appalachian Mountain Club** (AMC), www.outdoors.org, established in 1876, organizes a couple of summertime **trail-maintenance programs** at Baxter State Park. The one-week projects, including time to hike Katahdin, cost $130 for AMC members, $145 for nonmembers (food and lodging are included). No experience is necessary, but you need to be in reasonably good shape. For details and schedule, contact the AMC's White Mountains Trails Office, 603/466-2721, ext. 192.

Baxter Park headquarters periodically puts out calls for volunteers (for trail repair, carpentry projects, etc.). If you have time to spare for a great cause, download a volunteer application form from www.baxterstateparkauthority.com/volunteers/special.html.

Allagash Wilderness Waterway

In 1966, the state established a 92-mile stretch of the Allagash River as The Allagash Wilderness Waterway (AWW), a collection of lakes, ponds, and streams starting at Telos Lake and ending at East Twin Brook, about six miles before the Allagash meets the St. John River. Also recognized as a National Wild and Scenic River, the waterway's habitats shelter rare plants, 30 or so mammal species, and more than 120 bird species. You'll spot plenty of wildlife along the way.

Arranging a flexible schedule to do the Allagash gives you enough slack to wait out strong winds on the three largest lakes. Such a schedule also allows time for a leisurely pace, side trips, and fishing along the way.

Information

The Maine **Bureau of Parks and Lands,** in the Department of Conservation, www.state .me.us/doc/parks, manages operations on the Allagash Wilderness Waterway. During the season, rangers are stationed at key sites all along the route. For general information, including a useful free map and a list of outfitters, 207/941-4014 Mon.–Sat. 8 AM–5 PM. For seasonal water-level information, call the Forest Service at 207/435-7963 daily 8 AM–5 PM, late Apr.–mid-Dec.

A particularly lovely pictorial overview of the waterway is naturalist Dean Bennett's excellent book, *Allagash: Maine's Wild and Scenic River.*

WHEN TO GO

Canoeing season on the AWW usually runs late May (after "ice-out") to early October. Water and insect levels are high and water temperature is low in May and June; July and August are most crowded but have better weather; September can be chilly, but the foliage is fabulous. Average annual temperature in this area is 40°F; winter temperatures average 20°F. The AWW is accessible in winter for snowmobiling and ice fishing. Winter camping is permitted at the Chamberlain Thoroughfare Bridge parking lot, on a first-come, first-served basis.

CANOEING

Neophyte canoeists should think twice before setting out without a guide on multi-day canoe trips. You should have experience with Class II white-water before attempting either of these rivers. Even experienced paddlers who are unfamiliar with Maine's rivers ought to assess the pluses and minuses of a do-it-yourself expedition versus a guided trip. It's rare to find a deserted campsite. The costs of provisioning, arranging shuttles, camping fees, and gear rental can add up—and guides spare you from cooking and cleanup. Not a bad tradeoff.

Most guide services have their specialties, but few specialize in only one river. Some arrange trips all over the state; others go to Canada, Alaska, and beyond. Veteran guide services that offer trips on both the St. John and the Allagash include Mike Patterson and Edgar Eaton's **Wilds of Maine Guide Service,** 192 Congress St., Belfast 04915, 207/338-3932, www.wildsofmaine.com; **Gil Gilpatrick,** P.O. Box 461, Skowhegan 04976, 207/453-6959, www.gilgilpatrick.com; the Co-

rapids in the Allagash Wilderness Waterway

© KATHLEEN M. BRANDES

ALLAGASH WILDERNESS WATERWAY HIGHLIGHTS

The entire waterway is 92 miles, from Telos Lake northward to West Twin Brook, but shorter trips are possible from a half-dozen authorized put-ins along the way. There are 80 official campsites along the waterway; freelance camping is forbidden. The canoeing season is typically mid-May through September.

Allagash Lake, one of the state's most pristine lakes, feeds into Chamberlain Lake from the west, via Allagash Stream. No motors are allowed on Allagash Lake, making it especially tranquil. The side trip is six miles one-way, and water levels (too high or too low) can make it a rough go. At Lock Dam, ask about conditions. Between Chamberlain and Eagle Lakes, on a narrow spit of land seemingly in the middle of nowhere, stand two of the waterway's oddities— two old **steam engines,** relics rusted out and long abandoned. Once linked to the Eagle Lake and Umbazooksus Railroad, the short-run Lombard Hauler locomotives operated round-the-clock, six days a week, between 1927 and 1933, hauling 125,000 cords of pulpwood annually for the timber industry. The nonprofit **Allagash Alliance Group,** 207/273-6098, has begun long-range restoration of the engines and the site, known as the **Tramway National Historic District.** An exhilarating white-water run is the reward for tackling **Chase Rapids,** a nine-mile stretch starting just below Churchill Dam. You can usually expect Class II whitewater—sometimes Class III—if you launch with the dam's water release schedule. Two hours after the dam's been closed, the route can get pretty "bony," so you're likely to be hung up temporarily several times along the way. In the afternoon, wear sunglasses (well secured) to protect yourself from glare. For a fee, the Churchill rangers will portage your gear to the end of the rapids, so you only have to get yourselves and your canoes to the end of the run. If you're at all hesitant about making the run, or the water is too low, the rangers will also carry passengers to the end of the run.

Allagash Falls, eight miles before the end of the waterway and 13 miles before the river meets the St. John, has a dramatic, 40-foot drop. Needless to say, you'll need to portage here (on the right)—but only a third of a mile.

chrane family's **Allagash Canoe Trips,** P.O. Box 932, Greenville 04441, 207/237-3077, www.allagashcanoetrips.com; and Blaine Miller's **Allagash Guide Inc.,** 292 River Rd., Norridgewock 04957, 207/634-3748, www.allagashguide.com.

If you're planning to visit a sporting camp within reasonable distance of the Allagash, check to see whether they arrange Allagash trips; a number of them do.

Two guide services well known for small groups and a special love of traditional woods lore and gear are Garrett and Alexandra Conover's **North Woods Ways,** 2293 Elliottsville Rd., Willimantic 04443, 207/997-3723, www.northwoodsways .com, and Ray and Nancy Reitze's **Earthways,** 159 Earthways Rd., Canaan 04924, 207/426-8138, www.earthways.net. The Conovers run the Allagash early and late in the season, and the St. John in mid-May, but they provide woodstove-heated tents to combat the chill.

Costs vary for guided trips, usually including everything except transportation to Maine; figure on $150–175 a day per person.

CAMPING

There are 80 signposted campsites along the waterway; all are first-come, first served. July–Aug., when canoe traffic is fairly heavy, don't wait too late in the day to set up camp. Sites are $7 a night (including tax) for nonresidents, $5 a night for residents. Children under 10 are free. Fees are payable in advance at the ranger station where you enter the waterway. Theoretically, you're expected to stay only one night at any site, but an extension usually isn't a big problem.

SPORTING CAMP ALONG THE WATERWAY

Close to one of the major waterway access points, and roughly 50 miles north of Millinocket, **Nugent's Chamberlain Lake Camps,** Chamberlain Lake, mailing address HC76, Box 632, Greenville 04441, 207/944-5991, is reachable only by boat, floatplane, or snowmobile. You can drive as far as Chamberlain Thoroughfare Bridge (after paying a North Maine Woods fee at the Telos Checkpoint—$10 for residents, $14 for nonresidents), park, and arrange for Nugent's staff to pick you up ($35 per boatload). Built in 1936, the 12 clean cabins are determinedly rustic, without bathrooms; a common bathhouse serves the camps. Although housekeeping rates are available (bring your own sleeping bags and towels; no meals; $30 pp a night), opt for American Plan ($80 pp a day, including linens and meals) to save lugging victuals and to take advantage of the hearty family-style meals in the character-full main lodge. Kids 12 and under stay for half price. Boat rentals are $55 a day (plus gas). John Richardson and Regina Webster keep Nugent's open all year, catering to major clientele—a constant flow of snowmobilers and ice anglers in winter.

GETTING THERE

The Allagash Wilderness Waterway is accessible by private logging roads at specified points. You'll need to pay the North Maine Woods gate fees when you cross onto timber-company land ($4 per day for residents, $7 for nonresidents). You can get here from Greenville or Millinocket, or from the Aroostook County community of Ashland. Official **access points** with parking areas are Chamberlain Thoroughfare Bridge, Churchill Dam, Umsaskis Thoroughfare, and Michaud Farm. Winter access sites are different.

THE ST. JOHN RIVER

Like the Allagash, the St. John has long been associated with the timber industry—and the spring log drives when huge loads of giant logs were driven *upstream* and eventually to the mills. The history of the late-19th- and early-20th-century lumbering era is especially colorful, loaded with tales of unbelievably rugged conditions and equally rugged characters. It's only a memory now that the log drives have ended, but you'll see remnants of the industry along the way.

Information

North Maine Woods (NMW), P.O. Box 421, Ashland 04732, 207/435-6213, www.northmainewoods.org, is the nonprofit recreational manager for this area. The **Northwoods Maine Gate** fee is $5 pp per day for residents, and $8 for non-residents, plus a daily camping fee of $6 pp per night.

When to Go

The prime season for canoeing the St. John River is May–early June, although many years there's enough water until late June. North Maine Woods monitors daily water levels on the river, so you'll need to call a day in advance, 207/435-6213, to confirm that water flow is adequate, especially after mid-June. NMW suggests that 3,000 cfs (cubic feet per second) is the minimum for enjoyable canoeing—to avoid grounding out or extensive portaging—but experienced canoeists recommend a minimum of 2,000 cfs.

June brings out the blackflies at campsites, so be sure you are well prepared to combat them with high-powered (100 percent DEET) bug dope and tight-fitting, light-colored clothing.

Camping

Between Baker Lake and Allagash village, there are 28 riverside camping areas with a total of more than 60 sites. All are signposted. Most are on the left (west) side of the St. John; some require climbing the bank to reach level ground. Campsites are first-come, first-served. If a site is filled, you'll have to move on, anywhere from two to five more miles. Camping is allowed only at designated sites. About half of the sites have at least one sheltered picnic table, a real plus that saves rigging tarps for meals in rainy weather. Other facilities are outhouses and fire rings. Campsites are $6 per person per night (plus tax); fees are payable at the checkpoint where you enter North Maine Woods territory.

Note: Even though the St. John has no dams, a heavy rainstorm can swell the water level, causing the river to rise as much as three feet overnight. Keep this in mind when lashing your canoe for the night; secure it well, as high as possible.

Getting There

There are four main access points for the St. John, plus the final takeout point downriver at the top of Maine. From the southernmost point, **5th St. John Pond,** it's 143 miles to the town of Allagash.

The easiest way to get here is via one of Greenville's two flying services. Downstream are **Baker Lake** and **Moody Bridge,** the latter being best for low-water conditions; drive in via Ashland (about 3.5 hours on the American Realty Rd.). By the time you get to **Priestly Bridge,** you're more than halfway downriver—almost not worth the trip. Opt instead for starting at Baker Lake or Moody Bridge—or, if you're going with a guiding service, wherever your guides prefer to start. Shuttle arrangements can be complicated for St. John trips. If you're on your own hook, be sure all details are worked out in advance, and include logging-road user fees in your budget.

Greenville and Vicinity

Greenville (pop. 1,885) is the jumping-off point for the North Woods—ground zero for float- and skiplanes maintaining contact with remote hamlets and sporting camps. It's the big city for tinier communities in every direction, but it's a bit like a frontier town itself. Greenville looks out over Moosehead Lake—Maine's largest—from its southern end. Moosehead is 40 miles long and covers 117 square miles, but counting all the niches and notches, its shoreline runs to more than 400 miles.

The origin of the lake's name *has* to be from the large number of antlered critters hereabouts, especially along the shore toward Rockwood or Kokadjo. In addition to moose-watching, you can wear yourself out with all the recreational choices: swimming, boating, fishing, camping, hiking, white-water rafting, golfing, picnicking, birding, skiing, snowshoeing, and snowmobiling. In spring, summer, and fall, you can also cruise the lake in an antique steamer.

The most distinctive landmark here, at the lake's "waistline," is Mount Kineo, a 763-foot-high chunk of green-tinged rhyolite or felsite that erupted from the bowels of the earth about 425 million years ago. Smoothed by glacial activity on the west side, Kineo has sharp cliffs on its east side. The chert-like volcanic stone (not flint—Maine has no native flint) was a major reason Native Americans glommed on to the Moosehead area thousands of years ago—its hardness served them well for weapons and fishing and hunting tools. The surrounding woodlands yielded prime birch bark, supplying raw material for canoes, carry-alls, and even shelters. Stone tools and arrowheads still turn up occasionally, especially along the shore when the water level is low, but most have been carted off by amateur collectors. *Resist the urge to take home samples.*

Moosehead has been attracting outdoors enthusiasts, primarily hunters and anglers, since the 1880s. The long haul from lower New England, ending with the passenger train from Bangor, apparently was worth it for the clean air, prime angling, and chance to rough it. That era has long passed, and the clientele has changed noticeably, but Greenville's downtown still has a rustic air, and the outlying hamlets even more so.

Greenville was incorporated in 1836, just before the timber industry began to take off. Steamboats hauled huge corrals ("booms") of logs down the lake to the East Outlet of the Kennebec River (East and West Outlets are both on the west side of Moosehead), where river drivers took over. All that ended fairly recently, in the 1970s. The steamer *Katahdin* is a relic of that colorful era.

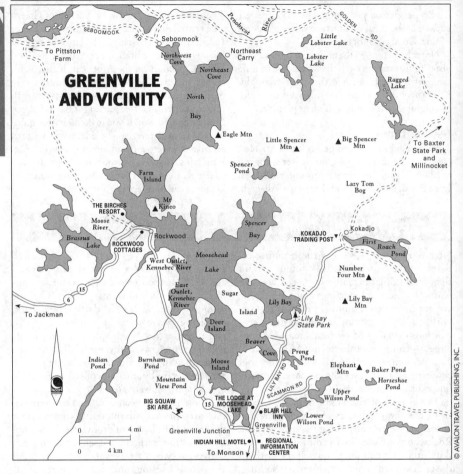

GREENVILLE AND VICINITY

© AVALON TRAVEL PUBLISHING, INC.

Greenville's lakeshore twin, Greenville Junction, once a busy rail crossroads, now has become one of those blink-and-you'll-miss-it places, but you can still eat and sleep there. Twenty miles northwest of Greenville, on Rte. 6/15, is the small and somewhat crowded hamlet of Rockwood, closest spot to Kineo, a scenic viewpoint for lakeside lodgings. One of the best views is from the public boat landing, on a loop road just off Rte. 6/15. Rte. 6/15 then continues west, along Brassua Lake and the aptly named Moose River, to Jackman—a lovely 30-mile drive popular with moosewatchers.

From Greenville, it's easy to access the fabled Golden Road, the 96-mile unpaved timber superhighway from Millinocket to the Quebec border. To enter the road on Moosehead's east side, take Lily Bay Rd. north from Greenville for 23 miles; the last section is unpaved but well maintained.

To reach the Golden Road via Moosehead's west shore—the route to Pittston Farm—take Rte. 6/15 northwest of Greenville for 20 miles to Rockwood. Then go another 18 or so unpaved miles northwest to Great Northern's Twenty-Mile Checkpoint,

© KATHLEEN M. BRANDES

Moosehead Lake Excursion boat

staffed 4 AM–11 PM, and pay the user fee: $8 for nonresident vehicle, $5 for Maine plates. It's only a few more miles to Pittston Farm, just south of the Golden Road.

Don't be surprised, when you make inquiries about the Moosehead area, to hear lots of references to "ice-out." It's almost a season—the time when winter's ice releases its grip on the lake and spring and summer activities can begin. Depending on the severity of the winter, ice-out occurs anywhere from early to late May. Fishermen arrive, plumbing begins to work, and a few weeks later, the blackfly larvae start to hatch. Spring is underway.

SIGHTS
Lake Cruises
A turn-of-the-century wooden vessel once used in the lumber industry, the steamboat *Katahdin* (locally called the *Kate*) has been converted to diesel and now runs cruises on 40-mile-long Moosehead Lake from her base at the bottom of the lake, next to the **Moosehead Marine Museum.** The best trip for children is the regular three-hour run, departing Tues., Thurs., Sat., and Sun. at 12:30 PM. Tickets are $30 adults, $26 seniors, $15 kids 11–16; kids under eleven are free. A five-hour **Mount Kineo cruise** ($35 adults, $31 seniors, $18 kids, plus $6 for buffet lunch) departs each Wed. at 10 AM. An all-day head-of-lake trip ($45 adults, $40 seniors, $25 kids) operates the last Saturday of September,

when it's chilly, but the fall foliage is fantastic. Indoor and outdoor seating; snack bar on board. No smoking or high-heeled shoes; the boat is wheelchair accessible. Cruises operate on a regular schedule July–Labor Day, but only on weekends Memorial Day weekend–June. There are also cruises during the September Fly-In and the first week in October. Reservations are advisable for the longer cruises; contact **Katahdin Cruises,** N. Main St., P.O. Box 1151, Greenville 04441, 207/695-2716, www .katahdincruises.com.

Flightseeing
Moosehead Lake from the air during fall-foliage season is incomparable—you'll bank over Mount Kineo, survey a palette of autumn colors, and very possibly see a moose or two. (They're easiest to spot in the sad-looking tracts clear-cut by the timber companies.) Most fun is the lakefront takeoff and landing. **Currier's Flying Service,** Pritham Ave., Rte. 6/15, Greenville Junction 04442, 207/695-2778, www.curriersflyingservice.com, offers a whole slew of on-demand trips over Mount Kineo, Squaw Mountain, and Katahdin. Costs range $35–90 pp (two-person minimum). Moose-watching trips, depending on their length, are $50–100 a person. Call to arrange a flight schedule; planes depart from Greenville Junction, where the Currier family also operates a small gift shop.

The veteran in this neck of the woods, **Folsom's Air Service,** P.O. Box 507, Greenville 04441, 207/695-2821, fax 695-2434, also does half a dozen daily flightseeing trips ($30–50 pp), weather permitting. Folsom's, Currier's, and Jack's Air Service (downtown Greenville) are available year-round for flights to remote wilderness camps.

PARKS AND RECREATION
Lily Bay State Park
Lining the eastern shore of Moosehead Lake, 925-acre Lily Bay State Park, Lily Bay Rd., HC 76, Box 425, Greenville 04441, 207/695-2700, www.campwithme.com, is the place to

go for moose-watching, fishing, picnicking, hiking, canoeing, swimming, birding, and camping at some of Maine's most desirable waterfront sites. July–Aug. weekends, campsite reservations are essential; two-night minimum. Call 207/287-3824, and have a MasterCard, Visa, or Discover card ready. Only the lucky will find a last-minute space, even though there are 93 sites in two clusters; no hookups. Park admission (for daytime use) is $3 adults, $1 children 5–11; seniors and kids under five are free. Nonresident camping fees are $16–22 per site per night, plus the reservation fee of $2 per site per night. The park is open daily 7 AM–11 PM, May 1–Oct. 15, but it's accessible in winter for excellent cross-country skiing and snowmobiling. From Greenville, head north on Lily Bay Rd. for eight miles; the park is on the left.

Lazy Tom Bog

Swampy Lazy Tom Bog is one of the region's best moose-watching haunts. Plan to go soon after sunrise or just before sunset. From Greenville, take Lily Bay Rd. north to Kokadjo, 18 miles. A mile later, when the road forks, take the left fork (signposted Spencer Pond Camps). Continue 0.5 mile to a small bridge. Park on either side of the bridge and have your camera ready, preferably with a long lens. If you want to emerge from your car, or even stick your lens through the open window, you may need to douse yourself with insect repellent. And try to keep the kids quiet.

Moose Safaris

Ed Mathieu is the chief honcho of **Moose Country Safaris,** Rte. 1, Box 524D, Sangerville 04479, 207/876-4907, www.moosecountrysafaris.com, usually operating in the Greenville area. Reservations are essential. Mid-May–mid-Oct., **moose safaris,** lasting about four hours, go out at 5:45 AM and 2 PM, by 4WD and canoe; there's a two-person minimum/maximum. Cost is $125 for two, including a box lunch with Ed's trademark moose cookies (edible ones; not what you might think). Moose Country Safaris also offers dogsledding and snowshoeing.

Both Evergreen Lodge and The Birches Resort also have moose safaris; Folsom's and Currier's do their moose-watching from the air.

Hiking

Except for early June, when blackflies torment woodland hikers as well as moose, the Greenville area is sublime for hiking. The chamber of commerce has a list that includes hiking directions for **Number Four Mountain, Big and Little Squaw Mountains, Big and Little Spencer Mountains,** and **Elephant Mountain** (a B-52 wreck site).

Mount Kineo

A hike up Mount Kineo is a must. Kineo is accessible by rough roads, via the east side of the lake, but just barely. It's far easier and better to rent a boat on the west side of the lake, in Rockwood (but beware of fluky lake winds), or take one of the Rockwood-to-Kineo shuttle services. Each Wednesday during the season, the steamboat *Katahdin* makes a 1.5-hour stop at the base of Mount Kineo—not enough time for a major hike, but ample for a sense of the site.

From the dock, the Indian and Bridle Trails lead to the top, but signposting is a bit lax; keep an eye out for blue blazes. The Bridle Trail is easier. Allow about three hours round-trip for the hike; carry a picnic. In winter, when Moosehead Lake freezes solid, you can get to the Kineo peninsula by snowmobile (weather and common sense determine the schedule), but you the trails are too full of snow for hiking.

Mountain Biking

The Moosehead area's hottest new sport is mountain biking. You can bring a bike and strike out on your own, rent a bike, or go with a guide or group. Remember, however, that bicycles are *not* allowed on logging roads; the huge lumber trucks are intimidating enough for passenger vehicles, never mind bicycles.

Mountain bike **rentals** are available from **Northwoods Outfitters,** Main St., P.O. Box 160, Greenville 04441, 207/695-3288, www.maineoutfitter.com, for $20–30 a day, depending on the type. They have baby seats and car carriers for rent, as well as canoes, kayaks, and camping equipment. The shop is open daily 8 AM–7 PM year-round. They're helpful with trail information and deliver free to Lily Bay State Park.

Twenty miles north of Greenville, **The Birches Resort,** P.O. Box 41, Rockwood 04478, 207/534-7305, www.birches.com, rents mountain bikes and sends you off on their network of mountain-bike trails. They also have group rides, including an early-morning moose-watching pedal for $35 a person, including breakfast. Check the website for snowmobiling and cross-country-skiing rates.

Canoeing and Kayaking

If you're not an experienced paddler, be cautious about canoeing or kayaking on Moosehead Lake. The sheltered bays and coves are usually safe, but you can have serious trouble in the open areas—*especially* the stretch between Rockwood and Kineo. Do *not* attempt it; even pros have been swamped by rogue winds on

that route. At Lily Bay State Park, you can launch a canoe from the waterfront campsites and easily make it to Sugar Island.

If you're on your own and need gear, **Northwoods Outfitters,** Main St., P.O. Box 160, Greenville 04441, 207/695-3288, www.maineoutfitter.com, has canoe rentals for $20 a day, kayaks for $35 (single) or $40 (tandem) a day. They offer free delivery to Lily Bay State Park. They also rent tents and provide shuttle service. Open daily 9 AM–7 PM in summer, Wed.–Mon. 8 AM–5:30 PM off-season.

White-water Rafting

The major white-water rafting operator in the Greenville area is Wilderness Expeditions, one of many outdoors enterprises based at the Birches Resort, in Rockwood. **Wilderness Expeditions,** P.O. Box 41, Rockwood 04478, 800/825-9453, www.birches.com, runs 14- to 16-mile day trips on the **Dead, Kennebec,** and **Penobscot Rivers,** between early May and Columbus Day. Costs range $69–115 pp, depending on the river and trip date (July–Aug. weekends are the most expensive). There are

© MARY LYONS

view of Mount Kineo from a Moosehead Lake cruise boat

also overnight rafting packages and a variety of family trips. A bus shuttles rafters from Rockwood to the put-in points, or can pick them up in downtown Greenville, or you can stay at the Wilderness Expeditions lodging nearer the rivers. There's a huge range of lodging rates—in cabins, tents, yurts, and lodges; with or without meals. No kids under 10 are allowed on the Kennebec or the Penobscot's Lower West Branch; no kids under 12 on the Dead or the Penobscot's Upper West Branch. Call or email for the brochure, with dates and details.

Fly-Fishing

The best local resource for fly fishers, hands down, is the **Maine Guide Fly Shop and Guide Service,** Main St., P.O. Box 1202, Greenville 04441, 207/695-2266, www.maine-guideflyshop.com. This veteran operation, owned by Dan Legere, will set you up with a guide and all the equipment you need to do it right. May– Sept., the shop is open Mon.–Sat. 7 AM–5:30 PM, Sun. 9 AM–5 PM. It's open Thurs.–Sun. other months 5 AM–5 PM.

Golf

The most popular, scenic, and windswept course in the area is the nine-hole **Kineo Golf Club,** built for the 500 or so guests at the turn-of-the-20th-century Mount Kineo House. At every turn, you'll see Mount Kineo or Moosehead Lake, or both. There are dynamite views. The course is open June–mid-Oct., and you'll need to get there by boat (see below).

Built in the 1920s, nine-hole **Squaw Mountain Village Golf Course,** Rte. 6/15, Greenville Junction 04441, 207/695-3609, is now part of a modern condo complex. Greens fees are low, the pace is unhurried. The course is open May–Columbus Day.

Snowmobiling

The biggest winter pursuit hereabouts is snowmobiling, thanks to an average 102-inch annual snowfall and 300 miles of Greenville-area trails connecting to the entire state network. It's pretty competitive trying to get a bed in winter if you don't plan ahead; be forewarned.

Incidentally, if you're curious about how people get around northern Maine in winter, check out the parking lot at the Greenville school complex (Pritham Ave.); the vehicle of choice is the snowmobile.

A particularly popular loop is the 160-mile **Moosehead Trail,** which circumnavigates Moosehead Lake: Greenville to Rockwood to Pittston Farm, Seboomook, Northeast Carry, Kokadjo, and back to Greenville. Or start at any access point along the route and go in either direction.

The chamber of commerce has snowmobile trail maps and can put you in touch with local snowmobile clubs. Thanks to these energetic clubs, trails are well maintained and signposted. **Snowmobile rentals** are available at the Birches Resort, Box 41, Rockwood 04478, 207/534-7305, but it's wise to call ahead and reserve; cost is about $125 a day, including helmets and handlebar and thumb warmers.

Downhill Skiing

Compared to the world-class ski resorts south and west of here, the **Big Squaw Mountain Resort,** Rte. 6/15, P.O. Box 430, Greenville 04441, 207/695-1000, www.bigsquawmountain.com, is small potatoes, but if slopeside frills and mega-prices don't fit your budget, here's your ticket. Best of all, we're not talking wimpy bunny slopes; there's a challenge for every alpine skill level. Summit views of Moosehead Lake are fantastic. Eighteen trails are served by a triple chairlift, a double chair, and a T-bar. Vertical drop is 1,750 feet. Snowmaking covers a third to half of the mountain. Big Squaw has had a roller-coaster career in recent years, and it's still in a transitional phase, but equipment maintenance has had high priority. The hotel decor is still leftover 1960s, but how can you beat a cafeteria (open 9 AM–4 PM) with 25-cent sodas and $2 hot dogs? And more than 250 beds in slopeside lodging at $89–99 d on weekends. And—get this—weekday adult lift tickets for $20.

In summer, the double chairlift whisks you up for that terrific view, but the lift tends to operate on a rather erratic schedule, so you can't always count on it. You'll need to call to check or ask at the chamber of commerce. The ski area is just off Rte. 6/15, on the west side of Moosehead Lake.

Cross-Country Skiing
The Birches Resort, Box 41, Rockwood 04478, 207/534-7305, has miles of groomed cross-country-ski trails winding through an 11,000-acre nature preserve. Call for rates and snow conditions. Ski rentals are available at The Birches Ski Touring Center. For lodging at the Birches, escape to one of their remote, heated trailside yurts for $35 pp in peak season (Jan.–Mar. and June–Sept.), $30 off-peak, two-person minimum both seasons. Skiers can use the hot tub and sauna, go on guided ski excursions, and avail themselves of ski packages.

SHOPPING
If you're entering Greenville from the south, cresting the last hill you'll see on your right the **Indian Hill Trading Post,** Rte. 15, Greenville 04441, 207/695-2104 or 800/675-4487, www.indianhill.com, a frontier mini-mall with camping gear, an ATM machine, fishing and hunting licenses, souvenirs, and an IGA supermarket that sells ice, liquor, groceries, and even live lobsters. It's open daily 7 AM–8 PM, all year. It's right next to the chamber of commerce information center, where you'll want to stop anyway.

In downtown Greenville, Mariette Sinclair has opened the **Great Eastern Clothing Co.,** Main St. and Pritham Ave., P.O. Box 1307, Greenville 04441, 207/695-0770, fax 695-2775, selling a tempting selection of casually chic women's clothing. The appealing shop is open daily in summer and fall and irregularly off season.

Also on the main drag is **Maine Mountain Soap and Candle Co.,** Main St., P.O. Box 130, Greenville 04441, 207/695-3926, with a huge array of flavors. The scents of blackberry, lemon, pine, and more all greet you at the door. It's hard to resist. Aromatherapy products are also available. The shop is open all year.

Up the west side of the lake in Rockwood is **Nee-Bur-Bann,** a small cabin next to the home of Mariette and Francis Tomer where they sell a good selection of their own and others' handcrafted Native American baskets, beadwork, and silver jewelry. The shop, whose name means "Northern Lights," is open all year by chance or appointment, so it's best to call ahead to be sure before driving the 20 miles from Greenville to Rockwood. On Rte. 6/15, follow signs to the turnoff for Abnaki Camps. Nee-Bur-Bann's driveway is the next right after the camps.

FESTIVALS AND EVENTS
Moosemainea, an annual, month-long, moose-oriented festival sponsored by the Moosehead Lake Region Chamber of Commerce, combines canoe, rowboat, and mountain-bike races; a family fun day; moose safaris; even a best-moose-photo contest. Register your own moose sightings on a huge map at the chamber of commerce. Events take place in Greenville and Rockwood mid-May–mid-June.

Greenville's **Fourth of July** celebration includes a huge fireworks display capping daytime community events.

The first full weekend in September, the **International Seaplane Fly-In Weekend** is a four-day event drawing seaplanes from all over New England for public breakfasts, a two-day craft fair, flightseeing, and more. At Greenville and Greenville Junction. Beds are *very* scarce during the Fly-In, so either book well ahead to be part of it or wait for another time to visit.

ACCOMMODATIONS
The Greenville area has about 2,000 beds for visitors, so even if you arrive on the spur of the moment, you're likely to find a place to sleep as long as you're flexible. August is a busy month; the September fly-in weekend is crowded, as is the fall-foliage season. Winter brings out snowmobilers by the dozens; rooms can be very scarce, especially in the motels. From mid- to

late May, before the blackflies emerge, Greenville is uncrowded; some back roads may still be tank traps, and the weather will be cool, but it's a peaceful time to be here.

Country Inns

Talk about an oasis! Elegance and comfort are bywords at Sandra and Bruce Hamilton's **The Lodge at Moosehead Lake,** Lily Bay Rd., P.O. Box 1167, Greenville 04441, 207/695-4400, www.lodgeatmooseheadbay.com, but the most astonishing feature might be the furniture. Each of the five guest rooms in the main building has a theme—Trout, Loon, Moose, Totem, and Bear-and each has handcarved beds and mirrors, plus lots of accessories, to carry it out. All but the Trout have dramatic views of Moosehead Lake. Jacuzzis and camouflaged VCRs are in each room, as well as in the three bi-level, water-view carriage-house suites—Allagash, Baxter, and Katahdin. In Allagash and Baxter, lumber-era boom chains hold swaying queen-size beds with incredible lake views; Katahdin has a fireplace in the *bathroom*. Elegantly rustic twig furniture completes the picture. Don't worry—it works, and it's comfortable. In the guest pantry are a small gift shop with clever moose-themed items and dozens of videos for guests to borrow. No smoking, no pets, no children under 14. All of this, of course, comes with a price: rooms and suites are $275–475 d in summer and fall, $205–375 off-season. Breakfast is included all year; an a la carte dinner menu is available June–Oct. Fri.–Mon., and in winter Fri.–Sat. only. Ask about the Lodge's multiday packages that include a variety of area excursions. The inn, open all year, is 2.5 miles north of downtown Greenville.

Just down the road, and up Blair Hill, is the **Blair Hill Inn,** Lily Bay Rd., P.O. Box 1288, Greenville 04441, 207/695-0224, www.blairhill.com, where Dan and Ruth McLaughlin (escapees from the software world) have eight second- and third-floor rooms in a magnificent 1891 manse with antique furnishings, ornate woodwork, walls covered with fine paintings, and eye-popping views of Moosehead Lake. Be sure to hike to the top of the hill

for an even more expansive view; afterward, slip into the outdoor Jacuzzi and survey it all from there. All rooms have private baths (and fresh flowers); most have a lake view and four-poster beds, and some have working fireplaces. Rates are $250–425 d June–Oct., $250–395 d other months. Fri.–Sat. in summer, 6–8:30 PM, the inn's restaurant serves prix-fixe five-course dinners ($50 pp) by reservation to guests and the public. The Inn creates such entrée choices as grilled venison medallions and Jamaican jerk-pork tenderloin; their greenhouse produces much of the fresh produce they serve. The inn is open all year. No smoking, no pets (Thistle the rabbit is in residence), no children under 10.

Another inn with a baronial air is the **Greenville Inn,** Norris St., P.O. Box 1194, Greenville 04441, 207/695-2206 or 888/695-6000, www.greenvilleinn.com, a gray-blue Victorian occupying a prime in-town hilltop. Completed in 1895, the building has incredible woodwork, Tiffany-style lamps, and myriad other elegant details on the ground floor. Five second-floor rooms and a suite (private baths), a more rustic Carriage House suite, and six well-laid-out cottages are $160–325 d, depending on the season. Cottages have mountain views; several inn rooms have water views. No smoking, no pets. No children under seven in inn rooms. The generous breakfast buffet has a European flair, as does the dinner menu; entrées are $20–29. Specialties are seafood and game—all attractively presented and served in three dining rooms (two with views of the sunset). Dinner is 5:30–9 PM, Memorial Day–Oct. (not every day in the shoulder months). Be sure to reserve ahead, especially in midsummer and fall, and save room for dessert. The inn is open all year; dinner is available for guests off-season only by advance reservation.

Bed-and-Breakfasts

Five miles south of Greenville, on 30 acres, the post-and-beam cedar **Evergreen Lodge,** Rte. 15, HC 76, Box 58, Greenville 04441, 207/695-3241 or 888/624-3993, www.evergreenlodgemoosehead.com, has six first- and second-floor rooms with private baths and a variety of decorating themes (one even has a Southwest flavor). The entire downstairs is available for guests, as are a hot tub and a grill on the deck. Rates are $110–150 d, including a full breakfast.

Motels

The **Kineo View Motor Lodge,** Rte. 15, P.O. Box 514, Greenville 04441, 207/695-4470 or 800/659-8439, www.kineoview.com, three miles south of Greenville, sits on a prime hilltop with a dead-on view of Mount Kineo and gorgeous sunsets. Opened in 1993, the modern, three-story motel has 12 good-size rooms with phones, TV, and balconies for $79–89 d, including free continental breakfast Memorial Day weekend–mid-Oct.; $55–69 d (no breakfast) other months. Two suites are $169. Innkeepers Diane and George Edmondson are especially cordial, and this is a great place to bring kids-there's lots of acreage to run around, including nature trails. Rooms have phones, TV, and private decks. Outside are picnic tables and a grill; the windowed ground floor has a hot tub for guests' use. Kineo View, open all year, is 0.5 mile east of Rte. 15.

Two miles closer to Greenville than Kineo View, with the best hilltop view of Moosehead Lake itself, the **Indian Hill Motel,** Rte. 15, P.O. Box 327, Greenville Junction 04442, 207/695-2623 or 800/771-4620, is a more typical one-story motel with 15 rooms for $65 d in summer, $70 d other months. Good-size rooms have phones, cable TV, and that splendid view. In the commercial complex across Rte. 15 are a supermarket and the chamber of commerce. Open all year.

You're practically *in* the lake at **Chalet Moosehead,** Birch St., P.O. Box 327, Greenville Junction 04442, 207/695-2950 or 800/290-3645, www.mooseheadlodging.com. A newish (spring 2000), two-story building is where you want to stay; first- and second-floor rooms have whirlpool tubs, fridges, TVs, phones, and private balconies with dynamite views. Cost is $67–140 d. The older, two-story section has seven basic rooms at $98 d in season, $67 d off

season; eight two-room efficiencies are $104 d in-season, $73 d off-season. Rooms have cable TV, phones, and views through picture windows. Kids five and under stay free; pets ($10) are allowed only in the older units. Dock space is free if you bring your own boat, and guests have free use of canoes, paddleboats, gas grills, and a private swimming area. Open all year.

Small Cottage Colonies

In Rockwood, 20 miles north of Greenville, on Moosehead's west shore, are two well-run small cottage colonies—nothing fancy, but well sited. Pets are allowed at both. **Rockwood Cottages,** Rte. 6/15, P.O. Box 176, Rockwood 04478, 207/534-7725, has eight two-bedroom housekeeping cottages, painted white and fully equipped (even cable TV). Weekly rate in summer is $480 d; half price for kids under six. Daily rate is $80 d for two people. No minimum stay. Canoe rentals are $20 a day. Waterfront sauna, picnic tables, and swimming area. Open May 1–Nov. 30. The six modern cottages at **Sundown Cabins,** Rte. 6/15, Box 129, Rockwood 04478, 207/534-7357, are close to the road yet comfortably quiet. Weekly rates are $475–800. One-week minimum is required July–Aug. Boat rentals are $125 a day. Open all year.

Wilderness Resort

Nailing down a category for the **Birches Resort,** P.O. Box 41, Rockwood 04478, 207/534-7305 or 800/825-9453, isn't easy, because this family-owned operation has a finger in every pie—from a wide range of lodging to first-rate dining to year-round recreational activities. The views, over the lake and Mount Kineo, are fantastic. Set the alarm to catch the sunrise.

The **main lodge** has four small, attractive second-floor rooms (shared bath, balconies) at $60–90 d, peak season. Rustic, sporting-camp-style **log cabins** (one, two, or four bedrooms), most with lakeside porches, are $135–255 per cabin peak season, $110–210 other months. Pets in cabins are extra; no pets in the main lodge. **Cabin tents and yurts** are $25–35 pp and share a shower house. American Plan rates (three meals) are also available for cabin, lodge, and cabin-tent guests—a good idea. You're a healthy drive from Greenville's restaurants, and the cuisine here competes favorably. The Birches' Inn at Pleasant Pond in Caratunk is relaxed, rustic, and recreationally well-equipped. It can accommodate 20 in its eleven rooms, and the rate is $70 d.

The lake-view **dining room**—featuring a humongous moose head, a stone fireplace, and a cedar-strip canoe suspended from the rafters-is open to guests and the public all year for breakfast, lunch, and dinner (dinner reservations are essential; this place packs 'em in). Prime ribs are a specialty. A limited lunch menu is served from the patio grill. Hours of operation vary seasonally, so call to check times.

Besides white-water rafting, snowmobiling, and cross-country skiing, the Birches organizes moose cruises on the lake, kayak lessons, mountain-bike rides, gear rentals, float plane adventures, and wilderness jeep tours. By the time you arrive, they'll have added something else. The Birches also has lodging and adventure facilities near Millinocket and at the Forks. Send for the current brochure. The Birches Resort is beyond the center of Rockwood; turn right off Rte. 6/15 at the Moose River, cross the river, and watch for signs on the right.

Sporting Camps

Genial hosts Andy and Carol Stirling are the third generation now running **West Branch Pond Camps,** Kokadjo, mailing address Box 1153, Greenville 04441, 207/695-2561, one of the quintessential old-time sporting camps. Lining the shore of First West Branch Pond, overlooking White Cap Mountain, are eight classically rustic cabins that have seen better days. But there *is* indoor plumbing. When the bell rings for meals, guests head to the 1890 lakeside lodge and vacuum up the hearty cuisine described in one upscale national magazine as "simple, soulful Yankee cooking." Thursday nights, the prime-rib dinner ($24 pp, including dessert) is open to the public by reservation. BYOL. Most guests stay for a week, and the many repeats make it tough to book

space, but the daily rate is $80 pp American Plan, $40 for kids 5–11. Fly-fishing, hiking, and canoeing are the major pursuits here; the Stirlings don't stay open for hunting season. Take Lily Bay Rd. from Greenville 17 miles; turn right onto an unpaved road (signposted for West Branch Ponds) and go 10 more miles. It's open May–Sept.

Campgrounds and Campsites

The **Maine Forest Service** supervises and maintains free campsites, with fireplaces and outhouses, many on the shores of Moosehead Lake. Most are accessible only by boat-first come, first served. For information, contact the Maine Forest Service office in downtown Greenville, 207/695-3721.

At the northern end of Moosehead Lake, about 5.5 miles south of the Golden Road, **Seboomook Wilderness Campground,** Seboomook Village, mailing address HC85, Box 560, Rockwood 04478, 207/280-0555, www.seboomookwildernesscampground.com, has 84 wooded and open tent, RV, and cabin sites, many right on the water. Everything is very rustic. Request a site on the eastern side, away from the long-term RV area. Facilities include a small, shallow beach, free hot showers, and a grocery store/lunch counter. Sites are $14 a day. Seboomook's store is open all winter for snowmobilers and cross-country skiers; campsites are open mid-May–Nov. The campground is about 28 unpaved miles north of Rockwood; you'll need to pay a user fee ($8 for non-Maine plates, $5 for Maine plates) at Great Northern's Twenty-Mile Checkpoint just before Pittston Farm.

Seasonal Rentals

Folsom's Air Service, P.O. Box 507, Greenville 04441, 207/695-2821, fax 695-2434, rents rustic housekeeping cottages and camps on remote fishing ponds, and they'll fly you in with your gear.

FOOD

The range of dining experiences in and near Greenville is amazingly broad. From pure rustic to local color to upwardly mobile to gourmet cuisine—take your pick. No need to starve here.

Inexpensive to Moderate

Across from the *Katahdin* steamboat dock, **Auntie M's Family Restaurant,** N. Main St., Greenville 04441, 207/695-2238, is a throwback to the 1950s—a locally colorful, casual hangout with booths and tables. A peanut butter and jelly sandwich goes for $1.95, a hearty bowl of homemade chili for $3.95, a side order of gravy for 50 cents. Breakfast is served all day. For something really different, order a stack of chocolate-chip pancakes ($4.50). Open all year, 5 AM–4 PM, until 7:30 PM in summer.

Also popular among local residents for breakfast and lunch is the **Boom Chain Restaurant,** Main St., Greenville 04441, 207/695-2602, named after part of the gear that hauled timber down the lake. Ever had beans-and-toast ($1.50) for breakfast? It's open all year, daily, 6 AM–2 PM.

Fish is the dominant theme at the **Rod-N-Reel Café,** Pritham Ave., Greenville 04441, 207/695-0388—from the name to the decor to the menu—but you can get steaks, chicken, and pasta as well. The menu is loaded with typos, and iceberg lettuce invades the salads, but the service is great and so are the burgers. (They stress they're not responsible if you order your meat well done.) Lunch for two won't set you back more than $16; dinner entrées are $8–20 (with extras). Friday and Saturday are prime rib nights ($13–21). Save room for turtle cheesecake. Open all year, Wed.–Mon. from 11 AM, for lunch and dinner.

On the outskirts of town, the **Lost Lobster Seafood Cafe,** N. Main St., Greenville 04441, 207/695-3900, is the ideal lunch spot on a warm, sunny day. Seems weird to be eating a lobster roll (about $9) this far inland (is that why they call it the Lost Lobster?), but when you sit on the deck and gaze out at Big Squaw Mountain, it won't matter where you are. Beer and wine are available from the unique "lobsterboat bar"; early-bird specials are in effect at this very popular place from 3–5:30 PM daily. Open mid-May–mid-Oct. for lunch and dinner.

In Kokadjo, eighteen miles up the east side of the lake, is the **Kokadjo Trading Post,** Lily Bay Rd., Kokadjo, mailing address Box 1210, Greenville 04441, 207/695-3993, where a sign next to the door reads Parking for Italians Only. Fred and Marie Candeloro opened this chummy Italian-restaurant-cum-convenience-store in 1993, and they've gained a loyal following. In winter, the parking lot is wall-to-wall snowmobiles. Marie's fantastic seafood chowder isn't always on the menu, but order it if it is. Bay scallops may not sound Italian, but they're delicious here. The operation is open all year, daily 7 AM–9 PM.

In Greenville Junction, with fantastic lake views, is **Kelly's Landing,** Rte. 6/15, P.O. Box 336, Greenville Junction 04442, 207/695-4438 or 800/498-9800 in Maine. Hearty home cooking is the rule, and you can eat on the deck in good weather. The big, open dining room, its walls lined with hunting trophies, is open daily, all year, for breakfast, lunch, and dinner. Entrées run $6–16, with a kids' menu available. The Sunday breakfast buffet is a mega-bargain at $9. There's always a crowd here, and boaters can tie up at the dock.

Trust me. If you continue on up Rte. 6/15 from Greenville, 20 miles to Rockwood, and then another 20 miles on an unpaved road, you're guaranteed to have an adventure at **Pittston Farm,** Seboomook Rd., T2 R4, mailing address P.O. Box 525, Rockwood 04478, 207/280-0000. You may even spot some moose on the way; drive defensively. (A few miles before the farm, you'll need to stop at the timber-company checkpoint and pay the road fee: $5 for Maine plates, $8 for non-Maine plates.) This unincorporated territory, officially called the Pittston Academy Grant, once was a major center for timber operations along the Penobscot River. Now the 100-acre riverside farm is known as *the* place to go—by car, flying service, or snowmobile—for meals fit for lumberjacks. Dress down (suspenders will fit right in) and prepare to line up for dinner and eat at a big table; buffet-style meals are available at either 5 and 6:30 PM or just 5 PM, but not all year. Cost is $12, and plates are huge; seconds are allowed. BYOL. It's hearty home cooking, definitely meat-oriented, and you won't eat alone. Ken and Mary Twitchell feed as many as 300 people a day on a holiday weekend; snowmobilers pile in here by the dozens. Reservations are advisable. No credit cards are accepted. Breakfast (great doughnuts) and lunch are also available. During snowmobiling season (Jan.–March), three meals are served daily. May–Sept., it's open Wed.–Sat. 10 AM–8 PM, Sun. noon–8 PM. Oct.–Nov. (hunting season), it's open for breakfast, lunch, and dinner, 5 AM–8 PM. (If all that sounds confusing, it is; call ahead to be sure.) Basic accommodations in the farmhouse (shared baths) go for $47.50 pp, including meals. Don't miss the resident tropical birds and the mini-herd of llamas—and don't fall for the $10 bill polyurethaned to the floor.

INFORMATION AND SERVICES

The regional information center is the **Moosehead Lake Region Chamber of Commerce,** Indian Hill, Rte. 15, P.O. Box 581, Greenville 04441, 207/695-2702, fax 695-3440, www .mooseheadarea.com, on a panoramic hilltop as you enter Greenville from the south. The modern office has **public restrooms** and a gift shop stocked with such moose-erie as T-shirts, moose magnets, bumper stickers, and boxer shorts. It's open Tues.–Sat. 10 AM–4 PM, subject to change; call ahead. The chamber annually publishes a very helpful, free *Visitor's Guide.* The Greenville Downtown Merchants Association produces a map showing locations of shops, restaurants, and lodgings in the small downtown area.

DeLorme Mapping produces a widely available foldout *Map & Guide of Moosehead Lake,* with excellent detail and information on sightseeing and recreational pursuits.

The **Shaw Public Library,** N. Main St.,

Greenville 04441, 207/695-3579, its archives loaded with North Woods lore, is open all year, Tues. 10 AM–6 PM, Wed. 1–5 PM, Thurs. 5–7 PM, Fri. 10 AM–6 PM, and Sat. 9 AM–1 PM.

Newspaper

The Moosehead Messenger, 207/695-3077 or 800/696-3077, published every Wed., covers Greenville and points north.

Emergencies

Greenville is on the boundary of Penobscot and Piscataquis Counties; the Piscataquis County Sheriff, 800/432-7372, handles **police** duties. However, for emergencies in Greenville or Rockwood, dial 911 for fire, police, or ambulance.

State agencies with offices in Greenville are the **Maine Warden Service** (MWS), 207/695-3756, and the **Maine Forest Service** (MFS), Lakeview St., Greenville 04441, 207/695-3721. The Greenville MWS office, with jurisdiction for all search-and-rescue missions of Maine's acreage, undertakes at least one search-and-rescue mission a week. The MFS, besides fire-spotting duty, also is responsible for a number of public campsites in the region.

The **Charles A. Dean Memorial Hospital,** Pritham Ave., Greenville 04441, 207/695-2223, maintains a round-the-clock emergency room. Although the hospital is small, it's the first stop for remote-area trauma cases, such as injured hikers and snowmobile accident victims, so the staff is experienced with emergency situations.

Public Restrooms

The Greenville area is more considerate than most in the matter of public restrooms. In Greenville, the **chamber of commerce office** has restrooms, as does the Moosehead Marine Museum, next to the *Katahdin* wharf. Greenville Junction, there are restrooms at **Junction Wharf;** in Rockwood, there are restrooms at the **public boat landing.** Lily Bay State Park has outhouses, but of course you'll have to pay the day-use fee to enter the park.

Getting Around

Three Greenville **flying services** operating small pontoon- or ski-equipped planes act as the lifelines to remote North Woods sporting camps, campsites, rivers, lakes, and ponds inaccessible overland. In some cases, road access exists, but you'll jeopardize your vehicle, your innards, and maybe your life along the way. Veteran of them all is **Folsom's Air Service,** P.O. Box 507, Greenville 04441, 207/695-2821, fax 695-2434, based at the southeastern corner of Moosehead Lake. Founded in 1946, when everyone walked, canoed, or flew, Folsom's had a huge clientele. The Folsom's headquarters radiophone was their only link to the outside world. Now, with logging roads (albeit bumpy), snowmobiles, and cellular phones, the business has changed markedly, but many visitors still opt for the convenience of the planes. Round-trip rates to more than 60 locations are $50–300 pp; they'll even fly to Augusta, Bangor, and Portland. Canoe transport is also available (extra charge). **Currier's Flying Service,** Pritham Ave., Rte. 6/15, Greenville Junction 04442, 207/695-2778, www.curriersflying-service.com, and **Jack's Air Service,** Pritham Ave., Greenville 04441, 207/695-3020, based

in downtown Greenville, also provide on-demand charter service to remote locales. All three firms have flat hourly rates if you want to create your own itinerary.

You don't need a plane to get to Kineo, but you will need a boat. First, drive the 20 miles along Rte. 6/15 to Rockwood, where the lake is narrowest—about 4,000 feet across. The *Kineo Launch,* a sturdy transport vessel, has been operating since the spring of 1997. It runs back and forth continuously from the Rockwood public landing (on the village loop just off the highway) to Kineo. Just show up and climb aboard. Cost is $10 pp, round-trip. It is open Memorial Day to Labor Day.

Many of the **roads** in the Greenville area are unpaved; paper-company roads tend to be the best maintained, because access is essential for their huge log trucks and machinery. But others, especially roads leading to sporting camps, can become tank traps in spring—April and May—and after a heavy downpour. Before setting out during those times—especially if you don't have a 4WD vehicle—be sure to check on road conditions. Ask the chamber of commerce, the Maine Forest Service, the county sheriff, or the sporting camp owners.

Dover-Foxcroft Area

Located at the bottom of Piscataquis (Piss-CAT-uh-kwiss) County, Dover-Foxcroft is the county seat, hub for the surrounding towns of Milo, Brownville Junction, Sangerville, Guilford, Abbot, and Monson. Here's an area that's often overlooked—probably because Greenville, Moosehead Lake, and Baxter State Park are just up the road. But it's easy to spend a couple of exploring days here—notably for dramatic Gulf Hagas Reserve and Borestone Mountain Sanctuary, but also for a handful of out-of-the-way towns few visitors get to appreciate.

One town growing steadily in renown is Monson (pop. about 749), 20 miles northwest of Dover-Foxcroft and 15 miles south

of Greenville. Incorporated in 1822, Monson has an old reputation and a new one. The old one comes from its slate quarries, first mined in the 1870s, which shipped slate around the nation for sinks, roof tiles, blackboards, and even urinals. A considerable Finnish community grew up here to work the quarries; their descendants still celebrate traditional holidays. Although the industry has declined, and only two companies still operate, Monson slate monuments adorn the gravesites of John F. Kennedy and Jacqueline Kennedy Onassis. You can still see an abandoned quarry pit on Pleasant Street, near Lake Hebron, on the western side of town.

Monson's current fame comes from

Appalachian Trail through-hikers, whose energetic grapevine carries the word about the town's hospitality to the rugged outdoorsfolk nearing the end of their arduous trek from Springer Mountain, Georgia. The Monson stopover comes just before the AT leg known as the "100-Mile Wilderness," so it's a place to regroup, clean up, and rev up for the isolated week or 10 days ahead.

Sangerville (pop. 1,324), incorporated in 1813, is the birthplace of the infamous Sir Harry Oakes, a colorful adventurer who acquired a fortune in Canadian gold mining. Murdered in bed in his Nassau (Bahamas) mansion in 1943, gazillionaire Oakes was interred in Dover-Foxcroft. His killer was never found. Also born in Sangerville was Sir Hiram Maxim, inventor of the Maxim gun.

SIGHTS AND RECREATION

Low's Covered Bridge

In 1987, the raging Piscataquis River, swollen by spring rains, wiped out 130-foot-long Low's Covered Bridge, near Sangerville. Named after settler Robert Low, the original bridge was built in 1830 and replaced in 1843 and 1857. The current incarnation, a well-made replica, reopened in 1990, at a cost of $650,000. It's one of only nine covered bridges now in Maine. Close to Rte. 16/6/15, the bridge is 3.7 miles east of Guilford and 4.5 miles west of Dover-Foxcroft.

Katahdin Iron Works

Only a lonely stone blast furnace and a charcoal kiln remain at Katahdin Iron Works, the site of a once-thriving 19th-century community where iron mining produced 2,000 tons of ore a year and steam trains brought tourists to the three-story Silver Lake House to "take the waters" at Katahdin Mineral Springs. Today most visitors drive down the unpaved 6.5 miles from Rte. 11 and stop just across the road, at the North Maine Woods **KI Checkpoint,** for hiking in Gulf Hagas Reserve. Entrance to the KI site (as it's known locally) is free, but the best way to appreciate the

site and its fascinating history is to contact local historian/author Bill Sawtell, a fount of information, to schedule one of his fact-filled, 45-minute, $5 pp (minimum two people) tours: **Bill Sawtell,** P.O. Box 272, Brownville 04414, 207/965-3971; best to call in the morning. Wear sturdy shoes to follow him around. The site is officially open Memorial Day to Labor Day. Katahdin Iron Works is 11.5 miles northwest of Brownville Junction. (Bill Sawtell also gives tours of Brownville's historic sights.)

Gulf Hagas Reserve

Hiking in and around Gulf Hagas Reserve, a spectacular 400-foot-high, 3.5-mile-long wooded, rocky gorge along the West Branch of the Pleasant River, requires registering first at the **KI Checkpoint,** 207/965-8135, operated by North Maine Woods, the forest recreation-management association. (KI is short for Katahdin Ironworks.) The checkpoint is one of the entrances into the **KI Jo-Mary Multiple Use Forest,** a working forest of over 200,000 acres. (Jo-Mary is the name of a legendary Indian chief.) The checkpoint is open 6 AM–9 PM (sometimes later on midsummer weekends) early May–Columbus Day. The staffers have maps of the reserve ($1) and KI Jo-Mary ($2); *do not* hike Gulf Hagas without the map. Access is $8 for nonresidents, $5 for Maine residents; seniors and kids under 15 are free. No bicycles, motorcycles, or ATVs can go beyond this point. Camping at one of the 60 scenic primitive sites in this area costs an extra $7 per night (residents or nonresidents). It's wise to call the checkpoint ahead of time to reserve one of the sites, which have outhouses, picnic tables, and fire rings. The policy is carry-in, carry-out. There's also a commercial campground here.

You'll need to drive about seven miles from the checkpoint to one of the two parking areas; remember that logging trucks have the right-of-way on this road. As you walk from your vehicle toward the gulf, you'll go through **The Hermitage,** a 35-acre Nature Conservancy preserve of old-growth pines. Gulf Hagas

Reserve, a National Natural Landmark, is no cakewalk. Almost weekly, rangers have to rescue injured or lost hikers who underestimate the terrain. Ledges are narrow, with 100-foot dropoffs, and rain can make them perilous. Leave rambunctious children at home; the section beyond **Screw Auger Falls** is particularly dangerous for kids under 12. Wear waterproof hiking boots—you have to cross a stream to gain access to the reserve.

Caveats aside, the hike is fantastic—especially mid-Sept.–early Oct., when the leaves are gorgeous and the bugs have retreated. Carry a compass and a flashlight and allow six to eight hours for the 8.3-mile canyon circuit (although there are shortcuts if you tucker out before the end). Most hikers do the loop clockwise. North Maine Woods trails are blue-blazed; a spur of the AT is white-blazed. The trails are open mid-May–late Oct., but atypical weather can affect the schedule. The checkpoint is 11.5 miles northwest of Brownville Junction (6.5 miles northwest of Rte. 11).

Peaks-Kenny State Park

Get organized to arrive at Peaks-Kenny State Park, Sebec Lake Rd., Dover-Foxcroft 04426, 207/564-2003, well before 11 AM on weekends in June, July, and August—after that, you may be turned away or have to wait. This particularly scenic park on 14-mile-long Sebec Lake has 50 picnic sites, a playground, lifeguard-staffed sand beach, nine miles of hiking trails, an amphitheater for special nature programs, and 56 campsites. On July–Aug. weekends, camping reservations are essential (two-night minimum). Call 207/287-3824, using Master-Card or Visa. Day-use admission is $4 adults, free for seniors and kids under five. Nonresident camping fees are $20 per site per night, resident fee $15 per site per night plus the reservation fee of $2 per site per night; no hookups. Leashed pets are allowed. Canoe rentals are $3 an hour. The park is open 7 AM–10 PM, May 15–Sept. 30. Take Rte. 153 north from Dover-Foxcroft, about six miles, following signs for the park.

Borestone Mountain Sanctuary

Owned and maintained by the Maine Audubon Society, www.maineaudubon.org, Borestone Mountain Sanctuary in Elliotsville Township, near Monson, is a 1,600-acre preserve that provides a wonderful hiking experience for all ages. The two-mile, moderately difficult trail to the rocky, open summit delivers ample rewards at the top: full-circle views, including Lake Onawa below, and the mountains of the 100-Mile Wilderness. Foliage season is especially dramatic here. Allow 4–5 hours for the four-mile round-trip, including a halfway-up stop at the Sunrise Pond visitors center. Pets are not permitted. Admission is $4 adults, $1 children 6–18. The sanctuary is officially open June–Sept., 207/631-4050, 8 AM to sunset Oct.–May, 207/781-2330. From Rte. 6/16/15 at the northern edge of Monson, take the Elliotsville Rd. (partly unpaved) northeast 8.5 miles to the trailhead.

Lake Onawa

Four-mile-long Lake Onawa is the mountain-ringed setting for the charming hamlet of **Onawa,** once linked to civilization only by train. Then came the road, and passenger service ceased, leaving Onawa as a summer colony with a year-round population of three. A prime attraction is an incredible 126-foot-high wooden railroad trestle (pronounced "trussel" around here) that challenges even bravehearted souls. Acrophobes, forget it. There's a walkway alongside, but it's still scary; don't attempt it on a windy day. Bungee jumpers haven't yet discovered the trestle, but it *was* featured in one of Stephen King's films. During World War II, the trestle was protected by black security guards, among them Edward Brooke, the late U.S. senator from Massachusetts. The 1,400-foot-long trestle, officially the Ship Pond Stream Viaduct, soars over Ship Pond Stream, at the southern end of the lake, about 0.5 mile beyond the cluster of cottages. To reach Onawa, follow directions (above) for Borestone Mountain, but turn right off Elliotsville Rd. at the Big Wilson Stream bridge, then the next left onto Onawa Rd. Continue about three miles to the settlement.

Northern Maine Riding Adventures

Under the heading of Northern Maine Riding Adventures, 64 Garland Line Rd., Dover-Foxcroft 04426, 207/564-3451, www.mainetrailrides.com. Maine Guides Judy Cross-Strehlke and Bob Strehlke operate pack trips, summer camps, a riding school, and adventure-based learning programs out of their 70-acre farm. The most popular day-trip is the six-hour Borestone Mountain/Drew Valley Ride over toward the mountain and to Onawa. Lunch (bring your own) is under the soaring trestle. Cost is $185 pp (minimum two persons, maximum eight). Another popular expedition is the Hi-Cut Trail Ride ($155 pp; discount for families), suitable for every level of rider (age nine and up) and ascending 900 feet to panoramic views. The ride takes 5–6 hours, including time to down a box lunch along the way. Group minimum is two; maximum is 10. Campsites ($15) and a yurt ($25) are available for lodging on the farm. No credit cards. Prices for other trips range from $75 (half day) to $700 (three days, including lodging). It's pricey, since kids pay as much as adults, but you'll have a well-run adventure. Reservations are required for the trips, which operate mid-May–late Oct., depending on weather and demand. The farm is six miles southeast of Dover-Foxcroft and six miles northeast of Dexter, off Rte. 7.

FESTIVALS AND EVENTS

The last Saturday in April, the early-season **Piscataquis River Canoe Race** covers eight miles of mostly flat water, between Guilford and Dover-Foxcroft. An hour-long, family-oriented race goes under Low's Covered Bridge. Starting time is 11 AM, next to the Guilford Industries factory.

The **Piscataquis Valley Fair** takes place the fourth weekend in August. A family-oriented traditional county fair, it features agricultural exhibits, a pig scramble, a homemade ice-cream parlor, fireworks, and a carnival. It's at the Piscataquis Valley Fairgrounds, Fairview Ave. (just south of Rte. 6/15, east side of town), in Dover-Foxcroft.

ACCOMMODATIONS

Bed-and-Breakfasts

On a prominent hilltop and surrounded by gardens, the dark-red-painted **Guilford Bed and Breakfast,** Elm St., Rte. 6/15/16, Guilford 04443, 207/876-3477, fax 876-3615, has an inviting feel. The interior adds to the appeal, with interesting antiques, six second- and third-floor guest rooms (private and shared baths; air-conditioning on the third floor), and three common rooms. Rates are $75–105 d. Since innkeepers Lynn and Harry Anderson have a catering business, count on gourmet breakfasts, maybe stuffed French toast, served on the wraparound porch in summer. They'll also do dinner by advance reservation. No pets (cat and dog in residence), no smoking; well-behaved older children welcome. The Guilford Bed and Breakfast is open all year.

Just beyond the Dover-Foxcroft area, but close enough, the **Brewster Inn,** 37 Zion's Hill Rd., Dexter 04930, 207/924-3130, is an attractively updated 19-room National Historic Register mansion designed by John Calvin Stevens and once owned by Maine Governor Ralph Brewster. The B&B's five rooms and two suites ($59–119 d) all have private baths, phones, air-conditioning, cable TV, and stories to tell. The knotty-pine Games Room was the governor's private hideout, and guess who once slept in the Truman Room? In the aptly named Honeymoon Suite are a stained-glass window, four-poster bed, fireplace, and double whirlpool. Breakfast is a generous buffet. Innkeepers Michael and Ivy Brooks have filled the house with family antiques—plus Ivy's lace collection and Michael's eclectic antique radio collection. Outside are tennis courts and lovely gardens. No pets, no smoking; well-behaved children are welcome. Open all year. (The biggest problem in Dexter is finding a good spot for dinner.) Dexter is 13 miles south of Dover-Foxcroft and 15 miles from I-95.

Hostel

Headquarters for Appalachian Trail through-hikers, a home-away-from-home since 1977, is the legendary **Shaw's Boarding Home,** Pleasant St., Monson 04464, 207/997-3597, www .shawslodging.com. To weary hikers, Pat and Keith Shaw's welcoming, no-frills operation feels like the Hyatt Regency. Short-haul hikers are also welcome, and snowmobilers in winter; couch potatoes will feel totally out of place. The Shaws can accommodate nearly three dozen guests in varied arrangements—private rooms in the main house ($30 pp), bunkhouse beds ($20 pp), and bunks in the adjoining barn ($12 pp). A lumberjack-quality breakfast is $6 or all you can eat for $8. For small fees, the Shaws provide shuttle and mail-drop service and laundry facilities; parking for short-haulers is $1 a day. The hostel is a block west of Main St. (Rte. 15) and is open all year.

Campgrounds

Within the boundaries of the KI Jo-Mary Multiple Use Forest is a single commercial campground, the **Jo-Mary Lake Campground,** Upper Jo-Mary Lake, TB R10 WELS, mailing address P.O. Box 329, Millinocket 04462, 207/723-8117 or 800/494-0031, located on the southern shore of five-mile-long Upper Jo-Mary Lake. Despite being remote, the campground has 60 sites, flush toilets, hot showers, laundry facilities, a snack bar, plenty of play space for kids, and a sandy beach. Sites are about $17 a night per family. July–Aug., there's a Wednesday night beanhole bean supper (beans baked underground). The campground, open mid-May–late Sept., is 15 miles southwest of Millinocket and 20 miles north of Brownville. From Brownville Junction, take Rte. 11 northwest about 15 miles, turn left onto an unpaved road, and stop at the Jo-Mary Checkpoint. After paying the user fee ($8 for nonresidents, $5 for Maine residents; seniors and kids under 15 are free), continue six miles northwest to the campground.

FOOD

A popular local favorite, **The Covered Bridge Restaurant,** Rte. 15, Guilford 04443, 207/564-2204, is just across the street from Low's Covered Bridge, midway between Dover-Foxcroft and Guilford. Dinner entrées—hearty home cooking—run $6–16. An all-you-can-eat fish fry is $6.95. They now have a liquor license, and they accept credit cards. Breakfast is only served on weekends. Seasonal hours, Tues.–Thurs. 11 A.M.–8 PM, Fri. 11 AM–9 PM, Sat. 7 AM to 9 PM, Sun. 7 AM–7 PM.

If you feel like rubbing shoulders with AT through-hikers—especially in September, when they're close to finishing up—plan to have a meal at the chummy **Appalachian Station Restaurant,** 1 Tenney Hill Rd., Rte. 15, Monson 04464, 207/997-3648. Plenty of local color here, too—what one patron calls "the real goddam thing." No liquor license, no credit cards. Open all year, Tues.–Fri. 5:30 AM–7 PM (to 9 PM Thurs.–Fri.), Sat. 6 AM–9 PM, and Sun. 6 AM–7 PM.

INFORMATION AND SERVICES

Based in a riverside log cabin, the **Southern Piscataquis County Chamber of Commerce,** 100 South St., Rte. 7, P.O. Box 376, Dover-Foxcroft 04426, 207/564-7533, www.nconline.net-spcc, is open daily 9 AM–4 PM, June–Aug.; weekdays 9 AM–4 PM other months.

For information about Gulf Hagas Reserve and the KI Jo-Mary Multiple Use Forest, contact **North Maine Woods,** P.O. Box 421, Ashland 04732, 207/435-6213, www.northmainewoods.org.

Newspapers

The *Piscataquis Observer,* 207/564-8355, published Wednesdays in Dover-Foxcroft, covers this area thoroughly. The *Bangor Daily News* is the daily newspaper focusing on this area.

Emergencies

In Dover-Foxcroft, Guilford, and Monson, dial 911 for police, fire, or ambulance services. **Mayo Regional Hospital,** 75 W. Main St., Dover-Foxcroft 04426, 207/564-8401, has round-the-clock emergency care. The nearest major medical facility is **Eastern Maine Medical Center,** emergency-room 207/973-8000, in Bangor.

Kennels

All Breed Groom and Board, Downs Rd., Sebec, mailing address RFD 2, Box 640, Dover-Foxcroft 04426, 207/564-3656 or 564-8688, boards both dogs and cats at very reasonable rates. (They also breed English springer spaniels.) The kennel is open all year, Tues.–Sat. 8 AM–6 PM, Sun.–Mon. 8–10 AM and 4–6 PM. It's on a side road north of Rte. 6/16, about midway between Dover-Foxcroft and Milo.

Kennebec and Moose River Region

The mighty Kennebec, Maine's fourth-largest river, defines this region. The river wends its way through Somerset and Kennebec Counties from Jackman through Bingham, Skowhegan, Waterville, Augusta, and Richmond, and then on toward the sea at Bath. Many of these inland communities seldom see out-of-towners, since most visitors tend to concentrate on the region's lovely lakes districts—Belgrade Lakes, China Lakes, and Winthrop Lakes, all favorite summer destinations for as long as anyone can remember.

In 1976, timber companies stopped float-ing logs down the Kennebec to their lumber mills. Since then, white-water rafting has mushroomed, focusing long-overdue attention on the beautiful Upper Kennebec Valley and creating a whole new crowd of enthusiasts for this region. And there's no sign of a let-up. When I first rafted the Kennebec, in 1985, it was still a rather volatile yet unsophisticated business; regulations were still a bit loose, and the competition was scrappy. Since then, however, a number of fly-by-night firms have gone belly-up, and those that remain range from deliberately small operations to four-season

©MARY LYONS

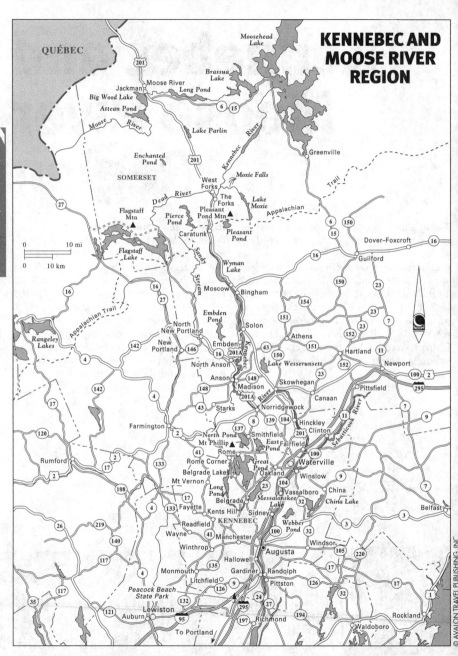

Kennebec/Moose River

KENNEBEC AND
MOOSE RIVER
REGION

QUÉBEC

Moosehead
Lake

Brassua
Lake

201

Moose River   Long Pond

Jackman

Big Wood Lake

Attean Pond

6   15

Moose   River

Lake Parlin

Greenville

Enchanted
Pond

201

SOMERSET

Kennebec River

West
Forks

Moxie Falls

Trail

The
Forks

Lake
Moxie

Appalachian

6   150

Dead   River

27

Flagstaff
Mtn

Pierce
Pond

Pleasant
Pond Mtn

Pleasant
Pond

15

Dover–Foxcroft   16

Caratunk

0   10 mi

0   10 km

Flagstaff
Lake

Sandy   Stream

Wyman
Lake

16

Guilford

16

Moscow   Bingham

150

23

27

Embden
Pond

Solon

154

151

23

Rangeley
Lakes

Appalachian Trail

16

North
New Portland

142

New
Portland

146

Embden

16   201A

North Anson

Kennebec

43

Athens

151

152

23

7

Lake Wesserunsett

152

Hartland

11

Newport

100   2

295

4

Anson

148

Madison

201A

Skowhegan

23

Canaan

Pittsfield

142

148

Norridgewock

River

17

43   Starks

8   139   104

11

7

Farmington

2

North Pond
Mt Phillip

137

Smithfield

Hinckley
Clinton

201

9

120

17

41

Rome

East
Pond

Fairfield

100

Sebasticook River

Rome Corner

133

Great
Pond

Waterville

Rumford

2

Mt Vernon

Belgrade Lakes

Oakland

Winslow

9

7

108

Long
Pond

Belgrade

104

Messalonskee
Lake

Vassalboro

China

4

133

Fayette

Sidney

China Lake

Belfast

26

219

Kents Hill

KENNEBEC

Webber
Pond

3

3

140

Readfield

100

32

117

Wayne

41

Manchester

Windsor

105

220

4

Winthrop

Augusta

17

Monmouth

135

Hallowell

Gardiner   Randolph

126

17

117

Litchfield

126

Pittston

32

35

Peacock Beach
State Park

132

9

24

27

1

121

Auburn   Lewiston

95

295

197   Richmond

194

Rockland

To Portland

Waldoboro

© AVALON TRAVEL PUBLISHING, INC.

enterprises with a variety of other sports options and all the amenities anyone could want. Visit the Forks and you'll understand.

When you see the terrain, you'll also begin to understand some of the awful rigors endured by Col. Benedict Arnold (before his change of heart and alliance) and his men when they chose a route through the Kennebec Valley to attack the British in Quebec City in 1775.

The Arnold Trail

"A tragic masterpiece of bad timing, bad maps, and bad luck" is author Ogden Tanner's summation of the "March on Quebec" spearheaded by Col. Benedict Arnold. Although he later betrayed the Revolutionary cause, Arnold was in good graces when he set out that fall with 1,100 adventurers to remove the English from their Quebec stronghold. In Pittston (six miles south of Augusta), the expedition assembled 220 locally made bateaux, then continued up the Kennebec River to Augusta, Skowhegan, and Norridgewock—cutting a swath through the Kennebec/Moose River region before portaging westward at Carrying Place Township to the Western Lakes and Mountains region and on into Canada. Afflicted by disease, hunger, cold, insects, and unforgiving terrain, the group was devastated before dragging into Quebec City in December 1775. From Pittston to the Carrying Place (10 miles north of Bingham), Arnold Trail historical markers note the expedition's rest stops, obstacles, and other details. Even though Arnold's expedition has been little more than a footnote to history, it's an incredible story, and one best appreciated during a visit to this region.

Augusta and Vicinity

As the state capital, Augusta is where everything is supposed to happen. A lot does happen here, but don't be surprised to find the imposing State House and lovely governor's mansion the centerpieces of a relatively sleepy city. With a population of only 20,280, Augusta is the seventh-largest city in Maine and no megalopolis, but it *is* the heart of state government and central Maine.

Pilgrims first settled here on the banks of the Kennebec River in the 17th century (in 1997, the city celebrated its bicentennial with considerable fanfare), and Boston merchants established Fort Western in the mid-18th century. Augusta was named the capital in 1827.

Augusta's housing costs are low, and the population is particularly diverse for Maine. As real estate on the coast moves out of reach for the average person, Augusta and the surrounding area are experiencing an infusion of new vitality.

The three best-known communities south of Augusta—Hallowell, Gardiner, and Richmond—all scale down hillsides to the river, making their settings especially attractive. In Hallowell (pop. 2,600), settled in 1762, the main thoroughfare still retains the air of its former days as a prosperous port and source of granite and ice. The entire downtown, with brick sidewalks and attractive shops and restaurants, is a National Historic District.

Six miles south of Augusta, Gardiner (pop. 6,729), the "Tilbury Town" of noted author Edwin Arlington Robinson, claims more National Historic Register buildings than any of its neighbors. The Gardiner Historic District includes more than

Cumston Hall, Monmouth

© KATHLEEN M. BRANDES

45 downtown buildings; lots more are beyond the district. Besides Robinson, another prominent Gardiner resident was Laura Howe Richards, author of *Captain January* and daughter of Julia Ward Howe, who wrote "The Battle Hymn of the Republic." (The yellow Federal-style home where Richards and her husband raised seven children, at 3 Dennis St., is not open to the public.) Most outstanding of Gardiner's mansions (also not open to the public) is "Oaklands," a Gothic Revival home built in 1836 by the

THE RUSSIANS WERE COMING

In the 1950s, the sleepy Kennebec River town of Richmond, 12 miles south of Maine's state capital, became the center of a unique and unlikely colony, as several hundred Russian-speaking refugee families settled among the area's villages and rolling farmland. The Kennebec Valley, economically depressed and remote from other Russian immigrant centers in the United States, seems an improbable choice for a Slavic enclave. Yet Richmond soon boasted a Russian restaurant, a Russian bootmaker's shop, and even onion domes—on St. Alexander Nevsky, Maine's first Russian Orthodox church. For the first time, Russian was heard on Richmond's streets, and Russian-speaking children enrolled in local schools.

The settlement was the brainchild of Baron Vladimir von Poushental, a swashbuckling veteran of the tsar's World War I air force. Fleeing the Bolshevik Revolution, he landed in New York, where his personality and family connections gained him entrée to a series of managerial jobs, if not to the wealth he had enjoyed as a Russian noble. An expert marksman and dedicated hunter, von Poushental in 1947 decided to retire to a modest cabin in the Kennebec Valley, where he had hunted and fished for many years. There he began buying up abandoned farms and promoting the valley's attractions to fellow Russian émigrés. The climate and countryside resembled Russia's, he said, and land was cheap. For a few thousand dollars, a refugee could buy a house and 30 acres. To create a nucleus for the settlers, the baron donated a 400-acre farm to the aging veterans of Russia's White armies, and he helped them establish a retirement home and an Orthodox chapel.

And so they came: Ukrainians, Russians, Byelorussians, and Cossacks; professors, farmers, artists, and carpenters. Some came directly from Europe's displaced-persons camps, others from homes and jobs in U.S. cities where they had lived for years. The settlers shared a common language, their Orthodox faith, a zest for life, and a hatred of the Soviet regime. The younger émigrés worked, raised families, and became part of the larger American community around them. Their elderly parents felt more comfortable associating with other Russian-speakers.

Today the bootmaker and restaurant are gone. Most of the elderly—the old émigrés from pre-Communist Russia—are dead, their Cyrillic gravestones dotting the Richmond cemetery. A few old-timers, still hardy, stand each Sunday through the long Orthodox service, and they bake *pirozhki* or sweets for church sales on special occasions, like the town's late-July celebration of Richmond Days.

Their grandchildren, Russian-Americans, have merged successfully into mainstream America. Most have married outside their ethnic group, and many have taken jobs outside the Kennebec Valley, not necessarily by choice. Yet a fair number still live and work in the area. In a way that might have surprised even von Poushental (who died in 1978), the colony he sponsored took root and flourished in a part of America he loved.

—Robert S. Jaster, author of *Russian Voices on the Kennebec: The Story of Maine's Unlikely Colony* grandson of founding father Dr. Sylvester Gardiner, a wealthy land speculator.

Just over the border in Sagadahoc County, Richmond (pop. 3,400), also flush with handsome buildings, was the site of a Russian émigré community in the 1950s. Here's a town that awaits rediscovery.

West of Augusta, the town of Monmouth (pop. 3,500) is the site of Cumston Hall, a dramatic, turn-of-the-20th-century structure that now houses the Theater at Monmouth as well as the municipal offices and public library.

SIGHTS

Maine State House

From almost every vantage point in Augusta, your eye catches the prominent dome of the Maine State House, centerpiece of the government complex on the west side of the Kennebec River. Occupying the corner of State and Capitol Sts., the State House dates originally from 1832, when it was completed to the design of famed Boston architect Charles Bulfinch, who modeled it on his Massachusetts

State House design. Only a dozen years had passed since Maine had separated from Massachusetts, and Augusta became the state capital in 1827. Granite for the building came from quarries in nearby Hallowell; total construction cost was $145,000. Atop the oxidized copper dome stands a gold-gilded sculpture of "Lady Wisdom." In the early 20th century, space needs forced a major expansion of the building, leaving only the eight-columned front portico as the Bulfinch legacy. When a $32 million renovation began in 1999, a new public entrance was added, and the interior was changed to hide pipes and wires, install new sprinklers, and heating and air-conditioning systems, making the inside functional while retaining most of the original exterior.

Visitors are welcome to wander around the State House, but check first to see whether the legislature is in session. If so, parking becomes scarce, the hallways become congested, and access may be restricted. Best place to enter the building is on the west side, facing the more modern state office building, and marked "Maine State House." Pick up the useful brochure

Kennebec/Moose River

Maine State Capitol building in Augusta

© MARY LYONS

for a self-guided tour, or, better still, take a free guided tour, available weekdays 9 AM–1 PM. Call ahead, 207/287-2301 (tours are organized by the Maine State Museum), to arrange it, or ask at the kiosk.

Maine State Museum

If the Smithsonian is the nation's attic, welcome to Maine's attic—and a well-organized one at that. At the Maine State Museum, State House Complex, 83 State House Station, Augusta 04333, 207/287-2301, www.mainestatemuseum.org, gears and tools spin and whir in the intriguing *Made in Maine* industrial exhibits—focusing on quarrying, ice harvesting, fishing, agriculture, lumbering, and ship-building. A spiraled archaeological exhibit covers the past 12 millennia of Maine's history. Some displays are interactive and all exhibits are wheelchair-accessible. During the winter, the museum sponsors a free lecture series, and special programs occur throughout the year. A small gift shop stocks historical publications, and Maine-related gifts and toys. The museum is part of the state government complex that includes the State House and the Maine State Library. The museum and library share a building, separated by a parking lot from the State House. The museum is open all year, Mon.–Fri. 9 AM–5 PM, Sat. 10 AM–4 PM, and Sun. 1–4 PM. Best of all, admission is way less than a movie: $2 for adults, $1 for children 6–18 and seniors, free under 6, maximum for a family $6.

The Blaine House

In 1833, a year after the State House was ready for business, retired sea captain James Hall finished his elegant new home across the street. But it was not until 29 years later, when prominent politico James G. Blaine assumed ownership, that the house became the hotbed of state and national political ferment. No underachiever, Blaine was a Maine congressman and senator, Speaker of the U.S. House, U.S. secretary of state under two presidents, and Republican candidate for the presidency. Two decades after his death, Blaine's widow donated the family home to the state of Maine; it's been the **governor's mansion** ever since.

Free, half-hour guided tours of the ground-floor public areas of the Blaine House, State and Capitol Sts., Augusta 04333, 207/287-2121, occur Tues.–Thurs. 2–4 PM, all year. A special event occasionally cancels the tour schedule, so it's wise to call ahead to avoid being disappointed.

Old Fort Western

Built in 1754 for the French and Indian Wars and restored as recently as 1988, Old Fort Western, 16 Cony St., Augusta 04330, 207/626-2385, www.oldfortwestern.org—reputedly the nation's oldest remaining stockaded fort—has witnessed British, French, and Native Americans squabbling over this Kennebec riverfront site. Benedict Arnold and his troops camped here during their 1775 march on Quebec. Today, costumed interpreters help visitors travel through time to the 18th century; hands-on demonstrations—butter churning, musket drill, barrel building, weaving, even vinegar making—occur daily from July Fourth to Labor Day. Admission is $5 adults, $4 seniors (55 and over), $3 children 6–16; kids under six are free. Hours: Memorial Day weekend to Labor Day: 1 PM–4 PM daily; Labor Day to Columbus Day: 1 PM–4 PM weekends only; Nov.–Jan.: first Sun. of month 1–3 PM; Mar.: Maple Syrup Day, fourth Sun. of the month 1–3 PM. The museum is on the east bank of the Kennebec in downtown Augusta, next to Augusta City Hall.

PARKS AND PRESERVES

On the east side of State St., between the State House and the river, is 10-acre **Capitol Park,** a great place for a picnic after visiting the Maine State Museum, the State House, and the Blaine House. In the park is the **Maine Vietnam Veterans Memorial,** a dramatic, you-are-there, walk-through monument erected in 1985.

On the east side of the Kennebec River, across from the old Augusta Mental Health Institute, is a wonderful oasis. The **Pine Tree State Ar-**

boretum, 153 Hospital St., Rte. 9, P.O. Box 344, Augusta 04332, 207/621-0031, devotes 224 acres to more than 600 trees and shrubs. Bring a picnic (carry-in, carry-out) and wander the nearly six-mile trail network. If you're a birder, bring binoculars. Well-designed planting clusters include hosta and rhododendron collections, a rock garden, an antique apple orchard, and the Governors Grove—with a white pine dedicated to each Maine governor. Stop first at the Viles Visitor Center to pick up a trail map. The grounds are open daily, sunrise to sunset, all year; the visitors center is open Mon.–Fri. 8 AM–4 PM. Leashed pets are allowed; no smoking on the grounds. During the winter, the trails are groomed for cross-country skiing.

Next to the arboretum parking lot is **Cony Cemetery** (also known as Knight Cemetery), one of Augusta's oldest, with gravestones dating from the late 18th century. Old-cemetery buffs will want to check it out, but rubbings are not permitted.

About 12 miles south of Augusta, 100-acre **Peacock Beach State Park,** Rte. 201, Richmond 04357, 207/582-2813, on long, narrow Pleasant Pond, is an underutilized pocket park great for swimming and picnicking; a lifeguard is on duty in summer. Admission is $2 adults, $1 children 5–11; free for kids under five. Open Memorial Day–Labor Day, 9 AM–sunset.

You can walk, bike, ski, or run the **Kennebec River Rail Trail,** keeping an eye peeled for bald eagles, salmon, and just the general flow of the Kennebec. The Friends of KRRT, P.O. Box 2195, Augusta 04338, www.KRRT.org, plan a 6.5-mile trail, of which 1.6 miles are already built. Contact them for information, or pick up maps at local businesses and tourism offices.

Swan Island

The Maine Department of Inland Fisheries and Wildlife (IF&W) has established a byzantine reservation system to limit visitors to its **Steve Powell Wildlife Management Area** on 1,755-acre, four-mile-long **Swan Island,** www.state.me.us/ifw/education/swanisland,

in the middle of the Kennebec River. Don't be daunted; it's worth the effort. The entire island is on the National Register of Historic Places. Well-marked trails are everywhere; one trail takes 30 minutes, another takes three hours and goes the length of the lovely wooded island. Plan to take the free, hour-long ranger-guided tour. No license is needed for fishing, but even private boats need permission to land here (near the campground); small boats are not recommended because of 10-ft. tidal variations; bikes are permitted on center main road only; cars and pets are not allowed.

To get here, you'll take a small ferry the very short distance from a dock in Richmond, next to the town-owned Waterfront Park on Rte. 24. The boat operates May 1–Labor Day. Call for reservations and an informational brochure, 207/547-5322, Mon.–Fri. 7:30–11:30 AM. Day-use admission is $5 adults, $4 seniors, and $3.50 for kids 4–12; children three and under are free. Pack a picnic lunch; fireplaces at the campground are available for day use if no campers are using

a colonial house on Swan Island

© MARY LYONS

them, but bring tinfoil for cooking. Alcohol is *not* allowed on the island.

The island, settled in the early 1700s, once had as many as 95 resident farmers, fishermen, ice-cutters, and ship-builders. Now there are derelict antique houses, a herd of whitetail deer, wild turkeys, nesting bald eagles, plenty of waterfowl and other birds, and the primitive campground.

Swan Island's campground has 10 well-spaced lean-tos (each sleeping six) with picnic tables, fireplaces, and outhouses; firewood and potable water are provided. Cost is $8 a night for adults, $7 for seniors, and $6.50 for children. (Add the state's 7 percent lodging tax to those rates.) Kids three and under are free. There's a two-night maximum. The policy is carry-in, carry-out, so bring trash bags. A rickety flatbed truck with benches meets campers at the island dock and transports them the 1.5 miles to the campground. The same truck does the island tour.

RECREATION
Bicycling
Bike routes with decent shoulders are all too rare in Maine, so take advantage of Rte. 27 between Augusta and Belgrade Lakes. It's mostly wide, flat, and fairly open, making it an easy 18-mile one-way trip to Belgrade Lakes village. Most of the area back roads are beautiful, with lakes, ponds, and old farms, but check road conditions for safety. A variety of rides are available at www.bikemaine.org/trails/kennebec.htm.

Golf
Ten miles north of Augusta and 12 miles south of Waterville, the highly rated **Natanis Golf Club,** Webber Pond Rd., Vassalboro 04989, 207/622-3561, www.natanisgc.com, has been the site of many a Maine golf tournament. Named after a trusted Indian guide, the Natanis club has two separate eighteen-hole courses. The attractive clubhouse has a pro shop, café/lounge, and wraparound porch. Call or email for tee times. On the east bank of the Kennebec in Augusta, take Rte.

201 to Webber Pond Rd. and continue to the club entrance.

Kids Stuff
"Small is beautiful" fits the **Children's Discovery Museum,** 265 Water St., Vickery Building, Augusta 04330, 207/622-2209, with interactive activities and imaginative playthings for kids to age 10. Besides the post office, supermarket, diner, and "construction zone" exhibits, there's a communications center with computers and a ham radio. Adults must accompany all children. Admission is $4 pp; children under one are free. The museum is open Mon.–Fri. 9 AM–4 PM, Sat. 10 AM–4 PM, and Sun. 1–4 PM. On the ground floor of the same building is the **Vickery Café,** 261 Water St., Augusta 04330, 207/623-7670, serving up PB&J sandwiches and lots of other child-friendly fare. It's open all year, Mon.–Fri. 7 AM–2:30 PM, but unfortunately not on weekends.

Richmond Sauna
Meriting a recreational category of its own—or maybe it should qualify as entertainment—the **Richmond Corner Sauna,** 81 Dingley Rd., Richmond 04357, 207/737-4752 or 800/400-5751, www.richmondsauna.com, is one of those funky places you either like or you don't. But it's been here since 1976. And maybe you'll like it. Finnish-American owner Richard Jarvi has built up a loyal clientele for his authentic, wood-heated sauna house—six private rooms and a group one. In between and afterward, there's a pool and a hot tub. If nudity bothers you, don't come, but no one seems to gawk. If you're too relaxed to drive after the sauna, the casual main house, built in 1831, has five B&B rooms at $75 d (shared baths; sauna and continental breakfast included). The sauna is open all year, Tues.–Sun. 5–9 PM in winter, 6–10 PM in summer. Cost is $20 pp. From downtown Richmond, take Rte. 197 west about five miles and turn left (south) onto Rte. 138. Take an immediate left onto Dingley Rd., where you'll see the sign.

ENTERTAINMENT

On the northern edge of Augusta, across from the Augusta Civic Center (Rte. 27), is the 10-screen **Hoyts Cinema,** 23 Marketplace Dr., Augusta 04330, 207/623-8183. There's something for everyone, and matinees as well. Check local newspapers or call for schedules.

The **Gaslight Theater,** a talented community-theater group, performs periodically throughout the year at the **Hallowell City Hall Auditorium,** Winthrop St., Hallowell 04347, 207/626-3698, www.gaslighttheater.org. Call for schedule, or stop in at Hallowell's town office.

Six miles south of Augusta, the 1864 **Johnson Hall Performing Arts Center,** 280 Water St., P.O. Box 777, Gardiner 04345, 207/582-7144, www.johnsonhall.org, is the year-round site of just about anything anyone wants to present—plays, lectures, art camps, after-school programs, classes, concerts, and more. Call or see website for a current schedule.

Maine's enduring Shakespearean theater is the **Theater at Monmouth,** Main St., Rte. 132, P.O. Box 385, Monmouth 04259, box office 207/933-9999 or 800/769-9698 in Maine, www.theateratmonmouth.org, based in Monmouth's architecturally astonishing Cumston Hall. Completed in 1900, the Romanesque Victorian structure has columns, cutout shingles, stained glass, and a huge square tower. The interior is equally stunning, with frescoes and a vaulted ceiling. The theater's summer season, performed by professionals in rotating repertory, runs early July–Aug. Shakespeare gets the nod for at least two of the four plays. Tickets are $10–26.

FESTIVALS AND EVENTS

During the school year, the **University of Maine at Augusta** campus on the outskirts of the city schedules lectures, concerts, and other performances. Check with the school, 207/621-3000, ext. 3442 (student activities) or 877/862-1234 (information center), for current information.

The Augusta area seems to claim more country fairs than any other part of the state; don't miss an opportunity to attend at least one. Each has a different flavor, but there are always lots of animals, games, and junk food, often a carnival, and sometimes harness racing.

Late June–mid-Aug., free **New England Music Camp Concerts** are offered by students Saturday and Sunday (3 PM), with chamber-music recitals by students and faculty on Wednesday (8 PM) and Friday (7:30 PM). Weekend concerts are at the outdoor "Bowl-in-the-Pines" (bring a blanket or folding chair); Wednesday and Friday performances take place in Alumni Hall. The famed camp was founded in the 1930s. New England Music Camp, Lake Messalonskee, Sidney, 207/465-3025, www.nemusiccamp.com.

The small, four-day **Pittston Fair** features agricultural exhibits, a carnival, and even a woodsman contest at the Pittston Fairgrounds, East Pittston, in mid-July. The third Saturday in July, **Old Hallowell Day** includes a craft fair, a parade, food booths, and a road race in downtown Hallowell. The **Monmouth Fair** fills four days with agricultural exhibits, a carnival, and crafts in early August.

The last week of August, the Windsor Fairgrounds come alive with the week-long **Windsor Fair,** with agricultural exhibits, harness racing, demolition derby, beauty pageant, and carnival.

The three-day **Litchfield Fair** has farm exhibits, animal pulling, a carnival, and more, the second weekend in September.

SHOPPING

Augusta has two major shopping areas—not exactly malls, but clusters of stores—**Capitol Shopping Center,** in town on Western Ave., and the **Marketplace at Augusta,** across from the Augusta Civic Center on Rte. 27 north of the city.

For a different kind of shopping experience, head a mile south of Augusta to **Hallowell,** where boutiques, restaurants, and nearly a dozen antiques shops line historic Water St. It's a prime destination for anyone in search of anything from gifts to collectibles to fine antiques.

Art Galleries and Crafts

The **Harlow Gallery,** 160 Water St., P.O. Box 213, Hallowell 04347, 207/622-3813, headquarters for the Kennebec Valley Art Association, serves as a magnet not only for its member artists but also for friends of art. It's a happening place. Open Wed.–Fri. noon–4 PM, Sat.–Sun. 11 AM–4 PM.

Hand-painted stoneware pottery and W.A. Mitchell Furniture are among the high-end beautiful crafts at **The Potter's House,** 335 Water St., Gardiner,. 207/582-3632, www.thepottershouse.com, part of Gardiner's downtown renaissance, a few doors up from A-1 to Go. Open Mon.–Sat. 11 AM–5 PM.

New and Used Books

The megabookstores, following the Wal-Mart trend, have entered Maine like gorillas, so underdog defenders are quick to lambaste them, but it's impossible to ignore the quality, value, and service at **Barnes & Noble Booksellers,** 9 Marketplace Dr., Augusta 04330, 207/621-0038. Besides, with its heavy schedule of special events, it even qualifies in the entertainment category in a community not overloaded with evening options. In addition to carrying about 150,000 titles, Barnes & Noble stocks an excellent selection of Maine books, even self-published ones. The "woody" decor, random easy chairs, café (with Starbucks coffee and world-class chocolate chip cookies), and public restrooms encourage browsing and lingering. The store is open all year, Mon.–Sat. 9 AM–11 PM, Sun. 10 AM–10 PM. It's at the northern edge of Augusta, just off Rte. 27 on the hill across from the Augusta Civic Center.

The apt slogan at **Merrill's Bookshop,** 134 Water St., second floor, Hallowell 04347, 207/623-2055, is "Good literature from Edward Abbey to Leane Zugsmith." John Merrill has an eye for unusual rare and used books, so you may walk out with a personal treasure. The shop is open Tues.–Sat. 10 AM–5 PM, all year.

Fine Jewelry

More than half a dozen goldsmiths market their exquisite jewelry at **David-Brooks Goldsmiths,** 190 Water St., Hallowell 04347, 207/622-9895 or 800/734-2666, and they'll also accept custom orders. Prices are high, but definitely worth it. Open Tues.–Fri. 9 AM–5 PM (Sat. to 4 PM), all year.

Hussey's General Store

What do power tools, fishing gear, and bridal gowns have in common? Not what you may think. They're all in the front window at Hussey's General Store, 510 Ridge Rd., corner of Rtes. 32 and 105, Windsor 04363, 207/445-2511, a country store with a difference. There isn't much that Hussey's doesn't have, and that bridal department does a steady business. Hussey's is open all year: Sunday hours are 9 AM–5 PM, year-round. Mon.–Sat. hours are: Jan. 1–May 1, 8 AM–6 PM; May 1–June 1, 8 AM–7 PM; June 1–Oct. 1, 8 AM–8 PM; and Oct. 1–Jan. 1, 8 AM–7 PM. From Augusta, take Rte. 105 about 11 miles east to Rte. 32; Hussey's is on the corner. If you're at the Windsor Fairgrounds, the store is only about two miles farther north on Rte. 32.

Farmers Markets

Three of the local farmers markets are open May–Oct. At the Turnpike Mall on Western Ave., the **Augusta Farmers Market** operates Wed. and Sat. 9 AM–noon. It's a large market with produce, syrup, crafts, chicken, eggs, and such exotica as rabbit meat. There's also an **Augusta River Market,** at the old Edwards Mill site on the north end of Water St., operating June–Sept., on Sat. 8:30 AM–1 PM, selling produce, baked goods, jams, some crafts, and more.

A mile down the river, at the southern end of Hallowell, across from the public boat landing, the **Hallowell Sunday Market** sets up (obviously) on Sun., 11 AM–3 PM.

West of Augusta, the **Winthrop Farmers Market** is set up in the municipal building parking lot (Main St. in Winthrop) Sat. 9 AM–1 PM, and, beginning in June, Tues. 9 AM–6 PM.

ACCOMMODATIONS

Most of the lodgings in the Augusta area are motels; chain motels are well represented. The emphasis here, at the center of state government, seems to be on convenience, efficiency, and anonymity. Close to the Augusta Civic Center, on the northern outskirts of town, recommended chain motels are the 99-room **Comfort Inn Civic Center,** 281 Civic Center Dr., Augusta 04330, 207/623-1000 or 800/808-1188 ($100–114 d), and the 102-room **Holiday Inn Civic Center,** 110 Community Dr., Augusta 04330, 207/622-4751 or 800/694-6404 ($112–125 d).

On the western side of the city, close to I-95 exit 30 but also closest to downtown and the Capitol complex, is the **Best Western Senator Inn,** 284 Western Ave., Augusta 04330, 207/622-5804 or 877/772-2224, www.senatorinn.com. Recent upgrades—including a good restaurant (great Sun. brunch), full-service spa, and indoor and outdoor heated pools—have made this the best of the chain choices. A full cooked breakfast is included in the rates ($109–139 d); pets are allowed in certain rooms with security deposit and pet fee. Luxury spa suites with fireplaces are available. Nearby are the **Augusta Hotel,** 390 Western Ave., Augusta 04330, 207/622-6371, and the **Super 8 Motel,** 395 Western Ave., Augusta 04330, 207/626-2888. At all three of these motels, request a room farthest from traffic noise. The Senator and the Augusta Hotel have on-site restaurants; **Margarita's,** 207/622-7874, at the Augusta Hotel, is one of several in a popular New England Tex-Mex chain.

Bed-and-Breakfasts

On a back road only 10 minutes from the State House, 130-acre **Maple Hill Farm Bed and Breakfast Inn and Conference Center,** 11 Inn Rd. (off the Outlet Rd.), Hallowell 04347, 207/622-2708 or 800/622-2708, www.MapleBB.com, feels like worlds away. Eight rooms (all with wireless high speed Internet, phones, cable TV, VCR, A/C, and individual heat control) in the informal, renovated 1890s farmhouse overlook woods, fields, gardens, and even the Camden Hills. Innkeeper Scott Cowger—a state legislator, avid bicyclist, and Hallowell enthusiast—pays close attention to guests' needs. His favorite line is, "I can cus-

tomize your day," specializing in outdoor activities and day-trips. Four of the rooms have double whirlpool tubs, five have gas fireplaces, three have private decks. Rates, depending on room type and season, are $75–190. Breakfast is a custom-cooked affair off a menu, and features the inn's own fresh eggs as an option. Coffee, tea, and baked goodies are available any time in the inn's common guest kitchen. The high standard of hospitality and concern for guests' comfort here has garnered numerous awards for Maple Hill Farm, including a *Travel & Leisure* mention as one of "30 Great U.S. Inns." Call if you are bringing children. No pets are permitted because of the delightful farm animals, including llamas, cows, and goats. The Gathering Place, with state-of-the-art A/V equipment, and dining facilities, is ideal for weddings and conferences. The eco-aware inn has a wind-generating turbine and energy-saving methods in place. Maple Hill Farm is three miles west of downtown Hallowell, next to an 800-acre wildlife preserve with an extensive trail network.

Cottage Colonies

A cross between a cottage colony and a sporting camp, **Echo Lake Lodge & Cottages,** Rte. 17, Fayette, 207/685-9550, has occupied these wooded acres since 1937. All of the rustic white cottages have kitchen facilities. This is an especially kid-friendly place, and families have been returning here for years, so reserve well ahead. Request a cottage with a screened porch to ward off mosquitoes. The main lodge has seven B&B rooms rented by the night. Occasionally, usually at the last minute, you can rent a cottage for a single day. Open seasonally, Echo Lake is 15 miles west of Augusta.

FOOD
Special Bakeries

Hand-in-hand with the microbrewery explosion in Maine came a microbakery explosion—a feast of designer bread and pastries. Run, don't walk, to sample their ethnic specialties, incredible flatbreads, and unique, just-invented combinations. Two super examples are on the outskirts of Augusta.

The specialty at **Black Crow Bakery,** Plains Rd., RR3, Box 1550, Litchfield 04350, 207/268-9927, is a Tuscan loaf that's as pretty as it is tasty. It's available Tues.–Sat. Except for cheese focaccia (available Thurs.), all their other exotic breads are sourdough-based—200–300 loaves a day. Try the fantastic Apricot Almond loaf (available Sat.). A modern mixer is Mark and Tinker Mickalide's only high-tech tool; they operate a very traditional bakery in their 1810 farmhouse's former summer kitchen, even grinding their own grains on Maine granite. The shop is open all year, Tues.–Sat. 7 AM–7 PM. It's across from the Legion Hall, between I-495 and the Litchfield Fairgrounds.

Chris Szigeti-Johnson's **Upper Crust Bakery,** 207 Highland Ave., Gardiner 04345, 207/582-2220, has some specialties with a Central European flavor, like Hungarian pockets, and her Linzertorte is beyond delicious. She makes custom cakes, like Yule logs and wedding cakes, and takes mail orders. After 17 years in Manchester, Chris now works out of her home, so hours are flexible to suit her customers. Call for info or to order, or see her website, www.uppercrustbakery.com.

While you're on an upscale-bread kick, **Slates,** 161 Water St., Hallowell 04347, 207/622-9575, also has an excellent bakery, open 7 AM–6 PM Mon.–Sat. (to 4 PM Sun.).

If you'd rather have old-fashioned high-cal fare, head for **MacDonald's Bakery,** 339 Water St., Gardiner 04345, 207/582-5450, where hundreds of doughnuts disappear out the door before 10 AM and the most popular item is a six-inch éclair for under $1.23. The bakery is open all year, Tues.–Sat. 5:30 AM–6 PM. On Mon., it's open only 10 AM–noon, when everything in the store is half-price.

Gourmet-to-Go (or Stay)

In downtown Gardiner, on the corner by the A-1 Diner, is **A-1 to Go Community Market & Cafe,** 347 Water St., Gardiner 04345, 207/582-5586, a stylish café cum bakery/deli counter serving both breakfast and lunch. There are takeout selections (fresh and frozen) as well as an array of wines, gourmet foods, and ingredients to choose from. You won't be able to find many of the items anywhere else in the area. There are soup, salad, and panini lunches, coffee, fantastic desserts, and lots of exotic (nonalcoholic) drinks to choose from. A cup of soup is $3.50, a panini is $5.75–$7.50; takeout dinners like chicken Marbella or tofu with Korean garlic sauce will run you about $7.99–10.00/lb. Neil Andersen and staff are friendly, knowledgeable, and helpful. When you leave—a hard thing to do—take a selection from the international array of fine dark chocolates with you. Open all year, 7 AM–7 PM Mon.–Sat.

Inexpensive to Moderate

If you're traveling with children, **The Ground Round,** 110 Community Dr., Augusta 04330, 207/623-0022, is better than McDonald's at keeping them distracted, although the atmosphere is a bit frenetic. The menu is burger-centric, always reliable. The waitresses know how to finesse the kids. Part of the Holiday Inn complex at the Augusta Civic Center, the Ground Round is open daily, 6:30 AM–11 PM, (to midnight or so Fri.–Sat.) all year.

The best grownup food in the Augusta area is at **Slates,** 167 Water St., Hallowell 04347, 207/622-9575, the Energizer bunny of local restaurants. Founded in 1979, it just keeps improving. Dinner entrées—mostly creative seafood and chicken, and a few token tournedos—are in the $11–19 range. The Saturday and Sunday brunches are fabulous: grilled fish and meats, unique omelets and benedicts, huevos rancheros, stuffed croissants, homemade granola, salads. Reservations only for six or more, except dinner, where reservations are taken for any size party. Open for breakfast Mon.–Fri. 7:30–11 AM; for lunch Mon.–Fri. 11:30 AM–2:30 PM; for dinner Tues.–Sat. 5:30–9 PM (to 9:30 Fri.–Sat.); and for brunch Sat. 9 AM–2:30 PM and Sun. 9:30 AM–2 PM.

It's the 20-oz. pint glass, not politics, that

Kennebec/Moose River

helped christen **The Liberal Cup,** 115 Water St., Hallowell 04347, 207/623-2739, a brew-pub and restaurant where owner Geoffrey Houghton, who studied in Britain, makes six different great beers. Homemade is true of the food, too; the place is packed with diners sampling the salads, salmon, steak, fish and chips, and shepherd's pie. Even the salad dressings are made on the premises. Lunch and dinner are served year-round 11:30 AM–1 AM.

Hard by the Kennebec River in downtown Gardiner, adorned with flowerboxes, is the first-rate **A-1 Diner,** 3 Bridge St., Gardiner 04345, 207/582-4804. It's the real thing, a genuine classic diner, with moderate prices and some added attractions—like air-conditioning and a yuppified eclectic menu. How about tilapia with pesto? Or Transylvania eggplant casserole? Or wild mushroom ragout? Board specials are $9–13. There are great soups, too. (There's also a regular diner menu.) Sunday brunch draws a big crowd. Open all year, Mon.–Sat. 7 AM–8 PM (to 9 PM Fri.–Sat.), Sun. 8 AM–1 PM.

Downriver from Augusta, the **Railway Café,** 64 Main St., Richmond 04357, 207/737-2277, has been the favorite local gathering spot since 1984. Looking at the original 19th-century woodwork and tin ceiling, who'd guess it had once been a funeral parlor? If you're here on Friday (and sometimes other days), order the lobster stew, *loaded* with lobster meat. Dinner entrées—steak, seafood, grilled chicken, pizza—run $6–14. The café is open all year, Mon.–Fri. 5:30 AM–8 PM (to 9 PM Fri.), Sat. 7 AM–9 PM, and Sun. 7 AM–4 PM.

INFORMATION AND SERVICES

The information center of the **Kennebec Valley Chamber of Commerce,** 21 University Dr., P.O. Box 676, Augusta 04332, 207/623-4559, fax 626-9342, www.augustamaine.com, is open all year, Mon.–Fri. 8:30 AM–5 PM (answering machine on weekends). It's located in the Augusta Civic Center complex at the northern edge of the city.

A mile south of Augusta is the state headquarters of the **Maine Tourism Association,** 327 Water St., Hallowell 04347, 207/623-0363, www.mainetourism.com, a nonprofit organization that sounds like the official state tourism office, but it isn't. It's contracted by the state to handle some tourism functions, including operating seven information centers around the state. The main office is devoted primarily to administration, but helpful brochures are available. It's open weekdays 8 AM–5 PM.

The Romanesque Revival **Lithgow Public Library,** Winthrop and State Sts., Augusta 04330, 207/626-2415, www.lithgow.lib.me.us, one of Maine's handsomest libraries, was built in 1896 of Maine granite. Do not miss the gorgeous reading room, with a Tiffany clock, stained-glass windows, and French-inspired decor. The library is open all year, Mon.–Thurs. 9 AM–8 PM, Fri.–Sat. 9 AM–5 PM. July–Aug., Sat. hours are 9 AM–noon.

The **Maine State Library,** Maine State Cultural Building, Augusta 04333, 207/287-5600, in the State House complex, includes the Maine State Museum and the State Archives, 207/287-5790, within its walls. Stocked with hundreds of magazines, the reading room is a convenient place to peruse esoteric articles, rest your feet, or wait for a friend; there are also public restrooms. The library is open Mon.–Fri. 9 AM–5 PM (to 9 PM Thurs.), mid-June–early Sept. It's also open Sat. noon–5 PM, and to 9 PM Tues.–Wed., in addition to Thurs. early Sept.–mid-June. The library provides an Internet research tool—**Marvel! Virtual Library**—which can be accessed at home by members of any library in the state.

Newspapers

Founded in 1825, the *Kennebec Journal,* 207/623-3811 or 800/537-5508, began publication only five years after Maine became a state. It's published every day except Christmas. Each Friday, the paper's eight-page *What's Happening* supplement carries ads, calendar listings, and local color galore. Also in Augusta is the Thursday *Capital Weekly,* 207/621-6000, with local news, features, and extensive calendar listings.

Emergencies
In Augusta, Hallowell, Gardiner, and Manchester, dial 911 for fire, police, and ambulance services. The major medical facility for the area is the respected **MaineGeneral Medical Center,** 6 E. Chestnut St., Augusta 04330, emergency room 207/626-1206, with round-the-clock emergency-room care.

Kennels
About seven miles west of Augusta, the **Barks and Meows,** Rte. 202, Manchester 04351, 207/623-4976, operates year-round, boarding dogs for $14–15 a day and cats and exotics for $10 a day. Proof of vaccination is required. Owner is June E. Gilley, a licensed veterinary technician. Hours are Mon., Tues., Thurs., Fri., 8–10 AM and

4–6 PM, closed Wed., Sat. 8–10 AM, Sun. 4–6 PM. Grooming and holidays are by appointment.

GETTING THERE AND AROUND
US Airways Express, 800/428-4322, www.usairways.com, operates flights all year between Boston's Logan Airport and the Augusta State Airport, a distance of 148 miles. It's a busy route, especially on midsummer weekends, so be sure to book well ahead.

Vermont Transit, connected with Greyhound, 207/772-6587 or 207/622-1601, operates bus service between Portland and Augusta. **Concord Trailways**, 800/639-3317, with a new Augusta terminal, has scheduled daily runs between Augusta and Logan.

Augusta-based **Al's & Double R's Taxi Service,** 207/622-5846 or 623-3431, has a fleet of radio-equipped taxis operating daily all year.

Belgrade Lakes Area

The Belgrade Lakes area is one of those Proustian memories-of-childhood places, where multigenerational family groups return year after year for idyllic summer visits full of nothing but playing, going for hikes or swims, fishing, listening for the loons, watching sunsets, and dreading the return to civilization. Today's boomer generation, recalling carefree days at one of the many Belgrade-area summer camps, now send their own kids to camp here, or they rent a lakefront cottage and devote their energies to re-creating those youthful days.

Belgrade's chain of lakes comprises seven major lakes and ponds: Long Pond, North Pond, Great Pond, East Pond, Salmon Pond, McGrath Pond, and Messalonskee Lake (also known as Snow Pond). Camps and cottages are sprinkled around their shores, and each has a boat-launch ramp where you can put in a canoe, kayak, or powerboat. Incidentally, the village of Belgrade Lakes, heart of the region, has its own post office but is part of the towns of Belgrade and Rome.

Since the Belgrade Lakes area is tucked in between Waterville and Augusta, those cities

serve as the easily accessible commercial and cultural hubs for Belgrade visitors.

Directly west of Belgrade Lakes village is the charming, out-of-the-way hamlet of Mount Vernon (pop. 1,430), founded in 1792 and worth a visit by car or bike.

SIGHTS
Great Pond Mailboat
Remember the movie *On Golden Pond?* Well, author Ernest Thompson found his inspiration summering on the shore of Great Pond. (He's still here, although Hollywood's version was filmed in New Hampshire.) You can join the real-life postman on his rounds, feeding the 100-plus lakefront mailboxes—but you'll be in a 24-foot pontoon boat instead of a Chris-Craft. Mailbox creativity is half the entertainment, and one cottager's dog—named Kibble—dashes to the dock to pick up the mail in his mouth. Bring binoculars, a camera, a jacket, and a sandwich, and settle in aboard the stable, 10-passenger boat. Reservations are

essential, especially in July and August; call a day or two ahead. Occasionally, you can luck out and find space available without a reservation. If your kids can behave for the duration of a four-hour excursion, by all means try this one. But leave them ashore if they're restless types (there's only an emergency Porta-Potti on board). Operated by the Great Pond Mail Boat, 207/215-7520, the mail boat departs Mon.–Sat. at 10 AM, June–Sept., from the dock next to the post office in Belgrade Lakes village. Cost is $15 per passenger. By reservation, and for at least four persons, Capt. Norman Shaw also will do 90-minute late-afternoon and sunset cruises for $15 per passenger.

D.E.W. Animal Kingdom

Allow at least an hour to visit the 42-acre D.E.W. (Domestic/Exotic/Wild) Animal Kingdom, 918 Pond Rd., Rte. 41, Box 2820, Mount Vernon 04352, 207/293-2837, west of Belgrade Lakes village. Kids love the hands-on stuff at Julie and Bob Miner's innovative nonprofit zoo, where they raise and rehabilitate exotic and not-so-exotic animals, enhancing rare and endangered breeds. Among the residents are bobcats, lions and tigers, plus pettable creatures. The zoo, on Rte. 41, is in West Mount Vernon, midway between Mount Vernon village and Kents Hill. It's open Tues.–Sun. and on holidays. Admission is $8 per person, except for "Infants and over 100," who, presumably, are free.

RECREATION

Just north of Day's Store in Belgrade Lakes village is a cute little picnic area on Long Pond, **Belgrade Peninsula Park,** open 5:30 AM–10:30 PM, next to an old dam. Late in the day, it's a great spot for sunset-watching and fishing, no camping or fires permitted. It was restored by the Belgrade Lakes Conservation Corps in 1996, and there is space for five (carefully parked) cars. Another scenic standout, with a super photo op of Long Pond and Belgrade Lakes village, is the state-maintained overlook at **Blueberry Hill,** on the west side of Long

Pond. From Rte. 27, just south of Belgrade Lakes village, take Castle Island Rd. west about three miles to Watson Pond Rd. Turn right (north) and continue about 1.5 miles. (Another 2.8 miles north of Blueberry Hill is the trailhead for French's Mountain.)

Golf

Golf has taken center stage here ever since the opening of the splendid **Belgrade Lakes Golf Club,** West Rd., P.O. Box 500, Belgrade Lakes 04918, 207/495-4653, www.belgradelakesgolf.com, in 1998. Designed by noted British expert Clive Clark, the course is an 18-hole standout, and the view from the elegant clubhouse is dazzling. Caddies are available to encourage walking. Tee times are necessary, but they're well spaced; greens fees are pricey. Open late Apr.–late Oct., if the weather cooperates.

Swimming

Rental cottages on the Belgrade Lakes have direct access to the water, but even close to shore it can be too deep for little kids. In that case, head for the beach at Sunset Camps. In the hamlet of Smithfield, northeast of Belgrade Lakes village, the owners of **Sunset Camps,** Rtes. 8 and 137, P.O. Box 68, Smithfield 04978, 207/362-2611, www.sunsetcamps.com, allow public access for swimming and other activities; cost is $2 pp. When it's hot, get there early. (Sunset Camps is a sporting camp, with 18 housekeeping cabins.) Pick up lunch at the snack bar, then rent a canoe and paddle around North Pond.

Hiking

Proactive in protecting much of the region's beautiful land for hiking and responsible enjoyment, the **Belgrade Regional Conservation Alliance** (BRCA), P.O. Box 250, Belgrade Lakes 04918, www.belgradelakes.org, 207/495-6039, has a terrific trail map and hiking guide to the Kennebec Highlands available—although it doesn't show every protected acre, since the alliance is managing to protect land faster than they can print maps. Says the alliance: "The Kennebec Highlands' 6,000 acres contain the highest peaks in Kennebec County, miles of pristine streams, several wetlands, and five undeveloped ponds."

The two good hikes below—included on the map, which can also be obtained at local general stores like Day's or at EMS in Augusta—are just north of Belgrade Lakes village, in the town of Rome. Neither is particularly high, but their summits are isolated enough to provide panoramic vistas; a fall-foliage hike is wonderful. The map and trail guide also give detailed information for other hikes—on Round Top Trail, Sanders Hill Trail, and the Mountain.

For lots of gain and and little pain, a good family hike, head for **French Mountain,** on the west side of Long Pond. To reach the trailhead from Rte. 27, go about 4.2 miles north of Belgrade Lakes village and turn left onto Watson Pond Rd. Go less than a mile; the trail (signposted) begins on the left. Allow about 20 minutes to reach the summit, with fantastic views of Long Pond, the village, and Great Pond. Take a picnic (and a litter bag) and stretch out on the ledges.

A marginally tougher, yet still-easy hike is **Mount Philip,** a 755-footer with summit views of Great Pond. Allow about 20 minutes to reach the top from the Rte. 225 trailhead. From Rte. 27, north of Belgrade Lakes village, turn right onto Rte. 225 at Rome Corner (Logan's Country Antiques is at the fork). Continue another 1.5 miles to the trailhead (on the left), across from a Hemlock Trail sign. Park as far off the road as possible. Head on up the blue-blazed trail to the summit.

Fishing

Fishing is a big deal here, particularly in May, June, and September (the season runs Apr. 1–Oct. 1). Among the 20 species in the seven major lakes and ponds are landlocked salmon, brown trout, black bass, pickerel, white perch, and eastern brook trout. You'll have to stick to bag, weight, and length limits. Pick up tackle and nonresident fishing licenses at Day's Store, Main St., Belgrade Lakes 04918, 207/495-2205 or 800/993-9500.

Getting Afloat

The most entertaining way to get afloat in the Belgrade Lakes is the Great Pond Mailboat, but the next best choice is to rent a canoe or kayak or take a guided paddle. About five miles south of Belgrade Lakes village (across from the turn to Oakland), Ralph Ardito's **Belgrade Canoe & Kayak,** Rte. 27, Belgrade 04917, 207/495-2005 or 888/226-6311, has a hefty inventory of Old Town kayaks, canoes, and accessories for sale and rents canoes and kayaks. You can try them outside in the store's demo pond, or on a local streams tour. Nine miles north of the Augusta Civic Center.

At Mike and Louise Pooler's **Belgrade Boat Rentals and Storage,** Foster Point Rd. on Great Pond in Pinkham's Cove, P.O. Box 471, Belgrade 04917, 207/495-3415, either Old Town lake kayaks or 16-foot Gazelle canoes can be rented for three days for $75; $110 for a week.

The **Great Pond Marina,** Rte. 27, P.O. Box 405, Belgrade Lakes 04918, 207/495-2213, www.greatpondmarina.com, rents canoes or kayaks ($30 a day), pontoon boats ($200 a day), and personal watercraft ($245 a day); all require hefty deposits, and you'll be charged $40 an hour for returning late. Pickup and delivery charges are extra. The marina is a mile south of Belgrade Lakes village.

A canoe trip with lobster picnic is one way **Maine Wilderness Tours,** 207/465-4333, www.mainewildernesstours.com, gets people afloat. There are others, and lodging can be had, too.

SHOPPING
You-Name-It

Cars and canoes are about the only things you can't buy at **Day's Store,** Main St., Rte. 27, P.O. Box 277, Belgrade Lakes 04918, 207/495-2205 or 800/993-9500, www.go2days.com, a legendary institution since 1960. From firewater to fishing tackle, sandwiches (including the Long Pond Grinder) to souvenirs—and over a dozen kinds of homemade fudge—it's a general store par excellence. Don't expect fancy; the local flavor provides its character. Long Pond is at its back door, providing access by boat or car. The store is open daily 7 AM–9 PM, in summer, more limited hours the rest of the year. Day's is in the center of the village; you can't miss it.

Gifts and Crafts

A few doors south of the Village Inn in Belgrade Lakes is the seasonal branch of Waterville's **Maine Made & More Shop,** Main St., Rte. 27, Belgrade Lakes 04918, 207/495-2274, a summer landmark since 1980. Here's the place to stock up on tasteful gifts and crafts: jams and maple syrup, cards and guidebooks, T-shirts and sweatshirts, stuffed moose, and even shoes. The shop is open summers, Mon.–Sat. 9 AM–8 PM, Sun. 10 AM–6 PM.

ACCOMMODATIONS

The Belgrade Lakes Region actually extends its reach into the Waterville area, so be sure to see details on the Pressey House Lakeside Bed and Breakfast and Alden Camps, under *Accommodations* in the *Waterville and Vicinity* section. Both are on Belgrade lakes, in Oakland.

Inns

The five rooms and one suite at **Wings Hill Inn & Restaurant,** Rte. 27, P.O. Box 386, Belgrade Lakes 04918, 866/495-2400, www.wingshillinn.com, are $130–165 in season. The rooms have decks, some of which are private. The chef-owners provide a sumptuous complimentary full breakfast, and fresh-baked treats with afternoon tea.

The Village Inn, Main St., Rte. 27, P.O. Box 282, Belgrade Lakes 04918, 207/495-3553, www.villageinnducks.com, has six rooms and two suites, in a two story building attached to the restaurant.

Sporting Camps

Distant from most of Maine's sporting camps, a classic Belgrade-area operation nonetheless retains the flavor of those much farther north. And it's a heck of a lot easier to reach when driving from the south.

Established in 1910, **Bear Spring Camps,** 60 Jamaica Point Rd., Rome, www.bearspringcamps.com, is one of the state's largest sporting camps, with 32 rustic cottages on 400 wooded acres. All have baths and Franklin stoves and overlook the North Bay of nine-mile-long Great Pond; each has its own dock, and rental motorboats are available. Other facilities include a sandy beach, tennis court, and hiking trails. Cabins are $625–2,525 a week, AP; meals are important here. (They'll even cook up the fish you catch.) Cabins are available only by the week mid-June–Labor Day, and reservations are tough to come by. Some guests stay a month, and they book a year ahead. No pets. Open mid-May–Sept. (they're not open during hunting season). Bear Spring Camps is on Rte. 225, four miles east of Rte. 27.

Seasonal Rentals

Seasonal rentals are the preferred lodging in the Belgrade Lakes Area. It must relate to the children's summer camps in this area—you may not be able to go home again, but you *can* spend a week or two trying to recapture the aura. The **Belgrade Reservation Center,** 262 Augusta Rd. (Rte. 27), P.O. Box 284, Belgrade Lakes 04918, 207/495-2104, www.belgradelakeandcountry.com, based in the Lake & Country Real Estate building on the southern outskirts of Belgrade Lakes Village, has the best selection of rentals. Cottages with 1–5 bedrooms are $305–1,500 per week, mid-May–mid-Oct.

FOOD

If you're looking for picnic fare, or a quick bite, stop in at **Day's Store** Main St., Rte. 27, P.O. Box 277, Belgrade Lakes 04918, 207/495-2205 or 800/993-9500, www.go2days.com, and pick up pizza, sandwiches, and/or baked goodies.

Almost across the street is a restaurant that attracts patrons from all over central Maine. It's hard to imagine, from its average-looking exterior, that superb duckling is the menu highlight at the **Village Inn,** Main St., Rte. 27, Belgrade Lakes 04918, 207/495-3553 or

888/581-1154, www.villageinnducks.com. Even the distinctly casual interior, overlooking the inlet to Great Pond, doesn't give it away. (Don't worry—the ducks in the inlet aren't destined for your plate.) The kitchen wizards use a unique two-day roasting technique, and you can choose nine interesting sauces. A two-duck-breast dinner is $22.95, half a roast duck $19.95, and one quarter $15.95, and you can even order some by mail. Since 1991, the restaurant reputedly has sold more roasted-duck dinners than any other place in the United States, so they must be doing something right. The extensive menu (entrées $16–30) has tons of other options, including pasta dishes and steak. Reservations are encouraged. The Village Inn is open for dinner and Sunday lunch early and late season Wed.–Sat. 5–9 PM and Sun. 11:30 AM–8 PM. From June 21–Sept. 4, the schedule is dinner daily 5–9 PM, and Lunch Wed.–Sun., 11:30 AM–2:30 PM. It's in the center of Belgrade Lakes village, and if you can't waddle to the car, you can stay over.

The innkeepers, Tracey and Christopher Anderson, at **Wings Hill Inn & Restaurant,** Rte. 27, P.O. Box 386, Belgrade Lakes 04918, 866/495-2400, www.wingshillinn. com, met while attending culinary school, fortunately for diners at the inn. The five courses on their $40 prix-fixe menu, served Thurs.–Sun., seatings at 6 and 8 PM, change weekly, but give appetizers, choices of soup, salad, main courses like Grilled pork or Slow-Roasted Cornish Hen, and desserts like Brown Sugar Creme Brulee. On Thursday and Sunday, there might be a three-course

option for $30. BYOL. Reservations strongly recommended. If you've overindulged, you can stay here, too.

Off the beaten track a bit, **The Olde Post Office Cafe,** 366 Pond Rd.-Village Center, Mount Vernon 04352, 207/293-4978, gets high marks for its fine foods and coffees. A shredded pork sandwich is $6.75, Cobb salad $7.50. There are breakfast specials and prepared meal items, salads, and spreads can come home with you. Hours: Mon.–Sat. 6 AM–2 PM, Sun. 8 AM–2 PM.

INFORMATION

The **Belgrade Lakes Region Information Center,** P.O. Box 72, Belgrade 04917, 207/495-2744, www.belgrademaine.com, is a cute little log cabin just south of Messalonskee Stream on the east side of Rte. 27, about 10 miles north of Augusta. It's open only mid-June–mid-Sept., 9 AM–5 PM, and staffed by volunteers, some long-term residents of the area with interesting local lore to relate. When the office is closed, brochures are left outside, under the overhang, which is lit at night, and where people can leave their name and number for a call-back. Safest bet is to call or write in advance for regional information.

Summertime in the Lakes, a free tabloid with ads, features, and calendar listings, is an especially helpful local publication that appears weekly during the summer. Copies are available at the information center and at most of the restaurants and shops in the region.

Waterville and Vicinity

Second-largest community in Kennebec County, the city of Waterville boasts a population of 16,000. When you throw in its sister town of Winslow, the head count jumps to nearly 24,000. A key player in Waterville life today is prestigious Colby College, whose students and faculty give the college-town flavor to this mill town incorporated in 1802.

As early as 1653, Europeans set up a trading entrepôt here, calling it Teconnet—the earlier version of today's Ticonic Falls, on the Kennebec—and commerce with the Indians thrived until the onset of the Indian Wars two decades later. In the late 19th century, a contingent of Lebanese immigrants arrived, finding employment in the town's mills, and many of their descendants have become respected community members. Best known of these is favorite son and former U.S. Senate Majority Leader George J. Mitchell, who still returns to spend time with his many relatives here.

Waterville has long been overshadowed by Augusta, the Kennebec County seat 20 miles to the south, but commercial turnarounds and communal efforts like Waterville Main Street have led to rising optimism about the city's prospects. A welcome 1997 addition was the opening of the $33.5 million Donald V. Carter Memorial Bridge over the Kennebec, relieving some of the Winslow-Waterville congestion on the Rte. 201 bridge, 1.25 miles upriver.

SIGHTS
Colby College

Crowning Mayflower Hill, two miles from downtown Waterville, Colby College, Mayflower Hill, Waterville 04901, 207/872-3000, www.colby.edu, is a must-see. Colby's 1,800 students attend a huge variety of liberal-arts programs on a 714-acre campus noted for its handsome Georgian buildings. Founded by Baptists in 1813 as the all-male Maine Literary and Theological Institution, Colby received its current name in 1867 and went coed in 1871. Campus tours are available by prior arrangement through the Admissions Office, 207/859-4828 or 800/723-3032, open weekdays 8:30 AM–4:30 PM.

The **Colby College Museum of Art,** 207/872-3228, in the Bixler Art and Music Center, has earned an especially distinguished reputation for its remarkable permanent collection of 18th-, 19th-, and 20th-century American art. Colby's museum is a stop on the Maine Art Museum Trail, which highlights the state's seven major art museums. In 1996, the museum opened its $1.5-million Paul J. Schupf Wing to house 415 paintings and sculptures created by artist Alex Katz over a 50-year period. In July 1999, the architecturally stunning $1.3 million Lunder Wing opened, expanding the museum's exhibit space to 28,000 square feet. Other significant holdings include works by Gilbert Stuart, Winslow Homer, and John Marin; special solo and group shows are mounted throughout the year. And don't miss the tasteful gift shop. Museum hours are Tues.–Sat. 10 AM–4:30 PM, Sun. noon–4:30 PM. Admission is free. The museum is on the east side of the campus's main quadrangle, just north of Mayflower Hill Drive.

Also on the campus is the 128-acre **Perkins Arboretum and Bird Sanctuary,** with three nature trails. Bring a picnic and blanket and stretch out next to Johnson Pond. In winter, there's ice-skating on the pond.

Fort Halifax

Left over from a fort built in 1754, the two-story Fort Halifax blockhouse, Bay St., Winslow 04901, stands sentinel where the Sebasticook River meets the Kennebec. Oldest blockhouse in the nation, it was built of doweled logs during the French and Indian Wars. In 1984, after rampaging Kennebec floodwaters swept away the building, more than three dozen of the giant timbers were retrieved downstream. Energetic fundraising allowed the blockhouse to be meticulously restored. The surrounding park is a great place for a picnic.

Two-Cent Bridge

Spanning the Kennebec from Benton Avenue in Winslow to Front Street in Waterville (walk down Temple Street in Waterville), the 700-foot-long Two-Cent Bridge (officially the Ticonic Footbridge) was built in 1903 for pedestrian commuters to the Scott Paper mill in Winslow, who paid two cents to cross. Closed in 1973, the bridge was recently reopened and is the forerunner of a Head of Falls waterfront redevelopment effort. Possibly the only toll pedestrian bridge left in the U.S., its replica toll booth is a "stand still" museum. A stroll over the bridge gives a good scenic of "Empire Falls."

Redington Museum

Home of the Waterville Historical Society, the Redington Museum and Apothecary, 64 Silver St., Waterville 04901, 207/872-9439, has a particularly intriguing 19th-century pharmacy, as well as Native American artifacts. The Federal-style Redington House was built in 1814 by early settler Asa Redington for his son, Silas. Admission is $3 adults, $2 children under 12. The museum is open Memorial Day week to Labor Day (closed holidays); tours are at 10 and 11 AM and 1 and 2 PM.

PARKS AND RECREATION

Waterville can serve as a convenient base for **white-water rafting** trips out of the Forks, on the upper Kennebec River. See below for details.

Golf

Public access is limited at the semiprivate 18-hole **Waterville Country Club,** Country Club Rd., Oakland 04963, 207/465-9861, so you'll need to call for a starting time. The course, covering both sides of Country Club Road, is particularly well kept up, and facilities include a pro shop and driving range. There's a certain degree of stuffiness here; greens fees are moderate. Open mid-April–Oct., the course is a mile from I-95 exit 127. Also see Belgrade Lakes Area, above, for information on the fabulous **Belgrade Lakes Golf Club,** and Augusta and Vicinity for information on the tournament-level **Natanis Golf Club.**

Kids Stuff

Across North St. from MaineGeneral Medical Center's Thayer Unit, the **North Street Playground** has very creative playground equipment plus ball fields, free tennis courts (207/877-7520), and an outdoor pool (207/877-6699—when pool open, approximately June–Aug.).

INSIDE OUT Playground and Preschool, Waterville Regional Arts and Community Center, 93 Main St., Waterville 04901, 207/877-8747, www.insideoutplayground.org, is just what it sounds like—an indoor play center for children up to age 8. On the fourth floor of a town-owned building known for short as "The Center," this nonprofit enterprise is "designed to enhance the growth of children through the power of play"—there's a castle, a ship, and bikes, balls, and tumbling mats. It's open all year, Mon.–Thurs. 9 AM–5 PM (to 7 PM Fri.–Sat.). Cost is $5 per child for the day; supervising parents play free, as do babies under one, and twins are "two for one."

ENTERTAINMENT

Curiously, one of Maine's premier art-film houses is in downtown Waterville. The two-screen **Railroad Square Cinema,** 17 Railroad Sq., Waterville 04901, 207/873-6526, www.railroadsquarecinema.com, is the home of the Maine International Film Festival (MIFF), which has brought such luminaries as Sissy Spacek and Peter Fonda to town to receive Mid-Life Achievement Awards. For Festival passes, 207/873-7000. The Festival takes place in the summer, but a MIFF in the Morning series takes place from January to March. Shows change weekly; there are matinees most weekends and occasional weekdays. Conveniently attached to the theater is the casual **Buen Apetito.**

Flagship Cinemas, 247 Kennedy Memorial Dr., Shaw's Plaza, 207/873-0033 (movie hotline), www.flagshipcinemas.com, has eight screens, internet ticketing, and a "Super Bargain Tuesday."

FESTIVALS AND EVENTS

During the academic year, and less often in summer, Colby College is the venue for exhibits, lectures, concerts, performances, and other events. Check with the school, 207/859-4353, or visit www.colby.edu/news, for the schedule.

The refurbished turn-of-the-20th-century **Waterville Opera House,** is located above City Hall at 1 Common St. Mailing address: 93 Main St., Waterville 04901; 207/873-5381, ticket hotline 207/873-7000. Once the haunt of vaudevillians, the Opera House is now the site of plays, dance performances, and concerts throughout the year. Call for a schedule.

At various locations between Waterville and Jackman the first Saturday in June, **National Trails Day** features organized noncompetitive biking, hiking, and canoeing.

A gathering of New England's best fiddlers, the **East Benton Fiddlers' Convention** draws close to 2,000 enthusiasts to open-air performances at the Littlefield farm in East Benton. The convention happens the last Sun. in July, noon–dusk. Call 207/453-2017 for directions.

Downtown Waterville is the site of late July's **Taste of Greater Waterville.** The food-focused one-day festival, usually held on a Wednesday, is organized by more than two dozen restaurants. In Castonguay Square and surrounding streets, there's alfresco dining, plus music for kids and adults.

SHOPPING
New, Used, and Children's Books

Conveniently located downtown (facing the square), **Re-Books,** 25 E. Concourse, Waterville 04901, 207/877-2484, is a basement-level shop with a fairly extensive selection of hardcovers and paperbacks. Amiable proprietor Robert Sezak's specialties include poetry, philosophy, mysteries, Judaica, photography, sci-fi, and language titles. The shop is open all year, Tues., Wed., Thurs., Sat. 10 AM–5 PM; Mon. and Fri. noon–5 PM.

The **Children's Book Cellar,** 52 Main St., Waterville 04901, 207/872-4543, is *really* into kids, with a great selection of books and toys. The shop is open all year, Tues.–Sat. 9 AM–5 PM. It's closed Mondays in winter, but in summer it's open Monday eves.

Colby College's **Seaverns Bookstore,** Roberts Union, Colby College, Waterville 04901, 207/872-3609 or 800/727-8506, has general books and lots of Colby-logo sweatshirts, T-shirts, and other wearables. Bookstore hours vary, depending on whether or not school is in session. Roberts Union is on the northern side of the campus.

Crafts and Gifts

Paula and George Gordon's **Maine Made & More Shop,** 93 Main St., Waterville 04901, 207/872-7378, spotlights the work of Maine individuals and companies, but you'll find far more than crafts, and everything's high quality. The shop is open all year, Mon.–Thurs. 9 AM–6 PM, Fri. 9 AM–8 PM, Sat. 9 AM–5:30 PM, and Sun. noon–5 PM. There are seasonal branches of the shop in Belgrade Lakes and Boothbay Harbor, and a year-round one in Augusta.

Johnny's Selected Seeds

If you're a gardener, farmer, horticulturalist, or just plain curious, take a 15-minute drive east of Waterville to visit **Johnny's Selected Seeds** research farm on Foss Hill Rd., Albion 04910, and take a self-guided tour of the 40 acres of trial gardens from Mon.–Fri. 8 AM–4 PM in season. Or visit their store (207/861-3999) and headquarters, 955 Benton Ave., Winslow 04901, 207/861-3900, www.johnnyseeds.com, open 8:30 AM–5 PM Mon.–Fri., Feb. 1–July 1. Starting mid-Feb., Sat. hours are added through June, 9 AM–4 PM. July 1–Jan., the store is open three days: Mon., Thurs, Fri., 8:30 AM–3:30 PM. The eponymous seed source has a national reputation. More than 2,000 varieties of herbs, veggies, and flowers are grown in the trial gardens, which were started in 1973. Known for high-quality seeds and service, the company makes good on anything that doesn't sprout. Call ahead for tours.

Farmers Market

The **Fairfield Farmers Market** begins its season in mid-May and continues to late October. Look for it on Main St. in Fairfield (a few miles north of Waterville), Wed. 2–6 PM and Sat. 9 AM–1 PM.

ACCOMMODATIONS

Most lodgings in Waterville are chain motels. The **Best Western, Comfort Inn, and Holiday Inn** are on Main St., right off I-95, exit 130, and the **Econo Lodge, Budget Host, and Hampton Inn** are on Kennedy Memorial Drive. The Holiday, Comfort, and Hampton Inns have indoor pools, the Best Western a year-round outdoor hot tub; the Holiday Inn and Best Western have a restaurants, the Hampton Inn and the Econo Lodge serve a complimentary continental breakfast, the Comfort Inn a full hot breakfast. The stars of *Empire Falls,* including Paul Newman, stayed at the Comfort Inn.

Just west of Waterville, and technically in the Belgrade Lakes region, is **The Pressey House Lakeside Bed & Breakfast,** 32 Belgrade Rd., Oakland 04963, 207/465-3500, a stunning mid-19th-century octagonal house at the head of nine-mile-long Messalonskee Lake (also known as Snow Pond). Five good-size rooms (private baths) are $110–175 d mid-May–mid-Oct., $95–120 d other months, including a full breakfast. No smoking, no pets. Relax on the patio or borrow the canoe, paddleboat, or motorboat to explore the lake. The Pressey House, a five-minute drive from I-95 exit 127, is open all year.

Most of Maine's traditional sporting camps are farther north or west, deep in the woods. **Alden Camps,** 3 Alden Camps Cove, Oakland 04963, 207/465-7703, fax 465-7912, is more accessible—but it's worth your life to get a reservation. (It's also technically in the Belgrade Lakes region.) Founded in 1909, Alden Camps has an incredibly loyal following, unto fourth-generation guests. The 18 rustic cottages face great sunrises across three-mile-long East Pond (aka East Lake). Weekly rates, mid-June–late Aug., are $612–810 pp, AP, depending on cottage size. Rates early and late in the season are $462–582 pp, AP. Children are $96–426 a week, depending on age. Most guests spend a week. Each no-frills cottage has a screened porch, electricity, bath, fridge, and daily maid service. The crew of college kids aims to please, and former staffers now show up as guests. Meals are hearty, and the Friday-night lobsterbake/clambake—open to the public, call for reservations—is a longstanding tradition. BYOL. The dining room is also open to the public for dinner by reservation Memorial Day–Labor Day, but nonguest space is very limited July–Aug. The 40-acre spread on Rte. 137 has clay tennis courts, a sandy beach, a waterskiing boat, boat rentals, and a kids' play area. Pets are allowed for $25 a day (a kennel would be far cheaper). Alden Camps is seven miles off I-95 exit 127. Open mid-May–late Sept.

FOOD

In a local twist on the traditional Maine public suppers—thanks to Waterville's substantial Lebanese community—**St. Joseph Maronite Church,** 3 Appleton St., Waterville 04901, 207/872-8515, puts on a Lebanese supper at least once a year (the second Sunday after Easter). If you enjoy Eastern Mediterranean home cooking, be there. Call the church for details.

The rest of the year, the best source of Lebanese goodies is a block away from the church. The little **Lebanese Cuisine,** 34 Temple St., Waterville 04901, 207/873-7813, has homemade spinach and meat pies, hummus, tabbouleh, and kibbe. Eat here or get it to go. The bakery is open all year, Mon.–Fri. 9:30 AM–4 PM, Sat. 9 AM–1 PM.

Lunch

A popular hangout, **Big G's Deli,** Outer Benton Ave., Winslow 04901, 207/873-7808, has enormous "name" sandwiches such as the Miles Standwich (nearly a whole turkey dinner), all on homemade bread. Price range is $5–7. Order at the counter and try for a seat—or get it to go for the mother of all picnics. No credit cards. Open all year except Thanksgiving and Christmas, Sun.–Thurs. 6 AM–7 PM, Fri.–Sat. 6 AM–9 PM. On the east side of the Kennebec, Big G's is about a mile north of the Rte. 201 bridge to Waterville.

Inexpensive to Moderate

Linked like a Siamese twin to the Railroad Square Cinema, **Buen Apetito,** Railroad Sq., Waterville 04901, 207/872-9500, serves popular Tex-Mex meals, while the nearby Grand Central Café serves popular brick-oven pizza.

Just across the Waterville/Winslow bridge, with deck tables overlooking the Kennebec, is the **Lobster Trap and Steakhouse,** 25 Bay St., Rte. 201, Winslow 04901, 207/872-0529. Lobster stew is famous here, so is the surf-and-turf. Generally, entrées are $10–16, lobsters are higher. When the weather turns sour, there's plenty of room inside this casual place. The Lobster Trap is open 11 AM–9 PM daily.

A Vegetarian Chef is just one of a full menu page of salad choices at **The Last Unicorn,** 8 Silver St., Rte. 201, Waterville 04901, 207/873-6378. Creative appetizers, an extensive wine and cocktail list, Borealis bread, and Sunday brunch are some of the best features of this friendly place. Soups and desserts are made daily, most dressings and spreads are made on premises, and the house dressings, sauces, and Boursin are sold retail. Lunch salad or sandwich ranges $5–8; dinner entrées $14–18. The menu says "creative and intriguing cuisine." You'll probably agree. Open Mon.–Thurs. 11 AM–9 PM, Fri.–Sat. 11 AM–10 PM, Sun. 11 AM–9 PM, brunch till 2:30 PM.

You can have *Saturday* brunch at **The Bread Box Cafe,** 137 Main St., Waterville 04901, 207/873-4090. Try the raspberry waffle, crisp with fresh-tasting fruit, or anything with home fries. Two can eat lunch for $25, if they're willing to skip desserts like chocolate mousse or creme caramel. Open for dinner, too.

There's good stuff seasonally at the **Riverside Farm Market,** 291 Fairfield St., Oakland 04963, 207/465-4439. Order scones or muffins, or lunch—soups, salads, quiche, and sandwiches—at the deli/baked goods counter. Sit inside or on the porch. Open Mon.–Sat. 9 AM–6 PM.

Jorgensen's Cafe, 103 Main St., Waterville 04901, 207/872-8711, is a downtown institution, with a French-language club meeting there on Saturday mornings. But you can hear French spoken at other times, too, while sipping one of what seem to be hundreds of kinds of coffee set out on a center counter, and enjoying a bagel, muffin, or breakfast sandwich. Lunch consists of a unique variety of specialty sandwiches, with every kind of deli meat available, plus quiche, salads, and soups. There's also an unusually interesting selection of gourmet gifts, implements, and sweets. In summer, sit at a table outside. Open all year, 7 AM–5 PM; to 8 PM in summer and for the Dec. holidays, and to 6 PM in fall.

It's hidden away downstairs, but lots of people find—and recommend—**The Freedom Cafe,** 18 Silver St., Waterville 04901, 207/859-8742, www.freedomcafefood.com, with a southern Creole accented menu that changes weekly. Owners James and Janice Swinton—she's the chef—might be serving St. Louis Style BBQ Back Ribs, Jambalaya, Buttermilk Fried Chicken, Beef Ribeye with Herb Butter, au jus, or Shrimp and Crab Cake with Tropical Salsa, made, like the desserts, on the premises from fresh ingredients. Full meals range $17–20. The wine list includes vintages from the Winterport Winery in Maine. Open Thurs.–Sat. 5 –9 PM.

Another eatery that comes highly recommended by locals is the **Asian Cafe,** 53 Bay St., Winslow 04901, 207/877-6688, serving Japanese, Korean, Thai, and Vietnamese cuisine daily 11 AM–10 PM. Don't over-order appetizers. They're huge!

Kennebec/Moose River *(vertical sidebar text)*

INFORMATION AND SERVICES

The **Mid-Maine Chamber of Commerce,** 1 Post Office Sq., Elm and Main Sts., Waterville 04903, 207/873-3315, www.midmainechamber.com, has its headquarters in an elegant 1911 Greek Revival building. The office is open all year, Mon.–Fri. 9 AM–5 PM.

The **Waterville Public Library,** 73 Elm St., Waterville 04901, 207/872-5433, with about 94,000 volumes, is open all year, Mon.–Fri. 10 AM–7 PM, plus Sat. 10 AM–3 PM during the school year. Closed Sat. in summer.

The **Miller Library,** Colby College, Waterville 04901, 207/859-5100, has state-of-the-art computer technology and 900,000 volumes, including a huge Irish literature collection and a room dedicated to poet Edwin Arlington Robinson.

Newspapers

The *Morning Sentinel,* 207/873-3341, published daily, is the Waterville/Winslow area's major source of information and events, although the *Bangor Daily News* also provides coverage.

Emergencies

For police, fire, and ambulance services in **Fairfield, Oakland, Waterville, and Winslow,** dial 911. The **MaineGeneral Medical Center,** 149 North St., Waterville 04901, emergency-room 207/872-1300, has round-the-clock emergency-room care. (It's under the same administrative umbrella as Augusta's MaineGeneral Medical Center.)

Getting Around

Pine Tree Taxi Co., 207/465-2304, provides 24-hour taxi service in the Waterville area and will "go anywhere," including to and from Bangor International Airport.

Community Organizations

You can't take a picture of community spirit, but Waterville seems to embody it. Some unique organizations are the grass-roots volunteer consortium, *REM,* and *Hardy Girls, Healthy Women,* standouts in efforts to build a healthy community.

Skowhegan Area

The Abnaki named Skowhegan (skow-HE-gun), "the place to watch for fish," because that's just what the early Native Americans did at the Kennebec River's twin waterfalls here. Their spears were ready when lunch came leaping up the river. The island between the falls later formed the core for European settlement of Skowhegan (pop. 9,000), largest town and county seat in Somerset County. Named for England's Somersetshire, the county was incorporated in 1823 and covers 3,633 square miles.

Favorite daughter Margaret Chase Smith, one of Maine's pre-eminent politicians, put Skowhegan on the map, and even since her 1995 death, admirers and historians have made pilgrimages to her former home. During her years in the U.S. Congress and Senate,

"The Lady from Maine" would return to her constituents—and she was never too busy to autograph placemats at her favorite local restaurant or to wave from her chair in her house's streetside solarium. Older local residents still recall the day President Dwight D. Eisenhower and his entourage visited Mrs. Smith, in 1955, when "Ike" spoke to an enthusiastic crowd at the Skowhegan Fairgrounds.

Another local institution is the nationally and internationally renowned Skowhegan School of Painting and Sculpture, founded in 1946 as a summer residency program. One of America's few art schools offering workshops in fresco painting, Skowhegan provides 65 artists with a bucolic, 300-acre lakeside setting for honing their skills and interacting with peers and prominent visiting artists. Acceptance is highly competitive for the nine-week program, and only on a one-time basis. Skowhegan's annual summer lecture series, featuring big names in the art world, is open to the public.

In the early 18th century, the town of Norridgewock (NORE-ridge-wok) was a French and Indian stronghold against the British. A century earlier, French Jesuit missionaries had moved in among the Norridgewock Indians at their settlement here and converted them to Catholicism. Best known of these was Father Sebastien Râle, beloved of his Indian parishioners. In 1724, taking revenge for Indian forays against them, a British militia detachment marched in and massacred the priest and his followers, a major milestone during what was known as Dummer's War. Today, a granite monument to Father Râle stands at the crime scene, Old Point, along the Kennebec about two miles south of downtown Madison, close to the Madison/Norridgewock town boundary.

Meaning "smooth water between rapids," Norridgewock (pop. 3,340) was the last bit of civilization for Benedict Arnold and his men before they headed into the Upper Kennebec wilderness on their March to Quebec in 1775. Stopping for almost a week, they spent most of their time caulking their leaky bateaux. Today the town has a slew of handsome 18th- and 19th-century homes.

SIGHTS
Margaret Chase Smith Library
Beautifully sited on Neil Hill, high above the Kennebec River, the Margaret Chase Smith Library, 56 Norridgewock Ave., Skowhegan 04976, 207/474-7133, fax 474-8878, bulges with fascinating memorabilia from the life and times of one of Maine's best-known politicians, who spent 32 years in the U.S. House and Senate and died in 1995. Over the entrance door is her signature red rose; inside is a 20-minute video describing her career. In 2000, the library held a special commemoration of the 50th anniversary of Sen. Smith's "declaration of conscience" speech, in which she cou-

rageously castigated Sen. Joseph McCarthy for his "Red Scare" witch-hunting tactics. Ask if a staff member is available to show you Sen. Smith's house, connected to the library on the 15-acre estate. (She was born at 81 North Ave. in Skowhegan.) The library is open all year, Mon.–Fri. 10 AM–4 PM, except for the week between Christmas and New Year's Day. Admission is free, but donations are welcome. The complex is 0.5 mile west of Rte. 201 (Madison Ave.).

Skowhegan History House
When you enter the handsome red-brick Skowhegan History House, 40 Elm St., Skowhegan 04976, 207/474-6632, with only a half-dozen rooms, you'll find it hard to believe that blacksmith Aaron Spear built it in 1839 for his family of 10 children. Must have been mighty cozy sleeping. Skowhegan treasures—antique clocks, china, and other furnishings—now fill the two-story structure, with a commanding view over the Kennebec River. Open Tues.–Fri. 1–5 PM, early June–late Sept. Admission is free, but donations are welcome. The house is just west of Rte. 201, at the junction of Elm and Pleasant Sts.

The Skowhegan Indian Monument
On High Street, next to a parking lot just east of Madison Ave. (Rte. 201), stands the giant wooden **Skowhegan Indian.** Rising 62 feet above its pedestal, the statue was carved in 1969 by Maine sculptor Bernard Langlais, who died in 1977. Nationally known for his work, Langlais dedicated the monument to the Native Americans who first settled this area. One hand holds a spear, the other holds a stylized fishing weir. The Langlais home in Cushing, where the sculpture was created, still has an open-air gallery of the artist's work, although it's not open to the public.

Skowhegan Historic District
Bounded roughly by Water and Russell Streets, and Madison Ave., the Skowhegan Historic District, close to the Kennebec River, contains 38 turn-of-the-20th-century buildings

from the town's heyday as a commercial center. After trains arrived in 1856, the wireless telegraph in 1862, and telephones in 1883, Skowhegan saw incredible prosperity. It's worth a walkabout to admire the architectural details of a bygone era.

L.C. Bates Museum

Located in a Romanesque National Historic Register building on the Good Will-Hinckley School campus, The L.C. Bates Museum, Rte. 201, Hinckley 04944, 207/238-4250, fax 238-4007, www.gwh.org, has a broadly eclectic collection with a natural-history focus. Among the treasures in the dozen or so rooms are hundreds of mounted rare birds, priceless Native American artifacts, and a trophy marlin caught by Ernest Hemingway. Maine's only similarly offbeat museums are the Wilson Museum in Castine and the Nylander Museum in Caribou.

A nine-mile nature-trail network winds through the 2,400-acre campus—established in 1889 as a school for disadvantaged children. Behind the museum, visit the arboretum and nature trails, open dawn to dusk. "Forest Walking Trails" maps are available in the museum. Alongside the trails are monuments to prominent conservationists. For a small fee, kids can attend Saturday-morning natural-history workshops May–Nov. The museum is open Wed.–Sat. 10 AM–4:30 PM, Sun. 1–4:30 PM, Apr.–mid-Nov., and the rest of the year by chance or appointment. Admission is $2.50 adults, $1 students and young children. The turreted brick-and-granite building is five miles north of I-95, exit 133, between Fairfield and Skowhegan, and is visible from Rte. 201 at the southern end of the campus.

South Solon Meetinghouse

This place is nothing short of amazing. As you drive out the East Madison Road from Skowhegan, headed north, you'll pass Lake Wesserunsett and soon come to the hamlet (little more than a crossroads) of South Solon. Here you'll find a serene white clapboard building, a traditional mid-19th-century New England meetinghouse. Then you go inside and

it's *totally* frescoed with interdenominational religious scenes. One of the founders of the Skowhegan School of Painting and Sculpture rescued the church from ruin in the 1930s; in the 1950s, fresco artists selected in a stiff competition were given a free hand to have a go at the place. The riot of color followed, until every square inch of walls and ceiling was covered. (A fresco program still continues at the Skowhegan School.) If the door is locked when you get there, call Andy Davis at 207/643-2555; better still, call ahead.

PARKS AND RECREATION

Skowhegan is the base for **Kennebec Valley Trails** (KVT), P.O. Box 144, Skowhegan 04976, 207/474-9606, an energetic membership organization promoting an ambitious long-range plan for multi-use recreational trail systems throughout the Kennebec Valley. KVT publishes *The Kennebec River: A Guide for Paddlers and Friends,* an extensive guide to the river, its history, and its environs, and *Take a Ride: Road and Mountain Biking Guide to the Upper Kennebec Valley.* The organization annually sponsors **National Trails Day** events the first Saturday in June. If you'd like to order a guidebook or become a member, contact KVT.

Coburn Park

Donated to the town by Abner Coburn, 13-acre Coburn Park, a wonderful riverside oasis, has a lily pond, memorial gardens (including a Hospice garden and a Margaret Chase Smith rose garden), a summer concert series at the gazebo, pagodas, and more than a hundred species of trees and shrubs. Bring a picnic, grab a table, and enjoy. The park is on Water St. (Rte. 2), at the eastern edge of town.

Lake George Park

Eight miles east of Skowhegan, along Rte. 2 (Canaan Road), is 257-acre state-owned Lake George Regional Park, 207/474-1292, with facilities for swimming and picnicking, plus a boat launch, restrooms, ball fields, hiking trails, and cross-country trails. Open seasonally, 8 AM–sunset. No pets, alcohol, or camping. $3 adults, $1 children 5–11, children under 5 and seniors over 65 free.

Arnold's Way Rest Area

About three miles north of Solon, close to the Solon/Bingham town line and just north of the area known as Arnold's Landing, is this especially attractive state rest area with covered picnic tables, grills, and an outhouse. Interpretive panels here mark the beginning of two dozen along the Old Canada Road Scenic Byway at Moscow, the Forks, Parlin Pond, and Attean, helping motorists get a feel for area history and pursuits like logging.

Traditional Skills Courses

In Canaan, east of Skowhegan, Master Maine Guide Ray Reitze, Jr., and his wife, Nancy, operate **Earthways Guided Canoe Trips and School of Wilderness Living,** 159 Earthways Rd., Canaan 04924, 207/426-8138, www.earthways.net, with an extensive schedule of canoe trips on the St. John, Allagash, Poland Pond ($625–725), and classes on traditional skills like basket-making, flint knapping, snowshoe lacing, and traditional medicine. Primitive campsites are available on their "campus" in Canaan. Ray, who learned woods lore as a youth from a Native American elder, has written a book about his spiritual philosophy, *And We Shall Cast Rainbows Upon the Land.*

Golf

The 18-hole **Lakewood Golf Course,** Rte. 201, Madison 04950, 207/474-5955, on the west side of Lake Wesserunsett, dates from 1925. Trickiest hole is the eighth, with a good-size pond between you and the green. Tee times are advisable here, especially in fall when the foliage is spectacular; carts are available. Open Apr.–early Nov. The course is five miles north of Skowhegan.

Downhill Skiing

Skowhegan is an easy drive from the top-flight skiing at Sugarloaf/USA, but you'll put a far smaller dent in your wallet at a small, family-operated ski area just down Rte. 2 to the east. **Eaton Mountain Ski Area,** Rte. 2, HC 71, Box 128, Skowhegan 04976, 207/474-2666, has 20 trails, novice to expert, served by a double chairlift. Vertical drop is 622 feet. There's night skiing, plus snowboard and tubing parks, ski school, rentals, and a cafeteria and lounge. Thanks to top-to-bottom snowmaking, the season is roughly Dec.–early April, although the lodge is the site of year-round concerts and other events. The access road is about five miles east of Skowhegan.

ENTERTAINMENT

A blast from the past is the refurbished **Strand Cinema,** 19 Court St., Skowhegan 04976, 207/474-3451, which opened in late 1929 as the Strand Theater. It still has the largest film screen in the state, and, supposedly, some ghosts. Films are screened daily, usually at 6:45 PM. Tickets are $5, children and matinees $3.50, and there's audio equipment for the hearing-impaired.

For another dose of nostalgia, plan to catch a flick at the 350-car **Skowhegan Drive-In,** Waterville Rd., Rte. 201, Skowhegan 04976, 207/474-9277, a landmark since 1954. Nightly double features (starting at dusk or whenever the sun disappears) are $5 pp; kids under 12 are free. Gates open at 7:30 PM. The drive-in, located at the southern end of town, is open Thurs.–Sun. late May–late June, then daily until Labor Day. The show goes on, rain or shine, except in fog.

Built in 1901, the **Lakewood Theater,** Rte. 201, Madison, 207/474-7176, mailing address P.O. Box 331, Skowhegan 04976, www.lakewoodtheater.org, on the shores of Lake Wesserunsett six miles north of Skowhegan, has had a roller-coaster history, but it's now in a decidedly "up" phase, thanks to the State Theater of Maine Company. Maine's oldest summer theater presents nine musicals, comedies, and light dramas each season, late May–mid-Sept. Performances are Thurs.–Sat. at 8 PM, plus matinees every other Wed. at 2 PM and Sun.

at 4 PM. On matinee Wednesdays, there is also a 6:45 PM evening performance. Tickets are $20/22 adults, $14 children 5–17. For an extra $5, you can have cabaret seating on the side balconies. Special children's plays ($5 per ticket) are performed at 10 AM on four summer Saturdays. You'll find food just steps from the theater at the Lakewood Inn Restaurant.

FESTIVALS AND EVENTS

Mid-June–early Aug., the evening (usually Fri.) **Barbara Fish Lee Lecture Series** draws nationally and internationally noted artists to participate in its lecture/presentation series at the Old Dominion Fresco Barn, Skowhegan School of Painting and Sculpture. Contact the school (207/474-9345) for dates and times.

Mega-omelettes made in world's largest omelette pan, a parade, a craft fair, live entertainment, a carnival, and fireworks are among the features of the **Central Maine Egg Festival.** The biggest day is Saturday. It's held at Manson Park in Pittsfield in mid-July.

Billed as America's oldest country fair, and Maine's largest outdoor event, going back more than 175 years, the **Skowhegan State Fair** is a 10-day extravaganza with agricultural exhibits galore, live entertainment, harness racing, food booths, a carnival, and a demolition derby at the Skowhegan Fairgrounds, Rte. 201, Skowhegan, early–mid-Aug. Skowhegan also hosts the **Flavor of Skowhegan,** in mid- to late July, when Commercial Street is closed off for restaurateurs to serve "Dinner on the Street."

Mid-September's low-key **New Portland Lions Club Fair,** in North New Portland, features agricultural and craft exhibits, animal-pulling events, and a carnival.

SHOPPING
Antiquarian Books
No old-book fan should miss **C.J. Seams Books,** 103 Main St., Rte. 201A, Madison 04950, 207/696-8361. Ask Colby Seams for a specific title and he'll negotiate his rabbit warren of a shop and pull it right out. Impressive. Hardcover mysteries and lots of fiction are specialties, but there's so much more in this funky shingled emporium. It's open May–Oct., Tues.–Sat. 10 AM–5 PM.

Factory Outlet
Discounts of up to 50 percent are typical for athletic-shoe seconds at the **New Balance Factory Store,** 12 Walnut St., Skowhegan 04976, 207/474-6231. The store also carries sportswear, socks, sports bags, and such. Open all year, Mon.–Sat. 9 AM–6 PM, Sun. 11 AM–5 PM. The outlet is just off Rte. 201 (W. Front St.), south of the Kennebec. The turn is next to Skowhegan Savings Bank.

Natural Foods and Farmers Markets
The Spice of Life, 338 Madison Ave., Rte. 201, Skowhegan 04976, 207/474-8216, stocks vitamins, spices, bulk grains, and other health-food items. The shop is in the Skowhegan Village Shopping Center, a mile north of downtown. In summer, it's open Mon.–Fri. 9 AM–6 PM, Sun. 10 AM–5 PM. Winter hours are the same, except for a 3 PM closing on Friday.

In downtown Skowhegan, next to the chamber of commerce, the **Skowhegan Farmers Market** operates from early July–Oct., 9 AM–1 PM Sat. Heavy emphasis on organic products.

East of I-95 exit 150, the **Pittsfield Farmers Market** sets up shop at Hathorn Park, Rte. 152 (Hartland Ave.), every Mon. and Thurs. 2–6 PM, May–Oct. Among the goodies are grass-fed beef, free-range eggs, fresh fruits, herbs, honey, and lots more.

ACCOMMODATIONS
Bed-and-Breakfast
Helen's Bed & Breakfast, 2 Prospect St., Rte. 201, Skowhegan 04976, 207/474-0066, is a lovely 19th-century brick house just off Rte. 201 with four rooms (all with private baths; $40–60 d). Guests share the large deck and yard. No smoking. Open Apr.–Dec.

Motels

Also convenient to downtown Skowhegan, the **Towne Motel,** 172 Madison Ave., Rte. 201 North, Skowhegan 04976, 207/474-5151 or 800/843-4405, fax 207/474-6407, www. townemotel.com, has 33 rooms with phones, air-conditioning, cable TV, hi-speed Internet access, and free continental breakfast. The outdoor pool is great for kids. Pets are welcome in some rooms. Rates are $69–89 July–mid-Oct., $43–66 other months. Open all year.

Sporting Camps

On the west side of Lower Pierce Pond, **Cobb's Pierce Pond Camps,** Pierce Pond, mailing address P.O. Box 124, North New Portland 04961, 207/628-2819, winter 207/628-3612, is far from an easy destination—but it's worth the effort once you get there. This traditional sporting camp, founded in 1902, has been a mecca for anglers, family vacationers, and deer hunters ever since, and it can be tough to get a reservation. Amazingly, the 11 rustic cabins have generator-created electricity and flush toilets. Meals are served family-style in the main lodge; it's all very chummy. BYOL and they'll supply the "pond ice"—from big blocks cut out of the frozen pond last winter. Daily rates are $95 pp, less for children, AP. Call in advance to discuss pets. Cobb's is open May–Nov. From Rte. 16 in North New Portland, just east of Gilman Stream, take the Long Falls Dam Rd. north about 23 mostly unpaved miles and watch carefully for signs. At the end of the road, you'll be picked up by boat for the quick run to the camps.

Campgrounds

About 1.5 miles north of downtown Skowhegan, **Yonder Hill Family Campground,** 221 Lakewood Rd., Rte. 201, Madison 04950, 207/474-7353 or 207/474-6688, www.yonderhill.com, has 100 mostly wooded sites on its 35 acres. Rates are by the day, month, or season, and the site-tent, pop-up, RV, Adirondack shelter, or all-season cabin. Facilities include a giant pool, playground, recreation hall, and laundry room. Most leashed pets

are allowed; no credit cards. Open mid-May–mid-Sept.

Ten miles east of downtown Skowhegan, **Skowhegan/Canaan KOA Campground,** Rte. 2, Box 87, Canaan 04924, 207/474-2858 or 800/562-7571, www.smorefuncampground. com, has 80 acres with 100 mostly open sites, a lodge, and cabins, ranging from $20 for a tent site to $99 for the lodge. As with other KOA locations, don't expect wilderness camping; there are even cable TV hookups. Other features at this well-maintained winner of facilities and operations awards include a heated pool, playground, free hot showers, and a laundry room. Pet friendly; boat and bike rentals are available, plus activities like hayrides and ice-cream socials. Open mid-May–mid-Oct.

How often do you find a campground on the National Historic Register? That's the case at **The Evergreens Campground & Restaurant,** Rte. 201A, P.O. Box 114, Solon 04979, 207/643-2324, www.evergreenscampground. com, a prehistoric site used by Native Americans some 4,000 years ago. Many stone tools and weapons excavated here are now in the Maine State Museum in Augusta; a small collection is displayed at the campground. The campground has mostly wooded sites ($7.50 pp for tent sites, $24 d for RV sites), some right on the Kennebec River. Cottages are $30 pp. Pets are allowed; rental canoes and kayaks are available by the day. There is a small launch fee for people bringing their own boats, and a guest fee. The restaurant has a bar and a riverfront deck. Directly across the river (technically in Embden) is a huge outcrop covered with ancient Indian petroglyph; eagles can often be seen on this shore. The campground, a mile south of the center of Solon, is open all year, catering to snowmobilers in winter.

FOOD
Groceries

In Solon, the staff is so cordial at the **Solon Corner Market,** Main St., Solon 04979, 207/643-2458, you'll probably want to buy one of their embroidered baseball caps.

Everything's here—groceries, pizza, newspapers, info, all the fixings for a picnic—and they're now an agency liquor store. Open Mon.–Fri. 6 AM–8 PM (to 9 PM Thurs.–Fri.), Sat. 7 AM–9 PM, and Sun. 8 AM–8 PM.

Inexpensive to Moderate

Right on the river, the **Old Mill Pub and Restaurant,** 39 Water St., Skowhegan 04976, 207/474-6627, in a handsome antique brick building, gets high marks for its buffalo wings. Weather permitting, you can drink and dine on the deck. Prices are moderate, particularly for the early-bird specials, served 4–6 PM daily. It's open all year, Mon.–Thurs. 11:30 AM–9 PM (to 10 PM Fri.–Sat.) and Sun. noon–8 PM. Closed Sun. Nov.–Mar. Friday night there's live music; it gets pretty noisy.

Moderate to Expensive

Two doors from the Towne Motel, in a historic home, the **Heritage House Restaurant,** 182 Madison Ave., Skowhegan 04976, 207/474-5100, is Skowhegan's best dining choice. Dinner entrées run $10–20. Apricot Mustard Chicken Breast is a specialty. Reservations are advisable on weekends. The Heritage House is open all year, Tues.–Fri. for the lunch buffet (11:30 AM–2 PM) and Sun.–Thurs. 5–9 PM, Fri.–Sat., 5–10 PM, for dinner.

Elegance is the by-word at the restored **Lakewood Inn Restaurant**, Rte. 201, P.O. Box 331, Skowhegan 04976, 207/858-4403, open to theatergoers and the public. There's a "Bette Davis table," and Lana Turner and John Travolta have also frequented the premises. Open Wed., Thurs., Fri., and Sat. at 5 PM, Sun. at 1:30 PM, and on show days. There's a two-for-one entrée special on Wednesday, and a brunch buffet on show Wednesdays, 11 AM–2 PM.

INFORMATION AND SERVICES

The **Skowhegan Area Chamber of Commerce,** 23 Commercial St., Skowhegan 04976, 207/474-3621, or 888/772-4392, www.skowheganchamber.com, operates a small freestanding **information center** on the corner of Rtes. 201 and 2 in downtown Skowhegan. If you're coming from the south, it's a pretty zippy turn to make—watch out for other traffic—but there's a parking lot right there. It's open all year, Mon.–Fri. 9 AM–4 PM and occasional Sat. in summer—call ahead. Be sure to request the chamber's informational regional map and community profile.

The **Skowhegan Free Public Library,** 9 Elm St., Skowhegan 04976, 207/474-9072, is open all year. Winter hours are Mon., Tues, Wed., Fri., 10 AM–6 PM, Thurs. to 7 PM, Sat. to 2 PM. In summer, hours are Mon.–Fri., 10 AM–6 PM, closed Sat. The library is half a block west of Madison Avenue (Rte. 201).

Newspapers

The Somerset Gazette, 207/474-0606, fax 207/474-0303, is a folksy, free tabloid published every Friday in Skowhegan. Each summer, it publishes a free newsprint entertainment guide with local historical features and info on events and recreational activities.

Most Skowhegan-area residents rely on Waterville's *Central Maine Morning Sentinel* for daily news, although the *Bangor Daily News* also provides some coverage of this area.

Emergencies

In **Skowhegan, Norridgewock, and Madison,** for fire, police, or ambulance services, dial 911. **Redington-Fairview General Hospital,** Fairview Ave., Rte. 104, Skowhegan 04976, 207/474-5121, has round-the-clock emergency care.

Bingham to Jackman

Until the arrival of white-water rafting in the mid-1970s, the Upper Kennebec Valley was best known to fishermen, hunters, timber truckers, and families who'd been summering here for generations. And long before that, long before dams changed the river's flow patterns, Native Americans used the Kennebec as a convenient chute from the interior's dense forests to summer encampments on the coast. In 1775, Col. Benedict Arnold led more than a thousand men up this river in a futile campaign to storm the ramparts of Quebec City.

If you're history-minded—or just interested in "heritage touring"—consider following the **Kennebec-Chaudière International Corridor,** a historic route that stretches from Bath, Maine, to Quebec City. Benedict Arnold used it; Native Americans used it (on foot and by canoe); and enterprising 19th-century traders found it invaluable for moving their wares between the United States and Canada. Along the route are museums, churches, dramatic scenery, and French and American cultural centers. For details, and a helpful map and booklet, visit www.kennebec-chaudiere.com, or call 800/782-6497. Even more helpful is *Following Their Footsteps: A Travel Guide & History of the 1775 Secret Expedition to Capture Quebec,* by Stephen Clark. The 160-page book (Clark Books, Shapleigh, Maine) includes history, maps, canoe routes, and an appendix of places to visit along the way.

The valley's main artery, Rte. 201, often paralleling the Kennebec River, is now the most convenient driving route from Maine to Quebec City (about a six-hour drive from Rockland, Maine), but those motorists dash through like a horse headed for the barn. It's rafting that has awakened thousands to the attractions of the valley and spurred a tourism boomlet.

Midway between Skowhegan and The Forks, 23 miles in each direction, Bingham (pop. 989 in the 2000 census) is also right on the 45th parallel and thus equidistant between the North Pole and the equator (3,107 miles in each di-

rection). This quiet valley town is a low-key commercial center with attractive, manicured homes, as well as a stopping point for many whitewater rafters en route to Caratunk and The Forks. The town was named for William Bingham, an influential Colonial-era banker and land speculator who made a fortune in privateering. Roscoe Vernon ("Gadabout") Gaddis, TV's pioneering Flying Fisherman, built Bingham's funky grass airfield, the Gadabout Gaddis Airport, site of an annual September fly-in, with plane rides and aerobatics.

Just north of Bingham is Moscow, home of the 155-foot-high Wyman Dam, harnessing the Kennebec River for hydroelectric power. Backed up behind the dam is gorgeous Wyman Lake, lined with birches, evergreens, frequent pullouts (great for shutterbugs), and a small lakeside picnic area on the west side of Rte. 201.

Appropriately named, The Forks stands at the junction of the Kennebec and Dead Rivers, making it obvious why rafting companies have set up shop here. The tiny year-round population of 35 supports an ever-expanding transient population for the whitewater-rafting trade from late April to mid-October.

Surrounded by mountains, Jackman (pop. 718) is the valley's frontier town, the last outpost before the Quebec provincial border, 16 miles northward. In the middle of town, the Moose River links Jackman to the town of Moose River (pop. 219), just to the north.

From Bingham to Jackman, Rte. 201 is better known as "Moose Alley." Even though state transportation officials have built rumble strips into the road and littered the roadsides with flashing yellow lights and cautionary Moose Crossing signs, drivers still barrel along, and every year fatalities occur. Those who drive carefully, though, have a treat in store: moose sightings are relatively frequent, especially early and late in the day. If you notice a car or two pulled off the road, it's likely someone has spotted a moose. (Another Moose Alley in this area—a pretty sure bet for spotting one of the behemoths—is Rte. 6/15 from Jackman east to Rockwood.

SIGHTS
Moxie Falls

Here's a big reward for little effort. One of New England's highest waterfalls, Moxie Falls, with drops of as much as 100 feet, is one of the easiest to reach. From Rte. 201, just south of the Kennebec River bridge in The Forks, drive 1.8 miles east on Lake Moxie Rd. to the signposted parking area. From here, via an easy, wide trail, plus steps and a boardwalk, it's 0.6 mile to the falls in Moxie Stream. Allow a relaxed hour for the round-trip; if it's hot, cool off in the stepped pools. Avoid the falls in June, when blackflies will have you for lunch. Don't forget a camera.

Fall-Foliage Bonanza

High on everyone's list of "best roads to drive in fall" is **Route 201,** the officially designated Old Canada Road Scenic Byway between Solon and the Canadian border. Every curve in the winding, two-lane road reveals a red, gold, and green palette any artist would die for.

Among the must-sees along the route are the **Attean View Rest Area,** just south of Jackman (have your picnic here, and climb the Owl's Head trail for an even more spectacular view), and the neat little hamlet of **Caratunk** (pop. 108), a smidgen east of Rte. 201 on the way to Pleasant Pond. Include a stop at the folksy **Caratunk General Store**-cum-post office.

RECREATION

Recreation is The Big Focus in this part of Maine. Among the opportunities in the Upper Kennebec Valley are hiking, canoeing, bicycling, fishing, and snowmobiling—just for a start—but the big business is whitewater rafting, headquartered in and around The Forks. The umbrella organization for 11 whitewater rafting companies is **Raft Maine,** P.O. Box 3, Bethel 04217, 207/824-3694 or 800/723-

8633, www.raftmaine.com. The group provides info, sends out brochures, and fields reservation requests.

White-water Rafting

Carefully regulated by the state, the rafting companies have come a long way since the sport took off in 1976; outfitters have created sprawling base-camp complexes and diversified year-round into such other adventure sports as mountain biking, canoeing, kayaking, camping, rock climbing, horseback riding, snowmobiling, and cross-country skiing. The state strictly monitors the number of rafts allowed on the rivers; on midsummer weekends, there's a near-capacity crowd. More than 80,000 rafters run Maine's rivers each season (compared with only 600 in 1976).

The focus of whitewater rafting in this region is the **East Branch of the Kennebec River,** a 12-mile run from the Florida Power and Light/Maine Hydro Harris Station hydroelectric dam, below Indian Pond, to The Forks. The dam's controlled water releases produce waves of up to eight feet, but the only major whitewater (Class IV and V) is at Magic Falls, near the beginning of the trip. By the end of the run, you're just floating along. Kennebec trips operate between early May and mid-October. Information about the Harris Dam water-release schedule is available round-the-clock by calling FPL's "flow line" at 800/557-3569.

Most of the rafting companies also organize trips on the more challenging and oddly named **Dead River,** but serious water releases occur only half a dozen times during the season, mostly on spring weekends. Competition is stiff for space on the infrequent Dead River trips, an exhilarating 16-mile run through Class III to Class V whitewater from below Grand Falls to The Forks. Biggest thrill is Poplar Hill Falls. In July and August, the Dead River lives up to its placid name, and outfitters organize moderately priced Sport-Yak and family rafting trips. Many of the companies described below also operate rafting trips on the **West Branch of the Penobscot River,** from base or outpost camps near Millinocket.

In spring, when ice has barely left the rivers, you'll need to bring or rent a wetsuit; in fall, you'll float past brilliant riverside colors; in both these seasons, as well as on weekdays, prices are the lowest. September is a great time to be here. No matter when you come, expect to get wet; wear fleece or wool or polypropylene, *not* cotton. When you make your reservation, each of the outfitters sends a list of what to bring and wear.

Cost of a one-day Kennebec River trip ranges from $80 to $130 pp, depending on whether it's a weekday, weekend, or midsummer. Prices include a hearty cookout or lunch either along the river or back at base camp. Cost of the one-day Dead River trip ranges from $90 to $140 pp. Scads of economical package rates are available—covering lodging, meals, and other activities—especially early and late in the season. Be forewarned that all outfitters have **age minimums:** 10 on the upper Kennebec and 15 on the Dead. Some also impose a weight minimum. (Minimum age on the more challenging upper Penobscot River is 15; Penobscot trip costs range from $75 to $120.)

If you want to make more than a day of it—definitely a good plan, since trips start early in the morning and you'll be exhilarated but dog-tired at the end of the day—spend a night or two, maybe one night before and one night afterward. Most of the whitewater rafting companies have been building and refurbishing like mad, building hot tubs and creating beds and restaurants for every budget. The camaraderie is contagious when everyone around you is about to go rafting or has just done it.

Rafting Outfitters

One of the early rafting firms, established in the early 1980s, is **North Country Rivers,** Rte. 201, P.O. Box 633, Bingham 04920, 207/672-4814 or 800/348-8871, www.northcountryrivers.com, based next to Gadabout Gaddis Airport. Solid experience, competitive rates, no frills; Kennebec, Dead, and Penobscot trips. North Country Rivers offers camping packages (lodging, rafting, and meals) for $89 to $149 pp, as well as good-size modern cabins for $40 pp per night.

The pioneer of Maine's rafting companies, and one of the largest operations, is **Northern Outdoors,** Rte. 201, P.O. Box 100, The Forks 04985, 207/663-4466 or 800/765-7238, www.northernoutdoors.com, established in 1976. Northern Outdoors runs trips on the Kennebec, Dead, and Penobscot Rivers; their trip prices are the highest, but you get what you pay for. From The Forks Resort Center, four miles south of town, buses transport rafters (about half an hour) to the Harris Station put-in. This first-rate, well-run enterprise also offers family-oriented activities, including freshwater fishing trips, rock climbing, camping overnights, lake kayaking, and snowmobiling. The center has a whole range of lodging possibilities—campsites, condos, cabin tents, log cabins, and luxurious "club cabins"—all priced according to the number of occupants. Also here are tennis courts, an outdoor pool, hot tub, brewpub, and restaurant serving three meals a day. Open all year.

Five miles east of The Forks is **Moxie Outdoor Adventures,** Lake Moxie Camps, Lake Moxie Rd., HC 63, Box 60, The Forks 04985, 207/663-2231 or 800/866-6943, www.moxierafting.com, which runs Kennebec, Dead, and Penobscot trips from a traditional sporting-camp base on lovely Lake Moxie (also called Moxie Pond), east of Moxie Falls. Canoes and kayaks are available, there's great hiking, and guests tend to linger here. Rustic cabins, platform tents, and primitive campsites are the lodging options; opt for American Plan. Moxie also organizes rafting trips in Massachusetts.

A smaller operation than most, **Professional River Runners of Maine,** Rte. 201, P.O. Box 92, West Forks 04985, 207/663-2229 or 800/325-3911, www.proriverrunners.com, does Kennebec, Dead, and Penobscot trips, as well as spring trips on New York's Hudson and Moose Rivers. Campsites are available at their base here, and they'll arrange other lodging on request. They'll also organize a "wilderness island campout," with two days of rafting and an evening lobster cookout. This is a good company for family trips.

On the banks of the Dead River, **Magic Falls Rafting Company,** P.O. Box 9, West Forks 04985, 207/663-2220 or 800/207-7238, www.magicfalls.com (winter: Rte. 4, Box 2820, Winslow 04901, 207/873-0938), does Kennebec, Dead, and Penobscot trips and also offers rock climbing with certified instructors. A unique "rock and roll" package covers a day of rafting and a day of climbing. Accommodations include lodge rooms, cabin tents, and basic tent sites.

Three other Kennebec, Dead, and Penobscot rafting outfitters have their headquarters elsewhere and a variety of base camps here in the Kennebec Valley. **New England Outdoor Center,** based at a huge complex in Millinocket, has an impressive resort facility on Wyman Lake in Caratunk, managing its Kennebec and Dead River trips. **Wilderness Expeditions,** based at The Birches Resort in Rockwood, has a lodge and campground at The Forks for its Kennebec and Dead trips and another lodge close to Baxter State Park for its Penobscot trips.

Canoeing and Kayaking

If you're a neophyte canoeist, or have never done a multiday trip, or you want to go *en famille,* your baptismal expedition probably ought to be the three-day **Moose River Bow Trip,** an easy, 45-mile loop (ergo, "bow") with mostly flatwater. Of course, you can do this yourself, but you don't even need to arrange a shuttle, but a guided trip has its advantages—not the least of which is that the guides provide the know-how for the beginners, they do the cooking and cleanup, and they're a big help for portaging. Allow $100–110 pp a day for a guided trip.

The Moose River trip has become so popular in recent years that campsite maintenance has backslid a bit and some guides prefer to go elsewhere, but it's still a fine, fun expedition. Veteran guide services that do this trip include Mike Patterson's **Wilds of Maine Guide Service Inc.,** 192 Congress St., Belfast 04915, 207/338-3932, www.wildsofmaine.com, and **Allagash Canoe**

Trips, P.O. Box 932, Greenville 04441, 207/237-3077, www.allagashcanoetrips.com.

Experienced guides Andy and Leslie McKendry operate **Cry of the Loon Kayak Adventures,** P.O. Box 238, Jackman 04945, 207/668-7808, www.cryoftheloon.net, from mid-May to early October. Lots of options are available, including a three-day Moose River Bow ($325 pp, with only one portage). Maximum group is eight, minimum four. Leslie's gourmet meals are included in the cost. Andy and Leslie will also do one-day guided trips ($60 pp with lunch), or they'll customize a multi-sport trip for you, with kayaking, rafting, rock climbing, and hiking. If you want to be on your own, they rent Old Town kayaks for $25 a day and Old Town canoes for $20 a day. Avoid June, when the blackflies descend; water level can be a problem in August for the bow trip. Cry of the Loon's base is on Rte. 15, 6.5 miles east of Jackman.

Hiking

The **Appalachian Trail,** extending 2,158 miles from Springer Mountain, Georgia, to the summit of Maine's Katahdin, crosses the Upper Kennebec Valley near Caratunk, just south of The Forks. The *Appalachian Trail Guide to Maine* provides details for reaching several sections of the white-blazed trail accessible to short-haul hikers. Crossing the 70-yard-wide Kennebec at this point would be a major obstacle were it not for the seasonal free ferry service operated for AT hikers by Rivers and Trails Northeast. The designated boatman is Steve Longley, 207/663-4441 or 888/356-2863, www.riversandtrails.com. Since the mid-1980s, he's been one of the "old reliables" along the AT. The ferry schedule tends to be two hours in the morning from late May through mid-July, four hours a day from mid-July through September, and two hours in the morning in early October.

If you're spending any time in the woods from mid-October through November, *do not go out* without at least a hunter-orange cap to signal your presence to hunters; a hunter-orange vest is even better. Even though some properties are posted No Hunting, don't take a chance; one scofflaw can make a life-and-death difference. If you're skittish, or don't have the proper clothing, hike on Sunday, when hunting is banned.

Mountain Biking

The major highway in the valley (Rte. 201) is winding and fairly narrow, so plan to bike primarily on the side roads—some paved, some not. The **Kennebec Valley Trail** is an easy 12-mile multiuse loop trail that follows a disused railroad bed (no tracks) from Bingham south to Solon. Best place to pick up the trail is at the Gadabout Gaddis Airport, on the southern outskirts of Bingham. The route roughly parallels the river and Rte. 201. Endpoint is the Williams Dam public landing, alongside the Kennebec in Solon. (Or do this loop in reverse, starting in Solon.)

In the Jackman area, an easy-to-moderate 10-mile trip is the **Sandy Bay Loop,** beginning seven miles north of downtown Jackman. Jackman's chamber office has a recreational map detailing this route and others in the area. Mountain biking is becoming a big deal here.

Snowmobiling

The **Jackman/Moose River** area has more than 100 miles of groomed snowmobile trails, and the mountain setting makes it particularly appealing. In fact, the town looks a bit less raw and frontierish under a fresh coat of snow. The trail network connects east to the Moosehead Lake area and west to the Sugarloaf/USA area.

Skiing

For cross-country skiing, head for the 30-mile network of groomed trails at The Birches Resort (www.birches.com), a 30-mile drive east on Rte. 6/15. (See Greenville and Vicinity in the Katahdin/Moosehead chapter.)

The nearest downhill skiing is at Sugarloaf/USA, but there's no east-west road; you'll have to go south to North Anson and take Rte. 16 northwest to Sugarloaf.

ACCOMMODATIONS

If you're planning to be in this area during snowmobiling season, especially in Jackman, be sure to book well in advance; the lodgings get chockablock full of snow-sledders.

Inns

The only lodging in The Forks not established as part of a rafting company, **Inn by the River,** Rte. 201, The Forks, mailing address HCR 63, Box 24, West Forks 04985, 207/663-2181 or 866/663-2181, www.innbytheriver.com, has now expanded to offer rafting, fishing, eco-tours, and snowmobiling. Most of its clients are those looking for a bit of casual elegance. Everything's new, modern, and efficient here. Guests collect in the handsome great room, and there's even a pub. Ten rooms (private baths) go for $75-160 d in summer and fall; two-night minimum during holidays. The more expensive rooms have whirlpools and screened balconies. Dinner is available nightly in summer, but you'll need to reserve ahead. Children are welcome. No smoking. Open all year, but call ahead in winter. Inn by the River is .5 mile south of the Kennebec River bridge in The Forks.

Sporting Camps

Legendary on the Appalachian Trail hikers' grapevine, since the AT goes right through here, **Harrison's Pierce Pond Camps,** Pierce Pond Stream, P.O. Box 315, Bingham 04920, 207/672-3625 (off-season 207/279-8424), serves up 12-pancake breakfasts to hungry trekkers as well as to camp guests. And the rest of the meals are just as impressive. Started in 1934, Harrison's has long catered to fishermen but encourages families in July and August, when fishing slacks off. Special summer rates (early July to mid-August; three-night minimum) are $65 pp a day, half-price for kids 4–12. All meals are included. The huge lodge/dining hall has great views of the stream and waterfalls. Boat rentals are available; pets are allowed. Nine rustic log cabins have kerosene lamps and separate bathhouses; a few have toilet and sink (for a slightly higher rate). Vehicle access is an adventure in itself: about 20 miles (well signposted) northwest of Bingham, on paved and unpaved roads. Open May–Sept., but closed to lodging (AT breakfasts still go on) for 10 days in mid-August.

Attean Lake Lodge, Birch Island, P.O. Box 457, Jackman 04945, 207/668-3792, www.atteanlodge.com, has certain trappings of a traditional sporting camp, but it's more like an upscale rustic cottage colony. Owned by the Holden family since 1900, it's located on Birch Island in the center of island-and-rock-sprinkled Attean Lake (also called Attean Pond). Brad and Andrea Holden now make it all work-flawlessly. Fourteen well-maintained log cabins (some old, some new; two to six beds) have bathrooms, fireplaces, gas or kerosene lamps, and porches with fantastic views of the lake and surrounding mountains. Guests tend to collect in the new main lodge, with its cathedral ceiling, stone fireplaces, and window-walled dining room. Kids love the sandy beach. Meals have plenty of creativity (swordfish with ginger sauce, for instance). Motorboats are $30 a day, canoes are $10 a day; free use of kayaks, paddleboats, and a sailboat. From July through Labor Day, rates for two adults are $280 per day, AP (wine and beer are available), but nobody stays just one night. (Early and late in the season, rates are $240 d per day; children's rates are much lower.) Book well ahead; this is a popular getaway, and many families have been coming for years. Some guests barely leave the island the whole time they're here, but be sure to paddle across the pond and climb **Sally Mountain** (about 1.5 miles round trip) for views that stretch as far as Katahdin. (In fall, the foliage vistas are fabulous.) Access to the island is via the lodge launch, a five-minute run. Open Memorial Day through September.

Campgrounds

FPL Energy/Maine Hydro operates a campground next to its Harris Station on the East Branch of the Kennebec, where all the Upper Kennebec rafting trips begin. **Indian Pond Campground,** HC 63, Box 52, The Forks 04985, 800/371-7774, has 27 tent and RV sites (no hookups), including picnic tables and fire rings. Other facilities include showers, restrooms, RV dump station, laundry machines, and boat launch. Cost is $17 a site (for two); kids under 10 stay free. Leashed pets are allowed. You can hike from here to Magic Rock and watch Kennebec rafters surging through Magic Falls. If hydroelectric plants pique your interest, ask at the gatehouse about a tour of Harris Station. To reach the campground from Rte. 201 in The Forks, take Lake Moxie Rd. (also Moxie Pond Rd.) about five miles east; turn left (north) onto Harris Station Rd. and continue eight miles to the campground gatehouse. Open mid-April to mid-October.

On Heald Stream in Moose River, a mile east of downtown Jackman, the 24-acre **Moose River Campground,** P.O. Box 98, Jackman 04945, 207/668-3341, has 51 tent and RV sites close to a picturesque old dam site. Now crumbling from disuse, the dam once was part of a thriving, turn-of-the-20th-century lumber mill that employed more than 700 workers to turn out 35 million board feet annually. Open and wooded campsites are $32 (for four); canoe rentals are available. Facilities include a snack bar, heated swimming pool, trout pond, laundry room, and children's play area. Open mid-May to mid-Oct.

For a totally peaceful camping experience, book one of the fifteen waterfront sites (no hookups) at **Loon Echo Campground,** Lake Parlin, P.O. Box 711, Jackman 04945, 207/668-4829, www.campmaine.com/loonecho, 14 miles north of The Forks and 12 miles south of Jackman. It's the way camping used to be. Former teachers Bill and Holly Erven can provide all kinds of information on hiking, rafting, fishing, and more. Kayaks, canoes, and fishing gear are available for rent. Quiet time is strictly enforced. If you're here in late July, you can even help with the annual loon count on Lake Parlin. Sites are $19 for two (children under 12 are free). Loon Echo is open May through Labor Day.

FOOD

Bingham's headquarters for inexpensive, down-home cooking is **Thompson's Restaurant,** Upper Main St., Rte. 201, Bingham 04920, 207/672-3245, where *everyone* eventually shows up. Doughnuts are superb, portions are huge.

During snowmobile season, it's mobbed. This friendly two-room operation is open all year, Mon.–Sat. 5 AM–8 PM and Sun. 7 AM–8 PM. No credit cards.

If you're staying in Jackman and don't mind a 60-mile round-trip for dinner, it's worth heading east on Rte. 6/15 to Rockwood for moderate-priced dinners at **The Birches Resort** (207/534-7305 or 800/825-9453, www.birches.com). Be sure to call for a reservation; you don't want to drive that far and not have a table. The pre-dinner slot is prime time for moose-watching along this route. Afterward, unless there's a moon, the road is terminally dark, so drive *very* carefully.

INFORMATION AND SERVICES

Staffers at the Bingham and Jackman information centers are especially outgoing and helpful, but their hours are limited. It's wise to request their publications in advance, then hope to find the offices open when you arrive.

The **Upper Kennebec Valley Chamber of Commerce,** Murray St., P.O. Box 491, Bingham 04920, 207/672-4100, www.upperkennebecvalley.com, has a well-stocked new information center in the former Scott Paper building, half a block off Main St. (Rte. 201). The office, which has public restrooms, is open Memorial Day weekend through Sept., daily 9 AM–5 PM.

If your aim is to go rafting, you're likely to end up in The Forks at some point, so get in touch in advance with **The Forks Area Chamber of Commerce,** The Forks 04985, 207/663-4430, www.forksarea.com.

The **Jackman/Moose River Region Chamber of Commerce,** Lakeside Town Park, Main St., Rte. 201, P.O. Box 368, Jackman 04945, 207/668-4171 or 888/633-5225, www.jackmanmaine.org, has a small log-cabin information center with public restrooms out back. The hours vary considerably. Be sure to request a copy of the *Jackman/Moose River Region recreational map,* showing canoeing, biking, hiking, and snowmobile trails, plus driving routes and good moosewatching spots.

The umbrella organization for 11 whitewa-ter rafting companies is **Raft Maine,** P.O. Box 3, Bethel 04217, 207/824-3694 or 800/723-8633, www.raftmaine.com, which provides info, sends out brochures, and fields reservation requests. The toll-free number rotates like Russian roulette, connecting you to the next-in-line rafting outfitter. If you prefer, contact individual outfitters directly (see above).

Emergencies
Throughout the Upper Kennebec Valley, call 911 for police, health, and fire emergencies. The **Jackman Region Health Center,** Main St., Rte. 201, Jackman 04945, 207/668-2691, a division of Waterville and Augusta's Maine-General Medical Center, has a round-the-clock emergency room, but you'll need to go at least as far as Skowhegan for anything major.

Money and Customs
The **Border Trust Company,** Main St. (Rte. 201) at Nichols Rd., P.O. Box 400, Jackman 04945, 207/668-2251, is a convenient place to change Canadian and U.S. dollars. If you're headed *into* Canada, they'll be happy to see your U.S. dollars, but they'll stretch farther if you change them. Remember to carry appropriate identification if you're planning to cross the border. U.S. citizens need to have a photo ID—a passport would be better, particularly for reentry. Other nationals will need a passport and visa, however, provisions of the Homeland Security Act are tightening border-crossing requirements. Check on the requirements before you go. The customs post on Rte. 201 is open round-the-clock. Border Trust is open Mon.–Thurs. 9 AM–3 PM and Fri. 9 AM–5 PM. The drive-up window opens at 8:30 AM Mon.–Sat. and closes at 5 PM weekdays and at noon on Saturday. There's also an ATM.

Laundry
At the **Jackman Landing Campground,** Big Wood Lake, P.O. Box 567, Jackman 04945, 207/668-3301, close to the center of town, the laundry facilities are open to the public round-the-clock, all year, whether or not you're renting a campsite.

Western Lakes and Mountains

When I tire of the summertime coastal grid-lock or I get the winter blahs, the place I'm most likely to go for refuge is Maine's Western Lakes and Mountains—about 4,500 outstandingly scenic square miles of Franklin, Oxford, Androscoggin, and Cumberland Counties. The recreational variety is astonishing. Here are the two skiing powerhouses—Sunday River and Sugarloaf/USA—plus four smaller, family-oriented ski areas: Saddleback, Shawnee Peak, Mount Abram, and Lost Valley. While downhill may be the specialty, most of these also have miles of nordic trails.

Major "urban" destinations in the region are Bethel, Lewiston-Auburn, and Farmington. Of Maine's nine covered bridges (seven originals and two carefully built replicas), you'll find five in the Western Lakes and Mountains—including the picturesque "Artist's Covered Bridge," near Sunday River, my favorite because you can ski through the forest and suddenly come upon it. And one of the most rugged stretches of the 2,158-mile Appalachian Trail, which runs from Georgia to Maine, occurs in this area, right along the New Hampshire border.

Sprawling, mountainous Oxford County, with its back to New Hampshire, has fabulous trails for hiking and rivers for canoeing—and boasts the state's lowest population density. There's gold—and all kinds of other minerals—in the Oxford Hills; the official state gemstone, tourmaline (an intriguing stone that turns up in green, blue, or pink), is most prevalent in western Maine. Grab a digging tool or

© MARY LYONS

gold pan and have a go at amateur prospecting. You're unlikely to find more than a few flakes or some pretty specimens of sparkly pyrite ("fool's gold"), but the fun is in the adventure anyway.

East of Oxford County, Franklin County comprises Sugarloaf/USA and the lovely Rangeley Lakes recreational area. Farmington is the county seat. Mostly rural Androscoggin, fourth-smallest of the state's 16 counties, takes its commercial and political cues from Lewiston and Auburn, the state's second-largest population center.

Directly west of Portland, and partly in Cumberland County, are Sebago and Long Lakes, surrounded by towns and villages that swell with visitors throughout the summer. Also here are most of the state's youth summer camps—some many generations old. During the annual summer-camp parents' weekend in July, Bridgton's tiny, besieged downtown feels like Times Square at rush hour.

For tackling the many miles of trails in this region, you may find several guidebooks helpful—especially *AMC Maine Mountain Guide, 50 Hikes in the Maine Mountains, Guide to the Appalachian Trail in Maine,* and *Hikes in and around Maine's Lake Region.* If you can afford only one, pick up the *Hikes* booklet, a handy, inexpensive publication written by a local resident.

An excellent resource for exploring the historical/cultural/natural resources in this region is a foldout map/brochure produced by a consortium spearheaded by the Maine Mountain Counties Regional Heritage Program. The *Franklin Heritage Loop* brochure includes information on museums, hikes, historic sites, events, and visitor services in the areas around Farmington, Sugarloaf, and Rangeley Lakes. Request a copy at one of the chambers of commerce, or contact MMC/Heritage, P.O. Box 508, Farmington 04938, 207/778-3885, www.discovermainemountains.com.

Farmington Area

Farmington (pop. 6,880) is a sleeper of a town—home to a respected University of Maine campus, one of Maine's best art galleries, a first-class hospital, and an unusual opera museum. What's more, mountain towns and scenery stretch out and beyond in every direction. Less than an hour's drive north of town is the stunning Carrabassett Valley, made famous by the year-round Sugarloaf/USA resort. Off to the northwest are the fabled Rangeley Lakes, and a drive southwest leads to Bethel, home of Sunday River Ski Resort, mineral quarries, and the White Mountain National Forest. Farmington itself is a bit thin on interesting lodgings, but otherwise it's an ideal base for exploring western Maine.

Farmington was incorporated in 1794 and became the county seat for Franklin County 44 years later. It remains the judicial hub but also is the commercial center for the nearby towns of Wilton, Weld, New Sharon, Temple, and Industry. To the south and west are Jay,

Livermore Falls, Livermore, Dixfield, Mexico, and Rumford.

In Rumford and Jay, your nose will tell you it's paper-mill territory, part of Maine's economic lifeline. Residents have become inured to the aroma, but visitors may need a chance to adjust. Livermore is the site of the Norlands Living History Center, a unique participatory museum that rewards you with a real "feel" for the past.

And, lest we forget, Farmington's leading candidate for favorite son is Chester Greenwood, who, in 1873, rigged beaver fur, velvet, and a bit of wire to create "Champion ear protectors"—earmuffs to you—when he was only 15. The clever fellow patented his invention and then went on to earn a hundred more patents for such things as doughnut hooks and shock absorbers. His early-December birthday inspires the quirky annual Chester Greenwood Day celebration in downtown Farmington.

Western Lakes & Mountains

Western Lakes & Mountains

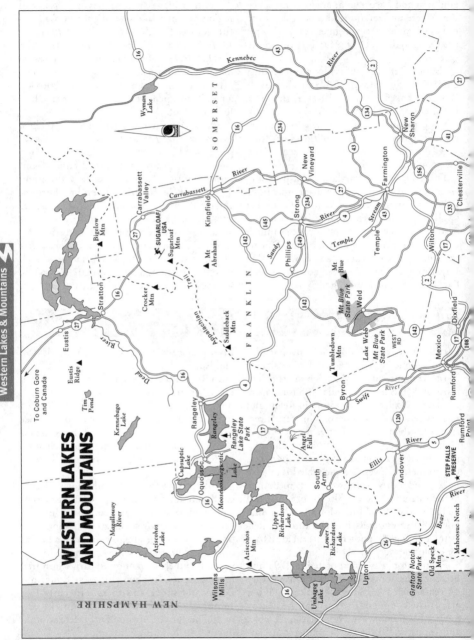

WESTERN LAKES AND MOUNTAINS

© AVALON TRAVEL PUBLISHING, INC.

Western Lakes & Mountains

SIGHTS

Nordica Homestead Museum

Gem-encrusted gowns, opera librettos, lavish gifts from royalty, and family treasures fill the handful of rooms in the Nordica Homestead Museum, 116 Nordica Ln. (nearly a mile off Fairbanks Rd., on Holly Rd.) Farmington 04938, 207/778-2042, birthplace of Lillian Norton (1857–1914)—Madame Lillian Nordica, legendary turn-of-the-20th-century Wagnerian opera diva. Her influence still pervades the house, where scratchy recordings play in the background and newspaper clips line the walls. No opera buff should miss this. A caretaker is on hand to answer questions. Admission is $2 adults, $1 children over five; even the kids get a kick out of the costumed mannequins, and there's lots of space on the grounds for letting off steam. The museum is open June–Labor Day, Tues.–Sat. 10 AM–noon and 1–5 PM, Sun. 1–5 PM. Closed Mon. Also open by appointment from Labor Day–mid-Oct. and in May. Take Rte. 4/27 north from Farmington and turn right (east) onto Holley Rd.; the farm is half a mile down the road.

University of Maine at Farmington

Founded in 1864 as Western State Normal School, with 31 teacher trainees, the University of Maine at Farmington (UMF), 86 Main St., Rte. 4, Farmington 04938, 207/778-7000, now has about 2,000 students tackling their studies in more than three dozen buildings. UMF's Education Department has always been topnotch, with a 100 percent placement record for its graduate teachers.

The university's administration building, **Merrill Hall,** on Main Street, is a 19th-century National Historic Register gem. Inside, **Nordica Auditorium,** named after the favorite-daughter diva, is the year-round setting for plays and concerts.

Living History at Norlands

Abandon your 21st-century mindset and drop into the 19th century at **Norlands Living History Center,** 290 Norlands Rd., Livermore 04253, 207/897-4366, www.norlands .org. The quickest way to do this is to take a 1.5-hour guided tour of the 430-acre farm officially known as **Washburn-Norlands.** The best way to do it, however, is to sign up for a three-day/two night family live-in program—when you don the clothing and identity of a real 19th-century Mainer and immerse yourself in quilting, farming, storytelling, cooking, and other chores. The ultimate in role-playing! Reservations required; $125 ages 6–12, $150 ages 13–18, $175 adults. The program is available June 17–19 and Aug. 5–7. It's a retro experience the kids certainly won't forget—and the parents won't either.

Regular guided tours of the house, barn, and schoolhouse are $8 adults, $4 children. Check the website for summer hours. Otherwise, tours are available by appointment or by chance. Throughout the year, Norlands has a number of special weekend events, all family-oriented, which also include tours. Norlands, a name from a Tennyson poem, was the 19th-century home of the politically potent Washburn family. Two Washburns became state governors of different states and four became U.S. congressmen. The farm is four miles east and north of downtown Livermore and two miles north of Rte. 108.

Weld Historical Society Museum

Three carefully preserved 19th-century buildings and a reconstructed Grange Hall in the village center are the domain of the Weld Historical Society Museum, Rte. 156, P.O. Box 31, Weld 04285, 207/585-2542 or 207/585-2586. Among the local memorabilia are old photos, antique tools and furniture, vintage clothing, even medical paraphernalia. The summer highlight is the museum's **Heritage Day Fair,** held the last Saturday in July. The museum is open July and Aug., Wed. and Sat. 2–4 PM, other times by appointment. Out back, by the way, is Weld's only public toilet. The museum is just east of the Rte. 142 junction. Donations are encouraged.

Mainely Critters Museum

Far from your typical museum—if "museum" is the correct term—Mainely Critters, Rte. 2, RR 1, Box 510, Dixfield 04224, 207/562-8231, is a quirky place, the brainchild of taxidermists Vance and Diane Child. The big blue building houses their collection of road-killed and other Maine creatures, all restored and displayed in lifelike settings. Among the specimens are raccoons, skunks, black bears, foxes, even a bull moose. Friends and motorists drift in regularly with future exhibits. Admission is free, but donations are welcome. A small gift shop features animal-oriented items. The museum is about seven miles east of downtown Dixfield. Open year-round, Mon.–Fri. 8 AM–5 PM, by appointment Sat.–Sun.

PARKS AND RECREATION

Fortunately for visitors as well as residents, the Farmington area is well endowed with parks and playgrounds. At the southern edge of Farmington, town-owned **Hippach Field,** Intervale Rd., Rte. 4/27, Farmington 04938, 207/778-3464, has playing fields, a playground, lighted tennis courts, and, in winter, a pond for ice-skating. There's even a skateboard park.

Just northeast of Hippach Field, at the head of Intervale Rd., is **Abbott Park,** a lovely oasis with interesting plantings, a pond, and little wooden bridges. It's a great spot for a picnic.

In Wilton, it's easy to spend an entire day at town-owned **Kineowatha Park,** 45 acres on the shore of Wilson Lake. Among the facilities are a beach, tennis courts, playing fields, playground, picnic tables, and even a lodge with a snack bar.

Mount Blue State Park

Mount Blue State Park, 299 Center Hill Rd., Weld 04285, 207/585-2261 (campground 585-2261), www.campwithme.com, covering 5,021 acres, is one of Maine's best-kept

secrets—crowded in summer, but mostly with Mainers. Yet it offers multilevel hiking, superb swimming, wooded campsites, mountain scenery, and daily interpretive natural-history programs in summer. There are movies on weekends, guided hikes, weekly guest speakers, even gold-panning expeditions—you'll never be bored. The park is split into two sections; swimming and camping are on Lake Webb's west side; the Center Hill section, including the trail to Mount Blue itself, is on the lake's east side. The main entrance, with a two-mile access road, is eight miles from Weld, on the lake's west side. Day-use admission is $3 adults, $1 children 5–11. Camping fees are extra (nonresidents pay $20 per site per night, residents pay $15). Reservations for the 136 wooded campsites are handled through the state-park reservation system; from out-of-state call 207/287-3824 at least two weeks ahead, and have your Visa or MasterCard handy. You can book reservations online as of February 1st at www.campwithme.com. Reservation fee is $2 per site per night; two-night minimum. No hookups. Canoe rentals are $3 an hour. Camping is available May 15–Sept. Winter activities include showshoeing, snowmobiling, and more than a dozen miles of groomed cross-country-ski trails. There is also an ice rink. Adults $1.50, children under 12 are free.

Swimming

Five miles northeast of downtown Farmington is the hamlet of **Allens Mills** (officially the town of **Industry**), where you can swim in aptly named **Clearwater Lake.** Follow Broadway (Rte. 43) from Farmington until you reach a T-junction at the lake, where there's a little boat landing and access for swimming.

Canoeing and Kayaking

If you just want to paddle around, with no major energy investment, a good choice is 800-acre **Clearwater Lake.** To get there from Farmington, follow Broadway (Rte. 43) until you reach the T-junction and boat landing at the lake.

Hiking

You're getting into western Maine's serious mountains here, so there are plenty of great hiking opportunities, running the gamut from a cakewalk to a workout.

In Weld, a deservedly popular hiking route goes up 3,187-foot **Mount Blue,** in the eastern section of Mount Blue State Park. From Rte. 142 in Weld village, follow signs and take Maxwell Rd., then Center Hill Rd. about 2.5 miles to the parking area for Center Hill itself. (There's no fee in this part of the park.) You can stop for a picnic (sweeping views even at this level, plus picnic tables and outhouses), follow the mile-long self-guided nature-trail loop (pick up a brochure here), then go on. (It's also a great spot for sunset-watching.) Continue up the unpaved road 3.5 miles to the parking lot for the Mount Blue trailhead. Allow about three hours for the steepish three-mile round-trip (easy, then moderately difficult). In midsummer, carry plenty of water. Pray for clear air on the summit; vistas of the Longfellows and beyond are awesome. Climb the stanchions of the old fire tower, now used for cellular-phone communications.

Other good hikes around Weld, on the west side of Lake Webb, are **Tumbledown Mountain** (3,068 feet via several route options; nesting peregrines can restrict access in early summer) and **Little Jackson Mountain** (3,434 feet). Tumbledown, moderately strenuous, attracts the been-there-done-that set. A much easier hike, but likely to be more crowded, is 2,386-foot **Bald Mountain,** with a scoured summit fine for picnics if it's not too blustery. Allow about two hours for the three-mile round-trip, including lunch break. To reach the trailhead from Weld, take Rte. 156 southeast about 5.5 miles. There's limited parking on the right; watch for the sign.

Seasonal Camping

Troll Valley, 283 Red Schoolhouse Rd., Farmington 04938, 207/778-3656. Troll Valley is open May 1–Oct. 31st, with 25 sites, bathrooms, and showers. They offer tenting and can accommodate RVs of up to 45 feet in length. Pull-through sites and pumping dump stations are also available. The maximum amperage is 50.

Golf

Nine-hole **Wilson Lake Country Club,** Weld Rd., Rte. 156, Wilton 04294, 207/645-2016, www.wilsonlakecc.com, established in 1931, is a sleeper of a course—not as well known as it should be. Tee times are a good idea. Facilities include a pro shop and snack bar. The scenic, wooded course, northwest of downtown Wilton, is open May–Oct. There's also a fabulous (but pricey) course at Sugarloaf/USA.

Fitness Center

A rainy-day godsend is the $4.5-million University of Maine at Farmington **Health and Fitness Center,** 152 Quebec St. (corner of Quebec and Lincoln Sts.), Farmington 04938, 207/778-7495, www.hfc.umf.maine.edu. It's open to the public for weight training, indoor jogging, tennis, and swimming in a six-lane heated pool. Call ahead to reserve a court time. In summer, it's open Mon.–Thurs. 5:30 AM–9 PM, Fri. 5:30 AM–7 PM, Sat. 8 AM–7 PM, and Sun. 10 AM–9 PM. Winter hours begin at the same time but the closing times are later. Cost is a bargain-basement $7 pp, valid all day.

Kids Stuff

Behind the W.G. Mallett School, 1 Quebec St., Farmington 04938, is a kids' paradise. **Castlemania,** centered on an intriguing wooden castle, owes its existence to a whole crew of dedicated volunteer fundraisers and builders. The Leathers-designed creative playground is three blocks east of Main St. The playground is off-limits during school hours.

Skiing

Most gonzo downhill skiers and snowboarders head right for the championship slopes at Sugarloaf/USA, but if you're still on the learning curve, or your budget is tight, the local alternative is family-oriented **Titcomb Mountain Ski Area,** Morrison Hill Rd., P.O. Box 138, West Farmington 04992, 207/778-9031, www.skiblackmtofme.org, run by the Farmington Ski Club. This all-volunteer operation has 17 trails, two T-bars, a handle tow, snow-making, ski lessons and rentals. An all-day adult lift pass is $19. The vertical drop is 340 feet. For $9, you can put on your cross-country skis or snow shoes and negotiate nine miles of groomed nordic trails (novice, intermediate, and advanced). Alpine lifts are open Mon.– Fri. 3–6 PM, with later hours on Wed. and Fri. nights, as well as Sat.–Sun. 9 AM–4 PM. There are extended hours over school vacation.

Also distinctly family-friendly, with great rates, **Black Mountain,** P.O. Box 239, 39 Glover Rd, Rumford 04276, 207/364-8977, offers alpine skiing, cross-country, snowboarding, snow tubing, lessons and more. This is a tobacco-free facility and proud of it. There are nine trails, including night skiing on six trails Thurs.–Sat. nights. Snowmaking covers most of the slopes; the vertical drop is 470 feet. Offerings include ski rentals, lessons, and a small snack bar. Off to the west of the lodge are six miles of groomed cross-country trails ($8 for a day pass).

ENTERTAINMENT

The multiplex at **Narrow Gauge Cinemas,** Front St., Farmington 04938, 207/778-4877, is open daily, all year, with periodic matinees Saturday and Sunday. Tickets are $5 adults.

Throughout the year, something is always happening at the **University of Maine at Farmington:** lectures, concerts, plays, you-name-it. Contact the college for schedule and details, 207/778-7000. At Meetinghouse Park, on Main St. in downtown Farmington, **band concerts** are held at 7:30 PM periodically throughout the summer; take a folding chair or a blanket. The Old Crow Band holds forth in a green-and-white octagonal bandstand. Check locally for the schedule.

FESTIVALS AND EVENTS

Besides the events listed here, the nearby Sugarloaf area is also busy with activities particularly during skiing season.

Farm tours, wagon or sleigh rides, a country dinner, and maple syrup tasting all figure in **Norlands Maple Days,** at the Norlands Living History Center, Livermore, on the third or fourth weekend in March.

In late June, on a Saturday, 10 AM–4 PM, the **Strawberry Festival** is an old-fashioned summer fair with guided tours, craft booths, hay-wagon rides, music, and superb strawberry shortcake at the Norlands Living History Center, Livermore.

July is the month to visit Farmington. While every town has some variation on the **Independence Day celebration,** Farmington puts on a whoop-de-do affair on that day. And the last Friday of the month, **Moonlight Madness** combines sidewalk sales, a street dance, a chicken barbecue, and an art show in downtown Farmington.

The second weekend in August, the three-day **Wilton Blueberry Festival** is (obviously) a blueberry-oriented celebration (always crowded), including a parade, road races, games, craft booths, a book sale, a museum open house, live entertainment, lobster-roll lunch, chicken barbecue, and a pig roast in downtown Wilton.

The third week of September is given over to the **Farmington Fair,** a week-long country fair (one of the last of the season) with agricultural exhibits, a parade, harness racing, and live entertainment at the Farmington Fairgrounds. The last weekend of September is Norlands Living History Center's **Autumn Celebration,** with woodsmen's events, harvest demonstrations, wagon rides, guided tours, a baked-bean supper, and a barn dance. A new wrinkle in recent years has been a Civil War reenactment during the weekend.

The first Saturday in December, Farmington honors a native son on **Chester Greenwood Day.** Festivities commemorating the inventor of earmuffs include a road race, an oddball earmuff parade, a polar-bear swim, and other activities. That same weekend, Livermore's Norlands Living History Center celebrates **Christmas at Norlands,** an old-fashioned celebration with sleigh rides, carol singing, guided tours, and a country luncheon.

Western Lakes & Mountains

SHOPPING

Art Galleries

Savvy art connoisseurs make pilgrimages to Farmington to check out one of Maine's best galleries, the **Tom Veilleux Gallery,** 30 Broadway, Farmington 04938, 207/778-0784. Tom Veilleux has been dealing in early-20th-century painters—most with a Maine connection—since 1979, selling several hundred paintings a year. Even if your wallet's a little thin, it's worth climbing to the bright second-floor gallery for a look at his high-quality inventory. Summer hours are Tues.–Sat. 11 AM–4 PM; other seasons are less predictable. The gallery is always open by appointment, so call ahead if you're on a mission.

New and Used Books

It's hard to resist the cheerful, welcoming ambience at **Devaney Doak and Garrett Booksellers,** 193 Broadway, Farmington 04938, 207/778-3454, not to mention the upholstered chairs, classical background music, and a children's corner piled high with books, toys, and games. Cookbooks are a specialty, along with literary journals, lots of Maine books, unusual cards, and even designer coffees. Owner Kenny Brechner does the ordering (and the website book reviews); his eclectic taste is evident. And how many independent bookshops have a website with hilarious parody reviews? Check out www.ddgbooks.com. The shop is open Mon.–Wed. 10 AM–5 PM, Thurs. 10 AM–5:30 PM, Fri. 10 AM–6:30 PM, Sat. 9 AM–5 PM, and Sun. noon–3 PM.

Around the corner, **Twice-Sold Tales,** 155 Main St., Farmington 04938, 207/778-4411, has a well-chosen and well-organized selection; Maine titles are a specialty, and prices are reasonable. Ask owner Jim Logan, an avid outdoorsman, about hiking options in Farmington and beyond. Open Open daily July, Aug., and Dec.; all other months open Tues.–Sat. 10–5 (call ahead in Jan.).

Gourmet Goodies

In downtown Farmington, Nina Gianquinto's **Up Front and Pleasant Gourmet,** 157 Front St., Farmington 04938, 207/778-5671, has all kinds of condiments, cheeses, homemade pasta, Borealis breads, exotic coffees, plus a huge wine selection. Be sure to try the locally made York Hill Farm goat cheese. No credit cards. Open all year, Mon.–Wed. 10 AM–5 PM, Thurs.–Fri. 10 AM–6 PM, and Sat. 10 AM–3 PM.

Farmers Market

Each Fri. 9 AM–2 PM, May–Oct., the **Sandy River Farmers Market** sets up its tables at the Better Living Center parking lot, 13 Front St. Along with a lively, can-do spirit, you'll find herbs, homemade bread, cheeses, and organic meats and produce.

ACCOMMODATIONS

Farmington is not overrun with extraordinary places to stay, but at least the prices are reasonable, and there are several lodging options in surrounding communities.

The **Farmington Motel,** 489 Farmington Falls Rd, Farmington 04938, 207/778-4680 or 800/654-1133 outside Maine, gets the nod for inexpensive, clean lodging in the area, but don't expect lots of amenities. All 37 rooms and two suites have phones, air-conditioning, and cable TV. No pets. Biggest plus is behind the motel: a nature trail leading down to the Sandy River, where you can launch a canoe or just sit on the shore. The motel, 1.5 miles southeast of downtown Farmington, is open all year. Call for rate information.

In Weld village, west of Farmington and northwest of Wilton, you'll find Fred and Cheryl England's **Lake Webb House Bed & Breakfast,** 19 Church St., Weld 04285, 207/585-2479, a cheerful sight with a wraparound porch and lovely gardens. Four second-floor rooms share a bath ($70–80 d in summer, lower off season; only three rooms are available in winter). Breakfast includes goodies from the family's **Morning Glory Bake Shop,** 207/585-2479, www.lakewebbhouse.com, a wholesale business open for retail Memorial Day to Labor Day, Mon.–Sat. 8 AM–5 PM and

Sun. 8 AM–noon. In part of the garage is a seasonal gift shop, with quilts, carvings, and other handmade items. The B&B is open all year. No pets, no smoking.

About a mile south of the center of Weld, on the east shore of Lake Webb, **Kawanhee Inn**, 12 Annâs Way, Rte. 142, Weld 04285, 207/585-2000. www.MaineInn.net. Since 2004, new owners have operated the inn. The owners have done a lot of "refreshing" to restore the inn to its rustic charm. Sunsets in this mountain-and-lake setting are spectacular; loons' cries add to the magic. A deluxe continental breakfast is included for all lodgers, as well as complimentary use of canoes, kayaks, and paddleboats. The 10 second-floor rooms in the large main lodge go for $85–140 per day (shared and private baths) with a two-night minimum stay on weekends. There is also a colony of cabins; eight are on the water, and one is on two acres of land, with 3 bedrooms and a full kitchen. Cabins are available by the week or the night, with weekly rates between $850–1,150. Eight have fieldstone fireplaces and screened porches facing the lake. The cabins range in size from 1–3 bedrooms. Call regarding pets. The sandy beach is great for kids, and superb hiking is close by. The lodge's lake-view dining room is open to the public. Reservations are suggested. Closed Mondays. The dining room earns high marks. Entrées start at $17. The menu offers wonderful appetizers, try a couple as your meal! There is also a bistro menu. The bar is rustic with a "live-edge" (the natural shape of the tree it was made from). With a day's notice, box lunches can be ordered, starting at $8. Non smoking in the lodge. Kawanhee Inn is open Memorial Day weekend through Columbus Day weekend. Devotees keep returning here, so book well ahead for midsummer (when the dining room is open). In mid-September, nights are coolish and it's pretty quiet, but the foliage is incredible.

Campgrounds
Besides the campground at Mount Blue State Park, on the other side of Lake Webb is **Dum-** mer's Beach Campground, Rte. 142, Weld 04285, 207/585-2200; winter: 401/433-1388. winter, is a large (200 sites) family-owned campground with a half-mile-long sandy beach. Request a waterfront site for best sunset-watching. July–Aug., the preferred minimum stay is a week, but last-minute cancellations usually create a few vacancies. There are three nightly rates per family; $13 for tenting, $22 for the section back from the beach, and $25 for beach front. They can accommodate tents and campers with hook-ups. Leashed pets are allowed. The campground is open Memorial Day weekend to Labor Day.

FOOD
Ice Cream
Across from Hippach Field, there's always a line at **Gifford's Ice Cream,** Intervale Rd., Rte. 4/27, Farmington 04938, 207/778-3617, a longtime take-out spot. Besides about four dozen terrific ice-cream flavors, they also have foot-long hot dogs. Open mid-Mar.–early Nov., 11 AM–10 PM in summer, to 9 PM in spring and fall.

Inexpensive to Moderate
Close to Gifford's is another local institution, the gen-u-ine classic **Farmington Diner,** 313 Main St., Farmington 04938, 207/778-4151. The huge portions, instantaneous service, and *really* good prices are an answer to a budgeteer's prayer. Without a thick haze of smoke, it's no longer the same—thank goodness. No credit cards. The diner is open all year, Mon.–Sat. 5 AM–8 PM (to 9 PM Fri.–Sat.) and Sun. 7 AM–8 PM.

The most creative menu in Farmington is at **The Homestead Bakery Restaurant,** 186 Broadway, Farmington 04938, 207/778-6162, where everything's first-rate and there's plenty of ethnic variety—Mediterranean, Mexican, Thai, plus vegetarian. Industrial-strength garlic infuses some of the choices. Open for breakfast and lunch Mon.–Fri. 7 AM–2 PM, and for brunch Sat.–Sun. 11 AM–2 PM. Open for dinner Mon.–Sat. 5–9 PM.

Western Lakes & Mountains

Brewpub

Tucked away on a side street not far from the Sandy River, **The Granary Brewpub,** 147 Pleasant St., Farmington 04938, 207/779-0710, www.thegranarybrewpub.com, packs them in, especially when the university is in session. Home of the Narrow Gauge Brewing Company (call 207/778-5363 for a free tour), with such specialty microbrews as Iron Rail Ale and Clearwater Cream Ale. The extensive menu of dinner entrées ranges $13.95–28.95. Sunday brunch is served 11–3. Lunch and kids' menus are available, as is inexpensive pub food. Most weekends, there's live music; Tuesday is open-mike night. Open all year, daily 11 AM–10 PM (sometimes later on weekends).

INFORMATION AND SERVICES

The office of the **Farmington-Wilton Chamber of Commerce,** 575 Wilton Rd. (Rtes. 2 and 4), Farmington 04938, 207/778-4215, fax 778-2438, www.farmingtonwiltonchamber.org, is in the historic **Red Schoolhouse** in West Farmington. The joint *Farmington-Wilton Four-Season Guide* is especially useful.

The 1903 **Cutler Memorial Library,** 117 Academy St., Farmington 04938, 207/778-4312, www.farmington.lib.me.us, is worth a look just for its intriguing glass floor and domed rotunda, but the staff is especially helpful, too. Genealogical research is a specialty here. The National Historic Register library is open all year, Tues.–Fri. 10 AM–6:30 PM, Sat. 10 AM–2 PM (July–Aug. 10–noon on Sat.).

The University of Maine at Farmington's **Mantor Library,** 207/778-7210, is located at the corner of South and High Sts. in Farmington. Hours during the academic year: Mon.–Thurs. 8 AM–11 PM; Fri. 8 AM–5 PM; Sat.

9 AM–5 PM, Sun. 1–11 PM. UMF's **bookstore,** where you can pick up typical logo-stamped gear, is at 111 South St., 207/778-7325. It's open 8 AM–4:30 PM Mon.–Fri.

Newspapers

The Franklin Journal, 207/778-2075, is published every Tuesday and Friday. The "On the Menu" section of the "What's Happening" column lists public suppers—always a source of hearty food, low prices, and local color. In summer, the paper produces a helpful tabloid supplement highlighting activities in Farmington and beyond. Under the same ownership is *The Livermore Falls Advertiser,* 207/897-4321, published each Thursday. The preferred daily paper here is the *Lewiston Sun-Journal,* which maintains a Farmington office.

Emergencies

In Farmington, dial 911 for police, fire, and ambulance service. To reach the **Franklin County Sheriff,** dial 800/492-0120. **Franklin Memorial Hospital,** 111 Franklin Health Commons, Farmington 04938, emergency-room 207/779-2250, with a particularly fine reputation, has round-the-clock emergency-room care. Behind the hospital is a fitness trail with exercise stations.

Laundry

Across the street from the F.L. Butler Restaurant, the **Depot Laundry,** 185 Front St., Farmington 04938, 207/778-0803, is open all year, daily 6 AM–7 PM.

Public Restrooms

Across from Meetinghouse Park, downtown, there's a public restroom in the basement of the **Franklin County Courthouse,** N. Main St., Farmington, accessible on weekdays.

Sugarloaf Area

The thread tying together the Sugarloaf area is the lovely Carrabassett River, which winds its way through the smashingly scenic Carrabassett Valley from the area more or less around Sugarloaf/USA to North Anson, where it meets the mighty Kennebec. On both sides of the valley, the Longfellow and Bigelow Ranges boast six out of 10 of Maine's 4,000-footers—a hiker's paradise.

Flanking the west side of the valley is the huge Sugarloaf/USA resort—only a germ of an idea half a century ago. In 1951, Kingfield businessman Amos Winter and some of his pals, known locally as the "Bigelow Boys," cut the first ski trail from the snowfields on Sugarloaf Mountain, dubbing it "Winter's Way." A downhill run required skiing three miles to the base of the trail, then strapping on animal skins for the uphill trek. Three runs on wooden skis would be about the max in those days. By 1954, the prophetically named Winter and some foresighted investors had established the Sugarloaf Mountain Ski Club. . . and the rest, as they say, is history. In 1996, the giant American Skiing Company, owner of Sunday River Ski Resort and other properties, purchased Sugarloaf/USA, so it now operates under the ASC umbrella.

Sugarloaf/USA is the mega-taxpayer in the relatively new town of Carrabassett Valley (year-round population 367). It bills itself as a year-round resort, which is true, but winter is definitely the peak season, when the headcount is highest and so are the prices. Everything's open and humming from November well into May; in 1997, spring skiing even extended into June. More than 350,000 skiers hit the slopes here each year.

Before Amos Winter brought fame and fortune to his hometown and the valley, Kingfield was best known as a timber center and the birthplace of the Stanley twins (designers of the Stanley Steamer). Today it's an appealing slice-of-life rural town (pop. 1,245), with handsome old homes and off-mountain beds and restaurants.

Farther up the valley, old-timers reminisce over the towns of Flagstaff and Dead River—already historic two centuries before they were consigned to the history books in the 1950s. That's when the Long Falls Dam, built on the Dead River, backed up the water behind it, inundated the towns, and created 20,000-acre Flagstaff Lake. The hydroelectric dam now controls the water flow for spring white-water rafting on the Dead River. In Stratton village, the Dead River Historical Society's museum contains fascinating memorabilia from the two submerged villages.

Flagstaff owes its name to Col. Benedict Arnold, whose troops en route to Quebec in 1775 flew their flag at the site of today's Cathedral Pines Campground. After struggling up the Kennebec River to the spot known as The Carrying Place, the disheartened soldiers turned northwest along the Dead River's North Branch at Flagstaff and then on through the Chain of Ponds to Canada.

Route 27, from Kingfield to the Canadian border at Coburn Gore, is an officially designated Scenic Highway, a 54-mile stretch that's most spectacular in mid- to late September. But there's no pot of gold at the end—not much to Coburn Gore except a customs outpost, a convenience store (with fuel), and a few unimpressive dwellings.

SIGHTS

Stanley Museum

Children of all ages love antique cars, so this museum is a must. The small but captivating Stanley Museum, 40 School St., Kingfield 04947, 207/265-2729, www.stanleymusuem.org, has two meticulously restored Stanley Steamers, designed at the turn of the 20th century by the Kingfield-born Stanley twins, Francis Edgar and Freelan Oscar. These versatile overachievers also gained fame with the invention of the photographic dry plate, eventually selling out to George Eastman. Freelan

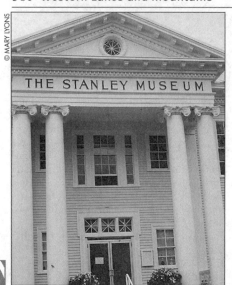

© MARY LYONS

Western Lakes & Mountains

Stanley, the first to climb Mount Washington by car, later became a noted violinmaker. Also in the museum, based in the yellow, Georgian-style Stanley School, are hundreds of superb photographs (and glass-plate negatives) by the twins' clever sister, Chansonetta Stanley Emmons, and work by Chansonetta's artist-daughter, Dorothy. The museum gift shop contains auto-related books, pamphlets, and other specialty items. The museum is open June–Oct. Tues.–Sun. 1–4 PM; Nov.–May Tues.–Fri. 1–4 PM by appointment. Admission is $4 adults, $3 seniors, and $2 children under 12 years of age.

Western Maine Children's Museum
Not open often enough, but definitely worth a look-see, The Western Maine Children's Museum, Rte. 27, RR1, Box 2153, Carrabassett Valley 04947, 207/235-2211, practices a please-touch philosophy. Kids can try on vintage clothing, play puppeteer, make sand pictures, enter a ski gondola and a wigwam, climb into a cave with real crystals, and otherwise amuse themselves. Workshops are held some weekends. Admission is $2.50 for children; adults and children under one year are free.

The museum is open Sept.–Apr., Sat.–Mon. 1–5 PM; May–Aug. open Mon. 1–5 PM. The museum shares a building with the Carrabassett Public Library.

Nowetah's American Indian Museum
A bold, in-your-face sign announces the driveway to Nowetah's American Indian Museum, Rte. 27, Box 40, New Portland 04954, 207/628-4981, an astonishing repository of hundreds of Maine Indian baskets and bark objects—plus porcupine-quill embroidery, trade beads, musical instruments, soapstone carvings, and other Native American esoterica. Susquehanna-Cherokee owner Nowetah Timmerman loves explaining unique details about the artifacts she's displayed here since 1969. Admission is free. In the museum's gift shop are many craft items made by Nowetah and her seven children (one daughter is now a lawyer), and she runs a thriving mail-order business. Since she lives next door, the museum is open daily 10 AM–5 PM, all year. It's 16 miles north of Farmington and just south of New Portland village; you can't miss the sign.

Bridge to the Past
Now here's a most unusual landmark—about seven miles south of Kingfield and not far from Nowetah's museum. Twenty-five-foot-tall shingled towers announce the entrance to the **Wire Bridge** suspended over the Carrabassett River in New Portland. Built in 1841–42 at a cost of $2,000, with steel supports imported from England, the bridge is on the National Historic Register. Locals often refer to it as the "Rustproof Wire Bridge," for its stainless-steel construction, or "Floodproof Wire Bridge," for its longtime survival despite nasty spring floods. To find the bridge from Rte. 146 in New Portland, turn north onto Wire Bridge Rd. and follow signs for less than a mile.

PARKS
Picnic and Rest Areas
Several riverside and viewpoint rest areas on or near Rte. 27 make picnicking almost

mandatory in the Carrabassett Valley—especially in September, when the leaf colors are fabulous. The mountains, the foliage parade, the rock-clogged river—all really splendid. On Rte. 27, roughly halfway between Kingfield and the Sugarloaf access road, a lovely picnic area is sandwiched between the highway and the Carrabassett River, just north of Hammond Field Brook.

About 12 miles north of the Sugarloaf access road, turn left (west) onto Eustis Ridge Rd. and go two miles to the **Eustis Ridge Picnic Area,** a tiny park with an expansive view of the Bigelow Range.

Finally, on Rte. 27, about 23 miles north of Sugarloaf, there's another scenic picnic area, this one alongside the Dead River (east side of the highway).

Riverside Park

Carrabassett Valley's well-maintained, town-owned Riverside Park has tennis courts, a swimming pool, playing fields, playground, picnic tables, restrooms, and access to a Carrabassett River swimming hole. It's just off Rte. 27, near Valley Crossing. The park is also a great picnic-and-swim destination after a bike ride along the old narrow-gauge railbed.

SUMMER RECREATION

The Carrabassett Valley is drop-dead gorgeous in summer, and people "from away" are finally beginning to recognize it. Traffic has increased dramatically in recent years, largely because of active four-season promotion of the area by Sugarloaf/USA and its golf club. The only hitch is that "four seasons" is a bit of a misnomer; spring (aka June, more or less) is all too short here, usually muddy and thick with blackflies. Concentrate on the other three seasons, all outstanding. Since 2003 **The Kingfield POPS** concert has become one of Maine's premier annual summer evening cultural events of the summer. The event takes place around July 4th. Presented by the Bangor Symphony Orchestra, this is the place to enjoy incredible panoramic scenic views, a family-friendly atmosphere, and

an outstanding orchestral performance. As a fun, family-style festival the Kingfield POPS features the Western Mountain Trash Can Band and other area talent, the Bangor Symphony Orchestra instrument petting zoo, the No Frowns Clowns, other family activities and plenty of delicious food. Bring blankets and picnic if you choose. For more information or to order tickets, contact the Bangor Symphony Orchestra at 207/942-5555 or 800/639-3221 or visit www.bangorsymphony.com.

Summer activities for Sugarloaf/USA are coordinated primarily at the **Sugarloafer Shop in Village West. 207/237-6718,** 207/237-6830, www.sugarloaf.com/outdoor. Here you can plan hiking and mountain-biking excursions, rent a canoe or bike, and sign up for fly-fishing lessons.

Golf

Designed by Robert Trent Jones, Jr., and regularly ranked in national golf magazines as Maine's top course, the 18-hole, par-72 **Sugarloaf Golf Club & Golf School,** Sugarloaf/USA, 800-THE-LOAF, www.sugarloaf.com meanders through woods and alongside the Carrabassett River, in the shadow of the Longfellow Range. It's actually a town-owned course, but managed by Sugarloaf. An active bug-suppression program makes golfing pleasant even in June, when blackflies normally could dampen the fun. You get what you pay for; greens fees are steep. Tee times are essential—a week or two in advance for weekends. Sugarloaf's golf school offers multiday programs all summer, with special weeks designed for Women's Golf School and Junior Golf Camp. Club rentals and private lessons are available; carts are mandatory. A driving range, a pro shop, and a café round out the facilities. The course is open mid-May–late Oct., but an extended snow season can affect the season opening.

Mountain Biking

Sugarloaf/USA, with its incredible 53-mile mountain-bike trail network, has cornered the market in this sport, too. A free trail map is available at the Sugarloafer Shop. There is no charge to use the trails.

A fun (and scenic) family or beginners' excursion is the **Narrow Gauge Trail,** beginning on the east side of Rte. 27 at the foot of the Sugarloaf access road and continuing seven miles, gradually downhill, to Riverside Park in Carrabassett Valley. The trail follows the abandoned narrow-gauge railway bed, along the river. Pack a picnic and wear a bathing suit under your biking duds; you'll be passing swimming holes along the way. **The Sugarloafer Shop,** 207/237-6718, rents mountain bikes, does repairs, and provides free trail maps and advice for trails on and off the mountain. The staff is especially helpful. Informal group rides originate from here most Wednesday nights, contact the shop to inquire. Guided rides are also available with advance reservations.

Swimming

Along the Carrabassett River between Kingfield and the Sugarloaf access road are half a dozen swimming holes used by generations of local residents. Several spots have natural water slides and room for shallow dives. They're not all easy to find, and parking is limited, but a refreshing river dip on a hot day is hard to beat. Check with the Sugarloaf Area Chamber of Commerce for exact locations.

On mountain-rimmed Flagstaff Lake in Eustis, about 11 miles north of Sugarloaf, the town-owned beach next to the Cathedral Pines Campground has a playground and changing rooms. There are no lifeguards, but there's also no admission fee. (Do not use the campground's beach unless you're staying there.)

Hiking

An easy family hike, combining a picnic and swim, goes to the twin cascades of **Poplar Stream Falls.** On Rte. 27 in Carrabassett Valley, leave your car at Valley Crossing and walk northeast 1.5 miles to the falls. Pack a picnic and let the kids have a swim.

Just east of Stratton (eight miles northwest of Sugarloaf) is the dedicated hiker's dream: 35,000-acre **Bigelow Preserve**—all public land, thanks to conservationists who organized a statewide referendum and yanked it from developers' hands in 1976. Within the preserve are the multiple peaks of the **Bigelow Range**—the Horns Peaks (3,810 and 3,831 feet), West Peak (4,150 feet), Avery Peak (4,088 feet), and Little Bigelow (3,040 feet), as well as 3,213-foot Cranberry Peak. In the fall, when the hardwoods all change colors, the vistas are incomparable. In winter, snowmobilers crisscross the preserve, and cross-country skiers often take advantage of their trails, especially along the East Flagstaff Road, where you can stop for hot chocolate at volunteer-staffed Bigelow Lodge. The trailhead for Cranberry Peak (6.6 miles round-trip; moderate to strenuous) is next to Rte. 27 at the southern end of Stratton village.

About five miles southeast of Stratton, the **Appalachian Trail** crosses Rte. 27 and continues north and then east across the Bigelow peaks, the spine of the Bigelow Range. You can access the AT here, or drive back northwest half a mile on Rte. 27 and go 0.9 mile on the rugged, unpaved Stratton Brook Rd. to another AT trailhead. In any case, if you do the whole AT traverse, 16.5 miles from Rte. 27 to East Flagstaff Rd., you'll probably want to arrange a shuttle at East Flagstaff Rd. (via the Long Falls Dam Rd. from North New Portland), or opt for the Round Barn camping area on Flagstaff Lake, to save a re-traverse. The white-blazed AT route is strenuous; four free campsites with lean-tos are spotted along the way. (The most-used campsite is Horns Pond; space can be tight there.)

Depending on your enthusiasm, your stamina level, and your time frame (and maybe the weather), there are lots of options for short hikes along the AT or on a number of side trails. Preserve maps usually are available at the Sugarloaf Area Chamber of Commerce, but for planning ahead, request a copy of the Bigelow Preserve map/brochure from the **Maine Bureau of Parks and Lands,** 22 State House Station, Augusta 04333, 207/287-3821, or the regional office of the Bureau of Public Lands, 207/778-8231. Also helpful is the *Appalachian Trail Guide to Maine.*

MOOSE-WATCHING

Early July–early Sept., Sugarloaf/USA operates a weekly **Moose Cruise,** 207/237-2000, departing from the Grand Summit Hotel around 8:30 PM Wed. and Sat. (time depends on when dusk arrives). Cost is $20 adults, $10 kids 12 and under. After a 10-minute moose video and a free glass of champagne or beer, the "Moose Express" van heads off to make the rounds of the well-known moose haunts. Invest in bug repellent and don't forget binoculars and a camera. Also, if you arrive close to dusk at the Sugarloaf Check-In Center, hang around the bog near the center and you may spot a moose.

For moose-watching on your own, the best bet is to head up Rte. 27 to Rte. 16 and go west. Early or late in the day, perhaps en route to dinner in Rangeley, you're almost guaranteed to see a moose in the boggy areas or near the sand and salt piles stored for winter use. Just remember to drive slowly and watchfully. No one wins when you hit a moose.

WINTER RECREATION

The big story in this area, of course, is **Sugarloaf/USA,** 207/237-2000 or 800/843-5623, www.sugarloaf.com, a major New England ski resort centered on 4,237-foot Sugarloaf, Maine's highest skiing mountain. Even though the resort attracts national and international ski and snowboard champions, Sugarloaf has always been especially family-friendly, with day care, reduced kids' rates, and all kinds of children's ski and entertainment programs.

The heart (and soul) of the operation is **Sugarloaf Village,** halfway up the access road (Sugarloaf Rd.) from Rte. 27. Here you'll find administration buildings, the Grand Summit Resort Hotel, the Sugarloaf Inn, the Base Lodge, a tiny chapel, and a whole commercial complex with more than three dozen restaurants and shops—a mini-community. Spreading out from here are side roads leading to clusters of condos.

First stop for overnight condo visitors is the

Check-In Center, where you'll register and pick up your key. If you've decided to wing it and show up without a reservation, this is where you inquire about vacancies. Condo prices and amenities vary widely.

Downhill Skiing and Snowboarding

Sugarloaf covers 7,000 acres, of which 1,400 are skiable, with 94 percent snowmaking capability. The 133 trails and glades in the 54-mile network are served by 15 lifts, ranging from a T-bar to detachable high-speed quads. Vertical rise is 2,820 feet and the longest run is 3.5 miles. For snowboarders, the resort has recently constructed a state-of-the-art Superpipe.

If you're here just for the day, your first stop on the mountain will be the **Base Lodge,** the locale for lift tickets, trail maps, ski rentals, and ski-school signups. Snowboard rentals are handled in the Snowboard Rental Shop, in the next building. Skiing hours are weekdays 8:30 AM–3:50 PM and weekends 8 AM–3:50 PM. Check the website to confirm lift hours of operation (www.sugarloaf.com). Be prepared for *big* crowds on weekends and holidays, but crowd control is fairly efficient, and lift lines are reasonably tolerable after the initial rush.

Adult full-day **lift tickets** for the 2004–2005 season were $58 for adults, $53 for teens, and $39 for kids 6–12; children five and under ski free. Save 10 percent per ticket by purchasing tickets online. Most lodging packages include lift tickets; multiday tickets are less expensive, as are "mid-mountain" tickets, which are restricted to the lower slopes.

Nordic Skiing, Snowshoeing, and Ice-Skating

On Rte. 27, about a mile south of the Sugarloaf access road, is the entrance to the **Sugarloaf Outdoor Center,** 207/237-6830, geared in winter toward cross-country skiing, snowshoeing, and ice-skating. Some sections of the 63-mile nordic trail network are on Maine Public Reserve Land and some are on Penobscot Indian Nation land. All the trails have tongue-twisting Indian names such as Bunawabskeg, Gwipdez, and Jezhawuk. All-day passes are

$15 adults, $10 seniors and children 6–12. The Outdoor Center is on the shuttle route, so you can leave your car on the mountain. Or ski to the center: an easy cross-country trail links the Snowbrook condos to the Outdoor Center; a moderately difficult trail begins higher up near the Base Lodge and hooks up with the Snowbrook route.

Also at the Outdoor Center is an Olympic-size outdoor ice-skating rink, lighted on weekend nights and holiday weeks. The huge, modern, glass-walled lodge looking out on Sugarloaf Mountain has ski, snowshoe, and skate rentals, plus the **Klister Kitchen,** a casual café serving moderately priced homemade soups, sandwiches, and baked goodies.

Skating fee is $5 adults, $4 children 6–12. Ice-skating hours are 9 AM–4 PM weekdays and 9 AM–9 PM weekends.

At the lodge, you can sign up for a 90-minute **group or private cross-country clinic,** but it's a good idea to call ahead and check on times. A learn-to-ski package, including ski rental, a group lesson, and a trail pass, is under $40.

The Outdoor Center also rents headlamps for their occasional **guided moonlight ski tours** through the woods, a really special experience. Although it's usually a Saturday night, the schedule is unpredictable, so you'll need to contact the Outdoor Center or Guest Services for days and times. Cost is $15 a person.

Mushing

Providing an exciting taste of Jack London-style adventure, 8–12 enthusiastic Samoyeds—bound along a wooded route in the shadow of Sugarloaf Mountain. Musher Troy Haskell, owner of **Fallen Snow Dogsledding Company,** Rte. 27, Carrabassett Valley, mailing address 888 Bog Rd., New Portland 04961, 207/491-2655, www.fallensnowdogsleddingco.com, stands on the sled in back, while riders sit bundled up in front of him. (Wear glasses or goggles—the dogs kick up the snow.) Winter trips operate weather (and snow) permitting; the season begins around early December and ends in early April, and the schedule varies be-

tween weekend and midweek. The cost is $35 per person. The ride is 2–3 miles long. Every ride includes a stop for a snack and hot chocolate at the halfway point and a warm blanket for the ride. Children are welcome! All children under 12 years of age must be accompanied by an adult. For reservations call Kate or Troy, or visit the website.

ENTERTAINMENT

There's no night skiing at Sugarloaf, but no problem staying busy. Every night in winter, there's live music somewhere, so you can hopscotch from The Bag to Geppetto's to Theo's and back again. The musical grand finale for the season is Reggae Ski Week in April.

If you're staying at a Sugarloaf condo and want to distract the kids with TV, **K-Two Video Network,** 207/237-4865, has video rentals. Sugarloaf organizes evening **children's entertainment** Mon.–Sat. Dec.–early Apr. Separate programs—typically films, skating, or games—are geared to ages 5–12 and 13–18.

The nearest **cinema** is in Farmington, 38 miles south of Sugarloaf/USA—too far after a day of skiing.

FESTIVALS AND EVENTS

Sugarloaf/USA has a huge schedule of events throughout the ski season and also a sprinkling of summer activities. A couple of recurring highlights are listed below, but the resort also hosts many one-of-a-kind events throughout the season, so it's best to check with the resort when you know the timing of your visit.

The last full week in January is **White White World Week,** Sugarloaf's winter carnival, with discount lift tickets, reduced lodging rates, ski races, fireworks, a torchlight parade, and other special events.

Sugarloaf hosts the **Maine Special Olympics Winter Games,** the annual skiing, showshoeing, and skating event for Maine's Special Olympians, the first weekend of February. Volunteers are welcome to lend a hand.

Sugarloaf meets the Caribbean during **Reggae Ski Week,** with West Indian cuisine, spring skiing, reggae bands day and night, and lots of boisterous fun the second week of April. Bring earplugs.

ACCOMMODATIONS

When you've had a long day of skiing or snowboarding, a bed close to the slopes can be mighty tempting—plus you can be upward bound quickly in the morning. But such convenience doesn't come cheaply, so your budget may dictate where you decide to stay. Basically, the choices are on the mountain at Sugarloaf/USA, in Carrabassett Valley near the Sugarloaf access road, or farther afield in Kingfield, Eustis, and beyond.

Once or twice during the winter season, when international ski or snowboard races bring in big-name champions, beds are scarce to nonexistent. Beds are also very hard to come by during Christmas week, February Presidents' Day week, and Sugarloaf's Reggae Ski Week in April.

Many of the lodgings in the region around Sugarloaf provide discount passes for nordic skiing out of the Sugarloaf Outdoor Center. It's a nice little perk, so if you're planning any cross-country skiing, be sure to ask when you're inquiring about a room.

Sugarloaf/USA

Accommodations are available all year at the resort; to book lodgings at Sugarloaf/USA, call 800/843-5623.

The clusters of on-mountain **condo "villages"** each have different features (studios to multiple bedrooms), different characters, and different prices. Midwinter rates range $120–365 a night per condo unit in midweek, $160–450 a night per condo unit on weekend nights. Lift tickets, ski clinics, and taxes are included. Lots of special packages, even including transportation, are available. Summer rates are markedly lower, and if you're eminently flexible, you can usually even take a chance and show up at the resort without a reservation.

The **Sugarloaf Inn,** conveniently located in front of the Sawduster double chairlift, has 42 attractive rooms with rates in the same ranges as the condos. The high-end Shipyard Restaurant (best on the mountain) and the casual Shipyard Brewhaus are also here.

All reservations booked by Sugarloaf include use of the **Sugarloaf Sports and Fitness Club,** 207/237-6946, in the Sugartree condo complex on Mountainside Rd. The club has a pool, indoor and outdoor hot tubs, a fitness room, racquetball courts, evening aerobics classes, three or four massage therapists, restrooms, locker rooms, a climbing wall, and a snack bar with great pizza and the cheapest bottled beer on the mountain. You can even buy a bathing suit or get a haircut. In the winter, the club opens at 8 AM and closes around 10 PM; summer hours are 11 AM–7 PM. Day visitors can use club facilities for a fee.

Right in the center of Sugarloaf Village is the imposing **Grand Summit Resort Hotel,** 207/237-2222 or 800/527-9879, fax 207/237-2874, with 119 rooms and suites, and two penthouses. Amenities include microwave, refrigerator, and VCR. Guests have use of a small health club. No pets, no smoking. Late Jan.–early Apr., rates can go as high as $800 double occupancy. Early and late in the winter season, rates are considerably less. The suites and penthouses, of course, are the high end. Open all year.

Kingfield and Eustis

The renovated **Herbert Grand Hotel,** 246 Main St., Rte. 27, P.O. Box 67, Kingfield 04947, 207/265-2000 or 800/843-4372, www.herbertgrandhotel.com, is a three-story grand hotel completed in 1918, where you can meet kindred spirits in the lobby. The property changed hands in 2001. Owner Marcie Herrick has re-done the 26 guest rooms, lobby and dining room, as well as the landscaping. All rooms have private baths, some with Jacuzzis. Winter rates range $90–186, including continental breakfast. There is a two-night minimum on weekends during the ski season. Spring, summer, and fall rates range $73–148, a true bargain, including continental breakfast. Multi-night stay specials are offered year round. Pets are allowed. The hotel's dining room—**Herbert Restaurant**—serves a continental breakfast to guests only. It's open to the public for dinner several nights a week. Call for reservations. The menu is imaginative. Dress is informal. Herbert Grand Hotel is 18 miles south of Sugarloaf/USA.

Bed-and-Breakfasts: Geared to skiers, hikers, and bikers, the **River Port Inn Bed & Breakfast,** 322 Main St., Rte. 27, Kingfield 04947, 207/265-2552, is a comfortable 1840s farmhouse where you can bring home a take-out meal and spread it out in a huge dining room. There's cross-country skiing right from the yard, and a deepwater swimming hole adjoins the property. Snowmobiling, biking, river walks, and hiking are all within a five-mile radius. Five bedrooms upstairs share one bath; three downstairs rooms share a bath. Rates start at $89. Generous continental breakfast is included; multi-night special rates are available. No smoking, no credit cards, no pets. Open all year.

Next door to One Stanley Avenue and under the same ownership, **Three Stanley Avenue,** 3 Stanley Ave., P.O. Box 169, Kingfield 04947, 207/265-5541, www.stanleyavenue.com, has been a B&B since the early 1980s. The antiques-filled yellow Victorian has three first-floor rooms (private baths) and three second-floor rooms sharing two baths. It's all very welcoming, with comfortable wicker chairs on the front porch and a traditional gazebo (ex-bandstand) in the back yard. Rooms are $65–70 double, with private bath in winter (Dec.–Mar.; two-night minimum), $60–65 double, with shared bath. Summer rates are lower. Open all year.

Built in 1892 by Stratton businessman Oramendal Blanchard, and now on the National Historic Register, **The Widow's Walk,** 171 Main St., Rte. 27, P.O. Box 150, Stratton 04982, 207/246-6901 or 800/943-6995, www.widowswalkbnb.com, has been a standout on the Appalachian Trail grapevine since avid hikers and skiers Mary and Jerry Hopson opened it in 1978. The camaraderie here is contagious, inevitably focusing on the outdoors. The B&B, known for years as "The Castle" for its distinctive turret, has four no-frills rooms (sharing two baths) in one section and two basic rooms (shared bath) in another. All are on the second floor and are $50 double in winter; two-day minimum. Summer and fall B&B rates are a bargain at $30 per double. No smoking, no pets (dog and cats in residence). Open all year; however, it may be closed at times during the summer. Call ahead. The B&B is about eight miles northwest of the Sugarloaf access road.

Sporting Camp: A wonderful, old-time traditional sporting camp, **Tim Pond Camps,** Box 22, Eustis 04936, 207/243-2947, in winter P.O. Box 89, Jay 04239, 207/897-4056, www.timpondcamps.com, has been operating since 1877, when guests took so long to get here that they stayed the whole summer. Harvey and Betty Calden have owned this idyllic lakeside retreat since 1980. Eleven rustic log cabins (all with full baths and maid service) are nestled in the woods on either side of a modern-rustic lodge (the original lodge burned), where everyone gathers three times a day for great comfort food; the dinner bell rings promptly at 5:30 PM (BYOL). Daily rates are $135 pp, AP, including use of a classic Rangeley boat and late-day moose-watching runs; half price for children under 12. Be forewarned, though, that it's worth your life to get a reservation here—about 90 percent of the guests are repeats, and most stay at least a week. Fly-fishing for brook trout is the prime pursuit, but it's just a fine place to relax and listen to the loons. Here's how one avid fisherman describes the schedule: "Fish, eat breakfast, fish, eat lunch, fish, eat supper, fish, sleep." July is the best month for families. Cabins have bathrooms, electricity (until 10 PM), daily maid service, and fascinating guest journals. Tim Pond Camps is at the northern end of mile-long Tim Pond, on a dirt road about 10 miles west of Rte. 27 in Eustis. It's open mid-May–mid Oct., then again in Nov.

Campgrounds: Located right on the

45th parallel, 40-acre **Deer Farm Campground,** 495 Tufts Pond Rd., Kingfield 04947, 207/265-2241 or 207/265-4599, www.deerfarmcamps.com. Has 47 well-maintained sites. Wooded tent sites: $16.50/night. Cabin rentals: $225/week. Sites with water and electric: $18/night; $108/week. Facilities include laundry, a small store, and a playground. Tufts Pond is close enough for swimming, and lots of easy hiking trails fan out from the campground. Canoe rentals are $3/hour. Pets are allowed. No credit cards. Take Rte. 27 north of Kingfield about a mile; turn left onto Tufts Pond Rd. and continue another two miles northwest to the campground. Open mid-May–mid-Oct.

With 115 wooded sites (most with hookups) on 300 acres, **Cathedral Pines Campground,** Rte. 27 North, P.O. Box 146, Eustis 04936, 207/246-3491, www.eustismaine.com, has one of Maine's most scenic locations—amid gigantic red pines and surrounded by mountains on the shore of Flagstaff Lake. Look for the marker that designates this site as one of Benedict Arnold's stops during his march to Quebec city in 1775. Facilities include a recreation hall, bathhouse, laundry, swimming beach, basketball, playground, canoe rentals, and paddleboat rentals. Pets are allowed. The campground is 26 miles south of the Quebec border. Open mid-May–Sept.

FOOD

You can bounce around to different Sugarloaf-area restaurants in the winter season and even catch a twofer night here and there. Considering the cost of lift tickets, ski rentals, lodging, and just getting here, the discount dinners are a real asset.

Sugarloaf/USA

You certainly won't starve if you stick with the food at one of the dozen or so eateries at Sugarloaf/USA, and the range of choices means you won't bust your budget, but do yourself a favor and explore the dining options in Carrabassett Valley, Stratton, Eustis, and Kingfield.

Over holidays and winter weekends, though, be sure to make advance dinner reservations if you're heading off mountain.

Bullwinkle's Grill, 800/843-5623, is a casual, popular lunch place at the top of the Bucksaw; it is a rustically elegant restaurant. They have expanded both their physical space as well as their menu. Lunch is served every day. Dinner is served on Saturday nights 6 PM to 8:30 PM. You are brought to and from Bullwinkle's in a Snocat. Dinner lasts three hours. Call for reservations.

At the geographic extreme, close to the bottom of Sugarloaf's access road, a bright, 200-seat brewpub named **Theo's,** Sugarloaf Rd., 207/237-2211, shares quarters with the glass-walled **Sugarloaf Brewing Company.** Try the pizza! Up to eight of their brews are available at any given time; best seller is Carrabassett Pale Ale. The seasonal Amos Winter Ale is super. Theo, by the way, is for Theodore Johnsen, a Portland boat-builder (and ski-maker) who wrote *The Winter Sport of Skeeing* in 1905. Brewery tours daily 2–4 PM, subject to staff availability. No tours mid-Apr.–mid-May or mid-Oct.–mid-Nov., when lunch is not available in the restaurant.

For ample sandwiches, homemade soups, salads, and other deli fare, **D'Ellies,** Village West, 207/237-2490, is one of Sugarloaf Village's most popular eateries. It's open daily, all year, for breakfast and lunch. To avoid the swarming noontime rush, call in your sandwich order in the morning, before heading for the lift line, and place your lunch order. Name a time and it'll be ready.

In summer, the café at the Sugarloaf Golf Club is a bit pricey, but the sandwiches are hefty and you can't knock the convenience after a round of golf. **Strokes Cafe,** 207/237-6035, is open daily 8 AM–8 PM during the golf season (usually mid-May–late Oct.).

Inexpensive to Moderate

Drive down the mountain from Sugarloaf/USA and you'll find restaurants in Carrabassett Valley, in Stratton and Eustis to the north, and in Kingfield, to the south.

Reservations are a good idea at **Hug's,** Rte. 27, Carrabassett Valley 04947, 207 /237-2392, an "in" Italian restaurant camouflaged by a nondescript gray exterior. To enjoy one of the area's best moderately priced menus, try the artichoke-heart appetizer with eggplant, spinach, and feta, or shiitake mushroom ravioli with walnut pesto alfredo. Entrées run $11–20; kids' portions are available. Beer and wine only. Hug's, a mile south of the Sugarloaf Rd., is open for dinner Tues.–Sun. 5– 9 PM, Nov.–Apr.

Six miles south of the Sugarloaf access road is **Tufulio's,** Rte. 27, Carrabassett Valley 04947, 207/235-2010, producers of the valley's best pizza. The shrimp-and-artichoke pesto pizza is tops. Also on the menu are seafood, chicken, and plenty of pasta dishes. In summer, you can eat on the deck. The wine list is ambitious, and there's plenty of beer on tap. Located at Valley Crossing, Tufulio's is open daily 4 PM–9:30 PM.

A mile north of Kingfield, **Nostalgia Tavern,** Rte. 27, Kingfield 04947, 207/265-2559, has a loyal local clientele and not one but *two* twofer nights (Tues. and Thurs.). The simple menu—heavy on sandwiches, burgers, and dogs—shows a sense of humor, and peanut-butter sandwiches come in five flavors (under $3). Open all year, Tues.–Sun. 11 AM–9 PM.

Popular with the Kingfield crowd, **Longfellow's Restaurant,** 247 Main St., Rte. 27, Kingfield 04947, 207/265-4394, is a rustic, homey eatery across from the Herbert Hotel in the center of Kingfield. The daily specials are a good bet; offers chicken, seafood, beef entrées, and standard pasta dishes. Kid-size portions are available; Tuesday is twofer night. The coffee list is huge. Open daily, all year, 11 AM–9 PM.

Everyone eventually shows up at the **Kingfield Woodsman** (usually just referred to as the "Woodsman"), Rte. 27, Kingfield 04947, 207/265-2561, best choice in the area for local color, especially at breakfast, which starts early. The rustic eatery has been a local landmark since the mid-1970s. Open Mon.–Fri. 5 AM–2 PM, Sat. 7 AM–2 PM, and Sun. 7 AM–

1 PM (no lunch or brunch on Sun., just breakfast).

Eight miles north of the Sugarloaf access road, the **White Wolf Restaurant,** Main St., Rte. 27, Stratton 04982, 207/246-2922, gets you off the mountain and into congenial, casual surroundings with an imaginative menu ($11–22) for entrées, usually including venison and buffalo). It's open all year, Mon.– Fri. 11 AM–9 PM and Sat.–Sun. 7 AM–9 PM. Reservations are a good idea. During May's mud season, "The Wolf" usually shuts down Mon.–Tues.

Moderate to Expensive

The best restaurant in the entire area is **One Stanley Avenue,** 1 Stanley Ave., Kingfield 04947, 207/265-5541, a Kingfield magnet since 1972. Cocktails in the Victorian lounge precede a dining experience: unobtrusive service, understated decor, and entrées ($18–30) such as roast duck with rhubarb glaze, chicken with fiddleheads, and saged rabbit. Dill-flavored Shaker dumplings come with every entrée. Reservations are essential on winter weekends; the restaurant attracts Sugarloaf's higher-end ski crowd. Open for dinner Tues.–Sun., mid-Dec.–mid-Apr., 5–9:30 PM, One Stanley Avenue is 18 miles south of Sugarloaf.

Consistent, creative cuisine has drawn customers from as far as Rangeley to the **Porter House Restaurant,** Rte. 27, Eustis 04936, 207/246-7932, a back-of-beyond 1908 farmhouse along the highway to Canada. An extra touch is the choice of antique-filled dining rooms. Specialties include Porter House steak, bacon-wrapped filet mignon, and roast duckling. Although it tends to be a "grownup" place, kids can order a sirloin burger or a hot dog. You'll probably be out of luck if you show up without a reservation, and it's a bit far to drive for a disappointment, so call ahead. Dress is casual or formal, your choice. Open all year Wed.–Sun. 5–9 PM, the Porter House is 12 miles northwest of Sugarloaf/USA and 23 miles east and north of Rangeley; allow 30– 40 minutes from Rangeley—enough time for moose-watching.

INFORMATION AND SERVICES

The **Sugarloaf Area Chamber of Commerce,** Rte. 27, RR 1, Box 2151, Carrabassett Valley 04947, 207/235-2100, www.carrabassettvalley.org, handles information requests for the whole valley, including Sugarloaf/USA, and publishes a helpful map/guide as well as annual dining and lodging brochures. The office, across the road from Ayotte's Country Store, also handles reservations for lodging in the valley as well as on the mountain (800/843-2732). It's open most days, all year, 9 AM–4 PM. Request copies of the chamber's two helpful free brochures, updated annually: *Sugarloaf Region Dining Guide* and *Sugarloaf Region Lodging Guide.*

For information only on **Sugarloaf/USA,** write to Sugarloaf/USA, 5092 Access Rd., Carrabassett Valley 04947, 207/237-2000, www.sugarloaf.com, or contact Guest Services on the main floor of the Base Lodge, 207/237-6939. There isn't much the Guest Services staff can't handle; they're real pros, knowledgeable about the resort as well as about off-mountain museums, dining, and special events. During the ski season, the free tabloid *Sugarloaf This Week,* published biweekly, carries comprehensive information about on-mountain activities. It's available everywhere on the mountain.

The recorded **Snowphone** hotline (207/237-6808) has up-to-the-minute info on snow conditions and special events at Sugarloaf/USA. If you're staying hereabouts (on the mountain or in the valley) and have cable TV, tune to channel 17 (WSKI) for weather, snow, trail, and lift updates, plus an entertainment rundown.

Emergencies

For police, fire, and ambulance services in **Kingfield, Carrabassett Valley, Sugarloaf/ USA,** and **Eustis,** dial 911. Sugarloaf/USA has a **first-aid clinic** in the basement of the interfaith chapel at the west end of the upper parking area in Sugarloaf Village; during the ski season, a doctor or physician's assistant is on duty. The nearest major medical facility is in Farmington, 38 miles south of Sugarloaf.

Money

On the mountain at Sugarloaf/USA, there is an ATM in the Base Lodge, and at the Sugarloaf Grocery Store located next to D'ellies.

Getting Around

The free **Sugarloaf Shuttle** operates frequently on the mountain, with condo and parking lot pickups, daily, 8 AM–midnight, during the ski season. If they are on-call you can call the shuttle service at 207/237-6853.

The **Carrabassett Valley Ski Shuttle** operates Fri.–Sun. and holiday weeks throughout the ski season; other days, it's on call, 207/237-2000, 8 AM–midnight, and still free. Last bus Fri.–Sat. nights is usually 12:30 or 1 AM. Pick up a schedule at the Check-In Center or at Guest Services in the Base Lodge. In summer, the **Sugarloaf Bike Shuttle,** less extensive than the winter operation, provides continuous service (for a fee) Fri.–Sun. 9 AM– 4 PM, early July–early Sept. The route begins on Main St. in Sugarloaf Village and ends 35 minutes later at Carrabassett Valley's Riverside Park, terminus of the seven-mile Narrow Gauge (trail 9) bike path.

Western Lakes & Mountains

Rangeley Lakes Area

Incorporated in 1855, the town of Rangeley (pop. 1,075) and the surrounding Rangeley Lakes region have seen ups and downs in the past century or so—grand hotels and great fires, regression and renewal. The uncrowded streets, slower pace, and countless recreational opportunities are changing the face of western Maine. Centerpiece of a vast system of lakes and streams, and surrounded by mountains, Rangeley is loaded with potential for year-round activities. Summer sees swimming, golf, tennis, canoeing, biking, hiking, fishing, even panning for gold; in winter there's snowmobiling, ice fishing, snowshoeing, and downhill and nordic skiing. But there's more—Rangeley Friends of the Arts cultural events, old-fashioned annual festivals and fairs, the unique Wilhelm Reich Museum, a flightseeing service, and shops that carry antiques, books, sportswear, and crafts. In 2005 Rangeley celebrated its 150th anniversary, with a long list of festivities.

And then there's history, even prehistory—excavations have revealed evidence of human habitation in this area as long ago as 9000 BC. More than 8,000 stone tools and other artifacts were uncovered at the Vail site, on the edge of Aziscohos Lake. Native Americans certainly left their linguistic mark here, too, with tongue-twisting names applied to the lakes and other natural features. Mooselookmeguntic means "where hunters watch moose at night"; Umbagog means "shallow water"; Mollychunkamunk (aka Upper Richardson Lake) means "crooked water"; Oquossoc means "landing place"; and Kennebago means "land of sweet water." The town's more prosaic name comes from 19th-century landowner Squire James Rangeley.

Rangeley is a catchall name. First applied to the town (formerly known as the Lake Settlement), it now also refers to the lake and the entire region. "I'm going to Rangeley" could indicate a destination anywhere in the extensive network of interconnecting lakes, rivers, and streams backing up to New Hampshire. The Rangeley Lakes make up the headwaters of the Androscoggin River, which technically begins at Umbagog Lake and flows seaward for 167 miles to meet the Kennebec River in Merrymeeting Bay, near Brunswick and Topsham.

Southeast of Rangeley, the town of Phillips was the birthplace of fly-fishing legend Cornelia T. ("Fly Rod") Crosby (1854–1946), recipient of the first Registered Maine Guide license issued by the state—the imprimatur for outdoors professionals. Crosby, who wrote columns for the local paper, was a fanatic angler and hunter who always kept a china tea set neatly stowed in her gear.

While most visitors reach Rangeley via Rte. 4 from the Farmington area, another popular route is Rte. 17 from the Rumford/Mexico area. Between Mexico and Byron, the shoulders are ample enough for bicycles. When you reach Byron on the Swift River, you enter the 35-mile Rangeley Lakes Scenic Byway, stretching from Byron north to Oquossoc and then southward down Rte. 4 through Rangeley to Madrid. The label is unquestionably deserved, especially in autumn, when the vibrant colors are unforgettable. The two-lane road winds through the rural woods of western Maine, opening up periodically to reveal stunning views of lakes, streams, forested hillsides, and the Swift River. You might even see a moose. Highlights are two sign-posted viewpoints—Height of Land and the Rangeley Scenic Overlook—surveying Mooselookmeguntic and Rangeley Lakes, respectively. Height of Land, 11 miles south of Oquossoc, adjoins the Appalachian Trail. Have your camera handy; it's a photogenic standout.

Along Rte. 17 (about 23 miles south of Oquossoc) is Coos Canyon, in the town of Byron, where gold was found in the early 1800s on the east branch of the Swift River. Amateur prospectors still flock to the area, but don't get your hopes up—it's more play than profit.

SIGHTS

Wilhelm Reich Museum

Controversial Austrian-born psychoanalyst/ natural scientist Wilhelm Reich (1897–1957), noted expert on sexual energy, chose Rangeley for his residence and research. Hour-long guided tours of The Wilhelm Reich Museum, Dodge Pond Rd., P.O. Box 687, Rangeley 04970, 207/864-3443, his handsome field-stone mansion, include a slide presentation covering Reich's life, eccentric philosophy, experiments, and inventions such as the orgone accumulator and the cloudbuster. Reich is buried on the estate grounds. Views are spectacular from the roof of the museum, also known as **Orgonon,** so bring binoculars and a camera. A nature-trail system, including a bird blind, winds through the wooded acreage. Museum hours are Wed.–Sun. July–Aug., and Sun. only 1–5 PM in Sept. There are free natural science programs each Sun. 2–4 PM. Admission to the museum (no charge for being on the grounds) is $6 adults; children 12 and under are free. The museum is west of Rangeley, 0.8 mile north of Rte. 4.

Bennett Bridge

Spanning the Magalloway River beneath Aziscohos Mountain, the 92-foot-long Bennett Covered Bridge (also known as the Bennett-Bean Bridge), built in 1898–99, sees far fewer visitors than most of Maine's eight other covered bridges. The setting, in the hamlet of Wilsons Mills, makes for great photos, so it's worth detouring on the unpaved road next to the Aziscoos Valley Camping Area, 0.3 mile west of Rte. 16 and 28 miles west of Rangeley.

Flightseeing

Lake Region Air, 2602 Main St., Rte. 4, P.O. Box 1313, Rangeley 04970, www.lakeregionair.com, 207/864-5307, does on-demand 15-minute mini-tours via floatplane. A 15 minute flight is $70 (two person minimum) and $100 for a 30 minute flight. Longer flights can be arranged. Reservations aren't always needed, but call ahead to be sure. Best deal, but unpre-

dictable time-wise, is the two-hour **fire warden's flight,** (two persons maximum). Trips depend on weather, fire danger, and other factors; call for details and rate. You may need to stand by for a phone call. The office is open daily 9 AM–5 PM.

Rangeley Lakes Region Logging Museum

The Rangeley Lakes Region Logging Museum, Rte. 16, Rangeley 04970, 207/864-7311,is an eclectic assortment of lumberjack paraphernalia and lumber-camp paintings. The annual Logging Festival Days is held on the last Friday and Saturday in July. Activities include the Burying of the Beans—logging "camp style"; music, entertainment, a Logger's Hall of Fame, and a parade of floats, bands, and logging equipment. The festivities continue with woodsmen's competitions of chain-sawing, pulp-piling, axe-throwing, and more. The museum is open 11 AM–2 PM in July and August. Donations are welcomed.

PARKS AND PRESERVES

In downtown Rangeley, overlooking both lake and mountains **Lakeside Park** has grills and picnic tables (some covered), tennis courts, a playground with plenty of swings, lots of lawn for running, and a busy boat-launching ramp. The park is open 5 AM–10 PM. Access is from Main St. (Rte. 4), near the Parkside and Main Restaurant and the chamber of commerce office.

Rangeley is another Maine region where foresighted conservationists have jumped in and helped set aside recreational land for everyone to enjoy. The most visible standard-bearer is the **Rangeley Lakes Heritage Trust** (RLHT), Rte. 4, P.O. Box 249, Oquossoc 04964, 207/864-7311, an energetic membership organization that oversees thousands of acres of protected land, including 10 islands and more than 20 miles of lake and river frontage. The RLHT office, in the Stony Batter Station building, across from The Gingerbread House in Oquossoc, is open all year, Mon.–

Fri. 9 AM–4:30 PM, plus Sat. 9 AM–noon Memorial Day weekend to Labor Day.

Rangeley Lake State Park

With 1.2 miles of lake frontage and panoramic views toward the mountains, nearly 1000-acre Rangeley Lake State Park, South Shore Dr., HC 32, Box 5000, Rangeley 04970, 207/864-3858, gets high marks for picnicking, swimming, fishing, birding, boating, and camping. The swimming "beach" is a large patch of grass. None of the 50 campsites are at water's edge, but a dozen have easy shore access. For camping reservations from out-of-state, call 207/287-3824 at least two business days in advance (MasterCard and Visa only). Maine residents should call 800/332-1501. If you're doing any boating, stay close to shore until you're comfortable with the wind conditions; the wind picks up very quickly on Rangeley Lake, especially in the south and southeast coves near the park. Day-use admission is $3 adults, $1 children 5–11. For those under five and over 65, admission is free. Nonresident camping is $20 per site per night (plus $2 per site per night for a reservation); no hookups, but there are hot showers. The park, located four miles off Rte. 17, is open mid-May–Sept., but it's accessible in the winter for cross-country skiing and snowmobiling.

Hunter Cove Wildlife Sanctuary

Loons, ducks, and other waterfowl are the principal residents of Hunter Cove Wildlife Sanctuary, a small preserve previously owned by the Maine Audubon Society, transferred to the Rangeley Lakes Heritage Trust in July 2004. While walking the three miles of easy blazed trails, best in a clockwise direction, keep an eye out for blue-flag iris, which blossoms throughout the summer. You may even spot a moose. If you launch a canoe into Hunter Cove and paddle under the Mingo Loop Road bridge early in the season, you'll come face-to-face with nesting cliff swallows. To reach the sanctuary, take Rte. 4 west of downtown Rangeley for about 2.5 miles, turning left into the preserve across the road from Dodge Pond. It's signposted. The

preserve is open daily, sunrise to sunset. Admission is free.

Smalls Falls Rest Area

One of Maine's most accessible cascades, Smalls Falls is right next to Rte. 4, at a state rest area 12 miles south of Rangeley. Pull into the parking area and walk a few steps to the overlook. Bring a picnic. For more of a challenge, ascend a bit farther to Chandler's Mill Stream Falls. The rest area is officially open mid-May–Oct., but it's easy to park alongside the highway early and late in the season.

RECREATION

The Rangeley Lakes area earned its vaunted reputation from world-class fishing and other summer pursuits, but it's now become a year-round destination thanks to snowmobiling and skiing. Diehard anglers will always show up in May and early June, but most everyone else stays away then, preferring not to become lunch for hungry blackflies.

The **Rangeley Parks and Recreation Department,** 15 School St., Rangeley 04970, 207/864-3326, sponsors a huge number of activities for residents as well as visitors. Among the **summer programs** are canoeing, swimming, tennis, and golf lessons; hiking and canoe trips; children's workshops; a tennis tournament; and day trips for seniors. Pre-registration is required for many of the activities, and most programs require at least a minimal fee. Contact the department or check with the chamber of commerce.

Guided Wildlife and Water Excursions

Do-it-yourself moose spotting is a favorite pastime in this area, if you're out and about. The likelihood of spotting one of these big critters can be quite high, depending if conditions are ripe. Rte. 16, between Rangeley and Stratton, is well known as "Moose Alley," especially in the boggy areas close to the road. If you're heading that way for dinner, allow time for a slow drive and plenty of gawking. Keep your camera handy. Drive slowly in any case—no one wins in a moose-car collision, and fatal accidents are not uncommon on this unlighted stretch.

Maine Professional Guide **Rich Gacki, Recreation Resources, Inc.,** P.O. Box 695, Rangeley 04970, 207/864-5136, has 20 years experience as a guide. Rich leads guided canoe trips on the Kennebago River in search of moose and other wildlife. To reserve a space, give Rich a call. May–late Oct., Rich also leads three-hour, on-demand guided nature hikes and sailing excursions and/or lessons. In winter, he leads cross-country-skiing and snowshoeing trips on the network of trails in the area. He's a certified ski instructor, so lessons can be part of the deal. He tailors each trip to the skill level of his clients. Call to schedule.

Hiking

Centerpiece of a 1,953-acre parcel of Maine Public Reserve Land, **Bald Mountain** is a relatively easy two-hour round-trip hike that ascends less than 1,000 feet, yet the minimal effort leads to stunning views of Mooselookmeguntic and Upper Richardson Lakes—not to mention the surrounding mountains. Even three-year-olds can tackle this without terrorizing their parents. Pack a picnic. The trailhead is on Bald Mountain Road in Oquossoc, about a mile south of Rte. 4 and roughly across from the entrance to Bald Mountain Camps. Park well off the road.

Dropping 90 feet straight down, dramatic **Angel Falls** is one of New England's highest cascades, reached after a fairly short easy-to-moderate hike. Even in midsummer, you'll be fording running water, so wear rubberized or waterproof shoes or boots. Best time to come is autumn, when most of the rivulets have dried up and the woods are brilliantly colorful. Allow an hour to 1.5 hours for the 1.5-mile round-trip hike. The trail is mostly red-blazed, with the addition of orange strips tied at crucial points. From Oquossoc, take Rte. 17 south 17.9 miles to the unpaved Bemis Track, on the right. Follow the road along Berdeen Stream about 3.6 miles until you see a steep road descending to a gravel pit on the left. Park alongside the Bemis Track and walk down the hill. This is a popu-lar hike, so you should see other cars. The trail leads off to the left.

A distinctive landmark on the western slope of Saddleback Mountain, **Piazza Rock** is a giant cantilevered boulder 600 feet off the Appalachian Trail. The hike up is easy to moderate, not a cakewalk but fine for families, along the white-blazed AT from Rte. 4. From downtown Rangeley, go seven miles southeast on Rte. 4 and park in the new lot on the south side of the highway. Piazza Rock is 1.2 miles northeast of the highway.

If you continue on the AT from Piazza Rock, it's another four miles to the summit of 4,116-foot **Saddleback Mountain,** but most hikers take the shorter route up the mountain from the ski area's Base Lodge. To get there from Rangeley, go south on Rte. 4 to Dallas Hill Rd., then go 2.5 miles to Saddleback Mountain Rd. From the lodge, follow the orange trail markers. Expect a stiff breeze and 360-degree vistas. A trail map is available at the lodge.

Other excellent hikes west and north of Rangeley are **Aziscohos Mountain** and **West Kennebago Mountain.** Both are easy to moderate, have terrific views from their summits, and require three or four hours round-trip from their trailheads. West Kennebago has a fire tower.

Biking

In downtown Rangeley, **Railroad Trail Loop** is a multiuse trail network. The loop starts in town. It is a 12.5-mile circuit via paved and unpaved roads and an abandoned railroad bed. (The Chamber of Commerce also has copies.) You can begin the loop close to the shop, but be prepared for some steep sections near the Saddleback Access Road. **The Rangeley Lakes Trails Center** is opening a 45-kilometer groomed trail network on lower Saddleback Mountain, Saddleback Mountain Road, for hiking, biking, nature-watching, and cross-country skiing in winter, 207/864-4309. **Seasonal Cycles** 2593 Main St., Rangeley, 207/864-2100, has all-terrain bike rentals. The location is convenient to the Railroad Loop Trail. Ask about other suggested rides.

Swimming

Although many lodgings have lake swimming access, not all do. If you're ready for a swim, head for downtown Rangeley's **Lakeside Park** or **Rangeley Lake State Park.** In summer, a lifeguard is on duty at Lakeside Park weekdays 11 AM–5 PM and weekends 9 AM–5 PM.

Also see the *Sugarloaf Area* section, above, for information on swimming at Cathedral Pines in Eustis, east of Rangeley via Rte. 16.

Getting Afloat

Canoeing, kayaking, and motorboating are splendid throughout this region; kayaking is the relative newcomer, but it's fast becoming a very popular sport here. Be forewarned, though, that Rangeley and Mooselookmeguntic Lakes are much larger than they look, and they have wide-open expanses where flukey winds can kick up suddenly and mightily and swamp boats. Fatalities have occurred in just such circumstances—as recently as 1999. Check on wind conditions before you head out. Do not take chances.

If you're looking for a pristine lake where motorboats are banned, opt for **Saddleback Lake, Loon Lake, Little Kennebago Lake,** or **Quimby Pond,** all fairly close to Rangeley.

Good choices for **canoeing** around Rangeley are Rangeley Lake (especially around Hunter Cove), the Cupsuptic River, the lower Kennebago River, and Mooselookmeguntic Lake. For canoeing slightly farther afield, Upper and Lower Richardson Lakes are wonderfully scenic, as is Umbagog Lake (um-BAY-gog), straddling the Maine-New Hampshire border. The Rangeley Lakes Area Chamber of Commerce has produced a suggested canoeing itinerary for the Rangeley Lakes chain, including information about wilderness campsites en route. Some of the campsites require advance reservations and fire permits.

Besides being a fishing-gear supplier and a place that has camping, fishing, and hunting gear, water toys, outdoor clothing, and unique gifts, **River's Edge Sports,** Rte. 4, P.O. Box 347, Oquossoc 04964, 207/864-5582, www.riversedgesports.org, also rents canoes

and kayaks, starting at $20 a day. For $40, including canoe rental, they'll shuttle you and the canoe up the Kennebago River to the start of an idyllic three- to four-hour downstream paddle to Rte. 16. Leave your car at the end. The shop is open all year, daily 8 AM–6 PM, except in April when hours are 9 AM–5 PM. They are adjacent to the Public Boat Launch at the Rangeley Outlet. River's Edge Sports is Franklin County's largest sports shop.

Kayak and canoe rental places are plentiful in the Rangeley area.

The best place to rent a sturdy motorboat is **Oquossoc Cove Marina,** Rte. 4, P.O. Box 335, Oquossoc 04964, 207/864-3463. Cost is about $150 a day. Oquossoc Cove Marina is owned by the same owners of Oquossoc Marine, whose fine reputation means their boats are much in demand, so reserve well ahead. Restroom and picnic facilities are available. **Ecopelagicon,** 7 Pond St., P.O. Box 899, Rangeley 04970 207/864-2771, www.ecopelagicon.com, rents kayaks for use on Haley Pond for a short paddle or to take to your camp. Rentals are small and mid size recreational and tandem kayaks and include paddle, life jacket and tie downs. Rentals available by the hour, day or week. Call for rates. Delivery and pick-up is available for a fee. Open daily 10 AM–5 PM, Memorial Day to Columbus Day; 10 AM–7 PM July–Aug.; hours vary in winter. **Haines Landing Marina,** on Mooselookmeguntic Lake, offers motorboat, canoe, and kayak rentals. They're located at P.O. Box 1195, Rangeley, Maine 04970, 207/864-2393 (207/864-5040 in winter).

Golf

Noted golfers have been teeing off at **Mingo Springs Golf Course,** Country Club Rd., P.O. Box 399, 207/864-5021, since 1925, when the course started with nine holes. Today's 18-hole, par-70 course boasts panoramic vistas of lakes and mountains—and sometimes an annoying breeze. Facilities include lessons, a pro shop, and cart rentals. Tee times are advisable, particularly on weekends. Golf-and-lodging packages are available at the adjacent Country Club Inn. Open Memorial Day weekend to early October. Take Rte. 4 west of Rangeley and turn left onto Mingo Loop Rd.; follow the signs.

Mingo Springs is almost as scenic as the Sugarloaf Golf Course, and a bit less expensive, but it can be hard to resist the temptation to play a round on Sugarloaf's championship course.

A nine-hole course is **Evergreen Golf Course,** Dallas Hill Rd., Rangeley, 207/864-9055.

Narrow Gauge Railroad

The **Sandy River & Rangeley Lakes Railroad,** Phillips, Maine, 207/788-3621 or 207/639-3742, www.srrl-rr.org, operates on the first and third Sundays of each month, June through the second week in October. Open additional days for special events, so call ahead. The station is on Mill Hill Road (aka Bridge Street). The 50-minute excursion includes the train ride and some walking. The ride travels through woods and fields, with a glimpse of the Sandy River. As the passenger car sways, you hear the noise of the tracks and enjoy your trip on the "two-footer" rails of the past.

Winter Sports

Neighboring Sugarloaf/USA dominates the **Alpine Skiing (downhill) World** in this part of Maine, but the Rangeley area has its own first-rate, low-key, family-oriented ski resort—with lift and lodging prices that put less of a dent in your wallet. Seven miles southeast of Rangeley, **Saddleback,** P.O. Box 490, Rangeley 04970, 207/864-5671, 866/918-2225, www.saddlebackmaine.com, has 54 novice to expert trails served by two double chairlifts, two T-bars, one quad, plus two snowboard parks. Vertical drop on the mountain is an impressive 2,000 feet. Daily lift tickets for adults are $39, with weekday specials at $25. Children 13–18 years old are $31; 7–12 years old are $29. Children 6 and younger are free, as are senior adults over 70 years of age. On-mountain facilities include the Base Lodge (with a pub), ski school, rentals, a cafeteria (open daily during ski season), inexpensive day care, and three attractive condo

complexes. Some townhouse accommodations sleep as many as 10, making the price a bargain. Ski season is mid-Dec.–early Apr.; lifts operate daily 9 AM–4 PM. Service begins at 8:30 AM on weekends and holidays.

Cross-country skiing

Cross-country ski trails are available on Saddleback Mountain at **Ski Nordic at Saddleback,** P.O. Box 490, Rangeley 04970, 207/864-5671, snow hotline 207/864-3380, with about 72 kilometers of groomed trails (and backcountry access). Rental skis are available at the Saddleback Base Lodge.

The **Rangeley Lakes Trails Center,** located on lower Saddleback Mountain, Saddleback Mountain Rd., 207/864-4309, built for the 2005–06 season, is a network of 45 kilometers of groomed trails for cross-country skiing, hiking, biking, and nature-watching. Maps are available at the center.

At **Orgonon, the Wilhelm Reich Museum,** 207/864-3443, west of downtown Rangeley, the summer nature trails are accessible for free nordic skiing weekdays 9 AM–4 PM. Maine Guide **Rich Gacki of Recreation Resources, Inc.** leads guided cross-country-skiing tours (207/864-5136). **River's Edge Sports,** Rte. 4, P.O. Box 347, Oquossoc 04964, 207/864-5582, rents cross-country skis. They're open daily 8 AM–6 PM.

The Rangeley area, linked to the statewide system of **snowmobile trails,** has its own 150-mile groomed network, thanks to the diligent efforts of local snowmobile clubs. **River's Edge Sports,** Rte. 4, Oquossoc 04967, 207/864-5582,www.etravelmaine.com/riversedge/, rents snowmobiles.

ENTERTAINMENT

Under new ownership since May 2005, the **Lakeside Theater,** Main St., Rangeley 04970, 207/864-5000, originally opened in the summer of 1996 as a nonprofit community cinema. It screens films with surround sound and state-of-the-art equipment. Built with extra elevation, all 187 seats have unencumbered vantage points. Call for times. Adult tickets are $6. During summer on Thursday and Sunday nights, independent films are shown. Off-season, films are only shown weekend evenings.

Rangeley Friends of the Arts (RFA), P.O. Box 333, Rangeley 04970, 207/864-2958, www.rangeleyarts.com, is a local cultural organization that promotes the arts in the region through concerts, events, scholarships, and school programs. Call for event information.

The Clubhouse, Main St., Rangeley 04970, 207/864-9955, draws a crowd Fri.–Sat. nights, starting at 9 PM, when there's live music or a deejay.

FESTIVALS AND EVENTS

The fourth weekend in January, the **Snowmobile Snodeo** brings games, a snowmobile parade, and fireworks to Lakeside Park, Rangeley.

At Rangeley's **Wilhelm Reich Museum,** 207/864-3443, there are nature trails. Natural science programs are held each Sun. 2–4 PM during the summer. Call for topics.

Rangeley goes all out with its **Independence Day** celebration (fireworks, chicken barbecue, parade, and live music), held on the Fourth or a day before or after. Be here for it if you're anywhere near the area. The festivities are held in Lakeside Park, Rangeley. The third Sunday in July, the **Old-Time Fiddlers' Contest** draws great musicians and includes a barbecue. Bring your own chair or blanket and expect lots of foot-stomping fun. It runs 1–5 PM at Rangeley Inn Green. The last weekend in July, **Logging Museum Festival Days** includes a parade, bean-hole bean supper, lumberjack events, and the Little Miss Woodchip contest. It's held on the Rangeley Logging Museum grounds, Rte. 16.

On the first Thursday in August, the **Sidewalk Art Show** is an all-day street festival featuring dozens of artists displaying a wide range of talents along Rangeley's Main Street. During the second full week of August, **Phillips Old Home Days** is a down-home community-pride celebration with live music, a carnival, a parade, a barbecue, and a road race. Downtown Rangeley comes alive the third Thursday in August for the **Annual Blueberry Festival,** a day-long celebration of the blueberry harvest, with sales of blueberry-everything.

Held the first Saturday in October, the **Logging Museum Apple Festival** is a day-long, apple-theme celebration including cider pressing. It's held on the Rangeley Logging Museum grounds, Rte. 16.

SHOPPING
Antiques Plus
Old fishing and hunting gear, antique tools, and postcards are the specialties at **Gearsyl Antiques,** 3779 Main St. (Rtes. 4 and 16), Rangeley, Maine 04970, 207/864-5784, a two-story barn roughly midway between Rangeley and Oquossoc. Art and Sylvia Guerin live in the farmhouse, so the shop is open all year, daily 9 AM–5 PM.

Books, Gifts, and Crafts
The new-book selection is distinguished at **Books, Lines, and Thinkers,** Main St., P.O. Box 971, Rangeley 04970, 207/864-4355, bltbooks@rangeley.org, thanks to owner Wess Connally, a former high school English teacher in Rangeley. The small, user-friendly shop has lots of great reading. He's combined his shop with Birds of a Feather Gallery, so there's plenty of great artwork and crafts. The schedule is a bit unpredictable, with Wednesdays and Thursdays by chance, so call ahead. Wess organizes and leads a book-discussion group year-round, and visitors are welcome.

The Rangeley area's best selection of sportswear and gifts comes from the **Alpine Shop,** 2504 Main St., Rangeley 04970, 207/864-3741. Patagonia, Woolrich, and Teva are just a few of the brand names; the Icelandic sweater selection is impressive; and the Maine-themed gifts are (mostly) tasteful. The shop is open all year, daily 9 AM–5:30 PM in winter, 9 AM–8:30 PM July–Aug.

Ecopelagicon: A Nature Store, 3 Pond St., Rangeley 04970, 207/864-2771, is a kind of miniaturized (and less expensive) Nature Company, emphasizing eco-oriented gifts, books, toys, games, and cosmetics. Don't miss it. The shop, half a block off Main St., is open daily 10 AM–5 PM, Memorial Day weekend through Christmas; July–Aug. it stays open to 8 PM.

In downtown Rangeley, you can't miss the house and shop of **Rodney Richard, the Mad Whittler,** 123 Main St., Rte. 4, P.O. Box 183, Rangeley 04970, 207/864-5595, behind all the wood shavings and works-in-progress. If Rodney's performing his magic with the chainsaw and jackknife, you can stand by and watch, or perhaps purchase one of his woodcarvings. His son, Rodney Jr., a chip off the old block, has earned his own reputation as an accomplished woodcarver, specializing in loons. Rodney Sr. has achieved national and international renown as a folk artist and master carver. His work has traveled to dozens of museums and appears in collections as far afield as Archangel in Russia. He's also the prime mover behind Rangeley's fledgling Logging Museum. Look for the Open pennant outside his shop in July and August; other times, call ahead to make sure someone is home.

Just up the hill west of town, **Sunrise View Farm,** Cemetery Hill, Rte. 4, 2963 Main St., Rangeley 04970, 207/864-2117, has cornered one of the best views in the area. It's hard to concentrate on the herbs, flowers, jams, and herbal gifts when all of Rangeley is spread out before you. The farm shop is open all year. Memorial Day to Labor Day hours are Mon.–Sat. 10 AM–5 PM. For other times call ahead.

Farther north on Rte. 4, in Oquossoc, is the whimsically named **Stony Batter Station.** Among the shops and offices in this handsome building (across from the Gingerbread House) is **The Gallery at Stony Batter Station,** Rte. 4, P.O. Box 291, Oquossoc 04964, 207/864-3373. The gallery has expanded from two rooms to four themed rooms, all with imaginative displays. One room has antiques, another has lamps and custom lamp shades, while a third has gourmet foods and candles, and the forth has a wide assortment of gift items

including blueberry ware, soaps/lotions, stationery, garden gifts, birdhouses, balsam, and the popular birch-twig photo frames. The shop is open 10 AM–4 PM daily in summer, Thurs.–Sun. in winter.

ACCOMMODATIONS
Inns and Bed-and-Breakfasts

Entering Rangeley from the south, you can't miss the three-story **Rangeley Inn and Motor Lodge,** 2443 Main St., P.O. Box 160, Rangeley 04970, 207/864-3341 or 800/666-3687, on the edge of downtown's Haley Pond. Thirty-five rooms in the turn-of-the-century main section and 15 modern rooms in the motel annex (overlooking the pond) are $84–129. All have private baths; some rooms have whirlpools. The large lobby has comfortable chairs and lots of woody touches. The huge, tin-ceiling dining room is open to the public Thurs.–Sat. for dinner. Entrées run $17–30, with an interesting wine list; a children's menu is also available. Reservations are advisable, and a must on summer weekends. The adjoining pub serves less expensive and better-than-average tavern fare. It's open most of the year, but closed for part of April and November. Call ahead.

Next to the stunning Mingo Springs Golf Course, the **Country Club Inn,** 56 Country Club Rd., P.O. Box 680, Rangeley 04970, fax 207/864-3831, claims the same fabulous lake-and-mountain panorama as the golf course. The inn opened in 1976. Nineteen lake-view rooms (private baths) go for $117 d, including breakfast, or $173 d MAP. A room-only rate ($99 d) is also available, as is a two-night all-inclusive golf package. Off-season, the B&B rate is $91 d. Decor is updated-1960s; the inn is superbly maintained and run, and there's an outdoor pool. Children are welcome, but no pets. The dramatic windowed dining room is open to the public by reservation for breakfast and dinner Wed.–Sun., late June to Columbus Day, but tables for the public can be scarce when the inn is fully booked. Call well ahead, especially on summer weekends. The inn, located

2.2 miles west of downtown Rangeley, is open mid-May–mid-Oct. and late Dec.–Mar.

A genuine veteran in the B&B trade, Joanne Koob has been running **Oquossoc's Own Bed & Breakfast,** 32 Rangeley Ave., P.O. Box 27, Oquossoc 04964, 207/864-5584, since 1980. Repeat customers are the rule at this lively, informal place. Joanne provides a cozy living room, a spare refrigerator. Croquet and volleyball gear is available by request. Joanne's professional kitchen is the heart of her catering business. Five attractively decorated second- and third-floor rooms share two baths ($70/day for a double, $40/day for a single). Smoking is only allowed outside. Kids under six stay free. It's located at the junction of Rtes. 4 and 17. Open all year.

Twenty-one miles southeast of Rangeley, **The Elcourt Bed and Breakfast,** Pleasant St., P.O. Box 214, Phillips 04966, 207/639-2741 or 888/231-8389, gets gold stars for the hearty country breakfast served to classical music. Cordial innkeepers Court and Elsie Dill cater to hikers, snowmobilers, and skiers at their comfortably old-fashioned village B&B; children and well-behaved pets are also welcome. Three rooms share 2.5 baths ($45–65 d); smoking allowed on the open porch only. No credit cards. Out back are lovely formal gardens. It's usually open all year, but call ahead to confirm. On Toothacre Pond in Phillips 04966, Elsie also runs **Clover Cove Cottage,** 1 Walker Rd., 207/639-2741 or 888/231-8389, which is owned by her sister. The two-story cottage has an open first-floor plan, with lots of windows overlooking the pond. It's a great spot to listen to loons. There are three bedrooms, a full bath, and full kitchen. It sleeps nine. Rates start at $500/week. Call for nightly rates and availability. Rowboats, canoes, kayaks, and paddleboats are available for guest use.

Cabin Colony

On a quiet cove about four miles west of town, **Hunter Cove on Rangeley Lake,** 334 Mingo Loop Rd. (office), Hunter Cove Rd. (cabins), Rangeley 04970, 207/864-3383, www.huntercove.com, has eight rustically modern waterfront cabins on six acres. Each has one or two bedrooms, screened porch, woodstove, and even color TV. Rates are $140–200 d; two-night minimum. Weekly rates (required July–Aug.) are $800–1,050 (up to four persons); pets are $10 a day. The pricier cabins have hot tubs in the living room. Open all year, with lower rates off season and mid-week. From here, it's an easy paddle to the western edge of the Hunter Cove Wildlife Sanctuary, and Mingo Springs Golf Course is nearby.

Sporting Camps

Stephen Philbrick is the third-generation owner of **Bald Mountain Camps,** Bald Mountain Rd., P.O. Box 332, Oquossoc 04964, office 207/864-3671, 207/864-3778 or 888/392-0072, www.baldmountaincamps.com, a family-oriented traditional sporting camp on the shore of Mooselookmeguntic Lake. Established in 1897 and now run by Steve and his wife Fernlyn, the superb operation has more than 90 percent repeat guests, some of whom have been returning since the 1930s. It's tough to get a reservation, especially July–Aug. Fifteen rustic, waterfront log cabins can accommodate 2–8 people. Cabins are completely furnished, each offering a private porch, fireplace, living room, individual bedrooms, full housekeeping services, and porter service. Three meals a day are served daily in the lake-view lodge. No alcohol is served, so BYOA. A highlight is the Friday-night cookout, with lobster, ribs, corn, steamed clams, and blueberry pancakes for dessert. The informal dining room is open to the public for dinner (book well ahead) by reservation only. Among the activities are swimming (sandy beach), fishing, tennis, canoeing, motorboating, sailing, and waterskiing. There's a playground for kids. Rates range $115–135 per day, per person, depending on the season. Children are less. Open mid-May–late September.

More rustic and remote than Bald Mountain Camps, **Grant's Kennebago Camps,** P.O. Box 786, Rangeley 04970, 207/864-3608 or 800/633-4815, www.grantscamps.com, is a classic sporting camp built in 1905 on remote, five-mile-long Kennebago Lake. Expect to hear lots of loons and see plenty of moose—*if* you can get a reservation. Seriously dedicated fly-fishers fill up the beds in May and Sept.; families take their places July–Aug., when a boat, motorboat, mountain bikes, sailboat, hiking packs, and Windsurfer are included in the cabin price. Daily rates for the 18 rustic cabins, with private bathrooms and hot showers, are $145 pp (three or more nights) to $165 pp (for two nights or less); all include three meals a day in the dining room overlooking the water. Children under 12 are $58 a night; however, children under four are free. Pets are $15 a night, per pet. The main lodge's lakeview dining room is open to the public for all meals by reservation (BYOL), but the hearty cuisine makes it a popular place, so call well ahead. Canoe rentals are $15 a day. July–Aug., Grant's arranges a daily moose run on the Kennebago River for $30 per person. (Non-guests can also go on the moose run, for a higher fee; call for details.) Access is via a gated nine-mile road from Rte. 16, west of Rangeley. The gate is only open 7 AM–6 PM; if you're coming just for dinner, Grant's will arrange for access. Open mid-May–mid-Oct.

Campgrounds and Campsites

In addition to the nonprofit and commercial campgrounds described here, the Rangeley Lakes Region Chamber of Commerce maintains a list of no-fee and low-fee **remote wilderness campsites** throughout the Rangeley Lakes.

The **Maine Forest Service,** Rte. 16, P.O. Box 267, Oquossoc 04964, 207/864-5545, responsible for more than a dozen no-fee primitive campsites, will provide a copy of its list upon request. The office also issues fire permits.

The **Stephen Phillips Memorial Preserve Trust,** P.O. Box 21, Oquossoc 04964, 207/864-2003, oversees 70 primitive tent sites on the mainland and on several islands in Mooselookmeguntic Lake. Cost is $16 per site (for two). The best option is to reserve one of the 18 waterfront sites on **Students Island,** which is accessible only

by boat. Two nature trails cross and circle the island. The campsites are open May–Sept.

About 18 miles west of Oquossoc, **Aziscoos Valley Camping Area,** Rte. 16, HC 10, Box 302, Wilsons Mills 03579, 207/486-3271, has 34 open and wooded tent and RV sites in the shadow of two mountains and close to the Bennett Covered Bridge. Site #5 is right next to the bridge. Swimming, canoeing, and fishing are all popular pursuits here. Rates are $10–16 per family. Leashed pets are allowed, but noise levels are strictly enforced. Facilities include a laundry room; recycling is mandatory. The campground is open mid-May–Oct.

At the southeast corner of Aziscohos Lake, **Black Brook Cove Campground,** Lincoln Pond Rd., P.O. Box 319, Oquossoc 04964, 207/486-3828, provides three different kinds of camping experiences. The Main Campground has 30 tent and RV sites with hookups; the secluded East Shore Area has 26 wooded waterfront sites for small, self contained units and tents—perfect for campers who enjoy a wilderness setting. These wooded waterfront sites are 3.5 miles from the main campground and 100 feet from the water. Each site has a picnic table and a fire ring. Twenty-acre, boat-accessible Beaver Island, out in the lake, has nine wilderness sites, with another seven wilderness sites around the lake. The remote sites include outhouses. Rates are $18 per family per site, plus a hookup fee. The Main Campground facilities include coin-operated hot showers, a private beach, a convenience store, and rental boats and canoes. The well-maintained campground, about 16 miles west of Oquossoc, is open mid-Apr.–mid-Oct.

The wilderness setting on the Swift River is a big plus at **Coos Canyon Campground & Cabins,** 445 Swift River Rd., Byron 04275, 207/364-3880, where sites includes a fire ring and picnic table. Most have a stone fireplace and rustic swing. Hookups (electricity and water) are available, and RVs are allowed. Most toilet facilities are outhouses; however, there are two flush toilets, and coin-operated hot showers. Sites are $12 per night. There are four lean-tos that run $15–20. Rates are based on a family of four. There is a charge for additional persons. An added attraction is the chance to try your hand at gold-panning in the river. Campground owners Roger and Judy Boucher are local experts, and they'll tell you where to go. At their store, they give **gold-panning lessons** (for campers and non-campers) with a $5 pp refundable deposit, plus $5 to rent a pan and trowel. If you're not camping here, call ahead to be sure they're available for a lesson. The campground is 21 miles south of Oquossoc, 14 miles north of Mexico, across from the Byron rest area. The office and the store are open Mon.–Thurs. and Sat. 9 AM–5 PM, Fri. 9 AM–7 PM, and Sun. 9 AM–2 PM. The campground is open year-round. Cabins are $100 per night for two persons, $10 for each additional person.

Seasonal Rentals

The **Morton & Furbish Agency,** P.O. Box 1209, Rangeley 04970, 207/864-5777 or 888/218-4882, has a wide selection of weekly and monthly rental cottages, camps, houses, and condos for winter and summer use. Costs range $500–1,000 per week.

The chamber of commerce can assist with seasonal rentals.

FOOD

Check the local newspaper for announcements of **public suppers,** featuring chicken, beans, spaghetti, or just potluck. Most suppers benefit charitable causes, cost under $10 pp, and provide an ample supply of local color.

Lunch and Picnics

"Meet me at the Frosty" is Rangeley's summertime one-liner, a ritual for locals and visitors. **Pine Tree Frosty,** Main St., Rangeley 04970, 207/864-5894, a tiny takeout near Haley Pond and the Rangeley Inn, serves ever-popular Gifford's ice cream, in dozens of flavors, plus good-size lobster rolls and superb onion rings. Tables outside are convenient for picnics. The Frosty is open mid-May–Labor Day, daily 11 AM–8:30 PM.

Inexpensive to Moderate

The Clubhouse, Main St., Rangeley 04970,

207/864-9955, is a busy, locally popular restaurant—as much for the weekend entertainment as the menu. In winter, it's jammed to the rafters with snowmobilers. It's open all year, daily 6 AM–9 PM. **The Red Onion,** Main St., Rte. 4, Rangeley 04970, 207/864-5022, is a barn of a place where you can also get award-winning chili and German pizza (sauerkraut, bacon, and onions). Portions are large; Saturday is prime-rib night. The "Onion" is open all year, daily 11 AM–9:30 PM, unless, as they say, "high winds, low humidity, and plain laziness" inspire them to close the doors.

Moderate to Expensive

The Gingerbread House, Rte. 4, Oquossoc 04964, 207/864-3602, underwent an incredible transformation in early 1997, going from a chummy, old-fashioned place to a casually upmarket, bright, open restaurant. The only hints of the former incarnation are the exterior gingerbread and the gussied-up antique soda fountain. On the menu are regional American items, with culinary flair (dinner entrées $14–24). Breakfast is especially popular, as is the ice-cream takeout (Annabelle's Ice Cream). Open all year, Mon.–Sat. 6 AM–9 PM and Sun. 6 AM–6 PM.

Several sporting camps in the Rangeley area open their dining rooms to the public, primarily for dinner, during the summer. Grab the opportunity to sample the sporting-camp ambience and the retro comfort food that brings guests back from one generation to the next.

INFORMATION AND SERVICES

The knowledgeable staffers at the **Rangeley Lakes Region Chamber of Commerce,** Lakeside Park, P.O. Box 317, Rangeley 04970, 207/864-5364 or 800/685-2537, www.rangeleymaine.com, cope with the craziest of questions. They'll also help you find a place to sleep. Request copies of their annual guides to lodgings and services; their useful *Maine's Rangeley Lakes Map* costs $4. The office is open Mon.–Sat. 9 AM–5 PM all year, plus Sun. 10 AM–2 PM July–Aug.

The **Rangeley Public Library,** Lake St., Rangeley 04970, 207/864-5529, housed in a wonderful old stone building just off Main St., is open Tues.–Fri. 10 AM–4:30 PM and Sat. 10 AM–2 PM. **Maine Guide Services** has guides available to lead all sorts of excursions—anything from a moose safari to hiking, fishing, hunting, or skiing and snowmobiling in the winter. There are many excellent licensed and experienced Maine guides who can truly get you in touch with the wonders of Maine. Rates are usually by the day or the week. Inquire at the Rangeley Lakes Region Chamber of Commerce.

Newspapers

The Rangeley Highlander, 207/864-3756, published every other Friday, a folksy, community-oriented paper, carries helpful ads, features, and calendar listings. It provides a real flavor of small-town life.

The *Original Irregular* newspaper, based in Kingfield, 207/265-2773, produces the free, tabloid-style *Rangeley Lakes Area Summertime Guide,* a very useful collection of ads, features, and events listings.

Emergencies

For police, fire, and ambulance services in **Rangeley** and **Oquossoc,** dial 911. The modern **Rangeley Region Health Center,** Dallas Hill Rd., P.O. Box 569, Rangeley 04970, 207/864-3303, after-hours 800/398-6031, opened in 1995, provides health care for residents and visitors and acts as the first-care provider in emergencies, but serious accident victims are transported via an excellent ambulance service to Franklin Memorial Hospital in Farmington, about 40 miles southeast of Rangeley. The health center is open Mon.–Fri. 8:30 AM–noon and 1–5 PM, plus Thurs. 5–7:30 PM and Sat. 9 AM–noon.

Bethel and Vicinity

A fantastic mountain-valley locale, classic antique homes, unique boutiques, a 19th-century prep school (Gould Academy), and one of New England's hottest ski resorts give Bethel (pop. 2,380) year-round appeal, much of it outdoors-oriented. Winter—the peak season—brings alpine and nordic skiing, snowshoeing, snowboarding, dogsledding, skijoring, snowmobiling, ice-skating, ice-fishing, and ice climbing. Summer—gaining in popularity, except perhaps during early June's blackfly season—means stupendous hiking, swimming, mountain biking, rock climbing, rockhounding in local quarries, fishing, camping, picnicking, golfing, and even llama trekking. Autumn has most of the summer's assets (well, maybe not swimming)—plus a fabulous blanket of colorful foliage.

The Sunday River Ski Resort, 207/824-3000, www.sundayriver.com, six miles from downtown Bethel, can take credit for many of the changes that have occurred in recent years in the Bethel area. Begun on a small scale by entrepreneur Les Otten, the mega-resort is now the flagship of the giant American Skiing Company (ASC), the nation's largest ski-resort corporation. And there's no sign of a let-up; ASC has expanded well beyond New England into the Western U.S. ski market. Frequent-skier cards and all-mountain season passes encourage diehards to try all the resorts.

But let's back up a bit. Bethel's "modern" history dates from 1774, when settlers from Sudbury, Massachusetts, called it Sudbury Canada, a name reflected in the annual August Sudbury Canada Days festival. Another present-day festival, Mollyockett Day, commemorates one of the area's most intriguing historical figures, a Pequawket Indian woman named Mollyockett. She practiced herbal medicine among turn-of-the-19th-century settlers, including a baby named Hannibal Hamlin. Her remedies proved effective snatching from death in1809 Abraham Lincoln's future vice president. (The incident actually occurred in the Hamlin home on Paris Hill, southeast of Bethel.) Mollyockett died August 2, 1816, and is buried in the Woodlawn Cemetery on Rte. 5 in Andover.

Meanwhile, the name Bethel surfaced in 1796, when the town was incorporated. Agriculture sustained the community for another half a century, until the Atlantic and St. Lawrence Railroad connected Bethel to Portland in 1851 (and later to Montreal) and access to major markets shifted the economic focus toward timber and wood products, which remain significant even today.

North of Bethel, Andover (pop. 945) has become a word-of-mouth favorite among through-hikers and section hikers on the Appalachian Trail, which snakes by about eight miles to the west. It's Maine's southernmost town near the AT, and the hikers pile into Andover for a break in Aug. and Sept. after negotiating the Mahoosuc Range, one of the toughest parts of the AT.

East of Bethel are the communities of Locke Mills (officially in the town of Greenwood, pop. 725) and Bryant Pond (in the town of Woodstock, pop. 1,240), both with summer and winter recreational attractions. Northeast of Bethel is Rumford (pop. 6,750), a paper-manufacturing center whose favorite son was former Secretary of State Edmund Muskie.

SIGHTS

Covered Bridges

Often called the **Artist's Covered Bridge** because so many artists have committed it to canvas—an 1872 wooden structure stands alongside a quiet country road north of the Sunday River Ski Resort. In winter, one of the Sunday River Inn's cross-country-skiing trails ends at the bridge—a great way to see it. Kids love running back and forth across the unused bridge, and in summer they can swim below in the Sunday River. The bridge is 5.7 miles northwest of Bethel; take Rte. 2 toward Newry, turn left at the Sunday River Rd., then bear right at the fork. The bridge is well signposted, just beyond a small cemetery.

About 20 miles north of Bethel, the **Lovejoy Bridge,** in South Andover, built in 1867, is one of the lesser-visited of Maine's nine covered bridges. It's also the shortest. Spanning the Ellis River, a tributary of the Androscoggin, the 70-foot-long bridge is 0.25 mile east of Rte. 5, but not visible from the highway; it's about 7.5 miles north of Rumford Point. In summer, local kids use the swimming hole just below the bridge.

Artist's Covered Bridge

© MARY LYONS

Dr. Moses Mason House

Listed on the National Historic Register, the 1813 Federal-style Dr. Moses Mason House, Bethel Common, 14 Broad St., P.O. Box 12, Bethel 04217, 207/824-2908, not only is a beautifully restored eight-room museum but also serves as the headquarters of the very active **Bethel Historical Society.** Particularly significant are the hall murals painted by noted itinerant muralist Rufus Porter or his nephew Jonathan Poor. Dr. Moses Mason, a local physician, was elected to the U.S. Congress a dozen years after Maine statehood and served two terms as a Maine congressman. The museum is open Tues.–Sun. 1–4 PM, July–Labor Day; Tues.–Fri. Sept.–June; and by appointment other months. Admission is $3 adults, $1.50 children.

Bethel Historic District

At the Dr. Moses Mason House, or at the chamber of commerce, pick up a copy of the Bethel Historical Society's *Walking Tour of Bethel Hill Village,* detailing information on 29 buildings and monuments in the downtown area's Historic District, 10–14 Broad St., P. O. Box 12, Bethel, 04217, 207/824-2908, www .bethelhistorical.org. Officially, more than 60 structures are included in the district. Follow the self-guided route (allow about an hour) to appreciate the 19th- and 20th-century architecture that gives real cachet to Bethel's heart.

Flightseeing

Bethel Air Service, Northwest Bethel Rd., P.O. Box 786, Bethel 04217, 207/824-4321, runs on-demand scenic flights daily, all year, but the best time is mid-Sept.–early Oct., for the parade of leaf colors. A 20-minute flight along the Sunday River and over the Jordan Bowl is $25 a person. Call for reservations. Based at the airport on the outskirts of town, the air service is open daily 8 AM–8 PM in summer, 8 AM–5 PM in winter.

Paper Mill Tours

About 25 miles northeast of Bethel, the **Mead Westvaco Papers Group,** 35 Hartford St.,

© MARY LYONS

covered bridge, Newry

Western Lakes & Mountains

Rumford 04276, schedules fascinating two-hour mill tours July–Aug., beginning at 10 AM each Wednesday. Reservations are required for the free tours (207/369-2045). Be prepared to wear a hardhat and earplugs. No open-toed shoes, no children under 12. Once or twice a summer, there's a free half-day forest-and-mill tour(call for exact date); full-day forest tours, 7:15 AM–3 PM, occur Wednesdays July–Aug. Reservations are required for all tours.

PARKS AND PRESERVES

Step Falls Preserve

The Nature Conservancy's first Maine acquisition (in 1962), 24-acre Step Falls Preserve, Rte. 26, Newry, mailing address The Nature Conservancy, Maine Chapter, Fort Andross, 14 Maine St., Brunswick 04011, 207/729-5181, is ideal for family hiking—an easy, one-hour round-trip through the woods alongside an impressive series of cascades and pools. Pick up a trail map at the box in the parking area. Bring

© MARY LYONS

headquarters of the Bethel Historical Society at the 1813 Dr. Moses Mason House

a picnic and have lunch on the rocks along the way. The waterfalls are most dramatic in late spring; the foliage is most spectacular in fall; the footing can be dicey in winter. Trailhead for the preserve is on Rte. 26, eight miles northwest of Rte. 2 and 10 miles southeast of the New Hampshire border. Watch for The Nature Conservancy oak-leaf sign on the right, next to Wight Brook.

Grafton Notch State Park

Nestled in the mountains of western Maine, 3,192-acre Grafton Notch State Park, Rte. 26, Grafton Township, mailing address HC 61, Box 330, Newry 04261, 207/824-2912, off-season 207/624-6080, boasts splendid hiking trails, spectacular geological formations (some, such as **Screw Auger Falls,** almost in the drive-by category), and plenty of space for peace and quiet. It's hard to say enough about this lovely park, a must-visit. Bring a picnic.

The best (but not easiest) hike here is the **Table Rock Loop,** a 2.5-mile, moderate-to-strenuous two-hour circuit from the main trailhead (signposted Hiking Trails) at the edge of Rte. 26. The trailhead parking area is four

miles inside the park's southern boundary and 0.8 mile beyond the Moose Cave parking area. Part of the route follows the white-blazed Appalachian Trail, otherwise the trail is orange- and blue-blazed. Some really steep sections are indeed a challenge, but it's well worth the climb for the dramatic mountain views from aptly named Table Rock.

Another favorite hike, moderate to strenuous, goes up **Old Speck Mountain** (4,180 feet), third highest of 10 Maine 4,000-footers and part of the Mahoosuc Range. The 28-foot-high viewing platform on the recently restored fire tower gets you above the wooded summit for incredible 360-degree views of the White Mountains, the Mahoosuc Range, and other mountains and lakes. Allow a solid seven hours for the eight-mile round-trip from the trailhead on the west side of Rte. 26 in Grafton Notch. The route follows the white-blazed Appalachian Trail most of the way; the tower is about 0.25 mile off the AT. Although there's a route map at the trailhead (same location as for the Table Rock hike), the best trail guide for this hike is in John Gibson's *50 Hikes in Southern and Coastal Maine,* second edition.

Park admission is $2 adults, $1 children 5–11;

payment is on the honor system. Fee boxes are posted at Screw Auger Falls and the main hiking trailhead. The park is officially open mid-May–mid-Oct., but Screw Auger Falls is easily accessible off season.

If you're driving along Rte. 26 early or late in the day, keep a lookout for moose; have your camera ready and exercise extreme caution. You'll usually spot them in boggy areas, munching on aquatic plants, but when they decide to cross a highway, watch out—unlike the rest of us, they don't look both ways. And their eyes don't reflect headlights, so be vigilant after dark. Moose-car collisions are too often fatal—to both moose and motorists.

The Mahoosuc Range

South and east of Grafton Notch State Park is a 27,253-acre chunk of Maine Public Reserve Land known as **The Mahoosucs,** or the Mahoosuc Range, where the hiking is rugged and strenuous but the scenic rewards are inestimable. The Appalachian Trail traverses much of the reserve, and AT hikers insist that the mile-long Mahoosuc Notch section, between Old Speck and Goose Eye Mountains, is one of their biggest challenges on the 2,158-mile Georgia-to-Maine route, requiring steep ascents and descents, with insecure footing, gigantic boulders, and narrow passages. If you're an experienced hiker, go for it, and use reliable guidebooks and maps, preferably USGS maps. The best overview of the reserve is *Recreational Opportunities in the Mahoosuc Mountains,* a free foldout map/brochure available from the Bureau of Parks and Lands, 22 State House Station, Augusta 04333, 207/287-3821, or the Western Region Office, Bureau of Parks and Lands. PO Box 327, 129 Main St., Farmington 04938, 207/778-8231. The helpful brochure lists and characterizes trails, lists campsites, and provides info on wildlife, vegetation, and water supplies.

White Mountain National Forest

Just under 50,000 acres (49,800 to be exact) of the 770,000-acre White Mountain National Forest, www.fs.fed.us/r9/white, lie on the Maine side of the New Hampshire border. Rte. 113, roughly paralleling the border, bisects the **Caribou-Speckled Mountain Wilderness,** the designated name for this part of the national forest. It's all dramatically scenic, with terrific opportunities for hiking, camping, picnicking, swimming, and fishing.

A drive along Rte. 113, north to south between Gilead and Stow, is worth a detour. It takes about 30 minutes nonstop, but bring a picnic and enjoy the mountain views from the tables at the Cold River Overlook, about a mile south of the Evans Notch highpoint. Rte. 113 is too narrow for bikes in midsummer, when logging trucks and visitor traffic can be fairly dense. Save this bike tour for a fall weekday, and take it south to north for a good downhill run from Evans Notch. The road is closed in winter.

RECREATION

Hiking

Much of the hiking in this area is within the various parks and preserves, but a fun family hike not in that category is the easy-to-moderate ascent of **Mt. Will** in Newry, on the outskirts of Bethel. The Bethel Conservation Commission has developed a 3.2-mile loop trail that provides mountain and river views; allow about 2.5 hours to do the loop. At the chamber of commerce information center, pick up a Mt. Will trail-map brochure, which explains three different hiking options. There also may be maps at the trailhead, which is on the west side of Rte. 2/26, 1.9 miles north of the Riverside Rest Area—a terrific spot, incidentally, for a post-hike picnic next to the Androscoggin River.

Canoeing

The rivers in the Bethel area are a paddler's dream, ranging from beginner/family stretches to whitewater sections for intermediate and advanced canoeists. Fortunately, the major artery, the **Androscoggin River,** seldom has low-water problems, and you'll see lots of islands, as

LLAMA TREKKING

In 1988, Steve Crone introduced llama trekking to Maine, and he's still at it, even more enthusiastically, offering one-day and multiday trips in the White Mountain National Forest. Be forewarned, though: You'll be hiking *with* the llamas, not *on* them; they tote the gear. Schedules can vary, so call well ahead to reserve. Most popular choice is the **Scenic Day Trek,** a four-to-six-hour hike departing about 9:30 AM from the Telemark Inn, 10 miles west of Bethel. Cost is $85 adults, $65 children under 14, including a buffet lunch en route.

Basic rooms are available at Steve's casually rustic **Telemark Inn Wilderness Lodge** ($95 d in spring, summer, and fall, including breakfast), where lots of possible lodging/ trekking packages incorporate nature hikes, mountain biking, canoeing, or llama treks. Three- to seven-day activity packages are $425–825 per adult, $285–625 for kids, including meals; a six-day mountains-and-lakes llama trek is $950 per adult.

In winter, cross-country skiing and sleigh rides are on the schedule. Steve has also introduced *skijoring,* a fun sport best compared to mushing without a sled. Strap on your skis, strap yourself into a harness, and a couple of huskies whisk you off on the trails. For more information, contact the Telemark Inn Wilderness Lodge, King's Hwy., RFD 2, Box 800, Bethel 04217, 207/836-2703, www.telemarkinn.com.

well as eagles, moose, and a beaver dam. West of Bethel, there's even an old cable from a onetime ferry crossing. The best source of information on the Androscoggin is Bethel Outdoor Adventures (BOA), 121 Mayville Rd., Rte. 2, Bethel 04217, 207/824-4224 or 800/533-3607, www.betheloutdooradventure.com, a firm founded in 1990. They'll provide canoe rentals ($52 for the day, including the shuttle), maps, shuttle service, and trip-planning advice. In addition, the BOA staff, especially owners Jeff and Pattie Parsons, can advise on canoeing the Ellis, Little Androscoggin, and Sunday

Rivers. They also offer kayak ($35 full day) and mountain-bike ($27/day) rentals.

Also see *Festivals and Events,* below, for information on the annual Androscoggin River Source to the Sea Canoe Trek, a celebration of the river's revival from years of unbridled pollution caused primarily by paper-mill runoff.

Just east of Locke Mills, before the Littlefield Beaches Campground, 207/875-3290, www.littlefieldbeaches.com, you can put in at **Round Pond,** on the south side of Rte. 26, and continue on into North and South Ponds. Bring a picnic and before you head out, enjoy it across the road at the lovely state rest area, with grills and covered picnic tables in a wooded setting.

Veteran professional guides Polly Mahoney and Kevin Slater of **Mahoosuc Guide Service,** 1513 Bear River Rd., Newry 04261, 207/824-2073, www.mahoosuc.com, lead wilderness canoe trips not in the Bethel area but on the Allagash, Penobscot, and St. John Rivers, as well as in Quebec. With extensive wilderness backgrounds in such locales as Labrador and the Yukon Territory, management experience with Outward Bound, a flair for camp cooking, and a commitment to Native American traditions, Polly and Kevin are ideal trip leaders. Request a brochure with their schedules and rates.

Golf

Thanks to its spectacular setting, the 18-hole championship course at the **Bethel Inn & Country Club,** Bethel Common, Bethel 04217, 207/824-2175, www.bethelinn.com, wows every golfer who plays here. Starting times are definitely needed, and caddies are available. In summer, luncheon is served on the inn's Millbrook Terrace, overlooking the course. (The restaurant is named after one of the course's little challenges—a dam between tee and green on the third hole.) Special golf packages are available, including meals, greens fees, and several lodging options. Best bargains are mid-Sept.–Oct., when the fall foliage is a bonus. The course is open early May–Oct.

There is a world-class 18-hole course at Sunday River Ski Resort, 207/824-3000, www .sundayriver.com.

Winter Sports

Sprawling octopus-like over eight mountains, **Sunday River Ski Resort,** Sunday River Rd., Newry, mailing address P.O. Box 450, Bethel 04217, 207/824-3000 or 800/543-2754, snow phone 207/824-6400, www.sundayriver.com, defines the winter sports scene in this area, with world-class downhill skiing and snowboarding, ice-skating, access to nordic skiing, phenomenal snowmaking capability, slopeside lodging, and every possible amenity. The mega-resort has nine quads, four triples, two doubles, and three surface lifts serving 127 trails and glades, including more than 14 miles of expert terrain. Highest vertical drop is 2,340 feet, about 500 feet lower than at Sugarloaf/USA—long a competitive rival but now under the same American Skiing Company corporate umbrella.

Sunday River's trademarked Perfect Turn ski clinics, pegged as "skier development," have created hordes of enthusiastic new skiers and smoothed the style of intermediate skiers. And the resort's Learn-to-Ski in One Day Program is more than just a slogan. It works.

Sunday River has day-care facilities in three locations (reservations advised), ski school for kids, an excellent inventory of top-of-the-line rental skis and snowboards, free on-mountain trolley-bus service, and plenty of places, with a wide range of prices, to grab a snack or a meal. Call or check web for current ticket prices.

The ski season usually runs mid-Oct. to early May, weather permitting (average annual snowfall is 155 inches). Lift hours are weekdays 9 AM–4 PM, weekends and holidays 8 AM–4 PM. Especially on weekends and during school vacations, make every effort to avoid the opening and closing hours for buying lift tickets, renting skis, or heading home; the congestion can be maddening. There's only one road on and off the mountain, so expect delays early and late in the day.

Mt. Abram: For anyone weak in the wallet or overawed by Sunday River, there's help about 12 miles to the east. **Mt. Abram,** Howe Hill Rd., off Rte. 26, Locke Mills 04255, 207/875-5002, www.skimtabram .com, a low-key, well-managed, family-oriented ski area where the vertical drop is a respectable-enough 1,030 feet. Two double-chairlifts and three T-bars serve 36 trails, almost half of which are intermediate level. Winter 2005, adult weekend lift tickets were a reasonable $41 a day (on Thursdays, lift tickets are half price). Snowmaking coverage is about 75 percent, top to bottom, and 12 trails are lighted for night skiing Thurs.–Sat. and during school vacations (adults $15). In addition to a ski school, rentals, a 600-foot snow-tubing park, and ice-skating rink, Mt. Abram has such facilities as day care (by reservation only), cafeteria, and the Westside Lodge. Unlike other ski areas, Mt. Abram has not been distracted by rushing to build slopeside housing, although there are a few condos near the mountain's base. See *Accommodations,* below, for help finding lodging close to the mountain.

Nordic Skiing: The **Sunday River Cross Country Ski Center,** 23 Skiway Rd., RR2, Box 1688, Bethel 04217, 207/824-2410, www.sundayriverinn.com, based at the independent Sunday River Inn, is not officially part of the Sunday River operation, but it's conveniently only 0.5 mile away. Nearly 25 miles of lovely, well-groomed wooded trails extend out from the center. The best one leads from the lodge to the Artist's Covered Bridge. A clever innovation is the free *Kids' Trail Map,* showing locations of special surprises along the trails (totem pole, wind chimes, and more). Trail passes range from $8 for a child under 12, to $16 for an adult; ski rentals, for $10–16, are available in the small lodge, which also has a snack bar.

Right in downtown Bethel, the **Bethel Inn Touring Center,** Bethel Common, P.O. Box 49, Bethel 04217, 207/824-6276, www.caribourecreation.com, uses its scenic golf course for nearly 25 miles of novice-to-advanced cross-country trails. The ski shop has a wax room and snack bar with seating areas. Ski rentals are available ($16 for the day, as are private and group lessons. Trail passes are $16 adults, $11 children.

About 30 miles of trails wind through a thousand acres at **Carter's Cross-Country Ski Center,** Middle Intervale Rd., Bethel 04217, 207/539-4848, www.cartersxcski.com, owned and managed by Carter's Cross-Country Ski Center in Oxford, 207/539-4848. In winter, the Bethel location operates a lodge, a ski shop, and snack bar and rents skis and snowshoes. Daily rates are $12 adults, $8 for children, and $20 for racing skis.

The Telemark Inn, www.telemarkinn.com, (see *Accommodations* below) also maintains cross-country trails. Snow fun at the Telemark doesn't stop there; snowshoeing, dog sledding, ice-skating and skijoring (which combines cross-country skiing and dog sledding) are other options at this unique operation.

Ice-Skating: Picture an old-fashioned Currier & Ives winter landscape, with skaters skimming a snow-circled pond, and you'll come close to the scene on Bethel Common in winter. Bring a camera. The groomed ice-skating area, in the downtown Historic District, usually is ready for skaters by Christmas vacation. Also see details above on Sunday River Ski Resort and Mt. Abram, both of which have ice-skating rinks.

Mushing: When they're not off leading three- or four-day dogsledding trips in the Mahoosucs or on Umbagog Lake ($450–525 pp), or even with the Inuit in Nunavut (formerly Baffin Island; $4,500 pp) or the Cree in Quebec ($2,900 pp), Kevin Slater and Polly Mahoney of **Mahoosuc Guide Service,** 1513 Bear River Rd., Newry 04261, 207/824-2073, www.mahoosuc.com, will bundle you in a deerskin blanket and take you on a one-day dogsled trip on Umbagog Lake, beyond Grafton Notch State Park. Wear goggles or sunglasses; the dogs kick up the snow. A campfire lunch and warm drinks are included in the $225 pp fee. Trips are only available Tues.–Thurs., mid-Dec.–mid-Mar., and they're *very* popular; book well in advance.

ENTERTAINMENT

The **Mahoosuc Arts Council** (MAC), P.O. Box 534, Bethel 04217, 207/824-3575, www.mahoosucarts.org, sponsors more than a dozen performances throughout the year, plus about a dozen art residencies and other cultural events in local schools. An additional source of MAC schedule information is the Bethel Area Chamber of Commerce.

The four-screen **Casablanca Cinema,** Cross St., Rtes. 2 and 26, Bethel 04217, 207/824-8248, www.compuflare.com/casablanca, was the first step in the ambitious Bethel Station development project—a Renaissance that hasn't occurred, but the cinema continues. In addition to one or two nightly showings on each screen, there usually are two matinees on Saturday and Sunday. Monday is bargain day ($4 tickets). Regular rates are $6 adult evenings, $4 children. Open all year.

At **Sunday River Ski Resort,** there's live entertainment in several locations weekends and during school vacations.

FESTIVALS AND EVENTS

During the ski season, both Sunday River Ski Resort and Carter's Cross Country Ski Center in Bethel schedule a number of ski races, festivals, and other special events. Check with the resort and the center or with the Bethel Area Chamber of Commerce, 207/824-2282 or 800/442-5826, www.bethelmaine.com. For more happenings within reasonable driving distance, see the events listings for the Rangeley Lakes Area, Oxford Hills, and Sebago and Long Lakes.

On the nearest March or April Saturday to April Fools' Day, Bethel's **April Fools' Pole, Paddle, and Paw Race** pits two-person triathlon teams against one another in nordic skiing, canoeing, and snowshoeing. Events begin at the Sunday River Cross-Country Ski Center.

The first or second weekend of June, the annual three-day **Trek Across Maine: Sunday River to the Sea** draws nearly 2,000 cyclists for the 180-mile bike expedition from

Bethel to Rockport, proceeds from which benefit the Maine Lung Association. Registrations are accepted on a first-come, first-served basis, and the trek usually is fully booked by April. Pledges are required, and there's a registration fee. Call 800/458-6472 for details. Don't like cycling? Perhaps the **Androscoggin River Source to the Sea Canoe Trek** is more your style: The annual 19-day paddle (last weekend in June to mid-July) from the New Hampshire headwaters to Fort Popham, near Bath—about 170 miles—is open to all canoeists, who can participate on any leg of the journey. A contribution is requested, to benefit the Androscoggin Land Trust, 207/527-2918, www.androscogginriver.net.

Bethel's **Annual Gem, Mineral, and Jewelry Show** is a long-running event with exhibits, demonstrations, and sales of almost everything imaginable in the rock-and-gem line—even guided field trips to nearby quarries. Hours are Sat. 9 AM–5 PM and Sun. 10 AM–4 PM; admission is $2. It takes place at Telstar Regional High School the second weekend in July. The third Saturday in July, on Bethel Common in downtown Bethel, **Mollyockett Day** commemorates a legendary turn-of-the-19th-century Native American healer with a parade, children's activities, a craft fair, food booths, and fireworks. There's also usually an oddball race—a couple of years it was wheeled beds, another year it was spouse-carrying.

Andover presents a parade, live entertainment, children's games, art and flower shows, antique cars, a barbecue, and a beanhole bean supper the first weekend in August as part of **Andover Old Home Days.** The second weekend that month at the Moses Mason House in Bethel, **Sudbury Canada Days** commemorates Bethel's earliest settlers with traditional crafts, an art show, parade, croquet, bean supper, and contradance.

Maine artisans take center stage in the annual display and sale at the **Blue Mountains Arts and Crafts Festival,** held the second weekend in October at the Sunday River Ski Resort, Newry.

SHOPPING

Books

Books-N-Things of Bethel, 85 Main St., P.O. Box 112, Bethel 04217, 207/824-0275 or 800/851-3219, provides the kind of personal service that no chain bookstore could ever achieve. Besides carrying a select inventory in her two-room shop, Sandy Dennis is ready with suggestions and will order anything. The shop, open all year, is in the carriage house of the historic Holidae House B&B, owned by Sandy and her husband.

Gifts and Crafts

Check out the strikingly unusual designs and glazes at **Bonnema Potters,** 146 Main St., P.O. Box 53, Bethel 04217, 207/824-2821, mainebiz.com, located in a handsomely restored studio across the street from the Sudbury Inn. Best of all are the earth colors used on tiles, dishes, vases, and lamps. The shop is open year-round daily 9:30 AM–5 PM, closed Wed.

If something a bit more offbeat appeals, stop in for Moose-Drop earrings, allegedly the genuine article, at **Maine Line Products,** 23 Main St., P.O. Box 356, Bethel 04217, 207/824-2522, source of whimsical souvenirs for your whimsical friends. In the same vein is the "Lobsta Parts Jewelry," but Maine Line also carries serious gifts, such as jams, syrup, fudge, buckets, and wind chimes. The shop is open all year, Mon.–Sat. 9 AM–5 PM (to 8 PM in summer), Sun. 10 AM–4 PM In 1997, owner Richard Whitney expanded his Maine Line empire to a former supermarket on Rte. 26 in Locke Mills, 800/874-0484, The "branch" shop, triple the size of the Bethel store, is open all year, same hours as in Bethel.

Gems and Minerals

At **Mt. Mann Jewelers,** 57 Main St. Place, P.O. Box 597, Bethel 04217, 207/824-3030, www.mtmann.com, Jim Mann wears the hats of owner, miner, gemcutter, and jeweler, and he's full of information in every category. Here's the Bethel area's best place to see Maine's special gems: **tourmaline** (the official state mineral), aquamarine, amethyst, and morganite. The shop also has a basement "crystal cave," where kids can "discover" minerals and learn to identify them. For $0.50, Jim has free maps to area mines and quarries open to the public. Inquire about guided quarry tours. The shop is open all year, 9 AM–5 PM Tues.–Fri. and 10 AM–5 PM Sat.

Also see **Oxford Hills** for information on Perham's of West Paris, Maine's mother of all rock shops.

Natural Foods and Farmers Markets
The **Good Food Store,** Rte. 2, P.O. Box 467, Bethel 04217, 207/824-3754 or 800/879-8926, www.goodfoodbethel.com, stocks a huge array of goodies, from organic produce to healthful munchies to cookbooks to gourmet condiments. Create an instant picnic with sandwiches, beer, and wine. If you're renting a condo and don't feel like cooking or eating out, you can pick up homemade soups, stews, and casseroles to go. The barn-based shop is open all year, daily 9 AM–8 PM.

Each Sat., 9 AM–noon, mid-June–mid-Oct., the **Bethel Farmers Market** sells good-for-you produce and other items on Rte. 26, Railroad St., next to Bethel Family Health Care, at the southern edge of town.

ACCOMMODATIONS

Conveniently, the **Bethel Area Chamber of Commerce Reservations Service,** 800/442-5826, www.bethelmaine.com, provides toll-free lodging assistance for more than a thousand beds in B&Bs, motels, condos, and inns in Bethel, at Sunday River Ski Resort, and farther afield. If you're planning a winter visit, however, particularly during Thanksgiving and Christmas holidays, February school vacation, and the month of March, don't wait until the last minute. Procrastination will put you in a bed 40 miles from the slopes.

Keep in mind that peak season (ergo highest room rates) in this part of Maine is in *winter,* not summer. Some lodgings also have

higher rates for fall foliage in September and October.

Sunday River Lodging
On the mountain at Sunday River Ski Resort, lodging options include 425 rooms and suites in two full-service hotels—the **Grand Summit** and the new **Jordan Grand Hotel**—as well as more than 700 slopeside condos and townhouses in seven different clusters. Nicest (and priciest) of the latter are the Locke Mountain Townhouses. The spiffy Jordan Grand, has restaurants and cafés, indoor/outdoor heated pool, tennis courts, video game room, and lots of extra amenities. Most of its rooms have full kitchen facilities. Except for dorm rooms, lodging packages include lift tickets. Prices for accommodations and activity packages vary widely (207/824-3000; reservations: 800/543-2754; www.sundayriver.com).

Country Inns
The **Bethel Inn & Country Club,** Bethel Common, P.O. Box 49, Bethel 04217, 207/824-2175 or 800/654-0125, www.bethelinn.com, centerpiece of a classic New England village scene, has 57 inn rooms and 40 modern one- and two-bedroom townhouses. Numerous packages are available, some include discounted Sunday River tickets and free skiing on the inn's trails; two-night minimum (three nights during Christmas and February vacations). Most summer packages include free golf on the inn's course. two-night minimum. Children are free, summer and winter. Lowest rates are mid-May to mid-June and November to mid-December. Other packages are available. Rooms vary widely in decor and quality; upgrading is an ongoing process here. If you can afford it, spring for a room in the new wing of the main inn. With six rate seasons, and six accommodation types, plus packages, rates vary widely. A standard summer room is $178 d, luxury townhouse $259 for the unit, during the winter holiday a standard room is $238 d, $319 for the townhouse. "Traditional Inn" rates are MAP (townhouses are not), including dinner in the inn's elegant restaurant

(candlelight and piano music; no blue jeans or T-shirts). The restaurant is open to the public daily, with New England cuisine and a good wine list, and dinner reservations are advisable. The inn's Millbrook Tavern and Terrace serves light meals in an informal setting; a pianist usually appears around 9 PM Friday and Saturday. All rooms include free use of the health club, with saunas, outdoor heated pool, and workout room. In winter, there's a free daily shuttle to Sunday River Ski Resort. Open all year, but the restaurant may be closed some nights in April and November.

Only 0.5 mile from Sunday River Ski Resort, the **Sunday River Inn,** 23 Skiway Rd., RR2, Box 1688, Bethel 04217, 207/824-2410, www.sundayriverinn.com, caters to families with its casual, homey atmosphere and generous buffet-style meals included in the MAP. Most of the 18 rooms have shared baths, $80 d., private bath rooms are $95. A big plus is the Sunday River Cross Country Ski Center right on the premises; cross-country trail passes are included in the room rates. Ice skating, hot tub, and sauna are further enticements. Dorm bunks (BYO sleeping bag) are available for $55. Children 2–12 are half price, children under 2, $10. Dinner is ample, served buffet style; BYOL. Open only in winter.

Bed-and-Breakfasts

Queen Victoria would feel right at home if she dropped into **The Victoria,** 32 Main St., P.O. Box 249, Bethel 04217, 207/824-8060 or 888/774-1235, www.thevictoria-inn.com, amid lots of lace and floral prints. Built in 1895, the Victoria became a B&B in 1998, and fifteen rooms are divided between the main house (five rooms, all with private baths) and the carriage house (10 rooms, also with private baths). A good hangout is the carriage house's second-floor cathedral-ceilinged sitting room, looking off to the woods. You'd never know you were in downtown Bethel. Four suites in the carriage house are perfect for families. Rates for standard, superior, and deluxe guest are: Apr.–mid-June from $89 d weekday standard room to $215 d for the top suite on the weekend;

mid-June–mid-Oct., weekday standard room $99 d to top weekend suite $249 d.; lowest winter room $79 d. (mid-week), weekend and holiday rate for top suite is $279 d. A delicious breakfast is included. The Victoria's restaurant quickly became a magnet after it opened in three dining areas on the first floor. Reservations are essential. The restaurant is open Wed.–Mon., all year.

About midway between Bethel and the Sunday River ski area is GaryBrearley's **Briar Lea B&B,** 150 Mayville Rd., Rte. 2/26, Bethel04217, 207/824-4717 or 877/311-1299. Decor and details are topnotch in the 1845 house. Six attractive second- and third-floor rooms (private baths) are $99–109 d.; add $10 at the height of ski season. Full breakfast is included. In summer, request a back-facing room if noise bothers you—the highway is loud. Pets are allowed at the inn for $10 extra. Open all year. **The Jolly Drayman English Pub and restaurant** occupies two rooms on the first floor; it's open to the public Wed.–Mon. for moderately priced breakfasts and excellent dinners. Dinner reservations are essential on weekends at this popular spot. Reduced-rate ski packages are available, and you can save time by buying your lift tickets here.

The hospitality, the breakfasts, and the bottomless cookie jar arelegendary at the **Chapman Inn,** Bethel Common, Broad and Main Sts.,P.O. Box 206, Bethel 04217, 207/824-2657 or 877/530-1498, Sandra Frye and Fred Nolte's informal B&B (built 1865) in the heart of historic Bethel and just 10 minutes from the Sunday River ski area. Nine rooms (private and shared baths) are $59–109 d, depending on the season. The on-site sauna is a big hit after skiing, biking, or hiking. A 24-bed dormitory wing, popular with skiers, has rustic accommodations, a game room with cable TV, and reasonable rates ($33 pp, including breakfast). No pets. Open all year.

How about a B&B with a bookstore? Sandy and Scott Dennis took over the **Holidae House,** 85 Main St., Bethel 04217, 207/824-3400 or 800/882-3306, www.holidae-house.com, and installed their Books-N-Things shop in the carriage house. This B&B is another of Bethel's elegant Victorian manses, with a tin ceiling in the dining room and antiques and reproductions throughout. Seven first- and second-floor rooms all have intriguing details (#4 has stars on the ceiling), as well as private baths, phones, TV, and air-conditioning. Rates are $55–98 d. depending on room and season. Other options are a studio apartment (with kitchen facilities) and a three-bedroom apartment. Breakfast is continental and geared to vegetarians. No pets. Open all year.

Established in 1982, **A Prodigal Inn and Gallery,** 162 Mayville Rd., Rte. 2, Bethel 04217, 207/824-8884 or 800/320-9201, www.prodigalinn.com, was the first B&B in western Maine (then called the Douglass House). Tom and Marcey White, originally from Texas, purchased it from longtime innkeeper Barbara Douglass, who lived in the house for 52 years. The original family, the Twitchells, who helped found Bethel and built the house, lived in the house for 150 years. Six suites are $120–155 d, according to room and season, including a gourmet breakfast and homemade goodies for afternoon tea or snack. The "Gallery" refers to the bronze statuary created by Tom, a sculptor.

Down in the valley, where the Sunday River runs through its idyllic setting close to the ski area, the **Black Bear B&B,** 829 Sunday River Rd., Newry 04261, mailing address P.O. Box 55, Bethel 04217, 207/824-0908 800/222-2160, www.bbearbandb.com, exudes warmth. New owner is Julie Bullard. Guests have two lounges with books galore (and TV and internet if you must). Hot chocolate is always available. Outside, a hot tub awaits in winter, a heated swimming pool and tennis in summer. Six Colonial-style rooms with private bath are $85–125 d., including a full country breakfast. Open all year.

The Norseman Inn and Motel

Two buildings—a 200-year-old inn and a century-old converted barn—make up **The Norseman Inn and Motel,** Rte. 2, 134 Mayville Rd., P.O. Box 934, Bethel 04217, 207/824-2002, www.norsemaninn.com, two miles north of Bethel. Family-run and family-oriented, it's one of Bethel's most popular motel-style lodgings. The inn has eight rooms and a fireplace suite. In the barn/motel are 22 first- and second-floor rooms. Rates are categorized by midweek, weekend, and five separate seasons, inn range is $78–158, motel $45–158, suite $98–168. No pets. Also in the barn are a game room and coin-operated laundry room. A complimentary continental breakfast is served seasonally in one of the inn's lovely old first-floor rooms, next to a fireplace built of stones from all over the world. Open all year.

The Maine Houses

In a category all their own are the **Maine House,** the **Maine Farm House,** and the **Maine Mountain View House,** Lake Rd., Bryant Pond, 207/846-9131 or 800/646-8737, www.themainehouses.com, three attentively renovated buildings within shouting distance of each other in Bryant Pond, three miles from Mt. Abram ski area. Under a quirkily successful arrangement without resident innkeepers or managers, the houses cater primarily to groups but also are open to families or even individuals. Everyone shares the spacious kitchen facilities, typically with interesting dynamics. The Maine House, right on Lake Christopher with its own small beach, has nine rooms (7.5 baths) in a variety of configurations, and a steam room; the Maine Farm House, a more modern facility closer to Rte. 26, has seven rooms with private baths, and some handicapped-access. The Maine Mountain View House, just across Rte. 26, has seven rooms, seven baths, an indoor spa, and two living and dining rooms. All kinds of price configurations are possible, depending on sleeping arrangements and season; minimums are imposed during school-vacation weeks, call or check website for more information. Kids under 14 stay free in parents' room. No pets. Linens are provided. Open all year. The houses are just off Rte. 26 in Bryant Pond.

Campgrounds

Riverside Campground, 121 Mayville Rd., Rte. 2, Bethel 04217, 207/824-4224, newest campground in the area and closest to downtown Bethel, has 48 RV ($22 with full hookup) and tent sites ($16) on the banks of the Androscoggin River north of downtown Bethel. The family-oriented campground is under the same ownership as **Bethel Outdoor Adventures** (BOA), www.betheloutdooradventure.com, a recreational backup operation providing gear rentals and guided tours. Rent a canoe, kayak (day rate $52 canoe, $35 kayak, including shuttle service) or mountain bike ($27/day); BOA will shuttle you upriver on the Androscoggin for a leisurely downstream paddle. Both the campground and BOA are open daily, May–Oct.

Well-maintained **Littlefield Beaches Campground,** Rte. 26, Locke Mills, mailing address RR2, Box 4300, Bryant Pond 04219, 207/875-3290, www.littlefieldbeaches.com, has mini-golf, horseshoes, playgrounds, canoe/kayak rentals, general store, laundry, weekly cottage rental, seasonal sites and more; it caters primarily to the RV trade with 130 sites, and has a terrific 40-acre location with a sandy beach on South Pond. Facilities include a playground, store, and coin-operated laundry room. Canoe and paddleboat rentals are available. Rules are enforced, including the campground's ban on water scooters (PWCs). Pets are allowed, but not on the beach; the store has pooper-scoopers you can borrow. Rates are $26 and $28, the latter for a waterfront site. Open mid-May–Sept.

On Rte. 113, west of Bethel, is the seven-acre **Hastings Campground,** one of several campgrounds in the White Mountain National Forest. The 24-site campground is primitive, with no hookups or showers, but does have vault toilets, hand pump for water, fishing and hiking, and is handicapped-accessible. Rte. 113 is especially scenic, so this is a prime location for extensive hiking in the national forest. Trail information and maps are available from the Evans Notch Ranger District office (see *Information and Services*

below). The campground is in Gilead, three miles south of Rte. 2. Base rate for a campsite is $16. For reservations call 877/444-6777. Open mid-May–mid-Oct.

Seasonal Rentals

For weekly or monthly seasonal rentals, winter or summer, contact **Rentals Unlimited,** 2 Main St., Bethel 04217, 207/824-4044 or 800/535-2220, www.rentalsunltd.com. Options include B&Bs, inns, condos, motels, and private houses. For school-vacation weeks, be sure to call well ahead, or your choices will be more limited than unlimited.

Maine Street Realty & Rentals, 207/824-2114, www.mainestreetrealty.com, also can arrange seasonal rentals.

FOOD

On the mountain at Sunday River Ski Resort, your choices are snack bars, pubs, an Italian restaurant, a steakhouse, and casually fancy hotel restaurants. Off the mountain, in addition to the listings below, dining options include the **Bethel Inn, The Victoria,** and the **Briar Lea's Jolly Drayman English Pub and Restaurant.**

Part of a Maine chain founded in Orono, **Pat's Pizza,** Rte. 2, Bethel 04217, 207/824-3637, has a quasi-lumberjack theme. Choose from more than four dozen hot and cold subs ($3–7), or 14-inch pizzas in the $7–15 range; gourmet 14-inchers are about $15. "Little Logger Portions" are for kids under 12. Pat's is open all year, daily 11 AM–9 PM (to 10 PM Fri.–Sat.).

Inexpensive to Moderate

A homey atmosphere (a wall of books in one room), reliable food, and friendly service have made **Mother's,** 43 Main St., P.O. Box 771, Bethel 04217, 207/824-2589, a popular destination ever since it opened. The something-for-everyone menu includes a great crab-cake sandwich for lunch; dinner entrées are in the $10–20 range (try the meatloaf). On the first floor of a renovated home with about 75 seats in small, separate dining rooms and an enclosed porch (plus outdoor porch in summer), Mother's is open daily, 11:30 AM–2:30 PM and 5–9 PM, year-round.

Down the street from Mother's, **Café Di Cocoa,** 125 Main St., Bethel 04217, 207/824-5282, is a meat-free, seafood-free zone, vegetarian all the way. Its name is cleverly derived from that of co-owner: Cathy diCocco. Mediterranean and other ethnic specialties (most under $15) demand your attention. Then there's the café's trademark "gentle dining," a Saturday-night (6:45 PM) candlelight-dinner experience during ski season. The five-course, *prix fixe* dinner (BYOL) is by reservation only. Great baked goods come out of these kitchens, too. The café is open all year except May: weekends for breakfast, Thurs.–Sun. for lunch, Thurs.–Fri. for dinner (plus Sat. when there's gentle dining).

A new vegan café and bakery, **Taste of Eden,** 188 Mountain View Mall, Bethel, 207/824-8939, concentrates on food from scratch, everything is homemade from whole foods, even condiments; wheat-free dishes are usually on the menu. Breakfast and lunch are served all day; a typical price is $4.99 for an entrée, $3.50 for a soup. Open Sun.–Thurs. 7 AM–4 PM, Fri. 7 AM–2 PM.

Glass walls surround the bustling brewery at the **Sunday River Brewing Company,** 1 Sunday River Rd. at Rte. 2, P.O. Box 847, Bethel 04217, 207/824-4253, producer of Reindeer Rye, Black Bear Porter, and Brass Balls Barley Wine. This is a lively place, probably because the menu is step above typical pub fare. Entrées average $15, but there are lots of options for less than that. Live music Fri. and Sat. nights in winter, sometimes also in summer. Free half-hour brewery tours are available only by appointment. The brewpub, at the junction of Rte. 2 and Sunday River Rd., is open all year, daily 11:30 AM–12:30 AM (food service ends at 10 PM).

Moderate to Expensive

Although **The Sudbury Inn,** 151 Main St., Bethel 04217, 207/824-2174 or 800/395-7837, www.sudburyinn.com, has guest rooms, it's best known for its kitchen. This warmly retrofitted 1873 hostelry has several separate dining areas. Entrée range is $18–29 (more if you order lobster), but there's no surcharge for sharing; the rack of lamb is superb. Reservations are essential at this popular spot, especially on weekends and holidays. The restaurant is open daily 5–9 PM, all year. On the lower level is the **Suds Pub,** 207/824-6558, a very relaxing hangout with a moderately priced menu of appetizers, burgers, soups, salads, pizza, and a few entrées. Thursday night, there's live music until 1 AM, something to remember if you're spending the night in one of the inn's 17 guest rooms and suites ($79–199 d, including breakfast; private baths), and there is a separate apartment for $240–350 d. The inn is open year round.

INFORMATION AND SERVICES

Next door to the Casablanca Cinema, at the Bethel Station, is the handsome **Bethel Area Chamber of Commerce,** Cross St., P.O. Box 1247, Bethel 04217, 207/824-2282 or 800/442-5826, www.bethelmaine.com, among the state's most energetic chamber organizations. The office is open all year; summer hours are Mon.–Fri. 9 AM–6 PM, Sat., 9 AM–5 PM, Sun. noon–5 PM. The building has public restrooms.

Located just north of Bethel, the Evans Notch Information Center for the Evans Notch Ranger District of the **White Mountain National Forest,** is at 18 Mayville Rd., Rte. 2, RR2, Box 2270, Bethel 04217, 207/824-2134, www.fs.fed.us/r9/white. Trail maps, campsite information, bird checklists, and other helpful wildlife brochures are all available here. Even in summer, the office may be closed at unexpected times; call for hours.

Newspapers

Published every Thursday since 1895, *The Bethel Citizen,* 207/824-2444, www.bethelcitizen.com, thoroughly covers Bethel and the surrounding area, with extensive calendar listings. The *Citizen* also produces two extremely useful tabloid-style supplements, *Vacation in Bethel,* in winter and summer editions. Both are free and widely available at shops, lodgings, restaurants, and the chamber of commerce. The preferred daily newspaper is the *Lewiston Sun-Journal,* www.sun-journal.com.

Emergencies

For emergencies in Bethel, call 911. **The Bethel Family Health Center,** Railroad St., P.O. Box 977, Bethel 04217, 207/824-2193 or 800/287-2292, is a medical facility, not a hospital, but a physician or physician's assistant is always on call for emergencies. The **Rumford Hospital,** 420 Franklin St., P.O. Box 619, Rumford 04276, 207/369-1000, 24 miles from downtown Bethel, has a round-the-clock emergency room, 364-4581. The nearest major medical center is in Lewiston, 46 miles from Bethel.

At Sunday River Ski Resort, the **Western Maine Mountain Clinic,** South Ridge Base Area, 207/824-4900, is staffed for medical emergencies daily 9 AM–6 PM. Half a dozen **first-aid centers** are scattered throughout the resort.

Special Courses

Thanks to the Bethel area's spectacular scenery and relatively rugged terrain, two excellent outdoors-oriented programs have become well

established here. The Rockland-based **Hurricane Island Outward Bound School,** part of the national Outward Bound network, operates mountain-oriented wilderness courses from its center in Newry, 207/824-3152, course information 800/341-1744, www.hurricaneisland.org, a few miles beyond the Sunday River access road.

Eight miles southeast of Bethel, **The Maine Conservation School,** P.O. Box 188, Bryant Pond 04219, 207/665-2068, www.meconservationschool.org, founded in the 1960s, covers 100 acres on the shore of Lake Christopher. Environmental education is the focus for weekend and week-long hands-on programs for students and teachers, and the school does an impressive job of instilling a conservation ethic in children and adults. Activities include hiking, survival skills, wildlife studies, and conservation work projects. Maine Guide trainings are also given.

In downtown Bethel, at the end of Broad St., is the onetime Gehring estate that houses the **NTL Institute,** 207/824-2151, www.ntl.org, established here in 1947 to offer courses in personal and professional development and human dynamics. The NTL bookstore is open to the public weekdays from early June–Sept.

Oxford Hills

Sandwiched between the Lewiston/Auburn area and the Bethel area, with Sebago and Long Lakes off to the south, the Oxford Hills region centers on Norway and South Paris. The town of Norway (pop. 4,740) shares the banks of the Little Androscoggin River with the community of South Paris, the major commercial center for the town of Paris.

From here it gets really complicated, although it's unlikely to affect a visitor. Oxford County's official seat is Paris (pop. 4,360), but all the relevant county offices are in South Paris. Next, throw into the mix the town of West Paris (pop. 1,620)—which is, in fact, mostly *north* of Paris and South Paris. Within the boundaries of West Paris is the hamlet of North Paris. Fortunately, there's no East Paris,

but there is the tiny enclave of Paris Hill, a pocket paradise many people never discover.

West Paris gained its own identity when it separated from Paris in 1957, but its traditions go way back. The Pequawket Indian princess Mollyockett, celebrated hereabouts as a healer, supposedly buried a golden treasure under a suspended animal trap, hence the name of Trap Corner for the junction of Rtes. 26 and 219. No such cache has been uncovered, but the corner is the site of the incredible gemstone collection at Perham's of West Paris. More recent traditions in West Paris come from Finland, home of many 19th- and early-20th-century immigrants who gravitated to a new life in this area. Finnish names are common on the town's voting registers.

Norway, fortunately, is far less complicated. The name, incidentally, comes not from Europe, or Norwegian settlers, but rather from a variation on a Native American word for waterfalls—cascades on the town's Pennesseewassee (PENN-a-see-WAH-see) Lake (called Norway Lake locally), which powered 19th-century mills. European settlement began in 1786.

Norway was the birthplace of C.A. Stephens (1844–1931), who for 55 years wrote weekly stories for a 19th-century boys' magazine, *Youth's Companion.* Colorfully reflective of rural Maine life, the entertaining tales were collected in *Stories from the Old Squire's Farm,* published in 1995.

Waterford (pop. 1,460) is a must-see, especially the National Historic District known as Waterford Flat or Flats—too pretty to believe, with classic homes and tree-lined streets alongside Keoka Lake in the shadow of Mount Tire'm. It's a 19th-century village frozen in time.

SIGHTS

Paris Hill and Hamlin Memorial Library

On Rte. 26, just beyond the northern edge of **South Paris,** a sign on the right marks one end of Paris Hill Road, a four-mile loop that reconnects farther along with Rte. 26. As you head uphill, past an old cemetery, you'll arrive at a Brigadoon-like enclave of elegant 18th- and 19th-century homes—a National Historic District with dramatic views off to the White Mountains and the lakes below. Centerpiece of the road is Paris Hill Common, a pristine park in front of the birthplace (not open to the public) of former Vice President Hannibal Hamlin (1809–91). South of the green stands the Hamlin Memorial Library P.O. Box 43, Paris Hill, Paris 04271, 207/743-2980, www.hamlin.lib.me.us (ex-Oxford County Jail), the only Paris Hill building open to the public, where you can bone up on the history of this pocket paradise.

Most children (and adults) get a kick out of entering a public library that once was a town jail. This one, built in 1822, held as many as 30 prisoners until 1896. Three prisoners somehow escaped in the 1830s, abandoning one of their pals stuck in the wall opening they had created. In 1902, the jail became the library, retaining the telltale signs of jail—bar hinges in the granite walls. Admission is free to the library's upper-level museum section, but donations are welcomed. The library has no heat, so be sure to dress warmly if you're here early or late in the season. Hours are Wed. 1:30–5:30 PM, Thurs.–Fri. 11:30–5:30, and Sat. 10 AM–2 PM.

If you're in the area on the first December weekend in an even-numbered year, inquire about the **Biennial Holiday House Tour,** when a dozen of these elegant homes, decorated exquisitely for Christmas, are open to the public, all to benefit the Paris Hill Community Club.

Perham's of West Paris

And now for something completely different. Welcome to rock-hound heaven! Perham's of West Paris, 194 Bethel Rd., Rte. 26, P.O. Box 280, West Paris 04289, 207/674-2342 or 800/371-4367, is part museum, part shop, and part counseling service. You can admire shelf after shelf of spectacular rare gems, buy cut and uncut gems and minerals, and get do-it-yourself advice for a family outing in the mineral-rich quarries of the Oxford Hills. Established in 1919 at the Trap Corner crossroads, Perham's sells books, videos, rock tumblers, metal detectors, gold pans, and all the tools you'll need for treasure-hunting. Request a free map of the five quarries they own. And good luck! The shop, at the junction of Rtes. 26 and 219, is open all year, 9 AM–5 PM daily May–Dec., Tues.–Sun. Jan.–Apr. Closed Thanksgiving, Christmas, and New Year's.

Global Maine

Posted almost casually on an undistinguished corner in western Maine is a roadside landmark that inevitably appears in any travel book or slide show with a sense of the whimsical. Nine markers direct bikers, hikers, or drivers to Maine communities bearing the names of international locales: **Norway, Paris, Denmark, Naples, Sweden, Poland, Mexico, Peru,** and **China.** All are within 94 miles of the sign, which stands at the junction of Rtes. 5 and 35 in the burg of Lynchville (part of Albany Township), about 14 miles west of Norway. If you approach the sign from the south on Rte. 35, you're likely to miss it; it's most noticeable when coming from the north on Rte. 35 or the west on Rte. 5.

PARKS AND PRESERVES
McLaughlin Garden

In 1997, a little miracle happened in South Paris. For more than 60 years, Bernard McLaughlin had lovingly tended his two-acre perennial garden alongside Rte. 26, eventually surrounded by commercial development, and he'd always welcomed the public into his floral oasis. In 1995, at the age of 98, McLaughlin died, stipulating in his will that the property be sold. Eager developers eyed it, but loyal flower fans dug in their heels, captured media attention, created a nonprofit foundation, and managed to purchase the property—the beginning of the little miracle. The McLaughlin Garden, 97 Main St., Rte. 26 and Western Ave., South Paris, mailing address: the McLaughlin Foundation, P.O. Box 16, South Paris 04281, 207/743-8820, www. mclaughlingarden.org, lives on, with its 98 varieties of lilacs, plus lilies and irises and so much more. Mid-May–late Sept., the gardens are open daily for self-guided tours. Admission is free, but donations are welcomed. The Garden Café, 207/739-2228, is open June–Aug., Wed.–Sat. 11 AM–3 PM. A gift shop in the house's front parlor carries gardening items and high-end crafts and gifts, mostly Maine-made. The shop is open daily 10 AM–5 PM in-season.

Snow Falls

A 300-foot gorge on the Little Androscoggin River is the eye-catching centerpiece of Snow Falls Rest Area, an easy-off-easy-on roadside park where you can commandeer a table alongside the waterfall. What better place for a relaxing picnic (no grills, some sheltered tables). Trucks whiz by on the highway, but the water's noise usually drowns them out. The rest area is on Rte. 26, about six miles north of the center of South Paris.

RECREATION

The most popular Oxford Hills hikes are particularly family-friendly—no killer climbs or even major ascents, no bushwhacking, just darned good exercise and some worthwhile views. From July to mid-August, don't be surprised to encounter clusters of summer campers, since camp counselors all over this region regularly gather up their kids and take them out on the trail or paddling the ponds. If you're spending more than a day hiking in this area, pick up a copy (at bookstores and gift shops) of *Hikes in and around Maine's Lake Region,* by Marita Wiser; it's the best available advice on this area.

Hiking

It's hard to resist a hike up **Mount Tire'm** (1,104 feet)—if only to disprove its name. Actually, it's supposedly a convolution of a Native American name. The only steep section is at the beginning, after the memorial marker dedicated to 19th-century Waterfordite Daniel Brown, for whom the trail (unblazed) is named. Allow an hour or so for the 1.5-mile round-trip, especially if you're carrying a picnic. From downtown Waterford (Rte. 35), take Plummer Hill Rd. about 300 feet beyond the community center; the trailhead is on the west side of the road; watch for the marker.

Straddling the Paris-Buckfield-Hebron town boundaries, **Streaked** (STREAK-ed) **Mountain** (1,770 feet) has a moderate, then easy trail to an expansive summit with an abandoned fire tower, wireless towers, and vistas as far as Mount Washington. Pack a picnic. If you're here in early August, take along a small pail to collect wild blueberries. Late Sept.–early Oct., it's indescribable, but remember to wear a hunter-orange hat or vest once hunting season has started—or tackle the trail on a Sunday, when there's no hunting. Allow about 1.5 hours for the one-mile round-trip, especially if you're picnicking and blueberrying. To reach the trailhead from South Paris, take Rte. 117 west to Streaked Mountain Rd., on the right (south). Turn and go about 0.5 mile. Park well off the road. (You can also climb Streaked from the east, but it's a much longer hike that requires waterproof footwear.)

Other good Oxford Hills hikes are **Hawk Mountain** (in Waterford; easy; 360-degree summit) and **Singlepole Ridge** (or Singlepole Mountain; in Paris; moderate).

Golf

At nine-hole **Paris Hill Country Club,** 355 Paris Hill Rd., Paris 04271, 207/743-2371, founded in 1899, you'll find a low-key atmosphere, reasonable greens fees, cart rentals, and a snack bar. No tee times are needed. The rectangular course has all straight shots; the challenges come from slopes and unexpected traps. Just off Rte. 26 on the outskirts of South Paris, and part of the Paris Hill Historic District, the club is open May–Oct.

It's not just golfers who patronize the nine-hole **Norway Country Club,** Lake Rd., Rte. 118, P.O. Box 393, Norway 04268, 207/743-9840; this is a popular spot to have lunch or kick back on the club porch. The mountain-lake scenery, especially in the fall, is awesome. Starting times not required; first-come, first-served. Established in 1929, the club is a mile west of Rte. 117. It's open late Apr.–mid-Oct.

Spectator Sports

If you're partial to guerrilla warfare on wheels, the place to be is **Oxford Plains Speedway,** Rte. 26, P.O. Box 208, Oxford 04270, 207/539-8865, www.oxfordplains.com, Maine's center for stock-car racing. From late April to mid-September, souped-up high-performance vehicles careen around the track in pursuit of substantial money prizes. All races begin at 6:30 PM.

Sauna

For anyone addicted to the sauna ritual, **Dave's Sauna Bath,** 20 Paris Hill Rd., South Paris 04281, 207/743-7409, is the best in this part of Maine—the adopted homeland of thousands of Finns. Dave Graiver has six saunas open daily 4–9 PM, all year. He charges $7 for "as long as you can stand it."

Winter Sports

Alpine skiing isn't an Oxford Hills sport, but not far away are the slopes at Sunday River Ski Resort, Mt. Abram, and Shawnee Peak.

The best Oxford Hills locale for **cross-country skiing** is Carter's Cross-Country Ski Center, Rte. 26, Box 710, Oxford 04270, 207/539-4848, www.cartersxcski.com/ox-fordtrails.html, with about 21 miles of groomed novice, intermediate, and advanced trails amid lovely frozen-lake scenery in the Welchville section of Oxford. Facilities include ski and snowshoe rentals, a well-equipped ski shop, plus snack bar, solarium, and sauna. Trail pass is $12 adults, $10 seniors, $8 students under 18. Kids under six are free.

ENTERTAINMENT

Marcel Marceau wannabes come to study at the nationally famed **Celebration Barn Theater,** 190 Stock Farm Rd., South Paris 04281, 207/743-8452, www.celebrationbarn.com, established in 1972 by the late mime master Tony Montanaro. Mime, juggling, dance, clowning, storytelling, and improv comedy performances are open to the public in the 125-seat barn on assorted Fridays and Saturdays (8 PM), July–Aug. Reservations are advisable. Ticket prices range from $8–10 for adults; $5–8 for children 12 and under. Pack a picnic supper and arrive early. The theater (signposted) is just off Rte. 117.

FESTIVALS AND EVENTS

For other events within a reasonable distance, see the events listings for Bethel and Vicinity, Sebago and Long Lakes, and the Lewiston/Auburn Area.

Wall-to-wall paintings are for sale along Main St. in downtown Norway for the **Sidewalk Art Festival,** the second Saturday in July, in which nearly 100 artists participate. The Norway Memorial Library holds its annual book sale at the same time, www.norway. lib.me.us. **Founders' Day** brings craft and antiques exhibits, music, and an antique-car open house on Paris Hill Common, Paris Hill, the third Saturday in July. Tickets are $7 adults, $3 kids. The name of North Waterford's **World's Fair** seems sort of cheeky for this three-day country medley of egg-throwing contests, talent show, live music, dancing, and more the fourth weekend in July.

Offering nonstop bluegrass, Friday evening to Sunday afternoon, the Record family's annual **Bluegrass Festival** draws about 3,000 spectators to the Rose-Beck Farm, 486 E. Oxford Rd., South Paris, the third weekend in August.

The family-oriented, four-day agricultural **Oxford County Fair,** "The Horse-Powered Fair," held in mid-September, features 4-H exhibits, a beauty pageant, a pig scramble, live entertainment, an apple-pie contest, and plenty of crafts and food booths at the Oxford County Fairgrounds.

SHOPPING
Art Galleries
The **Matolcsy Art Center,** 265 Main St., Norway 04268, 207/743-5411, showcase for the impressive Western Maine Art Group, sponsors exhibits, demonstrations, workshops, classes, and art auctions, as well as Norway's annual Sidewalk Art Festival. Founded in 1967 by Lajos Matolcsy (Ma-TOLL-she), the center occupies an old schoolhouse in downtown Norway. It's open July–Aug. and staffed by volunteers. Watch for "open" sign or call for hours.

Books, Gifts, and Crafts
Books-N-Things of Oxford, 1570 Main St., Suite 3, Oxford Plaza, Rte. 26, Oxford 04270, 207/743-7197, www.oxfordbooksnthings.com,

is one of those full-service bookstores that inspires you to buy more than you ever planned. It's open all year, daily 9 AM–8 PM in summer, Mon.–Sat. 9 AM–6 PM off-season.

Just beyond the Celebration Barn Theater, **Christian Ridge Pottery,** Christian Ridge Rd., South Paris 04281, 207/743-8419, www. applebaker.com, produces functional ceramic designs and *objets,* including a trademarked apple baker and a bagel cutter. You can see the work in progress at the shop, open Mon.–Sat. 10 AM–5 PM and Sun. noon–5 PM, Memorial Day weekend–Dec. Other months, it's open Mon.–Sat. 10 AM–4 PM.

Natural Foods and Farm Stands
Fare Share Market and Natural Foods Co-op, 443 Main Street, Norway 04268, 207/743-9044, www.faresharecoop.org, a membership organization, is also open to the public. Lots of bulk grains and locally grown (in season) organic produce, wine and beer. Open all year, Mon.–Fri. 10 AM–6 PM, Sat. 10 AM–4 PM.

Local produce, honey, organic meat, perennials, preserves, syrup, cheese, and baked goods are all part of the stock at **Norway Farmers Market,** which sets up downtown at Main and Deering Sts., in the parking lot of L.M.Longley's, Thurs. 2–6 PM.

ACCOMMODATIONS
Bed-and-Breakfasts
For a complete change of pace, back in time and back of beyond, **Morrill Farm Bed and Breakfast,** 85 Morrill Farm Rd., Sumner 04292, 207/388-2059, www.bbonline.com/ me/morrillfarm, a late-18th-century farm with three rustic second-floor rooms (shared bath) in the ell connecting the house and the barn. On the 217-acre spread are nature/cross-country-skiing trails, river fishing, and a menagerie of domestic farm animals. Rates are $75 d. Pets are kenneled on site for $15 a day. The farm is north and east of Norway/South Paris, a mile from Rte. 219 (West Sumner Road). Turn north on Greenwoods Rd. at Roll-In

Western Lakes & Mountains

Variety and continue a mile to Morrill Farm Rd. Dec.–Mar., open only by advance reservation to groups, with a two-day minimum.

Waterford

Waterford—that lovely little enclave flanked by Norway/South Paris, Bridgton/Naples, and the Lovells—has a couple of fine places to put your head.

Barbara and Rosalie Vanderzanden's traditionally elegant **Waterford Inne,** 258 Chadbourne Rd., Box 149, Waterford 04088, 207/583-4037, www.waterfordinne.com, an antiques-filled 19th-century farmhouse on 25 open and wooded acres, is a prime getaway spot. Five lovely rooms and a suite are $90 d (shared bath) or $110–150 d (private bath). A delicious breakfast is included; children are welcome. Pets are allowed for $15 extra. By advance reservation, the Vanderzandens will prepare a four-course dinner for guests and the public (about $35 pp; BYOL); spring for it, they do a wonderful job. No credit cards. The inn is close to East Waterford, 0.5 mile west of Rte. 37. Open all year.

You have to love bears (and who doesn't?) if you stay at the **Bear Mountain Inn,** Rte. 35, South Waterford 04081, 207/583-4404, www.bearmtninn.com, a beautifully updated 1820s B&B on 53 acres overlooking Bear Pond (it's really a lake). This is one of those places it's hard to leave—especially after you settle in on the pond-view terrace. And then there are the canoes and kayaks, and the beach. Enthusiastic innkeeper Lorraine Blais, a professional decorator, has created five bear-themed rooms (private and shared baths) for $120–160 d, plus luxury and family suites for $220–295, including breakfast. Two-night minimum on weekends. Across the road from the inn is a trail up Bear Mountain, and Hawk Mountain is just around the corner. Lorraine can set you up with all kinds of special activities—trail-riding, fishing, mountain biking in summer; snowmobiling, dogsledding, and ice-fishing in winter. No children under eight. No pets; there are cats, dogs, goats, and rabbits (not in the inn). Open all year.

FOOD

General Stores and Restaurants

Many people flock to **The Lake Store,** 14 Waterford Rd., Rtes. 117 and 118, Norway Lake, Norway 04268, 207/743-6562, just to check out the crazy collection of Coca-Cola memorabilia, but you can also load up with picnic fixings, pizza, liquor, groceries, and videos. Summer hours are daily 5 AM–9 PM; winter hours are daily 5 AM–7 PM and Sun. 6 AM–7 PM.

Across the road from Perham's of West Paris, **Trap Corner Store and Restaurant,** 227 Bethel Rd., Rtes. 26 and 219, West Paris 04289, 207/674-3300, serves up hearty comfort food in a casual, down-home atmosphere. No credit cards. It's open all year, Tues.–Sun. 6 AM–2 PM.

What's the most intriguing short-order menu item at **Melby's Market and Eatery,** Rte. 35, P.O. Box 28, North Waterford 04267, 207/583-4447 or 800/281-4437? The buffalo burger, made from bison raised right down the road at the Jones farm. A popular item, especially in summer, is Maine-made Gifford ice cream. Melby's has all the usual general-store stuff, plus 59 seats for eating in. The store is open all year, daily 6 AM–9 PM.

Inexpensive to Moderate

Located in a brick streetcar barn built in 1895, **The Trolley House Food and Spirits,** Main St., Norway 04268, 207/743-2211, specializes in seafood and Black Angus beef, but chicken and pasta are also available; Friday and Saturday are prime-rib nights. Dinner entrées are in the $13–19 range. The two dining rooms are air-conditioned. Open all year, Mon.–Sat., 11 AM–2 PM for lunch and 4:30–9 PM for dinner.

Moderate to Expensive

An unassuming exterior on a busy intown thoroughfare camouflages the pleasant interior at **Maurice Restaurant Français,** 109 Main St., Rte. 26, P.O. Box 317, South

Paris 04281, 207/743-2532, www.mauricer
estaurant.com. A veteran in this area, the
popular restaurant serves creditable French
cuisine in the $13–24 price range. Reserva-
tions are a good idea, especially on weekends.
Open all year, Mon.–Fri. 11:30 AM–1:30 PM
and 4:30–8:30 PM (to 9 PM Fri.), plus 4:30–
8:30 PM Sat. and 11 AM–2 PM and 4:30–
8:30 PM Sun.

INFORMATION AND SERVICES

The information center for the well-organized
Oxford Hills Chamber of Commerce, 213
Main St., South Paris 04281, 207/743-2281,
www.oxfordhillsmaine.com, is easy to find in
the midst of the South Paris commercial district. The center is open 9 AM–4 PM weekdays.
At other times, you can pick up brochures in
the kiosk out front.

Newspapers
Maine's oldest weekly, the *Advertiser Democrat,*
207/743-7011, www.advertiserdemocrat.com,
published each Thursday in Norway since
1826, carries local features, ads, and extensive
calendar listings. The daily newspaper providing best coverage of this area is the *Lewiston
Sun-Journal,* Norway office 207/743-9228,
www.sunjournal.com.

Emergencies
For police, fire, and ambulance emergencies,
in Norway, Oxford, South Paris, and Waterford, call 911.

Stephens Memorial Hospital, 181 Main St.,
Norway 04268, 207/743-5933, www.mainehealth
.com/wmh_about/wmhaffiliates_stephens.htm, a
well-regarded community hospital, has round-
the-clock emergency-room care. The nearest
major medical center is in Lewiston.

Fryeburg Area

Fryeburg (pop. 3,000), a crossroads community
on busy Rte. 302, is best known as the funnel
to and from the factory outlets, hiking trails,
and ski slopes of New Hampshire's North Conway and the White Mountains. Except during early October's annual extravaganza, the
giant Fryeburg Fair, Fryeburg seldom ends up
on anyone's itinerary. Too bad. The mountain-
ringed community has lots of charm, historic
homes, the flavor of rural life, and access to
miles of Saco River canoeing waters.

Incorporated in 1763, Fryeburg is Oxford County's oldest town; even earlier, it
was known as Pequawket, an Indian settlement and trading post—until skirmishes with
white settlers routed the Native Americans in
1725 during Dummer's War (also known as
Lovewell's War). Casualties were heavy on both
sides; Lovewell and the Pequawket chief were
among the fatalities.

In 1792, Fryeburg Academy, a private school
on Main Street, was chartered; the school's
Webster Hall is named after famed states-
man Daniel Webster, whose undistinguished

teaching career at the school began and ended
in 1802. Among the students at the time was
Rufus Porter, who later gained renown as a
muralist, inventor, and founder of *Scientific
American* magazine. Today the school is one
of a handful of private academies in Maine that
provide public secondary education, a uniquely
successful private/public partnership.

Just north of Fryeburg is the town of Lovell,
with three hamlets—known collectively as
"The Lovells"—strung along Rte. 5, on the
east side of gorgeous Kezar Lake. Anyone who
has discovered Kezar Lake yearns to keep it
a secret, but the word is out. The mountain-
rimmed lake is *too* beautiful.

Other areas relatively convenient to Fryeburg for restaurants, recreation, and other activities are Sebago and Long Lakes, Oxford
Hills, and Bethel.

SIGHTS
Covered Bridges
Two of Maine's nine covered bridges are within

striking distance of Fryeburg. In the hamlet of East Fryeburg, just west of Kezar Pond, 116-foot-long **Hemlock Bridge** was built in 1857. Beneath the bridge runs the "Old Saco," or "Old Course," a former channel of the Saco River. Best time to visit is July–Oct.; mud or snow can prevent car access other months, and June is buggy. From the Rte. 5/302 junction in Fryeburg, take Rte. 302 east 5.5 miles to Hemlock Bridge Road. Turn left (north) and go about three miles on a paved, then unpaved road to the bridge. Or paddle under the bridge on a detour from canoeing on the Saco River.

A bit farther south, 183-foot-long **Porter Covered Bridge,** linking Oxford and York Counties and the towns of Porter and Parsonsfield, spans the Ossipee River. Officially known as the **Parsonsfield-Porter Historical Bridge,** it was built in 1798, then rebuilt once or twice between 1858 and 1876. The bridge is just east of Rte. 160, about 0.5 mile from the center of Porter. From Fryeburg, take Rte. 5/113 to East Brownfield, then Rte. 160 to Kezar Falls and Porter.

RECREATION
Canoeing
The **Saco River,** headwatered in Crawford Notch, New Hampshire, meanders 84 miles from the Maine border at Fryeburg to the ocean at Saco and Biddeford. Its many miles of flatwater, with intermittent sandbars and a few portages, make it wonderful for canoeing, camping, and swimming, but there's the rub: the summer weekend scene on the 35-mile western Maine stretch looks like bumper boats at Disneyland. Aim for midweek in late September, and early October, when the foliage is spectacular, the current is slower, noise levels are lower, and the crowds are busy elsewhere. For a relaxing trip, figure about two miles an hour and you can do the Fryeburg-to-Hiram segment with two overnight stops, including a couple of interesting side-trip paddles—to Hemlock Bridge, Pleasant Pond, and Lovewell's Pond. If you put in at Swan's Falls in Fryeburg, you won't have to deal with portages between there and Hiram.

The handiest reference is the ***AMC River Guide: Maine.*** For multiday trips, you'll need to get a **fire permit** (free), or stay at one of the commercial campgrounds. Fire permits are available at some local stores.

Saco River Canoe & Kayak, Rte. 5, P.O. Box 111, Fryeburg 04037, 207/935-2369, located close to the convenient put-in at Swan's Falls, rents Old Town Discovery canoes and tandem kayaks ($35 a day weekends, $23 midweek) and provides delivery and pickup service along a 50-mile stretch of the Saco River. Shuttle costs range $5–22 per canoe, (depending on location). Safety-conscious owners Fred and Prudy Westerberg know their turf and provide helpful advice for planning short and extended canoe trips. Open mid-May–late Oct.

Besides Saco River Canoe, you can rent canoes and/or arrange shuttle service from **Woodland Acres Campground** and **River Run Campground**, even if you aren't staying with them.

If crowds on the Saco become a bit much, head east or north with your canoe or kayak to the area's lakes and ponds, even to **Brownfield Bog.** Prime canoeing spots are **Lovewell Pond** and **Kezar Pond** in Fryeburg; **Kezar Lake** in Lovell; and **Virginia Lake** in Stoneham. (If a north wind kicks up on Kezar Lake, stay close to shore.) Most spectacular is mile-long Virginia Lake, nudged up against the White Mountain National Forest. A house on the wooded shoreline is a rarity. The access road (off Rte. 5 between North Lovell and East Stoneham) is a mechanic's delight, but persevere—tranquility lies ahead.

Hiking
Easiest (and therefore busiest) trail in the area is the 20-minute stroll up (barely up) **Jockey Cap,** named for a cantilevered ledge that's long since disappeared. At the top of the trail, with a 360-degree view of lakes and mountains, is a monument to Adm. Robert Peary, the arctic explorer who once lived in Fryeburg. The metal edge of the monument is a handy cheat sheet—profiles and names of all the mountains you're seeing, more than four dozen of them.

The trail is fine for kids, but keep a close eye on the littlest ones; the dropoff is perilous on the south side. The trailhead is on Rte. 302, about a mile east of downtown Fryeburg, on the left, between the Jockey Cap Country Store and the Jockey Cap Motel.

The 60-acre **Hiram Nature Study Area,** established by Central Maine Power alongside the Hiram Dam on the Saco River, has two linked loop trails covering just over a mile. Take the Base Trail, leading down to the river. En route are signs identifying trees, shrubs, wildflowers, and other botanical specimens. Bring a picnic. From Fryeburg, take Rte. 5/113 southeast to Hiram, then continue about two miles south of Hiram village to the signposted road into the preserve.

Allow about half an hour to reach the summit of **Sabattus Mountain** in Lovell, north of Fryeburg. This is an especially good family hike, easy and short enough for small children. Carry a picnic and enjoy the views at the top—on the ledges of the more open second summit. You'll see the White Mountains, Pleasant Mountain, and skinny Kezar Lake; in fall, it's fabulous. To reach the trailhead from Fryeburg, take Rte. 5 north to Center Lovell. About 0.8 mile after the junction of Rtes. 5 and 5A, turn right onto Sabattus Rd. Go about 1.6 miles, bearing right at the fork onto an unpaved road. Continue a very short distance to a parking area on the left; the trailhead is across the road. Round-trip hike is about 1.5 miles.

Other good hikes in this area are **Mount Tom** (easy, about 2.5 hours round-trip; just east of Fryeburg), **Burnt Meadow Mountain** (moderately difficult, about four hours round-trip to the north peak; good views of the Presidential Range; near Brownfield); and **Mount Cutler** (moderately difficult, about two hours round-trip; near Hiram).

FESTIVALS AND EVENTS

Anything happening in Bethel and Vicinity, Oxford Hills, or Sebago and Long Lakes is also within easy reach of the Fryeburg area, especially in the daytime.

The **Ossipee Valley Fair** is an old-fashioned, four-day agricultural fair with tractor pulling, animal exhibits, live entertainment, food booths, games, and a carnival. In South Hiram the second weekend in July.

The Big Event in these parts is the **Fryeburg Fair,** the last country fair of the season (first week of Oct., sometimes including a few days in Sept.), Maine's largest agricultural fair, and an annual event since 1851. A parade, a carnival, craft demonstrations and exhibits, harness racing, pig scrambles, children's activities, ox pulling, and live entertainment are all here, as are plenty of food booths (it's sometimes called the "Fried-burg" Fair). Over 300,000 turn out for eight days of festivities, so expect traffic congestion. The fair runs Sun.–Sun., and the busiest day is Saturday. No dogs are allowed on the 180-acre site. Spectacular fall foliage and mountain scenery just add to the appeal. At the Fryeburg Fairgrounds (officially the West Oxford Agricultural Society Fairgrounds), Rte. 5, Fryeburg.

ACCOMMODATIONS

If you're planning to be in the area during the Fryeburg Fair, you'll need to reserve beds or campsites months ahead, in some cases a year in advance. Don't procrastinate.

Bed-and-Breakfasts

Named after the famed polar explorer who lived here in the late 19th century, the **Admiral Peary House,** 9 Elm St., Fryeburg 04037, 207/935-3365 or 877-4ADMPRY, www.admiralpearyhouse.com, has seven Peary-themed rooms (private baths and air-conditioning) that go for $95–189, depending on season and amenities. Some rooms have fireplaces and/or Jacuzzis. Tennis enthusiasts Nancy and Ed Greenberg encourage guests to use their clay court, or wander the perennial gardens or borrow a bike. You'll have the run of several comfortable first-floor rooms, good when the weather closes in. No small children, no pets. Open all year, but advance reservations preferred.

In the center of town, **The Oxford House Inn,** 548 Main St., Rte. 302, Fryeburg 04037, 207/935-3442 or 800/261-7206, www.oxfordhouseinn.com, has four second-floor rooms with private baths ($110–175 d). Breakfasts, served in the mountain-view porch/dining room, are every bit as creative as the inn's dinner menus. Open all year.

Cottage Colony

The *New York Times* once headlined a story on **Quisisana,** Kezar Lake, Center Lovell 04016, 207/925-3500, www.quisianaresort.com, winter address P.O. Box 142, Larchmont, NY 10538, 914/833-0293, as "Where Mozart Goes on Vacation." Amen. By day, the staff at this elegantly rustic 47-acre retreat masquerades as waiters and waitresses, chambermaids, boat crew, and kitchen help; each night, presto, they're the stars of musical performances worthy of Broadway and concert-hall ticket prices. Since 1947, it's been like this at "Quisi"—with a staff recruited from the nation's best conservatories. (The resort was founded in 1917.) Veteran managers literally attuned to guests' needs keep it all working smoothly.

The frosting on all this culture is the setting—a beautifully landscaped pine grove on the shores of sandy-bottomed Kezar Lake, looking off to the White Mountains and dramatic sunsets. No wonder that reservations for the 38 neat white cottages are hard to come by. The New York-heavy clientele knows to book well ahead, often for the same week, and new generations have followed their parents here. A week at Quisisana, late June to late Aug., averages $2,500 d, AP. No credit cards; beer and wine only. Quisisana's season begins in mid-June and ends in late August. Lower rates (and daily rates) prevail the last two weeks in June, after which a one-week minimum (Sat.–Sat.) prevails.

Campgrounds

Canoeing is the major focus at **Woodland Acres Campground,** Rte. 160, RR1, Box 445, Brownfield 04010, 207/935-2529, www.woodlandacres.com, with a 100-canoe fleet available for rent ($38 a day, including shuttle service to one location; reduced rates for additional canoes). They make it

all very convenient, even suggesting more than half a dozen day-long and multiday canoe trips for skill levels from beginner to expert. This well-maintained campground on the Saco River has 109 wooded tent and RV sites ($26–34 a night per family; two-night weekend minimum). Riverfront sites are the best, but you'll need to stay a week in July and August unless you luck out with a cancellation. Facilities include a rec hall, beach, camp store, and free hot showers. Leashed pets are allowed ($5). From Fryeburg, take Rte. 5/13 southeast to Rte. 160. Turn left (north) and go a mile to the campground. Open mid-May–mid-Oct.

Also in Brownfield, and also geared toward canoeists, is **River Run,** Rte. 160, P.O. Box 90, Brownfield 04010, 207/452-2500, www.riverruncanoe.com, with 22 large primitive tent sites on 130 acres next to the Saco River's Brownfield Bridge; no hookups. Sites are $7 a person. Canoe rentals and shuttle service are available, canoes run about $21 a day Mon.–Thurs., and $35 on weekends and holidays, with the shuttle price about $8–10. At the end of the season, River Run sells its rental canoes at greatly reduced rates; call to find out when the bargains begin. The campground is open mid-May–Sept.; after Labor Day, reservations are required.

The Appalachian Mountain Club maintains a wilderness campground on the Saco River. The **AMC Swan's Falls Campground,** Rte. 5, Fryeburg 04037, 207/935-3395, www.outdoors.org, just north of Fryeburg, has 18 campsites and one lean-to, picnic tables and toilets. Reservation requests, including numbers of people and equipment in party, dates and arrival time, are processed starting April 15, and need to be mailed to Campground Manager, AMC-Swan's Falls Campground, P.O. Box 378, Fryeburg 04037-0378 (207/935-3395). The AMC has information volunteers and staff stationed at the campground to answer questions and provide info about river conditions. This is a very busy canoe and kayak access point on the Saco River. Open mid-May–mid-Oct.

FOOD

Chef/co-owner John Morris's creative menu (entrées $22–30) at **The Oxford House Inn,** 548

Main St., in downtown Fryeburg, 207/935-3442, www.oxfordhouseinn.com, has earned the inn restaurant a first-rate reputation. The back porch/dining room (where B&B guests have breakfast) has wonderful mountain views. Dinner reservations are wise, especially July–Aug. and during the Fryeburg Fair. Open for dinner daily 6–9 PM, July–Oct., and Thurs.–Sun. the rest of the year.

What do you do for an encore when you've won a country inn in an essay contest and become a cover story in the *New York Times Magazine*? You prove you deserved it, and that's what's happened at the **Center Lovell Inn & Restaurant,** 1107 Main St., P.O. Box 261, Center Lovell 04016, 207/925-1575 or 800/777-2698, www.centerlovellinn.com. Janice Sage has been here since 1993, serving an enthusiastic clientele drawn to the wide-ranging continental menu, which changes weekly (entrées average $18–27).

Save room for one of the pastry chef's incredible desserts. Best tables are on the glassed-in porch, where you can watch the sun slip behind the mountains. The inn serves dinner daily 6–9 PM May–Oct.; reservations are advised, especially in midsummer. Dec.–Mar., dinner is served Fri.–Sat., as well as daily during school vacation weeks. The inn has five second-floor rooms (private and shared baths) in the 1805 main building, plus five more (private and shared baths) in the adjacent Harmon House. Room rates are $90–120 d without meals. Suites are $203. The inn and its restaurant are open May–Oct. and Dec.–Mar.

INFORMATION AND SERVICES

Check with the **Fryeburg Town Office,** 2 Lovewell's Pond Rd., Fryeburg 04037, 207/935-2805, open weekdays only.

Sebago and Long Lakes

Maine's Lakes region, the area along the shores of Sebago and Long Lakes, includes the two major hubs of Bridgton (pop. 4,210) and Naples (pop. 3,170) as well as the smaller communities of East Sebago and Harrison and the larger communities of Raymond, Casco, and Windham. All are in Cumberland County.

Settled in 1768, Bridgton was incorporated in 1794; Naples was not incorporated until 1834. When the summer-vacation boom began in the mid-19th century, and then erupted after the Civil War, visitors flowed into this area—via stagecoach, the Cumberland and Oxford Canal, and later the Bridgton and Saco Railroad.

The 28-lock canal, opened in 1830 and shut down in 1870, connected the Fore River in Portland with Sebago and Long Lakes. Its only working remnant is the Songo Lock in Naples, on the Songo River between Brandy Pond and Sebago Lake.

Sebago is an apt Native American word meaning "large, open water"; it's the state's second-largest lake (after Moosehead), and flukey winds can kick up suddenly and toss around little boats, so be prudent. Now a major water source for Greater Portland, the lake reportedly served as the crossroads for major Native American trading routes, and artifacts still occasionally surface in the Sebago Basin area.

Engage in a heart-to-heart with an adult vacationing in this area and you're likely to find someone trying to recapture the past—the carefree days at summer camp in the Sebago and Long Lakes region. The shores of Sebago, Long, and Highland Lakes shelter dozens of children's camps that have created several generations of Maine enthusiasts—"people from away" who still can't resist an annual visit. Unless your own kids are in camp, however, or you're terminally masochistic, do *not* appear in Bridgton, Naples, or surrounding communities on the last weekend in July. Parents, grandparents, and surrogate parents all show up then for the midseason summer-camp break, and there isn't a bed or restaurant seat to be had in the entire county, maybe beyond. Gridlock is the rule.

The rest of the time, congestion can occur on a regular basis in the center of Naples, where traffic backs up half a mile when the drawbridge on the causeway opens for boat traffic passing between Brandy Pond and Long Lake. Openings are on the hour—every hour on weekends, every other hour on weekdays. Plan accordingly.

Aside from those minor glitches, this mountain-lake setting has incredible locales for canoeing, swimming, hiking, fishing, golfing, camping, biking, ice-skating, snowshoeing, and skiing. (Maine's first ski lift opened in 1938 on Pleasant Mountain, now the Shawnee Peak ski area.) If rain descends, head for Bridgton's historic Magic Lantern movie theater. And be sure to check the schedule for Harrison's Deertrees Theatre—a fascinating National Historic Register building now restored for summertime plays and concerts.

These lakes are terribly convenient to Portland—Sebago is the large body of water you'll see to the west as you descend into the Portland Jetport.

SIGHTS

Narramissic, The Peabody-Fitch Farm

Built in 1797 and converted to Federal style in 1828, the Peabody-Fitch Farm is the crown jewel of the Bridgton Historical Society. Still undergoing restoration—now to the pre-Civil War era—the homestead includes a carriage house, ell, barn, blacksmith shop, and historic gardens. The barn has its own story: it's known as the "Temperance Barn" because the landowners were avowed teetotalers, so the volunteer barn-raisers earned only water for their efforts. Narramissic is a relatively recent name, given to

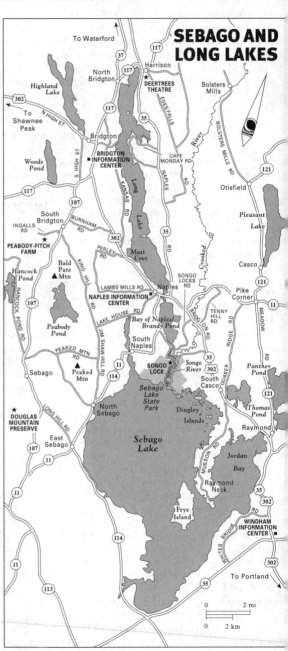

SEBAGO AND LONG LAKES

it by the 20th-century owner who donated it to the historical society in 1986. The name is a Native American word meaning "hard to find," reflecting her lengthy search for a family summer home. But it also suits the circuitous route, fortunately signposted, to the South Bridgton farm from downtown Bridgton (Main St. to Rte. 117 to Rte. 107 to Ingalls Rd.). A season highlight is the Woodworkers' Show in July. The farm is open July–Aug.; call ahead for hours and admission prices. Contact the **Bridgton Historical Society,** P.O. Box 44, Bridgton 04009, 207/647-3699, for more information.

Shades of Mississippi

Berthed in downtown Naples, Maine, is a 90-foot Mississippi sternwheeler replica that operates narrated cruises throughout the summer: the *Songo River Queen II,* Bay of Naples Causeway, Rte. 302, P.O. Box 1226, Naples 04055, 207/693-6861, www.songoriverqueen.net. Opt for the 2.5-hour Songo River trip, which departs at 9:45 AM and 3:45 PM; you'll cross Brandy Pond and head downriver, transiting the 19th-century **Songo River Lock** via a hand-turned swing bridge that raises and lowers the river level by five feet. Kids love it, and the lockkeeper plays to his audience. Cost is $12 adults, $10 children. The other option is a one-hour Long Lake cruise ($7 adults, $6 kids), at 1, 2:30, and 7 PM. Cruises operate daily, rain or shine, July–Labor Day (two Songo cruises, three Long Lake trips). In June and September, the boat only operates weekends, making one Songo Lock cruise daily at 9:45 AM. On a clear day, you can even spot Mount Washington, centerpiece of the White Mountains; bring binoculars and a camera. On board are restrooms and a snack bar.

Presidential Maine

Inspired by a famous western Maine signpost giving directions to nine Maine towns named for foreign cities and countries, Boy Scouts in Casco decided to create some competition— a directional sign for 10 Maine towns named for U.S. presidents. The marker stands next to the Village Green in **Casco,** at the corner of

Rte. 121 and Leach Hill Rd., pointing to towns such as Washington (76 miles), Lincoln (175 miles), Madison, and Monroe. There's even a Clinton (84 miles).

If you're here in the fall, take time to detour briefly to Casco's "million-dollar view." Continue south from the signpost less than two miles on Rte. 121 to Rte. 11 (Pike Corner), turn right (west) and go about half a mile to Quaker Ridge Rd. and turn left (south). Views are spectacular along here, especially from the Quaker Hill area—worth bringing a panorama camera.

Rufus Porter Museum

The artist's murals and paintings (c. 1828) are the focus at the Rufus Porter Museum and Cultural Heritage Center, 67 N. High St., Bridgton 04009, 207/647-2828, the beginning of plans to put an art barn on the property in order to become an artistic facility exposing arts of the 19th and 20th century to fuller appreciation.

PARKS AND PRESERVES
Sebago Lake State Park

Fourth largest of Maine's state parks, 1,400-acre Sebago Lake State Park, 11 Park Access Road, Naples 04055, 207/693-6613 late June–Labor Day, www.campwithme.com, 207/693-6231 off-season, is one of the most popular—so don't anticipate peace and quiet here in July and August. Swimming and picnicking are superb, fishing is so-so, personal watercraft are an increasing hazard. During the summer, park officials organize lectures, hikes, and other activities; the schedule is posted at the gate. Day-use admission is $4 adults, $1 children 5–11; children under five are free. More than 70,000 campers sleep at the 250 sites each year, so far-ahead reservations are essential for midsummer, 207/287-3824 with Visa or MasterCard; two-night minimum, no hookups. Nonresident rate is $20 per night. No pets in campground, and pets are allowed on leash in the picnic area. The park is mid-May to Oct, but there's winter access to 4.5 miles of groomed cross-country-skiing trails—mostly beginner terrain. It's ideal, too, for snowshoeing.

You can access the park's separate picnicking and camping areas from Rte. 302 in Casco. Take State Park Rd. to the fork, where you go left to the picnic area or right to Songo Lock and the camping area. (Both sections have sandy beaches, now slightly diminished after major storms in 1996.) Or, from downtown Naples, take Rte. 11/114 to Thompson Point Rd. and follow the signs.

Douglas Mountain Preserve

The Douglas Mountain Preserve was formerly owned by The Nature Conservancy, and was deeded to the town of Sebago in 1997. Fortunately or unfortunately, Douglas Mountain (also called Douglas Hill) is one of southern Maine's most popular hikes, so you probably won't be alone. Park in the lot on the left. Walk farther up, take a brochure from the registration box, and follow the easy Woods Trail to the 1,415-foot summit-30 minutes maximum. At the top is a 0.75-mile nature-trail loop, plus a 16-foot stone tower with a head-spinning view. In the fall, the vistas are incomparable. Be ecosensitive and stick to the trails in this 169-acre preserve. No pets. The trails are accessible dawn to dusk.

RECREATION

Hiking

Six interconnecting trails provide access to the main summit (2,000 feet) of **Pleasant Mountain,** but one of the most popular—and relatively easiest for kids—is the Ledges (or Moose) Trail. In late July, allow four hours for the 3.5-mile round-trip, so you can pick blueberries on the open ledges midway up. At the top is a disused fire tower—and plenty of space for spreading out a picnic overlooking panoramic vistas of woods, lakes, and mountains. The mountain straddles the Denmark/Bridgton town line, as well as the Cumberland/Oxford county line. From Bridgton, drive 5.75 miles west on Rte. 302 to Mountain Rd. (just after the causeway over Moose Pond). Turn left (south) at signs for Shawnee Peak ski area and go 3.3 miles to the trailhead

for the Ledges (or Moose) Trail; parking is limited. An alternative access route, from the west side of the mountain, is via the Wilton Warren Rd., also south of Rte. 302.

Swimming

Besides two sandy beaches at Sebago Lake State Park, other swimming locations are the **Naples Town Beach; Crystal Lake Beach** in Harrison; **Salmon Point** and the **Town Beach on Highland Lake** in Bridgton; and **Tassel Top Beach** in Raymond.

Golf

Bridgton Highlands Country Club, Highland Ridge Rd., RR3, Box 1065, Bridgton 04009, 207/647-3491, www.bridgtonhighlands.com. This 18 hole course, is outstandingly scenic and very popular, especially at the height of summer. Starting times are needed. Greens and cart fees are not cheap, but no one seems to object. Also here are a handsome clubhouse, tennis courts, a pro shop, and a snack bar. The course, about two miles from downtown Bridgton, is open mid-Apr.–Oct.

Less expensive but also scenic is the **Naples Golf and Country Club,** Rte. 114, Naples 04055, 207/693-6424, www.naplesgolfcourse.com, established in 1922. Light meals are available at the clubhouse, and there's a pro shop. On midsummer weekends, call for a starting time. The course, across from the Naples Golf Driving Range, adjoins Bay of Naples Family Camping. It's open mid-April–Oct.

The championship-level **Point Sebago Golf Club,** Rte. 302, RR 1, Box 712, Casco 04015, 207/655-2747, www.pointsebago.com/golf/golf.html, is part of a once-low-key campground transformed into the 800-acre Club Med-style **Point Sebago Resort.** Call for starting times at the 18-hole course, which is open to the public. Golf-and-lodging packages are available. Open May to mid-Oct. For info and reservations for campsites or cottages, call 800/655-1232, or go to www.pointsebago.com.

Getting Afloat

In addition to cruises on the *Songo River Queen*

II, and the mail-boat rides, you can rent your own pontoon boat, powerboat, or, if you must, a water scooter (officially, a personal watercraft, PWC, often referred to by the trademark-name Jetski). Water scooters have become a major itch on huge Sebago Lake, as well as many other Maine lakes, and there's no gray area in the opinion department. Biggest objections are noise pollution and excessive speed. The state requires PWCs to be licensed as powerboats, but regulations are weak, the state legislature has taken little action, and inadequate funding has led to inadequate enforcement. Each year, fatalities occur, spurring towns to try (usually unsuccessfully) to ban or limit PWCs. If you *do* rent one, play by the rules, exercise caution, and operate at sensible speeds.

Naples Marina, Rtes. 302 and 114, Naples 04055, 207/693-6254, behind Rick's Café, rents pontoon boats and runabouts, and fishing boats. **Causeway Marina,** Rte. 302, Naples 04055, 207/693-6832, www.causewaymarina.com, rents canoes, powerboats, pontoon boats, water-skiing boats and gear, and PWCs. Both marinas are open daily during the summer.

If you've brought a **canoe or kayak,** don't launch it into Sebago Lake; save it for the smaller lakes and ponds, where the winds are more predictable and the boat traffic is less congested. Long Lake is also a possibility, if you put in at Harrison, on the east side.

Downhill Skiing

Judicious marketing, reasonable rates, top-to-bottom snowmaking, and 16 trails lighted for night skiing have made **Shawnee Peak,** Rte. 302, Bridgton 04009, 207/647-8444, www.shawneepeak.com, an increasingly popular destination. Its proximity to Portland (45 miles) boosts the appeal for day-trip skiing. Vertical drop is 1,300 feet; one quad, two triples, a double, and a surface lift serve 38 trails, about half intermediate. An array of special rates depend on the day and season, special packages are rampant. Lift tickets range from a low of $19 for midweek night Jr./Sr. skiing, to a high of $45 for day weekend/holiday adult. When

you've had your fill of night skiing, there's always the **Blizzards Pub,** in the base lodge, and it is a lively spot to kick back. Fri.–Sat. nights, there's usually live entertainment. Lodging information is available through Shawnee Peak's main phone line. The ski area is six miles west of downtown Bridgton.

ENTERTAINMENT

Tucked away on a back road in Harrison, east of Long Lake, dramatic-looking, 278-seat **Deertrees Theatre and Cultural Center,** Deertrees Rd., P.O. Box 577, Harrison 04040, 207/583-6747, www.deertreestheatre.org, is a must-see even if you don't attend a performance. The acoustically superior National Historic Register building, constructed of rose hemlock in 1936, has seen the likes of Rudy Vallee, Ethel Barrymore, Tallulah Bankhead, and Henry Winkler; restoration of the rustic building in the 1990s has given it an exciting new life. Each summer season (June to Labor Day) includes five concerts in the acclaimed annual Sebago-Long Lake Chamber Music Festival, plus jazz, ragtime, pops, and classical programs. The theater is off Rte. 117 (signposted) in the Harrison woods. Tours are available (handicapped accessible), contact the box office in advance if possible.

One of a dying species, **Bridgton Drive-In,** Rte. 302, Bridgton 04009, 207/647-8666, www.driveins.com, screens a double feature each night July–Aug., beginning at dusk. Tickets are $6 adults, $3 children 11 and under. Sound comes via the FM radio in your car. The drive-in is 2.5 miles south of downtown Bridgton.

Nearest first-run multiplex is in North Windham. The seven-screen **Windham Five Star Cinema,** 207/892-7000, www.fivestarcinemas.com, is at the Windham Mall on Rte. 302. Matinees are $5.50 before 6 PM; evenings are general admission $7.50, seniors and children $5.50.

FESTIVALS AND EVENTS

The **Shawnee Peak** ski area, 207/647-8444, www.shawneepeak.com, has a full schedule of family-oriented special events, including races, throughout the winter; call or check web for information.

Nearly a hundred teams compete in the **Mushers Bowl,** two days of dogsled and skijoring races on Highland Lake, a great spectator event in West Bridgton the first full weekend in February. Be sure to leave your own pets at home.

Bridgton's **Pondicherry Days** festivities take place in mid-August. The name comes from the former Pondicherry Mills factory, which once operated here. The third Saturday in July, Bridgton is the scene of the Annual Art in the Park exhibition and sale, a mad success since its inception. Bridgton's annual **Chickadee Quilters Show** www.guiltguilds.com/maine. htm, features exhibits and sales of magnificent quilts and wall hangings at the Bridgton Town Hall in July. Mid-July–early Aug., the **Sebago-Long Lake Chamber Music Festival** brings Tuesday-night (8 PM) chamber-music concerts to Harrison's Deertrees Theatre. Advance booking is essential for this popular series, founded in 1975, 207/583-6747, www.sebagomusicfestival.org. Single adult tickets cost $20, $10 for students and children. Also mid-July–mid-Aug., Sunday-evening **band concerts** around the gazebo behind the Naples Information Center are free. Bring a chair or blanket to the Village Green, Rte. 302, Naples. In mid-September, **Brewfest** brings meisters from all over Maine to the Village Green in Casco to display their art.

SHOPPING

Interesting shops fill historic buildings along the main drag in downtown Bridgton, best source in this region for crafts, gifts, and more—especially the work of Maine artisans.

Art and Antiques

More than 20 dealers sell their wares at **Wales & Hamblen,** 134 Main St., Bridgton 04009, 207/647-3840. Inventory includes antiques as well as "tomorrow's antiques." The quirky old National Historic Register Victorian building in downtown Bridgton is open Memorial Day weekend through October. Call for current hours.

Art central: **Gallery 302,** 112 Main St. Bridgton 04009, 207/647-ARTS, in yet another example of adaptive reuse, has turned a former hardware store into the home of the Bridgton Art Guild.

Carol Honaberger's **Lamp and Shade Shop,** 95 Main St. Bridgton 04009, 207/647-5576, has cornered the market in antique lighting fixtures and custom-made new lampshades. They'll also repair damaged fixtures or convert any kind of treasured *objet* into a serviceable lamp. The shop is open daily, Memorial Day to Columbus Day; other months, the schedule can be erratic, so call ahead to be sure.

Books

Bridgton Books, 140 Main St., Bridgton 04009, 207/647-2122, an independent bookstore, carries an excellent selection of books (20,000 titles, including new, selected used, and a large bargain book section), cards, and bargain music CDs—a browser's (and buyer's) delight. The bookstore, which also sells and rents audio books and will special order at no extra charge, is open all year, Mon.–Sat. 9:30 AM–5:30 PM, Sun. 11 AM–4:30 PM, with extended hours in summer.

Crafts and Gifts

A onetime Unitarian church and its church hall make terrific settings for the carefully chosen and superbly eclectic inventory at **Craftworks,** 79 Main St., Bridgton 04009, 207/647-5436, a Bridgton landmark since the early 1970s. In the church building are clothing, jewelry, and pottery; in the church hall are garden and kitchen specialty items, plus wine and gourmet goodies. Both buildings are open 9 AM–8:30 PM daily June–Aug., with shorter hours in spring and fall.

Across the street, a collection of boutiques inhabits another creative reuse building. **The Shops at the Maine Difference,** 148 Main St., Bridgton 04009, include **Mainely Gift Baskets,** 207/647-5200.

The Sheep Shop, 2056 N. High St., Rte. 302, Bridgton 04009, 207/647-3548,, is the ultimate source for sheepskins in six colors, washable wool blankets, sheepskin vests and jackets, sheepskin toys, Christmas ornaments, and wool and wool/mohair yarns. The Berry family's shop is open Tues.–Sat. 10 AM–4 PM, Sun. 10 AM–2 PM, or by appointment.

Cry of the Loon, Rte. 302, P.O. Box 40, South Casco 04077, 207/655-5060, has three floors of gifts, a tasteful, eclectic mix of gourmet condiments, Maine crafts, furniture, and much more. It's definitely worth a stop. Right around the corner from Migis Lodge, with a discriminating clientele, the shop is open daily 9 AM–5:30 PM.

Sportswear and Sporting-Gear Rentals

No matter what the season, there isn't much you can't rent, sports-wise, at the **Sportshaus,** 103 Main St., Bridgton 04009, 207/647-5100. In summer, the shop rents mountain bikes, canoes and kayaks, Sunfish, and in-line skates. For an extra fee, they'll deliver. If you want to try waterskiing, a demo is $20 pp. In winter, you can rent downhill skis, snowboards, cross-country skis, and snowshoes. Rates are lower for additional days and weekdays, as well as for kids. The shop is open Mon.–Sat. 9 AM–7 PM, 9 AM–6 PM on Sun.; it's closed Sun.–Mon. in spring and fall.

Sportshaus also has a seasonal branch, 207/647-3000, on Rte. 302 near the Shawnee Peak ski area. It's open daily Dec.–Feb. 8 AM–8 PM, and Oct.–Nov. and Mar. 9 AM–5 PM.

Farmers Markets

The **Naples Farmers Market** sets up on the Naples Village Green, off Rte. 302, each Thurs., 8 AM–1 PM, early May–mid-Sept., bringing to market organic vegetables and fruits, herbs, flower arrangements, shellfish and crabmeat, baked goods, preserves and other gifts of the earth and sea. The **Bridgton Farmers Market** is open Sat. 8 AM–1 PM, on Depot St., in front of the community center. Pick up veggies, lamb, goat cheese, baked goods, crabmeat, shellfish, flowers, jams, relishes, and more, all locally produced. It runs mid-May–Sept.

ACCOMMODATIONS

Bed-and-Breakfasts

On a busy corner in downtown Bridgton, convenient to all the shops, **The Bridgton House Bed & Breakfast,** 2 Main Hill, Bridgton 04009, 207/647-8175 or 866/779-3335, www.bridgtonhouse.com, built in 1815, has been tastefully updated. Five rooms, some with private baths. If you're highly noise-sensitive, request a back-facing room. Rates of $110 d private bath, and $90 d shared bath, include full breakfast and afternoon tea or snacks. Pets only by arrangement. Innkeepers Bill and Tina Berghof have small children and welcome more; they are making a specialty of catering to visiting families. Open mid-June–Labor Day, then weekends in fall by appointment.

Just around the corner from the Bridgton House and off the main road, **The Noble House,** 37 Highland Rd., P.O. Box 180, Bridgton 04009, 207/647-3733, www.noblehouse.com, is a turn-of-the-20th-century Victorian with nine warmly decorated rooms (six with private baths). Guests have use of a comfortable sitting room with TV and VCR. Rick and Julie Welcheck, new owners as of 2003, serve a generous breakfast, a good jump-start for the day. Be sure to wander across the road and down to their private lakefront oasis, where you can go for a paddle. Rates are $99–209 d (the latter for the honeymoon suite), lower off season. No pets. Open all year.

Book a room at the **Songo Locks Bed & Breakfast,** 120 Songo Locks Rd., Naples 04055, 207/693-6955, then pull up a riverside lawn chair and watch the world go by—to and from the historic, hand-cranked Songo Lock close by the B&B. (The lock operates May 1–Oct. 15, 8 AM–8 PM). The pine-paneled, carpeted guest rooms overlook the Songo River, too, as does the windowed dining area, where the blueberry pancakes are legendary. Five rooms share three baths ($75 d). An entrance to Sebago Lake State Park is just across the road—for swimming and cross-country skiing. Extras for guests include canoes and

Western Lakes & Mountains

a state park pass. No pets; children are welcome. The B&B, open all year, is four miles from downtown Naples. It's just behind the Songo Locks Snack Bar, a favorite munchie stop for boaters and bikers (open mornings for breakfast, closing about 8 PM, Memorial Day to just after Labor Day).

Built in 1870, the secluded **Greenwood Manor Inn,** 52 Tolman Rd., Harrison 04040, 207/583-4445, www.greenwood manorinn.com, is at the tip of Long Lake and in the foothills of the White Mountains, between Bridgton and Harrison. Enjoy the 108-acre grounds, lovely gardens, and guest canoes, while staying in one of the seven guest rooms or two suites, $120–209 d., depending on time of year and accommodation. Rates include homecooked country breakfast. Open all year.

At the head of Long Lake, close to Crystal Lake, and with the classic to-die-for Maine porch, **Harrison House Bed & Breakfast,** 16 Waterford Rd., Rte. 35, Harrison 04040, 207/583-6564, is set back just enough from a busy crossroads. A porch swing lets you survey the activity. Five good-size first- and second-floor rooms have featherbeds and quilts (four of the rooms have detached but private baths), for $85–95 d. Homemade baked goods and jams, and maybe "decadent French toast," make breakfast a treat. Open year-round.

Motel

Maplewood Inn & Motel, 549 Roosevelt Trail (Rte. 302), Casco, 207/655-7586, www.shindamen.com, has spacious hotel-style motel rooms, with an outdoor pool, complimentary continental breakfast (during high season), fridges and microwaves and high-speed Internet in each room. There are inn rooms, as well. From off-season to high season, inn rates are $50–95, motel rates $54–103. Motel rates include breakfast, which inn guests can purchase.

Cottage-Colony Resort

On the east side of Sebago Lake is a cottage-colony resort so popular that reservations are truly scarce. Persevere. July–Aug. are the sticking points; other months are not as booked up.

At **Migis Lodge,** Migis Lodge Rd., P.O. Box 40, South Casco 04077, 207/655-4524, www.migis.com, guests often confirm their next-year's July or August booking before they depart for home. The rustic elegance of 100-acre Migis, along with attentive service and a fabulous lakeside setting, have drawn big-name guests over the years—ever since the resort was established in the early 20th century as lodging for the parents of summer campers. Men wear jackets for dinner, and there is a supervised meal and playtime for children during dinner hours. All this comes at a price, which includes almost everything but tax and tips: sailboats, island cookouts, waterskiing, tennis courts, even a cinema. Daily rates for the 35 lake-view cottages (one to six bedrooms) are $280–410 d per person, per night, AP; one-week minimum. In the main lodge, six rooms have private baths, private balconies and lake views, and are $280–350 d per person, per night, also AP. Shorter stays are allowed at the fringes of the season. No credit cards, no pets. Open mid-June–mid-Oct. Migis is down an unpaved road off Rte. 302.

Campgrounds

Camping is especially popular in this part of Maine, and many campgrounds have long-term RV or "immobile" home rentals (also known as "seasonal sites"), so you'll need to plan well ahead and reserve sites in advance. Be forewarned, though, that if you're looking for a wilderness camping experience, especially in midsummer, you probably ought to head for the hills. Many of the campgrounds in this area feature nonstop organized fun, which is fine for enthusiastic families, but the intense activity can be overwhelming. Most campground managers do a creditable job of maintaining order and quiet, but even the best ones are chockablock in July and August.

Bay of Naples Family Camping, Rte. 11/114, Box 240, Naples 04055, 207/693-6429 or 800/348-9750 outside Maine, www.bayofnaples.com, has a fine track record for noise-level control. It also has such nice touches as a private sand beach, two playgrounds, and an outside slate sink at the shower house for dishwashing. The 23-acre campground on the Bay of Naples (also known as Brandy Pond, between Long and Sebago Lakes) has 130 good-size wooded sites at $25 for two adults, or family of four; the tenting area is separate. Pets are not allowed. Open late May–mid-Oct., the campground is a mile off Rte. 302, next to the Naples Golf and Country Club, www.visitmaine.net/golf.htm.

Three miles west of Naples, the Van Der Zee family does a creditable job of maintaining order at **Four Seasons Family Camping Area,** Rte. 302, Naples 04055, 207/693-6797, on the shores of Long Lake. (Despite its name, though, it's only open mid-May–mid-Oct.) More than a hundred open and shady sites are $28–46 per family. Facilities include ball fields, a volleyball court, and a great sand beach.

Seasonal Rentals

Krainin Real Estate, Rte. 302, P.O. Box 464, South Casco 04077, 207/655-3811 or 800/639-2321, www.krainin.com, handles weekly (Sat.–Sat.) and monthly rentals for cottages on Sebago and Long Lakes as well as many of the surrounding smaller lakes and ponds. Krainin also arranges rentals on **Frye Island,** a thousand-acre summer community in the middle of Sebago Lake that's accessible only by car ferry. Office hours are Mon.–Sat. 9 AM–5 PM, Sun 10 AM–4 PM.

FOOD

See the "Public Suppers" listings in *The Bridgton News,* www.bridgtonnews.com for details on chicken barbecues, potluck buffets, baked-bean suppers, and public breakfasts—all to benefit good local causes and all under $10 (less for kids).

Inexpensive to Moderate

If you get an outdoor table at **Rick's Café,** Rte. 302, on the Causeway, Naples 04055, 207/693-3759, www.rickscafe.us, you'll be right in the middle of all the action in downtown Naples. The café, with a reasonably priced menu and evidence of creativity, is open daily 11 AM–11 PM, (Fri.–Sat. to 1 AM May–late-Sept.). Dinner service ends about 9 PM, and there's light fare until 11 PM. Most nights in summer, there's live entertainment, occasionally with a small cover charge.

Almost across the street from Rick's, **Sandy's at the Flight Deck,** Rte. 302, on the Causeway, Naples 04055, 207/693-3508, is practically *in* Long Lake, so you can watch floatplane takeoffs and all the boating traffic. An especially kid-friendly spot, the Flight Deck is open daily 7 AM–8 PM, mid-May–Labor Day, with shorter hours when schools are open.

A popular landmark since the 1970s, the **Naples Lobster Pound,** Rte. 302, Naples 04055, 207/693-6580, satisfies lobster cravings but also serves up steak and pizza. The gray building, with outdoor tables, is a mile south of the Naples Causeway. Open July–Labor Day, Mon.–Fri. 4–10 PM, Sat.–Sun. noon–10 PM.

Located in a Victorian farmhouse previously known as the Epicurean Inn, **Bray's Brewpub and Eatery,** Rtes. 302 and 35, Naples 04055, 207/693-6806, www.braysbrewpub.com, is the pioneer brewpub in this part of Maine. Dinner specialties are steaks, seafood, and ribs—$13–18. Most popular brew is Old Church Pale Ale, drawing raves from reviewers; four other "styles" are always available. If the brewmaster can spring free, he'll give a brewery tour on request—a 15-minute "quickie" or a 30-minute in-depth explanation of the process. Bray's is open all year, daily 11:30 AM–10 PM (to midnight Fri.–Sat.).

Around the other side of Long Lake, in a restored grist mill, the **Olde Mill Tavern,** Main St., Rte. 35, Harrison 04040, 207/583-9077, www.oldemilltavern.com, serves comfort food with flair, for mostly moderate prices (entrée range is $10–22). Every day has a special feature, and lobster is available year-round. Sunday brunch is a great breakfast-plus buffet. Most Saturdays, there's live entertainment. Reservations are advisable on weekends. The Olde

Mill is open year-round, summer hours are noon–9 PM weekdays, Fri.–Sat. to 10 PM, Sun. noon–8 PM. Winter hours are 4–8 PM.

INFORMATION AND SERVICES

The **Greater Bridgton Lakes Region Chamber of Commerce,** Portland Rd., Rte. 302, P.O. Box 236, Bridgton 04009, 207/647-3472, www.mainelakeschamber. com, has an attractive information center (with public restrooms) half a mile south of downtown Bridgton. From Memorial Day to the beginning of October, it's open daily 9 AM–5 PM, Sat.–Sun., 9 AM–4 PM. Other months, it's open 9 AM–5 PM Mon.–Fri., Sat. 9 AM–4 PM.

In Naples, the **Sebago Lakes Region Chamber of Commerce,** Rte. 302, Naples 04055, 207/693-3285, www.sebago-lakeschamber.com, operates a small brick information center on the Village Green, next to the 1831 Naples Town Hall on Rte. 302. It's open weekends 10 AM–3:30 PM in June, then daily 10 AM–3:30 PM July–Labor Day.

The **Sebago Lakes Region Chamber of Commerce,** 816 Roosevelt Trail, Rte. 302, P.O. Box 1015, Windham 04062, 207/892-8265, www.sebagolakeschamber.com, has a small seasonal information booth along the Rte. 302 commercial strip. It's open Memorial Day weekend to Labor Day, 9 AM–5 PM daily. Off-season, call Barbara Clark, Chamber Director, at 207/892-8265 for infro on Naples, Windham and other Sebago Lakes region towns.

Of interest is a good general website for the area, the "Maine Mountain Heritage Area," www.visitmainemountains.com.

The **Bridgton Public Library,** Main St., Bridgton 04009, 207/647-2472, www.publiclibraries.com/maine.htm, has a broad range of programs, services and materials for children and adults. The library is open Wed. noon–8 PM, Thurs.–Fri. 10 AM–6 PM, Sat. 10 AM–4 PM. Technologically in the forefront of small-town libraries, the **Naples Public Library,** Rte. 302, Naples 04055, 207/693-6841, www.publiclibraries.com/maine.htm, was the first public library in the state to be hooked into the Internet. Located in a Victorian farmhouse, the library is open Tues. and Thurs. 10 AM–7 PM, Sat. 10 AM–2 PM, Sun. noon–4 PM.

Newspapers

The Bridgton News, 207/647-2851, published each Thursday, covers the Bridgton/Naples area as well as communities on the east shores of Sebago and Long Lakes. Calendar listings are extensive; the special "Summer Scene" section focuses on area happenings and recreational activities. The daily newspaper of choice is the *Portland Press Herald.*

Emergencies

Throughout the Lakes Region, for emergencies, call 911 for fire, police, and ambulance. The **Northern Cumberland Memorial Hospital,** Hospital Dr., Bridgton 04009, 207/647-6000, a small acute-care facility, has round-the-clock emergency-room service.

Lewiston/Auburn Area

A river runs through the heart of Lewiston and Auburn—the Androscoggin River, head-watered in the Rangeley Lakes and coursing southeastward until it joins the Kennebec in Merrymeeting Bay, near Brunswick. Surging over Great Falls, the mighty Androscoggin spurred 19th-century industrial development of the Twin Cities, where giant textile mills drew their power from the river and their hardworking employees from the local community of Yankees, then Irish, French-Canadian, and other immigrants. The Quebecois and Acadian French, who flocked to mills in Lewiston, Biddeford, Sanford, Augusta, and Brunswick, today constitute Maine's largest ethnic minority. In Lewiston and Auburn, the French-accented voting registers reveal long lists of Plourdes and Pomerleaus, Carons and Cloutiers, and the spires of Catholic churches still dominate the skyline.

Long before white men harnessed the falls of the Androscoggin, Native Americans recognized the area for its prime salmon fishing and set up seasonal campsites and year-round settlements. Nowadays, their artifacts occasionally turn up along the riverbanks.

European settlers began putting down roots around 1770, earning their keep from small water-powered mills. Quakers established a community as early as 1773. By 1852, the giant Bates Mill (of bedspread fame) began manufacturing cotton, expanding by that century's end to an annual output of more than 10 million yards. During the Civil War, Bates was a prime supplier of fabric for soldiers' tents. In 1861, Lewiston was incorporated as a city; Auburn was incorporated in 1869.

By the early 20th century, with a dozen more mills on line, taking advantage of the convenient hydropower, the lower reaches of the Androscoggin became polluted, a stinky eyesore until the 1980s, when environmental activists took up the cause. The river isn't 100 percent pristine, but it's almost there. You can stroll the banks, fish the waters, paddle a canoe, and get up close without holding your nose.

Natural gems are found in the region. Auburn's Mt. Apatite has produced record-setting tourmalines, Maine's state gemstone, as well as quartz and feldspar. Now owned by the city, the mountain is open to the prospecting public.

Lewiston (pop. 36,325) and Auburn (pop. 22,440)—quaintly called "the *other* LA"—still are not typical vacation destinations, but they deserve more than a drive-through glance. Lewiston is the state's second-largest city and the home of Bates College, a highly selective private liberal-arts school and a magnet for visiting performers, artists, and lecturers.

Auburn, the Androscoggin County seat, began its industrial career with a single shoe factory in 1836, expanding swiftly in those heady days. By the turn of the 20th century, Auburn's shoe factories were turning out six million pairs a year.

Lewiston and Auburn occupy a pivotal location in southern Maine, with easy access to Portland (35 miles away) and Freeport (28 miles), the western mountains, and the state capital (30 miles).

SIGHTS
Bates College
Founded in 1855 on foresighted egalitarian principles, Bates College, www.Bates.edu, received its current name after major financial input from Benjamin Bates of the Bates Mill. Located on a lovely wooded, 109-acre campus in the heart of Lewiston, the college earns high marks for small classes, a stellar faculty, a rigorous academic program, and a low faculty-to-student ratio. The student body of 1,738 comes from almost every state and about four dozen foreign countries; diversity has always been evident, and a point of honor. Oldest campus building is red-brick **Hathorn Hall,** built in 1856 and listed on the National Historic Register; one of the newest

Western Lakes & Mountains

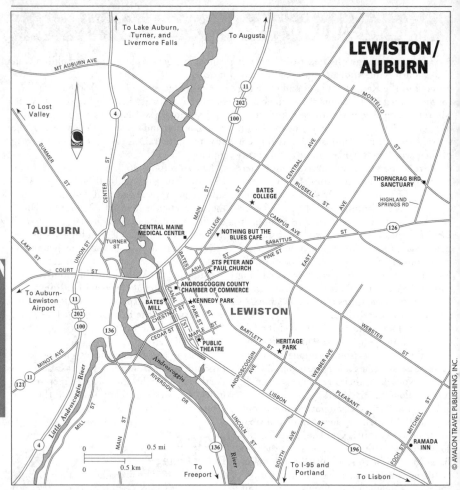

To Lake Auburn,
Turner, and
Livermore Falls

To Augusta

LEWISTON/
AUBURN

MT AUBURN AVE

To Lost
Valley

MONTELLO

11

202

100

THORNCRAG BIRD
SANCTUARY

HIGHLAND
SPRINGS RD

BATES
COLLEGE

126

AUBURN

CENTRAL MAINE
MEDICAL CENTER

NOTHING BUT THE
BLUES CAFÉ

STS PETER AND
PAUL CHURCH

ANDROSCOGGIN COUNTY
CHAMBER OF COMMERCE

To Auburn-
Lewiston
Airport

11

202

100

136

BATES
MILL

KENNEDY PARK

LEWISTON

WEBSTER

PUBLIC
THEATRE

HERITAGE
PARK

121

11

RIVERSIDE DR

Androscoggin River

RAMADA
INN

4

0   0.5 mi

0   0.5 km

136

To
Freeport

River

To I-95 and
Portland

To Lisbon

© AVALON TRAVEL PUBLISHING, INC.

buildings, the Olin Arts Center, built in 1986, is an award-winning complex overlooking manmade Lake Andrews.

Within the **Olin Arts Center,** Russell and Bardwell Sts., 207/786-6135, are the **Bates College Museum of Art,** 75 Russell St., 207/786-6158, and the 300-seat **Olin Concert Hall.** Most college-sponsored exhibits, lectures, and concerts at the Arts Center are free and open to the public (other organizations also use the concert hall). Monthly events calendars are published in the Lewiston papers. Each Thurs. at 6 PM, mid-July–mid-Aug., free **lakeside concerts** are presented outside the Arts Center; bring a picnic and a blanket or chair. The **Bates College Museum of Art,** with rotating exhibits, is open all year, Tues.–Sat. 10 AM–5 PM (free admission). A significant stop on the Maine Art Museum Trail, the Bates museum is best known for its holdings of prints, drawings, and paintings by Lewiston-born Marsden Hartley.

The college has won national and international acclaim for the summertime (mid-July–mid-Aug.) **Bates Dance Festival,** featuring modern-dance workshops, lectures, and performances. Sell-out student and faculty programs, most presented in 300-seat Schaeffer Theater, are open to the public. Call well ahead for tickets (207/786-6161).

Bates is the repository of the **Edmund S. Muskie Archives,** 70 Campus Ave., 207/786-6354, containing the papers of the Bates graduate (1936) and former Maine governor, U.S. senator, and U.S. secretary of state who died in 1996. The archives are open weekdays, 9 AM–4 PM.

Also open to the public at Bates are sporting events in Merrill Gym, Alumni Gym, and Underhill Arena; except for the outdoor track (for walking or jogging) and Lake Andrews (for ice-skating), none of the athletic facilities are open to the public.

At the western edge of the campus, at the corner of Mountain Ave. and College Sts., walk up **Mount David,** actually a grandly named hill, for a surprisingly good view of the Lewiston/Auburn skyline.

Bates Mill

Thanks to a progressive public/private partnership, the 19th-century Bates Mill complex, on Canal Street in downtown Lewiston, is being revitalized for a variety of new uses. Occupying 1.2 million square feet in twelve buildings spread over six acres, the mill once produced nearly a third of the nation's textiles. Maine Heritage Weavers now turns out the popular Bates bedspreads in one of the original buildings of the Bates Manufacturing Company here. Since 1992, much of the hulking brick complex has been undergoing a long-term makeover—offices, studios, shops, and restaurants have moved in, ever so slowly, helping the mill to reinvent itself.

Saints Peter and Paul Basilica

Most distinctive of Lewiston/Auburn's churches is the Gothic Revival Roman Catholic Saints Peter and Paul Basilica, 27 Bartlett St. (corner of Bartlett and Ash Sts.), Lewiston 04240, 207/777-1200, capable of seating more than 2,000 for its separate services in English and French. Dedicated in 1938, the recently designated basilica is the only one in New England.

Shaker Museum

Twelve miles southwest of Lewiston/Auburn, only a handful of Shakers remain in the world's last inhabited Shaker community. Nonetheless, the members of the United Society of Shakers, an 18th-century religious sect, keep a relatively high profile with a living-history museum, craft workshops, publications, mail-order herb and gift business, and even a music CD released in 1995. (See their website, www.shaker.lib.me.us, for the wonderful herb and herbal tea catalogue.) Each year, more than 8,000 visitors arrive at the 1,800-acre **Sabbathday Lake Shaker Community,** 707 Shaker Rd., Rte. 26, New Gloucester 04260, 207/926-4597, to glimpse an endangered lifestyle, and the Shakers welcome the public to their Sunday (10 AM) service (men and women enter through separate doors and sit separately). The 75-minute basic guided tour costs $6.50 adults, $2 children 2–12. Tours begin at 10:30 and are then given every hour on the half-hour, with the exception that the last tour of the day is at 3:15 PM. The village is open Mon.–Sat., Memorial Day weekend to Columbus Day.

Twice each year, on Saturdays in late May and mid-October, the Friends of the Shakers at Sabbathday Lake, a nonprofit group (annual membership for an individual is $15, a family $25), organizes **Friends' Work Day,** when three or four dozen volunteers show up at 10 AM to do spring and fall cleanup chores. The all-day work party includes a communal dinner. If you'd like to help, call the number above for exact dates.

PARKS AND PRESERVES

Thorncrag Bird Sanctuary

Imagine being able to birdwatch, hike, cross-country ski, and snowshoe on 310 acres within the city limits of Lewiston, in one of New England's largest bird sanctuaries. At the Thorncrag Bird Sanctuary, Montello St., Lewiston, mailing address Stanton Bird Club,

P.O. Box 3172, Lewiston 04240, 207/782-5238, www.avcnet.org/stanton/thorncrg.htm, pick up a trail map at the gate and head out on the three miles of well-maintained, color-coded, easy-to-moderate trails—past ponds, an old cellar hole, stone memorials and benches, and through stands of beech, hemlock, white pine, and mixed hardwoods. Bicycles are banned in the preserve, which is open dawn to dusk daily, year-round. Bring a picnic. Admission is free. Throughout the year, the **Stanton Bird Club** sponsors close to three dozen lectures and free, open-to-the-public field trips; call or see website for schedule. The club also sponsors an excellent junior naturalist program. From downtown Lewiston, take Sabattus St. (Rte. 126) east about three miles to Highland Springs Rd. Turn left (north) and continue to the end (Montello St.). You'll be facing the entrance to the sanctuary.

Range Ponds State Park

Brimming with swimmers when the temperature skyrockets, 777-acre Range (RANG) Ponds State Park, Empire Rd., Poland, mailing address P.O. Box 475, Poland Spring 04274, 207/998-4104, has facilities for swimming (including lifeguard and bathhouse) and picnicking, plus a playground and 2 miles of nature trails. (Part of the trail verges on a marsh; be prepared with bug repellent.) The beach, parking, restrooms, and picnic tables are handicapped-accessible. Most of the park's acreage once was the estate of Hiram Ricker, owner of Poland Spring Water (now owned by Perrier). Bring a canoe or kayak and launch it into Lower Range Pond. Admission is $3.50 adults, $1 children 5–11; the park is open mid-May–mid-Oct. From Lewiston/Auburn, take Rte. 202/11/100 south to Rte. 122. Turn right (east) and continue to the Empire Rd. in Poland Spring; the turnoff to the park is well signposted.

RECREATION

Golf

Prospect Hill Golf Course, 694 S. Main St., Auburn 04210, 207/782-9220, an 18-hole course, is open mid-Apr.–early Oct. Nine-hole **Apple Valley Golf Course,** 316 Pinewoods Rd., Lewiston 04240, 207/784-9773, is open mid-Apr.–mid-Nov. No credit cards at Apple Valley. Tee times aren't needed, but call ahead to reserve a cart.

About 11 miles north of Auburn, the eighteen-hole **Turner Highlands Country Club,** Rte. 117, Turner 04282, 207/224-7060, has a pastoral feel, with broad vistas. Tee times are necessary. The club's restaurant, Eli's, draws an enthusiastic crowd. The course is open May–Oct.

Tee times are necessary at the 18-hole **Poland Spring Country Club,** 41 Ricker Rd., Rte. 26, Poland Spring 04274, 207/998-6002, which was first laid out in 1893 on the grounds of the long-gone Poland Spring House, a health spa. Car rentals are available, and there are two restaurants. The course is open May–Oct.

Bicycling

The countryside in this area is mostly gentle, not much of a challenge for gonzo bikers but a decent workout for anyone looking for an average challenge. Although Rte. 202 between Lewiston and Augusta is a well-traveled highway, it has good, broad shoulders for biking—a rarity in Maine. Distance is about 30 miles one-way; a shorter pedal, as far as Greene or Monmouth and return, makes a good day-trip. One of the best vistas along Rte. 202 is from the hilltop near Highmoor Farm, just north of Rte. 106 near the Androscoggin/Kennebec county line.

Winter Sports

The championship alpine slopes of Sunday River Ski Resort are only 45 miles northwest of Lewiston/Auburn, but even closer is family-oriented **Lost Valley,** 200 Lost Valley Rd., off Young's Corner Rd., Auburn 04210, 207/784-1561, www.lostvalleyski.com, two miles from downtown Auburn. Vertical drop is only 240 feet. An unexpected thaw or winter rain sometimes sabotages business here, but top-to-bottom snowmaking (yes, 100 percent) lends a big assist. The crowds swarm in when the weather's right—especially for night skiing (to 9 PM Mon.–Sat.) on the lighted slopes. Lost Valley has 15 trails, a snowboard park, two double chairlifts, and a T-bar. Ski and snowboard rentals are available, the ski school is especially active, and the cafeteria usually teems with families. And where else can you get lift tickets for Lost Valley prices? Flex tickets come in two-, three-, four-, six- and eight-hour blocks; two-hour weekday tickets are $13 for adults or juniors, $18 on weekends. Lost Valley's season typically is mid-Dec.–mid-Mar. The ski area is just west of Lake Auburn.

ENTERTAINMENT

Established in 1991, **The Public Theatre, Lewiston/Auburn's Professional Theatre Company,** 31 Maple St., Lewiston 04240, mailing address 2 Great Falls Plaza, Box 7, Auburn 04210, box office 207/782-3200, has been presenting musicals and dramas for over a decade, leading the way in the Twin Cities cultural scene, and receiving recognition for the quality of its performances. The Theatre's performance of "A Christmas Carol" is a Yuletide tradition in the twin cities. Adult ticket prices are about $16, less for students and seniors.

Since 1973, **L/A Arts,** 221 Lisbon St., Lewiston 04240, 207/782-7228 or 800/639-2919, www.laarts.org, a respected nonprofit arts-sponsorship organization, has been bringing a whole range of cultural events to the area. The group sponsors an International Film Series (at Central Maine Community College; $7 a ticket), family shows (programs for parents and kids), a youth summer theatre program, free concerts in the parks, and a Cabaret Series (at the Ramada Inn). Their energy seems boundless. In early May (usually the first Saturday), L/A Arts holds its annual **art auction,** a fundraiser that draws bidders from around the state. Activities of both the Public Theatre and L/A Arts are listed in the *Lewiston Auburn Arts Calendar.*

The 10-screen **Hoyts Cinemas,** Auburn Plaza, 746 Center St., Auburn 04210, 207/786-8605, has bargain matinees before 6 PM and is open all year.

FESTIVALS AND EVENTS

Throughout the year, **Bates College,** 207/786-6255 weekdays, presents a full schedule of concerts, lectures, exhibits, sporting events, and other activities. Call for details or see www.bates.edu.

Each year, a community committee produces the *Lewiston Auburn Arts Calendar,* a free brochure listing concerts, plays, dances, and even lectures scheduled for the academic year in and around the Twin Cities, including some Bates events. Copies of the brochure are available at many locations or from the chamber of commerce.

The *second* Saturday of May brings the **Annual Thorncrag Community Day,** replete with flower and bird walks, kids' games, and other activities. At the Thorncrag Bird Sanctuary, Lewiston.

Auburn's Festival Plaza is the venue for **Auburn Community Band Concerts,** Wednesdays at 7 PM July–Aug.

Lewiston and Auburn celebrate the Fourth of July with the all-day **Liberty Festival** of nonstop music, children's games, and evening fireworks at Veteran's Park in Lewiston. The second weekend in July brings the **Moxie Festival,** a certifiably eccentric annual celebration of the obscure soft drink Moxie, invented in 1884 and still not consigned to the dustbin of history. Among the activities: a huge offbeat parade, food booths, a Moxie recipe contest, Chief Worumbo's Androscoggin Fun Race, a pancake breakfast, games, a carnival, live entertainment (including an appearance by Elvis), a chicken barbecue, a bubble-gum contest, a road race, and collectibles exhibits and sales. The biggest day is Saturday. It all happens in downtown Lisbon. The acclaimed annual **Bates Dance Festival,** at Bates College, Lewiston, mid-July–mid-Aug., features behind-the-scenes classes and workshops, as well as performances, which are open to the public.

Lewiston hosts the **Festival de Joie,** a three-day multicultural heritage celebration, the first weekend in August. The festival, at Railroad Park on Oxford St., next to the river in Lewiston, features live entertainment, dancing, cultural displays, a parade, bean supper, horse-drawn wagon rides, and more. Originally strictly a Franco-American event, it now encompasses all the ethnic groups that have settled in the area—Greek, Russian, French, African-American. Even Native Americans and Shakers are represented. The **Great Falls Balloon Festival,** the third weekend in August in both Lewiston and Auburn, involves a huge round of events and activities: live music on two big stages, a carnival, food booths, a craft show, games, and morning (6 AM) and evening (5:30 PM) hot-air-balloon launches (balloon rides available by advance reservation, 207/782-2637).

SHOPPING

Lewiston and Auburn have several shopping malls and minimalls; largest is the 46-store **Auburn Mall,** at 550 Center St. (Rte. 4), 207/786-2977, open Mon.–Sat. 10 AM–9 PM, Sun. 11 AM–5 PM.

Collectibles

Vintage clothing, antique and collectible glass and housewares, books, and antique jewelry are only a few of the possibilities in Danny Poulin's 3,000-square-foot space at **Orphan Annie's,** 96 Court St., Auburn 04210, 207/782-0638. Want more? The overflow warehouse, a block away at 10 Pleasant St., is open Mon. 10 AM–1 PM, with deals galore. Orphan Annie's is open all year, Mon.–Sat. 10 AM–5 PM, Sun. noon–5 PM.

Discount Shopping

Alongside the canal just off Lisbon Street in downtown Lewiston, the **Bates Mill Store,** 2 Cedar St., Lewiston 04240, 207/784-7626 or 800/552-2837 outside Maine, www.bates-bedspreads.com, is loaded with irregulars and closeouts of Bates spreads, blankets, towels, sheets, and more. The shop also does a big mail-order business in cotton bedspreads. Open all year, Mon.–Fri. 9 AM–4 PM, Sat. 10 AM–4 PM.

Marden's, Northwood Park Shopping Center, 750 Main St., Rte. 202, Lewiston 04240, 207/786-0313, almost belongs in a category by itself. The original store of a statewide chain, it's a huge collection of leftovers—maternity clothes, tools, lemonade mix, shoes, what-have-you. Each visit is an adventure, and the stock keeps changing. Prices are rock-bottom, great for bargain-hunters, but examine goods carefully before purchasing. Open all year, Mon.–Fri. 9 AM–8 PM, Sat. 9 AM–5 PM, Sun. 11 AM–5 PM.

Farmers Markets and Farm Shops

Look for the **Auburn Mall Farmers Market** in the Porteous back lot, near Turner St., at the Auburn Mall, 550 Center St., Rte. 4, each Thurs. 1–6 PM and Sat. 9 AM–3 PM. The market, one of the state's largest, with a huge selection, operates early May–Oct.

Named for the river running through town, **Nezinscot Farm Store,** N. Parish Rd., Rte. 117, Turner 04282, 207/225-3231, is worth the detour. Besides organically grown produce, the cookies and breads are fabulous. Shop hours are Mon.–Fri. 6 AM–6 PM, Sat. 8 AM–5 PM, and Sun. 9 AM–3 PM. Open all year. The farm is five miles east and north of the junction of Rtes. 4 and 117 (about 16 miles north of downtown Auburn). Call ahead if you're making a special detour.

ACCOMMODATIONS

Motels are the primary lodging type in the Lewiston/Auburn area, running the gamut from respectable national chains to no-tell motels. Two of interest are the **Ramada,** 490 Pleasant St., Lewiston 04240, 207/784-2331, and the recently-upgraded **Auburn Fireside Inn & Suites,** 1777 Washington St., Maine Turnpike Exit 75, 207/777-1777, with hot tubs and fireplaces in some of the suites, and relaxation suites equipped with a massage chair.

Out in the country, on the shores of Tripp Lake about 13 miles from Lewiston, Rose Aikman welcomes guests to her **Wolf Cove Inn Bed & Breakfast,** 5 Jordan Shore Dr., Poland 04274, 207/998-4976, www.wolfcoveinn.com, with ten rooms (eight with private baths, three with fireplaces) named after flowers—from Sweet Alyssum and Hollyhock at $85 d up to the Calla Lilly suite at $250 d. Off-season rates are $75–200 d. Paddle around in one of the inn's canoes or go for a swim in the lake, or both. Sunsets are magnificent here. No pets, no smoking. Open all year.

At the popular **Ware Street Inn,** 52 Ware St., Lewiston 04240, 207/783-8171, 877/783-8171, www.warestreeetinn.com, guests have the best of both worlds, an in-city accommodation right across the street from Bates, but surrounded by over an acre of gardens and trees. For the driven, there is total internet access, but if they want to slow down, they can use the lovely terrace or the video library—all rooms have VCRs. Friendly innkeeper Jan Barrett says "a really nice crowd comes here." It's easy to see why: with her concern for making people comfortable and bicyclist husband Mike's welcome to guests, including cyclists, who can store their bikes in the garage. There's a fireplace in the relaxed-elegant living room, entertainment specials in conjunction with the Nothing But the Blues Café. Rates for the six rooms range from $80–175 d., including a full breakfast. Open all year, except some holidays.

Campgrounds

On the shore of Lower Range Pond, 40-acre **Poland Spring Campground,** Rte. 26, P.O. Box 409, Poland Spring 04274, 207/998-2151, www.polandspringcamp.com, has 130 wooded tent and RV sites ($19–31 for two adults, three children, and one dog). Facilities include an outdoor pool, coin-operated showers, a general store, laundry, play areas, and rental canoes, kayaks, and rowboats. There's lots of organized fun; be prepared for campfires, ice cream parties, hay rides, barbecues, and other activities,

although noise rules are monitored. Reservations are recommended. The campground, open May 1–Columbus Day, is about 10 miles west of Auburn.

FOOD

Inexpensive to Moderate

The college crowd beats a path to **Nothing But the Blues Café,** 81 College St., Lewiston 04240, 207/784-6493, www.nbtbcafe.com, a casual, 32-seat restaurant not far from Bates. Entrées on the eclectic menu, emphasizing vegetarian and changing daily, are all under $11. Lunch portions are smaller, designed for speedy service. No liquor license; don't bring any. Open daily all year, Mon.–Sat. 11:30 AM–8 PM (to 9 PM Fri.–Sat.) and Sun. 11:30 AM–5 PM.

Locals rave about **Italian Bakery Products Co.,** 225 Bartlett St., Lewiston, 207/782-8312. It's a great little place to pick up baked goods like cannoli or Bismarck donuts, as well as sandwiches for lunch.

In the retrofitted Bates Mill, **DaVinci's Eatery,** Bates Mill, 35 Canal St., Lewiston 04240, 207/782-2088, www.davincieatery.com, specializes in pasta, and mostly northern Italian cuisine, and also features brick-oven pizza, but has a variety of other regional American and Italian entrées in the $10–17 range. The 150-seat restaurant, with liquor license, is open all year Mon.–Thurs. 11 AM–9 PM, Fri.–Sat. 11 AM–10 PM.

A few miles southeast of Lewiston is **Graziano's Casa Mia Restaurant,** Lisbon Rd., Rte. 196, Lisbon 04250, 207/353-4335, a locally colorful eatery lined floor-to-ceiling with classic autographed boxing portraits and a few ringers: Edmund Muskie, Frank Sinatra, Jimmy Carter, and the pope. Even if boxing is your least-favorite sport, you'll get a kick out of this traditional "tomato Italian" spot owned by Joe Graziano since 1968. The atmosphere in the sprawling, six-room restaurant is funky and friendly, average entrées range $10–14, with a couple of outliers, and the pasta and sauces are homemade, with some upscale touches. If you're into veal, eat it here. Children are welcome (the booths are convenient); the menu even has a "bambino corner," although there's pizza on the regular menu. Open all year, Tues.–Fri. 11 AM–9 PM (to 10 PM Fri.), Sat. 4–10 PM, Sun. 4–9 PM.

Eli's Restaurant, Turner Highlands Country Club, N. Parish Rd., Rte. 117, Turner 04282, 207/224-7090, www.elisrestaurant.com, in the bright, modernized clubhouse, has earned a fine reputation for creative regional cuisine with flair. Entrées are $7.25–10 for lunch, $8–23 for dinner. Reservations are a good idea. On Saturday "Couples Nights," two can wine and dine for $40 total. The restaurant is open mid-May–Oct.; summer hours are Tues.–Sat. 11 AM–9 PM, Sun. 11 AM–5 PM. Off-season there is a popular Sunday brunch. Turner is about 11 miles north of Auburn.

Moderate to Expensive

A newish spot for creative continental fare is **TJ's Restaurant,** 2 Great Falls Plaza, Auburn 04210, 207/784-7217. The 99-seat restaurant serves lunch and dinner for $13 and up.

The Sedgley Place, 54 Sedgley Rd., P.O. Box 517, Greene 04236, 207/946-5990, menu line 207/946-5989 or 800/924-7778, www.sedgleyplace.com, has a rather unusual dinner-by-reservation arrangement: First call the menu line to hear the current choices, then call back on the other number to reserve a table and order your preferences. The menu changes each week, usually featuring prime ribs as well as fish and poultry options (request vegetarian and children's portions ahead). The restaurant makes it a point to support local growers. Five-course dinners are $25.95 pp, but there are always $18.95 specials. Occasionally, there are wine tastings. Located in a lovely Federal-style homestead a mile southwest of Rte. 202 (6 miles north of Lewiston), the restaurant is open all year. Summer hours (Memorial Day weekend through Labor Day weekend): seatings Tues.–Thurs. and Sun. are at 5, 6, and 7 PM; Fri.–Sat. there is an additional seating at 8 PM. The menu line is always available, but reservations can be made only Tues.–Sun. 11 AM–9 PM.

Well-known for steaks, **Mac's Grill,** 1052 Minot Ave., Auburn 04210, 207/783-6885, www.macsgrill.com, has a wide variety of other menu items, from wraps and burgers to a seafood pasta bake, lots of salads, and stuffed chicken pomodoro. Sandwiches go for about $6; filet mignon for $22.50. Open daily 11:30 AM to 9 PM Sun.–Thurs., to 10 PM Fri.–Sat.

At the 99-seat **Blackwatch,** 84 Court St., Auburn 04210, 207/777-7443, www.blackwatchrest.com, casual fine dining centers on seafood and steaks, with entrées from $17–24. The menu changes often. Open for lunch 11 AM–2 PM weekdays, dinner 5–9 PM Mon.–Sat.

INFORMATION AND SERVICES

The **Androscoggin County Chamber of Commerce,** 179 Lisbon St., P.O. Box 59, Lewiston 04240, 207/783-2249, fax 783-4481, www.androscoggincounty.com, serves as the tourism information center for the entire county. The office is open Mon.–Thurs. 8 AM–5 PM and Fri. 8 AM–noon in summer, to 3 PMin winter. Parking can be a problem in this part of Lewiston, so use the Canal Street parking garage and take the fourth-floor walkway; you'll be right on the chamber's level. (Parking is cheap, and the chamber office will validate your ticket so you can park for free.) The website includes details on an exceptional historical walking tour, with photos of local landmarks.

Housed in a handsome granite Romanesque Revival building (1903), the **Lewiston Public Library,** 105 Park St., Lewiston 04240, 207/784-0135, www.lplonline.org, is one of the sponsors of the Great Falls Forum, presenting monthly lunches with expert speakers on various thought-provoking topics. Open Mon.–Thurs. 9 AM–8 PM, Fri. 9 AM–5 PM, and summer Sat. 9 AM–2 PM.

Newspapers

The daily newspaper of choice is the *Lewiston Sun-Journal,* 207/784-5411, www.sunjournal.com, plus the weekend *Sunday.* The Friday edition's "Encore" section contains extensive calendar listings spotlighting the Lewiston/Auburn area. Many residents also read the *Portland Press Herald,* published daily. Its Thursday "Go" section contains features and calendar listings that include the Lewiston/Auburn area.

Emergencies

For **police, fire, and ambulance services,** dial 911. The major medical facility is **Central Maine Medical Center,** 300 Main St., Lewiston 04240, 207/795-0111. Also here is **St. Mary's Regional Medical Center,** Campus Ave., Lewiston 04240, emergency-room 207/777-8120. Both hospitals have round-the-clock emergency rooms.

Getting Around

City Cab Co., 207/784-4521, provides 24-hour service in the Lewiston/Auburn area.

Know
Maine

MAINE COUNTIES

CANADA

QUÉBEC

AROOSTOOK

NEW BRUNSWICK

PISCATAQUIS

SOMERSET

PENOBSCOT

FRANKLIN

WASHINGTON

VT

HANCOCK

WALDO

OXFORD

KENNEBEC

ANDROSCOGGIN

KNOX

LINCOLN

SAGADAHOC

CUMBERLAND

YORK

NEW HAMPSHIRE

ATLANTIC OCEAN

0   50 mi

0   50 km

© AVALON TRAVEL PUBLISHING, INC.

The Land

Man is born to die. His works are short-lived. Buildings crumble, monuments decay, wealth vanishes...

With those words, Governor Percival P. Baxter in 1931 deeded to the people of Maine the first parcel of thousands of wilderness acres to remain "forever wild." Today, we know this natural treasure as Baxter State Park. Mile-high Katahdin, centerpiece of the park and the northern terminus of the Appalachian Trail, remains, as the governor stipulated, "the mountain of the people of Maine." Governor Baxter's incredible foresight preserved what surely could and likely would have been denuded, developed, and ultimately destroyed. And Baxter State Park is only the beginning of Maine's natural treasures.

The Pine Tree State boasts more than 17 million acres of forest covering 89 percent of the state; 5,900 lakes and ponds; 4,617 saltwater islands; 10 mountains over 4,000 feet and nearly a hundred mountains higher than 3,000 feet. The highest peak in the state is Katahdin, at 5,267 feet. (Katahdin is a Penobscot Indian word meaning "greatest mountain," making the name "Mt. Katahdin" redundant.)

Maine's largest lake is Moosehead, in Greenville, 32 miles long and 20 miles across at its widest point, with a maximum depth of 246 feet. Remote enough to have remained unspoiled, the area is fantastic for camping, fishing, boating, swimming, hiking, and moose-spotting.

Bounded by the Gulf of Maine (Atlantic Ocean), the St. Croix River, New Brunswick Province, the St. John River, Quebec Province, and the state of New Hampshire (and the only state in the Union bordered by only one other state), Maine is the largest of the six New England states, roughly equivalent in size to the five others combined—offering plenty of space to hike, bike, camp, sail, ski, swim, or just hang out. The state extends from 43° 05' to 47° 28' north latitude, and 66° 56' to 80° 50' west longitude. (Technically, Maine dips even farther southeast to take in five islands in the offshore Isles of Shoals.) It's all stitched together by 22,574 miles of highways and 3,561 bridges.

RIVERS TO THE GULF

Maine's 5,000-plus rivers and streams provide nearly half of the watershed for the Gulf of Maine. The major rivers are the Penobscot (350 miles), the St. John (211 miles), the Androscoggin (175 miles), the Kennebec (150 miles), the Saco (104 miles), and the St. Croix (75 miles). The St. John and its tributaries flow northeast; all the others flow more or less south or southeast.

The Penobscot and the Kennebec are navigable upstream—to Bangor and Augusta; on their upper reaches, dam-controlled flows make for splendid white-water rafting.

IN THE BEGINNING...

Maine is an outdoor classroom for Geology 101, a living lesson in what the glaciers did and how they did it. Geologically, Maine is something of a youngster; the oldest rocks, found in the Chain of Ponds area, not far from Sugarloaf/USA, are only 1.6 billion years old—more than two billion years younger than the world's oldest rocks.

But most significant is the great ice sheet that began to spread over Maine about 25,000 years ago, during the late Wisconsin Ice Age. As it moved southward from Canada, this continental glacier scraped, gouged, pulverized, and depressed the bedrock in its path. On it continued, charging up the north faces of mountains, clipping off their tops and moving southward, leaving behind jagged cliffs on the mountains' southern faces and odd deposits of stone and clay. By about 21,000 years ago, glacial ice extended well out over the Gulf of

Maine, perhaps as far as the Georges Bank fishing grounds.

But all that began to change with meltdown, beginning about 18,000 years ago. As the glacier melted and receded, ocean water moved in, covering much of the coastal plain and working its way inland up the rivers. By 11,000 years ago, glaciation had pulled back from all but a few minor corners at the top of Maine, revealing the south coast's beaches and the unusual geologic traits—eskers and erratics, kettleholes and moraines, even a fjord—that make the rest of the state such a fascinating natural laboratory.

TODAY'S LANDSCAPE

Seven distinct looks make up the contemporary Maine landscape. Along the southwest coast, from Kittery to Portland, are fine-sand beaches, marshlands, and only the occasional rocky headland. The Mid-Coast, from Portland to the Penobscot River, features one finger of rocky land after another, all jutting out into the Gulf of Maine and all incredibly scenic. The Down East coast, from the Penobscot River to Eastport and including fantastic Acadia National Park, has many similarities to the Mid-Coast (gorgeous rocky peninsulas, offshore islands, granite everywhere), but, except on Mount Desert Island, takes on a different look and feel by virtue of its slower pace, higher tides, and quieter villages.

The Down East mountains, roughly straddling "the Airline" (Route 9 from Bangor to Calais), are marked by open blueberry fields, serious woodlands, and mountains that seem to appear out of nowhere. The central upland—essentially a huge S-shape extending from the Portland area through Augusta, Waterville, and Skowhegan, then on up into Aroostook County, at the top of the state—is characterized by lakes, ponds, rolling fields, and occasional woodlands, interspersed with river valleys. Aroostook County is the state's agricultural jackpot. The northern region—essentially the valleys of the north-flowing St. John and Allagash

Rivers—was the last part of Maine to lose the glacier and is today dense forest, crisscrossed with logging roads (you can count the settlements on two hands). The mountain upland, taking in all the state's major elevations and extending from inland York County to Baxter State Park, is rugged, beautiful, and the premier region for skiing, hiking, camping, and white-water rafting.

CLIMATE

Whoever invented the state's oldest cliché—"If you don't like the weather, wait a minute"—must have spent several minutes in Maine. The good news is that if the weather is lousy, it's bound to change before too long. And when it does, it's intoxicating. Brilliant, cloud-free Maine weather has lured many a visitor to put down roots, buy a retirement home, or at least invest in a summer retreat.

The serendipity of it all necessitates two caveats: *Always pack warmer clothing than you think you'll need.* And *never arrive without a sweater or jacket—even at the height of summer.*

The National Weather Service separates Maine into three distinct climatological divisions—coastal, southern interior, and northern interior (several subdivisions also appear regularly in forecasts).

The **coastal** division, which includes Portland, runs from Kittery northeast to Eastport and about 20 miles inland. Here, the ocean moderates the climate, making coastal winters warmer and summers cooler than in the interior (relatively speaking, of course). From early June–August, the Portland area—fairly typical of coastal weather—may have 3–8 days of temperatures over 90°F, 25–40 days over 80°F, 14–24 days of fog, and 5–10 inches of rain. Normal annual precipitation for the Portland area is 44 inches of rain and 71 inches of snow (the snow total is misleading, though, since intermittent thaws clear away much of the base).

The **southern interior** division, covering the bottom third of the state, sees the warmest weather in summer, the most clear days each year, and an average snowfall of 60–90 inches. The **northern interior** part of the state, with the highest mountains, covers the upper two-thirds of Maine and boasts a mixed bag of snowy winters, warm summers, and the state's lowest rainfall.

Northeasters and Hurricanes

A northeaster is a counterclockwise, swirling storm that brings wild winds out of—you guessed it—the northeast. One can occur any time of year, whenever the conditions brew it up. Depending on the season, the winds are accompanied by rain, sleet, snow, or all of them together.

Hurricane season officially runs June–November but is most prevalent late August–September. Some years, the Maine coast remains out of harm's way; other years, head-on hurricanes and even glancing blows have eroded beaches, flooded roads, splintered boats, downed trees, knocked out power, and inflicted major residential and commercial damage. Winds—the greatest culprit—average 74–90 mph. A **hurricane watch** is announced on radio and TV about 36 hours beforehand, followed by a **hurricane warning,** indicating that the storm is imminent. Find shelter, away from plate-glass windows, and wait it out. If especially high winds are predicted, make every effort to secure yourself, your vehicle, and your possessions. Resist the urge to head for the shore to watch the show; rogue waves, combined with ultra-high tides, have been known to sweep away unwary onlookers.

Sea Smoke and Fog

Fog and sea smoke, two atmospheric phenomena resulting from opposing conditions, are only distantly related. But both can radically affect visibility and therefore be hazardous. In winter, when the ocean is at least 40°F warmer than the air, billowy sea smoke rises from the water, creating great photo-ops for camera buffs but especially dangerous conditions for mariners.

In any season, when the ocean (or lake or land) is colder than the air, fog sets in, creating perilous conditions for drivers, mariners, and pilots. Romantics, however, see it otherwise, reveling in the womblike ambience and the muffled moans of foghorns. Between April and October, Portland averages about 31 days with heavy fog, when visibility may be a quarter-mile or less.

Storm Warnings

The National Weather Service's official daytime signal system for wind velocity consists of a series of flags representing specific wind speeds and sea conditions. Beachgoers and anyone planning to venture out in a kayak, canoe, sailboat, or powerboat should heed these signals. The flags are posted on all public beaches, and warnings are announced on TV and radio weather broadcasts, as well as on cable TV's Weather Channel and the NOAA broadcast network.

Flora and Fauna

From this elevation, just on the skirts of the clouds, we could overlook the country, west and south, for a hundred miles. There it was, the State of Maine, which we had seen on the map, but not much like that. Immeasurable forest for the sun to shine on.... No clearing, no house. It did not look as if a solitary traveler had cut so much as a walking stick there. Countless lakes. . . and mountains. The forest looked like a firm grass sward, and the effect of these lakes in its midst has been well compared. . . to that of a mirror broken into a thousand fragments, and widely scattered over the grass, reflecting the full blaze of the sun.

—Henry David Thoreau, The Maine Woods

Looking out over Maine from Katahdin today, as Thoreau did in 1857, you get a view that is still a mass of green stretching to the sea, broken by blue lakes and rivers. Although the forest has been cut several times since Thoreau saw it, Maine is proportionately still the most forested state in the nation.

It also is clearly one of the best watered. Receiving an average of more than 40 inches of precipitation a year, Maine is abundantly endowed with swamps, bogs, ponds, lakes, streams, and rivers. These, in turn, drain from a coast deeply indented by coves, estuaries, and bays.

In this state of trees and water, nature dominates more than most—Maine is the least densely populated state east of the Mississippi River. Here, where boreal and temperate ecosystems meet and mix, lives a rich diversity of plants and animals.

THE ALPINE TUNDRA

Three continental storm tracks converge on Maine, and the state's western mountains bear the brunt of the weather they bring. Stretching from Katahdin in the north along most of Maine's border with Quebec and New Hampshire, these mountains have a far colder climate than their temperate latitude might suggest.

Timberline here occurs at only about 4,000 feet, and where the mountaintops reach above that, the environment is truly arctic—an alpine-tundra habitat where only the hardiest species can live. Beautiful, pale-green "map" lichens cover many of the exposed rocks like shapes cut from an atlas, and sedges and rushes take root in the patches of thin topsoil. As many as 30 alpine plant species—typically found hundreds of miles to the north—grow in crevices or hollows in the lee of the blasting winds. Small and low-growing to conserve energy in this harsh climate, such plants as **bearberry willow, Lapland rosebay, alpine azalea, diapensia, mountain cranberry,** and **black crowberry** reward the observant hiker with white, yellow, pink, and magenta flowers in late June and July.

Areas above tree line are generally inhospitable to most animals other than secretive **voles, mice,** and **lemmings.** Even so, summer or winter, a hiker is likely to be aware of at least one other species—the **northern raven.** More than any of the 300 or so other bird species that regularly occur in Maine, the raven is the bird of the state's wild places, its mountain ridges, rocky coasts, and remote forests. Solid black, like a crow, but larger and stockier and with a wedge-shaped tail and broad wings, the northern raven is a magnificent flyer—soaring, hovering, diving, and often turning loops and rolls as though playing in the wind. Known to be among the most intelligent of all animals, ravens are quite social, actively communicating with one another in throaty croaks as they range over the landscape in search of carrion and other available plant and animal foods.

At tree line and below, where conditions are moderate enough to allow black spruce and balsam fir to take hold, fauna becomes far more diverse. Among the wind- and ice-stunted trees, called *krummholz* (crooked wood), forage **northern juncos** and **white-throated**

STATE SYMBOLS

State Animal	Moose *(Alces alces americana)*
State Bird	Chickadee *(Parus atricapillus)*
State Cat	Maine Coon
State Fish	Landlocked Salmon *(Salmo salar)*
State Flower	White Pine Cone and Tassel *(Pinus strobus)*
State Fossil	*Pertica quadrifaria,* a six-foot-high plant that lived in Maine nearly 400 million years ago
State Herb	Wintergreen
State Insect	Honeybee *(Apis mellifera)*
State Mineral	Tourmaline
State Motto	*Dirigo* (Meaning "I lead" or "I direct"—in line with the late-19th-century political maxim, "As Maine goes, so goes the nation"—*dirigo* is emblazoned on the state flag.)
State Nickname	Pine Tree State (Pine is the most prominent tree species in Maine, and the source of wood for durable masts throughout the Great Age of Sail. A pine tree appears in the center of Maine's state seal.)
State Soil	Chesuncook

Know Maine

sparrows. The latter's plaintive whistle (often mnemonically rendered as "Old Sam Peabody, Peabody, Peabody") is one of the most evocative sounds of the Maine woods.

THE BOREAL OR NORTHERN FOREST

Mention the Maine woods and the image that is likely to come to mind is the boreal forests of **spruce** and **fir.** In 1857, Thoreau captured the character of these woods when he wrote, "It is all mossy and moosey. In some of those dense fir and spruce woods there is hardly room for the smoke to go up. The trees are a standing night, and every fir and spruce which you fell is a plume plucked from night's raven wing. Then at night the general stillness is more impressive than any sound, but occasionally you hear the note of an owl farther or nearer in the woods, and if near a lake, the semi-human cry of the loons at their unearthly revels."

Well adapted to a short growing season, low temperatures, and rocky, nutrient-poor soils, spruce and fir do dominate the woods on mountainsides, in low-lying areas beside watercourses, and along the coast. By not having to produce new foliage every year, these evergreens conserve scarce nutrients and also retain their needles, which capture sunlight for photosynthesis during all but the coldest months. The needles also wick moisture from the low clouds and fog that frequently bathe their preferred habitat, bringing annual precipitation to more than 80 inches a year in some areas.

In the lush boreal forest environment grows a diverse ground cover of herbaceous plants, including **bearberry, bunchberry, clintonia, starflower,** and **wood sorrel.** In older spruce-fir stands, mosses and lichens often carpet much of the forest floor in a soft tapestry of greens and gray-blues. Maine is extraordinarily rich in **lichens,** with more than 700 species identified so far—20 percent of the total found in all of North America. **Usnea** is a familiar one; its common name, old man's beard, comes from its wispy strands, which drip from the branches of spruce trees. The **northern parula,** a small blue, green, and yellow bird of the wood warbler family, weaves its ball-shaped pendulum nest from usnea.

The spruce-fir forest is prime habitat for many other species that are among the most sought-after by birders: **black-backed** and **three-toed woodpeckers,** the audaciously bold **gray jay** (or camp robber), **boreal chickadee, yellow-throated flycatcher, white-winged crossbill, Swainson's thrush,** and a half-dozen other gemlike wood warblers.

Among the more unusual birds of this forest type is the **spruce grouse.** Sometimes hard to spot because it does not flush, a spruce grouse is so tame that a careful person can actually touch one. Not surprisingly, the spruce grouse earned the nickname "fool hen" early in the 19th century, and no doubt it would have become extinct long ago but for its menu preference of spruce and fir needles, which render its meat bitter and inedible (you can get an idea by tasting a few needles yourself).

Few of Maine's 56 mammal species are restricted to the boreal forest, but several are very characteristic of it. Most obvious from its trilling, far-carrying chatter, is the **red squirrel.** Piles of cone remnants on the forest floor mark a red squirrel's recent banquet. The red squirrel itself is the favored prey of another coniferous forest inhabitant, the **pine marten.** An arboreal member of the mustelid family—which in Maine also includes **skunk, weasel, fisher,** and **otter**—the pine marten is a sleek, low-slung predator with blond to brown fur, an orange throat patch, and a long, bushy tail. Its beautiful pelt nearly led to the animal's obliteration from Maine through overtrapping, but with protection, the marten population has rebounded.

Nearly half a century of protection also allowed the population recovery of Maine's most prominent mammal, the **moose.** Standing 6–7 feet tall at the shoulder and weighing as much as 1,200 pounds, the moose is the largest member of the Cervidae or deer family. A bull's massive antlers, which it sheds and regrows each year, may span five or more feet and weigh 75 pounds. The animal's long legs

and bulbous nose give it an ungainly appearance, but the moose is ideally adapted to a life spent wading through deep snow, dense thickets, and swamps.

Usually the best place to observe a moose is at the edge of a body of water on a summer afternoon or evening. Wading out into the water, the animal may submerge its entire head to browse on the succulent aquatic plants below the surface. The water also offers a respite from the swarms of biting insects that plague moose (and people who venture into these woods without bug repellent). Except for a limited hunting season, moose have little to fear from humans and often will allow close approach. Be careful, however, and give them the respect their imposing size suggests; cows can be very protective of their calves, and bulls can be unpredictable, particularly during the fall rutting (mating) season.

Another word of caution about moose: When driving, especially in spring and early summer, be alert for moose wandering out of the woods and onto roadways to escape the flies. Moose are dark brown, their eyes do not reflect headlights in the way that most other animals' do, and they do not get out of the way—of cars or anything else. Colliding with a half-ton animal can be a tragedy for all involved. Pay particular attention while driving in Oxford, Franklin, Somerset (especially Rt. 201), Piscataquis, and Aroostook Counties, but with an estimated 25,000–30,000 moose statewide, they can and do turn up anywhere and everywhere—even in downtown Portland and on offshore islands.

Protection from unlimited hunting was not the only reason for the dramatic increase in Maine's moose population; the invention of the chain saw and the skidder have played parts, too. In a few days, one or two men can now cut and yard a tract of forest that a whole crew of lumbermen with saws and horses formerly took weeks to harvest. With the increase in logging, particularly the clear-cutting of spruce and fir (whose long fibers are favored for papermaking), vast areas have been opened up for regeneration by fast-growing, sun-loving hardwoods.

The leaves of these young **white birch, poplar, pin cherry,** and **striped maple** are a veritable moose salad bar.

THE TRANSITION ZONE: NORTHERN HARDWOOD FOREST

Although hardwoods have replaced spruce and fir in many areas, mixed woods of **sugar maple, American beech, yellow birch, red oak, red spruce, eastern hemlock,** and **white pine** have always been a major part of Maine's natural and social histories. This northern hardwood forest, as it is termed by ecologists, is a transitional zone between northern and southern ecosystems and rich in species diversity.

Dominated by deciduous trees, this forest community is highly seasonal. Spring snowmelt brings a pulse of life to the newly exposed forest floor as herbaceous plants race to develop and flower before the trees overhead leaf out and limit the available sunlight. (Blink and you can practically miss a Maine spring.) **Trout lily, goldthread, trillium, violets, gaywing,** and **pink lady's slipper** are among the many woodland wildflowers whose blooms make a walk in the forest so rewarding at this time of year. Deciduous trees, shrubs, and a dozen species of ferns also must make the most of their short (four-month) growing season. In the Maine woods, the buds of mid-May unfurl into a full canopy of leaves by the first week of June.

Late spring and early summer in the northern hardwood forest is also a time of intense animal activity. Runoff from the melting snowpack has filled countless low-lying depressions throughout the woods. These ephemeral swamps and vernal pools are a haven for an enormous variety of aquatic invertebrates, insects, amphibians, and reptiles. Choruses of spring **peepers,** Maine's smallest—but seemingly loudest—frog, alert everyone with their high-pitched calls that the ice is going out and breeding season is at hand. Measuring only about an inch in length, these tiny frogs with X-shaped patterns on their backs can be surprisingly difficult to see without some determined effort. Look on the branches of shrubs overhanging the water—males often use them as perches from which to call prospective mates. But then why stop with peepers? There are eight other frog and toad species in Maine to search for, too.

Spring is also the best time to look for **salamanders.** Driving a country road on a rainy night in mid-April provides an opportunity to witness one of nature's great mass migrations, as salamanders and frogs of several species emerge from their wintering sites and make their way across roads to breeding pools and streams. Once breeding is completed, most salamanders return to the terrestrial environment, where they burrow into crevices or the moist litter of the forest floor. The movement of amphibians from wetlands to uplands has an important ecological function, providing a mechanism for the return of nutrients that runoff washes into low-lying areas. This may seem hard to believe until one considers the numbers of individuals involved in this movement. To illustrate, the total biomass of Maine's **redback salamander** population—just one of the eight salamander species found here—is heavier than the combined weight of all the state's moose!

The many bird species characteristic of the northern hardwood forest are also most in evidence during the late spring and early summer, when the males are engaged in holding breeding territory and attracting mates. For most passerines—perching birds—this means singing. Especially during the early-morning and evening hours, the woods are alive with choruses of song from such birds as the **purple finch, white-throated sparrow, solitary vireo, black-throated blue warbler, Canada warbler, mourning warbler, northern waterthrush,** and the most beautiful singer of them all, the **hermit thrush.**

Providing abundant browse as well as tubers, berries, and nuts, the northern hardwood forest supports many of Maine's mammal species. The **red-backed vole, snowshoe hare, porcupine,** and **white-tailed deer** are relatively abundant and in turn are prey for **fox, bobcat, fisher,** and **eastern coyote.** Now well established since its expansion into Maine in the 1950s and 1960s, the eastern coyote has filled the niche at the top of the food chain once held by wolves and mountain lions before their extermination from the state in the late 19th century. **Black bears,** of which Maine has an estimated 25,000, are technically classified as carnivores and will take a moose calf or deer on occasion, but most of their diet consists of vegetation, insects, and fish. In the fall, bears feast on beechnuts and acorns, putting on extra fat for the coming winter, which they spend sleeping (not hibernating, as is often presumed) in a sheltered spot dug out beneath a rock or log.

Autumn is a time of spectacular beauty in Maine's northern hardwood forest. With the shortening days and cooler temperatures of September, the dominant green chlorophyll molecules in deciduous leaves start breaking down. As they do, the yellow, orange, and red pigments (which are always present in the leaves—and serve to capture light in parts of the spectrum not captured by the chlorophyll) are revealed. Sugar maples put on the most dazzling display, but beech, birches, red maple, and poplar add their colors to make up an autumn landscape famous the world over.

Ecologically, one of the most significant mammals in the Maine woods is the **beaver.** After being trapped almost to extinction in the 1800s, this large swimming rodent has recolonized streams, rivers, and ponds throughout the state. Well known for its ability as a dam builder, the beaver can change low-lying woodland into a complex aquatic ecosystem. The impounded water behind the dam often kills the trees it inundates, but these provide ideal nest cavities for **mergansers, wood ducks, owls, woodpeckers,** and **swallows.** The still water is also a nursery for a rich diversity of invertebrates, fish, amphibians, and Maine's seven aquatic turtle species, most common of which is the beautiful but very shy **eastern painted turtle.**

THE AQUATIC ENVIRONMENT

Small woodland pools and streams are, of course, only a part of Maine's aquatic environment. The state's nearly 6,000 lakes and ponds provide open-water and deep-water habitats for many additional species. A favorite among them is the **common loon,** symbol of north country lakes across the continent. Loons impart a sense of wildness and mystery with their haunting calls and yodels resonating off the surrounding pines on still summer nights. Adding to their popular appeal are their striking black-and-white plumage, accented with red eyes, and their ability to vanish below the surface and then reappear in another part of the lake moments later. The annual census of Maine's common loons since the 1970s indicates a relatively stable population of about 3,200 breeding pairs.

Below the surface of Maine's lakes, ponds, rivers, and streams, 69 freshwater fish species live in the state, of which 17 were introduced. Among these exotic transplants are some of the most sought-after game fish, including **smallmouth** and **largemouth bass, rainbow trout,** and **northern pike.** These introductions may have benefited anglers, but they have displaced native species in many watersheds.

Several of Maine's native fish have interesting histories in that they became landlocked during the retreat of the glacier. At that time, Maine was climatically much like northern Canada is today, and **arctic char** ran up its rivers to spawn at the edges of the ice. As the ice continued to recede, some of these fish became trapped but nevertheless managed to survive and establish themselves in their new landlocked environments. Two remnant subspecies now exist: the **blueback charr,** which lives in the cold, deep water of 10 northern Maine lakes, and the **Sunapee charr,** now found only in three lakes in Maine and two in Idaho. A similar history belongs to the **landlocked salmon,** a form of Atlantic salmon that many regard as the state's premier game fish and now widely stocked throughout the state and around the country.

M

Atlantic salmon still run up some Maine rivers every year to spawn, but dams and heavy commercial fishing at sea have depleted their numbers and distribution to a fraction of what they once were. Unlike salmon species on the Pacific coast, adult Atlantic salmon survive the fall spawning period and make their way back out to sea again. The young, or parr, hatch the following spring and live in streams and rivers for the next two or three years before migrating to the waters off Greenland. Active efforts are now underway to restore this species, including capturing and trucking the fish around dams. Salmon is just one of the species whose life cycle starts in fresh water and requires migrations to and from the sea. Called anadromous fish, others include **striped bass, sturgeon, shad, alewives, smelt,** and **eels.** All were once far more numerous in Maine, but fortunately pollution control and management efforts in the past three decades have helped their populations rebound slightly from their historic low numbers.

ESTUARIES AND MUDFLATS

Maine's estuaries, where fresh and salt water meet, are ecosystems of outstanding biological importance. South of Cape Elizabeth, where the Maine coast is low and sandy, estuaries harbor large salt marshes of **spartina** grasses that can tolerate the frequent variations in salinity as runoff and tides fluctuate. Producing an estimated four times more plant material than an equivalent area of wheat, these spartina marshes provide abundant nutrients and shelter for a host of marine organisms that ultimately account for as much as 60 percent of the value of the state's commercial fisheries.

The tidal range along the Maine coast varies 9–26 vertical feet, southwest to northeast. Where the tide inundates sheltered estuaries for more than a few hours at a time, spartina grasses cannot take hold, and mudflats dominate. Although it may look like a barren wasteland at low tide, a mudflat is also a highly productive environment and home to abundant marine life. Several species of tiny primitive

worms called **nematodes** can inhabit the mud in densities of 2,000 or more per square inch. Larger worm species are also very common. One, the **bloodworm,** grows up to a foot in length and is harvested in quantity for use as sportfishing bait.

More highly savored among the mudflat residents is the **soft-shelled clam,** famous for its outstanding flavor and an essential ingredient of an authentic Maine lobsterbake. But because clams are suspension feeders—filtering phytoplankton through their long siphon, or "neck"—they can accumulate pollutants that cause illness, including hepatitis. Many Maine mudflats are closed to clam harvesting because of leaking septic systems, so it's best to check with the state's Department of Marine Resources or the local municipal office before digging a mess of clams yourself.

For birds—and birders—salt marshes and mudflats are an unparalleled attraction. Long-legged wading birds such as **glossy ibis, snowy egret, little blue heron, great blue heron, tricolored heron, green heron,** and **black-crowned night heron** frequent the marshes in great numbers throughout the summer months, hunting the shallow waters for mummichogs and other small salt-marsh fish, crustaceans, and invertebrates. From mid-May to early June, and then again from mid-July until mid-September, migrating shorebirds pass through Maine to and from their subarctic breeding grounds. On a good day, a discerning birder can find 17 or more species of shorebirds probing the mudflats and marshes with pointed bills in search of their preferred foods. In turn, the large flocks of shorebirds don't escape the notice of their own predators—**merlins** and **peregrine falcons** dash in to catch a meal.

THE ROCKY SHORELINE AND THE MARINE ENVIRONMENT

On the more exposed rocky shores—the dominant shoreline from Cape Elizabeth all the way Down East to Lubec—where currents and waves keep mud and sand from accumulating, the plant and animal communities are entirely different from those in the inland aquatic areas. The most important requirement for life in this impenetrable, rockbound environment is probably the ability to hang on tight. **Barnacles,** the calcium-armored crustaceans that attach themselves to the rocks immediately below the high-tide line, have developed a fascinating battery of adaptations to survive not only pounding waves but also prolonged exposure to air, solar heat, and extreme winter cold. Glued in place, however, they cannot escape being eaten by **dog whelks,** the predatory snails that also inhabit this intertidal zone. Whelks are larger and more elongate than the more numerous and ubiquitous **periwinkle,** accidentally transplanted from Europe in the mid-19th century.

Also hanging onto these rocks, but at a lower level, are the brown algae—seaweeds. Like a marine forest, the four species of **rockweed** provide shelter for a wide variety of life beneath their fronds. A world of discovery awaits those who make the effort to go out onto the rocks at low tide and look under the clumps of seaweed and into the tidal pools they shelter. Venture into these chilly waters with mask, fins, and wetsuit and still another world opens for natural-history exploration. Beds of **blue mussels, sea urchins, sea stars,** and **sea cucumbers** dot the bottom close to shore. In crevices between and beneath the rocks lurk **rock crabs** and **lobsters.** Now a symbol of the Maine coast and the delicious seafood it provides, the lobster was once considered "poor man's food"—so plentiful that it was spread on fields as fertilizer. Although lobsters are far less common than they once were, they are one of Maine's most closely monitored species, and their population continues to support a large and thriving commercial fishing industry.

Sadly, the same cannot be said for most of Maine's other commercially harvested marine fish. When Europeans first came to these shores four centuries ago, **cod, haddock, halibut, hake, flounder, herring,** and **tuna** were abundant. No longer. Overharvested, their seabed habitat torn up by relentless dragging, these groundfish have all but disappeared. It

will be decades before these species can recover—and then only if effective regulations can be put in place soon.

The familiar doglike face of the **harbor seal,** often seen peering alertly from the surface just offshore, provides a reminder that wildlife populations are resilient—if given a chance. A century ago, there was a bounty on harbor seals because it was thought they ate too many lobsters and fish. Needless to say, neither fish nor lobsters increased when the seals all but disappeared. With the bounty's repeal and the advent of legal protection, Maine's harbor seal population has bounced back to an estimated 15,000–20,000. Scores of them can regularly be seen basking on offshore ledges, drying their tan, brown, black, silver, or reddish coats in the sun. Though it's tempting to approach for a closer look, avoid bringing a boat too near these haulout ledges, as it causes the seals to flush into the water and imposes an unnecessary stress on the pups, which already face a first-year mortality rate of 30 percent.

Positive changes in our relationships with wildlife are even more apparent with the return of birds to the Maine coast. Watching the numerous **herring gulls** and **great black-backed gulls** soaring on a fresh ocean breeze today, it's hard to imagine that a century ago, egg collecting had so reduced their numbers that they were a rare sight. In 1903, there were just three pairs of **common eiders** left in Maine; today, 25,000 pairs nest along the coast. With creative help from dedicated researchers using sound recordings, decoys, and prepared burrows, **Atlantic puffins** are recolonizing historic offshore nesting islands. **Osprey** and **bald eagles,** almost free of the lingering vestiges of DDT and other pesticides, now range the length of the coast and up Maine's major rivers.

LOOKING INTO THE FUTURE

Many Maine plants and animals, however, remain subjects of concern. Listed or proposed for listing as endangered or threatened species in the state are 178 vascular plants and 54 vertebrates. Too little is known about most of the lesser plants and animals to determine what their status is, but as natural habitats continue to decline in size or become degraded, it is likely that many of these species will disappear from the state. It is impossible to say exactly what will be lost when any of these species cease to exist here, but, to quote conservationist Aldo Leopold, "To keep every cog and wheel is the first precaution of intelligent tinkering."

It is clear, however, that life in Maine has been enriched by the recovery of populations of pine marten, moose, harbor seal, eider, and others. The natural persistence and tenacity of wildlife suggests that such species as the Atlantic salmon, wolf, and mountain lion will someday return to Maine—provided we give them the chance and the space to survive.

Flora and Fauna written by William P. Hancock, director of the Environmental Centers Department at the Maine Audubon Society, and former editor of *Habitat Magazine.*

History

PREHISTORIC MAINERS: THE PALEO-INDIANS

As the great continental glacier receded northwestward out of Maine about 11,000 years ago, some prehistoric grapevine must have alerted small bands of hunter-gatherers—fur-clad Paleo-Indians—to the scrub sprouting in the tundra, burgeoning mammal populations, and the ocean's bountiful food supply. Because come they did—at first seasonally, then year-round. Anyone who thinks tourism is a recent Maine phenomenon need only explore the shoreline in Damariscotta, Boothbay Harbor, and Bar Harbor, where heaps of cast-off oyster shells and clamshells document the migration of early Native Americans from woodlands to waterfront. "The shore" has been a summertime magnet for millennia.

Archaeological evidence from the Archaic period in Maine—roughly 8000–1000 BC—is fairly scant, but paleontologists have unearthed stone tools and weapons and small campsites attesting to a nomadic lifestyle supported by fishing and hunting (with fishing becoming more extensive as time went on). Toward the end of the tradition, during the late Archaic period, emerged a rather anomalous Indian culture known officially as the Moorehead phase but informally called the Red Paint People, due to their curious trait of using a distinctive red ocher (pulverized hematite) in burials. Dark red puddles and stone artifacts have led excavators to burial pits as far north as the St.

John River. Just as mysteriously as they had arrived, the Red Paint People disappeared abruptly and inexplicably around 1800 BC.

Following them almost immediately—and almost as suddenly—hunter-gatherers of the Susquehanna Tradition arrived from well to the south, moved across Maine's interior as far as the St. John River, and remained until about 1600 BC, when they, too, enigmatically vanished. Excavations have turned up relatively sophisticated stone tools and evidence that they cremated their dead. It was nearly 1,000 years before a major new cultural phase appeared.

The next great leap forward was marked by the advent of potterymaking, introduced around 700 BC. The Ceramic period stretched to the 16th century, and cone-shaped pots (initially stamped, later incised with coiled-rope motifs) survived until the introduction of metals from Europe. Houses of sorts—seasonal wigwam-style dwellings for fisherfolk and their families—appeared along the coast and on offshore islands.

THE EUROPEANS ARRIVE

The identity of the first Europeans to set foot in Maine is a matter of debate. Historians dispute the romantically popular notion that Norse explorers checked out this part of the New World as early as AD 1000. Even an 11th-century Norse coin found in 1961 in Brooklin (on the Blue Hill Peninsula) probably was carried there from farther north.

Not until the late 15th century, the onset of the great Age of Discovery, did credible reports of the New World (including what's now Maine) filter back to Europe's courts and universities. Thanks to innovations in naval architecture, shipbuilding, and navigation, astonishingly courageous fellows crossed the Atlantic in search of rumored treasure and new routes for reaching it.

John Cabot, sailing from England aboard the ship *Mathew,* may have been the first European to reach Maine, in 1498, but historians have never confirmed a landing site. No question remains, however, about the account of Giovanni da Verrazzano, an Italian explorer commanding *La Dauphine* under the French flag, who reached the Maine coast in May 1524, probably at the tip of the Phippsburg Peninsula. Encountering less-than-friendly native Indians, Verrazzano did a minimum of business and continued onward. His brother's map of the site labels it "The Land of Bad People." Esteban Gomez and John Rut followed in Verrazzano's wake, but nothing came of their exploits.

Nearly half a century passed before the Maine coast turned up again on European explorers' agendas. This time, interest was fueled by reports of a Brigadoon-like area called Norumbega (or Oranbega, as one map had it), a myth that arose, gathered steam, and took on a life of its own in the decades following Verrazzano's voyage.

By the early 17th century, when Europeans began arriving in more than twos and threes and getting serious about colonization, Native American agriculture was already underway at the mouths of the Saco and Kennebec Rivers, the cod fishery was thriving on offshore islands, native Indians far to the north were hot to trade furs for European goodies, and the birch-bark canoe was the transport of choice on inland waterways.

In mid-May 1602, Bartholomew Gosnold, en route to a settlement off Cape Cod aboard the *Concord,* landed along Maine's southern coast. The following year, merchant trader Martin Pring and his boats *Speedwell* and *Discoverer* explored farther Down East, backtracked to Cape Cod, and returned to England with tales that inflamed curiosity and enough sassafras to satisfy royal appetites. Pring produced a detailed survey of the Maine coast from Kittery to Bucksport, including offshore islands.

On May 18, 1605, George Waymouth, skippering the *Archangel,* reached Monhegan Island, 11 miles off the Maine coast, and moored for the night in Monhegan Harbor (still treacherous even today, exposed to the weather from the southwest and northeast and subject to meteorological beatings and heaving swells. Yachting guides urge sailors not to expect to anchor, moor, or tie up there). The next day, Waymouth crossed the bay and scouted the mainland. He took five native Indians hostage and sailed up the St. George River, near present-day Thomaston. As maritime historian Roger Duncan has put it, "The Plimoth Pilgrims were little boys in short pants when George Waymouth was exploring this coastline."

Waymouth returned to England and awarded his hostages to officials Sir John Popham and Sir Ferdinando Gorges, who, their curiosity piqued, quickly agreed to subsidize the colonization effort. In 1607, the *Gift of God* and the *Mary and John* sailed for the New World carrying two of Waymouth's captives. After returning them to their native Pemaquid area, Captains George Popham and Raleigh Gilbert continued westward, establishing a colony (St. George or Ft. George) at the tip of the Phippsburg Peninsula in mid-August 1607 and exploring the shoreline between Portland and Pemaquid. Frigid weather, untimely deaths (including Popham's), and a storehouse fire doomed what's called the Popham Colony, but not before the hundred or so settlers built the 30-ton pinnace *Virginia,* the New World's first such vessel. When Gilbert received word of an inheritance waiting in England, he and the remaining colonists returned to the Old World.

In 1614, swashbuckling Capt. John Smith, exploring from the Penobscot River westward to Cape Cod, reached Monhegan Island nine

© KATHLEEN M. BRANDES

plaque to Capt. John Smith, Monhegan Island

years after Waymouth's visit. Smith's meticulous map of the region was the first to use the "New England" appellation, and the 1616 publication of his *Description of New-England* became the catalyst for permanent settlements.

THE FRENCH AND THE ENGLISH SQUARE OFF

English dominance of exploration west of the Penobscot River in the early 17th century coincided roughly with French activity east of the river.

In 1604, French nobleman Pierre du Gua, Sieur de Monts, set out with cartographer Samuel de Champlain to map the coastline, first reaching Nova Scotia's Bay of Fundy and then sailing up the St. Croix River. In midriver, just west of present-day Calais, a crew planted gardens and erected buildings on today's St. Croix Island while de Monts and Champlain went off exploring. The two men reached the island Champlain named *l'Isle des Monts Deserts* and present-day Bangor before returning to face the winter with their ill-fated compatriots. Scurvy, lack of fuel and water, and a ferocious winter wiped out nearly half of the 79 men. In spring 1605, de Monts, Champlain, and other survivors headed southwest, exploring the coastline all the way to Cape Cod before heading northeast again and settling permanently at Nova Scotia's Port Royal (now Annapolis Royal).

Eight years later, French Jesuit missionaries en route to the Kennebec River ended up on Mount Desert Island and, with a band of French laymen, set about establishing the St. Sauveur settlement. But leadership squabbles led to building delays, and English marauder Samuel Argall—assigned to reclaim English territory—arrived to find them easy prey. The colony was leveled, the settlers were set adrift in small boats, the priests were carted off to Virginia, and Argall moved on to destroy Port Royal.

By the 1620s, more than four dozen English fishing vessels were combing New England waters in search of cod, and year-round fishing depots had sprung up along the coast between Pemaquid and Portland. At the same time, English trappers and dealers began usurping the Indians' fur trade—a valuable income source.

The Massachusetts Bay Colony was established in 1630 and England's Council of New England, headed by Sir Ferdinando Gorges, began making vast land grants throughout Maine, giving rise to permanent settlements, many dependent on agriculture. Among the earliest communities were Kittery, York, Wells, Saco, Scarborough, Falmouth, and Pemaquid—places where they tilled the acidic soil, fished the waters, eked out a barely-above-subsistence living, coped with predators and endless winters, bartered goods and services, and set up local governments and courts.

By the late 17th century, as these communities expanded, so did their requirements and responsibilities. Roads and bridges were built, preachers and teachers were hired, and militias were organized to deal with internecine and Native Indian skirmishes.

Even though England yearned to control the entire Maine coastline, her turf, realistically, was primarily south and west of the Penobscot River. The French had expanded out from their Canadian colony of Acadia, for the most part north and east of the Penobscot. Unlike the absentee bosses who controlled the English territory, French merchants actually showed up, forming good relationships with the Indians and cornering the market in fishing, lumbering, and fur trading. And French Jesuit priests converted many a Native American to Catholicism. Intermittently, overlapping Anglo-French land claims sparked locally messy conflicts.

In the mid-17th century, the strategic heart of French administration and activity in Maine was Ft. Pentagoet, a sturdy stone outpost built in 1635 in what is now Castine. From here, the French controlled coastal trade between the St. George River and Mount Desert Island and well up the Penobscot River. In 1654, England captured and occupied the fort and much of French Acadia, but, thanks to the 1667 Treaty of Breda, title returned to the French in 1670, and Pentagoet briefly became Acadia's capital.

A short but nasty Dutch foray against Acadia in 1674 resulted in Pentagoet's destruction ("levell'd with ye ground," by one account) and the raising of a third national flag over Castine.

THE INDIAN WARS (1675–1760)

Caught in the middle of 17th- and 18th-century Anglo-French disputes throughout Maine were the Wabanaki (People of the Dawn), the collective name for the state's major Native American tribal groups, all of whom spoke Algonquian languages. Modern ethnographers label these groups the Micmacs, Maliseets, Passamaquoddies, and Penobscots.

In the early 17th century, exposure to European diseases took its toll, wiping out three-quarters of the Wabanaki in the years 1616–19. Opportunistic English and French traders quickly moved into the breach, and the Wabanaki struggled to survive and regroup.

But regroup they did—less than three generations later, a series of six Indian wars began, lasting nearly a century and pitting the Wabanaki most often against the English but occasionally against other Wabanaki. The conflicts, largely provoked by Anglo-French tensions in Europe, were King Philip's War (1675–78), King William's War (1688–99), Queen Anne's War (1703–13), Dummer's War (1721–26), King George's War (1744–48), and the French and Indian War (1754–60). Not until a get-together in 1762 at Ft. Pownall (now Stockton Springs) did peace effectively return to the region—just in time for the heating up of the revolutionary movement.

COMES THE REVOLUTION

Near the end of the last Indian War, just beyond Maine's eastern border, a watershed event led to more than a century of cultural and political fallout. During the so-called Acadian Dispersal, in 1755, the English expelled from Nova Scotia some 10,000 French-speaking Acadians who refused to pledge allegiance to the British Crown. Scattered as far south as Louisiana and west toward New Brunswick and Quebec, the Acadians lost farms, homes, and possessions in this *grand dérangement*. Not until 1785 was land allocated for resettlement of Acadians along both sides of the Upper St. John River, where thousands of their descendants remain today. Henry Wadsworth Longfellow's epic poem *Evangeline* dramatically relates the sorry Acadian saga.

In the District of Maine, on the other hand, with relative peace following a century of intermittent warfare, settlement again exploded, particularly in the southernmost counties. The 1764 census tallied Maine's population at just under 25,000; a decade later, the number had doubled. New towns emerged almost overnight, often heavily subsidized by wealthy investors from the parent Massachusetts Bay Colony. With almost 4,000 residents, the largest town in the district was Falmouth (later renamed Portland).

In 1770, 27 Maine towns became eligible, based on population, to send representatives to the Massachusetts General Court, the colony's legislative body. But only six coastal towns could actually afford to send anyone, sowing seeds of resentment among settlers who were thus saddled with taxes without representation. Sporadic mob action accompanied unrest in southern Maine, but the flashpoint occurred in the Boston area.

On April 18, 1775, Paul Revere set out on America's most famous horseback ride—from Lexington to Concord, Massachusetts—to announce the onset of what became the American Revolution. Most of the Revolution's action occurred south of Maine, but not all of it.

In June, the Down East outpost of Machias was the site of the war's first naval engagement. The well-armed but unsuspecting British vessel HMS *Margaretta* sailed into the bay and was besieged by local residents angry about a Machias merchant's sweetheart deal with the British. Before celebrating their David-and-Goliath victory, the rebels captured the *Margaretta,* killed her captain, then captured two more British ships sent to the rescue.

In the fall of 1775, Col. Benedict Arnold—better known to history as a notorious turncoat—assembled 1,100 sturdy men for a flawed and futile "March on Quebec" to dislodge the English. From Newburyport, Massachusetts, they sailed to the mouth of the Kennebec River, near Bath, then headed inland with the tide. In

Pittston, six miles south of Augusta and close to the head of navigation, they transferred to a fleet of 220 locally made bateaux and laid over three nights at Ft. Western in Augusta. Then they set off, poling, paddling, and portaging their way upriver. Skowhegan, Norridgewock, and Chain of Ponds were among the landmarks along the grueling route. The men endured cold, hunger, swamps, disease, dense underbrush, and the loss of nearly 600 of their comrades before reaching Quebec in late 1775. In the Kennebec River Valley, Arnold Trail historical signposts today mark highlights (or, more aptly, lowlights) of the expedition.

Four years later, another futile attempt to dislodge the British, this time in the District of Maine, resulted in America's worst naval defeat until World War II—a little-publicized debacle called the Penobscot Expedition. On August 14, 1779, as more than 40 American warships and transports carrying more than 2,000 Massachusetts men blockaded Castine to flush out a relatively small enclave of leftover Brits, a seven-vessel Royal Navy fleet appeared. Despite their own greater numbers, about 30 of the American ships turned tail up the Penobscot River. The captains torched their vessels, exploding the ammunition and leaving the survivors to walk in disgrace to Augusta or even Boston. Each side took close to a hundred casualties, three commanders—including Paul Revere—were court-martialed, and Massachusetts was about $7 million poorer.

The American Revolution officially came to a close on September 3, 1783, with the signing of the Treaty of Paris between the United States and Great Britain. The U.S.–Canada border was set at the St. Croix River, but, in a massive oversight, boundary lines were left unresolved for thousands of square miles in the northern District of Maine.

TRADE TROUBLES AND THE WAR OF 1812

In 1807, President Thomas Jefferson imposed the Embargo Act, banning trade with foreign entities—specifically France and Britain. With

Know Maine

MAINE WOMEN IN HISTORY

Throughout Maine's history—as everywhere else—attention inevitably focuses on the role of men who have significantly affected the course of progress. In Maine, thanks to eager researchers (notably at the University of Southern Maine) and the annual celebration of Women's History Month, many key women have been identified, highlighted, and saluted. Portland and Brunswick have women's-history walking routes, and the **Maine Women Writers Collection** (open by appointment), at Westbrook College, includes an impressive and expanding inventory of female authors' books, articles, and memorabilia. Here are a few of the standouts—a colorful lot:

Dorothea L. Dix (1802–87), of Hampden, crusaded tirelessly in America and Europe for humane treatment of prisoners and proper care of the retarded and mentally ill. During the Civil War, she was superintendent of Army nurses.

Cornelia T. "Fly Rod" Crosby (1854–1946), of Phillips, was a skilled markswoman and angler who penned articles on hunting and fishing for her local paper, soon gaining a nationwide audience for her writings. Fly Rod Crosby also drew national attention in 1896 at a Madison Square Garden sportsmen's expo for modeling a then-risqué outfit that revealed (gasp!) seven or eight inches of her lower legs.

Lillian Norton (1857–1914), of Farmington, better known as the elegant diva Madame Nordica, won international acclaim in opera circles (and gossipy headlines in tabloid circles) at the turn of the 20th century.

Chansonetta Stanley Emmons (1858–1937), of Kingfield, lugged around a hefty camera to document life in western Maine. Always overshadowed by her famed automaker brothers, she received artistic notice and acclaim only after her death.

Josephine D. Peary (1863–1955), who summered on Casco Bay's Eagle Island and died in Portland, endured the arctic rigors of Greenland in the late 19th century with her husband, Adm. Robert E. Peary. She gave birth to their first child, Marie (called "Snow Baby" by the Inuit), in a primitive tar-paper dwelling on the second of their expeditions. In the 1950s, the National Geographic Society awarded Mrs. Peary its coveted Medal of Achievement.

Margaret Chase Smith (1897–1995), of Skowhegan, was the first woman elected in her own right to the U.S. Senate (1948) and the first woman nominated for the presidency by a major party (1964). In 1950, her "Declaration of Conscience" speech in the Senate catapulted her to national prominence as an intrepid opponent of McCarthyism.

Mollie Spotted Elk (Mary Alice Nelson) (1903–77), a Penobscot from Indian Island near Bangor, gained renown as an accomplished exotic dancer in 1920s New York and 1930s Paris, then returned to Indian Island in 1940 married to a French journalist (who died in 1941) and mother of a daughter, Jean.

And let's not forget to acknowledge the thousands of now-anonymous pioneering women who made their mark managing households during Colonial times, maintaining communications links during the Civil War, slaving away in textile mills and shoe factories during and after the Industrial Revolution, and propping up the shipbuilding efforts at Bath Iron Works during World War II, while the men were off at the front.

thousands of miles of coastline and harbor villages dependent on trade for revenue and basic necessities, Maine reeled. By the time the act was repealed, under President James Madison in 1809, France and Britain were almost unscathed, but the bottom had dropped out of New England's economy.

An active smuggling operation based in Eastport kept Mainers from utter despair, but the economy still had continued its downside. In 1812, the fledgling United States declared war on Great Britain, again disrupting coastal trade. In the fall of 1814, the situation reached its nadir when the British invaded the Maine coast and occupied all the shoreline between the St. Croix and Penobscot Rivers. Later that same year, the Treaty of Ghent finally halted the squabble, forced the British to withdraw from Maine, and allowed the locals to get on with economic recovery.

STATEHOOD

In October 1819, Mainers held a constitutional convention at the First Parish Church on Congress St. in Portland. (Known affectionately as "Old Jerusalem," the church was later replaced by the present-day structure.) The convention crafted a constitution modeled on that of Massachusetts, with two notable differences: Maine would have no official church (Massachusetts had the Puritans' Congregational Church), and Maine would place no religious requirements or restrictions on its gubernatorial candidates. When votes came in from 241 Maine towns, only nine voted against ratification.

For Maine, March 15, 1820, was one of those good news/bad news days: after 35 years of separatist agitation, the District of Maine broke from Massachusetts (signing the separation allegedly, and disputably, at the Jameson Tavern in Freeport) and became the 23rd state in the Union. However, the Missouri Compromise, enacted by Congress only 12 days earlier to balance admission of slave and free states, mandated that the slave state of Missouri be admitted on the same day. Maine had abolished slavery in 1788, and there was deep resentment over the linkage.

Portland became the new state's capital (albeit only briefly; it switched to Augusta in 1832), and William King, one of statehood's most outspoken advocates, became the first governor.

TROUBLE IN THE NORTH COUNTRY

Without an official boundary established on Maine's far northern frontier, turf battles were always simmering just under the surface. Timber was the sticking point—everyone wanted the vast wooded acreage. Finally, in early 1839, militia reinforcements descended on the disputed area, heating up what has come to be known as the Aroostook War, a border confrontation with no battles and no casualties (except a farmer who was shot by friendly militia). It's a blip in the historical timeline, but remnants of fortifications in Houlton, Ft. Fairfield, and Ft. Kent keep the story alive today. By March 1839, a truce was negotiated, and the 1842 Webster-Ashburton Treaty established the border once and for all.

MAINE IN THE CIVIL WAR

In the 1860s, with the state's population slightly more than 600,000, more than 70,000 Mainers suited up and went off to fight in the Civil War—the greatest per capita show of force of any northern state. Some 18,000 of them died in the conflict. Thirty-one Mainers were Union Army generals, the best-known being Joshua L. Chamberlain, a Bowdoin College professor, who commanded the Twentieth Maine regiment and later became president of the college and governor of Maine.

During the war, young battlefield artist Winslow Homer, who later settled in Prouts Neck, south of Portland, created wartime sketches regularly for such publications as *Harper's Weekly*. In Washington, Maine Sen. Hannibal Hamlin was elected vice president under Abraham Lincoln in 1860 (he was removed from the ticket in favor of Andrew Johnson when Lincoln came up for reelection in 1864).

MAINE COMES INTO ITS OWN

After the Civil War, Maine's influence in Republican-dominated Washington far outweighed the size of its population. In the late 1880s, Mainers held the federal offices of acting vice president, Speaker of the House, secretary of state, Senate majority leader, Supreme Court justice, and several important committee chairmanships. Best known of the notables were James G. Blaine (journalist, presidential aspirant, and secretary of state) and Portland native Thomas Brackett Reed, presidential aspirant and Speaker of the House.

In Maine itself, traditional industries fell into decline after the Civil War, dealing the economy a body blow. Steel ships began replacing Maine's wooden clippers, refrigeration techniques made the block-ice industry obsolete, concrete threatened the granite-quarrying trade, and the output from Southern textile mills began to supplant that from Maine's mills.

Despite Maine's economic difficulties, however, wealthy urbanites began turning their sights toward the state, accumulating land (including islands) and building enormous summer "cottages" for their families, servants, and hangers-on. Bar Harbor was a prime example of the elegant summer colonies that sprung up, but others include Grindstone Neck (Winter Harbor), Prouts Neck (Scarborough), and Dark Harbor (on Islesboro in Penobscot Bay). Vacationers who preferred fancy hotel-type digs reserved rooms for the summer at such sprawling complexes as Kineo House (on Moosehead Lake), Poland Spring House (west of Portland), or the Samoset Hotel (in Rockland). Built of wood and catering to long-term visitors, these and many others all eventually succumbed to altered vacation patterns and the ravages of fire.

As the 19th century spilled into the 20th, the state broadened its appeal beyond the well-to-do who had snared prime turf in the Victorian era. It launched an active promotion of Maine as "The Nation's Playground," successfully spurring an influx of visitors from all economic levels. By steamboat, train, and soon by car, people came to enjoy the ocean beaches, the woods, the mountains, the lakes, and the quaintness of it all. (Not that these features didn't really exist, but the state's aggressive public relations campaign at the turn of the 20th century stacks up against anything Madison Avenue puts out today.) The only major hiatus in the tourism explosion in the century's first two decades was 1914–18, when 35,062 Mainers joined many thousands of other Americans in going off bravely to the European front to fight in World War I. Two years after the cessation of hostilities, in 1920 (the centennial of its statehood), Maine women were the first in the nation to troop to the polls after ratification of the Nineteenth Amendment granted universal suffrage.

Maine was slow to feel the repercussions of the Great Depression, but eventually they came, with bank failures all over the state. Federally subsidized programs, such as the Civilian Conservation Corps (CCC) and the Works Progress Administration (WPA), left lasting legacies in Maine.

Politically, the state has contributed notables on both sides of the aisle. In 1954, Maine elected as its governor Edmund S. Muskie, only the fifth Democrat in the job since 1854. In 1958, Muskie ran for and won a seat in the Senate, and in 1980 he became secretary of state under President Jimmy Carter. Muskie died in 1996.

Elected in 1980, Waterville's George J. Mitchell made a respected name for himself as a Democratic senator and Senate majority leader before retiring in 1996, when Maine became only the second state in the union to have two women senators (Olympia Snowe and Susan Collins, both Republicans). Following his 1996 re-election, President Bill Clinton appointed Mitchell's distinguished congressional colleague and three-term senator, Republican William Cohen of Bangor, secretary of defense, a position he held through the rest of the Clinton administration. Mitchell spent considerable time during the Clinton years as the U.S. mediator for Northern Ireland's "troubles."

Economy and Government

Maine's relatively uninhabited, mostly rural and coastal land mass lends the state its renowned scenic beauty, but the lack of large urban centers also makes for a patchwork economy. In this sprawling state—as big as the rest of the New England states put together—small businesses and independent work dominate.

Many Mainers, especially in the less-populated northern regions, often hold two or three jobs to meet their families' needs. Perhaps they will cut a little firewood, make wreaths in the fall, or rake blueberries in season, sometimes to supplement factory wages. Younger, more mobile workers may move from ski instructing on the slopes in the winter, to working as lifeguards or waiters in summer resorts.

A few large companies employ significant numbers of residents, but some of them have cut their work forces in recent years. Once the paper industry was the largest overall employer of Mainers, but as paper companies have shut down or reduced their work forces, tourism has stepped into first place.

Tourism

Summer, defined as July and August, was once the only significant time of year for tourism. If the weather was bad on Fourth of July weekend or Labor Day, seasonal businesses suffered losses of up to half their annual income. Now more of the millions of tourists who arrive by plane, boat and car annually, visit increasingly in fall and winter, not only to enjoy the many delights of sailing, swimming and fishing, but activities such as leaf-peeping, skiing, snowmobiling, and ice-fishing.

Tourism jobs are harder to track because they cut across many areas such as transportation, meals, lodging, entertainment, other services and retail. Yet by 2001, estimates showed tourism supports roughly 58,000 Maine jobs, and conservatively, pumped $6.2 billion into the state economy. On a per-capita basis, the concentration of tourism-related jobs in Maine is nearly double that of other states.

If the state's natural resources—the evergreen woods, the convoluted 5,300-mile coastline and the wild Atlantic Ocean—attract tourists, they also underpin Maine's traditional industries of fishing, farming and timber. The woods provided the timber for Maine's healthy shipbuilding industry in the days of sail while the ocean provided the means of launching the ships, which carried more wood and other products, including ice and lime, around the world.

Paper and Other Forest Products

A combination of spruce and fir, the best woods for making paper, comprise 35 percent of the Pine Tree State's forests. Maine also boasts one of the finest white birch resources in the world. Nearly 89 percent of the state is covered by 17 million acres of woods, making Maine the most heavily forested state in the country. While paper is still the second-largest industry paying the highest average wage in the state, the paper companies, primary users of the resource, have been shutting down or cutting back for a number of years now. Still, Maine is the second-highest producer of paper, after Wisconsin, and a recent industry report predicted a rebound in paper sales, perhaps to be followed by an upsurge in paper manufacturing.

More than 96 percent of Maine timberlands are privately owned, giving Maine the lowest percentage of national forest land, with only 0.19 percent, compared to the national average of 46 percent. Only one million acres of Maine woods are publicly owned. Besides paper, other Maine forest products include firewood, hardwood and softwood sawlogs, and biomass for wood-burning energy plants. Secondary processing, from clothespins and golf tees to decking and furniture, is on the increase.

In recent years, forest products pumped $5.6 billion into the state economy, or 40.5 percent of the state's manufacturing sales. Maine's forests may assume more importance to the U.S. industry if national forests are restricted for cutting, and attempts are being made to ensure the future of the Maine resource through widespread "green" programs that certify loggers and companies for sustainable practices.

Fishing

Commercial fishing throughout New England has suffered ups and downs in the past decade because of downtrends in traditional stocks such as cod, haddock and scallops, followed by stringent federal regulations. Maine coastal communities have depended for hundreds of years on fishing, and although the fleet has been reduced, anglers still harvest groundfish, shrimp, clams, mussels, and other seafood in mostly seasonal fisheries. Sea urchins were not harvested at commercial levels until the mid-80s, when they commanded high prices to Japanese markets. Urchin landings peaked at above 40 million pounds worth, or more than $37 million in 1993. Since then, the resource has declined and catches have fallen to around 5 million pounds per year.

Lobster, for years Maine's most valuable seafood product, has also proven to be the state's most enduring fisheries resource. Along the convoluted 5,300-mile coastline, more than 7,000 residents hold lobster licenses. Nearly 1,200 lobstermen (and most women prefer to be called lobstermen) are considered full-time, dependent on their lobstering income for their livelihood. Some fish nearly year-round, weather permitting. Others are considered part-time, lobstering only in the summer when their other jobs, such as teaching or working in winter fisheries, are done.

It's easy to spot lobstering communities, their docks usually piled high with the colorful wire mesh traps. When traps are all in the water, colorful buoys, each with the owner's trademark color scheme and pattern, mark their location. Lobster boats come and go at the docks, refueling, offloading, or just sitting and facing the wind in the harbor, waiting for the next haul.

Maine lobstermen and women, rugged individualists all, rightly claim some credit for protecting the lobster resource through voluntary conservation measures. In 2004, Maine lobstermen harvested 63.2 million pounds of *Homarus americanus,* the favorite crustacean of tourists. Lobster landings continue to set records with recent catches of nearly 73 million pounds valued at around $300 million, beating out the previous record set in 2002, valued conservatively at $254 million. In 1990, the record catch totaled 28 million pounds, and in 1999, it soared to 52.3 million. Maine lobsters are enjoyed by diners in the shell, and, by those who don't want to work so hard, in lobster rolls up and down the coast all summer. However, lobsters are shipped live all over the country and the world to tanks in stores and restaurants.

Aquaculture

If fishing has gone down, aquaculture seemed poised to fill in the gaps, but the industry has been plagued by problems. Farming of Atlantic salmon started slowly in Penobscot and Cobscook Bays a little more than 20 years ago with a handful of independent farms, later consolidated by fewer but larger owners, some from Canada, Norway, and Chile. Harvests peaked at around 37 million pounds in 2000 and have declined steadily since. Several years ago a worldwide glut of farmed salmon depressed prices everywhere and strict environmental regulations governing escapes and other biological aspects of farming increased costs. Competition from the newer but fast-growing industry in Chile, where production costs are lower, offers a major challenge to the survival of North American salmon farming. But salmon is now recognized as one of the heart-healthiest foods on the market and worldwide sales are on the rise, offering hope for Maine's Down East salmon industry.

Shellfish such as oysters and clams are also farmed in Maine's tidal rivers, and seaweed for food and nutraceuticals is harvested wild and cultivated in Cobscook Bay. Wild blue mussels are plentiful along the shore and on the bottom, and many mussel beds are seeded by harvesters to increase the yield. Now mussels are also being raised on ropes to provide a cleaner, high-quality product.

Agriculture

A meal composed of Maine's primary seafood and agricultural products would be a tasty and nutritious one. A delicious banquet composed of lobster, salmon, mussels, and clams, served with Maine potatoes and broccoli with a sweet blueberry dish for dessert, would provide a powerhouse of Omega 3s, antioxidants, protein, and other nutrients.

Potatoes are still Maine's primary agricultural product. In recent years, Maine produced 1.79 billion pounds of potatoes valued at just under $100 million. Nearly 65 percent of Maine's potatoes are processed into chips and fries, and McDonald's restaurants in Maine serve only Maine potatoes. But demand has been dropping steadily for the round, white fresh potatoes that make up 15 percent of Maine's harvest from 65,000 acres of farms. Some growers are diversifying into unusual boutique varieties, aiming for niche markets. Still, schools in Aroostook County (known in Maine simply as "The County") still close for a few weeks each fall so children can help with the potato harvest as they have traditionally.

Broccoli, despite the dislike harbored for the vegetable by George H. W. Bush, former president and longtime Maine summer resident, is Maine's and "The County's" second biggest agricultural crop. Acreage for broccoli-growing increased from 284 acres in 1982 to 3,182 acres in recent years. Maine now ranks as the third-largest broccoli producer in the United States.

Blueberries

The state's favorite berry falls somewhere between wild harvest and agriculture. The smaller, low-bush blueberries, sweeter than the large, high-bush, cultivated varieties, grow wild in Maine, but the industry "encourages" them by burning fields, as Native Americans did centuries ago, and by applying pesticides—which

they did not. Maine is the largest producer of wild blueberries in the world, harvesting half of the state's 60,000 acres of blueberry fields annually. Less than one percent of the wild crop is sold fresh, while 99 percent of blueberries are frozen. Some frozen berries are later canned. Recent statistics show a total of 80.4 million pounds of blueberries valued at $28.5 million were harvested in Maine, although the industry generates nearly three times that for the state economy. Besides serving as a delicious ingredient in muffins, pies, ice cream, jam, cakes, wine, pancakes, and a wide range of other gourmet items, blueberries are now considered to provide an important antioxidant that may help prevent cancer.

Maple Syrup

Maple syrup is another Maine food product derived from a "wild" source. Producers, predominantly in Somerset County, tap maple trees in early spring, harvesting up to 60 gallons of sap from one big, healthy tree. Forty gallons of sap are needed to produce one gallon of the sweet stuff. Although Maine's output of maple syrup is a distant second to Vermont's, it is climbing each year, and topped 290,000 gallons in 2004.

Major Corporations

Governor after governor of Maine has tried to shorten the economic gap between the "three Maines." Southern Maine, nearer to the urban center of greater Boston, is more populous with more diversity of jobs, many more people and the sandy beaches that attract a multitude of tourists. The north has fewer people, little industry, and generally lower wages, except for the paper industry. The central region lies between the two in every respect. There are a few more population centers and a little more industry. Efforts to stimulate economic development in the less developed areas have experienced fluctuating degrees of success that largely mirror the state of the U.S. economy.

Bath Iron Works, which builds and repairs large ships, mainly for the Navy, has been Maine's biggest single employer for many years. In recent decades, cutbacks in military shipbuilding have reduced its production and therefore its work force. L.L. Bean, famous worldwide through its catalogs as a supplier of outdoor gear and sportswear, still keeps its Freeport store open seven days a week, 24 hours a day, as it has since it first opened. When L. L. Bean founded his emporium, the store provided access for hunters and anglers heading north at all hours. Now the late-night shoppers tend to be summer folks avoiding daytime crowds, or simply proving to themselves the store is open at 3 AM. The credit-card giant MBNA moved to Maine in 1993 and quickly developed a huge presence that included huge donations to libraries, museums, schools, hospitals, and small nonprofits. Recently, the company cut back its work force and shut down two facilities, but it still qualifies as one of the state's larger employers.

GOVERNMENT

The Maine political scene is not as unpredictable as the weather, but pundits are wary of forecasting what Mainers will do in an election. Although Maine has been traditionally Republican since the late 19th century, independent-minded voters here have an equally strong tradition of voting for the individual, not the party.

Four modern politicians illustrate Maine's independence: Margaret Chase Smith, Edmund Muskie, George Mitchell, and Bill Cohen. Republican Margaret Chase Smith, Maine's first woman senator, famously spoke out against Sen. Joseph McCarthy's activities on the Senate floor in the 1950s and was the first woman to have her name proposed for president. Edmund Muskie, the first important Democrat to come out of Maine, won every election he ever entered except an aborted bid for the presidency in 1972, then served as secretary of state. Democrat George Mitchell became Senate majority leader in 1989, and then retired from the Senate and helped broker the peace in Northern Ireland. Republican Senator Bill Cohen left the Senate and served as secretary of defense. In a manifestation of Maine's bipartisanship, while they served together in the Senate, Mitchell and Cohen worked together for the benefit of the state and the nation, and even wrote a book together.

Maine's governors serve four-year terms and are limited to two continuous terms. In the '70s, Maine elected an independent governor, James Longley, who ran for only one term. His son later ran successfully for the U.S. Congress and his daughter served three terms in the state Senate. In 1994, Maine elected another independent governor, Angus King, who served two terms. In 2005, Maine was represented by two women senators, Republicans Olympia Snowe and Susan Collins, and two Democratic Congressmen. Democratic governor John E. Baldacci was first elected to office as a Bangor City Councilman at the age of 23. He went on to serve in the State Senate, then four terms as a U.S. congressman. The Baldaccis became the first First Family to live in the governor's mansion, the Blaine House, since 1986.

Like many states, Maine has a hardworking, overburdened judiciary. It boasts the smallest number of general-jurisdiction judges of any state judiciary, ranks fifth from the bottom in money spent on judicial and legal services, but is the fifth most productive in resolving civil cases and 12th in resolving criminal cases. The state's Supreme Judicial Court has a chief justice and six associate justices.

Maine is ruled by a bicameral, biennial citizen legislature comprising 151 members in the House of Representatives and 35 members in the State Senate, including a relatively high percentage of women and a fairly high proportion of retirees. Members of both houses serve two-year terms. Along with the governor, they meet at the State House in Augusta to administer the state's more than $3 billion annual budget. In 1993, voters passed a referendum question limiting lawmakers to four terms.

While nearly two dozen Maine cities are ruled by city councils, some 450 smaller towns and plantations retain the traditional form of rule by annual town meeting. Generally held in March, town meetings provide entertainment along with democracy. Residents have the opportunity to speak to every issue on the warrant, air their differences, and vote publicly. Newspaper stories abound in colorful quotes from town meetings, such as, "I don't know of anyone's dog running loose except my own, and I've arrested her several times," or, "Don't listen to him; he's from New Jersey."

Economy and Government written by freelance magazine writer and former newspaper and wire service writer, Nancy Griffin.

The People

Maine's population didn't top the one-million mark until 1970. Thirty years later, according to the 2000 census, 1,274,923 residents live in the state. Cumberland County, comprising the Portland area, has the highest head count; far-inland Piscataquis County, whose largest town is Dover-Foxcroft, is the least populous.

Despite the longstanding presence of several substantial ethnic groups, plus four Native American tribes, diversity is a relatively recent phenomenon in Maine, and the population is more than 90 percent Caucasian. A steady influx of refugees, beginning after the Vietnam War, forced the state to address diversity issues, and that continues today.

NATIVES AND "PEOPLE FROM AWAY"

People who weren't born in Maine aren't natives. Even people who *were* may experience close scrutiny of their credentials. In Maine, there are natives and *natives*. Every day, the obituary pages describe Mainers who have barely left the houses in which they were born—even in which their grandparents were born. We're talking roots!

Along with this kind of heritage comes a whole vocabulary all its own—lingo distinctive to Maine or at least New England. (For help in translation, see *Glossary: A Down East Dictionary* at the end of this book.)

Part of the "native" picture is the matter of "native" produce. Hand-lettered signs sprout everywhere during the summer advertising native corn, native peas, even—believe it or not—native ice. In Maine, homegrown is well grown.

"People from away," on the other hand, are those whose families haven't lived here a generation or more. But people from away (also called flatlanders) exist all over Maine, and they have come to stay, putting down roots of their own and altering the way the state is run, looks, and *will* look. Senators Snowe and Collins are natives, but governor King was from away, as were most of his cabinet members. You'll find other flatlanders as teachers, corporate executives, artists, retirees, writers, town selectmen, and even lobstermen.

In the 19th century, arriving flatlanders were mostly "rusticators" or "summer complaints"—summer residents who lived well, often in enclaves, and never set foot in the state off-season. They did, however, pay property taxes, contribute to causes, and provide employment for local residents. Another 19th-century wave of people from away came from the bottom of the economic ladder: Irish escaping the potato famine and French-Canadians fleeing poverty in Quebec. Both groups experienced subtle and overt anti-Catholicism but rather quickly assimilated into the mainstream, taking jobs in mills and factories and becoming staunch American patriots.

The late 1960s and early 1970s brought bunches of "back-to-the-landers," who scorned plumbing and electricity and adopted alternative ways of life. Although a few pockets of diehards still exist, most have changed with the times and adopted contemporary mores (and conveniences).

Today, technocrats arrive from away with computers, faxes, cell phones, and other high-tech gear and "commute" via the Internet and modern electronics. Maine has played a national leadership role in telecommunications reform—thanks to the university system's early push for installation of state-of-the-art fiber optics.

Native Americans

In Maine, the *real* natives are the Wabanaki (People of the Dawn)—the Micmac, Maliseet, Penobscot, and Passamaquoddy tribes of the eastern woodlands. Many live in or near three reservations, near the headquarters for their tribal governors. The Penobscots are based on Indian Island, in Old Town, near Bangor. Passamaquoddies are at Pleasant Point, in Perry, near Eastport; and at Indian Township, in Princeton, near Calais. Other Native American population clusters—known as "off-reservation Indians"—are the Aroostook Band of Micmacs, based in Presque Isle, and the Houlton Band of Maliseets, in Littleton, near Houlton.

In 1965, Maine became the first state to establish a Department of Indian Affairs, but just five years later the Passamaquoddy and Penobscot tribes initiated a 10-year-long land-claims case involving 12.5 million Maine acres (about two-thirds of the state) weaseled from the Indians by Massachusetts in 1794. In late 1980, a landmark agreement, signed by President Jimmy Carter, awarded the tribes $80.6 million in reparations. Controversy has surrounded the settlement—including complaints about its inadequacy—but the pluses seem to have outweighed the minuses, as investments and capital distributions have allowed Native Americans to find jobs, upgrade their homes, improve their medical care, and seek higher educational opportunities. One can only hope that the funds will also spur the tribes to revive and maintain their splendid cultural traditions.

Several well-attended annual summer festivals—in Bar Harbor, Grand Lake Stream, and Perry—highlight Native American traditions and heighten awareness of Native American culture. Basketmaking, canoebuilding, and traditional dancing are all parts of the scene. Museums in Orono, Old Town, Perry, Augusta, Bar Harbor, Hinckley, and New Portland feature American Indian artifacts, interactive displays, historic photographs, and special programs. Gift shops have begun adding Native American jewelry and baskets, and the Wabanaki Arts Center Gallery, a gallery/shop located in Old Town, features exhibits and arts and crafts created by Maine tribal members exclusively.

Acadians and Franco Americans

Within about three decades of their 1755 expulsion from Nova Scotia in *le grand dérangement,* Acadians had established new communities and new lives in northern Maine's St. John Valley. Gradually, they explored farther into central and southern Maine and west into New Hampshire. The Acadian diaspora has profoundly influenced Maine and its culture, and it continues to do so today. Biddeford, Lewiston, Augusta, and Madawaska hold annual Acadian or Franco-American festivals; French is spoken on the streets of those cities, as well as in Bangor and Fort Kent; and Lewiston, Biddeford, and Fort Kent boast extensive Franco-American and Acadian research collections.

African Americans

Although Maine's African American population is small, the state has had an African American community since the 17th century; by the 1764 census, there were 322 slaves and free blacks in the District of Maine. Segregation remained the rule, however, so in the 19th century, the black community established its own parish, the Abyssinian Church, in Portland. Efforts are now underway to restore the long-closed church as an African American cultural center and gathering place for Greater Portland's black community. For researchers delving into "Maine's black experience," the University of Southern Maine, in Portland, houses the African American Archive of Maine, a significant collection of historic books, letters, and artifacts donated by Gerald Talbot, the first African American to serve in the Maine Legislature.

Finns, Swedes, and Lebanese

Finns came to Maine in several 19th-century waves, primarily to work the granite quarries on the coast and on offshore islands and the slate quarries in Monson, near Greenville. Finnish families clustered near the quarries in St. George and on Vinalhaven and Hurricane Islands—all with landscapes similar to those of their homeland. Today, names such as Laukka, Lehtinen, Hamalainen, and Harjula are interspersed among the Yankee names in the Mid-Coast region.

In 1870, an idealistic American diplomat named William Widgery Thomas established a model agricultural community with 50 brave Swedes in the heart of Aroostook County. Their enclave, New Sweden, remains today, as does the town of Stockholm, and descendants of the pioneers have spread throughout Maine.

At the turn of the 20th century, Lebanese (and some Syrians) began descending on Waterville, where they found work in the textile mills and eventually established St. Joseph's Maronite Church in 1927. One of these immigrants was the mother of former senator George Mitchell.

Russians, Ukrainians, and Byelorussians

Arriving after World War II, Slavic immigrants established a unique community in Richmond, near Augusta. Only a tiny nucleus remains today, along with an onion-domed church, but a stroll through the local cemetery hints at the extent of the original colony.

The Newest Arrivals: Refugees from War

War has been the impetus for the more recent arrival of Asians, Africans, Central Americans, and Eastern Europeans to Maine. Most have settled in the Portland area, making that city the state's center of diversity. Vietnamese and Cambodians began settling in Maine in the mid-1970s. A handful of Afghanis who fled the Soviet-Afghan conflict also ended up in Portland. Somalis, Ethiopians, and Sudanese fled their war-torn countries in the early to mid-1990s, and Bosnians and Kosovars arrived in the last half of the 1990s. With every new conflict comes a new stream of immigrants—world citizens are becoming Mainers, and Mainers are becoming world citizens.

The Arts

Every creative soul longs for inspiration and motivation to jump-start a painting or a poem, a statue or a novel. Maine has exerted a powerful lunar-like gravitational pull on creative types. The craggy shoreline, dense forests, and visually rich beauty—infused with hidebound Yankee traditions and an often harsh existence—have inspired artists and writers to create work of national and international repute.

Beginning around the mid-19th century, when people from away descended on Maine for their summer getaways, little pockets of creative energy flourished (largely but not exclusively along the coast), and art and literature reaped the benefits. These weren't Maine's first artists or earliest writers, but they represented a turning point, a stepped-up pace of artistic and literary activity.

FINE ART

In 1850, in a watershed moment for Maine landscape painting, Hudson River School artist par-excellence Frederic Edwin Church (1826–1900) vacationed on Mount Desert Island. Influenced by the luminist tradition of such contemporaries as Fitz Hugh Lane (1804–65), who summered in Castine, Church accurately but romantically depicted the dramatic tableaux of Maine's coast and woodlands that even today attract slews of admirers.

By the 1880s, however, impressionism had become the style du jour and was being practiced by a coterie of artists who collected around Charles Herbert Woodbury (1864–1940) in Ogunquit. His program made Ogunquit the best-known summer art school in New England. After Hamilton Easter Field established another art school in town, modernism soon asserted itself. Among the artists who took up summertime Ogunquit residence was Walt Kuhn (1877–1949), a key organizer of New York's 1913 landmark Armory Show of modern art.

Meanwhile, a bit farther south, impressionist Childe Hassam (1859–1935), part of writer Celia Thaxter's circle, produced several hundred works on Maine's remote Appledore Island, in the Isles of Shoals off Kittery, and illustrated Thaxter's *An Island Garden.*

Another artistic summer colony found its niche in 1903, when Robert Henri (born Robert Henry Cozad; 1865–1929), charismatic leader of the Ashcan School of realist/modernists, visited Monhegan Island, about 11 miles offshore. Artists who followed him there included Rockwell Kent (1882–1971), Edward Hopper (1882–1967), George Bellows (1882–1925), and Randall Davey (1887–1964). Among the many other artists associated with Monhegan images are William Kienbusch (1914–80), Reuben Tam (1916–91), and printmakers Leo Meissner (1895–1977) and Stow Wengenroth (1906–78).

But colonies were of scant interest to other notables, who chose to derive their inspiration from Maine's stark natural beauty and work mostly in their own orbits. Among these are genre painter Eastman Johnson (1824–1906); romantic realist Winslow Homer (1836–1910), who lived in Maine for 27 years and whose studio in Prouts Neck (Scarborough) still overlooks the surf-tossed scenery he so often depicted; pointillist watercolorist Maurice Prendergast (1858–1924); John Marin (1870–1953), a cubist who painted Down East subjects, mostly around Deer Isle and Addison (Cape Split); Lewiston native Marsden Hartley (1877–1943), who first showed his abstractionist work in New York in 1909 and later worked in Berlin; Fairfield Porter (1907–75), whose family summered on Great Spruce Head Island, in East Penobscot Bay; Andrew Wyeth (b. 1917), whose reputation as a romantic realist in the late 20th century sur-

passed that of his illustrator father, N. C. Wyeth (1882–1945).

On a parallel track was sculptor Louise Nevelson (1899–1988), raised in a poor Russian-immigrant family in Rockland and far better known outside her home state for her monumental wood sculptures slathered in black or gold. Two other noted sculptors with Maine connections were William Zorach and Gaston Lachaise, both of whom lived in Georgetown, near Bath.

Today, Maine has no major community known exclusively for its summer art colony. Sure, there are artistic clusters here and there, united by the urge for creative networking and moral support—especially when threatened with reduced government subsidy. Among these artistic pockets, all close to the ocean, are the Kennebunks, Portland, Monhegan Island, Rockland, Blue Hill, Deer Isle, and Eastport.

Year-round or seasonal Maine residents with national (and international) reputations include Lincolnville's Neil Welliver and Alex Katz, North Haven's Eric Hopkins, Deer Isle's Karl Schrag, Eustis's Marguerite Robichaux, Tenants Harbor's Jamie Wyeth (third generation of the famous family), Kennebunk's Edward Betts, Port Clyde's William Thon, and Cushing's Lois Dodd and Alan Magee.

The state's most prestigious summer art program—better known in Manhattan than in Maine—is the highly selective Skowhegan School of Painting and Sculpture, Box 449, Skowhegan 04976, 207/474-9345; off-season 200 Park Ave. S., New York, NY 10003, 212/529-0505, founded in 1946. From well over 1,000 applicants, 65 young artists are chosen each year to spend nine weeks (mid-June–mid-Aug.) on the school's 300-acre lakeside campus in East Madison. An evening lecture series is open to the public.

The two best collections of Maine art are at the **Portland Museum of Art,** 7 Congress Sq., Portland 04101, 207/775-6148; and the **Farnsworth Art Museum and Wyeth Center,** 16 Museum St., Rockland 04841, 207/596-6457. The Farnsworth, in fact, focuses only on Maine art, primarily from the 20th century. In

1996, both museums saw their already-impressive holdings greatly enhanced when philanthropic collector Elizabeth Noyce bequeathed her comprehensive Maine collection to them. As the home of the Wyeth Center, the Farnsworth features the works of N. C., Andrew, and Jamie Wyeth.

The **Ogunquit Museum of American Art,** appropriately, also has a very respectable Maine collection (in a spectacular setting). Other Maine paintings, not always on exhibit, are at the Bowdoin College Museum of Art, in Brunswick; Bates College Museum of Art, in Lewiston; and Colby College Museum of Art, in Waterville. Colby has a huge collection of works by painter Alex Katz.

CRAFTS

Any survey of Maine art, however brief, must include the significant role of crafts in the state's artistic tradition. As with painters, sculptors, and writers, craftspeople have gravitated to Maine—most notably since the establishment in 1950 of the **Haystack Mountain School of Crafts.** Started in the Belfast area, the school put down roots on Deer Isle in 1960. Each summer, internationally famed artisans—sculptors, glassmakers, weavers, jewelers, potters, papermakers, and printmakers—become the faculty for the unique school, which has weekday classes and 24-hour studio access for adult students on its handsome 40-acre campus. For information, write to Haystack Mountain School of Crafts, P.O. Box 518, Deer Isle 04627, 207/348-2306, fax 348-2307. Portland is the headquarters for the **Maine Crafts Association,** P.O. Box 8817, Portland 04103, 207/780-1807, www.mainecrafts.maine.org, which has more than 200 members and produces a very useful annual directory of artists and exhibits.

DOWN EAST LITERATURE

Maine's first big-name writer was probably the early 17th-century French explorer Samuel de Champlain (1570–1635), who scouted the Maine coast, established a colony in 1604 near present-day Calais, and lived to describe in detail his experiences. Several decades after Champlain's forays, English naturalist John Josselyn visited Scarborough and in the 1670s published the first two books accurately describing Maine's flora and fauna (aptly describing, for example, blackflies as "not only a pesterment but a plague to the country").

Today, Maine's best-known author is Bangor resident Stephen King (b. 1947), wizard of the weird. Many of his dozens of horror novels and stories are set in Maine, and several have been filmed for the big screen here. King and his author-wife, Tabitha, are avid fans of both education and team sports and have generously distributed their largesse among schools and teams in their hometown as well as other parts of the state.

Other best-selling contemporary authors writing in or about Maine include Carolyn Chute (b. 1948), resident of Parsonsfield and author of the raw novels *The Beans of Egypt, Maine* and *Letourneau's Used Auto Parts;* Cathie Pelletier (b. 1953), raised in tiny Allagash and author of such humor-filled novels as *The Funeral Makers* and *The Bubble Reputation;* and coastal-Maine resident Richard Russo (b. 1949), author of *Empire Falls,* winner of the 2002 Pulitzer Prize in Fiction, and named the year's best novel by *Time.*

Chroniclers of the Great Outdoors

John Josselyn was perhaps the first practitioner of Maine's strong naturalist tradition in American letters, but the Pine Tree State's rugged scenic beauty and largely unspoiled environment have given rise to many ecologically and environmentally concerned writers. Henry David Thoreau (1817–62), well known for poking around Walden Pond and other points south, undertook three Maine treks—in 1846, 1853, and 1857—and chronicled his trails, climbs, and canoe routes in *The Maine Woods,* published two years after his death.

The 20th century saw the arrival in Maine of crusader Rachel Carson (1907–64), whose 1962 wake-up call, *Silent Spring,* was based partly on Maine observations and research. The Rachel Carson National Wildlife Refuge, headquartered in Wells and comprising 10 chunks of environmentally sensitive coastal real estate, covers nearly 3,500 acres between Kittery Point and the Mid-Coast region.

The tiny town of Nobleboro, near Damariscotta, drew nature writer Henry Beston (1888–1968), author of, among other things, *The Outermost House* (about Cape Cod); his *Northern Farm* lyrically chronicles a year in Maine. Beston's wife, Elizabeth Coatsworth (1893–1986), wrote more than 90 books—including *Chimney Farm,* about their life in Nobleboro.

Fannie Hardy Eckstorm (1865–1946), born in Brewer to Maine's most prosperous fur trader, graduated from Smith College and became a noted expert on Maine (and specifically Native American) folklore. Among her extensive writings, *Indian Place-Names of the Penobscot Valley and the Maine Coast,* published in 1941, remains a sine qua non for researchers.

The out-of-doors and inner spirits shaped Cape Rosier adoptees Helen and Scott Nearing, whose 1954 *Living the Good Life* became the bible of Maine's back-to-the-landers.

Classic Writings on the State

Historical novels, such as *Arundel,* were the specialty of Kennebunk native Kenneth Roberts (1885–1957), but Roberts also wrote *Trending into Maine,* a potpourri of Maine observations and experiences (the original edition was illustrated by N. C. Wyeth). Kennebunkport's Booth Tarkington (1869–1946), author of the *Penrod* novels and *The Magnificent Ambersons,* described 1920s Kennebunkport in *Mary's Neck,* published in 1932.

A little subgenre of sociological literary classics comprises astute observations (mostly by women) of daily life in various parts of the state. Some are fiction, some nonfiction, some barely disguised *romans à clef.* Probably the best known chronicler of such observations is Sarah Orne Jewett (1849–1909), author of *The Country of the Pointed Firs,* a fictionalized

1896 account of "Dunnet's Landing" (actually Tenants Harbor); her ties, however, are in the South Berwick area, where she spent most of her life. Also in South Berwick, Gladys Hasty Carroll (1904–99) scrutinized everyday life in her hamlet, Dunnybrook, in *As the Earth Turns* (a title later "borrowed" and tweaked by a soap-opera producer). Lura Beam (1887–1978) focused on her childhood in the Washington County village of Marshfield in *A Maine Hamlet,* published in 1957, while Louise Dickinson Rich (1903–72) entertainingly described her experiences in the North Woods in *We Took to the Woods* and Down East in *The Peninsula.* Ruth Moore (1903–89), born on Gott's Island, near Acadia National Park, published her first book at the age of 40. Her tales, recently brought back into print, have earned her a whole new, appreciative audience. A native of northern Maine, from a mixed French and American family, Helen Hamlin (1917–2004) wrote *Nine Mile Bridge,* a gritty narrative of her three years at Churchill Lake, near the Allagash headwaters, where she taught school and her husband was a game warden. Her book, in a special edition, was re-published by Islandport Press in 2005. Elisabeth Ogilvie (b. 1917) came to Maine in 1944 and lived for many years on remote Ragged Island, transformed into "Bennett's Island" in her fascinating "tide trilogy": *High Tide at Noon, Storm Tide,* and *The Ebbing Tide.* Ben Ames Williams (1887–1953), the token male in this roundup of perceptive observers, in 1940 produced *Come Spring,* an epic tale of hardy pioneers founding the town of Union.

Seldom recognized for her Maine connection, antislavery crusader Harriet Beecher Stowe (1811–96) lived in Brunswick in the mid-19th century, where she wrote *The Pearl of Orr's Island,* a folkloric novel about a tiny nearby fishing community.

Mary Ellen Chase was a Maine native, born in Blue Hill in 1887. She became an English professor at Smith College in 1926 and wrote about 30 books, including some about the Bible as literature. She died in 1973.

Two books do a creditable job of excerpting Maine literature—something of a daunting task. The most comprehensive is *Maine Speaks: An Anthology of Maine Literature,* published in 1989 by the Maine Writers and Publishers Alliance. *The Quotable Moose: A Contemporary Maine Reader,* edited by Wesley McNair and published in 1994 by the University Press of New England, focuses on 20th-century authors.

A World of Her Own
For Marguerite Yourcenar (1903–87), Maine provided solitude and inspiration for subjects ranging far beyond the state's borders. Yourcenar was a longtime Northeast Harbor resident and the first woman elected to the prestigious Académie Française. Her house, now a shrine to her work, is open to the public in summer.

Essayists, Critics, and Humorists Native and Transplanted
Maine's best-known essayist is and was E. B. White (1899–1985), who bought a farm in tiny Brooklin in 1933 and continued writing for *The New Yorker. One Man's Meat,* published in 1944, is one of the best collections of his wry, perceptive writings. His legions of admirers also include two generations raised on his classic children's stories *Stuart Little, Charlotte's Web,* and *The Trumpet of the Swan.*

Now settled in Sargentville, not far from Brooklin but far from her New York ties, writer and critic Doris Grumbach (b. 1918) has written two particularly wise works from the perspective of a Maine transplant: *Fifty Days of Solitude* and *Coming into the End Zone.*

Maine's best exemplars of humorous writing are Artemus Ward (born Charles Farrar Browne; 1834–67) and John Gould (1909–2003), whose life in rural Friendship has provided grist for many a tale. Gould's hilarious columns in the *Christian Science Monitor* and his impressive book output made him the icon of Maine humor.

Pine Tree Poets
Born in Portland, Henry Wadsworth Longfellow (1807–82) is Maine's most famous poet; his marine themes clearly stem from his seashore childhood (in "My Lost Youth," he rhapsodized, "Often I think of the beautiful town/That is seated by the sea… ").

Widely recognized in her own era, poet Celia Thaxter (1835–94) held court on Appledore Island in the Isles of Shoals, welcoming artists, authors, and musicians to her summer salon. Today, she's best known for *An Island Garden,* published in 1894 and detailing her attempts at horticultural TLC in a hostile environment.

Self-effacing Edwin Arlington Robinson (1865–1935) would probably be the first to squirm if he knew his hometown of Gardiner now organizes an annual Edwin Arlington Robinson Poetry Festival. Edna St. Vincent Millay (1892–1950) had connections to Camden, Rockland, and Union and described a stunning Camden panorama in "Renascence."

Whitehead Island, near Rockland, was the birthplace of Wilbert Snow (1883–1977), who went on to become president of Connecticut's Wesleyan University. His 1968 memoir, *Codline's Child,* makes fascinating reading.

A longtime resident of York, May Sarton (1912–95) approached cult status as a guru of feminist poetry and prose—as well as an articulate analyst of death and dying during her terminal illness.

Among respected Maine poets today are Philip Booth (b. 1925), a resident of Castine; William Carpenter (b. 1940), of Stockton Springs; and Appleton's Kate Barnes (b. 1932), named Maine's Poet Laureate from 1996 to 1999. Although she comes by her acclaim legitimately, Barnes is also genetically disposed, being the daughter of writers Henry Beston and Elizabeth Coatsworth.

Maine Literature for Little Ones
Besides E. B. White's children's classics, *Stuart Little, Charlotte's Web,* and *The Trumpet of the Swan,* America's kids were also weaned on books written and illustrated by Maine island summer resident Robert McCloskey (1914–2003), notably *Time of Wonder, One*

Morning in Maine, and *Blueberries for Sal.* Neck-and-neck in popularity is prolific Walpole illustrator-writer Barbara Cooney (1917–99), whose award-winning titles include *Miss Rumphius, Island Boy,* and *Hattie and the Wild Waves.* Cooney produced more than 100 books, and it seems as if everyone has a different favorite.

C. A. (Charles Asbury) Stephens (1844–1931) for 60 years wrote for the magazine *Youth's Companion.* In 1995, a collection of his vivid children's stories was reissued as *Stories from the Old Squire's Farm.*

Maine can also lay partial claim to Kate Douglas Wiggin (1856–1923), author of the eternally popular *Rebecca of Sunnybrook Farm;* she spent summers at Quillcote, in Hollis, west of Portland.

Outdoor Recreation

You'll never have enough vacation to take advantage of all the outdoor recreational possibilities Maine offers in summer, fall, and winter. Below is a roundup of sites and activities; details appear in the specific regional chapters (see *Suggested Reading* for specialized recreational guides). For a uniquely Maine resource, staff members at L.L. Bean pride themselves on their knowledge of the outdoors and are, even at the height of summer, incredibly helpful. Depending on your recreational interest, stop in at the appropriate department and pick their brains.

ACADIA NATIONAL PARK

Nearly three million visitors show up each year at Maine's only national park, and officials fret about overcrowding, but there's still plenty of room in these 47,000 or so acres for a fantastic, all-around recreational experience: camping (530 sites), hiking, rock climbing, bicycling, canoeing/kayaking, cross-country skiing, and snowshoeing. Included within park jurisdiction are several less-crowded spaces on parts of three offshore islands and the Schoodic Peninsula, just north of the main chunk of the park. During the summer, there's an ambitious schedule of nature walks, hikes, cruises, and lecture programs (some wheelchair accessible). Canoe, kayak, and bike rentals are available in island towns. For park information, contact Acadia National Park, P.O. Box 177, Bar Harbor 04609, 207/288-3338, www.nps.gov/acad. From May through October, the visitors center

in Hulls Cove provides orientation and information; November through April, the park headquarters office (Rte. 233, same phone) serves as a scaled-down info center.

STATE PARKS

Despite occasional midsummer overcrowding at some locations and recurring budget constraints, Maine's 32 state parks are spectacularly situated and maintained for fishing, swimming, hiking, canoeing, picnicking, birding, and camping. The state also supervises 12 state historic sites, over half a million acres of Public Reserved Lands, and two river corridors: the Allagash Wilderness Waterway and the Penobscot River Corridor. For more information, contact the Bureau of Parks and Lands, Maine Department of Conservation, 22 State House Station, Augusta 04333, 207/287-3821, www .parksandlands.com.

In 1930, Maine Governor Percival P. Baxter, determined to preserve a chunk of Maine real estate for Maine residents and posterity, began accumulating acreage—including Katahdin, Maine's highest mountain—to create Baxter State Park. Under separate jurisdiction from the state park system, this recreational wilderness covers 204,733 acres containing 46 mountain peaks and 175 miles of trails. One unpaved road (20 mph limit) traverses the park; no pets or operation of audio devices, including radios and cell phones, are allowed; no gasoline or drinking water is available; and camping (the only way to stay in Baxter—at tentsites, lean-tos, or rustic log cabins) is carry-in, carry-out. Competition is fierce on mid-summer weekends; it's pure luck to find space. The reward? Rare alpine flowers, unique rock formations, wildlife sightings, and incomparable hiking, canoeing, and photography. Day use is free for Maine residents; $12 per vehicle for nonresidents. Information: Baxter State Park Authority, 64 Balsam Dr., Millinocket 04462, 207/723-5140.

SAILING

With 5,500 miles of in-and-out coastline, several thousand offshore islands, and countless nooks and crannies for dropping anchor, Maine is a sailor's paradise. If you've brought your own yacht or chartered one here, you'll quickly discover some scenic standouts and never run out of places to go. The most popular cruising centers are Boothbay Harbor, Rockland, North Haven/Vinalhaven, Camden, Castine, Blue Hill, Northeast Harbor, and Southwest Harbor.

Start off on the right tack with the Maine sailors' bible, *A Cruising Guide to the Maine Coast, 4th ed.,* by Hank and Jan Taft and Curtis Rindlaub, available in hardcover and paperback. Don't try to cover the whole coast; choose beginning and ending points and take the circuit in small doses.

Fog is the biggest enemy of overambitious itineraries; the farther Down East you go (toward Canada), the sparser the facilities and the greater the likelihood of fog. One of the best cruising months is September, with crisp air, fine breezes, minimal fog, and uncrowded harbors. If you belong to a yacht club elsewhere, bring your membership card; Maine clubs offer reciprocal privileges.

If you're not lucky enough to have your own boat or enough spare change to charter one, see *Getting Afloat,* later in this chapter, for other ways to escape to sea.

CANOEING AND KAYAKING

Thanks to the inspiration and creativity of Native Americans, we're able to explore Maine's streams, lakes, rivers, estuaries, and coastline in canoes and kayaks. If you wish to do it on your own, you'll want to rely on three excellent resources: the *AMC River Guide: Maine* by Katherine Yates and Carey Phillips, *Quiet Water Maine* by Alex Wilson and John Hayes, and *Kayaking the Maine Coast* by Dorcas Miller. See the Suggested Reading list for details.

Best places to rent canoes are Andover, Belgrade Lakes, Blue Hill, Brownfield, Fryeburg, Jackman, Machias, Medway and Millinocket (near Baxter State Park), Mount Desert Island, Rangeley, Rockport, Rockwood (on Moosehead Lake), Scarborough, and Somesville. Kayak rentals are almost universally available in coastal towns, and there are also many guided trips.

Native Trails, Inc., a nonprofit organization spearheaded by Mike Krepner, P.O. Box 240, Waldoboro 04572, 207/832-5255, has information available on a variety of Native American canoe routes inside and outside Maine. **Northern Forest Canoe Trail, Inc.,** a nonprofit located in Waitsfield, Vermont, is mapping and promoting the 740-mile Northern Forest Canoe Trail—a historic traditional canoe route stretching from Old Forge, NY, in the Adirondacks to Fort Kent in northern Maine. The goal is to celebrate the diverse natural and human history of the region, where waterways were once the primary routes of communication. For information, contact the Northern Forest Canoe Trail, 802/496-2285, www.northernforestcanoetrail.org.

Each summer, **L.L. Bean Outdoor Discovery Schools** offers a variety of kayaking courses, trips, and tours, from a Half-Day Kayak Tour to a Three-Day Island Kayak Camping Trip, and everything in between. These programs allow beginners and experienced paddlers to select courses suitable to their skill and interests. Courses begin at the L.L. Bean Paddling Center at Flying Point in Freeport, where you'll receive personal attention from expert instructors. The L.L. Bean PaddleSports Festival occurs in mid-June in Freeport. For more information, contact the L.L. Bean Outdoor Discovery Schools at 888/552-3261 or visit www.llbean.com/ods.

Maine Sport Outdoor Adventures, 207/236-8797 or 800/722-0826, a program of **Maine Sport Outfitters,** Rte. 1, P.O. Box 956, Rockport 04856, 207/236-7120 or 888/236-8797, www.MaineSport.com, operates sea-kayaking programs, including ocean tours of Camden and Rockport Harbors, instructional programs, and custom tours of Penobscot and Muscongus Bays. Beginners are welcome, and kayak and camping gear are available for rent.

Maine is also, of course, the home of the **Old Town Canoe Factory Outlet Store,** 239 Main St., Old Town 04468, 207/827-1530, just north of Bangor. Old Town has built classic canoes since 1898, and even if a canoe isn't on your shopping list, you can still enjoy a visit to the outlet store. Or, if you are interested in making your own traditional wood-and-canvas canoe, you can complete one in a seven-day workshop led by Dave Mussey of **Maine Journeys,** 2839 Ohio St., Glenburn 04401, 207/884-6278. Dave's wife, Fran Doonan, can teach you to make traditional brown ash baskets to carry your gear on your trip.

WHITE-WATER RAFTING

From late April to mid-October, fleets of multi-person self-bailing rafts operated by more than a dozen outfitters bump and grind down the Kennebec, Dead, and Penobscot Rivers in western Maine's mountains. Begun in the mid-1970s, white-water rafting has become a multimillion-dollar industry—much of it headquartered in and around the Forks, a nondescript hamlet at the junction of the Kennebec and the Dead. All outfitters are state-licensed and state-monitored, and all three rivers are dam-controlled; two have scheduled daily water releases during the season. Trips require busing to put-in sites. Since the Forks is about a three-hour drive north of Portland, and rafting trips get going early, consider spending pre- and post-rafting nights nearby.

Trip options range from half-day runs to multi-day, three-river experiences. All offer real upper-arm workouts, hearty outdoor cookouts,

and post-trip video reruns. Best prices are midweek. On spring and fall trips (also cheaper), wetsuits may be mandatory (rentals are available). Spring brings wildest (and iciest) water, fall (late September and early October) the best scenery. Several outfitters offer adventure packages, combining rafting with mountain biking, hiking, or rock climbing; many have year-round sports facilities.

Rank beginners and family groups (although no kids under 10) should opt for the 12-mile Kennebec River trip, starting just below Harris Station (a hydroelectric dam) and ending at the Forks. Four miles of Class IV rapids through the Kennebec Gorge—including the quaintly named Magic Falls—precede a rather leisurely coast downstream to the takeout.

The thrills multiply on the 14-mile Penobscot River trip (no kids under 15), starting below McKay Station (another hydro dam), heading into Ripogenus Gorge, and negotiating Class IV and V rapids named Exterminator, Bone Cruncher, and Cribwork. Beyond are Class III and IV rapids, with some quiet spots in between, en route to the takeout, at Pockwockamus Falls.

Even more challenging, especially in May, is the 16-mile Dead River trip, with plenty of Class IV and V whitewater. Dam releases are less frequent on the Dead—only five in the spring and three in the fall.

Companies with top reputations are **Northern Outdoors,** oldest in Maine, Rte. 201, P.O. Box 100, The Forks 04985, 207/663-4466 or 800/765-7238, fax 207/663-2244; **New England Outdoor Center,** Rice Farm, P.O. Box 669, Millinocket 04462, 207/723-5438 or 800/766-7238; and **Magic Falls Rafting Company,** P.O. Box 9, West Forks 04985, 800/207-7238. **Raft Maine,** an industry association comprising more than a dozen rafting companies, maintains a reservations clearinghouse at 800/723-8633, fax 207/824-3694, www.raftmaine.com. Cost ranges are $80–120 per person on the Kennebec, $90–135 on the Dead, and $90–120 on the Penobscot. Maine residents should ask about the special discounts available on a dozen or so weekdays in June, early July, and mid-September.

SWIMMING

Southern Maine's beaches, stretching from York to South Portland, provide the state's best saltwater swimming and sunning spots. Some beaches are municipal, some are parts of state parks. Remember that the Atlantic water is chilly but warms up (relatively speaking) as the tide comes in. Water temperatures are highest in August, but the closer you get to Canada, the colder the water. Sand Beach, in Acadia National Park, gets several stars for its setting—but none for water temperature.

Warmer water is a better bet in the state's countless freshwater lakes and ponds. Several of the best swimming spots are within state parks. Outdoor municipal swimming pools and indoor YMCA and health-club pools draw crowds year-round.

FISHING AND HUNTING

The best general reference on hunting and fishing is the *Maine Guide to Hunting and Fishing,* a booklet published annually by the Maine Tourism Association, 327 Water St., Hallowell 04347, 207/623-0363, www.mainetourism.com, and containing articles, regulations, and ads for lodgings, restaurants, and gear. For copies of official regulations, contact the **Maine Department of Inland Fisheries and Wildlife,** 284 State St., 41 State House Station, Augusta 04333, 207/287-8000; recorded seasonal information: 207/287-8003.

In Maine, recreational fishing can involve anything from dangling a baited line off a creaky dock to fly-fishing remote inland streams to heading offshore aboard a sport-fishing "party boat." No license is needed for saltwater fishing. Adult (16 and over) freshwater-fishing licenses for nonresidents of Maine cost $12 for one day, $24 for three days, $37 for seven days, and $53 for a season pass. Fees for noncitizens of the United States ("nonresident aliens" in the regulations) are higher—a season pass, for example, runs $75.

Unless you know someone who can show you the ropes, the best way to experience Maine's fishing and/or hunting possibilities is to book a trip at one of Maine's several dozen sporting camps, where you can get information, swap stories with kindred spirits, and sign on with a registered guide—a licensed specialist who'll provide a boat, gear, and expertise. Some guides operate independently, some work with sporting-camp owners or outfitters. For a list of available guides, and the services they offer, contact the **Maine Professional Guides Association,** P.O. Box 336, Augusta 04332, 207/751-3797, www.maineguides.org.

BICYCLING

As elsewhere, mountain biking and bicycle touring in Maine mushroomed in the 1990s. And in the 21st century, cyclists have benefited from the state's significant progress in paving shoulders. While some sections of road still remain narrow, Maine offers many wonderful back roads, lesser levels of traffic than most of New England, and even some excellent off-road options.

Leading the charge for paved shoulders and user-friendly cycling, and acting as Maine's bicycling clearinghouse, is the **Bicycle Coalition of Maine,** P.O. Box 5275, Augusta 04332, 207/623-4511, www.BikeMaine.org. The BCM produces a free annual event calendar listing rides, races, bike shops (for repairs and rentals), and bike clubs all over the state. To support the cause (and receive discounts), join the BCM.

Great news for bicyclists is the publication of two very helpful documents by the Maine DOT—the *Maine Bike Map* and the *Explore Maine Bike Guide.* The map is helpful for planning rides with information about traffic levels and which roads have paved shoulders. The guide is a book of 25 loop rides with color maps and directions. Both publications are available for free by contacting the **Maine Department**

of Transportation, 16 State House Station, Augusta 04333, 207/624-3252. Cue sheets can also be downloaded from the Maine DOT website at www.ExploreMaine.org/bike.

Bike shops and bike clubs around the state sponsor group rides, usually on summer evenings and weekends. Some are scheduled, some impromptu; some require shuttling to starting points; and some combine cycling and socializing.

Best places for bike rentals are Auburn, Augusta, Bar Harbor, Camden, Ellsworth, Kennebunkport, Machias, Ogunquit, Orono, Portland (several choices), Presque Isle, Rockport, Rockland, Searsport, Southwest Harbor, and Woolwich (next to Bath).

Maine law now requires that any bicyclist under the age of 16 wear a helmet—and it certainly behooves every adult to do the same. A list of rental shops around Maine is available at www.BikeMaine.org.

An annual ride of passage for cyclists is the 180-mile **Trek Across Maine: Sunday River to the Sea,** a three-day, pedal-at-your-own-pace marathon from Bethel to Rockland, benefiting the American Lung Association of Maine (ALAM). Drawing 1,600 cyclists of all ages, the scenic trek, in early June, wins high praises for its top-notch organization. Registration begins early in the year, and participants have to guarantee minimum pledges of $450 (higher pledges earn incentive prizes). For information contact ALAM, 122 State St., Augusta 04330, 800/458-6472, www.mainelung.org.

Another popular event is the **Maine Bike Rally,** which takes place the weekend after July 4th and moves to different communities every two years. Riders can choose from a smorgasbord of 30 rides both on- and off-road; camping and meals are included for $75. In late July, based in Rockland, the **Maine Lobster Ride and Roll** offers 50- and 100-mile coastal routes, and includes a lobster roll at the end of the ride.

HIKING

Maine's pioneer ecotourist, Henry David Thoreau, was a big believer in "going afoot," and who's to disagree when thousands of miles of hiking trails await? You can stroll the shorelines, wander the woods, bushwhack in the boonies, and conquer Katahdin. There's no central clearinghouse for hiking information, but a couple of contacts and a couple of specialized publications can provide more than enough dope.

Best hiking contact for **Acadia National Park** is the park's visitors center, P.O. Box 177, Bar Harbor 04609, 207/288-3338, www.nps.gov/acad. For state parks and public lands, contact the **Maine Bureau of Parks and Lands,** 22 State House Station, Augusta 04333, 207/287-3821, www.parksandlands.com (they have hiking maps for state parks). Dozens of spectacular hiking sites come under the jurisdiction of **The Nature Conservancy,** 14 Maine St., Fort Andross, Brunswick 04011, 207/729-5181, www.nature.org, and the **Maine Audubon Society,** 20 Gilsland Farm Rd., Falmouth 04105, 207/781-2330, www.maineaudubon.org. Both are membership organizations, but their properties are open to nonmembers. Ask Maine Audubon for its schedule of moderately priced, always excellent in-state field trips. They're very popular, so make reservations well in advance.

The best hiking reference books are *50 Hikes in the Maine Mountains,* by Cloe Chunn, *50 Hikes in Coastal and Southern Maine,* by John Gibson, and an Appalachian Mountain Club (AMC) publication: *Maine Mountain Guide.* Other good resources include *A Walk in the Park: Acadia's Hiking Guide,* by Tom St. Germain; and *Katahdin: A Guide to Baxter State Park & Katahdin,* by Stephen Clark.

GOLF

You can tee off at more than 140 golf courses in Maine (59 of them have 18 holes)—along the shore, on islands, and deep in the mountains. There's lots of variety here. An informal poll lists the most scenic courses as Kebo Valley (in Bar Harbor, the nation's eighth oldest), Sugarloaf/USA (Carrabassett Valley), Mingo Springs (Rangeley), Point Sebago (Casco), Belgrade

Lakes, the Ledges (York), Dunegrass (Old Orchard Beach), and Samoset Resort (Rockport). The same poll lists the toughest as the Woodlands (private, in Falmouth), Samoset Resort, Kebo Valley, Sable Oaks (South Portland), Martindale (also private, in Auburn), and Sugarloaf/USA. The official **Maine State Golf Association** is at 374 U.S. Rte. 1, Yarmouth 04096, 207/846-3800, www.mesga.org. See the Maine Golf Trail, and order a "Golf Trail Guide," at www.visitmaine.com.

If lousy weather sets in and you're in the Portland area, head for Fore Season Indoor Golf, 1037 Forest Ave., Portland 04103, 207/797-8835, an indoor facility with six computerized golf simulators where you can play virtual golf at any of over 30 international PGA-tour courses. Call for tee times and reservations.

OTHER SUMMER ACTIVITIES

The mountains of western Maine's Oxford County are pockmarked with disused quarries just waiting for enthusiastic rockhounds. The best source of maps, information, tools, and gear is area landmark **Perham's of West Paris,** Rtes. 26 and 219, P.O. Box 280, West Paris 04289, 207/674-2341 or 800/371-4367, open every day, with the exception of Thanksgiving, Christmas, and Mondays from January 1 to May 1. They'll give you free quarry maps, sell you equipment, and point you in the right direction. (Skip quarry areas during the fall hunting season; hunting is allowed there.) You can also buy gold-panning gear and head for the Swift River in Byron—best locale for sifting out bits of the precious metal. Don't get overeager, though; the prize nuggets have long since been retrieved. A helpful guide is *A Collector's Guide to Maine Mineral Localities,* by W. B. Thompson et al.

SPECTATOR SPORTS

Portland is the best spot for professional sports, since it's home to the **Portland Sea Dogs,** Double-A Affiliate of the Boston Red Sox, and the **Portland Pirates,** AHL affiliate of the Washington Capitols. The Sea Dogs play early April through early September at Hadlock Field, 271 Park Ave., Portland 04102. For a home-game schedule and ticket info, 800/936-3647 or visit www.seadogs.com. Home ice for the Pirates, who play throughout the winter, is the 6,733-seat Cumberland County Civic Center, One Civic Center Sq., Portland 04101. Box office: 207/775-3458, www.portlandpirates.com.

During the winter, basketball is the game of choice, played by high school and college athletes in every corner of the state. University of Maine ice-hockey and basketball teams have garnered many awards and tons of loyal fans. Check sports pages in the *Portland Press Herald* and the *Bangor Daily News* for full schedules of games.

SKIING AND SNOWBOARDING

In the winter of 1870–71, a handful of Swedish immigrants in Aroostook County's New Sweden introduced the sport of skiing, and it's been downhill ever since. Maine now has two major ski resorts—**Sunday River Ski Resort,** in Bethel, and **Sugarloaf/USA,** in Carrabassett Valley (both operate under the umbrella of the giant American Skiing Company). On their websites (www.sundayriver.com and www.sugarloaf.com, respectively), you'll find trail maps, skiing advice, and information on weather and snow conditions, accommodations, and online discounts. Both resorts are full-service, year-round destinations, with lots of lodgings, restaurants, ski and gift shops, instruction, and entertainment.

Saddleback, adjacent to Sugarloaf/USA, came under new ownership in 2003 and immediately invested millions of dollars in snowmaking, lifts, and base facilities. It expects a new trailside hotel to bring it national prominence.

A dozen good medium-size and small ski areas specialize in child-friendliness and reasonable lift prices in Auburn, Bridgton, Camden, Farmington, Greenville, Hermon, Lee, Locke Mills, Mars Hill, Rangeley,

Rumford, and Skowhegan. All of these ski areas except Greenville and Rangeley have **night skiing.**

The state clearinghouse for ski (and snowboard) information is **Ski Maine,** P.O. Box 7566, Portland 04112, 207/761-3774, www.skimaine.com. The website is particularly useful, since it provides up-to-date ski conditions and event calendars.

Cross-country skiing has taken on a life of its own in Maine, especially in years when the weather gods cooperate. Sugarloaf has its own Ski Touring Center, and the privately owned Sunday River Inn Ski Touring Center supplements the downhill and snowboarding facilities at Sunday River Ski Resort. Both centers rent skis, offer lessons, and have miles of mapped and groomed trails of varying difficulty. In the winters when snow piles up along the coast (not every year), there's no more splendid cross-country spot than Acadia National Park, where trails follow some 50 miles of carriage roads through woods, across stone bridges, and along seaview ledges. For information about Acadia snow conditions, 207/288-3338.

The **Maine Nordic Ski Council,** P.O. Box 645, Bethel 04217, 800/754-9263, www.mnsc.com, an industry association, produces an annual brochure with info on more than a dozen ski centers. Up-to-date snow conditions are listed on their website.

Snowboarding parks are now known as Terrain Parks, and almost every ski area has one, because the space needed is small. There's new enthusiasm at community ski areas because of the appeal the parks have for kids as mountain "playgrounds." The phenomenal growth in snowboarding since the late 1980s means dramatic changes lie ahead at all of the ski areas, with new gimmicks continually being added to attract neophytes and satisfy daredevils. Stay tuned.

SNOWMOBILING

Once considered a rough-and-ready, exclusive pursuit for hard-driving, hard-drinking good ol' boys, snowmobiling (or snowsledding) is, after snowboarding, one of Maine's fastest-growing winter sports. Development of ultraprotective sportswear, establishment of the Maine Snowmobile Association, and coordination of an astonishing, 13,000-mile trail system have opened the pastime to a far broader clientele. Park rangers, preachers, schoolkids, and eight-to-fivers have long commuted by snowmobile in the North Woods, but weekends used to bring out a different species. Now everyone's at it seven days a week. As the snow gets deeper, motels fill up, their parking lots overrun with the machines. All snowmobiles must be registered by the state. Season registration is $34 for Maine residents, $69 for nonresidents.

Best and most scenic locales for snowmobiling are Rockwood and Greenville (both on Moosehead Lake), Millinocket (next to Baxter State Park), Jackman, Bethel, and Rangeley, where snowmobile rentals, restaurants, and accommodations are all available. Aroostook County, at the top of Maine, is prime snowmobiling country—often with the best snow in the state—but you'll spend a long time going and coming.

Serving as the clearinghouse and advocacy group for nearly 300 local snowmobile clubs is the **Maine Snowmobile Association (MSA),** 7 Noyes Pl., P.O. Box 80, Augusta 04332, 207/622-6983, www.mesnow.com. Weekday trail-condition updates are found at the website.

OTHER WINTER SPORTS

Most every corner of Maine has a popular spot for **ice-skating,** and some communities make a real effort to keep the ice clear and maintain smooth skating surfaces. There's no central information source; see the regional chapters for recommendations.

Snowshoes—awkward-looking, functional footwear originally made of wood and hides—have been around at least since the Stone Age, allowing access through the deepest snowdrifts; in northern Maine's pre-snowmobile days, snowshoes were essential to survival. Nowadays, however, **snowshoeing** has gained new popularity as a low-impact, low-cost winter sport. No lift tickets needed, no fancy gear required (recreational snowshoes—metal or wood—cost $100–150). L.L. Bean's Outdoor Discovery Schools, 888/552-3261, www.llbean.com, hold snowshoeing courses, as does the Outdoor Center at Sugarloaf/USA, 207/237-2000 or 207/237-6808 (snow phone). Both rent snowshoes.

The Camden Snow Bowl ski area has Maine's only **toboggan chute.** Because of unpredictable snow and ice in this coastal town, be sure to call ahead for conditions—the 400-foot speedway ends on Hosmer Pond, and if it isn't frozen, there's no go. Best time to come is February, when the **National Toboggan Championships** are held here. For details, call 207/236-3438.

Sometimes dubbed "chess on ice," because of the amount of strategy involved, the Scottish national sport of curling has dozens of enthusiastic supporters at Maine's only curling rink, the **Belfast Curling Club,** operating from early November to late March. Leagues play regularly on weeknights, and the club holds tournaments (called bonspiels) and open houses several times during the season. Info: Belfast Curling Club, Belmont Ave., Rte. 3, Belfast 04915, 207/338-1466 or 207/548-0142.

Entertainment and Events

Next to ecotourism, cultural tourism (for lack of a better term) has become Maine's focus in recent years. And why not? The state boasts enough arts-related sites and activities to keep residents and visitors on the move from New Year's Day to Christmas. The flavor varies a bit from summer to winter and back again—due partly to demand, partly to weather—but unless you'd rather be navel-gazing in the North Woods, shunning the outside world, you can tap into a mix of activities and have no problem staying busy.

MUSEUMS AND HISTORIC SITES

If museums and history intrigue you, you'll have no dearth of options in Maine. The best museums and sites for **kids** are the Children's Museum of Maine, in Portland; the Maine Discovery Museum, in Bangor; the Maine State Museum, in Augusta; and Fort Knox State Historic Site, near Bucksport.

Best **art** museums are the Portland Museum of Art, the Farnsworth Art Museum and Wyeth Center in Rockland, and the art museums at Bowdoin College in Brunswick and Colby College in Waterville.

Best **marine** museums are the Maine Maritime Museum, in Bath, and the Penobscot Marine Museum (Maine's oldest), in Searsport. The Owls Head Transportation Museum in Owls Head, near Rockland, focuses on wheeled and winged vehicles—it's the best such collection in the state and even beyond.

Maine's most **eclectic** and **one-of-a-kind** museums—where every display case holds a surprise—include the Nylander Museum, in Caribou; the Wilson Museum, in Castine; and the L.C. Bates Museum, in Hinckley.

Unique **history** museums include the 1770 Burnham Tavern, in Machias; the 1754 Old Fort Western, in Augusta; the 1870s Norlands Living History Center, in Livermore; and the 1885 Franklin D. Roosevelt Cottage, on Campobello Island, near Lubec. The Old York Historical Society also has a sprawling collection of historic museum buildings.

Self-explanatory are the **collections** in the Webb Museum of Vintage Fashion, in Island Falls; the Lumberman's Museum, in Patten; the Seashore Trolley Museum, in Kennebunkport; the Wendell Gilley Museum of Bird Carving, in Southwest Harbor; and the Peary-MacMillan Arctic Museum, at Bowdoin College, in Brunswick. Music boxes fill the Musical

Know Maine

FESTIVALS, FAIRS, AND OTHER EVENTS

While there is a great concentration of activity in summer, hundreds of special events occur all year long in Maine. In addition to an endless round of concerts, plays, art shows, and other cultural offerings, here's a sampling of the most intriguing, enduring, and enjoyable festivals and fairs that turn up on Maine's annual calendar. These and lots more are described in the regional sections. Also check calendars of events in free tabloids and on local bulletin boards for other goings-on. A good way to sample local flavor is to attend commemorations—especially centennials—of town foundings, town separations, and other noteworthy events. Everyone turns out, enthusiasm is contagious, and the eats are always homemade. If you're basing your itinerary on specific events, be sure to call ahead to confirm dates and times. (See www.mainetourism.com or www.maineevents.com for up-to-date information on what's happening around the state.)

January
Snodeo (parade and fireworks), Rangeley, 207/864-5364; **Maine WinterFest,** Falmouth and Freeport, 207/772-2811.

February
Heritage Day, Dr. Moses Mason House, Bethel, 207/824-2908; **Log Drivers' Cookout,** Island Falls, 207/463-2077; **National Toboggan Championships,** Camden, 207/236-3438; **Winter Fest,** Millinocket, 207/723-4443.

March
Can-Am Sled Dog Races, Fort Kent, 207/444-5439; **Maple Sunday at Norlands,** (maple syrup festivities), Washburn-Norlands Living History Center, Livermore, 207/897-4366; **Maine Maple Sunday,** statewide, 207/287-1132.

April
Fishermen's Festival, Boothbay Harbor, 207/633-2353; **Piscataquis River Canoe Race,** Guilford to Dover-Foxcroft, 207/564-7533; **Bradbury Mountain Hawk Watching Days,** Pownal, 207/781-2330.

May
Memorial Day celebrations—parades, dinners, crafts fairs—statewide; **Moose Mainea** (a month-long tribute to the favorite local beast, including the Tour De Moose), Greenville, 207/695-2702; **Lilac Festival & Plant Sale, Lilac Lap,** McLaughlin Gardens, South Paris, 207/743-8820.

June
Acadian Festival, Madawaska, 207/728-7000; **Greek Heritage Festival,** Portland, 207/774-0281; **La Kermesse Franco-American Festival,** Biddeford, 207/282-2894; **Midsummer Festival** (commemorating Scandinavian heritage), New Sweden, 207/896-3306; **National Trails Day,** statewide; **Old Port Festival,** Portland, 207/772-6828; **Strawberry Festival,** Wiscasset, 207/882-7184; **Windjammer Days,** Boothbay Harbor, 207/633-2353.

July

Juried Arts and Crafts Show, Camden, 207/236-4404; **Great Schooner Race,** Penobscot Bay, 800/807-9463; **Belfast Bay Festival,** Belfast, 207/338-5719; **Central Maine Egg Festival,** Pittsfield, 207/257-4209; **Folk Art Festival,** Grand Lake Stream, 207/796-8199; **Fourth of July celebrations,** statewide, but best locations include Bar Harbor, Bath, Bethel, Boothbay Harbor, Eastport, Greenville, Jonesport, Rangeley, Thomaston, and York; **Mollyockett Day** (townwide festivities commemorating a Native American maiden), Bethel, 207/824-3575; **Native American Festival & Maine Basketmakers Market,** College of the Atlantic, Bar Harbor, 207/288-3519; **North Atlantic Blues Festival,** Rockland, 207/593-1189; **Open Farm Day,** statewide, 207/287-3702; **World's Fair** (a tongue-in-cheek country fair), North Waterford, 207/345-8061; **Yarmouth Clam Festival,** Yarmouth, 207/846-3984.

August

Bangor State Fair, Bangor, 207/947-5555; **Beach Olympics,** Old Orchard Beach, 207/934-2500; **Festival de Joie,** Lewiston, 207/782-6231; **International Festival,** Calais (cooperative activities with St. Stephen, New Brunswick), 800/422-3112; **Lobster Festival,** Winter Harbor, 207/963-7658; **Maine Antiques Festival,** Union, 207/563-1013; **Maine Highland Games** (Scottish festival), Brunswick, 207/688-4483; **Maine Lobster Festival,** Rockland, 207/596-0376; **Olde Bristol Days** (great small-town celebration), Pemaquid Peninsula, 207/563-8340; **Blueberry Festival,** Rangeley, 207/864-5364; **Machias Wild Blueberry Festival,** Machias, 207/255-6665.

September

Cornish Apple Festival, Cornish, 207/625-7447; **Blue Hill Fair,** Blue Hill, 207/374-3701; **Common Ground Country Fair** (Maine's best country fair, focusing on environmental consciousness and 100 percent–organic everything), Unity, 207/568-4142; **Salmon Festival,** Eastport, 207/853-4644; **International Seaplane Fly-In,** Greenville, 207/695-2702; **Laudholm Farm Nature Crafts Festival** (high-quality juried crafts fair), Wells, 207/646-4521; **Maine Healing Arts Festival,** Winthrop, 207/336-2065; **Windjammer Weekend,** Camden, 207/236-4404.

October

Fall Festival Arts and Crafts Show, Camden, 207/236-4404; **Fall Foliage Festival,** Boothbay Railway Village, Boothbay, 207/633-4727; **Fryeburg Fair** (the state's biggest, best, and most popular agricultural fair), Fryeburg, 207/935-3268; **Harvestfest,** York Village, 207/363-4422.

November

Christmas crafts fairs, statewide, in locations such as Augusta, Bangor, Farmington, Fort Kent, Greenville, Kennebunk, Lewiston, Portland, Rockport, and Waterville; **Festival of Lights Celebration,** Rockland, 207/596-0376.

December

Chester Greenwood Day (commemorating the inventor of earmuffs), Farmington, 207/778-4215; **Christmas at Norlands,** Washburn-Norlands Living History Center, Livermore, 207/897-4366; **Christmas by the Sea,** Camden, 207/236-4404; **Christmas Prelude,** Kennebunk/Kennebunkport, 207/967-0857; **Harbor Lights Festival,** Boothbay Harbor, 207/633-2353; **New Year's Portland** (the best place in the state to ring in the New Year), 207/772-6828.

Know Maine

Wonder House in Wiscasset, and operatic costumes fill the Nordica Homestead Museum, in Farmington (birthplace of early-20th-century opera diva Madame Lillian Nordica). The Shaker Museum, in New Gloucester, represents the life and work of the nation's only remaining Shaker colony.

ARTS AND CRAFTS

Ask an artist why she or he creates in Maine and you'll hear, "It's the light," "It's the setting," or "It's the support network." (You *won't* often hear, "It's the money.") Whatever the reason, the creative juices generate superb work that fills galleries large and small from Kittery to Fort Kent. The best statewide resource for finding studios, shops, and galleries is the free annual *Maine Guide to Craft Artists and Culture,* published by the Maine Crafts Association, P.O. Box 8817, Portland 04103, 207/780-1807, www.mainecrafts .org. Included in the directory is a month-by-month calendar of shows, workshops, and related events.

Two educational institutions that draw recognized craftspeople from around the country and beyond are the **Haystack Mountain School of Crafts,** P.O. Box 518, Deer Isle 04627, 207/348-2306, fax 348-2307, www.haystack-mtn.org, which offers courses for talented artisans in a huge variety of media, and the **Watershed Center for the Ceramic Arts,** 19 Brick Hill Rd., Newcastle 04553, 207/882-6075, www.watershedcenter-ceramicarts.org, a retreat providing ceramic artists with summer residencies, lectures, and studio space.

THEATER

Professional and semiprofessional companies and community troupes command stages throughout the year, but summer brings out most of the thespians and their audiences. Among the best and longest-running summer theaters (with emphasis on musicals) are Ogunquit Playhouse, in Ogunquit;

Maine State Music Theater, in Brunswick; and Lakewood Theater, in Madison (near Skowhegan). Shakespeare and other high literary lights take center stage at the Theater at Monmouth (between Lewiston and Augusta), where Italianate Cumston Hall provides the perfect setting for Shakespeare productions. Bangor's riverfront Maine Shakespeare Festival is a spin-off of the city's Penobscot Theatre Company. Each summer, Acadia Repertory Company presents a range of contemporary and classic plays in the idyllic village of Somesville (near Bar Harbor). Recently restored after decades of decline is the historic Deertrees Theater, in Harrison, a comfortably rustic performance space for plays and concerts. The Portland Opera Repertory Theatre gives three performances of a major opera (*Carmen* in 2005) in the city's Merrill Auditorium each July, and smaller-scale, semi-staged operas in towns across Maine late June–mid-July.

Maine is home, too, to many community theater groups using nonprofessional yet extremely capable talent. Among the best are Camden Civic Theatre, in Camden; Belfast Maskers, in Belfast; Gaslight Theater, in Hallowell; The Public Theater, in Lewiston; and the Sanford Maine Stage Company, in Sanford.

During the winter, Bangor's Penobscot Theatre enters its real season, and in Portland, the options include Portland Stage Company, Portland Players, and the Lyric Theater (the latter two perform on weekends in South Portland). The Children's Theatre of Maine also performs weekends in Portland.

Also during the winter, the drama departments of Maine's universities and colleges mount theatrical performances. Check newspaper listings for schedules at the University of Maine campuses (especially Orono, Portland, and Machias) and at Bowdoin, Bates, and Colby Colleges.

DANCE

Although performance dance groups have sprung up in spots, and Bates College puts on a nationally acclaimed dance festival each summer in Lewiston, Portland is the state's center of dance, boasting classical companies such as the Maine State Ballet and the Portland Ballet. Check listings for their performance schedules.

If you're more interested in participating than spectating, Maine Ballroom Dance, 614A Congress St., 207/773-0002, holds weekly dances (Sat. 8 PM–midnight) in Portland— and a renewed interest in ballroom (including Latin) dancing has spurred classes and dances in other parts of the state.

Check newspapers, bulletin boards, and telephone poles for notices of contradances—once described as "brief whirling encounters of the safest kind." Vaguely comparable to square or line dancing, old-fashioned/new-fashioned contradances involve a chunk of exercise, a bit of potluck, and a chance to schmooze with like-minded souls. Held in town, American Legion, and grange halls, most are "chem-free." Dress up or down and get into the spirit. The best statewide information source is Down East Friends of the Folk Arts (DEFFA), 13 Pinkham's Flats Rd., Lamoine 04605, www .deffa.org, which publishes the monthly *DEFFA Newsletter,* listing contradances, Scottish and English dances, Celtic music, and other folk events.

MUSIC

Scheduled and impromptu concerts—jazz, blues, classical, rock, folk, funk, zydeco, and what-have-you—occur statewide throughout the summer. (The pace slows slightly in winter but definitely doesn't stop.) Best summertime options for classical music are the chamber-music series in Rockport (Bay Chamber Concerts), Machias (Machias Bay Chamber Concerts), Harrison (Sebago/Long Lake Chamber Music Festival), Portland (Portland Chamber Music Festival), and Damariscotta (Salt Bay Chamberfest); and the concert series in Bar Harbor (Arcady Music Festival, Bar Harbor Music Festival), Brunswick (Bowdoin Summer Music Festival), Blue Hill (Kneisel Hall Chamber Music Festival), and Hancock

(the Pierre Monteux School). In the Portland area, the Portland String Quartet and the Portland Symphony Orchestra perform year-round—less often but sometimes alfresco in summer. The Portland Concert Association and Rockport Bay Chamber Concerts present regular winter series; season tickets provide substantial discounts and priority seating, but individual tickets are available.

The Center for Cultural Exchange in downtown Portland (1 Longfellow Sq., Portland 04101, 207/761-0591) has been a bonanza for world-music lovers, bringing in musicians and dancers from all over the globe—even the Throat Singers of Tuva.

The best resource for all of the above is www.mainemusic.org, rated a Top 100 website by *Portland Magazine,* with extensive fresh listings, an event search, and discussion board. It's updated regularly, with lots of good links.

For a unique musical immersion, plan well ahead and book a week at **Quisisana,** on the shores of western Maine's spectacular Kezar Lake. Aspiring (and ultra-talented) musicians earn their keep by day and perform opera, piano concerts, and more each night in the lakeside music hall—much to the delight of enthusiastic guests at the decades-old summer resort. Even the rustic cabins have musical names. One newspaper described Quisisana as "Where Mozart Goes on Vacation." The only problem here is getting a reservation; the regulars are incredibly loyal. Quisisana, Center Lovell 04016, 207/925-3500; or, off-season, P.O. Box 142, Larchmont, NY 10538, 914/833-0293, http://quisisanaresort.com.

NIGHTLIFE

For a year-round concentration of live entertainment and nightlife, Portland is the place to be. On any given night (and especially on weekends), you can find jazz, blues, folk, hip-hop, oldies, rock, country, grunge, and all the latest buzzword music styles—plus comedy improv, karaoke, poetry slams, and "exotic dance" spots. A good source for entertainment ads and listings is the *Portland Phoenix,* a free tabloid available in shops and restaurants throughout the Portland area. The tabloid *Go,* a supplement in Thursday's *Portland Press Herald,* also carries a list of club and disco schedules. Both websites, www.portlandphoenix.com and www.mainetoday.com (Blethen Maine Newspapers, Inc., *Press Herald* publisher), carry mega-listings for movies, music, theater, and other arts and entertainments.

Accommodations

Depending on your lifestyle, your wallet, and the condition of your back, getting a night's rest in Maine can entail anything from luxurious resorts to the remotest of campsites.

BED-AND-BREAKFASTS AND COUNTRY INNS

Hundreds of licensed bed-and-breakfasts—from cozy mom-and-pop enterprises to antiques-filled mansions—welcome visitors to Maine. If you don't mind sacrificing a bit of privacy in your comings and goings, B&Bs are prime venues for swapping tips on sightseeing, restaurants, and lodging; bumping into former colleagues; or launching lasting friendships or even new careers.

Although Maine and other American B&Bs are European in inspiration, there are differences: Prices are relatively higher here than in Europe; here, you're more likely to find a private bath; here, too, many hosts are not area natives, though they compensate with congeniality and enthusiasm for their adopted turf. Most hosts pride themselves on their breakfasts, which can be continental, buffet-style, or sumptuous (and anything-with-blueberries tends to be the preferred specialty du jour).

The round-the-clock demands of operating a B&B lead to burnout for hosts who overdo it, so don't be surprised if an establishment has changed hands by the time you arrive. A sign posted at one B&B sums it up well: "Open 24 hours year-round. Additional services: caterer, chauffeur, moneylender, tutor, nurse, seamstress, psychologist, laundress, etc." Consider "etc." the operative word. The longest-tenure B&B hosts hire inn-sitters, night managers, or at least enough staff to share the chores.

Few allow pets or smoking indoors, many are not equipped for small children, and few have in-room TVs or telephones. When planning overnight stays, be considerate; if your schedule demands a very early departure, for instance, try to find more anonymous lodgings where you won't disturb hosts or other guests.

Throughout Maine, you'll also find superb specimens of country inns—and not just in rural areas. In general, while you're likely to run into the same congeniality in the inns that exists at B&Bs, and while prices tend to be in the same range, country inns often have more rooms and staff, and most rooms have private baths. Most inns also have dining rooms open to the public for dinner and sometimes lunch.

Prices for a high-season double-occupancy room at a Maine B&B or inn range from about $70 to well over $200. About half of Maine's B&Bs are closed Nov.–May; except in the ski areas around Bethel and Kingfield, the year-round operations usually have reduced rates in winter. For a free copy of the *Maine Guide to Inns & Bed & Breakfasts,* an annual booklet covering about 160 establishments, contact the Maine Tourism Association, 327 Water Street, Hallowell 04347, 207/623-0363, www.mainetourism.com. In southern Maine, Donna Little operates a B&B reservations service: **Bed & Breakfast of Maine,** 377 Gray Rd., Falmouth 04105, 207/797-5540, fax 797-7599.

FARM BED-AND-BREAKFASTS

For a moderate price, these rural slice-of-life digs offer guests a chance to hobnob with honest-to-goodness farmers and resident menageries of sheep, cows, goats, ducks, llamas, chickens, geese, deer, or turkeys. Price for a high-season double ranges from $50 with shared bath to $150 with private bath and other amenities. Most of the farms welcome children but prohibit pets and smoking. For pictures of, and links to, nearly 20 farm B&Bs, visit the **Maine Farm Vacation B&B Association** website at www.MaineFarmVacation.com.

SPORTING CAMPS

These traditional log-cabin colonies—ranging from rustic to semi-elegant—cater to fans of fishing, hiking, rafting, swimming, canoeing, rock-climbing, bird-watching, nature photography, cross-country skiing, snowmobiling, and hunting. Deer, moose, and bear are frequent visitors. Most sporting camps are located "up back"—above Bangor in the remote northern two-thirds of the state. Some camps are accessible by state roads, some by logging roads, a few only by boat or floatplane (or, in winter, snowmobile or skiplane). Some serve legendary (always hearty) meals on the American Plan, others have do-it-yourself cooking facilities; some boast modern conveniences, others have outhouses and gas lights.

Facilities at sporting camps include canoe and boat rentals, guide service, and nonresident freshwater fishing licenses. Cabins accommodating 2–12 people are arranged in complexes of as few as five or as many as 20 buildings. During the summer, most sporting camps stipulate a one-week minimum stay, and early reservations are essential. Best months for families are July and August. Many guests return year after year, generation after generation—although most don't go to the extreme of the man who bequeathed mantelpiece ornaments to the cabin he'd enjoyed every summer for 50 years.

For a free directory of its 60-plus members, contact **Maine Sporting Camp Association,** P.O. Box 119, Millinocket 04462, 207/723-6622, www.mainesportingcamps.com. An entertaining survey of more than 80 Maine sporting camps and their owners appears in

Alice Arlen's *Maine Sporting Camps,* an illustrated paperback.

HOTELS, MOTELS, RESORTS, CONDOMINIUMS

Just as in every other state, hotels and motels abound in Maine. The state's resort complexes can be counted on two hands. Condominium rentals are clustered primarily in York County, the Camden/Rockport area, and the Sunday River and Sugarloaf/USA areas. Hint: Although best known as ski resorts, Sunday River and Sugarloaf/USA are year-round destinations, and off-season rates are in effect for their condos in summer—a great time to be in Maine's western mountains. Names and telephone numbers (including many toll-free numbers) of over 600 members of the **Maine Innkeepers Association** are listed in the organization's annual directory. For a free copy, contact the association at 304 US Rte. 1, Freeport 04032, 207/865-6100, www.maineinns.com.

CAMPGROUNDS AND CAMPSITES

Maine is a camper's nirvana, with countless camping facilities ranging from wilderness outposts to state-of-the-art RV resorts.

Federal Campgrounds and Campsites

Straddling the Maine–New Hampshire border, the **White Mountain National Forest** covers 53,000 acres—6,000 of them roadless—in Maine; it also encompasses five Forest Service campgrounds, some boasting well water, trash pickup, and toilets, in addition to tentsites and fireplaces. For information about camping, hiking, or the national forest itself, contact the Evans Notch Visitors Center, White Mountain National Forest, 18 Mayville Rd., Bethel 04217, 207/824-2134, www.fs.fed.us/r9/white. For camping reservations, call toll-free 877/444-6777.

Three National Park Service campgrounds lie within **Acadia National Park,** including lean-tos on Isle au Haut. Blackwoods, on

Mount Desert Island, and Duck Harbor, on Isle au Haut, require reservations during the high season; Seawall, on Mount Desert Island, operates on a first-come, first-served basis. Specifics about camping and the park itself are available by contacting Information, Acadia National Park, P.O. Box 177, Bar Harbor 04609, 207/288-3338, www.nps.gov/acad.

Along the 276-mile Maine segment of the **Appalachian Trail,** some 40 campsites—each about a day's hike apart—have tenting areas or lean-tos. The Maine Appalachian Trail Club, P.O. Box 283, Augusta 04330, www.matc.org, maintains most (266.8 miles) of the Maine section, and produces the essential *Appalachian Trail Guide to Maine,* which includes seven strip maps.

State Campgrounds and Campsites

Various branches of the state government supervise and/or maintain campsites and campgrounds all over Maine. Unfortunately, even though their territories overlap, there is no single source for information on all campsites owned and operated by the state.

Details on camping along the **Allagash Wilderness Waterway** and in 32 of Maine's **state parks** are available from the Bureau of Parks and Lands, 22 State House Station, Augusta 04333, 207/287-3821, www.parksandlands .com. A reservation system is in effect for the campsites, and, even though there's an extra charge, reservations are definitely advisable mid-June–Labor Day. In 2004, over 11,000 campsite reservations were processed. Only a small number of sites in each park are allocated on a first-come, first-served basis; the rest are by reservation. Some state parks, such as Sebago Lake, Camden Hills, and Lily Bay, fill up quickly.

For reservations, at least seven days ahead of the first night you want to stay (minimum stay is two nights, maximum 14 nights), call 207/287-3824 (from outside Maine) or 800/332-1501 (within Maine) 9 AM–4 PM weekdays Feb. 1–early Sept. Have your Visa or MasterCard ready. Online reservations, at www.CampWithMe.com, are encouraged.

Nonresident camping fees range from $11–17 per site per night, which includes the state's 7 percent lodging tax. Camping fees for Maine residents are about 25 percent cheaper. Reservation fee is $2 per site per night. Sebago Lake and Lily Bay State Parks open for camping on May 1; the others open May 15. All close either September 30 or October 15.

Be forewarned that alcohol is not allowed in state parks or on the grounds of state historic sites.

For info on primitive campsites on nearly 0.5 million acres of **public lands,** contact the Bureau of Parks and Lands, 22 State House Station, Augusta 04333, 207/287-3821.

The **Maine Forest Service** maintains a list of primitive campsites which require fire permits and have fire rings, but no toilet facilities. Contact one of the Maine Forest Service regional offices about sites within their geographic area: Augusta, 207/624-3700; Old Town, 207/827-1800; or Ashland, 207/435-7963.

Owned by Maine residents but administered separately from the state park system, **Baxter State Park** contains 10 campgrounds offering a variety of accommodations—wilderness sites, campground tentsites, bunkhouses, lean-tos, and 22 prized log cabins. Depending on their location, some campgrounds open as early as May 15; all close by October 15. Winter camping is allowed at specified sites Dec. 1–March 31, but rigid safety rules are strictly enforced, and no park roads are plowed. Pets, radios, and cell phones are prohibited in the park. The Baxter State Park Authority, 64 Balsam Dr., Millinocket 04462, 207/723-5140, began a new trial reservation system in 2005. In-person reservations could be made at Park HQ on January 18 for 20 percent of the sites in each campground. A Rolling Reservation System was instituted, whereby you can walk in or mail in for reservations four months or less prior to date wanted, or call the Park 10 days or fewer prior to date wanted. Detailed instructions can be found at www.baxterstateparkauthority.com/camping. Plan ahead and be flexible; choice dates and locations fill up quickly.

Comfy Camping at Mattawamkeag

An hour east of Baxter, the Town of Mattawamkeag operates the relatively plush **Mattawamkeag Wilderness Park and Campground,** (campsites and lean-tos, plus hot showers and bathrooms, and a recreation building with fireplace). In scenic country, the park has white-water canoeing opportunities, nearly 15 miles of hiking trails, a gorge, and waterfalls. For information, contact the Mattawamkeag Wilderness Park, Rte. 2, Box 5, Mattawamkeag 04459, 207/736-4881, www.mainerec.com/mattpark.

Wilderness Commercial Campsites

Responsible for recreation management on three million acres of paper-company land, **North Maine Woods, Inc.,** publishes maps of and information on its authorized campsites (equipped with toilets and fire rings) and designated fire-permit campsites (primitive sites requiring Maine Forest Service fire permits). Camping permits are issued at the checkpoint huts when you enter the paper company's private roads, but quotas are in effect, so it's best to call or write for reservations: **North Maine Woods, Inc.,** P.O. Box 421, Ashland 04732, 207/435-6213, www.northmainewoods.org.

Commercial Campgrounds

The annual *Maine Camping Guide* lists locations and facilities for about 230 commercial campgrounds throughout the state. For a free copy of the booklet, contact the **Maine Campground Owners Association,** 10 Falcon Rd., Ste. 1, Lewiston 04240, 207/782-5874, fax 782-4497, www.campmaine.com.

HOSTELS

For the young and the young at heart, Maine has an unusual hostel affiliated with Hostelling International (HI), near the skiing areas of Western Maine. It's the **SnowBoarding House** in West Bethel, 646 West Bethel Rd., Bethel 04217, 207/824-4224, www.BethelOutdoorAdventure.com, with rates from $19. On the coast, near Acadia National Park, the downtown Bar Harbor **Mount Desert Island Youth Hostel** recently underwent a thorough restoration, which director Ron Gamble terms "quite spectacular." The seasonal (Apr. 1–Nov. 1) accommodation now has a shower room, an organic garden, maid service, and a Weber grill, among other luxuries. Not yet affiliated with HI, it's located at 321 Main St., 207/288-5587, www.barharborhostel.com. Rates are $24–27 per person per night; prepaid credit-card reservations are accepted.

If you're not already a Hostelling International member, sign up: 301/495-1240, fax 301/495-6697, www.hiusa.org. A year's membership is $28 for adults (over 18), free for youths under 18, $18 for senior citizens (over 55), $250 for a life membership. Once you're enrolled, contact HI hostels directly, or book online.

Several unofficial hostels—inns with dorm-style rooms—are located in the ski areas of western Maine.

SEASONAL RENTALS

You'll find advertisements for cabins, cottages, condos, RV sites, and campsites—for rent by the week, month, or season—in every corner of the state (Realtors who handle seasonal rentals are listed in the appropriate regional chapters of this book). Remember that highest prices will prevail in July and August. A good source of independent rentals is the classified section of the monthly *Down East* magazine, P.O. Box 679, Camden 04843, 800/766-1670, www.downeast.com. The March, April, and May issues usually contain the most comprehensive listings. Also helpful is the *Maine Guide to Camps & Cottages,* a free booklet published annually by the Maine Tourism Association, 327 Water Street, Hallowell 04347, 207/623-0363, www.mainetourism.com. Short- and long-term winter condo rentals are available in the ski areas around Bethel (near Sunday River), Sugarloaf/USA, and Rangeley (home of Saddleback); inexpensive dormitory accommodations also rent by the week around Sunday River, Shawnee Peak, Mt. Abram, Saddleback, and Sugarloaf/USA.

SUGARING OFF—MAINE'S MAPLE SYRUP

March in Maine brings warmer days and cold nights—the ideal climate for maple-syrup production. For decades, maple trees all over Maine sprouted faucet-like taps (inserted into half-inch holes drilled into the trees), from which hung metal buckets. The taps released the tree sap, drop by drop, into the buckets. This is still true on some farms; many, however, have changed to a system of plastic tubing which moves the syrup right from the trees to a central collection point. The best syrup comes from the sugar or rock maple—*Acer saccharum*. On Maine Maple Sunday (the fourth Sunday in March), several dozen syrup producers open their rustic sugarhouses to the public for "sugaring-off" parties—to celebrate the sap harvest and share the final phase in the production process. Wood smoke billows from the sugarhouse chimney while everyone inside gathers around huge kettles used to boil down the watery sap. (A single gallon of syrup starts with 30–40 gallons of sap.) Finally, it's time to sample the syrup every which way—on pancakes and waffles, in tea, on ice cream, in puddings, in muffins, even just drizzled over snow. Most producers also have containers of syrup for sale.

The state annually publishes a list of Maine Maple Sunday sites. For a copy, contact the Maine Department of Agriculture, 28 State House Station, Augusta 04333; 207/287-3491, or visit www.getrealmaine.com.

If you can't be in Maine during March, the syrup is available in supermarkets, convenience stores, and specialty shops around the state. Look for organic syrup certified by the Maine Organic Farmers and Gardeners Association (MOFGA)—a guarantee that the tapped trees are free of fertilizers and pesticides and the processing is chemical-free.

Maine maple syrup has a life beyond blueberry pancakes or sourdough waffles; here's a traditional Franco-American recipe for a scrumptious dessert.

Maple Walnut Pie

9-inch pie shell
2 tbsp. unsalted butter
4 whole eggs
2 c. maple syrup
2 tsp. apple-cider vinegar
¼ c. chopped walnuts

Preheat the oven to 400°F. Bake the pie shell according to directions. Allow to cool. Melt butter and set aside to cool. In a medium-size bowl, beat eggs with an electric beater until thick, about three minutes. Continuing to beat the eggs, add maple syrup slowly but steadily. Add melted butter and vinegar and blend thoroughly. Pour maple mixture into the pie shell and bake about 40 minutes, until the top is light brown. (Watch for signs of burning.) Remove pie from oven and place on a rack to cool. Before serving, decorate the edges of the pie with the chopped walnuts. Make sure your dentist isn't watching. *Bon appetit!*

Food and Drink

Say the word Maine and what comes to mind, gustatorily speaking? Lobsters, potatoes, and blueberries? Of course, but don't overlook mussels, farm-raised venison and lamb, maple syrup, fiddlehead ferns, and baked beans. And if you're in Maine on the Fourth of July, the traditional dinner is salmon and peas—Atlantic salmon, that is, and peas fresh from the garden. Throughout the summer, food-oriented festivals celebrate the state's comestible bounty; they highlight salmon (Eastport), strawberries (South Berwick, Wiscasset, and lots of other small communities), blueberries (Machias and Union), potatoes (Houlton and Fort Fairfield), eggs (Pittsfield), clams (Yarmouth), and lobsters (Rockland, Winter Harbor, Bar Harbor).

LOBSTER GALORE

You won't find it on the official roster of state symbols, but there's no question about the state's favorite menu item—lobster. Whether you eat it indoors in a fancy restaurant or alfresco at one of the dozens of coastal lobster "pounds" or wharves (where you can dress down and make a mess), lobster wins high honors for low fat, low calories, and low cholesterol. You'll have plenty of choices as to how it's prepared—steamed, boiled, or broiled in the shell; in a lobster roll (chopped up with a hint of mayo in a hamburger or hot-dog roll); or dressed up in designer sauces. Mainers dispute the advantages of hard-shell versus soft-shell, but July–Sept., most newcomers prefer the ease of eating (and the lower price) of the soft-shelled variety—called shedders, since they've recently shed their carapaces and grown new ones.

For some peculiar reason, eat-on-the-wharf lobster shacks become scarce as you head Down East into Washington County, in Maine's northeast corner. Odd, because the Sunrise Coast's prime geography deserves dining-on-the-dock, even when the fog sweeps in. Sure, you can buy fresh lobsters in that area, but you'll usually have to cook them yourself. Or go to a regular restaurant, where it's awkward to be messy.

If you're camping or renting or cringe at the thought of cooking lobsters, contact a nearby lobster pound (look under "Lobsters" in the Yellow Pages) and ask them to steam or boil the crustaceans for you (some will even deliver, along with all the fixins).

For the ultimate lobster feeding frenzy, plan to be in Rockland the first weekend in August, when volunteers at the annual Maine Lobster Festival stoke up the world's largest lobster cooker and hand out thousands of pounds of lobsters nonstop to more than 50,000 enthusiastic diners.

BLUEBERRIES

What's black and blue and red all over? Maine's wild-blueberry barrens (fields), depending on what time of year you find them. They're black in fall and spring, when growers torch their fields to jump-start the crop. By August, after a summer full of a million rented bees pollinating the blossoms, a blue haze forms over the knee-high shrubs—interspersed with bent-over bodies carrying old-fashioned short-handled rakes to harvest the ripe berries. And they're red after harvest, when they turn brilliant red, then maroon.

Although most of the Down East barren barons harvest their crops for the lucrative wholesale market—averaging 65 million pounds annually—a few growers let you pick your own blueberries in mid-August. Contact the Wild Blueberry Commission (207/581-1475, wildblueberries.maine.edu) or the state Department of Agriculture (207/287-3491, www.getrealmaine.com) for locations, recipes, and other wild-blueberry information.

BEANHOLE BEANS

"To be happy in New England," wrote one Joseph P. MacCarthy at the turn of the 20th century, "you must select the Puritans for your ancestors. . . [and] eat beans on Saturday night." There is no better way to check this out than to attend a "beanhole" bean supper—a real-live legacy of colonial times, with dinner baked in a hole in the ground.

Generally scheduled, appropriately, for a Saturday night (check local newspapers), a beanhole bean supper demands plenty of advance preparation from its hosts—as well as a secret ingredient or two (don't even think about trying to pry the recipe out of the cooks). The supper always includes hot dogs, coleslaw, relishes, home-baked breads, and homemade desserts, but the beans are the star attraction. (Typically, the suppers are also alcohol-free.) Not only are they feasts; they're also bargains, never setting you back more than about $8.

As one example, at **Cushing,** a mid-coast community best known as "Wyeth country," the beans at the Broad Cove Church's annual mid-July beanhole bean supper, served family style at long picnic tables, are legendary—attracting nearly 200 eager diners. Minus the secrets, here's what happens:

Early Friday morning: Church volunteers load 10 pounds of dry pea and soldier (yelloweye) beans into each of four large kettles and add water to cover. The beans are left to soak and soften for six or seven hours. Two or three volunteers uncover the churchyard's four rock-lined beanholes (each about three feet deep), fill the holes with hardwood kindling, ignite the wood, and keep the fires burning until late afternoon, when the wood is reduced to red-hot coals.

Early Friday afternoon: The veteran chefs parboil the beans and stir in the seasonings. Typical additions are brown sugar, molasses, mustard, salt, pepper, and salt pork (much of the secret is in the exact proportions). When the beans are precooked to the cooks' satisfaction, the kettle lids are secured with wire and the pots are lugged outdoors.

Friday mid-afternoon: With the beans ready to go underground, some of the hot coals are quickly shoveled out of the pits. The kettles are lowered into the pits and the coals replaced around the sides of the kettles and atop their lids. The pits are covered with heavy sheet metal and then topped with a thick layer of sand and a tarpaulin. The round-the-clock baking begins, and no one peeks before it's finished.

Saturday mid-afternoon: Even the veterans start getting nervous just before the pits are uncovered. Was the seasoning right? Did too much water cook away? Did the beans dry out? Not to worry, though—failures just don't happen here.

Saturday night: When a pot is excavated for the first of three seatings (about 5 PM), the line is already long. The chefs check their handiwork and the supper begins. No one minds waiting for the second and third seatings—while others eat, a sing-along gets underway in the church, keeping everyone entertained.

The best place to simply *appreciate* blueberries is Machias, site of the renowned annual Wild Blueberry Festival, held the third weekend in August. While harvesting is underway in the surrounding fields, you can stuff your face with blueberry-everything—muffins, jam, pancakes, ice cream, pies. Plus you can collect blueberry-logo napkins, T-shirts, fridge magnets, pottery, and jewelry.

POTATOES

Native to South America, the potato is king in northern Maine—more specifically, in Aroostook County, where 92 percent of the state's spuds are grown. Potatoes grow in about 65,000 acres, appear on every restaurant menu and family table, are peddled by the bagful in countless roadside stands, and are stored in huge, half-buried barns. Annual festivals celebrate the arrival on the plants of delicate pink and white summer blossoms and, later in the year, the annual potato harvest. In September, schools in the county even close down for a week or two while students and teachers help with the harvest. The most unusual dish you'll find in potato country is *poutine,* a mound of French fries smothered with brown gravy and melted cheese. Who knows what it does to your arteries, but it's a traditional favorite of northern Maine's French-speaking Acadians. The **Maine Potato Board,** 744 Main St., P.O. Box 669, Presque Isle 04769, 207/769-5061, www.mainepotatoes.com, offers online contests and recipes.

OTHER MAINE SPECIALTIES

For a few weeks in May, right around Mother's Day (the second Sunday in May), a wonderful delicacy starts sprouting along Maine's woodland streams: **fiddleheads,** the still-furled tops of the ostrich fern *(Matteuccia struthiopteris).* Tasting vaguely like asparagus, fiddleheads have been on May menus ever since Native Americans taught the colonists to forage for the tasty vegetable. Don't go fiddleheading unless you're with a pro, though; the lookalikes are best left to the woods critters. Cookbook writers have

dreamed up a zillion ways to prepare these treats, but nothing beats steaming them for 5–7 minutes and serving them with lemon butter. If you find them on a restaurant menu, indulge.

As with fiddleheads, we owe thanks to Native Americans for introducing us to **maple syrup,** one of Maine's major agricultural exports. The 2004 production figure was 290,000 gallons. The syrup comes in four different colors/flavors (from light amber to extra-dark amber), and inspectors monitor syrup quality strictly.

FARMERS MARKETS

After a tentative beginning in the 1970s and 1980s, farmers markets have become ritual stops for locals and visitors in Maine communities from Kittery to Fort Kent. Their biggest asset is serendipity—you never know what you'll find. Everything is locally grown and often organic, and it's hard to resist walking away with far more than you need. Herbs, unusual vegetables, seedlings, baked goods, meat, free-range chicken, goat cheese, herb vinegars, berries, exotic condiments, honey, and jams are just a few of the possibilities. Some markets also offer live entertainment, crafts booths, cookbook signings, prepared foods, even petting zoos. Maine has a short growing season, but green-thumbers make the most of it. Community-supported agriculture (CSA), where people pre-buy shares in farm production, has been growing throughout the state, and Open Farm Day in July, and Maine Maple Syrup day in March, make visitors more aware of the value of Maine's farms. Although each farmers market has its own schedule, most are set up (usually outdoors) one or two days a week. The season varies, depending on location. July and August are the big months, but some open as early as April and others run as late as November. For a list of all the markets, contact the Maine Department of Agriculture, 207/287-3491, www.mainefoodandfarms.com. The newest entry in this category, on a grand scale, is the Portland Public Market, modeled on Seattle's Pike Place Market.

RESTAURANTS FOR EVERY TASTE AND BUDGET

Note: Maine now has laws banning smoking in *nearly all* public places, including restaurants and bars. Smoking is only allowed in motel or hotel rooms, Indian-run casinos, private residences not used for daycare, and privately chartered buses. Initially controversial, the new regulations have literally cleared the air.

Naturally, the golden arches and their clones have saturated Maine, so expect to bump into all the eat-and-run household words: Burger King, McDonald's, KFC, Wendy's, Dunkin' Donuts, Pizza Hut, Taco Bell. Depending on your interests and budget, however, you'll also find old-fashioned and updated diners (Moody's in Waldoboro, A-1 Diner in Gardiner, Farmington Diner in Farmington, and the state's best-known 24-hour truck stop, Dysart's, near Bangor). In out-of-the-way spots, you can eat in country stores or family-oriented restaurants (usually labeled as such), or sporting camps with public dining rooms (primarily in the Rangeley and Greenville areas) but also near Millinocket.

Don't overlook roadside takeout stands. Most are Maine institutions with long-standing (literally) clienteles. If you spot a waiting line and have the time, join the crowd. Some of the best are Flo's Steamed Hot Dogs in Cape Neddick (the legendary sauce is now bottled for retail sale), Red's Eats in Wiscasset, Wasses Wagon in Rockland (which now has "branch wagons"), and Scott's Place in Camden. Superb takeout ice cream comes from Brown's in York Beach, Round Top in Damariscotta, Dorman's in Rockland, and Spencer's in Bradley (north of Bangor).

You'll find great sandwiches and other gourmet takeout fare (and, usually, shorter waiting lines) at such emporia as Aurora Provisions in Portland, Clayton's in Yarmouth, A-1 to Go in Gardiner, Market on Main in Rockland, the Market Basket in Rockport, and the Vinery at Arborvine in Blue Hill. In Waldoboro, Laura Cabot Catering packs picnics with a few hours advance notice.

Ethnic cuisine is easiest to find in greater Portland, which allegedly has the nation's highest number of restaurant seats per capita. Here you can dine around the world from menus Indian, Japanese, Chinese, French, Italian (both north and south), Vietnamese, Greek, Thai, and Mexican. Beyond Portland, there are Indian restaurants in Biddeford, Brunswick, and Bangor; a German restaurant in Topsham; Pakistani (Bahaar) and Japanese restaurants in Bangor; and Thai, Chinese, and Mexican restaurants of varying quality all over the state.

At the upper end of the food-and-money chain are inn/hotel dining rooms catering to the platinum-card and/or trust-fund set: The Colony in Kennebunkport, Black Point Inn in Prouts Neck (Scarborough), Inn by the Sea in Cape Elizabeth, Spruce Point Inn in Boothbay, Whitehall Inn in Camden, the Claremont in Southwest Harbor, and Asticou Inn in Northeast Harbor.

Maine won't win any national prizes for having the most haute-cuisine restaurants, but don't miss the standouts. Among the best are the White Barn Inn (Kennebunkport); Arrows, and Provence (both in Ogunquit); Back Bay Grill, Fore Street, Hugo's, Street and Company (all in Portland); Robinhood Free Meetinghouse (Georgetown, near Bath); Primo (Rockland); Castine Inn (Castine); Arborvine (Blue Hill); The Edge (Lincolnville), George's, and the Burning Tree (Bar Harbor); and Le Domaine (Hancock).

PUBLIC SUPPERS

These are a guaranteed way to sample an array of Down East home cooking, meet "real Mainers" (and maybe other adventurous fellow travelers), and be finished before the sun sets. Check calendars in local newspapers for listings of public suppers (or their variations—chowder suppers, potluck suppers, beanhole bean dinners). These events are designed to help swell the coffers of the various volunteer organizations who sponsor them—fire department auxiliaries, historical societies, church groups, festival committees. Count on a minimal charge, but feel free to add a little extra. Reservations are seldom required, but you may have to call for directions. Also, be sure to arrive on time—the regulars know who makes the best pie, and it disappears fast.

ALCOHOLIC BEVERAGES

As is customary in the United States, Maine's minimum drinking age is 21 years—and bar owners, bartenders, and serving staff can be held accountable for serving underage imbibers. Owners and employees also may be held liable for accidents caused by *legal* drinkers. Stiff anti-drunk-driving efforts in Maine (including random roadblocks, license revocation or suspension, hefty fines, and jail terms) have reduced but by no means halted the fatalities. If your blood alcohol level is 0.08 percent or higher, you are legally considered to be operating under the influence. Because of individual differences in size and metabolism, even printed blood-alcohol charts cannot guarantee what blood-alcohol level will result from a particular number of drinks. Best bet for avoiding problems: Don't drink and drive. Minimum fine for a first offense is $500.

Maine has removed itself from the business of retailing liquor at state-run stores. Now, all forms of alcoholic beverages can be bought at supermarkets and other retail venues.

The policy in restaurants varies. Many lobster pounds encourage patrons to bring their own. Restaurants that do not serve alcohol themselves but are helpful to alcohol-toting guests—supplying corkscrews and maybe even setups—are noted in the listings in this book with a designation of BYOL. When an establishment doesn't allow liquor (rare) that, too, is noted.

Getting There

Maine has two major airports, two major bus networks, a toll highway, Amtrak service on the Downeaster, and some ad hoc local transportation systems that fill in the gaps.

BY AIR

Maine's major airline gateways are **The Portland International Jetport** (PWM), 207/774-7301, www.portlandjetport.org, and **Bangor International Airport** (BGR), 207/992-4623 or 866/359-2264, www.flybangor.com. The "international" in their names is a bit misleading; neither has direct scheduled service to international destinations. Charter flights from Europe often stop at Bangor for refueling and customs clearance, and sometimes bad weather or air rage diverts flights there, but Boston's Logan Airport is the nearest facility with direct flights to Europe and other worldwide destinations.

You'll want to fly into Bangor if you're headed for the North Woods, Bar Harbor and Acadia National Park, or the Down East coastal counties of Washington and Hancock. But Portland is the more logical airport choice if you're visiting southern Maine—the beaches, Portland, or the coastal towns up to Damariscotta—or the Bethel area of western Maine. If your destination is the Camden-Rockport area, which is equidistant between the two, your choice is a toss-up (you may want to make your decision based on flight schedules). Being on the coast, the Portland airport is more subject to fog shutdowns than Bangor, but many Bangor flights originate (or stop) in Boston, where fog delays can afflict Logan Airport even more.

Airlines serving both Portland and Bangor are **Continental,** 800/523-3273; **Delta,** 800/221-1212; **US Airways,** 800/428-4322; and **Northwest,** 800/225-2525. **United Express,** 800/864-8331, and **Independence Air,** 800/359-3594, also serve Portland, while **American Airlines,** 800/433-7300, flies into Bangor.

Augusta State Airport, 207/626-2306, the base for state-government flights, has commercial service to and from Boston via **US Airways Express,** 800/428-4322. Other airports accessible via US Airways Express from Boston are **Hancock County-Bar Harbor Airport,** near Bar Harbor; **Knox County Regional Airport** at Owls Head, near Rockland and Camden; and Northern Maine Regional Airport, in

Know Maine

Presque Isle. Colgan Air is the local affiliate of US Airways Express.

An increasingly popular choice for bargain-hunters is the Manchester Airport, in Manchester, New Hampshire, a rapidly expanding alternative to Logan, now served by all the Maine carriers, as well as **Air Canada,** 888/247-2262, **Delta Connection Comair,** 800/354-9822, and **Southwest Airlines,** 888/435-9792, which operates economical flights into Manchester, New Hampshire. Ground transportation (see below) is available from Manchester to the Portland Jetport.

All the airlines increase their flight frequency during the summer to accommodate stepped-up demand.

Airport Facilities

Portland's three-story terminal received a $10 million facelift in 1996, and is still in the process of a multimillion dollar improvement. In 2002, a new five-story garage was added; this was followed by major improvements to the main runway, including lengthening, repaving, and adding center runway lights to minimize delays caused by fog and weather. Amenities include a business center with wi-fi technology, newsstand/gift shop, Starbucks coffee shop, restaurant/lounge, large waiting area with comfortable seats, ATM, and plenty of coin- and card-operated telephones. Alamo, Avis, Budget, Hertz, and National car-rental agencies are quartered in an atrium in the garage. Visitor information is dispensed from a desk (not always staffed, unfortunately) located between the gates and the baggage-claim area. No need to rush out to grab your luggage, though—Portland has one of the slowest baggage-claim operations in the country. After you arrive, plan to stop at the restrooms, browse through the gift shop, and pick up tourism information—and even then you may still have to wait for your luggage. Complaints to management elicit the response that Portland is the terminus of many airline routes, and the airline companies (who provide the baggage handlers) give low priority to locations that don't require fast turnaround. As a result, carry-on luggage is a plus here. However, as part of its improvement campaign, the airport

is expanding the claim area and adding a carousel, plus planning changes to present carousels. Baggage-handling offices surround the luggage carousels, but if you have an emergency, contact Jetport management at 207/773-8462.

Bangor's airport has scaled-down versions of Portland's facilities but all the necessary amenities: Avis, Budget, Hertz, and National rental cars (with Enterprise and Thrifty nearby); newsstand/gift shop; Red Baron Lounge and The Coffee Shop; The Grasshopper Shop, mini-version of a popular Bangor emporium; and waiting area. Baggage claim tends to be more efficient than Portland's, but if you need help, contact Airport Director Rebecca Hupp at 207/992-4600.

Ground Transportation

Portland's Metro Bus Line, 207/774-0351, provides scheduled service throughout the city. Free shuttle service is available to 19 local accommodations, and the airport is also served by close to three dozen livery, limo, van, and taxi providers. If you need a taxi at the Portland Jetport, make arrangements with the "starter," located in the baggage-claim area.

If you're planning to arrive in Portland and head directly up the coast anywhere between the airport and Belfast, call ahead to Mid-Coast Limo, 207/236-2424 or 800/937-2424, www.midcoastlimo.com, for their daily shuttle service.

Mermaid Transportation, in Portland, 207/885-5630 or 800/696-2463, operates van service by reservation between Logan Airport and the Portland Jetport, and Manchester Airport and Portland. Cost is $53 one way; children under 15 are free when accompanied by an adult; bicycles (in a box) are $15. For an extra charge, pickups and dropoffs can be arranged at residences or park-and-ride areas. Web reservations can be made at www.gomermaid.com until 3 PM the day before the ride; later reservations available by phone.

BY CAR

The major highway access to Maine is the **Maine Turnpike,** which links up with I-95 at the New Hampshire border. Other busy access points are **Rte. 1,** also from New Hampshire; **Rte. 302,** from North Conway, NH, entering Maine at Fryeburg; **Rte. 2,** from Vermont and New Hampshire, entering at Bethel; **Rte. 201,** from Quebec, entering north of Jackman; and a handful of crossing points from New Brunswick into Aroostook and Washington Counties in northern Maine.

BY BUS

Concord Trailways, 800/639-3317, www.concordtrailways.com, departs downtown Boston (South Station Transportation Center) and Logan Airport for Portland about a dozen times daily, making pickups at Logan airline terminals B, C, and D. The Portland bus terminal is at the Portland Transportation Center, Thompson Point Road, across from the Doubletree Inn parking lot, just off Rte. 22 (Congress St. W.) or take I-295 exit 5 northbound, 5A southbound. (If you're headed for downtown Portland from the bus terminal, board the Metro city bus at the terminal and show your Concord Trailways bus ticket to receive a free trip.) Three daily express buses continue on from Portland to Bangor; two nonexpress buses go along the coast as far as Searsport, then head inland to the Bangor Transportation Center, near the airport entrance. Vermont Transit, 800/552-8737, www.vermonttransit.com, operates a seasonal service between Bangor and Bar Harbor, with a stop in Ellsworth. In Bangor, once-a-day connections are available to Ellsworth, Machias, Calais, Houlton, Presque Isle, and Caribou.

BY RAIL

It took 30 years of determined citizen effort, led by Wayne Davis' Train Riders Northeast, to persuade Amtrak to restore long-abandoned Boston-to-Portland passenger rail service, but on December 14, 2001, it happened: Maine's then-governor, Angus King, broke a bottle of champagne over the train, and several hundred riders, including Maine senators Susan Collins and Olympia Snowe, rode the inaugural run from Boston. Four times a day, Downeaster passenger trains make a 2.5-hour round-trip between Boston and Portland, with Maine stops in Wells, Saco/Biddeford, and, from late April to October 31, Old Orchard Beach. For fares and schedules, including discounts and special tours and promotions, on what *Travel & Leisure* magazine calls "the most charming train on the continent," go to www.thedowneaster .com, or 800/USA-RAIL. Tickets can also be bought from Quik-Trak ticketing machines, which accept credit and debit cards, in all Amtrak stations, or through travel agents.

Getting Around

BY AIR

State, county, and municipal airports are sprinkled all over Maine—from Presque Isle to Eastport to Bar Harbor, Augusta, and Lewiston. (Each is described in the relevant regional chapter of this book.)

Penobscot Island Air, 207/596-7500, based at Knox County Regional Airport in Owls Head, near Rockland, flies to several airstrip-equipped islands in Penobscot Bay. Several firms in the Katahdin/Moosehead Lake region and in Rangeley operate summer floatplanes and winter skiplanes to provide access to wilderness sporting camps. For a sightseeing treat during fall-foliage season (late Sept. and early Oct. in that area), reserve a seat on a scenic flight where you'll fly low over sparkling lakes, multicolored forests, and, unfortunately, the clear-cuts, too. Keep an eye out for moose and don't forget your camera!

BY BUS

Ground transportation exists in Maine, but it's far from adequate. For instance, there's no bus service to western Maine from Portland, and only two long-distance companies cover the state. Smoking is not permitted on buses.

Concord Trailways, 800/639-3317, www .concordtrailways.com, has the best intrastate bus network, with routes designed to assist students, island-ferry passengers, and day-trippers. Buses from Boston's Logan Airport stop at the Portland Transportation Center, and follow a mostly coastal route through Brunswick, Bath, Wiscasset, Damariscotta, Waldoboro, Rockland, Camden, Belfast, and Searsport, ending in Bangor, then following the same route in reverse. (During the school year, the route also includes Bowdoin College in Brunswick and the University of Maine campus in Orono.)

Vermont Transit, 800/552-8737, www.vermonttransit.com, a division of Greyhound Bus Lines, follows an inland route, linking Lewiston, Augusta, and Waterville with Bangor, Houlton, and Caribou. Vermont and Concord compete only on the Portland-Bangor run, where Vermont's fares tend to be slightly lower than Concord's. Several express buses operate daily between Portland and Bangor.

Buses to and from Caribou and Calais coordinate with the Bangor bus schedules. The Caribou line, stopping in Medway (near Millinocket), Houlton, and Presque Isle, is operated by **Cyr Bus Lines,** headquartered in Old Town, near Bangor, 207/827-2335 or 800/244-2335. The Calais line, stopping in Ellsworth, Gouldsboro, Machias, Perry, and flag stops along the way, is operated by **West's Coastal Connection,** P.O. Box 82, Milbridge 04658, 207/546-2823 or 800/596-2823, and leaves the Bangor Airport twice a day, year-round.

Major cities such as Portland, South Portland, Lewiston/Auburn, Augusta, and Bangor have **city bus service,** with some wheelchair-accessible vehicles. A number of smaller communities have established **local shuttle vans** or **trolley-buses,** but most of the latter are seasonal. Trolley-buses operate (for a fee) in the Yorks, Ogunquit, Wells, the Kennebunks, Old Orchard Beach, Portland, Bath, Boothbay, Rockland, and Sunday River. Mount Desert Island has the unique **Island Explorer,** a free summer

(from late June) bus service, and Bethel is served by the Mountain Explorer.

BY CAR

No matter how much time and resourcefulness you summon up, you'll never really be able to appreciate Maine without a car. The state has more than 22,000 miles of paved (mostly two-lane) roads and countless miles of unpaved country roads and logging routes (used by giant timber trucks). Down every little peninsula jutting into the Atlantic lies a picturesque village or park or ocean view. Inland, roads wind over the hills and through the woods. Even I-95, the state's major artery, boasts scenic vistas that bring photographers to a screeching halt. (Of course, a radar-equipped cop or a moose can deliver the same result for any driver.)

Between Kittery, at the New Hampshire border, and Houlton, at the Canadian one, lie 305 miles of I-95, with the last toll at Augusta. The Maine Turnpike Authority, 877/682-9433 or 800/675-PIKE (travel conditions), www.maineturnpike.com (includes traffic web cams), and the Maine Department of Transportation, 800/877-9171, www.state. me.us/mdot, have instituted a new exit numbering and interstate designation system designed to reduce motorist confusion. Initial reaction has been positive; the system gives drivers a better sense of how many miles it will take to get *there* from *here*. Exit numbers are now based on mileage, and the entire turnpike, from Kittery to Houlton, is named I-95, while the Scarborough-to-Gardiner bumpout is all I-295. Additionally, the turnpike widening project which delayed and dismayed so many of Maine's 50 million annual visitors, as well as resident commuters, is finished. From Kittery to Scarborough, three lanes are moving traffic more smoothly and reducing accidents, though not doing much for tollbooth congestion at the York Toll Plaza in summer. Service areas are infrequent on the 'pike, and aren't on both sides of the highway, so stop when you see one (even if you might not need it); don't wait for the next one.

Maximum speed on I-95, the Maine Turnpike, is 65–55 mph on some stretches. In snow, sleet, or dense fog, the limit drops to 45 mph (only rarely does the highway close). On other roads, the speed limit is usually 55 mph in rural areas and posted in built-up areas. A menu of travel information to help you "know before you go," including road conditions and weather, can be accessed at **511, Maine's Travel Info line,** or, outside Maine, by calling 866/282-7578. The information is also accessible on the web at www.511Maine.gov.

Two lanes wide from Kittery in the south to Fort Kent at the top, U.S. 1 is the state's most congested road, particularly in July and August. Mileage distances can be extremely deceptive, since it will take you much longer than anticipated to get from point A to point B. If you ask about distances, chances are good that you'll receive an answer in hours rather than miles. Plan accordingly. If you're trying to make time, it's best to take the turnpike (I-95); if you want to see Maine, take U.S. 1 and lots of little offshoots. (Acadia National Park visitors often can make better time from the New Hampshire border by taking I-95 to the Bangor area, then heading southeast on U.S. 1A.)

Although the turnpike itself can become mega-congested on summer weekends, and especially summer *holiday* weekends, the recently completed widening to three lanes up to Scarborough has even former opponents of the widening project conceding that traffic flows much more smoothly. Conveying a portion of Maine's 50 million annual visitors, more than 300,000 vehicles use the turnpike on Memorial Day, Fourth of July, and Labor Day weekends. Worst times on the turnpike are Friday 4–8 PM (northbound), Saturday 11 AM–2 PM (southbound; weekly cottage rentals run from Saturday noon to Saturday noon), and Sunday 3–7 PM (southbound). On three-day holiday weekends, avoid heading southbound on Monday between 3 and 7 PM.

Rental cars are available at the Portland, Bangor, and most smaller airports, and at some city locations. All the major chains are represented in Maine, including Alamo, Avis, Budget, Enterprise, Hertz, National, and Thrifty. If you're planning to arrive on a July or August weekend, or a summer holiday weekend, call well ahead for a reservation or you may be out of luck.

Almost all **gas stations** in Maine are self-serve—at the rare pump marked Full, an attendant will pump the gas for you—and almost all allow you to pay at the pump with a credit or gas card. (Many also have ATMs, but you'll usually have to pay a bank surcharge.)

Important Driving Regulations: Seat belts are mandatory in Maine. You cannot be stopped for not wearing one, but if you're stopped for any other reason, you can be fined if you're not buckled in. Maine allows **right turns at red lights,** after you stop and check for oncoming traffic. In rare cases, you'll see a No Turn on Red sign—in which case, heed it. *Never* pass a **stopped school bus** in either direction. Wait until the bus's red lights have stopped flashing and all children are well off the road. Drivers in Maine are required to turn on their car's **headlights** any time the windshield wipers are operating.

Roadside Assistance: Since Maine is enslaved to the automobile, it's not a bad idea for vacationers to carry membership in AAA or some other similar program in the event of breakdowns, flat tires, and other car crises. Contact your nearest AAA office or AAA Northern New England, 425 Marginal Way, Portland 04101, 207/780-6800 or 800/482-7497. The emergency-road-service number is 800/222-4357.

BY RAIL

Except for the southern Maine Amtrak service, the Downeaster, riding the rails within Maine means hopping aboard one of a handful of excursion lines or visiting the Boothbay Railway Museum or Kennebunkport's Seacoast Trolley Museum. In downtown Portland, the **Maine Narrow Gauge Railroad Co. & Museum,** based on the waterfront, offers short rides in

Know Maine

spiffed-up antique railway cars. The **Maine Eastern Railroad** runs weekend excursion trains from Brunswick and Bath to Rockland in summer and fall. Financial difficulties have plagued the **Sandy River & Rangeley Lakes Railroad,** in the mountains of western Maine, but the train still operates periodically out of Phillips in the summer, and a manager has been hired.

HITCHHIKING

Even though Maine's public transportation network is woefully inadequate and the crime rate is fourth-lowest in the nation, it's still risky to hitchhike or pick up hitchhikers. Sure, pick up a schoolchild in an out-of-the-way village, or kids headed home from the beach; just use common sense.

SPECIAL-INTEREST TOURS

In addition to the one-size-fits-all bus tours described below, Maine has become a hot ticket on the ecotourism circuit, with organized trips specializing in bicycling, walking and hiking, canoeing and kayaking, birding, llama trekking, dogsledding, and winter camping.

Bus Tours

Major national bus-tour companies include Maine on their New England itineraries, but most offer only summer coastal trips (usually Kennebunkport to Bar Harbor) or fall-foliage tours (inland, then across to New Hampshire and Vermont). Neither itinerary offers much chance to see what Maine has to offer. **Cyr Northstar Tours,** P.O. Box 368, Old Town 04468, 207/827-2010 or 800/244-2335, offers mostly out-of-state tours from Maine, but it's worth checking out their one-day in-state options, especially the spring Moosehead Excursion, which includes lunch and a narrated cruise, for $98 a person.

Walking Tours

Boothbay Harbor, Monhegan, and Camden are the locales for eight five-day, four-night, easy-to-moderate walks organized by **Country Walkers,** P.O. Box 180, Waterbury, VT 05676, 802/244-1387 or 800/464-9255, fax 802/244-5661, www.countrywalkers.com, a well-managed firm started in 1980. Lodging is at country inns. Cost, excluding airfare, is about $1,900.

Bicycle Tours

For an extensive menu of homegrown cycling tours, request a catalog from **Summer Feet: Maine Coast Cycling Adventures,** P.O. Box 10822, Portland, ME 04101, 207/828-0342 or 866/857-9544, www.summerfeet.net. A tour operator in its sixth year, Summer Feet schedules 30–40 departure dates for eight coastal and foliage itineraries, each 3–6 days long. Lodging is at B&Bs. Costs (including bike rental but not airfare) range from $650–1,900.

A three-day **Maine Coast and Country Bike Tour** is offered once a month during June, July, August, and September by L.L. Bean's Outdoor Discovery Schools, 888/552-3261. Participants cruise along the rocky coast down hidden coves, along working waterfronts, past historic villages and active farms—and get to see the Maine many visitors miss. Highlights include lodging at a historic bed-and-breakfast, a kayaking option, and an evening lobster bake. Bean provides the bikes and safety equipment.

Canoeing Tours

Approaching legend status as Maine wilderness guides are Alexandra and Garrett Conover, highly skilled traditionalists who lead five- to eight-day trips in wood-and-canvas canoes on the St. John, Allagash, and Penobscot (West Branch) Rivers, plus paddles on Loon Lake, Caucomgomoc Stream, and the area around isolated Chesuncook Village. Costs range from $775–1,125 (excluding airfare). The Conovers also do some winter snowshoeing trips. Their company is **North Woods Ways,** Willimantic, mailing address RR 2, Box 159A, Guilford 04443, 207/997-3723. The Conovers celebrated their 25th wedding anniversary in

Know Maine

2005 with a Winter Walk for the Wilds over 200 miles of frozen waterways, from Greenville to Allagash Village; they guided schoolchildren on portions of the walk, and helped educate others about wilderness issues via local and Internet publicity.

Mike Patterson is a Registered Master Maine Guide who can handle most any kind of outdoor pursuit, but his specialty is canoe trips, Mar.–Oct., on all Maine's major rivers: the Allagash, St. John, Machias, St. Croix, Penobscot (east and west branches), and Moose. Costs average $150–200 per person per day. Neophytes should consider the St.Croix River Trip, a classic, easy, four-day trip providing a fine wilderness canoeing experience. In addition to running his own company, Mike also runs trips to Costa Rica, Arizona, Utah, the Rio Grande, and the Canadian Yukon, and teaches clinics in the almost-lost art of canoe poling. **Wilds of Maine Guide Service Inc.,** 192 Congress St., Belfast, ME 04915, 207/338-3932, www.wildsofmaine.com.

Other Specialty Tours

Year-round outdoor experiences and women-only trips are the stock-in-trade of Kevin Slater and Polly Mahoney's **Mahoosuc Guide Service,** based in western Maine's mountains. Five- to seven-day wilderness canoe trips ($375–1925) tackle Maine's northern rivers, and there are special trips, like Foliage and Canoeing with the Cree, as well as Maine Guide trainings. During their superb weekend dogsledding trips ($425–750) Jan.–Mar., accommodations are in woodstove-heated tents. Some of their huskies are Iditarod veterans. Polly also leads women-only dogsledding and canoe trips. Mid-Dec.–mid-Mar., become a dilettante musher on a one-day midweek trip ($200; it's very popular) on frozen Umbagog Lake. A hearty campfire lunch is part of the deal. Mahoosuc Guide Service, 1513 Bear River Rd., Newry 04261, 207/824-2073, www.mahoosuc.com.

Also in western Maine is the **Telemark Inn,** site of the state's original llama treks. Owner Steve Crone organizes a variety of outdoor excursions including wilderness canoe trips, moose tours, and fully-catered llama treks lasting 1–4 days. The inn has six guest rooms with hand-built cabinetry, as well as mountain-bike trails, cross-country-skiing packages, a swimming hole and waterfall, meals, sleigh and trail rides, and gear rental—lots of options for a real getaway. Three-day packages—lodging, breakfast and lunch, and guided day activities—are $450 per adult, $300 per child. There are also five- ($700/500) and seven-day ($950/650) packages. The Telemark Inn, King's Hwy., RFD 2, Box 800, Bethel 04217, 207/836-2703, www.telemarkinn.com.

Getting Afloat

Know Maine

MAINE STATE FERRY SYSTEM

Unless you're lucky enough to have your own boat, the only way to reach Vinalhaven, North Haven, Matinicus, Islesboro, Swans Island, and Frenchboro (Long Island) is via the state ferry system. All of the state ferries carry cars, trucks, bicycles, strollers, pets (leashed or caged), groceries, lumber, and what-have-you. Ferry captains are real pros, accustomed to dodging obstacles and battling the elements, including pea-soup fog and choppy seas. The biggest bottleneck tends to be periodic reconstruction of dock and terminal facilities, but the service continues nonetheless, with only minor delays.

For various reasons, the ferry service has been known to increase fares without much warning, so consider the following rates ballpark figures. (Reservations, bicycles, and cars all cost extra.) Round-trip fares for **Vinalhaven, North Haven, Swans Island,** and **Frenchboro** in 2005 were $12 adult, $5.25 children (5–11), $11.50 for an adult bicycle (without rider), $5.75 for a child's bicycle, and $34.50 for a car (including driver). **Islesboro** fares for the same categories were $6, $2.50, $5.75, $3, and $17.50. Children under 5 are free.

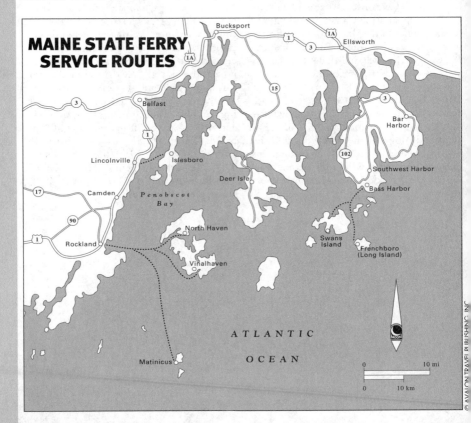

Nonrefundable **vehicle reservations** are strongly recommended for July and August weekends but cannot be made more than 30 days in advance. Call the ferry service and reserve by credit card, or send your request, along with a check for the full fare plus the reservation fee ($46 round-trip for vehicle with driver), to the terminal from which you will be departing (see addresses below). Or, if you're in the area, you can reserve by stopping in at the terminal a few days or a week ahead. Reservations are held until 15 minutes before departure.

A different schedule prevails on each of the state ferry routes, but keep in mind that except for one Vinalhaven boat, the final ferry from the mainland each day *remains on the island,* so don't miss the last departure or you'll have an unexpected island stay (and beds can be scarce).

State ferries depart from Rockland for **Matinicus** only 27 times a year, making the 23-mile crossing in 135 minutes. The schedule is dependent on tides, weather, and vessel availability, and fares are subject to change, so check with the Rockland terminal, 207/596-2202. Matinicus reservations can be made up to three months in advance, and are held till 30 minutes prior to loading.

Maine State Ferry Service parking lots at Rockland, Lincolnville, and Bass Harbor are $7 daily May 1–Labor Day; weekly, monthly, and summer rates are also available. Off-season parking is free.

For comprehensive recorded **statewide ferry and other transportation information, schedule, etc.,** contact Maine State Ferry Service, 517A Main St., P.O. Box 645, Rockland 04841, 207/596-2202 or 800/491-4883, www.state.me.us/mdot/opt/ferry.

Vinalhaven and North Haven

Vinalhaven and North Haven boats—as well as Matinicus ones—depart from Rockland's North End, across U.S. 1 from the Navigator Motor Inn and the Old Granite Inn (watch for distinctive five-sided blue directional signs). Schedules vary, depending on the day and the season. From March through October,

the *Captain Charles Philbrook* and the *Governor Curtis* make six trips a day to and from Vinalhaven, covering the 15 miles in 75 minutes. Earliest boats in either direction depart at 7 AM, latest ones at 4:30 PM. The *Captain Neal Burgess* makes three round-trips a day to North Haven year-round, beginning at 8 AM in North Haven and 9:30 AM in Rockland. Crossing time for the 12.5 miles is 70 minutes. Last boat from North Haven departs at 3:45 PM, last boat from Rockland at 5:15 PM. You can reach offices of the Maine State Ferry Service at P.O. Box 191, Vinalhaven 04863, 207/863-4421; or P.O. Box 225, North Haven 04853, 207/867-4441.

The Vinalhaven and North Haven routes see heavy vehicle traffic, so it is essential to arrive at the ferry terminal well in advance if you plan to take a car to either island and you don't have a reservation. (The same goes for the return trip.) Don't push your luck.

Lodgings are limited on both islands, so call ahead to reserve beds, especially during late July and early August. Local innkeepers are extremely accommodating and can help with alternative arrangements when fog or heavy seas cancel a trip, but the islands reach saturation that time of year.

The roads on Vinalhaven and North Haven are narrow and shoulderless—as in so much of Maine—but the islands are still manageable for **bicycling.** Remember to obey the rules of the road and use common sense, though. Park your car at the Rockland ferry terminal and take your bicycle on the ferry—that's far cheaper than taking a car. Nearest bike rentals are at Maine Sport Outfitters, Rte. 1, P.O. Box 956, Rockport 04856, 800/722-0826 (Outdoor Adventures) or 888/236-8797 (reservations and availability), www.mainesport.com. The $18 daily rate for a hybrid bike includes helmet, lock, and maps of local rides; a car rack is $12 the first day, $4 each additional day.

Another option is to go along just for the ride, without car or bike, and make a simple day of it—the Penobscot Bay scenery alone is worth the trip. Between boats on Vinalhaven,

Know Maine

you can explore the downtown Carver's Harbor area, hike Lane's Island Preserve, swim at Lawson's Quarry, and picnic in Grimes Park.

Islesboro

Just three miles off Lincolnville (five miles north of Camden), Islesboro is a quick, 20-minute trip via the *Margaret Chase Smith.* Mid-Apr.–mid-Oct., the vessel makes nine round-trips Tues.–Sat., eight Mon., departing on most half-hours from Islesboro (beginning at 7:30 AM) and on most hours (beginning at 8 AM) from Lincolnville. Last boat off the island is at 4:30 PM. On Sunday, when there are eight round-trips, the captain and crew can sleep in: Boats begin at 8:30 AM from Islesboro and 9 AM from Lincolnville. Off-season, fewer trips operate in the middle of the day.

To explore this 10-mile-long, relatively level island best known as an exclusive summer colony, you *will* want a car or bicycle; except for visiting a small museum, there's little to do around Islesboro's ferry terminal. However, roads are narrow and winding—and some islanders resent the influx of two-wheelers—so be particularly conscientious and sensible here. You can leave your car on the mainland, at one of the parking lots near the ferry landing. Information: Maine State Ferry Service, P.O. Box 214, Lincolnville 04849, 207/789-5611; or Islesboro Terminal, Islesboro 04848, 207/734-6935.

Swans Island and Frenchboro

The Bass Harbor ferry terminal, tucked into the southwestern corner of Mount Desert Island, serves as the base for boats to Swans Island and Frenchboro. The ferry system's distinctive five-sided blue signs appear all over Mount Desert, so you'll have no trouble finding Bass Harbor's terminal. Allow some time to check out Bass Harbor, maybe even spend the night.

Getting to Swans Island, six miles offshore, takes 40 minutes aboard the *Captain Henry Lee,* which makes six round-trips Monday, Tuesday, Friday, and Saturday, and five on Wednesday, Thursday, Sunday, early Apr.–Oct. Schedules vary Apr.–May and on Thursdays;

check carefully. Here, too, you'll want a car or bicycle—preferably a mountain bike—to negotiate unpaved side roads.

There is fee parking opposite the Bass Harbor ferry terminal. Information: Maine State Ferry Service, P.O. Box 114, Bass Harbor 04653, 207/244-3254, or P.O. Box 213, Swans Island 04685, 207/526-4273.

Frenchboro, the only hamlet on sparsely populated Long Island, is just over eight miles off Bass Harbor, 50 minutes and 50 years away. The *Captain Henry Lee* serves the island with infrequent trips, but there are no lodgings and no campgrounds. You should go for the ride and a glimpse of a remote island harbor, but you're on your own if you decide not to return on the boat. Each Wednesday, the boat leaves Bass Harbor at 9 AM, returning from Frenchboro at 10 AM Thursday, it departs Bass Harbor at noon, then returns from Frenchboro via Swans Island at 1 PM. Mid-Apr.–Oct., on Sunday, the ferry departs Bass Harbor at 12:15 PM and returns from Frenchboro at 1:15 PM. Each Friday, early Apr.–Oct., a small passenger-only vessel, the *R. L. Gott,* makes two round-trips. The first departs Bass Harbor at 8 AM and the second returns from Frenchboro at 6 PM, allowing a nine-hour stay on the island. A round-trip ticket is $12.

CASCO BAY LINES

Residents of the Casco Bay islands—Portland's bedroom communities—cheerfully commute to work and school on the brightly-colored ferries of **Casco Bay Lines,** Commercial and Franklin Sts., P.O. Box 4656, Old Port, Portland 04112, 207/774-7871, www.cascobaylines.com, the nation's oldest continuously operating ferry system. Boats serve **Cliff, Great Chebeague, Little and Great Diamond, Long,** and **Peaks Islands.** No smoking is allowed aboard the vessels; dogs (leashed) and bicycles require their own tickets. An interesting quirk and potential bargain: All tickets are round-trip, and they're collected when you board in Portland. If you manage to get to one of the islands by some other means—such as via the Chebeague

Transportation Company (see below)—there's no charge for going from island to island or returning to Portland on a Casco Bay Lines vessel. The Lines are re-examining their one-pay policy as of this writing, however, and also say it's easy to get stuck on an island if you aren't very conversant with schedule ins and outs. Not all the islands have places to stay, so beware of becoming an overnight Robinson Crusoe, or bring cash for water taxi or private boat hire. Or bring your own boat. You can ship kayaks—and just about anything else—on the ferries for an extra charge.

Most frequent is the Peaks Island run, a 20-minute trip. Round-trip fare is $6.25 in summer, less in winter. Bikes are $5.25 extra (you can also rent one on Peaks, often on the honor system—go up the hill from the ferry, turn left, and you will see a bunch of bikes on the right).

The best Casco Bay Lines trip is the year-round **mailboat run,** which makes a three-hour loop, stopping at five islands, twice daily. (An extra early-morning weekday trip also operates between mid-June and Labor Day.) Cost is $13 for adults, $11.50 for seniors, $6.50 for children ages 5–9. Also popular is the seasonal, narrated, Bailey Island day cruise, including the history and sights of Casco Bay, probably some seals and seabirds, and time for a lobster or picnic lunch at the Island.

OTHER OFFSHORE SERVICES

Small municipal and private ferry services provide transportation to islands up and down the coast. **Chebeague Transportation Company,** 207/846-3700, www.chebeaguetrans.com, runs its passenger ferry year-round between Cousins Island in Yarmouth and Great Chebeague Island, a 15-minute hop. (Parking for CTC passengers is in Cumberland, linked to the wharf by a shuttle bus.) Round-trip tickets are $12 for adults, $3 for children 1–11, $3 for dogs, $6 for bikes. From Boothbay Harbor, New Harbor, and Port Clyde, boats depart for Monhegan Island. The only year-round service to Monhegan, and the shortest

route, used for passengers and freight, is via Port Clyde, 12 miles down the St. George Peninsula from Thomaston. Round-trip tickets are $27 for adults, $14 for children ages 2–12, $2 for pets. Mainland parking is $4 a day. Don't take a bicycle; the island has banned them. Reservations are essential in summer; contact the **Monhegan-Thomaston Boat Line,** P.O. Box 238, Port Clyde 04855, 207/372-8848, www.monheganboat.com.

Passenger ferries for the 45-minute run to Isle au Haut depart Mon.–Sat. year-round from Stonington, on Deer Isle. There are two boats on Sundays in the summer, but no Sunday boats in the winter. Round-trip adult tickets are $32, kids under 12 are $16. Bikes are $16 round-trip, pets are $8, and a 10-foot kayak is $30 (plus $4 for each additional foot). The Boat Company also offers bicycles for rental on Isle au Haut. Mon.–Sun. mid-June–Labor Day, the ferry makes two runs to and from Duck Harbor, the Isle au Haut section of Acadia National Park. No bikes, canoes, or kayaks can be carried to the park. Contact the **Isle au Haut Company,** Sea Breeze Ave., P.O. Box 709, Stonington 04681, 207/367-5193, www.isleauhaut.com.

The Cranberry Cove Ferry passenger line runs the *Island Queen* to the Cranberry Isles, off Mt. Desert Island, starting from the Upper Town Dock (Clark Point Rd.) in Southwest Harbor, proceeding to the Manset Town Dock, and making a loop between Great Cranberry, Islesford (Little Cranberry Island), and Great Cranberry. Mid-May–mid-Oct. there are six trips daily, with summer-schedule additions according to demand. Round-trip fare is $18 for adults, $12 for kids 3–11. Bikes are $5 extra. Contact the **Cranberry Cove Boating Co.,** Upper Town Dock, Southwest Harbor 04679, 207/244-5882. The same company also runs the Bar Harbor Ferry passenger service between Bar Harbor and Winter Harbor. The *Katherine, Schoodic,* or *St. Croix* departs from the Bar Harbor Inn Pier, landing at Winter Harbor Marine, in Winter Harbor. Late June–Labor Day, the Island Explorer bus meets the ferry,

Know Maine

providing free service to Schoodic Point (part of Acadia National Park) and Winter, Birch, and Prospect Harbors. Round-trip rates are $24 for adults, $15 for children, and $5 for bicycles; commuter rates are available. There are six trips daily in season, with additional peak trips added when needed. Tel. 207/288-2984, www.barharborferry.com (both ferries).

MAINE–NOVA SCOTIA CRUISE FERRY

An oceangoing car-and-passenger cruise ferry links Bar Harbor with Yarmouth, in western Nova Scotia, making twice-daily trips throughout the summer. It's worth considering cruising one way and driving the other. Taking your car aboard is expensive, but you're saving the cost of a long drive from Bar Harbor. When making plans, remember that Yarmouth is on Atlantic time—an hour later than Maine's eastern time.

The sleek car-and-passenger catamaran ferry known as *The Cat,* the fastest car ferry in North America, dashes from **Bar Harbor** to Yarmouth in under three hours, carrying up to 900 passengers and 240 cars. In summer (late June–late Sept.) the CAT sails twice a day, stopping for an hour or so. With two sailings a day, passengers can spend the day in Nova Scotia and take the evening boat back. Special round-trip rates for these day cruises are $59 for adults and $25 for youths 6–13. Off-season, there is one sailing a day, with a 3.5-hour layover. Summer one-way tickets are $169 for car-plus-driver (includes port fees, but fuel surcharges may apply), lower off-season. Summer youth fare is $39; kids up to age five ride free. Pets are not allowed on the passenger deck, but are kenneled on a first-come, first-served basis on the vehicle deck. For more information, contact **Bay Ferries,** 207/288-3395 or 888/249-7245, www.catferry.com.

Note: The *Scotia Prince* no longer offers service between Portland and Yarmouth.

WINDJAMMER CRUISES

Taking a windjammer cruise means swinging aboard an antique or replica wooden sailing vessel, stowing your duffel bag, and letting the wind carry you away—overnight or for three or four or six days.

Named for their ability to "jam" into the wind when they carried freight up and down the New England coast, windjammers trigger images of the Great Age of Sail. Most are rigged as schooners, with two or three soaring wooden masts. Windjammers are 45–132 feet long and carry 20–40 passengers.

You're aboard for the experience, not for luxury, so expect basic accommodations with few frills. Most boats have shared showers and toilets and in-cabin sinks. Quarters are tight, but you'll want to spend as much time as possible on deck anyway. Deck tarps provide shelter from rain or sun. No matter when you go, even in midsummer, be sure to pack raingear and warm clothing—including a hat and gloves if you're especially cold-sensitive.

Highlights of a windjammer cruise include stupendous scenery, hearty food, sing-alongs, sunsets to die for, and a grand finale lobster-bake on a deserted shore.

Home base for all Maine's cruising windjammer schooners is the Mid-Coast region—nearly two dozen vessels sail out of Camden, Rockport, and Rockland.

When you book a cruise, you receive all the details and directions, but for a typical six-day trip, you arrive at the boat by 7 PM for the captain's call to meet your fellow passengers. You sleep aboard at the dock that night, then depart midmorning Monday and spend five nights and days cruising Penobscot Bay, following the wind, the weather, and the whims of the captain. (Many of the windjammers have no engines, only a motorized yawlboat used as a pusher and a water taxi.) You might anchor in a deserted cove and explore the shore, or you might pull into a harbor and hike, shop, and bar-hop. Food aboard is always excellent. When the cruise ends on Saturday morning, most passengers find it hard to leave.

Costs for three- to six-day cruises range from $395–915, with all meals. Windjammer cruising is *not* designed for infants or small children, although four vessels (*Nathaniel Bowditch, Isaac H. Evans, Timberwind, J. & E. Riggin*) have special family cruises allowing children as young as five. Best source of information about 14 of the windjammers is the **Maine Windjammer Association,** P.O. Box 1144, Blue Hill 04614, 800/807-9463, www .sailmainecoast.com.

SAILING EXCURSIONS

All along the coast, from York to Mount Desert Island, small sailing vessels offer daytime excursions lasting anywhere from two hours to an entire day. Depending on the type of sailing, the size of crew, and the amenities you prefer, you can choose a small sloop, a classic yacht, or a windjammer schooner. Best places for sailing excursions are York Harbor, Kennebunkport, Portland, Boothbay Harbor, East Boothbay, Rockland, Rockport, Camden, Bar Harbor, Northeast Harbor, and Southwest Harbor.

POWERBOAT EXCURSIONS

Maine's coast, lakes, and rivers are all sites for an incredible variety of excursions in motorized boats. In Naples, you can cruise Long Lake and transit the historic Songo River Lock aboard the restored sternwheeler *Songo River Queen II.* On Great Pond (inspiration for the film *On Golden Pond*), in Belgrade Lakes, you can board a pontoon boat and ride

along as the mail carrier delivers mail to dockside boxes. Greenville is the home of the SS *Katahdin* (better known locally as the *Kate*), a onetime workhorse of the lumber industry that now cruises stunning Moosehead Lake. Jonesport and Cutler, way Down East, are the departure points for day-long boat trips to the famed puffin colony on Machias Seal Island. You can learn about the lobster industry aboard lobsterboats based in Ogunquit, Kennebunkport, Boothbay Harbor, Camden, and Bar Harbor. From Portland and South Freeport, you can cruise out to Eagle Island, former home of arctic explorer Adm. Robert Peary. (The island is now a state historic site, with trails and picnic spots.) Or you can just go along for scenic rides aboard boats leaving Ogunquit, Kennebunk, Bath, Boothbay Harbor, New Harbor, Rockland, Camden, Belfast, Northeast Harbor and Bass Harbor (both on Mount Desert Island), Greenville (on Moosehead Lake), and Cutler.

WHALE-WATCHING

The best venues for whale-watching trips are Kennebunkport, Portland, Boothbay Harbor, Bar Harbor, and Eastport. There's a bonus in Bar Harbor, where the College of the Atlantic sponsors the Allied Whale conservation program ("Adopt a Finback"), and a catamaran runs to the whale grounds at speeds up to 40 mph. Since whale-watching sometimes involves riding the swells while waiting for the behemoths to surface, be sure to arm yourself against seasickness.

Information and Services

TOURISM INFORMATION AND MAPS

Maine Online

The Maine Office of Tourism has established a Maine home page on the World Wide Web (www.visitmaine.com). You'll find chamber of commerce addresses, articles, photos, information on lodgings and events in Maine's eight regions, and access to a variety of Maine tourism businesses. But hundreds of other Maine pages are also up and running, so surf away. The state's toll-free **information hotline** is 888/MAINE-45 (888/624-6345).

Local Chambers of Commerce and Tourism Offices

Tourism is Maine's second-largest source of revenue, so almost every community of any size has some kind of information office, ranging from York's mansion-like quarters to tiny log cabins. Some are staffed by volunteers and open only in summer. Most of these communities also produce annual booklets, brochures, or maps loaded with tourism info. In remote areas, local shopkeepers, lodging hosts, and town-office employees are the best alternative information sources. If you haven't planned ahead, ask them for suggestions for places to sleep, eat, shop, and play. No question is too foolish—and you can bet they've heard it before. Contact information for local tourism offices is found in the Maine Tourism Association's *Maine Invites You* magazine, available in visitor information centers; at www.visitmaine.com; and in the regional chapters of this book.

Maps

Maine is the home of DeLorme, publisher of *The Maine Atlas and Gazetteer.* Despite an oversize format inconvenient for hiking and kayaking, this 96-page paperbound book just about guarantees that you won't get lost. Scaled at one-half inch to the mile, it's meticulously compiled from aerial photographs, satellite images, U.S. Geological Survey maps, GPS readings, and timber-company maps and is revised annually. DeLorme products are available nationwide in book and map stores, but you can also order direct, 800/561-5105, www.delorme.com. The atlas is $19.95 and shipping is $5 (Maine residents need to add 5 percent sales tax).

DeLorme also publishes an annual edition of *The Maine Map and Guide,* a standard folding map with detailed insets of major cities and towns, and helpful information on the reverse. It's available in supermarkets, convenience stores, gift shops, bookstores, sporting-goods stores, and some tourist offices. If you're headed for L.L. Bean and share my addiction to geography, stop in Yarmouth (just off I-95 exit 17 and across Rte. 1 from the visitor information center) at the DeLorme Store, 2 DeLorme Dr., P.O. Box 298, Yarmouth 04096, 207/846-7000. The store's 42-foot rotating globe—quaintly named "Eartha"—is alone worth the visit.

Guidebooks

The Suggested Reading list in the back of this book will steer you toward special-focus guides that supplement (but of course do not replace) *Moon Handbooks Maine.* Now out of print but still fascinating as background reading is *Maine: A Guide "Downeast,"* the 1970 edition of the original 1937 Federal Writers' Project volume. It's even more fun if you can pick up a copy of the first edition, an encyclopedic 500-page compendium produced by a talented team of underemployed researchers/writers. Read the history and architecture sections, and check out the old photos. The first edition can be hard to find in Maine's used-book stores, which of course is where everyone looks for it, so start by checking with out-of-state used-book dealers.

Where Is It?

Billboards are banned in Maine, but there's no lack of signage. State-sanctioned direc-

MAINE VISITOR INFORMATION CENTERS

The Maine Tourism Association, a private, nonprofit corporation, is contracted by the state to operate the information centers listed below, all at high-traffic locations. All have knowledgeable staff members, free restrooms, extensive racks of free brochures, and maps and booklets. All are open daily (except Easter, Thanksgiving, and Christmas) 9 AM–5:30 PM, but 8 AM–6 PM between Memorial Day and Columbus Day (early October, same weekend as Canadian Thanksgiving). All but one (Fryeburg) are open year-round.

To receive a free Maine map and 280-page *Maine Invites You* magazine—filled with articles, photos, and ads, as well as addresses of all of the state's chambers of commerce/tourism offices—contact: **Maine Tourism Association,** 327 Water St., Hallowell 04347, 207/623-0363, www.mainetourism.com; or the Maine Office of Tourism, 59 State House Station, Augusta 04333-0059, 888/624-6345, www. visitmaine.com.

Kittery: Accessible from both I-95 and Rt. 1 (near New Hampshire border), 207/439-1319

Yarmouth: I-295 Exit 17 (near Freeport on U.S. Rt. 1), 207/846-0833

Fryeburg: 85 Main St., (Rt. 302 near New Hampshire border; seasonal, May–Oct.), 207/935-3639

Hampden: I-95 northbound at mile 175, 207/862-6628; I-95 southbound at mile 179, 207/862-6638 (both near Bangor)

Calais: Inside the Downeast Heritage Museum, 39 Union St. (near St. Stephen, New Brunswick, border), 207/454-2211

Houlton: 28 Ludlow Rd. (near New Brunswick border), 207/532-6346

tional signs, generally restricted to a standard horizontal format, are posted along roadsides everywhere. Searching for a B&B in the boonies? Watch for a sign with the name and mileage as you get closer. In the more populated areas, the signs approach overkill, and it can be hard to pick out your target, but in remote terrain the placards are a blessing for the uninitiated. Some businesses have creatively adopted variant colors, but blue generally indicates businesses, brown signifies museums, state parks, and historic sites. State town-to-town mileage signs are green, as are the Maine turnpike and interstate signs.

CUSTOMS PROCEDURES

Customs procedures, once easygoing on the Maine–Canada border, are in flux and being tightened under homeland security regulations. Check the new requirements when planning your trip.

Duty-free limits for Canadians returning home range from C$20 to 300, depending on time spent in the United States, frequency of visits, and exclusions. More information, including publications and forms, can be found at www.cbsa-asf.gc.ca or 800/959-2221.

Canadians visiting the United States for at least 72 hours may bring in gifts valued as high as US$100, but no more than twice a year. Here's an odd regulation, obviously easy to circumvent: Canadians can carry one liter of beer, wine, or liquor as a personal effect but not as a gift.

Visitors are also allowed to bring in 200 cigarettes, 50 cigars (though not Cuban ones), or 4.4 pounds of tobacco. Duty is assessed on items over and above the personal exemptions. A brochure titled "Visiting the United States" is available at www.cbp.gov/xp/cgov/travel/vacation/kbyg, as is "Know Before You Go," directed to U.S. residents.

There is no limit on the amount of money

Know Maine

or travelers checks a nonresident may bring into the United States. If the amount exceeds $10,000, however, it's necessary to fill out an official report form.

In general, no fruit, vegetables, or plant materials can be taken across the border in either direction. A strict customs official once confiscated a flourishing 20-year-old jade plant a friend was carting across the border, and I suspect it's still adorning his living room.

TIME AND MONEY

Time Zone

All of Maine is in the eastern time zone—same as New York, Washington, D.C., Philadelphia, and Orlando, Florida. Eastern standard time (EST) runs from the last Sunday in October to the first Sunday in April; eastern daylight time (EDT), one hour later, prevails otherwise. If your itinerary also includes Canada, remember that the provinces of New Brunswick, Nova Scotia, and Prince Edward Island are on Atlantic time—one hour later than eastern.

Every day during the summer, cruise ferries travel between Yarmouth, Nova Scotia, and Bar Harbor, losing and gaining an hour en route. Their schedules are printed in local time at each terminus—EST in Maine, Atlantic time in Nova Scotia. And Campobello Island, site of the Roosevelt Campobello International Park, operates exclusively on Atlantic time.

Currency

Since much of Maine borders Canada, don't be surprised to see a few Canadian coins mixed in with American ones when you receive change from a purchase. In such cases, Canadian and U.S. quarters are equivalent, although the exchange rate is in fact drastically different. In 2005, a U.S. dollar would get you $1.24 Canadian. Most services (including banks) will accept a handful of Canadian coins at par, but you'll occasionally spot No Canadian Currency signs. Until the early 1980s, the two currencies were exchangeable one-for-one, but they've been drawing apart ever since. The mid-1990s disparity led to a tourism vacuum

afflicting such southern Maine communities as Ogunquit and Old Orchard Beach—longtime destinations of French-Canadian vacationers.

It's not absolutely necessary to exchange currency when traveling between the two countries, but Canadian dollars are worth considerably less in the United States (and U.S. dollars are worth considerably more in Canada). Also, the farther south of Canada you roam, the more likely you'll find resistance to Canadian currency in restaurants and shops. It's easier to convert it.

Banks and Automated Teller Machines

Typical Maine banking hours are 9 AM–4 PM weekdays, an hour later Thursdays and Fridays. Drive-up windows will often open as much as an hour earlier and stay open an hour or so after lobbies close. Most banks have at least one area branch with Saturday morning hours. But as long as you have an automated teller machine (ATM) or debit card or a credit card, you can go almost anywhere in Maine (a few coastal islands even have ATMs, but most do not) at any time and withdraw money from your personal checking, savings, or credit-card account. Unfortunately, some banks charge a usurious fee for ATM transactions—though other banks and credit unions have begun to form fee-free networks, like ACCESS. Depending on your schedule and location, it can be more trouble than it's worth to shop around. Grocery stores and post offices now allow cash withdrawals with purchases.

Major banks in Maine are TD Banknorth, KeyBank, and Bank of America.

If you need to exchange foreign currency—other than Canadian dollars—do it at or near border crossings or in Portland. In small communities, such transactions are more complicated; you may end up spending more time and money than necessary.

Credit Cards and Travelers Checks

Bank credit cards have become so preferred and so prevalent that it's nearly impossible to rent a car or check into a hotel without one (the alternative is payment in advance or a hefty cash deposit). MasterCard and Visa are most widely accepted in Maine, Discover and American Express are next most popular; Carte Blanche, Diners Club, and EnRoute (Canadian) lag far behind. The Japan Credit Bureau card is gaining acceptance, particularly in Freeport—a magnet for Japanese travelers. Be aware, however, that small restaurants, shops, and B&Bs off the beaten track might not accept credit cards; you may need to settle your account with a personal check, cash, or travelers check.

With the popularity of credit cards, travelers checks have lost favor, but if you decide to carry them, be sure they are in U.S. dollar amounts.

Major petroleum firms—Mobil/Exxon, Texaco, Citgo, Getty, and Gulf—have filling stations in Maine. Most accept their own credit cards as well as MasterCard, Visa, and Discover. Most have pay-at-the-pump options. The Irving Corporation, a Canadian firm with countless stations in Maine, accepts Master-Card, Visa, AMEX, Discover, Debit, Wright Express, Voyager, and Irving Light Fleet.

Taxes
Maine charges a 5 percent sales tax on items such as gifts, snacks, books, clothing, and video rentals, and a 7 percent tax on all bar, restaurant, and lodging bills. Bear in mind, especially when making reservations by phone, that restaurants and lodgings usually do *not* include the 7 percent tax when quoting their prices. A whopping 10 percent tax is added to car-rental rates.

Tipping
The longtime restaurant tipping standard—15 percent of the total bill—still prevails in most of Maine. One exception is Portland, where a big-city 20 percent rate isn't unusual in the upscale restaurants. Of course, the restaurant tip always should depend on the quality of the service. If you've ever worked in a restaurant, you know how much tips are appreciated—but they need to be earned. Don't penalize a waitperson for the kitchen's mistakes or incompetence, but do reduce the tip if the service is sloppy.

Taxi drivers expect a 15 percent tip; airport porters expect at least $1 per bag, depending on the difficulty of the job. If a porter simply unloads a suitcase from a car for curbside check-in, 50 cents is plenty; if he has to escort you to a ticket counter—and especially if he arranges for speedier service—a dollar per bag is appropriate.

Tipping in lodgings is another matter. I find inappropriate the increasingly popular envelope-in-the-room strategy. Expense-account travelers can be cavalierly generous, but independent travelers should not have to support low wage scales. I know that's what happens in restaurants, but it probably started the same way and gradually became the rule; I support halting the envelope practice now.

Special Discounts
AAA, the American Automobile Association, is the largest discounter for tourism, arranging special rates for its members at lodgings, restaurants, shops, museums, ski resorts, and amusement parks. Sometimes there are unadvertised discounts as well. Contact the AAA office nearest your home or AAA Northern New England, 425 Marginal Way, Portland 04101, 207/780-6800 or 800/482-7497, www.aaanne.com.

Anyone planning to spend time in the state parks—especially families—should consider buying a **state park day-use season pass,** issued by the Bureau of Parks and Lands, 22 State House Station, Augusta 04333, 207/287-3821, but also available at the gates of all major state parks. A $60 vehicle pass allows everyone in the car (or van or camper) free daytime use; a $30 individual pass applies only to the pass-holder. A (free) Senior Citizen Pass admits those over 65 to day-use areas free. There is also a gift bloc admission pass: 50 one-time day-use vehicle passes for $250.

Another bargain is the **Golf Privilege Card,** issued by the American Lung Association of Maine (ALAM) for $70. The card provides free or substantially reduced greens fees to over 80 Maine public and private courses (over 200 rounds of golf). The card also gives access to courses in New Hampshire and Canada, and a variety of driving ranges. It's available through ALAM, 122 State St., Augusta 04330, 207/622-6394 or 800/499-5864, www.maineelung.org, beginning early in the year, or at Play It Again Sports locations in Auburn, Augusta, Bangor, Brunswick, and Portland.

If you're planning to spend any time sampling restaurants in the southern Maine area, consider joining the **Portland Dine Around Club,** P.O. Box 15338, Portland 04112, 207/775-4711, www.dineportland.com. Membership gets you $10–25 off the lower-priced entrée when two people dine at 170 or so respected restaurants with a wide variety of menus, decor, and price ranges. There are also movie, sports, and entertainment deals. Two or three nights out and your membership card has earned its $29.95 price tag. Some limitations apply, but it's still a bargain.

Some of Maine's larger telephone directories contain a special section of discount coupons—more than 50 in Portland, for instance. If you can put your hands on a directory, browse the bargains, clip coupons, and take advantage of deals on pizzas, ice cream cakes, jewelry, motels, and more.

Bear in mind, when looking for bargains, that the cost of off-season lodging is inevitably lower—sometimes dramatically so—than during the busiest months of June, July, and August. Some lodgings extend their high-season rates to mid-October (to take in the foliage season), and lodgings in western Maine, near the ski areas, turn the tables—winter is the high season.

COMMUNICATIONS AND MEDIA
Postal and Shipping Services
Post offices in major cities are generally open Mon.–Fri., 8 AM–5 PM, and 8 AM–noon on Saturday. Hours at post offices in smaller communities vary, but they usually open no later than 9 AM and close no earlier than 4 PM, Mon.–Fri. Smaller community post offices have varying Saturday hours, and some close at lunchtime daily, so it is always best to check

first about the hours of operation before heading out. You can find out the exact hours of the post office closest to you by either calling 800/ASK-USPS or by visiting the Postal Service's website at www.usps.com and clicking on Find Post Office. You can also buy postage and prepare your own shipping labels on the website. Stamps can be purchased at some gift shops and supermarkets and at vending machines in some post office lobbies (most of these only carry domestic postage). You can also purchase stamps in advance of your trip by calling 800/STAMP24.

Maine also has three Automated Postal Centers (APCs) where customers can mail packages using debit and credit cards, buy stamps, find out zip code information, and purchase special services. The hours of operation for the APC at the Main Branch of the Portland Post Office, 125 Forest Ave. in Portland, are 5 AM–9 PM, seven days a week. The hours of operation at the APC at Downtown Station in Portland, 400 Congress St., Portland, are 7 AM–7 PM Mon.–Fri. and 7 AM–1 PM Sat. The hours of operation for the APC at the Scarborough Post Office, 31 Gorham Rd., Scarborough, are 6 AM–5:30 PM Mon.–Fri. and 6 AM–4 PM Sat.

First-class postage (as of 2005) is 37 cents for domestic letters (weighing up to one ounce) and 23 cents for each additional ounce. First-class postcards, domestically, cost 23 cents to mail. Sending an airmail letter overseas costs 80 cents for the first ounce, and 40 cents for each additional half-ounce. An airmail postcard stamp costs 70 cents for all countries except Canada and Mexico; a self-contained aerogram also costs 70 cents. A regular letter to Canada is 60 cents for the first ounce; a postcard is 50 cents.

Cities and large towns have strategically placed Express Mail, UPS, and Federal Express boxes. To contact Federal Express, call 800/463-3339, www.fedex.com; to contact UPS, call 800/742-5877, www.ups.com. Another national/international delivery service available in Maine is DHL Express, 800/225-5345, www.dhl-usa.com.

With franchises all over the state, the UPS

Store provides every imaginable type of packing and shipping assistance, as well as photocopy and fax services. You can even rent a short-term mailbox if you plan to stay in one area several days or longer. If you want to arrange for an address and/or phone/fax number in advance, call for UPS Store locations, 800/789-4623.

If you expect to receive mail while in Maine, have your correspondents address it to you c/o General Delivery in the town or city where you expect to be and mark it "Hold for arrival on [your estimated arrival date]." Be sure to give them that post office's correct zip code (every post office has a national zip code directory; overseas residents can check with the nearest U.S. embassy or consulate).

Area Codes

Maine still has only one telephone area code—**207**—and in-state phone rates are relatively high. Calling out-of-state (dial 1 plus the area code before the number) often is cheaper! Directory assistance is 411. From outside Maine, calls require use of the number 1 plus the 207 area code. Any number with an area code of 800, 888, 877, 866, or 855 is toll-free.

Cell Phones

When you're on vacation, a ringing telephone should be the absolute last thing you want to think about, but needs do arise, and cellular phones, alas, have become a fact of life. Transmission towers are now sprinkled everywhere in Maine; only a few pockets—mostly down peninsulas and in remote valleys and hollows—are out of cellular-phone range. (Keep in mind, however, that if you're planning to hike or camp in Baxter State Park, even in a cabin, you won't be allowed to use your phone or any other kind of electronic equipment. Baxter authorities work hard—and effectively—to maintain the park's "forever wild" philosophy.)

Newspapers, TV, and Radio

Maine's daily newspapers are the *Portland Press Herald*, Augusta's *Kennebec Journal*, the *Bangor Daily News, Lewiston Sun Journal, Biddeford Journal Tribune, Brunswick Times Record,* and Waterville's *Morning Sentinel.* Local weeklies number in the dozens. Blethen Maine Newspapers, owner of three major Maine dailies, has a useful website (www.mainetoday.com) of current activities, events, weather reports, and news stories.

Every major community in the more populous areas of the state has a weekly "shopper," supplemented in summer by special weekly tourist tabloids. You'll see these free publications everywhere: restaurants, convenience stores, gift shops, bookstores, supermarkets, art galleries, and more. Check these for up-to-date ads and listings of such local activities as concerts, lectures, public suppers, films, hikes, art and museum exhibits, and festivals.

Along the coast, most newspapers publish a daily or weekly tide calendar, essential information for anyone planning to fish, swim, dive, sail, or kayak. The daily papers have a particularly informative weather half-page. The 6 PM and 11 PM TV newscasts always include tide, sunrise, and sunset details in their weather segments.

Portland and Bangor are Maine's TV centers; each has affiliates of ABC, CBS, and NBC networks. Maine Public Broadcasting Network airs its TV programs on channels 10, 12, 13, or 26, depending on your location. MPBN radio transmits over seven different frequencies around the state.

In 1995, Maine licensed its 100th radio station, virtually saturating the airwaves and creating stiff commercial competition. Most now have grabbed programming niches—country, classical, news, sports, big band, talk, oldies, rock. Many pride themselves on being community-oriented, broadcasting information about sports and cultural activities, lost animals, community schedule changes, weather warnings, and more. The most intriguing operation is WERU (89.9 FM), a community radio station headquartered on U.S.1/ME3 in East Orland (www.weru.org). A few paid staffers, countless volunteer DJs and hosts, and thousands of supportive listeners keep programming on the air round-the-clock. Affectionately dubbed Radio

USEFUL CONTACTS

Acadia National Park, P.O. Box 177, Bar Harbor 04609, 207/288-3338 (general information) or 800/365-2267 (camping reservations), www.nps.gov/acad.

Allagash Wilderness Waterway, 207/941-4014 (general information), www.maine.gov/doc/parks/index.html.

Allied Whale, College of the Atlantic, 105 Eden St., Bar Harbor 04609, 207/288-5644 (whale research; Adopt-a-Finback program), www.coa.edu/alliedwhale.

American Automobile Association, 800/222-4357 (a variety of options, including road conditions and emergency road service for members), www.aaa.com.

Amtrak, 800/872-7245, www.amtrak.com (Boston-to-Portland rail service).

Appalachian Mountain Club, Maine Chapter, Attn: John Dolloff, 795 Lawrence Road, Pownal 04069, 207/415-6702, home.gwi.net/amcmaine.

Bangor International Airport, 207/992-4623 or 866/fly-bangor, www.flybangor.com.

Baxter State Park Headquarters, 64 Balsam Dr., Millinocket 04462, 207/723-5140 (general information by phone; reservations by mail or in person), www.baxterstateparkauthority.com.

Bay Ferries, 888/249-7245, www.nfl-bay.com (fast ferry, Bar Harbor to Yarmouth, Nova Scotia).

Bicycle Coalition of Maine, P.O. Box 5275, Augusta 04332, 207/623-4511, www.BikeMaine.org (statewide advocacy group).

Casco Bay Lines, Commercial and Franklin Sts., P.O. Box 4656, Portland 04112, 207/774-7871, fax 774-7875, www.CascoBayLines.com (ferries to Casco Bay islands).

Center for Maine History, 489 Congress St., Portland 04101, 207/774-1822, www.mainehistory.org (museum; research).

Concord Trailways, 800/639-3317, www.concordtrailways.com (bus service between Boston's Logan Airport and inland and coastal Maine).

DeLorme, Two DeLorme Dr., P.O. Box 298, Yarmouth 04096, 800/561-5105, www.delorme.com (map store; publisher of invaluable *Maine Atlas and Gazetteer*).

Greater Portland Landmarks, 165 State St., Portland 04101, 207/774-5561, www.portlandlandmarks.org (Portland-area historic preservation and site information, including Portland Observatory; guided tours).

Greater Portland Visitor Information Center, 245 Commercial St., Portland 04101, 207/772-5800, and at the Airport Terminal, www.visitportland.com.

Hurricane Island Outward Bound School, 75 Mechanic St., Rockland 04841, 866/746-9771, www.hurricaneisland.org (sailing and wilderness courses).

Island Institute, P.O. Box 648, 386 Main St., Rockland 04841, 207/594-9209 or 800/339-9209, fax 594-9314, www.islandinstitute.org (clearinghouse/advocate for Maine's islands).

Kennebec River water-flow information, 800/287-0999.

L.L. Bean, 95 Main St. (Rte. 1), Freeport 04032; Outdoor Discovery Program, 888/552-3261, www.llbean.com/odp.

Maine Appalachian Trail Club, P.O. Box 283, Augusta 04332, www.matc.org.

Maine Archives and Museums, P.O. Box 5024, Augusta 04333, 207/287-5709, www.mainemuseums.org.

Maine Association of Sea Kayaking Guides and Instructors (MASKGI), www.MaineSeaKayakGuides.com (contacts for guides, instructors, gear, and trips).

Maine Audubon Society, 20 Gilsland Farm Rd., Falmouth 04105, 207/781-2330, www.maineaudubon.org.

Maine Bureau of Parks and Lands, 286 Water Street, Key Bank Plaza, 22 State House Station, Augusta 04333, 207/287-3821 (general information); 800/332-1501 in Maine, or 207/287-3824 or fax 287-

6170 (state park camping reservations), www.state.me.us/doc/parks.

Maine Campground Owners Association, 10 Falcon Rd., Ste. 1, Lewiston 04240, 207/782-5874, fax 782-4497, www.campmaine.com (commercial campground information clearinghouse).

Maine Coast Heritage Trust, 1 Main St., Topsham 04086, 207/729-7366, www.mcht.org (conservation organization and land-trust clearinghouse).

Maine Crafts Association, P.O. Box 8817, Portland 04104, 207/780-1807, www.mainecrafts.org.

Maine Department of Inland Fisheries and Wildlife, 284 State St., 41 State House Station, Augusta 04333, 207/287-8000 (general information); 287-8003 (automated 24-hour info line), www.state.me.us/ifw.

Maine Forest Service, 207/287-2791 (campfire-permit information), www.state.me.us/doc/mfs.

Maine Island Trail Association, P.O. Box C, 328 Main St., Rockland 04841, 207/596-6456; or 58 Fore Street, Bldg. 30, 3rd fl., Portland 04101, 207/761-8225, www.mita.org (conservation-oriented coastal waterway route for sea kayakers and other boaters).

Maine Lobster Promotion Council, 207/947-2966, www.mainelobsterpromo.com.

Maine Nordic Ski Council, P.O. Box 645, Bethel 04217, 800/754-9263, www.mnsc.com (information clearinghouse for cross-country skiing).

Maine Office of Tourism (Maine state tourism department), www.visitmaine.com.

Maine Outdoor Adventure Club (Portland and Bangor areas), www.moac.org.

Maine Snowmobile Association, P.O. Box 80, Augusta 04332, 207/622-6983, www.mesnow.com.

Maine Sporting Camp Association, P.O. Box 89, Jay 04239, www.mainesportingcamps.com.

Maine State Ferry Service, 207/596-2202 for general schedule information,

or 800/491-4883 for a daily recorded update (ferries to six offshore islands), www.state.me.us/mdot/opt/ferry/ferry.htm.

Maine State Police, 800/482-0730, www.state.me.us/dps/msp/msp.htm.

Maine Tourism Association, 325B Water St., Hallowell 04347, 207/623-0363, fax 623-0388, www.mainetourism.com (state tourism information clearinghouse).

Maine Turnpike Authority, 800/675-7453 (road conditions), www.maineturnpike.com.

Maine Windjammer Association, P.O. Box 1144, Blue Hill 04614, 800/807-9463, www.sailmainecoast.com.

National Weather Service, 207/688-3210 (recorded local and marine weather), www.nws.noaa.gov.

Nature Conservancy, Maine Chapter, Fort Andross, 14 Maine St., Brunswick 04011, 207/729-5181, fax 729-4118, www.nature.org.

North Maine Woods, Inc., P.O. Box 425, Ashland 04732, 207/435-6213, www.north-mainewoods.org (timberlands recreational management; campsite reservations).

Poison Control Center, 800/222-1222.

Portland International Jetport, 207/874-8877, fax 207/774-7740, www.portlandjetport.org.

Portland Sea Dogs (AA baseball), Hadlock Field, Portland, 800/936-3647, www.portlandseadogs.com.

Raft Maine, P.O. Box 3, Bethel 04217, 207/824-3694 or 800/723-8633, www.raftmaine.com (whitewater-rafting clearinghouse).

Ski conditions, 207/773-7669 (recorded info), www.skimaine.com.

U.S. Customs, 207/780-3328, www.cbp.gov/xp/cgov/travel.

White Mountain National Forest, Evans Notch Ranger District, 18 Mayville Rd., Rte. 2, RR2, Box 2270, Bethel 04217, 207/824-2134, www.fs.fed.us/r9/white.

Free Spirit, the station broadcasts in-depth interviews, extensive calendar information, and an eclectic blend of music.

Down East Available for $4.95 a copy at newsstands, supermarkets, bookstores, and gift shops everywhere in Maine, *Down East* magazine has been the state's chief booster since 1954. The monthly publication carries a potpourri of articles about places, people, trends, gardens, and history, plus glossy photos, travel tips, boatyard news, calendar items, pages of real estate ads, and dozens of classifieds for seasonal house and cottage rentals. During the year, special supplements focus on such subjects as Maine travel, gardens, antiques, and boating.

Down East, 207/594-9544, is the oldest sibling of a publishing family, Down East Enterprise, Inc., that also includes Down East Books as well as fishing and hunting magazines. A mail-order catalog offers Maine books, gifts, and crafts. Headquarters for all this output is a rambling, Shingle-style estate on the east side of Route 1 in Rockport, midway between Rockland and Camden. Weekdays 8:30 AM–4:30 PM, you can stop in and browse for magazines, books, and gifts. *Down East* subscriptions are available from P.O. Box 679, Camden 04843, or 800/727-7422, www.downeast.com.

PUBLIC RESTROOMS

Unfortunately, public restrooms are in shorter supply in Maine than they ought to be, although some of the most visitor-oriented communities (such as Kennebunkport, Camden, Rockland, Bar Harbor, Southwest Harbor) have recognized the need and built facilities. Sad to say, some businesses post No Public Restrooms on their doors—and mean it. If you're traveling with kids, you're accustomed to being resourceful, but here are some general tips. Irving gas stations and McDonald's and Burger King fast-food joints would prefer that you patronize their establishments, but, even if you don't, you can use their restrooms. Some but not all other gas stations also have restrooms; you may

need to ask at the office for a key. Restaurants are required to have restrooms, but it may be less awkward to buy a cup of coffee before using the facilities. Public buildings, such as hospitals, courthouses, police stations, town offices, libraries, and ferry terminals, have public restrooms, usually wheelchair-accessible. Most municipal parks and state-maintained roadside rest areas have seasonal pit or vault toilets—but often no running water.

WHAT TO PACK
Clothing and Gear

No matter what your itinerary, you won't be able to make do in Maine with a couple of bathing suits, shorts, sandals, and coverups; the weather is just too unpredictable. Of course, Maine *is* the home of L.L. Bean, so you could just stop in Freeport as soon as you arrive and buy an entire vacation wardrobe there. Seriously, though, in summer you'll need to pack shorts, swimwear, raingear, jeans and other long pants, cotton and wool sweaters, warm nightwear, and a warm jacket. For hiking, you'll want sturdy shoes, a brimmed hat, and a waterproof daypack. If you have a yen for freshwater swimming, throw in a pair of Reefrunners for navigating wet grass and slippery rocks. In spring and fall, skip the shorts, swimwear, and Reefrunners, double up on all the rest, and add a pair of gloves or mittens, a wool hat, and rubber-bottomed shoes or boots. In winter, double up even more, but always make sure to pack clothing you can don or doff in layers.

The dress code in summer is relaxed and informal. Unless you plan to plug into the cocktail-party circuit, or you just feel more comfortable dressing up for dinner, you don't need to pack fancy clothes (a handful of restaurants require jackets, but most of those keep a few extras on hand). On the other hand, evenings are cool, so shorts won't do. Footwear is required in all restaurants. Unless you're canoeing the Allagash Wilderness Waterway or hiking the 100-Mile Wilderness on the Appalachian Trail, you'll rarely be far from laundry facilities, so you shouldn't need to pack masses of underwear.

If you're planning to camp, get out your camping checklist and load up all those items. If you'll be doing any wilderness camping, keep in mind that even though most lean-tos are built facing away from the prevailing wind, it doesn't hurt to pack an extra tarp for wind shifts and shelter on cold nights.

Other **important gear:** flashlight, compass and/or GPS, Swiss Army knife, small first-aid kit, binoculars, sunglasses, lip balm, sunscreen, camera (with an extra battery), whistle, small waterproof carryall, plastic water bottle with a belt hook or strap, health-insurance card, hiking maps and guides, and, perhaps most important of all, bug dope! If you plan to spend any time outdoors in Maine between early May and late September, insect repellent is critical for keeping at bay the state's abundant winged annoyances—especially blackflies, mosquitoes, and midges. Ben's and Cutter's work well, and Avon Skin-So-Soft lotion has become an inadvertent favorite recently (supermarkets and convenience stores seldom carry Avon products, but all carry the clone Skintastic, produced by the manufacturer of Off!). Home remedies (try at your own risk) include eating garlic, drinking alcohol, or rubbing cider vinegar, tansy leaves, or crushed lemon thyme on your skin. Caution is advised when using repellents. Find more specific precautions at www.state.me.us/agriculture/pesticides/public/repellents, and information on specific ingredients at 800/442-6305 (Maine Poison Center) or 800/858-7378 (National Pesticide Information Center). Natural foods stores sell non-chemical preparations, and Old Time Woodsman Fly Dope is DEET-free.

Not much daunts blackflies, but you can lower your appeal by not using perfume, aftershave lotion, or scented shampoo, and by wearing light-colored clothing.

Health and Safety

There's too much to do in Maine, and too much to see, to spend even a few hours laid low by illness or mishap. Be sensible—get enough sleep, wear sunscreen and appropriate clothing, know your limits and don't take foolhardy risks, heed weather and warning signs, carry water and snacks while hiking, don't overindulge in food or alcohol, always tell someone where you're going, and watch your step. If you're traveling with children, quadruple your caution.

Hospitals

All the hospitals in Maine's major population centers—primarily in southern and central Maine—feature round-the-clock emergency-room services with doctors and dentists on duty or on call. In these areas, dial 911 to get help. In sparsely populated corners of the state, regional acute-care hospitals serve large areas, but even small communities have volunteer ambulance corps with certified emergency medical technicians (EMTs) and sometimes paramedics. Coastal hospitals have helipads for acute-care transfers and for emergency evacuations from offshore islands. For emergencies on the islands, ferries and lobsterboats are commandeered. Floatplanes (skiplanes in the winter) provide evacuation services in the remote North Woods, where park rangers and game wardens are essential parts of the response network.

Walk-in, quick-care clinics can be found in such areas as Kennebunk, Old Orchard Beach, Portland, Wells, and Westbrook. No appointments are necessary, but you should rely on these facilities only for minor cuts and bruises, earaches, allergy shots, low-grade fevers, and other ailments that would relegate you to the bottom of an emergency-room triage list.

Pharmacies

The major pharmacy chains are Rite-Aid and CVS; many Shop 'n Save and Shaw's supermarkets also have pharmacy departments. All carry prescription and nonprescription (over-the-counter) medications, and are open seven days a week, but not around the clock. Some independent pharmacists post emergency numbers on their doors and will go out of their way to help, but your best bet for a middle-of-the-night medication crisis is the nearest hospital emergency room.

If you take regular medications, be sure to pack an adequate supply, as well as a new prescription in case you lose your medicine or unexpectedly need a refill.

Alternative Health Care

Nontraditional health-care options are available throughout the state, with concentrations around Portland, Camden/Rockland, and the Blue Hill Peninsula. Holistic practitioners, as well as certified massage therapists and acupuncturists, are listed in the Yellow Pages of local phone books. Also, check the bulletin boards and talk to the managers at food co-ops and health-food stores. They always know where to find homeopathic doctors and other holistic healers.

Warnings During Hunting Season

During Maine's fall hunting season (October to Thanksgiving weekend)—and especially during the November deer season—walk or hike only in wooded areas marked No Hunting, No Trespassing, or Posted. And even if an area *is* closed to hunters, don't decide to explore the woods during deer or moose season without wearing a "hunter orange" (read: eye-popping fluorescent) jacket or vest. If you take your dog along, be sure it, too, has an orange vest. Deer hunters are required to wear two items of orange clothing—a hat and usually a vest. Orange gear is available in sporting-goods stores, hardware stores, and some supermarkets and convenience stores, especially in traditional hunting areas. To be completely safe, stick to one of the state parks (although some of Baxter State Park is open for hunting) or get your exercise on Sunday—when hunting is illegal.

During hunting season, moose and deer are on the move and made understandably skittish by the hunters invading their turf. At night, particularly in remote wooded areas, they often end up alongside or in the roads, so ratchet up your defensive-driving skills. Reduce your normal speed, use high beams when there's no oncoming traffic, and remain extra-alert. In a moose-vs.-car encounter, no one wins, and human fatalities are common. An encounter between a deer and a car may be less dangerous to humans (although the deer usually dies), but some damage is inevitable.

AFFLICTIONS

Lyme Disease

A bacterial infection that causes severe arthritis-like symptoms, Lyme disease (named after the Connecticut town where it was first identified, in 1975) has been documented in Maine since 1986. (In Europe, the disease is known as borreliosis.) An average of more than 200 Maine cases were reported from 2002 to 2004, a huge increase from the 3 cases reported in 1989. Of the Center for Disease Control's reported 23,763 overall cases in 2002, 95 percent were from twelve states, one of which is Maine. In the first seven months of 2005, 40 cases were reported and confirmed by the state Bureau of Health, possibly reflecting better public awareness and prevention techniques. Health officials monitor the situation carefully and issue cautionary warnings during prime tick season—mid-May into August. Atlanta's Centers for Disease Control and Prevention (www.cdc.gov/) has cited the wooded, marshy areas of Maine's southernmost counties, York and Cumberland, as high-risk areas. From there northward, the risk is considered moderate.

Lyme disease is spread by bites from tiny deer ticks (not the larger dog ticks, which don't carry it), which feed on the blood of deer, mice, songbirds, and humans. Symptoms include joint pain, extreme fatigue, chills, a stiff neck, headache, and a distinctive ring-like rash. Treatment in the early stages is a fairly expensive round of antibiotics. Except for the rash, which occurs only in about 60 percent of victims, the symptoms mimic those of other

Know Maine

ailments, such as the flu, so the disease is hard to diagnose. The rash, which expands gradually and usually is not painful, may appear from three days to a month after a bite. If left untreated, Lyme disease eventually can cause heart and neurological problems and debilitating arthritis. Preventive measures are essential. LYMErix, a three-step vaccine, was taken off the market in 2002.

Best advice is to take precautions: Wear a long-sleeved shirt and long pants, and tuck the pant legs into your socks. Light-colored clothing makes the ticks easier to spot. Buy tick repellent at a supermarket or convenience store and use it liberally on your legs. Spray it around your cuffs and beltline. Permethrin, which kills ticks on contact, may be used to treat clothing in some cases, although special cautions apply to use with children, and it should not be applied to bare skin. While you're hiking, try to keep to the center of trails, away from long grasses. After any hike, check for ticks—especially behind the knees, and in the armpits, navel, and groin. Monitor children carefully. If you find a tick or suspect you have been bitten, head for the nearest hospital emergency room. If you spot a tick on you (or anyone else), remove it with tweezers and save it for analysis. Not all deer ticks are infected with the disease. For a brochure on avoiding and reporting Lyme disease, contact the Arthritis Foundation's Northern New England Chapter, 800/639-6650. Further information can be found at the State of Maine's Lyme Disease Resource Center website, www.maine.gov/dhhs/boh/ddc/lyme.

Rabies

Incidents of rabies—a life-threatening, nerve-attacking disease for which there is no cure unless treated immediately—have increased dramatically in Maine since 1994. No human has ever survived an untreated case of rabies, and the disease is horrible, so *do not* approach, or let any child approach, any of the animals known to transmit it: raccoons, skunks, squirrels, bats, and foxes. Domestic dogs are required to have biennial rabies inoculations,

which provide a front line of defense for humans. If you're bitten by any animal, especially one acting suspiciously, head for the nearest hospital emergency room. The virus travels along nerve roots to the brain, so a facial bite is far more critical, relatively speaking, than a leg bite. Treatment (a series of injections) is not as painful as it once was, but it's very expensive—and much better than the alternative. For statewide information about rabies, contact the Maine Division of Disease Control in Augusta, 207/287-3960.

Allergies

If your medical history includes extreme allergies to shellfish or bee sting, you know the risks of eating a lobster or wandering around a wildflower meadow. However, if you live in a landlocked area and are new to crustaceans, you might not be aware of the potential hazard. Statistics indicate that less than two percent of adults have a severe shellfish allergy, but for those victims, the reaction sets in quickly. Immediate treatment is needed to keep the airways open. If you have a history of severe allergic reactions to *anything,* be prepared when you come to Maine dreaming of lobster feasts—ask your doctor for a prescription for EpiPen (epinephrine), a preloaded, single-use syringe containing enough of the drug to tide you over until you can get to a hospital.

Seasickness

Samuel Butler, the 19th-century author of *Erewhon,* wrote, "How holy people look when they are sea-sick." And he wasn't kidding. Seasickness conjures visions of the pearly gates and an overwhelming urge for instant salvation. Fortunately, even though the ailment seems to last forever, it's only temporary—depending on where you are, what remedies you have, and how your system responds. If you're planning to do any boating in Maine—particularly sailing—you'll want to be prepared. (Being prepared may keep you from succumbing, since fear of seasickness just about guarantees you'll get it.)

Seasickness allegedly stems from an inner-ear imbalance caused by boat motion, but researchers have had difficulty explaining why some people on a vessel become violently ill and others have no problem at all.

To prevent seasickness, try to stay in good shape. Get enough sleep and food, and keep your clothing warm and dry (not easy, of course, on a heeling sailboat). Some veteran sailors swear by salted crackers, sips of water, and bites of fresh ginger. Ginger root powder, available from health food stores. has gotten good press in at least one medical journal. If you start feeling queasy, keep your eyes on the horizon and stay as far away as possible from odors from the engine, the galley, the head, and other seasick passengers. If you become seasick, keep sipping water to prevent dehydration.

Dramamine, Marezine, and Bonine, taken several hours before a boat trip, have long been the preventives of choice. They do cause drowsiness, but anyone who's been seasick will tell you they'd rather be drowsy. Another popular preventive is the scopolamine patch (available by prescription under the trademark Transderm Scop), which gradually releases medication into the bloodstream for up to three days. Behind an ear is the best location for the little adhesive disc. Wash your hands after you touch it—the medication can cause temporary blurred vision if you inadvertently rub your eyes. Children, pregnant women, the elderly, and those taking some common medications, or with common medical conditions, should not use scopolamine. Discuss side effects and appropriateness with the physician who gives you the prescription.

And some people swear by the pressure bracelet, which operates somewhat on the principle of acupressure, telling your brain to ignore the fact that you're not on terra firma. Great success has been reported with these prophylactics in the last decade. Before embarking, especially if the weather is at all iffy, go ahead and put on a patch or a bracelet. Any such preventive measure also improves your mental attitude, relieving anxiety. The British medical journal *Lancet* has had some good things to say about the practice of using ginger powder as an anti-seasickness measure.

Sunstroke

Since Maine lies between 43° and 48° north latitude, sunstroke is not a major problem, but don't push your luck by spending an entire day frying on the beach in south coastal Maine. Not only do you risk sunstroke and dehydration, but you're also asking for skin cancer down the road. Early in the season, slather yourself, and especially children, with plenty of PABA-free sunblock. (PABA can cause skin rashes and eruptions, even on people not abnormally sensitive.) Depending on your skin tone, use sun protection factor (SPF) 15 or higher. If you're in the water a long time, slather on some more. Start with a half hour of solar exposure and increase gradually each day. If you don't get it right, watch for symptoms of sunstroke: fever, profuse sweating, headache, nausea or vomiting, extreme thirst, and sometimes hallucinations. To treat someone with sunstroke, find a breezy spot and place a cold, wet cloth on the victim's forehead. Change it frequently so it stays cold. Offer lots of liquids—strong tea or coffee, fruit juice, water, soft drinks (no alcohol).

Hypothermia and Frostbite

Wind and weather can shift dramatically in Maine, especially at higher elevations, creating prime conditions for contracting hypothermia and frostbite. At risk are hikers, swimmers, canoeists, kayakers, sailors, skiers, even cyclists.

When body temperature plummets below the normal 97–98.6°F, hypothermia is likely to set in. Symptoms include disorientation, a flagging pulse rate, prolonged shivering, swelling of the face, and cool skin. Quick action is essential to prevent shock and keep body temperature from dropping into the 80s, where cardiac arrest can occur. Emergency treatment begins with removal of as much wet clothing as possible without causing further exposure. Wrap the victim in anything dry—blankets, sleeping bag, clothing, towels, even large plastic trash bags—to keep body heat from escaping. Be sure the neck and head are covered. Or practice the buddy system—climb into a sleeping bag with the victim and provide skin contact. Do not rub the skin, apply hot water, or elevate the legs. If he or she is conscious, offer high-sugar snacks and nonalcoholic hot drinks (but, again, no alcohol; it dilates blood vessels and disrupts the warming process). As quickly as possible, transport the victim to a hospital emergency room.

When extremities begin turning blue or gray, with red blotches, frostbite may be setting in. As with hypothermia, add warmth slowly but do not rub frostbitten skin. Offer snacks and warm, nonalcoholic liquids.

To prevent hypothermia and frostbite, dress in layers and remove or add them as needed.

Wool, waterproof nylon (such as Gore-Tex), and synthetic fleece (such as Polartec) are the best fabrics for repelling dampness. Polyester fleece lining wicks excess moisture away from your body. If you plan to buy a down jacket, be sure it has a waterproof shell; down will just suck up the moisture from snow and rain. Especially in winter, always cover your head, since body heat escapes quickly through the head; a ski mask will protect ears and nose. Wear wool- or fleece-lined gloves and wool socks.

Even during the height of summer, be on the alert for mild hypothermia when children stay in the ocean too long. Bouncing in and out of the water, kids become preoccupied, refuse to admit they are cold, and fall prey to wind chill.

Glossary: A Down East Dictionary

To help you translate some of the lingo in off-the-beaten-track Maine (e.g., country stores and county fairs, farmstands and flea markets), here's a sampling of local terms and expressions, followed by a list of place-names that have difficult or unusual pronunciations.

Airline, The—the 98-mile stretch of Route 9 between Bangor and Calais

alewives—herring

ayuh—yes

barrens—as in "blueberry barrens"; fields where wild blueberries grow

beamy—wide (as in a boat or a person)

beans—shorthand for the traditional Saturday-night meal, which always includes baked beans

blowdown—a forest area leveled by wind

blowing a gale—very windy

camp—a vacation house (small or large), usually on fresh water and/or in the woods

chance—serendipity or luck (as in "open by appointment or by chance")

chicken dressing—chicken manure

chowder (pronounced "chowdah")—soup made with lobster, clams, or fish, or a combination thereof; lobster version sometimes called lobster stew

coneheads—tourists (because of their presumed penchant for ice cream)

cottage—a vacation house (anything from a bungalow to a mansion), usually on salt water

County, The—Aroostook County, northernmost in Maine

culch (also cultch)—"stuff," the contents of attics, basements, and some flea markets

cull—a discount lobster, usually minus a claw

cunnin'—cute (usually describing a baby or small child)

dinner (pronounced "dinnah")—the noon meal

dinner pail—lunchbox

dite—a very small amount

dooryard—the yard near a house's main entrance

Down East—with the prevailing wind; the old coastal sailing route from Boston to Nova Scotia

downcellar—in the basement

downstate—the rest of Maine, according to residents of The County

dry-ki—driftwood, usually remnants from the logging industry

ell—a residential structural section that links a house and a barn; formerly a popular location for the "summer kitchen," to spare the house from woodstove heat

exercised—upset; angry

fiddleheads—unopened ostrich-fern fronds, a spring delicacy

finest kind—top quality; good news; an expression of general approval; also, a term of appreciation

flatlander—a person not from Maine, often but not exclusively someone from the Midwest

floatplane—a small plane equipped with pontoons for landing on water; the same aircraft often becomes a ski-plane in winter

flowage—a water body created by damming, usually beaver handiwork (also called "beaver flowage")

frappe—a thick drink containing milk, ice cream, and flavored syrup, as opposed to a milk shake, which does not include ice cream (But beware: A frappe offered in other parts of the United States is an ice-cream sundae topped with whipped cream!)

from away—not native to Maine

galamander—a wheeled contraption formerly used to transport quarry granite to building sites or to boats for onward shipment

gore—a sliver of land left over from inaccurate boundary surveys; Maine has Misery Gore, Coburn Gore, Moxie Gore, and more. Hibberts Gore, for instance, has a population of one.

got done—quit a job; was let go

harbormaster—local official who monitors water traffic and assigns moorings; often a very political job

hardshell—lobster that hasn't molted yet (more scarce, thus more pricey in summer)

hod—wooden "basket" used for carrying clams

ice-out—the departure of winter ice from ponds, lakes, rivers, and streams; many communities have ice-out contests, awarding prizes for guessing the exact time of ice-out, in April or May

Italian—long bread roll sliced and filled with peppers, onions, tomatoes, sliced meat, shredded lettuce, olive oil, seasonings, and more, according to taste; veggie versions available; elsewhere known as a hoagie, submarine, poor boy, hero, or grinder

lobster car—a large floating crate for storing lobsters

Maine Guide—a member of the Maine Professional Guides Association, trained and tested for outdoor and survival skills; also Registered Maine Guide

market price—restaurant menu term for "the going rate," usually referring to what you'll pay for lobster

molt—what a lobster does when it sheds its shell for a larger one; the act of molting is called ecdysis (as a stripper is an ecdysiast)

money tree—a collection device for a monetary gift

mud season—mid-March to mid-April, when back roads and unpaved driveways become virtual tank traps

nasty neat—extremely meticulous

near—stingy

notional—stubborn, determined

off island—the mainland, to an islander

place—another word for a house (as in "Herb Pendleton's place")

pot—trap, as in "lobster pot"

public landing—see "town landing"

rake—hand tool used for harvesting blueberries

rusticator—a summer visitor, particularly in bygone days

scooch (or **scootch**)—to squat; to move sideways

sea smoke—heavy mist rising off the water when the air temperature suddenly becomes much colder than the ocean temperature

select—a lobster with claws intact

Selectmen—the elected men and women who handle local affairs in small communities; the First Selectman chairs meetings; in some towns, "people from away" have tried to propose substituting a gender-neutral term, but in most cases the effort has failed

shedder—a lobster with a new (soft) shell; generally occurs in July and August (more common then, thus less expensive than hardshells)

shire town—county seat

shore dinner—the works: chowder, clams, lobster, and sometimes corn-on-the-cob, too; usually the most expensive item on a menu

short—a small, illegal-size lobster

slumgullion—tasteless food; a mess

slut—a poor housekeeper

slut's wool—dust balls found under beds, couches, etc.

snapper—an undersize, illegal lobster

softshell—see "shedder"

some—very (as in "some hot")

spleeny—overly sensitive

steamers—clams (before or after they are steamed)

sternman—a lobsterman's helper (male or female)

summer complaint—a tourist

supper (pronounced "suppah")—evening meal, eaten by Mainers around 5 or 6 PM (as opposed to flatlanders and summer people, who eat dinner between 7 and 9 PM)

tad—slightly; a little bit

thick-o'-fog—zero-visibility fog

to home—at home

tomalley—a lobster's green insides; considered a delicacy by some

town landing—shore access; often a park or a parking lot, next to a wharf or boat-launch ramp

upattic—in the attic

Whoopie! Pie—the trademarked name for a high-fat, calorie-laden, cake-like snack that only kids and dentists could love

wicked cold!—frigid

wicked good!—excellent

williwaws—uncomfortable feeling

Know Maine

CAN YOU GET THERE FROM HERE?

Countless names for Maine cities, towns, villages, rivers, lakes, and streams have Native American origins; some are variations on French; and a few have German derivations. Below are some pronunciations to give you a leg up when requesting directions in Maine.

Arundel—Uh-RUN-d'l
Bangor—BANG-gore
Bethel—BETH-l
Bremen—BREE-m'n
Calais—CAL-us
Carmel—CAR-m'l
Damariscotta—dam-uh-riss-COTT-uh
Harraseeket—Hare-uh-SEEK-it
Hebron—HE-brun
Isle au Haut—i'll-a-HO, I'LL-a-ho (subject to plenty of dispute, depending on whether or not you live in the vicinity)
Katahdin—Kuh-TA-din
Kokadjo—Ko-KAD-joe
Lubec—Loo-BECK
Machias—Muh-CHIGH-us
Maranacook—Muh-RAN-uh-cook
Matinicus—Muh-TIN-i-cuss
Medomak—Muh-DOM-ick
Megunticook—Muh-GUN-tuh-cook
Monhegan—Mun-HE-gun
Mount Desert—Mount Duh-ZERT (subject to dispute; some say Mount DEZ-ert)
Narraguagus—Nare-uh-GWAY-gus
Passagassawaukeag—Puh-sag-gus-uh-WAH-keg
Passamaquoddy—Pass-uh-muh-QUAD-dee
Piscataquis—Piss-CAT-uh-kwiss
Saco—SOCK-oh
Schoodic—SKOO-dick
Skowhegan—Skow-HE-gun
Steuben—Stew-BEN
Topsham—TOPS-'m
Umbagog—Um-BAY-gog
Wiscasset—Wiss-CASS-it
Woolwich—WOOL-itch
Wytopitlock—Wit-a-PIT-luck

Suggested Reading

TRAVEL

Arlen, A. *Maine Sporting Camps: A Year-Round Guide to Vacationing at Traditional Hunting & Fishing Lodges.* 3d ed. Woodstock, VT: Countryman Press, 2003. A survey of more than 90 Maine sporting camps; the only book on the subject.

Barry, C. *Portland Undercover: How to Visit New England's Hippest City Without Looking Like a Tourist.* Portland: Casco Bay Weekly, 2000. A witty take on the Portland scene.

Bumsted, L. *Hot Showers! Maine Coast Lodgings for Kayakers and Sailors.* 2d ed. Brunswick, ME: Biddle-Audenreed Press, 2000. Excellent, well-researched resource (although getting out of date) for anyone cruising the shoreline and yearning for alternatives to a sleeping bag.

Clark, S. *Katahdin: A Guide to Baxter State Park & Katahdin.* 5th ed. Harpers Ferry, WV: Appalachian Trail Conference Books, 2003. The only comprehensive guidebook—and in a pocket-size format as well—to Baxter and Katahdin.

Curtis, W., and T. Seymour. *Maine: Off the Beaten Path.* 6th ed. Guilford, CT: Globe Pequot, 2004. Great collection of offbeat and unexpected locales; a good supplementary guide for would-be explorers.

Dwelley, M. J. *Spring Wildflowers of New England.* 2d ed. Camden, ME: Down East Books, 2000. Out of print for several years, this beautifully illustrated gem is an essential guide for exploring spring woodlands.

Dwelley, M. J. *Summer and Fall Wildflowers of New England.* 2d ed. Camden, ME: Down East Books, 2004. Flowers are grouped by color; more than 700 lovely colored-pencil drawings simplify identification.

English, N. *The Coast of Maine Book: A Complete Guide.* 5th ed. Woodstock, VT: Countryman/Great Destinations, 2002. Lively writing style and useful information arranged by regions within topics.

Nangle, H. *Moon Handbooks Coastal Maine.* 2d ed. Emeryville, CA: Avalon Travel Publishing, 2005. A Maine native and veteran travel writer is the ideal escort for exploring the coast.

Pierson, E. C., J.E. Pierson, and P.D. Vickery. *A Birder's Guide to Maine.* Camden, ME: Down East Books, 1996. No ornithologist, novice or expert, should explore Maine without this valuable guide.

Taft, H., J. Taft, and C. Rindlaub. *A Cruising Guide to the Maine Coast.* 4th ed. Peaks Island: Diamond Pass Publishing, 2001. Don't even consider cruising the coast without this volume.

Thompson, W. B., et al. *A Collector's Guide to Maine Mineral Localities.* 3d ed. Augusta, ME: Maine Geological Survey, 1998. For amateur rock hounds, details on and directions to abandoned quarries and other sites.

Vietze, A. *Insiders' Guide to the Maine Coast.* Guilford, CT: Globe Pequot, 2004. Longtime *Down East* magazine editor Andy Vietze, who really *is* an insider, shares the results of his zillions of explorations.

Know Maine

LITERATURE, ART, AND PHOTOGRAPHY

Bennett, D. *Allagash: Maine's Wild and Scenic River.* Camden, ME: Down East Books, 1994. Elegant portrait of the Allagash Wilderness Waterway, by a veteran Maine naturalist.

Bunting, W. H., comp. *A Day's Work: A Sampler of Historic Maine Photographs, 1860-1920.* 2 vols. Gardiner, ME: Tilbury House, 1997 and 2000. Extensive captions accompany an incredible photograph collection.

Curtis, J. and W., and F. Lieberman. *Monhegan: The Artists' Island.* Camden, ME: Down East Books, 1995. Fascinating island history interspersed with landscape and seascape paintings and drawings by more than 150 artists, including Bellows, Henri, Hopper, Kent, Porter, Tam, and Wyeth.

Peavey, E. *Maine & Me: Ten Years of Down East Adventures.* Camden, ME: Down East Books, 2004. A collection of perceptive, funny stories covering the whole state-Rangeley, Matinicus, Monhegan, Fort Kent, and lots more-by one of Maine's most entertaining writers.

Silliker, Bill. *Wild Maine: Discoveries of a Maine Wildlife Photographer.* Camden, ME: Down East Books, 2004. Stories and superb nature photography by Maine's best-known wildlife photographer—who died suddenly in 2003.

Spectre, P.H. *Passage in Time.* New York: W.W. Norton, 1991. A noted marine writer cruises the coast aboard traditional windjammers; gorgeous photos complement the colorful text.

Thompson, C. *Maine Lighthouses: A Pictorial Guide.* 3d ed. Mt. Desert, ME: CatNap Publications, 2001. What they look like, how to find them (sometimes only by boat), with some historical and contemporary background info.

Thoreau, H. D. *The Maine Woods.* New York: Penguin Books, 1988 ed. [orig. pub. 1864]. A Maine classic, first published two years after the author's death; mid-19th-century exploration of Maine's wilderness around Greenville, Chesuncook, Katahdin, and more.

Van Riper, F. *Down East Maine: A World Apart.* Camden, ME: Down East Books, 1998. Maine's Washington County, captured with incredible insight and compassion by a master photographer/insightful wordsmith.

Villani, R. *Forever Wild: Maine's Magnificent Baxter State Park.* Camden, ME: Down East Books, 1991. Spectacular photos of Baxter in every season, taken by an accomplished professional.

REFERENCE

Gould, J. *Maine Lingo: Boiled Owls, Billdads, and Wazzats.* Camden, ME: Down East Books, 1975. A seasoned student of local jargon—the late, great columnist John Gould—provides advice on "speaking Maine."

The Maine Atlas and Gazetteer. Yarmouth, ME: DeLorme, updated annually. You'll be hard put to get lost if you're carrying this essential volume; 78 full-page (oversize format) topographical maps with GPS grids.

HISTORY

Acadian Culture in Maine. Washington, DC: National Park Service, North Atlantic Region, 1994. A project report on Acadians and their traditions in the Upper St. John Valley.

Duncan, R. F. *Coastal Maine: A Maritime History* New York: W.W. Norton, 1992.

Accessible maritime history from a distinguished historian and cruising sailor.

Isaacson, D., ed. *Maine: A Guide "Down East."* 2d ed. n.p.: Maine League of Historical Societies and Museums, 1970, O.P. Revised version of the Depression-era WPA guidebook. Still interesting for background reading.

Jaster, R. S. *Russian Voices on the Kennebec: The Story of Maine's Unlikely Colony.* Orono: University of Maine Press, 1999. A riveting account of the founding of a Russian-speaking colony in Richmond, Maine, in the 1950s. Superb historical photographs.

Judd, R. W., E. A. Churchill, J. W. Eastman, eds. *Maine: The Pine Tree State from Prehistory to the Present.* Orono: University of Maine Press, 1995. The best available Maine history, with excellent historical maps.

Paine, L. P. *Down East: A Maritime History of Maine.* Gardiner, ME: Tilbury House, 2000. A noted maritime historian provides an enlightening introduction to the state's seafaring tradition.

MEMOIRS

Dawson, L. B. *Beside the St. George's: Maine's Forgotten Ways.* Westford, MA: Impatiens Press, 2004. Witty, charming stories of growing up on the Cushing peninsula.

Hamlin, H. *Nine Mile Bridge: Three Years in the Maine Woods.* Yarmouth and Frenchboro, ME: Islandport Press, 2005 [orig. pub. 1945]. Hamlin's experiences as a teacher at a remote lumber camp near the headwaters of the Allagash, where her husband was a game warden.

Lunt, D. L. *Hauling by Hand: The Life and Times of a Maine Island.* Yarmouth and Frenchboro, ME: Islandport Press, 1999. A sensitive history of Frenchboro (aka Long Island), eight miles offshore, written by an eighth-generation islander, now a journalist.

Wass, P. B. *Lighthouse in My Life: The Story of a Maine Lightkeeper's Family.* Camden, ME: Down East Books, 1987. Offshore adventures, growing up on Libby Island, near Machias.

NATURAL HISTORY

Bennett, D. *Maine's Natural Heritage: Rare Species and Unique Natural Features.* Camden, ME: Down East Books, 1988.

Conkling, P. W. *Islands in Time: A Natural and Cultural History of the Islands of the Gulf of Maine.* 2d ed. Camden, ME: Down East Books, and Rockland, ME: Island Institute, 1999. A thoughtful overview by the founder of Maine's Island Institute.

Kendall, D. L. *Glaciers & Granite: A Guide to Maine's Landscape and Geology.* Unity, ME: North Country Press, 1993. Explains why Maine looks the way it does.

RECREATION

AMC Maine Mountain Guide. 9th ed. Boston: Appalachian Mountain Club Books, 2005. The definitive statewide resource for going vertical. Includes GPS-friendly maps and nearly 200 summits.

Chunn, C. *50 Hikes in the Maine Mountains: Day Hikes and Overnights from the Rangeley Lakes to Baxter State Park.* 3d ed. Woodstock, VT: Countryman Press/Backcountry, 2002. Well-researched and well-written guide (complements the Gibson guide, below).

Cobscook Trails: A Guide to Walking Opportunities Around Cobscook Bay and the Bold Coast. 2d ed. Whiting, ME: Quoddy Regional Land Trust. Essential handbook for exploring this part of the Sunrise Coast. Excellent maps.

Know Maine

Gibson, J. *50 Hikes in Coastal and Southern Maine.* 3d ed. Woodstock, VT: Countryman Press/Backcountry, 2001. Well-researched, detailed resource by a veteran hiker (complements the Chunn guide, above).

The Maine Island Trail: Stewardship Handbook and Guidebook. Portland, ME: Maine Island Trail Association (58 Fore St., Portland 04101, www.mita.org), updated annually. Available only with MITA membership (annual dues $45), providing access to more than 100 islands along the 325-mile watery trail.

Miller, D. *Kayaking the Maine Coast: A Paddler's Guide to Day Trips from Kittery to Cobscook.* Woodstock, VT: Countryman Press/Backcountry, 2000. A well-researched volume by a veteran kayaker and writer. With her book and a copy of *Hot Showers!* (see above), you're all set.

Stone, H. *25 Bicycle Tours in Maine: Coastal and Inland Rides from Kittery to Caribou.* 3d ed. Woodstock, VT: Countryman Press/Backcountry, 1998. The title says it all.

Wilson, A., and J. Hayes. *Quiet Water Maine.* 2nd ed. Boston: Appalachian Mountain Club Books, 2005. Comprehensive handbook, with helpful maps, for inland paddling.

Yates, K. and C. Phillips. *AMC River Guide: Maine.* 2nd ed. Boston: Appalachian Mountain Club Books, 1991. Detailed guide to canoeing or kayaking about 4,000 miles of Maine's large and small rivers. In a convenient small format.

ACADIA REGION

Abrell, D. *A Pocket Guide to the Carriage Roads of Acadia National Park.* 2d ed. Camden, ME: Down East Books, 1995. The best guide to the carriage-road system. A dozen excellent hiking or biking loops in a portable format.

Blagden, T., Jr., and C. R. Tyson, Jr. *First Light.* Englewood, CO: Westcliffe Publishers, and Bar Harbor, ME: Friends of Acadia, 2003. Spectacular is too tame a word for this large-format book containing Blagden's photos of Acadia as you've never seen it before.

Brandes, K. *Moon Handbooks Acadia National Park.* Emeryville, CA: Avalon Travel, 2004. Focuses on Acadia but also covers the rest of Mount Desert Island, as well as the Schoodic Peninsula, the Blue Hill Peninsula, Deer Isle, and Isle au Haut.

Brechlin, E. D. *A Pocket Guide to Paddling the Waters of Mount Desert Island.* Camden, ME: Down East Books, 1996. Registered Maine Guide Brechlin recommends 17 places to paddle your kayak or canoe.

Helfrich, G. W., and G. O'Neil. *Lost Bar Harbor.* Camden, ME: Down East Books, 1982. Fascinating collection of historic photographs of classic, turn-of-the-20th-century "cottages," many obliterated by Bar Harbor's Great Fire of 1947.

Kong, D., and D. Ring *Hiking Acadia National Park.* Guilford, CT: Globe Pequot/Falcon, 2001. Excellent hiking guide, with useful, accurate descriptions of 94 trails on Mount Desert Island, Isle au Haut, and the Schoodic Peninsula. The authors list their 25 favorites and advocate for Leave No Trace principles.

Minutolo, A. *A Pocket Guide to Biking on Mount Desert Island.* Camden, ME: Down East Books, 1996. A third-generation islander's expert advice covering the whole island (not just Acadia).

Monkman, J. and M. *Discover Acadia National Park: A Guide to Hiking, Biking, and Paddling.* 2d ed. Boston: Appalachian Mountain Club Books, 2005. Well-planned and well-written guide in the AMC tradition, including foldout map.

Roberts, A. R. *Mr. Rockefeller's Roads.* Camden, ME: Down East Books, 1990. The fascinating story behind Acadia's scenic carriage roads, written by the granddaughter of John D. Rockefeller, Jr. (who created them).

St. Germain, T. A., Jr. *A Walk in the Park: Acadia's Hiking Guide.* 10th ed. Bar Harbor: Parkman Publications (P.O. Box 826, Bar Harbor, ME 04609), 2000. The best Acadia National Park hiking guide, in a handy Michelin-type vertical format. Part of the proceeds go to Friends of Acadia's Acadia Trails Forever campaign to maintain and rehabilitate the park's trails.

Wilmerding, J. *The Artist's Mount Desert: American Painters on the Maine Coast.* Princeton, NJ: Princeton University Press, 1995. A respected art historian's perspective on Mount Desert's magnetic attraction to such noted artists as Thomas Cole, Frederic Church, and Fitz Hugh Lane.

Know Maine

Index

Acknowledgments

Many, many people lent a hand with information and support for the first and second editions of this book, including Mary Lyons, who has turned herself inside-out to update the material for the third edition. I am grateful to all.

For help with the first and second editions, I would like to thank particularly Richard E. Winslow III, Dale Kuhnert, Nancy Marshall, Bill Hancock, Joan Grant, Nancy Griffin, Robert Jaster, Molly Sholes, Pat Messler, Barbara Feller-Roth, Hilary Nangle, and Michael Drons. Also very helpful were Peter Randall, Richard Kelly, Deborah Wade, Georgia Hansen, Ellen Devine, Terry Dodge, Lurelle Cheverie, Jean Hendrick, Marion Bowman, Sue Palmer, Sally MacVane, Marilis Hornidge, Sherry Streeter, Jon Wilson, Charlotte Cushman, Kristen Lindquist, Jean Hoekwater, Joan Howard, Cathy and George Wilson, and Maureen and Gene Hart, Sally M. Littlefield, and the always-supportive members of Maine Media Women.

Thank-yous also go to Carolyn and Keith May, Peter and Eileen Spectre, Craig and Paula Dickinson, Dana Winchenbach, Sandra Garson, Charlene Williams, Rose Whitehouse, Anne Ball, Igor and Karen Sikorsky, Don Kleiner, Anne Carpenter, Robin Zinchuk, Virginia Farnsworth, Sheila Jans, Owen Lawlor, and the many helpful readers who have taken the time to email or snailmail tidbits and updates.

Past and present staff members at Avalon Travel Publishing with whom I have worked have always been especially supportive. I'm particularly grateful to Rebecca Browning, Pauli Galin, Amanda Bleakley, Gina Birtcil, Naomi Adler Dancis, Gregor Krause, Erin Van Rheenen, and Bill Newlin.

—Kathleen M. Brandes

As Kathy Brandes has written, you find out who your friends are when you do a project of this size, and I did! Thank you to all of them; they are wonderful, and I am grateful.

Special thanks for information, general helpfulness, above-and-beyond-ness, and/or encouragement, to: Nancy Abel, Jim Amaral, Sue Antal, Michael Auglis, Steve Balboni, Tom Bergh, Charles Blair, Tom Bradbury, Kathy Brandes, Martin Brown, Mary Chaney, Robin Cogger, Meghan Conley, Scott Cowger, Jim Crocker, Elaine Eskesen, Carolyn Farkas-Noe, Dennis Grannis-Phoenix, Capt. Tom Farnon, Capt. Laura Fish, Carrie Fisher, Suzanne M. Foster, Dianne Goodwin, Jeff Gordon, Nancy Griffin, Norma Harrop, Maureen Hart, Scott W. Hood, Jeanice Holmes, Marilis Hornidge, Mari M. Huotari, Ruth Kisseloff, Alvion Kimball, Jaimie A. Kleinstiver, Jeff Kuller, Anthony Liss, Mike Little, Sandra Lucas, Norma Harrop, Don Hudson, Mary May, Jeanne M. McGurn, Mac McKeever, Ryan McKisson, Meg Maiden, Peter Michaud, Jeffrey Miller, Heather O'Bryan, Megan Pinette, Trudi Price, Marietta Ramsdell, Robert "Bos" Savage, Anita Taggersell, Susan B. Tompkins, Bob and Juanita Topper, Marty Welt, Charlene Williams, Cathy and George Wilson, David Winslow, Janice Yankowski, Joan and Lee Yeaton, Marjorie Yesley, Janice Zenter.

And thank you to the people at Avalon for their professionalism and dedication to the beau ideal of travel: Rebecca Browning, Elizabeth McCue, Gerilyn Attebery, and Kevin Anglin.

—Mary Lyons

Updated by Mary Lyons, with the assistance of Liza Reilly, Susan Auglis, Nancy Bloch, Jean Hardy, Sandra Lucas, Maryann McGinn, Judith Reilly, and Leslie Sanford.

ALSO AVAILABLE FROM

MOON HANDBOOKS®
The Cure for the Common Trip

USA

Acadia National Park
Alaska
Arizona
Big Island of Hawai'i
Boston
California
Cape Cod, Martha's
 Vineyard & Nantucket
Charleston & Savannah
Chesapeake Bay
Coastal California
Coastal Carolinas
Coastal Maine
Coastal Oregon
Colorado
Columbia River Gorge
Connecticut
Florida Gulf Coast
Four Corners
Georgia
Grand Canyon
Hawaii
Hudson River Valley
Idaho
Illinois
Kaua'i
Las Vegas
Maine
Maryland & Delaware
Massachusetts
Maui
Michigan
Minnesota
Montana
Monterey & Carmel
Nevada
New Hampshire
New Mexico
New Orleans
New York State

North Carolina
Northern California
Northern California Wine
 Country
O'ahu
Ohio
Oregon
Pennsylvania
Rhode Island
San Juan Islands
Santa Fe-Taos
Silicon Valley
Smoky Mountains
South Carolina
Southern California
Tahoe
Tennessee
Texas
Utah
Virginia
Washington
Wisconsin
Wyoming
Yellowstone & Grand
 Teton
Yosemite
Zion & Bryce

THE AMERICAS

Alberta
Atlantic Canada
British Columbia
Canadian Rockies
Vancouver & Victoria
Western Canada

Acapulco
Baja
Cabo
Cancún & Cozumel
Guadalajara
Mexico City
Oaxaca
Pacific Mexico
Puerto Vallarta
Yucatán Peninsula

Argentina
Belize
Brazil
Buenos Aires
Chile
Costa Rica
Cuba
Dominican Republic
Ecuador
Guatemala
Havana
Honduras
Nicaragua
Panama
Patagonia
Peru
Virgin Islands

ASIA & THE PACIFIC

Australia
Fiji
Hong Kong
Micronesia
Nepal
New Zealand
South Korea
South Pacific
Tahiti
Thailand
Tonga-Samoa
Vietnam, Cambodia &
 Laos

www.moon.com

With expert authors, suggested routes and activities, and intuitive organization, Moon Handbooks ensure an uncommon experience—and a few new stories to tell.

ALSO FROM
AVALON TRAVEL PUBLISHING
www.travelmatters.com

 MOON METRO

Map-based Moon Metro unfolds each city neighborhood by neighborhood, with insider recommendations on the best spots to eat, sleep, shop, and explore.

www.moon.com

 *Rick Steves*

More Savvy. More Surprising. More Fun.

As the #1 authority on European travel, Rick gives you inside information on what to visit, where to stay, and how to get there— economically and hassle-free.

www.ricksteves.com

 **LIVING ABROAD**

DREAM. PLAN. MAKE IT HAPPEN.

With authors who have made the move themselves, these guides show readers how to make their dream of living in another country a reality.

www.livingabroadin.com

ROAD TRIP USA

OPEN ROAD. ENDLESS POSSIBILITIES.

See what the interstates have left behind. **ROAD TRIP USA** takes you off the beaten path, onto classic blacktop, and into the soul of America.

www.roadtripusa.com

 **THE DOG LOVER'S COMPANION**

The Inside Scoop on Where to Take Your Dog

A special breed of guidebook for travelers and residents who don't want to leave their canine pals behind.

www.dogloverscompanion.com

ⒻOGHORN OUTDOORS®

YOUR ADVENTURE STARTS HERE

Foghorn authors are recreation experts who provide readers with the most up-to-date information on enjoying the outdoors.

www.foghorn.com

AVAILABLE AT BOOKSTORES AND THROUGH ONLINE BOOKSELLERS

U.S. ~ Metric Conversion

1 inch	=	2.54 centimeters (cm)
1 foot	=	.304 meters (m)
1 yard	=	0.914 meters
1 mile	=	1.6093 kilometers (km)
1 km	=	.6214 miles
1 fathom	=	1.8288 m
1 chain	=	20.1168 m
1 furlong	=	201.168 m
1 acre	=	.4047 hectares
1 sq km	=	100 hectares
1 sq mile	=	2.59 square km
1 ounce	=	28.35 grams
1 pound	=	.4536 kilograms
1 short ton	=	.90718 metric ton
1 short ton	=	2000 pounds
1 long ton	=	1.016 metric tons
1 long ton	=	2240 pounds
1 metric ton	=	1000 kilograms
1 quart	=	.94635 liters
1 US gallon	=	3.7854 liters
1 Imperial gallon	=	4.5459 liters
1 nautical mile	=	1.852 km

To compute Celsius temperatures, subtract 32 from Fahrenheit and divide by 1.8. To go the other way, multiply Celsius by 1.8 and add 32.

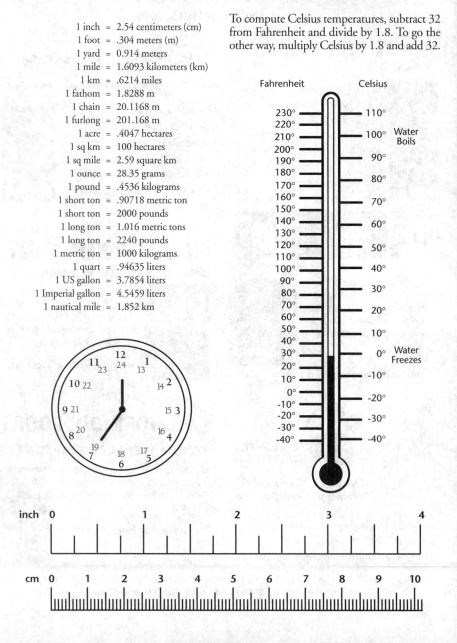